Volume A
To 1850

Out of Many

A History of the American People

Third Edition

John Mack Faragher
Yale University

Mari Jo Buhle
Brown University

Daniel Czitrom
Mount Holyoke College

Susan H. Armitage
Washington State University

Prentice Hall, Upper Saddle River, New Jersey 07458

Library of Congress Cataloging–in–Publication Data
Out of many: a history of the American people / John Mack Faragher
. . . [et al.]. — 3rd ed., Combined ed.
p. cm.
Includes bibliographical references and index.
ISBN 0-13-949760-9
1. United States—History. I. Faragher, John Mack
E178.1.0935 2000 98–34110
973—dc21 CIP

Editorial Director: Charlyce Jones Owen
Executive Editor: Todd R. Armstrong
Development Editor: David Chodoff
Production Editor: Louise Rothman
Creative Director: Leslie Osher
Art Director: Anne Bonanno Nieglos
Editor-in-Chief of Development: Susanna Lesan
Marketing Manager: Sheryl Adams
Interior and Cover Designer: Thomas Nery
Cover Art: John L. Krimmel, Painting, (1786–1821), oil on on canvas, H. 16⅜" x 25⅝". (AN:59.131) Courtesy, Winterthur Museum, *Election Day in Philadelphia* (1815)—detail.

AVP, Director of Production and Manufacturing: Barbara Kittle
Manufacturing Manager: Nick Sklitsis
Manufacturing Buyer: Lynn Pearlman
Photo Researcher: Barbara Salz
Photo Editor: Lorinda Morris-Nantz
Copy Editor: Sylvia Moore
Editorial Assistant: Holly Jo Brown
Line Art Coordinator: Guy Ruggiero
Cartographers: Alice and William Thiede/ CARTO-GRAPHICS
Electronic Page Layout: Scott Garrison and Rosemary Ross

Credits and acknowledgments for materials borrowed from other sources and reproduced, with permission, in this textbook appear on pages C–1 – C–3.

This book was set in 11/12 Weiss by the HSS in-house formatting and production services groups and was printed and bound by RR Donnelley & Sons Company. The cover was printed by Phoenix Color Corp.

Printed in the United States of America
10 9 8 7 6 5 4 3 2 1

ISBN 0-13-010031-5

Prentice-Hall International (UK) Limited, *London*
Prentice-Hall of Australia Pty. Limited, *Sydney*
Prentice-Hall Canada Inc., *Toronto*
Prentice-Hall Hispanoamericana, S.A., *Mexico*
Prentice-Hall of India Private Limited, *New Delhi*
Prentice-Hall of Japan, Inc., *Tokyo*
Pearson Education Asia Pte. Ltd., *Singapore*
Editora Prentice-Hall do Brasil, Ltda., *Rio de Janeiro*

To our students,
our sisters,
and our brothers

Brief Contents

1
A Continent of Villages, to 1500 1

2
When Worlds Collide, 1492–1590 25

3
Planting Colonies in North America, 1588–1701 49

4
Slavery and Empire, 1441–1770 73

5
The Cultures of Colonial North America, 1700–1780 103

6
From Empire to Independence, 1750–1776 132

7
The Creation of the United States, 1776–1786 162

8
The United States of North America, 1787–1800 193

9
An Agrarian Republic, 1790–1824 228

10
The Growth of Democracy, 1824–1840 261

11
The South and Slavery, 1790s–1850s 294

12
Industry and the North, 1790s–1840s 324

13
Coming to Terms with the New Age, 1820s–1850s 351

14
The Territorial Expansion of the United States, 1830s–1850s 386

Contents

Preface xxi
Community and Diversity xxviii

1 A Continent of Villages, to 1500 1

■ AMERICAN COMMUNITIES: **Cahokia: Thirteenth-Century Life on the Mississippi** 1

Settling the Continent 3
- Who Are the Indian People? **3**
- Migration from Asia **3**
- Clovis: The First American Technology **5**

The Beginning of Regional Cultures 6
- Hunting Traditions of the Plains and Forests **6**
- Desert Culture in Western America **7**
- ■ History and the Land The Regions of Native North America **8**
- Forest Efficiency **9**

The Development of Farming 10
- Mexico **10**
- The Resisted Revolution **11**
- Increasing Social Complexity **12**
- The Religions of Foragers and Farmers **12**
- Earliest Farmers of the Southwest **13**
- The Anasazis **14**
- Farmers of the Eastern Woodlands **14**
- Mississippian Society **15**
- The Politics of Warfare and Violence **16**

North America on the Eve of Colonization 17
- The Indian Population of America **17**
- The Southwest **17**
- The South **19**
- The Northeast **21**

Chronology 22 Conclusion 22 Review Questions 23
Recommended Reading 23 Additional Bibliography 24

2 When Worlds Collide, 1492–1590 25

■ AMERICAN COMMUNITIES: **The English and the Algonquians at Roanoke** 26

The Expansion of Europe 28
- European Communities **28**
- The Merchant Class and the Renaissance **29**
- The New Monarchies **30**
- Portuguese Explorations **30**
- Columbus Reaches the Americas **31**

The Spanish in the Americas 33
- The Invasion of America **33**
- The Destruction of the Indies **34**
- Intercontinental Exchange **36**
- The First Europeans in North America **37**
- The Spanish New World Empire **39**

French and English Explorations and Encounters 39
- The Political Impact of the Reformation **40**
- The French Colony in Florida **40**
- Fish and Furs **41**
- Social Change in Sixteenth-Century England **43**
- England Turns toward Colonization **44**

Conclusion 45 Chronology 46 Review Questions 46
Recommended Reading 46 Additional Bibliography 47

3 Planting Colonies in North America, 1588–1701 49

AMERICAN COMMUNITIES: Communities Struggle with Diversity in Seventeenth-Century Santa Fé 50

THE SPANISH AND FRENCH IN NORTH AMERICA 52
- New Mexico 52
- The First Communities of New France 53

ENGLAND IN THE CHESAPEAKE 54
- Jamestown and the Powhatan Confederacy 54
- Tobacco, Expansion, and Warfare 55
- Maryland 56
- Indentured Servants 57
- Community Life in the Chesapeake 58

THE NEW ENGLAND COLONIES 58
- The Social and Political Values of Puritanism 58
- Early Contacts in New England 58
- Plymouth Colony and the Mayflower Compact 59
- The Massachusetts Bay Colony 59
- Indians and Puritans 60
- New England Communities 61
- The Politics of Gender in Massachusetts 62
- Dissent and New Communities 63

THE RESTORATION COLONIES 64
- Early Carolina 64
- From New Netherland to New York 64
- The Founding of Pennsylvania 65

CONFLICT AND WAR 66
- King Philip's War 67
- Bacon's Rebellion 68
- Wars in the South 68
- The Glorious Revolution in America 69
- King William's War 69

CHRONOLOGY 70 CONCLUSION 70 REVIEW QUESTIONS 70
RECOMMENDED READING 71 ADDITIONAL BIBLIOGRAPHY 71

4 Slavery and Empire, 1441–1770 73

AMERICAN COMMUNITIES: African Slaves Build Their Own Community in Coastal Georgia 74

THE BEGINNINGS OF AFRICAN SLAVERY 76
- Sugar and Slavery 76
- West Africans 77

THE AFRICAN SLAVE TRADE 78
- The Demography of the Slave Trade 78
- Slavers of All Nations 79
- The Shock of Enslavement 79
- The Middle Passage 81
- Arrival in the New World 82
- Political and Economic Effects on Africa 82

THE DEVELOPMENT OF NORTH AMERICAN SLAVE SOCIETIES 83
- Slavery Comes to North America 83
- The Tobacco Colonies 84
- The Lower South 85
- Slavery in the Spanish Colonies 86
- French Louisiana 87
- Slavery in the North 87

BECOMING AFRICAN AMERICAN 88
- The Daily Life of Slaves 88
- Families and Communities 88
- African American Culture 89
- The Africanization of the South 90
- Violence and Resistance 91

SLAVERY AND THE STRUCTURE OF EMPIRE 92
- Slavery the Mainspring 92
- The Politics of Mercantilism 94
- Wars for Empire 94
- British Colonial Regulation 95
- The Colonial Economy 97

SLAVERY AND FREEDOM 98
- The Social Structure of the Slave Colonies 98
- White Skin Privilege 99

CHRONOLOGY 100 CONCLUSION 100 REVIEW QUESTIONS 101
RECOMMENDED READING 101 ADDITIONAL BIBLIOGRAPHY 102

5 The Cultures of Colonial North America, 1700–1780 103

■ AMERICAN COMMUNITIES: From Deerfield to Kahnawake: Crossing Cultural Boundaries 104

NORTH AMERICAN REGIONS 106
- Indian America 106
- The Spanish Borderlands 108
- ■ **History and the Land** Regions in Eighteenth-Century North America 108
- The French Crescent 111
- New England 112
- The Middle Colonies 113
- The Backcountry 114
- The South 115
- Traditional Culture in the New World 116
- The Frontier Heritage 117

DIVERGING SOCIAL AND POLITICAL PATTERNS 119
- Population Growth 119
- Social Class 120
- Economic Growth and Increasing Inequality 121
- Contrasts in Colonial Politics 123

THE CULTURAL TRANSFORMATION OF BRITISH NORTH AMERICA 123
- The Enlightenment Challenge 124
- A Decline in Religious Devotion 125
- The Great Awakening 126
- Great Awakening Politics 128

CHRONOLOGY 128 CONCLUSION 129 REVIEW QUESTIONS 129
RECOMMENDED READING 129 ADDITIONAL BIBLIOGRAPHY 130

6 From Empire to Independence, 1750–1776 132

■ AMERICAN COMMUNITIES: The First Continental Congress Shapes a National Political Community 133

THE SEVEN YEARS WAR IN AMERICA 135
- The Albany Conference of 1754 135
- Colonial Aims and Indian Interests 135
- Frontier Warfare 137
- The Conquest of Canada 137
- Indians and Europeans Struggle over the West 139

THE IMPERIAL CRISIS IN BRITISH NORTH AMERICA 141
- The Emergence of American Nationalism 141
- Politics, Republicanism, and the Press 142
- The Sugar and Stamp Acts 143
- The Stamp Act Crisis 143
- Repeal of the Stamp Act 145

"SAVE YOUR MONEY AND SAVE YOUR COUNTRY" 145
- The Townshend Revenue Acts 145
- Nonimportation: An Early Political Boycott 146
- The Massachusetts Circular Letter 147
- The Politics of Revolt and the Boston Massacre 148

FROM RESISTANCE TO REBELLION 149
- Intercolonial Cooperation 149
- The Boston Tea Party 150
- The Intolerable Acts 151
- The First Continental Congress 152
- Lexington and Concord 153

DECIDING FOR INDEPENDENCE 154
- The Second Continental Congress 155
- Fighting in the North and South 156
- No Turning Back 157
- The Declaration of Independence 158

CHRONOLOGY 159 CONCLUSION 159 REVIEW QUESTIONS 160
RECOMMENDED READING 160 ADDITIONAL BIBLIOGRAPHY 160

7 The Creation of the United States, 1776–1786 162

■ AMERICAN COMMUNITIES: **A National Community Evolves at Valley Forge 163**

THE WAR FOR INDEPENDENCE 165
- The Patriot Forces **165**
- The Loyalists **167**
- The Campaign for New York and New Jersey **168**
- The Northern Campaigns of 1777 **169**
- The Politics of the French and Spanish Alliance **170**
- Indian Peoples and the Revolution **172**
- The War in the South **173**
- Yorktown **175**

THE UNITED STATES IN CONGRESS ASSEMBLED 175
- The Articles of Confederation **176**
- Financing the War **176**
- Negotiating Independence **177**
- The Crisis of Demobilization **178**
- The Problem of the West **179**
- ■ **History and the Land** The Northwest Territory and the Land Survey System of the United States **180**

REVOLUTIONARY POLITICS IN THE STATES 182
- The Broadened Base of Politics **182**
- The First State Constitutions **183**
- Declarations of Rights **184**
- A Spirit of Reform **184**
- African Americans and the Revolution **185**
- Economic Problems **187**
- State Remedies **188**
- Shays' Rebellion **189**

CONCLUSION 189 CHRONOLOGY 190 REVIEW QUESTIONS 190
RECOMMENDED READING 191 ADDITIONAL BIBLIOGRAPHY 191

8 The United States of North America, 1787–1800 193

■ AMERICAN COMMUNITIES: **Mingo Creek Settlers Refuse to Pay the Whiskey Tax 194**

FORMING A NEW GOVERNMENT 196
- Nationalist Sentiment **196**
- The Constitutional Convention **196**
- Ratifying the New Constitution **198**
- Shaping the Bill of Rights **200**

THE NEW NATION 200
- The Washington Presidency **200**
- An Active Federal Judiciary **201**
- Hamilton's Controversial Fiscal Program **202**
- The Beginnings of Foreign Policy **203**
- The United States and the Indian Peoples **204**
- Spanish and British Hostility **205**
- Domestic and International Crises **206**
- Jay's and Pinckney's Treaties **207**
- Washington's Farewell Address **208**

FEDERALISTS AND REPUBLICANS 208
- The Rise of Political Parties **208**
- The Adams Presidency **209**
- The Alien and Sedition Acts **210**
- The Revolution of 1800 **211**

"THE RISING GLORY OF AMERICA" 213
- Art and Architecture **213**
- The Liberty of the Press **215**
- The Birth of American Literature **215**
- Women on the Intellectual Scene **218**

CHRONOLOGY 218 CONCLUSION 219 REVIEW QUESTIONS 219
RECOMMENDED READING 219 ADDITIONAL BIBLIOGRAPHY 220

Immigration & Community: The Changing Face of Ethnicity in America, To 1800 222

9 An Agrarian Republic, 1790–1824 228

■ AMERICAN COMMUNITIES: Expansion Touches Mandan Villages on the Upper Missouri 229

THE GROWTH OF AMERICAN COMMUNITIES FROM COAST TO COAST 231
- Russian America: Sitka **231**
- Northern New Spain: Los Angeles **232**
- A French Legacy: New Orleans and St. Louis **232**
- Trans-Appalachia: Cincinnati **233**
- Atlantic Ports: From Charleston to Boston **234**

A NATIONAL ECONOMY 235
- The Economy of the Young Republic **235**
- Shipping and the Economic Boom **235**

THE JEFFERSON PRESIDENCY 237
- Republican Agrarianism **237**
- Jefferson's Government **238**
- An Independent Judiciary **239**
- Opportunity: The Louisiana Purchase **239**
- Incorporating Louisiana **241**
- Texas and the Struggle for Mexican Independence **241**

RENEWED IMPERIAL RIVALRY IN NORTH AMERICA 242
- Problems with Neutral Rights **242**
- The Embargo Act **242**
- Madison and the Failure of "Peaceable Coercion" **242**
- A Contradictory Indian Policy **243**
- ■ **History and the Land** Indian Resistance, 1790–1816 **245**
- Indian Resistance **246**

THE WAR OF 1812 247
- The War Hawks **247**
- The Campaign against Canada **248**
- War in the South **248**
- The Naval War **248**
- The Hartford Convention **249**
- The Treaty of Ghent **249**

DEFINING THE BOUNDARIES 250
- Another Westward Surge **250**
- The Second Great Awakening on the Frontier **253**
- The Election of 1816 and the Era of Good Feelings **253**
- The Diplomacy of John Quincy Adams **254**
- The Panic of 1819 **256**
- The Missouri Compromise **256**

CHRONOLOGY 258 CONCLUSION 259 REVIEW QUESTIONS 259
RECOMMENDED READING 259 ADDITIONAL BIBLIOGRAPHY 260

10 The Growth of Democracy, 1824–1840 261

■ AMERICAN COMMUNITIES: Martin Van Buren Forges a New Kind of Political Community 262

THE NEW DEMOCRATIC POLITICS 264
- The Expansion and Limits of Suffrage **264**
- The Election of 1824 **266**
- Organizing Popular Politics **267**
- The Election of 1828 **268**

THE JACKSON PRESIDENCY 269
- A Popular Figure **269**
- The Spoils System and the New Politics **269**
- The Nation's Leader vs. Sectional Spokesmen **270**
- A Strong Executive **271**

INTERNAL IMPROVEMENTS: BUILDING AN INFRASTRUCTURE 271
- The Transportation Revolution **271**
- Canals and Steamboats **273**
- Railroads **275**
- The Legal Infrastructure **276**
- Commercial Agriculture in the Old Northwest **276**
- Effects of the Transportation Revolution **277**

JACKSON AND HIS OPPONENTS: THE RISE OF THE WHIGS 279
- The Nullification Crisis **279**
- Indian Removal **280**
- The Bank War **282**
- Jackson's Reelection in 1832 **283**
- Whigs, Van Buren, and the Election of 1836 **283**
- The Panic of 1837 **284**

THE SECOND AMERICAN PARTY SYSTEM 285
- Whigs and Democrats **285**
- The Campaign of 1840 **286**
- The Whig Victory Turns to Loss: The Tyler Presidency **287**

AMERICAN ARTS AND LETTERS 287
- The Spread of the Written Word **287**
- Creating an American Culture **288**
- Artists and Builders **290**

CHRONOLOGY 291 CONCLUSION 291 REVIEW QUESTIONS 292

RECOMMENDED READING 292 ADDITIONAL BIBLIOGRAPHY 292

11 The South and Slavery, 1790s–1850s 294

AMERICAN COMMUNITIES: Natchez-under-the Hill 295

KING COTTON AND SOUTHERN EXPANSION 297
- The Cotton Gin and Expansion into the Old Southwest **297**
- The Question of Slavery **298**
- The Internal Slave Trade **299**
- The Economics of Slavery **299**
- Cotton Culture **300**

TO BE A SLAVE 301
- The Maturing of the American Slave System **301**
- The Challenge to Survive **302**
- From Cradle to Grave **303**
- House Servants **304**
- Artisans and Skilled Workers **305**
- Field Work **305**

THE AFRICAN AMERICAN COMMUNITY 306
- Slave Families **306**
- African American Religion **307**
- Freedom and Resistance **308**
- Slave Revolts **309**
- Free African Americans **310**

YEOMEN AND POOR WHITE PEOPLE 311
- Yeomen **311**
- Poor White People **312**
- Yeoman Values **313**

PLANTERS 313
- Small Slave Owners **313**
- The Old Planter Elite **314**
- The Natchez "Nabobs" **315**
- Plantation Life **315**
- The Plantation Mistress **316**
- Coercion and Violence **317**

THE DEFENSE OF SLAVERY 317
- Developing Proslavery Arguments **318**
- After Nat Turner **318**
- Changes in the South **320**

CHRONOLOGY 320 CONCLUSION 321 REVIEW QUESTIONS 321

RECOMMENDED READING 322 ADDITIONAL BIBLIOGRAPHY 322

12 Industry and the North, 1790s–1840s 324

AMERICAN COMMUNITIES: Women Factory Workers Form a Community in Lowell, Massachusetts 325

PREINDUSTRIAL WAYS OF WORKING 327
- Rural Life: The Springer Family **327**
- The Family Labor System **327**
- Urban Artisans and Workers **328**
- Patriarchy in Family, Work, and Society **329**
- The Social Order **329**

THE MARKET REVOLUTION 330
- The Accumulation of Capital **330**
- The Putting-Out System **331**
- British Technology and American Industrialization **332**
- Slater's Mill **333**
- The Lowell Mills **334**
- Family Mills **335**
- "The American System of Manufactures" **336**
- Other Factories **337**

FROM ARTISAN TO WORKER 338
- Personal Relationships **338**
- Mechanization and Women's Work **339**
- Time, Work, and Leisure **339**
- The Cash Economy **340**
- Free Labor **341**
- Early Strikes **341**

A NEW SOCIAL ORDER 342
- Wealth and Class **342**
- Religion and Personal Life **343**
- The New Middle-Class Family **344**
- Family Limitation **345**
- Motherhood **345**
- Sentimentalism **346**
- Transcendentalism and Self-Reliance **347**

CHRONOLOGY 348 CONCLUSION 348 REVIEW QUESTIONS 349

RECOMMENDED READING 349 ADDITIONAL BIBLIOGRAPHY 350

13 Coming to Terms with the New Age, 1820s–1850s 351

■ AMERICAN COMMUNITIES: Seneca Falls: Women Reformers Respond to the Market Revolution 352

URBAN AMERICA 354
- The Preindustrial City 354
- The Growth of Cities 354
- Patterns of Immigration 355
- Class Structure in the Cities 355
- ■ **History and the Land** The Growth of Cities, 1820–1860 356
- Sanitation and Living Patterns 356
- Ethnic Neighborhoods 357
- Urban Popular Culture 358
- Civic Order 360
- Urban Life of Free African Americans 361

THE LABOR MOVEMENT AND URBAN POLITICS 362
- The Tradition of Artisanal Politics 362
- The Union Movement 363
- Big-City Machines 364

SOCIAL REFORM MOVEMENTS 365
- Evangelism, Reform, and Social Control 365
- Education and Women Teachers 366
- Temperance 367
- Moral Reform, Asylums, and Prisons 368
- Utopianism and Mormonism 369

ANTISLAVERY AND ABOLITIONISM 371
- The American Colonization Society 371
- African Americans' Fight against Slavery 371
- Abolitionists 372
- Abolitionism and Politics 375

THE WOMEN'S RIGHTS MOVEMENT 375
- The Grimké Sisters 376
- Women's Rights 376

CHRONOLOGY 377 CONCLUSION 378 REVIEW QUESTIONS 378
RECOMMENDED READING 378 ADDITIONAL BIBLIOGRAPHY 379

Immigration & Community: The Changing Face of Ethnicity in America, 1800–1860 380

14 The Territorial Expansion of the United States, 1830s–1850s 386

■ AMERICAN COMMUNITIES: Texans and Tejanos "Remember the Alamo!" 387

EXPLORING THE WEST 389
The Fur Trade **389**
Government-Sponsored Exploration **390**
Expansion and Indian Policy **391**

THE POLITICS OF EXPANSION 392
Manifest Destiny, an Expansionist Ideology **392**
The Overland Trails **394**
Oregon **396**
The Santa Fé Trade **397**
Mexican Texas **398**
Americans in Texas **399**
The Texas Revolt **400**
The Republic of Texas **401**
Texas Annexation and the Election of 1844 **402**

THE MEXICAN-AMERICAN WAR 403
Origins of the War **404**
Mr. Polk's War **404**
The Press and Popular War Enthusiasm **406**

CALIFORNIA AND THE GOLD RUSH 406
Russian-Californio Trade **406**
Early American Settlement **407**
Gold! **408**
Mining Camps **409**

THE POLITICS OF MANIFEST DESTINY 410
The "Young America" Movement **410**
The Wilmot Proviso **411**
The Free-Soil Movement **412**
The Election of 1848 **412**

CHRONOLOGY 414 CONCLUSION 414 REVIEW QUESTIONS 415
RECOMMENDED READING 415 ADDITIONAL BIBLIOGRAPHY 416

APPENDIX A-1

CREDITS C-1

INDEX I-1

MAPS

Chapter 1
Migration Routes from Asia to America 5
■ **History and the Land** The Regions of Native North America 8
Native North American Trade Networks, ca. C.E. 1400 16
Indian Settlement before European Colonization 18
Southwestern Indian Groups on the Eve of Colonization 19
Southern Indian Groups on the Eve of Colonization 19
Northeastern Indian Groups on the Eve of Colonization 21

Chapter 2
Western Europe in the Fifteenth Century 30
The Invasion of America 33
European Exploration, 1492–1591 38
The Roanoke Area in 1585 45

Chapter 3
New Mexico in the Seventeenth Century 52
New France in the Seventeenth Century 54
European Colonies of the Atlantic Coast, 1607–1639 63
The Restoration Colonies 64
Spread of Settlement: British Colonies, 1650–1700 67

Chapter 4
The African Slave Trade 78
Slave Colonies of the Seventeenth and Eighteenth Centuries 79
Triangular Trade across the Atlantic 98

Chapter 5
Growing Use of the Horse by Plains Indians 107
■ **History and the Land** Regions in Eighteenth-Century North America 108
The French Crescent 111
Spread of Settlement: Movement into the Backcountry, 1720–1760 115

Chapter 6
The War for Empire in North America, 1754–1763 136
European Claims in North America, 1750 and 1763 139
Demonstrations against the Stamp Act, 1765 145
The Quebec Act of 1774 152
The First Engagements of the Revolution 153

Chapter 7
Campaign for New York and New Jersey, 1775–1777 169
Northern Campaigns, 1777–1778 170
Fighting in the West, 1778–1779 173
Fighting in the South, 1778–1781 174
North America after the Treaty of Paris, 1783 178
State Claims to Western Lands 179
■ **History and the Land** The Northwest Territory and the Land Survey System of the United States 180

Chapter 8
The Ratification of the Constitution, 1787–1790 199
Spread of Settlement: The Backcountry Expands, 1770–1790 204
Spanish Claims to American Territory, 1783–1795 207
The Election of 1800 211

Immigration & Community: The Changing Face of Ethnicity in America, to 1800
Ethnic Groups in Eighteenth-Century British North America 224

Chapter 9
America in 1800 233
Louisiana Purchase 240
■ **History and the Land** Indian Resistance 1790–1816 244
The War of 1812 247
Spread of Settlement: Westward Surge, 1800–1820 250
Major Migration Routes, 1800–1820 252
John Quincy Adams's Border Treaties 255
The Missouri Compromise 257

Chapter 10
Population Trends: Westward Expansion, 1830 265
The Growth of Universal White Manhood Suffrage 266
The Election of 1824 267
The Election of 1828 269

Travel Times, 1800 and 1857 **272**
The Impact of the Erie Canal on Household Textile Manufacture **274**
Commercial Links: Rivers, Canals, Roads, 1830, and Rail Lines, 1850 **278**
Southern Indian Cessions and Removals, 1830s **281**
The Election of 1840 **287**

Chapter 11
The South Expands, 1790–1850 **297**
Agriculture, Industry, and Slavery, 1850 **301**
Cotton Production, 1820–1860 **302**
Slave Population, 1820–1860 **303**
Population Patterns in the South, 1850 **318**

Chapter 12
Lowell, Massachusetts, 1832 **334**
The Growth of Cotton Textile Manufacturing, 1810–1840 **335**

Chapter 13
■ **History and the Land** The Growth of Cities, 1820–1860 **356**
Reform Movements in the Burned-Over District **370**
The Mormon Migration, 1830–1847 **372**

Immigration & Community: The Changing Face of Ethnicity in America, 1800–1860
The Distribution of Foreign-born Residents of the United States in 1860 **382**

Chapter 14
Exploration of the Continent, 1804–1830 **391**
Indian Territory before the Kansas-Nebraska Act of 1854 **393**
The Overland Trails, 1840 **394**
Texas: From Mexican Province to U.S. State **401**
The Mexican-American War, 1846–1848 **403**
Territory Added, 1845–1853 **405**
California in the Gold Rush **407**

Charts, Graphs, and Tables

Chapter 1
Overview Origins of Some Indian Tribal Names **4**

Chapter 2
North America's Indian and Colonial Populations in the Seventeenth and Eighteenth Centuries **36**
Intercontinental Exchange **37**
The African, Indian, and European Population of the Americas **39**

Chapter 3
Population Growth of the British Colonies in the Seventeenth Century **57**
Overview Conflict and War **66**

Chapter 4
Estimated Number of Africans Imported to British North America, 1701–1775 **80**
Africans as a Percentage of Total Population of the British Colonies, 1650–1770 **84**
Tobacco and Rice Exports to England **85**
British Colonial Trade in the Americas, 1714–1773 **92**
Overview The Colonial Wars **95**
Value of Colonial Exports by Region, Annual Average, 1768–1772 **97**

Chapter 5
Monthly Frequency of Successful Conceptions **116**
Estimated Total Population of New Spain, New France, and the British North American Colonies, 1700–1780 **120**
Distribution of Assessed Taxable Wealth in Eighteenth-Century Chester County, Pennsylvania **122**
Wealth Held by Richest 10 Percent of the Population: Northern and Southern British Colonies Compared, 1770 **122**

Chapter 6
Overview The Thirteen Repressive British Measures **151**

Chapter 7
Postwar Inflation, 1777–1780: The Depreciation of Continental Currency **187**
The Trade Deficit with Great Britain **188**

Chapter 8
Overview The First American Party System **209**
Housing Values, 1798 **215**

Immigration & Community: The Changing Face of Ethnicity in America, To 1800
The Ancestry of the British Colonial Population **223**

Chapter 9
American Export Trade, 1790–1815 **235**
Western Land Sales **251**

Chapter 10
Overview The Second American Party System **286**
Pre–Civil War Voter Turnout **288**
The Burgeoning of Newspapers **288**

Chapter 11
Cotton Exports as a Percentage of All U.S. Exports, 1800–1860 **300**
Slaveholding and Class Structure in the South, 1830 **313**

Chapter 12
Wealth in Boston, 1687–1848 **330**
Occupations of Women Wage Earners in Massachusetts, 1837 **339**
Wealth in New York City, 1828–1845 **342**

Chapter 13
Participation of Irish and German Immigrants in the New York City Workforce for Selected Occupations, 1859 **359**
Per Capita Consumption of Alcohol, 1800–1860 **368**

Immigration & Community: The Changing Face of Ethnicity in America, 1800–1860
Immigration to the United States 1820–1860 **381**

Chapter 14
Overland Emigration to Oregon, California, and Utah, 1840–1860 **396**
Where the Forty-Niners Came From **407**
Overview Expansion Causes the First Splits in the Second American Party System **411**

PREFACE

Out of Many, A History of the American People, third edition, offers a distinctive and timely approach to American history, highlighting the experiences of diverse communities of Americans in the unfolding story of our country. These communities offer a way of examining the complex historical forces shaping people's lives at various moments in our past. The debates and conflicts surrounding the most momentous issues in our national life—independence, emerging democracy, slavery, westward settlement, imperial expansion, economic depression, war, technological change—were largely worked out in the context of local communities. Through communities we focus on the persistent tensions between everyday life and those larger decisions and events that continually reshape the circumstances of local life. Each chapter opens with a description of a representative community. Some of these portraits feature American communities struggling with one another: African slaves and English masters on the rice plantations of colonial Georgia, or Tejanos and Americans during the Texas war of independence. Other chapters feature portraits of communities facing social change: the feminists of Seneca Falls, New York, in 1848; the sitdown strikers of Flint, Michigan, in 1934; and the African Americans of Montgomery, Alabama, in 1955. As the story unfolds we find communities growing to include ever larger groups of Americans: The soldiers from every colony who forged the Continental Army into a patriotic national force at Valley Forge during the American Revolution; the movie-goers who dreamed a collective dream of material prosperity and upward mobility during the 1920s; and the Americans linked in ever-growing numbers in the virtual communities of cyberspace as the twenty-first century begins.

Out of Many is also the only American history text with a truly continental perspective. With community vignettes from New England to the South, the Midwest to the far West, we encourage students to appreciate the great expanse of our nation. For example, a vignette of seventeenth-century Santa Fé, New Mexico illustrates the founding of the first European settlements in the New World. We present territorial expansion into the American West from the point of view of the Mandan villagers of the upper Missouri River of North Dakota. We introduce the policies of the Reconstruction era through the experience of African Americans in the Sea Island of South Carolina. This continental perspective drives home to students that American history has never been the preserve of any particular region.

In these ways *Out of Many* breaks new ground, but without compromising its coverage of the traditional turning points that we believe are critically important to an understanding of the American past. Among these watershed events are the Revolution and the struggle over the Constitution, the Civil War and Reconstruction, and the Great Depression and World War II. In *Out of Many*, however, we seek to *integrate* the narrative of national history with the story of the nation's many diverse communities. The Revolutionary and Constitutional period tried the ability of local communities to forge a new unity, and success depended on their ability to build a nation without compromising local identity. The Civil War and Reconstruction formed a second great test of the balance between the national ideas of the revolution and the power of local and sectional communities. The Depression and the New Deal demonstrated the impotence of local communities and the growing power of national institutions during the greatest economic challenge in our history. *Out of Many* also looks back in a new and comprehensive way—from the vantage point of the beginning of a new century and the end of the Cold War—at the salient events of the last fifty years and their impact on American communities. The community focus of *Out of Many* weaves the stories of the people and of the nation into a single compelling narrative.

SPECIAL FEATURES

With each edition of *Out of Many* we have sought to strengthen its unique integration of the best of traditional American history with its innovative community-based focus and strong continental perspective. A wealth of special features and pedagogical aids reinforces our narrative and helps students grasp key issues.

- **Community and Diversity.** *Out of Many*, third edition, opens with an introduction, titled "Community and Diversity," that acquaints students with the major themes of the book, providing them with a framework for understanding American history.
- **Immigration and Community: The Changing Face of Ethnicity in America.** This feature, new to this edition, highlights

the impact of the immigrant experience on the formation of American communities. There are four Immigration and Community features in the book. The first covers the colonial period through 1800, the second covers from 1800 to 1860, the third covers from 1860 to 1930, and the last covers the period since 1930. Each is six pages long and opens with an overview of the character of immigration during the period in question. This overview is followed by a section called "In Their Own Words" that consists of extracts from primary sources written by immigrants themselves and by native-born Americans in response to the new arrivals. Study questions at the end of each Immigration and Community feature ask students to relate issues raised in the overview and documents to broader issues in American history.

- **History and the Land.** These features focus on the geographical dimension of historical change to give students an appreciation of the relationship between geography and history. Each elucidates an important historical trend or process with a map and a brief explanatory essay.
- **American Communities.** Each chapter opens with an American Communities vignette that relates the experience of a particular community to the broader issues discussed in the chapter.
- **Maps.** *Out of Many*, third edition, has more maps than any other American history textbook. Many maps include topographical detail that helps students appreciate the impact of geography on history.
- **Overview tables.** Overview tables, also new to this edition, provide students with a summary of complex issues.
- **Graphs, charts and tables.** Every chapter includes one or more graphs, charts, or tables that help students understand important events and trends.
- **Photos and illustrations.** The abundant illustrations in *Out of Many*, third edition, include many images that have never before been used in an American history text. None of the images is anachronistic—each one dates from the historical period under discussion. Extensive captions treat the images as visual primary source documents from the American past, describing their source and explaining their significance.
- **Chapter-opening outlines and key topics lists.** These pedagogical aids provide students with a succinct preview of the material covered in each chapter.
- **Chronologies.** A chronology at the end of each chapter helps students build a framework of key events.
- **Review Questions.** Review questions help students review, reinforce, and retain the material in each chapter and encourage them to relate the material to broader issues in American history.
- **Recommended Reading and Additional Bibliography.** The works on the short, annotated Recommended Reading list at the end of each chapter have been selected with the interested introductory student in mind. The extensive Additional Bibliography provides a comprehensive overview of current scholarship on the subject of the chapter.

CLASSROOM ASSISTANCE PACKAGE

In classrooms across the country, many instructors encounter students who perceive history as merely a jumble of names, dates, and events. *Out of Many*, third edition, brings our dynamic past alive for these students with a text and accompanying print and multimedia classroom assistance package that combine sound scholarship, engaging narrative, and a rich array of pedagogical tools.

PRINT SUPPLEMENTS

Instructor's Resource Manual

A true time-saver in developing and preparing lecture presentations, the *Instructor's Resource Manual* contains chapter outlines, detailed chapter overviews, lecture topics, discussion questions, readings, and information on audio-visual resources.

Test Item File

Prepared by Gisela Ables, Mike McCormick, and David Aldstadt, Houston Community College

The *Test Item File* offers a menu of more than 1,500 multiple-choice, identification, matching, true-false, and essay test questions and 10–15 questions per chapter on maps found in each chapter. The guide includes a collection of blank maps that can be photocopied and used for map testing purposes or for other class exercises.

Prentice Hall Custom Test

This commercial-quality computerized test management program, available for Windows, DOS, and Macintosh environments, allows instructors to select items from the Test Item File and design their own exams.

Transparency Pack

Prepared by Robert Tomes, St. John's University

This collection of more than 160 full-color transparency acetates provides instructors with all the maps, charts, and graphs in the text for use in the classroom. Each transparency is accompanied by a page of descriptive material and discussion questions.

Study Guide, Volumes I and II

Prepared by Elizabeth Neumeyer, Kellogg Community College, and S. Ross Doughty, Ursinus College

Each chapter in the *Study Guide* includes a chapter commentary and outline, identification terms, multiple-choice questions, short essay questions, map questions, and questions based on primary source extracts.

Documents Set, Volumes I and II

Prepared by John Mack Faragher, Yale University, and Daniel Czitrom, Mount Holyoke College

The authors have selected and carefully edited more than 300 documents that relate directly to the themes and content of the text and organized them into five general categories: community, social history, government, culture, and politics. Each document is approximately two pages long and includes a brief introduction and study questions intended to encourage students to analyze the document critically and relate it to the content of the text. The Documents Set is available at a substantial discount when packaged with *Out of Many*.

Retrieving the American Past: A Customized U.S. History Reader

Written and developed by leading historians and educators, this reader is an on-demand history database that offers 52 compelling modules on topics in American History, such as: Women on the Frontier, The Salem Witchcraft Scare, The Age of Industrial Violence, and Native American Societies, 1870–1995. Approximately 35 pages in length, each module includes an introduction, several primary documents and secondary sources, follow-up questions, and recommendations for further reading. By deciding which modules to include and the order in which they will appear, instructors can compile the reader they want to use. Instructor-originated material—other readings, exercises—can be included. Contact your local Prentice Hall Representative for more information about this exciting custom publishing option.

Understanding and Answering Essay Questions

Prepared by Mary L. Kelley, San Antonio College

This brief guide suggests helpful study techniques as well as specific analytical tools for understanding different types of essay questions and provides precise guidelines for preparing well-crafted essay answers. The guide is available free to students when packaged with *Out of Many*.

Reading Critically About History

Prepared by Rose Wassman and Lee Rinsky, both of DeAnza College

This brief guide provides students with helpful strategies for reading a history textbook. It is available free when packaged with *Out of Many*.

Themes of the Times

Themes of the Times is a newspaper supplement prepared jointly by Prentice Hall and the premier news publication, *The New York Times*. Issued twice a year, it contains recent articles pertinent to American history. These articles connect the classroom to the world. For information about a reduced-rate subscription to *The New York Times*, call toll-free: (800) 631–1222.

MULTIMEDIA SUPPLEMENTS

History on the Internet

This brief guide introduces students to the origin and innovations behind the Internet and World Wide Web and provides clear strategies for navigating the web to find historical materials. Exercises within and at the end of the chapters allow students to practice searching the wealth of resources available to the student of history. This 48-page supplementary book is free to students when packaged with *Out of Many*.

Out of Many CD-ROM

This innovative electronic supplement takes advantage of the interactive capabilities of multimedia technology to enrich students' understanding of the geographic dimension of history with animated maps, timelines, and related on-screen activities tied to key issues in each chapter of *Out of Many*.

Out of Many Companion Website

Address: http://www.prenhall.com/faragher

With the *Out of Many* Companion Website, students can now take full advantage of the World Wide Web and use it in tandem with the text to enrich their study of American history. The Companion Website ties the text to related material available on the Internet. Its instructional features include chapter objectives, study questions, news updates, and labeling exercises.

The American History CD-ROM

This vast library of more than 2500 images was compiled by Instructional Resources Corporation for instructors for creating slide shows and supplementing lectures. Among its resources are 68 film sequences, 200 works of art, and more than 100 maps. It also includes an overview of historical periods narrated by Charles Kuralt.

ACKNOWLEDGMENTS

In the years it has taken to bring *Out of Many* from idea to reality and to improve it in successive editions, we have often been reminded that although writing history sometimes feels like isolated work, it actually involves a collective effort. We want to thank the dozens of people whose efforts have made the publication of this book possible.

At Prentice Hall, Todd Armstrong, Executive Editor, gave us his full support and oversaw the entire publication process. David Chodoff, Senior Development Editor, greatly helped to strengthen the book's most distinctive features with his careful attention to detail and clarity. Susanna Lesan, now Editor-in-Chief of Development, worked with us on the first edition of the text; without her efforts this book would never have been published. Louise Rothman, Production Editor, oversaw the entire complicated production process in an exemplary fashion. Barbara Salz, our photo researcher, expertly tracked down the many pertinent new images that appear in this edition.

Among our many other friends at Prentice Hall we also want to thank: Phil Miller, President; Charlyce Jones Owen, Editorial Director; Sheryl Adams, Marketing Manager; Leslie Osher, Creative Design Director; Anne Nieglos, Art Director; Patterson Lamb, Copy Editor; and Holly Jo Brown, Editorial Assistant.

Although we share joint responsibility for the entire book, the chapters were individually authored: John Mack Faragher wrote chapters 1–8; Mari Jo Buhle wrote chapters 18–20, 25–26, 29–30; Daniel Czitrom wrote chapters 17, 21–24, 27–28, 31; and Susan Armitage wrote chapters 9–16.

Historians around the country greatly assisted us by reading and commenting on our chapters for this and previous editions. We want to thank each of them for the commitment of their valuable time.

Donald Abbe, Texas Tech University, TX
Richard H. Abbott, Eastern Michigan University, MI
Guy Alchon, University of Delaware, DE
Don Barlow, Prestonsburg Community College, KY
William Barney, University of North Carolina, NC
Alwyn Barr, Texas Tech University, TX
Debra Barth, San Jose City College, CA
Peter V. Bergstrom, Illinois State University, IL
William C. Billingsley, South Plains College, TX
Peter H. Buckingham, Linfield College, OR
Bill Cecil-Fronsman, Washburn University of Topeka, KS
Victor W. Chen, Chabot College, CA
Jonathan M. Chu, University of Massachusetts, MA
P. Scott Corbett, Oxnard College, CA
Matther Coulter, Collin Country Community College, TX
Virginia Crane, University of Wisconsin, Oshkosh, WI
Jim Cullen, Harvard University, MA
Thomas J. Curran, St. John's University, NY
Richard V. Damms, Ohio State University, OH
Elizabeth Dunn, Baylor University, TX
Emmett G. Essin, Eastern Tennessee State Unversity, TN
Mark F. Fernandez, Loyola University, IL
Leon Fink, University of North Carolina, Chapel Hill, NC
Michael James Foret, University of Wisconsin, Stevens Point, WI
Joshua B. Freeman, Columbia University, NY
Glenda E. Gilmore, Yale University, CT
Don C. Glenn, Diablo Valley College, CA
Lawrence Glickman, University of South Carolina, SC
Kenneth Goings, Florida Atlantic University, FL
Mark Goldman, Tallahassee Community College, FL
Gregory L. Goodwin, Bakersfield College, CA
Gretchen Green, University of Missouri, Kansas City, MO
Emily Greenwald, University of Nebraska at Lincoln, NE
Mark W. T. Harvey, North Dakota State University, ND
James A. Hijiya, University of Massachusetts at Dartmouth, MA
Raymond M. Hyser, James Madison University, VA
John Inscoe, University of Georgia, GA

John C. Kesler, Lakeland Community College, OH
Peter N. Kirstein, Saint Xavier University, IL
Frank Lambert, Purdue University, IN
Susan Rimby Leighow, Millersville University, PA
Janice M. Leone, Middle Tennessee University, TN
Glenn Linden, Southern Methodist University, Dallas, TX
George Lipsitz, University of California, San Diego, CA
Judy Barrett Litoff, Bryant College, RI
Jesus Luna, California State University, CA
Larry Madaras, Howard Community College, MD
Lynn Mapes, Grand Valley State University, MI
John F. Marszalek, Mississippi State University, MS
Scott C. Martin, Bowling Green State University, OH
Robert L. Matheny, Eastern New Mexico University, NM
Thomas Matijasic, Prestonsburg Community College, KY
M. Delores McBroome, Humboldt State University, CA
Gerald McFarland, University of Massachusetts, Amherst, MA
Sam McSeveney, Vanderbilt University, TN
Warren Metcalf, Arizona State University, AZ
M. Catherine Miller, Texas State University, TX
Norman H. Murdoch, University of Cincinnati, OH
Gregory H. Nobles, Georgia Institute of Technology, GA
Dale Odom, University of Texas at Denton, TX
Sean O'Neill, Grand Valley State University, MI
Edward Opper, Greenville Technical College, Greenville, SC
Charles K. Piehl, Mankato State University, MN
Carolyn Garrett Pool, University of Central Oklahoma, OK
Christie Farnham Pope, Iowa State University, IA
Susan Porter-Benson, University of Missouri, MO
Russell Posner, City College of San Francisco, CA
John Powell, Penn State University, Erie, PA
Sarah Purcell, Central Michigan University, MI
Joseph P. Reidy, Howard University, DC
Marilyn D. Rhinehart, North Harris College, TX
Leo P. Ribuffo, George Washington University, DC
Judy Ridner, California State University at Northridge, CA
Neal Salisbury, Smith College, MA
Roberto Salmon, University of Texas-Pan American, TX
Steven Schuster, Brookhaven Community College, TX
Megan Seaholm, University of Texas, Austin, TX
Nigel Sellars, University of Oklahoma, Norman, OK
John David Smith, North Carolina State University, NC
Patrick Smith, Broward Community College, FL
Mark W. Summers, University of Kentucky, KY
John D. Tanner, Jr., Palomar College, CA
Robert R. Tomes, St. John's University, NY
Michael Miller Topp, University of Texas at El Paso, TX
John Trickel, Richland Community College, IL
Steve Tripp, Grand Valley State University, MI
Fred R.Van Hartesveldt, Fort Valley State University, GA
Philip H. Vaughan, Rose State College, OK
Robert C. Vitz, Northern Kentucky University, KY
F. Michael Williams, Brevard Community College, FL
Charles Regan Wilson, University of Mississippi, MS
Harold Wilson, Old Dominion University, VA
William Woodward, Seattle Pacific University, WA
Loretta E. Zimmerman, University of Florida, FL

Each of us depended on a great deal of support and assistance with the research and writing that went into this book. We want to thank: Kathryn Abbott, Nan Boyd, Krista Comer, Crista DeLuzio, Keith Edgerton, Carol Frost, Jesse Hoffnung Garskof, Jane Gerhard, Todd Gernes, Melani McAlister, Cristiane Mitchell, J. C. Mutchler, Tricia Rose, Gina Rourke, and Jessica Shubow.

Our families and close friends have been supportive and ever so patient over the many years we have devoted to this project. But we want especially to thank Paul Buhle, Meryl Fingrutd, Bob Greene, and Michele Hoffnung.

About the Authors

Chris Freitag

JOHN MACK FARAGHER

John Mack Faragher is Arthur Unobskey Professor of American History at Yale University. Born in Arizona and raised in southern California, he received his B.A. at the University of California, Riverside, and his Ph.D. at Yale University. He is the author of *Women and Men on the Overland Trail* (1979), which won the Frederick Jackson Turner Award of the Organization of American Historians, *Sugar Creek: Life on the Illinois Prairie* (1986), and *Daniel Boone: The Life and Legend of an American Pioneer* (1992). He is also the editor of *The American Heritage Encyclopedia* (1988).

MARI JO BUHLE

Mari Jo Buhle is Professor of American Civilization and History at Brown University, specializing in American women's history. She is the author of *Women and American Socialism, 1870–1920* (1981) and *Feminism and its Discontents: A Century of Struggle with Psychoanalysis* (1998). She is also coeditor of *Encyclopedia of the American Left*, second edition (1998). She currently serves as an editor of a series of books on women and American history for the University of Illinois Press. Professor Buhle held a fellowship (1991–1996) from the John D. and Catherine T. MacArthur Foundation.

DANIEL CZITROM

Daniel Czitrom is Professor and Chair of History at Mount Holyoke College. He received his B.A. from the State University of New York at Binghamton and his M.A. and Ph.D. from the University of Wisconsin, Madison. He is the author of *Media and the American Mind: From Morse to McLuhan* (1982), which won the First Books Award of the American Historical Association. His scholarly articles and essays have appeared in the *Journal of American History, American Quarterly, The Massachusetts Review*, and *The Atlantic*. He is currently completing *Mysteries of the City: Culture, Politics, and the Underworld in New York, 1870–1920*.

SUSAN H. ARMITAGE

Susan H. Armitage is Professor of History at Washington State University. She earned her Ph.D. from the London School of Economics and Political Science. Among her many publications on western women's history are three coedited books, *The Women's West* (1987), *So Much To Be Done: Women on the Mining and Ranching Frontier* (1991), and *Writing the Range: Race, Class, and Culture in the Women's West* (1997). She is the editor of *Frontiers: A Journal of Women's Studies*.

C O M M U N I T Y & D I V E R S I T Y

One of the most characteristic features of our country has always been its astounding variety. The American people include the descendants of native Indians, colonial Europeans, Africans, and migrants from virtually every country and continent. Indeed, as we enter the new century the nation is absorbing a tide of immigrants from Latin America and Asia that rivals the great tide of immigrants from eastern and southern Europe that arrived at the beginning of the twentieth century. Moreover, the United States is one of the world's largest nations, incorporating more than 3.6 million square miles of territory. The struggle to make a nation out of our many communities is what much of American history is all about. That is the story told in this book.

Every human society is made up of communities. A community is a set of relationships that link men, women, and their families into a coherent social whole, more than the sum of its parts. In a community people develop the capacity for unified action. In a community people learn, often through trial and error, how to transform and adapt to their environment. The sentiment that binds the members of a community together is the origin of group identity and ethnic pride. In the making of history, communities are far more important than even the greatest of leaders, for the community is the institution most capable of passing a distinctive historical tradition to future generations.

Communities bind people together in multiple ways. They can be as small as the local neighborhood, in which people maintain face-to-face relations, or as large as the imagined entity of the nation. This book examines American history from the perspective of community life—an ever widening frame that has included larger and larger groups of Americans.

Networks of kinship and friendship, and connections across generations and among families, establish the bonds essential to community life. Shared feelings about values and history establish the basis for common identity. In communities, people find the power to act collectively in their own interest. But American communities frequently took shape as a result of serious conflicts among groups, and within communities there often has been significant fighting among competing groups or classes. Thus the term community,

John L. Krimmel, Painting, (1786–1821), oil on canvas, H. 16⅜" x W. 25⅝". (AN:59.131) Courtesy, Winterthur Museum, *Election Day in Philadelphia* (1815).

John L. Krimmel, Election Day in Philadelphia (1815).

as we employ it here, includes tension and discord as well as harmony and agreement.

For years there have been persistent laments about the "loss of community" in modern America. But community has not disappeared—it is continually being reinvented. Until the late eighteenth century, community was defined primarily by space and local geography. The closer one gets to the present, the more community is reshaped by new and powerful historical forces such as the nation state, the marketplace, industrialization, the corporation, mass immigration, and electronic media.

The American Communities vignettes that open each chapter of *Out of Many* reflect this shift. Most of the vignettes in the pre–Civil War chapters focus on geographically-defined communities, such as the ancient Indian city at Cahokia, or the experiment in industrial urban planning in early nineteenth-century Lowell, Massachusetts. In the post–Civil War chapters different and more modern kinds of communities make their appearance—the community of Hollywood movie audiences in the 1920s, or the "virtual communities" made possible by new computer technologies. Also, the nearer we get to the present, the more we find Americans struggling to balance their membership in several communities simultaneously. These are defined not simply by local spatial arrangements, but by categories as varied as racial and ethnic groups, occupations, political affiliations, and consumer preferences.

Ralph Fasanella, Sunday Afternoon—Stickball Game, 1953

The title for our book was suggested by the Latin phrase selected by John Adams, Benjamin Franklin, and Thomas Jefferson for the Great Seal of the United States: *E Pluribus Unum*—"Out of Many Comes Unity." These men understood that unity could not be imposed by a powerful central authority but had to develop out of mutual respect among Americans of different backgrounds. The revolutionary leadership expressed the hope that such respect could grow on the basis of a remarkable proposition: "We hold these truths to be self-evident, that all men are created equal; that they are endowed by their Creator with certain unalienable rights; that among these are life, liberty, and the pursuit of happiness." The national government of the United States would preserve local and state authority but would guarantee individual rights. The nation would be strengthened by guarantees of difference.

Out of Many—that is the promise of America, and the premise of this book. The underlying dialectic of American history, we believe, is that as a people

William Hahn, *Market Scene, Sansome Street, San Francisco.* Crocker Art Musuem, Sacramento, CA. E.B. Crocker Collection.

William Hahn, Market Scene, Sansome Street, San Francisco.

we need to locate our national *unity* in the celebration of the *differences* that exist among us; these differences can be our strength, as long as we affirm the promise of the Declaration. Protecting the "right to be different," in other words, is absolutely fundamental to the continued existence of democracy, and that right is best protected by the existence of strong and vital communities. We are bound together as a nation by the ideal of local and cultural differences protected by our common commitment to the values of our revolution.

Today—with the many social and cultural conflicts that abound in the United States—some Americans have lost faith in that vision. But our history shows that the promise of American unity has always been problematic. Centrifugal forces have been powerful in the American past, and at times the country has seemed about to fracture into its component parts. Our transformation from a collection of groups and regions into a nation has been marked by painful and often violent struggles. Our past is filled with conflicts between Indians and colonists, masters and slaves, Patriots and Loyalists, Northerners and Southerners, Easterners and Westerners, capitalists and workers, and sometimes the government and the people. Americans often appear to be little more than a contentious collection of peoples with conflicting interests, divided by region and background, race and class.

Our most influential leaders also sometimes suffered a crisis of faith in the American project of "liberty and justice for all." Thomas Jefferson not only believed in the inferiority of African Americans, but he feared that immigrants from outside the Anglo-American tradition might "warp and bias" the development of the nation "and render it a heterogeneous, incoherent, distracted mass." We have not always lived up to the American promise, and there is a dark side to our history. It took the bloodiest war in American history to secure the human rights of African Americans, and the struggle for full equality continues nearly a century and a half later. During the great influx of immigrants in the early twentieth century, fears much like Jefferson's led to movements to *Americanize* the foreign born by forcing them, in the words of one leader, "to give up the languages, customs, and methods of life which they have brought with them across the ocean, and adopt instead the language, habits, and customs of this country, and the general standards and ways of American living." Similar thinking motivated Congress at various times to bar the immigration of Asians and other ethnic groups into the country, and to force assimilation on American Indians by denying them the freedom to practice their religion or even to speak their own language. Such calls for restrictive unity resound in our own day.

But other Americans have argued for a more idealistic version of *Americanization*. "What is the American, this new man?" asked the French immigrant Michel Crévecoeur in 1782. "A strange mixture of blood which you will find in no other country," he answered; in America, "individuals of all nations are melted into a new race of men." A century later Crévecoeur was echoed by historian Frederick Jackson Turner, who believed that "in the crucible of the frontier, the immigrants were Americanized, liberated, and fused into a mixed race, English in neither nationality nor characteristics. The process has gone on from the early days to our own."

The process by which diverse communities have come to share a set of common American values is one of the most fundamental aspects of our history. It did not occur, however, because of compulsory *Americanization* programs, but because of free public education, popular participation in democratic politics, and the impact of popular culture. Contemporary America does have a common culture: we laugh at the same television sitcoms and share the same aspirations to own a home and send our children to college—all unique American traits.

To a degree that too few Americans appreciate, this common culture resulted from a complicated process of mutual discovery that took place when different ethnic and regional groups encountered one another. Consider just one small and unique aspect of our culture, the barbecue. Americans have been barbecuing since before the beginning of written history. Early settlers adopted this technique of cooking from the Indians—the word itself comes from a native term for a framework of sticks over a fire on which meat was slowly cooked. Colonists typically barbecued pork, fed on Indian corn. African slaves lent their own touch by introducing the use of hot sauces. Thus the ritual that is a part of nearly every American family's Fourth of July silently celebrates the heritage of diversity that went into making our common culture.

The American educator John Dewey recognized this diversity early in this century. "The genuine American, the typical American is himself a hyphenated character," he declared, "international and interracial in his make-up." The point about our "hyphenated character," Dewey believed, "is to see to it that the hyphen connects instead of separates." We, the authors of *Out of Many*, share Dewey's perspective on American history. "Creation comes from the impact of diversity," wrote the American philosopher Horace Kallen. We also endorse Kallen's vision of the American promise: "A democracy of nationalities, cooperating voluntarily and autonomously through common institutions, . . . a multiplicity in a unity, an orchestration of mankind." And now, let the music begin.

CHAPTER ONE

A CONTINENT OF VILLAGES

TO 1500

Painting of aerial view of Cahokia Mounds circa A.D. 1100–1150. By William R. Iseminger, Cahokia Mounds State Historic Site.

Chapter Outline

SETTLING THE CONTINENT

Who Are the Indian People?

Migration from Asia

Clovis: The First American Technology

THE BEGINNING OF REGIONAL CULTURES

Hunting Traditions of the Plains and Forests

Desert Culture in Western America

Forest Efficiency

THE DEVELOPMENT OF FARMING

Mexico

The Resisted Revolution

Increasing Social Complexity

The Religions of Foragers and Farmers

Earliest Farmers of the Southwest

The Anasazis

Farmers of the Eastern Woodlands

Mississippian Society

The Politics of Warfare and Violence

NORTH AMERICA ON THE EVE OF COLONIZATION

The Indian Population of America

The Southwest

The South

The Northeast

AMERICAN COMMUNITIES

Cahokia: Thirteenth-Century Life on the Mississippi

As the sun rose over the rich floodplain, the people of the riverbank city set about their daily tasks. Some went to shops where they manufactured tools, crafted pottery, worked metal, or fashioned ornamental jewelry—goods destined to be exchanged in the far corners of the continent. Others left their densely populated neighborhoods for the outlying countryside, where in the summer heat they worked the seemingly endless fields that fed the city. From almost any point people could see the great temple that rose from the center of their city—the temple where priests in splendid costumes acted out public rituals of death and renewal.

This thirteenth-century city was not in preindustrial Europe but in North America. It flourished long before the first European explorer arrived. Its residents lived and worked on the alluvial soil of the Mississippi River, across from present-day St. Louis, at a place archaeologists have named Cahokia. In its heyday, in the mid-1200s, Cahokia was an urban cluster of perhaps 30,000 people. Its farm fields were abundant with corn, beans, and pumpkins, crops no European had ever seen. The temple, a huge earthwork pyramid, covered fifteen acres at its base and rose as high as a ten-story building. On top were the sacred residences of chiefs and priests, who dressed in elaborate headdresses made from the plumage of American birds.

By the fourteenth century, Cahokia had been abandoned, but its great central temple mound and dozens of smaller ones in the surrounding area, as well as hundreds more throughout the Mississippi Valley, remained to puzzle the European immigrants who resettled the valley in the eighteenth and nineteenth centuries. Treasure seekers plundered the mounds, and most were eventually dynamited and plowed under for farmland. Only a few were saved, inside parks or estates. Cahokia's central mound survived because in the nineteenth century its summit became the site of a monastery, now long gone.

The Europeans who first explored and excavated these mounds were convinced they were the ruins of a vanished civilization, but could not believe they were the work of Native Americans. The first comprehensive study of Cahokia, published in 1848 under the sponsorship of the Smithsonian Institution, noted that "the mound-builders were an agricultural people, considerably advanced in arts, manners, habits, and religion." But because "Indians were hunters averse to labor, and not known to have constructed any works approaching [the] skillfulness of design or [the] magnitude" of Cahokia, surely these wonders must have been constructed by a "lost race."

The Smithsonian scientists were wrong. Thanks to modern archaeology and anthropology we now know that it was the ancestors of contemporary Native Americans who began to construct massive earthworks in the Mississippi Valley as early as 1300 B.C.E. (Before the Common Era) at a place called Poverty Point in Louisiana. The vast urban complex of Cahokia flourished from the tenth to the fourteenth century and at its height stretched six miles along the Mississippi. Its residents were not nomadic hunters but farmers, members of an agricultural society—which archaeologists call the Mississippian—that had developed highly productive techniques of cultivation. Hundreds of acres of crops fed the people of Cahokia, which was the most populated urban community north of the Valley of Mexico. Mississippian farmers constructed ingenious raised plots of land on which they heaped compost in wide ridges for improved drainage and protection from unseasonable frosts. To their square houses of wood and mud they attached pens in which they kept flocks of domesticated turkeys and, perhaps, small herds of young deer that they slaughtered for meat and hides. Cahokia was at the center of a long-distance trading system that linked it to Indian towns over a vast area. Cahokia's specialized artisans were renowned for the manufacture of high-quality flint hoes, exported throughout the Mississippi Valley. Copper came to the city from Lake Superior, mica from the southern Appalachians, conch shells from the Atlantic coast.

The archaeological evidence suggests that Cahokia was emerging as a state supported by tribute and taxation. Like the awe-inspiring public works of early urban societies in other parts of the world—the pyramids of ancient Egypt, the acropolis of Athens—the great temple mound of Cahokia reflected the city's wealth and power. The great mound and other colossal public works at Cahokia were monuments of a society dominated by an elite class of priests and rulers. From their residences and temples atop the mound the city's elite could look down on their awe-struck subjects. There is no indication, however, that the Mississippian peoples had developed a system of writing that would permit us to glimpse their own version of their history.

As the words of the 1848 Smithsonian report on Cahokia make clear, the stereotypical view of Indians that emerged in the nineteenth and twentieth centuries was that they all lived in isolated hunting bands. But the great variety of lifeways Indian peoples developed in their long occupation of North America belies this stereotype. All Native Americans lived in strong vibrant communities that ranged from small hunting bands to large agricultural cities like Cahokia and splendid imperial capitals like that of the Aztecs of Mexico. Before the coming of the Europeans, North America was, as one historian phrases it, "a continent of villages," a land with thousands of local communities. Over many centuries the Indian peoples of North America developed a variety of community types, each with its own system of family and social organization, each integrated with its natural surroundings. The wonders of Cahokia are but one aspect of the little-understood history of the Indians of the Americas.

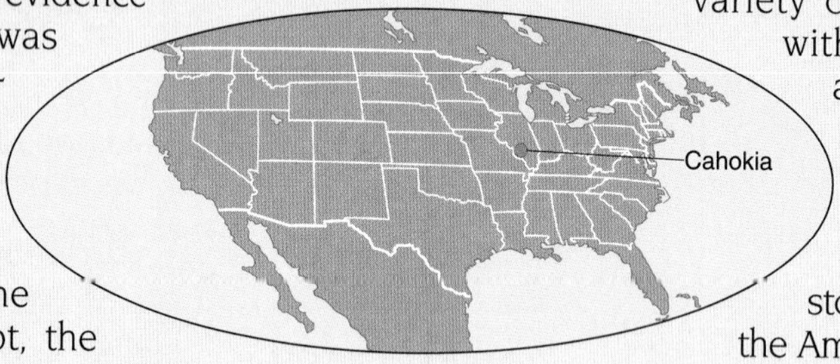

Key Topics

- The peopling of the Americas by migrants from Asia
- The adaptation of native cultures to the distinctive regions of North America
- The increase in complexity of many native societies following the development of farming
- The nature of Indian cultures in the three major regions of European invasion and settlement

SETTLING THE CONTINENT

"Why do you call us Indians?" a Massachusetts native complained to Puritan missionary John Eliot in 1646. More than a hundred years earlier, Christopher Columbus had mistaken the Arawaks of the Caribbean for the people of the East Indies and called them *Indios*. By the middle of the sixteenth century this Spanish word had passed into English as "Indians" and was widely used to refer to all the native peoples of the Americas. Today anthropologists often use the term "Amerindians," and many people prefer "Native Americans." But most indigenous Americans refer to themselves as "Indian people."

Who Are the Indian People?

At the time of their first contacts with Europeans, near the close of the fifteenth century, the native inhabitants of the Western Hemisphere represented more than 2,000 distinct cultures, spoke hundreds of different languages, and lived and worked in scores of different environments. Just as the term "European" includes such different peoples as the English, French, and Spanish, so "Indian" covers an enormous diversity of peoples. For example, the people of the mid-Atlantic coast called themselves *Lenni Lenape*, meaning "true men"; those of the northern Great Plains were *Lakota*, or "the allies"; and the hunters of the Southwest used the name *Dine* (pronounced "dee-nay"), meaning simply "the people." Interestingly, Europeans came to know these three groups by rather different names: the *Delawares* (from the principal river of the mid-Atlantic region), the *Sioux*, and the *Apaches* (both of which meant "enemy" in the language of a neighboring tribe).

Once Europeans realized that the Americas were in fact a "New World" rather than part of the Asian continent, they began debating how people might have moved there from Europe and Asia, where the Judeo-Christian Bible indicated human life had begun. Over the succeeding centuries writers proposed elaborate theories of transoceanic migrations that linked native Americans variously to ancient Greeks, Carthaginians, Tartars, Chinese, and Welsh; one theory even held they were the survivors of the mythical Atlantis. Common to all these theories was a belief that the Americas had been populated for a few thousand years at most and that native American societies were the degenerate offspring of a far superior Old World culture.

A number of Spanish observers thought more deeply about the question of Indian origins. In 1590 Joseph de Acosta reasoned that because Old World animals were present in the Americas, they must have crossed by a land bridge that could have been used by humans as well. A few years later, Enrico Martín speculated that since no such land passage had been found between the Americas and Europe, it must exist in the unexplored far northwest of the continent, and thus the people using it must have been Asian. In the 1650s Bernabé Cobo, who had lived most of his life in the Caribbean, argued that the great variety of native American languages showed that Indian peoples must have lived on the continent for centuries. But, he continued, their physical similarities suggested that "it was doubtless one nation or family of men which passed to people this land." Here were the principal elements of the migration hypothesis: Indian peoples were descended from a common stock of Asian migrants, they arrived by way of a northwestern land passage, and they had experienced a long and independent history in the Americas.

Certainly no single physical type characterized all the native peoples of the Americas. Although most had straight, black hair and dark, almond-shaped eyes, their skin ranged in color from mahogany to light brown and few fit the "yellow men" or "redskin" descriptions given them by colonists and settlers of the eighteenth and nineteenth centuries. Indeed, it was only when Europeans compared Indian peoples with natives of other continents, such as Africans, that they seemed similar enough to be classified as a group.

Migration from Asia

The theory most widely held today is that the native American peoples moved to this hemisphere from Asia some 25,000 to 30,000 years ago—about the

OVERVIEW

Origins of Some Indian Tribal Names

Cherokee	A corruption of the Choctaw *chiluk-ki,* meaning "cave people," an allusion to the many caves in the Cherokee homeland. The Cherokees called themselves *Ani-Yun-Wiya,* or "real people."
Cheyenne	From the Sioux *Sha-hiyena,* "people of strange speech." The Cheyennes called themselves *Dzi-tsistas,* meaning "our people."
Hopi	A shortening of the Hopis' own name for themselves, *Hópitu,* which means "peaceful ones."
Mohawk	From the Algonquian *Mohawaúuck,* meaning "man-eaters." The Mohawks called themselves *Kaniengehaga,* "people of the place of the flint."
Pawnee	From the Pawnee term *paríki,* which describes a distinctive style of dressing the hair with paint and fat to make it stand erect like a horn. The Pawnees called themselves *Chahik-sichahiks,* "men of men."

time that Japan and the countries of Scandinavia were being settled. Evidence supporting this view includes a common dental pattern found among the most ancient human fossils in the Americas and those in northeastern Asia. The most distinctive marker of modern native American peoples is blood type, for although the vast majority have type O blood and a few have type A, almost none have type B. Because modern Asian populations exhibit all three blood types, scientists have postulated that migrations to the New World took place before the evolution of type B, which they believe occurred about 30,000 years ago. Studies of genetic evolution suggest that it took at least 20,000 years to evolve the variety of physical traits found among native American populations today. And modern linguists, agreeing essentially with Cobo's observation, cited earlier, estimate that it would require about 25,000 years to develop, from a common base, the nearly 500 distinct languages of the Americas.

At the time of the proposed migration from Asia to the Americas, the Northern Hemisphere was experiencing the Ice Age that characterized the geological epoch known as the Pleistocene. Huge glaciers locked up massive volumes of water, and sea levels were as much as 300 feet lower than they are today. Asia and North America were joined by a huge subcontinent of ice-free, treeless grassland, 750 miles wide from north to south. Geologists have named this area Beringia, from the Bering Straits. Summers there were warm, winters were cold, dry, and almost snowfree. This was a perfect environment for large mammals—mammoth and mastodon, bison, horse, reindeer, camel, and saiga (a goatlike antelope).

Beringia also attracted Stone Age hunter-gatherers who lived in small, nomadic bands and subsisted almost entirely on these animals. The animals provided them not only with food but with hides for clothing and shelter, dung for fuel, and bones for tools and weapons. Hunting bands were driven to expand their territories by the powerful force of their own population growth and the pressure it placed on local resources. Today's few remaining hunting-and-gathering peoples have an annual population growth rate of 0.5 percent, which would double their populations only every 140 years. Ancient Asian hunters, with seemingly limitless open country into which they could move, likely had growth rates that were much higher, and their expansion into new territory was correspondingly rapid. Following the big game, and accompanied by a husky-like species of dog, hunting bands gradually penetrated Beringia, moving as far east as the Yukon River basin of northern Canada.

Until recently most scientists dated the first migrations at about 15,000 years ago, but there is growing evidence that people were moving from Asia considerably earlier. Because much of Beringia was later submerged beneath rising seas, definitive archaeological evidence of migration from Asia is difficult to find. No fossil human bones have yet been uncovered there. But in 1966, field excavations in the Yukon basin uncovered what appeared to be fossilized bone tools estimated to be 27,000 years old. Fieldworkers found that these tools fit perfectly into their hands and had worn edges exactly where one would expect them to be. Later digs in the area produced the jawbones of several dogs estimated to be at least 30,000 years old. The most persuasive evidence for an earlier migration,

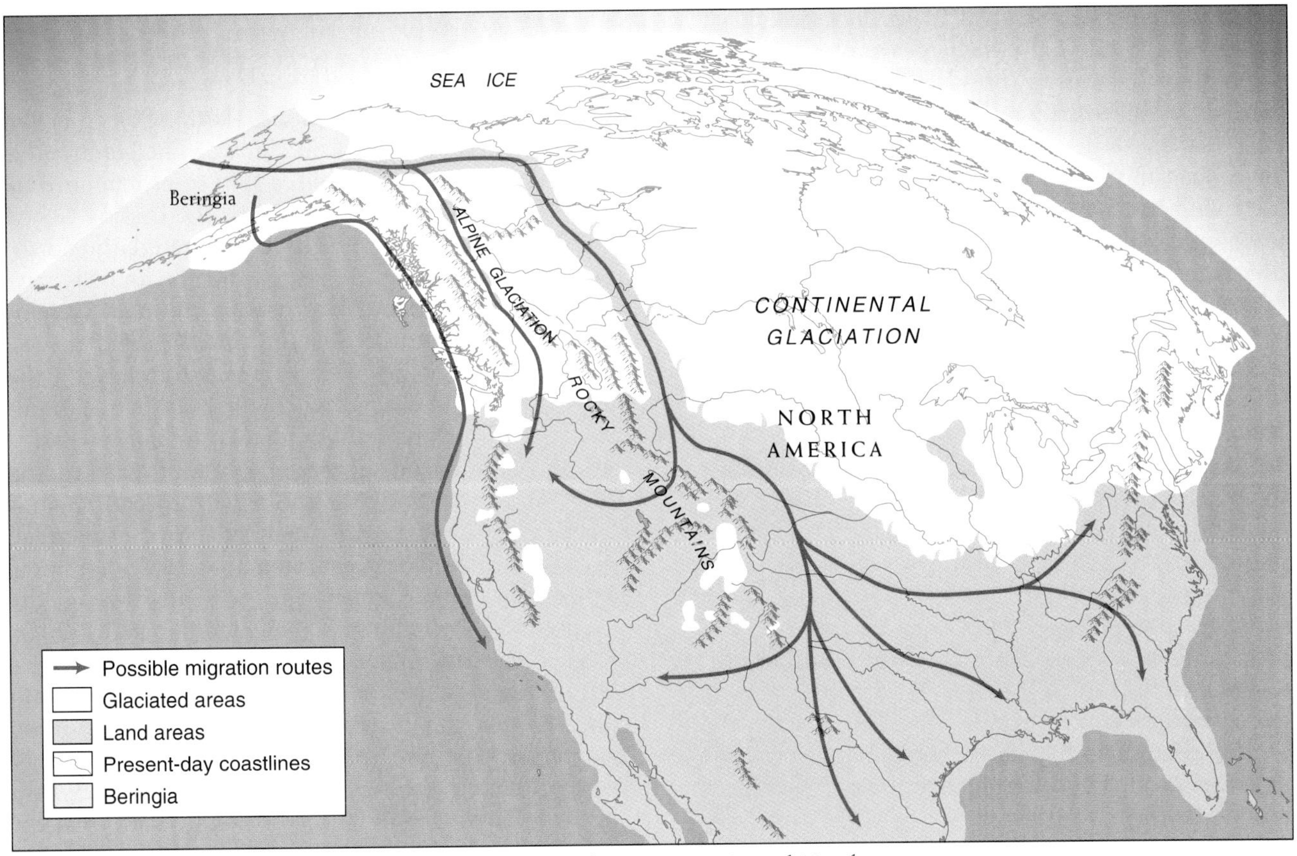

Migration Routes from Asia to America *During the Ice Age, Asia and North America were joined where the Bering Straits are today, forming a migration route for hunting peoples. Either by boat along the coast, or through a narrow corridor between the huge northern glaciers, these migrants began making their way to the heartland of the continent as much as 30,000 years ago.*

however, comes from the other end of the hemisphere, in South America. Archaeologists working at separate sites in the Amazon basin and in southern Chile in the early 1990s found striking evidence of human toolmaking, house-building, and rock painting that date from at least 12,000 years ago. The ancestors of those peoples must have crossed Beringia many thousands of years before. The consensus today is that the migration from Asia probably began about 30,000 years ago.

Huge glaciers to the south of Beringia blocked passage during most of the last Ice Age, but occasionally a narrow land corridor opened up along the eastern base of the Rocky Mountains. As early as 25,000 years ago, hunting bands following this corridor south could have emerged onto the northern Great Plains—a hunter's paradise teeming with animals of great variety. Migrants probably also moved south in boats, following the Pacific coastline. Rapid population growth would have permitted these groups to populate the entire Western Hemisphere in a few thousand years. Remarkably, the oral traditions of many Indian peoples depict a long journey from a distant place of origin to a new homeland. Europeans have recorded the Pima people of the Southwest singing this "Emergence Song":

> *This is the White Land; we arrive singing,*
> *Headdresses waving in the breeze.*
> *We have come! We have come!*
> *The land trembles with our dancing and singing.*

Clovis: The First American Technology

The earliest tools found at North American archaeological sites, crude choppers and scrapers made of stone or bone, are similar to artifacts from the same period found in Europe or Asia. About 12,000 years ago, however, a much more sophisticated style of toolmaking seems to have developed. Named after the site of its discovery in 1932, near Clovis, New Mexico, the Clovis tradition was a powerful new and more sophisticated technology, unlike anything found in the archaeology of the Old World. In the years since the initial discovery, archaeologists have unearthed Clovis artifacts at sites ranging from Montana to Mexico,

Nova Scotia to Arizona. All these finds date back to within one or two thousand years of one another, suggesting that Clovis spread quickly throughout the continent. This discovery has led, in turn, to speculation that the settlement of North America might then have been entering its final phase, as the continent filled with people. Scientists theorize that it was to feed their expanding populations that communities were driven to find a more efficient way to hunt and developed this greatly improved technology.

The evidence suggests that Clovis users were mobile peoples who traveled in communities numbering perhaps thirty to fifty individuals from several interrelated families. They returned to the same hunting camps year after year, migrating seasonally within territories of several hundred square miles. Near Delbert, Nova Scotia, archaeologists discovered the floors of ten tents arranged in a semicircle, their doors opening south to avoid the prevailing northerly winds. Both this camp and others found throughout the continent were placed so that they overlooked watering places that would attract game. Clovis blades have been excavated amid the remains of mammoth, camel, horse, giant armadillo, and sloth. Hunters apparently drove these animals into shallow bogs, killed them with spears, and butchered them on the spot.

These Clovis points are typical of thousands that archaeologists have found at sites all over the continent, dating from a period about 12,000 years ago. When inserted in a spear shaft, these three- to six-inch fluted points made effective weapons for hunting mammoth and other big game.

THE BEGINNING OF REGIONAL CULTURES

About 15,000 years ago a global warming trend began to alter the North American climate. The giant continental glaciers began to melt, a shift so pronounced by 8000 B.C.E. that it is used to mark the passing of the Pleistocene epoch. As the glaciers retreated, the northern latitudes were colonized by plants, animals, and humans. Meltwater created the lake and river systems of today and raised the level of the surrounding seas, flooding Beringia as well as vast stretches of the Atlantic and Gulf coasts and creating fertile tidal pools and offshore fishing banks. These monumental transformations produced new patterns of wind, rainfall, and temperature, reshaping the ecology of the entire continent and producing the distinct North American regions of today. The great integrating force of a single continental climate faded, and, with its passing, the continental Clovis culture fragmented into many different regional patterns.

Regions have ever since played an important role in American history. Variations in climate and geography combine to form the distinct regions of North America: the Arctic and Subarctic, the Northwest, the Great Plains, the Northeast, California, the Great Basin, the Southwest, the South, the Caribbean, and Mexico. Within these regions, human communities have had to adapt to nature, evolving their own ways of life. Indian peoples were the first in North America to embark on the long journey toward regionally distinct cultures, developing a wide variety of food sources to support their growing populations.

Hunting Traditions of the Plains and Forests

One of the most important effects of this massive climatological shift was the stress it placed on the big-game animals best suited to an Ice Age environment. The archaeological record details the extinction of thirty-two classes of large New World animals, including not only the mammoth and mastodon but the horse and camel, both of which evolved in America and then migrated to Asia across Beringia. It seems likely that lowered reproduction and survival rates of large animals forced hunting bands to intensify their efforts, and the combined effects of warmer climate and increased hunting eventually led to what some archaeologists have called the "Pleistocene Overkill."

As the other large-mammal populations declined, hunters on the Great Plains concentrated on the herds of American bison, more commonly called buffalo. To hunt these animals people needed a weapon they could throw quickly with great accuracy and velocity at fast-moving targets over distances of as much as a hundred yards. The Folsom technology, a refinement of the Clovis tradition, featured points that were more delicate and lighter in weight, but deadlier.

Folsom points were named for the site of their first major excavation, at Folsom, New Mexico, where the tools uncovered were judged to be about 10,000 years old. In one dramatic find, a Folsom point was discovered embedded between the fossilized ribs of an ancient species of bison. Hunters probably hurled the lances to which these points were attached with wooden spear-throwers, achieving far greater velocity than they could with their arms alone. By 7000 B.C.E., Folsom had evolved into a technology that archaeologists call Plano, and the points are often found with grinding tools suitable for processing vegetable foods. This association indicates that peoples of the Great Plains were in the process of developing a varied diet.

Archaeological finds also suggest the growing complexity of early Indian communities. Folsom and Plano hunters frequently stampeded herds of bison or other animals into canyon traps or over cliffs. At one such kill site in southeastern Colorado, estimated to be 8,500 years old, archaeologists uncovered the remains of nearly 200 bison that had been slaughtered and then systematically butchered on a single occasion. This job would have required at least 150 men and women and a sophisticated division of labor, which in turn probably involved the cooperation of a number of communities. Taking food in such quantities indicates a knowledge of basic preservation techniques: these people must have been among the first to make jerky, or dried strips of meat, and pemmican, a mixture of dried meat, animal fat, and berries that can keep into the winter when stored in hide containers. These characteristic products of the Great Plains later became the staple foods of European fur traders in the North American West.

The passing of the Pleistocene epoch and the submergence of Beringia were preceded by a second wave of Beringia migrants—the Athapascans, or Na-Dene people. After entering North America they moved southeast from Alaska, following the melting glacier that had formerly blocked passage. From 7,000 to 4,000 years ago, they settled the forests of the continent's Northwest. Although they eventually adopted a technology for making weapons and tools similar to that of neighboring peoples, the Na-Dene maintained a separate cultural and linguistic identity. The ancestors of the Athapascan-speaking Navajos and Apaches later migrated from this northern country, journeying across the Great Plains to the Southwest.

In a final migration from Asia that took place about 5,000 years ago, the Inupiat—more commonly known as Eskimos—and the Aleuts, other hunting peoples, crossed the flooded Bering Straits by boat. The Eskimos colonized the polar coasts of the Arctic, the Aleuts the Aleutian Islands (later named for them) and the southern coast of Alaska.

When in 1927 archaeologists at Folsom, New Mexico, uncovered this dramatic example of a projectile point embedded in the ribs of a long-extinct species of bison it was the first proof that Indians had been in North America for many thousands of years.

Desert Culture in Western America

As the glaciers began to retreat, people developed new ways of finding food. During what archaeologists call the Archaic period (which corresponds to the late phases of the Stone Age in Eurasia and Africa), varying modes of subsistence evolved in different regions of North America. Between about 10,000 and 2,500 years ago, desert foraging began in the arid Great Basin, fishing along the Northwest coast of the Pacific, and hunting and gathering in the forests of the humid eastern half of the continent.

In the Great Basin of present-day Utah and Nevada the warming trend associated with the end of the Ice Age created a desert where once there had been enormous inland seas. Here, Indian people developed Desert Culture, a way of life based on the pursuit of small game and intensified foraging for plant foods. Small communities or bands of desert foragers migrated seasonally within a small range. They collected seeds,

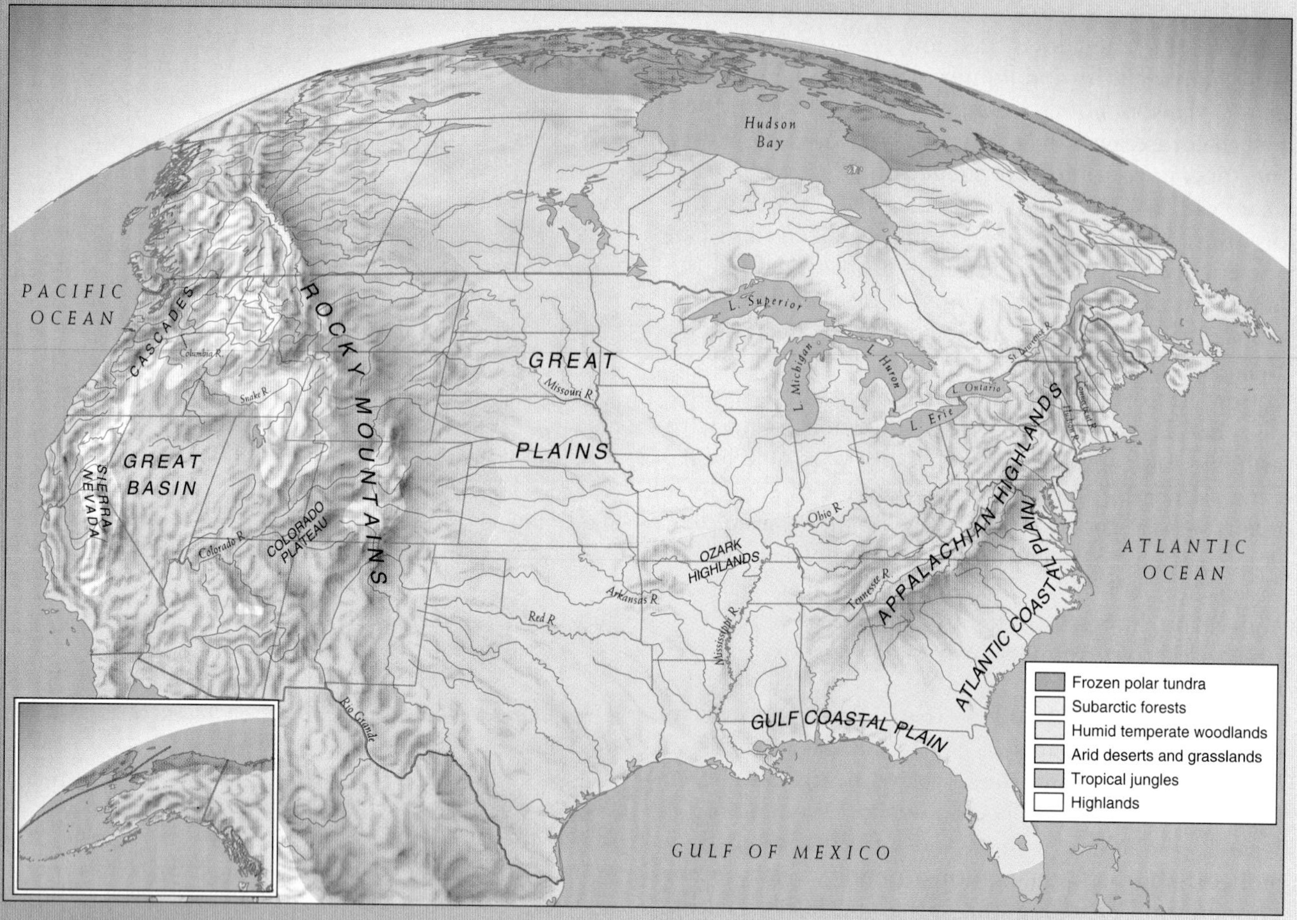

The Regions of Native North America

Occupying more than a third of the continent, the United States is alone among the world's nations in encompassing all five general classes of global climate: tropical jungles, arid deserts and grasslands, temperate woodlands, subarctic forests, and frozen polar tundra. The country also contains some of the world's largest lakes, most extensive grasslands, and mightiest rivers.

All peoples must adjust their diet, shelter, and other material aspects of their lives to the physical conditions of the world around them; thus a knowledge of the way in which geography and

fiber, and prickly pear from the yucca one season, then moved to highland mesas to gather grass seed, acorns, juniper berries, and piñon nuts, and next to mountain streams to spear and net fish. This strategy required considerable skill in handicrafts: fiber baskets for collecting, pitch-lined baskets for cooking, nets and traps, and stone grinders for processing seeds and nuts, as well as stone knives, hammers, and mauls.

Archaeologists know that desert foragers lived in caves and rock shelters, for their artifacts are found there today. In addition to stone tools these artifacts include objects of wood, hide, and fiber, wonderfully preserved for thousands of years in the dry climate. The Desert Culture persisted into the nineteenth century among modern Shoshoni and Ute communities. Although these people were once scornfully labeled "Diggers" because of their practice of gathering edible roots and were ridiculed for their "primitive" life ways, we now appreciate the very sophisticated adjustments they made to a harsh environment.

Descriptions of the culture of the modern Shoshonis suggest that the force of community was strong among the people of the desert. An emphasis on sharing and gift giving, the condemnation of hoarding, and the limitations posed by a nomadic lifestyle on the accumulation of material goods prevented individuals or families from acquiring excessive wealth. Thus, desert communities were characterized by general social equality. Decisions were made by consensus among the adults, and lead-

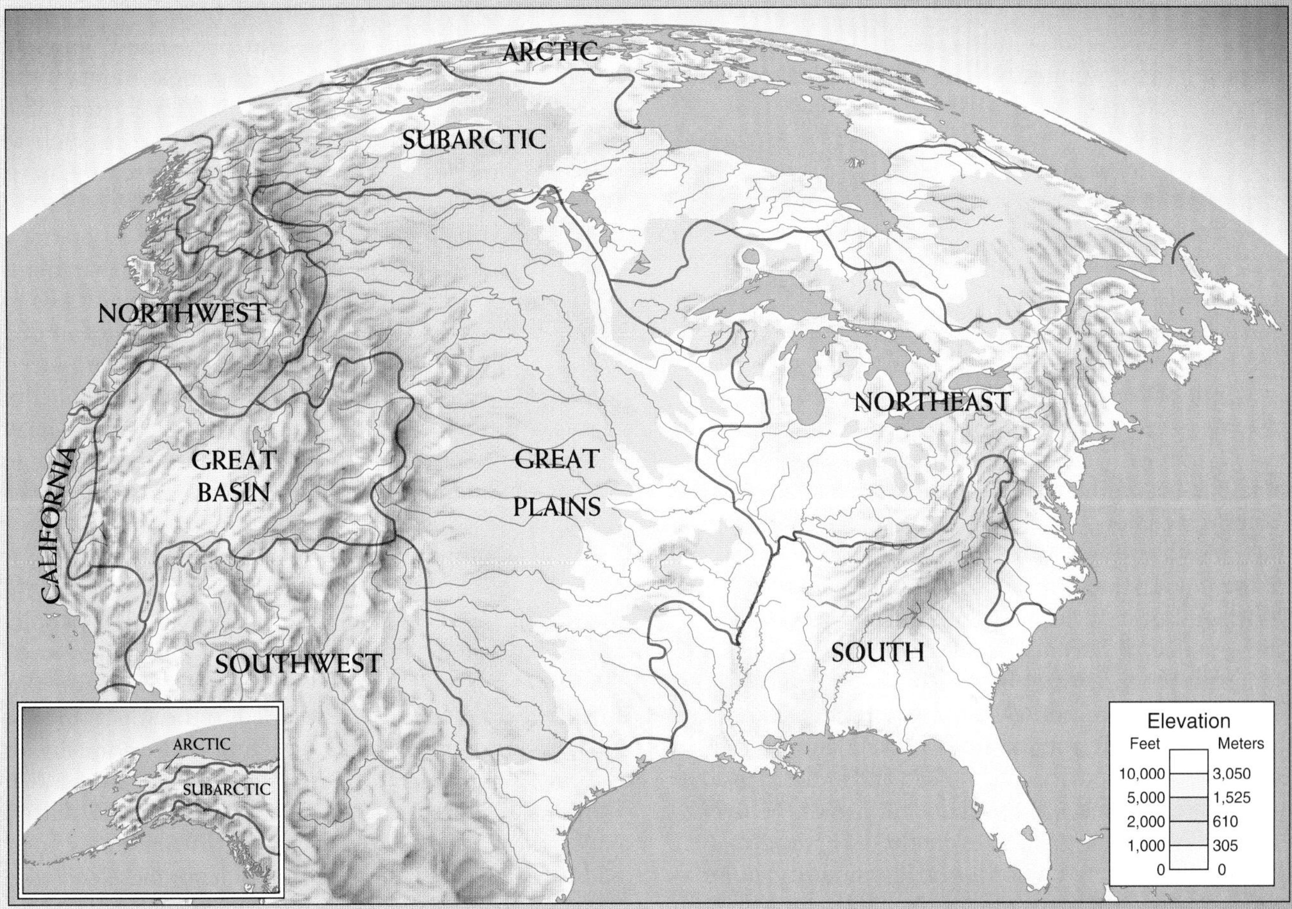

climate combine to form regions is a prerequisite to understanding the cultures of the peoples of America. Using the concept of "culture areas," anthropologists divide the continent into several fundamental regions, which have played an important role in the history of the continent for the past 10,000 years.

The Indian peoples of North America were first to develop distinct cultures suited to the regions in which they lived. Just as regions shaped the lifeways and history of Indian peoples, after the coming of the Europeans they nurtured the development of regional American cultures.

ership tended to be informal, based on achievement and reputation. The men of one band generally married women from another, and wives came to live with the people of their husbands, creating important linkages between groups that contributed to the sense of shared ethnic identity.

The innovative practices of the Desert Culture gradually spread from the Great Basin to the Great Plains and the Southwest, where foraging techniques began to supplement intensive hunting. About 6,000 years ago, archaeologists estimate, colonists from the Great Basin carried Desert Culture farther west to California. There, in the natural abundance of the valleys and coasts, Indian peoples developed an economy capable of supporting some of the densest populations and the first permanently settled communities in North America. Another dynamic center in the West developed along the Northwest Pacific coast, where native American communities developed a way of life based on the exploitation of abundant fish and sea mammals. This Old Cordilleran Culture became the basis for the historic cultures of the Plateau and Northwest, which also included densely populated sedentary communities.

Forest Efficiency

Similar trends were at work east of the Mississippi. Before European settlers destroyed countless acres of forest during the eighteenth and nineteenth centuries, the whole of eastern North America was a vast woodland. Hardwoods grew in the north, southern pine in the south. The Winnebagos of the Great Lakes region sang of these forests:

Pleasant it looked,
this newly created world.
Along the entire length and breadth
of the earth, our grandmother
extended the green reflection
of her covering
and the escaping odors
were pleasant to inhale.

Archaic forest communities achieved a comfortable and secure life based on what archaeologists call "forest efficiency"—a sophisticated exploitation of their rich and diverse resources. Archaic Indian communities of the forest hunted small game and gathered seeds, nuts, roots, and other wild plant foods. They also developed the practice of burning the woodlands and prairies to stimulate the growth of berries, fruits, and edible roots. The resulting meadows and forest edge produced harvestable foods and attracted grazing animals, which were then hunted for their meat and hides. Another important resource was the abundant fish of the rivers.

Archaeological sites in the East suggest that during the late Archaic period community populations grew and settlements became increasingly permanent, providing convincing evidence of the viability of forest efficiency. The artifacts these people buried with their dead—axes, fishhooks, and animal bones with males, nut-cracking stones, beads, and pestles with females—reflect the different roles of men and women in their society.

THE DEVELOPMENT OF FARMING

The exploitation of a wide variety of food sources during the Archaic period eventually led many Indian people to develop and adopt the practice of farming. The dynamic center of this development in North America was the highlands of Mexico, from which the new technology spread north and east.

Mexico

At the end of the Stone Age, people in four different parts of the world developed farming systems, each based on a different crop: rice in Southeast Asia, wheat in West Asia, maize (or Indian corn) in Mexico, and potatoes in the Andean highlands of South America. In Mexico a great variety of other crops—most importantly beans and squash, but also tomatoes, peppers, avocados, cocoa (chocolate), and vanilla—supplemented maize. Today the two American staples—maize and potatoes—contribute more to the world's food supply than do wheat and rice. These "miracle crops" fueled the expansion of European human and livestock populations in the three centuries after 1650. Without these and other New World crops such as tobacco, American cotton, and rubber—each the basis of important new industries and markets—the history of the modern world would have been far different.

Archaeological evidence suggests that plant cultivation in the highlands of central Mexico began about 5,000 years ago. Ancient Mexicans developed crops that responded well to human care and produced larger quantities of food in a limited space than did plants occurring naturally. Maize was particularly productive; over time it was adapted to a wide range of American climates, and farming spread throughout the temperate regions of North America.

As farming became increasingly important, it radically reshaped social life. Where a foraging society might require 100 square miles to support 100 people, a farming society required only one square mile. Population growth and the need for people to remain near their fields throughout the year led to the appearance of villages and permanent architecture and eventually to the emergence of large, densely settled communities like Cahokia. Autumn harvests had to be stored during winter months, and the storage and distribution of food had to be managed. The division of labor increased with the appearance of specialists like toolmakers, craftsworkers, administrators, priests, and rulers as well as farmers and food processors. Ultimately, unequal access to wealth and power resulted in the emergence of classes.

By 1000 B.C.E., urban communities governed by permanent bureaucracies had begun to form in Mesoamerica, the region stretching from central Mexico to Central America. By the beginning of the first millenium C.E. (Common Era) highly productive farming was supporting complex urban civilizations in the Valley of Mexico (the location of present-day Mexico City), the Yucatan Peninsula, and other parts of Mesoamerica. Like many of the ancient civilizations of Asia and the Mediterranean, these Mesoamerican civilizations were characterized by the concentration of wealth and power in the hands of an elite class of priests and rulers, the construction of impressive temples and other public structures, and the development of systems of mathematics and astronomy, and several forms of hieroglyphic writing. The civilizations of Mesomerica were also marked by warfare between states and by terrifying public rituals of human sacrifice.

The great city of Teotihuacan in the Valley of Mexico, which emerged about 100 B.C.E., had a population of as many as 200,000 at the height of its power around C.E. 500. Teotihuacan's elite class of religious and political leaders controlled an elaborate state-sponsored trading system that stretched from present-day

Mesoamerican maize cultivation, as illustrated by an Aztec artist for the Florentine Codex, *a book prepared a few years after the Spanish conquest. The peoples of Mesoamerica developed a greater variety of cultivated crops than those of any other region in the world, and their agricultural productivity helped sustain one of the world's great civilizations.*

Arizona south to Central America and may have included coastal shipping connections with the pre-Inca civilizations of Peru. The city had a highly specialized division of labor. Artisans manufactured tools and produced textiles, stoneware, pottery, and obsidian blades; the bureaucratic elite collected taxes and tribute; farmers left the city every day to work the fields that fed its people; and armies of workers constructed such monumental edifices as the Pyramids of the Sun and Moon, which still dominate the city's ruins.

Teotihuacan began to decline in the sixth century, and by the eighth century it was mostly abandoned. A new empire, that of the Toltecs, dominated central Mexico from the tenth to the twelfth century. By the fourteenth century a people known as the Aztecs, migrants from the north, had settled in the Valley of Mexico and begun a dramatic expansion into a formidable imperial power (see Chapter 2).

The Mayan peoples of the Yucatan peninsula developed a group of competing city-states that flourished from about 300 B.C.E. until about C.E. 900. The achievements of the Mayans included Mesoamerica's most advanced writing and calendrical systems and a sophisticated knowledge of mathematics that included the concept of zero.

The Resisted Revolution

Historians once described the development of farming as the "Neolithic Revolution" (*neolithic* means "New, or Later, Stone Age"). They believed that agricultural communities offered such obvious advantages that neighboring peoples must have rushed to adopt this way of life. Societies that remained without a farming tradition must simply have been too "primitive" to achieve this breakthrough; vulnerability to fickle nature was the penalty for their ignorance. This interpretation was based on a scheme of social evolution that viewed human history as the story of technological progress, in which savage hunters gradually developed into civilized farmers.

But there is very little evidence to support the notion that such a "revolution" occurred during a short, critical period. The adoption of farming was a gradual process, one that required hundreds, even thousands of years. Moreover, ignorance of cultivation was never the reason that cultures failed to take up farming, for all hunter-gatherer peoples understand a great deal about plant reproduction. When the Menomini Indians of the northern forests of Wisconsin gathered wild rice, for example, they purposely allowed some of it to fall back into the water to ensure a crop for the next season, and Desert Paiutes of the Great Basin systematically irrigated stands of their favorite wild food sources.

The way today's remaining hunter-gatherers view the farming way of life is instructive. Foragers generally look upon their own method of getting food as vastly superior to any other. The food sources of desert gatherers, for example, are considerably more varied and higher in protein than those of desert farmers, whose diets concentrate almost exclusively on grains. Because foragers took advantage of natural diversity, they were also less vulnerable to climatological stress; although gathering communities frequently experienced periods of scarcity and hunger, unlike farming societies they were rarely devastated by famine. Foragers also point out that farming requires much more work. Why sweat all day in the fields producing tasteless corn, they argue, when in an hour or two one can gather enough sweet prickly pear to last a week? Indeed, rather than freeing men and women from the tyranny of nature, farming tied people to a work discipline unlike anything previously known in human history. Finally, foragers consider their migratory ways far more interesting than village life, which they claim is dull and monotonous, preferred only by those whose possessions are too cumbersome to move.

As the techniques of large-scale agriculture became available, cultures in different regions assessed its advantages and limitations. In California and the Pacific Northwest, acorn gathering or salmon fishing made the cultivation of food crops seem a waste of time. In the Great Basin, several peoples attempted to farm, but without success. Before the invention of modern irrigation systems, which require sophisticated engineering, only the Archaic Desert Culture could prevail in this harsh environment. In the neighboring Southwest, however, farming resolved certain ecological dilemmas and transformed the way of life. Like the development of more sophisticated traditions of tool manufacture, farming represented another stage in the economic intensifications that kept populations and available resources in balance. It seems that where climate favored cultivation, people tended to adopt farming as a way of increasing the production of food, thus continuing the Archaic tradition of squeezing as much productivity as they could from their environment. But in a few areas farming resulted in a truly revolutionary transformation, pushing in the direction of an urban civilization like that of central Mexico or Cahokia on the banks of the Mississippi.

Increasing Social Complexity

Farming created the basis for much greater social complexity within Indian communities. Most important were elaborate systems of kinship. Greater population density prompted families to group themselves into clans responsible for different social, political, or ritual functions. These clans became an important mechanism for binding together the people of several communities into a tribe. A tribe, based on ethnic, linguistic, and territorial unity, was led by a leader or chief from an honored clan, who was often advised by councils of elders, all of whom were also clan leaders. In all likelihood, the city of Cahokia was governed by such a system. The tribal council sometimes arbitrated disputes between individuals or families, but most crimes—theft, adultery, rape, murder—were avenged by the aggrieved kinship group itself.

The primary function of the ruling council was to supervise the economy—to see that the harvest was collected and stored and that the food stores were distributed to the clans. Differences in wealth—small by the standards of modern societies—could develop between the families of a farming tribe, but these inequalities were kept in check by a system of redistribution that followed the principles of sharing characteristic of foraging communities. Nowhere in North America did Indian cultures develop a concept of the private ownership of land. Invariably, land was a common resource of the people and thus worked collectively.

Indian communities practiced a rather strict division of labor by gender that in its details varied greatly from culture to culture. Among foraging peoples, hunting was generally the work of men, whereas the gathering of food and the maintenance of home-base camps were the responsibility of women. This pattern probably originated during the early years of the Archaic period. But the development of farming disrupted these patterns. In Mexico, where communities became almost totally dependent on crops, both men and women worked in the fields. Where hunting remained important, the older division of labor continued, with women responsible for field work. In general, however, Indian patterns contrasted in important ways with the norms of colonizing Europeans, prompting much misunderstanding. When English colonists saw Indian women working in the cornfields, for example, they thought them greatly oppressed; Indians, on the other hand, thought colonial men who labored in the fields were performing "women's work."

In most North American Indian farming communities, women and men belonged to separate social groupings, each with its own rituals and lore. Membership in these societies was one of the most important elements of a person's identity. Marriage ties, on the other hand, were relatively weak, and in most Indian communities divorce was easy. The couple simply separated, the children almost always remaining with the mother. Indian women were free to determine the timing of reproduction as well as to use herbs to prevent pregnancy, induce abortion, or ease the pain of childbirth. The status and role of Indian women were strikingly different from European patterns, in which the rule of men over women and fathers over households was the norm.

Farming communities were far more complex than foraging communities, but they were also less stable. Growing populations demanded increasingly large surpluses of food, and this need frequently led to social conflict and warfare among farming communities. Moreover, farming systems were especially vulnerable to climatological disruptions such as drought, as well as to ecological crises of their own creation, such as soil depletion or erosion.

The Religions of Foragers and Farmers

The religions of Indian peoples were shaped primarily by the two great traditions of foraging and farming. The first, rooted deep in the Archaic past, is sometimes called the Hunting Tradition. This complex of beliefs centered in the relationship of hunters and prey and celebrated the existence of a "Master of Animals," often portrayed as the sacred bear. Associated with this tradition was the vision quest, a practice in which young men and women sought out personal protective spirits by going alone into the wilderness, exposing themselves to the elements, fasting, and inducing hallucinations and dreams. An individual who developed a special sensitivity to spiritual forces might

The creation of man and woman depicted on a pot (dated about C.E. 1000) *from the ancient villages of the* Mimbres River *of southwestern* New Mexico, *the area of* Mogollon *culture.* Mimbres *pottery is renowned for its spirited artistry.* Such *artifacts were usually intended as grave goods, to honor the dead.*

Arizona State Museum, University of Arizona

Human figures dance on this characteristic piece of red-on-buff pottery of the Hohokams *(dated about* C.E. 1000). *The* Hohokams, *located on the floodplain of the* Gila River *near present-day* Phoenix, Arizona, *were the first irrigation farmers of* North America. *The* Pima *and* Papago *people of* Arizona *may be descended from them.*

become a shaman—a "medicine" man or woman of the community. The Hunting Tradition was important throughout the continent but was strongest in the northern latitudes, where hunting played a prominent role in the economy.

With the northward spread of maize farming came a second religious complex, known as the Agrarian Tradition, which emphasized and celebrated the notion of fertility in ritual festivals marking the annual change of seasons. At Cahokia, archaeological evidence of posts used to mark the summer and winter solstices suggests that the Agrarian Tradition was honored there. Because this tradition was associated with the greater social complexity of the farming way of life, it was generally characterized by organized cults and priesthoods rather than by individualistic shamans. At its most elaborate, it featured a war-sacrifice-cannibalism ideology that glorified violence and included the ritual consumption of enemy flesh, a tradition whose origins may be related to those of the awe-inspiring sacrificial rituals performed by the priests and leaders of the Mesoamerican city-states.

Although religious beliefs were probably as distinctive as the local communities that held them, some combination of the Hunting and Agrarian traditions characterized most of the Indian cultures of North America. Natural and supernatural forces were thought to be inseparable, a system of belief called *pantheism*; people were thought to share a basic kinship with animals, plants, inanimate objects, and natural forces. Although many native religions recognized the existence of a paramount spiritual force, they were also generally polytheistic, with numerous gods and spirits.

The Earliest Farmers of the Southwest

Farming communities began to emerge in the arid Southwest during the first millenium B.C.E. Among the first to develop a settled farming way of life were the Mogollon people, who lived along what is today the southern Arizona–New Mexico border from around 250 B.C.E. to around C.E. 1450. Living along mountain ridges and near streams in permanent villages of ingenious pit houses well suited to the region's temperature extremes, these people used digging sticks to cultivate maize, beans, and squash. Some of the Mogollon pit structures may have been what Southwestern peoples today call *kivas,* which are used for community religious rituals.

From about C.E. 300 to 1500 the people of the Hohokam ("those who are gone," in the language of the modern Pimas and Papagos of the area) culture flourished in the region along the floodplain of the Salt and Gila Rivers in southern Arizona. The Hohokams, who lived in agricultural villages, built and maintained the first irrigation system in America north of Mexico, channeling river water many miles to desert fields of maize, beans, squash, tobacco, and cotton. They made jewelry from shells and developed a process for etching shells with animal designs. They shared many traits with Mesoamerican civilization to the south, including platform mounds for religious ceremonies and large courts for ball playing. One thoroughly excavated Hohokam community site is a place the Pimas call Skoaquik, or Snaketown. Located near present-day Phoenix, Snaketown includes the

In Chaco Canyon, in northern New Mexico, lie the ruins of Pueblo Bonito, built in the twelfth century C.E. *during the golden age of the Anasazis, an agricultural people who created a complex urban civilization amid the arid landscape of the Colorado Plateau. Until the invention of the modern construction techniques, Pueblo Bonito held the record as the world's largest apartment house.*

remains of a hundred pit houses spread over 300 acres. The number and variety of goods from central Mexico uncovered at the site—rubber balls, mirrors of pyrite mosaics, copper bells, and fashionable ear ornaments—suggest that it may have housed a community of merchants who traded Mesoamerican manufactured goods for locally mined turquoise.

The Anasazis

The best-known farming culture of the Southwest is that of the Anasazis ("ancient outsiders," in the Navajo language), which developed around the first century C.E. several hundred miles to the north of the Hohokam communities in the Four Corners area, where today Arizona, New Mexico, Utah, and Colorado meet on the eastern portion of the great plateau of the Colorado River. Around 750, possibly in response to population pressure and an increasingly dry climate, the Anasazis began a shift from pit-house villages to densely populated, multistoried apartment complexes called *pueblos* ("towns" in Spanish, for they were named by Spanish invaders). These complexes clustered around central plazas with circular underground *kivas*. The Anasazis grew high-yield varieties of maize in terraced fields irrigated by canals flowing from mountain catchment basins. To supplement this vegetable diet they hunted animals for their meat, using the bow and arrow that first appeared in the region about C.E. 500.

Anasazi culture extended over an area larger than California. The sites of more than 25,000 Anasazi communities are known in New Mexico alone. Only a few have been excavated, so there is much that archaeologists do not yet understand. The most prominent of the Anasazi centers was Pueblo Bonito in Chaco canyon. Completed in the twelfth century, this complex of 650 interconnected rooms is a monument to the golden age of the Anasazis. Hundreds of miles of arrow-straight roads and an interpueblo communication system consisting of mountaintop signaling stations connect Chaco Canyon to outlying sites, making it the center of a food distribution, trading, and ceremonial network.

During the thirteenth century, drought conditions in the Southwest worsened. Growing Anasazi populations redoubled their efforts to improve their production methods, building increasingly complex irrigation canals, dams, and terraced fields. Many large fields were mulched with small stones to retain moisture more effectively. But these measures were not sufficient. Scientific analysis of the varying size of the growth rings of ancient tree trunks reveals that between 1276 and 1293 there was a prolonged and devastating drought that must have resulted in repeated crop failures and eventual famine.

The Anasazis were confronted with an additional difficulty—the arrival of bands of Athapascan migrants who for a thousand years or more had been gradually moving south from Subarctic regions. If the Athapascans were anything like their immediate descendants, the Navajos and the Apaches, they must have been fierce fighters. By the fourteenth and fifteenth centuries, the Athapascans were raiding Anasazi farming communities, taking food, goods, and possibly slaves. The dramatic Anasazi cliff dwellings at Mesa Verde, Colorado, constructed about this time, may have been built as a defense against these raiders. Gradually the Anasazis abandoned the Four Corners area altogether. Their movements have not yet been fully traced, but most seem to have resettled in communities along the Rio Grande, joining with local residents to form the Pueblo people of modern times.

Farmers of the Eastern Woodlands

Archaeologists date the beginning of the farming culture of eastern North America, known as Woodland, from the first appearances of pottery in the region about 3,000 years ago. The Woodland culture was based on a sophisticated way of life that combined gathering and hunting with the cultivation of a few crops. People lived most of the year at permanent community sites but left them seasonally to take advantage of resources at different locations. Their crops included sunflowers and other locally domesticated plants. The discovery of clay pipes in archaeological excavations suggests that the early Woodlands people may also have cultivated tobacco, which was first domesticated in the Caribbean region.

Woodlands peoples began cultivating maize during the first millenium C.E., but even before then they had begun to adopt an increasingly settled existence and a more complex social organization in some regions. Between 1700 and 700 B.C.E. the people of the Poverty Point culture in the lower Mississippi Valley erected a remarkable site consisting of a series of concentric semicircular earth mounds covering an area about a mile square. The people of the Adena culture (the name is taken from a site on the upper Ohio River) occupied the Ohio River basin from present-day Indiana to Pennsylvania from before 1000 B.C.E. to about C.E. 250. They lived in permanent or semipermanent villages and built large burial mounds.

Between about 200 B.C.E. and fifth century C.E. the Hopewell people settled in the Mississippi-Ohio Valley. Hopewell communities were devoted to mortuary cults, in which the dead were honored through ceremony, display, and the construction of enormous and elaborate burial mounds. In support of this tradition, Hopewell chiefs mobilized an elaborate trade network that acquired obsidian from the Rocky Mountains, copper from the Great Lakes, mica from the Appalachians, and shells from the Gulf coast. Hopewell artisans converted these materials into distinctive and artistically sophisticated goods that played an important role in Hopewell trade and were buried with the dead in Hopewell graves.

Mississippian Society

The Hopewell culture collapsed in the fifth century, perhaps as a result of shifting climate patterns. Local communities continued to practice their late Archaic subsistence strategies, but abandoned the expensive cultural displays demanded by the Hopewell mortuary cult. Following the collapse of Hopewell, however, several important innovations were introduced in the East. The bow and arrow, developed on the Great Plains, appeared east of the Mississippi about the seventh century, greatly increasing the efficiency of hunting. Also between 450 and 800, maize farming spread widely in the east. Indian farmers had developed a new variety of maize called Northern Flint, with large cobs and plentiful kernels that matured in a short enough time to make it suitable for cultivation in temperate northern latitudes. Also about this time a shift from digging sticks to flint hoes took place, further increasing the productive potential of maize farming.

It was on the basis of these innovations that, in the seventh or eighth century, the powerful new Mississippian culture arose. The Mississippians were master maize farmers who lived in permanent villages along the floodplain of the Mississippi River. Cahokia, the most important of these, was the urban heart of Mississippian America. Cahokia's dense urban center with its monumental temple, its residential neighborhoods, and its surrounding farmlands were mirrored in many other regional centers, each with thousands of residents. There were cities on the Arkansas River near Spiro, Oklahoma; on the Black Warrior River at Moundville, Alabama; at Hiwassee Island on the Tennessee River; and along the Etowah and Ocmulgee Rivers in Georgia. Like Cahokia, these centers of civilization were probably characterized by a sophisticated division of labor that

The Great Serpent Mound in southern Ohio, the shape of an uncoiling snake more than 1,300 feet long, is the largest effigy earthwork in the world. Monumental public works like these suggest the high degree of social organization of the Mississippian people.

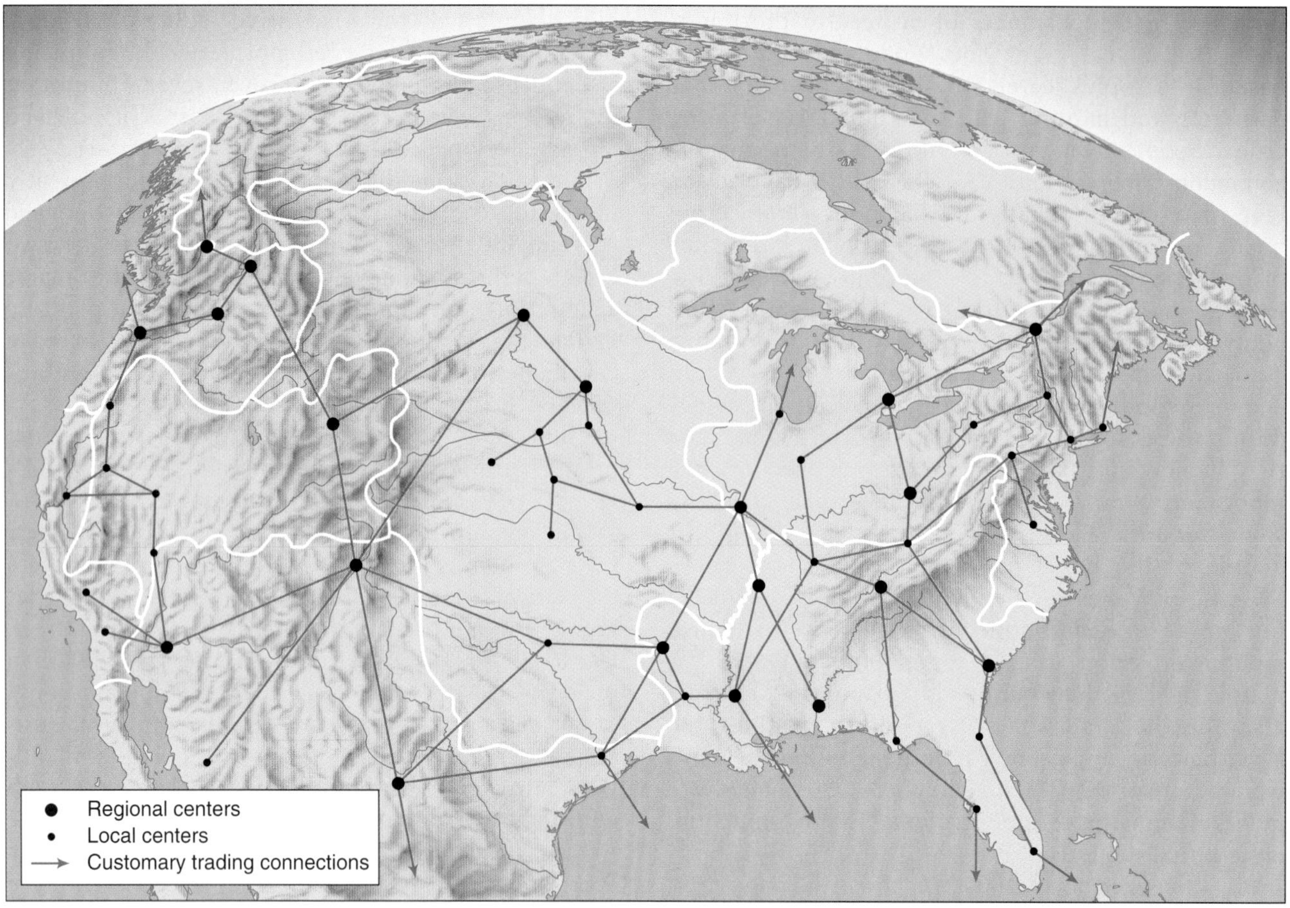

Native North American Trade Networks, ca. C.E. 1400 *By determining the places of origin of artifacts found at ancient sites, historians have devised a conjectural map of Indian trade networks. Among large regional centers and smaller local ones, trade connected Indian peoples of many different communities and regions.*

included artisans, priests, and an elite class of rulers. The Great Serpent Mound, the largest effigy earthwork in the world, was constructed by Mississippian peoples in southern Ohio.

Linked by the vast water transportation system of the Mississippi and its many tributaries, these communities became the earliest city-states north of Mexico, hierarchical chiefdoms that extended political control over the farmers of the surrounding countryside. With continued population growth, these cities engaged in vigorous and probably violent competition for the limited space along the rivers. It may have been the need for more orderly ways of allocating territories that stimulated the evolution of political hierarchies. The tasks of preventing local conflict, storing large food surpluses, and redistributing foodstuffs from farmers to artisans and elites required a leadership class with the power to command. Mound-building and the use of tribute labor in the construction of other public works testified to the power the chiefs wielded from their sumptuous quarters atop the commanding mounds. If politics is defined as the organized contest for power among people and groups, then the Mississippians and the Anasazis were the first truly political societies north of Mexico.

Mississippian culture reached its height between the eleventh and thirteenth centuries C.E., the same period in which the Anasazis were constructing their desert cities. Both groups adapted the technology that was spreading northward from Mexico to their particular environments, both developed impressive artistic traditions, and their feats of engineering reflect the beginnings of science and technology. These were complex societies characterized by urbanism, social stratification, craft specialization, and regional trade. Except for a formal system of writing, they had all the traits of European and Asian civilizations.

The Politics of Warfare and Violence

The late thirteenth century marked the end of several hundred years of climatological conditions that were very favorable to maize farming and the beginning of a century and a half of cool, dry conditions.

Although the changes in climate in the Mississippi Valley were not as severe as those that devastated the Anasazis of the Southwest, over the long term they significantly lowered the potential of farming to support growing urban populations. Some archaeologists have suggested that this extended drought sharpened political conflict in both areas and greatly increased violence and social disorder.

Warfare among Indian peoples certainly predated the colonial era. Organized violence was probably rare among hunting bands, which could seldom muster the manpower for more than a small raid against an enemy. Certain hunting peoples, though, such as the southward-moving Athapascans, undoubtedly engaged in systematic raiding of settled farming communities. Warfare was also common among farming societies fighting to gain additional lands for cultivation. The first Europeans in what is now the South of the United States described highly organized combat among large tribal armies. The bow and arrow was a deadly weapon of war, and the practice of scalping seems to have originated among warring tribes, who believed one could capture a warrior's spirit by taking his hair. (During the period of colonial warfare, the practice of scalping spread widely among both European colonists and the Indian tribes of other regions.) Sculpted images of human sacrifice found at Mississippian sites suggest that these peoples, like the inhabitants of Mexican city-states, not only waged war but practiced human sacrifice and cannibalism.

The archaeological remains of Cahokia reveal that during the thirteenth and fourteenth centuries the people of that great city surrounded its central sections with a heavy log stockade. This defensive structure suggests that there may have been a great deal of violent warfare with other nearby communities. Indeed, the fourteenth century may have been a period of intense conflict and war among competing city-states throughout the valleys of the Mississippi, each based on the domination of farming countrysides by metropolitan centers. Eventually conditions in the upper Mississippi Valley deteriorated so far that Cahokia and many other sites were abandoned altogether, and as the cities collapsed, people relocated in smaller, decentralized communities. Nevertheless, as we will see, among the peoples of the South, Mississippian patterns continued into the period of colonization.

NORTH AMERICA ON THE EVE OF COLONIZATION

The first Europeans to arrive in North America found a continent populated by more than 350 native societies speaking nearly as many distinct languages. Although anthropologists of the early twentieth century estimated that the population of the entire area north of Mexico was little more than a million, historians have now raised this estimate substantially.

The Indian Population of America

In determining the precolonial population of the Americas, today's historical demographers consider a number of factors—the population densities that different technological and economic systems could support, the archaeological evidence, the very earliest European accounts, and the estimated impact of epidemic diseases. (For a discussion of epidemics among Indian peoples, see Chapter 2.) Although estimates vary, most historians now believe that the population of America north of Mexico in the early sixteenth century numbered between 7 and 10 million. Moreover, probably another 25 million were concentrated in the complex societies of the Mexican highlands. Thus at the time of their first contact with European explorers and settlers, the peoples of the Western Hemisphere numbered some 60 to 70 million, about the same as Europe's population.

Population density in North America varied widely according to ways of life. Only scattered bands populated the Great Basin, the Great Plains, and Subarctic regions, but the Northwest and what is today California were densely settled because the foraging peoples of those areas maintained highly productive fishing and gathering economies. The Southwest, South, and Northeast contained the largest populations, and it was in these areas that European explorers, conquerors, and colonists first concentrated their efforts.

The Southwest

The single overwhelming fact of life in the Southwest is aridity. Summer rains average only ten to twenty inches annually, and on much of the dry desert cultivation is impossible. Several rivers, however, flow southward out of pine-covered mountain plateaus to the Gulf of Mexico and the Gulf of California. Narrow bands of green vegetation in parched sands of brown and red, they have made irrigation farming possible.

On the eve of European colonization, Indian farmers in the Southwest had been cultivating fields for nearly 3,000 years. In the floodplain of the Gila and Salt Rivers lived the Pimas and Papagos, descendants of the ancient Hohokams. Working small irrigated fields along the Colorado River and even on the floor of the Grand Canyon were the Yuman peoples. These desert farmers cultivated corn, beans, squash, sunflowers, and cotton, which they traded throughout the Southwest. They lived in dispersed

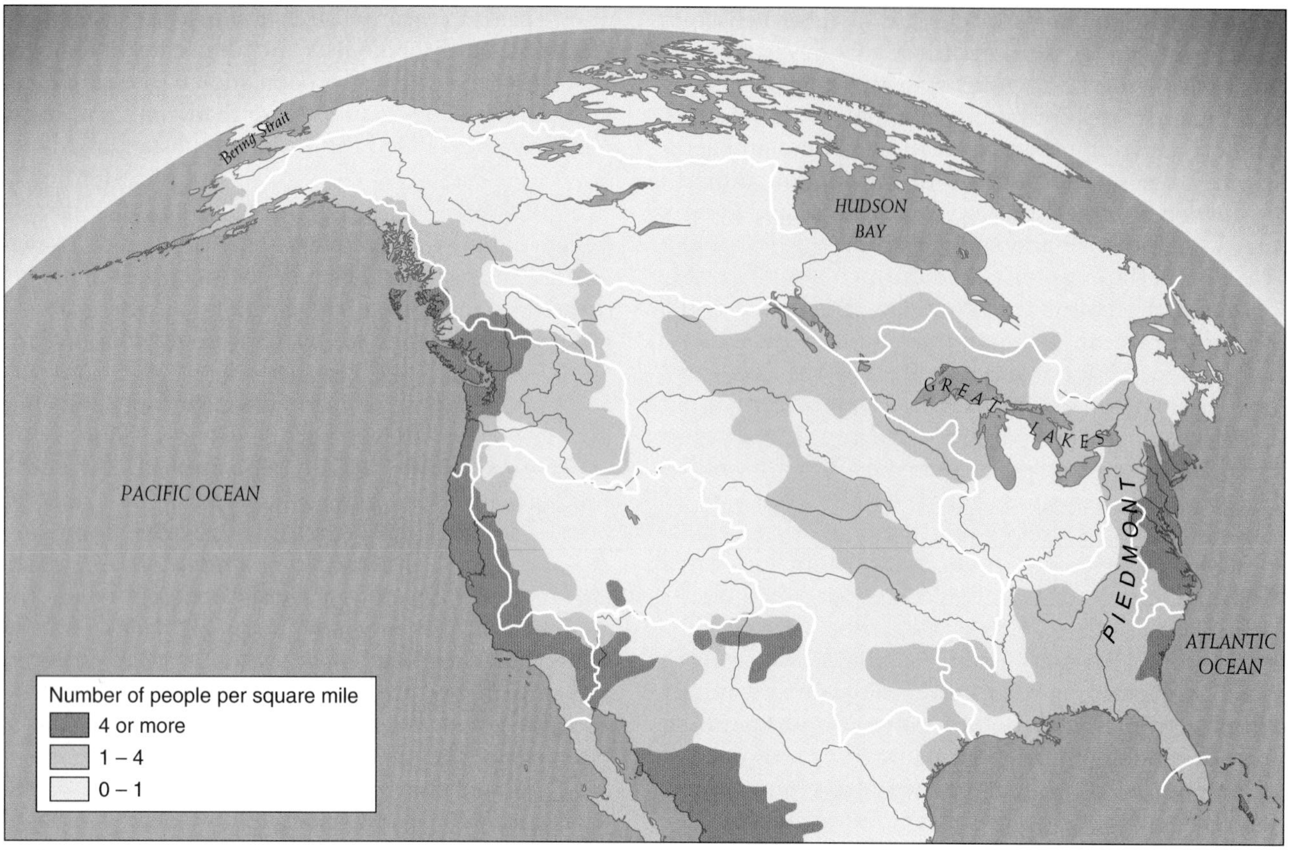

Indian Settlement before European Colonization *Based on what is called the "carrying capacity" of different subsistence strategies—the population density they could support—historical demographers have mapped the hypothetical population density of Indian societies in the fifteenth century, before the era of European colonization. Populations were most dense in farming societies or in coastal areas with marine resources and least dense in extreme environments like the Great Basin.*

settlements that the Spanish called *rancherias* (meaning "settlements"), which were separated by as much as a mile. That way, say the Pimas, people avoid getting on each other's nerves. Rancherias were governed in general by councils of adult men whose decisions required unanimous consent, although a headman was chosen to manage the irrigation works. Ceremonies focused, appropriately, on rainmaking; one ritual required everyone to drink cactus wine until thoroughly drunk, a state of presumed purification that was thought to bring rain.

East of the Grand Canyon, in their unique dwellings of stacked, interconnected apartments, lived the Pueblo peoples, who inherited this architectural form, as well as their farming techniques and religious practices, from their Anasazi forebears. Although the many Pueblo peoples spoke several languages, as a group they shared a commitment to communal village life that differentiated them from the individualistic desert farmers. A strict communal code of behavior regulating personal conduct was enforced by the Pueblos through a maze of matrilineal clans and secret religious societies; unique combinations of these clans and societies formed the governing systems of different Pueblo villages. Seasonal public ceremonies in the village squares featured colorful impersonations, with singing, chanting, and dancing, of ancestral sacred spirits called *kachinas*. "Clowns" mimicked in slapstick style those who did not conform to the communal ideal, pretending to drink urine or eat dirt, for example, in front of the home of a person who kept an unclean house.

The Pueblos inhabit the oldest continuously occupied towns in the United States. The village of Oraibi, Arizona, dates from the twelfth century, when the Hopis ("peaceful ones") founded it in the isolated central mesas of the Colorado Plateau. Using dry-farming methods and drought-resistant plants, these western Pueblo Indians produced rich harvests of corn and squash amid shifting sand dunes. On a mesa top about fifty miles southwest of present-day Albuquerque, New Mexico, Anasazi immigrants from Mesa Verde built Acoma, the "sky city," in the late thirteenth century. The Pueblo people established approximately

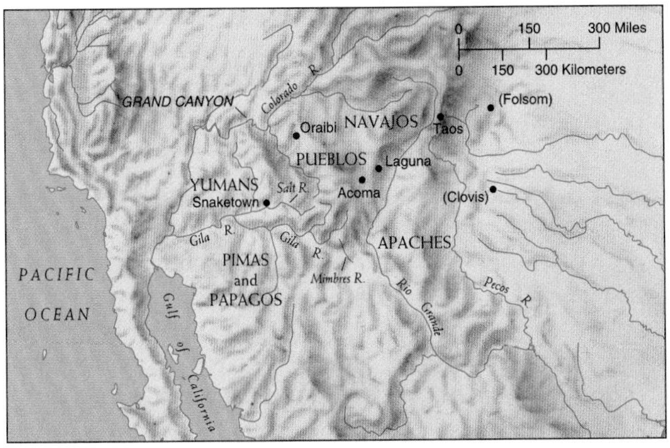

Southwestern Indian Groups on the Eve of Colonization *The Southwest was populated by desert farmers like the Pimas, Papagos, Yumans, and Pueblos, as well as by nomadic hunters and raiders like the Apaches and Navajos.*

seventy other villages during the next two hundred years; fifty of these were still in existence in the seventeenth century when the Spanish founded Santa Fé, and two dozen survive today, including the large Indian towns of Laguna, Isleta, Santo Domingo, Jémez, San Felipe, and Taos (see the map on p. 52).

In the arid deserts and mountains surrounding these towns were bands of nomadic hunters, some of whom had lived in the region thousands of years. But there were also the Athapascans who, as we have seen, began arriving in the fourteenth and fifteenth centuries and who hunted and foraged, traded meat and medicinal herbs with farmers, and frequently raided and plundered these same villages and rancherias. Gradually, some of the Athapascan people surrounding the Pueblo villages adopted their neighbors' farming and handicraft skills; these people were the Navajos. Others, who came be known as the Apaches, were more heavily influenced by the hunting and gathering traditions of the Great Basin and Great Plains and remained nomadic.

The South

The South enjoys a mild, moist climate with short winters and long summers, ideal for farming. From the Atlantic and Gulf coasts, a broad fertile plain extends inland to the Piedmont, a plateau separating the coastal plains from the Appalachian Mountains. The transition between plateau and coastal plain is marked by the fall line, an area of rapids and waterfalls in the descending rivers. The upper courses of the waterways originating in the Appalachian highlands offered ample rich bottomland for farming, and the extensive forests, mostly of yellow pine, offered abundant animal resources. In the sixteenth century, large populations of Indian peoples farmed this rich land, fishing or hunting to supplement their diets. They lived in communities ranging from villages of twenty or so dwellings to large towns of a thousand or more inhabitants.

Mississippian cultural patterns continued among the peoples of the South. They were organized into confederacies of farming towns, the most powerful living along the river floodplains. Because most of these groups were quickly decimated in the first years of European colonization, they are poorly documented. We know the most about the Natchez, farmers of the rich lands in the lower Mississippi delta who survived into the eighteenth century before being destroyed in a war with the French. Overseeing the Natchez was a ruler known as the Great Sun, who lived in royal splendor on a ceremonial mound in his village capital. When out among his subjects he was carried on a litter, the path before him swept by his retinue of servants and wives. Natchez society was class based. Noble families were represented on the Great Sun's council of advisers and appointed village peace and war chiefs. The majority of people, however, were a subordinate group known as the "Stinkards." Persistent territorial conflict with other confederacies elevated warfare to an honored status among the Natchez, and public torture and human sacrifice of enemies were commonplace. The Natchez give us our best glimpse at what life may have been like in ancient Cahokia.

The Indians of Florida also lived in sophisticated chiefdoms characterized by class systems, monarchs, and priests. Archaeological evidence implies that central towns dominated farmers in the countryside, demanding from them large quantities of maize, squash, and other cultivated plants grown on fields large enough to support populations numbering in the tens of thousands. As in the Natchez villages and the city of Cahokia, life in these Florida towns centered around the ceremonial mounds where the ruling families resided. Honored clans

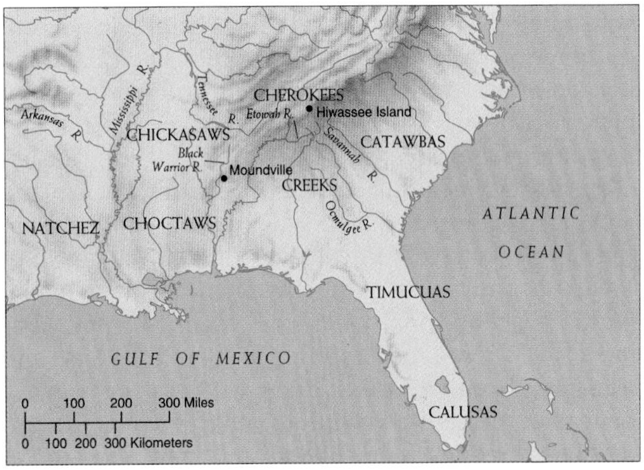

Southern Indian Groups on the Eve of Colonization *On the eve of colonization the Indian societies of the South shared many traits of the complex Mississippian farming culture.*

Neg. No. 324281, photographed by Rota, engraving by de Bry. Courtesy Department Library Services, American Museum of Natural History.

The New Queen Being Taken to the King, *engraved by Theodor de Bry in the sixteenth century from a drawing by Jacques le Moyne, an early French colonist of Florida. The communities of Florida were hierarchical, with classes and hereditary chiefs, some of whom were women. Here le Moyne depicted a "queen" being carried on an ornamental litter by men of rank.*

lived in the plaza below, with ordinary people on the fringes of town and in the countryside.

Eventually, these chiefdoms proved highly vulnerable to conquest, but the looser confederacies of the interior were considerably more resilient. Among the latter the most prominent were the Choctaws of present-day Mississippi and Alabama, the Chickasaws in western Tennessee, and the Creeks of Georgia, each confederacy, including several dozen towns. On the mountain plateaus lived the Cherokees, who made up the single largest confederacy, of more than sixty towns. Farming was somewhat less important in the highlands than along the coast, hunting somewhat more so. There were no ruling classes or kings, and leaders were either women or men. Most peoples reckoned their descent matrilineally (that is, through their mothers, grandmothers, and so on), and at marriage husbands left the homes of their mothers to reside with the families of their wives. Women controlled household and village life and were influential as well in the matrilineal clans that linked communities together. Councils of elderly men governed the confederacies but were joined by clan matrons for annual meetings at the central council house. These gatherings could last days or even weeks, since all clan members, male and female, were given the opportunity to speak.

All the peoples of the South farmed the same crops, hunted in the same kind of piney woods, and lived in similar villages. They celebrated a common round of agricultural festivals that brought clans together from surrounding communities. At the harvest festival, for example, people thoroughly cleaned their homes and villages. They fasted and purified themselves by consuming the "black drink," a vision-inducing libation made from roasted leaves of the cassina plant. They extinguished old fires, lit new ones, and then celebrated the new crop of sweet corn with dancing and other festivities. During the following days, villages, clans, and groups of men and women competed against each other in the ancient stick-and-ball game that the French named lacrosse; in the evenings men and women played chunkey, a gambling game.

The Northeast

The Northeast, the colder sector of the eastern woodlands, has a varied geography of coastal plains and mountain highlands, great rivers, lakes, and valleys. After C.E. 500, cultivation became the main support of the Indian economy in those places where the growing season was long enough to bring a crop of corn to maturity. In such areas of the Northeast—along the coasts and in the river valleys—Indian populations were large and dense.

The Iroquois of present-day Ontario and upstate New York, who have lived in these areas for at least 4,500 years, were among the first northeastern peoples to adopt cultivation. As they shifted from primary reliance on fishing and hunting to maize farming, they apparently relocated their villages from river floodplains to hilltops. There Iroquois women produced crops of corn, beans, squash, and sunflowers sufficient to support fifty longhouses, each occupied by a large matrilineal, extended family. Some of those houses were truly long; archaeologists have excavated the foundations of 400-foot-long dwellings that may have housed dozens of families. Typically, these villages were surrounded by substantial wooden walls, clear evidence of intergroup conflict and warfare.

Population growth and the resulting intensification of farming in Iroquois country stimulated the development of chiefdoms there as elsewhere. By the fifteenth century several centers of population, each in a separate river system, had coalesced from east to west across upstate New York. These were the five Iroquois chiefdoms or "nations": the Mohawks, Oneidas, Onondagas, Cayugas, and Senecas. Iroquois oral histories collected during the nineteenth century recall this as a period of persistent violence, possibly the consequence of conflicts over territory.

Historians believe that the Iroquois founded a confederacy to control this violence. The confederacy outlawed warfare among the member nations and established regulated forms of gift exchange and payment to replace revenge. According to Iroquois oral history, Chief Deganawida—known as the lawgiver—founded the confederacy. It is said that he "blocked out the sun" as a demonstration of his powers; it may be that these events took place during the full solar eclipse that was visible in the Northeast in 1451. Deganawida's message was proclaimed by his supporter, Hiawatha, a great orator, who convinced all the five Iroquois nations to join. As a model, the confederacy used the powerful metaphor of the longhouse; each nation, it was said, occupied

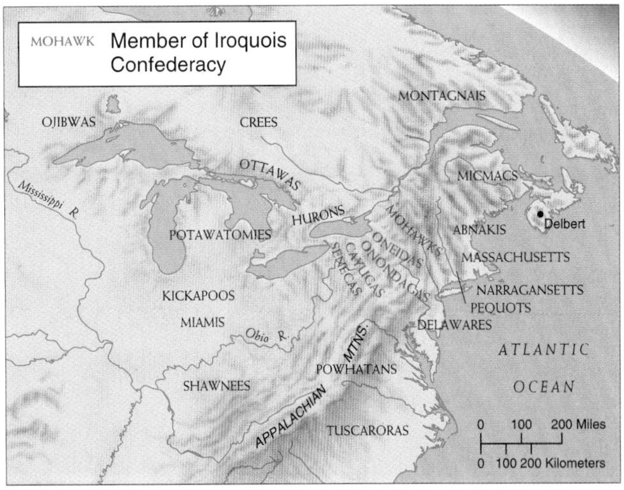

Northeastern Indian Groups on the Eve of Colonization *The Indians of the Northeast were mostly village peoples. In the fifteenth century five Iroquois groups—the Mohawks, Oneidas, Onondagas, Cayugas, and Senecas—joined together to form the Iroquois Five Nation Confederacy.*

a separate hearth but acknowledged descent from a common mother. As in the longhouse, women played important roles in choosing the male leaders who would represent their lineages and chiefdom on the Iroquois council. The confederacy suppressed violence among its members but did not hesitate to encourage war against outside groups such as the neighboring Hurons or the Eries, who constructed defensive confederacies of their own at about the same time. The Iroquois Confederacy would become one of the most powerful contenders in the struggles among competing Indian and European forces during the colonial period.

The Iroquois spoke Iroquoian. The other major language group of the Northeast was Algonquian, whose speakers belonged to at least fifty distinct cultures. In contrast to the Iroquois, most Algonquian peoples were patrilineal. In general, they lived in less extensive dwellings and in smaller villages than the Iroquois, often without palisade fortifications. The Algonquian peoples north of the Great Lakes and in northern New England were hunters and foragers, organized into bands with loose ethnic affiliations. Several of these peoples, including the Micmacs, Crees, Montagnais, and Ojibwas (also known as Chippewas), were the first to become enmeshed in the early fur trade with European newcomers. Among the Algonquians of the Atlantic coast from present-day Massachusetts south to Virginia, as well as among those in the Ohio Valley, farming led to the development of settlements as densely populated as those of the Iroquois, although the abundance of coastal and riverine resources made

CHRONOLOGY

30,000–15,000 B.C.E.	First humans in the Americas
13,000 B.C.E.	Global warming trend begins
10,000 B.C.E.	Clovis technology
9000 B.C.E.	Extinction of big-game animals
8000 B.C.E.	Beginning of the Archaic period
7000 B.C.E.	First cultivation of plants in the Mexican highlands
5000 B.C.E.	Athapascan migrations to America begin
4000 B.C.E.	First settled communities along the Pacific coast
3000 B.C.E.	Inupiat and Aleut migrations begin
1500–1000 B.C.E.	Maize and other Mexican crops introduced into the Southwest
1000 B.C.E.	Beginning of Adena culture
	First urban communities in Mexico
250 B.C.E.	Beginning of Mogollon culture in the Southwest
200 B.C.E.–C.E. 400	Hopewell culture flourishes
650	Bow and arrow, flint hoes, and Northern Flint corn in the Northeast
775–1150	Hohokam site of Snaketown reaches its greatest extent
1000	Tobacco in use throughout North America
1150	Founding of Hopi village of Oraibi, oldest continuously occupied town in the United States
1200	High point of Mississippian and Anasazi cultures
1276	Severe drought begins in the Southwest
1300	Arrival of Athapascans in the Southwest
1451	Founding of Iroquois Confederacy

the bow and arrow and the fishing spear as important to these people as the hoe.

Algonquian communities, although relatively autonomous from one another, also began to form confederacies during the fifteenth and sixteenth centuries. Among these groupings were those of the Massachusetts, Narragansets, and Pequots of New England, the Delawares and the peoples of Powhatan's confederacy on the mid-Atlantic coast, and the Shawnees, Miamis, Kickapoos, and Potawatomis of the Ohio Valley.

CONCLUSION

Over the thousands of years that elapsed between the settlement of the North American continent and the invasion of Europeans at the end of the fifteenth century, Indian peoples developed hundreds of distinctive cultures that were fine-tuned to the geographic and climatological possibilities and limitations of their homelands. In the northern forests they hunted game and perfected the art of processing furs and hides. Along the coasts and rivers they harvested the abundant runs of fish and learned to navigate the waters with sleek and graceful boats. In the arid Southwest they mastered irrigation farming and made the deserts bloom, while in the humid Southeast they mastered the large-scale production of crops that could sustain large cities with sophisticated political systems. North America was not a "virgin" continent, as so many of the Europeans believed. Indians had transformed the natural world, making it over into a human landscape.

"Columbus did not discover a new world," writes the historian J. H. Perry. "He established contact between two worlds, both already old." North America had a rich history, one that Europeans did not understand and later generations of Americans have too frequently ignored. The European colonists who came to settle encountered thousands of Indian communities with deep roots and vibrant traditions. In the confrontation that followed, Indian communities viewed the colonists as invaders and called upon their traditions and their gods to help them defend their homelands.

REVIEW QUESTIONS

1. List the evidence for the hypothesis that the Americas were settled by migrants from Asia.
2. Discuss the impact of environmental change and human hunting on the big-game populations of North America.
3. Review the principal regions of the North American continent and the human adaptations that made social life possible in each of them.
4. Define the concept of "forest efficiency." How does it help to illuminate the major development of the Archaic period?
5. Why did the development of farming lead to increasing social complexity? Discuss the reasons why organized political activity began in farming societies.
6. What were the Hunting and Agrarian Traditions? In what ways did the religious beliefs of Indian peoples reflect their environmental adaptations?
7. What factors led to the organization of the Iroquois Confederacy?

RECOMMENDED READING

Tom D. Dillehay and David J. Miltzer, eds., *The First Americans: Search and Research* (1991). A summary of the most recent archaeological findings, suggesting a much earlier migration to the Americas. For the newest discoveries, see recent issues of *National Geographic* and *Scientific American*.

Thomas E. Emerson, *Cahokia and the Archaeology of Power* (1997). The fascinating story of North America's first metropolis.

Brian M. Fagan, *The Great Journey: The Peopling of Ancient America* (1987). An anthropologist's account of the Asian migration to the Americas.

Stuart J. Fiedel, *Prehistory of the Americas* (1987). The best introduction for the nonspecialist, covering the first migrations, the development of technologies, and the spread of farming.

Alvin M. Josephy Jr., ed., *America in 1492* (1992). Important essays by the leading scholars of the North American Indian experience. Includes beautiful illustrations and maps as well as an excellent bibliography.

Alvin M. Josephy Jr., *500 Nations: An Illustrated History of North American Indians* (1995). A magnificent volume that includes historic illustrations as well as fascinating computer re-creations of the pre-European human landscape of America.

Alice B. Kehoe, *North American Indians: A Comprehensive Account* (1992). The best general anthropological survey of the history and culture of the Indians of North America. Organized by culture areas, the new edition covers all the peoples of the continent and includes the most recent scholarship.

Robert Silverberg, *Mound Builders of Ancient America: The Archaeology of a Myth* (1968). A brilliant history of opinion and theory about the mound builders, combined with a review of the best archaeological evidence then available.

William C. Sturtevant, general editor, *Handbook of North American Indians,* 20 vols. proposed (1978–). The most comprehensive collection of the best current scholarship. The completed series will include a volume for each of the culture regions of North America; volumes on origins, Indian-white relations, languages, and art; a biographical dictionary; and a general index.

Russell Thornton, *American Indian Holocaust and Survival: A Population History since 1492* (1987). The best introduction to the historical demography of North America. In a field of great controversy, it provides a judicious review of all the evidence.

ADDITIONAL BIBLIOGRAPHY

Settling the Continent

Larry D. Agenbroad, et al., eds., *Megafauna and Man* (1990)
John Bierhorst, ed., *The Red Swan: Myths and Tales of the American Indians* (1976)
Warwick M. Bray, et al., *The New World: The Making of the Past* (1977)
Mark Nathan Cohen, *The Food Crisis in Prehistory: Overpopulation and the Origins of Agriculture* (1977)
E. James Dixon, *Quest for the Origins of the First Americans* (1993)
Henry F. Dobyns, *Native American Historical Demography: A Critical Bibliography* (1976)
Richard Erdoes and Alfonso Ortiz, eds., *American Indian Myths and Legends* (1984)
Jonathon E. Ericson, et al., eds., *Peopling of the New World* (1982)
Brian M. Fagan, *Ancient North America: The Archaeology of a Continent*, Second Edition (1995)
Jeffrey Goodman, *American Genesis: The American Indian and the Origins of Modern Man* (1981)
Ted Hirschfield, *Middle Mississippians: Encounters with the Prehistoric Amerindians* (1996).
Lee Eldridge Huddleston, *Origins of the American Indians: European Concepts, 1492–1729* (1967)
Jesse D. Jennings, ed., *Ancient North Americans* (1983)
George Kubler, *Esthetic Recognition of Ancient Amerindian Art* (1991)
William S. Laughlin and Albert B. Harper, eds., *The First Americans: Origins, Affinities, and Adaptations* (1979)
James L. Phillips and James A. Brown, eds., *Archaic Hunters and Gatherers in the American Midwest* (1983)
Hanns J. Prem, *The Ancient Americas: A Brief History and Guide to Research* (1997).
Heather Anne Pringle, *In Search of Ancient North America: An Archaeological Journey to Forgotten Cultures* (1996).
Paul Shao, *The Origin of Ancient American Cultures* (1983)
Richard Shutler Jr., ed., *Early Man in the New World* (1983)
Richard F. Townsend, ed., *The Ancient Americas: Art from Sacred Landscapes* (1992)
Waldo R. Wedel, *Prehistoric Man on the Great Plains* (1961)
Gordon R. Willey, *An Introduction to American Archaeology* (1966)

The Beginning of Regional Cultures

Michael A. Adler, ed., *The Prehistoric Pueblo World, A.D. 1150–1350* (1996).
Frances R. Berdan, *The Aztecs of Central Mexico* (1982)
David S. Brose, et al., *Ancient Art of the American Woodland Indians* (1985)
David S. Brose and N'omi Greber, eds., *Hopewell Archaeology* (1979)
Michael D. Coe, *Mexico* (1967)
Linda S. Cordell, *Prehistory of the Southwest* (1984)
Munro Edmondson, ed., *Sixteenth-Century Mexico: The Works of Sahagun* (1974)
Richard I. Ford, ed., *Prehistoric Food Production in North America* (1985)
Melvin L. Fowler, *Perspectives in Cahokia Archeology* (1975)
Emil W. Haury, *The Hohokam* (1976)
William F. Keegan, ed., *Emergent Horticultural Economies of the Eastern Woodlands* (1987)
A. L. Kroeber, *Cultural and Natural Areas of Native North America* (1939)
Barker H. Morrow and V. B. Price, eds., *Anasazi Architecture and American Design* (1997)
Timothy R. Pauketat and Thomas E. Emerson, eds., *Cahokia: Domination and Ideology in the Mississippian World* (1997)
W. H. Wills, *Early Prehistoric Agriculture* (1988)
Eric Wolf, *Sons of the Shaking Earth* (1959)

The Eve of Colonization

James Axtell, ed., *The Indian Peoples of Eastern America: A Documentary History of the Sexes* (1981)
Elizabeth M. Brunfiel and John W. Fox, *Factional Competition and Political Development in the New World* (1993)
Lyle Campbell and Marianne Mithun, eds., *The Languages of Native America* (1979)
Olive P. Dickason, *Canada's First Nations: A History of Founding Peoples* (1992)
Edward P. Dozier, *The Pueblo Indians of North America* (1970)
Harold E. Driver, *Indians of North America* (1961)
James A. Ford, *A Comparison of Formative Cultures in the Americas* (1969)
Charles Hudson, *The Southeastern Indians* (1976)
Mallory McCane O'Connor, *Lost Cities of the Ancient Southeast* (1995)
Alfonso Ortiz, ed., *New Perspectives on the Pueblos* (1972)
Howard S. Russell, *Indian New England before the Mayflower* (1980)
Bruce D. Smith, *The Mississippian Emergence* (1990)
Frank G. Speck, *Penobscot Man* (1940)
Robert F. Spencer and Jesse D. Jennings, et al., *The Native Americans: Ethnology and Backgrounds of the North American Indians* (1977)
John R. Swanton, *The Indians of the Southeastern United States* (1946)
Bruce Trigger, *The Children of Aaeaentsic: A History of the Huron People to 1660* (1976)
Wilcomb E. Washburn, *The Indian in America* (1975)
J. Leitch Wright Jr., *The Only Land They Knew* (1981)

CHAPTER TWO

WHEN WORLDS COLLIDE

1492–1590

The French, under the command of Jean Ribault, discover the River of May (St. Johns River) in Florida on 1 May 1562. Colored engraving, 1591, by Theodor de Bry after a now lost drawing by Jacques Le Moyne de Morgues; the Granger Collection.

Chapter Outline

THE EXPANSION OF EUROPE

European Communities

The Merchant Class and the Renaissance

The New Monarchies

Portuguese Explorations

Columbus Reaches the Americas

THE SPANISH IN THE AMERICAS

The Invasion of America

The Destruction of the Indies

Intercontinental Exchange

The First Europeans in North America

The Spanish New World Empire

FRENCH AND ENGLISH EXPLORATIONS AND ENCOUNTERS

The Political Impact of the Reformation

The French Colony in Florida

Fish and Furs

Social Change in Sixteenth-Century England

England Turns toward Colonization

AMERICAN COMMUNITIES

The English and the Algonquians at Roanoke

It was late August 1590 when English ships sailed through Hatteras Inlet into Pamlico Sound, off the coast of present-day North Carolina, and made their way north through rough seas to Roanoke Island, where Governor John White had left the first English community in North America three years before. Anxiously, White went ashore in search of the sixty-five single men and twenty families including that of his own daughter, son-in-law, and granddaughter Virginia Dare, the first English baby born in America. Finding the houses "taken down" and possessions "spoiled and scattered about," White suddenly noticed some writing on a tree trunk: "in fair capital letters was graven CROATOAN." Because this was the name of a friendly Indian village fifty miles south and because White found no sign of a cross, which he had instructed the colonists to leave if they were in trouble, he felt sure that his people awaited him at Croatoan, and he returned to his ship, anxious to speed to their rescue.

The Roanoke settlement had been sponsored by Walter Raleigh, a wealthy adventurer who sought profit and prestige by organizing an English colony in the New World. When his men returned from a reconnoitering expedition to the area in 1584, they reported that the coastal region was densely populated by a "very handsome and goodly people." These Indians, the most southerly of the Algonquian coastal peoples, enjoyed a prosperous livelihood farming, fishing, and hunting from their small villages of one or two dozen communal houses. At an island the Indians called Roanoke, the English had been "entertained with all love and kindness" by a chief named Wingina. The leader of several surrounding villages, Wingina welcomed the English as potential allies in his struggle to extend his authority over still others. So when Raleigh's adventurers asked the chief's permission to establish a settlement on the island, he readily granted it, even sending two of his men back to England to assist in preparations for the enterprise. Manteo and Wanchese, the Indian emissaries, worked with Thomas Harriot, an Oxford scholar, and John White, a trained artist. The four men learned one another's language, and there seems to have been a good deal of mutual respect among them.

But when an all-male force of Englishmen returned the subsequent year, 1585, to establish the colony of Virginia (christened in honor of England's virgin queen, Elizabeth I), the two Indian ambassadors offered Wingina conflicting reports. Although Manteo, from the village of Croatoan, argued that the English technology and weaponry would make these men powerful allies, Wanchese described the disturbing inequalities of English society and warned of potential brutality. Wanchese was right to suspect English intentions, for Raleigh's plans were based not on respect for the Indians but on the expectation of exploiting them. He had directed the mission's commander to "proceed with extremity" should the Indians prove difficult and "bring them all in subjection to civility," meaning that they should be made serfs to English colonial masters. Raleigh anticipated that his colony would return profits through a lucrative trade in furs, or a flourishing plantation agriculture, or, best of all, mines of gold or silver. In any case, the Indians would supply the labor.

A colony like this—some 100 soldiers and adventurers with plunder foremost in their minds—was incapable of supporting itself. After building a rough fort on the island, the English went to Wingina for supplies of food. With his harvest in the storage pits, with fish running in the streams and game in the woods, Wingina did the hospitable thing. It was, after all, the duty of a chief to distribute presents and thus to create obligations on the part of recipients. But as fall turned to winter and the stores declined, the constant English demands began to tax the Indians' resources. Rather than hunt or fish, the colonists were out exploring for precious metals. They attacked several outlying villages, burning Indian homes and cornfields and kidnapping Indian women. By spring—traditionally the "starving season" for the Indians, before the crops were up or the game fat—Wingina and his people had had enough. But before the Indians could act, the English caught wind of the rising hostility, and in May 1586 they surprised the Roanoke villagers, killing several of the leading men and beheading Wingina. With the plan of using Indian labor now clearly impossible, the colonists returned to England.

John White and Thomas Harriot, who had spent their time exploring the physical and human world of the coast and recording their findings in notes and sketches, were appalled by this turn of events. Back in England Harriot insisted to Raleigh that the attack on the villagers came "upon causes that on our part might easily enough have been borne" and argued that "through discreet dealing" the Indians might "honor, obey, fear and love us." White proposed a new plan for a colony of real settlers, a community of English families who might live in harmony with the Indians. Harriot and White clearly thought English civilization was superior to the civilization of the Indians, but their vision of colonization was considerably different from that of the plunderers.

In 1587 Raleigh arranged for White to return to America as governor of a new family colony. But despite good intentions, the colonists could not overcome the legacy of violence and hatred left by the former expedition. Within a month one of White's colonists had been shot full of arrows by attackers under the leadership of Wanchese, who after Wingina's death became the most militant opponent of the English among the Roanoke Indians. White retaliated by attacking Wanchese's village, but the Indians fled into the forest with few casualties. Knowing that their entire mission hung in the balance but lacking a vessel large enough to carry them all back to England, the colonists begged White to return home in their only seaworthy ship to press Raleigh for support. Reluctantly, White set sail but arrived in England to find war threatening between England and Spain. Three anxious years elapsed before White was able to return to Roanoke, only to find the settlement destroyed and the colonists gone.

As White and his crew set their sights for Croatoan that August morning in 1590, a great storm blew up. "We drove fast into the shore," White wrote, and all hands feared imminent shipwreck. Several times they dropped anchor, but each time the cable broke. Finally, White and the ship's captain agreed that they would have to leave the sound for deeper waters. It proved to be White's last glimpse of America. Tossed home to England on a stormy sea, he never returned. The English settlers of Roanoke became known as the Lost Colony, their disappearance and ultimate fate one of the enduring mysteries of colonial history.

The Roanoke experience is a reminder of the underlying assumptions of New World colonization. "The English would act just as the Spanish had done in creating their empire," writes the historian and geographer Carl Sauer; they had "naked imperial objectives." It also suggests the wasted opportunity of the Indians' initial welcome. But in an unexpected way, the Roanoke story also emphasizes the importance of community. Many historians believe that the lost colonists lived out the rest of their lives in an Algonquian village. Many years later an English settler reported that a group of coastal North Carolina Indians had told him that "several of their Ancestors were white People," that "the English were forced to cohabit with them for Relief and Conversation, and that in the process of Time, they conformed themselves to the Manners of their Indian Relations." Thus it may be that Virginia Dare and the other children married into Indian families, creating the first mixed community of English and Indians in North America.

Key Topics

- The European background of American colonization
- Creation of the Spanish New World empire and its first extensions to North America
- The large-scale intercontinental exchange of peoples, crops, animals, and diseases
- The French role in the beginnings of the North American fur trade
- England's first overseas colonies in Ireland and America

THE EXPANSION OF EUROPE

There may have been numerous unrecorded contacts between the peoples of America and the Old World before the fifteenth century. Archaeological excavations at L'Anse aux Meadows on the fogbound Newfoundland coast provide evidence for a tenth- or eleventh-century landing in North America by the Norse people from Scandinavian countries. But earthshaking consequences were triggered by the contact with the Americas established in 1492 by Christopher Columbus. Within a generation of Columbus's first voyage, intercontinental exchanges of peoples, crops, animals, and germs had reshaped the Atlantic world. To appreciate these remarkable changes it is important to understand how Europe was transformed during the several centuries that preceded the voyage of Columbus.

European Communities

Western Europe was an agricultural society, the majority of its people peasant farmers. Farming and livestock raising had been practiced in Europe for thousands of years, but great advances in the technology of farming took place during the late Middle Ages. Water mills, iron plows, improved devices for harnessing ox and horse power, and systems of crop rotation greatly increased productivity. Over several centuries farmers more than doubled the quantity of European land in cultivation. The increased supply of food helped the population of western Europe nearly triple between the eleventh and fourteenth centuries.

Rural Europeans lived in family households clustered in farming villages. Men performed the basic field work; women were responsible for child care, livestock, and food preparation. In the European pattern, a daughter usually left the home and village of her family to take up residence among her husband's people. A woman's family gave her a dowry, or a gift of money at the time of marriage, but in general women were excluded from inheritance. Divorce was almost unknown.

This was a world of social contrasts. Europe was dominated by a social system historians have called "feudalism." The land was divided into hundreds of small territories, each ruled by a family of lords monopolizing wealth and power. From the peasants of their districts the noble lords commanded labor service and tribute in the form of crops. Thus the nobility was the main beneficiary of medieval economic expansion, accumulating great estates and building imposing castles. A relatively small class of freehold farmers prospered as well, but the majority of peasants experienced little improvement in their standard of living.

The majority of Europeans were Christians, united under the authority of the Roman Catholic Church, whose complex organization spanned thousands of local communities with a hierarchy that extended from parish priests all the way to the pope in Rome. At the core of Christian belief was a set of communal values: love of God the father, loving behavior toward other people, and the fellowship of all believers. Nevertheless, the Catholic Church itself was one of the most powerful landowners in Europe, devoting a large portion of its considerable resources to awe-inspiring display rather than the amelioration of poverty and suffering. Counseling the poor and downtrodden to place their hopes in heavenly rewards, the Church provided legitimization for the power relationships of Europe.

Europe was also home to numerous communities of Jews, a people who dispersed from their homeland in Palestine after a series of unsuccessful revolts against Roman rule in the first century C.E. Both church and civic authorities subjected the Jews to discriminatory treatment. Restricted to ghettos and forbidden from owing land, many Jews turned adversity to advantage, becoming merchants who specialized in long-distance trade. But Jewish success only seemed to stimulate Christian hostility, culminating in a series of expulsions in the thirteenth and fourteenth

A French peasant labors in the field before a spectacular castle in a page taken from the illuminated manuscript Tres Riches Heures, *made in the fifteenth century for the duc de Berry. In 1580 the essayist Montaigne talked with several American Indians at the French court who "noticed among us some men gorged to the full with things of every sort while their other halves were beggars at their doors, emaciated with hunger and poverty" and "found it strange that these poverty-stricken halves should suffer such injustice, and that they did not take the others by the throat or set fire to their houses."*

centuries: the Jews were forced out of England in 1290, France in 1394, and Spain in 1492. Religious tolerance was unknown in early modern Europe.

For the great majority of Europeans, those were the bad old days. Most rural people survived on bread and porridge, supplemented with seasonal vegetables and an occasional piece of meat or fish. Infectious diseases abounded; perhaps a third of all children died before their fifth birthday, and only half the population reached adulthood. Famines periodically ravaged the countryside. In the fourteenth century a series of crop failures resulted in widespread starvation and death. Malnutrition paved the way for disease. Between 1347 and 1353 the widespread epidemic of bubonic plague known as the Black Death swept in from Asia and wiped out a third of Europe's population. In many places Jews were accused of spreading the plague by poisoning wells, and there were violent attacks on the ghettos.

By 1500, however, Europe's agricultural economy, strengthened by the technological breakthroughs of the Middle Ages, had recovered and its population had nearly returned to its former peak of about 30 million. Europe's social structure was hierarchical and authoritarian, but its agricultural system had the technological capacity for far greater growth than the farming economy of the Americas.

The Merchant Class and the Renaissance

The economic growth of the late Middle Ages was accompanied by the expansion of commerce, especially trade in basic goods such as minerals, salt, timber, fish, cereals, wool, and wine. Commercial expansion stimulated the growth of markets and towns: the heart of this dynamic European commercialism lay in the city-states of Italy.

During the late Middle Ages, the cities of Venice, Genoa, and Pisa launched armed, commercial fleets that seized control of Mediterranean trade. The merchants of these cities became the principal outfitters of the Crusades, a series of great military expeditions promoted by the Catholic Church to recover Palestine from the Muslims. When the Crusaders conquered the Holy Land at the end of the eleventh century they delivered the silk and spice trades of Asia into the hands of the Italian merchants. Tropical spices—cloves, cinnamon, nutmeg, and pepper—were in great demand, for they made the European diet far less monotonous for the lords who could afford them. Asian civilization also supplied a number of technical innovations that further propelled European economic growth. From China alone came the compass, gunpowder, and the art of printing with movable type. These were, according to the seventeenth-century English philosopher Francis Bacon, "the three greatest inventions known to man."

Contact with Muslim civilization provided Western scholars with access to important ancient Greek and Roman texts that had been lost to them during the Middle Ages but that had been preserved in the great Muslim libraries. The revived interest in classical antiquity that resulted triggered during the fourteenth and fifteenth centuries a period of intellectual and artistic flowering known as the Renaissance. The revolution in learning made possible by the printing press, the beginning of regular postal service,

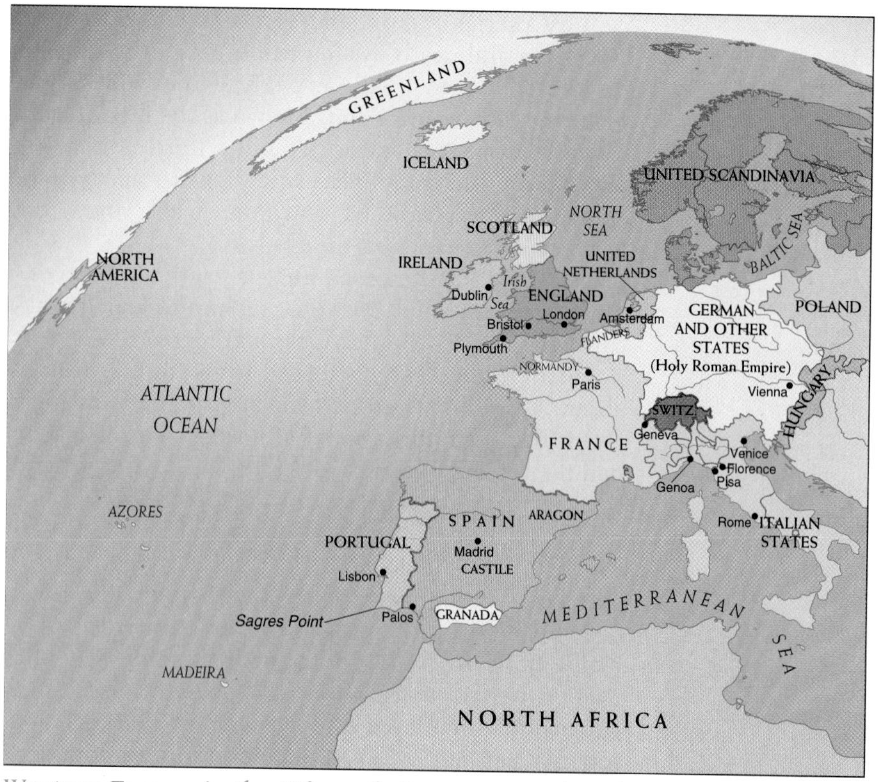

Western Europe in the Fifteenth Century *By the middle of the century, the monarchs of western Europe had unified their realms and begun to build royal bureaucracies and standing armies and navies. These states, all with extensive Atlantic coastlines, sponsored the voyages that inaugurated the era of European colonization.*

and the growth of universities helped spread the Renaissance throughout the elite circles of Europe.

The Renaissance celebrated human possibility. "The nature of all other beings is limited," the Italian intellectual Pico della Mirandola wrote in 1486; "but you, constrained by no limits, in accordance with your own free will, shall ordain for yourself the limits of your nature." This human-centered perspective was evident in architecture. The Gothic style of medieval cathedrals, whose soaring forms were intended to take human thoughts heavenward, gave way to styles borrowed from ancient Greece and Rome, which were thought to encourage rational reflection. In painting and sculpture there was a new focus on the human body. Artists modeled muscles with light and shadow to produce heroic images of men and women. These new artistic trends were aspects of what became known as *humanism*, a revolt against religious authority in which human life on earth took precedence over the afterlife of the soul. This outlook was a critical component of the inquisitive and acquisitive spirit that motivated the exploration of the Americas.

The New Monarchies

The Renaissance flowered amid the ruins that had been wrought by the plague. Famine and disease led to violence, as groups fought for shares of a shrinking economy. In Flanders—a cultural and linguistic region now spread across portions of France, Belgium, and the Netherlands—during the 1320s, peasants rose against both the noble lords and the Church, beginning a series of rebellions that culminated in the great English Peasants' Revolt of 1381. "We are made men in the likeness of Christ," one rebel cried out, "but you treat us like savage beasts!" Meanwhile civil and international warfare among the nobility greatly reduced the power of the landed classes and the Catholic Church was seriously weakened by an internal struggle between French and Italian factions.

During this period of social and political chaos, the monarchs of western Europe began to replace the lords as the new centers of power, building their legitimacy by promising internal order as they unified their realms. They built royal bureaucracies and standing armies and navies. In many cases, these new monarchs found support among the increasingly wealthy merchants, who in return sought lucrative royal contracts and trading monopolies. This alliance between commerce and political power was another of the important developments that prepared the way for European expansion.

Portuguese Explorations

Portugal, a narrow land along the western coast of the Iberian Peninsula with a long tradition of seafaring, became the first of these new kingdoms to explore distant lands. Lisbon, the principal port on the sea route between the Mediterranean and northwestern Europe, was a bustling, cosmopolitan city with large enclaves of Italian merchants. By 1385 local merchants had grown powerful enough to place their own favorite, João I, on the throne, and he laid ambitious plans to establish a Portuguese trading empire.

A central figure in this development was the son of the king, Prince Henry, known to later generations as "the Navigator." In the spirit of Renaissance learning, Henry established an institute of eminent geographers, instrument makers, shipbuilders, and seamen on Sagres Point, the southwestern tip of Portugal. By the mid-fifteenth century, principally as a result of their efforts, all educated Europeans knew the world was "round." (The idea that Europeans believed the world to be flat was invented in the nineteenth century.) The men of Sagres studied the seafaring techniques of Asia and the Muslim world. Incorporating these with European designs, they developed a new ship called the caravel, a faster, more maneuverable, and more seaworthy vessel than any previously known in Europe.

Using this new ship, the Portuguese plied the Atlantic coast of northwestern Africa, where gold mines and a long-established slave trade offered lucrative trading. By the time of Prince Henry's death in 1460, they had colonized the Atlantic islands of the Azores and the Madeiras and had founded bases along the West African Gold Coast. In 1488 the Portuguese captain Bartolomeu Días rounded the southern tip of Africa, known as the Cape of Good Hope, and ten years later Vasco da Gama, with the aid of Arab pilots, followed the same route to reach India. The Portuguese eventually erected strategic trading posts along the coasts of Africa, India, and China. Marrying native women and fitting into indigenous communities rather than trying to dominate them as the Roanoke colonists later would, Portuguese traders created the first and longest-lasting outposts of European world colonization, eventually gaining control of much of the Asian spice trade. Most important for the history of the Americas, however, was their establishment of the slave trade that spanned the Atlantic. (For a full discussion of slavery, see Chapter 4.)

Columbus Reaches the Americas

In 1476, Christopher Columbus, a young Genoan sailor, was shipwrecked off Sagres Point in Portugal. Making his way to Lisbon, he joined his brother, a chart maker in the Italian community there. Over the next ten years Columbus worked as a seafaring merchant seaman, visiting ports from Iceland in the North Atlantic to the Gold Coast in the south. He married and settled on the Portuguese island colony of Madeira in the Atlantic, and it was there that he developed the idea of opening a new route to Asia by sailing west across the ocean. Such a venture would require royal backing, but when he approached the various monarchs of Europe with his idea, their advisers laughed at his geographic ignorance, pointing out that his calculation of the distance to Asia was much too short. They were right, Columbus was wrong, but it turned out to be an error of monumental good fortune.

Columbus finally sold his idea to the monarchs of Castile and Aragon, Isabella and Ferdinand. This royal couple, who through marriage had joined their kingdoms to form the state of Spain, had just conquered the southern Iberian province of Granada, formerly held by the Moors of North Africa. Their victory completed the *Reconquista* (Reconquest), the centuries-long struggle between Catholics and Muslims for the control of Iberia. Through these many generations of warfare, the Spanish had developed a military tradition that thrived on conquest and plunder. Military service was a popular means by which ordinary men could enrich themselves and rise into the ranks of the noble class. The Catholic monarchs of Spain were eager for new lands to conquer, and observing the successful Portuguese push to the south, they also became interested in opening lucrative trade routes of their own with Asia. Columbus's name for his under-

This ship, thought to be similar to Columbus's Niña, *is a caravel, a type of vessel developed by the naval experts at Henry the Navigator's institute at Sagres Point, in Portugal. To the traditional square-rigged Mediterranean ship, they added the "lateen" sail of the Arabs, which permitted much greater maneuverability. Other Asian improvements, such as the stern-post rudder and multiple masting, allowed caravels to travel farther and faster than any earlier ships, and made possible the invasion of America.*

taking, "the Enterprise of the Indies," suggested its commercial motive, but his expedition symbolized hopes of both trade and conquest. It did not envision the establishment of a colonial community. Like the adventurers who later peopled the first English colony of Roanoke, the Spanish had material gain in mind.

Columbus's ships left the port of Palos, Spain, in August 1492, pushed west across the Atlantic by the prevailing trade winds. By October flocks of birds and bits of driftwood announced the ships' approach to land, which turned out to be a small, flat island somewhere in the Bahamas. Although scholars disagree on the precise location, many believe it to be a spot now known as Samana Cay. Columbus, however, believed he was somewhere near the Asian mainland. He explored the northern island coasts of Cuba and Hispaniola (now Haiti and the Dominican Republic) before heading home, fortuitously catching the westerly winds that blow from the American coast toward Europe north of the tropics. One of Columbus's most important contributions was the discovery of the clockwise circulation of the Atlantic winds and currents that ultimately carried thousands of ships back and forth between Europe and the Americas.

Leading Columbus's triumphal procession to the royal court were a number of Taino Indians, dressed in bright feathers with ornaments of gold. The natives, Columbus noted, were "of a very acute intelligence" but had "no iron or steel weapons." "Should your majesties command it," Columbus announced to Ferdinand and Isabella, "all the inhabitants could be made slaves." Columbus also reported that "there are many spices and great mines of gold and of other metals." In fact, none of the spices familiar to Europeans grew in the Caribbean, and there were only small quantities of the precious metal in the riverbeds of the islands. But the sight of the little gold ornaments worn by the Indians had infected Columbus with a bad case of gold fever. He had left a small force behind in a rough fort on what is now the isolated northern coast of Haiti with instructions to continue the search for gold—the first European foothold in the Americas.

This image accompanied Columbus's account of his voyage, which was published in Latin and reissued in many other languages and editions that circulated throughout Europe before 1500. The Spanish King Ferdinand is shown directing the voyage to a tropical island, where the natives flee in terror. Columbus's impression of native Americans as a people vulnerable to conquest shows clearly in this image.

The Spanish monarchs, enthusiastic about Columbus's report, financed a convoy of 17 ships and 1,500 men that left in late 1493 to begin the colonization of the islands Columbus described as "rich for planting and sowing, for breeding cattle of every kind, for building towns and villages." As later at Roanoke, it was expected that Indians would provide the labor for these enterprises. But on his return to Hispaniola, Columbus found his fort in ruins, his men killed by Indians who, like the Algonquians at Roanoke, lost patience with the demands and brutality of the invading Europeans. Columbus destroyed the nearby native villages, enslaving the Tainos and demanding tribute from them in gold. He took slaves back to Spain, but most soon sickened and died, and the supply of gold quickly ran out. By the time of Columbus's third voyage the Spanish monarchs had become so dissatisfied with these results that they ordered the admiral home in leg irons.

Columbus made a fourth and final trip to the Caribbean that was characterized by the same violent slave raiding and obsessive searching for gold. He died in Spain in 1506, still convinced that he had opened the way to Asia, a belief that persisted among many Europeans well into the sixteenth century. But others had already begun to see the discoveries from a different perspective. Amerigo Vespucci of Florence, who voyaged to the Caribbean in 1499, was the first European to describe the lands as *mundus novus*, a New World. When European geographers named these continents in the first decade of the sixteenth century, they called them America, after Vespucci.

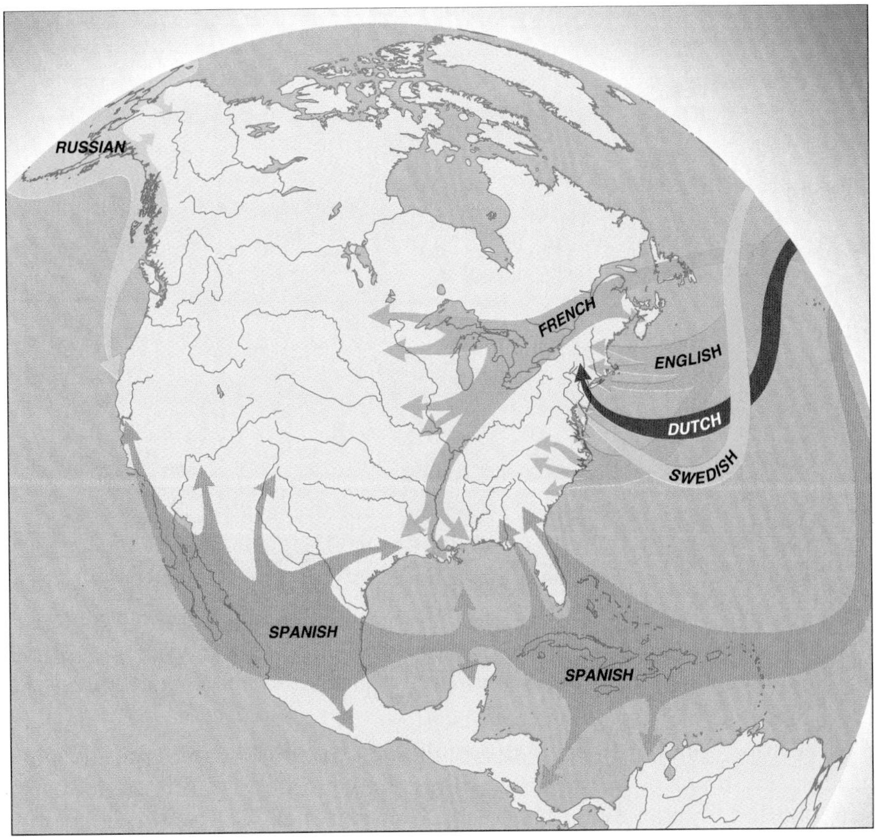

The Invasion of America *In the sixteenth century the Spanish first invaded the Caribbean and used it to stage their successive wars of conquest in North and South America. In the seventeenth century, the French, English, and Dutch invaded the Atlantic coast. The Russians, sailing across the northern Pacific, mounted the last of the colonial invasions in the eighteenth century.*

THE SPANISH IN THE AMERICAS

A century after Columbus's death, before the English had planted a single New World colony of their own, the Spanish had created a huge and wealthy empire in the Americas. In theory, all law and policy for the empire came from Spain; in practice, the isolation of the settlements permitted a good deal of local autonomy. The Spanish created a caste system, in which a small minority of settlers and their offspring controlled the lives and labor of millions of Indian and African workers. At the same time, theirs was a society in which colonists, Indians, and Africans mixed to form a new people.

The Invasion of America

The first stages of the Spanish invasion of America included frightful violence. Armies led by conquistadors marched across the Caribbean islands, plundering villages, slaughtering men, and capturing women. The Spanish crown created a system known as *encomienda*, in which colonial lords were given the right to the labor of a community of Indians; it was supposed to be a reciprocal relationship, with the lord protecting the Indians as well as exploiting them, but in practice it amounted to simply another form of slavery. Rather than work, one observer noted, many Indians took poison, "and others hanged themselves." Faced with labor shortages, slavers raided what King Ferdinand labeled the "useless islands" of the Bahamas and soon had entirely depopulated them. The depletion of gold on Hispaniola led to the invasion of the islands of Puerto Rico and Jamaica in 1508, and Cuba in 1511. Meanwhile, rumors of wealthy societies farther west led to scores of probing expeditions. The Spanish invasion of Central America began in 1511, and two years later Vasco Nuñez de Balboa crossed the Isthmus of Panama to what he called the "South Sea," the Pacific Ocean. In 1517 Spaniards landed on the coast of Mexico, and within a year they had made contact with the Aztec empire.

The warlike Aztecs had migrated to the high Valley of Mexico from the harsh deserts of the American Southwest during the thirteenth century in the wake of the collapse of the Toltec Empire (see Chapter 1). They settled the marshy lake district of the valley and built the city of Tenochtitlán. By the early fifteenth century the Aztecs had come to dominate

The Cruelties used by the Spaniards on the Indians, *from a 1599 English edition of* The Destruction of the Indies *by* Bartolomé de las Casas. *These scenes were copied from a series of engravings produced by* Theodore de Bry *that accompanied an earlier edition.*

the farming communities of the highlands, in the process building a powerful state. Tribute flowed into Tenochtitlán from all over Mexico and Central America. In public rituals designed to appease their gods, Aztec priests brutally sacrificed captives atop grand pyramids. By 1519, when Hernán Cortés, a veteran of the conquest of Cuba, landed on the Mexican coast, the population of the Aztec capital numbered as much as 300,000, five times the size of the largest city in Spain.

Within two years Cortés and his army had overthrown the Aztec empire, a spectacular military accomplishment that has no parallel in the annals of conquest. The Spanish had superior arms, and they also had horses, which the Indians found terrifying, mistaking mounted men for four-legged monsters. But these were not the principal causes of the Spanish success. Cortés skillfully exploited the resentments of the many native peoples who lived under Aztec domination, forging Spanish-Indian alliances that became a model for the subsequent European colonization of the Americas. Here, as at Roanoke and dozens of other sites of European invasion, colonists found Indians eager for allies to support them in their conflicts with their neighbors. Still, the Aztecs were militarily powerful, successfully driving the Spaniards from Tenochtitlán and putting up a bitter and prolonged defense when they returned to besiege the capital. But in the meantime the Aztecs were hit by a devastating smallpox epidemic that killed thousands and undermined their ability to resist. In the aftermath of conquest, the Spanish unmercifully plundered Aztec society, providing the Catholic monarchs with wealth beyond their wildest imagining. Later, the discovery of rich silver mines and the exploitation of Mexican labor through the encomienda system turned Spain into the mightiest state in Europe.

The Destruction of the Indies

Like the Aztecs, the other Indian peoples of the Americas resisted Spanish conquest, but most proved a poor match for mounted warriors wielding steel swords and accompanied by vicious bloodhounds. The record of the conquest, however, includes many brave Indian leaders and thousands of martyrs. The Carib people (from whose name "Caribbean" is derived) successfully defended the outermost islands until the end of the sixteenth century, and in the arid lands of northern Mexico the nomadic tribes known collectively as the Chichimecs proved equally difficult to subdue.

Among the Europeans who protested the horrors of the conquest, the most famous may have been Bartolomé de las Casas, a Spanish Catholic priest who had participated in the plunder of Cuba in 1511 but who several years later suffered a crisis of conscience and began to denounce the conquest. The Christian mission in the New World was to convert the Indians, he argued, and "the means to effect this end are not to rob, to scandalize, to capture or destroy them, or to lay waste their lands." Long before the world recognized the concept of universal human rights, Las Casas was proclaiming that "the entire human race is one," a statement that has earned him a reputation as one of the towering moral figures in the early history of the Americas. Las Casas's powerful supporters at court made repeated but unsuccessful attempts to reform the treatment of Indians.

In his brilliant history of the conquest, *The Destruction of the Indies* (1552), Las Casas blamed the Spanish for millions of deaths—in effect, for genocide. Translated into several languages and widely circulated throughout Europe, Las Casas's book was used by other European powers to condemn Spain in an effort to cover up their own dismal colonial records. Later scholars, questioning the accuracy of Las Casas's estimates of huge population losses, condemned his work as contributing to a "Black Legend" of the Spanish conquest. But many of today's historians find Las Casas's figures more believable. Demographic studies suggest that the Tainos of Hispaniola numbered in the hundreds of thousands when Columbus arrived; fifty years later they were reduced to a few hundred, and soon they disappeared from the face of the earth. Over the sixteenth century, the approximately 25 million people thought to have inhabited the highlands of Mexico were reduced to only one million.

Las Casas was incorrect, however, in attributing most of these losses to warfare. To be sure, thousands of lives were lost in battle, but these deaths were but a small proportion of the overall population decline. Thousands more starved because their economies were destroyed or their food stores taken by conquering armies. Even more important, native birth rates fell drastically after the conquest. Indian women were so "worn out with work," one Spaniard wrote, that they avoided conception, induced abortion, and even "killed their children with their own hands so that they [should] not have to endure the same hardships."

But by far the greatest loss of life resulted from the introduction of Old World diseases. The people of the Americas, separated from Asia, Africa, and Europe by the rising oceans following the Ice Age, were isolated from the virulent epidemic diseases that developed along with civilization, diseases such as smallpox, measles, pneumonia, and malaria. Pre-Columbian America was blessed with a remarkably disease-free environment, but the Indian peoples also lacked the antibodies necessary to protect them from European bacteria and viruses. A shipload of colonists carried smallpox to Hispaniola in 1516, causing an epidemic in the Caribbean that by 1520 crossed into Mexico and eventually spread along the trading network through both North and South America. This was the epidemic that provided Cortés with the critical edge in overcoming the Aztecs. Such devastating outbreaks of disease, striking for the first time against a completely unprotected population, are known as "virgin soil epidemics." After the conquest, Mexicans sang of an earlier time:

> *There was then no sickness.*
> *They had then no aching bones.*
> *They had then no high fever.*
> *They had then no smallpox.*
> *They had then no burning chest.*
> *They had then no abdominal pains.*
> *They had then no consumption.*
> *They had then no headache.*
> *At that time the course of humanity was orderly.*
> *The foreigners made it otherwise when they arrived here.*

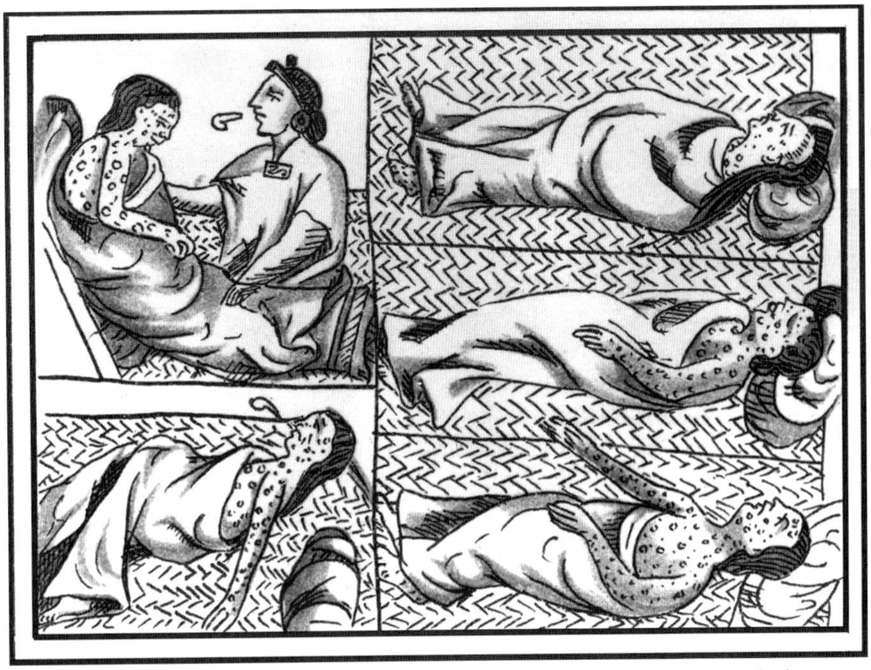

This drawing of victims of the smallpox epidemic that struck the Aztec capital of Tenochtitlán in 1520 is taken from the Florentine Codex, *a postconquest history written and illustrated by Aztec scribes. "There came amongst us a great sickness, a general plague," reads the account, "killing vast numbers of people. It covered many all over with sores: on the face, on the head, on the chest, everywhere.... The sores were so terrible that the victims could not lie face down, nor on their backs, nor move from one side to the other. And when they tried to move even a little, they cried out in agony."*

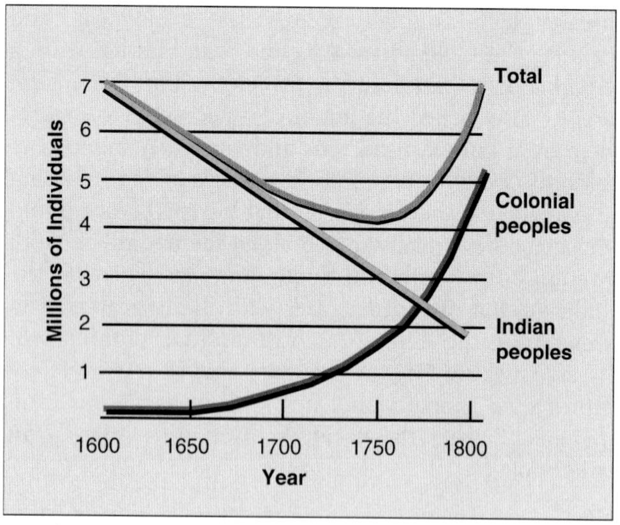

North America's Indian and Colonial Populations in the Seventeenth and Eighteenth Centuries *The primary factor in the decimation of native peoples was epidemic disease, brought to the New World from the Old. In the eighteenth century the colonial population overtook North America's Indian populations.*

Source: *Historical Statistics of the United States* (Washington, D.C.: Government Printing Office, 1976), 8, 1168; Russell Thornton, *American Indian Holocaust and Survival* (Norman: University of Oklahoma Press, 1987), 32.

Warfare, famine, lower birth rates, and epidemic disease knocked the population of Indian America into a downward spiral that did not swing upward until the twentieth century. By that time the native population had fallen by 90 percent. It was the greatest demographic disaster in world history. The outstanding difference between the European colonial experience in the Americas and elsewhere—Africa and Asia, for example—was this radical reduction in the native population.

It is possible that the New World sent one disease back across the Atlantic. On the basis of considerable evidence, archaeologists have concluded that syphilis was present in ancient America but not in the Old World before 1492. The first recorded epidemic of venereal syphilis in Europe took place in Spain in 1493, and many historians think it may have been carried home by the sailors on Columbus's ships. By 1495 the disease was spreading rapidly among Europe's armies, and by the sixteenth century it had found its way to Asia and Africa.

Intercontinental Exchange

The passage of diseases between the Old and New Worlds was just one part of the large-scale intercontinental exchange that marks the beginning of the modern era. The most obvious exchange was the vast influx into Europe of the precious metals plundered from the Aztec and Incan empires of the New World. "The best thing in the world is gold," wrote Columbus, and Cortés remarked, "We Spaniards suffer from a disease of the heart, the specific remedy for which is gold." Most of the booty was melted down, destroying forever thousands of priceless Indian artifacts. Even more important were the silver mines the Spanish discovered and operated in Mexico and Peru. Between 1500 and 1550 the amount of silver coin circulating in Europe tripled, then tripled again before 1600. The result was runaway inflation, which stimulated commerce and raised profits but lowered the standard of living for most people. During the sixteenth century, for example, rising prices depressed the value of European wages by more than 50 percent.

But of even greater long-term importance were the New World crops brought to Europe. Maize, or corn, from Mexico—the staff of life for most North Americans—became a staple human crop in Mediterranean countries, an important feed crop for livestock elsewhere in Europe, and the primary provision for the slave ships of Africa. Over the next few centuries, potatoes from Peru provided the margin between famine and subsistence for the peasant peoples of northern Europe and Ireland. And, of course, tomatoes transformed the cuisine of Italy. These "miracle crops" provided abundant food sources that went a long way toward ending the persistent problem of famine in Europe.

Although the Spanish failed to locate valuable spices such as black pepper or cloves in the New World, new tropical crops more than compensated. Tobacco, which was first prescribed as an antidote to disease when it appeared in Europe about 1550, soon became widely used as an intoxicant. American vanilla and chocolate both became highly valued commodities, and American cotton proved superior to Asian varieties for the production of cheap textiles. These native crops, together with crops brought from the Old World to the New, like sugar, rice, and coffee, supplied the basis for important new industries and markets that altered the course of world history.

Columbus introduced domesticated animals into Hispaniola and Cuba, and this breeding stock later supplied the conquistadors of Mexico. The movement of Spanish settlement into northern Mexico was greatly aided by an advancing wave of livestock, for not only did these animals supply the colonists with animal power and meat but they disturbed native fields and forests, disrupting Indian societies and preparing the way for conquest. Horses, used by Spanish stockmen to tend their cattle, also spread northward. Eventually they reached the Great

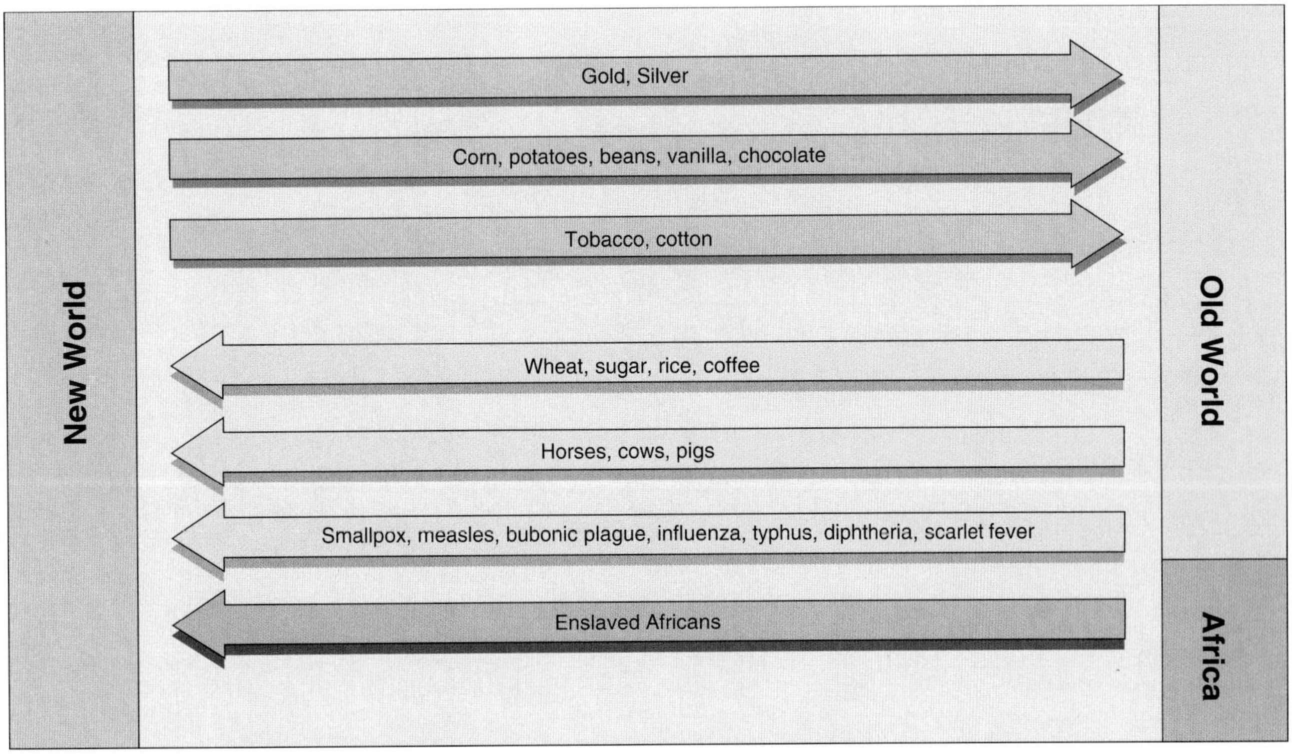

Intercontinental Exchange *The exchange between continents of crops and animals, microbes and men, marks the beginning of the modern era of world history.*

Plains of North America, where they transformed the lives of the nomadic hunting Indians.

The First Europeans in North America

Juan Ponce de León, governor of Puerto Rico, was the first conquistador to attempt to extend the Spanish conquest to North America. In 1513 he landed on the southern Atlantic coast, which he named Florida in honor of the Easter season, in Spanish called *pascua florida*. Florida is thus the oldest European place-name in the continental United States. Warriors from some of the powerful Indian chiefdoms of the South beat back Ponce de León's attempts to take slaves and finally killed him in battle in 1521. Seven years later another Spanish attempt to colonize Florida, under the command of Pánfilo de Narváez, also ended in disaster. Most of Narváez's men were lost in a shipwreck, but a small group of them survived, living and wandering for several years among the Indian peoples of the Gulf coast and the Southwest until they were finally rescued in 1536 by Spanish slave hunters in northern Mexico. One of these castaways, Alvar Núñez Cabeza de Vaca, published an account of his adventures in which he told of a North American empire known as Cíbola, with golden cities "larger than the city of Mexico."

Cabeza de Vaca's report inspired two Spanish attempts to penetrate the mystery of North America. Hernán de Soto, a veteran of the conquest of Peru, landed in Florida in 1539 with a Cuban army of more than 700 men and thousands of hogs and cattle. As he pushed hundreds of miles through the heavily populated South, he commandeered food and slaves from the Mississippian Indian towns in his path. De Soto failed, though, to locate another Aztec empire. In present-day Alabama, thousands of warriors of the powerful Alibamu chiefdom besieged his army, and a few months later the ancestors of the modern Chickasaws chewed the Spaniards apart. His army depleted by half, de Soto desperately drove his men westward, crossing the Mississippi and marching deep into present-day Arkansas before returning to the banks of the great river, where he died in 1542. Some 300 of de Soto's dispirited survivors eventually reached Mexico on rafts in 1543. They told of the great farming fields of the Mississippians but also emphasized the ferocity of the warriors. The native peoples of the South had successfully turned back Spanish invasion. If this were the end of the story, de Soto's expedition would be barely remembered, but his army also introduced epidemic diseases to the South that drastically undermined and depopulated the societies there. When Europeans finally returned to colonize the region in the seventeenth century, they found the descendants of the Mississippian chiefdoms living in much simpler tribal confederacies.

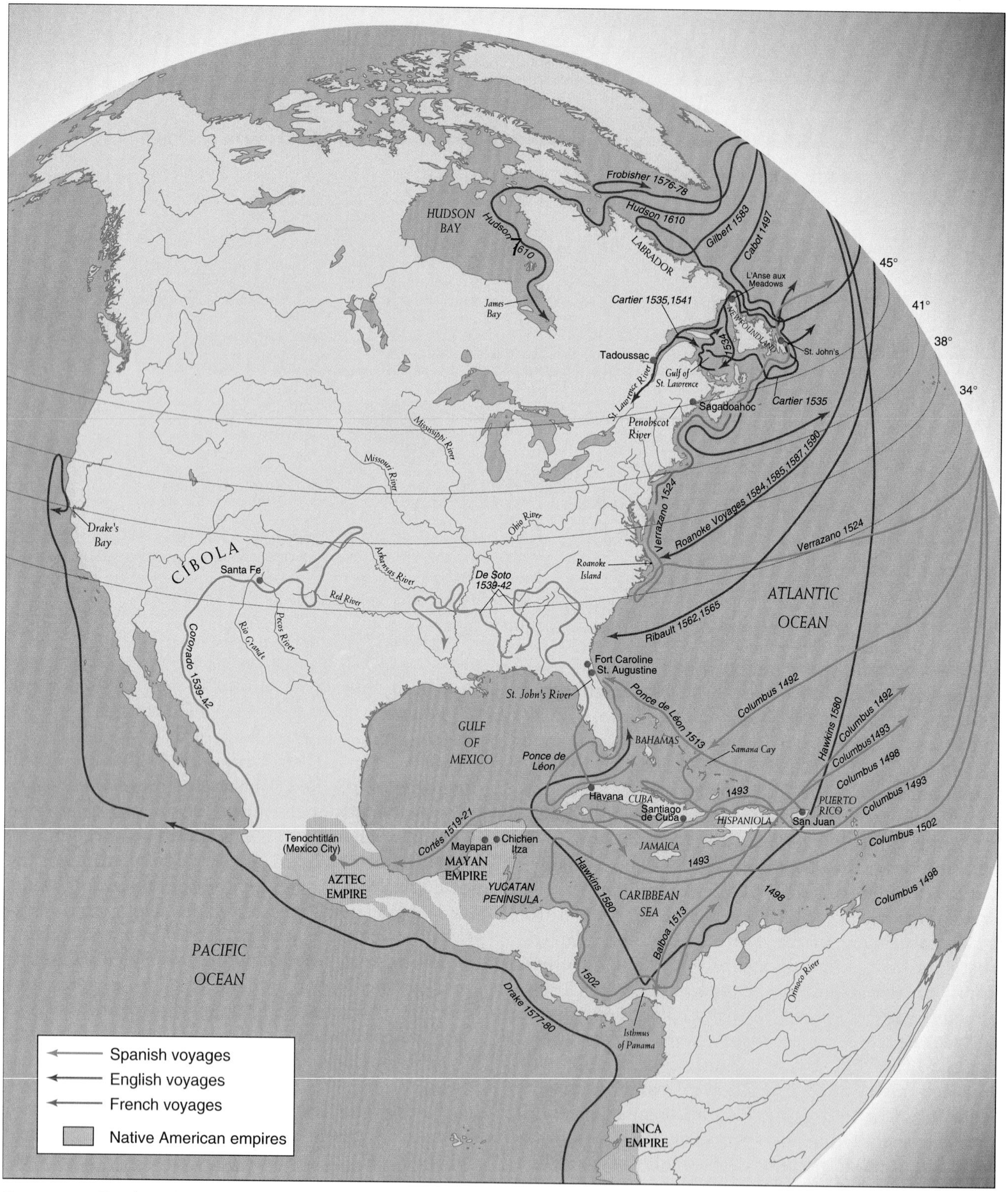

European Exploration, 1492–1591 *By the mid-sixteenth century Europeans had explored most of the Atlantic coast of North America and penetrated into the interior in the disastrous expeditions of de Soto and Coronado.*

The year following the beginning of the de Soto expedition, 1540, Spanish officials in Mexico launched a second attempt to find and conquer the cities of Cíbola, this one aimed at the North American Southwest. Francisco Vásquez de Coronado led 300 mounted men and infantry and 800 Indian porters north along well-marked Indian trading paths, passing through the settlements of Piman Indians near the present border of the United States and Mexico and finally reaching the Pueblo villages along the Rio Grande. The initial resistance of the Pueblo people was quickly quashed. But Coronado was deeply disappointed by these towns "of stone and mud, rudely fashioned." He led his army as far north as the Great Plains, where they observed great herds of "shaggy cows" (buffalo) and made contact with nomadic hunting peoples, but returned without gold. When Coronado and his men failed to find the "new Mexico" for which they had been looking, Spain lost all interest in the Southwest for the next fifty years.

The Spanish New World Empire

Despite these setbacks, by the late sixteenth century the Spanish had control of a powerful empire in the Americas. A century after Columbus, some 200,000 Europeans, most of them Spaniards, had settled in the Americas. Another 125,000 Africans had been forcibly resettled on the Spanish plantations of the Caribbean, as well as on the plantations of Brazil, which the Portuguese had colonized under the terms of the Treaty of Tordesillas, a 1494 agreement between Spain and Portugal setting a line of demarcation between their respective colonial domains. Most of the Spanish settlers resided in the more than 200 urban communities founded during the conquest, including cities such as Santo Domingo in Hispaniola; Havana, Cuba; Mexico City, built atop the ruins of Tenochtitlán; Quito, Peru (today in Ecuador), in the north of the conquered empire of the Incas; and Lima, Peru, near the empire's center. The few Spaniards who lived in the countryside supervised Indian or African workers in mining, ranching, or agriculture.

Because European women constituted only about 10 percent of the immigrants, from the beginning male colonists married or simply lived with African or Indian women. The result was the growth of large mixed-ancestry groups. The Spanish communities were characterized by what has been called a "frontier of inclusion," with a great deal of sexual mixing and marriage between male colonists and native women. Hundreds of thousands of Indians died, but Indian genes were passed on to generations of mestizo (European-Indian) and mulatto (European-African) peoples, who became the majority population in the mainland Spanish American empire.

Populated by Indians, Africans, Spanish colonists, and their mixed offspring, the New World colonies of Spain constituted one of the largest empires in the history of the world. In theory, the empire was a highly centralized and bureaucratic system, but in operation there was significant local autonomy. The Council of the Indies, composed of the king's principal advisers, formulated all the laws and regulations of the empire, but the Council was in Spain. In the colonies, halfway around the globe, passive resistance and sometimes outright defiance of central authority were commonplace.

FRENCH AND ENGLISH EXPLORATIONS AND ENCOUNTERS

With the Spanish empire at the height of its power in the sixteenth century, the merchants and monarchs of other important European seafaring states looked across the Atlantic for opportunities of their own. In the early sixteenth century France was first to sponsor intensive expeditions to the New World. At first the French attempted to plant settlements on the coasts of Brazil and Florida, but Spanish opposition ultimately persuaded them to concentrate on the northern regions. It was the second half of the

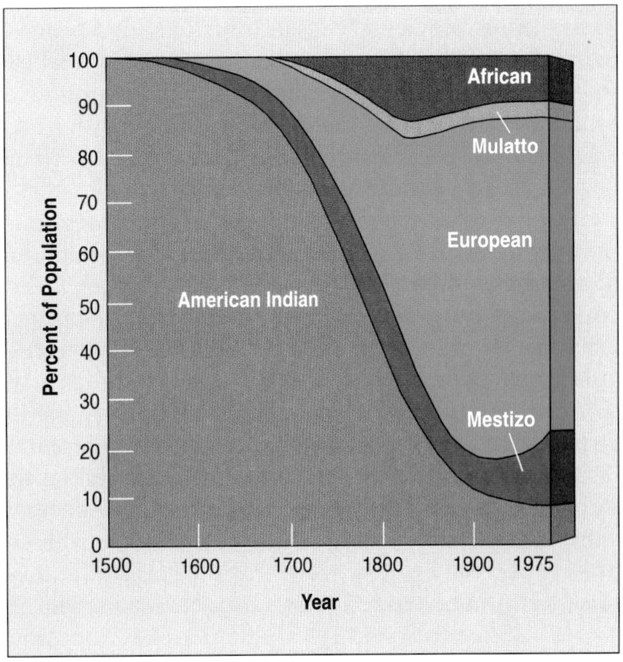

The African, Indian, and European Population of the Americas *In the 500 years since the European invasion of the Americas, the population has included varying proportions of native, European, and African peoples, as well as large numbers of persons of mixed ancestry.*

Source: Colin McEvedy and Richard Jones, *Atlas of World Population History* (New York: Penguin, 1978), 280.

sixteenth century before England developed plans to colonize North America. With the Spanish in Florida and the French establishing close ties with coastal tribes as far south as present-day Maine, the English focused on the middle latitudes.

The Political Impact of the Reformation

The religious revolt against Catholicism known as the Reformation began in 1517 when the German priest Martin Luther publicized his differences with Rome. Luther declared that eternal salvation was a gift from God, not something earned by good works or service to the Roman Catholic Church. He also emphasized the importance of individual Bible study, underlining the impact of the revolution in printing and literacy and undercutting the authority of priests. As a result of his attacks on the Catholic hierarchy Luther was excommunicated in 1521. But his ideas reflected a growing climate of dissatisfaction throughout Europe with the power and prosperity of the Catholic Church. And when German princes who wished to strengthen their independence from Rome subscribed to Luther's views, the controversy became political, inaugurating a series of bloody religious wars that ravaged Europe for the next century.

Protestantism, as Luther's protest movement came to be called, aroused considerable enthusiasm in France. Catholic persecution of French Protestants in the 1520s, however, caused John Calvin, a prominent reformer even more radical than Luther, to flee to Switzerland. Calvin settled in Geneva, where he organized a model Christian community that by the 1530s was in control of the entire city-state. A former lawyer, Calvin was the most systematic of the early Protestant theologians. His doctrine of predestination proposed that God had chosen a small number of men and women for "election," or salvation, while condemning the vast majority to eternal damnation. Calvinists were encouraged to examine themselves closely for "signs of election," which were usually thought to be prominence and prosperity. The virtues of thrift, industry, sobriety, and personal responsibility, which Calvin argued were essential to the Christian life, likewise promoted material success. This conjunction of spiritual and secular values proved powerful in the growth of the spirit of enterprise that characterized early European capitalism.

Sixteenth-century England also became deeply involved in struggles to reform the Catholic Church. At first King Henry VIII of England (reigned 1509–47) supported the Church against the Protestants. But in England, too, there was great public resentment of the ostentatious display of the Church and the drain of tax money to Rome. When the pope refused to grant Henry an annulment of his marriage to Catherine of Aragon, daughter of Isabella and Ferdinand of Spain, who had not produced a surviving male heir, the king exploited this popular mood. Taking up the cause of reform in 1534, he declared himself head of a separate Church of England. He later confiscated monastic property—the Catholic Church owned about a quarter of the country's land—and used the revenues to begin constructing a powerful English state system, including a standing army and navy. Working through Parliament, Henry carefully enlisted the support of the merchants and landed gentry for his program, parceling out a measure of royal prosperity in the form of titles, offices, lands, and commercial favors. By the mid-sixteenth century he had forged a solid alliance with the wealthy merchant class.

England and France moved in very different directions during the Reformation. Calvin's French followers—known as the Huguenots—were concentrated among merchants and the middle class, but they also included many of the nobility. In 1560 a group of Huguenot nobles tried to seize power, and their defeat initiated nearly forty years of religious struggle, during which France became known as the enemy of the new Protestant faith that was becoming so popular in England. One event that established France's fierce opposition to Protestantism was the St. Bartholomew's Day Massacre of August 24, 1572, in which some 6,000 Huguenots in Paris and thousands more throughout the country were slain at the direction of the French crown. Although in 1589 the Huguenot Henry IV became king of France, he found it impossible to govern until he converted to Catholicism. Henry's Edict of Nantes of 1598 guaranteed freedom of worship and the civil rights of Huguenots, but Henry's conversion, in effect, made Roman Catholicism the official religion of France.

The French Colony in Florida

Efforts by Huguenot leaders to establish a refuge for French Protestants in the New World led to the establishment of a French colony in Florida. In 1562 Jean Ribault and 150 Protestants from Normandy landed on Parris Island, near present-day Beaufort, South Carolina, and began constructing a fort and crude mud huts. Ribault soon returned to France for supplies, where he was caught up in the religious wars. The French colonists nearly starved, finally resorting to cannibalism before being rescued by a passing British ship. In 1564 another French expedition established the Huguenot colony of Fort Caroline on the St. Johns River in Florida, near the present-day city of Jacksonville. When Ribault arrived the next year, he reported that the people of the nearby Timucua villages were friendly and

Jacques Le Moyne, *Rene de Loudonniere and Chief Athore*, 1564, watercolor, The New York Public Library, N.Y.

This watercolor of Jacques le Moyne, painted in 1564, depicts the friendly relations between the Timucuas of coastal Florida and the colonists of the short-lived French colony of Fort Caroline. The Timucuas hoped that the French would help defend them against the Spanish, who plundered the coast in pursuit of Indian slaves.

hospitable, welcoming the French colonists into their homes and honoring them with food and drink. It seems possible that at Fort Caroline the Huguenots enjoyed the kinds of relations with the Indians that John White later hoped for at Roanoke.

The Spanish, however, saw Fort Caroline as a threat. Uninterested in settlement, the Spanish had established a foothold along the Atlantic coast of Florida simply to protect their fleets riding the offshore Gulf Stream home to Spain. Fort Caroline was manned not only by Frenchmen but by French Protestants—deadly enemies of the Catholic monarchs of Spain. "We are compelled to pass in front of their port," wrote one official of New Spain, "and with the greatest ease they can sally out with their armadas to seek us." In 1565 the Spanish crown sent Don Pedro Menéndez de Avilés, captain general of the Indies, to crush the Huguenots. He established the Spanish fort of St. Augustine on the coast, south of the French, then marched overland through the swamps to surprise them with an attack from the rear. "I put Jean Ribault and all the rest of them to the knife," Menéndez wrote triumphantly to the king, "judging it to be necessary to the service of the Lord Our God and of Your Majesty." More than 500 Frenchmen lay dead on the beaches of Florida; the French attempt to plant a colony along the South Atlantic coast had ended in disaster. Today, St. Augustine claims the distinction of being the oldest continuously occupied European city in North America.

Fish and Furs

For the French overseas empire, far more significant than these efforts at colonization was the entrance of French fishermen into the waters of the North Atlantic. It is possible that fishing ships from England, France, Spain, and Portugal had discovered the great fishing grounds off North America's northern coast long before Columbus's voyages. In the Grand Banks, the waters teemed with "so great multitudes of certain big fishes," in the words of one early seaman, "that they sometimes stayed my ships." By 1500, hundreds of ships and thousands of sailors were regularly fishing the coastal waters of the North Atlantic, many

Louis Nicholas, Northern Indian, *Capitaine de la Nation*, from the *Codex Canadensis*, 1701, by Charles Becard. National Archives of Canada/The Thomas Gilcrease Institute of American History and Art, Tulsa, Oklahoma

In his sketch of this "Capitaine" of the Illinois nation (drawn about 1700), the French artist Charles Becard de Granville carefully noted the tattooing of the warrior's face and body, his distinctive costume and feather headdress, his spear and tobacco pipe.

making landfall to take on wood and fuel and to dry their catch. Fishermen were not particularly interested in conquest, and in their contacts with Indian people they established relationships based on the exchange of goods and ideas. Thus the pattern of colonial history in the early Northeast contrasted dramatically with that in the Spanish New World empire—and with later English colonization.

The first official voyages of exploration in the North Atlantic used the talents of experienced European sailors and fishermen. With a crew from Bristol, England, the Genoan navigator John Cabot reached Cape Breton Island or Newfoundland in 1497, and in 1524 the Tuscan captain Giovanni da Verrazano sailed with a crew from France, exploring the North American coast from Cape Fear (in today's North Carolina) to the Penobscot River (in Maine). Anxious to locate a passageway to the spice trade of Asia, the French king next commissioned the experienced captain Jacques Cartier. In 1534 and 1535 Cartier reconnoitered the St. Lawrence River, which led deep into the continental interior, and established France's imperial claim to the lands of Canada.

The northern Indians found the Europeans odd—particularly their beards—but immediately appreciated the usefulness of the textiles, glass, copper, and ironware the Europeans possessed. Seeing Cartier's ship, the Micmacs waved him ashore. "The savages showed marvelous great pleasure in possessing and obtaining iron wares and other commodities," he noted in his report. For his part, Cartier was interested in the fur coats the Indians wore. Europeans, like Indians, used furs for winter clothing. But the growing population of the late Middle Ages had so depleted the wild game of Europe that the price of furs had risen beyond the reach of most people. The North American fur trade thus filled an important demand and produced high profits. Cartier attempted to found a French colony on the St. Lawrence in 1541, but the unremitting winter and the hostility of the Indians forced him to abandon the effort. For the rest of the sixteenth century relations between Europeans and Indians in the Northeast were dominated by commerce, not conquest.

By no means were Indians simply the victims of European traders. Indian traders had a sharp eye for quality, and because of the unbridled competition among the Europeans, they could demand good exchange rates. But the trade also had negative consequences for Indian people. Epidemic European diseases soon began to ravage their communities. Intense rivalry broke out between tribes over hunting territories, resulting in deadly warfare. By the 1580s, disease and violence had turned the St. Lawrence Valley into a virtual no-man's land. Moreover, as European manufactured goods, such as metal knives, kettles, and firearms, became essential to their way of life, the Indians became dependent upon European suppliers. Ultimately, the fur trade was stacked in favor of Europeans.

By the end of the sixteenth century over a thousand ships per year were trading for furs along the northern coast. The trade between Indians and Europeans of many nations grew increasingly important as the century progressed. The village of Tadoussac on the St. Lawrence, where a wide bay offered Europeans safe anchorage, became the customary place for several weeks of trading each summer, a forerunner of the western fur-trade rendezvous of the nineteenth century. Among European traders, the French were probably the most numerous, and later, in the early seventeenth century, they had to move to consolidate their hold by planting colonies along the St. Lawrence.

Social Change in Sixteenth-Century England

Henry VIII of England died in 1547. He was succeeded by his young and sickly son Edward VI, who six years later followed his father to the grave, then by his Catholic daughter Mary, who attempted to reverse her father's Reformation from the top. She added her own chapter to the century's many religious wars, martyring hundreds of English Protestants and gaining the title of "Bloody Mary." But upon Mary's death in 1558, her Protestant half-sister Elizabeth I (reigned 1558–1603) ascended to the throne. Although she outlawed Catholicism, Elizabeth sought to end the religious turmoil by tolerating a variety of views within the English church. Criticized by radical Protestants for not going far enough and condemned by Catholics for her "pretended title to the kingdom," Elizabeth nevertheless gained popularity among the English people with her moderate approach. The Spanish monarchy, the head of the most powerful empire in the world, declared itself the defender of the Catholic faith and vowed to overthrow her. England and Spain now became the two principal rivals in the Catholic-Protestant confrontation.

In the 1570s several of Elizabeth's closest advisers began to argue that the time had come for England to enter the competition for American colonies. Their analysis linked colonization to social change at home.

The Armada Portrait of Elizabeth I, *painted by an unknown artist in 1648. The queen places her hand on the globe, symbolizing the rising seapower of England. Through the open windows we see the battle against the Spanish Armada in 1588 and the destruction of the Spanish ships in a providential storm, interpreted by the queen as an act of divine intervention.*

Elizabeth I, Armada portrait, c. 1588 (oil on panel) by English School. Private collection/Bridgeman Art Library, London/New York

Algonquian Indian village of Pomeiooc (North Carolina); watercolor, c. 1585, by John White; The Granger Collection.

In July 1585, John White sketched the Algonquian village of Pomeiooc, a palisaded enclosure with an easily guarded entrance. The eighteen longhouses would have made this a rather large community. Note the house with the pyramid-shaped roof. It is thought to have been a ceremonial or religious center.

As New World inflation caused the prices of European goods to rise steeply, English landlords, their rents fixed by custom, sought ways to increase their incomes. Seeking profits in the woolen trade, for example, many fenced off lands traditionally used as common pasture for villagers in order to provide grazing lands for their sheep. The result of this practice, called "enclosure" was the dislocation of farmers; between 1500 and 1650 a third of all the common lands in England were affected. Deprived of their traditional livelihoods, thousands of families left the countryside for the cities, and the roads were crowded with the homeless. In a state paper written for the queen, Richard Hakluyt argued that New World colonies could be populated by these "multitudes of loiterers and idle vagabonds." Such colonies, he said, could provide bases from which to raid the Spanish in the Caribbean, Indian markets for English goods, and plantations for growing tropical products, freeing England from a reliance on the long-distance trade with Asia. He urged Elizabeth to begin the planting of colonies "upon the mouths of the great navigable rivers" from Florida to the St. Lawrence.

England Turns toward Colonization

Elizabeth's first overseas priority, however, was Ireland, not America. Fearing Spanish subversion on that neighboring Catholic island, she urged enterprising supporters such as Walter Raleigh and his half-brother Humphrey Gilbert to subdue the Irish and settle English families on their land. During the 1560s both those men, and many other colonists as well, did precisely that, invading the island across the Irish Sea and viciously attacking the Irish defenders of their homeland, forcing them to retreat beyond the line of English settlement along the coast.

The English believed the Irish to be "savages," and indeed the Irish fought so ferociously in resisting the English invasions that an image of the "wild Irish" became fixed in the minds of English colonists. Gilbert retaliated with even greater brutality, ordering his soldiers to behead those they captured and line the walk to his quarters with their heads, "so that none should come into his tent for any cause but commonly he must pass through a lane of heads." Their own barbarism did not dissuade the English from considering the Irish an inferior race, and the notion that civilized people could not mix with such "savages" was an assumption that English colonists would carry with them to the Americas.

Like the invasion of Ireland, England's first ventures in the New World were made against the backdrop of its conflict with Spain. The goal of these ventures was to punish the Spanish, particularly to break the Spanish trading monopoly with tropical America. In 1562 John Hawkins inaugurated English participation in the slave trade, violating Spain's prohibition on foreign commerce with its colonies by transporting African slaves to the Caribbean and bringing back valuable tropical goods. In 1567 the Spanish attacked Hawkins, giving English privateers such as Francis Drake an excuse for launching devastating and lucrative raids against Spanish New World ports and fleets. The voyages of these English "Sea Dogs" greatly enriched their investors, including the queen herself. From a voyage that cost several thousand English pounds, Drake was said to have returned with booty valued in the millions. Thus, like the Spanish, the English began their American adventures by slaving and plundering.

It was not until the 1570s that Elizabeth finally authorized and invested in several private attempts at exploration and colonization in North America. In the late 1570s Martin Frobisher conducted three voyages of exploration in the North Atlantic, bringing back an Eskimo man, woman, and child and samples of worthless ores. Fresh from the Irish wars, Raleigh and Gilbert teamed up to plan their first American colonizing venture in 1578, but it failed to get off the ground. In 1583 Gilbert sailed with a flotilla of ships from Plymouth, England, and landed at St. John's Bay, Newfoundland, where he claimed the territory for his queen even though he found fishermen from several other nations there. But Gilbert's ship was lost on the return voyage.

Raleigh followed up Gilbert's efforts with plans to establish a colony to the south, in the more hospitable climate of the mid-Atlantic coast, but, as described in the opening of this chapter, the Roanoke enterprise of 1584–87 eventually failed as well. Nevertheless, it left as a considerable legacy the scientific work of Thomas Harriot and John White, who mapped the area, surveyed its commercial potential, and studied the Indian residents. Harriot's *Briefe and True Report of the Newfound Land of Virginia* (1588) was addressed mainly to the problem of identifying the "merchantable commodities" that would support settlement, for without products a colonial system was impossible. A later edition of this book included engravings based on White's watercolors of the people and landscape of Virginia. Together Harriot and White provided the most accurate and sensitive description we have of North American Indians at the moment of their contact with Europeans.

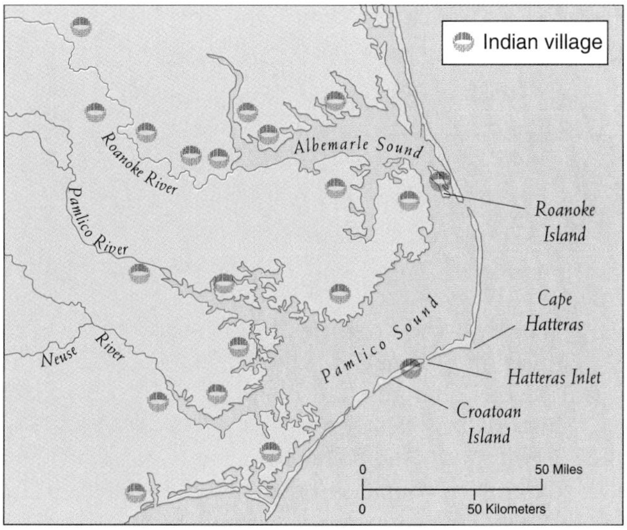

The Roanoke area in 1585 *The surveys of Thomas Harriot and John White revealed that the Roanoke area was densely settled with Indian villages. The information on this map is taken from their report.*

King Philip II of Spain was outraged at these English incursions into territory that, in the Treaty of Tordesillas of 1493, the pope had reserved for Spain. Philip had previously authorized the destruction of the French colony in Florida, and England's expanding colonial interests turned the competition between Catholic Spain and Protestant England into war. In 1588 Philip sent the Spanish Armada, a fleet of 130 ships carrying 30,000 men, to invade the British Isles. Countered by men such as Drake and Hawkins, who commanded smaller and more maneuverable ships, and frustrated by an ill-timed storm that the English chose to interpret as an act of divine intervention, the Armada foundered. Half the ships were destroyed, their crews killed or captured. The war continued until 1604, but the Spanish monopoly of the New World was broken in the English Channel.

CONCLUSION

The European colonization of the Americas opened with Columbus's voyage in 1492. For Indian people, assaulted by invasion and disease, the consequences were disastrous. But first in the Caribbean, then most spectacularly in Mexico, the Spanish succeeded in constructing the world's most powerful empire on the backs of Indian and imported African laborers. The New World colonies of Spain were characterized by a great deal of mixing between the mostly male colonists and native women; in this sense they were communities of "inclusion."

Inspired by the Spanish success, in the second half of the sixteenth century both the French and the English attempted to colonize the coast of North America but by the century's end had not succeeded in establishing any lasting communities. Instead, a very different kind of colonial encounter was taking place in Northeast North America, one based on commerce rather than conquest. In the next century the French would turn this development to their advantage in Canada. Along the mid-Atlantic coast in Virginia, however, the English would put their Irish experience to use, pioneering an altogether new kind of American colonialism.

CHRONOLOGY

1000	Norse settlement at L'Anse aux Meadows
1347–53	Black Death in Europe
1381	English Peasants' Revolt
1488	Bartolomeu Días sails around the African continent
1492	Christopher Columbus first arrives in the Caribbean
1494	Treaty of Tordesillas
1497	John Cabot explores Newfoundland
1500	High point of the Renaissance
1508	Spanish invade Puerto Rico
1513	Juan Ponce de León lands in Florida
1514	Bartolomé de las Casas begins preaching against the conquest
1516	Smallpox introduced to the New World
1517	Martin Luther breaks with the Roman Catholic Church
1519	Hernán Cortés lands in Mexico
1534	Jacques Cartier first explores the St. Lawrence River
1539–40	Hernán de Soto and Francisco Vásquez de Coronado expeditions
1550	Tobacco introduced to Europe
1552	Bartolomé de Las Casas's *Destruction of the Indies* published
1558	Elizabeth I of England begins her reign
1562	Huguenot colony planted along the mid-Atlantic coast
1565	St. Augustine founded
1572	St. Bartholomew's Day Massacre in France
1583	Humphrey Gilbert attempts to plant a colony in Newfoundland
1584–87	Walter Raleigh's colony on Roanoke Island
1588	English defeat the Spanish Armada
1590	John White returns to find Roanoke colony abandoned

REVIEW QUESTIONS

1. Discuss the roles played by the rising merchant class, the new monarchies, Renaissance humanism, and the Reformation in the development of European colonialism.
2. Define a "frontier of inclusion." In what ways does this description apply to the Spanish empire in the Americas?
3. Make a list of the major exchanges that took place between the Old World and the New World in the centuries following the European invasion of America. Discuss some of the effects these exchanges had on the course of modern history.
4. In what ways did colonial contact in the Northeast differ from contacts in the Caribbean and Mexico?
5. In what ways might the English experience in Ireland have shaped expectations about American colonization?

RECOMMENDED READING

Cyclone Covey, translator and editor, *Cabeza de Vaca's Adventures in the Unknown Interior of America* (1983). The captivity narrative that lured the Spanish into North America. An eye-opening story of the peoples and places of the preconquest Southwest.

Alfred W. Crosby Jr., *The Columbian Exchange: Biological and Cultural Consequences of 1492* (1972). Pathbreaking account of the intersection of the biospheres of the Old and New Worlds.

David Ewing Duncan, *Hernando de Soto: A Savage Quest in the Americas* (1995). A well-written biography of the conquistador and the story of his brutal expedition through the Indian homelands of the Southeast.

Charles Gibson, *Spain in America* (1966). The best introductory history of Spain's American empire.

Lewis Hanke, *The Spanish Struggle for Justice in the Conquest of America* (1949; reprint, 1965). The classic account of Las Casas's attempts to rectify the wrongs committed by the Spanish against the Indians.

Miguel Leon-Portilla, *The Broken Spears: The Aztec Account of the Conquest of Mexico* (1962; expanded ed., 1992). The history of the Spanish conquest as told by the Aztecs, drawn from manuscripts dating as early as 1528, only seven years after the fall of Tenochtitlán.

Samuel Eliot Morison, *The European Discovery of America: The Northern Voyages, A.D. 500–1600* (1971) and *The Southern Voyages, A.D. 1492–1616* (1974). The most detailed treatment of all the important European explorations of the Americas.

Anthony Pagden, *Lords of All the Worlds: Ideologies of Empire in Spain, Britain and France c. 1500-c. 1850* (1995). An important comparative history of the European justifications for colonial conquest.

David Beers Quinn, *Set Fair for Roanoke: Voyages and Colonies, 1584–1606* (1985). The story of Roanoke—the Indian village, the English settlement, and the Lost Colony.

Kirkpatrick Sale, *The Conquest of Paradise: Christopher Columbus and the Columbian Legacy* (1990). A harsh view of Columbus, but important information on the world of the Caribbean and the disastrous effects of the encounter with Europeans.

Carl Ortwin Sauer, *Sixteenth Century North America: The Land and the People as Seen by the Europeans* (1971). An excellent source for the explorations of the continent, providing abundant descriptions of the Indians.

David E. Stannard, *American Holocaust: Columbus and the Conquest of the New World* (1992). A provocative argument that the Spanish inaugurated a genocidal policy against the Indians that has continued into the twentieth century.

Hugh Thomas, *Conquest: Montezuma, Cortés, and the Fall of Old Mexico* (1993). A fascinating account, written by a master of historical style, that incorporates the Aztec view as well as the words of the conquerors.

ADDITIONAL BIBLIOGRAPHY

The Expansion of Europe

James M. Blaut, *1492: The Debate on Colonialism, Eurocentrism, and History* (1992)

Fernand Braudel, *The Mediterranean and the Mediterranean World in the Age of Philip II* (1972)

———, *Civilization and Capitalism, 15th–18th Centuries*, 3 vols. (1981)

Carol Cipolla, *Before the Industrial Revolution: European Society and Economy, 1100–1700* (1976)

Patrick Collinson, *The Religion of Protestants: The Church in English Society, 1559–1625* (1982)

Ralph Davis, *The Rise of Atlantic Economies* (1973)

Andre Gunder Frank, *World Accumulation, 1492–1789* (1978)

Douglas North, *The Rise of the Western World: A New Economic History* (1973)

José Casas Pardo, ed., *Economic Effects of the European Expansion, 1492–1824* (1992)

J. H. Parry, *The Age of Reconnaissance* (1963)

———, *Europe and a Wider World: The Establishment of the European Hegemony: Trade and Expansion in the Age of the Renaissance* (1966)

Geoffrey Vaughn Scannell, *The First Imperial Age: European Overseas Expansion c. 1400–1715* (1989)

The Spanish in the Americas

Warner Bowden, *American Indians and Christian Missions: Studies in Cultural Conflict* (1982)

Fredi Chiapelli, ed., *First Images of America: The Impact of the New World on the Old* (1976)

Nobel David Cook and W. George Lovell, *Secret Judgments of God: Old World Disease in Colonial Spanish America* (1991)

Henry F. Dobyns, *Their Number Become Thinned: Native American Population Dynamics in Eastern North America* (1983)

J. H. Elliott, *The Old World and the New, 1492–1650* (1970)

Anthony Grafton, *New Worlds, Ancient Texts: The Power of Tradition and the Shock of Discovery* (1992)

Hugh Honour, *New Golden Land: European Images of America from the Discoveries to the Present Time* (1975)
Charles Hudson, *Knights of Spain, Warriors of the Sun: Hernando De Soto and the South's Ancient Chiefdoms* (1997)
Charles Hudson and Carmen Chaves Tesser, eds., *The Forgotten Centuries: Indians and Europeans in the American South, 1521–1704* (1994)
René Jara and Nicholas Spadaccini, eds., *Amerindian Images and the Legacy of Columbus* (1992)
Elizabeth A. H. John, *Storms Brewed in Other Men's Worlds: The Confrontation of Indians, Spanish, and French in the Southwest, 1540–1795* (1975)
James Lang, *Conquest and Commerce: Spain and England in the Americas* (1975)
James Lockhart and Stuart B. Schwartz, *Early Latin America: A History of Colonial Spanish America and Brazil* (1983)
Peter Mason, *Deconstructing America: Representations of the Other* (1990)
Jerald T. Milanich and Charles Hudson, *Hernando de Soto and the Indians of Florida* (1993)
James Howlett O'Donnell III, *Southeastern Frontiers: Europeans, Africans, and American Indians, 1513–1840: A Critical Bibliography* (1982)
Edmundo O'Gorman, *The Invention of America: An Inquiry into the Historical Nature of the New World and the Meaning of its History* (1961)
David M. Traboulay, *Columbus and Las Casas: The Conquest and Christianization of America, 1492–1566* (1994)
Ronald Wright, *Stolen Continents: The Americas through Indian Eyes since 1492* (1992)

Northern Explorations and Encounters

Alfred Goldsworthy Bailey, *The Conflict of European and Eastern Algonkian Cultures, 1504–1700* (1969)
Carl Bridenbaugh, *Vexed and Troubled Englishmen, 1590–1642* (1968)
Peter Clark and Paul Slack, *English Towns in Transition, 1500–1700* (1976)
Susan Danforth, *Encountering the New World, 1493–1800* (1991)
G. R. Elton, *England under the Tudors* (1974)
C. H. George and Katherine George, *The Protestant Mind of the English Reformation* (1961)
John Guy, *Tudor England* (1988)
Karen Ordahl Kupperman, *Roanoke: The Abandoned Colony* (1984)
Peter Laslett, *The World We Have Lost* (1965)
E. B. Leacock and N. O. Laurie, eds., *North American Indians in Historical Perspective* (1971)
Anthony McFarlane, *The British in the Americas, 1480-1815* (1994).
David B. Quinn, *North America from Earliest Discovery to First Settlements* (1977)
———, *The Roanoke Voyages, 1584–1590*, 2 vols. (1955)
Bernard W. Sheehan, *Savagism and Civility: Indians and Englishmen in Colonial Virginia* (1980)
Russell Thornton, *American Indian Holocaust and Survival* (1987)
Margo Todd, ed., *Reformation to Revolution: Politics and Religion in Early Modern England* (1995)
Marcel Trudel, *The Beginnings of New France, 1524–1663* (1973)
Keith Wrightson, *English Society, 1580–1680* (1982)

Biography

Joe Armstrong, *Champlain* (1987)
Carole Levin, *The Heart and Stomach of a King: Elizabeth I and the Politics of Sex and Power* (1994)
Richard Lee Marks, *Cortés: The Great Adventurer and the Fate of Aztec Mexico* (1993)
Samuel E. Morison, *Admiral of the Ocean Sea: A Life of Christopher Columbus* (1942)
A. L. Rowse, *Eminent Elizabethans* (1983)
John Ure, *Prince Henry the Navigator* (1977)
Henry Raup Wagner, *The Life and Writings of Bartolomé de las Casas* (1967)

CHAPTER THREE

PLANTING COLONIES IN NORTH AMERICA

1588–1701

Navajo painted "Mural" depicting Spanish horsemen, Canyon del Muerto at Canyon de Chelly National Monument, Arizona. Jerry Jacka Photography.

Chapter Outline

THE SPANISH AND FRENCH IN NORTH AMERICA

New Mexico

The First Communities of New France

ENGLAND IN THE CHESAPEAKE

Jamestown and the Powhatan Confederacy

Tobacco, Expansion, and Warfare

Maryland

Indentured Servants

Community Life in the Chesapeake

THE NEW ENGLAND COLONIES

The Social and Political Values of Puritanism

Early Contacts in New England

Plymouth Colony and the Mayflower Compact

The Massachusetts Bay Colony

Indians and Puritans

New England Communities

The Politics of Gender in Massachusetts

Dissent and New Communities

THE RESTORATION COLONIES

Early Carolina

From New Netherland to New York

The Founding of Pennsylvania

CONFLICT AND WAR

King Philip's War

Bacon's Rebellion

Wars in the South

The Glorious Revolution in America

King William's War

AMERICAN COMMUNITIES

Communities Struggle with Diversity in Seventeenth-Century Santa Fé

On a hot August day in 1680, frantic messengers rode into the small mission outpost of El Paso with the news that the Pueblo Indians to the north had risen in revolt; corpses of more than 400 colonists lay bleeding in the dust. Two thousand Spanish survivors huddled inside the Palace of Governors in Santa Fé, surrounded by 3,000 angry Indian warriors. The Pueblo leaders had sent two crosses inside the palace—white for surrender, red for death. Which would the Spaniards choose?

Spanish colonists had been in New Mexico for nearly a century. Franciscan priests came first, followed by a military expedition from Mexico in search of precious metals. In 1609, in the picturesque foothills of the Sangre de Cristo Mountains, colonial authorities founded La Villa Real de la Santa Fé de San Francisco—"the royal town of the holy faith of St. Francis"—soon known simply as Santa Fé. Colonization efforts included converting the Pueblo Indians to Christianity, making them subjects of the king of Spain, and forcing them to work for the colonial elite who lived at the edges of the town.

In the face of overwhelming Spanish power—the military might that had retaken Spain from the Moors of North Africa and conquered the great Aztec and Incan civilizations farther south—the Pueblos adopted a flexible attitude. Although 20,000 converted to Christianity, most thought of the new religion as simply an appendage to their already complex culture. The Christian God was but one more of their numerous deities. They incorporated Church holidays into their own religious calendar and celebrated them with native dances and rituals.

Most ethnographers agree that the Pueblos were a sexually spirited people. Many of their public dances included erotic displays, and some ended in public lovemaking. Symbolizing the powerful force that brought the separate worlds of men and women together, sexual intercourse was emblematic of community. Indeed, the celibacy of the Franciscan priests not only astounded the Pueblos but horrified them; they saw the priests as only half-persons.

The Pueblos also found the Franciscan practice of subjecting themselves to prolonged fasts and tortures like self-flagellation completely inexplicable. "You Christians are crazy," one Pueblo chief told a priest. "You go through the streets in groups, flagellating yourselves, and it is not well that the people of this pueblo should be encouraged to commit such madness." The missionaries, for their part, were outraged by what they considered Pueblo sacrileges, and they invaded underground kivas, destroying sacred Indian artifacts, publicly humiliating holy men, and compelling whole villages to perform penance by working in irrigation ditches and fields. When the Spanish governor of New Mexico executed three Pueblo priests and publicly whipped dozens more for secretly practicing their religion, one of these priests, Popé of San Juan Pueblo, vowed to overthrow the Spanish regime and began organizing a conspiracy among more than twenty Indian towns.

Popé's job was not difficult, for there were plenty of local grievances. For example, the Hopis of northern Arizona still tell of a missionary who capped his ever-escalating demands on them with the order that all the young women of the village be brought to live with him. When the revolt of 1680 began throughout the entire colony, the Hopis surrounded the missionary's house. "I have come to kill you," the chief announced. "You can't kill me," the priest cried from behind his locked door. "I will come to life and wipe out your whole tribe." "My gods have more power than you have," the chief shouted back. He and his men broke down the door, hung the missionary from the beams, and lit a fire beneath his feet.

From within Santa Fé's Palace of Governors the Spanish sent back the red cross, signaling that they would fight to the death. But after a siege lasting five days the Pueblos agreed to allow most of them to flee south to El Paso, "the poor women and children on foot and unshod," in the words of one Spaniard's account, and "of such a hue that they looked like dead people." The Indians then ransacked the missions and churches, desecrating the holy furnishings with human excrement and leaving the mutilated bodies of priests lying upon their altars. They transformed the governor's chapel into a traditional kiva, his palace into a communal dwelling. On the elegant inlaid stone floors where the governor had held court, Pueblo women now ground their corn.

Santa Fé became the capital of a Pueblo confederacy led by Popé. Popé first forced Christian Indians to the river to scrub away the taint of baptism and then ordered the general population to destroy everything Spanish. But the latter command met with resistance. The colonists had introduced horses and sheep, fruit trees and wheat, new tools and new crafts—all things that the Indians found useful. In addition, the Pueblos sorely missed the support of the Spanish in their struggle against the Navajos and Apaches, the Pueblos' traditional enemies. Equipped with stolen horses and weapons, these nomadic tribespeople had become considerably more dangerous, and their raids on the unprotected Pueblo villages became much more destructive after the colonists fled. With chaos mounting, Popé was deposed in 1690, and many Indians found themselves thinking the unthinkable: If only the Spanish would come back!

Come back they did, beginning in 1692, and after six years of fighting succeeded in reestablishing Spanish authority. But both sides had learned a lesson, and over the next generation the colonists and the Indians reached an implicit understanding. Pueblos dutifully observed Catholicism in the missionary chapels, while missionaries tolerated the practice of traditional religion in the Indians' underground kivas. Royal officials guaranteed the inviolability of Indian lands, and Pueblos pledged loyalty to the Spanish monarch. Pueblos turned out for service on colonial lands, and colonists abandoned the system of forced labor. Together the Spanish and the Pueblos held off the nomadic tribes for the next 150 years. Colonist and Indian communities remained autonomous, but they were learning to live with one another.

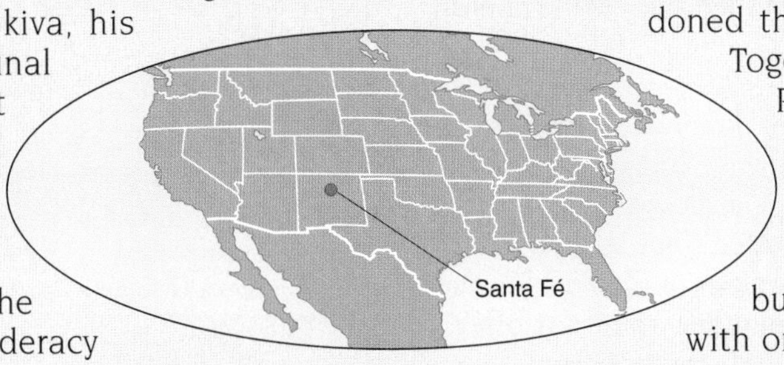

KEY TOPICS

- A comparison of the European colonies established in North America in the seventeenth century
- The English and Algonquian colonial encounter in the Chesapeake
- The role of religious dissent in the planting of the New England colonies
- The restoration of the Stuart monarchy and the creation of new proprietary colonies
- Indian warfare and internal conflict at the end of the seventeenth century

THE SPANISH AND FRENCH IN NORTH AMERICA

At the end of the sixteenth century the Spanish and the French were the only European powers directly involved in North America. The Spanish had built a series of forts along the Florida coast to protect the Gulf Stream sea lanes used by the convoys carrying wealth from their New World colonies. The French were navigating the St. Lawrence River in pursuit of fur trade. Early in the seventeenth century both were drawn into planting far more substantial colonies—New Mexico and New France—in North America. Because neither France nor Spain was willing or able to transport large numbers of its citizens to populate these colonies, both relied on a policy of converting Indians into subjects, and in New Mexico and New France there was a good deal of cultural and sexual mixing between colonists and natives. These areas became "frontiers of inclusion," where native peoples were part of colonial society, and they contrasted dramatically with the "frontiers of exclusion" established later by the English.

New Mexico

After the 1539 expedition of Francisco Vásquez de Coronado failed to turn up vast Indian empires to conquer in the northern Mexican deserts, the Spanish interest in the Southwest faded. But although the densely settled farming communities of the Pueblos may not have offered wealth to plunder, they did offer a harvest of souls, and by the 1580s Franciscan missionaries had entered the area. Soon, however, rumors drifted back to Mexico City of rich mines along the Rio Grande, and the hopes of Spanish officials that they might find another Aztec empire in what they had called "New Mexico" were rekindled. In 1598 Juan de Oñate, a member of a wealthy mining family, led 130 predominantly Indian and mestizo soldiers and their families, along with some 20 missionaries, north into New Mexico with the intent of mining both gold and souls.

Moving north into the upper Rio Grande Valley, Oñate encountered varying degrees of resistance by the Pueblo Indians. At Acoma, a pueblo set high atop a great outcropping of rock, Oñate met with considerable hostility, and he laid siege to the town. Indian warriors killed dozens of Spaniards with their arrows, and women and even children bombarded the attackers with stones. But in the end, the Spanish succeeded in climbing the rock walls and laying waste the town, killing 800 men,

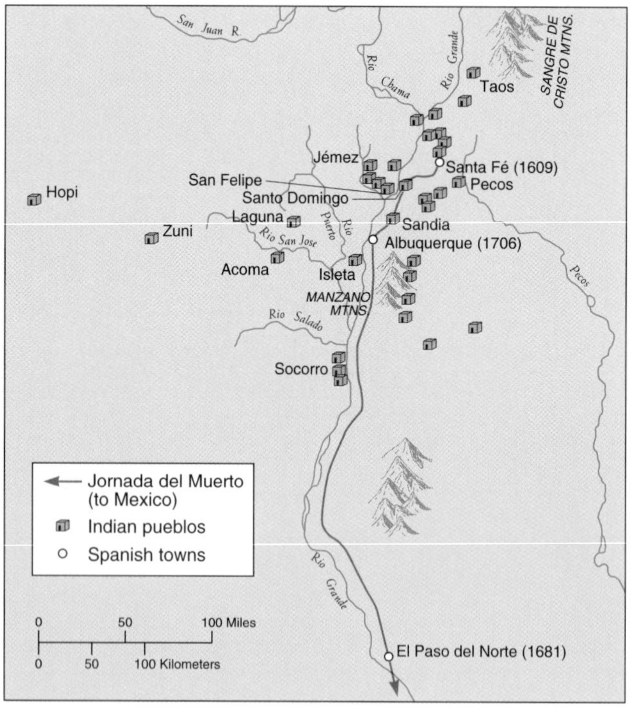

New Mexico in the Seventeenth Century *By the end of the seventeenth century, New Mexico contained 3,000 colonial settlers in several towns, surrounded by an estimated 50,000 Pueblo Indians living in some fifty farming villages. The isolation and sense of danger among the Hispanic settlers are evident in their name for the road linking the colony with New Spain,* Jornada del Muerto, *"the Road of Death."*

women, and children. The Spanish cut off one foot of each surviving Indian warrior and carried off more than 500 persons into slavery. "If you who are Christians cause so much harm and violence," a Pueblo Indian asked one of the priests, "why should we become Christians?" For their part, the Spanish authorities in Mexico recalled Oñate in 1606 for his failure to locate the fabled gold mines.

This illustration, taken from Samuel de Champlain's 1613 account of the founding of New France, depicts him joining the Huron attack on the Iroquois in 1609. The French and their Huron allies controlled access to the great fur grounds of the West. The Iroquois then formed an alliance of their own with the Dutch, who had founded a trading colony on the Hudson River. The palm trees in the background of this drawing suggest that it was not executed by an eyewitness but rather by an illustrator more familiar with South American scenes.

The Spanish were about to abandon the colony, but after publicizing a surge in Christian conversions among the Indians, the Church convinced the monarchy to subsidize New Mexico as a special missionary project. In 1609 the new governor, Don Pedro de Peralta, founded the capital of Santa Fé, and from this base the Franciscans penetrated all the surrounding Indian villages.

The colonial economy of New Mexico, based on small-scale agriculture and sheep raising, was never very prosperous. The Spanish settlers were not inclined to work—as one Spanish official put it, "One comes to the Indies not to plow and sow, but only to eat and loaf"—and forced the Indians to labor for them. After the initial conquest, few new colonists came up the dusty road from Mexico. Population growth was almost entirely the result of natural increase deriving from unions between colonial men and Indian women. By the late seventeenth century this northernmost outpost of the far-flung Spanish American empire contained some 3,000 mostly mestizo settlers in a few towns along the Rio Grande, surrounded by an estimated 50,000 Pueblo Indians in some fifty villages.

The First Communities of New France

In the early seventeenth century the French devised a strategy to monopolize the northern fur trade that had developed in the sixteenth century. In 1605, Samuel de Champlain, an agent of the royal Canadian Company, helped establish the outpost of Port Royal on what is now Nova Scotia, bordering the Bay of Fundy, and three years later he founded the town of Quebec at a site strategically located so that he could intercept the traffic in furs to the Atlantic. Champlain forged an alliance with the Huron Indians, who controlled access to the rich fur territories of the Great Lakes, and joined them in making war on their traditional enemies, the Five Nation Iroquois Confederacy. In his diplomacy, Champlain relied on the tradition of commercial relations that had developed between the French and the Indians. He sent agents and traders to live among native peoples, where they learned native languages and customs and directed the flow of furs to Quebec.

France encouraged families to settle the colony of Acadia, the tidal shores of the Bay of Fundy, and the colony of Canada, the narrow belt of fertile land along the St. Lawrence. It was the second of these that became the heart of New France. Small clusters of riverbank farmers known as *habitants* lived on the lands of *seigneurs*, or landlords. The little communities that emerged, with the manor house of the lord, the Catholic church, and perhaps a public building or two, resembled the towns of northern France. Although the growing season was short, *habitants* were able to produce subsistence crops by employing Indian farming techniques, and eventually they developed a modest export economy.

But the communities of Canada tended to look west toward the continental interior rather than east across the Atlantic. It was typical for the sons of *habitants* to take to the woods in their youth, working as agents for the fur companies or as independent traders, known as *coureurs de bois*, or "runners of the woods." Most eventually returned to take up farming, but others remained in Indian villages, where they married Indian women and raised families. Thus French traders were living on the Great Lakes as early as the 1620s, and from the late 1660s

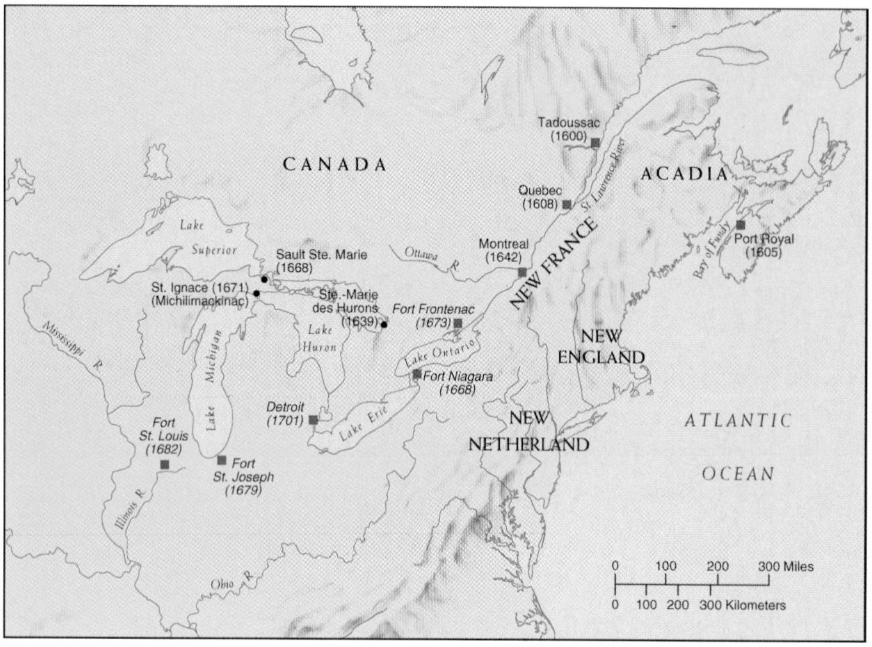

New France in the Seventeenth Century *By the late seventeenth century, French settlements were spread from the town of Port Royal in Acadia to the post and mission at Sault Ste. Marie, on the Great Lakes. But the heart of New France comprised the communities stretching along the St. Lawrence River between the towns of Quebec and Montreal.*

to the 1680s the French established outposts at strategic points on the lakes. By the 1670s French fur traders and missionaries were exploring the reaches of the upper Mississippi River. In 1681–82, fur trade commandant Robert Sieur de La Salle navigated the mighty river to its mouth on the Gulf of Mexico and claimed its entire watershed—a great inland empire—for France.

Thus although both the French and Spanish established societies of inclusion, in which settlers intermarried with native peoples, the early French colonial system differed from that of the Spanish. Whereas the French interest in the Indians was principally commercial, the Spanish organized Indian communities as a labor force for mines, plantations, and ranches. There were also important differences between Spanish and French missionary efforts. The Jesuits, arriving in 1625 and often accompanying French traders—and sometimes leading the way—introduced Christianity as a supplement to the Indian way of life. In contrast, the Franciscans of New Mexico insisted that Indian people accept European cultural norms.

The populations of Acadia and Canada grew throughout the seventeenth century but by 1700 still totaled only 15,000. Quebec City, the colony's administrative capital, was small by Spanish colonial standards, and Montreal, founded in 1642 as a missionary and trading center, remained little more than a frontier outpost. The real strength of New France lay in its extensive fur-trading system.

ENGLAND IN THE CHESAPEAKE

England first attempted to plant colonies in North America during the 1580s, in Newfoundland and on Roanoke Island in present-day North Carolina. Both attempts were failures. England's war with Spain, which lasted from 1588 to 1604, suspended colonization efforts, but at its close the English once again turned to the Americas.

Jamestown and the Powhatan Confederacy

Early in his reign, King James I (reigned 1603–25) issued royal charters for the colonization of the mid-Atlantic region, by then known as Virginia, to English joint-stock companies, which raised capital by selling shares. In 1607 a group of London investors known as the Virginia Company sent ships to the temperate latitudes of Chesapeake Bay, where a hundred men built a fort they named Jamestown, in honor of the king. It was destined to become the first permanent English settlement in North America.

The Chesapeake region was already home to an estimated 20,000 Algonquian people. The English colonists were immediately confronted by Powhatan, the powerful *werowance*, or leader, of a confederacy of Algonquian tribes. Powhatan had mixed feelings about the English. The Spanish had already attempted to plant a base nearby, bringing conflict and disease to his region. But he looked forward to valuable trade with the English as well as to their support for his struggle to extend his confederacy to outlying tribes. As was the case in Mexico and along the St. Lawrence, Indians tried to use Europeans to pursue ends of their own.

The English saw themselves as latter-day conquistadors. Abhorring the idea of physical labor, they survived the first year only with Powhatan's material assistance. Like the first Roanoke colonists (see Chapter 2), they were unable to support themselves. "In our extremity the Indians brought us corn," wrote John Smith, the colony's military leader, "when we rather expected they would destroy us." Jamestown grew so dependent on Algonquian stores that in 1609 Smith and his men began to plunder food from surrounding tribes. In retaliation, Powhatan decided to starve the colonists out. He now realized, as he said to Smith, that the

English had come "not for trade, but to invade my people and possess my country"—the approach not of the French but of the Spanish. During the winter of 1609–10 scores of colonists starved and a number resorted to cannibalism. By spring only 60 remained of the more than 900 colonists sent to Virginia.

Determined to prevail, the Virginia Company sent out a large additional force of men, women, and livestock, committing themselves to a protracted war against the Indians. By 1613 the colonists firmly controlled the territory between the James and York rivers. Worn down by warfare and disease, Powhatan accepted a treaty of peace in 1614. "I am old and ere long must die," he declared; "I know it is better to eat good meat, lie well, and sleep with my women and children, laugh and be merry than to be forced to flee and be hunted." He sent his daughter Pocahontas, fluent in English, on a diplomatic mission to Jamestown. She converted to Christianity and married John Rolfe, a leading settler. But Pocahontas died of disease while visiting England in 1617. Crushed by the news of her death, her father abdicated in favor of his brother Opechancanough and died the following year.

Tobacco, Expansion, and Warfare

Tobacco provided the Virginia colonists with the "merchantable commodity" for which Thomas Harriot, the scientist who accompanied the Roanoke expedition, had searched (see Chapter 2). In 1613 John Rolfe developed a hybrid of hearty North American and mild West Indian varieties, and soon the first commercial shipments of cured Virginia leaf reached England. The revenue from tobacco sales produced the first returns on the investment of the Virginia Company. Its cultivation quickly

The illustration on the left is a detail of John Smith's map of Virginia. It includes the names of many Indian villages, suggesting how densely settled was the Indian population of the coast of Chesapeake Bay. For the inset of Powhatan and his court in the upper left, the engraver borrowed images from John White's drawings of the Indians of the Roanoke area. The illustration on the right, from John Smith's memoirs (1624), was engraved by the artist Robert Vaughn. Seizing Chief Opechancanough, Powhatan's brother, by the scalplock, Smith attempts to obtain needed supplies from the Indians. Opechancanough later succeeded Powhatan and ruled the Chesapeake Algonquian Confederacy for a quarter century.

An eighteenth-century label for Virginia tobacco, featuring an African slave and a native American smoker. Tobacco was introduced to English consumers by Francis Drake in the 1580s, and despite King James's description of the habit as "loathsome to the eye, hateful to the nose, harmful to the brain, dangerous to the lungs," tobacco smoking developed into a craze that created strong consumer demand in the 1610s.

exhausted the soil, however, creating pressures for further expansion into Indian territory.

Because tobacco also required a great deal of hand labor, the company instituted what were called headright grants, or awards of large plantations on the condition that grant recipients transport workers from England at their own cost. Between 1619 and 1624 more than 4,500 English settlers arrived, many with families. But high rates of mortality—probably the result of epidemics of typhoid fever—kept the total population at just over a thousand. In populating their colony with families, the English had chosen a policy quite different from the Spanish practice of sending only male settlers. Moreover, the English emphasis on agriculture and lack of interest in trade with Indian peoples contrasted significantly with the French approach. With no need to incorporate Indians into the population, the English moved in the direction of exclusion, pushing Indian peoples to the periphery rather than incorporating them within colonial communities.

As the English pressed for additional lands, Opechancanough prepared the Chesapeake Algonquians for a final assault on the invaders. He encouraged a cultural revival under the guidance of the shaman Nemattanew, who instructed his followers to reject the English and their ways but to learn the use of firearms. The uprising, which began on Good Friday, March 22, 1622, completely surprised the English. Nearly 350 people, a quarter of the settlers, were killed before Jamestown could mobilize its forces. Yet the colony managed to hang on, and the attack stretched into a ten-year war of attrition. Horrors were committed by both sides, but English officials saw advantages in open warfare. As one wrote, "We may now by right of war, and law of nations, invade the country and destroy them who sought to destroy us, whereby we shall enjoy their cultivated places." Indian territory might now be obtained under the conventions of a "just war."

Long before it ended in 1632, the war bankrupted the Virginia Company. In 1624 the king converted Virginia into a royal colony, with civil authorities appointed by the crown, although the colony's House of Burgesses, created in 1619, continued to include representatives of Virginia's boroughs. Then, despite disease, famine, and warfare, the economy took off, and the English colonial population doubled every five years from 1625 to 1640, by which time it numbered approximately 10,000. Opechancanough emerged from the turmoil as undisputed leader of the still independent Chesapeake Algonquian Confederacy, but other smaller tribes, decimated by casualties and disease, were forced to accept English domination. By 1640 the native population of the Chesapeake had declined to about 10,000.

Numerical strength soon shifted in favor of the English. In 1644, Opechancanough organized a final desperate revolt, in which more than 500 colonists were killed. But the Virginians crushed the Algonquians in 1645, capturing and executing Opechancanough. The colonists then signed a formal treaty with the Indians, who were granted small reserved territories. By the 1670s, when the English population of Virginia numbered more than 40,000, only a dozen tribes and about 2,000 Algonquians remained from the 20,000 who inhabited the area when Jamestown was founded. Today, some 1,500 people who trace their roots to Powhatan's confederacy live in Chesapeake Indian communities near Richmond, Virginia, and Washington, D.C.

Maryland

In 1632, King Charles I (reigned 1625–49) granted 10 million acres at the northern end of Chesapeake Bay to the Calvert family, the Lords Baltimore, important supporters of the monarchy. The Calverts named their colony Maryland, in honor of the king's wife. The first party of colonists founded the settlement of St. Marys

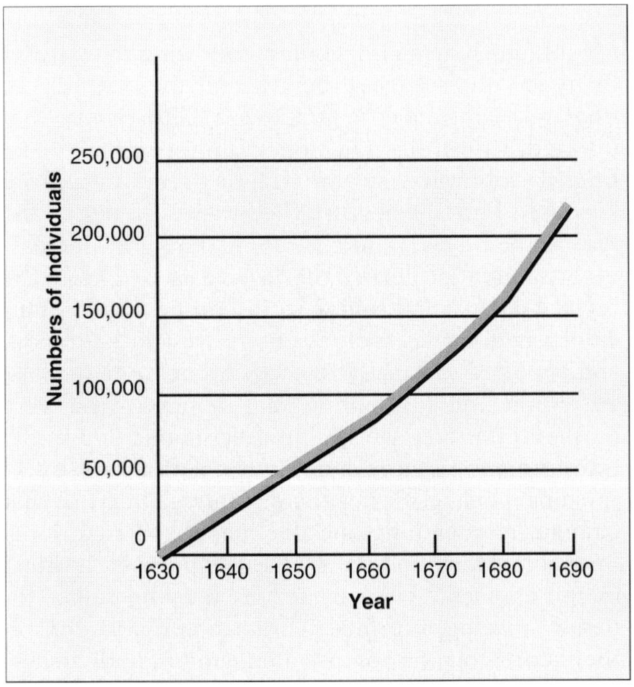

Population Growth of the British Colonies in the Seventeenth Century *The British colonial population grew steadily through the century, then increased sharply in the closing decade as a result of the new settlements of the Restoration colonies.*

near the mouth of the Potomac River in 1634. Two features distinguished Maryland from Virginia. First, it was a "proprietary" colony. The Calverts were sole owners of all the land, which they planned to carve into feudal manors that would provide them with annual rents, and they appointed all the civil officers. Second, because the proprietors were Catholics, they encouraged settlement by their coreligionists, a persecuted minority in seventeenth-century England. In fact, Maryland became the only English colony in North America with a substantial Catholic minority. Wealthy Catholic landlords were appointed to the governing council, and they came to dominate Maryland's House of Delegates, founded in 1635.

Despite these differences, Maryland quickly assumed the character of neighboring Virginia. Its tobacco plantation economy created pressures for labor and expansion that could not be met under the Calverts' original feudal plans. In 1640 the colony adopted the system of headright grants developed in Virginia, and settlements of independent planters quickly spread out on both sides of the bay. By the 1670s Maryland's English population numbered more than 15,000.

Indentured Servants

At least three-quarters of the English migrants to the Chesapeake came as indentured servants. In exchange for the cost of their transportation to the New World, men and women contracted to labor for a master for a fixed term. Most indentured servants were young, unskilled males, who served for two to seven years, but some were skilled craftsmen, and a few were women and children (the latter were expected to serve until they reached the age of twenty-one). A minority of these laborers were convicts or vagabonds bound into service by English courts for as long as fourteen years.

Masters were obliged to feed, clothe, and house these servants adequately. But work in the tobacco fields was backbreaking, and records include complaints of inadequate care. One Virginia ballad chronicled these complaints:

> *Come all you young fellows wherever you be,*
> *Come listen awhile and I will tell thee,*
> *Concerning the hardships that we undergo,*
> *When we get lagg'd to Virginia*
> *Now in Virginia I lay like a hog,*
> *Our pillow at night is a brick or a log,*
> *We dress and undress like some other sea dog,*
> *How hard is my fate in Virginia.*

Many servants tried to escape, but capture could mean a lengthening of their terms of service. On reaching the end of their service, servants were eligible for "freedom dues": clothing, tools, a gun, a spinning wheel, a little land, or perhaps food—something to help them get started on their own. Most former servants hoped to start farms in the backcountry and thus headed west, even though they thereby risked the danger of Indian attacks.

Reliance on indentured labor was unique to the English colonies. New France had little need for a systematic resort to servitude, for French colonists pretty much did their own labor. The Spanish, on the other hand, in places like Santa Fé, depended on the labor of Indians. African slaves were first introduced to the Chesapeake in 1619, but they were more expensive than servants, and as late as 1680 they made up less than 7 percent of the Chesapeake population. For many servants, however, the distinction between slavery and servitude may have seemed academic. Approximately two of every five servants died during their periods of indenture. In the hard-driving economy of the Chesapeake, many masters treated servants cruelly, and women especially were vulnerable to sexual exploitation. The harsh system of indentured labor prepared the tobacco masters of the Chesapeake for the transition to slavery that occurred during the second half of the seventeenth century. (Chapter 4 discusses the slave system and its implications for the economic and social aspects of American society as well as for slaves and masters themselves.)

Community Life in the Chesapeake

Most migrants were men, and male servants surviving their terms of indenture had a difficult time finding wives. Tobacco masters commonly received offers from men to pay off the indenture of a prospective wife, and free unmarried women often married as soon as they arrived. English men seemed to suffer a higher rate of mortality than English women in the disease-ridden environment of the early Chesapeake. Widows remarried quickly, sometimes within days. Their scarcity provided women with certain advantages. Shrewd widows bargained for remarriage agreements that gave them larger shares of the estate upon the death of their husband. So notable was the concentration of wealth in the hands of these widows that one historian has suggested that early Virginia was a "matriarchy." But because of high mortality rates, family size was smaller and kinship bonds—one of the most important components of community—were weaker than in England.

Visitors from England frequently remarked on the crude conditions of community life. Prosperous planters, investing everything in tobacco production, lived in rough wooden dwellings. Fifty miles inland, on the western edge of the settlements, freed servants lived with their families in shacks, huts, or even caves. Colonists spread across the countryside in search of new tobacco lands, creating dispersed settlements and few towns. Before 1650 there were relatively few community institutions such as schools and churches. The settlements of the Chesapeake, the site of England's premier colony in North America, looked temporary. Meanwhile, the Spanish in the Caribbean and Mexico were building communities that grew into great cities with permanent institutions.

In contrast to the colonists of New France, who were developing a distinctive American identity because of their commercial connections with native Americans, the population of the Chesapeake maintained close emotional ties to England. Colonial politics were shaped less by local developments than by a continuing relationship with the mother country. There was little movement toward a distinctively American point of view in the seventeenth-century Chesapeake.

THE NEW ENGLAND COLONIES

Both in climate and in geography, the northern coast of North America was far different from the Chesapeake. "Merchantable commodities" such as tobacco could not be produced there, and thus the region was far less favored for investment and settlement. Instead, it became a haven for Protestant dissenters from England, who gave the colonies of the North a distinctive character.

The Social and Political Values of Puritanism

Most English men and women, following to a greater or lesser degree the dictates of the Church of England, continued to practice a Christianity that differed little from traditional Catholicism. But the English followers of John Calvin (see Chapter 2), known as Puritans because they wished to purify and reform the English church from within, grew increasingly influential during the last years of Elizabeth's reign. Like Calvin's followers in Europe, the Puritans emphasized values such as enterprise and hard work and appealed especially to those groups—merchants, entrepreneurs, and commercial farmers—who were most responsible for the rapid economic and social transformation of England. But the Puritans were also the most vocal critics of the disruptive effects of that change, condemning the decline of the traditional rural community and the growing number of "idle and masterless men." They argued for reviving communities by placing reformed Christian congregations at their core to monitor the behavior of individuals. Puritanism was thus as much a set of social and political values as religious ones, a way of managing change in troubling times. By the early seventeenth century, Puritans controlled many congregations and had become an influential force at the universities in Oxford and Cambridge, training centers for the future political and religious leaders of England.

King James I, who assumed the throne after Elizabeth's death, abandoned her policy of religious tolerance. His persecution of the Puritans, however, merely stiffened their resolve and turned them toward overt political opposition. An increasingly vocal Puritan minority in Parliament complained that the Church of England was too "Catholic." These Puritans criticized King Charles I, James's son and successor, for supporting High Church policies—which emphasized the authority of the church and its traditional forms of worship—as well as for marrying a Catholic princess. In 1629, determined to rule without these troublesome opponents, Charles dissolved Parliament and launched a campaign of repression against the Puritans. "I am verily persuaded God will bring some heavy affliction upon this land," the Puritan leader John Winthrop despaired. This political turmoil provided the context for the migration of thousands of English Protestants to New England.

Early Contacts in New England

The northern Atlantic coast seemed an unlikely spot for English colonies, for the region was dominated by French and Dutch traders. In the early seventeenth century Samuel de Champlain established trading contacts with coastal Algonquians as far south as Cape Cod. The Dutch, following the explorations of Henry Hudson for the Netherlands, established settlements and a lucrative fur trade on the Hudson River. In 1613 the English, desperate to keep their colonial options open, dispatched a fleet from Jamestown that destroyed the French post at Port Royal on the Bay of Fundy and harassed the Dutch on the Hudson. The following year John Smith explored the northern coastline and christened the region "New England." The land was "so planted with Gardens and Corne fields," he wrote, that "I would rather live here than any where." But Smith's plans for a New England colony were aborted when he was captured and held captive by the French.

Then a twist of fate transformed English fortunes. From 1616 to 1618 a devastating plague ravaged the native peoples of the northern coast. Whole villages disappeared, and the trade system of the French and the Dutch was seriously disrupted. Indians perished so quickly and in such numbers that few remained to bury the dead. Modern estimates confirm the testimony of a surviving Indian that his people were "melted down by this disease, whereof nine-tenths of them have died." The native population of New England as a whole dropped from an estimated 120,000 to less than 70,000. So crippled were the surviving coastal societies that they could not provide effective resistance to the planting of English colonies.

Plymouth Colony and the Mayflower Compact

The first English colony in New England was founded by a group of religious dissenters known to later generations as the Pilgrims. The Pilgrims were English Separatists, people who believed the Anglican establishment so corrupt that they must establish their own independent church. One group of Separatists first moved to Holland in 1609, but, fearful that Dutch society was seducing their children, they soon began exploring the idea of emigrating to North America. Backed by the Virginia Company of London and led by Pilgrim William Bradford, 102 people embarked on the *Mayflower,* sailing from Plymouth, England, in September 1620.

The little group, mostly families but also a substantial number of single men hired by the investors, arrived in Massachusetts Bay at Plymouth, the site of the former Indian village of Patuxet. Soon the hired men began to grumble about Pilgrim authority, and to reassure them Bradford drafted a document known as the Mayflower Compact, in which all the men of the expedition did "covenant and combine [themselves] together into a civil body politic." Signed in November 1620, the Mayflower Compact was the first document of self-government in North America.

Weakened by scurvy and malnutrition, nearly half the Pilgrims perished over the first winter. Like the earlier settlers of Roanoke and Jamestown, however, the Pilgrims were rescued by Indians. Massasoit, the sachem, or leader, of the local tribe of Wampanoags, offered food and advice in return for an alliance with the newcomers against his enemies, the Narragansets, a powerful neighboring tribe to his immediate west.

The interpreter in these negotiations was an Indian named Squanto who had been kidnapped in 1614 by the captain of one English ship and who had returned to New England five years later as guide on another vessel. Finding that plague had wiped out his village of Patuxet, and knowledgeable in the ways of the Europeans, Squanto became an adviser to Massasoit. With the arrival of the Pilgrims, this last survivor of the Patuxets now resumed his former residence, but as guide and interpreter for the English. Squanto secured seed corn for the colonists and taught them how to sow and cultivate it.

Deeply in debt to its investors, always struggling to meet its payments through the Indian trade, fishing, and lumbering, the Plymouth colony was never a financial success. Most families raised their own crops and kept their own livestock, but produced little for export. Nevertheless, the Pilgrims succeeded in establishing the separate community they wanted. So strong was their communal agreement that the annual meeting of property-owning men reelected William Bradford to thirty consecutive terms as governor. By midcentury, however, the Plymouth population had dispersed into eleven separate communities, and the growth of diverse local interests had begun to disrupt this separatist retreat.

The Massachusetts Bay Colony

In England, the Puritan movement continued its struggle to reform the national church. The political climate of the late 1620s, however, convinced a number of influential Puritans that the only way to protect their congregations was to emigrate. Some went to Ireland, others to the Netherlands or the West Indies, but many decided on New England, where, according to John Winthrop—later the first governor of the colony—they could establish "a city on a hill," a model of reform for England. In 1629 a royal charter was granted to a group of wealthy Puritans who called their enterprise the Massachusetts Bay Company. The company was given exclusive rights to settle and to trade, as well as to "religiously, peaceably and civilly" govern the territory and the native people between the Merrimack and Charles rivers, from the Atlantic "to the south sea on the west part." An advance force of 200 settlers soon left for the fishing settlement of Naumkeag on Massachusetts Bay, which they renamed Salem.

The Puritan emigration to Massachusetts became known as the Great Migration, a phrase that would be repeated many times in American history.

The seal of the Massachusetts Bay Company featured an Indian (dressed more like a native of South America than southern New England) imploring Puritans to "Come over and help us." It was a cynical ploy, for English Puritans were less involved with mission efforts among the Indians than were any of the other colonists in North America.

Between 1629 and 1643 some 20,000 people relocated to New England. Boston, founded in 1630, was their central settlement; within five years it was ringed by towns as far as thirty miles inland. By 1640 settlements had spread seventy-five miles west, into the Connecticut River Valley.

Most colonists arrived in groups from long-established communities in the east of England and were frequently led by men with extensive experience in local English government. Taking advantage of a loophole in their charter, the Puritan leaders transferred company operations to America in 1629, and within a few years they had transformed the company into a civil government. The original charter had established a General Court composed of a governor and his deputy, a board of magistrates (advisers), and the members of the corporation, known as freemen. In 1632 Governor Winthrop and his advisers declared all male heads of household who were also church members to be freemen. Two years later the freemen established their right to select delegates to represent the towns in drafting the laws of the colony. These delegates and the magistrates later separated into two legislative houses. Thus the procedures of a joint-stock company provided the origins for democratic suffrage and the bicameral division of legislative authority in America.

Indians and Puritans

The Algonquian Indians of southern New England found the English considerably different from the French and Dutch traders who had preceded them. The principal concern of the English was not commerce—although the fur trade remained an important part of their economy—but the acquisition of land for their growing settlements. Massasoit attempted to use the colonists to his own advantage. But he soon found that when the English attacked his enemies, their true motive was expansion.

In 1623, on Massasoit's urging, the Pilgrim military commander Miles Standish attacked a group of Massachusetts Indians north of Plymouth. When Standish brought back the sachem's head and placed it on a pike outside the settlement's gates, the meaning of the gesture was not lost on the Wampanoags. If we are allies, one Indian asked, "how cometh it to pass that when we come to Patuxet you stand upon your guard, with the mouths of your pieces [guns] presented to us?" Even the Wampanoags were soon calling their English allies *wotowquenange*, or "cutthroats."

Ravaged by disease, the Wampanoags' northern neighbors, the Massachusetts, were ill prepared for the Puritan settlement that began in 1629. The English believed they had the right to take what they deemed "unused" lands—lands not being used, that is, in the "English way"—and depopulated Massachusetts villages became prime targets. As one colonist wrote: "Their land is spacious and void, and there are few and [they] do but run over the grass, as do also the foxes and wild beasts." Conflicts between settlers over title, however, made it necessary to obtain deeds to the land, and the English used a variety of tactics to pressure the Indians into signing quitclaims, or documents in which the signers relinquish all claim to specified properties. The English allowed their livestock to graze native fields, making them useless for cultivation. They fined Indians for violations of English law, such as working on the Sabbath, and then demanded land as payment. In addition, they made deals with dishonest sachems. For giving up the land that became Charlestown, for example, the "Squaw Sachem" of the Pawtuckets, one of a number of women Algonquian leaders, received twenty-one coats, nineteen fathoms of wampum, and three bushels of corn. Disorganized and demoralized, their populations reduced by disease and warfare, many of the coastal Algonquians surrendered their autonomy and placed themselves under the protection of the English.

Indian peoples to the west, however, remained a formidable presence. They blocked Puritan expansion until they were devastated in 1633–34 by an epidemic of smallpox that spread from the St. Lawrence south to Long Island Sound just as hundreds of English migrants were crowding into coastal towns. "Without this remarkable and terrible stroke of God upon the natives," recorded a town scribe, "we would with much more difficulty have found room, and at far greater charge have obtained and purchased land." In the aftermath of the epidemic, Puritans established many new inland towns.

By the late 1630s the most powerful tribes in the vicinity of the Puritans were the Narragansets of present-day Rhode Island and their traditional enemies the Pequots, principal trading partners of the Dutch. The Pequots lived on Long Island Sound near the mouth of the Connecticut River, where they controlled the production of wampum, woven belts of sea shells used as a medium of exchange in the Indian trade. In 1637 the Narragansets, in alliance with the English, who were looking for an excuse to smash the Dutch, inaugurated the Pequot War. Narraganset warriors and English troops attacked the main Pequot village, killing most of its slumbering residents, including women and children. Unaccustomed to such tactics, the shocked Narragansets cried out to the English: "It is too furious, it slays too many."

New England Communities

Back in England, the standoff between King Charles and the Puritans in Parliament erupted in armed conflict in 1642. The civil war that followed ended in the triumph of the Parliamentarians over royalist forces. The king was executed in 1649, and England proclaimed a "Commonwealth," headed by the Puritan leader Oliver Cromwell. With Cromwell's success, Puritans no longer had the same incentive to leave the country, and in fact many Puritans returned from New England to participate in the war.

New England's economy had depended on the sale of supplies and land to arriving immigrants, but in the 1640s the importance of this "newcomer market" declined with slackening immigration. Lacking a single exportable commodity like tobacco, New Englanders were forced to diversify into farming, fishing, and lumbering. Merchants began construction of what would become, by the end of the century, the largest shipping fleet in the colonies, and became active in the carrying trade between the Caribbean and Chesapeake colonies and Europe. Its diversified economy ultimately provided New England with considerable long-term strength.

The communities of New England were distinct from those of the Chesapeake because the vast majority of the Puritans had come in family groups with relatively few servants. The Puritan ideal was a family governed in the same way that kings ruled over society. "Surely there is in all children a stubbornness, and stoutness of mind arising from natural pride," one Puritan declared, "which must be broken and beaten down." Parents often participated in the choice of mates for their offspring, and children typically married in the order of their births, younger siblings waiting until arrangements had been made for their elders.

Unique among the seventeenth-century colonies in North America, Massachusetts built an impressive system to educate its young. In 1647 the colony required that towns with 50 families or more support a public school; those with 100 families were to establish a "grammar" school that taught Latin, knowledge of which was required for admission to Harvard College, founded in 1636. Connecticut enacted similar requirements. Literacy was higher in New England than elsewhere in the colonies, or even in much of Europe. Far fewer New England women than men could read and write, however, because girls were excluded from

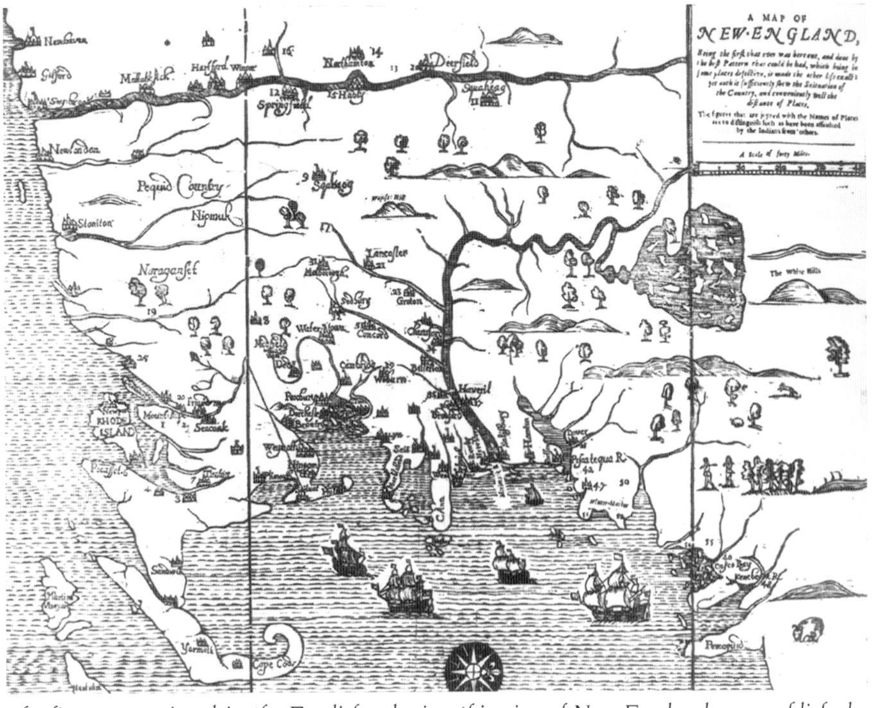

The first map printed in the English colonies, this view of New England was published in Boston in 1677. With north oriented to the right, it looks west from Massachusetts Bay, the two vertical black lines indicating the approximate boundaries of the Commonwealth of Massachusetts. The territory west of Rhode Island is noted as an Indian stronghold, the homelands of the Narraganset, Pequot, and Nipmuck peoples.

The Mason Children, by an unknown Boston artist, c. 1670. These Puritan children—David, Joanna, and Abigail Mason—are dressed in finery, an indication of the wealth and prominence of their family. The cane in young David's hand indicates his position as the male heir, while the rose held by Abigail is a symbol of childhood innocence.

Attributed to the Freake-Gibbs Painter, American, active Boston, Mass., c. 1670. *The Mason Children: David, Joanna, and Abigail*, 1670. Oil on canvas, 39 x 42½ in. The Fine Arts Museum of San Francisco, Gift of Mr. and Mrs. John D. Rockefeller 3rd, 1979.7.3.

the grammar schools. By 1639 the first printing press in the English colonies was in operation in Boston, and the following year it brought out the first American English publication, *The Bay Psalm Book*.

The Politics of Gender in Massachusetts

The Puritans stressed the importance of well-ordered communities and families. Colonists often emigrated in large kin groups that made up the core of the new towns. The Massachusetts General Court granted townships to proprietors representing the congregation, who then distributed fields, pasture, and woodlands in quantities proportional to the recipient's social status, so that wealthy families received more than humble ones. Settlers clustered their dwellings at the town center, near the meetinghouse that served as both church and civic center. Some towns, particularly those along the coast such as Boston, soon became centers of shipping. These clustered settlements and strong, vital communities made seventeenth-century New England quite different from Chesapeake society.

The family farm economy operated through the combined efforts of husband and wife. Men were generally responsible for field work, women for the work of the household, which included tending the kitchen garden (crops for household use), the dairy, and the henhouse, and securing fuel and water. Women managed an array of tasks, and some housewives independently traded garden products, milk, and eggs. One New England husband, referring to his wife's domestic management, said, "I meddle not with the geese nor turkeys, for they are hers for she hath been and is a good wife to me." Indeed, women traders helped to create and sustain many of the bonds of New England communities.

It is mistaken to regard the Puritans as "puritanical." Although adultery was a capital crime in New England, Puritans celebrated the sexual expression that took place within marriage. Courting couples were even allowed to lie in bed together, with their lower bodies wrapped in an apron, a custom known as "bundling," free to caress and pet. In the words of an old New England ballad:

> *She is modest, also chaste*
> *While only bare from neck to waist,*
> *And he of boasted freedom sings,*
> *Of all above her apron strings.*

There were certainly many loving Puritan households with contented husbands and wives. Anne Bradstreet, a Massachusetts wife and mother and the first published poet of New England, wrote about her husband and marriage:

> *If ever two are one, then surely we.*
> *If ever man were lov'd by wife, then thee;*
> *If ever wife was happy in a man,*
> *Compare with me ye women if you can.*

Nevertheless, the cultural ideal of the day was the subordination of women to men. "I am but a wife, and therefore it is sufficient for me to follow my husband," wrote Lucy Winthrop Downing, and her brother John Winthrop declared, "A true wife accounts her subjection [to be] her honor and freedom." Married women could neither make contracts nor own property, neither vote nor hold office. The extraordinarily high birth rate of Puritan women was one mark of their "subjection." The average woman, marrying in her early twenties and surviving through her forties, could expect to bear eight children. Aside from abstinence, there was no form of birth control. There was significant cultural suspicion about wives who failed to have children or widows who were economically independent.

These suspicions about women came to the surface most notably in periodic witchcraft scares. During the course of the seventeenth century, according to one historian, 342 New England women were accused by their neighbors of witchcraft. The majority of them were childless or widowed or had reputations among their neighbors for their assertiveness and independence. In the vast majority of cases these accusations were dismissed by authorities. But in Salem,

Massachusetts, in 1692, when a group of girls claimed that they had been bewitched by a number of old men and women, the whole community was thrown into a panic of accusations. Before the colonial governor finally called a halt to the persecutions in 1693, twenty people had been tried, condemned, and executed.

The Salem accusations of witchcraft probably reflected generalized social tensions that found their outlet through an attack on people perceived as outsiders. Salem was a booming port, but although some residents were prospering, others were not. Most of the victims came from the eastern, more commercial section of town, whereas the majority of their accusers lived on the economically stagnant western side. Most of the accused also came from families whose religious sympathies were with sects of Anglicans, Quakers, or Baptists, not Puritans. Finally, a majority of the victims were old women, suspect because they lived alone, without men. The Salem witchcraft trials exposed the dark side of Puritan ideas about women.

Dissent and New Communities

The Puritans emigrated in order to practice their variety of Christianity, but they had little tolerance for other religious points of view. Religious disagreements among them were not accommodated but soon provoked the founding of new colonies. Thomas Hooker, a minister in Cambridge, disagreed with Puritan leaders over the extent of their authority, and believed that suffrage should not be restricted to male church members only. In 1636 he led his followers west to the Connecticut River, where they founded the town of Hartford. Hooker helped write the Fundamental Orders that marked the beginning of the colony of Connecticut.

The second major dissenter was the clergyman Roger Williams, who came to New England in 1631 to take up duties for the congregation in Salem. Williams believed in religious toleration and the separation of church and state. (Chapter 5 discusses these issues at greater length.) He also preached that the colonists had no absolute right to Indian land but must bargain for it in good faith. Because the Puritans believed that theirs was the one true religion, because they believed in the absolute union of church and state, and because they had established their colony on what had been Indian land, they considered Williams's ideas highly dangerous, and in 1636 they banished him from the Bay colony. With a group of followers, Williams emigrated to the Narragansett country, where he purchased land from the Indians and founded the town of Providence.

The next year Boston shook with another religious controversy. Anne Hutchinson, a brilliant woman who had arrived in New England with her merchant husband in 1634, led religious discussion groups that

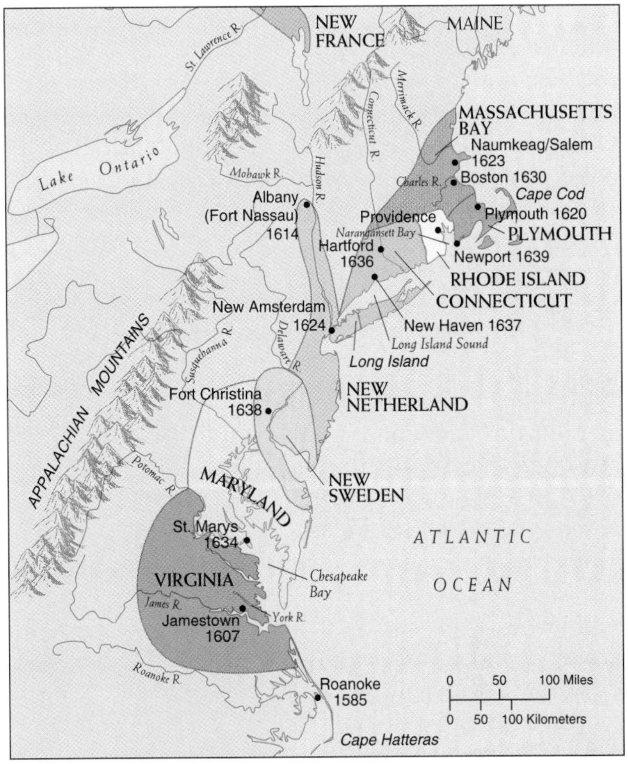

European Colonies of the Atlantic Coast, 1607–1639

Virginia on Chesapeake Bay was the first English colony in North America, but by the mid-seventeenth century Virginia was joined by settlements of Scandinavians on the Delaware River, and Dutch on the Hudson River, as well as English religious dissenters in New England. The territories indicated here reflect the vague boundaries of the early colonies.

criticized various Boston ministers for a lack of piety. The concentration of attention on good works, she argued, led people to believe that they could earn their way to heaven, a "popish" or Catholic heresy in the eyes of Calvinists. Hutchinson was called before the General Court, where the Puritan leaders made it clear that they would not tolerate a woman who publicly criticized men. Although she handled herself very skillfully, Hutchinson made the mistake of claiming that she had received a direct "revelation" from God, and so was excommunicated and banished. She and her followers moved to Roger Williams's settlement, where they established their own community in 1638.

A third group of dissenters, Samuel Gorton and his followers, were also banished from the Bay Colony and relocated, like the others, to the Narragansett haven. In 1644, Roger Williams received a charter creating the colony of Rhode Island, named for the principal island in Narragansett Bay, as a protection for these several dissenting communities. A new royal charter of 1663 guaranteed self-government and complete religious liberty and strengthened the colony's territorial claims for its approximately 2,000 English colonial inhabitants.

By the 1670s Massachusetts's population had grown to more than 40,000, most of it concentrated in and around Boston, although there were communities as far west as the lower Connecticut River Valley, New Hampshire—which was set off as a separate royal colony in 1680—and in the northern regions now the state of Maine (not separated from Massachusetts until 1820). Plymouth's 6,000 inhabitants were absorbed by Massachusetts in 1691. Connecticut's population totaled about 17,000.

THE RESTORATION COLONIES

The Puritan Commonwealth established in England after the execution of King Charles attempted to provide a measure of central control over colonial commerce with the passage in 1651 of an Act of Trade and Navigation, aimed specifically at excluding the Dutch from the carrying trade. But the regime was primarily concerned with affairs in England and left the colonies largely to their own devices. During this period colonial assemblies grew increasingly powerful and began to establish a tradition of independence. When Oliver Cromwell, Lord Protector of the Commonwealth, died in 1658, the Puritan new order failed to survive. England was desperate for political stability after decades of civil war and political strife. While retaining for itself certain significant powers of state, in 1660 a new royalist Parliament restored the Stuart monarchy, placing Charles II, son of the beheaded king, on the throne. One of Charles's most important acts was the establishment of several new proprietary colonies in North America, based on the model of the colony of Maryland. As this period in which the monarchy was reestablished was called the Restoration, these became known as the Restoration Colonies.

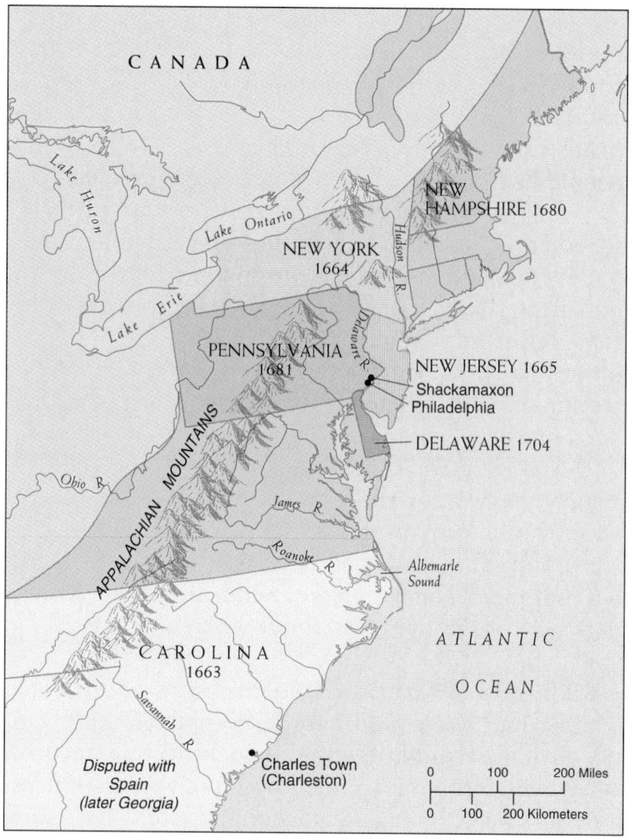

The Restoration Colonies *After the restoration of the Stuart monarchy in 1660, King Charles II of England created the new proprietary colonies of Carolina, New York, Pennsylvania, and New Jersey. New Hampshire was set off as a royal colony in 1680, and in 1704 the lower counties of Pennsylvania became the colony of Delaware.*

Early Carolina

In 1663 the king issued the first of the "Restoration" charters, which called for the establishment of the new colony of Carolina stretching from Virginia south to Spanish Florida. Virginians had already begun moving into the northern parts of this territory, and in 1664 the Carolina proprietors appointed a governor for the settlements in the area of Albemarle Sound and created a popularly elected assembly. By 1675, North Carolina, as it became known, was home to 5,000 small farmers and large tobacco planters.

Settlement farther south began in 1670 with the founding of coastal Charles Town (Charleston today). Most South Carolina settlers came from Barbados, a Caribbean colony the English had founded in 1627, which had grown rich from the production and sale of sugar. By the 1670s the island had become overpopulated with English settlers and Africans. The latter, imported as slaves to work the plantations, made up a majority of the population. Hundreds of Barbadians, both masters and their African slaves, relocated to South Carolina, lending a distinctly West Indian character to the colony. Adding to the diversity of the community was the arrival of several hundred French Huguenots after the revocation of the Edict of Nantes in 1685. By the end of the seventeenth century South Carolina's nonnative population numbered 6,000, some 2,500 of them enslaved Africans.

From New Netherland to New York

King Charles also coveted the lucrative Dutch colony of New Netherland, which extended from the trading town of Albany down the Hudson to the island city of New Amsterdam. The Netherlands was one of the great maritime trading powers of the seventeenth century, with sugar plantations in Brazil and trading posts in India, Indonesia, and China.

Establishing the colony of New Netherland in the 1620s, the Dutch forged a commercial alliance with the Iroquois Confederacy. The Iroquois, who occupied a strategic position between the coast and the interior, sought to channel the flow of furs through Dutch hands.

Once armed by the Dutch, the Iroquois embarked on a series of military adventures known as the Beaver Wars. They invaded the territories of neighboring peoples, and in the late 1640s they attacked and dispersed the Hurons, who had long controlled the flow of furs from the Great Lakes to the French in Montreal. As a result of these wars, the Dutch trading system was extended deep into the interior of the continent. Meanwhile, persistent conflict between the Iroquois and coastal Algonquians erupted in a series of brutal wars that resulted in the withdrawal of these Indian communities into the interior, opening the way for further Dutch expansion. In 1655 the Dutch succeeded in overwhelming a small colony of Swedes on the lower Delaware River, incorporating that region into their sphere of influence as well.

At that point the English began to challenge the Dutch. The two powers fought an inconclusive naval war in the English Channel during the early 1650s and then, a decade later, clashed along the West African coast. In 1664 Charles decided that the time had come to eliminate Dutch competition in North America. In 1664 an English fleet sailed into Manhattan harbor and forced the surrender of New Amsterdam without firing a shot. The next year, England declared war on the Netherlands, a conflict that lasted until 1667. Only five years of peace transpired before a third and final war broke out. These Anglo-Dutch wars marked the decline of the Dutch and the ascendance of the English in the Atlantic.

Charles granted the newly acquired colony of New Amsterdam to his brother James, the duke of York, renaming it New York in his honor. Otherwise the English government did little to disturb the existing order, preferring simply to reap the benefits of acquiring this profitable and dynamic colony. With settlers of various ethnic backgrounds, speaking many different languages and accommodating a wide range of religious sects, New York became the most heterogeneous colony in North America. In 1674 the colonists were granted the status of English subjects, and in 1683, after persistent appeals, the duke approved the creation of a representative assembly. The communities of the Delaware Valley became the proprietary colony of New Jersey in 1665 but continued to be governed by New York until the 1680s. By the 1670s the combined population of these settlements numbered over 10,000, with more than 1,500 people clustered in the governmental and commercial center of New York City.

The Founding of Pennsylvania

In 1676, proprietary rights to the western portion of New Jersey were sold to a group of English Quakers, among them William Penn, who intended to make the area a religious haven for the Society of Friends, as the Quakers were formally known. A dissenting sect, Quakers were committed to religious toleration and pacifism. Penn himself had been imprisoned four times for publicly expressing these views. But he was the son of the wealthy and influential English admiral Sir William Penn, a close adviser of the king. In 1681, to settle a large debt owed to Sir William, King Charles granted the younger Penn a huge territory west of the Delaware River. The next year Penn supervised the laying out of his capital of Philadelphia, which would become known as "The City of Brotherly Love."

This is the earliest known view of New Amsterdam, printed in 1651. Like the French, the Dutch intended to construct a fur trade network that extended far into the continent, thus the prominent position given to the Indians shown arriving with their goods. They paddle a dugout canoe of distinctive design known to have been produced by the Algonquian peoples in the vicinity of Long Island Sound. Twenty-five years after its founding, the Dutch settlement still occupied only the lower tip of Manhattan Island.

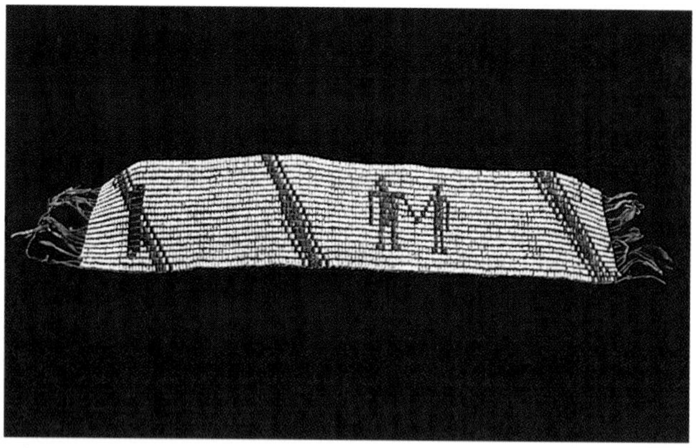

The Delawares presented William Penn with this wampum belt after the Shackamaxon treaty of 1682. In friendship, a Quaker in distinctive hat clasps the hand of an Indian. The diagonal stripes on either side of the figures convey information about the territorial terms of the agreement. Wampum belts like this one, made from strings of white and purple shells, were used to commemorate treaties throughout the colonial period and were the most widely accepted form of money in the northeastern colonies during the seventeenth century.

Penn wanted this colony to be a "holy experiment." In his first Frame of Government, drafted in 1682, he included guarantees of religious freedom, civil liberties, and elected representation. By attempting to deal fairly with the Algonquian Indians, Penn tried to achieve what it took the Spanish and the Pueblo Indians a great deal of bloodshed to accomplish. He refused to permit colonization until settlement rights were negotiated and lands purchased. In 1682 and 1683, he made an agreement with the sachem Tammany of the Delaware tribe at the Indian town of Shackamaxon on the Delaware River. In subsequent years Chief Tammany appeared in many popular stories and myths among the peoples of the mid-Atlantic region. By the time of the Revolution, his name had become emblematic of the American spirit of independence, and later it was adopted by a New York political club. Although Pennsylvania's relations with the Indians later soured, during Penn's lifetime his reputation for fair dealing led a number of Indian groups to take refuge in the Quaker colony.

During the first decade of Pennsylvania's settlement more than 10,000 colonists arrived from England, and agricultural communities were soon spreading from the Delaware into the fertile interior valleys. In 1704 Penn approved the creation of a separate government for the area formerly controlled by the Scandinavians and Dutch, which became the colony of Delaware. In the eighteenth century, Pennsylvania became known as America's breadbasket, and late in the century Philadelphia became the most important colonial port in North America.

CONFLICT AND WAR

Pennsylvania's ability to maintain peaceful relations with the Indians was the great exception of the late seventeenth century. Throughout all the colonial regions of the continent this proved to be a time of

OVERVIEW

CONFLICT AND WAR

King Philip's War	1675–76	The Indian peoples of southern New England and the Puritan colonies fight for the control of land
Bacon's Rebellion	1675–76	Backcountry settlers attack Indians, and colonial authorities try to suppress these attacks
Wars in the South	1670s–1720s	British colonists in the Carolinas incite Creeks, Cherokees, and other Indian tribes to attack and enslave the mission Indians of Spanish Florida
The Glorious Revolution in America	1689	Colonists in Massachusetts, New York, and Maryland rise up against the colonial governments of King James II
King William's War	1689–97	The first of a series of colonial struggles between England and France, these conflicts occur principally on the frontiers of northern New England and New York

persistent warfare between colonists and Indians and of violent conflicts within colonial communities themselves. The revolt of the Pueblo Indians in New Mexico, discussed in the opening of this chapter, was one of the most dramatic examples of such conflict, and the most effective instance of Indian resistance to colonization in the history of North America.

King Philip's War

Another Indian revolt, known as King Philip's War, which erupted in New England in 1675, turned out to be a disaster for Indian people. During the nearly forty years of relative peace that followed the Pequot War of 1637, the Algonquian and English peoples of New England lived in close if tense contact. Several Puritan ministers, including John Eliot and Thomas Mayhew, began to preach to Indian people, and several hundred Algonquian converts eventually relocated in Christian Indian communities called "praying towns." Outside the colonial boundaries, however, there remained a number of independent Indian tribes, including the Wampanoags and Narragansets of Rhode Island and the Abenakis of northern New England. The extraordinary expansion of the Puritan population, coupled with their hunger for land, created pressures for further expansion into those territories.

In 1671 the colonial authorities at Plymouth forced the Wampanoags to concede authority over their homeland territory. This humiliation convinced the Wampanoag sachem Metacomet (called King Philip by his English teachers), son of Massasoit, that his people must break their half-century alliance with Plymouth and take up armed resistance. The New England colonies, meanwhile, prepared for a war of conquest.

In the spring of 1675 Plymouth magistrates arrested three Wampanoag men and executed them for the murder of a Christian Indian. Fearing the moment of confrontation had arrived, Metacomet sent a diplomatic mission to the Narragansetts appealing for a defensive alliance. Arguing that an alliance amounted to an Indian conspiracy, the New England colonies and New York—each hoping for territorial gain—sent armed forces into Narraganset country, attacking and burning a number of villages. What became known as King Philip's War soon engulfed all of New England.

At first things went well for the Indians. They forced the abandonment of English settlements on the Connecticut River and torched several towns less than twenty miles from Boston. But by the beginning of 1676 their campaign was in collapse. A combined colonial army invaded Narraganset country, burning villages, killing women and children, and defeating a large Indian force in a battle known as the Great Swamp Fight. In western New England, Metacomet appealed to the Iroquois for supplies and support, but instead they attacked and defeated his forces. Metacomet retreated back to his homeland, where the colonists annihilated his army in August 1676. The victors killed Metacomet and triumphantly marched his head on a pike through their towns. The colonists sold his wife and son, among hundreds of other captives, into West Indian slavery.

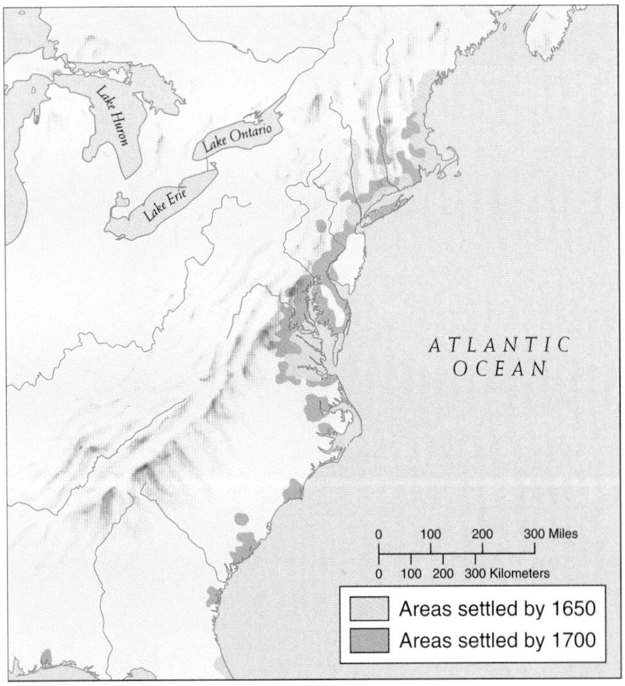

Spread of Settlement: British Colonies, 1650–1700

The spread of settlement in the English colonies in the late seventeenth century created the conditions for a number of violent conflicts, including King Philip's War, Bacon's Rebellion, the Southern Indian Wars, and King William's War.

In their decisive attack on Metacomet's army, the Iroquois had been motivated by interests of their own. Casting themselves in the role of powerful intermediaries between other tribes and the English colonies, the Iroquois wanted to subjugate all trading rivals. In a series of negotiations conducted at Albany in 1677, the Iroquois Confederacy and the colony of New York created an alliance known as the Covenant Chain, which sought to establish both Iroquois dominance over all other tribes and New York dominance over all other colonies. During the 1680s the Iroquois pressed their claims as far west as the Illinois country, fighting the western Algonquians allied with the French trading system.

King Philip's War, which marked the end of organized Indian resistance in New England, took an enormous toll on human life and property. Approximately 4,000 Algonquians and 2,000 English colonists were dead, and dozens of colonial and native towns

Metacomet, or King Philip, in a mid-eighteenth century engraving by Paul Revere of Boston. Like his father Massasoit, Metacomet tried to cooperate with English colonists but finally had to fight to maintain his authority. For many years after the war, the leaders at Plymouth kept his severed head on display. Because his remains never received an honored burial, say the descendants of the Wampanoags, Metacomet's ghost still rises and walks about his homeland.

lay in smoking ruins. Fearing attack from Indians close at hand, colonists also attacked and destroyed most of the Christian "praying towns." Measured against the size of the population, this was one of the most destructive wars in American history.

Bacon's Rebellion

At the same time as King Philip's War, another English-Indian confrontation took place to the south in the Chesapeake. In the 1670s the Susquehannock people of the upper Potomac River came into conflict with tobacco planters expanding from Virginia. Violent raids in 1675, led by wealthy backcountry settler Nathaniel Bacon, included the indiscriminate murder of Indians. The efforts of Virginia governor William Berkeley to suppress these unauthorized military expeditions so infuriated Bacon and his followers—many of them former indentured servants—that in the spring of 1676 they turned their fury against the colonial capital of Jamestown itself. Berkeley fled while Bacon pillaged and burned the town. When Bacon suddenly died of dysentery, however, his rebellion collapsed. Two years later, in a replay of these Virginia events, backcountry men in the Albemarle region of North Carolina overthrew the proprietary government in an episode of violence known as Culpeper's Rebellion. The rebels established a government of their own before being suppressed by English authorities.

Little immediate political change resulted from these two rebellions, but they marked an important change of direction for Virginia and North Carolina. During his tenure as "General of Virginia," Bacon had issued a manifesto demanding not only the death or removal of all Indians from the colony but also an end to the rule of aristocratic "grandees" and "parasites." The rebellion thus signaled a developing conflict of interests between the established Tidewater region, where the "Indian problem" had long since been settled, and frontier districts, where settler hunger for land created conflict with natives. Colonial authorities in Virginia and North Carolina, hoping to gain the support of backcountry men by enlarging the stock of available land, soon declared themselves in favor of armed expansion into Indian territory. But at the same time, planters' fears of disorder among former servants encouraged them to accelerate the transition to slave labor.

Wars in the South

There was also massive violence in South Carolina during the 1670s, as colonists there began the operation of a large-scale Indian slave trade. Charleston merchants encouraged Yamasees, Creeks, Cherokees, and Chickasaws to wage war on Indian tribes allied to rival colonial powers and to sell captives into slavery. Among the victims were the mission Indians of Spanish Florida, the Choctaw allies of the French, and the Tuscaroras, trading partners of the Virginians. The Florida mission Indians were hit so hard that by 1710 more than 12,000 of them had been captured and sold, thousands of others had been killed or dispersed, and the Spanish mission system, in operation for more than a century, lay in ruins.

This vicious slave trade extended well into the eighteenth century, resulting in the sale of thousands of southern Indians into captivity. Most of the men were shipped from Charleston to West Indian or northern colonies, but the Indian women remained in South Carolina. Many eventually formed relationships and had children with enslaved African men, forming a racial-ethnic group known as the mustees.

The Glorious Revolution in America

Dynastic change in England was another factor precipitating violence in North America. Upon Charles II's death in 1685, his brother and successor, James II, began a concerted effort to strengthen royal control over the colonies. During the preceding forty years colonial assemblies had grown powerful and independent, and King James was determined to reduce their status. He abolished the New York assembly, which had been particularly troublesome, and placed all power in the hands of the royal governor. Colonial assemblies continued to operate in the other colonies, but many became involved in bitter disputes with their governors.

In his most dramatic action, James abolished altogether the charter governments of the New England, New York, and New Jersey colonies, combining them into what he called the Dominion of New England. Edmund Andros, the royal governor of this dominion, imposed Anglican forms of worship in Puritan areas, violated traditions of local autonomy, and attempted to enforce the Navigation Acts (1651, 1660, 1663), which restricted colonial trade by preventing the colonies from trading directly with any nation other than England.

Within England, the same imperious style on the part of King James II alienated Parliament. In a bloodless transition in 1688, afterward known as the Glorious Revolution, some leaders in Parliament engineered replacing him with his daughter Mary and her Dutch husband, William of Orange. In 1689 the new monarchs agreed to a Bill of Rights, promising to respect traditional civil liberties, to summon and consult with Parliament annually, and to enforce and administer parliamentary legislation. These were significant concessions with profound implications for the future of English politics. England now had a "constitutional monarchy."

These changes unleashed the resentment against King James that had built up in the colonies, and a series of rebellions broke out against the authorities set in place by the king. In the spring of 1689, Governor Andros was attacked by an angry Boston mob, inflamed by rumors that he was a closet Catholic. He was able to escape their wrath but was arrested and deported by the local militia. When news of the Boston revolt arrived in New York, it inspired another uprising there. A group led by German merchant Jacob Leisler, and including many prominent Dutch residents, seized control of the city and called for the formation of a new legislature. In Maryland, rumors of a Catholic plot led to the overthrow of the proprietary rule of the Calvert family by an insurgent group called the Protestant Association.

The new monarchs carefully measured their response to these uprisings. When Jacob Leisler attempted to prevent the landing of the king's troops in New York, he was arrested, tried, and executed. But the monarchs consented to the dismantling of the Dominion of New England and the end of proprietary rule in Maryland. The outcome of the Glorious Revolution in America was mixed. All the affected English colonies quickly revived their assemblies and returned to their tradition of self-government. But to forestall such disorders in the future, in 1692 the crown decreed that Massachusetts, New York, and Maryland would be royal colonies, with appointed governors, thus extending the control of the monarchy over its troublesome colonists.

King William's War

The year 1689 also marked the beginning of nearly seventy-five years of armed conflict between English and French forces for control of the North American interior. The Iroquois-English Covenant Chain challenged New France to press ever harder in search of commercial opportunities in the interior. In the far North, the English countered French dominance with the establishment of the Hudson's Bay Company, a royal fur-trade monopoly that in 1670 was given exclusive rights to Rupert's Land, the watershed of the great northern Hudson Bay.

Hostilities began with English-Iroquois attacks on Montreal and violence between rival French and English traders on Hudson Bay. These skirmishes were part of a larger conflict between England and France called the War of the League of Augsburg in Europe and King William's War in the North American colonies. In 1690 the French and their Algonquian allies counterattacked, burning frontier settlements in New York, New Hampshire, and Maine and pressing the attack against the towns of the Iroquois. The same year, a Massachusetts fleet briefly captured the strategic French harbor at Port Royal, in Acadia, but a combined English colonial force failed in its attempt to conquer the French settlements along the St. Lawrence. This inconclusive war was ended by the Treaty of Ryswick of 1697, which established an equally inconclusive peace. War between England and France would resume only five years later.

The persistent violence of these years concerned English authorities, who began to fear the loss of their North American possessions either from outside attack or from internal disorder. To shore up central control, in 1701 the English Board of Trade recommended making all charter and proprietary

CHRONOLOGY

1598	Juan de Oñate leads Spanish into New Mexico
1607	English found Jamestown
1608	French found Quebec
1609	Spanish found Santa Fé
1620	Pilgrim emigration
1622	Indian uprising in Virginia
1625	Jesuit missionaries arrive in New France
1629	Puritans begin settlement of Massachusetts Bay
1637	Pequot War
1649	Charles I executed
1660	Stuart monarchy restored, Charles II becomes king
1675	King Philip's War
1676	Bacon's Rebellion
1680	Pueblo Revolt
1681–82	Robert Sieur de La Salle explores the Mississippi
1688	The Glorious Revolution
1689	King William's War
1698	Spanish reconquest of the Pueblos completed
1701	English impose royal governments on all colonies but Massachusetts, Connecticut, and Pennsylvania

governments into royal colonies. After a brief period under royal rule, William Penn regained private control of his domain, but Pennsylvania was the last remaining proprietary colony. Among the charter colonies, only Rhode Island and Connecticut retained their original governments. The result of this quarter-century of violence was the tightening of the imperial reins.

CONCLUSION

At the beginning of the seventeenth century the European presence north of Mexico was extremely limited: a Spanish base in Florida, a few Franciscan missionaries among the Pueblo Indians, and fishermen along the North Atlantic coast. By 1700, however, the human landscape of the Southwest, the South, and the Northeast had been transformed with the establishment of the Spanish colony of New Mexico, the French colonies of New France, and along the Atlantic coast a series of English colonies from New England in the North to the Carolinas in the South. More than a quarter million Europeans and Africans now resided in colonial enclaves. Indian tribal societies had been disrupted, depopulated, and in some cases destroyed. The policies of the various European colonizers differed significantly, and outside the colonial enclaves Indians still constituted the vast majority of the continent's inhabitants, but the profound changes of the seventeenth century had ominous implications for Indian peoples.

During the long civil war in England the English colonies had been left to run their own affairs, but with the Restoration in 1660, and the establishment of the constitutional monarchy in 1689, the English state began to supervise its troublesome colonists more closely, beginning a long struggle over the limits of self-government. The violence and warfare of the last decades of the century suggested that conflict would continue to play a significant role in the future of colonial America.

REVIEW QUESTIONS

1. Using examples drawn from this chapter, discuss the differences between colonizing "frontiers of inclusion" and "exclusion."
2. What factors turned England's Chesapeake colony of Virginia from stark failure to brilliant success?

3. Discuss the role of religious dissent in the founding of the first New England colonies and in stimulating the creation of others.
4. Compare and contrast William Penn's policy with respect to Indian tribes with the policies of other English settlers, in the Chesapeake and New England, and with the policies of the Spanish, the French, and the Dutch.
5. What were the principal causes of colonial violence and warfare of the late seventeenth century?

RECOMMENDED READING

James Axtell, *The European and the Indian: Essays in the Ethnohistory of Colonial America* (1981). A readable introduction to the dynamics of mutual discovery between natives and colonizers.

Carl Bridenbaugh, *Vexed and Troubled Englishmen, 1590–1642* (1968). A social history of the English people on the eve of colonization, emphasizing their religious and economic problems.

W. J. Eccles, *France in America* (1990). The most comprehensive introduction to the history of New France.

Andrew L. Knaut, *The Pueblo Revolt of 1680* (1995). The most complete and sophisticated account of the revolt.

Edmund S. Morgan, *American Slavery, American Freedom* (1975). A classic interpretation of early Virginia. Morgan argues that early American ideas of freedom for some were based on the reality of slavery for others.

Neal Salisbury, *Manitou and Providence: Indians, Europeans, and the Making of New England* (1982). One of the best examples of the new ethnohistory of Indians; a provocative intercultural approach to the history of the Northeast.

David J. Weber, *The Spanish Frontier in North America* (1992). A powerful overview that includes the history of New Mexico and Florida.

Peter H. Wood, et al., eds., *Powhatan's Mantle: Indians in the Colonial Southeast* (1989). Essays detailing the conflict and consort between colonists and natives in the South.

ADDITIONAL BIBLIOGRAPHY

The Spanish and French in North America

James Axtell, *The Invasion Within: The Contest of Culture in Colonial North America* (1985)

Gilberto Rafael Cruz, *Let There Be Towns: Spanish Municipal Origins in the American Southwest, 1610–1810* (1988)

W. J. Eccles, *The Canadian Frontier, 1534–1760* (1983)

The Chesapeake

Kathleen M. Brown, *Good Wives, Nasty Wenches, and Anxious Patriarchs: Gender, Race, and Power in Colonial Virginia* (1996)

Wesley F. Craven, *White, Red, and Black: The Seventeenth Century Virginian* (1971)

Carville Earle, *The Evolution of a Tidewater Settlement System: All Hallow's Parish, Maryland, 1650–1783* (1975)

Jack P. Greene and J. R. Poole, eds., *Colonial British America: Essays in the New History of the Early Modern Era* (1984)

Karen Ordahl Kupperman, *Settling with the Indians: The Meeting of English and Indian Cultures in America, 1580–1640* (1980)

Gloria L. Main, *Tobacco Colony: Life in Early Maryland, 1650–1720* (1982)

Thad W. Tate and David L. Ammerman, eds., *The Chesapeake in the Seventeenth Century* (1979)

New England

David Grayson Allen, *In English Ways: The Movement of Societies and the Transferal of English Local Law and Custom* (1981)

Bernard Bailyn, *The New England Merchants in the Seventeenth Century* (1955)

Emery Battis, *Saints and Sectaries: Anne Hutchinson and the Antinomian Controversy in the Massachusetts Bay Colony* (1962)

Theodore Dwight Bozeman, *To Live Ancient Lives: The Primitivist Dimension in Puritanism* (1988)

Francis J. Bremer, ed., *Puritanism: Transatlantic Perspectives on a Seventeenth-Century Anglo-American Faith* (1993)

Carl Bridenbaugh, *Fat Mutton and Liberty of Conscience: Society in Rhode Island, 1636–1690* (1974)

David Cressy, *Coming Over: Migration and Communication between England and New England in the Seventeenth Century* (1987)

William Cronon, *Changes in the Land: Indians, Colonists, and the Ecology of New England* (1983)

Bruce Colin Daniels, *Puritans at Play: Leisure and Recreation in Colonial New England* (1995)

John Demos, *A Little Commonwealth: Family Life in Plymouth Colony* (1970)

M. Etienne and E. Leacock, eds., *Women and Colonization* (1980)

Christopher Hill, *The World Turned Upside Down: Radical Ideas during the English Revolution* (1972)

Stephen Innes, *Labor in a New Land* (1983)

Francis Jennings, *The Invasion of America: Indians, Colonialism, and the Cant of Conquest* (1975)

Amy Scrager Lang, *Prophetic Women: Anne Hutchinson and the Problem of Dissent in the Literature of New England* (1987)

Michael Walzer, *The Revolution of the Saints: A Study in the Origins of Radical Politics* (1965)

Restoration Colonies

Wesley F. Craven, *The Southern Colonies in the Seventeenth Century, 1607–1689* (1949)
Melvin B. Endy Jr., *William Penn and Early Quakerism* (1973)
Michael Kammen, *Colonial New York: A History* (1975)
Sung Bok Kim, *Landlord and Tenant in Colonial New York: Manorial Society, 1664–1775* (1978)
H. T. Merrens, *Colonial North Carolina* (1964)
Gary B. Nash, *Quakers and Politics: Pennsylvania, 1681–1726* (1968)
Oliver Rink, *Holland on the Hudson: An Economic and Social History of Dutch New York* (1986)
Robert C. Ritchie, *The Duke's Province: A Study of New York Politics and Society, 1664–1691* (1977)
M. Eugene Sirmans, *Colonial South Carolina: A Political History, 1663–1763* (1966)
Jack M. Sosin, *English America and the Restoration Monarchy of Charles II: Transatlantic Politics, Commerce, and Kinship* (1980)

Conflict and War

Thomas J. Archdeacon, *New York City, 1664–1710* (1976)
Russell Bourne, *The Red King's Rebellion: Racial Politics in New England, 1675–1678* (1990)
Paul Boyer and Stephen Nissenbaum, *Salem Possessed* (1974)
Ramón A. Gutiérrez, *When Jesus Came, the Corn Mothers Went Away: Marriage, Sexuality, and Power in New Mexico, 1500–1846* (1991)
Richard R. Johnson, *Adjustment to Empire: The New England Colonies, 1675–1715* (1981)
D. W. Jordan, *Maryland's Revolution of Government, 1689–1692* (1974)
Carol F. Karlsen, *The Devil in the Shape of a Woman: Witchcraft in Colonial New England* (1987)
Yusuhide Kawashima, *Puritan Justice and the Indian: White Man's Law in Massachusetts, 1630–1763* (1986)
Almon Wheeler Lauber, *Indian Slavery in Colonial Times within the Present Limits of the United States* (1913)
David S. Lovejoy, *The Glorious Revolution in America* (1972)
Michael J. Publisi, *Puritans Besieged: The Legacies of King Philip's War in the Massachusetts Bay Colony* (1991)
Jack M. Sosin, *English America and the Revolution of 1688* (1982)
Wilcomb E. Washburn, *The Governor and the Rebel: A History of Bacon's Rebellion in Virginia* (1957)
Stephen S. Webb, *1676: The End of American Independence* (1980)
Thomas J. Wertenbaker, *Torchbearer of the Revolution: The Story of Bacon's Rebellion and its Leader* (1940)

Biography

Mary M. Dunn, *William Penn, Politics and Conscience* (1967)
J. A. Leo Lemay, *The American Dream of Captain John Smith* (1991)
Edmund S. Morgan, *Puritan Dilemma: The Story of John Winthrop* (1958)
Ann Sanford, *Anne Bradstreet, the Worldly Puritan* (1974)
Marc Simmons, *The Last Conquistador: Juan de Oñate and the Settling of the Far Southwest* (1991)
Robert S. Tilton, *Pocahontas: The Evolution of an American Narrative* (1994)
Alvin Gardner Weeks, *Massasoit of the Wampanoags* (1919)
Selma R. Williams, *Divine Rebel: The Life of Anne Marbury Hutchinson* (1981)

CHAPTER FOUR

SLAVERY AND EMPIRE

1441–1770

Painting of slaves in Antigua. From William Clark's *Ten Views Found in the Island of Antigua*, early 19th century. The British Library.

CHAPTER OUTLINE

THE BEGINNINGS OF AFRICAN SLAVERY

Sugar and Slavery

West Africans

THE AFRICAN SLAVE TRADE

The Demography of the Slave Trade

Slavers of All Nations

The Shock of Enslavement

The Middle Passage

Arrival in the New World

Political and Economic Effects on Africa

THE DEVELOPMENT OF NORTH AMERICAN SLAVE SOCIETIES

Slavery Comes to North America

The Tobacco Colonies

The Lower South

Slavery in the Spanish Colonies

French Louisiana

Slavery in the North

BECOMING AFRICAN AMERICAN

The Daily Life of Slaves

Families and Communities

African American Culture

The Africanization of the South

Violence and Resistance

SLAVERY AND THE STRUCTURE OF EMPIRE

Slavery the Mainspring

The Politics of Mercantilism

Wars for Empire

British Colonial Regulation

The Colonial Economy

SLAVERY AND FREEDOM

The Social Structure of the Slave Colonies

White Skin Privilege

AMERICAN COMMUNITIES

African Slaves Build Their Own Community in Coastal Georgia

Africans labored in the steamy heat of the coastal Georgia rice fields, the breeches of the men rolled up over their knees, the sack skirts of the women gathered and tied about their hips, leaving them, in the words of one shocked observer, "two thirds naked." Standing on the banks of canals that channeled water to the fields, African slave drivers, whips at the ready, supervised the work. Upriver, groups cut away cypress and gum trees and cleared the swampland's jungle maze of undergrowth; others constructed levees, preparing to bring more land under cultivation. An English overseer or plantation master could be seen here and there, but overwhelmingly it was a country populated by Africans.

These Georgia plantations were southern extensions of the South Carolina rice belt. Although slavery had been prohibited by Georgia's original colonial charter of 1732, the restriction was lifted when Georgia became a royal colony two decades later. By 1770, 15,000 African Americans lived on several hundred coastal plantations, and the population of the region was 80 percent African. The rice plantations were owned by a small elite, dominated by a tight circle of crown officials and their relatives and associates. Georgia's royal governor and lieutenant governor, for example, owned more than a dozen plantations with over 50,000 acres and 800 slaves. Plantations with names such as Mulberry Grove, New Settlement, and Walnut Hill were among the most recent, and most profitable, additions to the British New World empire.

Rice had become one of the most valuable commodities produced in mainland North America, surpassed in value only by tobacco and wheat. The growth of rice production in the Lower South was matched by an enormous expansion in the Atlantic slave trade. Having no experience in rice cultivation, English colonial planters pressed slave traders to supply them with Africans from rice-growing regions such as the Windward Coast of West Africa. In its workforce, its methods, and even its tools, southern rice culture was patterned on an African model.

Although in the eighteenth century the number of North American blacks who were "country-born" (native to America, and thus born into slavery) grew steadily, the majority on the rice plantations continued to be what were known as "salt-water" Africans. These men and women had endured the shock of enslavement. Ripped from their homeland communities in West Africa by slave raiders, they were brutally marched to coastal forts. There they were imprisoned, subjected to humiliating inspections of their bodies, and branded on the buttocks like animals. Packed into the holds of stinking ships, they endured a nightmarish passage across the Atlantic Ocean. When finally unloaded on a strange continent, they were sold at dockside auctions, then once again marched overland to their destinations on New World plantations. On the rice plantations of isolated coastal Georgia enslaved Africans suffered from overwork and numerous physical ailments caused by poor diet, minimal and inappropriate clothing, and inadequate housing. Mortality rates were exceptionally high, especially for infants. Colonial laws permitted masters to discipline and punish slaves indiscriminately. They were whipped, confined in irons, castrated, or sold to other landowners with little regard for their relations with family or friends.

Africans struggled to make a place for themselves in this inhospitable world. The knowledge of rice cultivation that many slaves brought with them to the rice coast gave them the bargaining power to win acceptance from their masters of the familiar work routines and rhythms of West Africa. Thus, low-country plantations operated according to the task system: once slaves finished their specific jobs, they could use their remaining time to hunt, fish, or cultivate family gardens. Masters frequently complained that "tasking" did not produce the same level of profit as the gang labor system of the sugar plantations, but African rice hands refused to work any other way.

Despite this small degree of control over the form of their servitude, slaves on the Georgia coast ran away, like slaves everywhere in the Americas. Readers of Savannah newspapers were urged to look out for fugitives: Statira, a woman of the "Gold Coast Country" with tribal markings upon her temples, or "a negro fellow named Mingo, about 40 years old, and his wife Quante, a sensible wench about 20 with her child, a boy about 3 years old, all this country born." Some fled in groups, heading for the Creek Indian settlements in northern Florida, or toward St. Augustine, where the Spanish promised them safe haven. Some struck out violently at their masters: in 1759, a group of nine Africans from a Savannah plantation killed their master and stole a boat, planning to head upriver. They were apprehended as they lay in wait to murder their hated overseers as well.

So slaves resisted. But like slaves throughout the New World, the majority of enslaved Africans and African Americans of the Georgia coast remained, and through their strategy and determination, built their own communities within the heartless world of slavery. Plantation slaves throughout the American South married, raised children, and gradually created African American kinship networks. They passed on African names and traditions and created new ones. These links between individuals and families formed the basis for reestablished communities.

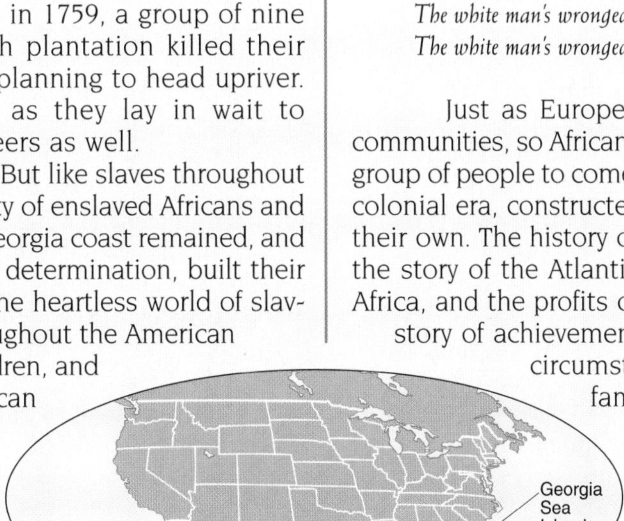

African American slave communities combined elements both of African languages and of English to form dialects that allowed newly arrived people from many different African ethnic groups as well as American-born slaves to communicate with one another. Neither individuals nor families alone can make a language; that is something only a community can do. The common African heritage and a common status as slaves supplied the basis for the African American community. Communities provided both newly arrived Africans and the American-born with the opportunity to build relationships. Without African American communities there could have been no African American culture.

Traveling through the Georgia and Carolina low country during the 1740s, an English missionary heard a clamor in the woods along the road. As he peered through the trees he was startled to see a group of slaves "dancing round the fire." The African American community was refitting traditional dance, song, and story to New World circumstances, just as it was reestablishing African arts such as woodworking, iron making, and weaving. Through their culture, the slaves shared a powerful awareness of their common oppression. They told or sang dialect tales of mistreatment, as in this song of Quow, the punished slave:

Was matter Buddy Quow?
I ble Obesha bang you....
Dah Backrow Man go wrong you, Buddy Quow,
Dah Backrow Man go wrong you, Buddy Quow.

[What's the matter Brother Quow?
I believe the overseer's beat you....
The white man's wronged you, Brother Quow,
The white man's wronged you, Brother Quow.]

Just as European settlers planted colonial communities, so Africans, who constituted the largest group of people to come to North America during the colonial era, constructed distinctive communities of their own. The history of African Americans includes the story of the Atlantic slave trade, the plunder of Africa, and the profits of the empire. But it is also a story of achievement under the most difficult of circumstances and of the making of families, kin networks, and communities. They "labor together and converse almost wholly among themselves," a minister wrote of low-country slaves. "They are, as 'twere, a nation within a nation."

KEY TOPICS

- The development of the slavery system
- The history of the slave trade and the Middle Passage
- Community development among African Americans in the eighteenth century
- The connections between the institution of slavery and the imperial system of the eighteenth century
- The early history of racism in America

THE BEGINNINGS OF AFRICAN SLAVERY

Household slaves had long been a part of the world of Mediterranean Europe. War captives were sold to wealthy families, who put them to work as servants or artisans. In the fifteenth century, Venetian and Genoese merchants led the traffic in captured Slavic peoples—the word "slave" derives from the name Slav—as well as Muslims and Africans. But many Europeans were disturbed by the moral implications of enslaving Christians, which most Slavs were, and in the early fifteenth century the pope excommunicated a number of merchants engaged in selling such captives. The trade in Africans and Muslims, however, continued.

One of the goals of Portuguese expansion in the fifteenth century was access to the lucrative West African trade in slaves that had been dominated by the Moors—today's Algerians, Libyans, and Moroccans—of northern Africa. The first African slaves to arrive in Lisbon were twelve men kidnapped by a Portuguese captain in 1441; three years later another Portuguese crew seized twenty-nine men and women off Cape Blanco and shipped them home. But Portuguese traders found it considerably more efficient to leave the kidnapping to Africans who were willing to sell captives in exchange for European commodities. By the 1450s a small but regular slave trade between Africa and Europe was in place.

Sugar and Slavery

The greatest market for these slaves was the large sugar plantations the Portuguese established on their island colony of Madeira, off the coast of northern Africa. Portuguese masters brutally exploited these Africans, working many of them to death, since profits were high and replacement costs low. Sugar and slaves had gone together since the fourteenth century, when Italian merchants first imported cane sugar from West Asia and set up the first sugar plantations on the islands of the Mediterranean. For the sake of sweetness, Europeans subjected Africans to the suffering of slavery.

One of the first products Columbus introduced to the New World was sugarcane, and soon sugar plantations were operating on the island of Hispaniola. At first the Spanish tried to use native Indian people as a slave labor force, but because disease and warfare had so reduced the indigenous population colonists soon turned to the African slaves who were already working in Spain. The introduction of horse-powered sugar mills around 1510 so increased the demand for labor that in 1518 Spain granted Portuguese slavers an *asiento* (license) to bring slaves to America directly from Africa. Meanwhile, the Portuguese, aided by Dutch financiers, created a center of sugar production in northeast Brazil that became a model of the efficient and brutal exploitation of African labor. By 1600 some 25,000 enslaved Africans labored on the plantations of Hispaniola and Brazil. "As a result of the sugar factories," a colonial Spanish official declared in 1535, "the land seems an...image of Ethiopia itself."

The Dutch, using their experience in Brazil, became responsible for the next extension of slavery in the Americas. In 1630 they seized Brazil and controlled this lucrative colony for the next twenty years. Skilled at finance and commerce, they greatly expanded the European market for sugar, converting it from a luxury item for the rich to a staple for European workers. Along with addictive tropical commodities such as tobacco, coffee, and tea, sugar became what one historian calls a "proletarian hunger-killer," helping to sustain people through increasingly long working days. As the market for sugar expanded, the Dutch expanded their sugar operations throughout the tropics, introducing it, for example, into the small island of Barbados, which soon became the most valuable of England's colonies. Once the profitability of sugar had been demonstrated, the English sought to expand their production by seizing the island of Jamaica from the Spanish in 1655 and making it over in the image of Barbados. Jamaica, much larger than Barbados, soon became the crown jewel of Britain's eighteenth-century empire.

The French repeated the process. They first developed sugar plantations on the small island of

Martinique, then seized the eastern half of Hispaniola from the Spanish and created a sugar colony called St. Domingue (today's Haiti). Caribbean sugar and slaves had become the centerpiece of the European colonial system.

West Africans

The men and women whose labor made these tropical colonies so profitable came from the long-established societies and local communities of West Africa. In the sixteenth century more than a hundred different peoples lived along the coast of West Africa, from Cape Verde south to Angola. In the north were the Wolofs, Mandingos, Hausas, Ashantis, and Yorubas; to the south the Ibos, Sekes, Bakongos, and Mbundus.

In all these societies the most important institution was the local community, which was organized by kinship. Decisions about production, storage, and distribution were generally made by clan leaders and village chiefs; local courts arbitrated disputes. Men frequently took a second or third wife. This marriage system, known as polygyny, produced very large composite families with complex internal relationships. Because of restrictions on sexual relations, however, West African women bore fewer children than the typical European woman, and many enjoyed considerable social and economic independence as tradeswomen.

West African societies were based on sophisticated farming systems many thousands of years old. Farmers cultivated millet, sorghum, and rice on the grassy savannas and fruits, root crops, and other vegetables in the tropical forests that straddled the equator. West Africans had mastered the art of iron making, but because their soils were rather thin and poor, they found no use for iron plows. Rather, like the native farmers of North America, Africans practiced "shifting cultivation": they cleared land by burning, used hoes or digging sticks to work in the ash, rich in nutrients, and when fertility declined after several years, they let their old fields lie fallow and moved on to clear new ones. Men worked at clearing the land, women at cultivation and the sale of surpluses in the lively West African markets.

Farming sustained large populations and thriving networks of commerce, and in some areas kingdoms and states developed. Along the upper Niger River, where the grassland gradually turns to desert, towns such as Timbuktu developed into trading centers. West African metal goods, gold, ivory, and textiles made their way from these towns to the Mediterranean on trans-Saharan caravans organized by Moors and other Muslim traders. The attempt to control the wealth this trade generated led to the rise and fall of a succession of military empires. The most extensive of these was the Mali Empire, whose greatest ruler, Mansa Musa, made Timbuktu a leading intellectual as well as commercial center. When the Portuguese first arrived in the fifteenth century, the most important state in the region was the powerful Muslim kingdom of Songhai (today the African nation of Mali), noted for the cavalry and army with which it controlled the flow of trade. There were also many lesser states and kingdoms along the coast, and it was with these that the Portuguese first bargained for Africans who could be sold as slaves.

Slavery had long been an established institution in Africa. Most enslaved men and women had been captured in war or condemned to servitude as criminal punishment. African slavery was not a permanent condition, however; most slaves were eventually incorporated into the families they served. They were allowed to marry, and their children were born free. "With us they did no more work than other members of the community, even their master," remembered Olaudah Equiano, an Ibo captured and shipped to America as a slave in 1756, when he was a boy of eleven. "Their food, clothing, and lodging were nearly the same as [the others'], except that they were not permitted to eat with those who were born free." When African merchants sold the first slaves to the Portuguese, they must have thought that European slavery would be similar. But as Equiano declared: "How different was their condition from that of the slaves in the West Indies!" Yet it was the West African familiarity with "unfree" labor that made it

This image of Mansa Musa (1312–37), *the ruler of the* Muslim *kingdom of* Mali *in* West Africa, *is taken from the* Catalan Atlas, *a magnificent map presented to the king of France in 1381 by his cousin, the king of Aragon. In the words of the* Catalan *inscription, Musa was "the richest, the most noble lord in all this region on account of the abundance of gold that is gathered in his land." He holds what was thought to be the world's largest gold nugget. Under Musa's reign, Timbuktu became a capital of world renown.*

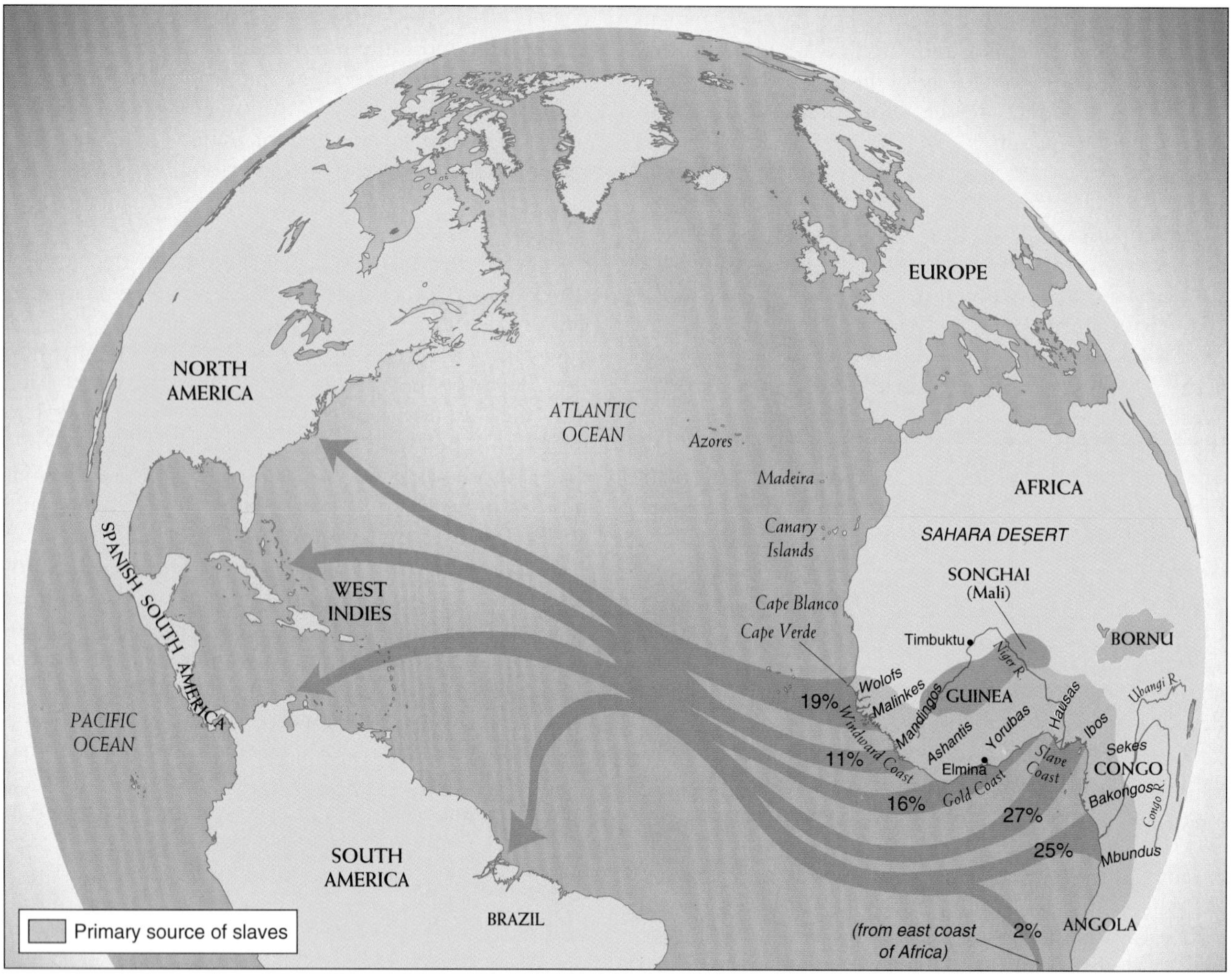

The African Slave Trade *The enslaved men, women, and children transported to the Americas came from West Africa, the majority from the lower Niger River (called the Slave Coast) and the region of the Congo and Angola.*

possible for African and European traders to begin the trade in human merchandise.

THE AFRICAN SLAVE TRADE

The movement of Africans across the Atlantic to the Americas was the largest forced migration in world history. Moreover, Africans made up the largest group of people to come to the Americas before the nineteenth century, outnumbering European immigrants by the astounding ratio of six to one. The Atlantic slave trade, which began with the Portuguese in the fifteenth century and did not end in the United States until 1808 (it continued elsewhere in the Americas until the 1870s) is a brutal chapter in the making of America.

The Demography of the Slave Trade

Scholars today estimate that slavers transported 10 to 11 million Africans to the Americas during the four centuries of the trade. Seventy-six percent arrived from 1701 to 1810—the peak period of colonial demand for labor, when tens of thousands of individuals were shipped from Africa each year. Of this vast multitude, about half were delivered to Dutch, French, or British sugar plantations in the Caribbean, a third to Portuguese Brazil, and 10 percent to Spanish America. A much smaller proportion—about one in twenty, or an estimated 600,000 men, women, and children—were transported from Africa to the British colonies of North America.

Among the Africans brought to the Americas, men generally outnumbered women two to one. Since most Africans were destined for field work, this ratio probably reflected the preferences of plantation owners. The majority of captured and transported Africans were young people, between the ages of fifteen and thirty, and nearly every ethnic group in West Africa was represented among them.

Slavers of All Nations

All the nations of western Europe participated in the slave trade. Dutch slavers began challenging Portuguese control at the end of the sixteenth century, and during the sugar boom of the seventeenth century Holland became the most prominent slave-trading nation. The English also entered the trade in the sixteenth century, beginning with the African voyages of John Hawkins. The Royal African Company, a slave-trading monopoly based in London, was chartered in 1672, but in 1698 England threw open the trade to independent merchants. Soon hundreds of ships from Bristol and Liverpool were competing with those from London. As a result, the number of slaves shipped to North America skyrocketed. The Dutch and Portuguese, however, continued to play important roles, alongside slave traders from France, Sweden, and several German duchies.

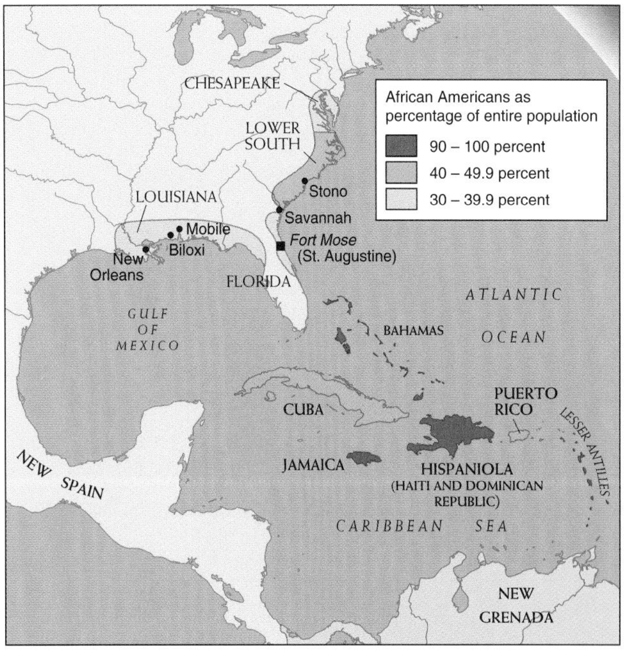

Slave Colonies of the Seventeenth and Eighteenth Centuries *By the eighteenth century the system of slavery had created societies with large African populations throughout the Caribbean and along the southern coast of North America.*

Portrait of a Negro Man, Olaudah Equiano, 1780s (previously attributed to Joshua Reynolds) by English School (18th c.). Royal Albert memorial Museum, Exeter, Devon, UK/Bridgeman Art Library, London/New York.

Portrait of Olaudah Equiano, *by an unknown English artist, ca.* 1780. *Captured in Nigeria in* 1756 *when he was eleven years old, Equiano was transported to America and eventually purchased by an English sea captain. After ten years as a slave, he succeeded in buying his own freedom and dedicated himself to the antislavery cause. His book,* The Interesting Narrative of the Life of Olaudah Equiano (1789), *was published in numerous editions, translated into several languages, and became the prototype for dozens of other slave narratives in the nineteenth century.*

For the most part the European presence in Africa was confined to outposts, although the Portuguese established a colony in Angola. By the early eighteenth century more than two dozen trading forts dotted the 220 miles of the Gold Coast alone. As the slave trade peaked in the middle of the century, however, the forts of trading companies gave way to small coastal clusters of huts where independent traders set up operations with the cooperation of local headmen or chiefs.

This informal manner of trading offered opportunities for small operators, such as the New England slavers who entered the trade in the early eighteenth century. Often bartering rum or salt fish for human beings, these Yankees earned a reputation for crafty dealings. They came by it honestly: "Water your rum as much as possible," one New England merchant instructed his captain, "and sell as much by the short measure as you can." At first, most New England slavers sailed principally from Massachusetts, but after 1750 the center shifted to Rhode Island. Many great New England fortunes were built from profits in the slave trade.

The Shock of Enslavement

The slave trade was a collaboration between European or American and African traders. Dependent on the favor of local rulers, many colonial slave traders lived permanently in coastal forts and married African women, reinforcing their commercial ties with family relations. In many areas a mixed-ancestry group became prominent in the coastal slave trade. Continuing the

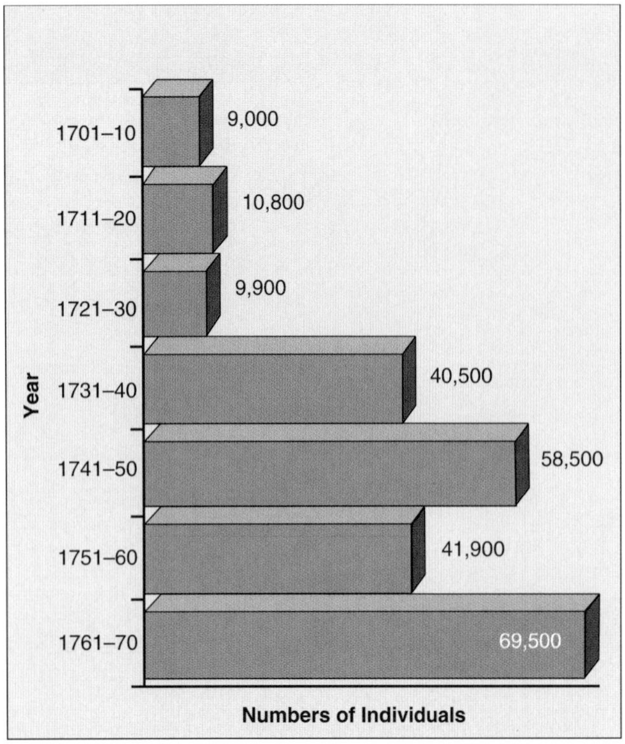

Estimated Number of Africans Imported to British North America, 1701–1775 *These official British statistics include only slaves imported legally and consequently undercount the total number who arrived on American shores. But the trend over time is clear. With the exception of the 1750s, when the British colonies were engulfed by the Seven Years War, the slave trade continued to rise in importance in the decades before the Revolution.*

Source: R. C. Simmons, *The American Colonies: From Settlement to Independence* (London: Longman, 1976), 186.

practice of the Portuguese, the grim business of slave raiding was left to the Africans themselves. Slaves were not at all reticent about condemning the participation of their fellow Africans. "I must own to the shame of my own countrymen," wrote Ottobah Cugoano, who was sold into slavery in the mid-eighteenth century, "that I was first kidnapped and betrayed by [those of] my own complexion."

Most Africans were enslaved through warfare. Sometimes large armies launched massive attacks, burning whole towns and taking hundreds of prisoners. More common were smaller raids in which a group of armed men attacked at nightfall, seized everyone within reach, then escaped with their captives. However, kidnapping, called *panyaring* in the jargon of the slave trade, was also common. One seaman, ashore while his slave ship awaited its cargo, amused himself by peeking at a young African woman bathing. Suddenly two raiders jumped from the bushes and dragged her off. He later saw them carry her on board and sell her to the captain, no questions asked.

As the demand for slaves increased in the eighteenth century with the expansion of the plantation system in the Americas, raids extended deeper and deeper into the African interior. The march to the coast was filled with terrors. One account describes a two-month trip in which many captives died of hunger, thirst, or exhaustion, several attempted suicide, and the whole party was forced to hide to avoid being seized by a rival band of raiders. The captives finally arrived on the coast, where they were sold to an American vessel bound for South Carolina.

Enslavement was an unparalleled shock. Venture Smith, an African born in Guinea in 1729, was eight years old when he was captured. After many years in North American slavery, he still vividly recalled the attack on his village, the torture and murder of his father, and the long march of his people to the coast. "The shocking scene is to this day fresh in my mind," he wrote, "and I have often been overcome while thinking on it." The horror was captured in the song of captives marching to the Slave Coast from the interior kingdom of Bornu, imploring the assistance of one of their gods, a song long remembered by African Americans and published by abolitionists in the nineteenth century:

Bornu-land was rich and good,
Wells of water, fields of food;
Bornu-land we see no longer,
Here we thirst, and here we hunger,
Here the Moor man smites in anger;
Where are we going, Rubee?
Where are we going? Where are we going?
Hear us, save us, Rubee!
Moons of marches from our eyes,
Bornu-land behind us lies;
Hot the desert wind is blowing,
Wild the waves of sand are flowing!
Hear us! Tell us, where are we going?
Where are we going, Rubee?

On the coast, European traders and African raiders assembled their captives. Prisoners waited in dark dungeons or in open pens called barracoons. To lessen the possibility of collective resistance, traders split up families and ethnic groups. Captains carefully inspected each man and woman, and those selected for transport were branded on the back or buttocks with the mark of the buyer. Olaudah Equiano remembered that "those white men with horrible looks, red faces, and long hair, looked and acted...in so savage a manner;...I had never seen among any people such instances of brutal cruelty." Equiano's narrative, written during the 1780s, after he had secured his freedom, is one of the few that

A slave coffle in an eighteenth-century print. As the demand for slaves increased, raids extended deeper and deeper into the African interior. Tied together with forked logs or bark rope, men, women, and children were marched hundreds of miles toward the coast, where their African captors traded them to Europeans.

provide an African account of enslavement. He and his fellow captives became convinced that they "had got into a world of bad spirits" and were about to be eaten by cannibals. A French trader wrote that many prisoners were "positively prepossessed with the opinion that we transport them into our country in order to kill and eat them."

The Middle Passage

In the eighteenth century English sailors christened the voyage of slave ships the Middle Passage, the middle part of a triangle from England to Africa, Africa to America, and America back to England. From coastal forts and barracoons, crews rowed small groups of slaves out to the waiting ships and packed them into shelves below deck only six feet long by two and a half feet high. "Rammed like herring in a barrel," wrote one observer, slaves were "chained to each other hand and foot, and stowed so close, that they were not allowed above a foot and a half for each in breadth." People were forced to sleep "spoon fashion," and the tossing of the ship knocked them about so violently that the skin over their elbows sometimes was worn to the bone from scraping on the planks.

Slavers debated the merits of various packing strategies. One camp argued that additional room lessened mortality and thus increased profits. But the great demand and the price for slaves in the mid-eighteenth century gave the upper hand to the "tight packers," those willing to risk life in order to carry as many men and women as possible. One ship designed to carry 450 slaves regularly crossed the Atlantic with more than 600. Their holds filled with human cargo, the ships headed toward Cape Verde to catch the trade winds blowing toward America. A favorable voyage from Senegambia to Barbados might be accomplished in as little as three weeks, but a ship from Guinea or Angola becalmed in the doldrums or driven back by storms might take as much as three months.

The voyage was marked by a daily routine. In the morning the crew opened the hatch and brought the captives on deck, attaching their leg irons to a great chain running the length of the bulwarks. After a breakfast of beans came a ritual known as "dancing the slave": while an African thumped an upturned kettle or plucked a banjo, the crew commanded men and women to jump up and down in a bizarre session of exercise. A day spent chained on deck was concluded by a second bland meal and then the stowing away. During the night, according to one seaman, there issued from below "a howling melancholy noise, expressive of extreme anguish." Down in the hold the groans of the dying, the shrieks of women and children, and the suffocating heat and stench combined to create, in the words of Olaudah Equiano, "a scene of horror almost inconceivable."

Among the worst of the horrors was the absence of adequate sanitation. There were "necessary tubs" set below deck, but Africans, "endeavoring to get to them, tumble over their companions," one eighteenth-century ship's surgeon wrote, "and as the necessities of nature are not to be resisted, they ease themselves as they lie." Efficient captains ordered crews to scrape and swab the holds daily, but so sickening was the task that on many ships it was rarely performed and the captive Africans were forced to lie in their own urine and feces. When first taken below deck, the boy Equiano remembered, "I received such a salutation in my nostrils as I had never experienced in my life," and "became so sick and low that I was not able to eat." Atlantic sailors said you could "smell a slaver five miles down wind." Many captives sickened and died in these conditions. Many others contracted dysentery, known as the "flux." Frequent shipboard epidemics of smallpox, measles, and yellow fever added to the misery. Historians estimate that during the Middle Passage of the eighteenth century at least one in every six Africans perished.

Slaves below deck on a Spanish slaver, a sketch made when the vessel was captured by a British warship in the early nineteenth century. Slaves were "stowed so close, that they were not allowed above a foot and a half for each in breadth," wrote one observer. The close quarters and unsanitary conditions created a stench so bad that Atlantic sailors said you could "smell a slaver five miles down wind."

The unwilling voyagers offered plenty of resistance. As long as ships were still within sight of the African coast, hope remained alive and the danger of revolt was great. One historian has found references to fifty-five slave revolts on British and American ships between 1699 and 1845. Once on the open sea, however, captives' resistance took a more desperate form. The sight of the disappearing coast of Africa "left me abandoned to despair," wrote Equiano; "I now saw myself deprived of all chance of returning to my native country, or even the least glimpse of hope of gaining the shore." He witnessed several Africans jump overboard and drown, "and I believe many more would very soon have done the same if they had not been prevented by the ship's crew." Captains took the precaution of spreading netting along the sides of their ships. "Could I have got over the nettings," Equiano declared, "I would have jumped over the side."

Arrival in the New World

As the ship approached its destination, the crew made the human cargo presentable, preparing it for market. All but the most rebellious of Africans were freed from their chains and allowed to wash themselves and move about the deck. One account describes the ship's surgeon plugging captives' rectums with clumps of hemp fiber to prevent potential buyers from seeing the bloody discharge, a symptom of the flux. To impress buyers, slavers sometimes paraded Africans off the ship to the tune of an accordion or the beat of a drum. But the toll taken by the Middle Passage was difficult to disguise. One observer described a disembarking group as "walking skeletons covered over with a piece of tanned leather."

Some cargoes were destined for a single wealthy planter or consigned to a merchant who sold the captives in return for a commission; in other cases the captain himself was responsible. Buyers painstakingly examined the Africans, who once again suffered the indignity of probing eyes and poking fingers. This caused "much dread and trembling among us," wrote Equiano, and "bitter cries." In ports like Charleston sales were generally made either by auction or by a method known as the scramble. In the scramble, standard prices were set in advance for men, women, boys, and girls. Then the Africans were driven into a corral, and at a signal the buyers rushed among them, grabbing their pick of the lot. The noise, clamor, and eagerness of the buyers, Equiano remembered, renewed all the terrible apprehensions of the Africans. "In this manner, without scruple, are relations and friends separated, most of them never to see each other again." Bought by a Virginian, Equiano was taken to an isolated tobacco plantation where he found himself unable to communicate with any of his fellow slaves, who came from other ethnic groups.

Political and Economic Effects on Africa

Africa began the sixteenth century with genuine independence. But as surely as Europe and America grew stronger as a result of the trade and the labor of slaves, so Africa grew weaker by their loss. In the short term, slave-trading kingdoms on the coast increased their power at the expense of interior states. Thus the interior West African state of Songhai gave way to the Gold Coast state of Akwamu. In the Niger delta the slaving states of Nembe, Bonny, and Kalabari arose, and to the south the kingdom of Imbangala drew slaves from central Africa. But these coastal states found that the slave trade was a viper that could easily strike back at them. "Merchants daily seize our own subjects, sons of the land and sons of our noblemen, they grab them and cause them to be sold," King Dom Affonso of the Kongo wrote to the Portuguese monarch in the sixteenth century; "and so great, Sir, is their corruption and licentiousness that our country is being utterly depopulated."

With the loss of millions of men and women over the centuries, the West African economy stagnated. Labor was drawn away from farming and other productive activities, and imported consumer goods such as textiles and metalwares stifled local manufacturing. African traders were expert at driving a hard bargain, and over several centuries they gained an increasing price for slaves—the result of rising demand and increased competition among European slavers. But even when they appeared to get the best of the transaction, the ultimate advantage lay with the Europeans, who in exchange for mere consumer goods got human capital—wealth-producing workers.

For every man or woman taken captive, at least another died in the chronic slave raiding. Many of the new West African states became little more than machines for supplying captives to European traders, and a "gun-slave cycle" pushed neighboring kingdoms into a destructive arms race. The resulting political and cultural demoralization prepared the way for the European conquest of Africa in the nineteenth century. The leaders of West Africa during the centuries of slave trading, writes the Nigerian poet Chinweizu, "had been too busy organizing our continent for the exploitative advantage of Europe, had been too busy with slaving raids upon one another, too busy decorating themselves with trinkets imported from Europe, too busy impoverishing and disorganizing the land, to take thought and long-range action to protect our sovereignty."

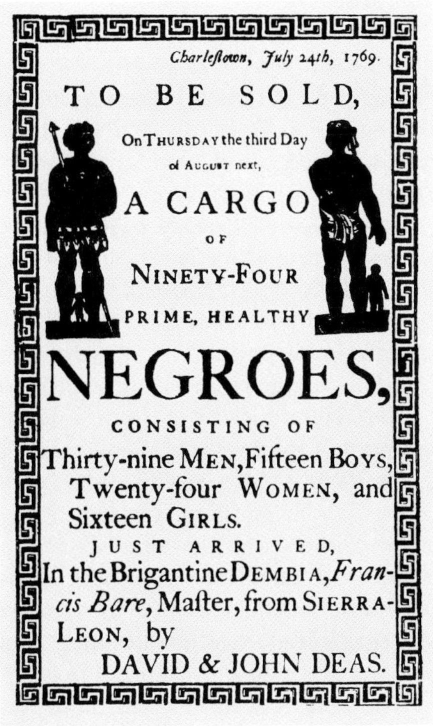

The announcement of the arrival of a consignment of slaves in Charleston, South Carolina, in 1769, where the most common method of sale was by auction. Men and women alike were subjected to intimate inspection before the bidding began. Buyers were quite interested in the ethnic origins of slaves but gave little concern to keeping family members together.

THE DEVELOPMENT OF NORTH AMERICAN SLAVE SOCIETIES

New World slavery was nearly two centuries old before it became an important system of labor in North America. There were slaves in each of the British colonies during the seventeenth century, but in 1700 they constituted only 11 percent of the colonial population. During the eighteenth century slavery greatly expanded, and by 1770 Africans and African Americans in British North America numbered 460,000, or more than 20 percent of the colonial population.

Slavery Comes to North America

The first Africans in Virginia arrived in 1619 when a Dutch slave trader exchanged "20 and odd Negroes" for badly needed provisions. But because slaves generally cost twice as much as indentured servants yet had the same appallingly short life expectancy—because of the frequent epidemics of diseases such as typhoid fever—they offered planters little economic benefit. Consequently, only a relatively small number were brought to Virginia over the next several decades. In fact, there are indications that those Africans who worked in the tobacco fields were not slaves at all, but servants.

An interesting case illustrates the ambiguous status of black Virginians. In 1654 the African John Castor told a local court that "he came unto Virginia for seven or eight years of indenture, yet Anthony Johnson his Master had kept him his servant seven years longer than he should or ought." Johnson claimed that "he had the Negro for his life." The court decided in the master's favor. But strange to say, Johnson himself was an African. He had arrived in 1621 as an indentured servant but achieved his freedom and succeeded in becoming a landowner. Property records reveal that other Africans acquired farms and servants or slaves of their own. Moreover, sexual relations among Africans, Indians, and Europeans produced a sizable group of free people of mixed ancestry known as mulattoes. It was only later that dark skin came to mean slavery, segregation, and lack of rights. Although there surely were slaves among the population in the early years, the first recorded instances of slavery date from around 1640.

In the last quarter of the seventeenth century, however, a number of developments encouraged the expansion of true slavery. As European immigrants discovered opportunities to establish themselves as free farmers in colonies such as Pennsylvania, it became increasingly difficult for southern masters to recruit them as indentured servants. Moreover, after Bacon's Rebellion and the other social conflicts of the 1670s, many colonial leaders began to worry about potential rebellions among former indentured servants in the back country. Because people were living longer, possibly the result of being better fed and more resistant to disease, more servants were surviving their indentures. But these improvements in living conditions also affected Africans, increasing their rates of survival, and planters began to see more advantage in the purchase of slaves. During these same years, the supply of slaves in North America increased when the Royal African Company inaugurated direct shipments from West Africa to the mainland.

Thus the workforce of indentured servants was gradually replaced by a workforce of slaves. By 1700 the number of African slaves had probably surpassed the number of indentured servants. There were some 19,000 Africans in Maryland and Virginia, about 22 percent of the population. In South Carolina, where indentured servants had never been an important part of the labor force, Africans constituted over 40 percent of the settler population by the end of the seventeenth century.

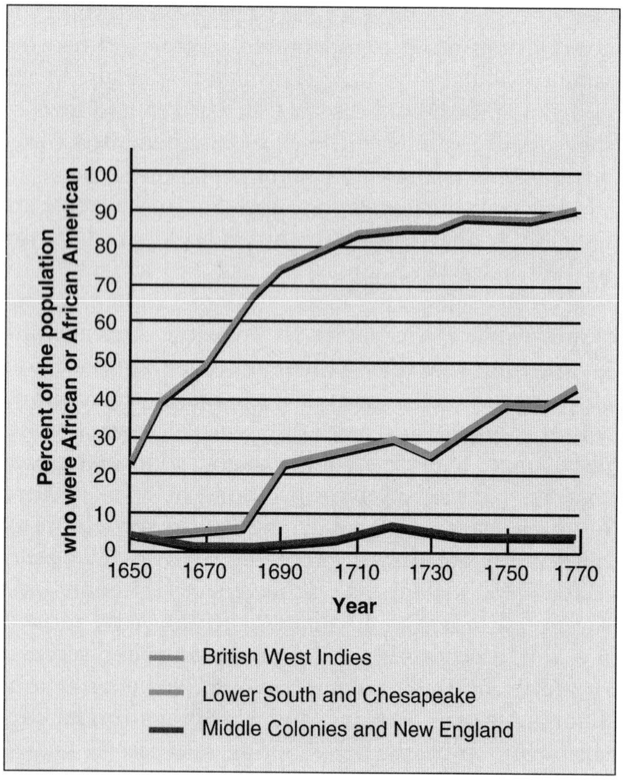

Africans as a Percentage of Total Population of the British Colonies, 1650–1770 *Although the proportion of Africans and African Americans was never as high in the South as in the Caribbean, the ethnic structure of the South diverged radically from that of the North during the eighteenth century.*

Source: Robert W. Fogel and Stanley L. Engerman, *Time on the Cross* (Boston: Little, Brown, 1974), 21.

As the proportions of slaves in the colonial population rose, colonists wrote slavery into law, a process best observed in the case of Virginia. In 1662 colonial officials declared that children inherited the status of their slave mothers; five years later they added that baptism could no longer alter conditions of servitude. Two important avenues to freedom were thus closed. The colony then placed life-threatening violence in the hands of masters, declaring in 1669 that the death of a slave during punishment "shall not be accounted felony." Such regulations accumulated piecemeal until, in 1705, they were gathered together in the comprehensive Virginia Slave Code that became a model for other colonies.

Thus the institution of slavery was strengthened just as the Atlantic slave trade reached flood tide in the eighteenth century. During that century's first decade, more Africans were imported into North America than the total number for the preceding ninety-three years of colonial history. The English colonies were primed for an unprecedented growth of plantation slavery.

The Tobacco Colonies

During the eighteenth century the European demand for tobacco increased more than tenfold. This demand was largely supplied by increased production in the Chesapeake. Tobacco plantations spread through all sections of the sea-level coastal region known as the Tidewater, extending from the colony of Delaware south through Maryland and Virginia into the Albemarle Sound region of North Carolina. Planters eventually extended their operations above the "fall line," where waterfalls or rapids mark the end of the Tidewater and the beginning of the foothill region known as the Piedmont. Tobacco was far and away the single most important commodity produced in North America, accounting for more than a quarter of the value of all colonial exports.

The expansion of tobacco production could not have taken place without an enormous growth in the size of the slave labor force. Unlike sugar, tobacco did not require large plantations and could be produced successfully on relatively small farms. But it was a crop that demanded a great deal of hand labor and close attention, and from the beginnings of Chesapeake colonization its cultivation had been the responsibility of indentured servants and slaves. As tobacco farming grew, slaveholding became widespread. By midcentury slaves were included in a majority of upcountry households and as many as three-quarters of the households in the Tidewater. Tobacco farms varied in size, from small establishments where farmers worked side by side with one or two slaves, to large, self-sufficient plantations with dozens of slaves. By 1770 more than a quarter of a million slaves labored in the colonies of the Upper South, and because of the exploding market for tobacco, their numbers were expanding at something like double the rate of the general population.

Shipments from Africa thus accounted for part of the growth of the slave population. From 1700 to 1770 a total of perhaps 80,000 Africans were imported into the Chesapeake colonies, but natural increase in this region was much more important. Indeed, in the 1730s the slave population of the Chesapeake was the first in the Western Hemisphere to achieve self-sustained growth. In the Caribbean and Brazil, where the profits from sugar plantations were high, many masters worked their slaves literally to death, replacing them with a constant stream of new arrivals from Africa. These landowners figured that they could make greater profits through extreme exploitation of the labor force than by creating the better living and working conditions that would allow Africans to reproduce at normal rates. In contrast, in Virginia lower rates of profit may have caused tobacco planters to pay more attention to the health of their labor force, establishing work routines that were not so deadly. Food supplies were also more plentiful in North America than in the Caribbean, where nearly every morsel had to be imported, and the better-fed Chesapeake populations of Africans were more resistant to disease. Historians continue to debate these important differences. But whatever the causes, self-sustained population growth among Chesapeake slaves had begun by the 1730s, and by the 1770s the majority of them were "country-born."

Benjamin Henry Latrobe, *An Overseer Doing His Duty*. Watercolor on paper. Collection of the Maryland Historical Society, Baltimore.

An Overseer Doing His Duty, *a watercolor sketch made by Benjamin Henry Latrobe during a trip to Virginia in 1798. The majority of masters in the tobacco region owned only one or two slaves and worked with them in the fields. In his portrayal of this overseer, relaxing as he supervises his workers, Latrobe clearly expressed his disgust for slavery.*

The Lower South

For fifty years after the founding of the South Carolina colony in 1670, the area outside the immediate region of Charleston remained a rough and dangerous frontier. English settlers raised cattle, often using slaves with experience in the pastoral economies of West Africa. Others engaged in the deerskin trade, bartering English goods with the numerous Indian people of the backcountry. But in terms of sheer profit, the most valuable part of the early Carolina economy was the Indian slave trade. Practicing a strategy of divide and conquer, in which they encouraged Indian tribes to fight one another, Carolinians enslaved tens of thousands of Indians before the 1730s. Because Indian slaves were dangerous as long as they were near their homelands, most were shipped off to other colonies.

By 1715, as the opening of this chapter illustrates, rice production had become the most dynamic sector of the South Carolina economy, and, like cattle grazing, it depended on the expertise of West Africans. Another important crop was added in the 1740s, when Elizabeth Lucas Pinckney, a young South Carolina woman, successfully adapted West Indian indigo to the low-country climate. It is likely that here as well, the assistance of West Indian slaves skilled in indigo culture was crucial. The indigo plant, native to India, produced

TOBACCO AND RICE EXPORTS TO ENGLAND (IN THOUSANDS OF POUNDS)

	Tobacco	Rice
1700	37,840	304
1725	21,046	5,367
1750	51,339	16,667
1775	55,968	57,692

Thomas Coram, *Residence and Slave Quarters of Mulberry Plantation*. Oil on paper, 10 × 17.6 cm. Gibbes Museum of Art, Carolina Art Association.

Residence and Slave Quarters of Mulberry Plantation, *by Thomas Coram, ca. 1770. The slave quarters are on the left in this painting of a rice plantation near Charleston, South Carolina. The steep roofs of the slave cabins, an African architectural feature introduced in America by slave builders, kept living quarters cool by allowing the heat to rise and dissipate in the rafters.*

a deep blue dye important in textile manufacture. Rice grew in the lowlands, but indigo could be cultivated on high ground. And because they had different seasonal growing patterns, the two crops harmonized perfectly. Rice and indigo production rose steadily over the next thirty years. By the 1770s they were among the most valuable commodities exported from the mainland colonies of North America.

Like tobacco, the expansion of rice and indigo production depended on the growth of African slavery. Before the importation of slaves to the United States ended in 1808, at least 100,000 Africans had arrived at Charleston. One of every five ancestors of today's African Americans passed through that port on his or her way to the rice and indigo fields.

By the 1740s many of the arriving Africans were being taken to Georgia, a colony created by an act of the English Parliament in 1732. Its leader, James Edward Oglethorpe, hoped to establish a buffer against Spanish invasion from Florida and to create a haven for poor British farmers who could then sell their products in the markets of South Carolina. Under Oglethorpe's influence, Parliament agreed to prohibit slavery in Georgia, but soon the colony's coastal regions were being settled by South Carolina planters with their slaves. In 1752 Oglethorpe and Georgia's trustees abandoned their experiment, and the colony was opened to slavery under royal authority. The Georgia coast had already become an extension of the Carolina low-country slave system.

By 1770 there were nearly 90,000 African Americans in the Lower South, about 80 percent of the population of coastal South Carolina and Georgia. The slave economy of the Lower South was dominated by large plantations, which had between fifty and seventy-five slaves each. The slaves' work was hard, but the task system, described at the beginning of this chapter, gave them a measure of control over their own lives. The African American communities of the Lower South, like those of the Chesapeake, achieved self-sustained growth by the middle of the eighteenth century.

Slavery in the Spanish Colonies

Slavery was basic to the Spanish colonial labor system, yet doubts about the enslavement of Africans were raised by both the Church and the crown. The papacy many times denounced slavery as a violation of Christian principles, and many priests condemned the institution. The

Catholic Church in Spanish America, however, owned slaves and profited from their labor. The slave system remained intact, and by later in the eighteenth century, when sugar production expanded in Cuba, it had become as brutal there as elsewhere in the Americas.

Still, the character of slavery varied with local conditions. One of the most benign forms operated in Florida, where Spanish colonization was undertaken primarily to create a buffer against the English. In 1699 the Spanish declared Florida a refuge for escaped slaves from the English colonies, offering free land to any fugitives who would help defend the colony and convert to Catholicism. Over the next half-century, refugee Indians and fugitive Africans established many communities in the countryside surrounding St. Augustine. North of the city, Fort Mose was manned by Negro troops commanded by their own officers. Slaves could be found in many Florida settlements, but the conditions of their servitude resembled the household slavery common in Mediterranean and African communities more than the plantation slavery of the British colonies.

In New Mexico, the Spanish depended on the forced labor of Indians. In the sixteenth century the colonial governor sent Indian workers to the mines of Mexico. And the requirement that Pueblo people labor for Spaniards was one of the causes of the Pueblo Revolt (see Chapter 3). During the eighteenth century, the Spanish were much more cautious in their treatment of the Pueblos, who were officially considered Catholics. But they captured and enslaved "infidel Indians" such as the Apaches or nomads from the Great Plains, using them as house servants and field workers.

French Louisiana

Slavery was also important in Louisiana, the colony founded by the French in the lower Mississippi Valley in the early eighteenth century. After Robert Sieur de La Salle's voyage down the Mississippi River in 1681–82, the French planned colonies to anchor their New World empire. In the early eighteenth century French Canadians established bases at Biloxi and Mobile on the Gulf of Mexico, but it was not until 1718 that they laid out the city of New Orleans on the Mississippi delta. Upriver, colonists established an alliance with the powerful Choctaw nation, and with their assistance defeated an opposing confederacy of Chickasaw and Natchez Indians during the 1720s and 1730s.

By 1750 several thousand French colonists, many from New France and the Caribbean, had established farms and plantations on the Gulf coast and in a narrow strip along the Mississippi River. Soon they were exporting rice, indigo, and tobacco, in addition to furs and skins for which they had traded with backcountry Indians. Like the Spanish in St. Augustine, however, the French were more interested in defending their access to the Mississippi against rival colonial threats than in commerce and export. Consequently, African slaves amounted to no more than a third of the colonial population of 10,000. It was not until the end of the eighteenth century that the colony of Louisiana became an important North American slave society.

Slavery in the North

North of the Chesapeake, slavery was much less important. Slaves worked on some farms, but almost never in groups, and they were principally concentrated in port cities. Slaves were first shipped to Philadelphia in the 1680s, and a visitor to the city in 1750 noted that slaves were bought "by almost everyone who could afford [them]." Together with a small group of free blacks, slaves then made up about 9 percent of the city's population.

It was the Quakers, many of whom had themselves kept slaves, who voiced the first antislavery sentiment in the colonies. In *Considerations on the Keeping of Negroes* (1754), John Woolman pointed to the Bible's declaration that all peoples were of one blood. He urged his readers to imagine themselves in the place of the African people:

> Suppose that our ancestors and we had been exposed to constant servitude in the more servile and inferior employments of life; that we had been destitute of the help of reading and good company; that amongst ourselves we had had few wise and pious instructors; that the religious amongst our superiors seldom took notice of us; that while others in ease have plentifully heaped up the fruit of our labour, we had received barely enough to relieve nature, and being wholly at the command of others had generally been treated as a contemptible, ignorant part of mankind. Should we, in that case, be less abject than they now are?

It was not until the Revolution, however, that antislavery sentiment became more widespread.

In New York slavery was somewhat more important. By 1770, New York and New Jersey were home to some 27,000 African Americans, about 10 percent of these colonies' respective populations. Black people were concentrated even more highly in New York City. A British naval officer stationed in the port during the 1750s observed that "the laborious people in general are Guinea negroes." In 1770, 3,000 slaves and 100 free blacks, about 17 percent of the population, lived in the city. The most important center of slavery in the North, however, was Newport, Rhode Island. In 1760 African Americans there made up about 20 percent of the population, a concentration resulting from that port's dominance of the midcentury slave trade. Moreover, the area was unique for the large slave gangs used in cattle and dairy operations in the Narragansett country, some of which were as large as Virginia plantations.

BECOMING AFRICAN AMERICAN

In 1774 a group of enslaved Massachusetts Africans spoke for tens of thousands of others when they petitioned the British authorities for their freedom. "We were unjustly dragged by the cruel hand of power from our dearest friends," they wrote, "and some of us stolen from the bosoms of our tender parents and from a populous, pleasant and plentiful country, and brought hither to be made slaves for life in a Christian land." Men and women from dozens of ethnic groups, representing many different languages, religions, and customs, had been transported across the Atlantic without any of their cultural possessions. In America they were subjected to the control of masters intent on maximizing their work and minimizing their liberty. Yet African Americans carved out lives of their own with a degree of independence. Their African heritage was not erased; it provided them with a fundamental outlook, the basis for a common identity.

The majority of Africans transported to North America arrived during the eighteenth century. They were met by a rapidly growing population of "country-born" slaves, or "creoles" (from the French créole and Spanish criollo, meaning "born" or "raised"), a term first used by slaves in Brazil to distinguish their children, born in the New World, from newly arrived Africans. The perspective of creoles was shaped by their having grown up under slavery, and that perspective helped them to determine which elements of African culture they would incorporate into the emerging culture of the African American community. That community was formed out of the relationship between creoles and Africans, and between slaves and their European masters.

The Daily Life of Slaves

Because slaves made up the overwhelming majority of the labor force that made the plantation colonies so profitable, it is fair to say that Africans built the South. As an agricultural people, Africans—both women and men—were accustomed to the routines of rural labor, and this experience was put to use on the plantations. Most Africans were field hands, and even domestic servants labored in the fields when necessary. As crop production expanded during the eighteenth century, and plantations became larger and more extensive, labor became specialized. On the eighteenth-century Virginia plantation of George Mason, for example, slaves worked as carpenters, coopers, sawyers, blacksmiths, tanners, curriers, shoemakers, spinners, weavers, knitters, and even distillers.

Masters provided their workers with rude clothing, sufficient in the summer but nearly always inadequate in the winter. Increasingly the plantations were supplied by cheap goods from the new industrial looms of England. Stiff shoes were a necessity in the cold months, but they so cramped the feet that everyone looked forward to shedding them in the spring and going barefoot all summer and fall. Hand-me-down clothes from the master's family offered slaves an opportunity to brighten their costumes, and many dressed in a variety of styles and colors. Similarly, they relieved the monotony of their rations of corn and pork with vegetables from their small gardens, game and fish from field and stream, and wild plant foods from the forests. On the whole, their diet must have been sufficient, for they not only survived but rapidly reproduced during the eighteenth century.

The growing African population, and larger plantations on which larger numbers lived and worked together, created the concentration necessary for the emergence of African American communities and African American culture. The typical slave served on a plantation with a workforce of ten or more. On small farms, Africans might work side by side with their owners and, depending on the character of the master, might enjoy living conditions not too different from those of other family members. But plantations offered possibilities for a more autonomous cultural life.

Families and Communities

The family was the most important institution for the development of community and culture. Slave codes did not provide for legal slave marriages, for that would have contradicted the master's freedom to dispose of his property as he saw fit. "The endearing ties of husband and wife are strangers to us," declared the Massachusetts slaves who petitioned for their freedom in 1774, "for we are no longer man and wife than our masters or mistresses think proper." How, they asked, "can a slave perform the duties of a husband to a wife or parent to his child? How can a husband leave master to work and cleave to his wife? How can the [wives] submit themselves to their husbands in all things? How can the [children] obey their parents in all things?" The creation and maintenance of slave family life were essential not only for reproduction but for the physical and psychological well-being of all family members and the development of African American culture.

Despite the barriers, many thousands of Africans in both the Chesapeake and the Lower South had created stable families by the 1730s. On large plantations throughout the southern colonies, travelers found Africans living in nuclear-family households in the slave quarters. But on smaller plantations, men frequently married women from neighboring farms, and with the permission of both owners visited their families in the evenings or on Sundays.

Generally, slave couples married when the woman became pregnant. "Their marriages are generally performed amongst themselves," one visitor to North Carolina wrote of the Africans he observed in the 1730s. "The man makes the woman a present, such as a brass ring or some other toy, which she accepts of, [and] becomes his wife." Common throughout the South was the postnuptial ritual in which the couple jumped over a broomstick together, declaring their relationship to the rest of the community. This custom may have originated in Africa, although versions of it were practiced in medieval Europe as well.

Recent studies of naming practices among eighteenth-century African Americans illustrate their commitment to establishing a system of kinship. Frequently sons were named for their fathers, perhaps a way of strengthening the paternal bonds of men forced to live away from their families. Children of both sexes were named for grandparents and other kin. African names were common; names such as Cudjo (Monday), Quow (Thursday), or Coffee (Friday) continued the African tradition of "weekday" names. Later in the century Anglo names became more general. Margery and Moody, slaves of Francis Jerdone of Louisa County, Virginia, named their six children Sam, Rose, Sukey, Mingo, Maria, and Comba, mixing both African and English traditions. Many Africans carried names known only within their community, and these were often African. In the sea island region of the Lower South, such names were common until the twentieth century.

Emotional ties to particular places, connections between the generations, and relations of kinship and friendship linking neighboring plantations and farms were the foundation stones of African American community life. Kinship was especially important. African American parents encouraged their children to use family terms in addressing unrelated people: "auntie" or "uncle" became a respectful way of addressing older men and women, "brother" and "sister" affectionate terms for age mates. Moreover, during the Middle Passage it was common for adults to address all children as "son" or "daughter." This tradition of "fictive kinship" may have been one of the first devices enslaved Africans used to humanize the world of slavery.

African American Culture

The eighteenth century was the formative period in the development of the African American community, for it was then that the high birth rate and the growing numbers of "country-born" provided the necessary stability for the evolution of culture. During this period, men and women from dozens of African ethnic groups molded themselves into a new people. Distinctive patterns in music and dance, religion, and oral tradition illustrate the resilience of the human spirit under bondage as well as the successful struggle of African Americans to create a spiritually sustaining culture of their own.

Eighteenth-century masters were reluctant to allow their slaves to become Christians, fearing that baptism would open the way to claims of freedom or give Africans dangerous notions of universal brotherhood and equality with masters. One frustrated missionary was told by a planter that a slave was "ten times worse when a Christian than in his state of paganism." Because of this attitude, a Protestant minister wrote from South Carolina in the 1770s, most slaves "are to this day as great strangers to Christianity, and as much under the influence of pagan darkness, idolatry and superstition, as they were at their first arrival from Africa." Thus, the majority of black Southerners before the American Revolution practiced some form of African religion. Many African Americans were not converted to Christianity until the Great Awakening, which swept across the South after the 1760s (see Chapter 5).

One of the most crucial areas of religious practice concerned the rituals of death and burial. In their separate graveyards, African Americans often decorated graves with shells and pottery, an old African custom. African Americans generally believed that the spirits of their dead would return to Africa. "Some destroy themselves [that is, commit suicide] through despair and from a persuasion they fondly entertain, that after death they will return to their beloved friends and native country," wrote one South Carolinian.

The burial ceremony, perhaps the most important of the slave rituals, was often held at night because slave owners objected to the continuation of African traditions. Historical knowledge of these secret proceedings comes from the accounts of a few white observers, from the stories and recollections of slaves, and from the reconstructions of twentieth-century anthropologists. The deceased person was laid out, and around the body men and women would move counterclockwise in a slow dance step while singing ancestral songs. The pace gradually increased, finally reaching a frenzied but joyful conclusion. Dance was a form of worship, a kind of prayer, a means of achieving union with the ancestors and the gods. The circle dance was a widespread custom in West Africa, and in America it became known as the ring shout. As slaves from different backgrounds joined together in the circle, they were beginning the process of cultural unification.

Music and dance may have formed the foundation of African American culture, coming even before a common language. Many eighteenth-century observers commented on the musical and rhythmic gifts of

Abby Aldrich Rockefeller Folk Art Center, Williamsburg, Virginia.

This eighteenth-century painting depicts a celebration in the slave quarters on a South Carolina plantation. The dance—known as "jumping the broomstick"—may have originated in Africa, and the stringed instrument was an African mbanza, *which evolved into the "banjo."*

The Africanization of the South

The African American community often looked to recently arrived Africans for religious leadership. Ancestor worship, divination, and magic were strengthened by constant African infusions through the eighteenth century. Many of these beliefs and practices had much in common with European folklore, especially magic and medicinal lore. In 1729 the governor of Virginia agreed to free one of his elderly slaves, "who has performed many wonderful cures of diseases," after the man revealed the secret formulas of his medical magic. Throughout the South, many whites had as much faith in slave conjurers and herb doctors as the slaves themselves did, one example of the many ways in which white and black Southerners came to share a common culture. Acculturation was by no means a one-way street; English men and women in the South were also being Africanized.

Slaves worked in the kitchens of their masters and thus introduced an African style of cooking into colonial diets already transformed by the addition of Indian crops. African American culinary arts are responsible for such southern specialties as barbecue, fried chicken, black-eyed peas, and various greens including collard and mustard. And the liberal African use of red pepper, sesame seeds, and other sharp flavors established the southern preference for highly spiced foods. In Louisiana, a combination of African, French, and Indian elements produced a most distinctive American regional cuisine, exemplified by gumbos (soups) and jambalayas (stews).

Mutual acculturation is also evident in many aspects of material culture. Southern basket weaving used Indian techniques and African designs. Woodcarving often featured African motifs. African architectural designs featuring high, peaked roofs (to drain off the heat) and broad, shady porches gradually became part of a distinctive southern style. The West African ironworking tradition was evident throughout the South, especially in the ornamentation of the homes of Charleston and New Orleans.

Even more important were less tangible aspects of culture. Slave mothers nursed white children as well as their own. As one English observer wrote, "each child has its [black] Momma, whose gestures and accent it will necessarily copy, for chil-

Africans. Olaudah Equiano remembered his people, the Ibos, as "a nation of dancers, musicians, and poets," and Thomas Jefferson, raised on a Virginia plantation, wrote that blacks "are more generally gifted than the whites, with accurate ears for tune and time." Many Africans were accomplished players of stringed instruments and drums, and their style featured improvisation and rhythmic complexity—elements that would become prominent in African American music. In America, slaves re-created African instruments—the banjo is an example—and mastered the art of the European violin and guitar. Fearing that slaves might communicate by code, authorities frequently outlawed drums. But using bones, spoons, or sticks or simply "patting juba" (slapping their thighs), slaves produced elaborate multirhythmic patterns.

One of the most important developments of the eighteenth century was the invention of African American language. An English traveler during the 1770s complained he could not understand Virginia slaves, who spoke "a mixed dialect between the Guinea and English." But such a language made it possible for "country-born" and "salt-water" Africans to communicate. The two most important dialects were Gullah and Geeche, named after two of the African peoples most prominent in the Carolina and Georgia low country, the Golas and Gizzis of the Windward Coast. These creole languages were a transitional phenomenon, gradually giving way to distinctive forms of so-called black English, although in certain isolated areas like the sea islands of the Carolinas and Georgia they persisted into the twentieth century.

dren, we all know, are imitative beings." In this way, many Africanisms passed into the English language of the South: "goober" (peanut), "yam," "banjo," "okay," "tote." Some linguists have argued that the Southern "drawl," evident among both black and white speakers, derived from the incorporation of African intonations of words and syllables.

African American music and dance also deeply affected white culture. These art forms offer a good example of mutual acculturation. At eighteenth-century plantation dances, the music was usually provided by Africans playing European instruments and their own, such as the banjo. African American fiddlers were common throughout the South by the time of the Revolution, but the banjo also became the characteristic folk instrument of the white South. Toward the end of the evening, the musicians were often told to play some "Negro jigs," and slaves were asked to demonstrate the African manner of dancing. They sometimes parodied the elegant and rigid dances of their masters, while whites in turn attempted to imitate African rhythmic dance styles. In such a back-and-forth fashion the traditions of both groups were gradually transformed.

Violence and Resistance

Slavery was based on the use of force and violence. Fear underlay the daily life of both masters and slaves. Some owners were humane, but even the kindest could be cruel, and slaves had no guarantees of benevolent treatment. Even the most broad-minded plantation owners of the eighteenth century thought nothing about floggings of fifty or seventy-five lashes. "Der prayer was answered," sang the Africans of South Carolina, "wid de song of a whip." Although the typical planter punished slaves with extra work, public humiliation, or solitary confinement, the threat of the lash was omnipresent. There were also sadistic masters who stabbed, burned, maimed, mutilated, raped, or castrated their slaves.

Yet African Americans demonstrated a resisting spirit. In their day-to-day existence they often refused to cooperate: they malingered, they mistreated tools and animals, they "accidentally" destroyed the master's property. Flight was also an option, and judging from the advertisements placed by masters in colonial newspapers, even the most trusted Africans ran away. "That this slave should run away and attempt getting his liberty, is very alarming," read the notice of one Maryland master in 1755. "He has always been too kindly used" and was "one in whom his master has put great confidence, and depended on him to overlook the rest of the slaves, and he had no kind of provocation to go off." A South Carolinian noted that his absent slave "may possibly have a ticket that I gave him, mentioning he was in quest of a runaway, [and] as I did not mention when he was to return, he may endeavour to pass by that." An analysis of hundreds of eighteenth-century advertisements for runaways reveals that 80 percent of them were men, most in their twenties, suggesting that flight was an option primarily for young, unattached men.

Runaways were sometimes called *maroons* from the Spanish *cimarrón*, meaning "wild and untamed." The African communities in Spanish Florida were often referred to as maroon colonies. Indeed, as a whole these mixed African and Creek Indian Florida peoples called themselves Seminoles, a name deriving from their pronunciation of *cimarrón*. Maroons also settled in the backcountry of the Lower South. In 1771, Georgia's governor warned that north of Savannah "a great number of fugitive Negroes had committed many robberies and insults," and he sent a detachment of

Thomas Moran, *The Slave Hunt*, 1862, oil on canvas, 86.4 x 111.8 cm. The Philbrook Museum of Art. Tulsa, Oklahoma

Fugitive slaves flee through the swamps in Thomas Moran's Slave Hunt *(1862). Many slaves ran away from their masters, and colonial newspapers included notices urging readers to be on the lookout for them. Some fled in groups or collected together in isolated communities called "maroon colonies," located in inaccessible swamps and woods.*

militia to destroy their camps. The "black Indian" violence continued, however, and reached catastrophic proportions during the Revolution. Although maroons were less common in the Upper South, a number of fugitive communities existed in the Great Dismal Swamp between Virginia and North Carolina. In the 1730s a group of escaped Africans built a community of grass houses and set up a tribal government there, but they were soon dispersed by the authorities.

The most direct form of resistance was revolt. In the Lower South, where slaves were a majority of the population, there were isolated but violent slave uprisings in 1704, 1720, and 1730. Then in 1738 a series of violent revolts throughout South Carolina and Georgia proved but a prelude to the largest slave rebellion of the colonial period. In September 1739, a group of twenty recently arrived Angolans sacked the armory in Stono, South Carolina. Arming themselves, they began marching toward Florida and freedom. Beating drums to attract other slaves to their cause, they grew to nearly a hundred. Along the way they plundered several planters' homes and killed some thirty colonists. Pausing in a field to celebrate their victory with dance and song, they were overtaken by the militia and destroyed in a pitched battle. That same year there was an uprising in Georgia, probably inspired by the Stono Rebellion, and the next year another took place in South Carolina. Attributing these revolts to the influence of newly arrived Africans, colonial officials shut off the slave trade through Charleston for the next ten years.

The second notable slave uprising of the colonial era occurred in New York City in 1712. Taking an oath of secrecy, twenty-three Africans vowed revenge for what they called the "hard usage" of their masters. They armed themselves with guns, swords, daggers, and hatchets, killed nine colonists, and burned several buildings before being surrounded by the militia. Six of the conspirators committed suicide rather than surrender. Those captured were hanged, burned at the stake, or broken on the wheel. In 1741 New York authorities uncovered what they thought was another conspiracy. Thirteen black leaders were burned alive, eighteen hanged, and eighty sold and shipped off to the West Indies. A family of colonists and a Catholic priest, accused of providing weapons, were also executed.

Wherever masters held slaves, fears of uprisings persisted. But compared with such slave colonies as Jamaica, Guiana, or Brazil, there were few slave revolts in North America. The conditions favoring revolt—large African majorities, brutal exploitation with correspondingly low survival rates, little acculturation, and geographic isolation—prevailed only in some areas of the Lower South. The very success of African Americans in British North America at establishing families, communities, and a stake in a culture of their own may have made them less likely to risk rebellion.

SLAVERY AND THE STRUCTURE OF EMPIRE

Slavery contributed enormously to the economic growth and development of Europe during the colonial era, and it was an especially important factor in Great Britain's industrial revolution in the eighteenth century. Slavery was the most dynamic force in the Atlantic economy during that century, creating the conditions for industrialization. But because colonists in the South single-mindedly committed their slave resources to the expansion and extension of the plantation system, they derived very little benefit from the economic diversification that characterized industrialization.

Slavery the Mainspring

The slave colonies accounted for 95 percent of exports from the Americas to Great Britain from 1714 to 1773. Most productive were the sugar plantations of the British West Indies (64 percent of total exports), followed by the rice, indigo, and tobacco fields of the mainland South (31 percent). Although approximately half of all Great Britain's American colonists lived in New England and the mid-Atlantic, the colonies in those regions

British Colonial Trade in the Americas, 1714–1773 (in thousands of British pounds sterling)

	Exports to Britain		Imports from Britain	
	£	%	£	%
British West Indies	96,808	64.0	41,653	38.8
Lower South and Chesapeake	47,192	31.2	27,561	25.7
Middle Colonies and New England	7,160	4.7	37,939	35.4
Total	151,160	99.9	107,153	99.9

Source: Eric Williams, *Capitalism and Slavery* (Chapel Hill: University of North Carolina Press, 1944), 225–26.

contributed less than 5 percent of total exports during this period. Moreover, there was the prime economic importance of the slave trade itself, which one economist of the day described as the "foundation" of the British economy, "the mainspring of the machine which sets every wheel in motion." According to another English writer, slavery was "the strength and sinews of this western world." This point is so important it bears repeating: it was the labor of African slaves that made the British empire in the Americas a success.

The profits of individual investors in the slave system varied widely, of course. Slave traders expected a return of 30 percent or more, but many ventures ended in financial disaster. Profits in sugar production during the boom of the seventeenth century easily exceeded 20 percent, but returns fell during the succeeding century. As late as 1776, however, the British economist Adam Smith wrote that "the profits of a sugar plantation in any of our West Indian colonies are generally much greater than those of any other cultivation that is known either in Europe or America." Economic historians estimate that annual profits during the eighteenth century averaged 15 percent of invested capital in the slave trade, 10 percent in plantation agriculture. Some of the first of England's great modern fortunes were made out of slavery's miseries.

Samuel Scott "Old Custom House Quay" Collection. By courtesy of the Board of Trustees of the Victoria and Albert Museum.

Eighteenth-century ships being unloaded of their colonial cargoes on London's Old Custom House Quay. Most of the goods imported into England from the American colonies were produced by slave labor.

The most obvious and direct economic effect of slavery was on the growth of transport: in the eighteenth century better than 10 percent of all English shipping was devoted to the African and American trades. Ships had to be outfitted and provisioned, trade goods had to be manufactured, and the commodities produced on slave plantations had to be processed. The multiplier effects of these activities are best seen in the growth of English ports such as Liverpool and Bristol. There the African and American trades provided employment for an army of ships' crews, dockmen, construction workers, traders, shopkeepers, lawyers, clerks, factory workers, and officials of all ranks down to the humblest employees of the customhouse. It was said of Bristol that "there is not a brick in the city but what is cemented with the blood of a slave."

The profits of the slave trade and slave production resulted in huge accumulations of capital, much of it invested in enterprises in these same cities. One historian estimates that in Great Britain alone during the eighteenth century the slave system generated capital valued at more than 300 million pounds. (Although converting monetary values over several centuries is always imprecise, the eighteenth-century British pound sterling was the equivalent in purchasing power of about $85 in 1990s currency; thus, £300 million would be worth about $25 billion.) This capital funded the first modern banks and insurance companies and eventually found its way into a wide range of economic activities. In the countryside surrounding Liverpool, capital acquired through slavery was invested in the cotton textile industry. Later, the demand for raw cotton to supply cotton textile factories led to the further expansion of American plantation slavery. The connections between slavery and the growth of industry were clear and dramatic.

The Politics of Mercantilism

When imperial officials argued that colonies existed solely for the benefit of the mother country, they had in mind principally the great wealth produced by slavery. To ensure that this wealth benefited their states, European imperial powers created a system of regulations that later became known as mercantilism. The essence of mercantilist policy was the political control of the economy by the state. Just as the new monarchs of western Europe had extended their control over the political affairs of their nations, so they sought to use politics to control the national and colonial economy. In the seventeenth century the French finance minister Jean-Baptiste Colbert formulated the most systematic political approach to mercantilism, and the French empire of Louis XIV became the strongest in the world. But in the eighteenth century mercantilist politics were most successfully applied in Great Britain, where the monarchy and Parliament established a uniform national monetary system, regulated workers and the poor by placing controls on wages and requiring the able-bodied to labor in workhouses, provided subsidies to encourage agriculture and manufacturing, and erected tariff barriers to protect themselves from foreign competition. England also sought to organize and control colonial trade to the maximum advantage of its own shippers, merchants, manufacturers, and bureaucrats. Mercantilists scoffed at the idea that the economy should be left to the free operation of the marketplace.

The mercantilists viewed the world economy as a "zero-sum" game in which total economic gains were equal to total losses. As an English mercantilist put it, "There is but a certain proportion of trade in the world." Profits were thought to result from successful speculation, crafty dealing, or simple plunder—all forms of stealing wealth. The institution of slavery proved the theory, for it was nothing more than a highly developed system by which masters stole the labor of slaves. The essence of the competition between nation-states, the mercantilists argued, was the struggle to acquire and hoard the wealth of the world. The nation that accumulated the largest treasure of gold and silver specie would become the most powerful.

Wars for Empire

The mercantilist era was thus a period of intense and violent competition among European nation-states. Wars usually arose out of Old World issues, spilling over into the New, but they also originated in conflicts over the colonies themselves. In the Anglo-Dutch Wars of the 1650s and 1660s, England replaced Holland as the dominant Atlantic power. Then, beginning with King William's War (1689–97), England and France (generally allied with Spain) opened a long struggle for colonial supremacy in North America that was not concluded until 1763. (For discussion of these conflicts, see Chapter 3.) The fighting took place principally at the peripheries of the empire, on the frontiers separating Spanish Florida from British Georgia and New France from New England.

In the southern region, these wars had everything to do with slavery. The first fighting of the eighteenth century took place during Queen Anne's War (known in Europe as the War of the Spanish Succession), a conflict that pitted Great Britain and its allies against France and Spain. In 1702 troops from South Carolina invaded Florida, plundering and burning St. Augustine in an attempt to destroy the refuge for fugitive slaves there. A combined French and Spanish fleet took revenge in 1706 by bombarding Charleston. But the British finally prevailed over the Spanish, and in 1713, as part of the Peace of Utrecht, Great Britain won the exclusive right to supply slaves to the Spanish colonies in the Americas, a very lucrative business.

The entrance of British slavers into Spanish ports provided an opportunity for illicit trade, and sporadic fighting between the two empires broke out a number of times over the next two decades. Robert Walpole, British prime minister from 1721 to 1748, wished to avoid the outbreak of full-scale war, but a faction in the House of Commons that wanted to bring even more slave colonies into the British orbit looked forward to smashing the Spanish in the Caribbean. In 1739, at the urging of these members of Commons, a one-eared sea captain by the name of Jenkins testified before the House to the indignities suffered by British merchant sailors at the hands of the Spanish. In a dramatic flourish he produced a dried and withered ear, which he claimed they had cut from his head. A public outrage followed, finally forcing Walpole to agree to a war of Caribbean conquest that the British called the War of Jenkins's Ear.

English troops allied with Creek Indians invaded Florida once again, laying waste the last of the old mission stations but failing to capture St. Augustine. In response, Spanish troops, including several companies of African Americans, invaded Georgia. Although the Spanish were defeated

OVERVIEW

The Colonial Wars

King William's War	1689–97	France and England battle on the northern frontiers of New England and New York.
Queen Anne's War	1702–13	England fights France and Spain in the Caribbean and on the northern frontier of New France. Part of the European conflict known as the War of the Spanish Succession.
War of Jenkins's Ear	1739–43	Great Britain versus Spain in the Caribbean and Georgia. Part of the European War of the Austrian Succession.
King George's War	1744–48	Great Britain and France fight in Acadia and Nova Scotia; the second American round of the War of the Austrian Succession.
French and Indian War	1754–63	Last of the great colonial wars pitting Great Britain against France and Spain. Known in Europe as the Seven Years War.

seventy-five miles south of Savannah, the campaign produced an agreement on the boundary between British Georgia and Spanish Florida that today separates those states. Elsewhere the British were not so lucky: in the Caribbean the imperial fleet suffered disaster at the hands of the Spanish navy.

In the northern region the principal focus of the imperial struggle was control of the Indian trade. In 1704, during Queen Anne's War, the French and their Algonquian Indian allies raided New England frontier towns such as Deerfield, Massachusetts, dragging men, women, and children into captivity in Canada. In turn, the English mounted a series of expeditions against the strategic French fortress of Port Royal, which they captured in 1710. At the war's conclusion in 1713, France was forced to cede Acadia, Newfoundland, and Hudson's Bay to Great Britain in exchange for guarantees of security for the French-speaking residents of those provinces. Thirty years of peace followed, but from 1744 to 1748 England again battled France in King George's War. The French attacked the British in Nova Scotia, Indian and Canadian raids again devastated the border towns of New England and New York, and hundreds of British subjects were killed or captured.

The French, allied with the Spanish and Prussians, were equally successful in Europe. What finally turned the tide of this war was the capture in 1745 of the French fortress of Louisburg on Cape Breton Island by an expedition of Massachusetts troops in conjunction with the royal navy. Deprived of the most strategic of their American ports, and fearful of losing the wealth of their sugar islands, the French agreed to a negotiated settlement in 1748. But despite the capture of Louisburg, the war had been fought elsewhere to a stalemate, so the treaty restored the prewar status quo, returning Louisburg to France. This disgusted merchants of New England, who wanted to expand their commercial influence in the maritime colonies, and left the North American conflict between France and Britain still simmering. Significantly, however, this was the first time that the concluding battle of a European war had been fought on North American soil, and it was a harbinger of things to come: the next war was destined to start as a conflict between French and British colonists before engulfing Europe (see Chapter 6).

British Colonial Regulation

Mercantilists used means other than war to win the wealth of the world. In the sixteenth century the Spanish monarchy became the first to create a state trading monopoly—the *Casa de Contratación*—to manage the commerce of its empire. This monopoly limited colonial trade to prescribed ports such as Seville or Veracruz, protected traders from attack and plunder, and established a system of great convoys in which merchant ships crossed the oceans under the protection of well-armed galleons. In the seventeenth century other European states followed the Spanish example. The British monarchy, for example, chartered the East India Company, the Hudson's Bay Company, and the Royal African Company as trading monopolies in their respective regions.

English manufacturers complained that the merchant-dominated trading monopolies paid too little attention to the export of their products to colonial markets. Reacting to these charges, between 1651 and 1696 Parliament passed a series of Navigation Acts (see also Chapter 3), which created the legal and institutional structure of Britain's eighteenth-century colonial system. These acts defined the colonies as both suppliers of raw materials and markets for English manufactured goods. Merchants from other nations were expressly forbidden to trade in the colonies, and all trade had to be conducted in ships built either in England or in the British colonies. The regulations specified a list of enumerated goods—colonial products that could be shipped only to England. These included the products of the southern slave colonies (sugar, molasses, rum, tobacco, rice, and indigo), those of the northern Indian trade (furs and skins), as well as the products essential for supplying the shipping industry (masts, tar, pitch, resin, and turpentine). The bulk of these products were not destined for English consumption, however; at great profit English merchants reexported them elsewhere.

England also placed limitations on colonial enterprises that might compete with those at home. A series of enactments—including the Wool Act of 1699, the Hat Act of 1732, and the Iron Act of 1750—forbade the colonial manufacture of those products. Moreover, colonial assemblies were forbidden to impose tariffs on English imports as a way to protect colonial industries. Banking was disallowed, local coinage prohibited, and the export of coin from England forbidden. Badly in need of a circulating medium, Massachusetts illegally minted copper coin, and several colonies issued paper currency, forcing Parliament to legislate against the practice. The colonists depended mostly on "commodity money" (furs, skins, or hogsheads of tobacco) and the circulation of foreign coin, the most common being the Spanish silver peso and the German silver thaler, which Americans pronounced "dollar." Official rates of exchange between commodity money, colonial paper, foreign currency, and English pounds allowed this chaotic system to operate without too much difficulty.

Certain British interests pressed for even more stringent restrictions. But as the colonies grew more populous, and as the trade in colonial products increased, the British came to agree that it made little sense to tamper with such a prosperous system. Prime Minister Walpole pursued a policy later characterized as one of "salutory neglect": any colonial rules and regulations deemed contrary to good business practice were simply ignored and not enforced. Between 1700 and 1760 the quantity of goods exported from the colonies to the mother country rose 165 percent, while imports from Britain to North America increased by more than 400 percent. In part because of the lax enforcement, but mostly because the system operated to the profit of colonial merchants, colonists

John Greenwood, *Sea Captains Carousing in Surinam*. 1757. Oil on bed ticking, 95.9 × 191.2 cm. The Saint Louis Art Museum, Museum Purchase.

The New England artist John Greenwood painted this amusing view of New England sea captains in Surinam in 1757. By the early eighteenth century New England merchant traders like these had become important participants in the traffic in slaves and sugar to and from the West Indies. Northern ports thus became important pivots in the expanding commercial network linking slave plantations with Atlantic markets.

complained very little about the operation of the mercantilist system before the 1760s.

The Colonial Economy

Despite seemingly harsh mercantilist regulations, then, this economic system benefited planters, merchants, and white colonists in general. Despite being restricted to English markets, southern slave owners made healthy profits on the sale of their commodities. They enjoyed a protected market, in which competing goods from outside the empire were heavily taxed. Moreover, agricultural products more than held their value against the price of manufactures, and planters found themselves with steadily increasing purchasing power.

Pennsylvania, New York, and New England, and increasingly the Chesapeake as well, produced grain and flour, meat and dairy products. None of these was included in the list of enumerated goods, and they could thus be sold freely abroad. They found their most ready market in the British West Indies and the Lower South, where food production was slighted in favor of sugar and rice. Most of this trade was carried in New England ships. Indeed, the New England shipbuilding industry was greatly stimulated by the allowance under the Navigation Acts for ships built and manned in the colonies. So many ships were built for English buyers that by midcentury nearly a third of all British tonnage was American made.

The greatest benefits for the port cities of the North came from their commercial relationship to the slave colonies. New England merchants had become important players in the slave trade by the early eighteenth century, and soon thereafter they began to make inroads as well into the export trade of the West Indian colonies. It was in the Caribbean that New England merchants most blatantly ignored mercantilist regulations. In violation of Spanish, French, and Dutch rules prohibiting foreign trade, New Englanders traded foodstuffs for sugar in foreign colonies. Then, in violation of British regulations prohibiting the importation of sugar from competing colonies, the enterprising Yankees mixed their contraband among legal shipments from the British West Indies. The Molasses Act of 1733, which Parliament enacted under pressure from British West Indian planters, placed a prohibitive duty on sugar products brought from foreign colonies to North America. Had these regulations been strictly applied, they surely would have caused conflict with the colonists, but in fact enforcement was lax. By 1750, more than sixty distilleries in Massachusetts Bay were exporting over 2 million gallons of rum, most of it produced from sugar obtained illegally. Because the restrictive rules and regulations enacted by Britain for its colonies were not enforced, the merchants and manufacturers of the port cities of the North prospered.

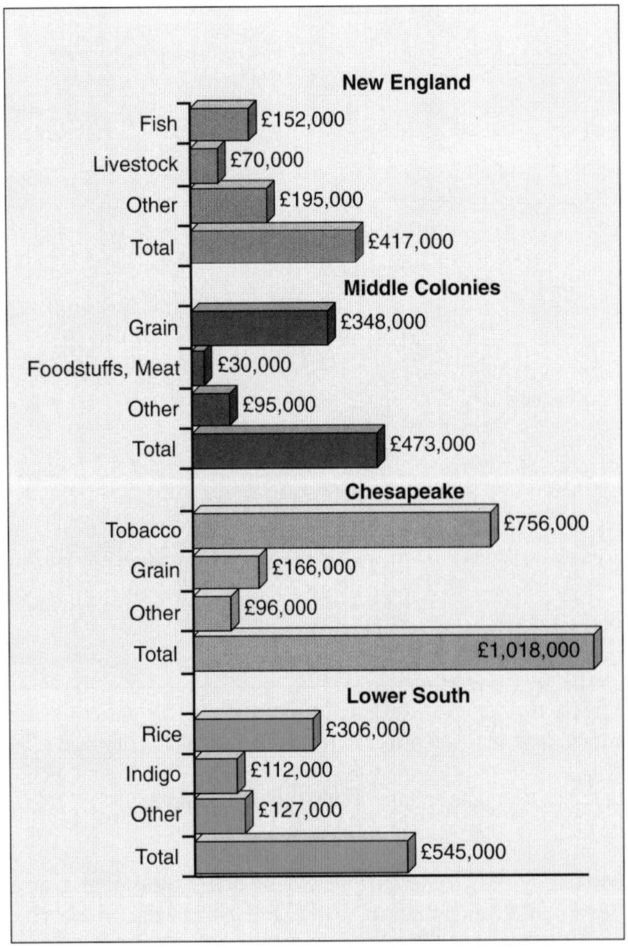

Value of Colonial Exports by Region, Annual Average, 1768–1772 *With tobacco, rice, grain, and indigo, the Chesapeake and Lower South accounted for nearly two-thirds of colonial exports in the late eighteenth century. The Middle Colonies, however, were also becoming major exporters of grain.*

Source: James F. Shepherd and Gary M. Walton, *Shipping, Maritime Trade and the Economic Development of Colonial America* (Cambridge, England: Cambridge University Press, 1972), 211–27.

As early as 1715, the exchange of New England fish, foodstuffs, and lumber for sugar and other tropical products from the West Indies accounted for more than half of the tonnage passing through the port of Boston. The volume of this trade remained steady over the next half-century, but Boston merchants greatly increased their commerce with the slave colonies of the Chesapeake and Lower South, shipping tobacco, rice, and indigo north, then reshipping it to England. A similar pattern is evident in the statistics of other northern ports. This carrying trade in the products of slave labor made it possible for New England and the Middle Colonies to earn the income necessary to purchase British imports despite the relative absence of valuable products from their own regions. Gradually, the commercial economies of the Northeast and the South were becoming integrated. From the 1730s

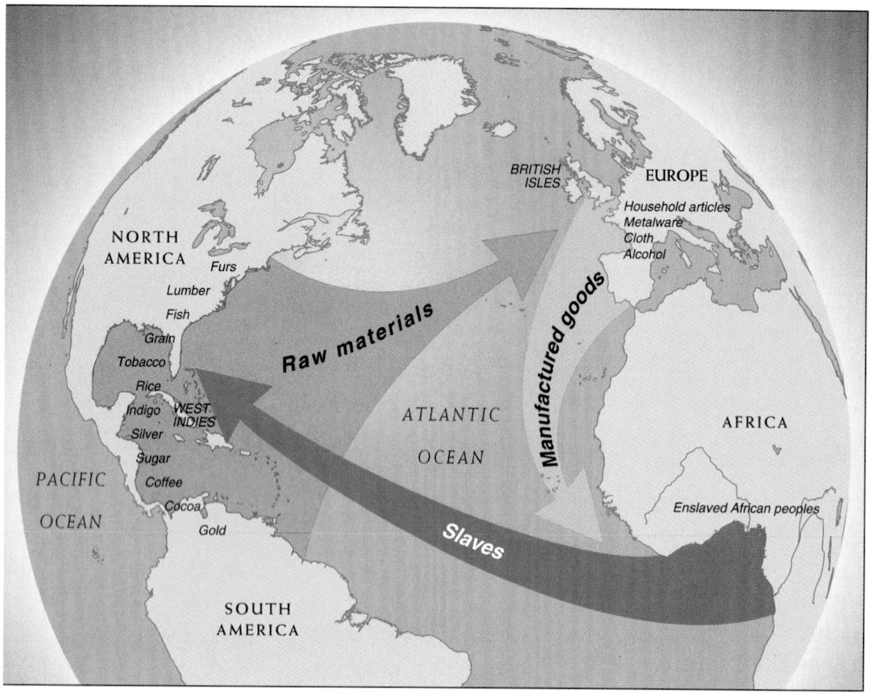

Triangular Trade across the Atlantic *The pattern of commerce among Europe, Africa, and the Americas became known as the "Triangular Trade." Sailors called the voyage of slave ships from Africa to America the "Middle Passage" because it formed the crucial middle section of this trading triangle.*

to the 1770s, for example, while the volume of trade between Great Britain and Charleston doubled, the trade between Charleston and northern ports grew sevenfold. The same relationship was developing between the Chesapeake and the North. Merchants in Boston, Newport, New York, and Philadelphia increasingly provided southern planters not only with shipping services but with credit and insurance as well. Like London, Liverpool, and Bristol—though on a smaller scale—the port cities of the North became pivots in the expanding trade network linking slave plantations with Atlantic markets. This trade provided northern merchants with the capital that financed commercial growth and development in their cities and the surrounding countryside. Slavery thus contributed to the growth of a score of northern port cities, forming an indirect but essential part of their economies.

SLAVERY AND FREEDOM

The prosperity of the eighteenth-century plantation economy thus improved the living conditions for the residents of northern cities as well as for a large segment of the population of the South, providing them with material opportunities unknown in the preceding century. The price, however, was the oppression and exploitation of millions of Africans and African Americans. Freedom for white men based on the slavery of African Americans is the most important contradiction in American history.

The Social Structure of the Slave Colonies

At the summit of southern colonial society stood a small elite of wealthy planters, in contrast with the mass of unfree men and women who formed the working population. Slavery had produced a society in which property was concentrated in the hands of a wealthy few. The richest 10 percent of southern colonists owned more than half the cultivated land and over 60 percent of the wealth. Although there was no colonial aristocracy—no nobility or royal appointments—the landed elite of the slave colonies came very close to constituting one.

Among the hundred wealthiest Virginians of the 1770s, for example, more than 80 percent had inherited their wealth from their fathers, and some were third- or fourth-generation colonials. Fewer than 10 percent were "self-made," and most of these men had acquired their fortunes through commerce or the law. The typical wealthy Virginia planter lived in a Tidewater county, owned several thousand acres of prime farmland and more than 100 slaves, resided in a luxurious plantation mansion, built perhaps in the fashionable Georgian style, and had an estate valued at more than 10,000 pounds. Elected to the House of Burgesses, and forming the group from which the magistrates and counselors of the colony were chosen, these "first families of Virginia"—the Carters, Harrisons, Lees, Fitzhughs, Burwells, Randolphs, and others—were a self-perpetuating governing class.

A similar elite ruled the Lower South, although wealthy landowners there spent relatively little time on their plantations. They resided instead in fashionable Charleston, where they constituted a close-knit group who controlled the colonial government. "They live in as high a style here, I believe, as any part of the world," wrote a visitor to Charleston.

A considerable distance separated this slave-owning elite from typical southern landowners. About half the adult white males were small planters and farmers. But although the gap between rich and middling colonists grew larger during the eighteenth century, the prosperity of the plantation economy created generally favorable conditions for this large landed class. Slave ownership, for example, became widespread among this group during the eighteenth century. In Virginia at midcentury, 45 percent of heads of household held one to four slaves, and even poorer farmers kept one or two.

Despite the prosperity that accompanied slavery in the eighteenth century, however, a substantial portion of colonists continued to own no land or slaves at all. Some rented land or worked as tenant farmers, some hired out as overseers or farm workers, and still others were indentured servants. Throughout the plantation region, landless white men constituted about 40 percent of the population. A New England visitor found a "much greater disparity between the rich and poor in Virginia" than at home.

White Skin Privilege

Yet all the white colonists of eighteenth-century North America shared the privileged status of their skin color. In the early seventeenth century there had been more diversity in views about race. For some, black skin was thought to be a sign of God's curse. "The blackness of the Negroes," one Englishman argued, "proceedeth of some natural infection." But not everyone shared those views. "I can't think there is any intrinsic value in one colour more than another," a second Englishman remarked, "nor that white is better than black, only we think it so because we are so." As slavery became increasingly important, however, Virginia officials took considerable care to create legal distinctions between the status of colonists and that of Africans, deliberately encouraging the growth of racism. Beginning in 1670, free Africans were prohibited from owning Christian servants. Ten years later, another law declared that any African, free or slave, who struck a Christian would receive thirty lashes on his bare back. One of the most important measures was designed to suppress intimate interracial contacts between white servants and enslaved Africans. A 1691 act "for prevention of that abominable mixture and spurious issue which hereafter may encrease in this dominion" established severe penalties for interracial sexual relationships.

Such penalties were rarely applied to masters, who frequently forced themselves on African women. But some slave women may have willingly established intimate relations with masters to better their condition or the opportunities for their children. The descendants of Sally Hemings, a slave owned by Thomas Jefferson, have long claimed that Jefferson fathered some of her children, and recent scientific tests comparing their DNA with that of descendents of Jefferson's paternal grandfather have confirmed their story. The Hemings children enjoyed a privileged position among Jefferson's slaves and were freed in his will.

Relationships between white masters or indentured servants and African slaves produced a rather large group of mulattoes. Since by law children inherited the bond or free status of their mothers, the children of African mothers became slaves, but a minority, the children of European women and African men, were free. According to a Maryland census of 1755, more than 60 percent of mulattoes were slaves. But mulattoes also made up three-quarters of a small free African American population. This group, about 4,000 in the 1770s, was denied the right to vote, to hold office, or to testify in court—all on the basis of racial

Alexander Spotswood Payne and His Brother, *John Robert Dandridge* Payne, *with Their* Nurse, ca. 1790. Oil on canvas, 142.2 × 175.2 cm. Virginia Museum of Fine Arts, Richmond, Gift of Miss Dorothy Payne.

Alexander Spotswood Payne and his brother John Robert Dandridge Payne with their African American nurse, painted by an unknown Virginia artist, ca. 1790. White and black Southerners lived in intimate contact. White children were breast-fed by African nannies, and interracial sex was very much a part of plantation life. But whiteness was the universal badge of freedom, blackness a mark of bondage. Despite their close association, said Thomas Jefferson, the two peoples were divided by "deep rooted prejudices entertained by the whites" and "ten thousand recollections, by the blacks, of the injuries they have sustained."

CHRONOLOGY

1441	African slaves first brought to Portugal
1518	Spain grants official license to Portuguese slavers
1535	Africans constitute a majority on Hispaniola
1619	First Africans brought to Virginia
1655	English seize Jamaica
1662	Virginia law makes slavery hereditary
1670	South Carolina founded
1672	Royal African Company organized
1691	Virginia prohibits interracial sexual contact
1698	Britain opens the slave trade to all its merchants
1699	Spanish declare Florida a refuge for escaped slaves
1702	South Carolinians burn St. Augustine
1705	Virginia Slave Code established
1706	French and Spanish navies bombard Charleston
1710	English capture Port Royal
1712	Slave uprising in New York City
1713	Peace of Utrecht
1721–48	Robert Walpole leads British cabinet
1733	Molasses Act
1739	Stono Rebellion War of Jenkins's Ear
1740–48	King George's War
1741	Africans executed in New York for conspiracy
1752	Georgia officially opened to slavery
1770s	Peak period of the English colonies' slave trade
1808	Importation of slaves into the United States ends

background. Denied the status of citizenship enjoyed by even the poorest of white men, free blacks were a pariah group who raised the status of poor white colonials by contrast. Racial distinctions were a constant reminder of the freedom of white colonists and the debasement of all blacks, slave or free.

Racism set up a wall of contempt between colonists and African Americans. Jefferson wrote of "the real distinctions which nature has made" between the races. "In memory they are equal to the whites," he wrote of the slaves, but "in reason much inferior." He gave no consideration to the argument of the freed slave Olaudah Equiano that "slavery debases the mind." Jefferson was on firmer ground when he argued that the two peoples were divided by "deep rooted prejudices entertained by the whites" and "ten thousand recollections, by the blacks, of the injuries they have sustained." Perhaps he knew of these feelings from his long relationship with Sally Hemings. "I tremble for my country when I reflect that God is just," Jefferson concluded in a deservedly famous passage, and remember "that his justice cannot sleep forever."

CONCLUSION

During the eighteenth century nearly half a million Africans were kidnapped from their homes and packed into ships for up to three months before arriving in British North America. They provided the labor that made colonialism pay. Southern planters, northern merchants, and especially British traders and capitalists benefited greatly from the commerce in slave-produced crops, and that prosperity filtered down to affect many of the colonists of British North America. Slavery was "the strength and sinews" of the British empire in North America. The focus of imperial warfare was seizing the slave colonies of other powers and putting them to the service of the mother country. Mercantilism was a system designed to channel the colonial wealth produced by slaves to the nation-state, but as long as profits were high, the British were content to wink at all colonists' violations of mercantilist regulations.

Although African Americans received nothing in return, their labor helped build the greatest accumulation of capital that Europe had ever seen. But despite enormous hardship and suffering, African Americans survived by forming new communities in the colonies, rebuilding families, restructuring language, reforming culture. African American culture added important components of African knowledge and experience to colonial agriculture, art, music, and cuisine. The African Americans of the British colonies lived better lives than the slaves worked to death on Caribbean sugar plantations, but lives of misery compared to the men they were forced to serve. As the slaves sang on the Georgia coast: "Dah Backrow Man go wrong you, Buddy Quow."

REVIEW QUESTIONS

1. Trace the development of the system of slavery and discuss the way it became entrenched in the Americas.
2. Describe the effects of the slave trade both on enslaved Africans and on the economic and political life of Africa.
3. Describe the process of acculturation involved in becoming an African American. In what ways did slaves "Africanize" the South?
4. Explain the connection between the institution of slavery and the building of a commercial empire.
5. In what ways did colonial policy encourage the growth of racism?

RECOMMENDED READING

Michael Craton, *Sinews of Empire: A Short History of British Slavery* (1974). An introduction to the British mercantilist system that emphasizes the importance of slavery. Includes a comparison of the mainland colonies with the Caribbean.

Philip D. Curtin, *The African Slave Trade: A Census* (1969). The pioneer work in the quantitative history of the slave trade. All subsequent histories of the slave trade are indebted to Curtin.

Herbert G. Gutman, *The Black Family in Slavery and Freedom, 1750–1925* (1976). A pathbreaking history of the development of the African American community in North America. The sections on the eighteenth century provide evidence of the development of multigenerational family and kin networks.

Winthrop D. Jordan, *White over Black: American Attitudes toward the Negro, 1550–1812* (1968). Remains the best and most comprehensive history of racial values and attitudes. A searching examination of British and American literature, folklore, and history.

Peter Kolchin, *American Slavery, 1619–1877* (1993). A survey that features comparisons with slavery in Brazil, the Caribbean, and serfdom in Russia. Includes a comprehensive bibliographic essay.

Walter Rodney, *How Europe Underdeveloped Africa* (1974). A highly influential book that traces the relationship between Europe and Africa from the fifteenth to the twentieth century and demonstrates how Europe's industrialization became Africa's impoverishment.

Mechal Sobel, *The World They Made Together: Black and White Values in Eighteenth-Century Virginia* (1987). Demonstrates the ways in which both Africans and Europeans shaped the formation of American values, perceptions, and identities.

Ian K. Steele, *Warpaths: Invasions of North America* (1994). A new synthesis of the colonial wars from the sixteenth to the eighteenth century that places Indians as well as empires at the center of the action.

Sterling Stuckey, *Slave Culture: Nationalist Theory and the Foundations of Black America* (1987). A study of the African origins of African American culture that concentrates on folklore. Includes important evidence on African American religion in the era before Christianization.

Hugh Thomas, *The Slave Trade: The Story of the Atlantic Slave Trade, 1440–1870* (1997). The horrifying history in brutal detail, told by a master historian.

ADDITIONAL BIBLIOGRAPHY

The African Slave Trade

Jay Coughtry, *The Notorious Triangle: Rhode Island and the African Slave Trade, 1799–1807* (1981)

Philip D. Curtin, *Economic Change in Precolonial Africa: Senegambia in the Era of the Slave Trade* (1975)

Basin Davidson, *The African Slave Trade* (1980)

Elizabeth Donnan, ed., *Documents Illustrative of the History of the Slave Trade to America* 4 vols. (1930–35)

J. E. Inikori, *Forced Migration: The Impact of the Export Slave Trade on African Societies* (1982)

Robert W. July, *A History of the African People* (1992)

Herbert S. Klein, *The Middle Passage: Comparative Studies in the Atlantic Slave Trade* (1978)

Robin Law, *The Slave Coast of West Africa, 1550–1750: The Impact of the Atlantic Slave Trade on an African Society* (1991)

Paul E. Lovejoy, ed., *Africans in Bondage: Studies in Slavery and the Slave Trade* (1986)

Daniel P. Mannix and Malcolm Crowley, *Black Cargoes: A History of the Atlantic Slave Trade* (1962)

David Northrup, ed., *The Atlantic Slave Trade* (1994)

J. A. Rawley, *The Transatlantic Slave Trade* (1981)

Edward Reynolds, *Stand the Storm: A History of the Atlantic Slave Trade* (1985)

A. C. De C. M. Saunders, *A Social History of Black Slaves and Freemen in Portugal, 1441–1555* (1982)

Jon Vogt, *Portuguese Rule on the Gold Coast, 1469–1682* (1979)

The Development of North American Slave Societies

L. R. Bailey, *Indian Slave Trade in the Southwest: A Study of Slave-Taking and the Traffic in Indian Captives* (1966)

T. H. Breen and Stephen Innes, *"Myne Owne Ground": Race and Freedom on Virginia's Eastern Shore* (1980)

Verner W. Crane, *The Southern Frontier, 1670–1732* (1929)

Richard S. Dunn, *Sugar and Slaves: The Rise of the Planter Class in the English West Indies, 1624–1713* (1972)

Laura Foner and Eugene D. Genovese, eds., *Slavery in the New World: A Reader in Comparative History* (1969)

Charles Joyner, *Down by the Riverside: A South Carolina Slave Community* (1984)

Alan Kulikoff, *Tobacco and Slaves: The Development of Southern Cultures in the Chesapeake, 1680–1800* (1986)

Daniel Littlefield, *Rice and Slaves: Ethnicity and the Slave Trade in Colonial South Carolina* (1981)

Paul E. Lovejoy, *Transformations in Slavery: A History of Slavery in Africa* (1983)

Edgar J. McManus, *Black Bondage in the North* (1973)

Gary B. Nash, *Red, White, and Black: The Peoples of Early North America* (1992)

Julia Floyd Smith, *Slavery and Rice Culture in Low Country Georgia, 1750–1860* (1985)

Brenda Stevenson, *Life in Black and White: Family and Community in the Slave South* (1996)

Peter H. Wood, *Black Majority: Negroes in Colonial South Carolina from 1670 through the Stone Rebellion* (1974)

Becoming African American

John B. Boles, *Black Southerners, 1619–1869* (1984)

Joseph E. Harris, ed., *Global Dimensions of the African Diaspora* (1982)

Annette Gordon-Reed, *Thomas Jefferson and Sally Hemings: An American Controversy*, (1997)

Gerald W. Mullin, *Flight and Rebellion: Slave Resistance in Eighteenth-Century Virginia* (1972)

Orlando Patterson, *Slavery and Social Death: A Comparative Study* (1982)

V. B. Thompson, *The Making of the African Diaspora in the Americas, 1441–1900* (1984)

The Structure of Empire

Joyce O. Appleby, *Economic Thought and Ideology in Seventeenth-Century England* (1978)

Eugene Genovese and Elizabeth Fox-Genovese, *Fruits of Merchant Capital: Slavery and Bourgeois Property in the Rise and Expansion of Capitalism* (1983)

E. J. Hobsbawn, *Industry and Empire: The Making of Modern English Society, 1750 to the Present Day* (1968)

Michael Kammen, *Empire and Interest: The American Colonies and the Politics of Mercantilism* (1970)

John J. McCusker and Russell R. Menard, *The Economy of British America, 1607–1787* (1985)

Barbara L. Solow, ed., *Slavery and the Rise of the Atlantic System* (1991)

Eric Williams, *Capitalism and Slavery* (1944)

Slavery and Freedom

David Brion Davis, *The Problem of Slavery in Western Culture* (1966)

Carl N. Degler, *Neither Black nor White: Slavery and Race Relations in Brazil and the United States* (1971)

Edmund S. Morgan, *American Slavery, American Freedom: The Ordeal of Colonial Virginia* (1975)

Joel Williamson, *New People: Miscegenation and Mulattoes in the United States* (1980)

Biography

Philip D. Curtin, ed., *Africa Remembered: Narratives of West Africans from the Era of the Slave Trade* (1967)

Paul Edwards, ed., *The Interesting Narrative of the Life of Olaudah Equiano, or Gustavus Vassa, the African, written by himself* (1987)

James B. Hedges, *The Browns of Providence Plantation* (1952)

Kenneth A. Lockridge, *The Diary and Life of William Byrd II of Virginia, 1674-1744* (1987)

Phinizy Spalding, *Oglethorpe in America* (1977)

Janet Whitman, *John Woolman, American Quaker* (1942)

CHAPTER FIVE

THE CULTURES OF COLONIAL NORTH AMERICA

1700–1780

Watercolor, fraktur of George and Lady Washington; Abby Aldrich Rockefeller Folk Art Center, Williamsburg, VA

Chapter Outline

NORTH AMERICAN REGIONS
Indian America
The Spanish Borderlands
The French Crescent
New England
The Middle Colonies
The Backcountry
The South
Traditional Culture in the New World
The Frontier Heritage

DIVERGING SOCIAL AND POLITICAL PATTERNS
Population Growth
Social Class
Economic Growth and Increasing Inequality
Contrasts in Colonial Politics

THE CULTURAL TRANSFORMATION OF BRITISH NORTH AMERICA
The Enlightenment Challenge
A Decline in Religious Devotion
The Great Awakening
Great Awakening Politics

AMERICAN COMMUNITIES

From Deerfield to Kahnawake: Crossing Cultural Boundaries

Two hours before daylight on February 29, 1704, the Reverend John Williams and his wife Eunice of Deerfield, Massachusetts, awoke to "horrid shouting and yelling" and the crash of axes and hatchets breaking open the doors and windows of their house. Leaping out of bed they knew immediately that the town was under attack by Indians and their French allies; this frontier settlement on the northwestern fringe of New England had already been attacked six times in the perennial fighting with New France. Never before, however, had the enemy penetrated the town's stockade. Suddenly the door burst open and "with painted faces and hideous exclamations" Indians began pushing inside. "I reached up my hands for my pistol," Williams remembered, "cocked it, and put it to the breast of the first Indian that came up." It misfired, and as the couple stood trembling in their night clothes, they were bound and dragged into the central hall with their seven children. In horror they were forced to watch the invaders club and kill their resisting six-year-old son, their screaming newborn infant daughter, and the black nursemaid. The family was hustled out into the frigid dawn and, with more than a hundred other captives, marched north through snow and ice toward Canada, leaving the frightful sight of the burning town behind.

The Deerfield raid became one of the most infamous events in the long series of colonial wars. One hundred and forty residents of the town managed to hold off the invasion and survive, but fifty others died in the attack. Among the captives, twenty-one were murdered along the way, in most cases because they were too weak to travel; the murdered included Mrs. Williams, who had not yet recovered from a difficult childbirth just six weeks before. The governor of Massachusetts ordered a day of fasting and prayed that "the Designs of the barbarous Salvages against us be defeated; our exposed Plantations preserved; and the poor Christian Captives in their hands returned." Authorities raised the bounty on Indian scalps from £10 to £100 and organized bloody raids of their own on the French and Indian settlements to the north.

Most of the Deerfield captives were delivered to the French authorities in Montreal. Within two years, fifty-nine of them had been ransomed and returned home to Deerfield, the Reverend Williams and four of his surviving children among them. Williams soon published an account of his captivity, *The Redeemed Captive Returning to Zion*. In colonial America, with its many peoples and cultures, readers were fascinated by the problems and dilemmas of crossing frontiers and boundaries. What was life like for you, people wanted to know, on the other side of the frontier? How were you changed by your experience? Did you remain loyal to your community? Can you still be trusted?

Questions of this sort were vitally important to the colonists, for over the years hundreds of Europeans who had been captured by Indians had chosen to remain with their captors rather than return home. Among the Deerfield captives, thirty-one—including ten-year-old Eunice Williams, her mother's namesake—remained in Canada. Eunice and many of the other Deerfield captives lived at Kahnawake, a community of Catholic Indians near Montreal. Like Deerfield, Kahnawake was a farming town of fifty or sixty homes clustered around a central church and surrounded by a stockade to protect it from enemy raiders. The differences between the two communities, however, were more striking than the similarities.

Founded in the seventeenth century by Jesuit missionaries as a refuge for Iroquois converts, Kahnawake not only became home to a great variety of Native American Catholics but also welcomed people of mixed Indian and European ancestry. The "great mixture of the blood of whites with that of aborigines is observable in the persons of the inhabitants," wrote one visitor, struck by the appearance of people who seemed to be Indians in all respects except their blue eyes. Such mixing was also evident in the community's culture, in the exotic mélange of European and Indian clothing, in the use of both Indian and French names, and in the special ways the community bent Catholic ritual to fit traditional Iroquois practices. Community members crossed boundaries in other ways, too: many residents were smugglers who engaged in the illegal trade of furs and other Indian products across the frontier into New York. According to the frustrated authorities in Montreal, Kahnawake operated as "a sort of republic," insisting on its freedom and independence.

As the historian John Demos writes, Kahnawake was "a unique experiment in bicultural living." Its residents were skilled at offering sympathetic sanctuary to traumatized captive children, and by the time Eunice Williams's father and siblings were ransomed she told the man who had come to fetch her that she was "unwilling to return." Soon she converted to Catholicism. Over the years the father sent several emissaries to retrieve her, but all she would say were two words of Iroquois: *jaghte oghte*, meaning "maybe not." She had apparently forgotten her English tongue, and she refused to acknowledge her English name, having taken another—A'*ongonte*, which in Iroquois means "she has been planted as a person." In 1713, at the age of sixteen, she married a Kahnawake Mohawk. Father and daughter would meet only once more, the following year, when he went to Kahnawake a final time to beg her to return. But she would "not so much as give me one pleasant look," Williams wrote mournfully. "She is yet obstinatly resolved to live and dye here."

And that is what happened. A'*ongonte* and her husband remained good Catholics, raising a family and working as traders. John Williams died in 1729, surrounded by his children and grandchildren but longing for his "unredeemed" daughter. It was not until 1739 that A'*ongonte* found the courage to bring her family south for a visit, for she feared being held in New England against her will. Her brother Stephen wrote in his diary that at long last "we had ye joyfull, Sorrowfull meeting of our poor Sister that we had been Sepratd from fer above 36 years." After that A'*ongonte* visited only rarely because of the continuing warfare. "We have a great desire of going down to see you," she wrote to her brother through an interpreter near the end of their lives in the 1770s, "but do not know when an oppertunity may offer.…I pray the Lord that he may give us grace so to Live in this as to be prepared for a happey meeting in the woreld to Come." And, perhaps as a sign of reconciliation, she signed the letter, "Loving Sister until death, Eunice Williams."

KEY TOPICS

- The similarities and differences among eighteenth-century Spanish, French, and English colonies
- The impact on British colonial culture of increasing European immigration
- Cultural changes in Indian America brought about by contact with European customs and lifestyles
- Patterns of work and class in eighteenth-century America
- Tensions between Enlightenment thought and the Great Awakening's call to renewed religious devotion

NORTH AMERICAN REGIONS

American colonial history too frequently is written as if only the British colonists along the Atlantic coast really mattered. But as the experience of the Deerfield community and the Williams family suggests, this is a mistake eighteenth-century colonists could not afford to make. In the first place, Indian America was a critically important part of the eighteenth-century world. From the fringes of colonial societies into the native heart of the continent, from the eastern foothills of the Appalachians to the western flank of the Sierra Nevada in California, hundreds of Indian cultures—despite being deeply affected by the spread of colonial culture—remained firmly in control of their homelands. And in addition to the British provinces stretching along the Atlantic coast, there were Hispanic colonists who defended the northern borderlands of the Spanish Caribbean and Mexican empire in isolated communities from Florida to California, and French communities that occupied the valley of the St. Lawrence River and scattered down the Mississippi Valley from the Great Lakes to the Gulf of Mexico. There were impressive similarities among these colonial societies, representing a continuation in the New World of traditional Old World beliefs, customs, and institutions, as well as a general pattern of European adaptation to American conditions.

Indian America

As the native peoples of the Atlantic coastal plain lost their lands to colonists through battles or treaties, and moved into or beyond the Appalachian Mountains, they became active in the European fur trade and dependent on firearms, metal tools, and other manufactured goods to maintain their way of life. Yet through the American Revolution they continued to assert a proud independence and gained considerable skill at playing colonial powers off against each other. The Iroquois Five Nations battled the French and

A portrait of the Delaware chief Tishcohan by Gustavus Hesselius, painted in 1732. In his purse of chipmunk hide is a clay pipe, a common item of the Indian trade. Tishcohan was one of the Delaware leaders forced by Pennsylvania authorities into signing a fraudulent land deal that reversed that colony's history of fair dealing with Indians over land. He moved west to the Ohio River as settlers poured into his former homeland.

their Indian allies in King William's War, but in 1701 they signed a treaty of neutrality with France that kept them out of harm's way during the next round of conflicts. The Catholic Iroquois of Kahnawake sometimes supported the French, as they did by mounting the Deerfield raid, but they also traded with the English. In the Lower South, the Creeks similarly traded with both the French and the English as a means of maintaining their autonomy.

In general, the French had significantly better relations with native peoples than the English, but inevitably as they pursued their expansionist plans they came into conflict with many Indian groups, and when opposed they could be just as cruel and violent as any other power. In the early eighteenth century the Fox Indians blocked French passage between the Great Lakes and the upper Mississippi, attempting to make themselves into middlemen in the fur trade. After several years of sporadic fighting, the French defeated the tribe in 1716. But Fox warriors rose again in 1726, and only with great violence and not until 1738 could the French force the tribe to sign a treaty. On the lower Mississippi the Natchez and Chickasaw tribes opposed the arrival of the French, engaging them in a series of bloody conflicts during the 1720s that concluded only when the French decimated the Natchez in 1731.

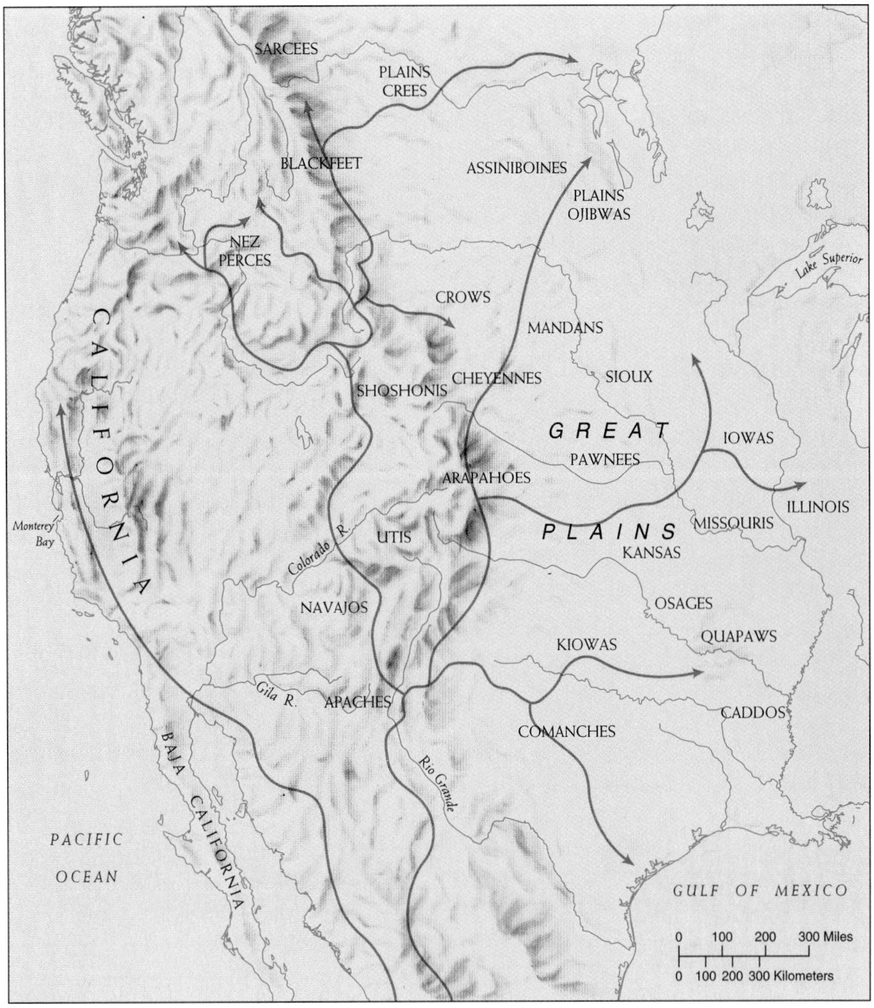

Growing Use of the Horse by Plains Indians *In the seventeenth and eighteenth centuries, Spanish settlers introduced horses into their New Mexican colony. Through trading and raiding, horses spread northward in streams both west and east of the Rocky Mountains. The horse, whose genetic ancestor had been native to the American continent in pre-Archaic times, offered the Indian peoples of the Great Plains the opportunity to create a distinctive hunting and warrior culture.*

The preeminent concern of the Indians of the eastern half of the continent was the tremendous growth of colonial population in the British Atlantic coastal colonies, especially the movement of settlers westward. In the 1730s and 1740s Pennsylvania perpetrated a series of fraudulent seizures of western lands from the Delawares. Particularly in the light of Pennsylvania's previous history of fair dealing with Indian peoples, these acts offered yet another disturbing sign of things to come. Thus Indian alliances with the French resulted not from any great love and affection on their part toward the French but from their great fear of British expansion.

Meanwhile, a long-term population decline continued among the Indian peoples of North America. The colonists were relatively immune from dramatic fluctuations in the death rate, but Indian America continued to take a terrific beating from epidemics of European disease. There was no systematic census of North American Indians before the nineteenth century, but historians estimate that from a high of 7 to 10 million native Americans north of Mexico in 1500 the population had probably fallen to around a million by 1800. Thus, during the eighteenth century the colonial population overtook and began to overwhelm the native population of the continent. Population loss did not affect all Indian tribes equally, however. Native peoples with a century or more of colonial contact and interaction had lost 50 percent or more of their numbers, but most Indian societies in the interior had yet to be struck by the horrible epidemics.

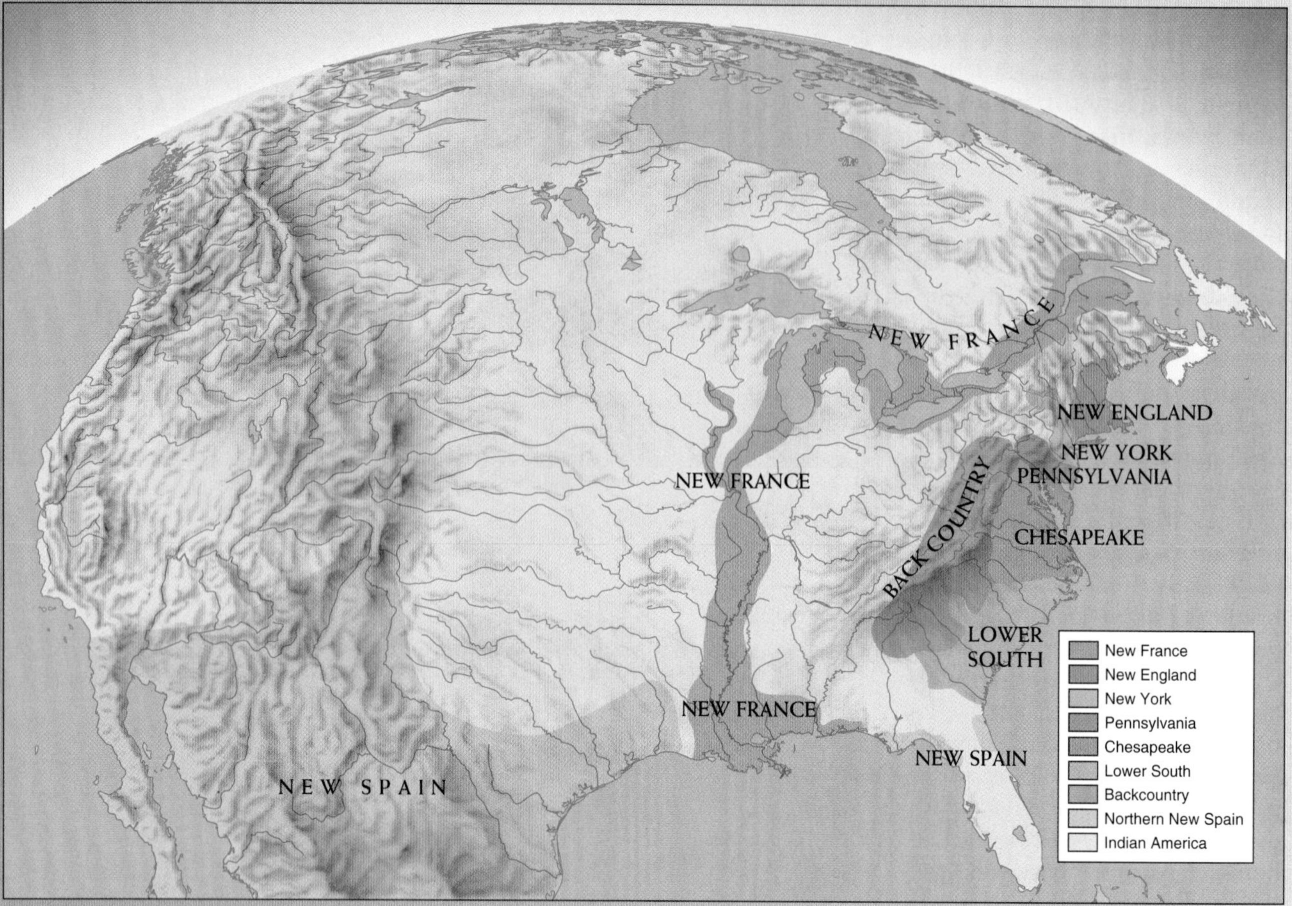

Colonization introduced other, less-distressing changes in Indian cultures. By the early eighteenth century, Indians on the southern fringe of the Great Plains were using horses stolen from the Spanish in New Mexico. Horses enabled Indian hunters to exploit the buffalo herds much more efficiently than before, and on the base of this more productive subsistence strategy many groups built a distinctive and elaborate nomadic culture. Great numbers of Indian peoples moved onto the plains during the eighteenth century, pulled by this new way of life, pushed by colonial invasions and disruptions radiating southwest from Canada and north from the Spanish borderlands. By midcentury, the New Mexicans had become regular victims of raids by mounted hunters of the Great Plains. The invention of nomadic Plains Indian culture was another of the dramatic cultural amalgamations and innovations of the eighteenth century. The mounted Plains Indian, so frequently used as a symbol of native America, was actually a product of the colonial era.

The Spanish Borderlands

In the mid-eighteenth century what is today the Sunbelt of the United States formed the periphery of the largest and most prosperous European colony on the North American continent—the viceroyalty of New Spain, which included approximately 1 million Spanish colonists and mestizos and at least 2 million Indians. The administrative capital of Mexico City was the most sophisticated metropolis in the Western Hemisphere, the site of one of the world's great universities, with broad avenues and spectacular baroque architecture. New Spain's northern provinces of Florida, Texas, New Mexico, and California, however, were far removed from this opulence. Officials of the viceroyalty of New Spain, who oversaw these colonies, thought of them as buffer zones, protecting New Spain from the expanding colonial empires of Spain's New World rivals.

In Florida, the oldest of European colonies in North America, fierce fighting among the Spanish, the British, and the Indians had by the early eighteenth century reduced the colonial presence to little more than the forts of St. Augustine on the Atlantic and Pensacola on the Gulf of Mexico, each surrounded by small colonized territories populated with the families of Spanish troops. In their weakened condition, the Spanish had no choice but to establish cooperative relations with the Creek and Seminole Indians who dominated the region,

Region	Population
New France	70,000
New England	400,000
New York	100,000
Pennsylvania	230,000
Chesapeake	390,000
Lower South	100,000
Backcountry	100,000
Northern New Spain	20,000
Indian America	1,500,000

Regions in Eighteenth-Century North America

By the middle of the eighteenth century, European colonists had established a number of distinctive colonial regions in North America. The northern periphery of New Spain, the oldest and most prosperous European colony, stretched from Baja California to eastern Texas, then jumped to the settlements on the northern end of the Florida peninsula; cattle ranching was the dominant way of life in this thinly populated region. New France was like a great crescent, extending from the plantation communities along the Mississippi near New Orleans to the French colonial communities along the St. Lawrence; in between were isolated settlements and forts, connected only by the extensive French trading network.

as well as the hundreds of African American runaways who considered St. Augustine a refuge from the cruel slave regimes in Georgia and Carolina. Like the community of Kahnawake, eighteenth-century Florida included a growing mestizo population as well as a considerable number of free African Americans and Hispanicized Indians from the old missions.

New Mexico, nearly 2,000 miles to the west, was similarly isolated from the mainstream of New Spain. One Spanish observer characterized the province as "little populated and poverty-stricken, although endowed with natural resources." At midcentury New Mexico included some 20,000 Pueblo Indians (their numbers greatly reduced by disease since their first contact with Europeans) and perhaps 10,000 colonists. The prosperity of these colonists, who supported themselves with subsistence agriculture, was severely constrained by a restrictive colonial economic policy that forced them to exchange their wool, pottery, buffalo hides, and buckskin for imported goods at unfavorable rates. Unlike the colonial population of Florida, however, the settlements of New Mexicans were gradually expanding, following the valleys and streams that led east and north from the original colonial outposts scattered along the upper Rio Grande.

The Spanish also founded new northern outposts during the eighteenth century. Concerned about French colonization of the Mississippi Valley, they established several military posts or *presidios* on the fringes of the colony of Louisiana and in 1716 began the construction of a string of Franciscan missions among the Indian peoples of Texas. By 1750 the settlement of San Antonio had become the center of a developing frontier province. The Spanish also established new colonial outposts west of New Mexico, in what is today southern Arizona. In the 1690s, Jesuit missionaries, led by Father Eusebio Kino, founded missions among the desert Indians of the lower Colorado and Gila River Valleys. Mission San Xavier del Bac near Tucson is acclaimed the most striking example of Spanish colonial architecture in the United States. Cattle ranching, introduced by the Jesuits, and farming as well spread along the lower Rio Grande Valley; in fact, ranching would continue to define the region's economy for the next 200 years.

Midcentury also found the Spanish considering new settlements along the California coast. Juan

The church of San Xavier del Bac, constructed in the late eighteenth century, is located a few miles south of the city of Tucson, where Jesuit Father Eusebio Kino founded a mission among the Pima Indians in 1700. Known as the White Dove of the Desert, it is acclaimed as the most striking example of Spanish colonial architecture in the United States.

Cabrillo, an associate of Hernán Cortés, had first explored the coastal waters in 1542 and was the first European to sail into the fine harbor at San Diego. In 1603 the explorer Sebastián Vizcaíno had come upon Monterey Bay. The Spanish did little to follow up on these finds, but in 1769, acting on rumors of Russian expansion along the northern Pacific coast (for a discussion of Russian America, see Chapter 9), officials in Mexico City ordered Gaspar de Portolá, governor of what is now Baja California, to establish a Spanish presence in the North. With him were Franciscan missionaries led by Junípero Serra, president of the missions in Baja. At the harbor of San Diego, Portolá and Serra founded the first mission and pueblo complex in present-day California. Portolá then proceeded overland, becoming the first European to explore the interior valleys and mountains, and in 1770 he and Serra established their headquarters at Monterey Bay on the central coast. Two years later Juan Bautista de Anza established an overland route across the blistering deserts connecting Arizona and California, and in 1776 he led a colonizing expedition that founded the pueblo of San Francisco. Over the next fifty years the number of California settlements grew to include twenty-one missions and a half-dozen presidios and pueblos, including the town of Los Angeles. Founded in 1781 by a group of mestizo settlers from Sinaloa, Mexico, by the end of the century Los Angeles, with a population of only 300, was California's largest town.

A distinguishing mark of these colonial communities was their close association with the mission system. For the Spanish, conquest demanded conversion, which, according to theory, would lead Indians toward "civilization." Like the efforts of the Jesuits at Kahnawake and elsewhere in New France, the Spanish experiment in cultural transformation was designed to make Indians over into Christians and loyal subjects by educating them and putting them to work raising cattle and crops. The most extensive mission project was in California, where under the direction of priests thousands of Indian laborers produced a flourishing local economy based on irrigation farming as well as horse, cattle, and sheep ranching. Near Los Angeles lay San Gabriel, one of the most prosperous missions, where large vineyards and orchards produced fine wines and brandies. Indian people also constructed the adobe and stone churches, built on Spanish and Moorish patterns, whose ruins symbolize California's colonial society.

But this experiment in culture change was deadly for Indian people. To keep the system functioning, the Franciscan missionaries resorted to cruel and sometimes violent means of controlling their Indian subjects: shackles, solitary confinement, and whipping posts. Indians resisted from the very beginning. In 1775 the villagers around San Diego rose up and killed several priests. The history of many missions was punctuated by revolts, but the arms and organization of Spanish soldiers were usually sufficient to suppress the uprisings. There were also smaller incidents of retaliation, as when at Mission Santa Cruz, on the central coast, a priest who thrashed Indians too often was murdered. Another form of protest was flight: whole villages sometimes fled to the inaccessible mountains.

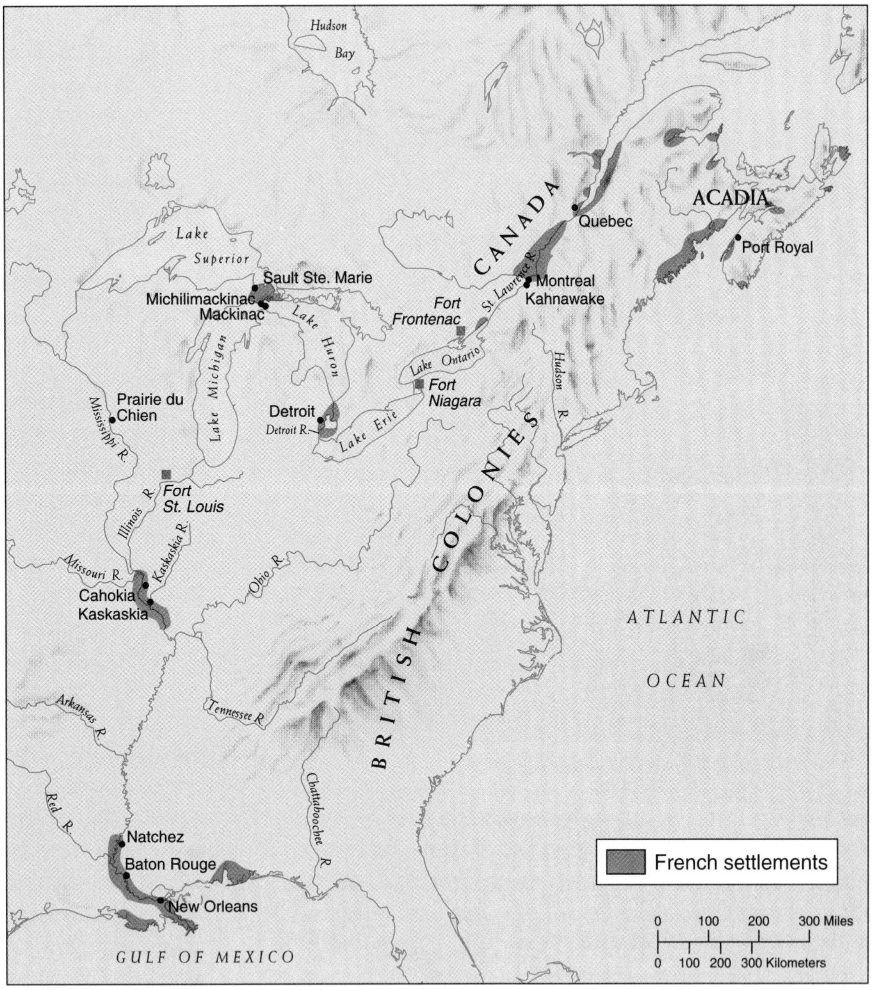

The French Crescent *The French empire in North America was based on a series of alliances and trade relations with Indian nations linking a great crescent of colonies, settlements, and outposts that extended from the mouth of the St. Lawrence River, through the Great Lakes, and down the Mississippi River to the Gulf of Mexico.*

Foreign observers noted the despondency of California's mission Indians. "I have never seen any of them laugh," one European visitor wrote. "I have never seen a single one look anyone in the face. They have the air of taking no interest in anything." The record of revolt suggests that there may have been more than a little guile in this mask of servility. But overwork, overcrowding, poor nutrition, poor sanitation, and epidemic disease took a terrible toll. The death rate, particularly high for children and women of child-bearing age, exceeded the birth rate, and California's native population fell by at least 25 percent.

As the prominence of mission settlements in California, Texas, and New Mexico suggests, the Catholic Church played a dominant role in the community life of the borderlands. In the eighteenth century, religion was no private affair. It was a deadly serious business dividing nations into warring camps, and the Spanish considered themselves the special protectors of the traditions of Rome. The object of colonization, one colonial promoter wrote in 1584, was "enlarging the glorious gospel of Christ, and leading the infinite multitudes of these simple people that are in error into the right and perfect way of salvation." Although these are the words of the English imperialist Richard Hakluyt, they could as easily have come from the Spanish padres Kino or Serra or the Jesuit missionaries at Kahnawake. There was no tradition of religious dissent. Certain of the truth of their "right and perfect way," the Spanish could see no reason for tolerating the errors of others.

The French Crescent

In France, as in Spain, Church and state were closely interwoven. During the seventeenth century the French prime ministers, Cardinal Richelieu and Cardinal Mazarin, laid out a fundamentally Catholic imperial policy, and under their guidance colonists constructed a second Catholic empire in North America. In 1674 Church and state collaborated in establishing the bishopric of Quebec. Under aggressive leadership that office founded local seminaries, oversaw the appointment and review of priests, and laid the foundation of the resolutely Catholic culture of New France. Meanwhile, Jesuit missionaries continued to carry Catholicism deep into the continent.

The number of French colonists rose at an impressive rate from fewer than 15,000 in 1700 to more than 70,000 at midcentury. During the eighteenth century the French used their trade network and alliances with the Indians to establish a great crescent of colonies, military posts, and settlements that extended from the mouth of the St. Lawrence River, southwest through the Great Lakes, then down the Mississippi River to the Gulf of Mexico. The maritime colony of Acadia, populated by fishermen and farmers, anchored the crescent on the northeast; the slave colony of Louisiana held the other end at the mouth of the Mississippi. Over this vast territory the French laid a thin colonial veneer, the beginning of what they planned as a

The persistence of French colonial long lots in the pattern of modern landholding is clear in this enhanced satellite photograph of the Mississippi River near New Orleans. Long lots, the characteristic form of property holding in New France, were designed to offer as many settlers as possible a share of good bottomland as well as a frontage on the waterways, which served as the basic transportation network.

great continental empire that would contain the Protestant British to a narrow strip of Atlantic coastline.

At the heart of the French empire in North America were the farming communities of the colony of Quebec along the banks of the St. Lawrence, including the towns of Montreal and Quebec City. There were also farming communities in the Illinois country, which shipped wheat down the Mississippi to supply the booming sugar plantations of Louisiana. By the mid-eighteenth century, those plantations—extending along the river from Natchez and Baton Rouge to New Orleans—had become the most profitable French enterprise in North America.

One of the most distinctive French stamps on the North American landscape were the "long lots" stretching back from the rivers that provided each settler family a share of good bottomland to farm as well as frontage on the waterways, the "interstate highway system" of the French Crescent. This pattern had first appeared with the seigneurial grants along the St. Lawrence, but French colonists transplanted it throughout their domain; aerial photographs reveal its persistence today. Long lots were laid out along the lower Mississippi in Louisiana and at sites on the upper Mississippi such as Kaskaskia and Prairie du Chien, as well as at the strategic passages of the Great Lakes, the communities of Mackinac, Sault Ste. Marie, and Detroit. In 1750 Detroit was a stockaded town with a military garrison, a small administrative center, several stores, a Catholic church, and 100 households of *métis* (French for mestizo) families. French and *métis* farmers worked the land along the Detroit River, not far from communities inhabited by more than 6,000 Ottawa, Potawatomi, and Huron Indians.

Communities of this sort that combined both French and Indian elements were in the tradition of the inclusive frontier. Detroit looked like "an old French village," said one observer, except that its houses were "mostly covered with bark," in Indian style. "It is not uncommon to see a Frenchman with Indian shoes and stockings, without breeches, wearing a strip of woolen cloth to cover what decency requires him to conceal," wrote another. "Yet at the same time he wears a fine ruffled shirt and a laced waistcoat, with a fine handkerchief on his head." Detroit had much of the character of the mixed community of Kahnawake on the St. Lawrence.

Family and kinship were also cast in the Indian pattern. Households frequently consisted of several related families, but wives limited their births, having on average only two or three children. There were arranged marriages and occasional polygamy, but women had easy access to divorce and enjoyed property rights. Yet the people focused their activities on commerce and identified themselves overwhelmingly as Catholic. More frequently than not choosing a path of mutual accommodation, the French and Indians established some of the most interesting and distinct of North American communities.

New England

Just as New Spain and New France had their official church, so did the people of New England: local communities in all the New England colonies but Rhode Island were governed by Puritan congregations. Under the plan established in Massachusetts, the local church of a community was free to run its own affairs under the guidance of the General Court (the governor and the representatives selected by the towns). The Puritan colonies allotted each congregation a tract of communal land. Church members divided this land among themselves on the basis of status and seniority, laying out central villages like Deerfield and building churches (called meetinghouses) that were maintained through taxation. Adult male church members constituted the freemen of the town, and thus there was very little distinction between religious and secular authority. At the town meeting the freemen chose their minister, voted on his salary and support, and elected local men to offices ranging from town clerk to fence viewer.

The Puritan tradition, however, was a curious mix of freedom and repression. Although local communities had considerable autonomy, they were tightly bound by the restrictions of the Puritan faith and the General Court. Contrary to the beliefs of many, the Puritans did not come to America to create a society where religion could be freely practiced but to establish their own version of the "right and perfect way," which placed severe restraints on individuals. The General Court, for example, passed a statute threatening that "if any man shall exceed the bounds of moderation, we shall punish him severely." Specifics were left to the imagination. Not only did the Puritans exile dissidents such as Roger Williams and Anne Hutchinson (see Chapter 3), they banned Anglicans and Baptists and jailed, tortured, and even executed members of the Society of Friends, commonly known as the Quakers.

One of the first formal arguments for religious toleration was made by the New Englander Roger Williams, leader of dissenting Rhode Island, in his book *The Bloudy Tenent of Persecution* (1644). "Forced worship," he wrote, "stinks in God's nostrils." This argument gained increasing appeal following the religious excesses of the English civil war. In 1661, lamenting "the sad experience" of the previous generation of religious conflicts, restored King Charles II ordered a stop to religious persecution in Massachusetts. The new climate of opinion was best expressed by the English philosopher John Locke in his *Letter on Tolerance* (1688). Churches were voluntary societies, he argued, and could work only through persuasion. That a religion was sanctioned by the state was no evidence of its truth, because different nations had different official religions. Consequently, the state had no legitimate concern with religious belief. Locke's ideas were embodied in the Toleration Act, passed by Parliament in 1689. New England at first resisted it, but under pressure from English authorities, Massachusetts and Connecticut reluctantly allowed other Protestant denominations to begin worshipping openly in 1700. In both colonies, however, the Puritan, or as it was now called, Congregationalist Church (because of its self-governing congregations) continued to be officially supported through taxation. (It would not be "disestablished" in Massachusetts until 1833.) By the 1730s there were Anglican, Baptist, and Presbyterian congregations in many New England towns.

The system of town and church government was well suited to population growth. As towns grew too large for the available land, groups of residents left together, "hiving off" to form new churches and towns elsewhere. An intricate network of roads and rivers knit the region together. Seventy-five years after the Indians of southern New England suffered their final defeat in King Philip's War (see Chapter 3), Puritan farm communities had taken up most of the available land of Massachusetts, Connecticut, and Rhode Island, leaving only a few communities of Pequots, Narragansets, and Wampanoags on restricted reservations. Northern Algonquians and Catholic Iroquois allied with the French in Quebec, however, maintained a defensive barrier preventing New Englanders from expanding northward into Maine, New Hampshire, and the region later called Vermont. Deerfield represented the far northern limit of safe settlement. By midcentury, then, as the result of growing population, New England was reaching the limit of its land supply.

The Middle Colonies

The colony of New York had one of the most ethnically diverse populations on the continent, in striking contrast to the ethnically homogeneous neighboring New England colonies of Connecticut and Massachusetts. At midcentury society along the lower Hudson River, including the counties in northern New Jersey,

The House of the Seven Gables in Salem, Massachusetts, was constructed in the seventeenth century. In this style of architecture, function prevailed over form as structures grew to accommodate their residents; rooms were added where and when they were needed. In England, wood for building was scarce, but the abundance of forests in North America created the conditions for a golden age of wood construction.

was a veritable mosaic of ethnic communities: the Dutch of Flatbush, the Huguenots of New Rochelle, the Flemish of Bergen County, and the Scots of Perth Amboy were but a few. African Americans, both slave and free, made up more than 15 percent of the lower Hudson population. Congregations of Puritans, Baptists, Quakers, and Catholics worshiped without legal hindrance. New York City also was home to the oldest Jewish community in the country, established in 1654; several hundred Jewish families attended services in North America's first synagogue, built in 1730. Among these communities there was a great deal of intermingling (as there was at places such as Kahnawake), but different ethnic and religious groups would long retain their distinctions, which made New York something of a cultural "salad bowl" if not a "melting pot."

New York City grew by leaps and bounds in the eighteenth century, but the elite who had inherited the rich lands and great manors along the upper Hudson chose to rent to tenants rather than to sell, diminishing the region's attractiveness to immigrants. By contrast, Pennsylvania was what one German immigrant called "heaven for farmers." The colony's Quaker proprietors were willing to sell land to anyone who could pay the relatively modest prices. Thus as the region around New York City filled up, immigrants by the thousand made the decision to land at Philadelphia, Pennsylvania's growing port city on the Delaware River. During the eighteenth century the population of this region and an extended area that encompassed portions of New Jersey, Delaware, and Maryland grew more dramatically than any other in North America. Here, immigration played the dominant role in achieving the astonishing annual growth rate of nearly 4 percent. Boasting some of the best farmland in North America, the region was soon exporting abundant produce through Philadelphia.

The Quakers who had founded Pennsylvania quickly became a minority, but, unlike the Puritans, they were generally comfortable with religious and ethnic pluralism. Many of the founders of the Society of Friends had been imprisoned for their beliefs in pre-Restoration England, and they were determined to prevent a repetition of this injustice in their own province. William Penn himself had been prominent in the struggle for religious toleration. "Force never yet made a good Christian," he argued. Indeed, the Quakers were opposed to all signs of rank, refusing to doff their hats to superiors but greeting all comers, whatever their station, with the extended handshake of brotherhood. To a remarkable extent, these attitudes extended to relations between the sexes as well. English founder George Fox had proclaimed that "in souls there is no sex," and among American Friends, women preached equally with men.

These Quaker attitudes were well suited to the ethnically and religiously diverse population of Pennsylvania. Although the Society of Friends remained the affiliation of the governing elite, it never became an established church. Most German immigrants were Lutherans or Calvinists, most North Britons Presbyterians, and there were plenty of Anglicans and Baptists as well. These churches constituted one of the cornerstones of Pennsylvania community life.

The institutions of government were another pillar of community organization. Colonial officials appointed justices of the peace from among the leading local men, and these justices provided judicial authority for the countryside. Property-owning farmers chose their own local officials. Country communities were tied together by kinship bonds and by bartering and trading among neighbors. The substantial stone houses and great barns of the Pennsylvania countryside testified to the social stability and prosperity of this system. The communities of the middle colonies, however, were more loosely bound than those of New England. Rates of mobility were considerably higher, with about half the population moving on in any given decade. Because land was sold in individual lots rather than in communal parcels, farmers tended to disperse themselves at will over the open countryside. Villages gradually developed at crossroads and ferries but with relatively little forethought or planning. It was Pennsylvania, which emphasized individual settlement, that provided the basic model for American expansion.

The Backcountry

By 1750 Pennsylvania's exploding population had pushed beyond the first range of the Appalachian highlands. Settlers occupied the northern reaches of the

This two-story log house, built in Pennsylvania in the early eighteenth century, is one of the oldest surviving examples of the method and style of log construction introduced in America by the Scandinavian colonists on the lower Delaware River. Learning New World farming and woodland hunting techniques from the Indians, these settlers forged a tradition of settlement that proved enormously successful for pioneers.

Great Valley, which extended southwest from Pennsylvania into Virginia. Although they hoped to become commercial farmers, these settlers began more modestly, planting Indian corn and raising hogs, hunting in the woods for meat and furs, and building log cabins. This strategy had originated with the settlers of the New Sweden colony on the lower Delaware River. Scandinavian immigrants brought their hunting traditions and introduced log cabin construction to North America. From the Delaware Indians they incorporated the methods of New World farming and woodland hunting, just as the Indians took from them the use of firearms and metal tools and began to build log structures of their own. These were some of the most successful cross-cultural adaptations of the eighteenth century.

The movement into the Pennsylvania and Virginia backcountry that began during the 1720s was the first of the great pioneer treks that would take Americans into the continental interior. Many, perhaps most, of these pioneers held no legal title to the lands they occupied; they simply hacked out and defended their squatters' claims from Indian tribes and all other comers. Many of these backcountry settlers came from the northern borders of England and Ireland, where there was considerable clan and ethnic violence, and adapted well to the violence of the backcountry. To the Delawares and Shawnees who had been pushed into the interior, or the Cherokees who occupied the Appalachian highlands to the south, however, these pioneers presented a new and deadly threat. Their rising fears and resentments over the expanding colonial population triggered much eighteenth-century warfare.

One of the distinctive characteristics of the backcountry was the settlers' disdain for rank. "The rain don't know broadcloth from bluejeans," they said. But the myth of frontier equality was simply that—myth. Most pioneers owned little or no land, while "big men" held great tracts and dominated local communities with their bombastic style of personal leadership. Here the men were warriors, the women workers. The story was told of one pioneer whose wife began to "jaw at" him. "He pulled off his breeches and threw them down to her, telling her to 'put them on and wear them.'"

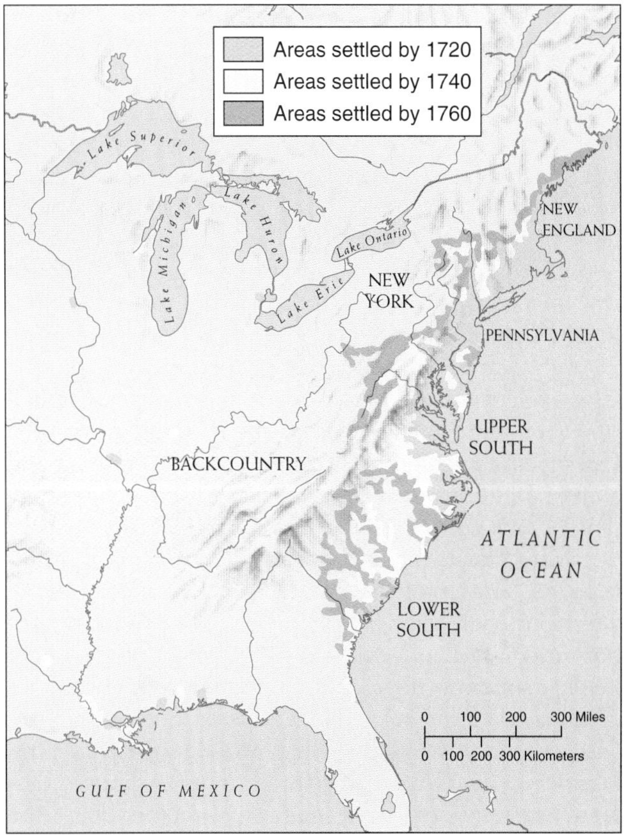

Spread of Settlement: Movement into the Backcountry, 1720–1760 *The spread of settlement from 1720 to 1760 shows the movement of population into the backcountry in the midcentury.*

The South

The Chesapeake and the Lower South were tri-racial societies, with intermingled communities of white colonists and black slaves, along with substantial Indian communities living on the fringes of colonial settlement. Much of the population growth of the region resulted from the forced migration of enslaved Africans, who by 1750 made up 40 percent of the population. Colonial settlement had filled not only the Tidewater area of the southern Atlantic coast but much of the Piedmont as well. Specializing in rice, tobacco, and other commercial crops, these colonies were overwhelmingly rural. Farms and plantations were dispersed across the countryside, and villages or towns were few.

English authorities made the Church of England the state religion in the Chesapeake colonies. Residents paid taxes to support the Church and were required to attend services. No other churches were allowed into Virginia and Maryland, and dissenters were excluded or exiled. Before the 1750s, the Toleration Act was little enforced in the South; at the same time, the Anglican establishment was internally weak. It maintained neither a colonial bishop nor local institutions for training clergy. In Carolina and Georgia, neither Anglicanism nor any other denomination rested on a firm foundation.

Along the rice coast, the dominant institution of social life was the large plantation. Transforming the tangle of woods and swamps along the region's rivers into an ordered pattern of dams, dikes, and flooded fields required a heavy capital investment, which meant that rice cultivation could be undertaken only by men of means. By midcentury, established plantations typically were dominated by a large main house, generally located on a spot of high ground overlooking the fields. Drayton Hall near Charleston, a mansion of the period that still survives, was built of pink brick in classically symmetrical style, with hand-carved interior moldings of imported Caribbean mahogany. Nearby, but a world apart, were the slave quarters, rough wooden cabins lining two sides of a muddy pathway near the outbuildings and barns. In this contrast between "big house" and "quarters" the Lower South was the closest thing in North America to the societies of the Caribbean sugar islands.

Grand plantation houses could be found in the Chesapeake as well. However, because tobacco, unlike rice, could be grown profitably in small plots, the Chesapeake included a greater variety of farmers and a correspondingly diverse landscape. Tobacco quickly drained the soil of its nutrients, and plantings had to be shifted to fresh ground every few years. Former tobacco land could be planted with corn for several years but then required twenty years or more of rest before reuse. The landscape was thus a patchwork of fields, many in various stages of ragged second growth. The poorest farmers lived in wooden cabins little better than the shacks of the slaves. More prosperous farm families lived with two or three slaves in houses that were nevertheless considerably smaller than the substantial homes of New England.

In the Lower South, where the plantations were little worlds unto themselves, there was relatively little community life outside the plantation. But by midcentury the Chesapeake had given rise to well-developed neighborhoods based on kinship networks and economic connections. Encouraging the developing sense of community more than any other institution was the county court, which held both executive and judicial power. On court day, white people of all ranks held a great gathering that included public business, horse racing, and perhaps a barbecue. The gentleman justices of the county, appointed by the governor, included the heads of the leading planter families. These men in turn selected the grand jury, composed of substantial freeholders. One of the most significant bonding forces in this free white population was the growing sense of racial solidarity that developed in response to the increasing proportion of African slaves dispersed throughout the neighborhoods.

Traditional Culture in the New World

In each of these North American colonial societies the family and kinship, the church, and the local community were the most significant factors in everyday life. Throughout the continent, colonists tended to live much as they had in their European homelands at the time their colonies were settled. Thus the residents of New Mexico, Quebec, and New England continued to be attached to the religious passions of the seventeenth century long after their mother countries had put those religious controversies aside in favor of imperial geopolitics. Nostalgia for Europe helped to fix a conservative colonial attitude toward culture.

These were oral cultures, depending on the transmission of information by the spoken word rather than through print, on the passage of traditions through storytelling and song, music and crafts. North American colonial folk cultures, traditional and suspicious of change, preserved an essentially medieval world view. The rhythms of life were regulated by the hours of sunlight and the seasons of the year. People rose with the sun and went to bed soon after it went down. The demands of the season determined their working routines. They farmed with simple tools and were subject to the whims of nature, for drought, flood, or pestilence might quickly sweep away their efforts. Experience told them that the natural world imposed limitations within which men and women had to learn to live. Even patterns of reproduction conformed to nature's cycle: in nearly every European colonial community of North America the number of births peaked in late winter, then fell to a low point during the summer; for African Americans, by contrast, births peaked in early summer. Historians have not yet

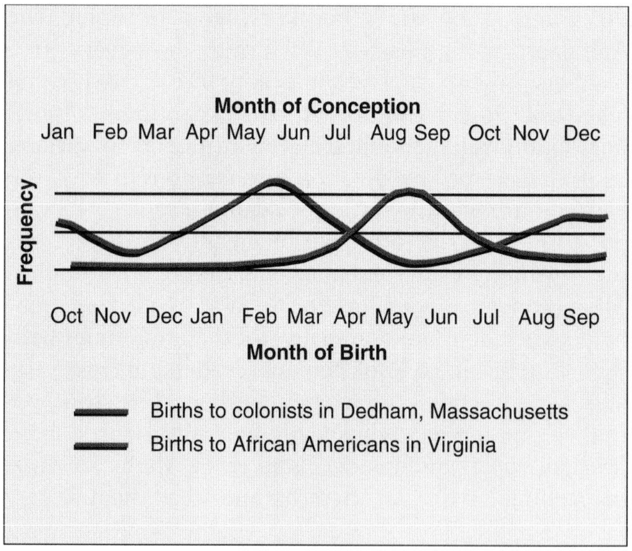

Monthly Frequency of Successful Conceptions
Human reproduction in colonial America corresponded to cycles. But European colonists and African American slaves had different patterns, with white births peaking in March, black births peaking in May and June. Historians do not yet know the cause of this variation, but it is probably tied to old English and African traditions.

Source: James A. Henretta and Gregory H. Nobles, *Evolution and Revolution: American Society, 1600–1820* (Lexington, Mass.: Heath, 1987), 37; Mechal Sobel, *The World They Made Together: Black and White Values in Eighteenth-Century Virginia* (Princeton: Princeton University Press, 1987), 67.

accounted for this intriguing pattern or provided an explanation for the differences between white and black families, but apparently there was some "inner" seasonal clock tied to old European and African patterns. Human sexual activity itself seemed to fluctuate with the rural working demands created by the seasons.

These were also communal cultures. In Quebec villagers worked side by side to repair the roads, in New Mexico they collectively maintained the irrigation canals, in New England they gathered in town meetings to decide the dates when common fields were to be plowed, sowed, and harvested. When in 1620 the Pilgrims and the other Mayflower passengers signed their compact, promising "due submission" to "the general good," they explicitly set down principles with which most North American colonists could agree. Even the artifacts of everyday life reveal this collective emphasis. Houses offered little privacy, with families often sleeping together in the same chamber, sitting together on benches rather than in chairs, and taking their supper from a common bowl or trencher. For most North American colonists of the mid-eighteenth century, the community was more important than the individual.

Throughout North America, most colonists continued the traditional European occupation of working the land. Plantation agriculture was designed to be a commercial system, in which crops were commodities for sale. Commercial farming also developed in some particularly fertile areas, notably southeastern Pennsylvania, which became known as the breadbasket of North America, as well as the country surrounding colonial cities such as New York, Boston, and Quebec. The majority of the farmers of eighteenth-century North America, however, grew crops and raised livestock for their own needs or for local barter, and communities were largely self-sufficient. Most farmers attempted to produce small surpluses as well, which they sold to pay their taxes and buy some manufactured goods. But rather than specializing in the production of one or two crops for sale, they attempted to remain as independent of the market as possible, diversifying their activities. The primary goal was ownership of land and the assurance that children and descendants would be able to settle within the community on lands nearby.

Rural households frequently practiced crafts or trades as a sideline. Farm men were also blacksmiths, coopers, weavers, or carpenters. Some farm women were independent traders in dairy products or eggs. Others became midwives and medicinal experts serving the community. In one Maine community, for example, the midwife Martha Ballard delivered 797 babies over twenty-seven years, and both male and female patients came to her for salves, pills, syrups, ointments, or advice.

In colonial cities, artisans and craftsmen worked at their trades full time. Artisans also followed tradition by organizing themselves according to the European craft system. In the colonial cities of the Atlantic coast, carpenters, iron makers, blacksmiths, shipwrights, and scores of other tradesmen had their own self-governing associations. Young men who wished to pursue a trade served several years as apprentices, working in exchange for learning the skills and secrets of the craft. After completing their apprenticeships they sought employment in a shop. Their search often required them to migrate to some other area, thus becoming "journeymen." Most craftsmen remained at the journeyman level for their whole careers. But by building a good name and carefully saving, journeymen hoped to become master craftsmen, opening shops and employing journeymen and apprentices of their own. As in farming, the ultimate goal was independence, control over one's work.

With the exception of midwifery, there were few opportunities for women outside the household. By law, husbands held managerial rights over family property, but widows received support in the form of a one-third lifetime interest, known as "dower," in a deceased husband's real estate (the rest of the estate being divided among the heirs). And in certain occupations, such as printing (which had a tradition of employing women), widows succeeded their husbands in business. As a result, some colonial women played active roles in eighteenth-century journalism. Ann Smith Franklin, Benjamin Franklin's sister-in-law, took over the operation of her husband's Rhode Island shop after his death. Widow Cornelia Smith Bradford continued to publish her deceased husband's Philadelphia paper and was an important force in publishing throughout the 1750s.

The Frontier Heritage

The colonial societies of eighteenth-century North America also shared perspectives unique to their frontier heritage. European colonists came from Old World societies in which land was scarce and monopolized by property-owning elites. They settled in a continent where, for the most part, land was abundant and cheap. This was probably the most important distinction between North America and Europe. American historians once tied the existence of this "free land" directly to the development of democracy. But although extensive lands were available in all the colonies of North America, the colonial experience encouraged assumptions that were anything but democratic.

One of the most important and widely accepted of these assumptions was that forced labor was legitimate. A woman of eighteenth-century South Carolina once offered advice on how to achieve a good

A carpenter and spinner from The Book of Trades, *an eighteenth-century* British *survey of the crafts practiced in colonial America. In colonial cities artisans organized themselves into the traditional European craft system, with apprentices, journeymen, and masters. There were few opportunities for the employment of women outside the household, but women sometimes earned income by establishing sidelines as midwives or spinners.*

living. "Get a few slaves," she declared, and "beat them well to make them work hard." In a land where free men and women could work for themselves on their own plot of ground, there was little incentive to work for wages. As a result, labor was in short supply throughout the colonies. Coercion was one of the few ways a landowner could secure an agricultural work force. In the Spanish borderlands, captured Apache children were made lifetime servants, and the Indian slave trade flourished through the eighteenth century. In Quebec one could see African American slaves from the French Caribbean working side by side with enslaved Indians captured by other tribes in the West and sold to French traders. In Philadelphia, according to Benjamin Franklin, wages for free workers were so high that most of the unskilled labor was "performed chiefly by indentured servants." All the colonists came from European cultures that believed in social hierarchy and subordination, and involuntary servitude was easily incorporated into their world view.

At least half the immigrants to eighteenth-century British America arrived as indentured servants. This system allowed poor immigrants to arrange passage across the Atlantic in exchange for four or five years of service in America. Usually indentured servants were single men, often skilled artisans. Sometimes families without means emigrated as "redemptioners." Under this system, they arranged with the ship's owner to pay their passage on arrival in North America. If no one in the colonies stepped forth to pay, they sold themselves into service for the payment. Thus family members were sometimes separated. In addition, during the eighteenth century the British sent over, mostly to the Chesapeake, some

50,000 convicts sentenced to seven or fourteen years at hard labor. One historian, accounting for the cost of passage and upkeep, estimates that indentured servants earned their masters, on average, about fifty pounds sterling over their terms of service, the equivalent of something like four or five thousand dollars in today's values.

All classes of bound laborers remained on board ship after arrival in America, awaiting inspection by potential buyers, who poked muscles, peered into open mouths, and pinched women. Although servants were not slaves, to the men and women lined up for inspection that may have seemed a distinction without a difference. There were other similarities between indentured servitude and slavery. The ocean crossing was frequently traumatic. One immigrant described a passage across the Atlantic to Philadelphia in which several hundred people were packed like sardines in the ship's hold. "The ship is filled with pitiful signs of distress," he wrote, "smells, fumes, horrors, vomiting, various kinds of sea sickness, fever, dysentery, headaches, heat, constipation, boils, scurvy, cancer, mouth-rot, and similar afflictions. In such misery all the people on board pray and cry pitifully together." In 1750 Pennsylvania was finally compelled to pass a law to prevent the overcrowding of ships filled with indentured passengers. Especially in the Chesapeake, the life of an indentured servant could be filled with harsh and grueling labor, just like a slave's. Running away was common, although it was usually unsuccessful and resulted in extra time to serve: in Pennsylvania a runaway was liable for five times the lost service, in Maryland ten times!

Unlike slaves, however, those servants who endured had a chance of freedom. "Freedom dues" might include a suit of clothes, tools, money, and sometimes land. The social mobility of former servants was limited, however. Of the thousands of men who came to the British colonies under indenture during the seventeenth and early eighteenth centuries, only about 20 percent achieved positions of moderate comfort. The majority died before their terms were completed, returned to England, or continued in miserable poverty. But opportunities for advancement increased somewhat with the overall prosperity of the eighteenth-century British colonies. By midcentury, the chances of moderate success for former servants were probably better than fifty-fifty. The majority of redemptioners, for example, appear to have become small farmers.

The expectation of property ownership was a second important assumption that flowed from the frontier heritage and abundance of land in colonial America. This expectation led to rising popular demands in all regions that more and more land be taken from the Indian inhabitants and opened to white settlement. Some colonists justified the resulting wars of dispossession by arguing, as Puritans did, that Indians deserved to lose their lands because they had failed to use them to their utmost capacity. Others simply maintained that Indians should be dispossessed because they were "savages." But whatever their specific justifications, the majority of colonists—whether British, Spanish, or French—accepted the violence and brutality directed against the Indians as an essential aspect of colonial life. Thus did the Puritan minister Cotton Mather praise Hannah Dustin, a New England woman who escaped her captors during King William's War by killing and scalping nine sleeping Indians, including two women and six children. With this as the model for the behavior of captive women, one can understand why Eunice Williams was hesitant to return to Deerfield after she had married an Indian.

DIVERGING SOCIAL AND POLITICAL PATTERNS

Despite these important similarities among the colonial regions of North America, the eighteenth century also marked a period when the experience of the British colonies began to diverge sharply from that of the French and Spanish. Immigration, economic growth, and provincial political struggles all pushed British colonists in a radically new direction.

Population Growth

All the colonial regions of North America experienced unprecedented growth in the eighteenth century. "Our people must at least be doubled every twenty years," wrote Benjamin Franklin in a remarkable 1751 essay on population, and he was very nearly right. In 1700 there were 290,000 colonists north of Mexico; fifty years later they had grown to approximately 1.3 million, an average annual growth rate of about 3 percent. Typical preindustrial societies grow at rates of less than 1 percent per year, approximately the pace of Europe's expansion in the eighteenth century. But the colonial societies of North America experienced what English economist Thomas Malthus, writing at the end of the eighteenth century, described as "a rapidity of increase probably without parallel in history."

High fertility played an important role in this extraordinary growth. It was common for women in the British colonies to bear seven or more children, and colonial women in the French villages along the St. Lawrence or the towns of New Mexico were equally fertile. In addition, mortality rates were relatively low: in most colonial areas there were fewer than 30 deaths for every 1,000 persons, a rate 15 or 20 percent lower than in Europe. Moreover, levels of infant mortality were low. Blessed with fertile lands and the effective-

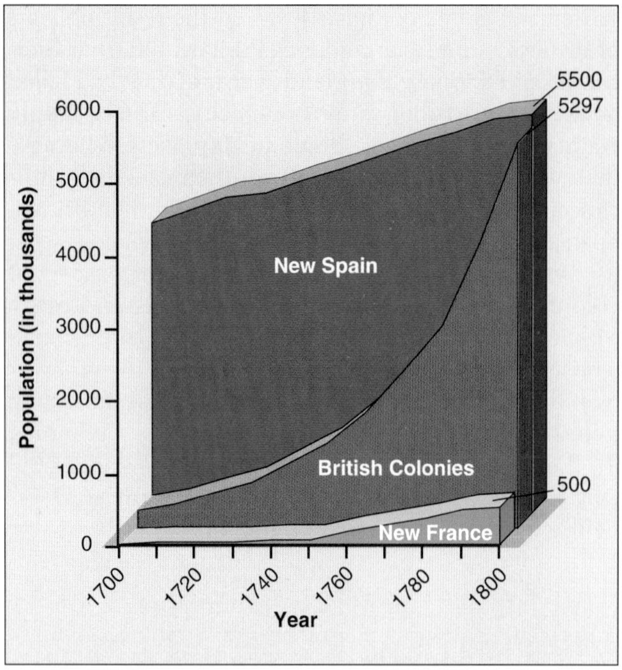

Estimated Total Population of New Spain, New France, and the British North American Colonies, 1700–1780 *Although the populations of all three North American colonial empires grew in the eighteenth century, the explosive growth of the British colonies was unmatched.*

Source: *Historical Statistics of the United States* (Washington, D.C.: Government Printing Office, 1976), 1168.

ness of Indian agricultural techniques, North America had no famines. For the colonists, North America was a remarkably healthy environment.

Yet although all North American colonial societies had high fertility rates, the British colonies grew far more rapidly than those of other nations. The reason for this contrast was the very different colonial policies on immigration. In New France and New Spain restrictive policies curbed the number of European immigrants. By contrast, English authorities allowed a massive immigration of their own subjects to North America in the seventeenth century. A total of 150,000 English men and women had relocated to the colonies by 1700, providing a substantial population base for further growth. In addition, the British were the only colonial power to encourage the immigration of foreign nationals to their colonies. (See "Immigration and Community: The Changing Face of Ethnicity in America, to 1800" on page 222.)

Social Class

Although traditional working roles were transferred to North America, attempts to transplant the European class system by creating monopolies on land were far less successful. In New France the landowning seigneurs claimed privileges similar to those enjoyed by their aristocratic counterparts at home; the Spanish system of encomienda and the great manors created by the Dutch, and after them the English along the Hudson River, also represented attempts to bring the essence of European feudalism to North America. But in most areas, because settlers had relatively free access to land, these monopolies proved difficult or impossible to maintain. There was, of course, a system of economic rank and an unequal distribution of wealth, prestige, and power. North American society was not aristocratic, but neither was it without social hierarchy.

In New Spain the official criterion for status was racial purity. *Españoles* (Spaniards) or *gente de razón* (literally, "people of reason") occupied the top rung of the social ladder, with mestizos, mulattoes, and others on descending levels; African slaves and Indians were at the bottom. In the isolated northern borderlands, however, these distinctions tended to disappear, with *castas* (persons of mixed background) enjoying considerably more opportunity. Mestizos who acquired land might suddenly be reclassified as españoles. "The only two castes we know of here are the gente de razón and Indians," observed a missionary in California, "and all the former are considered Spaniards." Similarily, census takers in eighteenth-century Texas listed everyone but Indians as españoles, producing curious listings such as "Spaniard from Canada" or "Spaniard from France." Even so, Spanish and French colonial societies were cut in the style of the Old World, with its hereditary ranks and titles. The landlords of New France and the Spanish borderlands may have lacked the means to accumulate real wealth, but they lived lives of elegance compared to the hard toil of the people who owed them labor service or rent.

The upper class of British colonial society—the wealthiest 10 percent of all whites—was made up of large landowners, merchants, and prosperous professionals. In the eighteenth century, property valued at £2,000 marked a family as well-to-do, and £5,000 was real wealth. Leading merchants, with annual incomes in excess of £500, lived in opulence. Despite their lack of titles, the wealthy planters and merchants in the British colonies lived far more extravagantly than the seigneurs of New France or the dons of the Spanish borderlands. What separated the culture of class in the British colonies from that of New France or New Mexico, however, was not so much the material conditions of life as the prevailing attitude toward social rank. In the Catholic cultures, the upper class attempted to obscure its origins, claiming descent from European nobility. But in British North America people celebrated social mobility. The class system was remarkably open, and the entrance

An eighteenth-century Mexican painting of a mixed family, an example of a genre of portraits depicting various racial castas. *Here, a Spanish father and Indian mother produce a* mestizo *child.*

of newly successful planters, commercial farmers, and merchants into the upper ranks was not only possible but frequent—although by midcentury most upper-class families had inherited, not earned, their wealth.

To be sure, there was a large lower class in the British colonies. Slaves, bound servants, and poor laboring families made up at least 40 percent of the population. For them the standard of living did not rise above bare subsistence. Most lived from hand to mouth, often suffering through seasons of severe privation. A small proportion of poor whites could expect their condition to improve during their lifetimes, but slaves were a permanently servile population. Enslaved African Americans stood apart from the gains in the standard of living enjoyed by immigrants from Europe. Their lives had been degraded beyond measure from the conditions prevailing in their native lands.

The feature of the class system most frequently commented on by eighteenth-century observers was not the character or composition of the lower ranks but rather the size and strength of the middle class, a rank entirely absent in the colonies of France and Spain. As one Pennsylvanian wrote at midcentury, "The people of this province are generally of the middling sort." More than half the population of the British colonies, and nearly 70 percent of all white settlers, might be so classified. Most were families of landowning farmers of small to moderate means, but the group also included artisans, craftsmen, and small shopkeepers.

At the low end, the colonial middle class included families whose standard of living was barely above subsistence; at the high end were those whose holdings approached real wealth. Households solidly in the center of this broad ranking owned land or other property worth approximately £500 and earned the equivalent of about £100 per year. They enjoyed a standard of living higher than that of the great majority of people in England and Europe. The low mortality of British Americans was important testimony to generally better living conditions. Touring the British Isles at midcentury, Benjamin Franklin was shocked at the squalid conditions of farmers and workers, and he wrote of his renewed appreciation of America, where everyone "lives in a tidy, warm house, has plenty of good food and fuel, with whole cloths from head to foot, the manufacture perhaps of his own family." For the majority of British colonists in North America it was possible to achieve "roast beef and apple pie" comfort.

Economic Growth and Increasing Inequality

One of the most important differences among North American colonial regions in the eighteenth century was the economic stagnation in New France and New Spain compared with the impressive economic growth of the British colonies. Weighed down by royal bureaucracies and overbearing regulations, neither the French Crescent nor New Spain evidenced much prosperity. In British North America, however, per capita production grew at an annual rate of .5 percent. Granted, this was considerably less than the average annual growth rate of 1.5 percent that prevailed during the era of industrialization, from the early nineteenth through the mid-twentieth century. But as economic growth steadily increased the size of the economic pie, most middle- and upper-class British Americans began to enjoy improved living conditions, better than those of any people in Europe. Improving standards of living and relatively open access to land encouraged British colonists to see theirs as a society where hard work and savings could translate into prosperity, thus producing an upward spiral of economic growth.

At the same time, this growth itself produced increasing social inequality. In the commercial cities, for example, prosperity was accompanied by a concentration of assets in the hands of wealthy families. In

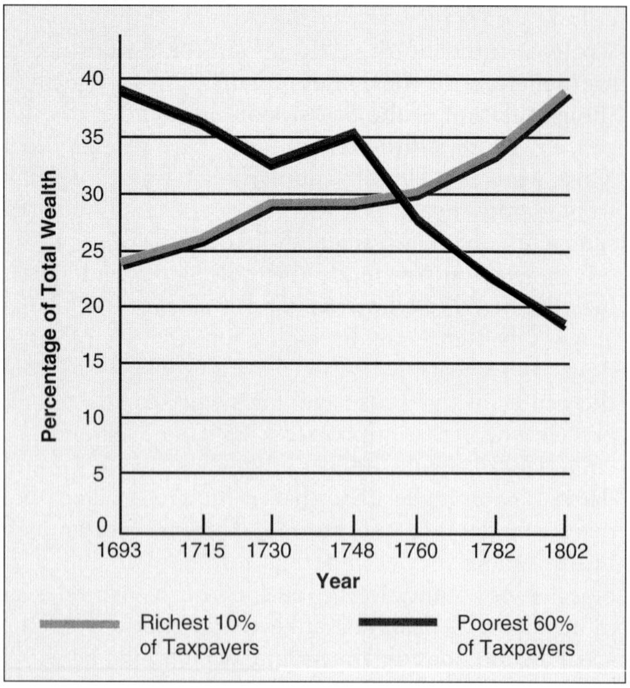

Distribution of Assessed Taxable Wealth in Eighteenth-Century Chester County *This graph charts the concentration of assets in the hands of wealthy families. From 1693 to 1802 the percentage of total wealth held by the richest 10% of taxpayers rose from 24% to 38%, while the percentage held by the poorest 60% of taxpayers fell from 39% to 18%. This pattern was typical for regions dominated by commerce.*

Source: James Lemon and Gary Nash, "The Distribution of Wealth in Eighteenth-Century America," *Journal of Social History* 2 (1968):1–24.

Boston and Philadelphia at the beginning of the century, the wealthiest 10 percent of households owned about half of the taxable property; by about midcentury this small group owned 65 percent or more. In the commercial farming region of Chester County in southeastern Pennsylvania, the holdings of the wealthiest tenth increased more modestly, from 24 to 30 percent during the first half of the century. But at the same time the share of taxable property owned by the poorest third fell from 17 to 6 percent. The general standard of living may have been rising, but the rich were getting richer and the poor poorer. The greatest concentrations of wealth occurred in the cities and in those regions dominated by commercial farming, whether slave or free, while the greatest economic equality continued to be found in areas of self-sufficient farming such as the backcountry.

Another eighteenth-century trend confounded the hope of social mobility in the countryside. As population grew, and as generations succeeded one another in older settlements, all the available land in the towns was taken up. Under the pressure of increased demand, land prices rose almost beyond the reach of families of modest means. As a family's land was divided among the heirs of the second and third generations, parcels became ever smaller and thus more intensively farmed. Eventually the soil was exhausted.

By the eighteenth century, many farm communities did not have sufficient land to provide those of the emerging generation with farms of their own. This problem was particularly acute in New England, where colonists were hemmed in by the French and Indians on the north and the great landed estates of the Hudson Valley on the west. There were notable increases in the number of landless poor in the towns of New England as well as the disturbing appearance of the "strolling poor"—homeless people who traveled from town to town looking for work or a handout. Destitute families crowded into Boston, which by midcentury was expending more than £5,000 annually on relief for the poor, who were required to wear a large red P on their clothing. In other regions, land shortages in the older settlements almost inevitably prompted people to leave in search of cheap or free land.

Young men unable to obtain land in hometowns often moved to the towns and cities of the seaboard, for New England also enjoyed a strong seafaring tradition. Fishing and shipping had first become important during the late seventeenth century, as merchants struggled to find a successful method of earning foreign exchange. The expanding slave market in the South opened new opportunities, prompting the growth of thriving coastal ports such as New Haven, Newport, Salem, and Boston. By midcentury New England had become the most urban of all North America's regions. Boston, the

Wealth Held by Richest 10 Percent of the Population: Northern and Southern British Colonies Compared, 1770

	North	South
Frontier	33	40
Rural subsistence farming	35	45
Rural commercial farming	45	65
Cities	60	65
Overall	45	55

Source: Jackson Turner Main, *The Social Structure of Revolutionary America* (Princeton: Princeton University Press, 1965), 276n.

largest city in the British colonies, was the metropolis of a region that included not only New England but also the maritime settlements of Nova Scotia and Newfoundland, where New England merchants dominated commerce and recruited seamen for their fishing and shipping fleets.

Contrasts in Colonial Politics

The administration of the Spanish and French colonies was highly centralized. French Canada was ruled by a superior council including the royal governor (in charge of military affairs), the *intendant* (responsible for civil administration), and the bishop of Quebec. New Spain was governed by the Council of the Indies, which sat in Spain, and direct executive authority over all political affairs was exercised by the viceroy in Mexico City. Although local communities enjoyed informal independence, the highly bureaucratized and centralized governments of the French Crescent and the Spanish Borderlands left little room for the development of vigorous traditions of self-government.

The situation in the British colonies was quite different. During the early eighteenth century the British government of Prime Minister Robert Walpole assumed that a decentralized administration would best accomplish the nation's economic goals. Contented colonies, Walpole argued, would present far fewer problems. "One would not strain any point where it can be of no service to our King or country," a British official advised the governor of South Carolina in 1722. "The government should be as easy and mild as possible." Each of the colonies was administered by royally appointed governors, its taxes and finances set by constituent assemblies. Those who owned property could vote for representatives to the assembly. Because many people—mostly white males—owned property, the proportion of adult white men able to vote was 50 percent or higher in all the British colonies. Proportionally, the electorate of the British colonies was the largest in the world.

That did not mean, however, that the British colonies were democratic. The basic principle of order in eighteenth-century British culture was the ideal of deference to natural hierarchies. The well-ordered family—in which children were to be strictly governed by their parents and wives by their husbands—was the common metaphor for civil order. The occupant of each rung on the social ladder was entitled to the respect of those below. Members of subordinate groups, such as women, the non-English, African American slaves, servants, and Indians—who in some colonies constituted nine of every ten adults in the population—could not vote or hold public office. Moreover, for the most part those men who did vote chose wealthy landowners, planters, or merchants to serve as their leaders. Thus, provincial assemblies were controlled by colonial elites.

The important political developments in eighteenth-century British North America, then, had nothing to do with what we commonly call democracy. To educated British colonists, the word "democracy" implied rule by the mob, the normal order of things turned upside-down. Over the century there was, however, an important trend toward stronger institutions of representative government. By midcentury most colonial assemblies had achieved considerable power over provincial affairs and enjoyed a parity of authority with governors and other imperial officials. They collected local revenues and allocated funds for government programs, asserted the right to audit the accounts of public officers, and in some cases even acquired the power to approve the appointment of provincial officials. Royal governors sometimes balked at such claims of power, but because the assemblies controlled the purse strings, most governors were unable to resist this trend.

The potential power of the assemblies was compromised somewhat by the competition among elite families for patronage and government contracts. The royal governors who were most successful at realizing their agendas were those who became adept at playing off one provincial faction against another. All this conflict had the important effect of schooling the colonial elite in the art of politics. It was not democratic politics, but schooling in the ways of patronage, coalition-building, and behind-the-scenes intrigue had important implications for the development of American institutions.

THE CULTURAL TRANSFORMATION OF BRITISH NORTH AMERICA

Despite broad similarities, therefore, the colonial regions of North America developed along divergent lines during the eighteenth century. The British colonies were marked by increasing ethnic diversity, economic growth, social tensions, and conflictual politics that proved to be training for self-government. The middle decades of the eighteenth century also witnessed significant cultural transformation as new ideas and writings associated with the Enlightenment made their way across the Atlantic on the same ships that transported European goods. In New Spain and New France, by contrast, colonial officials worked diligently to suppress these challenging new ideas. The Catholic Church effectively banned the works of hundreds of authors. In Mexico officials of the Inquisition conducted house-to-house searches in pursuit of prohibited texts that they feared had been smuggled into the country.

The Enlightenment Challenge

Drawing from the discoveries of Galileo, Copernicus, and the seventeenth-century scientists René Descartes and Sir Isaac Newton, Enlightenment thinkers in Britain and on the Continent argued that the universe was governed by natural laws that people could understand and apply to their own advantage. John Locke, for example, articulated a philosophy of reason in proposing that the state existed to provide for the happiness and security of individuals, who were endowed with inalienable rights to life, liberty, and property. Enlightenment writers emphasized rationality, harmony, and order, themes that stood in stark contrast to folk culture's traditional emphasis on the unfathomable mysteries of God and nature and the inevitability of human failure and disorder.

Enlightenment thinking undoubtedly appealed most to those whose ordered lives had improved their lot. The colonial elite had good reason to believe in progress. They sent their sons to college, where the texts of the new thinkers were promoted. Harvard, established in 1636, remained the only institution of higher education in British America until 1693, when Anglicans established the College of William and Mary at Williamsburg, soon to become the new capital of Virginia. Puritans in Connecticut, believing that Harvard was too liberal, founded Yale College in 1701. The curricula of these colleges, modeled on those of Oxford and Cambridge in England, were designed to train ministers, but gradually each institution introduced courses and professors influenced by the Enlightenment. In the 1730s Harvard endowed a chair of mathematics and natural philosophy and to fill it appointed John Winthrop, grandson of the Puritan leader and a disciple of Newton.

A mixture of traditional and Enlightenment views characterized the colonial colleges, as it did the thought of men like Cotton Mather. A conservative defender of the old order, Mather wrote a book supporting the existence of witches. On the other hand, he was also a member of the Royal Society, an early supporter of inoculation against disease, and a defender of the Copernican sun-centered model of the universe. On hearing a scientific lecture of Mather's that could have been construed as raising conflicts with a literal reading of the Bible, one old Boston minister noted in his diary, "I think it inconvenient to assert such problems."

This clergyman's views probably characterized a majority of the reading public. About half the adult men and a quarter

Peter Pelham, *Portrait of Cotton Mather*, c. 1725, oil painting, Courtesy American Antiquarian Society, Worcester, Massachusetts.

The Reverend Cotton Mather (1663–1728), pastor of Boston's Second Congregational Church and author of 450 books on theology, history, government, and science, combined both traditional and Enlightenment views. Although he defended the existence of witches, contributing to the hysteria of the Salem witchcraft trials, he also promoted Copernican science and inoculation against disease.

of the adult women of the British colonies could read, a literacy rate that was comparable to those of England and Scandinavia. In striking contrast, in the French and Spanish colonies reading was a skill confined to a tiny minority of upper-class men. In New England, where the Puritans were committed to Bible reading and had developed a system of public education, literacy rates were 85 percent among men and approximately 50 percent among women—the highest in the entire Atlantic world. But the tastes of ordinary readers ran to traditional rather than Enlightenment fare. Not surprisingly, the best-selling book of the colonial era was the Bible. In second place was that unique American literary form, the captivity narrative. The first publication of that genre was *Sovereignty and Goodness of God* (1682), Mary Rowlandson's story of her captivity among the Indians during King Philip's War, a kind of "pilgrim's progress" through the American wilderness. "It is good for me that I have been afflicted," she wrote, for "I have learned to look beyond present and smaller troubles, and to be quieted under them." Appearing in fifteen editions during the colonial period, Rowlandson's account stimulated the publication of at least 500 other such narratives, including the Reverend John Williams's *Redeemed Captive,* cited in the opening of this chapter, most with a lot less religion and a great deal more gore.

Another popular literary form was the almanac, a combination calendar, astrological guide, and sourcebook of medical advice and farming tips reflecting the concerns of traditional folk culture. The best remembered is Benjamin Franklin's *Poor Richard's Almanac* (1732–57), although it was preceded and outlived by a great many others. But what was so innovative about Franklin's almanac, and what made it so important, was the manner in which the author used this traditional literary form to promote the new Enlightenment emphasis on useful and practical knowledge. Posing as the simple bumpkin "Poor Richard," the highly sophisticated Franklin was one of the first Americans to bring Enlightenment thought to ordinary folk.

The growth of the economy in the British colonies and the development of a colonial upper class stimulated the emergence of a more cosmopolitan "Anglican" culture, particularly in the cities of the Atlantic coast. "The culture of minds by the finer arts and sciences," Franklin wrote in 1749, "was necessarily postponed to times of more wealth and leisure." And now, he added, "these times are come." A rising demand for drama, poetry, essays, novels, and history was met by urban booksellers who imported British publications. In Boston bookshops at midcentury one could buy the works of William Shakespeare and John Milton, the essays of Joseph Addison, Richard Steele, Jonathan Swift, and Samuel Johnson, and editions of the classics. In shops elsewhere around the colonies one might also find editions of novels such as *Moll Flanders* by Daniel Defoe and *Tom Jones* by Henry Fielding—but not in New England, where such works were considered indecent.

A Decline in Religious Devotion

While these new ideas flourished, religion seemed in decline. South of New England, the Anglican Church was weak, its ministers uninspiring, and many families remained "unchurched." A historian of religion has estimated that only one adult in fifteen was a member of a congregation. Although this figure may understate the impact of religion on community life, it helps keep things in perspective.

The Puritan churches of New England also suffered declining membership and falling attendance at services, and many ministers began to warn of Puritanism's "declension," pointing to the "dangerous" trend toward the "evil of toleration." By the second decade of the eighteenth century only one in five New Englanders belonged to an established congregation. When Puritanism had been a sect, membership in the church was voluntary and leaders could demand that followers testify to their religious conversion. But when Puritanism became an established church, attendance was expected of all townspeople, and conflicts inevitably arose over the requirement of a conversion experience. An agreement of 1662, known as the Half-Way Covenant, offered a practical solution: members' children who had not experienced conversion themselves could join as "half-way" members, restricted only from participation in communion. Thus the Puritans chose to manage rather than to resolve the conflicts involved in becoming an established religion. Tensions also developed between congregational autonomy and the central control that traditionally accompanied the establishment of a state church. In 1708 the churches of Connecticut agreed to the Saybrook Platform, which enacted a system of governance by councils of ministers and elders rather than by congregations. This reform also had the effect of weakening the passion and commitment of church members.

In addition, an increasing number of Congregationalists began to question the strict Calvinist theology of predestination—the belief that God had predetermined the few men and women who would be saved in the Second Coming. In the eighteenth century many Puritans turned to the much more comforting idea that God had given people the freedom to choose salvation by developing their faith and good works, a theological principle known as Arminianism (for the sixteenth-century Dutch theologian Jacobus Arminius). This belief was in harmony with the Enlightenment view that men and women were not helpless pawns but rational beings who could actively shape their own destinies. Also implicit in these new views was an image of God as a loving rather than a punishing father. Arminianism became a force at Harvard in the early eighteenth century, and soon a new generation of Arminian ministers began to assume leadership in New England's churches. These "liberal" ideas appealed to groups experiencing economic and social improvement, especially commercial farmers, merchants, and the comfortable middle class with its rising expectations. But among ordinary people, especially those in the countryside where traditional patterns lingered, there was a good deal of opposition to these "unorthodox" new ideas.

The Great Awakening

The first stirrings of a movement challenging this rationalist approach to religion occurred during the 1730s, most notably in the movement sparked by the Reverend Jonathan Edwards in the community of Northampton, in western Massachusetts. As the leaders of the community increasingly devoted their energies to the pursuit of wealth, the enthusiasm had seemed to go out of religion. The congregation adopted rules allowing church membership without evidence of a conversion experience and adopted a seating plan for the church that placed wealthy families in the prominent pews, front and center. But the same economic forces that made the "River Gods"—as the wealthy landowners of the Connecticut Valley were known—impoverished others. Young people from the community's poorer families grew disaffected as they were forced to postpone marriage because of the scarcity and expense of the land needed to set up a farm household. Increasingly they refused to attend church meeting, instead gathering together at night for "frolics" that only seemed to increase their discontent.

The Reverend Edwards made this group of young people his special concern. Believing that they needed to "have their hearts touched," he preached to them in a style that appealed to their emotions. For the first time in a generation, the meetinghouse shook with the fire and passion of Puritan religion. "Before the sermon was done," one Northampton parishioner remembered of one notable occasion, "there was a great moaning and crying through the whole house—What shall I do to be saved?—Oh I am going to Hell!—Oh what shall I do for Christ?" Religious fervor swept through the community, and church membership began to grow. There was more to this than the power of one preacher, for similar revivals were soon breaking out in other New England communities, as well as among German pietists and Scots-Irish Presbyterians in Pennsylvania. Complaining of "spiritual coldness," people abandoned ministers whose sermons read like rational dissertations for those whose preaching was more emotional.

These local revivals became an intercolonial phenomenon thanks to the preaching of George Whitefield, an evangelical Anglican minister from England, who in 1738 made the first of several tours of the colonies. By all accounts, his preaching had a powerful effect. Even Benjamin Franklin, a religious skeptic, wrote of the "extraordinary influence of [Whitefield's] oratory" after attending an outdoor service in Philadelphia where 30,000 people crowded the streets to hear him. Whitefield began as Edwards did, chastising his listeners as "half animals and half devils," but he left them with the hope that God would be responsive to their desire for salvation. "The word was sharper than a two-edged sword," Whitefield wrote after one of his sermons. "The bitter cries and groans were enough to pierce the hardest heart. Some of the people were as pale as death; others were wringing their hands; others lying on the ground; others sinking into the arms of their friends; and most lifting their eyes to heaven and crying to God for mercy. They seemed like persons awakened by the last trumpet, and coming out of their graves to judgement." Whitefield avoided sectarian differences. "God help us to forget party names and become Christians in deed and truth," he declared.

Historians of religion consider this widespread colonial revival of religion, known as the Great Awakening, to be the American version of the second phase of the Protestant Reformation. Religious leaders condemned the laxity, decadence, and officialism of established Protestantism and reinvigorated it with calls for piety and purity. People undergoing the economic and social stresses of the age, unsure about their ability to find land, to marry, to participate in the promise of a growing economy, found relief in religious enthusiasm.

In Pennsylvania, two important leaders of the Awakening were William Tennent and his son Gilbert. An Irish-born Presbyterian, the elder Tennent was an evangelical preacher who established a school in Pennsylvania to train like-minded men for the ministry. Tennent sent many enthusiastic ministers into the field, and his lampooned "Log College" ultimately evolved into the College of New Jersey — later Princeton University—founded in 1746. In the early 1740s, disturbed by what he called the "presumptuous security" of the colonial church, Tennent toured with Whitefield and delivered the famous sermon "The Dangers of an Unconverted Ministry," in which he called upon Protestants to examine the religious

Baptism by full immersion in the Schuylkill River of Pennsylvania, an engraving by Henry Dawkins illustrating events in the history of American Baptists, was published in Philadelphia in 1770. With calls for renewed piety and purity, the Great Awakening reinvigorated American Protestantism. The Baptists preached an egalitarian message, and their congregations in the South often included both white and black Protestants.

convictions of their own ministers. Among Presbyterians, open conflict broke out between the revivalists and the old guard, and in some regions the church hierarchy divided into separate organizations.

In New England similar factions known as the New Lights and the Old Lights accused each other of heresy. The New Lights railed against Arminianism, branding it a rationalist heresy, and called for a revival of Calvinism. The Old Lights condemned emotional enthusiasm as part of the heresy of believing in a personal and direct relationship with God outside the order of the church. Itinerant preachers appeared in the countryside stirring up trouble. The followers of one traveling revivalist burned their wigs, jewelry, and fine clothes in a bonfire, then marched around the conflagration, chanting curses at their opponents, whose religious writings they also consigned to the flames. Many congregations split into feuding factions, and ministers found themselves challenged by their newly awakened parishioners. In one town members of the congregation voted to dismiss their minister, who lacked the emotional fire they wanted in a preacher. When he refused to vacate his pulpit, they pulled him down, roughed him up, and threw him out the church door. Never had there been such turmoil in New England churches.

The Great Awakening was one of the first "national" events in American history. It began somewhat later in the South, developing first in the mid-1740s among Scots-Irish Presbyterians, then achieving its full impact with the organization work of Methodists and particularly Baptists in the 1760s and early 1770s. The revival not only affected white Southerners but introduced many slaves to Christianity for the first time. Local awakenings were frequently a phenomenon shared by both whites and blacks. The Baptist churches of the South in the era of the American Revolution included members of both races and featured spontaneous preaching by slaves as well as masters. In the nineteenth century white and black Christians would go their separate ways, but the joint experience of the eighteenth-century Awakening shaped the religious cultures of both groups.

Many other "unchurched" colonists were brought back to Protestantism by the Great Awakening. But a careful examination of statistics suggests that the proportion of church members in the general population probably did not increase during the middle decades of the century. Although the number of churches more than doubled from 1740 to 1780, the colonial population grew even faster, increasing threefold. The greatest impact was on families already associated with the churches. Before the Awakening, attendance at church had been mostly an adult affair, but throughout the colonies the revival of religion had its

CHRONOLOGY

1636	Harvard College founded
1644	Roger Williams's *Bloudy Tenent of Persecution*
1662	Half-Way Covenant in New England
1674	Bishopric of Quebec established
1680s	William Penn begins recruiting settlers from the European Continent
1682	Mary Rowlandson's *Sovereignty and Goodness of God*
1689	Toleration Act passed by Parliament
1690s	Beginnings of Jesuit missions in Arizona
1693	College of William and Mary is founded
1700s	Plains Indians begin adoption of the horse
1701	Yale College founded Iroquois sign treaty of neutrality with France
1704	Deerfield raid
1708	Saybrook Platform in Connecticut
1716	Spanish begin construction of Texas missions
1730s	French decimate the Natchez and defeat the Fox Indians
1732	Franklin begins publishing *Poor Richard's Almanac*
1738	George Whitefield first tours the colonies
1740s	Great Awakening gets under way in the Northeast
1740	Parliament passes a naturalization law for the colonies
1746	College of New Jersey (Princeton) founded
1760s	Great Awakening achieves full impact in the South
1769	Spanish colonization of California begins
1775	Indian revolt at San Diego
1776	San Francisco founded
1781	Los Angeles founded

deepest effects on young people, who flocked to church in greater numbers than ever before. For years the number of people experiencing conversion had been steadily falling, but now full membership surged. Church membership previously had been concentrated among women, leading Cotton Mather, for one, to speculate that perhaps women were indeed more godly. But men were particularly affected by the Great Awakening, and their attendance and membership rose. "God has surprisingly seized and subdued the hardest men, and more males have been added here than the tenderer sex," wrote one Massachusetts minister.

Great Awakening Politics

The Awakening appealed most of all to groups who felt bypassed by the economic and cultural development of the British colonies during the first half of the eighteenth century. Religious factions did not divide neatly into haves and have-nots, but the New Lights tended to draw their greatest strength from small farmers and less prosperous craftsmen. Many members of the upper class and the comfortable "middling sort" were shocked by the excesses of the Great Awakening, viewing them as indications of anarchy, and became even more committed to rational religion.

Some historians have suggested that the Great Awakening had important political implications. In Connecticut, for example, Old Lights politicized the religious dispute by passing a series of laws in the General Assembly designed to suppress the revival. In one town, separatists refused to pay taxes that supported the established church and were jailed. New Light judges were thrown off the bench, and others were denied their elected seats in the assembly. The arrogance of these actions was met with popular outrage, and by the 1760s the Connecticut New Lights had organized themselves politically and, in what amounted to a political rebellion, succeeded in turning the Old Lights out of office. These New Light politicians would provide the leadership for the American Revolution in Connecticut.

Such direct connections between religion and politics were relatively rare. There can be little doubt, however, that for many people the Great Awakening offered the first opportunity to actively participate in public debate and public action that affected the direction of their lives. Choices about religious styles, ministers, and doctrine were thrown open for public discourse, and ordinary people began to believe that their opinions actually counted for something. Underlying the debate over these issues were insecurities about warfare, economic growth, and the development of colonial society. The Great Awakening empowered ordinary people to question their leaders, an experience that would prove critical in the political struggles to come.

CONCLUSION

By the middle of the eighteenth century a number of distinct colonial regions had emerged in North America, all with rising populations pressing for more land to be seized from the Indians. Although colonists lived in traditional and local cultures, they were fascinated with the problems presented by frontiers and boundaries within the increasingly diverse continent. Some colonies attempted to ensure homogeneity, while others embraced diversity. Within the British colonies, New England in particular seemed bound to the past, whereas the Middle Colonies and the backcountry embraced both pluralism and expansion. These developments placed them in direct competition with the expansionist plans of the French and at odds with Indian peoples committed to the defense of their homelands.

The economic development of the British colonies introduced new social and cultural tensions that led to the Great Awakening, a massive revival of religion that was the first transcolonial event in American history. Thousands of people experienced a renewal of religious passions, but rather than resuscitating old traditions, the Awakening pointed people toward a more active role in their own political futures. These transformations added to the differences among the British colonies on the one hand, and those of the Spanish and French on the other.

REVIEW QUESTIONS

1. What were the principal colonial regions of North America? Discuss their similarities and their differences. Contrast the development of their political systems.
2. Why did the Spanish and the French close their colonies to immigration? Why did the British open theirs? How do you explain the ethnic homogeneity of New England and the ethnic pluralism of New York and Pennsylvania?
3. What were the principal trends in the history of Indian America in the eighteenth century?
4. Discuss the development of class differences in the Spanish, French, and British colonies in the eighteenth century.
5. Discuss the effects of the Great Awakening on the subsequent history of the British colonies.

RECOMMENDED READING

Edward Countryman, *Americans: A Collision of Histories* (1996). An important new synthesis that includes the many peoples and cultures of North America.

John Demos, *The Unredeemed Captive: A Family Story from Early America* (1994). A moving history of the Deerfield captives, focusing on the experience of Eunice Williams, the unredeemed captive.

W. J. Eccles, *The Canadian Frontier, 1534–1760* (1983). An introduction to the history of French America by a leading scholar on colonial Canada.

David Hackett Fischer, *Albion's Seed: Four British Folkways in America* (1990). An engaging history with fascinating details on the regions of New England, Pennsylvania, Virginia, and the Backcountry.

Jack P. Greene, *Pursuits of Happiness: The Social Development of Early Modern British Colonies and the Formation of American Culture* (1986). A distillation of a tremendous amount of historical material on community life in British North America.

James A. Henretta and Gregory H. Nobles, *Evolution and Revolution: American Society, 1600–1820* (1987). A useful synthesis of the newest social history of the British colonies. Includes an excellent bibliographic essay.

Jackson Turner Main, *The Social Structure of Revolutionary America* (1965). A detailed treatment of colonial social structure, with statistics, tables, and enlightening interpretations.

Colon McEvedy, *The Penguin Atlas of North American History to 1870* (1988). An unparalleled comparative perspective on the Spanish, French, and British regions of the continent, from precolonial times to the nineteenth century.

D. W. Meinig, *The Shaping of America: Atlantic America, 1492–1800* (1986). A geographer's overview of the historical development of the North American continent in the era of European colonialism. Provides a survey of the British and French colonies.

David J. Weber, *The Spanish Frontier in North America* (1992). A magnificent treatment of the entire Spanish borderlands, from Florida to California. Includes important chapters on colonial government and social life.

Robert Wells, *The Population of the British Colonies in America before 1776* (1975). The standard source on colonial population growth.

ADDITIONAL BIBLIOGRAPHY

North American Regions

Patricia Albers and Beatrice Medicine, eds., *The Hidden Half: Studies of Plains Indian Women* (1983)

Barbara Allen and Thomas J. Schlereth, eds., *Sense of Place: American Regional Cultures* (1990)

Richard L. Bushman, *From Puritan to Yankee: Character and the Social Order in Connecticut, 1690–1765* (1967)

Edward D. Castillo, ed., *Native American Perspectives on the Hispanic Colonization of Alta California* (1992)

Cornelia Hughes Dayton, *Women before the Bar: Gender, Law, and Society in Connecticut, 1639–1789* (1995)

John C. Ewers, *The Horse in Blackfoot Indian Culture* (1955)

Joseph W. Glass, *The Pennsylvania Culture Region: A View from the Barn* (1986)

Charles E. Hambrick-Stowe, *The Practice of Piety: Puritan Devotional Disciplines in Seventeenth-Century New England* (1982)

Robert F. Heizer, *The Destruction of California Indians* (1974)

Donald A. Hutslar, *The Architecture of Migration: Log Construction in the Ohio Country, 1750–1850* (1986)

Christine Leigh Hyrman, *Commerce and Culture: The Maritime Communities of Colonial Massachusetts* (1984)

Rhys Isaac, *Worlds of Experience: Communities in Colonial Virginia* (1987)

Francis Jennings, *The Ambiguous Iroquois Empire* (1984)

Terry G. Jordan and Matti Kaups, *The American Backwoods Frontier: An Ethnic and Ecological Interpretation* (1988)

Lyle Kohler, *A Search for Power: "The Weaker Sex" in Seventeenth-Century New England, 1650–1750* (1982)

A. C. Land, et al., eds., *Law, Society, and Politics in Early Maryland* (1977)

James T. Lemmon, *The Best Poor Man's Country: A Geographical Study of Early Southeastern Pennsylvania* (1972)

Kenneth Lockridge, *Literacy in Colonial New England* (1974)

James H. Merrell, *The Indians' New World: Catawbas and Their Neighbors from European Contact through the Era of Removal* (1989)

Gary B. Nash, *The Urban Crucible* (1979)

Charles Edwards O'Neill, *Church and State in French Colonial Louisiana: Policy and Politics to 1732* (1966)

Jacqueline Peterson and Jennifer S. H. Brown, eds., *The New Peoples: Being and Becoming Métis in North America* (1985)

Daniel K. Richter, *The Ordeal of the Longhouse: The Peoples of the Iroquois League in the Era of European Colonization* (1992)

Darrett B. Rutman and Anita H. Rutman, *A Place in Time: Middlesex County, Virginia, 1650–1750* (1984)

Marylynn Salmon, *Women and the Law of Property in Early America* (1986)

Sally Schwartz, *A Mixed Multitude: The Struggle for Toleration in Colonial Pennsylvania* (1987)

William S. Simmons, *Spirit of the New England Tribes: Indian History and Folklore, 1620–1984* (1986)

Daniel Blake Smith, *Inside the Great House: Planter Family Life in Eighteenth-Century Chesapeake Society* (1980)

Helen Horbeck Tanner, ed., *Atlas of Great Lakes Indian History* (1987)

Laurel T. Ulrich, *Good Wives: Image and Reality in the Lives of Women in Northern New England, 1650–1750* (1982)

Daniel H. Usner Jr., *Indians, Settlers, and Slaves in a Frontier Exchange Economy: The Lower Mississippi Valley before 1783* (1992)

Diverging Social and Political Patterns

Bernard Bailyn, *The Peopling of British North America: An Introduction* (1986)

Bruce C. Daniels, ed., *Power and Status: Essays on Officeholding in Colonial America* (1986)

Robert J. Dinkin, *Voting in Provincial America: A Study of Elections in the Thirteen Colonies, 1680–1776* (1977)

A. Roger Ekirch, *Bound for America: The Transportation of British Convicts to the Colonies, 1718–1775* (1987)

David W. Galenson, *White Servitude in Colonial America* (1981)

Jack P. Green, *The Quest for Power: The Lower Houses of Assembly in the Southern Royal Colonies, 1689–1776* (1963)

Thomas L. Purvis, *Proprietors, Patronage, and Paper Money: Legislative Politics in New Jersey, 1703–1776* (1986)

Sharon V. Salinger, *"To Serve Well and Faithfully": Labor and Indentured Servants in Pennsylvania, 1682–1800* (1987)

The Cultural Transformation of British North America

Patricia U. Bonomi, *Under the Cope of Heaven: Religion, Society, and Politics in Colonial America* (1986)

Henry Steele Commager, *The Empire of Reason: How Europe Imagined and America Realized the Enlightenment* (1977)

Alan Heimert and Perry Miller, eds., *The Great Awakening* (1967)

Jackson Maine, *The Social Structure of Revolutionary America* (1965)

Barbara B. Oberg and Harry S. Stout, eds., *Benjamin*

Franklin, Jonathan Edwards, and the Representation of American Culture (1993)
Frank Shuffelton, ed., *The American Enlightenment* (1993)

Biography

Milton J. Coalter, *Gilbert Tennent, Son of Thunder* (1986)
Verner W. Crane, *Benjamin Franklin and a Rising People* (1952)
Harry Kelsey, *Juan Rodriguez Cabrillo* (1986)
Martin J. Morgado, *Junípero Serra's Legacy* (1987)
Kenneth Silverman, *The Life and Times of Cotton Mather* (1984)
John Edwin Smith, *Jonathan Edwards: Puritan, Preacher, Philosopher* (1992)
Harry S. Stout, *The Divine Dramatist: George Whitefield and the Rise of Modern Evangelicalism* (1991)
Laurel Ulrich, *A Midwife's Tale: The Life of Martha Ballard, Based on Her Diary, 1785–1812* (1990)

CHAPTER SIX

FROM EMPIRE TO INDEPENDENCE

1750–1776

Bostonians protesting the Stamp Act in 1765 by burning the stamps in a bonfire: German colored engraving, 1784. The Granger Collection.

Chapter Outline

THE SEVEN YEARS WAR IN AMERICA

The Albany Conference of 1754

Colonial Aims and Indian Interests

Frontier Warfare

The Conquest of Canada

Indians and Europeans Struggle over the West

THE IMPERIAL CRISIS IN BRITISH NORTH AMERICA

The Emergence of American Nationalism

Politics, Republicanism, and the Press

The Sugar and Stamp Acts

The Stamp Act Crisis

Repeal of the Stamp Act

"SAVE YOUR MONEY AND SAVE YOUR COUNTRY"

The Townshend Revenue Acts

Nonimportation: An Early Political Boycott

The Massachusetts Circular Letter

The Politics of Revolt and the Boston Massacre

FROM RESISTANCE TO REBELLION

Intercolonial Cooperation

The Boston Tea Party

The Intolerable Acts

The First Continental Congress

Lexington and Concord

DECIDING FOR INDEPENDENCE

The Second Continental Congress

Fighting in the North and South

No Turning Back

The Declaration of Independence

AMERICAN COMMUNITIES

The First Continental Congress Shapes a National Political Community

Although Britain's North American colonies had enjoyed considerable prosperity during the late seventeenth and early eighteenth centuries, beginning with the Stamp Act in 1765 the British government began to put pressures on them, largely in the form of taxes and new trade restrictions, that drew increasing resistance. In convening the first Continental Congress in September 1774, the colonies made clear their displeasure with the government's actions. Fifty-six elected delegates from twelve of the colonies met at Philadelphia to draft a common response to what they called the Intolerable Acts—the closing of the port of Boston, the suspension of Massachusetts government, and several other measures of British repression—that were the latest attempt to force the colonies to accept the power of Parliament to make laws binding them "in all cases whatsoever." This was the first intercolonial meeting since the Stamp Act Congress of 1765 (discussed later in this chapter). If the colonies now failed to act together, they would be "attacked and destroyed by piece-meal," declared Arthur Lee of Virginia. "Every part will in its turn feel the vengeance which it would not unite to repel." Abigail Adams, the politically astute wife of John Adams of Massachusetts, agreed. "You have before you," she wrote to her husband, "the greatest national concerns that ever came before any people."

The opening minutes of the first session of the Continental Congress, on September 5, did not bode well. One delegate moved that they begin with prayer, but another responded that they were "so divided in religious sentiments, some Episcopalians, some Quakers, some Anabaptists, some Presbyterians and some Congregationalists, so that we could not join in the same act of worship." Were the delegates to be stymied from the very beginning by things that separated rather than united them? John Adams's cousin, fellow Massachusetts delegate Samuel Adams, jumped to his feet. He was no bigot, he said, "and could hear a prayer from any gentleman of piety and virtue who was at the same time a friend to his country." The delegates finally agreed to ask a local clergyman, a supporter of the American cause, to officiate. The minister took for his text the Thirty-fifth Psalm: "Plead my cause, O Lord, with them that strive with me; fight against them that fight against me." John Adams was delighted. The minister "prayed with such fervor, such Ardor, such Earnestness and Pathos, and in Language so elegant and sublime," he wrote home, that "it has had an excellent Effect upon every Body here."

This incident highlighted the most important task confronting those attending the Continental Congress: they had to develop trust in one another, for what they were doing was considered treason by the British authorities. And they had to find a way to support the common cause without compromising their local identities. At first it was as if the delegates were "ambassadors from a dozen belligerent powers of Europe," wrote John Adams. The delegates represented different colonies, whose traditions and histories were as distinct as those of separate countries. Moreover, these lawyers, merchants, and planters, who were leaders in their respective colonies, were strangers to one another. Their political opinions ranged from loyalty to the British crown and empire to a belief in the necessity of violent revolution. "Every man," Adams wrote, "is a great man, an orator, a critic, a statesman, and therefore every man, upon every question, must show his oratory, his criticism, and his political abilities." As a result, he continued, "business is drawn and spun out to an immeasurable length. I believe that if it was moved and seconded that we should come to a resolution that three and two make five, we should be entertained with logic and rhetorick, law, history, politicks and mathematics concerning the subject for two whole days."

During seven weeks of deliberations, however, the men of the Continental Congress succeeded in forging an agreement on both the principles and the policies they would have to follow in addressing the most serious crisis in the history of Britain's North American colonies. Equally important, the delegates found ways to work together and harmonize their interests. They immediately resolved that each colony would have one vote, thereby committing themselves to preserving provincial autonomy. They sent their most vexing problems to committees, whose members could sound each other out on the issues without speaking for the public record, and they added to their daily routine a round of dinners, parties, and late-night tippling. The greatest single accomplishment of the Continental Congress was the creation of a community of leadership for the united colonies. "It has taken us much time to get acquainted," John Adams wrote to Abigail, but he left Philadelphia thinking of his fellow representatives as "a collection of the greatest men upon this continent."

The First Continental Congress thus took the initial steps toward the creation of a national political community. The bonds of community can be local, regional, national, or international. In a town or village the feeling of association comes from daily face-to-face contact, but for larger groups these feelings must be created, or "imagined," as the historian Benedict Anderson puts it. The delegates took some of the first steps in this direction. In their final declaration they pledged to "firmly agree and associate, under the sacred ties of virtue, honor and love of our country." They urged their fellow Americans to "encourage frugality, economy, and industry, and promote agriculture, arts and the manufactures of this country," to "discountenance and discourage every species of extravagance and dissipation, especially all horse-racing, and all kinds of gaming, cock fighting, exhibitions of shows, plays, and other expensive diversions and entertainments." In other words, they called upon the common religious and cultural traditions of British Americans. They asked their countrymen to remember "the poorer sort" among them during the coming economic troubles. And in demanding that their fellow Americans "break off all dealings" and treat with contempt anyone violating the compact, the delegates were declaring who was "inside" and who was "outside" their community. Drawing boundaries is the essential first act in the construction of a new community.

Patrick Henry of Virginia, one of the delegates already committed to independence, was exuberant when the Continental Congress adjourned in late October. "The distinctions between Virginians, Pennsylvanians, New Yorkers, and New Englanders, are no more," he declared. "I am not a Virginian, but an American." Although Henry was a little premature in making this remark, he gave expression to an important truth. The Sugar Act, the Stamp Act, and the so-called Intolerable Acts that taxed and restricted colonists in various ways had also aroused a growing resistance among them. Great Britain had forced the colonists to recognize that they shared a community of interest distinct from that of the mother country. The delegates to the Continental Congress would become the core leaders of the national Revolutionary generation. Theirs was a first attempt to overcome local diversity and difference in pursuit of a common national goal. In the months and years to come the strength of local community would sometimes threaten to pull them apart, and the "imagined community" of America would be sorely tested as the colonies cautiously moved toward independence.

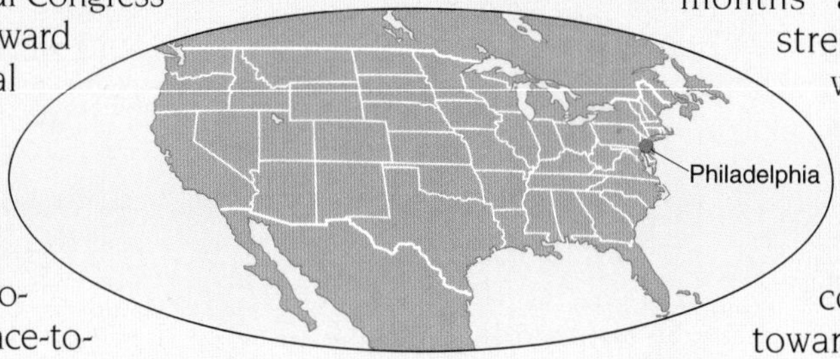

Key Topics

- The final struggle among Great Britain, France, and native American tribes for control of eastern North America
- American nationalism in the aftermath of the French and Indian War
- Great Britain's changing policy toward its North American colonies
- The political assumptions of American republicanism
- The colonies' efforts to achieve unity in their confrontation with Great Britain

THE SEVEN YEARS WAR IN AMERICA

The first attempt at cooperation among the leaders of the British colonies had taken place twenty years earlier, in July 1754, when representatives from New England, New York, Pennsylvania, and Maryland met to consider a joint approach to the French and Indian challenge. Even as the delegates met, fighting between French Canadians and Virginians began on the Ohio River, the first shots in a great global war for empire, known in Europe as the Seven Years War, that pitted Britain (allied with Prussia) against the combined might of France, Austria, Russia, and Spain. In North America, this war—which Americans remembered as the French and Indian War—became the final and most destructive of the armed conflicts between the British and the French before the French Revolution. Ultimately it decided the imperial future of the vast region between the Appalachian Mountains and the Mississippi River, and it laid the groundwork for the conflict between the British and the colonists that led to the American Revolution.

The Albany Conference of 1754

The 1754 meeting, which included an official delegation from the Iroquois Confederacy, took place in the New York town of Albany on the Hudson River. It was convened by officials of the British Board of Trade who wanted the colonies to consider a collective response to the continuing conflict with New France and the Indians of the interior. High on the agenda was the negotiation of a settlement with the leaders of the Iroquois Confederacy, who had grown impatient with colonial land grabbing. "Brother, you are not to expect to hear of me any more," the Iroquois chief Hendrick had declared in disgust to New York officials after a swindle that resulted in the loss of a vast tract. "And brother," he added as he departed, "we desire to hear no more of you." Because the powerful Iroquois Confederacy, and its Covenant Chain of alliances with other Indian tribes, occupied such a strategic location between New France and the British colonies, the British could ill afford Iroquois disaffection.

The Albany Conference made it clear that the British colonists were not yet ready to unite in common cause. Behind the scenes, while the negotiations took place, real estate agents bribed some minor Iroquois chiefs for their signatures on a "deed" to an enormous tract of land in Pennsylvania, turning the meeting into a vehicle for the very abuses the British were seeking to correct. Angered by these manipulations, the official Iroquois delegation walked out of the conference, refusing all offers to join a British alliance.

The Albany Conference did adopt Benjamin Franklin's Plan of Union, which proposed that Indian affairs, western settlement, and other items of mutual interest to all the colonies be placed under the authority of a grand council composed of representatives elected by the colonial assemblies and led by a royally appointed president. Franklin, who had been appointed by the British government as deputy postmaster general for all of British North America and charged with improving intercolonial communication and commerce, had become extremely sensitive to the need for cooperation among the colonies. Indeed, referring to the Iroquois Confederacy, he declared, "It would be a very strange thing if ignorant savages should be capable of forming a scheme for such a union, and yet a like union should be impracticable for ten or a dozen English colonies." But the colonial assemblies rejected the Albany Plan of Union. As one British official explained, each colony had "a distinct government, wholly independent of the rest, pursuing its own interest and subject to no general command."

Colonial Aims and Indian Interests

The absence of intercolonial cooperation proved to be one of the greatest weaknesses of the British North American empire, for the ensuing war was fought at a

The War for Empire in North America, 1754–1763 *The Seven Years War in America (also known as the French and Indian War) was fought in three principal areas: Nova Scotia and what was then Acadia, the frontier between New France and New York, and the upper Ohio River—gateway to the Great West.*

number of widespread locations. There were three principal flash points of conflict. The first was along the northern Atlantic coast. France had ceded to Britain its colony of Acadia in 1713 (which the British renamed Nova Scotia), but continued to occupy the fortress of Louisburg, from which it guarded its fishing grounds and the St. Lawrence approach to New France. New Englanders had captured this prize in 1745 during King George's War (see Chapter 4), but the French had reclaimed it upon the settlement of that conflict in 1748. They subsequently reinforced Louisburg to such an extent that it became known as the Gibraltar of the New World.

A second zone of conflict was the border region between New France and New York, from Niagara Falls to Lake Champlain, where Canadians and New Yorkers were in furious competition for the Indian trade. Unable to compete effectively against superior English goods, the French resorted to armed might, constructing fortifications on Lake George, south of Lake Champlain, and reinforcing their base at Niagara. This was the homeland of the Iroquois Confederacy, and the loyalty of these tribes would greatly affect the strategic balance here.

It was the Ohio country—the trans-Appalachian region along the Ohio River—that became the chief focus of British and French attention. This rich land was a prime target of British backcountry settlers and frontier land speculators. The French worried that their isolated settlements at places such as Detroit, Vincennes, and Kaskaskia would be overrun by the expanding British population and that the loss of the Ohio would threaten their entire Mississippi trading empire. To reinforce their claims, in 1749 the French sent a heavily armed force down the Ohio to warn off the British, and in 1752, supported by their northern Indian allies, they expelled a large number of British traders from the region. To prevent the British from returning to the West, in 1753 they began to construct a series of forts running south from Lake Erie to the junction of the Allegheny and Monongahela rivers, a site known as the Forks of the Ohio River.

The French "have stripped us of more than nine parts in ten of North America," one British official cried, "and left us only a skirt of coast along the Atlantic shore." In preparation for a general war, the British established the port of Halifax in Nova Scotia as a counterpart to Louisburg. In northern New York, they strengthened existing forts and constructed new ones. And finally, the British king decided to directly challenge the French claim to the upper Ohio Valley: he conferred an enormous grant of land on the Ohio Company, organized by Virginia and London capitalists, and the company made plans to build a fort at the Forks of the Ohio.

The impending conflict involved more than competing colonial powers, however, for the Indian peoples of the interior had interests of their own. In addition to its native inhabitants, the Ohio country had become a refuge for Indian peoples who had fled the Northeast—Delawares, Shawnees, Hurons, and Iroquois among them. Most of the Ohio Indians opposed the British and were anxious to preserve the Appalachians as a barrier to westward expansion. They were also disturbed by the French movement into their country, although the French outposts, unlike those of the British, did not become centers of expanding agricultural settlements.

The Iroquois Confederacy maintained an official position of neutrality between the rival colonial powers. Iroquois factions allied themselves with either the British or the French, and the confederacy as a whole sought to play off one power against the other, to its own advantage. In the South, the Creeks carved out a similar role for themselves among the British, the French in Louisiana, and the Spanish in Florida; the Cherokees and the Choctaws attempted, less successfully, to do likewise. It was in the interests of these Indian tribes, in other words, to perpetuate the existing colonial stalemate. Their position would be greatly undermined by an overwhelming victory for either side.

Frontier Warfare

At the Albany Congress the delegates received news that Colonel George Washington, a young militia officer from Virginia, had been forced to surrender his troops to a French force near the headwaters of the Monongahela River. The governor of Virginia had sent Washington to expel the French from the region granted to the Ohio Company. Having forced Washington's forces back, the French Canadians now commanded the interior country from their base at Fort Duquesne, which they had built at the Forks of the Ohio and named for the governor of French Canada.

Taking up the challenge, the British government dispatched two Irish regiments under General Edward Braddock across the Atlantic in 1755 to attack and destroy Fort Duquesne. Meanwhile, colonial militias (the equivalent of today's National Guard) commanded by colonial officers were to strike at the New York frontier and the north Atlantic coast. An army of New England militiamen succeeded in capturing two important French forts on the border of Nova Scotia, but the other two prongs of the campaign were complete failures. The offensive in New York was repulsed. And in the worst defeat of a British army during the eighteenth century, Braddock's force was destroyed by a smaller force of French and Indians on the upper Ohio, and Braddock himself was killed.

Braddock's defeat was followed by the outbreak of full-scale warfare between Britain and France in 1756. The fighting of the first two years was a near catastrophe for Great Britain. Canadians captured the British forts in northern New York. Indians pounded backcountry settlements, killed thousands of settlers, and raided deep into the coastal colonies, throwing British colonists into panic. "There is no surer way to sicken the people of the English colonies," a Canadian commander mused, "and to make them desire the return of peace." The continuing absence of colonial cooperation greatly hampered the British attempt to mount a counterattack. And when British commanders tried to exert direct control over provincial troops, they succeeded only in angering local authorities.

In this climate of defeat, the British enacted a draconian policy of retribution against the French-speaking farmers of Acadia, who had lived peacefully under British rule for over forty years. The Acadians' refusal to swear allegiance to the crown was now used as an excuse for their expulsion. In 1755 New England troops began the forcible removal of approximately 10,000 Acadians, selling their farms at bargain prices to immigrants from New England. Suffering terrible hardship and heartbreak, the Acadians were dispersed throughout the Atlantic world, although a substantial number of them ended up settling in Louisiana, then under Spanish control, where they became known as "Cajuns." The Acadian expulsion is one of the most infamous chapters in the British imperial record in North America.

The Conquest of Canada

In the darkest days of 1757, William Pitt, an enthusiastic advocate of British expansion, assumed the prime ministership of Great Britain. "I know that I can save this country," Pitt declared, "and that no one else can." Deciding that the global war could be won in North America, he subsidized the Prussians to fight in Europe and reserved Britain's own forces and resources for naval and colonial operations. Pitt committed the British to the conquest of Canada and the elimination of all French competition in North America. Such a goal could be achieved only at tremendous cost in men and money. By promising that the war would be fought "at His Majesty's expense," Pitt was able to buy colonial cooperation. A massive infusion of British currency and credit greatly stimulated the North American economy. Pitt dispatched more than 20,000 regular British troops across the Atlantic. Combining them with colonial forces, he massed more than 50,000 armed men against Canada.

The British attracted Indian support for their plans by "redressing the grievances complained of by the Indians, with respect to the lands which have been fraudulently taken from them," in the words of a British official. In 1758 officials promised the Iroquois Confederacy and the Ohio Indians that the crown would "agree upon clear and fixed boundaries between our settlements and their hunting grounds, so that each party may know their own and be a mutual protection to each other of their respective possessions."

Thus did Pitt succeed in reversing the course of the war. Regular and provincial forces captured Louisburg in July 1758, setting the stage for the penetration of the St. Lawrence Valley. A month later a

Benjamin West (1738–1820), *The Death of General Wolfe*, 1770. Oil on canvas, 152.6 x 214.5 cm. Transfer from the Canadian War Memorials, 1921 (Gift of the 2nd Duke of Westminster, Eaton Hall, Cheshire, 1918). National Gallery of Canada, Ottawa, Ontario.

The death of General James Wolfe, at the conclusion of the battle in which the British captured Quebec in 1759, became the subject of American artist Benjamin West's most famous painting, which was exhibited to tremendous acclaim in London in 1770.

force of New Englanders captured the strategic French fort of Oswego on Lake Ontario, thereby preventing the Canadians from resupplying their western posts. Encouraged by British promises, many Indian tribes abandoned the French alliance, and the French were forced to give up Fort Duquesne. A large British force soon took control of the French fort at the Forks of the Ohio, renaming the post Fort Pitt (Pittsburgh today) in honor of the prime minister. "Blessed be God," wrote a Boston editor. "The long looked for day is arrived that has now fixed us on the banks of the Ohio." The last of the French forts on the New York frontier fell in 1759. In the South, regular and provincial British troops invaded the homeland of the Cherokees and crushed them.

British forces now converged on Quebec, the heart of French Canada. In the summer of 1759, following General James Wolfe's order to "burn and lay waste the country," British troops plundered farms and shelled the city of Quebec. Finally, in an epic battle on the Plains of Abraham before the city's walls, the British prevailed over Quebec's defenders. More than 2,000 British, French, American, and Canadian men lost their lives in the battle, including both Wolfe and the French commander, the marquis de Montcalm. Canadian resistance continued for another year, but in 1760 British forces conquered Montreal, completing the destruction of the French Empire in America. "The great day is now come," declared the editor of the *Boston News-Letter*, "the fall of the American Carthage."

In the final two years of the war the British swept French ships from the seas, conquered important French and Spanish colonies in the Caribbean, achieved dominance in India, and even captured the Spanish Philippines. In the Treaty of Paris, signed in 1763, France lost all its possessions on the North American mainland. It ceded its claims east of the Mississippi to Great Britain, with the exception of New Orleans. This city had already been transferred, along with all other French claims to lands west of the Mississippi, to Spain—to keep these territories in the possession of a Catholic monarch. For its part, Spain ceded

Florida to Britain in exchange for the return of all its Caribbean and Pacific colonies. The imperial rivalry in eastern North America that had begun in the sixteenth century now came to an end with total victory for the British empire.

Indians and Europeans Struggle over the West

When the Ohio Indians heard of the French cession of the western country to Britain, they were shocked. "The French had no right to give away [our] country," they told a British trader. "They were never conquered by any nation." A new set of British policies soon shocked them all the more. Both the French and the British had long used gift giving as a way of gaining favor with Indians. The Spanish officials who replaced the French in Louisiana made an effort to continue the old policy. But the British military governor of the western region, General Jeffery Amherst, in one of his first official actions, banned presents to Indian chiefs and tribes, demanding that they learn to live without "charity." Not only were Indians angered by Amherst's reversal of custom, but they were also frustrated by his refusal to supply them with the ammunition they required for hunting. Many were left starving.

In this climate, hundreds of Ohio Indians became disciples of the Indian visionary Neolin (meaning "The Enlightened One," in Algonquian), known to the English as the Delaware Prophet. The core of Neolin's teaching was that Indians had been corrupted by European ways and needed to purify themselves by returning to their traditions and preparing for a holy war. "Drive them out," he declared of the settlers. A confederacy of tribes organized by a group of chiefs who had gained influence by adopting Neolin's ideas laid plans for a coordinated attack against the British in the spring of 1763. The principal figure among them was the Ottawa chief Pontiac, renowned as an orator and political leader. This combination of inspirational religious and political leadership was a pattern in the long history of Indian resistance to colonial expansion in North America. The first instance of this approach on the part of Indian tribes had taken place among the Algonquians of the Chesapeake in the early seventeenth century (see Chapter 3).

In May 1763 the Indian confederacy simultaneously attacked all the British forts in the West. Warriors overran Fort Michilimackinac, at the narrows between Lakes Michigan and Huron, by scrambling

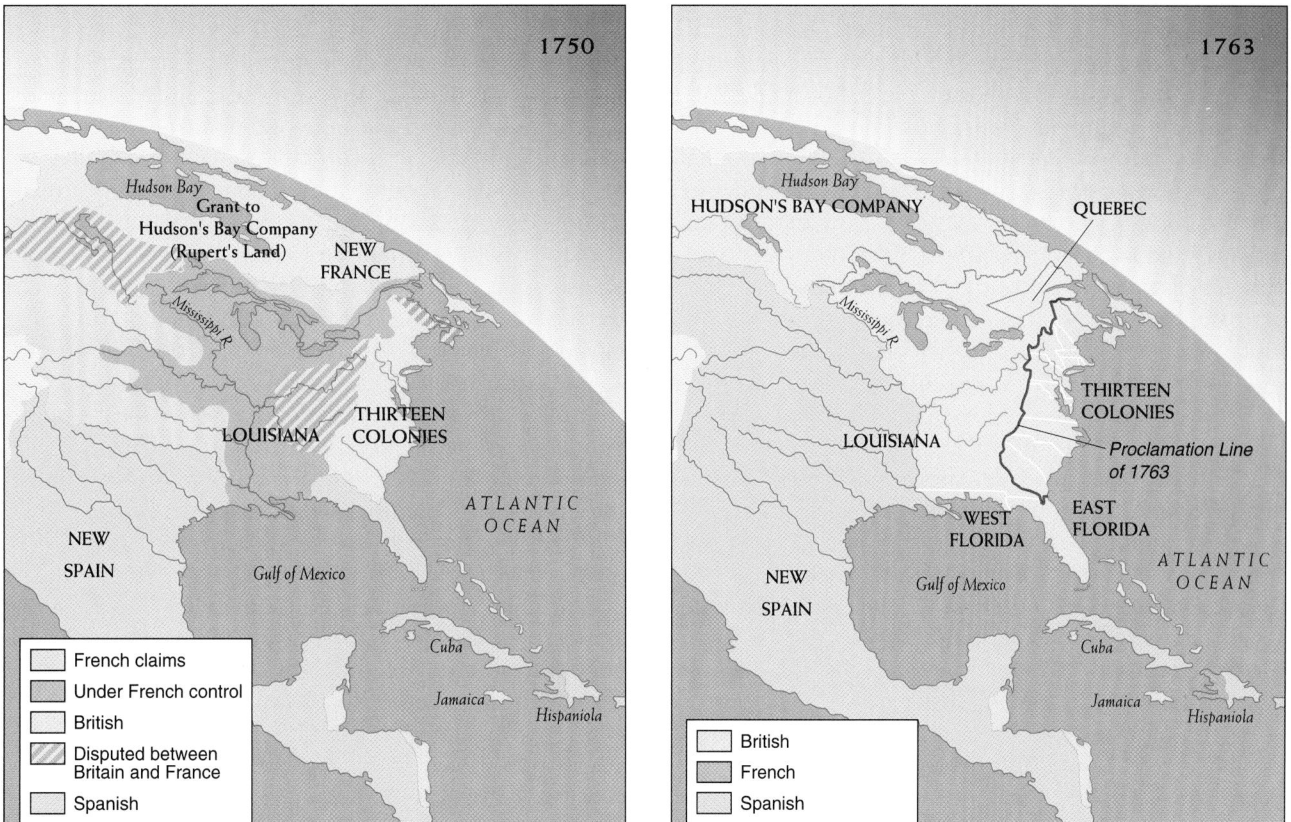

European Claims in North America, 1750 and 1763 *As a result of the British victory in the Seven Years War, the map of colonial claims in North America was fundamentally transformed.*

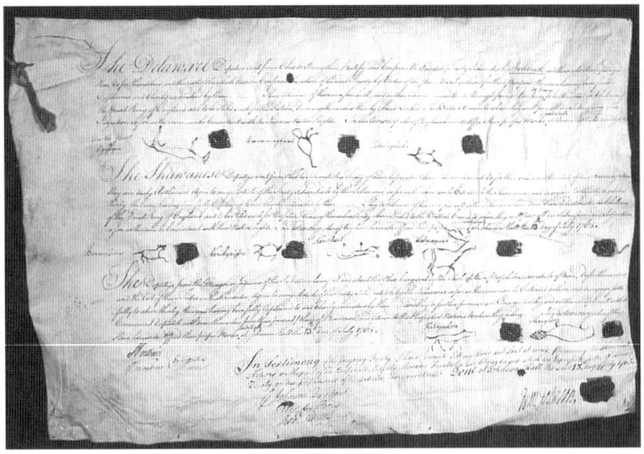

A treaty between the Delaware, Shawnee, and Mingo (western Iroquois) Indians and Great Britain, July 13, 1765, at the conclusion of the Indian uprising. The Indian chiefs signed with pictographs symbolizing their clans, each notarized with an official wax seal.

through the gates supposedly in pursuit of a lacrosse ball, cheered on by unsuspecting soldiers. In raids throughout the backcountry, Indians killed more than 2,000 settlers. At Fort Pitt, General Amherst proposed that his officers "send the smallpox among the disaffected tribes" by distributing infected blankets from the fort's hospital. This early instance of germ warfare resulted in an epidemic that spread from the Delawares and Shawnees to the southern Creeks, Choctaws, and Chickasaws, killing hundreds of people. Although they sacked and burned eight British posts, the Indians failed to take the key forts of Niagara, Detroit, and Pitt. Pontiac fought on for another year, but most of the Indians sued for peace, fearing the destruction of their villages. For their part, the British came to terms because they knew they could not overwhelm the Indian peoples. The war thus ended in stalemate.

Even before the uprising, the British had been at work on a policy they hoped would help resolve frontier tensions. In the royal Proclamation of 1763, the British government set the terms for continuing British policy toward the Indians. The proclamation set aside the region west of the crest of the Appalachian Mountains as "Indian Country," and any purchase of these protected Indian lands required the specific authorization of the crown. Indians were pleased with the proclamation, but land speculators and backcountry British Americans were outraged.

Colonists had expected that the removal of the French threat would allow them to move unencumbered into the West, regardless of the wishes of the Indian inhabitants. They could not understand why the British would award territory to Indian enemies who had slaughtered more than 4,000 settlers during the previous war. In an act emblematic of the anger backcountry settlers felt about these restrictions, a mob of Pennsylvanians known as the Paxton Boys butchered twenty Indian men, women, and children at the small village of Conestoga on the Susquehanna River in December 1763. When colonial authorities moved to arrest them, 600 frontiersmen marched into Philadelphia in protest. Negotiations led by Benjamin Franklin helped to prevent a bloody confrontation.

In fact, the British proved unable and ultimately unwilling to prevent the westward migration that was a dynamic part of the colonization of British North America. Within a few years of the war, New Englanders by the thousands were moving into the northern Green Mountain district, known as Vermont. In the Middle Colonies, New York settlers pushed ever closer to the homeland of the Iroquois, while others located within the protective radius of Fort Pitt in western Pennsylvania. Hunters, stock herders, and farmers crossed over the first range of the Appalachians in Virginia and North Carolina, planting pioneer communities in what are now West Virginia, western Virginia, and eastern Tennessee.

Moreover, the press of population growth and economic development turned the attention of investors and land speculators to the area west of the Appalachians. George Washington, now a prominent investor in western lands, believed that the Royal Proclamation of 1763 declaring an Appalachian boundary to western expansion was merely "a temporary expedient." In 1768 the Ohio Company sent surveyors to mark out their grant in the upper Ohio Valley. In response to demands by settlers and speculators, British authorities were soon pressing the Iroquois and Cherokees for cessions of land in Indian Country. No longer able to play off rival colonial powers, Indians were reduced to a choice between compliance and resistance. Weakened by the recent war, they chose to sign away lands. In the Treaty of Hard Labor in 1768, the Cherokees ceded a vast tract on the waters of the upper Tennessee River, where British settlers had already planted communities. In the Treaty of Fort Stanwix of the same year, the Iroquois gave up their claim to the Ohio Valley, hoping thereby to deflect English settlement away from their own homeland.

The individual colonies were even more aggressive. Locked in a dispute with Pennsylvania about jurisdiction in the Ohio country, in 1773 the Virginia governor, John Murray, earl of Dunmore, sent a force to occupy Fort Pitt. The next year, in an attempt to gain legitimacy for his dispute with Pennsylvania, Dunmore provoked a frontier war with the Shawnees. After defeating them he forced their cession of the upper Ohio River Valley to Virginia. The Iroquois and Ohio Indians angrily complained about the outcome of what came to be known as Dunmore's

War. The English king, they argued, had guaranteed that the boundary between colonial and Indian land "should forever after be looked upon as a barrier between us." But the Americans "entirely disregard, and despise the settlement agreed upon by their superiors and us." They "are come in vast numbers to the Ohio, and [give] our people to understand that they would settle wherever they pleased. If this is the case we must look upon every engagement you made with us as void and of no effect." This continuing struggle for the West would be an important issue in the coming Revolution.

THE IMPERIAL CRISIS IN BRITISH NORTH AMERICA

No colonial power of the mid-eighteenth century could match Great Britain in projecting empire over the face of the globe. During the years following its victory in the Seven Years War, Britain turned confidently to the reorganization of North America. This new colonial policy plunged British authorities into a new and ultimately destructive conflict with the colonists, who had begun to develop a sense of a separate identity.

The Emergence of American Nationalism

Despite the anger of frontier people over the Proclamation of 1763, the conclusion of the Seven Years War left most colonists proud of their place in the British empire. But during the war many had begun to note important contrasts between themselves and the mother country. The regular soldiers of the British army, for example, shocked Americans with their profane, lewd, and violent behavior. Colonists were equally shocked by the swift and terrible punishment that aristocratic officers used to keep these soldiers in line. David Perry of Massachusetts witnessed the punishment of two soldiers sentenced to 800 lashes apiece. "The flesh appeared to be entirely whipped from their shoulders," he wrote, "and they hung as mute and motionless as though they had long since been deprived of life." A military doctor stood nearby with a vial of smelling salts, periodically reviving the men and taunting them: "Damn you, you can bear it yet!" It was, Perry concluded, "a specimen of British cruelty." Those who had witnessed such scenes later found it easy to believe that the British wished to impose "slavery" on them.

Colonial forces, by contrast, were composed of volunteer companies. Officers tempered their administration of punishment, knowing they had to maintain the enthusiasm of these troops. Discipline thus fell considerably below the standards to which British officers were accustomed. "Riff-raff," one British general said of the colonials, "the lowest dregs of the people, both officers and men." The British made no secret of their poor opinion of colonial fighting men. "The Americans are in general the dirtiest, most contemptible, cowardly dogs that you can conceive," wrote General Wolfe. For their part, many colonial officers believed that the British ignored the important role the Americans had played in the Seven Years War. Massachusetts, for example, lost between 1,500 and 2,000 fighting men. This mutual suspicion and hostility was often expressed in name calling: British soldiers called New Englanders "Yankees," while colonists heckled the red-coated British with taunts of "Lobster."

If the the Seven Years War left many colonists seeing themselves as distinct from the British, it also strengthened a sense of intercolonial, American identity. Farm boys who never before had ventured outside the communities of their birth fought in distant regions with men like themselves from other colonies. Such experiences reinforced a developing nationalist perspective. From 1735 to 1775, while trade with Britain doubled, commerce among the colonies increased by a factor of four. People and ideas moved along with goods. The first stage lines linking seaboard cities began operation in the 1750s. Spurred by Postmaster Benjamin Franklin, many colonies built or improved post roads for transporting the mails.

One of the most important means of intercolonial communication was the weekly newspaper. Early in the eighteenth century the colonial press functioned as a mouthpiece for the government; editors who criticized public officials could land in jail. In 1735, for example, the New York City editor John Peter Zenger was indicted for seditious libel after printing antigovernment articles. But as it turned out, the Zenger case provided the precedent for greater freedom of the press. "Shall the press be silenced that evil governors may have their way?" Zenger's attorney asked the jury. "The question before the court is not the cause of a poor printer," he declared, but the cause "of every free man that lives under a British government on the main of America." Zenger was acquitted. By 1760, more than twenty highly opinionated weekly newspapers circulated in the British colonies, and according to one estimate, a quarter of all male colonists were regular readers.

The midcentury American press focused increasingly on intercolonial affairs. One study of colonial newspapers indicates that intercolonial coverage increased sixfold over the four decades preceding the Revolution. Editors of local papers increasingly looked at events from what they called a "continental" perspective. This trend accelerated during the Seven Years War, when communities demanded coverage of events

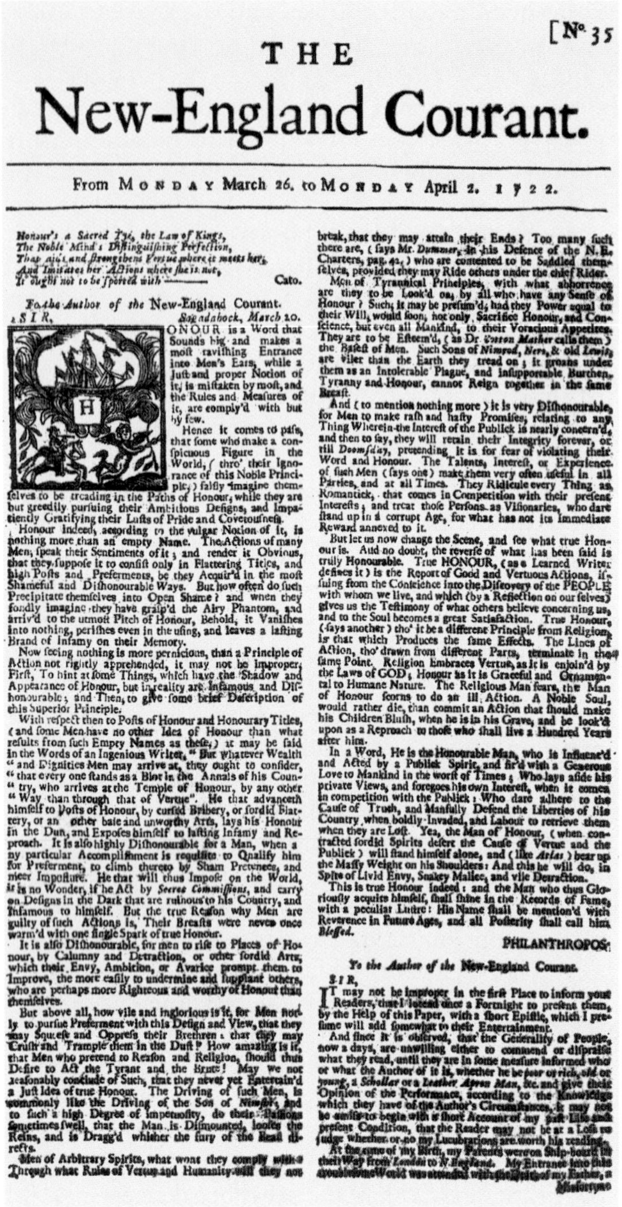

[No 35

THE

New-England Courant.

From MONDAY March 26. to MONDAY April 2. 1722.

Honour's a Sacred Tye, the Law of Kings,
The Noble Mind's Distinguishing Perfection,
That aids and strengthens Vertue where it meets her,
And Imitates her Actions where she is not,
It ought not to be sported with ——— Cato.

To the Author of the New-England Courant.

SIR, *Sagadahock, March* 20.

HONOUR is a Word that Sounds big and makes a most ravishing Entrance into Men's Ears, while a Just and proper Notion of it, is mistaken by most, and the Rules and Measures of it, are comply'd with but by few.

Hence it comes to pass, that some who make a conspicuous Figure in the World, (thro' their Ignorance of this Noble Principle,) falsly imagine themselves to be treading in the Paths of Honour, while they are but greedily pursuing their Ambitious Designs, and Impatiently Gratifying their Lusts of Pride and Covetousness.

Honour indeed, according to the vulgar Notion of it, is nothing more than an empty Name. The Actions of many Men, speak their Sentiments of it; and render it Obvious, that they suppose it to consist only in Flattering Titles, and high Posts and Preferments, be they Acquir'd in the most Shameful and Dishonourable Ways. But how often do such Precipitate themselves into Open Shame? and when they fondly imagine they have grasp'd the Airy Phantom, and arriv'd to the utmost Pitch of Honour, Behold, it Vanishes into nothing, perishes even in the using, and leaves a lasting Brand of Infamy on their Memory.

Now seeing nothing is more pernicious, than a Principle of Action not rightly apprehended, it may not be improper, First, To hint at some Things, which have the Shadow and Appearance of Honour, but in reality are Infamous and Dishonourable; and Then, to give some brief Description of this Superior Principle.

With respect then to Posts of Honour and Honourary Titles, (and some Men have no other Idea of Honour than what results from such Empty Names as these,) it may be said in the Words of an Ingenious Writer, "But whatever Wealth "and Dignities Men may arrive at, they ought to consider, "that every one stands as a Blot in the Annals of his Coun- "try, who arrives at the Temple of Honour, by any other "Way than through that of Vertue". He that advanceth himself to Posts of Honour, by cursed Bribery, or sordid Flattery, or any other base and unworthy Arts, lays his Honour in the Dust, and Exposes himself to lasting Infamy and Reproach. It is also highly Dishonourable for a Man, when any particular Accomplishment is requisite to Qualify him for Preferment, to climb thereto by Sham Pretences, and meer Imposture. He that will thus Impose on the World, it is no Wonder, if he Act by *Secret Commissions*, and carry on Designs in the Dark that are ruinous to his Country, and Infamous to himself. But the true Reason why Men are guilty of such Actions is, Their Breasts were never once warm'd with one single Spark of true Honour.

It is also Dishonourable, for men to rise to Places of Honour, by Calumny and Detraction, or other sordid Arts, which their Envy, Ambition, or Avarice prompt them to Improve, the more easily to undermine and supplant others, who are perhaps more Righteous and worthy of Honour than themselves.

But above all, how vile and inglorious is it, for Men hotly to pursue Preferment with this Design and View, that they may Squeese and Oppress their Brethren: that they may Crush and Trample them in the Dust? How amazing is it, that Men who pretend to Reason and Religion, should thus Desire to Act the Tyrant and the Brute! May we not reasonably conclude of Such, that they never yet Entertain'd a Just Idea of true Honour. The Driving of such Men, is commonly like the Driving of the Son of *Nimshi*, and to such a high Degree of impetuosity, do their Passions sometimes swell, that the Man is Dismounted, looses the Reins, and is Dragg'd whither the fury of the Beast directs.

Men of Arbitrary Spirits, what wont they comply with? Through what Rules of Vertue and Humanity will they not break, that they may attain their Ends? Too many such there are, (says Mr. *Dummer*, in his Defence of the N.E. Charters, pag. 42.) who are contented to be Saddled themselves, provided they may Ride others under the chief Rider.

Men of Tyrannical Principles, with what abhorrence are they to be Look'd on, by all who have any Sense of Honour? Such, it may be presum'd, had they Power equal to their Will, would soon, not only Sacrifice Honour, and Conscience, but even all Mankind, to their Voracious Appetites. They are to be Esteem'd, (as Dr *Cotton Mather* calls them) the Basest of Men. Such Sons of *Nimrod*, *Nero*, & old *Lewis*, are viler than the Earth they tread on; it groans under them as an Intolerable Plague, and insupportable Burthen. Tyranny and Honour, cannot Reign together in the same Breast.

And (to mention nothing more) it is very Dishonourable, for Men to make rash and hasty Promises, relating to any Thing Wherein the Interest of the Publick is nearly concern'd, and then to say, they will retain their Integrity forever, or till *Doomsday*, pretending it is for fear of violating their Word and Honour. The Talents, Interest, or Experience of such Men (says one) make them very often useful in all Parties, and at all Times. They Ridicule every Thing as Romantick, that comes in Competition with their present Interests, and treat those Persons as Visionaries, who dare stand up in a corrupt Age, for what has not its Immediate Reward annexed to it.

But let us now change the Scene, and see what true Honour is. And no doubt, the reverse of what has been said is truly Honourable. True HONOUR, (as a Learned Writer defines it) is the Report of Good and Vertuous Actions, issuing from the Conscience into the Discovery of the PEOPLE with whom we live, and which (by a Reflection on our selves) gives us the Testimony of what others believe concerning us, and to the Soul becomes a great Satisfaction. True Honour, (says another) tho' it be a different Principle from Religion, is that which Produces the same Effects. The Lines of Action, tho' drawn from different Parts, terminate in the same Point. Religion Embraces Vertue, as it is enjoin'd by the Laws of GOD; Honour as it is Graceful and Ornamental to Humane Nature. The Religious Man fears, the Man of Honour scorns to do an ill Action. A Noble Soul, would rather die, than commit an Action that should make his Children Blush, when he is in his Grave, and be look'd upon as a Reproach to those who shall live a Hundred Years after him.

In a Word, He is the Honourable Man, who is Influenc'd and Acted by a Publick Spirit, and fir'd with a Generous Love to Mankind in the worst of Times; Who lays aside his private Views, and foregoes his own Interest, when it comes in competition with the Publick: Who dare adhere to the Cause of Truth, and Manfully Defend the Liberties of his Country when boldly Invaded, and Labour to retrieve them when they are Lost. Yea, the Man of Honour, (when contracted sordid Spirits desert the Cause of Vertue and the Publick) will stand himself alone, and (like *Atlas*) bear up the Massy Weight on his Shoulders: And this he will do, in Spite of Livid Envy, Snakey Malice, and vile Detraction.

This is true Honour indeed: and the Man who thus Gloriously acquits himself, shall shine in the Records of Fame, with a peculiar Lustre: His Name shall be mention'd with Reverence in Future Ages, and all Posterity shall call him *Blessed*.

PHILANTHROPOS.

To the Author of the New-England Courant.

SIR,

IT may not be improper in the first Place to inform your Readers, that I intend once a Fortnight to present them, by the Help of this Paper, with a short Epistle, which I presume will add somewhat to their Entertainment.

And since it is observed, that the Generality of People, now a days, are unwilling either to commend or dispraise what they read, until they are in some measure informed who or what the Author of it is, whether he be poor or rich, old or young, a *Schollar* or a *Leather Apron Man*, &c. and give their Opinion of the Performance, according to the Knowledge which they have of the Author's Circumstances, it may not be amiss to begin with a short Account of my past Life and present Condition, that the Reader may not be at a Loss to judge whether or no my Lucubrations are worth his reading.

At the time of my Birth, my Parents were on Ship-board in their Way from *London* to *N. England*. My Entrance into this troublesome World was attended with the death of my Father, a *Misfortune*

James Franklin began publishing the New-England Courant *in Boston in 1721. When Franklin criticized the government, he was jailed, and the paper continued under the editorship of his brother Benjamin. The* Courant *ceased publication in 1726, and the Franklin brothers went on to other papers—James to the* Rhode Island State Gazette, *Benjamin to the* Pennsylvania Gazette *in Philadelphia. Before the Zenger case in 1735, few editors dared to challenge the government.*

in distant colonies where their men might be fighting. During these years the British colonists of North America first began to use the term "American" to denote their common identity. More than any earlier event, the Seven Years War promoted a new spirit of nationalism and a wider notion of community. This was the social base of the political community later forged at the Continental Congress.

Politics, Republicanism, and the Press

The pages of the colonial press reveal the political assumptions held by informed colonists. For decades, royal governors had struggled with colonial assemblies over their respective powers. As commentary on the meaning of these struggles, colonial editors frequently reprinted the writings of the radical Whigs of eighteenth-century England, pamphleteers such as John Trenchard and Thomas Gordon, political theorists such as John Locke, and essayists such as Alexander Pope and Jonathan Swift. These writers warned of the growing threat to liberty posed by the unchecked exercise of power. In their more emotional writings they argued that a conspiracy existed among the powerful—kings, aristocrats, and Catholics—to quash liberty and institute tyranny. Their political principles included extension of the ballot to greater numbers of men, apportionment of legislative representation on the basis of population, and responsiveness by representatives to their constituents. The only effective counterweight to the abuse of power, they argued, was the constant vigilance of the people and their exercise of public virtue—the sacrifice of self-interest for the public good. Outside the mainstream of British political opinion, these ideas came to define the political consensus in the British colonies, a point of view historians call "republicanism."

Republicanism declared that the truly just society provided the greatest possible liberty to individuals. As the power of the state, by its very nature, was antithetical to liberty, it had to be limited. John Locke argued that the authority of a ruler should be conditional rather than absolute and that the people had the inherent right to select their own form of governance and to withdraw their support if the government did not fulfill its trust. The best guarantee of good government, then, was the broad distribution of power to the people, who would not only select their own leaders but vote them out as well. In this view, republican government depended on the virtue of the people, their willingness to make the health and stability of the political community their first priority, and was possible only for an "independent" population that controlled its own affairs. As Thomas Jefferson once wrote, "Dependence begets subservience and venality, suffocates the germ of virtue, and prepares fit tools for the designs of ambition." Individual ownership of property, especially land, he argued, was the foundation of an independent and virtuous people.

This was a political theory that fit the circumstances of American life, with its wide base of property ownership, its tradition of representative assemblies, and its history of struggle with royal authority. Contrast the assumptions of republicans with those of British monarchists, who argued that the good society was one in which a strong state, controlled by a hereditary elite, kept a vicious and unruly people in line.

The Sugar and Stamp Acts

The emerging sense of American political identity was soon tested by British measures designed to raise revenues in the colonies. To quell Indian uprisings and stifle discontent among the French and Spanish populations of Quebec and Florida, 10,000 British regular troops remained stationed in North America at the conclusion of the Seven Years War. The cost of maintaining this force added to the enormous debt Britain had run up during the fighting and created a desperate need for additional revenues. Increased excise taxes at home, however, resulted in disruptive demonstrations in the South of England, and Parliament was flooded by petitions from landlords and merchants protesting any attempt to raise revenues at their expense. In 1764 the Chancellor of the Exchequer, George Grenville, decided to obtain the needed revenue from America and pushed through Parliament a measure known as the Sugar Act.

The Sugar Act placed a prohibitive duty on sugar imported into the colonies and revitalized the customs service, introducing stricter registration procedures for ships and adding more officers. In anticipation of American resistance, the legislation also increased the jurisdiction of the vice-admiralty court at Halifax, where customs cases were heard. Vice-admiralty courts were hated because they stood outside the tradition of the English common law; they made no presumption of innocence and provided the accused with no right to a jury trial. These new regulations promised not only to squeeze the incomes of American merchants but to cut off their lucrative smuggling operations. The merchants had already been hurt by an economic depression that accompanied the decline in public spending at the end of the Seven Years War. Colonial taxes, moreover, which had been raised during the war, remained at an all-time high. In many cities merchants as well as artisans protested loudly. Boston was especially vocal: in response to the sugar tax, the town meeting proposed a boycott of certain English imports. This movement for nonimportation soon spread to other port towns.

James Otis Jr., a Massachusetts lawyer fond of grand oratory, was one of the first Americans to strike a number of themes that would become familiar over the next fifteen years. A man's "right to his life, his liberty, his property" was "written on the heart, and revealed to him by his maker," he argued in language echoing the rhetoric of the Great Awakening. It was "inherent, inalienable, and indefeasible by any laws, pacts, contracts, covenants, or stipulations which man could devise." "An act against the Constitution is void," he declared; there could be "no taxation without representation."

But it was only fair, Grenville countered, that the colonists help pay the costs of the empire, and what better way to do so than by a tax? So in early 1765 Grenville, unswayed by American protests, followed the Sugar Act with a second and considerably more sweeping revenue measure, the Stamp Act. This tax required the purchase of specially embossed paper for all newspapers, legal documents, licenses, insurance policies, ship's papers, and even dice and playing cards.

The Stamp Act Crisis

During the summer and autumn of 1765 the American reaction to the Stamp Act created a crisis of unprecedented proportions. Unlike the Sugar Act, which struck only at merchants, the stamp tax affected lawyers, printers, tavern owners, and other influential colonists. It had to be paid in hard money, and it came during a period of economic stagnation. Many colonists complained, as one did, of being "miserably burdened and oppressed with taxes."

Of more importance for the longer term, however, were the constitutional implications. Although colonial male property-owners elected their own assemblies, they could not vote in British elections. But the British argued that Americans were subject to the acts of Parliament by the fact of "virtual representation." That is, members of Parliament were thought to represent not just their districts but all citizens of the empire. As one British writer put it, the colonists were "represented in Parliament in the same manner as those inhabitants of Britain are who have not voices in elections." But in an influential pamphlet of 1765, *Considerations on the Propriety of Imposing Taxes*, Maryland lawyer Daniel Dulany rejected this theory. Because Americans were members of a separate political community, he insisted, Parliament could impose no tax on them. Instead, he argued for "actual representation," emphasizing the direct relationship that must exist between the people and their political representatives.

It was just such constitutional issues that were emphasized in the Virginia Stamp Act Resolutions, pushed through the Virginia assembly by the passionate young lawyer Patrick Henry in May 1765. Two years before, Henry had established his reputation as a radical by arguing that George III had degenerated "into a tyrant, and forfeits all rights to his subjects' obedience." Now, speaking in favor of these resolutions in the Virginia House of Burgesses, Henry warned the king to heed the fate of earlier tyrants such as Caesar and Charles I, both of whom had lost their lives. To howls of "Treason!" from his conservative colleagues, Henry cried that he spoke in "the interest of his country's dying liberty." Although the Burgesses rejected the most radical of his resolutions, they were all reprinted throughout the colonies. By the end of 1765 the assemblies of eight other colonies had approved similar measures denouncing the Stamp Act and proclaiming their support of "no taxation without representation."

In Massachusetts, the leaders of the opposition to the Stamp Act came from a group of upper- and middle-class men who had long opposed the conservative leaders of the colony. These men had worked for years to establish a political alliance with Boston craftsmen and workers who met at taverns, in volunteer fire companies, or at social clubs. One of these clubs, known as the Loyall Nine, included Samuel Adams (see the opening of this chapter), an associate and friend of James Otis who had made his career in local politics. Using his contacts with professionals, craftsmen, and laboring men as well, Adams helped put together an anti-British alliance that spanned Boston's social classes. "If our trade may be taxed," he reasoned with working men, "why not our lands? Why not the produce of our lands and everything we possess or make use of?" In August 1765, Adams and the Loyall Nine were instrumental in organizing a protest of Boston workingmen against the Stamp Act.

Samuel Adams, a second cousin of John Adams, was a leader of the Boston radicals and an organizer of the Sons of Liberty. The artist of this portrait, John Singleton Copley, was known for setting his subjects in the midst of everyday objects; here he portrays Adams in a middle-class suit with the charter guaranteeing the liberties of Boston's freemen.

The working people of Boston had reasons of their own to be angry. While Boston's elite had prospered during the eighteenth century, the conditions for workers and the poor had worsened. Unemployment, inflation, and high taxes had greatly increased the level of poverty during the depression that followed the Seven Years War, and many were resentful. Concerted action by crowds, as when people took to the streets to demand fair prices for bread, or when posses formed to capture criminals, were commonplace in eighteenth-century communities throughout Europe and the colonies.

It was in this tradition that a large Boston crowd assembled on August 14, 1765, in the shade of a broad "liberty tree" and strung up effigies of several British officials, including Boston's stamp distributor, Andrew Oliver. The restless crowd then proceeded to vandalize Oliver's office and home. At the order of Oliver's brother-in-law, Lieutenant Governor Thomas Hutchinson, leader of the Massachusetts conservatives, the town sheriff tried to break up the crowd, but he was pelted with paving stones and bricks. Soon thereafter, Oliver resigned his commission. The unified action of Boston's social groups had its intended effect.

Twelve days later, however, a similar crowd gathered at the elegant home of Hutchinson himself. As the family fled through the back door, the crowd smashed through the front with axes. Inside they demolished furniture, chopped down the interior walls, consumed the contents of the wine cellar, and looted everything of value, leaving the house a mere shell. As these events demonstrated, it was not always possible to keep popular protests within bounds. During the fall and winter, crowds in commercial towns from Halifax in the North to Savannah in the South forced the resignation of many British tax officials.

In many colonial cities and towns, merchants, lawyers, and respectable craftsmen sought to moderate the resistance movement by seizing control of it. Groups calling themselves the Sons of Liberty encouraged moderate forms of protest. They circulated petitions, published pamphlets, and encouraged crowd actions only as a last resort; always they emphasized limited political goals. Then in October 1765 delegations from nine colonies (New Hampshire and Georgia declined the invitation to attend, and the governors of Virginia and North Carolina prevented their delegates from accepting) met at what has been called the Stamp Act Congress in New York City, where they passed a set of resolutions denying Parliament's right to tax the colonists, since taxation depended on representation. But the delegates also agreed that Parliament had the authority to pass laws regulating colonial trade. These moderate efforts defused the radicals, and there were few repetitions of mob attacks, but by the end of 1765 almost all the stamp distributors had resigned or fled, making it impossible for Britain to enforce the Stamp Act.

Repeal of the Stamp Act

In the fall of 1765, British merchants, worried about the effects of the growing nonimportation movement among the colonists, began increasingly to petition Parliament to repeal the Stamp Act. About 40 percent of England's exports went to the British colonies in North America. "I rejoice that America has resisted," said William Pitt, who was no longer prime minister but spoke for the merchant interests in Parliament. "It is my opinion that this kingdom has no right to lay a tax upon the colonies." Grenville demanded that the British army be used to enforce the act. "Tell me," he demanded of Pitt, "when the Americans were emancipated." Pitt's response was memorable: "I desire to know when they were made slaves." Parliament heard the testimony of several interested parties, including Benjamin Franklin, who warned that Grenville's proposal to use troops could bring on a rebellion.

It was not, however, until Grenville was replaced by Lord Rockingham, who opposed the Stamp Act, that in March 1766 a bill for repeal passed the House of Commons. This news was greeted with celebrations throughout the American colonies, and the nonimportation associations were disbanded. Overlooked in the mood of optimism was Parliament's assertion in this Declaratory Act of its full authority to make laws binding the colonies "in all cases whatsoever." The notion of absolute parliamentary supremacy over colonial matters was basic to the British theory of empire. Even Pitt, friend of America that he was, asserted "the authority of this kingdom over the colonies to be sovereign and supreme, in every circumstance of government and legislation whatsoever." The Declaratory Act signaled that the conflict had not been resolved, merely postponed.

"SAVE YOUR MONEY AND SAVE YOUR COUNTRY"

Colonial resistance to the Stamp Act was stronger in urban than in rural communities, stronger among merchants, craftsmen, and planters than among farmers and frontiersmen. When Parliament next moved to impose its will on the colonies, as it had claimed the right to do in the Declaratory Act, it placed new duties on imported goods, and the American opposition again adopted the tactic of nonimportation. But this time resistance spread from

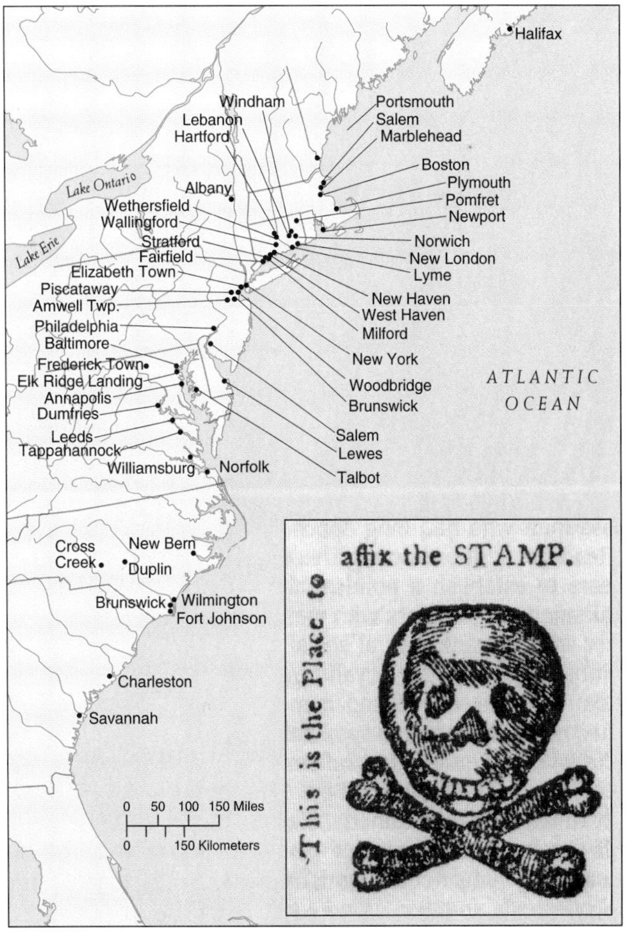

Demonstrations against the Stamp Act, 1765

From Halifax in the North to Savannah in the South, popular demonstrations against the Stamp Act forced the resignation of British tax officials. One newspaper editor cynically proposed that the stamp itself be in the form of a skull and crossbones (inset).

the cities and towns into the countryside. As the editor of the *Boston Gazette* phrased the issue, "Save your money and you save your country." It became the slogan of the movement.

The Townshend Revenue Acts

During the 1760s there was a rapid turnover of government leaders that made it difficult for Britain to form a consistent and even-handed policy toward the colonies. In 1767, after several failed governments, King George III asked William Pitt to again become prime minister. Pitt enjoyed enormous goodwill in America, and a government under his leadership stood a good chance of reclaiming colonial credibility. But, suffering from a prolonged illness, he was soon forced to retire, and his place as head of the cabinet was assumed by Charles Townshend, Chancellor of the Exchequer.

One of the first problems facing Townshend was the national debt. At home there were massive

British politicians bury the Stamp Act in this satirical engraving of 1766.

unemployment, riots over high prices, and tax protests. The large landowners forced a bill through Parliament slashing their taxes by 25 percent. The government feared continued opposition at home far more than opposition in America. So as part of his plan to close the budget gap, Townshend proposed a new measure for the colonies that placed import duties on commodities such as lead, glass, paint, paper, and tea. By means of these new Revenue Acts, enacted in 1767, Townshend hoped to redress colonial grievances against internal taxes like those imposed by the Stamp Act. The new acts provided for the collection of an external tax, that is, a duty imposed on goods at the customhouse, in colonial ports, before they entered colonial markets. In his presentation to the House of Commons, Benjamin Franklin had drawn the distinction between external taxes and internal taxes, and left the impression that colonists would be more accepting of external ones. For most colonial Americans, however, it proved to be a distinction without a difference.

The most influential response to these Revenue Acts came in a series of articles by John Dickinson, *Letters from a Farmer in Pennsylvania,* that were reprinted in nearly every colonial newspaper. In reality a wealthy Philadelphia lawyer, Dickinson posed in these articles as a humble husbandman. Parliament had the right to regulate trade through the use of duties, he conceded. It could place prohibitive tariffs, for example, on foreign products. But it had no constitutional authority to tax goods in order to raise revenues in America. As the preface to the Revenue Acts made clear, the income they produced would be used to pay the salaries of royal officials in America. Such an arrangement, Dickinson pointed out, would render those in charge of administering colonial affairs independent of elected representatives in the colonial assemblies and thus answerable to no one within the colonies themselves.

Other Americans saw the Revenue Acts as part of a British conspiracy to suppress American liberties. Their fears were confirmed by Townshend's stringent enforcement measures. He created a new and strengthened Board of Commissioners of the Customs and established vice-admiralty courts at Boston, Philadelphia, and Charleston to prosecute violators of the duties—the first time this hated institution had appeared in the most important American port cities. And to demonstrate his power, he also suspended New York's assembly. That body had refused to vote public funds to support the British troops garrisoned in the colony. Until the citizens of New York relented, Townshend declared, they would no longer be represented.

In response to these measures, some men argued for violent resistance. But Dickinson's essays had a great effect on the public debate, not only because of their convincing argument but because of their mild and reasonable tone. "Let us behave like dutiful children," Dickinson urged, "who have received unmerited blows from a beloved parent." As yet, no sentiment for independence existed in America. The colonial response was one of resistance to what were considered unconstitutional measures by the British authorities.

Nonimportation: An Early Political Boycott

Associations of nonimportation and nonconsumption, revived in October 1767 when the Boston town meeting drew up a long list of British products to boycott, became the main weapon of the resistance movement. Over the next few months other port cities, including Providence, Newport, and New York, set up nonimportation associations of their own. Towns such as Philadelphia, however, were unable to overcome conflicts between merchants and artisans. The economy had begun to improve since the earlier boycott, and many merchants saw little advantage in curtailing imports. Craftsmen, on the other hand, supported nonimportation with enthusi-

This British cartoon, A Society of Patriotic Ladies, *ridiculed the efforts of American women to support the Patriot cause by boycotting tea. The moderator of the meeting appears coarse and masculine, while an attractive scribe is swayed by the amorous attention of a gentleman. The activities under the table suggest that these women are neglecting their true duty.*

asm, because it meant that consumers would buy their products rather than foreign ones. Supported by workers, artisans took to the streets in towns and cities throughout the colonies to force merchants to stop importing British goods. The associations published the names of uncooperative importers and retailers. These people then became the object of protesters, who sometimes resorted to violence. Coercion was very much a part of the movement.

Adopting the language of Protestant ethics, nonimportation associations pledged to curtail luxuries and stimulate local industry. These values held great appeal in small towns and rural districts, which previously had been relatively uninvolved in the anti-British struggle. And in 1768 and 1769, colonial newspapers paid a great deal of attention to women's support for the boycott. Groups of women, some styling themselves Daughters of Liberty, organized spinning and weaving bees to produce homespun for local consumption. The actual work performed at these bees was less important than the symbolic message. "The industry and frugality of American ladies," wrote the editor of the *Boston Evening Post*, "are contributing to bring about the political salvation of a whole continent." Other women renounced silks and satins and pledged to stop serving tea to their husbands. Women sang:

> *Throw aside your topknots of pride,*
> *Wear none but your own country linen.*
> *Of economy boast, let your pride be the most,*
> *To show clothes of your own make and spinning.*

The poet Milcah Martha Moore urged American women to

> *Stand firmly resolv'd, and bid Grenville to see,*
> *That rather than freedom we part with our tea,*
> *And well as we love the dear draught when a-dry,*
> *As American patriots our taste we deny.*

Nonimportation appealed to the traditional values of rural communities—self-sufficiency and independence—and for the first time brought country people into the growing community of resistance.

Nonimportation was greatly strengthened in May 1769 when the Virginia House of Burgesses enacted the first provincial legislation banning the importation of goods enumerated in the Townshend Revenue Acts, and slaves and luxury commodities as well. Over the next few months all the colonies but New Hampshire enacted similar provisions. Because of these efforts, nonimportation was a great success. The value of colonial imports from Britain declined 41 percent the first year. In the largest port cities the decrease was even greater—54 percent in Philadelphia and over 80 percent in New York. The new Townshend duties, meanwhile, collected only about £20,000 in revenue. By 1770 English merchants were again protesting their hardship before Parliament.

The Massachusetts Circular Letter

Boston and Massachusetts were at the center of the agitation over the Townshend Revenue Acts. In February 1768 the Massachusetts House of Representatives approved a letter, drawn up by Samuel Adams, addressed to the speakers of the other provincial assemblies. Designed largely as a propaganda device and having little practical significance, the letter denounced the Townshend Acts, attacked the British plan to make royal officials independent of colonial assemblies, and urged the colonies to find a way to "harmonize with each other." Massachusetts governor Francis Bernard condemned the document for stirring up rebellion and dissolved the legislature. In Britain Lord Hillsborough, secretary of state for the colonies, ordered each royal governor in America to likewise dissolve his colony's assembly if it should endorse the letter. Before this demand reached America, the assemblies of New Hampshire, New Jersey, and Connecticut had commended Massachusetts. Virginia, moreover, had issued a circular letter encouraging a "hearty union" among the colonies and urging common action against the British measures that "have an immediate tendency to enslave us."

Hillsborough now ordered Massachusetts Governor Bernard to force the newly elected House of Representatives to rescind Adams's letter and delete all mention of it from its journal. The radicals could have asked for nothing better; resistance to the Townshend duties had been flagging, but there was great support for the prerogative and independence of the assembly. After protracted debate in June 1768, the representatives voted ninety-two to seventeen to defy Bernard, who immediately shut them down. The "Glorious Ninety-two" became heroes of the hour, and men in taverns throughout the colonies drank "ninety-two toasts" to the brave men of Massachusetts. The "rescinders," meanwhile, were condemned by public and press; in local elections the next year, seven of them lost their seats.

Throughout this crisis there were rumors and threats of mob rule in Boston. "I am no friend to riots, tumult, and unlawful assemblies," Samuel Adams declared, "but when the people are oppressed...they are not to be blamed." Because customs agents pressed on smugglers and honest traders alike, they enraged merchants, seamen, and dockworkers. In June 1768 a crowd assaulted customs officials who had seized John Hancock's sloop *Liberty* for nonpayment of duties. So frightened were the officials that they fled the city. Hancock, reportedly the wealthiest merchant in the colonies and a vocal opponent of the British measures, had become a principal target of the customs officers. In September, the Boston town meeting called on the people to arm themselves, and in the absence of an elected assembly it invited all the other towns to send delegates to a provincial convention. There were threats of armed resistance, but little support for it in the convention, which broke up in chaos. Nevertheless the British, fearing insurrection, occupied Boston with infantry and artillery regiments on October 1, 1768. With this action, they sacrificed a great deal of goodwill and respect and added greatly to the growing tensions.

The Politics of Revolt and the Boston Massacre

The British troops stationed in the colonies were the object of scorn and hostility over the next two years. There were regular conflicts between soldiers and radicals in New York City, often focusing on the Sons of Liberty. These men would erect "liberty poles" festooned with banners and flags proclaiming their cause, and the British troops would promptly destroy them. When the New York assembly finally bowed to Townshend in December 1769 and voted an appropriation to support the troops, the New York City Sons of Liberty organized a demonstration and erected a large liberty pole. The soldiers chopped it down, sawed it into pieces, and left the wood on the steps of a tavern frequented by the Sons. This act led to a riot in which British troops used their bayonets against a few thousand New Yorkers armed with cutlasses and clubs. Several men were wounded.

Confrontations also took place in Boston. In September 1769, James Otis provoked a melee by picking a fight in a tavern catering to British officers. The next month an encounter between a mob and soldiers ended with the troops' firing a volley into the air. The demonstrators were "mutinous desperadoes," wrote General Thomas Gage, guilty of "sedition." Samuel Adams played up reports and rumors of soldiers harassing women, picking fights, or simply taunting residents with versions of "Yankee Doodle." Soldiers were frequently hauled into Boston's courts, and local judges adopted a completely unfriendly attitude toward these members of the occupying army. In February 1770, an eleven-year-old boy was killed when a customs officer opened fire on a rock-throwing crowd. Although no soldiers were involved, this incident heightened the tensions between citizens and troops.

A persistent source of conflict was the competition between troops and townsmen over jobs. Soldiers were permitted to work when off duty, putting them in competition with day laborers. In early March 1770, an off-duty soldier walked into a ropewalk (a long narrow building in which ropes are made) in search of a job. The proprietor told him—using an obscenity—that he could clean the outhouse. The soldier left but returned with his friends, and a small riot ensued. Fighting continued over the next few days in the streets between the wharf and the Common, where the soldiers were encamped. On the evening of March 5, a crowd gathered at the Customs House and began taunting a guard, calling him a "damned rascally scoundrel lobster", and worse. A captain and seven soldiers went to his rescue, only to be pelted with snowballs and stones. Suddenly, without orders, the frightened soldiers began to fire. In what became known as the "Boston Massacre," three of the crowd fell dead immediately, and six more were wounded, two of these dying later. The first blood shed was that of Crispus Attucks, whose mother was Indian and father African American. The soldiers escaped to their barracks, but a mob numbering in the hundreds rampaged through the streets demanding vengeance.

Fearing for the safety of his men and the security of the state, Thomas Hutchinson, now governor of Massachusetts, ordered British troops out of Boston and arrested the soldiers who had fired the shots. The soldiers were tried later that year. Defending them were John Adams and Josiah Quincy Jr., two leaders of the radicals. Adams and Quincy established a reputation for fairness and statesmanship by convincing a jury of Bostonians that the soldiers had fired in fear of their lives. The Boston Massacre became infamous throughout the colonies, in part because of the circulation of an inflammatory print produced by the Boston engraver Paul Revere, which depicted the British as firing on a crowd of unresisting civilians. But for many colonists the incident was a disturbing reminder of the extent to which relations with the mother country had deteriorated. During the next two years, many people found themselves pulling back from the brink. "There seems," one Bostonian wrote, "to be a pause in politics."

The growth of American resistance was slowed as well by the news that Parliament had repealed most of the Townshend Revenue Acts on March 5, 1770—the same day as the Boston Massacre. The nonimportation measures almost immediately collapsed. Over the next three years, the value of British imports rose by 80 percent. The parliamentary retreat on the question of duties, like the earlier repeal of the Stamp Act, was accompanied by a face-saving measure—retention of the tax on tea "as a mark of the supremacy of Parliament," in the words of Frederick Lord North, the new prime minister.

In Paul Revere's version of the Boston Massacre, issued three weeks after the incident, the British fire an organized volley into a defenseless crowd. Revere's print—which he plagiarized from another Boston engraver—may have been inaccurate, but it was enormously effective propaganda. It hung in so many Patriot homes that the judge hearing the murder trial of these British soldiers warned the jury not to be swayed by "the prints exhibited in our houses."

FROM RESISTANCE TO REBELLION

The tax revolt in America was not an isolated incident, but the largest of numerous resistance movements to taxation—in Russa, the Netherlands, Corsica, Ireland, and Great Britain itself. There was a lull in the American controversy during the early 1770s, but the situation turned violent again in 1773, when Parliament infuriated the Americans with an ill-advised tax on tea. The Tea Act propelled the colonists on a swift track from resistance to outright rebellion. The groundwork for these developments, however, was laid during the quiet years that preceded them.

Intercolonial Cooperation

The Townshend Revenue Acts, although repealed, reflected Britain's intention of using customs revenues to pay the salaries of royal officials in the colonies. In June 1772, Governor Hutchinson inaugurated another controversy by announcing that his salary and those of other royally appointed Massachusetts officials would be paid by the crown. In effect, this made the executive and judiciary branches of the colony's government independent of elected representatives. In November, the Boston town meeting appointed a Committee of Correspondence to communicate with other towns regarding this challenge. A few weeks later the meeting issued what became known as the Boston Pamphlet—a series of declarations written by Samuel Adams and other radicals concluding that British encroachments on colonial rights were signs of a plot to enslave Americans.

In March 1773 the Virginia House of Burgesses appointed a standing committee for intercolonial correspondence "to obtain the most early and authentic intelligence" of British actions affecting America, "and to keep up and maintain a correspondence and communication with our sister colonies." The Virginia committee, including Patrick Henry, Richard Henry Lee, and young Thomas Jefferson, served as a model, and within a year all the colonies except Pennsylvania, where conservatives controlled the legislature, had created committees of their own. These committees became the principal channel for sharing information, shaping public opinion, and building intercolonial cooperation before the Continental Congress of 1774.

A British tax man is tarred and feathered and forced to drink tea, while the Boston Tea Party takes place in the background, in this image of 1774.

The information most damaging to British influence came from the radicals in Boston. Governor Hutchinson put himself at the center of controversy by declaring early in 1773 that the colonists were mistaken if they thought they enjoyed all the rights of Englishmen. Furthermore, even though they had removed themselves across the Atlantic, he argued, they were still subordinate to Parliament. "I know of no line that can be drawn," he asserted, "between the supreme authority of Parliament and the total independence of the colonies." This bold declaration outraged colonists, who during the years of agitation against taxes and duties had convinced themselves of the case against parliamentary supremacy.

In June, the Boston committee circulated a set of confidential letters from Hutchinson to the ministry in Britain, obtained in London by Benjamin Franklin from friends within the British government. Because Franklin had pledged to keep the letters to himself, he became the center of a scandal in London, and was dismissed from his position as postmaster general. But the British cause in the colonies suffered much more than Franklin's reputation. The letters revealed Hutchinson's call for "an abridgement of what are called English liberties" in the colonies. "I wish to see some further restraint of liberty," he had written, "rather than the connection with the parent state should be broken." This statement seemed to be the "smoking gun" of the conspiracy theory, and it created a torrent of anger against the British and their officials in the colonies.

The Boston Tea Party

It was in this context that the colonists received the news that Parliament had passed a Tea Act. Colonists were major consumers of tea, but because of the tax on it that remained from the Townshend duties, the colonial market for tea had collapsed, bringing the East India Company to the brink of bankruptcy. This company was the sole agent of British power in India, and Parliament could not allow it to fail. The British therefore devised a scheme in which they offered tea to Americans at prices that would tempt even the most patriotic back to the beverage. The radicals argued that this was merely a device to make palatable the payment of unconstitutional taxes—further evidence of the British conspiracy to corrupt the colonists.

In October a mass meeting in Philadelphia denounced anyone importing the tea as "an enemy of his country." A group calling itself the Committee for Tarring and Feathering plastered posters all over the city asking if the pilots of ships carrying the tea might like "ten gallons of liquid tar decanted on your pate—with the feathers of a dozen wild geese laid over that to enliven your appearance?" The Philadelphia consignees resigned in terror. Similar protests in New York City forced resignations there as well. The town meeting in Boston passed resolutions patterned on those of Philadelphia, but the tea agents there, among them two of Governor Hutchinson's sons, resisted the call to refuse the shipments.

The first of the tea ships arrived in Boston Harbor late in November. Mass meetings in Old South Church, which included many country people drawn to the scene of the crisis, resolved to keep the tea from being unloaded. Governor Hutchinson was equally firm in refusing to allow the ship to leave the harbor. On December 16, 1773, 8,000 people crowded into and around the church to hear the captain of one tea ship report to Samuel Adams that he could not move his ship. "This meeting can do nothing more to save the country," Adams declared. This was the signal for a disciplined group of fifty or sixty men, including farmers, artisans, merchants, professionals, and even apprentices, to march to the wharf disguised as Indians. There they boarded the ships and dumped into the harbor 45 tons of tea, valued at £18,000, all the while cheered on by Boston's citizens. "Boston Harbor's a tea-pot tonight," the crowd chanted.

Boston's was the first tea party, and other incidents of property destruction followed. When the New York Sons of Liberty learned that a cargo of tea had landed secretly in New York harbor, they, too, dressed themselves as Indians and dumped the tea chests over the sides. At Annapolis a ship loaded with tea was destroyed by fire, and arson also consumed a shipment stored at a warehouse in New Jersey. But it was the action in Boston at which the British railed. The government became convinced that something had to be done about the rebellious colony of Massachusetts. Strong measures were required, King George wrote to Lord North, for "we are now to dispute whether we have, or have not, any authority in that country."

The Intolerable Acts

During the spring of 1774 an angry Parliament passed a series of acts—termed by Americans the Intolerable Acts—that were calculated to punish Massachusetts and strengthen the British hand. The Boston Port Bill prohibited the loading or unloading of ships in any part of Boston harbor until the town fully compensated the East India Company and the customs service for the destroyed tea. The Massachusetts Government Act annulled the colonial charter: delegates to the upper house would no longer be elected by the assembly but henceforth be appointed by the king. Civil officers throughout the province were placed under the authority of the royal governor, and the selection of juries was given over to governor-appointed sheriffs. Town meetings, an important institution of the resistance movement, were prohibited from convening more than once a year except with the approval of the governor, who was to control their agendas. With these acts the

OVERVIEW

THE THIRTEEN REPRESSIVE BRITISH MEASURES

Legislation	Year	
Sugar Act	1764	Placed prohibitive duty on imported sugar; provided for greater regulation of American shipping to suppress smuggling
Stamp Act	1765	Required the purchase of specially embossed paper for newspapers, legal documents, licenses, insurance policies, ships' papers, and playing cards; struck at printers, lawyers, tavern owners, and other influential colonists. Repealed in 1766
Declaratory Act	1766	Asserted the authority of Parliament to make laws binding the colonies "in all cases whatsoever"
Townshend Revenue Acts	1767	Placed import duties, collectible before goods entered colonial markets, on many commodities including lead, glass, paper, and tea. Repealed in 1770
Tea Act	1773	Gave the British East India Company a monopoly on all tea imports to America, hitting at American merchants
Intolerable Acts	1774	
Boston Port Bill		Closed Boston harbor
Massachusetts Government Act		Annulled the Massachusetts colonial charter
Administration of Justice Act		Protected British officials from colonial courts by sending them home for trial if arrested
Quartering Act		Legalized the housing of British troops in private homes
Quebec Act		Created a highly centralized government for Canada

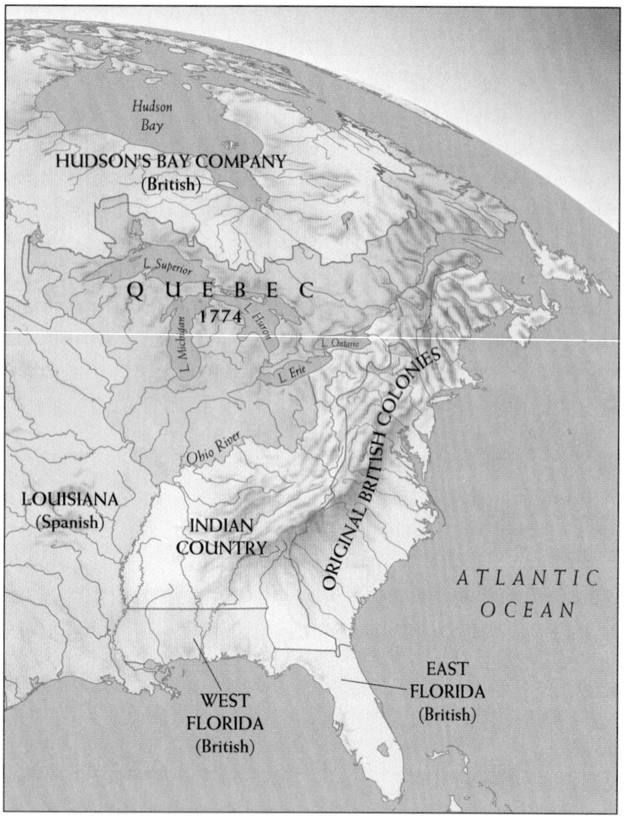

The Quebec Act of 1774 *With the Quebec Act, Britain created a centralized colonial government for Canada and extended that colony's administrative control southwest to the Ohio River, invalidating the sea-to-sea boundaries of many colonial charters.*

British terminated the long history of self-rule by communities in the colony of Massachusetts.

Additional measures affected the other colonies and encouraged them to see themselves in league with suffering Massachusetts. The Quartering Act legalized the housing of troops at public expense not only in taverns and abandoned buildings but in occupied dwellings and private homes as well. And the Administration of Justice Act sought to protect British officials from colonial courts, thereby encouraging them to pursue the work of suppression vigorously; those accused of capital crimes committed while putting down riots or collecting revenue, such as the soldiers involved in the Boston Massacre, were now to be sent to England for trial.

Finally, in the Quebec Act, the British authorized a permanent government for the territory taken from France in the late war. Originally, British officials had anticipated creating a popular assembly for Quebec, bringing it in line with the other colonies, but with the continuing American difficulties those plans were shelved. Instead Parliament established an authoritarian, antirepublican administration for Quebec, with a royal governor and an appointed council. To curry favor with the seigneurial class, the act confirmed the feudal system of land tenure along the St. Lawrence. And the Roman Catholic Church was granted religious toleration and confirmed in its traditional right to collect tithes, thus, in effect, establishing it as the state religion.

To the American colonists the Quebec Act was a frightening preview of what imperial authorities might have in store for them, and it confirmed the prediction of the Committees of Correspondence that there was a British conspiracy to destroy American liberty. The argument was made for them in Parliament by the radical Whig Charles James Fox: "To establish a perfectly despotic government, contrary to the genius and spirit of the British constitution," he warned his colleagues, "carries with it the appearance of a love of despotism, and a settled design to enslave the people of America." Moreover, the act extended Quebec's jurisdiction to the Ohio Valley, thus violating the "sea-to-sea" provisions of many of the colonies' charters. The British appeared to be giving the West back to the very people from whom it had been won.

In May, General Thomas Gage arrived in Boston to replace Hutchinson as governor. The same day, the Boston town meeting called for a revival of nonimportation measures against Britain. In Virginia, the Burgesses declared that Boston was enduring a "hostile invasion" and made provision for a "day of fasting, humiliation, and prayer, devoutly to implore the divine interposition for averting the heavy calamity, which threatens destruction to our civil rights and the evils of civil war." For this expression of sympathy, Governor Dunmore suspended the legislature, but the members adjourned to nearby Raleigh Tavern, where they voted for a Congress of all the colonies. Despite the governor's displeasure, throughout the colony on the first of June, funeral bells tolled, flags flew at half mast, and people flocked to the churches.

The First Continental Congress

It was amid this crisis that town meetings and colonial assemblies alike chose representatives for the Continental Congress described in the opening of this chapter. The delegates who arrived in Philadelphia in September 1774 included the most important leaders of the American cause. Cousins Samuel and John Adams, the radicals from Massachusetts, were joined by Patrick Henry and George Washington from Virginia and Christopher Gadsden of South Carolina. Many of the delegates were conservatives: John Dickinson and Joseph Galloway of Philadelphia, John Jay and James Duane from New York.

With the exception of Gadsden, a hothead who proposed an attack on British forces in Boston, the delegates wished to avoid war and favored a policy of economic coercion.

In one of their first debates, the delegates passed a Declaration and Resolves, in which they asserted that all the colonists sprang from a common tradition and enjoyed rights guaranteed "by the immutable laws of nature, the principles of the English constitution, and the several charters or compacts" of their provinces. Thirteen acts of Parliament, passed since 1763, were declared in violation of these rights. Until these acts were repealed, the delegates pledged, they would impose a set of sanctions against the British. These would include not only the nonimportation and nonconsumption of British goods but a prohibition on the export of colonial commodities to Britain or its other colonies.

To enforce these sanctions, the Continental Congress urged that "a committee be chosen in every county, city, and town, by those who are qualified to vote for representatives in the legislature, whose business it shall be attentively to observe the conduct of all persons." This call for democratically elected local committees in each community had important political ramifications. The following year, these groups, known as Committees of Observation and Safety, took over the functions of local government throughout the colonies. They organized militia companies, convened extralegal courts, and combined to form colony-wide congresses or conventions. By dissolving the colonial legislatures, royal governors unwittingly aided the work of these committees. The committees also scrutinized the activities of fellow citizens, suppressed the expression of Loyalist opinion from pulpit or press, and practiced other forms of coercion. Throughout most of the colonies the committees formed a bridge between the old colonial administrations and the revolutionary governments organized over the next few years. Committees began to link localities together in the cause of a wider American community. It was at this point that people began to refer to the colonies as the American "states."

Lexington and Concord

On September 1, 1774, General Gage sent troops from Boston to seize the stores of cannon and ammunition the Massachusetts militia had stored at armories in Charlestown and Cambridge. In response, the Massachusetts House of Representatives, calling itself the Provincial Congress, created a Committee of Safety empowered to call up the militia. On October 15 the committee authorized the creation of special units, to be known as "minutemen," who stood ready to be called at a moment's notice. The armed militia of the towns and communities surrounding Boston faced the British army, quartered in the city.

It was no rabble he was up against, Gage wrote to his superiors, but "the freeholders and farmers" of New England who believed they were defending their communities. Worrying that his forces were insufficient to suppress the rebellion, he requested reinforcements. The stalemate continued through the fall and winter. To raise their spirits, the New England militia ridiculed the British army:

> *And what have you got now with all your designing,*
> *But a town without victuals to sit down and dine in;*
> *And to look on the ground like a parcel of noodles,*
> *And sing, how the Yankees have beaten the Doodles.*
> *I'm sure if you're wise you'll make peace for a dinner,*
> *For fighting and fasting will soon make ye thinner.*

But King George was convinced that the time had come for war. "The New England governments are in a state of rebellion," he wrote privately. "Blows must decide whether they are to be subject to this country or independent." In Parliament, Pitt proposed withdrawing troops from Boston, but was overruled by a large margin. Attempting to find a balance between hard-liners and advocates of conciliation, Lord North organized majority support in the House of Commons for a plan in which Parliament would "forbear" to levy taxes for purposes of revenue once the colonies had agreed to tax themselves for the common defense. But simultaneously Parliament passed legislation severely restraining colonial commerce. "A great empire and little minds go ill together," Edmund Burke quipped in March 1775 in a brilliant speech in Parliament opposing this bill. "Let it be once understood that your government may be one thing and their privileges

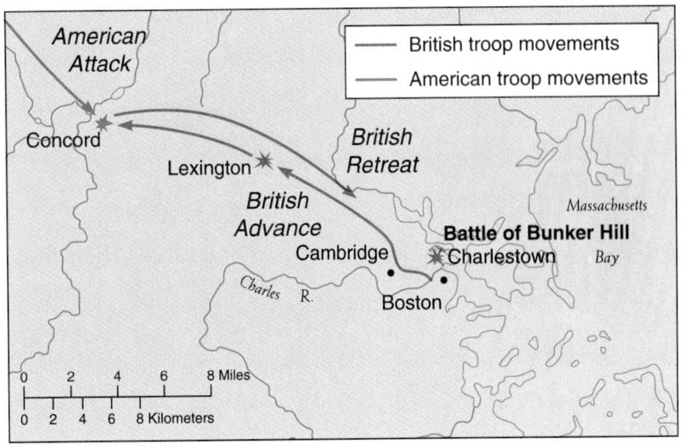

The First Engagements of the Revolution *The first military engagements of the American Revolution took place in the spring of 1775 in the countryside surrounding Boston.*

another, that these two things may exist without any mutual relation." Then he declared in prophetic words, "The cement is gone, the cohesion is loosened, and everything hastens to decay and dissolution."

In Virginia, at almost the same moment, Patrick Henry predicted that hostilities would soon begin in New England. "Gentlemen may cry peace, peace!—but there is no peace," he thundered in prose later memorized by millions of American schoolchildren. "Is life so dear, or peace so sweet, as to be purchased at the price of chains and slavery? Forbid it, Almighty God! I know not what course others may take, but as for me give me liberty or give me death!" Three weeks later, on April 14, General Gage received instructions to strike at once against the Massachusetts militia. "It will surely be better that the conflict should be brought on upon such ground," argued his superior, "than in a riper state of rebellion."

On the evening of April 18, 1775, Gage ordered 700 men to capture the store of American ammunition at the town of Concord. Learning of the operation, the Boston committee dispatched two men, Paul Revere and William Dawes, to alert the militia of the countryside. By the time the British forces had reached Lexington, midway to their destination, it was dawn. Some seventy armed minutemen had assembled on the green in the center of town, but they were disorganized and confused. "Lay down your arms, you damned rebels, and disperse!" cried one of the British officers. The Americans began to withdraw in the face of overwhelming opposition, but they took their arms with them. "Damn you, why don't you lay down your arms!" someone shouted from the British lines. "Damn them! We will have them!" No order to fire was given, but shots rang out, killing eight Americans and wounding ten others.

The British marched on to Concord, where they burned a small quantity of supplies and cut down a liberty pole. Meanwhile, news of the skirmish at Lexington had spread through the countryside and the militia companies of communities from miles around converged on the town. Seeing smoke, they mistakenly concluded that the troops were firing homes. "Will you let them burn the town!" one man cried, and the Americans moved to the Concord bridge. There they attacked a British company, killing three soldiers—the first British casualties of the Revolution. The British immediately turned back for Boston, but were attacked by Americans at many points along the way. Reinforcements met them at Lexington, preventing a complete disaster, but by the time they finally marched into Boston 73 were dead and 202 wounded or missing. The British troops were vastly outnumbered by the approximately 4,000 Massachusetts militiamen, who suffered 95 casualties. The engagement forecast what would be a central problem for the British: they would be forced to fight amid an armed population defending their own communities against outsiders.

Soon after the fighting at Lexington and Concord, the artist Ralph Earl and the engraver Amos Doolittle visited the location and interviewed participants. They produced a series of four engravings of the incident, the first popular prints of the battles of the Revolutionary War. This view shows the British soldiers marching back to Boston through the hail of sniper fire from colonial militiamen.

DECIDING FOR INDEPENDENCE

"We send you momentous intelligence," read the letter received by the Charleston, South Carolina, Committee of Correspondence on May 8, reporting the violence in Massachusetts. Community militia companies mobilized throughout the colonies. At Boston, thousands of militiamen from Massachusetts and the surrounding provinces besieged the city, leaving the British no escape but by sea; the siege would last for nearly a year. Meanwhile, delegates from twelve colonies reconverged on Philadelphia for the second session of the Continental Congress. What would be the political consequences of the armed struggle now under way?

The Second Continental Congress

The members of the Second Continental Congress, which opened on May 10, 1775, represented twelve of the British colonies on the mainland of North America. From New Hampshire to South Carolina, Committees of Observation and Safety had elected colonywide conventions, and these extralegal bodies in turn had chosen delegates. Consequently, few conservatives or Loyalists were among them. Georgia, unrepresented at the first session of the Continental Congress, remained absent at the opening of the second. This newest mainland colony depended heavily on British subsidies, and its leaders were cautious, fearing both slave and Indian uprisings. But in 1775 the political balance in Georgia shifted in favor of the radicals; observing the British attempt to curry favor with Indians elsewhere, Georgia frontier settlers came to believe that the Continental Congress would be more supportive in the matter of encroachments against the Creek Indians. Leaders from the backcountry then joined Whig merchants from Savannah to form a provincial Committee of Safety, and by the end of the summer the colony had delegates in Philadelphia.

The addition of Georgia made thirteen colonies in the revolutionary camp. But what of the other British possessions? The Continental Congress made overtures to a number of them. In one of their first acts, delegates called on "the oppressed inhabitants of Canada" to join in the struggle for "common liberty." After the Seven Years War, the British had treated Quebec as a conquered province, and French Canadians had little sympathy for the British empire. On the other hand, the Americans were traditional enemies, much feared because of their aggressive expansionism. Indeed, when the Canadians failed to respond positively and immediately, the delegates reversed themselves and voted to authorize a military expedition against Quebec to eliminate any possibility of a British invasion from that quarter. They thus killed any chance of the Canadians' joining the anti-British cause and set a course toward the development of separate nations.

Many of the other British colonies, however, harbored significant sympathy for the American struggle against parliamentary authority. For example, the population of Nova Scotia (not then a part of Canada) included many New Englanders who had relocated there after the expulsion of the Acadians. When the British attempted to recruit among them for soldiers to serve in Boston, one community responded that since "[we are] almost all of us born in New England, [we are] divided betwixt natural affection to our nearest relations and good faith and friendship to our king and country." But the British had established a naval stronghold at Halifax, and the province remained secure within the empire. The presence of the British military was decisive in several other locations as well. For example, the British army was able to keep Florida, where there was minimal local government, completely outside the revolutionary struggles. The popular assemblies of Jamaica, Grenada, and Barbados all formally declared themselves in sympathy with the Continental Congress, but the powerful British navy prevented them from sending representatives. Bermuda succeeded in sending a delegation to Philadelphia to plead for support, but so preoccupied were the Americans with more pressing matters that they found themselves unable to assist. Thus it was thirteen colonies against the empire.

Among the delegates at the Continental Congress were many familiar faces and a few new ones. One of the latter was Thomas Jefferson, a plantation owner and lawyer gifted with one of the most imaginative and analytical minds of his time who had served as a junior member of Virginia's Committee of Correspondence. All the delegates carried news of the enthusiasm for war that raged in their home provinces. "A frenzy of revenge seems to have seized all ranks of people," said Jefferson. George Washington attended all the sessions in uniform. "Oh that I was a soldier," an envious John Adams wrote to his wife, Abigail. The delegates agreed that defense was the first issue on their agenda.

On May 15 this Second Continental Congress resolved to put the colonies in a state of defense, but the delegates were divided on how best to do it. They lacked the power and the funds to immediately raise and supply an army. After debate and deliberation, John Adams made the practical proposal that the delegates simply designate as a "Continental Army" the militia forces besieging Boston. On June 14 the Congress resolved to supplement the New England militiamen with six companies of expert riflemen raised in Pennsylvania, Maryland, and Virginia. The delegates agreed that in order to emphasize their national aspirations, they had to select a man from the South to command these New England forces. All eyes turned to George Washington. Although Washington had suffered defeat at the beginning of the Seven Years War, he had subsequently compiled a distinguished record and had been promoted by the British command to brigadier, the highest rank of any native-born American. On June 15, Washington was elected commander in chief of all Continental forces by a unanimous vote. He served without salary. The Continental Congress soon appointed a staff of major generals to support him. On June 22, in a highly significant move, the Congress voted to finance the army with an issue of $2 million in bills of credit, backed by the good faith of the "Confederated Colonies." Thus began the long and complicated process of financing the Revolution.

During its first session in the spring of 1775, the Continental Congress had begun to move cautiously down the path toward independence. Few would admit, even to themselves, however, that this was their goal. John Adams, who was close to advocating independence, wrote that he was "as fond of reconciliation as any man" but found the hope of peaceful resolution unreasonable. "The cancer is too deeply rooted," he thought, "and too far spread to be cured by anything short of cutting it out entire." Still, on July 5, 1775, the delegates passed the so-called Olive Branch Petition, written by John Dickinson of Pennsylvania, in which they professed their attachment to King George and begged him to prevent further hostilities so that there might be an accommodation. The next day they approved a Declaration of the Causes and Necessities of Taking Up Arms, written by Jefferson and Dickinson. Here the delegates adopted a harder tone, resolving "to die freemen rather than to live slaves." Before the Second Continental Congress adjourned at the beginning of August, the delegates appointed commissioners to negotiate with the Indian nations in an attempt to keep them out of the conflict. They also reinstated Benjamin Franklin as postmaster general to keep the mails moving and protect communication among the colonies.

Fighting in the North and South

Both North and South saw fighting in 1775 and early 1776. In May 1775, a small force of armed New Englanders under the command of Ethan Allen of Vermont surprised the British garrison at Fort Ticonderoga on Lake Champlain, demanding—"in the name of Great Jehovah and the Continental Congress"—that

The Connecticut artist John Trumbull painted The Battle of Bunker Hill *in 1785, the first of a series that earned him the informal title of "the Painter of the Revolution." Trumbull was careful to research the details of his paintings but composed them in the grand style of historical romance. In the early nineteenth century he repainted this work, and three other Revolutionary scenes, for the rotunda of the Capitol in Washington,* D.C.

the commander surrender. The Continental Congress, in fact, knew nothing of this campaign, and when news of its arrived, members of the New York delegation were distressed at this New England violation of their territorial sovereignty. With great effort, the Americans transported the fort's cannon overland to be used in the siege of Boston.

At Boston the British hastened to reinforce Gage's forces and by the middle of June 1775 had approximately 6,500 soldiers in the city. By that time the American forces had increased to nearly 10,000. Fearing Gage would occupy the heights south of town, the Americans countered by occupying the Charlestown peninsula to the north. On June 17, British ships in the harbor began to fire on the American positions, and Gage decided on a frontal assault to dislodge them. In bloody fighting that, although it occurred at Breed's Hill, has since been known as the Battle of Bunker Hill, the British finally succeeded in routing the Americans, killing 140 men, but not before suffering over a thousand casualties of their own, including 226 dead. The fierce reaction in England to this enormous loss ended all possibility of any last-minute reconciliation. In August 1775, King George rejected the Olive Branch Petition and issued a royal proclamation declaring the colonists to be in "open and avowed rebellion." "Divers wicked and desperate persons" were the cause of the problem, said the king, and he called on his loyal subjects in America to "bring the traitors to justice."

In June 1775, the Continental Congress had also assembled its expeditionary force against Canada. One thousand Americans moved north up the Hudson River corridor, and in November General Richard Montgomery forced the capitulation of Montreal. Meanwhile, Benedict Arnold set out from Massachusetts with another American army, and after a torturous march through the forests and mountains of Maine, he joined Montgomery outside the walls of Quebec. Unlike the assault of British General Wolfe in 1759, however, the American assault failed to take the city. Montgomery and 100 Americans were killed, and another 300 were taken prisoner. Although Arnold held his position, the American siege was broken the following spring by British reinforcements who had come down the St. Lawrence. By the summer of 1776 the Americans had been forced back from Canada.

Elsewhere there were successes. Washington installed captured British artillery on the heights above Boston, placing both the city and its harbor within cannon range. General William Howe, who had replaced Gage, had little choice but to evacuate. In March, the British sailed out of Boston harbor for the last time, heading north to Halifax with at least 1,000 American Loyalists. In the South, American militia rose against the Loyalist forces of Virginia's Governor Dunmore, who had alienated the planter class by promising freedom to any slave who would fight with the British. After a decisive defeat of his forces, Dunmore retreated to British naval vessels, from which he shelled and destroyed much of the city of Norfolk, Virginia, on January 1, 1776. In North Carolina in February, the rebel militia crushed a Loyalist force at the Battle of Moore's Creek Bridge near Wilmington, ending British plans for an invasion of that province. The British decided to attack Charleston, but at Fort Moultrie in Charleston harbor an American force turned back the assault. It would be more than two years before the British would try again to invade the South.

No Turning Back

Hopes of reconciliation died with the mounting casualties. The Second Continental Congress, which was rapidly assuming the role of a new government for all the provinces, reconvened in September 1775 and received news of the king's proclamation that the colonies were in formal rebellion. Although the delegates disclaimed any intention of denying the sovereignty of the king, they now moved to organize an American navy. They declared British vessels open to capture and authorized privateering. The Congress took further steps toward de facto independence when it authorized contacts with foreign powers through its agents in Europe. In the spring of 1776, after a period of secret negotiations, France and Spain approved the shipping of supplies to the rebellious provinces. The Continental Congress then declared colonial ports open to the trade of all nations but Britain.

The emotional ties to Britain proved difficult to break. But in 1776 help arrived in the form of a pamphlet written by Thomas Paine, a radical Englishman recently arrived in Philadelphia. In *Common Sense*, Paine proposed to offer "simple fact, plain argument, and common sense" on the crisis. For years Americans had defended their actions by wrapping themselves in the mantle of British traditions. But Paine argued that the British system rested on "the base remains of two ancient tyrannies," aristocracy and monarchy, neither of which was appropriate for America. Paine placed the blame for the oppression of the colonists on the shoulders of King George, whom he labeled the "royal Brute." Appealing to the millennial spirit of American Protestant culture, Paine wrote: "We have it in our power to begin the world over again. A situation, similar to the present, hath not happened since the days of Noah until now." *Common Sense* was the single most important piece of writing during the Revolutionary era, selling more than 100,000 copies within a few months of its publication in January 1776. It reshaped popular thinking and put independence squarely on the agenda.

In April the North Carolina convention, which operated as the revolutionary replacement for the old colonial assembly, was first to empower its delegates to vote for a declaration of independence. News that the British were recruiting a force of German mercenaries to use against the Americans provided an additional push toward what now began to seem inevitable. In May the Continental Congress voted to recommend that the individual states move as quickly as possible toward the adoption of constitutions. When John Adams wrote, in the preamble to this statement, that "the exercise of every kind of authority under the said crown should be totally suppressed," he sent a strong signal that the delegates were on the verge of approving a momentous declaration.

The Manner in which the American Colonies Declared themselves INDEPENDENT of the King of ENGLAND, *a 1783 English print. Understanding that the coming struggle would require the steady support of ordinary people, in the Declaration of Independence the upper-class men of the Continental Congress asserted the right of popular revolution and the great principle of human equality.*

The Declaration of Independence

On June 7, 1776, Richard Henry Lee of Virginia offered a motion to the Continental Congress: "That these united colonies are, and of right ought to be, free and independent states, that they are absolved from all allegiance to the British crown, and that all political connection between them and the state of Great Britain is, and ought to be, totally dissolved." After some debate, a vote was postponed until July, but a committee composed of John Adams, Thomas Jefferson, Benjamin Franklin, Roger Sherman of Connecticut, and Robert Livingston of New York was asked to prepare a draft declaration of American independence. The committee assigned the writing to Jefferson.

The intervening month allowed the delegates to sample the public discussion and debate and receive instructions from their state conventions. By the end of the month, all the states but New York had authorized a vote for independence. When the question came up for debate again on July 1, a large majority in the Continental Congress supported independence. The final vote, taken on July 2, was twelve in favor of independence, none against, with New York abstaining. The delegates then turned to the declaration itself and made a number of changes in Jefferson's draft, striking out, for example, a long passage condemning slavery. In this and a number of other ways the final version was somewhat more cautious than the draft, but it was still a stirring document.

Its central section reiterated the "long train of abuses and usurpations" on the part of King George that had led the Americans to their drastic course; there was no mention of Parliament, the principal opponent since 1764. But it was the first section that expressed the highest ideals of the delegates:

> We hold these truths to be self-evident, that all men are created equal, that they are endowed by their creator with certain inalienable rights, that among these are life, liberty, and the pursuit of happiness. That to secure these rights, governments are instituted among men, deriving their just powers from the consent of the governed. That whenever any form of government becomes destructive of these ends, it is the right of the people to alter or to abolish it, and to institute a new government, laying its foundation on such principles, and organizing its powers in such form, as to them shall seem most likely to effect their safety and happiness.

There was very little debate in the Continental Congress about these "truths" and principles. The delegates were mostly men of wealth and position,

CHRONOLOGY

1713	France cedes Acadia to Britain
1745	New Englanders capture Louisburg
1749	French send an expeditionary force down the Ohio River
1753	French begin building forts from Lake Erie to the Ohio
1754	Albany Congress
1755	British General Edward Braddock defeated by a combined force of French and Indians Britain expels Acadians from Nova Scotia
1756	Seven Years War begins in Europe
1757	William Pitt becomes prime minister
1758	Louisburg captured by the British for the second time
1759	British capture Quebec
1763	Treaty of Paris Pontiac's uprising Proclamation of 1763 creates "Indian Country" Paxton Boys massacre
1764	Sugar Act
1765	Stamp Act and Stamp Act Congress
1766	Declaratory Act
1767	Townshend Revenue Acts
1768	Treaties of Hard Labor and Fort Stanwix
1770	Boston Massacre
1772	First Committee of Correspondence organized in Boston
1773	Tea Act Boston Tea Party
1774	Intolerable Acts First Continental Congress Dunmore's War
1775	Fighting begins at Lexington and Concord Second Continental Congress
1776	Americans invade Canada Thomas Paine's *Common Sense* Declaration of Independence

but realizing that the coming struggle for independence would require the steady support of ordinary people they asserted this great principle of equality and the right of revolution without examining the implications or the potential consequences. Surely no statement would reverberate more through American history. The ideal of equality would inspire the poor as well as the wealthy, women as well as men, blacks as well as whites, indeed, people of all races and creeds.

But it was the third and final section that may have contained the most meaning for the delegates: "For the support of this declaration, with a firm reliance on the protection of divine providence, we mutually pledge to each other our lives, our fortunes, and our sacred honor." In voting for independence, the delegates proclaimed their community but they also committed treason against their king. They could be condemned as traitors, hunted as criminals, and might soon stand on the scaffold to be executed for their sentiments. Yet on July 4, 1776, these men approved the text of the Declaration without dissent.

CONCLUSION

Great Britain emerged from the Seven Years War as the dominant power in North America. Yet despite its attempts at strict regulation and determination of the course of events in its colonies, it faced consistent resistance and often complete failure. Perhaps British leaders assumed that resistance would never be unified. After all, John Adams expressed the same doubts when he likened the delegates at the Continental Congress in 1774 to "ambassadors from a dozen belligerent powers." But the British underestimated the political consensus that existed among the colonists about the importance of "republican" government. They also underestimated the ability of the colonists to inform one another, to work together, to build a sentiment of nationalism that cut across the boundaries of ethnicity, region, and economic status. Through newspapers, pamphlets, Committees of Correspondence, community organizations, and group protest, the colonists discovered the concerns they shared, and in so doing they fostered a new, "American" identity. Without that identity it would have been difficult for them to consent to the treasonous act of declaring independence—especially when the independence they sought was from an international power that dominated much of the globe.

REVIEW QUESTIONS

1. How did overwhelming British success in the Seven Years War lead to an imperial crisis in British North America?
2. Outline the changes in British policy toward the colonies from 1750 to 1776.
3. Trace the developing sense of an American national community over this same period.
4. What were the principal events leading to the beginning of armed conflict at Lexington and Concord?
5. How were the ideals of American republicanism expressed in the Declaration of Independence?

RECOMMENDED READING

Benedict Anderson, *Imagined Communities: Reflections on the Origin and Spread of Nationalism*, revised edition (1991). An argument that the essential first act of national consciousness is the effort to create a community that encompasses more than just local individuals and groups.

Bernard Bailyn, *The Ideological Origins of the American Revolution* (1967). Whereas other accounts stress economic or social causes, this classic argument emphasizes the role of ideas in the advent of the Revolution. Includes an analysis of American views of the imperial crisis.

Eric Foner, *Tom Paine and Revolutionary America* (1976). Combines a biography of Paine with a community study of the Revolution in Philadelphia and Pennsylvania.

Lawrence H. Gipson, *British Empire before the American Revolution*, 8 vols. (1936–49). Although these volumes are heavy going, they offer what is still the best and most comprehensive treatment of the Seven Years War in America.

Robert A. Gross, *The Minute Men and Their World* (1976). This fascinating and readable history examines the coming of the Revolution from the viewpoint of a New England community.

Francis Jennings, *Empire of Fortune: Crowns, Colonies, and Tribes in the Seven Years War in America* (1988). The French and Indian War examined from the point of view of the Iroquois Confederacy. This is opinionated but exciting history.

Pauline Maier, *American Scripture: Making the Declaration of Independence* (1997). The deep background of this foundation of American democracy.

Richard L. Merritt, *Symbols of American Community, 1735–1775* (1966). A study of colonial newspapers that provides evidence for a rising sense of national community. The French and Indian War emerges as the key period for the growth of nationalist sentiment.

Richard White, *The Middle Ground: Indians, Empires, and Republics in the Great Lakes Region, 1650–1815* (1991). This well-researched history provides a fascinating account of the West from the point of view of imperialists, settlers, and Indians.

ADDITIONAL BIBLIOGRAPHY

The Seven Years War in America

Fred Anderson, *A People's Army: Massachusetts Soldiers and Society in the Seven Years' War* (1984)

Sylvia R. Frey, *The British Soldier in America: A Social History of Military Life in the Colonial Period* (1981)

Dougles E. Leach, *Roots of Conflict: British Armed Forces and Colonial Americans, 1677–1763* (1986)

Richard Middleton, *The Bells of Victory: The Pitt-Newcastle Ministry and the Conduct of the Seven Years' War, 1757–1762* (1985)

Robert C. Newbold, *The Albany Congress and Plan of Union of 1754* (1955)
Howard H. Peckham, *Pontiac and the Indian Uprising* (1947)
William Pencak, *War, Politics, and Revolution in Provincial Massachusetts* (1981)
Alan Rogers, *Empire and Liberty* (1974)
Noel T. St. John Williams, *Red Coats along the Hudson* (1997)

Imperial Crisis in British North America

Thomas C. Barrow, *Trade and Empire: The British Customs Service in Colonial America* (1967)
John Brewer, *Party Ideology and Popular Politics at the Accession of George III* (1976)
Don Cook, *The Long Fuse: How England Lost the American Colonies, 1760–1785* (1995)
Theodore Draper, *A Struggle for Power: The American Revolution* (1996)
Marc Egnal, *A Mighty Empire: The Origins of the American Revolution* (1988)
Alice Hanson Jones, *The Wealth of a Nation to Be* (1980)
John J. McCusker, *Rum and the American Revolution* (1989)
Richard L. Merritt, *Symbols of American Community, 1735–1775* (1966)
J. G. A. Pocock, *The Machiavellian Moment: Florentine Political Thought and the Atlantic Republican Tradition* (1975)
Caroline Robbins, *The Eighteenth-Century Commonwealthman* (1959)
Arthur M. Schlesinger, *The Colonial Merchants and the American Revolution* (1917)
W. A. Speck, *Stability and Strife: England, 1714–1760* (1977)
Peter David Garner Thomas, *Revolution in America: Britain and the Colonies, 1763–1776* (1992)
John W. Tyler, *Smugglers and Patriots: Boston Merchants and the Advent of the American Revolution* (1986)
Carl Ubbelohde, *The Vice-Admiralty Courts and the American Revolution* (1960)

From Resistance to Rebellion

David Ammerman, *In the Common Cause: American Response to the Coercive Acts of 1774* (1974)
T. H. Breen, *Tobacco Culture: The Mentality of the Great Tidewater Planters on the Eve of Revolution* (1985)
Richard D. Brown, *Revolutionary Politics in Massachusetts: The Boston Committee of Correspondence and the Towns, 1772–1774* (1970)
Richard L. Bushman, *King and People in Provincial Massachusetts* (1985)
H. Trevor Colbourn, *The Lamp of Experience: Whig History and the Intellectual Origins of the American Revolution* (1965)
Bernard Donoughue, *British Politics and the American Revolution: The Path to War, 1773–1775* (1964)
Jack P. Greene, *Understanding the American Revolution: Issues and Actors* (1995)
Dirk Hoerder, *Crowd Action in Revolutionary Massachusetts* (1977)
Benjamin W. Labaree, *The Boston Tea Party* (1974)
Pauline Maier, *From Resistance to Rebellion* (1972)
Edmund S. Morgan, *The Birth of the Republic, 1763–1789* (1956)
John Shy, *Toward Lexington: The Role of the British Army in the Coming of the American Revolution* (1965)
Peter David Garner Thomas, *Tea Party to Independence: The Third Phase of the American Revolution, 1773–1776* (1991)
Morton White, *The Philosophy of the American Revolution* (1978)
Gary Wills, *Inventing America* (1978)

Biography

Bernard Bailyn, *The Ordeal of Thomas Hutchinson* (1974)
Della Gray Barthelmas, *The Signers of the Declaration of Independence* (1997)
Richard R. Beeman, *Patrick Henry: A Biography* (1974)
Jeremy Black, *Pitt the Elder* (1992)
John Brooke, *King George III* (1974)
John E. Ferling, *The Loyalist Mind: Joseph Galloway and the American Revolution* (1977)
Milton E. Flower, *John Dickinson: Conservative Revolutionary* (1983)
William M. Fowler, Jr., *The Baron of Beacon Hill: A Biography of John Hancock* (1979)
William M. Fowler, Jr., *Samuel Adams: Radical Puritan* (1997)
David A. McCants, *Patrick Henry, the Orator* (1990)
Peter Shaw, *The Character of John Adams* (1976)
Peter D. G. Thomas, *Lord North* (1974)

CHAPTER SEVEN

THE CREATION OF THE UNITED STATES

1776–1786

William Ranney, *The Battle of Cowpens*. Oil on canvas. Photo by Sam Holland. Courtesy South Carolina State House.

Chapter Outline

THE WAR FOR INDEPENDENCE
The Patriot Forces
The Loyalists
The Campaign for New York and New Jersey
The Northern Campaigns of 1777
The Politics of the French and Spanish Alliance
Indian Peoples and the Revolution
The War in the South
Yorktown

THE UNITED STATES IN CONGRESS ASSEMBLED
The Articles of Confederation
Financing the War
Negotiating Independence
The Crisis of Demobilization
The Problem of the West

REVOLUTIONARY POLITICS IN THE STATES
The Broadened Base of Politics
The First State Constitutions
Declarations of Rights
A Spirit of Reform
African Americans and the Revolution
Economic Problems
State Remedies
Shays' Rebellion

AMERICAN COMMUNITIES
A National Community Evolves at Valley Forge

A drum roll ushered in a January morning in 1778, summoning the Continental Army to roll call. Along a two-mile line of log cabins, doors slowly opened and ragged men stepped out onto the frozen ground at Valley Forge. "There comes a soldier," wrote army surgeon Albigense Waldo. "His bare feet are seen through his worn-out shoes, his legs nearly naked from the tattered remains of an only pair of stockings, his breeches not sufficient to cover his nakedness, his shirt hanging in strings, his hair disheveled, his face meagre." The reek of foul straw and unwashed bodies filled the air. "No bread, no soldier!" The chant began as a barely audible murmur, then was picked up by men all along the line. "No bread, no soldier! No bread, no soldier!" At last the chanting grew so loud it could be heard at General Washington's headquarters, a mile away. The 11,000 men of the American army were surviving on little more than "firecake," a mixture of flour and water baked hard before the fire that, according to Waldo, turned "guts to pasteboard." Two thousand men were without shoes, others were without blankets and had to sit up all night about the fires to keep from freezing. Addressing the Continental Congress, Washington wrote, "Three or four days of bad weather would prove our destruction."

Valley Forge was to become a national symbol of endurance. After marching hundreds of weary miles and suffering a series of terrible defeats at the hands of a British force nearly twice their number, the soldiers of the Continental Army had retreated to this winter headquarters only to find themselves at the mercy of indifferent local suppliers. Contractors demanded exorbitant rates for food and clothing, rates the Congress had refused to pay, and as a result local farmers preferred to deal with the British, who paid in pounds sterling, not depreciated Continental currency.

The 11,000 men of the Continental Army, who had not been paid for nearly six months, were divided into sixteen brigades composed of regiments from nine states. An unsympathetic observer described them as "a vagabond army of ragamuffins," and indeed many of the men were drawn from the ranks of the poor and disadvantaged: indentured servants, landless farmers, and nearly a thousand African Americans, both slave and free. Most of the men came from thinly settled farm districts or small towns where precautions regarding sanitation had been unnecessary. Every thaw revealed ground covered with "much filth and nastiness," and officers ordered sentinels to fire on any man "easing himself elsewhere than at ye vaults." Typhoid fever and other infectious diseases spread quickly: along with dysentery, malnutrition, and exposure they claimed as many as 2,500 lives that winter. More than 700 women—wives, lovers, cooks, laundresses, and prostitutes—lived at Valley Forge that winter, and they were kept busy nursing the sick and burying the dead.

"What then is to become of this army?" Washington worried during the depth of the winter. But six months later the force he marched out of Valley Forge was considerably stronger for its experience there. Most important were the strong relationships that formed among the men, twelve of whom bunked together in each cabin, grouped by state regiments and brigade. In these units they fashioned "a band of brotherhood" and "shared with each other their hardships, dangers, and sufferings," wrote common soldier Joseph Plumb Martin, "sympathized with each other in trouble and sickness, assisted in bearing each other's burdens, [and] endeavored to conceal each other's faults." During the coming trials of battle, Washington, who referred to his staff as "family," would rely greatly on the bonds of affection his men had developed during the hard winter. As psychologists know today, it is this sense of community that contributes most to success in warfare.

To some American Patriots—as the supporters of the Revolution called themselves—the European-style Continental Army betrayed the ideals of the citizen-soldier and the autonomy of local communities, central tenets of the Revolution. Washington argued strongly, however, that the Revolution could not be won without a national army insulated from politics and able to withstand the shifting popular mood. Moreover, through the developing sense of community among these men—who came from hundreds of localities and a variety of ethnic backgrounds—the Continental soldiers became living examples of the egalitarian ideals of the Revolution. They were a popular democratic force that counterbalanced the conservatism of the new republic's elite leadership. The national spirit they built at Valley Forge would sustain them through four more years of war and provide momentum for the long process of forging a national political system out of the persistent localism of American politics. "I admire them tremendously!" wrote one European officer serving with Washington. "It is incredible that soldiers composed of men of every age, even children of fifteen, of whites and blacks, almost naked, unpaid, and rather poorly fed, can march so well and withstand fire so steadfastly." Asked to explain why his men served, another officer declared: "Nothing but virtue and that great principle, the love of our country."

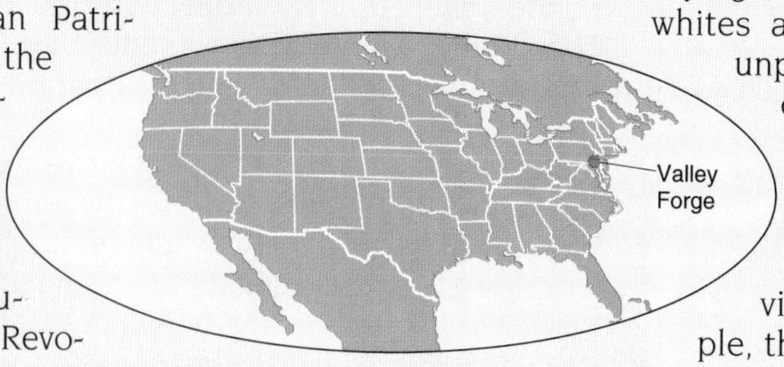

KEY TOPICS

- The major alignments and divisions among Americans during the American Revolution
- Major military campaigns of the Revolution
- The Articles of Confederation and the role of the Confederation Congress during the Revolutionary War
- The states as the setting for significant political change
- The economic crisis in the aftermath of the American Revolution

THE WAR FOR INDEPENDENCE

At the beginning of the Revolution, the British had the world's best-equipped and most disciplined army as well as a navy that was unopposed in American waters. But they greatly underestimated the American capacity to fight. With a native officer corps and considerable experience in the colonial wars of the eighteenth century, the Patriot forces proved formidable. The British also misperceived the sources of the conflict. Seeing the rebellion as the work of a small group of disgruntled conspirators, initially they defined their objective as defeating this Patriot opposition. In the wake of a military victory, they believed, they could easily reassert political control. But the geography of eastern North America offered no single vital center whose conquest would end the war. The Patriots had the advantage of fighting on their own ground and among a population thinly spread over a territory stretching along 1,500 miles of coastline and extending 100 miles or more into the interior. When the British succeeded in defeating the Patriots in one area, resistance would spring up in another. The key factor in the outcome of the war for independence, then, was the popular support for the American cause.

The Patriot Forces

Most American men of fighting age had to face the call to arms. From a population of approximately 350,000 eligible men, more than 200,000 saw action, though no more than 25,000 were engaged at any one time. More than 100,000 served in the Continental Army, under George Washington's command and the authority of the Continental Congress; the others served in Patriot militia companies.

These militias—armed bodies of men drawn from local communities—proved important in the defense of their own areas, where they had homes as well as local reputations to protect. Despite legend, however, the Revolutionary War was not won by these citizen-soldiers who exchanged plows for guns, or backcountry riflemen who picked off British soldiers from behind trees. In the exuberant days of 1776, many Patriots did believe that militias alone could win the war against the British. As one observer wrote, "The Rage Militaire, as the French call a passion for arms, has taken possession of the whole Continent." But, serving short terms of enlistment, often with officers of their own choosing, militiamen resisted discipline. Washington's deputy, General Nathanael Greene, declared that they lacked the fortitude "to stand the shocking scenes of war," having never been "steeled by habit or fortified by military pride." Indeed, in the face of battle militia companies demonstrated appalling rates of desertion. During the fierce fighting on Long Island, for example, three-quarters of Connecticut's 8,000 militiamen simply abandoned the field and headed home.

Initially, the Continental Congress refused to invoke a draft of men from all the colonies or to mandate army enlistments exceeding one year. As a result, and because men preferred the militia to the regular army, the states failed to meet their quotas for regiments in the Continental Army. Nevertheless, the final victory in the American Revolution was won essentially by the steady struggle of the Continental Army. And indeed, the Revolution had little in common with modern national liberation movements in which armed populations engage in guerrilla warfare. General Washington and his officers required a force that could directly engage the British, and from the beginning of the war Washington argued with a skeptical Congress that victory could be won only with a full commitment to a truly national army. This view conflicted with popular fears of a standing army: Would they not be defeating their own purpose, many Patriots wondered, by adopting the corrupt institutions of their British enemies?

The failings of the militias in the early battles of the war sobered Congress, however, and it both greatly enlarged state quotas for the army and extended the term of service to three years or the war's duration. To spur enlistment Congress offered bounties, regular wages, and promises of free land after victory. Although the states consistently failed to meet their quotas, by the spring of 1777 Washington's army had grown to nearly 9,000 men.

Discipline was essential in a conflict in which men fired at close range, charged each other with bayonets, and engaged in hand-to-hand combat. One Connecticut man wrote of the effects of cannon on his regiment: "The ball first cut off the head of Smith, a stout heavy man, and dashed it open, then took Taylor across the bowels; it then struck Sergeant Garret of our company on the hip, took off the point of the hip bone." "Oh! What a sight that was," he concluded, "to see within a distance of six rods those men with their legs and arms and guns and packs all in a heap." In New Jersey, a sergeant in the Continental Army witnessed British troops slaughtering Americans lying on the field: "The men that was wounded in the thigh or leg, they dashed out their brains with their muskets and run them through with their bayonets, made them like sieves. This was barbarity to the utmost."

According to the best estimates, a total of 25,674 American men died in the Revolution, approximately 6,000 from wounds suffered in battle, 10,000 from the effects of disease, and the rest as prisoners of war or missing in action. Regiments of the Continental Army experienced the highest casualty rates, sometimes 30 or 40 percent. Indeed, the casualty rate overall was higher than in any other American conflict up to the present day, with the exception of the Civil War. Although in most areas the war was confined to direct engagements between the armies, in the backcountry and in the South, where supporters and opponents of independence waged vicious campaigns of violence against each other, there were considerable noncombatant casualties.

Both the Continentals and the militias played important political roles as well. At a time when Americans identified most strongly with their local communities or their states, the Continental Army, through experiences like the Valley Forge winter, evolved into a powerful force for nationalist sentiment. Shortages of food and pay led to many army mutinies, in the most serious of which an officer was killed and two others wounded. But, when the mutineers in this instance set out, in January 1781, for Philadelphia, where they intended to address the Continental Congress, their purpose was not to abandon the American cause but to ask Congress to uphold its commitments to the soldiers who were fighting for the nation. En route to Philadelphia, the soldiers encountered British agents who tried to persuade them to go over to the king. Angry as these Continental soldiers were at the conditions under which their Congress expected them to fight, they were enraged at this attempt at subversion, and they hanged the British agents on the spot. The men from every colony who served in the Continental Army contributed mightily to the unity of purpose—the formation of a national community—that was essential to the process of nation making.

In most communities Patriots seized control of local government during the period of committee organizing in 1774 and 1775 (see Chapter 6), and with war imminent they pressed the obligation to serve in a Patriot militia upon most eligible men. In Farmington, Connecticut, in 1776, eighteen men were imprisoned "on suspicion of their being inimical to America" when they failed to join the muster of the local militia. After individual grilling by the authorities, they petitioned for pardon. "They appeared to be penitent of their former conduct," it was reported, and understood "that there was no such thing" as remaining neutral. Probably the most important role of the Patriot militias was to force even the most apathetic of Americans to think seriously about the Revolution, and to choose sides under the scrutiny of their neighbors.

As men marched off to war, many women assumed the management of family farms and businesses; Abigail Adams, for

Jean Baptiste Antoine de Verger, a French officer serving with the Continental Army, made these watercolors of American soldiers during the Revolution. Some 200,000 men saw action, including at least 5,000 African Americans; more than half of these troops served with the Continental Army.

example, ran the family's farm at Quincy for years. Adams wrote eloquently and often to her husband, John, on issues surrounding the American struggle for independence and, later, on the structure of the new republic. Some women participated even more directly in patriotic politics. The Boston home of Mercy Otis Warren, daughter of James Otis, was a center of Patriot political activity, and this dedicated revolutionary woman published a series of satires supporting the American cause and scorning the Loyalists. When the fighting shifted to their locales, women volunteered as seamstresses, cooks, nurses, and even spies.

When the months of fighting lengthened into years, many women left their homes to join husbands and lovers, fathers and brothers, in army encampments. Some were officially employed, but most took care of their own men, and many fought with them side by side. Best known among the women who stayed by their husbands' sides even in camp were Martha Washington and Catherine Greene, wives of the two most important American generals of the war. But less socially prominent women were remembered as well. Mary Ludwig Hays (later McCauley) earned the name "Molly Pitcher" for her courage in bringing water to the Patriots during the battle of Monmouth, in June 1778. When her husband was overcome by heat, Mary took his place at the cannon. When Margaret Corbin's husband died in battle, she stepped into his position. Other women, such as Deborah Sampson of Massachusetts, disguised themselves as men and enlisted.

Copley, John Singleton, U.S., 1738–1815. Mrs. *James Warren* (*Mercy Otis*), ca. 1763. Oil on canvas. 51 1/4 x 41 in. (130.1 x 104.1 cm). Bequest of Winslow Warren. Courtesy, Museum of Fine Art, Boston.

John Singleton Copley's portrait of Mercy Otis Warren captured her at the age of thirty-six, in 1765. During the Revolution her home in Boston was a center of patriotic political activity.

The Loyalists

Not all Americans were Patriots. Many sat on the fence, confused by the conflict and waiting for a clear turn in the tide of the struggle before declaring their allegiance. About a fifth of the population, perhaps as many as half a million people, remained loyal to the British crown. They called themselves Loyalists but were known to Patriots as "Tories," the popular name for the conservative party in England, which traditionally supported the authority of the king over Parliament. Loyalism was strongest in the Lower South, weakest in New England. British colonial officials were almost always Loyalists, as were most Anglican clergymen and many lawyers who had worked with colonial administrators. The British cause also attracted ethnic minorities who had been persecuted by the dominant majority, such as the Highland Scots of the Carolinas and western New York, and southern tenant farmers who had Patriot landlords. Many slaves and most Indians identified with the Loyalists, the first because the Patriot leadership in the South was drawn from the ranks of slave owners, the second because they feared aggressive expansion by independent American states. Other Loyalists were conservatives, fearful of political or social upheaval, or were temperamentally opposed to resistance to established authority.

Patriots passed state treason acts that prohibited speaking or writing against the Revolution. They also punished Loyalists with bills of attainder, by which persons were deprived, without trial, of their civil rights and property (a process later made illegal in the United States Constitution). In some areas, notably New York, South Carolina, Massachusetts, and Pennsylvania, Loyalists faced mob violence. One favorite punishment was the "grand Tory ride," in which a crowd hauled the victim through the streets astride a sharp fence rail. Another was tarring and feathering, in which men were stripped to "buff and breeches" and their naked flesh coated liberally with heated tar and then feathers. One broadside recommended that Patriots "then hold a lighted Candle to the feathers, and try to set it all on fire." The torment rarely went that far, but it was brutally painful nonetheless.

The most infamous American supporter of the British cause was Benedict Arnold, whose name has become synonymous, in the United States, with treason. Arnold was a hero of the early battles of the Revolution. But in 1779, angry and resentful about what he

A Patriot mob torments Loyalists in this print published during the Revolution. One favorite punishment was the "grand Tory ride," in which a crowd hauled the victim through the streets astride a fence rail. In another men were stripped to "buff and breeches" and their naked flesh coated liberally with heated tar and feathers.

perceived to be assignments and rank below his station, he became a paid informer of General Henry Clinton, head of the British army in New York City. In 1780 Patriots uncovered Arnold's plot to betray the strategic post of West Point, which he commanded. After fleeing to the British, who paid him a handsome stipend and pension, he became a brigadier general in the British army. The *bête noire* of the Revolution, Arnold became the most hated man in America. In his hometown of Norwich, Connecticut, a crowd destroyed the gravestones of his family, and in cities and towns throughout America thousands burned his effigy. During the last two years of the war he led British raids against his home state as well as against Virginia, and after the Revolution he lived in England until his death in 1801.

The British strategy for suppressing the Revolution depended on mobilizing the Loyalists, but in most areas this proved impossible. As noted earlier, the Loyalists were not a monolithic group but were divided in their opinions, and many were covertly sympathetic to Patriot arguments. Still, as many as 50,000 Loyalists fought for the king during the Revolution. Many joined Loyalist militias or engaged in irregular warfare, especially in the Lower South. In 1780, when Washington's Continentals numbered about 9,000, there were 8,000 American Loyalists serving in the British army in America.

As many as 80,000 Loyalists fled the country during and after the Revolution, taking up residence in England, the British West Indies, or Canada. Their property was confiscated by the states and sold at public auction. Although the British government compensated many for their losses, most Loyalists were unhappy exiles. "I earnestly wish to spend the remainder of my days in America," wrote William Pepperell, formerly of Maine, from London in 1778. "I love the country, I love the people." Former governor Thomas Hutchinson of Massachusetts wrote that he "had rather die in a little country farm-house in New England than in the best nobleman's seat in old England." Despite their disagreement with the Patriots on essential political questions, they remained Americans, and they mourned the loss of their country.

The Campaign for New York and New Jersey

During the winter of 1775–76 the British developed a strategic plan for the war. From his base at Halifax, Nova Scotia, Sir William Howe was to take his army to New York City, which the British navy would make impregnable. From there Howe was to drive north along the Hudson, while another British army marched south from Canada to Albany. The two armies would converge, cutting New England off from the rest of the colonies, and then turn eastward to reduce the rebellious Yankees into submission. Washington, who had arrived at Boston to take command of the militia forces there in the summer of 1775, anticipated this strategy, and in the spring of 1776 he shifted his forces southward toward New York.

In early July, as Congress was taking its final vote on the Declaration of Independence, the British began their operation at New York City, landing 32,000 men on Staten Island, a third of them Hessian mercenaries (from the German state of Hesse). The Americans, meanwhile, set up fortified positions across the harbor in Brooklyn. Attacking in late August, the British inflicted heavy casualties on the Americans, and the militia forces under Washington's command proved unreliable under fire. The battle of Long Island ended in disaster for the Patriots, and they were forced to withdraw across the East River to Manhattan.

The British now offered Congress an opportunity to negotiate, and on September 6, Benjamin Franklin, John Adams, and Edward Rutledge sat down with General Howe and his brother, Admiral Richard Howe, on Staten Island. But the meeting broke up when the Howes demanded revocation of the Declaration of Independence. The stage was set for another round of violence. Six days later the British invaded Manhattan island, and only an American stand at Harlem Heights prevented the destruction of a large portion of the Patriot army. Enjoying naval control of the harbor, the British quickly outflanked the American positions. In a series of battles over the next few months, they forced Washington back at White Plains and overran the American posts of Fort Washington and Fort Lee, on either side of the Hudson River. By November the Americans were fleeing south across New Jersey in a frantic attempt to avoid the British under General Charles Cornwallis.

With morale desperately low, whole militia companies deserted; others, announcing the end of their terms of enlistment, left for home. American resistance seemed to be collapsing all around Washington. "Our troops will not do their duty," he wrote painfully to Congress as he crossed the Delaware River into Pennsylvania. Upon receiving his message, the delegates in Philadelphia fled to Baltimore. "I think the game is pretty near up," Washington admitted to his brother. But rather than fall back further, which would surely have meant the dissolution of his entire force, he decided to risk a counterattack. On Christmas night Washington led 2,400 troops back across the Delaware, and the next morning defeated the Hessian forces in a surprise attack on their headquarters at Trenton, New Jersey. The Americans inflicted further heavy losses on the British at Princeton, then drove them all the way back to the environs of New York City.

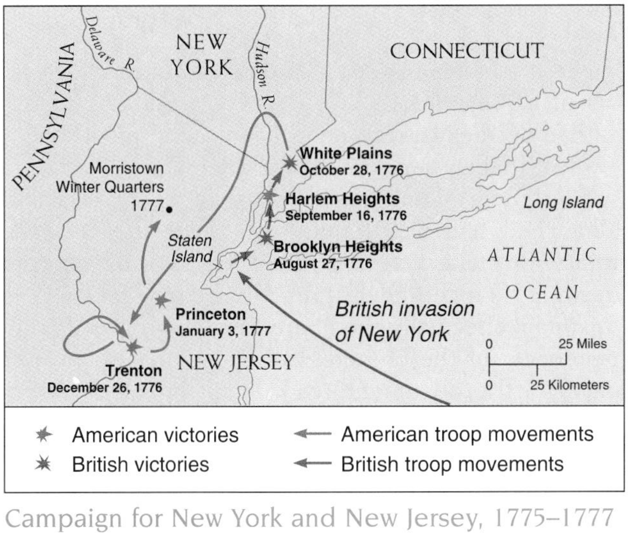

Campaign for New York and New Jersey, 1775–1777

Although these small victories of 1776 and early 1777 had little strategic importance, they salvaged American morale. As Washington settled into winter headquarters at Morristown, he realized he had to pursue a defensive strategy, avoiding direct confrontations with the British while checking their advances and hurting them wherever possible. "We cannot conquer the British force at once," wrote General Greene, "but they cannot conquer us at all." This last sentiment was more of a hope than a conviction, but it defined the essentially defensive American strategy of the Revolution. Most important to that strategy was the survival of the Continental Army.

The Northern Campaigns of 1777

The fighting with the American forces had prevented Howe from moving north up the Hudson, and the British advance southward from Canada had been stalled by American resistance at Lake Champlain. In 1777, however, the British decided to replay their strategy. From Canada they dispatched General John Burgoyne with nearly 8,000 British and German troops. Howe was to move his force from New York, first taking the city of Philadelphia, the seat of the Continental Congress, and then moving north to meet Burgoyne.

Fort Ticonderoga fell to Burgoyne on July 6, but by August the general found himself bogged down and harassed by Patriot militias in the rough country south of Lake George. After several defeats in September at the hands of an American army commanded by General Horatio Gates, Burgoyne retreated to Saratoga. There his army was surrounded by a considerably larger force of Americans, and on October 17, lacking alternatives, he surrendered his nearly 6,000 men. It would be the biggest British defeat until Yorktown, decisive because it forced the nations of Europe to recognize that the Americans had a fighting chance to win their Revolution.

The Americans were less successful against Howe. A force of 15,000 British troops left New York in July, landing a month later at the northern end of Chesapeake Bay. At Brandywine Creek the British outflanked the Americans, inflicting heavy casualties and forcing a retreat. Ten days later the British routed the Americans a second time with a frightful bayonet charge at Paoli that left many Patriots dead. When British troops occupied Philadelphia on September 26, Congress had already fled. Washington attempted a valiant counterattack at Germantown on October 4, but initial success was followed by miscoordination that eventually doomed the operation.

After this campaign the Continentals headed for winter quarters at Valley Forge, about twenty miles from Philadelphia, the bitterness of their defeats muted somewhat by news of the surrender at Saratoga. In taking Philadelphia, the British had gained the most important city in North America, but it proved to have

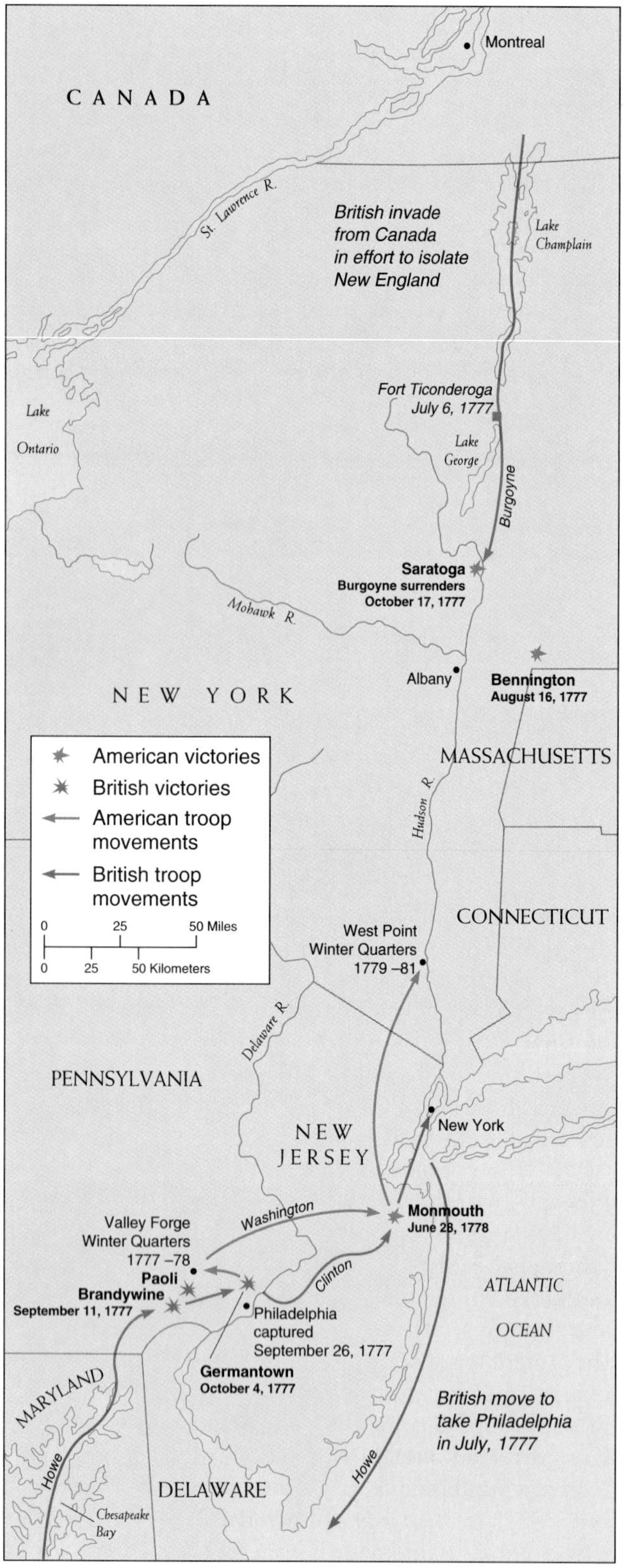

Northern Campaigns, 1777–1778

little strategic value. The Continental Congress moved to the Pennsylvania backcountry. In any event, central government was virtually nonexistent, and so the unified effort suffered little disruption. The British would have done better to move north instead, where they might have saved Burgoyne. At the end of two years of fighting, the British strategy for winning the war had to be judged a failure.

The Politics of the French and Spanish Alliance

During these first two years of fighting, the Americans were sustained by loans from France and Spain, allies in the Bourbon "family compact" of monarchies. Both saw an opportunity to win back North American territories lost to Great Britain in the Seven Years War that concluded in 1763. The Continental Congress maintained a diplomatic delegation in Paris headed by Benjamin Franklin. The urbane and cosmopolitan Franklin, who captured French hearts by dressing in homespun and wearing a "frontiersman" fur cap, maintained excellent relations with the Comte de Vergennes, the French foreign minister. Franklin negotiated with Vergennes for recognition of American independence and a Franco-American alliance against the British in addition to loans to finance the Revolution, but was unable to convince him. France, which wanted to weaken the British empire any way it could, was inclined to support the Americans, but it was reluctant to encourage a republican revolution being fought against monarchy and colonialism.

In England, meanwhile, there was rising opposition to the war among the Tories and the Whigs, their political opponents who took a less authoritarian view of things. "The measures toward America are erroneous," declared Lord Rockingham, "the adherence to them is destruction." William Pitt warned his countrymen to "beware the gathering storm" if and when France decided to support the Americans actively. When British Prime Minister Lord North received the news of Burgoyne's surrender, he dispatched agents to begin peace discussions with Franklin in Paris. The victory at Saratoga, as well as fears of British conciliation with the revolutionaries, finally persuaded Vergennes to intervene on the side of the United States. In mid-December of 1777 he informed Franklin that the king's council had decided to recognize American independence.

In February 1778 the American delegation submitted to Congress a treaty of commerce and alliance it had negotiated with the French. In the treaty, to take effect upon a declaration of war between France and Britain, the French pledged to "maintain effectually the liberty, sovereignty, and independence" of the United States. "Neither of the two parties," the document read, "shall conclude either truce or peace with Great Britain, without the formal consent of the other." The Americans had compelled France to guarantee to the United States all the "northern parts of America" conquered in the war, ending any thought of a rebirth of New France. But they promised to recognize any French acquisitions of British islands in the West Indies. In June, France declared war, and soon began fighting with Britain.

A year later Spain also entered the war. Spanish officials in New Orleans provided substantial ammunition and provisions for American forts in the West, including herds of cattle, driven to New Orleans by *vaqueros* (cowboys) from Texas. In New Spain the viceroy levied a special tax to pay for these supplies, and borderland colonists contributed their share. Father Junípero Serra, president of the California missions, prescribed a weekly prayer for American victory, and the scene of California Indian converts praying for the freedom of European colonists on the other coast is surely one of the most ironic of the era. But American attempts to establish a formal Spanish alliance met with failure. The Spanish feared the Americans as a danger to their own empire of New Spain but regarded the Revolution as an opportunity to regain Florida from the British and extend their control of the Mississippi Valley. "Its people are active, industrious, and aggressive," one Mexican official wrote of the United States, and "it would be culpable negligence on our part not to thwart their schemes for conquest."

The Spanish zealously pursued their strategy, attacking and taking the Mississippi River towns of Natchez and Baton Rouge in 1779, and the Gulf ports of Mobile in 1780 and Pensacola in 1781; their victory at Pensacola was won with the help of several companies of African Americans. Alarmed by the quick spread of American settlements west of the Appalachians, the Spanish attempted to establish a claim of their own to the British territory north of the Ohio by sending an expedition into the Northwest in 1781, which succeeded in taking the minor British post of St. Joseph, in present-day Michigan.

The first French ambassador to the United States arrived with instructions to do everything he could to prevent the Americans from enlarging their territory at the expense of the Spanish empire in the West. Vergennes also feared the potential power of an independent United States. Several years before, he had warned the British that once the Americans gained their independence they "would immediately set about forming a great marine," and use it in the Caribbean to "conquer both your islands and ours," then sweep south, where it would "not leave a foot of that hemisphere in the possession of any European power." American leaders understood that the treaty with France and the *modus vivendi* with Spain were merely expedients for all sides, and they recognized the dangers that France and Spain posed to the United States. But far more important was the prospect the French treaty offered of victory over Britain.

The entry of France into the war forced the British to rethink their strategy. At first Lord North took a conciliatory approach, sending a peace commission to America with promises to repeal the parliamentary legislation that had provoked the crisis in the first place and pledging never again to impose revenue taxes on the colonies. Three years earlier, such pledges would surely have forestalled the movement toward independence. But the Continental Congress now declared that any person coming to terms with the peace commission was a traitor; the only possible topics of negotiation were the withdrawal of British forces and the recognition of American independence. The peace commission was reduced to attempting to bribe members of Congress and finally to threatening a war of devastation, but to no avail.

Meanwhile the British realized that with France in the war their valuable West Indies colonies were at risk, and they rushed 5,000 men from New York to the Caribbean, where they beat back a French attack. Fearing the arrival of the French fleet along the North American coast, the new British commander in America, General Henry Clinton, evacuated Philadelphia in June 1778. In hot pursuit were Washington's Continentals. At the battle of Monmouth on June 28, the British blunted the American drive and retreated to New York. The Americans, centered at West Point, took up defensive positions surrounding the lower Hudson. Confidence in an impending victory now spread through the Patriot forces. But after a failed campaign with the French against the British forces at Newport, Rhode Island, Washington settled for a defensive strategy. Although the Americans enjoyed several small successes in the Northeast over the next two years, the war there went into a stall.

The war at sea was fought mostly between the British and the French, but Continental, state, and private vessels raided British merchant ships and conducted isolated naval patrols. The foremost American naval hero of the war was John Paul Jones, who, in 1777, raided the coast of Scotland. In 1779, while commanding the French ship *Bonhomme Richard* (named in honor of Franklin's "Poor Richard"), Jones engaged in a celebrated battle with the British warship *Serapis*. When the two ships locked together, the British captain hailed Jones, asking if he were ready to surrender. Jones's reply—"I have not yet begun to fight"—became one of the most quoted lines of the Revolution. Jones won his battle, though it had little military consequence. After the war Congress decommissioned the small American navy and dismissed its officers, including Jones, who went on to serve in the imperial Russian navy.

Gilbert Stuart. *Joseph Brant*, 1786. Oil on canvas, 30" × 25". New York State Historical Association, Cooper-

Joseph Brant, the brilliant chief of the Mohawks who sided with Great Britain during the Revolution, in a 1786 painting by the American artist Gilbert Stuart. After the Treaty of Paris, Brant led a large faction of Iroquois people north into British Canada, where they established a separate Iroquois Confederacy.

Indian Peoples and the Revolution

At the beginning of the conflict both sides solicited the support of the Indians. A committee of the Continental Congress reported that "securing and preserving the friendship of Indian nations appears to be a subject of the utmost moment to these colonies." Most concerned about the stance of the Iroquois Confederacy—long one of the most potent political forces in colonial North America—a delegation from Congress told the Iroquois that the conflict was a "family quarrel" and urged them to avoid it. British agents, on the other hand, pressed the Iroquois to unite against the Americans. Many Indian people were reluctant to get involved: "We are unwilling to join on either side of such a contest," an Oneida chief responded, "for we love you both—old England and new."

But ultimately the British were more persuasive, arguing that a Patriot victory would mean the extension of American settlements into Indian homelands. Native peoples fought in the Revolution for some of the same reasons Patriots did—for political independence, cultural integrity, and the protection of their land and property—but Indian fears of American expansion led them to oppose those who claimed the cause of natural rights and the equality of all men. Almost all the tribes that engaged in the fighting did so on the side of the British.

British officials marshaled the support of Cherokees, Creeks, Choctaws, and Chickasaws in the South, supplying them with arms from the British arsenal at Pensacola. The consequence was a ferocious Indian war in the southern backcountry. In the summer of 1776 a large number of Cherokees, led by the warrior chief Dragging Canoe (Tsiyu-Gunsini), attacked dozens of American settlements. It took hard fighting before Patriot militia companies managed to drive the Cherokees into the mountains, destroying many of their towns. Although the Cherokees eventually made an official peace, sporadic violence between Patriots and Indians continued along the southern frontier.

Among the Iroquois of New York, the Mohawk leader Joseph Brant succeeded in bringing

This American cartoon, published during the Revolution, depicts "the Scalp Buyer," Colonel Henry Hamilton, paying bounties to Indians. In fact, Indian warriors were not simply pawns of the British but fought for the same reasons the Patriots did—for political independence, cultural integrity, and protection of land and property.

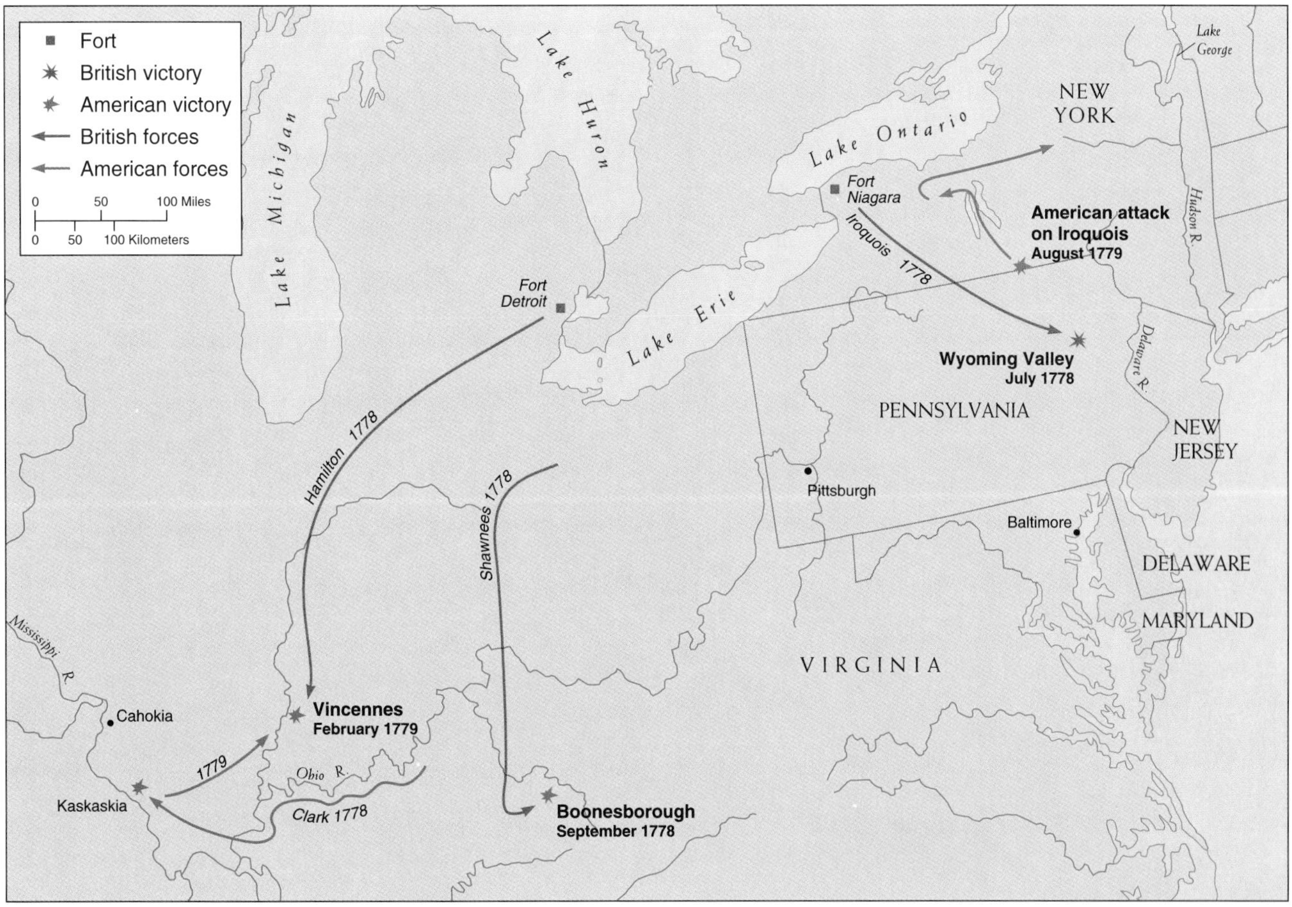

Fighting in the West, 1778–1779

most Iroquois warriors into the British camp, although he was opposed by the chiefs of the Oneidas and Tuscaroras, who supported the Patriots. In the summer and fall of 1778, Iroquois and Loyalist forces raided the northern frontiers of Pennsylvania and New York. In retaliation an American army invaded the Iroquois homelands in August 1779, defeating a strong force in the summer and destroying dozens of western villages and thousands of acres of crops during the fall. For the first time since the birth of their confederacy in the fifteenth century, the Iroquois were fighting each other.

Across the mountains the Ohio Indians formed an effective alliance under the British at Detroit in 1777, and during that year and the next American settlements in Kentucky such as Boonesborough were nearly destroyed by Indian attacks. Virginian George Rogers Clark countered by organizing an expedition of militia forces against the French towns in the Illinois country. In July 1778 Clark's men took the British post at Kaskaskia. The following February at Vincennes, Clark captured Colonel Henry Hamilton, British commander in the West, infamous as "the Scalp Buyer" because of the bounty he had placed on Patriots. But Clark lacked the strength to attack the strategic British garrison at Detroit. Raids back and forth across the Ohio River by Indians and Americans claimed hundreds of lives over the next three years. The war in the West would not end with the conclusion of hostilities in the Revolution; in fact, it would continue for another twenty years.

The War in the South

The hardest and most important fighting of the Revolution took place in the South. There the war had begun with a slave uprising. In late 1775 Lord Dunmore, the last royal governor of Virginia, issued a proclamation calling on slaves to desert their masters and take up arms with the British. More than 800 slaves responded to his call, terrifying Chesapeake planters. When Patriot forces effectively routed Dunmore's army in July 1776, they fought a large number of African American troops wearing sashes emblazoned with the words "Liberty to Slaves." Many of these black soldiers succumbed to smallpox, but at least 300 sailed with Dunmore when he departed.

In December 1778 General Clinton regained the initiative for Britain when he sent a force from New

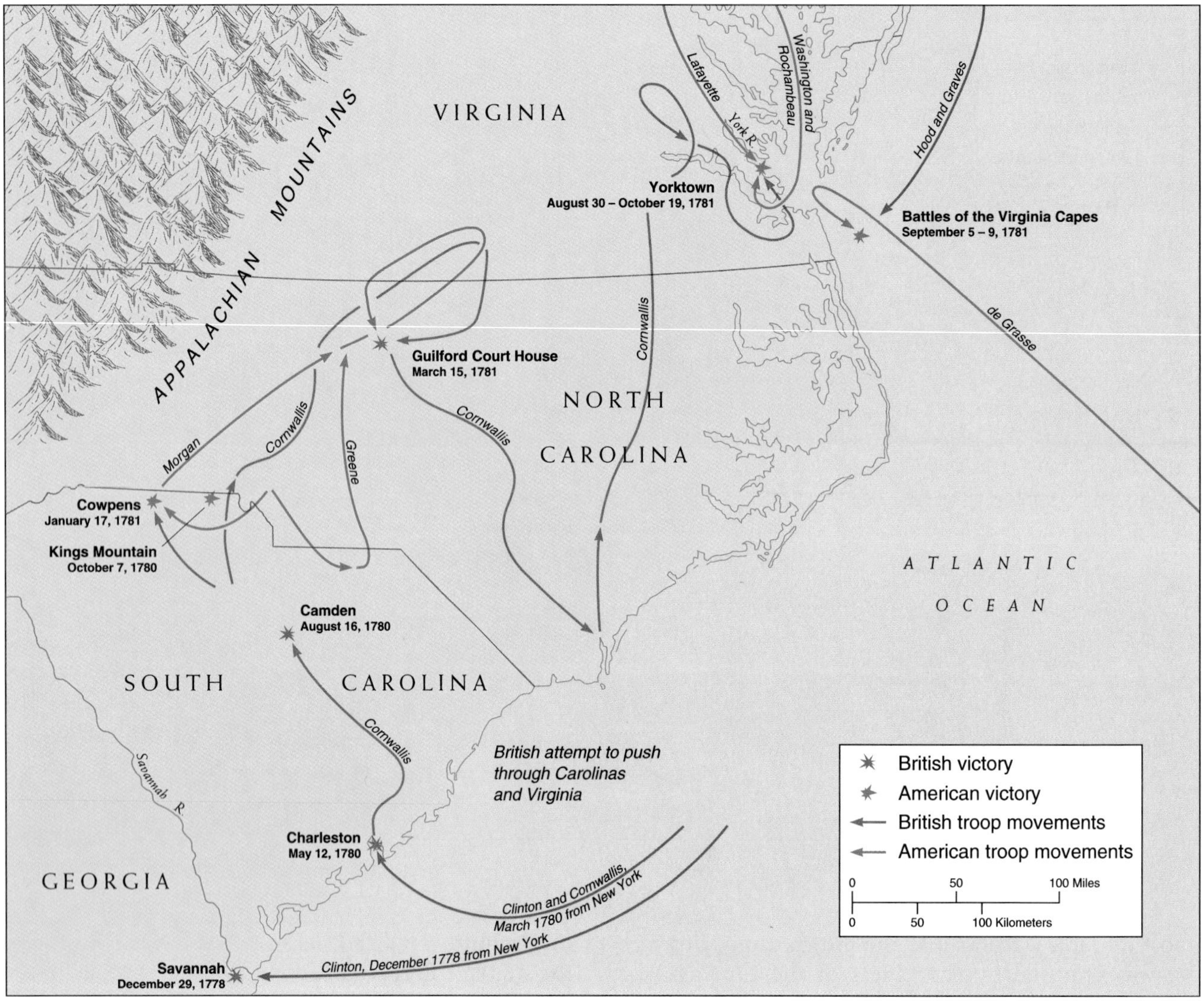

Fighting in the South, 1778–1781

York against Georgia, the weakest of the colonies. The British crushed the Patriot militia at Savannah and began to organize the Loyalists in an effort to reclaim the colony. Several American counterattacks failed, including one in which the French fleet bombarded Savannah. Encouraged by their success in Georgia, the British decided to apply the lessons learned there throughout the South. This decision involved a fundamental change from a strategy of military conquest to one of pacification: territory would be retaken step-by-step, then handed over to Loyalists who would reassert colonial authority loyal to the crown. In October 1779 Clinton evacuated Rhode Island, the last British stronghold in New England and, with 8,000 troops, moved south for an attack on Charleston. Outflanking the American defenders, in May Clinton forced the surrender of over 5,000 troops—the most significant American defeat of the war. Horatio Gates, the hero of Saratoga, led a detachment of Continentals southward, but in August they were defeated by Cornwallis at Camden, South Carolina. Patriot resistance to the British collapsed in the Lower South, and American fortunes were suddenly at their lowest ebb since the beginning of the war.

During the British campaign through the South, thousands of slaves responded to General Clinton's promise of liberty to those who would fight. In response, Maryland, Virginia, and North Carolina grudgingly began to recruit free persons of color and even slaves into their armed forces. Northern states, led by New England, had already solicited African American recruits, and Rhode Island had placed an African American regiment in the field. Some of these men served in the infantry, while many more were commissary workers or teamsters. By war's end at least 5,000 African Americans had served in Patriot militias or the Continental Army, and in the South some slaves won their freedom through military service. In the

Lower South, however, where the numerical superiority of slaves bred fears of rebellion among white people, there was no similar movement.

The southern campaign was marked by vicious violence between partisan militias of Patriots and Loyalists. "The Whigs and Tories persecute each other with little less than savage fury," wrote General Greene, appointed to succeed Gates after the disaster at Camden. "There is nothing but murders and devastations in every quarter." The violence peaked in September 1780 with Cornwallis's invasion of North Carolina, where the Patriots were stronger and better organized. There the British found their southern strategy untenable: plundering towns and farms in order to feed the army in the interior, where it was detached from lines of supply, had the effect of producing angry support for the Patriots. The Patriots won two important battles at Kings Mountain in October 1780 and the Cowpens in January 1781.

Into 1781 the Continentals and militias waged what General Greene called a "fugitive" war of hit and run against the British. "I am quite tired of marching about the country in quest of adventures," Cornwallis wrote; he declared himself "totally in the dark" about what to do next. He won a victory over the Patriots at Guilford Court House in March, but finally deciding that he would not be able to hold the Carolinas so long as Virginia remained a base of support and supply for the Americans, Cornwallis led his army northward in the summer of 1781. After marauding throughout the Virginia countryside he reached the Chesapeake, encamping at Yorktown to await expected reinforcements from New York. This withdrawal from North Carolina allowed Greene to reestablish Patriot control of the Lower South.

Yorktown

While the British raged through the South the stalemate continued in the Northeast. In the summer of 1780, taking advantage of the British evacuation of Rhode Island, the French landed 5,000 troops at Newport under the command of General Comte de Rochambeau. But it was not until the spring of 1781 that the general risked joining his force to Washington's Continentals north of New York. They planned a campaign against the city, but in August Washington learned that the French Caribbean fleet was headed for the Chesapeake. He sensed the possibility of a *coup de grâce* if only he and Rochambeau could move their troops south in coordination with the French naval operation, locking Cornwallis into his camp at Yorktown. Leaving a small force behind as a decoy, Washington and Rochambeau moved quickly down the coast to the Virginia shore.

More than 16,000 American and French troops had converged on the less than 8,000-man British garrison at Yorktown by mid-September. "If you cannot relieve me very soon," Cornwallis wrote to Clinton in New York, "you must expect to hear the worst." French and American heavy artillery hammered the British unmercifully until the middle of October. Cornwallis found it impossible to break the siege, and after the failure of a planned retreat across the York River, he opened negotiations for the surrender of his army. Two days later, on October 19, 1781, between lines of victorious American and French soldiers, the British troops came out from their trenches to surrender, marching to the melancholy tune of "The World Turned Upside Down":

> *If buttercups buzzed after the bee,*
> *If boats were on land, churches on sea,*
> *If summer were spring and t'other way round,*
> *Then all the world would be upside down.*

It must have seemed that way to Cornwallis, who, pleading illness, sent his second-in-command, General Charles O'Hara, to surrender. Refusing to acknowledge the presence of the Americans, O'Hara first approached General Rochambeau, but the Frenchman waved him toward General Washington. To the British, it was almost incomprehensible that they could be surrendering to former subordinates. Everyone knew this was an event of incalculable importance, but few guessed it was the end of the war, for the British still controlled New York.

In London, at the end of November, Lord North received the news "as he would have taken a ball in the breast," reported the colonial secretary. "Oh God!" he moaned, "it is all over!" British fortunes were at low ebb in India, the West Indies, Florida, and the Mediterranean; the cost of the war was enormous; and there was little support for it among the public and members of Parliament. King George wished to press on, but North submitted his resignation, and in March 1782 the king was forced to accept the ministry of Lord Rockingham, who favored granting Americans their independence.

THE UNITED STATES IN CONGRESS ASSEMBLED

The motion for independence, offered to the Continental Congress by Richard Henry Lee on June 7, 1776, called for a confederation of the states. The Articles of Confederation, the first written constitution of the United States, created a national government of sharply limited powers, an arrangement that reflected the concerns of people fighting to free themselves from a coercive central government. The weak Confederation government found it difficult to forge the unity and assemble the resources necessary to fight the war and win the peace.

The Articles of Confederation

The debate over confederation that took place in the Continental Congress following the Declaration of Independence made it clear that delegates favoring a loose union of autonomous states outnumbered those who wanted a strong national government. Not until the following year did a consensus finally emerge. In November 1777 the Articles of Confederation were formally adopted by the Continental Congress and sent to the states for ratification. The Articles created a national assembly, called the Congress, in which each state had a single vote. Delegates, selected annually in a manner determined by the individual state legislatures, were subjected to term limits, prohibited from serving in more than three years out of any six-year period. Similarly, a president, elected annually by Congress, was eligible to serve no more than one year out of any given three. Votes would be decided by a simple majority of the states, but major questions would require the agreement of nine states.

Congress was granted national authority in the conduct of foreign affairs, matters of war and peace, and maintenance of the armed forces. It could raise loans, issue bills of credit, establish a coinage, and regulate trade with Indian peoples, and it was to be the final authority in jurisdictional disputes between states. It was charged with establishing a national postal system as well as a common standard of weights and measures. Lacking the power to tax citizens directly, however, the national government was to apportion its financial burdens among the states according to the extent of their surveyed land. The Articles explicitly guaranteed the sovereignty of the individual states, reserving to them all powers not expressly delegated to Congress. Ratification or amendment required the agreement of all thirteen states. This constitution thus created a national government of specific, yet sharply circumscribed powers.

The legislatures of twelve states soon voted in favor of the Articles, but final ratification was held up for over three years by the state of Maryland. Representing the interests of states without claims to lands west of the Appalachians, Maryland demanded that states cede to Congress their western claims, the new nation's most valuable resource, for "the good of the whole." Excepted, however, would be the colonial grants made to land companies. The eight states with western claims were reluctant to give them up, and the remaining states included powerful land speculators among their most influential citizens. While the stalemate over western lands continued, Congress remained an extralegal body, but it agreed to work under the terms of the unratified document. It was 1781 before Virginia, the state with the largest western claims, broke the log-jam by promising to cede its lands. Maryland then agreed to ratification, and in March the Articles of Confederation took effect.

Financing the War

Congress financed the Revolution through grants and loans from friendly foreign powers and by issuing paper currency. The total foreign subsidy by the end of the war approached $9 million, but this was insufficient to back the circulating Continental currency that Congress had authorized, the face value of

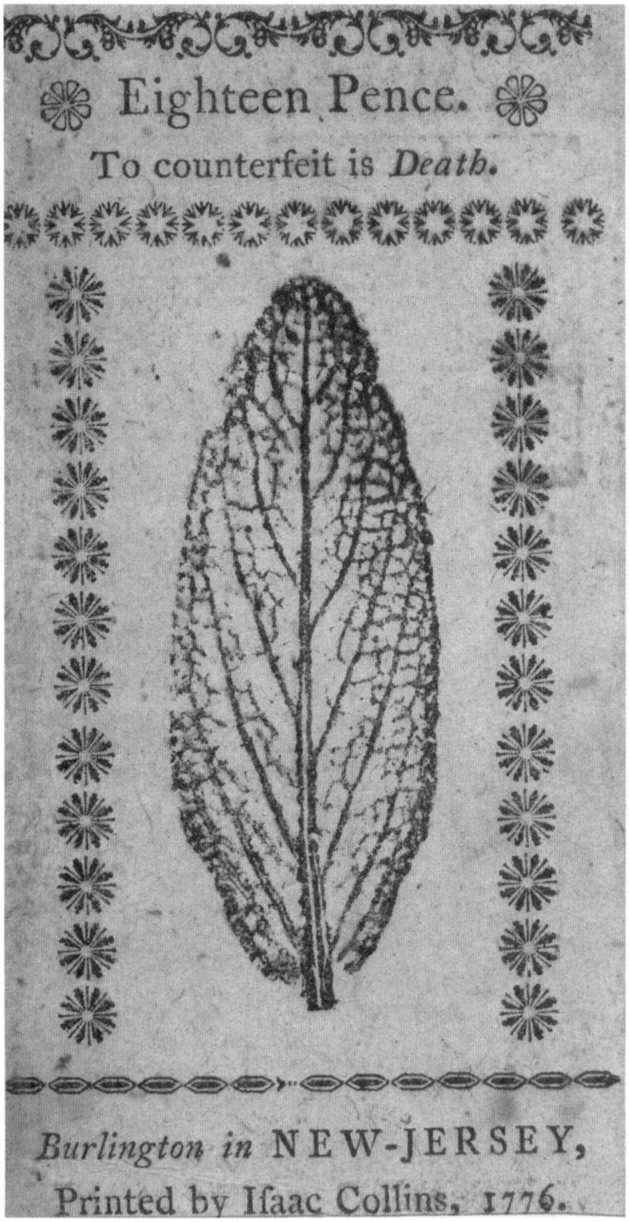

The Continental Congress printed currency to finance the Revolution. Because of widespread counterfeiting, engravers attempted to incorporate complex designs, like the unique vein structure in the leaf on this eighteen-pence note. In case that wasn't enough, the engraver of this note also included the warning: "To counterfeit is Death."

which had risen to nearly $200 million by the end of the war. Congress called on the states to raise taxes, payable in Continental dollars, so that this currency could be retired. But most of the states proved unwilling to do this. In fact, the states resorted to printing currency of their own, which totaled another $200 million by the end of the war. The results of this growth in the money supply were rapid depreciation of Continental currency and runaway inflation. People who received fixed incomes for services—Continental soldiers, for example, as well as merchants, landlords, and other creditors—were devastated. When Robert Morris, one of the country's wealthiest merchants, became superintendent of finance in May 1781, Continental currency had ceased to circulate. Things of no value were said to be "not worth a Continental."

Morris persuaded Congress to charter the Bank of North America in Philadelphia, the first private commercial bank in the United States. There he deposited large quantities of gold and silver coin and bills of exchange obtained through loans from Holland and France. He then issued new paper currency backed by this supply. Once confidence in the bank had developed, he was able to begin supplying the army through private contracts. He was also able to meet the interest payments on the debt, which in 1783 he estimated to be about $30 million.

Morris was associated with the nationalists who controlled Congress in the early 1780s. With their support, he proposed amending the Articles of Confederation to empower Congress to levy a 5 percent duty on imports. The Confederation would then have a source of revenue independent of state requisitions. By the fall of 1782, twelve states had approved the "impost amendment," but Rhode Island refused, objecting that state control of import duties was essential to its own revenues. The nationalists continued to press for an independent congressional revenue, but Morris, having failed in his effort, resigned office in 1784.

Negotiating Independence

Peace talks between the United States and Great Britain opened in April 1782, when Benjamin Franklin sat down with the British emissary in Paris. Congress had issued its first set of war aims in 1779. The fundamental demands were recognition of American independence and withdrawal of British forces. Negotiators were to press for as much territory as possible, including Canada, and guarantees of the American right to fish the North Atlantic. As for its French ally, Congress instructed the commissioners to be guided by friendly advice but also by "knowledge of our interests, and by your own discretion, in which we repose the fullest confidence." But as the British pushed through the South over the next two years and the Americans grew increasingly dependent on French loans and military might, the French ambassador in Philadelphia worked to limit potential American power. In June 1781, partly as a result of French pressure, Congress issued a new set of instructions: the commissioners were to settle merely for a grant of independence and withdrawal of troops, and to be subject to the guidance and control of the French in the negotiations.

Franklin, John Jay, and John Adams, the peace commissioners in Paris, were aware of French attempts to manipulate the outcome of negotiations. In violation of instructions and treaty obligations, and without consulting the French, they signed a preliminary treaty with Britain in November. The British were delighted at the thought of separating the wartime allies. In the treaty, Britain acknowledged the United States as "free, sovereign & independent" and agreed to withdraw its troops from all forts within American territory "with all convenient speed." They guaranteed Americans "the right to take fish" in northern waters. The American commissioners had pressed the British for Canada, but settled for territorial boundaries that extended to the Mississippi. Britain received American promises to erect "no lawful impediments" to the recovery of debts, to cease confiscating Loyalist property, and to try to persuade the states to compensate Loyalist exiles fairly. Finally, the two nations agreed to unencumbered navigation of the Mississippi. The American commissioners had accomplished an astounding coup. The new boundaries, they wrote to Congress, "appear to leave us little to complain of and not much to desire."

France was thus confronted with a *fait accompli*. When Vergennes criticized the commissioners, the Americans responded by hinting that resistance to the treaty provisions could result in a British-American alliance. France thereupon quickly made an agreement of its own with the British.

Spain, the Americans' reluctant ally, was also left out of the negotiations. But as a result of its successful military campaign against the British in the West, Spain now claimed sovereignty over much of the trans-Appalachian territory granted to the United States. The most important issue here was American use of the Mississippi, which depended on access to the Spanish-controlled port of New Orleans. Refusing to deal directly with the Americans, the Spanish arranged their own peace with Great Britain, winning the return of Florida. The final Treaty of Paris—actually a series of separate agreements among the United States, Great Britain, France, and Spain—was signed at Versailles on September 3, 1783.

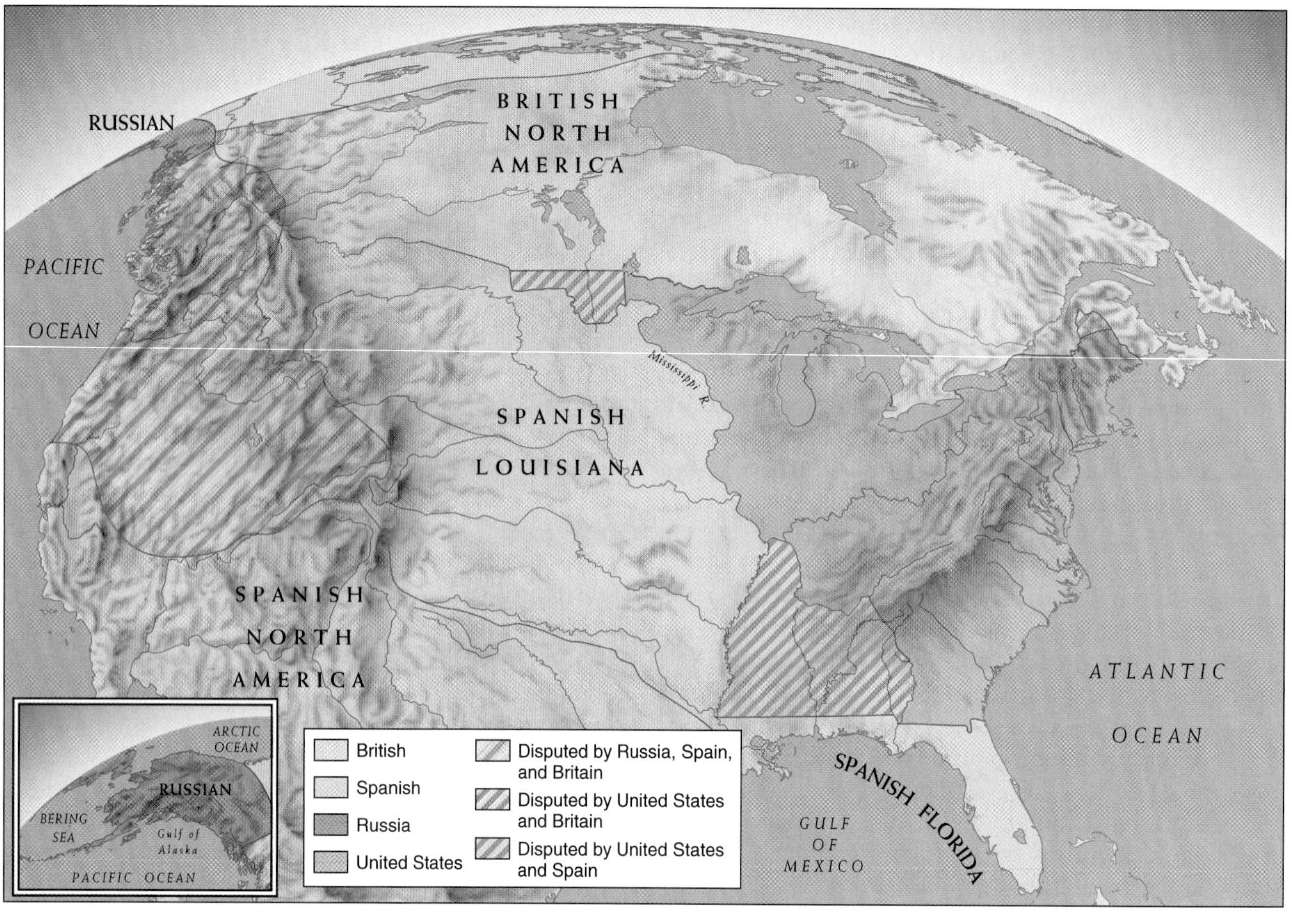

North America after the Treaty of Paris, 1783 *The map of European and American claims to North America was radically altered by the results of the American Revolution.*

The Crisis of Demobilization

During the two years between the surrender at Yorktown and the signing of the Treaty of Paris, the British continued to occupy New York City, Charleston, and a series of western posts. The Continental Army remained on wartime alert, with some 10,000 men and an estimated 1,000 women encamped at Newburgh, New York, north of West Point. The soldiers had long been awaiting their pay and were concerned about the postwar bounties and land warrants promised them. The most serious problem, however, lay not among the enlisted men but in the officer corps.

Continental officers had extracted a promise from Congress of life pensions at half pay in exchange for enlistment for the duration of the war. By 1783, however, Congress had still not made specific provisions for the pensions. With peace at hand, officers began to fear that the army would be disbanded before the problem was resolved, and they would lose whatever power they had to pressure Congress. In January 1783 a group of prominent senior officers petitioned Congress, demanding that the pensions be converted to a bonus equal to five years of full pay. "Any further experiments on their patience," they warned, "may have fatal effects." Despite this barely veiled threat of military intervention, Congress rejected their petition.

With the backing of congressional nationalists, a group of army officers associated with General Horatio Gates called an extraordinary meeting of the officer corps at Newburgh. But General Washington, on whom the officers counted for support, condemned the meeting as "disorderly" and called an official meeting of his own. There was enormous tension when the officers assembled on March 15; at stake was nothing less than the possibility of a military coup at the very moment of American victory. Washington strode into the room and mounted the platform. Turning his back in disdain on General Gates, he told the assembly that he wished to read a statement, and then pulled a pair of glasses from his pocket. None of his officers had seen their leader wearing glasses before. "Gentlemen, you must pardon me," said Washington when he noticed their surprise. "I have grown gray in your service and now find myself growing blind." He then went on to denounce any resort to force, but it was his offhand remark about growing gray that made the greatest impact. Who had sacrificed more than their commander in chief? After he left, the officers adopted resolutions rejecting intervention, and a week later, on Washington's urging, Congress decided to convert the pensions to bonuses after all.

Washington's role in this crisis was one of his greatest contributions to the nation. In December 1783 he resigned his commission as general of the army despite calls for him to remain. There is little doubt that he could have assumed the role of American dictator. Instead, by his actions and example, the principle of military subordination to civil authority was firmly established.

As for the common soldiers, they wanted simply to be discharged. "It is not in the power of Congress or their officers to hold them much, if any, longer," Washington wrote Alexander Hamilton in April. The next month, Congress voted the soldiers three months' pay as a bonus and instructed Washington to begin dismissing them. Some troops remained at Newburgh until the British evacuated New York in November, but by the beginning of 1784 the Continental Army had shrunk to no more than a few hundred men.

The Problem of the West

After Yorktown, the British abandoned their Indian allies in the West. When the Indians learned of the armistice, according to one British officer, they were "thunderstruck." Neither the Iroquois nor the Ohio tribes, who had fought with the British, considered themselves defeated, but the United States claimed that its victory over Great Britain was a victory over the Indians as well. A heavily armed American nation now pressed for large grants of territory according to the right of conquest. Even Patriot allies were not exempt. The Oneidas, for example, who had supported the Americans, suffered territorial demands along with the other Iroquois.

Even during the fighting the American migration to the West had continued, and after the treaty of peace settlers streamed over the mountains and down the Ohio River. The population of Kentucky (still a part of Virginia until admitted as a state in 1792) had grown to more than 30,000 by 1785; in 1790 it numbered 74,000, and the Tennessee area held another 36,000. Thousands of Americans pressed against the Indian country north of the Ohio River, and destructive violence continued along the frontier. British troops continued to occupy posts in the Northwest and encouraged Indian attacks on vulnerable settlements. To the southwest, Spain, refusing to accept the territorial settlement of the Treaty of Paris, closed the Mississippi River to Americans. Westerners who saw that route as their primary access to markets were outraged.

The American leadership saw the West as critical to the continued development of national community sentiment. John Jay, appointed secretary for

State Claims to Western Lands *The ratification of the Articles of Confederation in 1781 awaited settlement of the western claims of eight states. Vermont, claimed by New Hampshire and New York, was not made a state until 1791, after disputes were settled the previous year. The territory north of the Ohio River was claimed in whole or in part by Virginia, New York, Connecticut, and Massachusetts. All of them had ceded their claims by 1786, except for Connecticut, which had claimed an area just south of Lake Erie, known as the Western Reserve; Connecticut ceded this land in 1800. The territory south of the Ohio was claimed by Virginia, North Carolina, South Carolina, and Georgia; in 1802 the latter became the last state to cede its claims.*

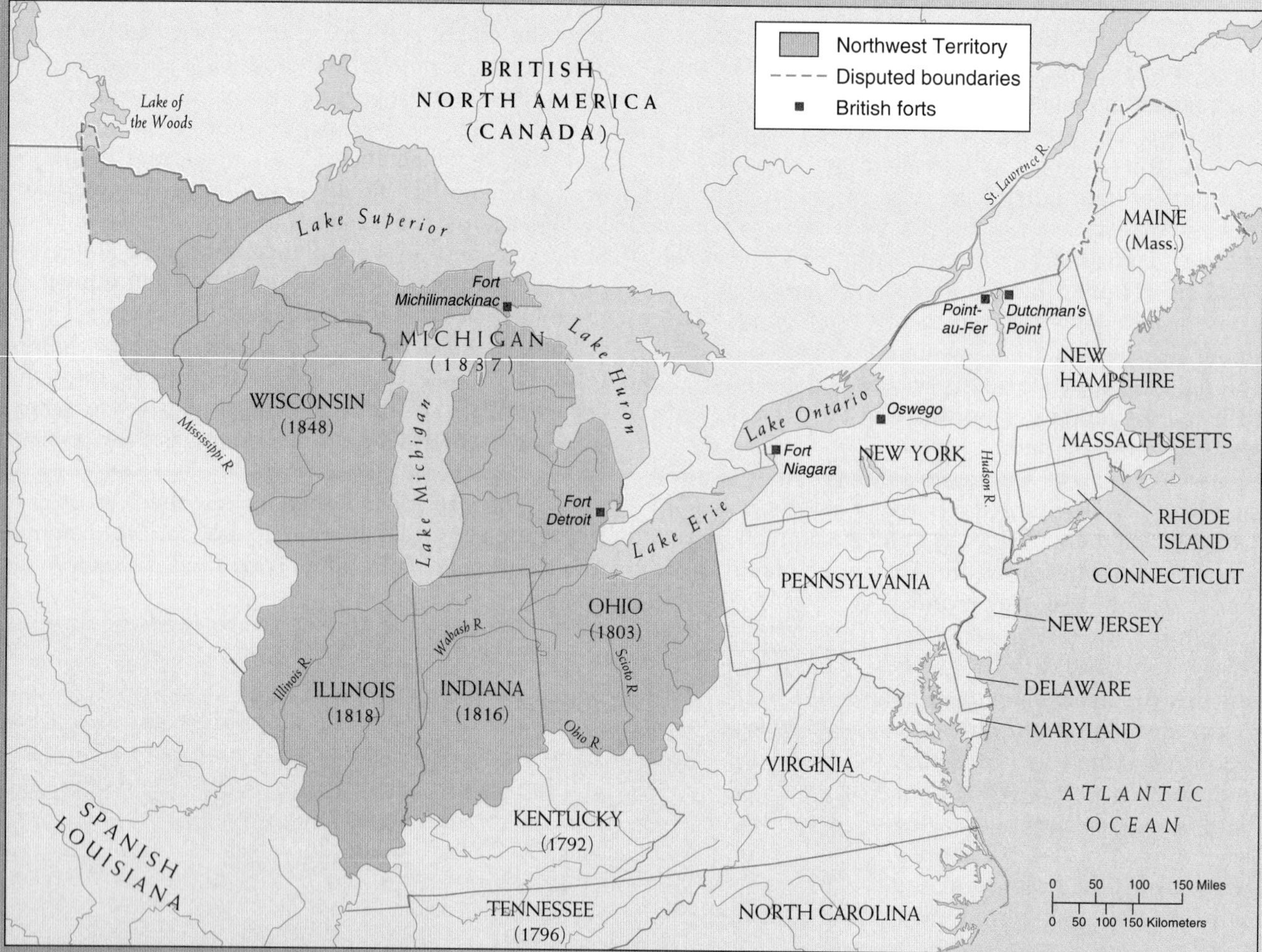

The Northwest Territory and the Land Survey System of the United States

The greatest achievement of the Confederation government was the passing of the Land Ordinance of 1785 and the Northwest Ordinance of 1787. The first act made provision for the federal survey of newly incorporated lands. To avoid the problem of overlapping surveys that could occur under the old system of "metes and bounds" surveying, the authors of the ordinance created an ordered system of survey, dividing the land into townships composed of thirty-six sections of one square mile (640 acres) each. (The differences are clearly evident in the contrast between the patterns of landholding in Ohio, on the left side of the photo, and Pennsylvania, on the right.) The income from section 16 was reserved for the support of local schools, and sections 8, 11, 26, and 29 were held off the market for later sale. First employed in the territory north of the Ohio River, this survey system was used for all the western territory of the United States and has been adopted by many other nations.

With the Northwest Ordinance, Congress established a system of government for the territory north of the Ohio. This legislation established the important principle of eventually bringing new territory

foreign affairs by the Confederation Congress in 1784, attempted to negotiate with the British, but he was told that British troops would not evacuate the Northwest until all outstanding debts from before the war were settled. Jay also attempted to negotiate with the Spanish for guarantees of territorial sovereignty and commercial relations, but he was told that first the United States would have to relinquish free navigation of the Mississippi. Congress would approve no treaty with such terms. Under these frustrating circumstances, some Westerners considered leaving the Confederation. Kentuckians threatened to rejoin the British. The Spanish secretly employed several prominent westerners, including George Rogers Clark and General James Wilkinson, as informants and spies. The people of the West "stand as it were upon a pivot," wrote Washing-

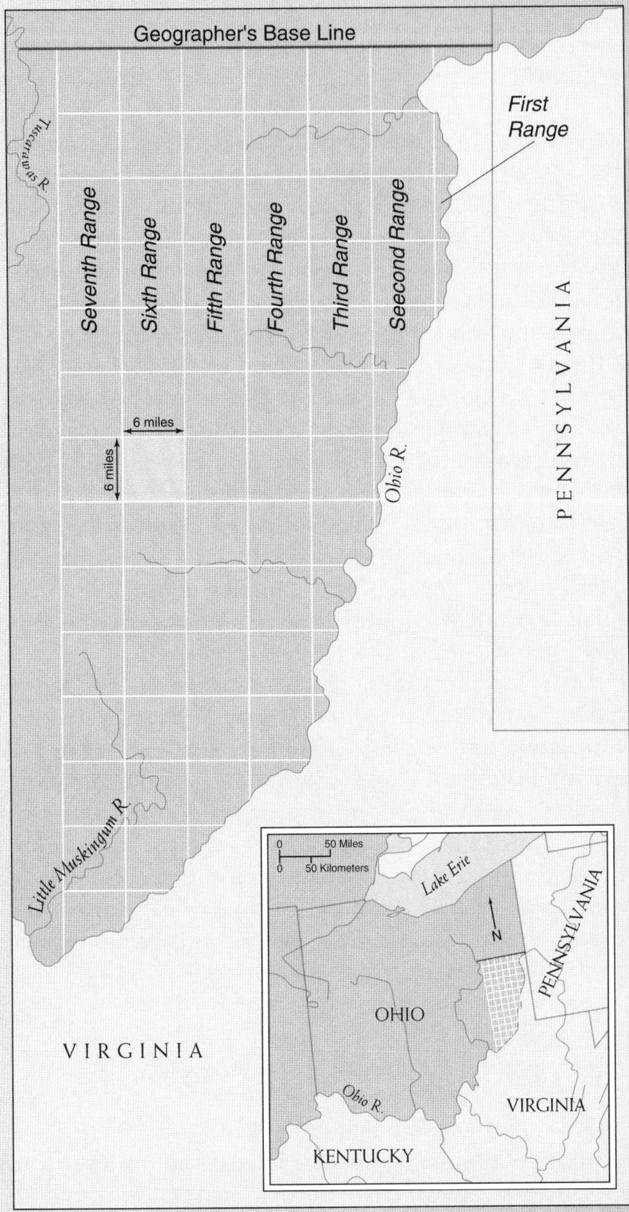

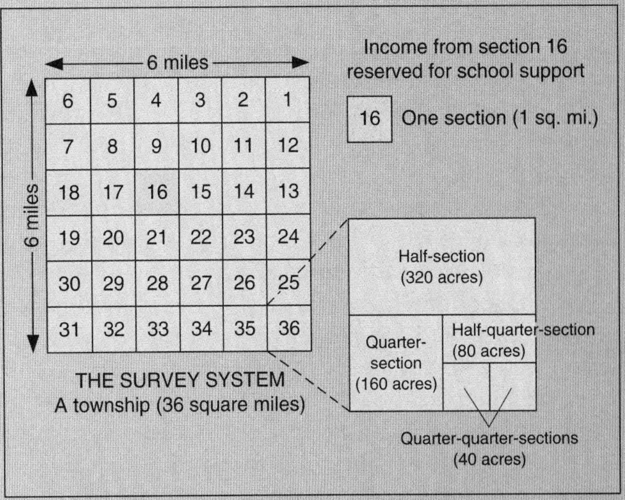

into the states on an equal basis with the original thirteen states. The Northwest Territory was eventually divided into the five states that are the focus of this map, and each was admitted to the Union on the date that appears below its name. The Northwest Ordinance also outlawed slavery north of the Ohio River.

Before that process could begin, however, the United States had to establish sovereignty over the country. The British did not abandon the posts that they had continued to occupy after 1783 until June 1, 1796, following the agreement between the United States and Great Britain in Jay's Treaty (1794).

ton in 1784 after a trip down the Ohio. "The touch of a feather would turn them any way." In the West, local community interest continued to override the fragile development of national community sentiment.

In the context of these problems, Congress took up the problem of extending national authority over the West in 1784. Legislation was drafted, principally by Thomas Jefferson, providing for "Government for the Western Territory." The legislation was a remarkable attempt to create a democratic colonial policy. The public domain was to be divided into states, and Congress was to guarantee the settlers in them immediate self-government and republican institutions. Once the population of a territory numbered 20,000, the residents could call a convention and establish a constitution and government of their own choosing. And once the population grew to equal that of the smallest of the original thirteen states, the territory could obtain statehood, provided it agreed to remain forever a member of the Confederation. Fortunately, Congress rejected Jefferson's proposal to provide the future states with names such as Assenisippia and Metropotamia. But it also rejected, by a vote of seven to six, his clause prohibiting slavery.

Passed the following year, the Land Ordinance of 1785 provided for the survey and sale of western lands. To avoid the chaos of overlapping surveys and land claims that had characterized Kentucky, the authors of the ordinance created an ordered system of survey, dividing the land into townships composed of thirty-six sections of one square mile (640 acres) each. This measure would have an enormous impact on the North American landscape, as anyone looking down from an airplane window on the Midwest or West can see. The Land Ordinance also reserved one section in each township for the support of schools; local officials could sell or rent this land to raise money to build schoolhouses or employ teachers. Jefferson argued that all the other land ought to be given away to actual settlers. But Congress, eager to establish a revenue base for the government, provided for the auction of public lands for not less than $1 per acre (the equivalent of $117 in 1990 currency).

In the second Treaty of Fort Stanwix in 1784 and the Treaty of Fort McIntosh in 1785, congressional commissioners forced the Iroquois and some of the Ohio Indians to cede a portion of their territory in what is now eastern Ohio. These treaties were not the result of negotiation; the commissioners dictated the terms by seizing hostages and forcing compliance. Quickly, Congress sent surveyors into the area to divide up the lands. The surveyors did not complete their work and make the lands available for settlers to purchase until the fall of 1788. In the meantime, Congress, desperate for revenue, sold a tract of more than 1.5 million acres to a new land company, the Ohio Company, for $1 million. Jefferson's vision of land for actual settlers seemed to be receding from view.

But thousands of Westerners refused to wait for the official opening of the public land north of the Ohio River. Instead they simply crossed the river and settled illegally. In 1785 Congress raised troops and evicted many of them, but once the soldiers left the squatters returned. The persistence of this problem convinced many congressmen to revise Jefferson's democratic territorial plan. It was necessary, explained Richard Henry Lee of Virginia, "for the security of property among uninformed and perhaps licentious people, as the greater part of those who go there are, that a strong toned government should exist."

In the Northwest Ordinance of 1787, Congress established a system of government for the territory north of the Ohio. Three to five states were to be carved out of the giant Northwest Territory and admitted "on an equal footing with the original states in all respects whatsoever." Slavery was prohibited. But the guarantee of initial self-government in Jefferson's plan was replaced by the rule of a court of judges and a governor appointed by Congress. Once the free white male population of the territory had grown to 5,000, these citizens would be permitted to choose an assembly, but the governor was to have the power of absolute veto on all territorial legislation. National interest would be imposed on the localistic western communities. The Northwest Territory was a huge region that included the future states of Ohio, Indiana, Illinois, Michigan, and Wisconsin. In an early instance of government in the hands of developers, Congress chose Arthur St. Clair, president of the Ohio Company, as the first governor of the Northwest Territory.

The creation of the land system of the United States was the major achievement of the Confederation government. But there were other important accomplishments. Under the Articles of Confederation, Congress led the country through the Revolution and its commissioners negotiated the terms of a comprehensive peace treaty. In organizing the departments of war, foreign affairs, the post office, and finance, the Confederation government created the beginnings of the national bureaucracy.

REVOLUTIONARY POLITICS IN THE STATES

Despite the accomplishments of the Confederation government, most Americans focused not on events in Philadelphia but on those in their own states. Although a strong national community feeling developed during the Revolutionary era, most Americans identified more strongly with their local communities and states than the American nation. People spoke of "these United States," emphasizing the plural, and were relatively unaffected by the national government. The states were the setting for the most important political struggles not only of the Confederation period but for long after.

The Broadened Base of Politics

The political mobilization that took place in 1774 and 1775 greatly broadened political participation. Mass meetings in which ordinary people expressed their opinions, voted, and gained political experience were common, not only in the cities but in small towns and rural communities as well. During these years, a greater proportion of the population began to participate in elections. South Carolina, for example, employed a system of universal white manhood suffrage for the selection of delegates to the Continental Congress, and many other states relaxed property qualifications. Compared with the colonial assemblies, the new state legislatures included more men from rural and western districts—farmers and artisans as well as lawyers, merchants, and large landowners. Many delegates to the Massachusetts provincial congress of 1774 were men from small farming communities who lacked formal education and owned little property.

This transformation was accompanied by a dramatic shift in the political debate. During the colonial period, when only the upper crust of colonial society had been truly engaged by the political process, the principal argument took place between Tory and Whig positions. Tory principles, articulated by royal officials, held that colonial governments were simply convenient instruments of the king's prerogative, serving at his pleasure. The Whig position, on the other hand, was represented by the American colonial elites, who, seeking to preserve and increase their own power, argued for stronger assemblies. They justified their position with arguments about the need for a government balanced with monarchic, aristocratic, and democratic elements, represented by the governor, the upper house, and the assembly, respectively. This debate was ended by the American Revolution. The Tory position lost all legitimacy, indelibly soiled by the taint of Loyalism and treason. There were still plenty of moderate Patriots who took a Whig position on balanced government. But farmers, artisans, and other ordinary people began to argue for a democratic government of the people themselves. For the first time in American history, democracy lost its negative connotations and became a term of approval. One of the most important consequences of the Revolution was a radical shift of the political discourse to the left.

An early post-Revolution debate focused on the appropriate governmental structure for the new states. The new thinking was indicated by the title of a New England pamphlet of 1776, *The People the Best Governors.* Power, the anonymous author argued, should be vested in a single, popularly elected assembly. There should be no property qualifications for either voting or holding office. The governor should simply execute the wishes of the people as voiced by their representatives in the assembly. Judges, too, should be popularly elected, and their decisions reviewed by the assembly. The people, the pamphlet concluded, "best know their wants and necessities, and therefore are best able to govern themselves." The ideal form of government, according to such democrats, was the community or town meeting, in which the people set their own tax rates, created a militia, controlled their own schools and churches, and regulated the local economy. State government was necessary only for coordination among communities.

Conservative Americans took up the Whig argument on the need for a balanced government. The "unthinking many," wrote another pamphleteer, should be checked by a strong executive and an upper house. Both should be insulated from popular control by property qualifications and long terms in office, designed to draw forth the wisdom and talent of the country's wealthiest and most accomplished men. The greatest danger, according to conservatives, was the possibility of majority tyranny, which might lead to the violation of property rights and to dictatorship. "We must take mankind as they are," one conservative wrote, "and not as we could wish them to be."

The First State Constitutions

Fourteen states—the original thirteen plus Vermont—adopted constitutions between 1776 and 1780. Each of these documents was shaped by debate between radicals and conservatives, democrats and Whigs, and reflected a political balance of power. The constitutions of Pennsylvania, Maryland, and New York typified the political range of the times: Pennsylvania instituted a radical democratic government something like that proposed in *The People the Best Governors,* Maryland created a conservative set of institutions designed to keep citizens and rulers as far apart as possible, and New York adopted a system somewhere in the middle.

In Pennsylvania, a majority of the political conservatives had become Loyalists, allowing the democrats to seize power in 1776. The election of delegates to the constitutional convention was open to every man in the militia, an arrangement that further strengthened the advocates of democracy. The document this convention adopted clearly reflected a democratic agenda. It created a unicameral assembly elected annually by all free male taxpayers. So that delegates would be responsive to their constituents, sessions of the assembly were open to the public and included roll-call votes—the latter somewhat rare in colonial assemblies. There was no governor, but rather an elected executive committee. Judges were removable by the assembly.

By contrast, the Maryland constitution, adopted the same year, was written by conservative planters. It created property requirements for office-holding that left only about 10 percent of Maryland men eligible to serve in the assembly, 7 percent in the senate. A powerful governor, elected by large property owners, controlled a highly centralized government. Judges and other high executive officers served for life. These two states, Maryland and Pennsylvania, represented the political extremes. Georgia, Vermont, and North Carolina followed Pennsylvania's example; South Carolina's constitution was much like Maryland's.

In New York, the constitutional convention of 1777 included a large democratic faction. But conservatives such as John Jay, Gouverneur Morris, and Robert R. Livingston, managing the convention with great skill, helped produce a document that reflected Whiggish principles while still appealing to the people. There would be a bicameral legislature, each house having equal powers. The lower house, or assembly, was democratically elected, but there were stiff property qualifications for election to the upper house, or senate, and senators represented districts apportioned by wealth, not population. The governor, also elected by property owners, had the power of veto, which could be overridden only by a two-thirds vote of both houses. Ultraconservatives wanted a constitution more like Maryland's, but Jay argued that "another turn of the winch would have cracked the cord"; conservatives, in other words, had gotten about as much as they could without alienating the mass of voters. Other states whose constitutions blended democratic and conservative elements were New Hampshire, New Jersey, and Massachusetts.

Declarations of Rights

One of the most important innovations of these constitutions was a guarantee of rights patterned on the Virginia Declaration of Rights of June 1776. Written by George Mason—wealthy planter and brilliant political philosopher—the Virginia declaration set a distinct tone in its very first article: "That all men are by nature equally free and independent, and have certain inherent rights,...namely, the enjoyment of life and liberty, with the means of acquiring and possessing property and pursuing and obtaining happiness and safety." The sixteen articles declared, among other things, that sovereignty resided in the people, that government was the servant of the people, and that the people had the "right to reform, alter, or abolish" that government. There were guarantees of due process and trial by jury in criminal prosecutions, and prohibitions of excessive bail and "cruel and unusual punishments." Freedom of the press was guaranteed as "one of the great bulwarks of liberty," and the people were assured of "the free exercise of religion, according to the dictates of conscience."

Eight state constitutions included a general declaration of rights similar to the first article of the Virginia declaration; others incorporated specific guarantees. A number of states proclaimed the right of the people to engage in free speech and free assembly, to instruct their representatives, and to petition for the redress of grievances—rights either inadvertently or deliberately omitted from Virginia's declaration. These declarations were important precedents for the Bill of Rights, the first ten amendments to the United States Constitution. Indeed, George Mason of Virginia was a leader of those democrats who insisted that the Constitution stipulate such rights.

A Spirit of Reform

The political upheaval of the Revolution raised the possibility of other reforms in American society. The 1776 constitution of New Jersey, by granting the vote to "all free inhabitants" who met the property requirements, enfranchised women as well as men. The number of women voters eventually led to male protests and a new state law explicitly limiting the right to vote to "free white male citizens."

The New Jersey controversy may have been an anomaly, but women's participation in the Revolution wrought subtle but important changes. In 1776 Abigail Adams had written her husband John Adams, away at the Continental Congress: "In the new code of laws which I suppose it will be necessary for you to make I desire you would remember the ladies, and be more generous and favourable to them than your ancestors." In the aftermath of the Revolution, there was evidence of increasing sympathy in the courts for women's property rights and fairer adjudication of women's petitions for divorce. And the postwar years witnessed an increase in opportunities for women seeking an education. From a strictly legal and political point of view, the Revolution may have done little to change women's role in society, but it did seem to help change expectations. Abigail Adams's request to her husband was directed less toward the shape of the new republic than toward the structure of family life. "Do not put such unlimited powers into the hands of husbands," she wrote, "for all men would be tyrants if they could." She had in mind a new, companionate ideal of marriage that contrasted with older notions of patriarchy. Men and women ought to be more like partners, less like master and servant. This new ideal took root in America during the era of the Revolution.

The most steadfast reformer of the day was Thomas Jefferson, who after completing work on the Declaration of Independence returned to Virginia to take a seat in the House of Delegates, convinced that the most important political work lay within his own state. In 1776 he introduced a bill that abolished the law of entails, which had confined inheritance to particular heirs in order that landed property remain undivided. Jefferson believed that entail and primogeniture (inheritance of all the family property by the firstborn son)—legal customs long

By giving the vote to "all free inhabitants," the 1776 constitution of New Jersey enfranchised women as well as men who met the property requirements. The number of women voters eventually led to male protests. Wrote one: "What tho' we read, in days of yore, / The woman's occupation / Was to direct the wheel and loom, / Not to direct the nation." In 1807 a new state law explicitly limited the right of franchise to "free white male citizens."

operating in aristocratic England—had no place in a republican society. The legislation had little practical effect, since relatively few estates were entailed, but the repeal was symbolically important, for it repudiated an aristocratic custom. By 1790, every state but one had followed Virginia's lead (Rhode Island acted in 1798).

Jefferson's other notable success was his Bill for Establishing Religious Freedom. Indeed, he considered this document one of his greatest accomplishments. At the beginning of the Revolution, there were established churches in nine of the thirteen colonies—the Congregationalists in Massachusetts, New Hampshire, and Connecticut, the Anglicans in New York and the South. (See also Chapter 5 for a discussion of colonial religion.) Established religion was increasingly opposed in the eighteenth century, in part because of Enlightenment criticism of the power it had over free and open inquiry but, more important, because of the growing sectarian diversity produced by the religious revival of the Great Awakening. Many Anglican clergymen harbored Loyalist sympathies, and as part of an anti-Loyalist backlash New York, Maryland, the Carolinas, and Georgia had little difficulty passing acts that disestablished the Anglican Church. In Virginia, however, many planters viewed Anglicanism as a bulwark against Baptist and Methodist democratic thinkers, resulting in bitter and protracted opposition to Jefferson's bill. Patrick Henry, grown conservative, defended state support for the church, and it was not until 1786 that the bill passed.

New England Congregationalists proved even more resistant to change. Although Massachusetts, New Hampshire, and Connecticut allowed dissenters to receive tax support, they maintained the official relationship between church and state well into the nineteenth century. Other states, despite disestablishment, retained religious tests in their legal codes. Georgia, the Carolinas, and New Jersey limited officeholding to Protestants; New York required legislators to renounce allegiance to the pope; and even Pennsylvania, where religious freedom had a long history, required officials to swear to a belief in the divine inspiration of the Old and New Testaments.

Jefferson proposed several more reforms of Virginia law, all of which failed to pass. He would have created a system of public education, revised the penal code to restrict capital punishment to the crimes of murder and treason, and established the gradual emancipation of slaves by law. (This, by the way, marked the third time Jefferson had tried to encourage an end to slavery; the first time in his antislavery clause in the Declaration of Independence, the second with his proposed "Government for the Western Territory" of 1784.) Other states witnessed more progress, but on the whole, the Revolutionary generation, like Jefferson, were more successful in raising these issues than in accomplishing reforms. The problems of penal reform, public education, and slavery remained for later generations of Americans to resolve.

African Americans and the Revolution

For most African Americans, there was little to celebrate in the American victory, because it perpetuated the institution of slavery. Few people were surprised when thousands of black fighters and their families departed with the British at the end of the war, settling in the West Indies, Canada, even Africa. Virginia and South Carolina were said to have lost 30,000 and 25,000 slaves, respectively, as a result of the war.

To many white Americans, as well, there was an obvious contradiction in waging a war for liberty

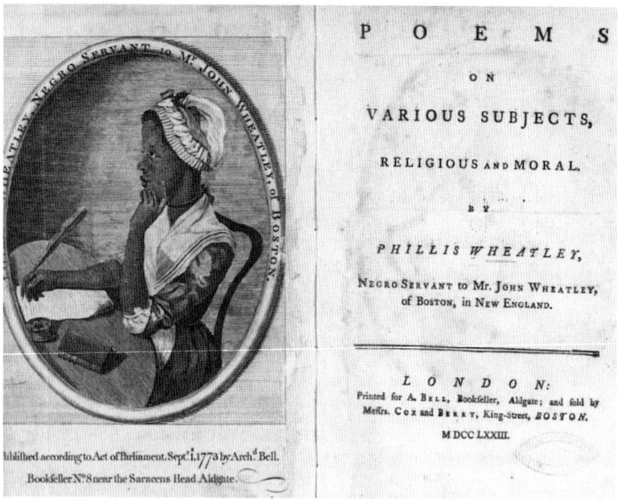

This portrait of the African American poet Phillis Wheatley was included in the collection of her work published in London in 1773, when she was only twenty. Kidnapped in Africa when a girl, then purchased off the Boston docks, she was more like a daughter than a slave to the Wheatley family, and later married and lived as a free woman of color before her untimely death in 1784.

while continuing to support the institution of slavery. Slavery was first abolished in the state constitution of Vermont in 1777, and in Massachusetts and New Hampshire in 1780 and 1784, respectively. Pennsylvania, Connecticut, and Rhode Island adopted systems of gradual emancipation during these years, freeing the children of slaves at birth. By 1786 every northern state but Delaware had provided for immediate or gradual emancipation of slaves, although as late as 1810, 30,000 African Americans remained enslaved in the North.

In the Upper South, revolutionary idealism, the Christian egalitarianism of Methodists and Baptists, and a shift from tobacco farming to the cultivation of cereal grains such as wheat and corn combined to weaken the commitment of many planters to the slave system. There was a great increase in manumissions—grants of freedom to slaves by individual masters—and a small but important movement encouraged gradual emancipation by convincing masters to free their slaves in their wills. George Washington not only freed several hundred of his slaves on his death but developed an elaborate plan for apprenticeship and tenancy for the able-bodied, lodging and pensions for the aged. Planters in the Lower South, however, heavily dependent on slave labor, resisted the growing calls for an end to slavery. Between 1776 and 1786 all the states but South Carolina and Georgia prohibited or heavily taxed the international slave trade, and this issue became an important point of contention at the Constitutional Convention in 1787 (see Chapter 8).

Perhaps the most important result of these developments was the growth of the free African American population. From a few thousand in 1750, the free African American population grew to more than 200,000 by the end of the century. The increase was most notable in the Upper South. The free black population of Virginia, for example, grew from less than 2,000 in 1780 to approximately 20,000 in 1800. Largely excluded from the institutions of white Americans, the African American community now had sufficient strength to establish schools, churches, and other institutions of its own. Initially this development was opposed. In Williamsburg, Virginia, for instance, the leader of a black congregation was seized and whipped when he attempted to gain recognition from the Baptist Association. But by the 1790s the Williamsburg African Church had more than 500 members, and the association reluctantly recognized it. In Philadelphia the Reverend Absalom Jones established St. Thomas's African Episcopal Church. The incorporation of the term "African" in the names of churches, schools, and mutual benefit societies reflected the pride that African Americans now took in their heritage. New York's African Marine Fund, to take one example, described itself as an organization for assisting "our African brethren and the descendants of our mother country."

A small group of African American writers rose to prominence during the Revolutionary era. Benjamin Banneker, born free in Maryland, where he received an education, was one of the most accomplished mathematicians and astronomers of late-eighteenth-century America. In the 1790s he published a popular almanac that both white and black Americans consulted. Jupiter Hammon, a Long Island slave, took up contemporary issues in his poems and essays, one of the most important of which was his *Address to the Negroes of the State of New York,* published in 1787. The most famous African American writer, however, was Phillis Wheatley, who came to public attention when her *Poems on Various Subjects, Religious and Moral* appeared in London in 1773, while she was still a domestic slave in Boston. Kidnapped as a young girl and converted to Christianity during the Great Awakening, Wheatley wrote poems that combined her piety with a concern for her people. "On Being Brought from Africa to America" is a good example:

'Twas mercy brought me from my pagan land,
Taught my benighted soul to understand
That there's a God, that there's a Saviour too;
Once I redemption neither sought nor knew.
Some view our sable race with scornful eye,
"Their colour is a diabolic dye."
Remember, Christians, Negros, black as Cain,
May be refin'd, and join th'angelic train.

"In every human breast God has implanted a principle, which we call love of freedom; it is impatient of oppression, and pants for deliverance," Wheatley wrote in a letter. "The same principle lives in us."

Economic Problems

During the Revolution, the shortage of goods resulting from the British blockade, the demand for supplies by the army and militias, and the flood of paper currency issued by Congress and the states combined to create the worst inflation that Americans have ever experienced. Continental dollars traded against Spanish dollars at the rate of 3 to 1 in 1777, 40 to 1 in 1779, and 146 to 1 in 1781, by which time Congress had issued more than $190 million in Continentals. Most of this paper ended up in the hands of merchants who paid only a fraction of its face value. There was a popular outcry at the incredible increase in prices, and communities and states in the North responded with laws regulating wages and prices.

The sponsors of wage and price schedules often attributed high prices to hoarding and profiteering. Although it is doubtful that such practices caused the inflation, many merchants did gouge their customers. There were demonstrations and food riots in many communities; men and women demanded fair prices, and when they did not receive them they broke into storehouses and took what they needed. People organized local committees to monitor economic activity and punish wrongdoers. Abigail Adams told of a Boston merchant who refused to sell coffee for the price demanded by the committee. "A number of females, some say a hundred, some say more," she wrote, "seized him by his neck and tossed him into the cart. Upon his finding no quarter he delivered the keys," and the women opened his warehouse and took the coffee. "A large concourse of men stood amazed, silent spectators of the whole transaction."

After the war the primary economic problem was no longer inflation but depression. Political revolution could not alter economic realities: the independent United States continued to be a supplier of raw materials and an importer of manufactured products, and Great Britain remained its most important trading partner. After the Treaty of Paris was signed in 1783, British merchants dumped their unsold goods on the American market, offering easy terms of credit. The production of exportable commodities, however, had been drastically reduced by the fighting.

With few exports to offset all the imports, the trade deficit with Great Britain for the period 1784–86 rose to approximately £5 million in British currency. The deficit acted like a magnet, drawing gold and silver coin from American accounts: according to one estimate, merchants exported £1.3 million in gold and silver coin to Britain during these two years. In turn, these merchants demanded immediate payment from their customers. Short of hard currency, the three commercial banks in the United States—the Bank of North America (Philadelphia), the Bank of New York, and the Bank of Massachusetts (Boston)—insisted on immediate repayment of old loans and refused to issue new ones. The country was left with very little coin in circulation. It all added up to a serious depression, which lasted from 1784 to 1788. At their lowest level, in 1786, prices had fallen 25 percent.

The depression struck while the country was burdened with the huge debt incurred during the Revolution. The total debt owed by the national and state governments amounted to more than $50 million in 1785. (To place this figure in perspective, consider that this debt was approximately sixty-four times greater than the value of American exports for the year 1785; by contrast, the national debt in 1990—considered a crippling burden—was only five times greater than the

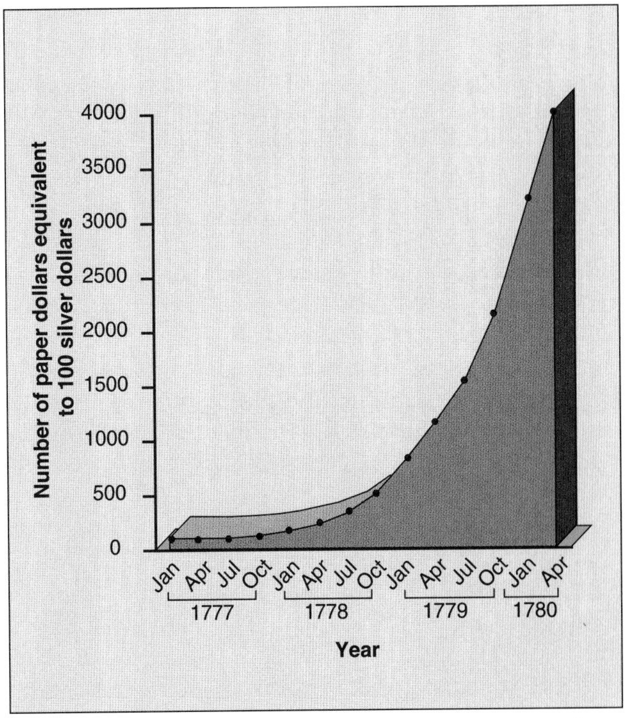

Postwar Inflation, 1777-1780: The Depreciation of Continental Currency (number of paper dollars equal to 100 silver dollars) *The flood of Continental currency issued by Congress, combined with the shortage of goods resulting from the British blockade, combined to create the worst inflation Americans have ever experienced. Things of no value were said to be "not worth a Continental."*

Source: John McCusker, "How Much Is That in Real Money?" *Proceedings of the American Antiquarian Society,* N.S. 102 (1992): 297–359.

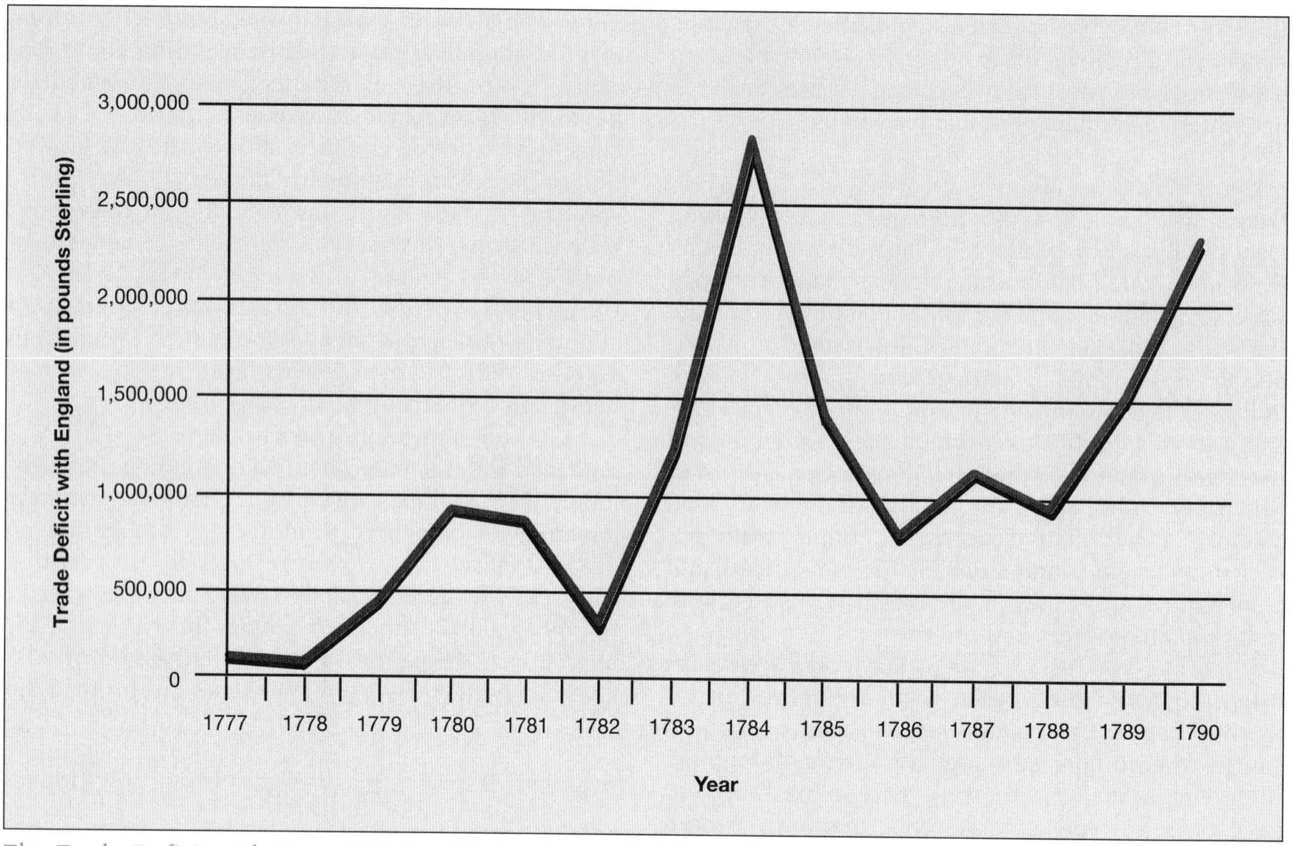

The Trade Deficit with Great Britain *The American trade deficit with Great Britain rose dramatically with the conclusion of the Revolution.*

Source: *Historical Statistics of the United States* (Washington, D.C.:Government Printing Office, 1976), 1176.

value of exports for that year.) Not allowed to raise taxes on its own, the Confederation Congress requisitioned the states for the funds necessary for debt repayment. The states in turn taxed their residents. At a time when there was almost no money in circulation, people rightly feared being crushed by the burden of private debt and public taxes. Thus the economic problem became a political problem.

State Remedies

Where there were manufacturing interests, as in the Northeast, states erected high tariffs to curb imports and protect "infant industries." But shippers could avoid these duties simply by unloading their cargo in nearby seaboard states that lacked tariffs; domestic merchants then distributed the products overland. To be effective, commercial regulation had to be national. Local sentiment had to give way to the unity of a national community. The "means of preserving ourselves," wrote John Adams, [will] "never be secured entirely, until Congress shall be made supreme in foreign commerce, and shall have digested a plan for all the states."

The most controversial economic remedies were those designed to relieve the burden on debtors and ordinary taxpayers. In some areas, farmers called for laws permitting payment of taxes or debts in goods and commodities, a kind of institutionalized barter. More commonly, farmers and debtors pressed their state governments for "legal tender" laws, laws that would require creditors to accept at specified rates of exchange a state's paper currency—regardless of its worth—for all debts public and private. Understandably, creditors opposed such a plan. But farmers were strong enough to enact currency laws in seven states during the depression. For the most part, these were modest programs that worked rather well, resulted in little depreciation, and did not produce the problems feared by creditors. In most instances, the notes were loaned to farmers, who put up the value of their land as collateral.

It was the radical plan of the state of Rhode Island, however, that received most of the attention. A rural political party campaigning under the slogan "To Relieve the Distressed" captured the legislature in 1786 and enacted a currency law. The supply of paper money issued in relation to the population was much greater under this program than in any other state. The law declared the currency legal tender for all debts. If creditors refused to accept it, people could satisfy their obligations by depositing the money with a county judge, who would then advertise the debt as paid. "In the state of Rogue Island," wrote a shocked merchant, "fraud and injustice" had been "enjoined by solemn law." Conservatives pointed to Rhode Island as an example of the evils that could accompany unchecked democracy. But such programs were perhaps the only alternative without effective national legislation, which required the development of national community sentiment and national political authority.

Shays' Rebellion

In 1786 a rural uprising of communities in Massachusetts shook the nation. Farmers in the western part of the state had been hit particularly hard during the depression, when country merchants pressed them to pay their debts in hard currency they did not possess. About a third of all male heads of household were sued for debt during the 1780s, and the county jails filled with debtors who could not pay. Dozens of towns petitioned the state government for relief, but the legislature, dominated by urban and merchant interests, rejected legal tender and paper currency laws. During the spring and summer of 1786, farmers throughout the rural parts of the state mustered their community militia companies and closed the courts—precisely what they had done during the Revolution. "Whenever any encroachments are made either upon the liberties or properties of the people," declared one rebel, "if redress cannot be had without, it is virtue in them to disturb government."

This uprising quickly became known as Shays' Rebellion, after Daniel Shays, a captain in the Revolution who was one of the leaders of what became known as the Committee of the People. Although the rebellion was most widespread in Massachusetts, similar disorders occurred in every other New England state except Rhode Island, where the farmers had already taken power. There were a number of incidents outside New England as well. A "tumultuary assemblage of the people" closed the court of one Maryland county, and in York, Pennsylvania, 200 armed men stopped a farm auction whose proceeds were marked for debt payment. "Following the example of the insurgents in Massachusetts," a conservative wrote, debtor associations in Virginia prevented auctions and, according to James Madison, officials throughout the state watched "prisons and courthouses and clerks' offices willfully burnt."

The crisis ended when a militia force raised in communities from eastern Massachusetts marched west and crushed the "Shaysites" in January 1787 as they attacked the Springfield armory. Fifteen rebels were subsequently sentenced to death; two were hanged before the remainder were pardoned, and several hundred farmers had to swear an oath of allegiance to the state. In fact, these men had wanted little more than temporary relief from their indebtedness, and rural discontent quickly disappeared once the depression began to lift in 1788.

The most important consequence of Shays' Rebellion was its effect on conservative nationalists unhappy with the distribution of power between the states and national government under the Articles of Confederation. The uprising "wrought prodigious changes in the minds of men respecting the powers of government," wrote the Secretary of War Henry Knox. "Everybody says they must be strengthened and that unless this shall be effected, there is no security for liberty and property." It was time, he declared, "to clip the wings of a mad democracy."

National Portrait Gallery, Smithsonian Institution/Art Resource, NY

A mocking pamphlet of 1787 pictured Daniel Shays and Job Shattuck, two leaders of Shays' Rebellion. The artist gives them uniforms, a flag, and artillery, but the rebels were actually an unorganized group of farmers armed only with clubs and simple muskets. When the rebellion was crushed, Shattuck was wounded and jailed, and Shays along with many others left Massachusetts to settle in a remote region of Vermont.

CONCLUSION

The Revolution was a tumultuous era, marked by violent conflict between Patriots and Loyalists, masters and slaves, settlers and Indian peoples. The advocates of independence emerged successful, largely because of their ability to pull together and to begin to define their national community. But fearful of the power of central authority, Americans created a relatively weak national government. People identified strongly with their local and state communities, and these governments became the site for most of the struggles over political direction that characterized the Revolution and its immediate aftermath.

By the mid-1780s, however, many nationalists were paraphrasing Washington's question of 1777: "What then is to become of this nation?" The economic crisis that followed the Revolution sorely tested the

CHRONOLOGY

1775	Lord Dunmore, royal governor of Virginia, appeals to slaves to support Britain
1776	July: Declaration of Independence
	August: battle of Long Island initiates retreat of Continental Army
	September: British land on Manhattan Island
	December: George Washington counterattacks at Trenton
1777	Slavery abolished in Vermont
	September: British General William Howe captures Philadelphia
	October: British General John Burgoyne surrenders at Saratoga
	November: Continentals settle into winter quarters at Valley Forge
	December: France recognizes American independence
1778	June: France enters the war
	June: battle of Monmouth hastens British retreat to New York
	July: George Rogers Clark captures Kaskaskia
	December: British capture Savannah
1779	Spain enters the war
1780	February: British land at Charleston
	July: French land at Newport
	September: British General Charles Cornwallis invades North Carolina
1781	February: Robert Morris appointed superintendent of finance
	March: Articles of Confederation ratified
	October: Cornwallis surrenders at Yorktown
1782	Peace talks begin
1783	March: Washington mediates issue of officer pensions
	September: Treaty of Paris signed
	November: British evacuate New York
1784	Treaty of Fort Stanwix
	Postwar depression begins
1785	Land Ordinance of 1785
	Treaty of Fort McIntosh
1786	Jefferson's Bill for Establishing Religious Freedom
	Rhode Island currency law
	Shays' Rebellion

resources of local communities, and increasingly people found that local problems were really national problems. Conservative and moderate Patriots, who had been thrown on the defensive by the radical shift of the political debate to the left, saw this as their opportunity to successfully reenter the fray. Led by their Whiggish arguments, increasing numbers of Americans would seek to answer Washington's question by attempting to reform the national government and build a strong new national community.

REVIEW QUESTIONS

1. Assess the relative strengths of the Patriots and the Loyalists in the American Revolution.
2. What roles did Indian peoples and African Americans play in the Revolution?
3. Describe the structure of the Articles of Confederation. What were its strengths and weaknesses?
4. How did the Revolution affect politics within the states?
5. What were the issues in Shays' Rebellion? How do they help to illustrate the political conflict in the nation during the 1780s?

RECOMMENDED READING

Edward Countryman, *The American Revolution* (1985). The best short introduction to the social and political history of the Revolution. Informed by the great outpouring of studies during the twenty years preceding its publication.

Thomas Fleming, *Liberty! The American Revolution* (1997). This well-written account—derived from a public television series—includes wonderful contemporary images.

Merrill Jensen, *The New Nation: A History of the United States during the Confederation, 1781–1789* (1950). Still the standard work on the 1780s.

Charles Patrick Neimeyer, *America Goes to War: A Social History of the Continental Army* (1996). A detailed look at the men who fought and won the Revolution.

Mary Beth Norton, *Liberty's Daughters: The Revolutionary Experience of American Women, 1750–1800* (1980). A provocative and comprehensive history of women in the Revolutionary era. Treats not only legal and institutional change but also the more subtle changes in habits and expectations.

Charles Royster, *A Revolutionary People at War* (1979). A pathbreaking study of the Continental Army and popular attitudes toward it. Emphasizes the important role played by the officer corps and the enlisted men in the formation of the first nationalist constituency.

John Shy, *A People Numerous and Armed* (1976). A series of studies of the local and state militias, demonstrating that their most important contribution was political, not military.

David P. Szatmary, *Shays' Rebellion: The Making of an Agrarian Insurrection* (1980). An excellent study of the famous farmers' rebellion that stimulated conservatives to write the Constitution. Includes a great deal of general background material on the Confederation period, as well as excellent coverage of the specifics of the revolt.

Alfred F. Young, ed., *The American Revolution: Explorations in American Radicalism* (1976). Includes provocative essays on African Americans, Indians, and women.

ADDITIONAL BIBLIOGRAPHY

The War for Independence

Ira Berlin and Ronald Hoffman, eds., *Slavery and Freedom in the Age of the American Revolution* (1983)

Richard Buel Jr., *The Way of Duty: A Woman and Her Family in Revolutionary America* (1984)

Robert M. Calhoon, *The Loyalists in Revolutionary America, 1760–1781* (1973)

Charles E. Claghorn, *Women Patriots of the American Revolution* (1991)

Lawrence D. Cress, *Citizens in Arms: The Army and the Militia in American Society to the War of 1812* (1982)

Paul Finkleman, ed., *Slavery, Revolutionary America, and the New Nation* (1989)

William M. Fowler, *Rebels under Sail: The American Navy during the Revolution* (1976)

Barbara Graymont, *The Iroquois in the American Revolution* (1972)

Ronald Hoffman and Peter J. Albert, eds., *Arms and Independence: The Military Character of the American Revolution* (1984)

Ronald Hoffman and Peter J. Albert, eds., *Women in the Age of the American Revolution* (1989)

Ronald Hoffman and Thad W. Tate, eds., *An Uncivil War: The Southern Backcountry during the American Revolution* (1985)

Mark E. Kann, *A Republic of Men: The American Founders, Gendered Language, and Patriarchial Politics* (1998)

Paul C. Nagel, *The Adams Women: Abigail and Louise Adams, Their Sisters and Daughters* (1987)

Gary B. Nash, *Race and Revolution* (1990)

Mary Beth Norton, *The British Americans: The Loyalist Exiles in England, 1774–1789* (1972)

James O'Donnell, *Southern Indians in the American Revolution* (1973)

Howard W. Peckham, *The Toll of Independence: Engagements and Battle Casualties of the American Revolution* (1974)

Benjamin Quarles, *The Negro in the American Revolution*, rev. ed. (1996)

Jack M. Sosin, *The Revolutionary Frontier, 1763–1783* (1967)

James W. St. G. Walker, *The Black Loyalists* (1976)

Anthony F. C. Wallace, *The Death and Rebirth of the Seneca* (1970)

The United States in Congress Assembled

Robert A. Becker, *Revolution, Reform and the Politics of American Taxation, 1763–1783* (1980)

Richard Beeman, et al., eds., *Beyond Confederation: Origins of the Constitution and American National Identity* (1987)

E. Wayne Carp, *To Starve the Army at Pleasure: Continental Army Administration and American Political Culture, 1774–1783* (1984)

Jack Eblen, *The First and Second United States Empires* (1968)

E. J. Ferguson, *The Power of the Purse: A History of American Public Finance, 1776–1790* (1960)

Calvin C. Jillson, *Congressional Dynamics: Structure, Coordination, and Choice in the First American Congress, 1774–1789* (1994)

Jackson Turner Main, *Political Parties before the Constitution* (1973)

Jack N. Rakove, *The Beginnings of National Politics: An Interpretive History of the Continental Congress* (1979)
Gerald Sourzh, *Benjamin Franklin and American Foreign Policy* (1969)
Gordon S. Wood, *The Creation of the American Republic, 1776–1787* (1969)

Revolutionary Politics in the States

Willi Paul Adams, *The First American Constitutions: Republican Ideology and the Making of the State Constitutions* (1980)
Roger H. Brown, *Redeeming the Republic: Federalists, Taxation, and the Origins of the Constitution* (1993)
Donald S. Lutz, *Popular Consent and Popular Control: Whig Political Theory in the Early State Constitutions* (1980)
Jackson Turner Main, *The Sovereign States, 1775–1789* (1973)
Anne M. Ousterhout, *A State Divided: Opposition in Pennsylvania to the American Revolution* (1987)

Biography

Silvio A. Bedini, *The Life of Benjamin Banneker* (1972)
John Mack Faragher, *Daniel Boone: The Life and Legend of an American Pioneer* (1992)
Douglas Southall Freeman, *George Washington*, 7 vols. (1948–57)
Edith Belle Gelles, *Portia: The World of Abigail Adams* (1992)
Lowell Hayes Harrison, *George Rogers Clark and the War in the West* (1976)
Isabel Thompson Kelsay, *Joseph Brant, 1743–1807: Man of Two Worlds* (1984)
James Kirby Martin, *Benedict Arnold, Revolutionary Hero* (1997)
Willard Sterne Randall, *George Washington: A Life* (1997)
William Henry Robinson, *Phillis Wheatley and Her Writings* (1984)
Rosemarie Zagarri, *A Woman's Dilemma: Mercy Otis Warren and the American Revolution* (1995)

CHAPTER EIGHT

THE UNITED STATES OF NORTH AMERICA

1786–1800

A late 18th century American printer's cut reflecting confidence in the Constitution. The Granger Collection.

Chapter Outline

FORMING A NEW GOVERNMENT
Nationalist Sentiment
The Constitutional Convention
Ratifying the New Constitution
Shaping the Bill of Rights

THE NEW NATION
The Washington Presidency
An Active Federal Judiciary
Hamilton's Controversial Fiscal Program
The Beginnings of Foreign Policy
The United States and the Indian Peoples
Spanish and British Hostility
Domestic and International Crises
Jay's and Pinckney's Treaties
Washington's Farewell Address

FEDERALISTS AND REPUBLICANS
The Rise of Political Parties
The Adams Presidency
The Alien and Sedition Acts
The Revolution of 1800

"THE RISING GLORY OF AMERICA"
Art and Architecture
The Liberty of the Press
The Birth of American Literature
Women on the Intellectual Scene

AMERICAN COMMUNITIES
Mingo Creek Settlers Refuse to Pay the Whiskey Tax

On a hot July afternoon in 1794, the federal marshal and the federal tax collector arrived at the backcountry farm of William Miller in Mingo Creek, a community south of Pittsburgh. Like most of his neighbors, Miller had failed to pay the federal excise tax on his homemade whiskey still, and these men had come to serve him with a notice to appear in federal court in Philadelphia. "I felt myself mad with passion," said the farmer, knowing that the fine and the cost of the trip back east would "ruin" him. As the men argued, thirty or forty of Miller's neighbors suddenly appeared, armed with muskets and pitchforks. Members of the Mingo Creek Democratic Society, they had come to fight off this infringement on their liberty. There was an angry confrontation, and someone fired a gun into the air. No one was hit, and after a heated verbal exchange, the two officials rode off. But the farmers were fuming, and they decided to make a "citizen's arrest" of the officials the next day.

At Mingo Creek, poverty was the outstanding fact of life. A third of the farm families owned no land and rented or simply squatted on the acres of others. The tax collector or "exciseman" was one of the great landlords of Mingo Creek, not only controlling most of the local wealth but monopolizing political office as well. Other landlords lived outside the community, the most powerful being President George Washington himself, who owned thousands of acres in the West, much of it in the vicinity of Mingo Creek. The president had evicted so many squatters from his land that local people considered him a grasping speculator. Washington returned the compliment by describing these frontier settlers as "a parcel of barbarians" who were little better than "dogs or cats."

Farm families lived in miserable mud-floored log huts scattered along the creeks of the Monongahela Valley. But despite appearances, the farmers of Mingo Creek were bound together in networks of family and clan, work and barter, religion and politics. The militiamen acted together in what they perceived to be the interests of their community.

Like all the western territories, this was a violent place in a violent time. No-holds-barred fights at local taverns were frequent, and travelers remarked on the presence of one-eyed men, the victims of brutal gougings. Everyone knew of men or women lost in the continuing Indian wars. In 1782 militia companies from the area took their revenge by massacring ninety-six unresisting Christian Indians at Gnadenhutten, north of the Ohio River, hacking their bodies and bringing home their scalps as trophies. The new federal government had committed over 80 percent of its operating budget to defeating the Indians, but the failure of its campaigns left backcountry families resentful.

It was to help pay the costs of these campaigns that Congress had placed the tax on whiskey in 1791. The tax applied to the owners of stills, whether they produced commercially or simply for family and neighbors. Corn was not worth the cost of shipping it east, but whiskey made from corn was another matter, and many a farm family depended on the income from their stills. Farmers throughout America protested that the excise ran counter to Revolutionary principles. "Internal taxes upon consumption," declared the citizens of Mingo Creek, are "most dangerous to the civil rights of freemen, and must in the end destroy the liberties of every country in which they are introduced." Hugh Henry Brackenridge, editor of the *Pittsburgh Gazette*, argued for a tax on the "unsettled lands which all around us have been purchased by speculating men, who keep them up in large bodies and obstruct the population of the country." In other words, Congress should tax land speculators, like President Washington, instead.

Protest followed the course familiar from the Revolution. At first citizens gathered peacefully and petitioned their representatives, but when the tax collectors appeared there was vigilante action. Faces blackened or covered with handkerchiefs, farmers tarred and feathered the tax men. Although the immediate issue was taxation, larger matters were at stake. The Mingo Creek Democratic Society was part of Thomas Jefferson's political movement that supported republicanism and the French Revolution, in opposition to the conservative principles of the Washington administration. The tax protesters made this linkage explicit when they raised banners proclaiming the French slogan of "Liberty, Equality, Fraternity" and adding their own phrase, "and No Excise!" In North Carolina the rebels sang:

Some chaps whom freedom's spirit warms
Are threatening hard to take up arms,
And headstrong in rebellion rise
'Fore they'll submit to that excise:
Their liberty they will maintain,
They fought for't, and they'll
fight again.

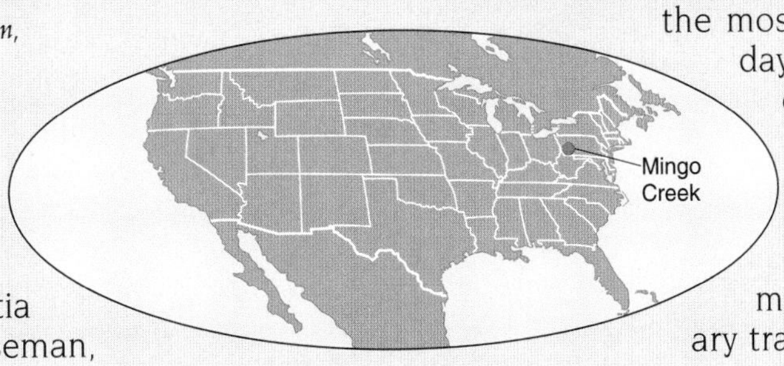

But it was only in western Pennsylvania that the protests turned to riot. When the Mingo Creek militia went to arrest the exciseman, several of their number were killed in the confrontation. The exciseman and his family escaped from their house as it was consumed by a fire set by the farmers. In a community meeting afterward, the farmers resolved to attack and destroy Pittsburgh, where the wealthy and powerful local landlords resided. Terrified residents of the town saved the day by welcoming the rebels with free food and drink. "It cost me four barrels of whiskey that day," declared one man, but "I would rather spare that than a single quart of blood." Destruction was averted, but an angry farmer rode through the street waving a tomahawk and warning: "It is not the excise law only that must go down. A great deal more is to be done. I am but beginning yet."

Declaring the Whiskey Rebellion "the first ripe fruit" of the democratic sentiment sweeping the country, President George Washington organized a federal army of 13,000 men, larger than the one he had commanded during the Revolution, and ordered the occupation of western Pennsylvania. Soldiers dragged half-naked men from their beds and forced them into open pens, where they remained for days in the freezing rain. Authorities arrested twenty people and sent them in irons to Philadelphia, where a judge convicted two of treason and sentenced them to death. The protest gradually died down, and Washington pardoned the felons, sparing their lives.

Federal power had prevailed over the local community. In his Farewell Address to the nation the following year Washington warned of an excessive spirit of localism that "agitates the community with ill-founded jealousies and false alarms; kindles the animosity of one part against another; foments occasionally riot and insurrection." But resistance to the excise remained widespread, and no substantial revenue was ever collected from the tax on whiskey. More important, the whiskey rebels had raised some of the most important issues of the day: the power and authority of the new federal government; the relation of the West to the rest of the nation; the nature of political dissent; and the meaning of the Revolutionary tradition.

KEY TOPICS

- The tensions and conflicts between local and national authorities in the decades after the American Revolution
- The struggle to draft the Constitution and to achieve its ratification
- Establishment of the first national government under the Constitution
- The beginning of American political parties
- The first stirrings of an authentic American national culture

FORMING A NEW GOVERNMENT

Eight years before the Whiskey Rebellion a similar rural uprising, Shays' Rebellion (see Chapter 7), had solidified beliefs that the powers of the federal government must be increased lest the budding nation wither. The action at Mingo Creek was the first test of the sovereignty of the newly formed central government, whose strength grew out of the Constitution forged in 1787 by delegates from all the colonies. In putting down the Whiskey Rebellion, federal forces exercised powers that the delegates to the Constitutional Convention agonized over but ultimately granted to the national community they wanted to build.

Nationalist Sentiment

Nationalists had long argued for a strengthened union of the states. Even before ratification of the Articles of Confederation, Alexander Hamilton, a New York lawyer and close associate of George Washington who had served during the Revolution as his aide, was advocating a "solid, coercive union" having "complete sovereignty" over the civil, military, and economic life of the states, along with permanent revenues from taxes and duties. But after emerging victorious from the Revolutionary War, most Americans turned their attention back to the states.

In general, the nationalists were drawn from the elite circles of American life. "Although there are no nobles in America, there is a class of men denominated 'gentlemen,'" the French ambassador to America wrote home in 1786. "They are creditors, and therefore interested in strengthening the government, and watching over the execution of the law. The majority of them being merchants, it is for their interest to establish the credit of the United States in Europe on a solid foundation by the exact payment of debts, and to grant to Congress powers extensive enough to compel the people to contribute for this purpose." In addition to merchants, the ambassador identified others who leaned toward national government: former officers in the Continental Army whose experience with the Continental Congress had made them firm believers in a stronger central government, and conservatives who wanted to restrain what they considered the excessive democracy of the states.

The economic crisis that followed the Revolutionary War (see Chapter 7) provided the nationalists with their most important opportunity to organize. In March 1785 a group of men from Virginia and Maryland, including James Madison, George Mason, and George Washington, drafted an agreement to present to legislatures recommending uniform commercial regulations, duties, and currency laws. Early the next year, at Madison's urging, the Virginia legislature invited all the states to send representatives to a commercial conference to be held at Annapolis.

Only five states sent strong nationalist delegates to the Annapolis Convention in September 1786. Hamilton, who played a leading role at the meeting, drew up a report calling on Congress to endorse a new convention to be held in Philadelphia to discuss all matters necessary "to render the constitution of the federal government adequate to the exigencies of the union." By this time, although there were still serious disagreements between localists and nationalists about the powers of the national government, most Americans agreed that the Articles needed strengthening, especially in regard to commercial regulation and the generation of revenue. Early in 1787, the Confederation Congress cautiously endorsed the plan for a convention "for the sole and express purpose of revising the Articles of Confederation."

The Constitutional Convention

Fifty-five men from twelve states assembled at the Pennsylvania State House in Philadelphia where the convention opened in late May 1787. Rhode Island, where radical localists held power (see Chapter 7), refused to send a delegation. A number of prominent men were missing. Thomas Jefferson and John Adams were serving as ambassadors in Europe, and crusty Patrick Henry declared that he "smelt a rat." Henry had become a localist, and perhaps what bothered him was the predominantly cosmopolitan cast of the meeting. But most of America's best-known leaders were present: George Washington, Benjamin Franklin, Alexander Hamilton, James Madison, George Mason, and Robert Morris. Twenty-nine of them were college educated, thirty-four were lawyers, twenty-four had served in Congress, and twenty-one were veteran officers of the Revolution. At least nineteen owned slaves, and there were also land speculators and merchants. But there were no ordinary farmers or artisans present, and certainly no women, African Americans, or Indians. The Constitution was framed by white men who represented America's social and economic elite.

George Washington presides over a session of the Constitutional Convention, meeting in Philadelphia's State House (now known as Independence Hall), in an engraving of 1799.

On their first day of work, the delegates agreed to vote by states, as was the custom in the Confederation Congress. They chose Washington to chair the meeting, and to ensure candid debate they decided to keep their sessions secret. James Madison took voluminous daily minutes, however, providing us with a record of what happened behind the convention's locked doors. Madison, a conservative young Virginian with a profound knowledge of history and political philosophy, had arrived several days before the convention opened, and with his fellow Virginians had drafted what became known as the Virginia Plan. Presented by Virginia Governor Edmund Randolph on May 29, it set the convention's agenda.

The authors of the Virginia Plan proposed scrapping the Articles of Confederation in favor of a "consolidated government" having the power to tax and to enforce its laws directly rather than through the states. "A spirit of locality," Madison declared, was destroying "the aggregate interests of the community," by which he meant the great community of the nation. Madison's plan would have reduced the states to little more than administrative districts. Representation in the bicameral national legislature would be based on population: the members of the House of Representatives were to be elected by popular vote, but senators would be chosen by state legislators so that they might be insulated from democratic pressure. The Senate would lead, controlling foreign affairs and the appointment of officials. An appointed chief executive and a national judiciary would together form a Council of Revision having the power to veto both national and state legislation.

The main opposition to these proposals came from the delegates from small states, which feared being swallowed up by the large ones. After two weeks of debate, William Paterson of New Jersey introduced an alternative, a set of "purely federal" principles known since as the New Jersey Plan. He proposed increasing the powers of the central government but retaining a single-house Congress in which the states were equally represented. After much debate and a series of votes that split the convention down the middle, the delegates finally agreed to what has been called the Great Compromise: proportional representation by population in the House, representation by states in the Senate. The compromise allowed the creation of a strong national government while still providing an important role for the states.

Part of this agreement was a second, fundamental compromise that brought together the delegates from North and South. To boost their power in the new government, the southern delegates wanted to include slaves in the population to be counted for the purpose of determining state representation, but to exclude them when it came to apportioning taxes. Ultimately it was agreed that five slaves would be counted as the equal of three freemen—the "three-fifths rule." Furthermore, the representatives of South Carolina and Georgia demanded protection for the international slave trade, and after bitter debate the delegates included a provision preventing any prohibition of the importation of slaves for twenty years. Another article legitimized the return of fugitive slaves from free states. Although the word "slave" does not appear anywhere in the Constitution (the framers avoided it with such phrases as "other persons" and "persons held to labor," these provisions nonetheless amounted to national guarantees for southern slavery. Many delegates were opposed to slavery and regretted having to give in on this issue, but they agreed with Madison, who wrote that "great as the evil is, a dismemberment of the union would be worse."

There was still much to decide regarding the other branches of government. Madison's Council of Revision was scratched in favor of a strong federal judiciary with the implicit power to declare acts of Congress unconstitutional. Demands for a powerful chief executive raised fears that the office might prove to be, in the words of Edmund Randolph of Virginia, "the fetus of monarchy." But there was considerable support for a president with veto power to check the legislature. In fact, according to James McHenry, a delegate from Maryland, twenty-one delegates favored some form of monarchy, and Alexander Hamilton went on record supporting the creation of a constitutional monarch. To keep the president independent of Congress, the delegates decided he should be elected; but fearing that ordinary voters could never "be sufficiently informed" to select wisely, they insulated the process from popular choice by creating the electoral college. Voters in the states would not actually vote for president. Rather, in a manner to be determined by its legislature, each state would select a slate of "electors" equal in number to the state's total representation in the House and Senate. Following the general election, the electors in each state would meet to cast their ballots and elect the president.

In early September the delegates turned their rough draft of the Constitution over to a Committee of Style that shaped it into an elegant and concise document setting forth the general principles and basic framework of government. But Madison, known to later generations as "the Father of the Constitution," was gloomy, believing that the revisions of his original plan doomed the Union to the kind of inaction that had characterized government under the Articles of Confederation. It was left for Franklin to make the final speech to the convention. "Can a perfect production be expected?" he asked. "I consent, Sir, to this Constitution, because I expect no better, and because I am not sure that it is not the best." The delegates voted their approval on September 17, 1787, and transmitted the document to Congress, agreeing that it would become operative after ratification by nine states. Some congressmen were outraged that the convention had exceeded its charge of simply modifying the Articles of Confederation, but Congress called for a special ratifying convention in each of the states.

Ratifying the New Constitution

The supporters of the new Constitution immediately adopted the name Federalists to describe themselves. Their outraged opponents objected that the existing Confederation already provided for a "federal" government of balanced power between the states and the Union and that the Constitution would replace it with a "national" government. But in this, as in much of the subsequent process of ratification, the Federalists (or nationalists) grabbed the initiative, and their opponents had to content themselves with the label Anti-Federalists. Mercy Otis Warren, a leading critic of the Constitution, commented on the dilemma in which the Anti-Federalists found themselves. "On the one hand," she wrote, "we stand in need of a strong federal government, founded on principles that will support the prosperity and union of the colonies. On the other, we have struggled for liberty and made costly sacrifices at her shrine and there are still many among us who revere her name too much to relinquish, beyond a certain medium, the rights of man for the dignity of government."

The critics of the Constitution were by no means a unified group. Because most of them were localists, they represented a variety of social and regional interests. But most believed the Constitution granted far too much power to the center, weakening the autonomy of communities and states. As local governments "will always possess a better representation of the feelings and interests of the people at large," one critic wrote, "it is obvious that these powers can be deposited with much greater safety with the state than the general government."

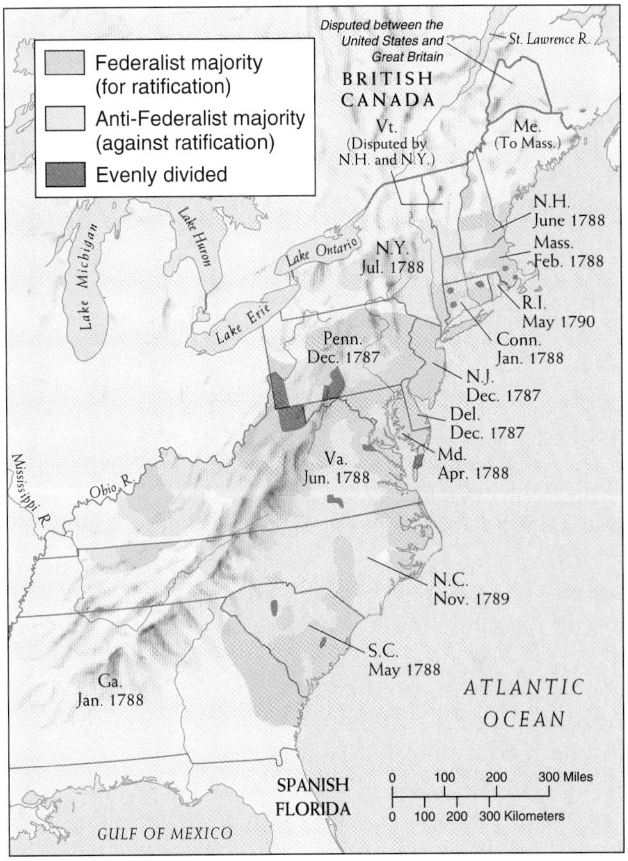

The Ratification of the Constitution, 1787–1790

The distribution of the vote for the ratification of the Constitution demonstrated its wide support in sections of the country linked to the commercial economy and its disapproval in more remote and backcountry sections. (Note that Maine remained a part of Massachusetts until admitted as a separate state in 1820.)

All the great political thinkers of the eighteenth century had argued that a republican form of government could work only for small countries. As the French philosopher Montesquieu had observed, "In an extensive republic, the public good is sacrificed to a thousand private views." But in *The Federalist,* a series of brilliant essays in defense of the Constitution written in 1787 and 1788 by Madison, Hamilton, and John Jay, Madison stood Montesquieu's assumption on its head. Rhode Island had demonstrated that the rights of property might not be protected in even the smallest of states. Asserting that "the most common and durable source of factions has been the various and unequal distribution of property," Madison concluded that the best way to control such factions was to "extend the sphere" of government. That way, he continued, "you take in a greater variety of parties and interests; you make it less probable that a majority of the whole will have a common motive to invade the rights of other citizens; or, if such a common motive exists, it will be more difficult for all who feel it to discover their own strength and to act in unison with each other." Rather than a disability, Madison argued, great size is an advantage: interests are so diverse that no single faction is able to gain control of the state, threatening the freedoms of others.

It is doubtful whether Madison's sophisticated argument, or the arguments of the Anti-Federalists for that matter, made much of a difference in the popular voting in the states to select delegates for the state ratification conventions. The alignment of forces generally followed the lines laid down during the fights over economic issues in the years since the Revolution. For example, in Pennsylvania—the first state to convene a ratification convention, in November 1787—48 percent of the Anti-Federalist delegates to the convention were farmers. By contrast, 54 percent of the Federalists were merchants, manufacturers, large landowners, or professionals. What tipped the Pennsylvania convention in favor of the Constitution was the wide support the document enjoyed among artisans and commercial farmers, who saw their interests tied to the growth of a commercial society. As one observer pointed out, "The counties nearest [navigable waters] were in favor of it generally, those more remote, in opposition."

Similar agrarian-localist and commercial-cosmopolitan alignments characterized most of the other states. The most critical convention took place in Massachusetts in early 1788. Five states—Delaware, Pennsylvania, New Jersey, Georgia, and Connecticut—had already voted to ratify, but the states with the strongest Anti-Federalist movements had yet to convene. If the Constitution lost in Massachusetts, its fate would be in great danger. At the convention, Massachusetts opponents of ratification enjoyed a small majority. But several important Anti-Federalist leaders, including Samuel Adams, were swayed by the enthusiastic support for the Constitution among Boston's townspeople, and on February 6 the convention voted narrowly in favor of ratification. To no one's surprise, Rhode Island rejected the Constitution in March, but Maryland and South Carolina approved it in April and May. On June 21, New Hampshire became the ninth state to ratify.

Anti-Federalist support was strong in New York, Virginia, and North Carolina. North Carolina voted to reject and did not join the union until the next year; it was followed by a still reluctant Rhode Island in 1790. In New York, the delegates were moved to vote their support by a threat from New York City to secede from the state and join the Union separately if the convention failed to ratify. The Virginia convention was almost evenly divided, but promises to amend the Constitution to protect individual rights persuaded enough delegates to produce a victory for the Consti-

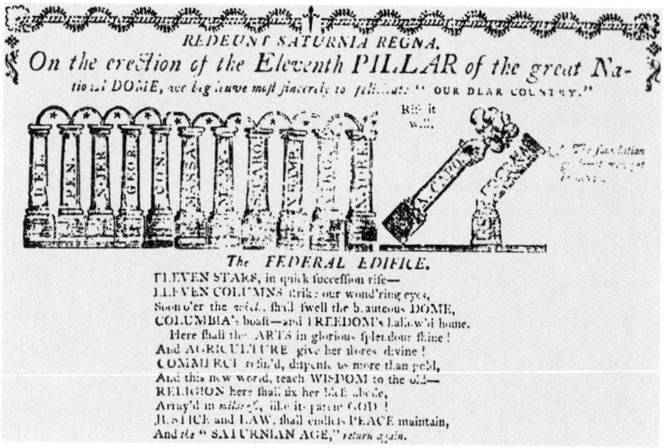

A cartoon published in July 1788 when New York became the eleventh state to ratify the Constitution. After initially voting to reject, North Carolina soon reconsidered, but radical and still reluctant Rhode Island did not join the Union until 1790.

tution. The promise of a Bill of Rights, in fact, was important in the ratification vote of five of the states.

Shaping the Bill of Rights

Although the Bill of Rights—the first ten amendments to the Constitution—was adopted during the first session of the new federal Congress, it was first proposed during the debates over ratification. The Constitutional Convention had considered a Bill of Rights patterned on the declarations of rights in the state constitutions (see Chapter 7) but rejected it as superfluous, agreeing with Madison that the federal government would exercise only those powers expressly delegated to it. However, George Mason, author of Virginia's Declaration of Rights, refused to sign the Constitution because it failed to contain similar provisions. He played an important role in getting the Virginia ratifying convention to endorse a set of constitutional amendments. Campaigning for a seat in the new Congress, Madison was pressed to affirm his willingness to propose and support a set of amendments guaranteeing "essential rights."

The various state ratification conventions had proposed a grab bag of more than 200 potential amendments. Madison set about transforming these into a series that he introduced into the new Congress in June 1789. Congress passed twelve and sent them to the states in September, and ten survived the ratification process to become the Bill of Rights in 1791.

The First Amendment prohibits Congress from establishing an official religion and provides for the freedoms of speech and the press and the right of assembly and petition. The other amendments guarantee the right to bear arms, limit the government's power to quarter troops in private homes, and restrain the government from unreasonable searches or seizures; they assure the people their legal rights under the common law, including the prohibition of double jeopardy, the right not to be compelled to testify against oneself, and due process of law before life, liberty, or property can be taken. Finally, the unenumerated rights of the people are protected, and those powers not delegated to the federal government are reserved to the states.

The first ten amendments to the Constitution have been a restraining influence on the growth of government power over American citizens. Their provisions have become an admired aspect of the American political tradition throughout the world. The Bill of Rights is the most important constitutional legacy of the Anti-Federalists.

THE NEW NATION

Ratification of the Constitution was followed by the first federal elections—for the congress and the presidency—and in the spring of 1789 the new federal government assumed power in the temporary capital of New York City. The inauguration of George Washington as the first president of the United States took place on April 30, 1789, on the balcony of Federal Hall, at the corner of Wall and Broad Streets. Reelected without opposition in 1792, Washington would serve until 1797.

The activities of the first federal government were far removed from the everyday lives of most Americans, but as the Whiskey Rebellion demonstrated, there were moments when the two intersected dramatically. Moreover, the first years under the new federal Constitution were especially important for the future, because they shaped the structure of the American state in ways that would be enormously significant for later generations.

The Washington Presidency

During its first month, the Congress debated what to call the president of the United States. Believing that no government could long endure without the awe and veneration of its citizens, Vice President John Adams, sitting as the president of the Senate, proposed "His Highness the President of the United States." But a majority in the House of Representatives saw this title as a dangerous flirtation with "monarchism." When someone proposed that the nation's coinage be stamped with a bust of the president, men of republican persuasion protested that such veneration would be too much like the customs of the British empire. The president himself finally resolved the controversy by declaring the whole topic had been raised "without any privity of knowledge of it on my part," and by custom he came to be addressed simply as "Mr. President." This issue encapsulated an important conflict of these early years—the desire of some nationalists to add to the power of executive authority, versus the faith of localists in a strong Congress.

Although he dressed in plain American broadcloth at his inauguration and claimed to be content with a plain republican title, Washington was counted among the nationalists. He was anything but a man of the people, by nature reserved and solemn, choosing to ride about town in a grand carriage drawn by six horses and escorted by uniformed liverymen. In the tradition of British royalty, he delivered his addresses personally to Congress and received from both houses an official reply. These customs were continued by John Adams, Washington's successor, but ended by Thomas Jefferson, who denounced them as "rags of royalty," and began the practice, continued throughout the nineteenth century, of sending written presidential messages to Congress. On the other hand, Washington worked hard to adhere to the letter of the Constitution, refusing, for example, to use the veto power except where he thought the Congress had acted unconstitutionally, and personally seeking the "advice and consent" of the Senate.

Congress quickly moved to establish departments to run the executive affairs of state, and Washington soon appointed Thomas Jefferson his secretary of state, Alexander Hamilton to run the Treasury, Henry Knox the War Department, and Edmund Randolph the Justice Department, as attorney general. The president consulted each of these men regularly, and during his first term met with them as a group to discuss matters of policy. By the end of Washington's presidency the secretaries had coalesced in what came to be known as the cabinet, an institution that has survived to the present despite the absence of constitutional authority or enabling legislation giving it formal recognition. Washington was a powerful and commanding personality, but he understood the importance of national unity, and in his style of leadership, his consultations, and his appointments he sought to achieve a balance of conflicting political perspectives and sectional interests. These intentions would be sorely tested during the eight years of his administration.

An Active Federal Judiciary

The most important piece of legislation to emerge from the first session of Congress was the Judiciary Act of 1789, which implemented the judicial clause of the Constitution and set up a system of federal courts.

Daniel Huntington's Republican Court *emphasized the similarities between American republican government and the royal courts of Europe. When Vice President John Adams proposed that the president be addressed as "His Highness," democrats in the Congress argued this was a dangerous flirtation with "monarchism," and Thomas Jefferson urged that the government give up such "rags of royalty."*

Congress provided that the Supreme Court consist of six justices (later increased to nine) and established three circuit and thirteen district courts. Strong nationalists argued for a powerful federal legal system that would provide a uniform code of civil and criminal justice throughout the country. But the localists in Congress fought successfully to retain the various bodies of law that had developed in the states. They wanted to preserve local community autonomy. The act gave federal courts limited original jurisdiction, restricting them mostly to appeals from state courts. But it thereby established the principle of federal judicial review of state legislation, despite the silence of the Constitution on this point.

Under the leadership of Chief Justice John Jay, the Supreme Court heard relatively few cases during its first decade. Still, it managed to raise considerable political controversy. In *Chisholm v. Georgia* (1793) it ruled in favor of two South Carolina residents who had sued the state of Georgia for the recovery of confiscated property. Thus did the Court overthrow the common law principle that a sovereignty could not be sued without its consent, and supported the Constitution's grant of federal jurisdiction over disputes "between a state and citizens of another state." Many localists feared that this nationalist ruling threatened the integrity of the states. In response, they proposed the Eleventh Amendment to the Constitution, ratified in 1798, which declared that no state could be sued by citizens from another state. The Supreme Court nevertheless established itself as the final authority on questions of law when it invalidated a Virginia statute in *Ware v. Hylton* (1796) and upheld the constitutionality of an act of Congress in *Hylton v. U.S.* (1796).

Hamilton's Controversial Fiscal Program

Fiscal and economic affairs pressed upon the new government. Lacking revenues, and faced with the massive national debt contracted during the Revolution, it took power in a condition of virtual bankruptcy. At the urging of James Madison, whose first official position in the United States government was floor leader for the Washington administration in the House of Representatives, Congress passed the Tariff of 1789, a compromise between advocates of protective tariffs (duties so high that they made foreign products prohibitively expensive, thus "protecting" American products) and those who wanted moderate tariffs that produced income. Duties on imported goods, rather than direct taxes on property or incomes, would constitute the bulk of federal revenues until the twentieth century.

After setting this system of duties in place, Congress turned to the problem of the debt. In January 1790, Hamilton submitted a "Report on the Public Credit," in which he recommended that the federal government assume the obligations accumulated by the states during the previous fifteen years and redeem the national debt—owed to both domestic and foreign leaders—by agreeing to a new issue of interest-bearing bonds. To raise the revenue required to retire the debt, Hamilton recommended an excise tax on the manufacture of distilled liquor.

By this means, Hamilton sought to inspire the confidence of domestic and foreign investors in the public credit of the new nation. Congress endorsed his plan to pay off the $11 million owed to foreign creditors but balked at funding the domestic debt of $27 million and assuming the state debts of $25 million. The funding of the domestic debt aroused debate because necessity had forced many individuals to sell off at deep discounts the notes, warrants, and securities the government had issued them during the Revolution. Yet Hamilton now advocated paying these obligations at face value, providing any speculator who held them with fabulous profits. The assumption of state debts aroused even greater debate because some states, mostly those in the South, had already arranged to liquidate their debts, whereas others had left theirs unpaid.

Congress remained deadlocked on these issues for six months, until congressmen from Pennsylvania and Virginia arranged a compromise. Final agreement, however, was stalled by a sectional dispute over the permanent location of the new national capital. Southerners supported Washington's desire to plant it on the Potomac River, but northerners argued for Philadelphia. In return for Madison's pledge to obtain enough southern votes to pass Hamilton's assumption plan—which Madison had earlier opposed as a "radically immoral" windfall for speculators—northern congressmen agreed to a location for the new federal district on the boundary of Virginia and Maryland. In July 1790, Congress passed legislation moving the temporary capital from New York to Philadelphia until the expected completion of the federal city, in 1800, in a "District of Columbia" that would be under the jurisdiction of Congress. Two weeks later it adopted Hamilton's credit program. This was the first of many sectional compromises.

Hamilton now proposed the second component of his fiscal program, the establishment of a Bank of the United States. The bank, a public corporation funded by private capital, would serve as the depository of government funds and the fiscal agent of the Treasury. Congress narrowly approved it, but Madison's opposition raised doubts in the president's mind about the constitutionality of the measure, and Washington solicited the opinion of his cabinet. Here for the first time were articulated the classic interpretations of constitutional authority. Jefferson took a "strict constructionist" position, arguing that the powers of the federal government must be limited to those specifically enumerated in the Constitution. This position came closest to the basic agreement of the men who had drafted the document. Hamilton, on the other hand, reasoned that the Constitution "implied" the power to use whatever means were "necessary and proper" to carry out its enumerated powers—a "loose constructionist" position. Persuaded by Hamilton's opinion, Washington signed the bill, and the bank went into operation in 1791.

Hamilton's "Report on Manufactures," submitted to Congress in December 1791, was the capstone to his comprehensive economic program. It contained an ambitious plan involving the use of government securities as investment capital for "infant industries," federal bounties to encourage innovation, and high protective tariffs. This system, Hamilton hoped, would promote the development of an industrial economy. Congressmen from farming areas, whose previous objections to Hamilton's preference for the "monied interests" had not prevailed, were finally able to frustrate him on this proposal. Hamilton's views, they argued, would limit them to roles exactly like those they had played within the British empire; in effect they would be exchanging British for Boston and New York masters. Of equal importance, the plan failed to inspire American capitalists, who continued to be more interested in investments in shipping or in land speculation than in industrial production.

Many of Hamilton's specific proposals for increased tariff protection became part of a revision of duties that took place in 1792. Moreover, his fiscal program as a whole dramatically restored the financial health of the United States. Foreign investment in government securities increased and along with domestic capital provided the Bank of the United States with enormous reserves. Its bank notes became the most important circulating medium of the North American commercial economy, and their wide acceptance greatly stimulated business enterprise. "Our public credit," Washington declared toward the end of his first term, "stands on that ground which three years ago it would have been considered as a species of madness to have foretold."

The Beginnings of Foreign Policy

The Federalist political coalition, forged during the ratification of the Constitution, was sorely strained by these debates over fiscal policy. By the middle of 1792, Jefferson, representing the southern agrarians, and Hamilton, speaking for northern capitalists, were locked in a full-scale feud within the Washington administration. Hamilton conducted himself more like a prime minister than a cabinet secretary, greatly offending Jefferson, who considered himself the president's heir apparent. But the dispute went deeper than a mere conflict of personalities. Hamilton stated the difference clearly when he wrote that "one side appears to believe that there is a serious plot to overturn the State governments, and substitute a monarchy to the present republican system," whereas "the other side firmly believes that there is a serious plot to overturn the general government and elevate the separate powers of the States upon its ruins." The conflict between Hamilton and Jefferson was to grow even more bitter over the issue of American foreign policy.

The commanding event of the Atlantic world during the 1790s was the French Revolution, which had begun in 1789. Most Americans enthusiastically welcomed the fall of the French monarchy. After the people of Paris stormed the Bastille, the new French republic sent Washington the key to the prison's doors as a symbol of the relationship between the two revolutions. But with the beginning in 1793 of the Reign of Terror, whose bloody guillotine claimed the lives of hundreds of aristocrats, American conservatives began to voice their opposition. The execution of King Louis XVI, and especially the onset of war between revolutionary France and monarchical Great Britain in 1793, firmly divided American opinion.

Most at issue was whether the Franco-American alliance of 1778 required the United States to support France in its war with Britain. All of Washington's cabinet agreed on the importance of American neutrality. With France and Britain prowling for each other's vessels on the high seas, the vast colonial trade of Europe was delivered up to neutral powers, the United States prominent among them. Neutrality, in other words, meant windfall profits. Jefferson believed it highly unlikely that the French would call on the Americans to honor the 1778 treaty; the administration should simply wait and see. Hamilton argued, however, that so great was the danger that Washington should immediately declare the treaty "temporarily and provisionally suspended."

These disagreements revealed two contrasting perspectives on the course the United States should chart in international waters. Hamilton believed in the necessity of an accommodation with Great Britain, the most important trading partner of the United States and the world's greatest naval power. Jefferson and Madison, on the other hand, looked for more international independence, pinning their hopes on the future of western expansion. There was room for compromise between these two points of view, but in the debate over the French Revolution positions tended to become polarized.

The debate in the United States grew hotter with the arrival in April 1793 of French ambassador Edmond Genêt. Large crowds of supporters greeted him throughout the nation, and among them he solicited contributions and distributed commissions authorizing American privateering raids against the British. Understandably, a majority of Americans still nursed a hatred of imperial Britain, and many had considerable sympathy for republican France. Like Hamilton, however, conservatives favored a continuation of traditional commercial relations with Britain and feared the anti-aristocratic violence of the French. Washington sympathized with Hamilton's position, but most of all he wished to preserve American independence and neutrality. Knowing he must act before "Citizen" Genêt (as the ambassador was popularly known) compromised American sovereignty and involved the United States in a war with Britain, the president issued a proclamation of neutrality on April 22, 1793. In it he assured the world that the United States intended to pursue "a conduct friendly and impartial towards the belligerent powers," while continuing to do business with all sides.

Hamilton's supporters applauded the president, but Jefferson's were outraged. "The cause of France is the cause of man," declared Hugh Henry Brackenridge of Pittsburgh, "and neutrality is desertion." Throughout the country those sympathetic to France organized Democratic Societies, political clubs modeled after the Sons of Liberty. Society members corresponded with each other, campaigned on behalf of candidates, and lobbied with congressmen. People interpreted the international question in the light of issues of local importance. Thus the members of the Mingo Creek Democratic Society used enthusiasm for the French Revolution as a way of organizing political opposition to the Washington administration. Brackenridge described the society's Mingo Creek chapter as "an engine of election," in other words, a political machine. In a speech to Congress, President Washington denounced what he called these "self-created societies," declaring them "the most diabolical attempt to destroy the best fabric of human government and happiness."

Citizen Genêt miscalculated, however, alienating even his supporters, when he demanded that Washington call Congress into special session to debate neutrality. Jefferson, previously a confidant of the ambassador, now denounced Genêt as "hot-headed" and "indecent towards the President." But these words came too late to save his reputation in the eyes of President Washington, and at the end of 1793 Jefferson left the administration. The continuing upheaval in France soon swept Genêt's party from power, and another minister from France arrived with a warrant for his arrest. Fearing the guillotine, Genêt claimed sanctuary and remained in the United States. The Citizen Genêt affair furthered the division of the Federalist coalition into one faction identifying with Washington, Hamilton, and conservative principles and another faction supporting Jefferson, Madison, democracy, and the French Revolution.

The United States and the Indian Peoples

Among the many problems of the Washington presidency, one of the most pressing concerned the West. The American attempt to treat the western Indian tribes as conquered peoples after the Revolution had resulted only in further violence and warfare. The Northwest Ordinance of 1787 (see Chapter 7) signaled a new approach. "The utmost good faith shall always be observed towards the Indians," it read. "Their lands and property shall never be taken from them without their consent; and in their property, rights, and liberty, they shall never be invaded or disturbed, unless in just and lawful wars authorized by Congress." Although the Constitution was silent regarding Indian policy, Congress endorsed this statutory recognition of the independent character of the Indian tribes when in 1790 it passed the Indian Intercourse Act, the basic law by which the United States would "regulate trade and intercourse with the Indian tribes." To eliminate the abuses of unscrupulous traders, the act created a federal licensing system; subsequent amendments authorized the creation of subsidized trading houses, or "factories," where Indians could obtain goods at reasonable prices. Trade abuses continued unabated for lack of adequate policing power, but

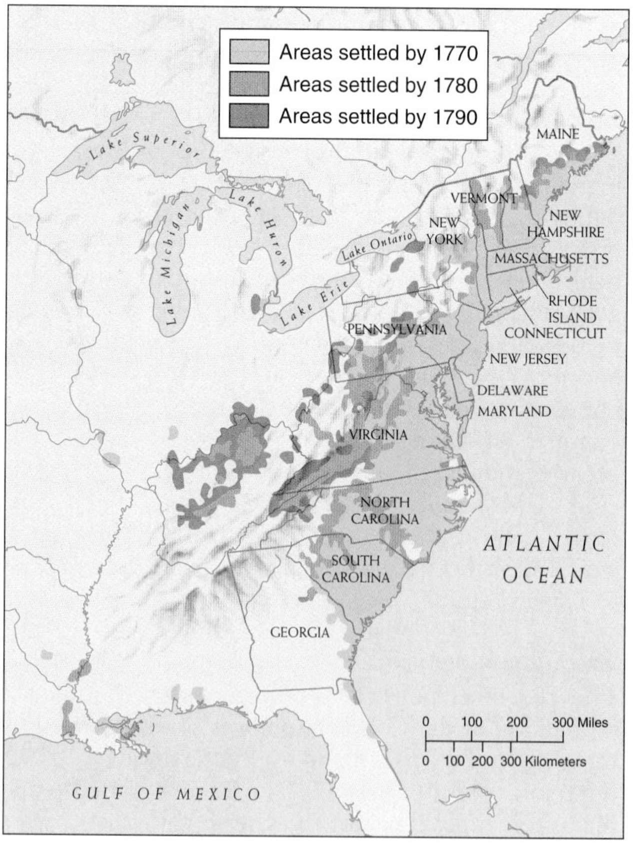

Spread of Settlement: The Backcountry Expands, 1770–1790 *From 1770 to 1790 American settlement moved across the Appalachians for the first time. The Ohio Valley became the focus of bitter warfare between Indians and settlers.*

these provisions indicated the good intentions of the Washington administration.

To clarify the question of Indian sovereignty, the Indian Intercourse Act declared public treaties between the United States and the Indian nations to be the only legal means of obtaining Indian land. Treaty making thus became the procedure for establishing and maintaining relations. Although the federal government frequently applied military pressure to secure the signing of such treaties, the process preserved a semblance of legality. In the twentieth century, a number of Indian tribes have successfully appealed for the return of lands obtained by states or individuals in violation of this provision of the Intercourse Act.

Little Turtle, a war chief of the Miami tribe of the Ohio valley, led a large pan-Indian army to victory over the Americans in 1790 and 1791. After his forces were defeated at the Battle of Fallen Timbers in 1794, he became a friend of the United States. This lithograph is a copy of an oil portrait, painted by the artist Gilbert Stuart, which no longer survives.

Yet conflict continued to characterize the relationship of Americans and Indian peoples, for one of the American government's highest priorities was the acquisition of Indian land to supply a growing population of farmers. American settlers along the Ohio River, wrote one army officer, "carry on private expeditions against the Indians and kill them whenever they meet them," and there was not a jury in the West, he added, that would dare to punish a man for these crimes. In defense of their homelands, villages of Shawnees, Delawares, and other Indian peoples confederated with the Miamis under their war chief Little Turtle. In the fall of 1790 Little Turtle lured an American expeditionary force led by General Josiah Harmar into the confederacy's stronghold in Ohio and badly mauled them. In November 1791 the confederation inflicted an even more disastrous defeat on a large American force under General Arthur St. Clair, governor of the Northwest Territory. More than 900 Americans were killed or wounded, making this the worst defeat of an army by Indians in North American history.

Spanish and British Hostility

The position of the United States in the West was made even more precarious by the hostility of Spain and Great Britain, which controlled the adjoining territory. Under the dynamic leadership of King Carlos III and his able ministers, Spain introduced liberal reforms to revitalize the rule-bound economy of its American empire; as a result the economy of New Spain experienced a period of rapid growth in the 1780s. Moreover, Spain had reasserted itself in North America, acquiring the French claims to Louisiana before the end of the Seven Years War, expanding into California, seizing the Gulf coast during the American Revolution, and regaining Florida from Britain in the Treaty of Paris in 1783. The Spanish were deeply suspicious of the Americans. The settlers, the Spanish governor of Florida declared, "were nomadic like Arabs,...distinguished from savages only in their color, language, and the superiority of their depraved cunning and untrustworthiness." Spain claimed for itself most of the territory south of the Ohio River and pursued a policy designed to block the expansion of the new republic.

Spain's anti-American policy in the West had several facets. Controlling both sides of the lower Mississippi, the Spanish closed the river to American shipping, making it impossible for western American farmers to market their crops through the port of New Orleans. The Spanish also sought to create a barrier to American settlement by promoting immigration to Louisiana and Florida. They succeeded in attracting several thousand of the Acadians deported by the British during the Seven Years War, who reassembled their distinctive communities in the bayou country of Louisiana (see Chapter 6). But otherwise the Spanish had little success with immigration and relied mostly on creating a barrier of pro-Spanish Indian nations in the lower Mississippi Valley. In exchange for supplies and Spanish recognition of them as "free and independent nations," the tribes of the South pledged themselves to "the preservation of the Dominion" of Spain in Louisiana and Florida. To consolidate these gains, in the early 1790s the Spanish constructed two new Mississippi River forts at sites that would later become the cities of Vicksburg and Memphis.

North of the Ohio River the situation was much the same. Thousands of Loyalists had fled the United States in the aftermath of the Revolution and settled in the country north of Lakes Ontario and Erie. They were understandably hostile to the new republic. In 1791 the British Parliament passed the Canada Act, creating the province of Upper Canada (later renamed Ontario) and granting the Loyalists limited self-government. To protect this province British troops remained at a number of posts within American territory at places such as Detroit, where they supplied the Indian nations with arms and ammunition, hoping to create a buffer to American expansion. In early 1794 the governor general of Canada told an assembly of Indian leaders from the Ohio country that war between Britain and the United States was almost certain, and that when it broke out, "a line must then be drawn by the warriors." British soldiers began constructing Fort Miami in the Maumee Valley, west of Lake Erie, well within American territory.

Domestic and International Crises

Washington faced the gravest crisis of his presidency in 1794. In the West, the inability of the federal government to subdue the Indians, to eliminate the British from the northern fur trade, or to arrange with the Spanish for unencumbered use of the Mississippi River stirred frontiersmen to loud protests. There were rumblings of rebellion and secession from western communities. This discontent was strengthened by Hamilton's federal excise tax on whiskey, which hit backcountry farmers hardest, as the opening of this chapter illustrates. "The people of the western counties," wrote an English commentator, find "themselves grievously taxed for the support of the government without enjoying the blessings of it." London and Madrid believed that American settlers in the Northwest and Southwest might quit the Union and join themselves to Canada or Florida, and both English and Spanish secret agents worked to enhance such possibilities with liberal bribes.

In the Atlantic, Great Britain declared a blockade of France, including the seizure of vessels trading with the French West Indies. From 1793 to the beginning of 1794 the British confiscated the cargoes of more than 250 American ships, threatening hundreds of merchants with ruin. The United States was being "kicked, cuffed, and plundered all over the ocean," declared Madi-

In this 1794 painting, President George Washington reviews some 13,000 troops at Fort Cumberland on the Potomac before dispatching them to suppress the Whiskey Rebellion. Washington's mobilization of federal military power dramatically demonstrated the federal commitment to the preservation of the Union and the protection of the western boundary.

son, and in Congress he introduced legislation imposing retaliatory duties on British ships and merchandise.

The Whiskey Rebellion, which broke out in the summer of 1794, thus came at a time when President Washington considered the nation to be under siege. The combination of Indian attack, international intrigue, and domestic insurrection, he believed, created the greatest threat to the nation since the Revolution. In April the president had dispatched Chief Justice John Jay to London to arrange a settlement with the British. At the same time, war seemed increasingly likely, and Washington feared that any sign of federal weakness in the face of western rebellion would invite British or Spanish intervention. With Hamilton's urging he took the decisive course described in the opening of this chapter: he raised a large militia even as he pursued halfhearted negotiations with local authorities and made preparations to occupy the area around Pittsburgh, including Mingo Creek. It is clear now that the president overreacted, for although there was riot and violence in western Pennsylvania, there was no organized insurrection. Nevertheless, his mobilization of federal military power dramatically demonstrated the federal commitment to the preservation of the Union, the protection of the western boundary, and the supremacy of the national over the local community.

This action was reinforced by an impressive American victory against the Indian confederacy. Following the disastrous defeat of St. Clair by Little Turtle, Washington appointed General Anthony Wayne to lead a greatly strengthened American army to subdue the Indian confederacy and secure the Northwest. At the battle of Fallen Timbers, fought in the Maumee country of northern Ohio on August 20, 1794, Wayne crushed the Indians. Retreating, the warriors found the gates of Fort Miami closed and barred, the British inside thinking better of providing the powerful American force with a reason to attack the fort. The victory set the stage for the Treaty of Greenville in 1795, in which the representatives of twelve Indian nations ceded a huge territory encompassing most of present-day Ohio, much of Indiana, and other enclaves in the Northwest, including the town of Detroit and the tiny village of Chicago.

Jay's and Pinckney's Treaties

The strengthened American position in the West encouraged the British to settle their dispute with the United States so that they might concentrate on defeating republican France. In November 1794 Jay and the British signed an agreement providing for British withdrawal from American soil by 1796, limited American trade with the British East and West Indies, and the status of most-favored-nation for both countries (meaning that each would enjoy trade benefits equal to those the other accorded any other state). The treaty represented a solid gain for the young republic. With only a small army and no navy to speak of, the United States was in no position to wage war.

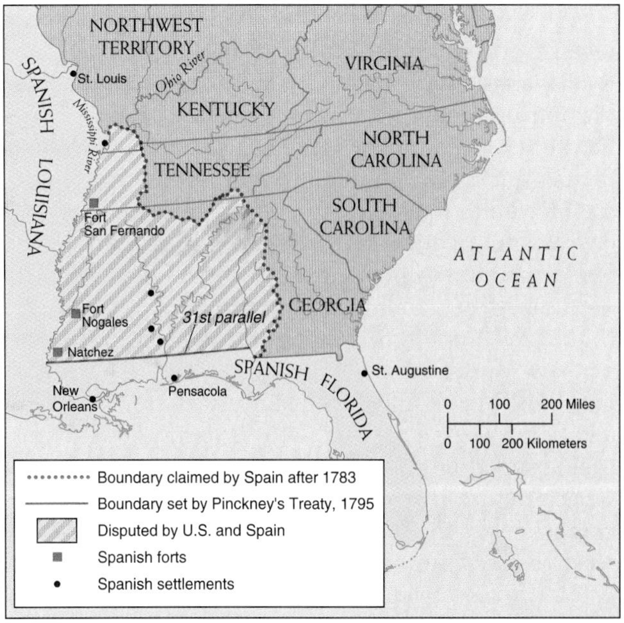

Spanish Claims to American Territory, 1783–1795

Before 1795 the Spanish claimed the American territory of the Old Southwest and barred Americans from access to the port of New Orleans, effectively closing the Mississippi River. This dispute was settled by Pinckney's Treaty in 1795.

As it did on all matters of importance, the Senate debated the treaty in secret session. Details leaked out in a piecemeal fashion that inflamed public debate. The treaty represented a victory for Hamilton's conception of American neutrality. The Jeffersonians might well have opposed any agreement with Great Britain, but they were enraged over this accommodation that virtually unleashed Britain to attack republican France with full force. The absence in the treaty of any mention of compensation for the slaves who had fled to the British side during the Revolution further alienated Southerners. Throughout the country Democratic Societies and Jeffersonian partisans organized protests and demonstrations. Upon his return to the United States, Jay joked, he could find his way across the country by the light of his burning effigies. Despite these protests, the Senate, dominated by supporters of Hamilton, ratified the agreement in June 1795. In the House, a coalition of Southerners, Westerners, and friends of France attempted to stall the treaty by threatening to withhold the appropriations necessary for its implementation and demanding that they be allowed to examine the diplomatic correspondence regarding the whole affair. By refusing this demand, the president established the precedent of executive privilege in matters of state.

The deadlock continued until late in the year, when word arrived that the Spanish had abandoned their claims to the territory south of the Ohio River. Having declared war on revolutionary France, Spain had suffered a humiliating defeat, and fearing the loss of its American empire now found it expedient to mollify the quarrelsome Americans. In 1795 American envoy Thomas Pinckney negotiated a treaty in which Spain agreed to a boundary with the United States at the thirty-first parallel and opened the Mississippi to American shipping, with the right to dock in the port of New Orleans. This treaty fit the Jeffersonian conception of empire, and congressmen from the West and South were delighted with its terms. But administration supporters demanded their acquiescence in Jay's Treaty before the approval of Pinckney's. With this compromise, the long political controversy finally reached a conclusion.

These two important treaties finally established American sovereignty over the land west of the Appalachians and opened to American commerce a vast market extending from Atlantic ports to the Mississippi Valley. From a political standpoint, however, the battle over Jay's Treaty was costly for Washington, for it provided the Jeffersonians an opportunity to claim that in exchange for British gold the administration had sold out American neutrality as well as the republican principles embodied by the French Revolution. Washington's role in the events of 1794 and 1795 brought the president down from his pedestal and subjected him to the rough-and-tumble of political warfare. In the opposition press, he was vilified as "the source of all the misfortunes of our country" and was even accused of having been a traitor during the Revolution. Sick of politics and longing to return to private life, Washington now rejected the offer of a third term.

Washington's Farewell Address

Just two months before the presidential election of 1796, Washington published his Farewell Address to the nation, an appeal for national unity. "With slight shades of difference," Washington said to his countrymen, "you have the same religion, manners, habits, and political principles," and "union ought to be considered as a main prop of your liberty." He warned against sectional loyalty and "the baneful effects of the spirit of party." In the increasingly polarized political debate, however, this appeal fell on deaf ears.

The second part of the address was considerably more influential. "Our detached and distant situation," Washington explained, invited the nation to "defy material injury from external annoyance." He argued not for American isolation, but rather for American disinterest in the affairs of Europe. "The great rule of conduct for us in regard to foreign nations is, in extending our commercial relations to have with them as little political connection as possible." Why, he asked "entangle our peace and prosperity in the toils of European ambition, rivalship, interest, humor, or caprice?" Thomas Jefferson, in his Inaugural Address of 1801, paraphrased this first principle of American foreign policy as "peace, commerce, and honest friendship with all nations, entangling alliances with none." Jefferson's statement underscored the extent to which Washington articulated principles agreed to by all the major political figures of his day.

FEDERALISTS AND REPUBLICANS

The framers of the Constitution envisioned a one-party state in which partisan distinctions would be muted by patriotism and public virtue. "Among the numerous advantages promised by a well constructed Union," Madison had written in *The Federalist,* is "its tendency to break and control the violence of faction." Not only did he fail to anticipate the rise of political parties or factions; he saw them as potentially harmful to the new nation. It is thus ironic that when Madison broke with the Washington administration on questions of fiscal policy, he was the first to take steps toward organizing a political opposition, which would become known as the Democratic Republican Party. At the height of the agitation of the Democratic Societies in 1794, Hamilton cried that "unless soon checked," the "spirit of faction" would "involve the country in all the horrors of anarchy." Yet in acting as Washington's political lieutenant, he did more than anyone else to solidify the "Friends of Order," as his supporters were first known, into a disciplined political party known as the Federalists. Despite the framers' intentions, in the twelve years between the ratification of the Constitution and the federal election of 1800 political parties became a fundamental part of the American system of government.

The Rise of Political Parties

Evident in the debates and votes of Congress from 1789 to 1795 were a series of shifting coalitions that pitted commercial against agrarian interests, representatives from the Atlantic seaboard against those from the frontier, Anglophiles against Francophiles. The greatest potential division, that of Northerners versus Southerners, inspired the greatest fears, and congressmen worked hard to achieve sectional compromise by agreeing to avoid the troublesome issue of slavery. Antislavery petitions submitted to Congress were dismissed by nearly unanimous votes, and a law for the apprehension of fugitive slaves by federal officers anywhere in the Union was approved by a large majority in 1793.

Overview

The First American Party System

Federalist Party	Organized by figures in the Washington administration who were in favor of a strong federal government, friendship with the British, and opposition to the French Revolution; its power base was among merchants, property owners, and urban workers tied to the commercial economy. A minority party after 1800, it was regionally strong only in New England.
Democratic Republican Party	Arose as the opposition to the Federalists; its adherents were in favor of limiting federal power, sympathetic to the French Revolution, and hostile to Great Britain; it drew strength from southern planters and northern farmers. The majority party after 1800.

These shifting coalitions first began to polarize into political factions during the debate over Jay's Treaty in 1795, when agrarians, Westerners, Southerners, and supporters of France came together in opposition to the treaty. In the House, Madison acted as a leader of this coalition when it met for the first time and attempted to implement a collective strategy. By the elections of 1796, people had begun to give names to the two factions. The supporters of Hamilton claimed the mantle of Federalism. "I am what the phraseology of politicians has denominated a FEDERALIST," declared one North Carolina candidate for office, "the friend of order, of government, and of the present administration." Forced to find another term, the Jeffersonian opposition used both Democrat (from the Democratic Societies) and Republican, a name carrying the implication that the Federalists were really monarchists at heart. "There are two parties at present in the United States," wrote a New York editor sympathetic to Jefferson, "aristocrats, endeavoring to lay the foundations of monarchical government, and Republicans, the real supports of independence, friends to equal rights, and warm advocates of free elective government." Hamilton insisted on labeling his opponents the Anti-Federalists, while others scorned them as anarchists, Jacobins, or sans-culottes—all labels from the French Revolution. Historians usually call the Jeffersonian coalition the Democratic Republicans.

These two political coalitions played a fitful role in the presidential election of 1796, which pitted John Adams, Washington's vice president, against Thomas Jefferson. Partisan organization was strongest in the Middle States, where there was a real contest of political forces, weakest in New England and the South, where sectional loyalty prevailed and organized opposition infrequent. When the ballots of the presidential electors, cast in their respective state capitals, were counted in the Senate, Adams was victorious. The authors of the Constitution, not anticipating this level of partisan competition, had provided that the runner-up—Jefferson in this case—would become vice president. Thus the new administration was born divided.

The Adams Presidency

Adams was put in the difficult situation of facing a political opposition led by his own vice president. He nevertheless attempted to conduct his presidency along the lines laid down by Washington, retaining most of the former president's appointees. This arrangement presented Adams with another problem. Although Hamilton had retired the year before, the cabinet remained committed to his advice, actively seeking his opinion and following it. As a result, Adams's authority was further undercut.

On the other hand, Adams benefited from the rising tensions between the United States and France. Angered by Jay's Treaty, the French suspended diplomatic relations at the end of 1796 and inaugurated a tough new policy toward American shipping. During the next two years they seized more than 300 American vessels and confiscated cargoes valued at an estimated $20 million. Hoping to resolve the crisis, Adams sent an American delegation to France. But in dispatches sent back to the United States the American envoys reported that agents of the French foreign ministry had demanded a bribe before any negotiations could be undertaken. Pressed for copies of these dispatches by suspicious Democratic Republicans in Congress, in 1798 Adams released them after substituting the letters X, Y, and Z for the names of the French agents. The documents proved a major liability for the Democratic Republicans, sparking powerful anti-French sentiment throughout the country. To the demand for a bribe, the American delegates had actually answered "Not a sixpence," but in the inflated rhetoric of the day the response became the infinitely more memorable: "Millions for defense, but not one cent for tribute!" The XYZ Affair, as it became known, sent Adams's popularity soaring.

Adams and the Federalists prepared the country for war during the spring of 1798. Congress authorized tripling the size of the army, and Washington came out of retirement to command the force. Fears of a French invasion declined after word arrived of the British naval victory over the French in August 1798 at Aboukir Bay in Egypt, but the "quasi-war" between France and the United States continued.

The Alien and Sedition Acts

In the summer of 1798 the Federalist majority in Congress, with the acquiescence of President Adams, passed four acts severely limiting both freedom of speech and the freedom of the press and threatening the liberty of foreigners in the United States. Embodying the fear that immigrants, in the words of one Massachusetts Federalist, "contaminate the purity and simplicity of the American character" by introducing dangerous democratic and republican ideas, the Naturalization Act extended the period of residence required for citizenship from five to fourteen years. The Alien Act and the Alien Enemies Act authorized the president to order the imprisonment or deportation of suspected aliens during wartime. Finally, the Sedition Act provided heavy fines and imprisonment for anyone convicted of writing, publishing, or speaking anything of "a false, scandalous and malicious" nature against the government or any of its officers.

The Federalists intended these repressive laws as weapons to defeat the Democratic Republicans. Led by Albert Gallatin, a Swiss immigrant and congressman from Pennsylvania (replacing Madison, who had retired from politics to devote his time to his plantation), the Democratic Republicans contested all the Federalist war measures and acted as a genuine opposition party, complete with caucuses, floor leaders, and partisan discipline. For the first time, the two parties contested the election of Speaker of the House of Representatives, which became a partisan office. The more effective the Democratic Republicans became, the more treasonous they appeared in the eyes of the Federalists. On at least one occasion acrimonious debate in the House gave way to fisticuffs. Matthew Lyon, Democratic Republican of Vermont, spit in the eye of Connecticut Federalist Roger Griswold. Griswold responded by attacking Lyon with a cane, Lyon defended himself with a pair of fire tongs, and the two had to be pulled apart. With the Revolution still fresh in memory, Americans had only a weak understanding of the concept of a loyal opposition. Disagreement with the administration was misconstrued by the Federalists as opposition to the state itself.

The Federalists thus pursued the prosecution of dissent, indicting leading Democratic Republican newspaper editors and writers, fining and imprisoning at least twenty-five of them. The most vilified was Congressman Lyon, scorned by Federalists as "Ragged Matt the Democrat." Lyon was convicted in July 1798 of publishing libelous statements about President Adams and thrown into a Vermont prison. Later that year, however, he conducted a campaign from his cell and was reelected to Congress.

From Virginia, Madison wrote that the Sedition Act "ought to produce universal alarm, because it is levelled against the right of freely examining public characters and measures, and of free commu-

In this contemporary cartoon, Congressional Pugilists, Congress Hall in Philadelphia, February 15, 1798, *Roger Griswold, a Connecticut Federalist, uses his cane to attack Matthew Lyon, Vermont Democratic Republican, who retaliates with fire tongs. During the first years of the American republic there was little understanding of the concept of a "loyal opposition," and disagreement with the policy of the Federalist administration was misconstrued as disloyalty.*

nication among the people thereon, which has ever been deemed the only effectual guardian of every other right." He and Jefferson anonymously authored resolutions, passed by the Virginia and Kentucky legislatures, that declared the Constitution to be nothing more than a compact between the sovereign states and advocated the power of those states to "nullify" unconstitutional laws. When threatened with overbearing central authority, the Democratic Republicans argued, the states had the right to go their own way. The Virginia and Kentucky Resolves, as they were known, had grave implications for the future of the Union, for they stamped the notion of secession with the approval of two of the founding fathers. The resolutions would later be used to justify the secession of the southern states at the beginning of the Civil War.

The Revolution of 1800

The Alien and Sedition Acts were overthrown by the Democratic Republican victory in the national elections of 1800. As the term of President Adams drew to a close, Federalists found themselves seriously divided. In 1799, by releasing seized American ships and requesting negotiations, the French convinced Adams that they were ready to settle their dispute with the United States. The president also sensed the public mood running toward peace. But the Hamiltonian wing of the party, always scornful of public sentiment, continued to beat the drums of war. When Federalists in Congress tried to block the president's attempt to negotiate, Adams threatened to resign and turn the government over to Vice President Jefferson. In the Convention of 1800, the United States abandoned its demand of compensation for seized cargoes in exchange for French abrogation of its 1778 alliance with the American colonies. "The end of war is peace," Adams declared, "and peace was offered me." Adams considered the settlement of this conflict with France to be one of the greatest accomplishments of his career, but it earned him the scorn of conservative Federalists, including Hamilton.

The Federalists also divided over a domestic controversy. Under their leadership Congress had enacted a direct tax on houses, similar to the earlier tax on whiskey. In eastern Pennsylvania in 1799 several dozen farmers, displaying symbols of the French Revolution, routed the tax collectors and freed from jail a tax resister, one John Fries, who had been involved in the Whiskey Rebellion. Adams sent federal troops to restore order, and for leading Fries's Rebellion, a court issued death sentences for three men, including Fries. The president's cabinet demanded that Adams enforce "exemplary rigor" by

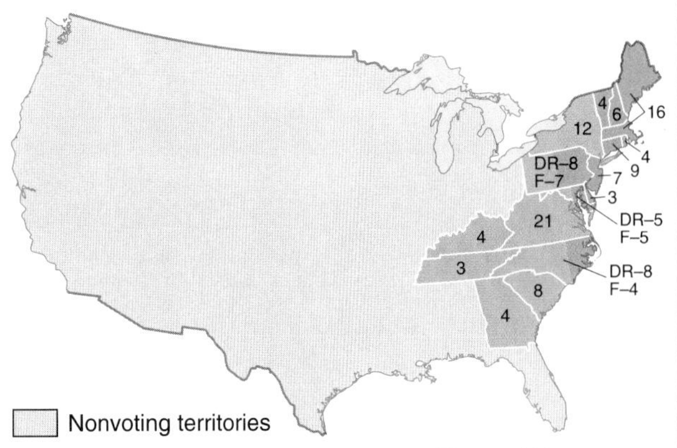

	Electoral Vote (%)
THOMAS JEFFERSON (Democratic-Republican)	**73 (53)**
John Adams (Federalist)	65 (47)

The Election of 1800 *In the presidential election of 1800, Democratic Republican victories in New York and the divided vote in Pennsylvania threw the election to Jefferson. The combination of the South and these crucial Middle States would keep the Democratic Republicans in control of the federal government for the next generation.*

allowing the sentence to be carried out, but in 1800 Adams responded to popular pressure and pardoned the three. To the jeers of conservative Federalists, Adams now dumped the Hamiltonians from his cabinet. During the war scare with France, Washington had insisted that Hamilton be appointed as second in command of the enlarged army. "You crammed him down my throat!" Adams cried. Now he denounced Hamilton as "a bastard, and as much an alien as Gallatin." Hamilton responded by circulating a private letter in which he condemned Adams for his "disgusting egotism," "distempered jealousy," and "vanity without bounds." This letter fell into the hands of Aaron Burr, leader of the New York Democratic Republicans, and he published it, to the consternation of the Federalists.

The Federalists divided at precisely the time when unity was necessary to prevent the Democratic Republicans from consolidating their strengths. The defusing of the crisis with France also helped the Democratic Republicans, who could claim opposition to Federalist warmongering. They captured the state governments of Pennsylvania and New York in 1799, the first important inroads of the party in the North. These states had been taken over, cried a shocked Federalist, by "the most God-provoking Democrats on this side of Hell." From Virginia, Jefferson proclaimed his hope that "with Pennsylvania we can defy the universe!"

The presidential election of 1800 was the first to feature campaign advertising. "T. Jefferson, President of the United States of America," reads the streamer on this election banner, illustrated with an American eagle and a portrait of Jefferson; "John Adams—no more." This was mild rhetoric in a campaign characterized by wild charges. The Republicans labeled Adams a warmonger and a monarchist, while the Federalists denounced Jefferson as an atheist, Jacobin, and sexual libertine.

The presidential campaign of 1800 was the first in which Democratic Republicans and Federalists operated as two national political parties. Caucuses of congressmen nominated respective slates: Adams and Charles Cotesworth Pinckney of South Carolina for the Federalists, Jefferson and Aaron Burr of New York for the Republicans. Both tickets thus represented attempts at sectional balance. The Republicans presented themselves as the party of traditional agrarian purity, of liberty and states' rights, of "government rigorously frugal and simple," in the words of Jefferson. They were optimistic, convinced that they were riding the wave of the future. Divided and embittered, the Federalists waged a defensive struggle for strong central government and public order, and resorted frequently to negative campaigning. They denounced Jefferson as an atheist, a Jacobin, and the father of mulatto children—the first two charges were without foundation, the last apparently true, according to the results of DNA matching tests. One campaign placard put the issue succinctly: "GOD—AND A RELIGIOUS PRESIDENT" or "JEFFERSON—AND NO GOD!"

The balloting for presidential electors took place between October and December 1800. Adams took all the New England states while Jefferson captured the South and West. Jefferson called it "the Revolution of 1800." Party discipline was so effective that one of the provisions of the Constitution was shown to be badly outmoded. By this clause, the candidate receiving a majority of electoral votes became president and the runner-up became vice president. But by casting all their ballots for Jefferson and Burr, Democratic Republican electors unintentionally created a tie and forced the election into the House of Representatives. Because the new Democratic Republican-controlled Congress would not convene until March 1801, the Federalist majority was given a last chance to decide the election. They attempted to make a deal with Burr, who refused but who also would not withdraw his name from consideration. Finally, on the thirty-fifth ballot the Federalists gave up and arranged with their opponents to elect Jefferson without any of them having to cast a single vote in his favor. Congressman Lyon, "Ragged Matt the Democrat," cast the symbolic final vote in a gesture of sweet revenge. The Twelfth Amendment, creating separate ballots for president and vice-president, would be ratified in time for the next presidential election.

With the rise of partisan politics came a transformation in political participation. In 1789 state regulations limited the franchise to a small percentage of the adult population. Women, African Americans, and Indians could not vote, but neither could a third to a half of all free adult males, who were excluded by tax-paying or property-owning requirements. And even among the eligible the turnout was generally low. The traditional manner of voting was by voice: at the polling place in each community individuals announced their selections aloud to the clerk of elections, who wrote them down. Not surprisingly, this system allowed wealthy men, landlords, and employers of the community to pressure poorer voters.

These practices began to change with the increasing competition between Democratic Republicans and Federalists. Popular pressure resulted in the introduction of universal white manhood suffrage in four states by 1800 and the reduction of property requirements in others. These changes inaugurated a movement that would sweep the nation over the next quarter-century, and as a consequence, voter turnout increased in all the states. The growth of popular interest in politics was a transformation as important as the peaceful transition from Federalists to Democratic Republicans in national government.

"THE RISING GLORY OF AMERICA"

In 1771 Philip Freneau and Hugh Henry Brackenridge read an epic poem, "The Rising Glory of America," to their graduating class at Princeton. They admitted that American contributions to learning and the arts had thus far been slim, but they were boundlessly optimistic about the potential of their country. Indeed, judged against the literary and artistic work of individuals in the colonial period, artists and others of the Revolutionary generation accomplished a great deal in their effort to build a national culture.

Art and Architecture

The first American to achieve prominence in the artistic world of Europe was Benjamin West, who painted portraits in his native Pennsylvania before leaving for the Continent and England, where he became popular as a painter of historical scenes. His *Death of General Wolfe* (1770) (see p. 138) was one of the more acclaimed paintings of its day and the first to elevate an American scene to the high status of monumental historical painting. In 1774 West was joined in London by John Singleton Copley, a Boston portraitist who left America because of his loyalist sentiments. Copley's work is renowned for the truth and straightforwardness of his depictions, as in his famous portrait of Samuel Adams (1771) (see p. 144). Both West and Copley remained in England after the Revolution. Their most promising student was Gilbert Stuart, whose work in the fashionable style of the day included a portrait of Mohawk leader Joseph Brant (see p. 172). Stuart returned to the United States in 1792 to paint what became the most famous portrait of President Washington.

The preeminent painter of the Revolution was Charles Willson Peale, who studied for a time with West in London. He returned to America, however, and during the Revolution turned his talents to producing wartime propaganda. Although the almond eyes and bloated torsos of his figures suggest his technical limitations, Peale's work has a naive charm. His paintings of Washington, for example, seem more revealing of character than Stuart's placid portrait. Inspired by nationalist zeal, Peale planned a public gallery of

Charles Willson Peale, *The Artist in His Museum*, 1822, oil on canvas, 103 3/4" x 79 7/8." Couresy of the Pennsylvania Academy of the Fine Arts, Philadelphia. Gift of Mrs. Sarah Harrison. (The Joseph Harrison, Jr. Collection).

In this self-portrait, American artist Charles Willson Peale dramatically lifts the curtain on his Philadelphia Museum. Peale's three sons—whom he named after the artists Raphael, Rembrandt, and Titian—and two of his nieces—Anna and Sarah—also became noted painters, constituting something of a first family of American art in the early years of the new republic.

heroes in Philadelphia that eventually grew into a famous museum of curios, reflecting his interest in natural history, archaeology, and exotic cultures. Federalists joked that its chaotic arrangement of exhibits mirrored Peale's Jeffersonian politics. Part science, part circus, the collection was purchased after Peale's death by the pioneer American entertainer P. T. Barnum.

John Trumbull of Connecticut, who had predicted America's rise to his Yale classmates, served as a soldier during the Revolution, then went to London to study with West. There he painted *The Battle of Bunker's Hill* (1785), the first of a series of Revolutionary scenes (see p. 156), four of which he repainted in the Capitol rotunda in the early nineteenth century. Influenced by the grand style of eighteenth-century historical painting, Trumbull was concerned above all else with documentary detail in his scenes of the birth of America.

Nationalism was also evident in architecture. The greatest architectural project of the day was the new federal capital city, named for President Washington. In 1790, after Congress had agreed on the site, Washington retained Pierre Charles L'Enfant, a French engineer who had served as an officer during the Revolution, to lay out the city. The survey was conducted by Andrew Ellicott, assisted by the African American mathematician Benjamin Banneker. L'Enfant took full advantage of the lay of the land and the Potomac River, placing the Capitol building on a hill "which stands as a pedestal waiting for a monument." He linked public buildings such as the president's house and the Capitol with radial avenues, allowing for what he called "a reciprocity of sight." And he planned a grand mall from the Capitol to the river, along which there would be public museums, academies, and assembly halls. Development during the nineteenth century obscured L'Enfant's original design, but it was revived in 1901. Jefferson recommended "the models of antiquity" for the public buildings of the federal city, a suggestion carried out in William Thornton's original design for the Capitol.

George Town and Federal City, *or City of Washington, a colored aquatint of* 1801 *by T. Cartwright. When President John Adams first occupied the White House in* 1800, *Washington was still a small village, its streets merely muddy pathways.*

"Architecture is worth great attention," declared Jefferson, for "as we double our numbers every twenty years, we must double our houses. It is, then, among the most important arts; and it is desirable to introduce taste into an art which shows so much." In New England, architect Asher Benjamin popularized an American variant of the Georgian style, emphasizing economy of decoration and recommending the use of indigenous materials when writing handbooks such as *The Country Builder's Assistant* (1797). A great deal of the urban building undertaken in coastal cities during the shipping boom of the 1790s was characterized by this restrained classicism, which was known as the Federal style.

But the majority of Americans lived in small, bare, even squalid conditions. A nationwide tax on houses produced the first comprehensive survey of the nation's housing in 1798. There was tremendous variation in living conditions. The wealthiest 10 percent lived in dwellings estimated to be worth more than half the total value of all houses. By contrast, the value of housing owned by the wealthiest tenth of Americans today is only 30 percent of the total. Forty percent of American houses in 1798 were valued at $99 or less (the equivalent of about $1,000 today), and were little more than shacks. In the expanding cities, many residents lived along dingy back alleys and in damp basements. In the country, the typical house was a one-story structure of two or three rooms. As the population continued to grow, and Americans continued to move west, many more people would be found in log hovels like those in the community along Mingo Creek.

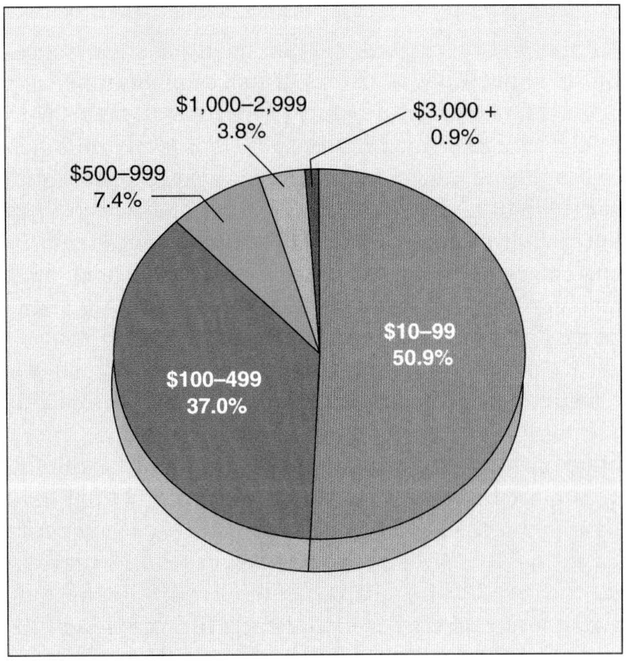

Housing Values, 1798 *In 1798 Congress enacted a direct tax on buildings, resulting in an inventory of American housing that has never been equaled. The data revealed an enormous gap between rich and poor. The majority lived in squalid cabins valued at $99 or less, while the wealthiest 10 percent of Americans lived in dwellings that, taken together, were worth just over half the total value of all the nation's houses.*

Source: Lee Soltow, "Egalitarian America and Its Inegalitarian Housing in the Federal Period," *Social Science History* 9 (1985): 199–213.

The Liberty of the Press

At the beginning of the Revolution in 1775 there were thirty-seven weekly or semiweekly newspapers in the thirteen colonies, only seven of which were Loyalist in sentiment. By 1789 the number of papers in the United States had grown to ninety-two, including eight dailies; three papers were being published west of the Appalachians. Relative to population, there were more newspapers in the United States than in any other country in the world—a reflection of the remarkably high literacy rate of the American people (see Chapter 5). In New England almost 90 percent of the population could read, and even on the frontier, where Brackenridge edited the *Pittsburgh Gazette*, about two-thirds of the males were literate.

During the political controversy of the 1790s, the press became the principal medium of Federalist and Democratic Republican opinion, and papers came to be identified by their politics. In 1789 John Fenno, aided by Alexander Hamilton, began publication of the *Federalist Gazette of the United States*, and in 1791 Jefferson encouraged Philip Freneau to establish the competing *National Gazette*. The columns of these papers broadcast the feud between the two cabinet secretaries.

The prosecutions under the Sedition Act, however, threatened to curb the further development of the media, and in their opposition to these measures Democratic Republicans played an important role in establishing the principle of a free press. In *An Essay on Liberty of the Press* (1799), the Virginia lawyer George Hay, later appointed to the federal bench by President Jefferson, wrote that "a man may say everything which his passions suggest." Were this not true, he argued, the First Amendment would have been "the grossest absurdity that was ever conceived by the human mind." In his first Inaugural Address Jefferson echoed this early champion of the freedom of expression. "Error of opinion may be tolerated," he declared, "where reason is left free to combat it."

The Birth of American Literature

During the post-Revolutionary years there was an enormous outpouring of American publications. In the cities the number of bookstores grew in response to the demand for reading matter. Perhaps even more significant was the appearance in the countryside of numerous book peddlers who supplied farm households with Bibles, gazettes, almanacs, sermons, and political pamphlets. One such peddler was Mason Locke Weems, a man trained as a doctor and ordained an Anglican minister, who gave up these careers in the early 1790s for book selling. Parson Weems, as he was known, wrote that he found his southern backcountry customers "uninformed, their minds bitter, and their manners savage," but that they cried out for "books, books, books!"

The literature of the Revolution understandably reflected the dominating political concerns of the times. Mercy Otis Warren and Hugh Henry Brackenridge wrote propagandistic dramas, and the poet Joel Barlow composed a nationalist epic, *The Vision of Columbus* (1787). *M'Fingal* (1782), a mock epic satirizing the British, was written by John Trumbull (a cousin of the painter), a leader of the literary group known as the Connecticut Wits. It sold copies enough to be considered the best-selling fictional work of the war. But the majority of "best-sellers" during the Revolutionary era were political. The most important were Thomas Paine's *Common Sense* (1776) and his series of stirring pamphlets, published under the running title *The American Crisis* (1776–83), the first of which began with the memorable phrase, "These are the times that try men's souls."

In the cause of reform, Paine later returned to England and published *The Rights of Man* (1791), a defense of the French Revolution. Banished from Britain for this expression of radical politics, he went to France, jumped into politics, and, in one of the periodic political turns of the revolution, found himself imprisoned for a time. From his jail cell Paine wrote *The Age of Reason* (1795), a powerful attack on organized religion that became one of the most popular American books of its day, loved by Jeffersonians and loathed by Federalists. Book-selling Parson Weems, for example, made a steady profit from the sale of Paine's work, though he offered pious sermons and religious tracts to placate those objecting to Paine's politics.

Some of the most interesting American books of the postwar years examined the developing American character. The French immigrant Michel-Guillaume Jean de Crèvecoeur, in *Letters from an American Farmer* (1782), proposed that the American, a product of many cultures, was a "new man" with ideas new to the world. John Filson, the author of the *Discovery, Settlement, and Present State of Kentucke* (1784), presented the narrative of one such new man, the Kentucky pioneer Daniel Boone. In doing so he took an important step toward the creation of that most American of literary genres, the western. In a satirical novel entitled *Modern Chivalry* (1792), featuring incidents from the Whiskey Rebellion, Pittsburgh editor Brackenridge dipped his pen "in the inkstand of human nature" and produced one of the first dialect portraits of "dat son o'd a whore," the American frontiersman. Brackenridge wrote with an appreciation for his crude characters but expressed frustration that the Revolution had failed to elevate the culture of ordinary people. By shunning simple celebration, however, he was one of the first to take a critical look at the American character.

The single best-selling book of the Revolutionary era

94 AN EASY STANDARD

tually promiſed to aſſiſt each other, if they ſhould happen to be aſſaulted. They had not proceeded far, before they perceived a Bear making towards them with great rage. There were no hopes in flight; but one of them, being very active, ſprung up into a tree; upon which the other, throwing himſelf flat on the ground, held his breath, and pretended to be dead; remembering to have heard it aſſerted, that this creature will not prey upon a dead carcaſe. The bear came up, and after ſmelling to him ſome time, left him, and went on. When he was fairly out of ſight and hearing, the hero from the tree calls out—Well, my friend, what ſaid the bear? He ſeemed to whiſper you very cloſely. He did ſo, replied the other, and gave me this good piece of advice; never to aſſociate with a wretch, who in the hour of danger will deſert his friend.

TABLE XXXIII.

Words in which *ch* have the ſound of *k*.

Christ	cho-rus	chol-ic	char-ac-ter
chyle	te-trarch	chol-er	cat-e-chiſm
ſcheme	cha-os	ſchol-ar	pen-ta-teuch
ache	cho-ral	mon-arch	ſep-ul-cher
	e-poch	or-chal	tech-nic-al
chaſm	o-cher		al-chy-my
chriſm	tro-chee	ſchir-rous	an-cho-ret
tach			brach-i-al
	an-chor	ſtom-ach	lach-ry-mal
chord	chriſ-ten		mach-i-nate
loch	chym-iſt	pa-tri-arch	ſac-char-ine
	ech-o	eu-cha-riſt	ſyn-chro-niſm
ſchool	chal-ice		mich-ael-mas
	ſched-ule	an-ar-chy	
choir	paſ-chal	chryſ-o-lite	chor-iſ-ter

OF PRONUNCIATION. 95

chron-i-cle	cha-lyb-e-rate	the-om-a-chy
or-cheſ-tra	a-nach-ro-niſm	
och-i-my	ſyn-ec-do-che	ar-chi-tec-ture
	pyr-rhich-i-us	an-ti-bac-chus
chi-me-ra	am-phib-ra-chus	
pa-ro-chi-al		cat-e-chet-ic-al
cha-mel-ion	mel-an-chol-y	
		bac-cha-nal-ian
tri-bach-us	chro-nol-o-gy	cat-e-chu-men
arch-an-gel	chi-rog-ra-phy	
me-chan-ic	cho-rog-ra-phy	ich-thy-ol-o-gy
ca-chex-y	chro-nom-e-ter	

FABLE VII.—*The* TWO DOGS.

HASTY and inconſiderate connections are generally attended with great diſadvantages; and much of every man's good or ill fortune depends upon the choice he makes of his friends.

A goodnatured Spaniel overtook a ſurly Maſtiff, as he was travelling upon the high road. Tray, although an entire ſtranger to Tyger, very civilly accoſted him; and if it would be no interruption, he ſaid, he ſhould be glad to bear him company on his way. Tyger

Pages from Noah Webster's famous American Spelling Book, *the largest seller of all American books during the nineteenth century. Believing that "the King's English" reflected aristocratic standards, Webster argued for spelling reform to create "the American language."*

was Noah Webster's *American Spelling Book* (1783), the famous "Blue-Backed Speller," which soon after its publication was selling 200,000 copies annually. It became the largest-selling of all American books, a good indicator of the remarkable literacy of the American people. With it, Webster launched a lifelong campaign for a distinctive American form of English, which culminated in his *American Dictionary of the English Language* (1828). In a belief that "the King's English" reflected aristocratic standards, Webster argued for a time that "the American language" must be guided by "republican principles," for example, spelling words as they sounded. "Ther iz no alternativ," he wrote. Eventually he abandoned the most radical of his suggestions, although many of his reforms stuck, dropping the "u" from the English spelling of "colour," for example, in favor of "color." The speller was the first in a graded series of textbooks that included a grammar and a reader designed to "diffuse the principles of virtue and patriotism." These texts included standard selections from not only British but also American writers. Webster compiled a list of important dates beginning with Columbus's voyage and ending with the British surrender at Yorktown—the first attempt at a distinctively American historical chronology.

Other writers produced more formal histories. Not surprisingly, Democratic Republican authors stressed the tradition of resistance to authority, whereas Federalists emphasized the importance, particularly during wartime, of central direction and unity. Fearing criticism by Federalist writers, Democratic Republican Mercy Otis Warren delayed publishing her *History of the Rise, Progress, and Termination of the American Revolution* (1805) until after Jefferson's victory in 1800.

Parson Weems found readers fascinated by the historical heroes of the Revolution, so he drew up plans for a series of "quarter of dollar books on subjects calculated to strike the popular curiosity, printed in very large numbers and properly distributed." When Washington died in December 1799, Weems was already at work on a short biography of the first president. "Washington, you know, is gone!" he wrote to his publisher. "Millions are gaping to read something about him. I am very nearly primed and cocked for 'em." His *Life of Washington* (1800, enlarged edition 1806), became the most popular history of the Revolution and introduced a series of popular and completely fabricated anecdotes, including the story of young Washington and the cherry tree. The book was a pioneering effort in mass culture, and Weems, as one historian puts it, was "the father of the Father of his Country."

Condemned by serious writers and scholars, even at the time of its publication, Weems's biography was loved by ordinary Americans of all political persuasions. In the mid-nineteenth century, Abraham Lincoln recalled that he had read Weems "away back in my childhood, the earliest days of my being able to read," and had been profoundly impressed by "the struggles for the liberties of the country." In praise of Washington, Weems wrote, "all parties join with equal alacrity and earnestness." Although Washington had in fact become a partisan leader of the Federalists during his second term, Weems presented him as a unifying figure for the political culture of the new nation, and this was the way he would be remembered. Jefferson echoed these sentiments in his Inaugural Address in 1801, when as a gesture of conciliation to his opponents he

In this 1792 cartoon from the Lady's Magazine, *the allegorical figure of "Columbia" receives a petition for the "Rights of Woman." In the aftermath of the Revolution, Americans debated the issue of an expanded role for women in the new republic. Many Federalists condemned "women of masculine minds," but there was general agreement among both conservatives and democrats that the time had come for better education for American women.*

CHRONOLOGY

1786	Annapolis Convention
1787	Constitutional Convention
1787–88	*The Federalist* published
1788	Constitution ratified First federal elections
1789	President George Washington inaugurated in New York City Judiciary Act French Revolution begins
1790	Agreement on site on the Potomac River for the nation's capital Indian Intercourse Act Judith Sargent Murray publishes "On the Equality of the Sexes"
1791	Bill of Rights ratified Bank of the United States chartered Alexander Hamilton's "Report on Manufactures" Ohio Indians defeat General Arthur St. Clair's army
1793	England and France at war; America reaps trade windfall Citizen Genêt affair President Washington proclaims American neutrality in Europe British confiscate American vessels Supreme Court asserts itself as final authority in *Chisholm v. Georgia*
1794	Whiskey Rebellion Battle of Fallen Timbers Jay's Treaty with the British concluded
1795	Pinckney's Treaty negotiated with the Spanish Treaty of Greenville Thomas Paine publishes The Age of Reason
1796	President Washington's Farewell Address John Adams elected president
1797–98	French seize American ships
1798	XYZ Affair "Quasi-war" with France Alien and Sedition Acts Kentucky and Virginia Resolves
1799	Fries's Rebellion
1800	Convention of 1800 Thomas Jefferson elected president Mason Locke Weems publishes *Life of Washington*

declared, "We have called by different names brethren of the same principle. We are all Republicans, we are all Federalists."

Women on the Intellectual Scene

One of the most interesting literary trends of the 1790s was the growing demand for books that appealed to women readers. Susanna Haswell Rowson's *Charlotte Temple* (1791), a tale of seduction and abandonment, ran up tremendous sales and remained in print for more than a century. Other romantic works of fiction included *The Power of Sympathy* (1789) by William Hill Brown, sometimes called the first American novel; the gothic novels of Charles Brockden Brown, such as *Arthur Mervyn* (1799); and *The Coquette* (1797) by Hannah Webster Foster. The young republic thus marked the first dramatic appearance of women writers and women readers. Although women's literacy rates continued to be lower than men's, they rose steadily as girls joined boys in common schools. This increase was one of the most important social legacies of the democratic struggles of the Revolutionary era.

Some writers argued that the new republican order ought to provide new roles for women as well as for men. The first avowed feminist in American history was Judith Sargent Murray, who publicly stated her belief that women "should be taught to depend on their own efforts, for the procurement of an establishment in life." She was greatly influenced by the English feminist Mary Wollstonecraft, but developed her line of thinking independently, as demonstrated by her essay "On the Equality of the Sexes," written in 1779 and finally published in 1790 in a Massachusetts magazine. "I expect to see our young women forming a new era in female history," Murray predicted. Federalists listened to such opinions with horror. "Women of masculine minds," one Boston minister sneered, "have generally masculine manners."

There seemed to be general agreement among all parties, however, that the time had come for better-educated and better-informed women. Republican institutions of self-government were widely thought to depend on the wisdom and self-discipline of the American people. Civic virtue, so indispensable for the republic, must be taught at home. The share that every male citizen had in the government of the country, Benjamin Rush said in 1787, required that women have "suitable education, to concur in instructing their sons in the principles of liberty and government." By placing her learning at the service of her family, the "republican mother" was spared the criticism leveled at independent-minded women such as Murray. "A woman will have more commendation in being the mother of heroes," said a Federalist, "than in setting up, Amazon-like, for a heroine herself." Thus were women provided the opportunity to be not simply "helpmates," but people "learned and wise." But they were also expected to be content with a narrow role, not to wish for fuller participation in American democracy.

CONCLUSION

In 1800, the population of Canada numbered about 500,000. Those of European background in New Mexico and the other Spanish North American colonies numbered approximately 25,000. And the Indian people of the continent numbered anywhere from 500,000 to a million. Overwhelming all these groups was the population of the United States, which stood at 5.3 million and was growing at the astounding annual rate of 3 percent. During the last years of the eighteenth century the United States had adopted a new constitution and established a new national government. It had largely repaid the debt run up during the Revolution and made peace with adversaries abroad and Indian peoples at home. Americans had begun to learn how to channel their disagreements into political struggle. The nation had withstood a first decade of stress, but tensions continued to divide the people. As some of the rebel supporters had promised at the beginning of the Whiskey Rebellion, "their liberty they will maintain, / they fought for't, and they'll fight again." At the beginning of the new century it remained uncertain whether the new nation would find a way to control and channel the energies of an expanding people.

REVIEW QUESTIONS

1. Discuss the conflicting ideals of local and national authority in the debate over the Constitution.
2. What were the major crises faced by the Washington and Adams administrations?
3. Describe the roles of Madison and Hamilton in the formation of the first American political parties.
4. What did Jefferson mean when he talked of "the Revolution of 1800"?
5. Discuss the contributions of the Revolutionary generation to the construction of a national culture.

RECOMMENDED READING

William N. Chambers, *Political Parties in a New Nation: The American Experience, 1776–1809* (1963). An introduction to the formation of the American party system. Though several decades old, it remains essential.

Stanley Elkins and Eric McKitrick, *The Age of Federalism* (1993). A massive and informative account of the politics of the 1790s, from the ratification of the Constitution to the election of Jefferson.

Joseph J. Ellis, *After the Revolution: Profiles of Early American Culture* (1979). A series of portraits of the more important cultural innovators in the young republic.

Reginald Horsman, *The Frontier in the Formative Years, 1783–1815* (1970). A sensitive survey of developments in the West, emphasizing that the "western question" was one of the most important facing the young republic.

Jackson Turner Main, *The Antifederalists: Critics of the Constitution, 1781–1788* (1961). A detailed examination of the localist tradition in early American politics. Includes a discussion of the ratification of the Constitution from the point of view of its opponents.

Willard Sterne Randall, *George Washington: A Life* (1997). The best one-volume biography of "the Father of his Country."

Thomas P. Slaughter, *The Whiskey Rebellion: Frontier Epilogue to the American Revolution* (1986). A detailed history of the rebellion in western Pennsylvania during the 1790s. Includes a thorough examination of the politics and culture of both the backcountry and the federal government at a moment of crisis.

James M. Smith, *Freedom's Fetters: The Alien and Sedition Laws and American Civil Liberties* (1966). Remains the best overview of the Federalist threat to liberty, as well as the Democratic Republican counterattack.

Gerald Stourzh, *Alexander Hamilton and the Idea of Republican Government* (1970). A solid biography of the ultimate Federalist man and his politics.

Gordon Wood, *The Creation of the American Republic, 1776–1787* (1969). This general survey provides the best overview of the Constitutional Convention.

ADDITIONAL BIBLIOGRAPHY

Forming a New Government

Douglass Adair, *Fame and the Founding Fathers*, ed. Trevor Colbourn (1974)

John K. Alexander, *The Selling of the Constitutional Convention: A History of News Coverage* (1990)

Charles A. Beard, *An Economic Interpretation of the Constitution of the United States* (1913)

Max Farrand, ed., *Records of the Federal Convention of 1787*, 4 vols. (1911–37)

Suzette Henberger, *Creatures of the Constitution: The Federalist Constitution and the Shaping of American Politics* (1994)

John P. Kaminski and Gaspare J. Saladino, eds., *The Documentary History of the Ratification of the Constitution* (1982)

Forrest McDonald, *Novus Ordo Seclorum: The Intellectual Origins of the Constitution* (1985)

Richard B. Morris, *Witnesses at the Creation: Hamilton, Madison, Jay and the Constitution* (1985)

Peter Onuf, *Origins of the Federal Republic* (1983)

Josephine F. Pacheco, ed., *Antifederalism: The Legacy of George Mason* (1992)

Herbert J. Storing, ed., *The Complete Anti-Federalist*, 7 vols. (1981)

Garry Wills, *Explaining America: The Federalist* (1981)

The New Nation

Harry Ammon, *The Genêt Mission* (1973)

Steven R. Boyd, ed., *The Whiskey Rebellion: Past and Present Perspectives* (1985)

Collin G. Calloway, *Crown and Calumet: British-Indian Relations, 1783–1815* (1987)

Gerald A. Combs, *The Jay Treaty: Political Battleground of the Founding Fathers* (1970)

Alexander De Conde, *Entangling Alliance: Politics and Diplomacy under George Washington* (1956)

Ralph Ketcham, *Presidents above Party: The First American Presidency, 1789–1829* (1984)

Charles R. Ritcheson, *Aftermath of Revolution: British Policy toward the United States, 1783–1795* (1969)

Wiley Sword, *President Washington's Indian War: The Struggle for the Old Northwest, 1790–1795* (1985)

J. Leitch Wright, *Britain and the American Frontier, 1783–1815* (1975)

Federalists and Republicans

Joyce Appleby, *Capitalism and a New Social Order: The Republican Vision of the 1790s* (1984)

Albert H. Bowman, *The Struggle for Neutrality: Franco-American Diplomacy during the Federalist Era* (1974)

Ralph Adams Brown, *The Presidency of John Adams* (1975)

Richard Buel Jr., *Securing the Revolution: Ideology in American Politics, 1789–1815* (1972)

Nobel E. Cunningham Jr., *The Jeffersonian Republicans: The Formation of Party Organization, 1789–1801* (1957)

Alexander De Conde, *The Quasi-War: Politics and Diplomacy of the Undeclared War with France, 1797–1801* (1966)

Drew McCoy, *The Elusive Republic: Political Economy in Jeffersonian America* (1980)

Andrew W. Robertson, *The Language of Democracy: Political Rhetoric in the United States and Britain, 1790–1900* (1995)

James Roger Sharp, *American Politics in the Early Republic: The New Nation in Crisis* (1993)

Alfred F. Young, *The Democratic Republicans of New York: The Origins, 1763–1797* (1967)

"The Rising Glory of America"

R. A. Burchell, ed., *The End of Anglo-America: Historical Essays in the Study of Cultural Divergence* (1991)

Emory Elliott, *Revolutionary Writers: Literature and Authority in the New Republic* (1982)

Michael Kammen, *A Season of Youth: The American Revolution and the Historical Imagination* (1978)

Linda Kerber, *Women of the Republic: Intellect and Ideology in Revolutionary America* (1980)

Kenneth Silverman, *A Cultural History of the American Revolution* (1976)

Biography

Robert C. Alberts, *Benjamin West: A Biography* (1978)

John R. Alden, *George Washington: A Biography* (1984)

Gay Wilson Allen, *St. John de Crèvecoeur: The Life of an American Farmer* (1987)

Aleine Austin, *Matthew Lyon, "New Man" of the Democratic Revolution, 1749–1822* (1981)

Lance Banning, *The Sacred Fire of Liberty: James Madison and the Founding of the Federal Republic* (1995)

Harvey Lewis Carter, *The Life and Times of Little Turtle: First Sagamore of the Wabash* (1987)
Jacob Ernest Cooke, *Alexander Hamilton* (1982)
Helen A. Cooper, *John Trumbull: The Hand and Spirit of a Painter* (1982)
Herbert Alan Johnson, *John Jay, Colonial Lawyer* (1989)
Dumas Malone, *Jefferson and His Time,* 6 vols. (1948–81)
Jules David Prown, *John Singleton Copley* (1966)
Edgar P. Richardson et al., *Charles Willson Peale and His World* (1983)
K. Alan Synder, *Defining Noah Webster: Mind and Morals in the Early Republic* (1990)
Mason Locke Weems, *The Life of Washington,* ed. Marcus Cunliffe (1962)

IMMIGRATION & COMMUNITY

The Changing Face of Ethnicity in America TO 1800

Immigration contributed to the growth of the population of the colonies that became the United States of America more than any other factor. Seventeenth-century migration to these colonies was mostly from England, although small but important groups of Dutch, Swedes, and French settled areas of New York, New Jersey, and Maryland.

By 1700 the population of British colonial North America had reached 250,000. The high levels of fertility characteristic of all the colonial societies of North America—British, Spanish, and French—contributed to the growth of population. But only the British encouraged immigration. The French and the Spanish adopted highly restrictive immigration policies. Dedicated to keeping its colonies exclusively Catholic, France turned down the requests of thousands of Protestant Huguenots who desperately sought to emigrate to Canada. The Spanish, fearful of depleting their population at home, severely limited the migration of their own subjects to their colonies and absolutely forbade the immigration of foreigners, with the exception of African slaves.

Yet a veritable flood of immigrants came to British North America during the eighteenth century. Scots, Scots-Irish, Germans, and French joined the English in the trans-Atlantic crossing. Slave traders also brought tens of thousands of Africans to the southern colonies. (For a full discussion of African migration, see Chapter Four.) By 1750 European and African migrants and their descendents outnumbered the Indian population of the continent, and by 1800 had grown to more than 5.3 million, an increase of more than twenty times the population in 1700 over the course of one hundred years.

William Penn was the first British colonial official to encourage the immigration of non-British western Europeans, in the 1680s sending agents to recruit settlers in Holland, France, and the German principalities along the Rhine River. His experiment proved so successful that the leaders of other British colonies soon were employing recruiting agents of their own in Europe. Further encouraging this development, most of the British colonies enacted liberal naturalization laws in the early eighteenth century, allowing immigrants who professed Protestantism and swore allegiance to the British crown to become free "denizens" with all the freedoms and privileges of natural-born subjects. In 1740 Parliament passed a general Naturalization Act that extended these policies to all the colonies. The new legislation continued to prohibit the naturalization of Catholic and Jewish immigrants, however, and these groups remained tiny minorities in the British colonies.

Still, immigration to what would become the United States was characterized by extraordinary ethnic diversity. The two largest migrating groups were the English and the Africans, each totaling, according to good historical estimates, perhaps 400,000 to 500,000 immigrants during the colonial period. There was also substantial emigration from the northern British Isles. Squeezed by economic hardship, an estimated 250,000 Highland Scots and Protestant Irish from the Ulster region (known in America as the "Scots-Irish") emigrated to North America during the eighteenth century. The Germans were another significant group; at least 100,000 of them settled in the British colonies, where they became known as the "Dutch" (from *Deutsch*, the German-language term for German). It should be noted that from half to two-thirds of Europeans came to British North America as indentured servants, or "redemptioners," or else convicts transported to the New World to serve out their sentences laboring on plantations. The Africans were not the only people to come involuntarily to America. A majority of immigrants during the colonial period came in a state of bondage.

The first federal census, conducted in 1790, provides a snapshot of the consequences of eighteenth-century immigration. Forty-nine percent of the population of the thirteen United States was English in origin, and nearly 20 percent was African; 15 percent were Irish or Scots, 7 percent German, 3 percent Dutch, and 2 percent French.

Many of the founders of the American republic worried that the different languages and traditions of these diverse peoples would fracture the nation. In the 1750s, for example, Benjamin Franklin wrote of his fears that German immigrants would not assimilate to English ways. "Why should Pennsylvania," he asked, "founded by English, become a colony of *aliens* who will shortly be so numerous as to Germanize *us* instead of Anglifying them?" Thomas Jefferson worried that immigrants from monarchical countries, untutored in the ways of democracy, would "warp and bias" the direction of American political development. Reflecting such fears, the nation's first Naturalization Act,

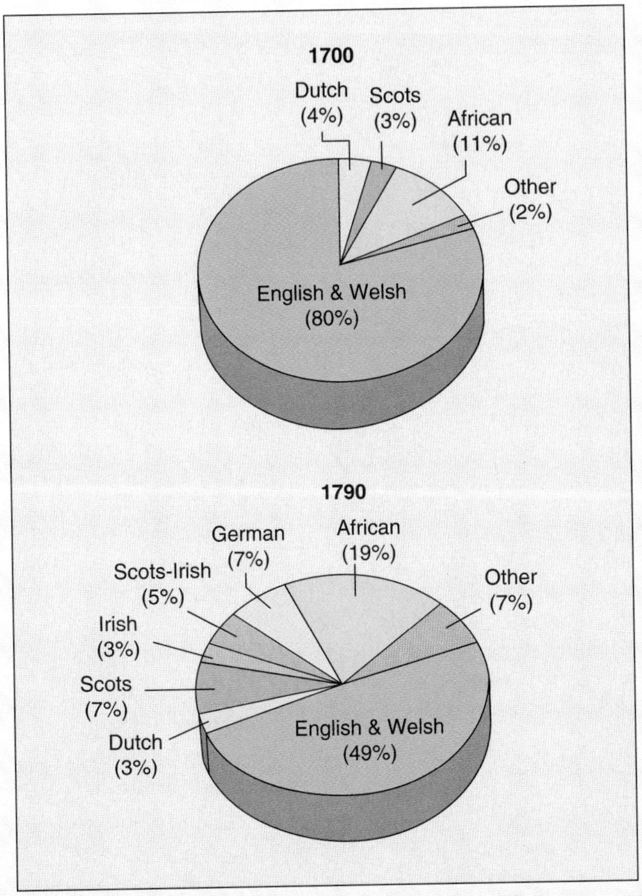

The Ancestry of the British Colonial Population

The legacy of eighteenth-century immigration to the British colonies was a population of unprecedented ethnic diversity.

Source: Thomas L. Purvis, "The European Ancestry of the United States Population," *William and Mary Quarterly* 61 (1984): 85–101.

passed in 1790, required a residency period of five years (a kind of probation period) before immigrants could apply for citizenship, and limited applications to "free white persons." In the nineteenth and early twentieth centuries this clause would be used to bar the naturalization of immigrants from Africa and Asia.

IN THEIR OWN WORDS

William Penn was the first colonial leader to actively seek out prospective immigrants for his colony. In 1681 he wrote a promotional account of Pennsylvania that was translated into several European languages and widely circulated.

> The place [Pennsylvania] lies 600 miles nearer the sun than England, for...[it] begins at about the latitude of Naples in Italy, or Montpellier in France. I shall say little in its praise, to excite desires in any, whatever I could truly write as to the soil, air and water. This shall satisfy me, that by the blessing of God, and the honesty and industry of man, it may be a good fruitful land....
>
> What persons will be fit to go? 1st. Industrious husbandmen and day-labourers, that are hardly able (with extreme labour) to maintain their families and portion [endow] their children.
>
> 2dly. Laborious handicrafts, especially carpenters, masons, smiths, weavers, tailors, tanners, shoemakers, shipwrights, etc., where they may be spared or are low in the world. And as they shall want no encouragement, so their labour is worth more there than here, and their provision cheaper.
>
> 3dly. A plantation [colony] seems a fit place for those ingenious spirits that being low in the world, are much clogged and oppressed about a livelihood, for the means of subsisting being easy there, they may have time and opportunity to gratify their inclinations, and thereby improve science and help nurseries of people.
>
> 4thly. A fourth sort of men for whom a plantation would be proper, takes in those that are younger brothers of small inheritances; yet because they would live in sight of their kindred in some proportion to their quality, and can't do it without a labour that looks like farming, their condition is too straight for them; and if married, their children are often too numerous for the estate, and are frequently bred up to no trades, but are a kind of hangers-on or retainers to the elder brother's table and charity....
>
> Lastly, there are another sort of persons, not only fit for, but necessary in plantations, and that is men of universal spirits, that have an eye to the good of posterity, and that both understand among a plain and well-intending people. Such persons may find room in colonies for their good counsel and contrivance, who are shut out from being of much use or service to great nations under settled customs. These men deserve much esteem, and would be hearkened to...[1]

Judith Giton (ca. 1665–1711) was twenty years old when she and many other Protestant Huguenots escaped French persecution to settle in South Carolina in 1685. In the following letter to her brother, written from America, she described the harrowing experience of immigration.

> For eight months we had suffered from the contributions and the quartering of the soldiers, on account of religion, enduring many inconveniences. We therefore resolved on quitting France at night, leaving the soldiers in their beds, and abandoning the house with its furniture....We passed into Holland, in order to go to England.

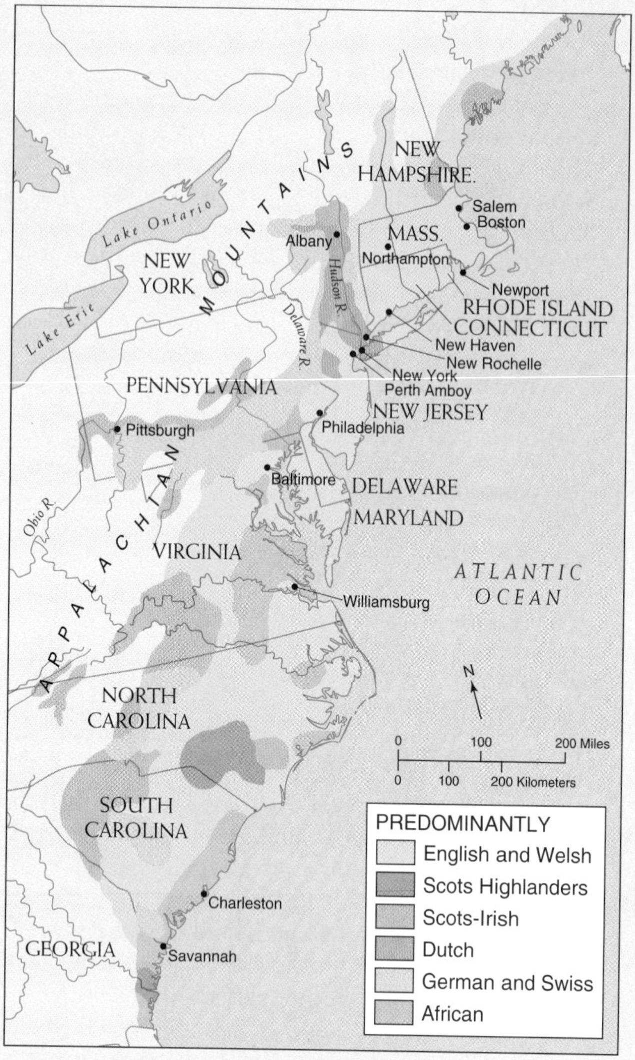

Ethnic Groups in Eighteenth-Century British North America *The first federal census, taken in 1790, revealed remarkable ethnic diversity. New England was filled with people from the British Isles, but the rest of the colonies were a patchwork. Most states had at least three different ethnic groups within their borders, and although the English and Scots-Irish were heavily represented in all colonies, in some they had strong competition from Germans (eastern and southern Pennsylvania) and from African peoples (Virginia and South Carolina).*

We were detained in London for three months, waiting for a vessel ready to sail for Carolina. Once embarked, we were miserably off indeed. The scarlet fever broke out in our ship, and many died, among them our aged mother.... Our vessel put in [at Bermuda] for repairs, having been badly injured in a severe storm. Our captain... was thrown into prison, and the ship was seized. It was with the greatest difficulty that we secured our passage in another ship, for our money had all been spent. After our arrival in Carolina, we suffered all sorts of evils. Our eldest brother died of a fever, eighteen months after coming here.... We ourselves have been exposed, since leaving France, to all kinds of afflictions, in the forms of sickness, pestilence, famine, poverty, and the roughest labor. I have been for six months at a time in this country without tasting bread, laboring meanwhile like a slave in tilling the ground. Indeed, I have spent three or four years without knowing what it was to eat bread whenever I wanted it. God has been very good to us in enabling us to bear up under trials for every kind.[2]

Robert Parke was a Presbyterian Scot who immigrated with his family from Ireland to Pennsylvania in the early 1720s. Letters home, like this one of Parke's, were an important means of advertising the advantages of American immigration.

Chester Township, the 10th Month 1725
Dear Sister Mary Valentine:

We have not had a day's sickness in the family since we came in to the country, blessed be God for it. My father in particular has not had his health better these ten years than since he came here, his ancient age considered. You write in your letter that there was a talk went back to Ireland that we were not satisfied in coming here, which was utterly false... for there is not one of the family but what likes the country very well and would if we were in Ireland again come here directly it being the best country for working folk and tradesmen of any in the world. But for drunkards and Idlers, they cannot live well anywhere. It is likewise an Extraordinarily healthy country....

Land is of all prices even from ten pounds, to one hundred pounds a hundred, according to the goodness or else the situation thereof, and grows more dear every year by reason of vast quantities of people that come here yearly from several parts of the world, therefore, you and your family or any that I wish well I would desire to make what speed you can to come here the sooner the better....[3]

Gottlieb Mittelberger came to Pennsylvania from Germany in 1750 and served as a schoolmaster and organist in Philadelphia for three years. In this famous account, written after his return to Europe, he paints a horrid picture of the voyage to America, the conditions for indentured servants, and warns his countrymen to remain content at home.

Both in Rotterdam and in Amsterdam the people are packed densely, like herrings so to say, in the large sea vessels. One person receives a place of scarcely 2 feet width and 6 feet length in the bedstead, while many a ship carries four to six hundred souls; not to mention the innumerable implements, tools, provisions, water-barrels and other things which likewise occupy much space.

On account of contrary winds it takes the ships sometimes 2, 3, and 4 weeks to make the trip from Holland to Kaupp [Cowes] in England.... When the ships have for the last time weighed their anchors near...Kaupp...., the real misery begins with the long voyage. For from there the ships, unless they have good wind, must often sail 8, 9, 10, to 12 weeks before they reach Philadelphia. But even with the best wind the voyage lasts 7 weeks.

But during the voyage there is on board these ships terrible misery, stanch, fumes, horror, vomiting, many kinds of seasickness, fever, dysentery, headache, heat, constipation, boils, scurvy, cancer, mouth-rot, and the like, all of which come from old and sharply salted food and meat, also from the very bad and foul water, so that many die miserably.

Add to this want of provisions, hunger, thirst, frost, heat, dampness, anxiety, want, afflictions and lamentations, together with other trouble, as *c.v.* the lice abound so frightfully, especially on sick people, that they can be scraped off the body. The misery reaches the climax when a gale rages for 2 or 3 nights and days, so that every one believes that the ship will go to the bottom with all human beings on board. In such a visitation the people cry and pray most piteously....

When the ships have landed at Philadelphia after their long voyage, no one is permitted to leave them except those who pay for their passage or can give good security; the others, who cannot pay, must remain on board the ships till they are purchased, and are released from the ships by their purchasers. The sick always fare the worst, for the healthy are naturally preferred and purchased first; and so the sick and wretched must often remain on board in front of the city for 2 or 3 weeks, and frequently die, whereas many a one, if he could pay his debt and were permitted to leave the ship immediately, might recover and remain alive....

The sale of human beings in the market on board the ship is carried on thus: Every day Englishmen, Dutchmen, and High-German people come from the city of Philadelphia and other places, in part from a great distance, say 20, 30, or 40 hours away, and go on board the newly arrived ship that has brought and offers for sale passengers from Europe, and select among the healthy persons such as they deem suitable for their business, and bargain with them how long they will serve for their passage money, which most of them are still in debt for. When they have come to an agreement, it happens that adult persons bind themselves in writing to serve 3, 4, 5 or 6 years for the amount due by them, according to their age and strength. But very young people, from 10 to 15 years, must serve till they are 21 years old.

One of Philadelphia's many wharves, featured in a hand-colored engraving of 1800. Attracted by the abundant and fertile farmland of the Pennsylvania countryside, more European immigrants passed through Philadelphia than any other North American port of the eighteenth century.

A master potter working with his indentured apprentices, from The Book of Trades, *a survey of eighteenth-century American crafts. Of all the Europeans who immigrated to British North America in the eighteenth century, half to two-thirds came as indentured servants*

Many parents must sell and trade away their children like so many head of cattle; for if their children take the debt upon themselves, the parents can leave the ship free and unrestrained; but as the parents often do not know where and to what people their children are going, it often happens that such parents and children, after leaving the ship, do not see each other again for many years, perhaps no more in all their lives....

It often happens that whole families, husband, wife, and children, are separated by being sold to different purchasers, especially when they have not paid any part of their passage money. When a husband or wife has died at sea, when the ship has made more than half of her trip, the survivor must pay or serve not only for himself or herself, but also for the deceased. When both parents have died over half-way at sea, their children, especially when they are young and have nothing to pawn or to pay, must stand for their own and their parents' passage, and serve till they are 21 years old. When one has served his or her term, he or she is entitled to a new suit of clothes at parting; and if it has been so stipulated, a man gets in addition a horse, a woman, a cow....

However hard he may be compelled to work in his fatherland, he will surely find it quite as hard, if not harder, in the new country. Besides, there is not only the long and arduous journey lasting half a year, during which he has to suffer, more than with the hardest work; he has also spent about 200 florins which no one will refund to him. If he has so much money, it will slip out of his hands; if he has it not, he must work his debt off as a slave and poor serf. Therefore let every one stay in his own country and support himself and his family honestly. Besides I say that those who suffer themselves to be persuaded and enticed away by the man-thieves, are very foolish if they believe that roasted pigeons will fly into the mouths in America or Pennsylvania without their working for them.[4]

Thomas Jefferson had doubts concerning the effect of mass immigration on American institutions. These comments come from his extended essay, *Notes on the State of Virginia,* published in 1784.

The present desire of America is to produce rapid population by as great importations of foreigners as possible. But is this founded in good policy?...Are there no inconveniences to be thrown into the scale against the advantage expected from a multiplication of numbers by the importation of foreigners? It is for the happiness of those united in society to harmonize as much as possible in matters which they must of necessity transact together. Civil government being the sole object of forming societies, its administration must be conducted by common consent. Every species of government has its specific principles. Ours perhaps are more peculiar than those of any other in the universe. It is a composition of the freest principles of the English constitution, with others derived from natural right and natural reason. To these nothing can be more opposed than the maxims of absolute monarchies. Yet, from such, we are to expect the greatest number of emigrants. They will bring with them the principles of the governments they leave, imbibed in their early youth; or, if able to throw them off, it will be in exchange for an unbounded licentiousness, passing, as is usual, from one extreme to another. It would be a miracle were they to stop precisely at the point of temperate liberty. These principles, with their language, they will transmit to their children. In proportion to their numbers, they will share with us the legislation. They will infuse into it their spirit, warp and bias its direction, and render it a heterogeneous, incoherent, distracted mass....

Suppose 20 millions of republican Americans thrown all of a sudden into France, what would be the condition of that kingdom? If it would be more turbulent, less happy, less strong, we may believe that the addition of half a million of foreigners to our present numbers would produce a similar effect here. If they come of themselves, they are entitled to all the rights of citizenship: but I doubt the expediency of inviting them by extraordinary encouragements.[5]

In contrast to Jefferson, the French immigrant J. Hector St. Jean de Crèvecoeur celebrated the American cultural blending that resulted from immigration. In his famous *Letters of an American Farmer* (1782), Crèvecoeur was the first to discuss the process by which immigrants were "melted" into a new kind of person, the American.

Whence came all these people? They are a mixture of English, Scotch, Irish, French, Dutch, Germans, and Swedes. From this promiscuous breed, that race, now called Americans, have arisen....

What then is the American, this new man? He is either an European, or the descendant of an European; hence that strange mixture of blood, which you will find in no other country. I could point out to you a man, whose grandfather was an Englishman, whose wife was Dutch, whose son married a French woman, and whose present four sons have now four wives of different nations. *He* is an American, who, leaving behind him all his ancient prejudices and manners, receives new ones from the new mode of life he has embraced, the new government he obeys, and the new rank he holds. He becomes an American by being received in the broad lap of our great Alma Mater.

Here individuals of all nations are melted into a new race of men, whose labours and posterity will one day cause great change in the world. Americans are the western pilgrims, who are carrying along with them that great mass of arts, sciences, vigour, and industry, which began long since in the east; they will finish the great circle. The Americans were once scattered all over Europe; here they are incorporated into one of the finest systems of population which has ever appeared, and which will hereafter become distinct by the power of the different climates they inhabit. The American ought, therefore, to love this country much better than that wherein either he or his forefathers were born. Here the rewards of his industry follow with equal steps the progress of his labour; his labour is founded on the basis of nature, *self-interest*; can it want a stronger allurement? Wives and children, who before in vain demanded of him a morsel of bread, now, fat and frolicsome, gladly help their father to clear those fields whence exuberant crops are to arise to feed and to clothe them all; without any part being claimed either by a despotic prince, a rich abbot, or a mighty lord. Here religion demands but little of him; a small voluntary salary to the minister, and gratitude to God; can he refuse these? The American is a new man, who acts upon new principles; he must therefore entertain new ideas, and form new opinions. From involuntary idleness, servile dependence, penury, and useless labour, he has passed to toils of a very different nature, rewarded by ample subsistence. This is an American.[6]

Questions

1. Identify the major immigrant groups of the colonial period and their proportion in the American population at the end of the eighteenth century.
2. What were the arguments made both in favor of and against immigration to British North America?
3. How would Jefferson respond to Crèvecoeur's argument about "the American, this new man"?

Sources

1. William Penn, "Account of the Province of Pennsilvania," in *Some Account of the Province of Pennsilvania in America* (London: Benjamin Clark, 1681)
2. Ruth Barnes Moynihan, Cynthia Russett, and Laurie Crumpacker, eds., *Second to None: A Documentary History of American Women* (Lincoln: University of Nebraska Press, 1993), 1, 54. Reprinted with permission of the publisher.
3. Robert Parke, "A Letter from Pennsylvania" (1725) from Charles A. Hanna, *The Scotch-Irish in America,* 2 volumes (1902), 2, 64–67
4. Gottlieb Mittelberger, *Journey to Pennsylvania in the Year 1750 and Return to Germany in the Year 1754*, translated by Carl Theo. Eben (Philadelphia: John Jos. McVey, 1898), 19–20, 22, 24–31.
5. Thomas Jefferson, *Notes on the State of Virginia* in *Thomas Jefferson: Writings* (New York, 1984), 210–212
6. J. Hector St. Jean de Crèvecoeur, *Letters from an American Farmer* (London, 1782)

CHAPTER NINE

AN AGRARIAN REPUBLIC

1790–1824

Applique quilt, late 18th–early 19th century, by Sarah Furman, with people and village at center. Henry Ford Museum and Greenfield Village.

CHAPTER OUTLINE

THE GROWTH OF AMERICAN COMMUNITIES FROM COAST TO COAST

Russian America: Sitka
Northern New Spain: Los Angeles
A French Legacy: New Orleans and St. Louis
Trans-Appalachia: Cincinnati
Atlantic Ports: From Charleston to Boston

A NATIONAL ECONOMY

The Economy of the Young Republic
Shipping and the Economic Boom

THE JEFFERSON PRESIDENCY

Republican Agrarianism
Jefferson's Government
An Independent Judiciary
Opportunity: The Louisiana Purchase
Incorporating Louisiana
Texas and the Struggle for Mexican Independence

RENEWED IMPERIAL RIVALRY IN NORTH AMERICA

Problems with Neutral Rights
The Embargo Act
Madison and the Failure of "Peaceable Coercion"
A Contradictory Indian Policy
Indian Resistance

THE WAR OF 1812

The War Hawks
The Campaign against Canada
War in the South
The Naval War
The Hartford Convention
The Treaty of Ghent

DEFINING THE BOUNDARIES

Another Westward Surge
The Second Great Awakening on the Frontier
The Election of 1816 and the Era of Good Feelings
The Diplomacy of John Quincy Adams
The Panic of 1819
The Missouri Compromise

AMERICAN COMMUNITIES

Expansion Touches Mandan Villages on the Upper Missouri

In mid-October 1804, news arrived at the Mandan villages, prominently situated on bluffs overlooking the upper Missouri, that an American expedition led by Meriwether Lewis and William Clark was coming up the river. The principal chiefs, hoping for expanded trade and support against their enemies the Sioux, welcomed these first American visitors. As the expedition's three boats and forty-three men approached the village, wrote Clark, "great numbers on both sides flocked down to the bank to view us." That evening the Mandans welcomed the Americans with an enthusiastic dance and gifts of food.

Since the fourteenth century, when they migrated from the East, the Mandans had lived along the Missouri, on the edge of the Great Plains in what is now North Dakota. They believed their homeland was "the very center of the world," and indeed it is in the heart of the North American continent. Mandan men hunted buffalo and Mandan women kept storage pits full with abundant crops of corn, beans, squash, sunflowers, and tobacco grown on the fertile soil of the river bottom. The Mandan villages were also the central marketplace of the northern Plains; at trading time in late summer they filled with Crows, Assiniboins, Cheyennes, Kiowas, and Arapahoes. Well before any of these people, or those of other tribes, had met a European, they were trading in kettles, knives, and guns acquired from the French and English to the east and leatherwork, glassware, and horses acquired form the Spanish in the Southwest.

The eighteenth century was a golden age for the Mandan, who with their closely related Hidatsa neighbors numbered about 3,000 in 1804. In each of their five villages, earth lodges surrounded a central plaza. One large ceremonial lodge was used for community gatherings, and each of the other earth lodges was home to a senior woman, her husband, her sisters (perhaps married to the same man as she, for the Mandans practiced polygamy), their daughters and their unmarried sons, along with numerous grandchildren. Matrilineal clans, the principal institution of the community, distributed food to the sick, adopted orphans, cared for the dependent elderly, and punished wrongdoers. A village council of male clan leaders selected chiefs who led by consensus and lost power when people no longer accepted their opinions.

Lewis and Clark had been sent by President Thomas Jefferson to survey the Louisiana Purchase and to find an overland route to the Pacific Ocean. They were also instructed to inform the Indians that they now owed loyalty—and trade—to the American government, thereby challenging British economic control over the lucrative North American fur trade. Meeting with the village chiefs, the Americans offered the Mandans a military and economic alliance. His people would like nothing better, responded Chief

Black Cat, for the Mandans had fallen on hard times over the past decade. "The smallpox destroyed the greater part of the nation" some twenty years before, the chief said. "All the nations before this malady [were] afraid of them, [but] after they were reduced the Sioux and other Indians waged war, and killed a great many." Black Cat was skeptical that the Americans would deter the Sioux, but Clark reassured him. "We were ready to protect them," Clark reported in his journal, "and kill those who would not listen to our good talk."

The Americans spent the winter with the Mandans, joining in their communal life and establishing firm and friendly relations with them. There were dances and joint hunting parties, frequent visits to the earth lodges, long talks around the fire, and, for many of the men, pleasant nights in the company of Mandan women. Lewis and Clark spent many hours acquiring important geographic information from the Mandans, who drew charts and maps showing the course of the Missouri, the ranges of the Rocky Mountains, and places where one could cross the Continental Divide. The information provided by the Mandans and other Indian peoples to the West was vital to the success of the expedition. Lewis and Clark's "voyage of discovery" depended largely on the willingness of Indian peoples to share their knowledge of the land with the Americans.

In need also of interpreters who could help them communicate with other Indian communities on their way, the Americans hired several multilingual Frenchmen who lived with the Mandans. They also acquired the services of Sacajawea, the fifteen-year-old Shoshoni wife of one of the Frenchmen, who became the only woman to join the westward journey. The presence of Sacajawea and her baby son was a signal, as Clark noted, to "all the Indians as to our friendly intentions"; everyone knew that women and children did not go on war parties.

When the party left the Mandan villages in March, Clark wrote, his men were "generally healthy, except venereal complaints which is very common amongst the natives and the men catch it from them." After an arduous journey across the Rockies, the party reached the Pacific Ocean at the mouth of the Columbia River, where they spent the winter. Overdue and feared lost, they returned in triumph to St. Louis in September 1806. Before long the Americans had established Fort Clark at the Mandan villages, giving American traders a base for challenging British dominance of the western fur trade. The permanent American presence brought increased contact, and with it much more disease. In 1837 a terrible smallpox epidemic carried away the vast majority of the Mandans, reducing the population to fewer than 150. Four Bears, a Mandan chief who had been a child at the time of the Lewis and Clark visit, spoke these last words to the remnants of his people. "I have loved the whites," he declared. "I have lived with them ever since I was a boy." But in return for the kindness of the Mandans, the Americans had brought this plague. "I do not fear death, my friends," he said, "but to die with my face rotten, that even the wolves will shrink with horror at seeing me, and say to themselves, that is Four Bears, the friend of the whites." "They have deceived me," he pronounced with his last breath. "Them that I always considered as brothers turned out to be my worst enemies."

In sending Lewis and Clark on their "voyage of discovery" to claim the land and the loyalty of the Mandans and other western Indian communities, President Jefferson was motivated by his vision of an expanding American republic of self-sufficient farmers. During his and succeeding presidencies expansion became a key element of national policy and pride. Yet, as the experience of the Mandans showed, what Jefferson viewed as enlargement of "the empire for liberty" had a dark side—the destruction, from disease and coerced displacement, of the communities created by America's first peoples. The effects—economic, political, and social—of continental expansion dominate the history of American communities in the first half of the nineteenth century.

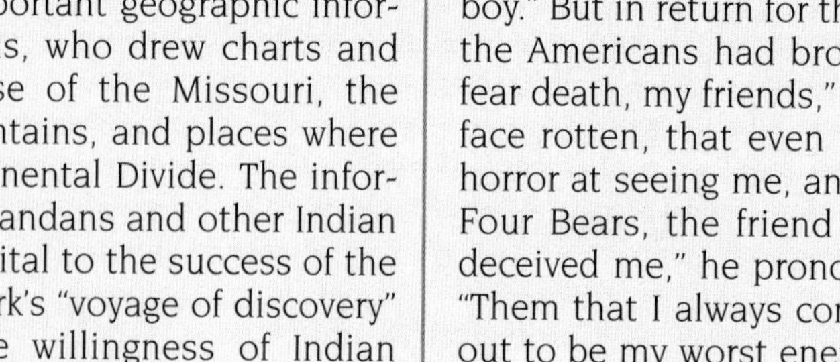

KEY TOPICS

- The development of America's economy in a world of warring great powers
- The role of Jefferson's presidency and his agrarian republicanism in forging a national identity
- The ending of colonial dependency by the divisive War of 1812
- Westward expansion becomes a nationalizing force

THE GROWTH OF AMERICAN COMMUNITIES FROM COAST TO COAST

At first glance, the United States of America in 1800 was little different from the scattered colonies of the pre-Revolution era. Two-thirds of the young nation's people still lived in a long thin line of settlement within fifty miles of the Atlantic coast. From New Hampshire to Georgia, most people lived on farms or in small towns, and, because they rarely traveled far from home, their horizons were limited and local.

As famed historian Henry Adams observed, at the beginning of the new century "nature was rather man's master than his servant." Travel in the young republic was slow and difficult, for the roads were poor, and a horse and carriage could go no more than three or four miles an hour. It took two days to travel from New York to Philadelphia, four days to Boston. Nevertheless, the new nation was already transforming itself, not held back by nature but plunging ahead into it. Between 1790 and 1800, according to the first and second federal censuses, the American population grew from 3.9 million to 5.3 million. Growth by migration was greatest in the trans-Appalachian West, a region that was already home to approximately 100,000 Indians. From 1800 to 1850, in an extraordinary burst of territorial expansion, Americans surged westward all the way to the Pacific. At the turn of the century few people would have predicted that within fifty years the nation would encompass the entire continent. In fact, in 1800 several European nations were still mounting significant attempts to settle parts of what is now the United States.

Russian America: Sitka

Russian settlement of what is now Alaska was an extension of its conquest of Siberia, which was driven by the fur trade. In 1741, commissioned by Tsar Peter the Great, the Danish-born naval officer Vitus Bering sailed east from Kamchatka across the sea that now bears his name, explored the Aleutian Islands, and made landfall on the southern coast of Alaska. Although Bering died in a shipwreck on his return voyage, his associates brought back a cargo of sea otter furs, news of the discovery of Alaska, and a navigational report on the Arctic waters of the northern Pacific. In the aftermath of these voyages, Russian and Siberian fur trappers, known as *promyshleniki*, became regular visitors to the Aleutian Islands and the Alaskan coast. By the late 1750s they were shipping a steady supply of furs from Russian America.

The Russians sometimes took furs by force, holding whole villages hostage and brutalizing the native Inuit and Aleut peoples. Within a decade, native resistance had broadened beyond sporadic and local efforts. In 1762, for example, the Aleuts destroyed a fleet of Russian ships from Kamchatka, beginning a series of attacks known as the Aleut Revolt. Finally crushing the Aleuts in 1766, the Russians promised to protect them from abuse, but by the end of the century, the precontact population of 25,000 Aleuts had been greatly reduced. At the same time, sexual relations and intermarriage between fur trappers and Aleut women created a large group of Russian creoles who assumed an increasingly prominent position in the Alaskan fur trade as navigators, explorers, clerks, and traders.

In 1784, the merchant trader Gregory Shelikhov set up a post on Kodiak Island, and over the next several years he established the first permanent Russian settlements in the Gulf of Alaska. In 1799, after his death, Shelikhov's company received a state charter as a quasi-governmental monopoly with rights to the lucrative trade in sea otter pelts. The Russian-American Company set up American headquarters first at Kodiak. When overhunting caused a scarcity of furs, the Russians moved their headquarters south to Sitka, in what is now the southeastern panhandle of Alaska. This was the homeland of the Tlingits, a warrior society, who destroyed the Russians' first fortress in the Tlingit Revolt of 1802. The Russians reestablished

From an engraving by Freidrich H. von Kittlitz, 1827.

This view shows Sitka, the center of Russian activities in Alaska, in 1827. Russian architectural styles and building techniques are apparent in the Church of St. Michael the Archangel in the right background, contrasting with the Asian and Indian origins of most of Sitka's inhabitants.

Sitka by force in 1804, and over the next generation established Russian settlements along the Pacific coast as far south as Fort Ross, which was just north of San Francisco Bay and well within what Spain considered Spanish territory.

Northern New Spain: Los Angeles

Spain had long been concerned about threats to its New World empire from other nations. Fearing incursions by the Russians and British, the Spanish sent naval squadrons north from Mexico to establish their claim to the Pacific coast. By the 1770s, Spain had explored and made claim to the mouth of the Columbia River, Nootka Sound (on Vancouver Island), and the coast of southeastern Alaska. But Spanish attempts to seal off the rich seaborne fur trade from other nations failed. The Russians were a strong presence in Alaska, and the British, already the major power in the land-based fur trade, built a trading post for sea otter furs at Nootka Sound in 1789 in spite of Spanish protests. Americans, who soon dominated the sea otter trade, made their first voyage to the Pacific Northwest in 1787.

In another effort to protect their rich colony of Mexico the Spanish pushed north into Alta (Upper) California, establishing a chain of twenty-one missions that stretched north from San Diego (1769) to Sonoma (1823). The largest of these missions was Los Angeles, which in 1800 had a largely mestizo population of 300. The town, which was the social center for the vast countryside surrounding it, functioned chiefly as a center of government authority (see Chapter 5). Despite Spain's desire to seal its territory from commerce with other nations, a brisk but illegal trade in otter skins, hides, and tallow developed between the United States and California after the first American ship, the *Lelia Bird*, arrived in 1803.

A French Legacy: New Orleans and St. Louis

For a half-century after its founding by Jean Baptiste le Moyne, Sieur de Bienville, in 1718, New Orleans was controlled by the French. Originally little more than a small port at the mouth of the Mississippi River, its location gave it access to the vast and vaguely defined continental interior that the French called Louisiana. New Orleans came under Spanish rule in 1763 as a result of the Seven Years War, but it continued to be a polyglot, French-dominated society. By 1800 it had a population of about 8,000, half white and half black. Two-thirds of the black population were slaves; the remainder were "free persons of color," who under French law enjoyed legal rights equal to those of white people. The white population was a mixture of French people of European and West Indian origin. Among them were French-speaking exiles from Acadia, who became known in New Orleans as Cajuns (see Chapters 6 and 8). But there were also Spanish, Germans, English, Irish, Americans, and native-born creoles, causing one observer to call the community "a veritable tower of Babel."

All these people were there because New Orleans was becoming a thriving international port. In 1801 it shipped more than $3 million worth of tobacco, sugar, rice, cotton, fruits, and vegetables to Europe. Every year, a greater proportion of the New Orleans trade was supplied by Americans living some distance up the Mississippi River. In 1801 alone, an observer in Natchez counted nearly 600 flatboats on their way to New Orleans from American settlements upriver. Pinckney's 1795 treaty with Spain guaranteed Americans free navigation of the Mississippi River and the right to deposit goods at the port of New Orleans. Nevertheless, Americans were uncomfortably aware that the city's crucial location at the mouth of the Mississippi meant that whatever foreign nation possessed New Orleans had the power to

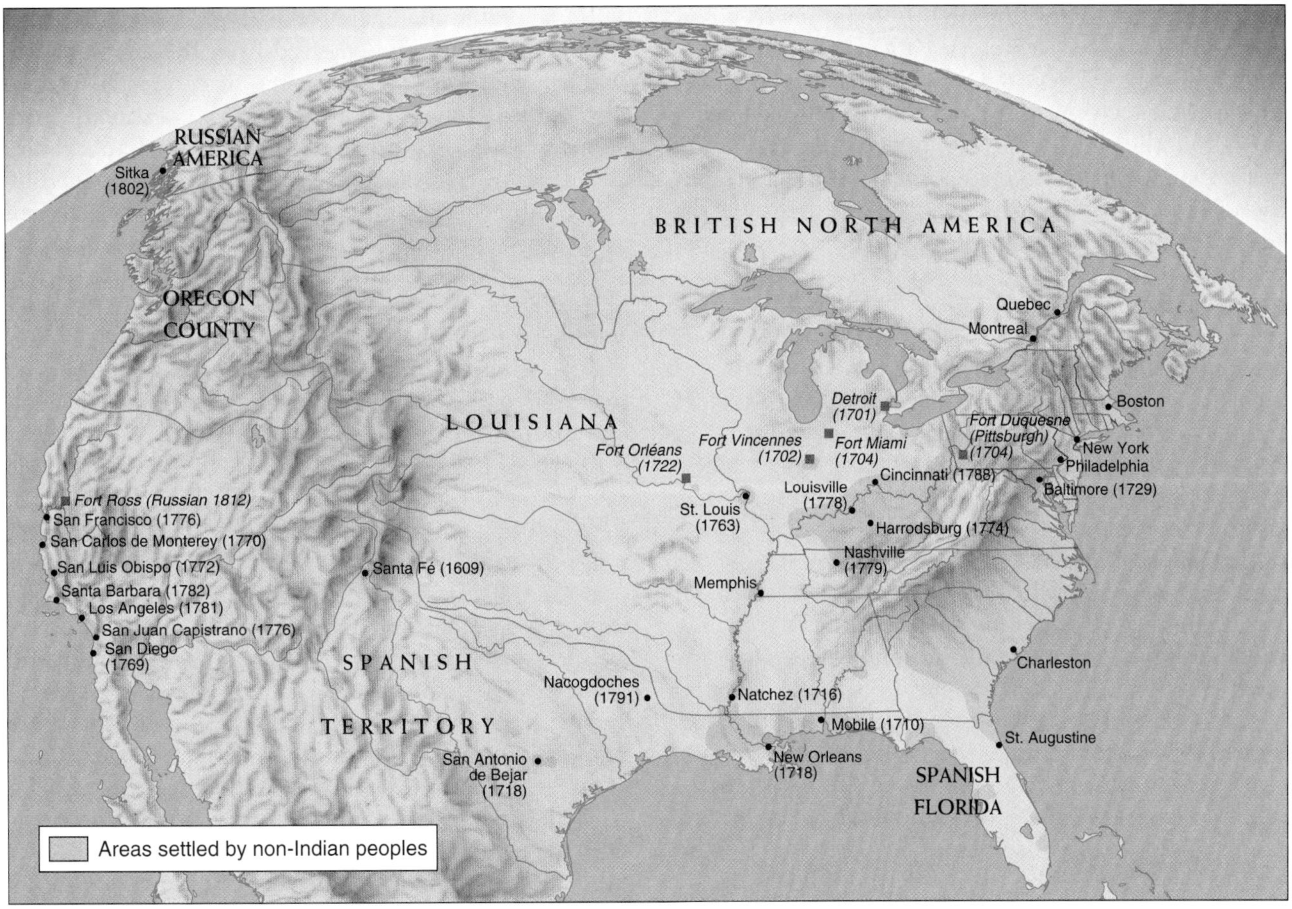

America in 1800 *In 1800, the new United States of America was surrounded by territories held by the European powers: British Canada, French Louisiana (secretly ceded that year to France by Spain), Spanish Florida, Spanish Mexico, and Russian Alaska expanding southward along the Pacific coast. Few people could have imagined that by 1850 the United States would span the continent. But the American settlers who had crossed the Appalachians to the Ohio River Valley were already convinced that opportunity lay in the West.*

choke off the flourishing trade in the vast Mississippi Valley river system.

More than 600 miles north was the small trading town of St. Louis, founded by the New Orleans trader Pierre Laclède in 1763. By 1800 the town had fewer than a thousand residents, three-quarters of whom were involved in the Indian trade of the Missouri River. Spanish officials tried to supervise that trade from their offices in the town, but real control rested in the hands of the Laclèdes and other French traders. Americans visiting this shabby little place laughed at Pierre Laclède's prediction that St.Louis would become "one of the finest cities in America," but he was right.

Trans-Appalachia: Cincinnati

Within the United States itself, the region of greatest growth was the area west of the Appalachian Mountains. By 1800, 500,000 people (the vast majority from Virginia and North Carolina) had found rich and fertile land along the splendid rivers of the interior—the Tennessee, the Cumberland, and the Ohio, all draining into the Mississippi River, which marked the western boundary of the United States. Soon there was enough population for statehood. Kentucky (1792) and Tennessee (1796) were the first trans-Appalachian states admitted to the Union.

Migration was a principal feature of American life. Probably 5 to 10 percent of all American households moved each year. In the rural areas of the Atlantic seaboard, a third of the households counted in the 1790 census had moved by 1800; in cities the proportion was closer to half. In the West, meanwhile, rates of migration rose to as high as two-thirds of the community every ten years. Most moves were between neighboring communities or towns, but many families underwent the painful process of long-distance relocation. Migration was generally a family affair, with groups of kin moving together to a new area. One observer wrote of a caravan moving across the mountains, "They had prepared baskets made of fine hickory withe or splints, and fastening two of them together with ropes they put a child in each basket and put it across a pack saddle." Once pioneers had managed to struggle by road over the Appalachians, they gladly took to the rivers, especially the Ohio River, to move farther west.

Cincinnati, strategically situated 450 miles downstream from Pittsburgh, was a particularly dramatic example of the rapid community growth and development that characterized the trans-Appalachian region. Founded in 1788, Cincinnati began life as a military fort defending settlers in the fertile Miami River valley of Ohio from resistance by Shawnee and Miami Indians. Conflict between these Indian peoples and the new settlers was so fierce that the district was grimly referred to as "the slaughterhouse." Trans-Appalachian settlement was not individual but communal: fear of attack led the white settlers to group together for protection. The basic form of settlement in early Kentucky was the "station," or fort; north of the Ohio River, compact settlements on the New England model were favored.

After the battle of Fallen Timbers broke Indian resistance in 1794, Cincinnati became the point of departure for immigrants arriving by the Ohio River on their way to settle the interior of the Old Northwest: Ohio, Indiana, and Illinois. In the boom years of settlement, the number of people passing through was so great that the entire town seemed to consist of hotels and eating places. In 1800, Cincinnati had a population of about 750 people. By 1810, it had tripled in size, confirming its boast to be "the Queen City of the West."

Cincinnati merchants were soon shipping farm goods from the fertile Miami Valley down the Ohio–Mississippi River system to New Orleans, 1,500 miles away. River hazards like snags and sandbars made the downriver trip by barge or keelboat hazardous, and the return trip upriver was slow, more than three months from New Orleans to Cincinnati. Frequently rivermen simply abandoned their flatboats in New Orleans and traveled home overland, on foot or horseback, by the long and dangerous Natchez Trace, an old Indian trail that linked Natchez with Nashville, Tennessee. Nevertheless, river traffic increased yearly, and the control of New Orleans became a key concern of western farmers and merchants. If New Orleans refused to accept American goods, Cincinnati merchants and many thousands of trans-Appalachian farmers would be ruined.

Atlantic Ports: From Charleston to Boston

Although only 3 percent of the nation's population lived in cities, the Atlantic ports continued, as in the colonial era, to dominate the nation economically and politically. Seaports benefited from the advantage of waterborne trade and communication over much slower land travel. Merchants in the seaboard cities found it easier to cross the Atlantic than to venture into their own backcountry in search of trade. In 1800 the nation's most important urban centers were all Atlantic seaports: Charleston (which had a population of 20,000), Baltimore (26,000), Philadelphia (70,000), New York (60,000), and Boston (25,000). Each had a distinctive regional identity.

Charleston, South Carolina, was the South's premier port. In colonial days, Charleston had grown rich on its links with the British West Indies and on trade with England in rice, long-staple cotton, and indigo. The social center for the great low-country plantation owners, Charleston was a multicultural city of white people, African Americans (2,000 of them free), Indian people, and the mixed race offspring of the three groups. One was as likely to hear French, Spanish, or Gullah and Geeche (African-based dialects of low-country slaves) as English. This graceful, elegant city was a center for the slave trade until 1808.

Baltimore was the major port for the tobacco of the Chesapeake Bay region and thus was connected with the slave-owning aristocracy of the Upper South. But proximity to the wheat-growing regions of the Pennsylvania backcountry increasingly inclined the city's merchants to look westward and to consider ways to tap the trade of the burgeoning Ohio country.

Philadelphia, William Penn's "City of Brotherly Love," was distinguished by the commercial and banking skills of Quaker merchants. These merchants had built international trade networks for shipping the farm produce of Pennsylvania's German farmers. Philadelphia served as the nation's capital in the 1790s and was acknowledged as its cultural and intellectual leader as well.

New York, still faintly Dutch in architecture and social customs, was soon to outgrow all the other cities. New York merchants were exceptionally aggressive in their pursuit of trade. Unlike their counterparts in Philadelphia and Boston, New Yorkers accepted the British auction system, which cut out the middleman and offered goods in large lots at wholesale prices at open auctions. Increasingly, British imports entered America through the port of New York. New York's shipping, banking, insurance, and supporting industries boomed, and as early as 1800 a quarter of all American shipping was owned by New York merchants.

Boston, the cockpit of the American Revolution, was also the capital of Massachusetts. The handsome State House, built on Beacon Hill, reflected the origins of Boston's merchant wealth: a carved wooden codfish occupied a place of honor in the new building. By the late eighteenth century, however, Boston's commercial wealth had diversified into shipbuilding and shipping, banking and insurance.

Though small in population, these Atlantic cities led the nation socially, politically, and above all economically. In 1800, the merchants in these seaports still primarily looked across the Atlantic to Europe. In the coming half-century, however, it was the cities that developed the strongest ties with the trans-Appalachian West that were to thrive.

A NATIONAL ECONOMY

In 1800, the United States was a producer of raw materials. The new nation faced the same challenge that developing nations confront today. At the mercy of fluctuating world commodity prices they cannot control, such countries have great difficulty protecting themselves from economic dominance by stronger, more established nations. In 1800, America was in just such a situation.

The Economy of the Young Republic

In 1800 the United States was predominantly rural and agricultural. According to the census of 1800, 94 in 100 Americans lived in communities of fewer than 2,500 people, and 4 in 5 families farmed the land, either for themselves or for others. Farming families followed centuries-old traditions of working with hand tools and draft animals, producing most of their own food and fiber, and most Americans dressed in cloth that had been spun, woven, and tailored by women in their own families. Seaboard farmers of the Middle States and those near urban centers engaged in commercial farming, but for most, crops were grown for home use rather than for sale. Production of a "surplus" to sell was a small sideline. Commodities such as whiskey and hogs (both easy to transport) provided small and irregular cash incomes or items for barter. As late as 1820, only 20 percent of the produce of American farms was consumed outside the local community.

In contrast to this pattern, the plantation agriculture of the South was wholly commercial and international. Slave owners, however, faced a growing dilemma: their heavy capital investment in African American slave labor was not matched by a growth in the demand for tobacco and rice, the traditional export crops. The tobacco trade, which accounted for about a third of the value of all colonial exports, remained at or below pre-Revolutionary levels, and the demand for rice had actually declined.

The demand for a third crop, cotton, was growing rapidly in response to the boom in the industrial production of textiles in England and Europe, but extracting the seeds from the fibers of the variety of cotton that grew best in the southern interior required an enormous investment of labor. The cotton gin, which mechanized this process, was invented in 1793, but not until the nineteenth century did cotton assume a commanding place in the foreign trade of the United States.

In 1790, increasing foreign demand for American goods and services hardly seemed likely. Trade with Britain, still the biggest customer for American raw materials, was considerably less than it had been before the Revolution. As an independent nation, the United States no longer benefited from British mercantilist trade privileges. Britain and France both excluded Americans from their lucrative West Indian trade and taxed American ships with discriminatory duties. It was difficult to be independent in a world dominated by great powers.

Shipping and the Economic Boom

Despite these restrictions on American commerce, the strong shipping trade begun during the colonial era and centered in the Atlantic ports became a major asset in the 1790s, when events in Europe provided America with extraordinary opportunities.

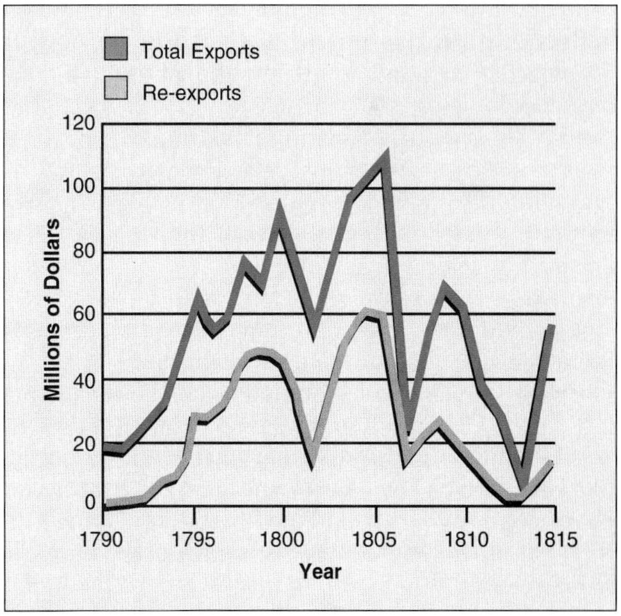

American Export Trade, 1790–1815 *This graph shows how completely the American shipping boom was tied to European events. Exports, half of which were reexports, surged when Britain and France were at war and America could take advantage of its status as neutral. Exports slumped in the brief period of European peace in 1803–1805 and plunged following the Embargo Act of 1807 and the outbreak of the War of 1812.*

Source: Douglass C. North, *The Economic Growth of the United States, 1790–1860* (New York: Norton, 1966), p. 26.

George Ropes. *Launching of the Ship* Fame, 1802. Oil on canvas. Accession no.108,332. Photograph by Mark Sexton. James Duncan Phillips Library, Peabody Essex Museum, Salem, Mass.

This picture shows the launching of the ship Fame *from Becket's Shipyard in Essex, Massachusetts, in 1802. Shipbuilding was a major* New England *industry, and a launching was a community event.*

The long series of European wars also allowed enterprising Americans to seize such lucrative international opportunities as the China trade. In 1784 the *Empress of China* set sail from New York for Canton with forty tons of ginseng. When it returned in 1785 with a cargo of teas, silks, and chinaware, the sponsors of the voyage, Philadelphia financier Robert Morris and his partners, made a 30 percent profit. Other merchants were quick to follow Morris's example, and to improve on it. In 1787 Robert Gray left Boston in the *Columbia,* sailing south around Cape Horn, then north to Nootka Sound in the Pacific Northwest, where he bought sea otter skins cheaply from the coastal Indians. Then, in 1789, Gray sailed west across the Pacific to China, where he sold the furs at fabulous profits before rounding the Cape of Good Hope and returning to Boston laden with tea. In his second voyage in 1792, Gray discovered the mouth of a major Northwest river, which he named for his ship. (When Lewis and Clark ventured west in 1804, part of their task was to chart the exact path of Gray's "Columbia's River.") Soon New England so dominated the seaborne trade in furs to China that the Pacific Northwest Indians called all Americans "Bostons."

The French Revolution, which began in 1789, soon initiated nearly twenty-five years of warfare between Britain and France. As the European powers converted their ships from international trade to military purposes, American vessels were ready to replace them. All along the Atlantic seaboard, urban centers thrived as American ships carried European goods that could no longer be transported on British ships without danger of French attack (and vice versa). Because America was neutral, its merchants had the legal right to import European goods and promptly reexport them to other European countries. In spite of British and French efforts to prevent the practice (see Chapter 8), reexports amounted to half of the profits in the booming shipping trade.

The vigorous international shipping trade had dramatic effects within the United States. The coastal cities all grew substantially from 1790 to1820. In 1790, only twelve cities in the United States held more than 5,000 people and only 3 percent of the population was urban; by 1820 city dwellers made up 7 percent of the population and thirty-five cities had a population exceeding 5,000. This rapid urbanization was a sign of vigorous economic growth (rather than a sign that poverty was pushing rural workers off the farms, as occurs in some third world countries today), for it reflected expanding opportunities in the cities. In fact, the rapid growth of cities stimulated farmers to produce the food to feed the new urban dwellers.

The active American participation in international trade fostered a strong and diversified shipbuilding industry. All the major Atlantic ports boasted expanding shipbuilding enterprises. The average size of full-rigged ships built in one shipyard in Portsmouth, New Hampshire, increased from 361 tons in 1825 to 2,145 tons in 1855. Demands for speed increased as well, resulting in what many people have regarded as the flower of American shipbuilding, the clipper ship. The narrow-hulled, many-sailed clipper ships of the 1840s and 1850s set records for ships of their size. In 1854, *Flying Cloud,* built in the Boston shipyards of Donald McKay, sailed from New York to San Francisco—a 16,000-mile trip that usually took 150 to 200 days—in a mere 89 days. The clipper ships' average of 300 miles a day made them competitive with steamships through the 1850s.

In every seaport, this booming trade stimulated the development of financial services, such as insurance companies, banks, and brokers, geared more to international than to local concerns. By 1820, the United States was well on its way to building a strong and diversified national economy. At the same time, the wealth, confidence, and power of the merchants in the seacoast cities greatly increased.

THE JEFFERSON PRESIDENCY

Thomas Jefferson began his presidency with a symbolic action worthy of a twentieth-century media-wise politician. At noon on March 4, 1801, he walked from his

modest boardinghouse through the swampy streets of the new federal city of Washington to the unfinished Capitol. George Washington and John Adams had ridden in elaborate carriages to their inaugurals. Jefferson, although accepting a military honor guard, demonstrated by his actions that he rejected the elaborate, quasi-monarchical style of the two Federalist presidents, and their (to his mind) autocratic style of government as well.

For all its lack of pretension, Jefferson's inauguration as the third president of the United States was a momentous occasion in American history, for it marked the peaceful transition from one political party, the Federalists, to their hated rivals, the Democratic Republicans. Beginning in an atmosphere of exceptional political bitterness, Jefferson's presidency was to demonstrate that a strongly led party system could shape national policy without leading either to dictatorship or to revolt. It was a great achievement.

Republican Agrarianism

Jefferson brought to the presidency a clearly defined political philosophy. Behind all the events of his administration (1801–09) and those of his successors in what became known as the Virginia Dynasty (James Madison, 1809–17; James Monroe, 1817–25) was a clear set of beliefs that embodied Jefferson's interpretation of the meaning of republicanism for Americans.

Jefferson's years as ambassador to France in the 1780s were particularly important in shaping his political thinking. Recoiling from the extremes of wealth and poverty he saw there, he came to believe that it was impossible for Europe to achieve a just society that could guarantee to most of its members the "life, liberty and...pursuit of happiness" of which he had written in the Declaration of Independence.

Tall, ungainly, and diffident in manner, Thomas Jefferson was nonetheless a man of genius. Jefferson designed and supervised every aspect of the building and furnishing of Monticello, his classical home atop a hill near Charlottesville, Virginia. The process took almost forty years (from 1770 to 1809), for Jefferson constantly changed and refined his design, subjecting both himself and his family to years of uncomfortable living in the partially completed structure. The result, however, was one of the most civilized—and most autobiographical— houses ever built.

The growth of the factory system in England horrified Jefferson, who deplored the squalor of teeming new factory towns such as Manchester in the north of England. He opposed industrialization in America: in the 1790s, when Alexander Hamilton and the Federalists had proposed fostering manufacturing in the United States, Jefferson had responded with outrage (see Chapter 8). He was convinced that the Federalist program would create precisely the same extremes of wealth and the same sort of unjust government that prevailed in Europe.

Jefferson believed that only America provided fertile earth for the true citizenship necessary to a republican form of government. What America had, and Europe lacked, was room to grow. Jefferson envisaged a nation of small family farms clustered together in rural communities—an agrarian republic. He believed that only a nation of roughly equal yeoman farmers, each secure in his own possessions and not dependent on someone else for his livelihood, would exhibit the concern for the community good that was essential in a republic. More romantically, Jefferson also believed that rural contact with the cycles and rhythms of nature was essential to the republican character. Indeed, Jefferson said that "those who labor in the earth are the chosen people of God," and so he viewed himself, though his "farm" was the large slave-owning plantation of Monticello.

Yet another European event influenced Jefferson's thinking. In 1798, the Englishman Thomas Malthus published a deeply pessimistic and widely influential *Essay on the Principle of Population.* Warning of an impending population explosion, Malthus predicted that the British population would soon outstrip the country's food supply. Unless this population growth was checked, misery and poverty would soon be widespread throughout Europe and even, Malthus warned, in America. Malthus's prediction alarmed many Americans, who had taken pride in having one of the fastest rates of population growth in the world, close to 40 percent per decade. Thomas Jefferson was not worried. He used Malthus to underline the opportunity created by America's vast land resources. The Malthusian prediction need not trouble the United States, Jefferson said, as long as the country kept expanding.

Jefferson's vision of an expanding agrarian republic remains to this day one of our most compelling ideas about America's uniqueness and special destiny. But expansionism contained some negative aspects. The lure of the western lands fostered constant mobility and dissatisfaction rather than the stable, settled communities of yeoman farmers that Jefferson envisaged. Expansionism caused environmental damage, in particular soil exhaustion—a consequence of abandoning old lands, rather than conserving them, and moving on to new ones. Finally, expansionism bred a ruthlessness toward Indian peoples, who were pushed out of the way for white settlement or who, like the Mandans, were devastated by the diseases that accompanied European trade and contact. Jefferson's agrarianism thus bred some of the best and some of the worst traits of the developing nation.

Jefferson's Government

Thomas Jefferson came to office determined to reverse the Federalist policies of the 1790s and to ensure an agrarian "republic of virtue." Accordingly, he proposed a program of "simplicity and frugality," promising to cut all internal taxes, reduce the size of the army (from 4,000 to 2,500 men), navy (from twenty-five ships to seven), and government staff, and to eliminate the entire national debt inherited from the Federalists. He kept all of these promises, even the last, although the Louisiana Purchase of 1803 cost the Treasury $15 million. This diminishment of government was a key matter of republican principle to Jefferson. If his ideal yeoman farmer was to be a truly self-governing citizen, the federal government must not, Jefferson believed, be either large or powerful. His cost-cutting measures simply carried out the pledge he had made in his Inaugural Address for "a wise

Thomas Jefferson based his republican agrarianism on the real lives of prosperous and independent farmers like this one, shown plowing his fields near Salem, North Carolina in 1787.

Ludwig Goettfried von Redeken. A *View of Salem in North Carolina,* 1787. Collection of the Wachovia Historical Society.

and frugal government, which shall restrain men from injuring one another, [and] shall leave them otherwise free to regulate their own pursuits."

Perhaps one reason for Jefferson's success was that the federal government he headed was small and unimportant by today's standards. For instance, Jefferson found only 130 federal officials in Washington (a grand total of nine in the State Department, including the secretary of state). The national government's main service to ordinary people was mail delivery, and already in 1800 there were persistent complaints about slowness, unreliability, and expense in the Postal Service! Everything else—law and order, education, welfare, road maintenance, economic control—rested with state or local governments. Power and political loyalty were still local, not national.

This small national government also explains why for years the nation's capital was so unimpressive. The French designer Pierre L'Enfant had laid out a magnificent plan of broad streets and sweeping vistas reminiscent of Paris. Congress planned to pay for the grand buildings with money from land sales in the new city, but few people besides politicians and boardinghouse keepers (a largely female occupation) chose to live in Washington. Construction lagged: the President's House lacked a staircase to the second floor until 1808, and although the House and Senate chambers were soon completed, the central portion of the Capitol was missing. Instead of the imposing dome we know so well today, the early Capitol consisted of two white marble boxes connected by a boardwalk. It is a telling indicator of the true location of national power that a people who had no trouble building new local communities across the continent should have had such difficulty establishing their federal city.

An Independent Judiciary

Although determined to reverse Federalist fiscal policies, Jefferson was much more moderate concerning Federalist officeholders. He resisted demands by other Democratic Republicans that "the board should be swept" and all Federalist officeholders replaced with party loyalists. During his term of office, Jefferson allowed 132 Federalists to remain at their posts, while placing Democratic Republicans in 158 others. This restrained use of patronage did much to attract moderate Federalists to the Democratic Republican party. Jefferson's restraint, however, did not extend to the most notorious Federalist appointees, the so-called midnight judges.

In the last days of the Adams administration, the Federalist-dominated Congress passed a Judiciary Act that created sixteen new judgeships and six new circuit courts. In one of his last acts in office, President Adams appointed Federalists—quickly dubbed the "midnight judges"—to the new positions. This last-minute action angered the Democratic Republicans, who feared that the losing Federalist Party was trying to use the judiciary to increase the power of the federal government over the states. Congress, controlled by the Democratic Republicans, repealed the Judiciary Act, depriving the new judges of their jobs. One of these hapless appointees, William Marbury, sued James Madison, Jefferson's secretary of state, to recover the position he had lost. This action provoked a landmark decision from the Supreme Court, head of the federal judiciary.

At issue was a fundamental constitutional point: Was the federal judiciary an independent and final authority on questions of law, as Supreme Court decisions during the Federalist administrations of the 1790s had asserted, or did the election of a Democratic Republican administration that favored states' rights curtail the powers of federal courts as well? In his celebrated 1803 decision, *Marbury v. Madison*, Chief Justice John Marshall, himself a strong Federalist and an Adams appointee, managed to find a way to please both parties. On the one hand, Marshall proclaimed that the courts had a duty "to say what the law is," thus unequivocally defending the independence of the judiciary and the principle of judicial review. On the other hand, Marshall conceded that the Supreme Court could not force the executive branch to appoint Marbury to a position that no longer existed. At first glance, Jefferson's government appeared to have won the battle over Adams's last-minute appointees. But in the long run, Marshall established the principle that only the federal judiciary could decide what was constitutional. This was a vital step in realizing the three-way balance of power among the branches of the federal government—executive (president), legislative (Congress), judiciary (courts)—envisaged in the Constitution. Equally important, during his long tenure in office (1801–35) Chief Justice Marshall consistently led the Supreme Court in a series of decisions that favored the federal government over state governments. Under Marshall's direction, the Supreme Court became a powerful nationalizing and unifying force.

Opportunity: The Louisiana Purchase

In 1800 the United States was a new and fragile democracy in a world dominated by two contending great powers: Britain and France. This rivalry appeared to threaten both American commerce and national security.

In 1799 the young general Napoleon Bonaparte seized control of France and began a career of military conquests. Four years later, Great Britain went to war against him. Following one year of peace, Britain and France were again at war by 1803, beginning a twelve-year duel that ended only with Napoleon's defeat at the battle of Waterloo in 1815. As had his predecessors, Napoleon looked at North America as a potential battleground on which to fight the British. In 1800, in a secret treaty, France reacquired the Louisiana Territory, the vast western drainage of the Mississippi and Missouri Rivers, from Spain, which had held the region since 1763. From Louisiana, if he chose, Napoleon could launch an attack to regain Canada from the British.

When President Jefferson learned of the secret agreement in 1801, he was alarmed. He feared that French control would threaten the growing American trade on the Mississippi River and force the young nation to take military action. In fact, in 1802 the Spanish commander at New Orleans (the French had not yet taken formal control) closed the port to American shippers, thus disrupting commerce as far away as Cincinnati. As Jefferson feared, Federalists in Congress clamored for military action to reopen the port, and he himself was determined to end this threat to American commerce.

Initially, Jefferson offered to buy New Orleans and the surrounding area for $2 million (or up to $10 million, if necessary). As it happened, Napoleon was eager to sell. A French army of 30,000 men had just withdrawn from the Caribbean island of Santo Domingo (now Haiti), defeated by yellow fever and an army of former slaves led by François Toussaint L'Ouverture. In the wake of the defeat, and in need of money for European military campaigns, Napoleon offered the entire Louisiana Territory, including the crucial port of New Orleans, to the Americans for $15 million. Exceeding his instructions, special American envoy James Monroe seized the opportunity and bought the entire Louisiana Territory from Napoleon in Paris in April 1803.

Louisiana Purchase *The Louisiana Purchase of 1803, the largest peaceful acquisition of territory in United States history, more than doubled the size of the nation. The Lewis and Clark expedition (1804–1806) was the first to survey and document the natural and human richness of the area. The American sense of expansiveness and continental destiny owes more to the extraordinary opportunity provided by the Louisiana Purchase than to anything else.*

Overnight, the size of the United States more than doubled. It was the largest peaceful acquisition of territory in United States history.

At home, Jefferson suffered brief qualms. The Constitution did not authorize the president to purchase territory, and Jefferson had always rigidly insisted on a limited interpretation of executive rights. But he had also long held a sense of destiny about the West and had planned the Lewis and Clark expedition before the Louisiana Purchase was a reality. In any case, the prize was too rich to pass up. Jefferson now argued that Louisiana was vital to the nation's republican future. "By enlarging the empire of liberty," Jefferson wrote, "we...provide new sources of renovation, should its principles, at any time, degenerate, in those portions of our country which gave them birth." In other words, expansion was essential to liberty.

Congress and the general public joined Jefferson in welcoming the purchase. Of course, the support was not unanimous. Some Federalists disputed Jefferson's claim that expansion would foster liberty and predicted that it would doom the republican form of government. As Federalist Fisher Ames dramatically warned, "By adding an unmeasured world beyond [the Mississippi]...we rush like a comet into infinity."

Incorporating Louisiana

The immediate issue following the Louisiana Purchase was how to treat the French and Spanish inhabitants of the Louisiana Territory. Many people thought that the only way to deal with a population so "foreign" was to wipe out its customs and laws and impose American ones as quickly as possible. But this did not happen. The incorporation of Louisiana into the American federal system was a remarkable story of adaptation between two different communities—American and French.

In 1803, when the region that is now the state of Louisiana became American property, it had a racially and ethnically diverse population of 43,000 people, of whom only 6,000 were American. French and French-speaking people were numerically and culturally dominant, especially in the city of New Orleans. There the French community effectively challenged the initial American plan of rapidly supplanting French culture and institutions with American ones. At a public ball held in New Orleans in January 1804, for example, American and French military officers almost came to blows over whether an English country dance or a French waltz would be played first.

Officials in Washington dismissed the reported conflict as mere frivolity, but the U.S. representative in New Orleans and governor of Lower Louisiana Territory, William Claiborne, did not. Over the next four years Claiborne came to accept the value of French institutions to the region. As a result, with Claiborne's full support, Louisiana adopted a legal code in 1808 that was based on French civil law rather than English common law. This was not a small concession. French law differed from English law in many fundamental respects, such as family property (communal versus male ownership), inheritance (forced heirship versus free disposal), and even contracts, which were much more strictly regulated in the French system. Remnants of the French legal system remain part of Louisiana state law to this day. In 1812, with the required 60,000 free inhabitants, Louisiana was admitted to the Union. New Orleans remained for years a distinctively French city, illustrating the flexibility possible under a federal system.

Texas and the Struggle for Mexican Independence

Spain objected, in vain, to Napoleon's 1803 sale of Louisiana to America. For years Spain had attempted to seal off its rich colony of Mexico from commerce with other nations. Now, American Louisiana shared one vague and disputed boundary with Mexico's northern province of Texas (a parcel of land already coveted by some Americans) and, on the east, a similarly uncertain boundary with Spanish Florida.

Soon Napoleon brought turmoil to all of Mexico. In 1808, he installed his brother Joseph Bonaparte as king of Spain, forcing Spain's king, Charles IV, to renounce his throne. For the next six years, as warfare convulsed Spain, the country's long-prized New World empire slipped away. Mexico, divided between royalists loyal to Spain and populists seeking social and economic justice for mestizos and Indians, edged bloodily toward independence. Two populist revolts—one in 1810 led by Father Miguel Hidalgo and the other in 1813 led by Father José María Morelos—were suppressed by the royalists, who executed both revolutionary leaders. In 1812 a small force, led by Mexican republican Bernardo Gutiérrez but composed mostly of American adventurers, invaded Texas, capturing San Antonio, assassinating the provincial governor Manuel Salcedo, and declaring Texas independent. A year later, however, the Mexican republicans were defeated by a royalist army that then killed suspected collaborators and pillaged the province so thoroughly that the local economy was devastated and the Mexican population declined to fewer than 2,000. Mexico's difficult path toward independence seemed, at least to some Americans, to offer yet another opportunity for expansion.

RENEWED IMPERIAL RIVALRY IN NORTH AMERICA

Fresh from the triumph of the Louisiana Purchase, Jefferson scored a major victory over the Federalist Charles Cotesworth Pinckney in the presidential election of 1804, garnering 162 electoral votes to Pinckney's 14. Jefferson's shrewd wooing of moderate Federalists had been so successful that the remaining Federalists dwindled to a highly principled but sectional group unable to attract voters outside of its home base in New England. Jefferson's Louisiana success was not repeated, however, and few other consequences of the ongoing struggle between Britain and France were so easy to solve. Their rivalry caused problems for America both on the high seas and on the nation's western borders.

Problems with Neutral Rights

In his first Inaugural Address in 1801, Jefferson had announced a foreign policy of "peace, commerce, and honest friendship with all nations, entangling alliances with none." This was a difficult policy to pursue after 1803, when the Napoleonic Wars resumed. By 1805 Napoleon had conquered most of Europe, but Britain, the victor at the great naval battle of Trafalgar, controlled the seas. The United States, trying to profit from trade with both countries, was caught in the middle. The British did not look kindly as their former colonists tried to evade their blockade of the French by claiming neutrality. Beginning in 1805, the British targeted the American reexport trade between the French West Indies and France by seizing American ships bringing French West Indian goods to Europe. Angry Americans viewed these seizures as violations of their neutral rights as shippers.

An even more contentious issue arose from the substantial desertion rate of British sailors. Many deserters promptly signed up on American ships, where they drew better pay and sometimes obtained false naturalization papers as well. The numbers involved were large: as many as a quarter of the 100,000 seamen on American ships were British. Soon the British were stopping American merchant vessels and removing any man they believed to be British, regardless of his papers. The British refusal to recognize genuine naturalization papers (on the principle "once a British subject, always a British subject") was particularly insulting to the new American sense of nationhood.

At least 6,000 innocent American citizens suffered forced impressment into the British navy from 1803 to 1812. In 1807 impressment turned bloody when the British ship *Leopard* stopped the American ship *Chesapeake* in American territorial waters and demanded to search for deserters. When the American captain refused, the *Leopard* opened fire, killing three men, wounding eighteen, and removing four deserters (three with American naturalization papers) from the damaged ship. An indignant public protested British interference and the death of innocent sailors. Had Congress been in session and the country militarily strong, public pressure might very well have forced a declaration of war against Britain then.

The Embargo Act

Fully aware that commerce was essential to the new nation, Jefferson was determined to insist on America's right as a neutral nation to ship goods to Europe. But Britain possessed the world's largest and strongest navy, one the small American navy could not effectively challenge. Jefferson first tried diplomatic protests, then negotiations, and finally threats, all to no avail. In 1806 Congress passed the Non-Importation Act, hoping that a boycott of British goods, which had worked so well during the Revolutionary War, would be effective once again. Presumably, denied their customary American markets British manufacturers would force a change in their government's policy. They did not. The boycott was suspended late in 1806 while the Jefferson administration tried to negotiate with the British; when that effort failed, the boycott was resumed.

Finally, in desperation, Jefferson imposed the Embargo Act in December 1807. This act forbade American ships from sailing to any foreign port, thereby cutting off all exports as well as imports. The act was directed at French as well as British disregard for the neutral rights of American vessels. Its intent was to force both countries to recognize those rights by depriving them of American-shipped raw materials. Jefferson hoped especially for a speedy change of British policy, because Britain's large navy caused much more harm to American shipping than did the smaller French navy.

But the results were a disaster for American trade. The commerce of the new nation, which Jefferson himself had done so much to promote, came to a standstill. Exports fell from $108 million in 1807 to $22 million in 1808, and the nation was driven into a deep depression. There was widespread evasion of the embargo. A remarkable number of ships in the coastal trade found themselves "blown off course" to the West Indies or Canada. Other ships simply left port illegally. Smuggling flourished. Pointing out that the American navy's weakness was due largely to the deep cuts Jefferson had inflicted on it, the Federalists sprang to life with a campaign of outspoken opposition to Jefferson's policy and found a ready audience in New England, the area hardest hit by the embargo.

Madison and the Failure of "Peaceable Coercion"

In this troubled atmosphere, Thomas Jefferson despondently ended his second term, acknowledging the failure of what he called "peaceable coercion." He was followed in office by his friend and colleague, James Madison of Virginia. Although Madison defeated the Federalist candidate—again Charles Cotesworth Pinkney—by 122 electoral votes to 47, Pinckney's share of the votes was three times what it had been in 1804, a reflection of the resentment New Englanders felt to the disproportionate hardships they suffered from the Embargo Act.

John Wesley Jarvis, *Black Hawk and His Son, Whirling Thunder*, 1833. Oil on canvas. 23 × 30 in. (60.3 × 76 cm). Gilcrease Museum, Tulsa, Oklahoma

This double portrait of two Sac Indians by John Wesley Jarvis, painted in 1833, symbolized the hopes of official American Indian policy. The traditional Indian ways represented by Whirling Thunder's attire would be superseded by the "civilized" attitude represented by his father Black Hawk's European dress.

Ironically, the Embargo Act had almost no effect on its intended victims. The French used the embargo as a pretext for seizing American ships, claiming they must be British ships in disguise. The British, in the absence of American competition, developed new markets for their goods in South America. And at home, as John Randolph sarcastically remarked, the embargo was attempting "to cure corns by cutting off the toes."

In March 1809 Congress admitted failure, and the Embargo Act was repealed. But the struggle to remain neutral in the confrontation between the European giants continued. The next two years saw passage of several acts—among them the Non-Intercourse Act of 1809 and Macon's Bill Number 2 in 1810—that unsuccessfully attempted to prohibit trade with Britain and France unless they ceased their hostile treatment of U.S. shipping. Frustration with the ineffectiveness of government policy mounted.

A Contradictory Indian Policy

The United States faced other conflicts than those with Britain and France over neutral shipping rights. In the West, the powerful Indian nations of the Ohio Valley were determined to resist the wave of expansion that had carried thousands of white settlers onto their lands. North of the Ohio River lived the Northwest Confederation of the Shawnees, Delawares, Miamis, Potawatomis, and several smaller tribes. To the south of the Ohio were the so-called "Five Civilized Tribes," the Cherokees, Chickasaws, Choctaws, Creeks, and (in Florida) the Seminoles.

According to the Indian Intercourse Act of 1790, the United States could not simply seize Indian land; it could only acquire it when the Indians ceded it by treaty. But this policy conflicted with the harsh reality of westward expansion. Commonly, settlers pushed ahead of treaty boundaries. When Indian peoples resisted the invasion of their lands, the pioneers fought back and called for military protection. Defeat of an Indian people led to further land cessions. The result for the Indians was a relentless cycle of invasion, resistance, and defeat.

Thomas Jefferson was deeply concerned with the fate of the western Indian peoples. Unlike most of the pioneers, who saw them simply as dangerous obstacles to be removed, Jefferson believed in coexistence and acculturation. His Indian policy was designed to solve the fundamental dilemma of expansion—the conflicting needs of white and Indian peoples. The Indians would cede the lands the pioneers craved, and in return white people would teach them how to farm and live like whites on their new, compressed reservations. Convinced that Indians had to give up hunting in favor of the yeoman-farmer lifestyle he so favored for all Americans, Jefferson directed the governors of the Northwest Territories to "promote energetically" his vision for civilizing the Indians.

Although he himself was notoriously indifferent to organized religion, Jefferson strongly supported efforts to Christianize Indian peoples and educate them in white ways. A number of denominations, among them the Moravians, Quakers, and Baptists, sent missionaries to the western Indians. Others formed special missionary societies, such as the Society for Propagating the Gospel among Indians (1797) and the American Board of Commissioners for Foreign

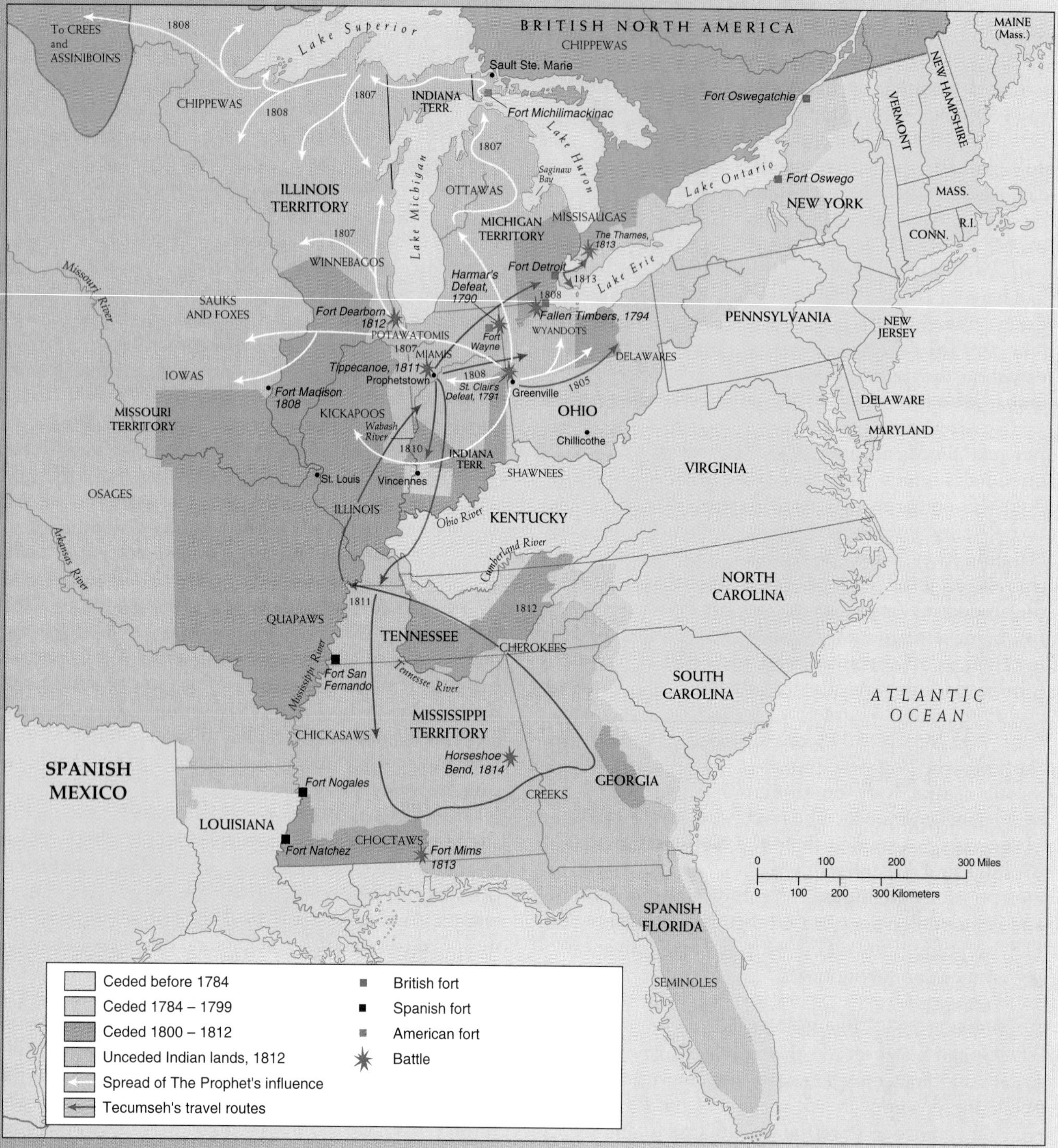

Missions (1810). The latter was a joint effort of the Congregationalist, Presbyterian, and Dutch Reformed churches. Jefferson's Indian civilization plan was never adequately funded by Congress or supported by territorial governors and settlers. Although missionaries promoted literacy and a knowledge of white ways, they were generally disdainful of Indian culture and created deep divisions within Indian tribes between those who converted to Christianity and those who actively resisted conversion and were unwilling to give up traditional ways, especially hunting. Thus missionary efforts unwittingly weakened tribes already disoriented by the loss of their lands and life ways.

After the Louisiana Purchase, Jefferson offered traditionalist Indian groups new lands west of the Mississippi River, claiming that they would be able to live there undisturbed by white settlers for centuries. But he failed to consider the pace of westward expan-

Tecumseh

Tenskwatawa, The Prophet

Indian Resistance, 1790–1816

American westward expansion put relentless pressure on the Indian nations in the Trans-Appalachian South and West. The Trans-Appalachian region was marked by constant warfare from the time of the earliest settlements in Kentucky in the 1780s to the War of 1812. Tecumseh's Alliance in the Northwest (1809–11) and the Creek Rebellion in the Southwest (1813–14) were the culminating struggles in Indian resistance to the American invasion of the Trans-Appalachian region. Tecumseh, a Shawnee military leader, and his brother Tenskwatawa, a religious leader called The Prophet, led a pan-Indian revitalization and resistance movement that posed a serious threat to American westward expansion. As the map shows, Tenskwatawa's message had wide appeal in the Northwest. Tecumseh traveled widely, attempting to build a military alliance on his brother's spiritual message. He achieved considerable success in the Northwest, but less in the Southwest, where many Indian peoples put their faith in accommodation. Tecumseh's death at the Battle of the Thames (1813) and British abandonment of their Shawnee allies at the end of the War of 1812 brought an end to organized Indian resistance in the Old Northwest. In the South, Andrew Jackson crushed Creek resisters in the Battle of Horseshoe Bend in 1814, and then demanded the cession of 23 million acres of land from both hostile and friendly Creek peoples.

sion. Less than twenty years later, Missouri, the first trans-Mississippi state, was admitted to the Union. The Indians living in Missouri, some of whom had been removed from the Old Northwest in accord with Jefferson's plan, were forced to move again to lands farther west. Western Indians like the Mandans, who had seemed so remote when Lewis and Clark wintered with them in 1804–05, were now threatened by further westward expansion.

In fact, Jefferson's Indian policy, because it did nothing to slow down the ever-accelerating westward expansion, offered little hope to Indian peoples. The alternatives they faced were stark: acculturation, removal, or extinction. Deprived of hunting lands, decimated by disease, increasingly dependent on the white economy for trade goods and annuity payments in exchange for land cessions, many Indian peoples despaired. Like the Mandans after Lewis and Clark's visit, they came to dread the effects of white contact. Nearly every tribe found itself bitterly split between accommodationists and traditionalists. Some, like groups of Cherokees and associated tribes in the South, advocated adapting their traditional agricultural lifestyles and pursuing a pattern of peaceful accommodation. In the Northwest Territory, however, many Indians chose the path of armed resistance.

Indian Resistance

The Shawnees, a seminomadic hunting and farming tribe (the men hunted, the women farmed) of the Ohio Valley, had resisted white settlement in Kentucky and Ohio since the 1750s. The decisive defeat of the Indian Confederacy led by Little Turtle, a Miami Indian, at Fallen Timbers (1794) and the continuing pressure of American settlement, however, left the Shawnees divided. One group, led by Black Hoof, accepted acculturation. Soon Quaker and Moravian missionaries were converting Black Hoof's band and teaching them farming. The rest of the tribe tried to maintain traditional ways. Most broke into small bands and tried to eke out a living by hunting, but their numbers were reduced by disease and the survivors further demoralized by the alcohol offered them illegally by private traders. One group of traditional Shawnees, however, led by the warrior Tecumseh, sought refuge farther west.

But there was no escape from white encroachment. Between 1801 and 1809, William Henry Harrison, governor of Indiana Territory, concluded fifteen treaties with the Delawares, Potawatomis, Miamis, and other tribes. These treaties opened eastern Michigan, southern Indiana, and most of Illinois to white settlement and forced the Indians into ever-smaller reservations. Many of these treaties were obtained by coercion, bribery, and outright trickery, and most Indians did not accept them.

In 1805 Tecumseh's brother, Tenskwatawa, known as The Prophet, began preaching a message of Indian revitalization: a rejection of all contact with the Americans, including use of American alcohol, clothing, and trade goods, and a return to traditional practices of hunting and farming. He preached an end to quarreling, violence, and sexual promiscuity and to the accumulation of private property. Wealth was valuable only if it was given away, he said. If the Northwest Indians returned to traditional ways, Tenskwatawa promised, "the land will be overturned so that all the white people will be covered and you alone shall inhabit the land."

This was a powerful message, but it was not new. Just six years earlier, Handsome Lake had led the Seneca people of upstate New York in a similar revitalization movement. Tecumseh, however, succeeded in molding his brother's religious following into a powerful pan-Indian military resistance movement. With each new treaty that Harrison concluded, Tecumseh gained new followers among the Northwest Confederation tribes. Significantly, he also had the support of the British, who, after 1807, began sending food and guns to him from Canada.

The pan-Indian strategy was at first primarily defensive, aimed at preventing further westward expansion. But the Treaty of Fort Wayne in 1809, in which the United States gained 3 million acres of Delaware and Potawatomi land in Indiana, led to active resistance. Confronting Harrison directly, Tecumseh argued that the land belonged to the larger community of all the Indian peoples; no one tribe could give away the common property of all. He then warned that any surveyors or settlers who ventured into the 3 million acres would risk their lives.

Tecumseh took his message of common land ownership and military resistance to all the Indian peoples of the Northwest Confederacy. He was not uniformly successful, even among the Shawnees. Black Hoof, for example, refused to join. Tecumseh also recruited, with mixed success, among the tribes south of the Ohio River. In councils with Choctaws, Chickasaws, Creeks, and Cherokees, he promoted active resistance:

> The white race is a wicked race. Since the days when the white race first came in contact with the red men, there has been a continual series of aggressions. The hunting grounds are fast disappearing, and they are driving the red man farther and farther to the west. Such has been the fate of the Shawnees, and surely will be the fate of all tribes if the power of the whites is not forever crushed. The mere presence of the white man is a source of evil to the red men. His whiskey destroys the bravery of our warriors, and his lust corrupts the virtue of our women. The only hope for the red man is a war of extermination against the paleface.

In November 1811, while Tecumseh was still recruiting among the southern tribes, Harrison marched to the pan-Indian village of Tippecanoe with 1,000 soldiers. The 600 to 700 Indian warriors at the town, urged on by Tenskwatawa, attacked Harrison's forces before dawn on November 7, hoping to surprise them. The attack failed, and in the battle that followed the Americans inflicted about 150 Indian casualties, while sustaining about as many themselves. Although Harrison claimed victory, the truth was far different. Dispersed from Tippecanoe, Tecumseh's angry followers fell on American settlements in Indiana and southern Michigan, killing many pioneers and forcing the rest to flee to fortified towns. Tecumseh himself entered into a formal alliance with the British. For western settlers, the Indian threat was greater than ever.

THE WAR OF 1812

Many westerners blamed the British for Tecumseh's attacks on pioneer settlements in the Northwest. British support of western Indians and the long-standing difficulties over neutral shipping rights were the two grievances cited by President Madison when he asked Congress for a declaration of war against Britain on June 1, 1812; Congress obliged him on June 18. But the war had other, more general causes as well.

The War Hawks

A rising young generation of political leaders, first elected to Congress in 1810, strongly resented the continuing influence of Britain, the former mother country, on American affairs. These War Hawks, who included such future leaders as Henry Clay of Kentucky and John C. Calhoun of South Carolina, were young Democratic Republicans from the West and South. They found all aspects of British interference, such as impressment and support for western Indians, intolerable. Eager to assert independence from England once and for all, these young men saw themselves finishing the job begun by the aging revolutionary generation.

The War Hawks were vehemently expansionist, and their dreams of expansion entailed control of peoples of other races—resistant Indians and rebellious African Americans—at the edges of the national boundaries. Southerners wanted to occupy Florida to prevent runaway slaves from seeking refuge with the Seminole Indians. Westerners wanted to invade Canada, hoping thereby to end threats from British-backed Indians in the Northwest such as Tecumseh. As resentments against England and frustrations over border issues merged, the pressure for war—always a strong force for national unity—mounted.

Unaware that the British, seriously hurt by the American trade embargo, were about to adopt a more conciliatory policy, President James Madison yielded to the War Hawks' clamor for action in June 1812, and his declaration of war passed the U.S. Senate by the close vote of 19 to 13, the House by 79 to 49. All the Federalists voted against the war. (The division along party lines continued in the 1812 presidential election, in which Madison garnered 128 electoral votes to 89 for his Federalist opponent, DeWitt Clinton.) The vote was sectional, with New England and the Middle States in opposition and the West and South strongly prowar. Thus the United States entered the War of 1812 more deeply divided along sectional lines than during any other foreign war in American history.

Nor was that the end of the difficulties. As a result of Jefferson's economizing, the American army and navy were small and weak. In contrast, the British,

The War of 1812 *On land, the War of 1812 was fought to define the nation's boundaries. In the North, American armies attacked British forts in the Great Lakes region with little success, and the invasion of Canada was a failure. In the South, the battle of New Orleans made a national hero of Andrew Jackson, but it occurred after the peace treaty had been signed. On the sea, with the exception of Oliver Perry's victory in the Great Lakes, Britain's dominance was so complete and its blockade so effective that British troops were able to invade the Chesapeake and burn the capital of the United States.*

after almost ten years' entanglement in the Napoleonic Wars, were in fighting trim. As a result, although the War of 1812 brought Americans a few moments of glory, it was on the whole an ignominious struggle that gained them little.

The Campaign against Canada

The American goal of expansion fared badly. Americans envisaged a quick victory over sparsely populated British Canada that would destroy British support for Tecumseh and his Northwest Indian allies, but instead the British-Indian alliance defeated them. In July 1812, a foray into western Canada by General William Hull of Michigan Territory was repulsed by a joint British and Indian force, which went on, in August, to capture Detroit, Fort Dearborn (site of Chicago), and Hull's army of 2,000 men. The American burning of York (now Toronto) in April 1813 achieved little, but in September, at the battle of Put-in-Bay, Captain Oliver H. Perry defeated a British naval squadron on Lake Erie, sending out the famous message, "We have met the enemy and they are ours." Without control of Lake Erie, the British could no longer assure their hold on Detroit. In October, William Henry Harrison retook Detroit and followed its retreating British and Indian defenders. Assisted by naval forces commanded by Perry, Harrison defeated them in the battle of the Thames. Among those slain in the battle was Tecumseh. Later attempts by the United States to invade Canada in the Niagara area failed, but so too did British attempts to invade the United States in the same area.

One reason for the failure of the Canadian invasion, aside from failure to appreciate the strength of the British-Indian forces, was that the New England states actively opposed the war. Massachusetts, Rhode Island, and Connecticut refused to provide militia or supplies, and other New England governors turned a blind eye to the flourishing illegal trade across the U.S.–Canadian border. Another reason was the reaction of Canadians themselves, the majority of whom were former Americans. Ironically, the most decisive effect of the abortive American attacks was the formation of a Canadian sense of national identity and a determination never to be invaded or absorbed by the United States.

War in the South

In the South, warfare similar to that waged against Tecumseh's pan-Indian resistance movement in the Northwest dramatically affected the southern Indian peoples. The first of the southern Indian peoples to battle the Americans were the Creeks, a trading nation with a long history of contacts with the Spanish and the French. When white settlers began to occupy Indian lands in northwestern Georgia and central Alabama early in the century, the Creeks, like the Shawnees in the Northwest, were divided in their response. Although many Creek bands argued for accommodation, a group known as the Red Sticks were determined to fight. During the War of 1812 the Red Sticks, allied with the British and Spanish, fought not only the Americans but other Indian groups.

In August 1813 the Red Sticks attacked Fort Mims on the Alabama River, killing more than 500 Americans and mixed-race Creeks who had gathered there for safety. Led by Andrew Jackson, troops from the Tennessee and Kentucky militias combined with the Creeks' traditional foes—the Cherokees, Choctaws, and Chickasaws—and some opposing bands of Creeks to exact revenge. Jackson's troops matched the Creeks in ferocity, shooting the Red Sticks "like dogs," one soldier reported. At the battle of Horseshoe Bend in March 1814, the Creeks were trapped between American cannon fire and their Indian enemies: more than 800 were killed, more than in any other battle in the history of Indian-white warfare. Jackson then marched on the remaining Red Stick villages, burning and killing as he went. Cornered, one remaining Red Stick leader, Red Eagle, personally confronted Jackson:

> General Jackson, I am not afraid of you. I fear no man, for I am a Creek warrior. I have nothing to request in behalf of myself....But I come to beg you to send for the women and children of the war party, who are now starving in the woods....If I could fight you any longer I would most heartily do so. Send for the women and children. They never did you any harm. But kill me, if the white people want it done.

At the end of the Creek War in 1814 Jackson demanded huge land concessions from the Creeks (including from some Creek bands that had fought on his side): 23 million acres, or more than half the Creek domain. The Treaty of Fort Jackson (1814) confirming these land concessions earned Jackson his Indian name, Sharp Knife.

The war failed to achieve another of its initial goals, that of capturing Florida from Spain. Mobile was captured in 1813, but although Jackson captured Pensacola in 1814, he was unable to hold it. In early 1815 (after the peace treaty had been signed but before news of it arrived in America), Andrew Jackson achieved his best-known victory, an improbable win over veteran British troops in the battle of New Orleans.

The Naval War

At sea the British navy quickly established a strong blockade, harassing coastal shipping along the Atlantic seaboard and attacking coastal settlements at will. In the most humiliating attack, the British burned Washington in the summer of 1814, forcing the president and Congress to flee. Dolley Madison, the president's wife, achieved a permanent footnote in history by saving a portrait of George Washington from the White House as she fled. The indignity of the burning of Washington was somewhat assuaged in September, when Americans beat back a British attack on Baltimore and Fort McHenry. Watching the "rockets' red glare" in the battle, onlooker Francis Scott Key was moved to write the words to the "Star-Spangled Banner." There were a few American naval successes. The American frigate *Constitution* destroyed two British men-of-war, the *Guerrière* and the *Java*, in classic naval battles but failed to lift the British blockade.

The Hartford Convention

America's occasional successes failed to diminish the angry opposition of the New England Federalists to the War of 1812. In late 1814, Federalist representatives from the five New England states met in Hartford, Connecticut, to air their grievances. At first the air was full of talk of secession from the Union, but soon cooler heads prevailed.

The Hartford Convention's final document contained a long list of grievances, but it did not mention secession. It did, however, insist that a state had the right "to interpose its authority" to protect its citizens against unconstitutional federal laws. This nullification doctrine was not new; Madison and Jefferson had proposed it in the Virginia and Kentucky Resolves opposing the Alien and Sedition Acts in 1798 (see Chapter 8). In any event, the nullification threat from Hartford was ignored, for peace with Britain was announced as delegates from the convention made their way to Washington to deliver their message to Congress. There the convention's grievances were treated not as serious business but as an anticlimactic joke.

The Treaty of Ghent

In 1814, as the long Napoleonic Wars in Europe were drawing to a close, the British decided to end their minor war with the Americans. The peace treaty, after months of hard negotiation, was signed at Ghent, Belgium, on Christmas Eve in 1814. Like the war itself, the treaty was inconclusive. The major issues of impressment and neutral rights were not mentioned, but the British did agree to evacuate their western posts, and late in the negotiations they abandoned their insistence on a buffer state for neutral Indian peoples in the Northwest.

For all its international inconsequence, the war did have an important effect on national morale. As one historian has said, Americans had fought "for their chance to grow up." Andrew Jackson's victory at New Orleans allowed Americans to believe that they had defeated the British. It would be more accurate to say that by not losing the war the Americans had ended their own feelings of colonial dependency. Equally important, they convinced the British government to stop thinking of America as its colony. As it turned out, the War of 1812 was the last war the United States and Britain were to fight against each other.

At the same time, the war was a dangerous risk to new and fragile ideas of national unity. It was one of America's most divisive wars, and what made the opposition so serious was its sectional nature. Had the conflict continued, it might have led to the secession of New England.

The only clear losers of the war were the Indian nations in the Northwest and their southern allies. With the death of Tecumseh in 1813 and the defeat of the southern Creeks in 1814, the last hope of a united Indian resistance to white expansion perished forever. Britain's abandonment of its Indian allies in the Treaty of Ghent sealed their fate. By 1815, American settlers were on their way west again.

The burning of Washington by the British was the worst indignity the young American nation suffered in the War of 1812. This contemporary woodcut shows Washington aflame on August 2, 1814.

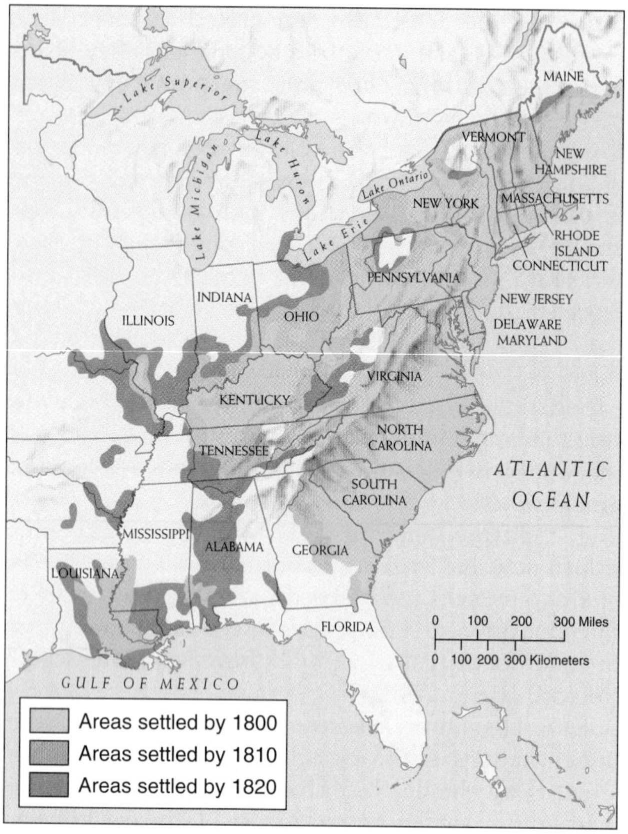

Spread of Settlement: Westward Surge, 1800–1820
Within a period of twenty years, a quarter of the nation's population had moved west of the Appalachian Mountains. The westward surge was a dynamic source of American optimism.

DEFINING THE BOUNDARIES

With the War of 1812 behind them, Americans turned, more seriously than ever before, to the tasks of expansion and national development. The so-called Era of Good Feelings (1817–23) found politicians largely in agreement on a national agenda, and a string of diplomatic achievements forged by John Quincy Adams gave the nation sharper definition. But the limits to expansion also became clear: the Panic of 1819 showed the dangers in economic growth, and the Missouri Crisis laid bare the sectional split that attended westward expansion.

Another Westward Surge

The end of the War of 1812 was followed by a westward surge to the Mississippi River that populated the Old Northwest (Ohio, Indiana, Illinois, Michigan, and Wisconsin) and the Old Southwest (western Georgia, Alabama, Mississippi, Louisiana). The extent of the population redistribution was dramatic: in 1790, 95 percent of the nation's population had lived in states bordering the Atlantic Ocean; by 1820 fully 25 percent of the population lived west of the Appalachians.

What accounted for the westward surge? There were both push and pull factors. Between 1800 and 1820, the nation's population almost doubled, increasing from 5.3 million to 9.6 million. Although many easterners were attracted to the rapidly growing seacoast cities, 2.5 million, most of them farmers, chose to go westward. Overpopulated farmland in all of the seaboard states pushed farmers off the land, while new land pulled them westward. Defeat and removal of Indians in the War of 1812 was another important pull factor. In the Southwest, the Creeks ceded a huge tract of land amounting to three-fifths of Alabama and one-fifth of Georgia in the Treaty of Fort Jackson (1814); in the Northwest, the threat to settlers posed by Tecumseh's alliance had been removed.

The most important pull factor, however, was the attractive price of western land. The Land Ordinance of 1785 priced western lands too high for all but speculators and the wealthy (see Chapter 7), but since that time realities had slowly forced Congress to

Settlement of the heavily forested Old Northwest and Old Southwest required much heavy labor to clear the land. One common laborsaving method settlers learned from Indians was to "girdle" the trees (cutting the bark all around), thereby killing them. Dead trees could be more easily chopped and burned.

enact land laws more favorable to the small farmer. The most sustained challenge came from "squatters," who repeatedly took up land before it was officially open for sale and then claimed a "preemption" right of purchase at a lower price that reflected the value of improvements made to the land. Congress sought to suppress this illegal settlement and ordered the expulsion of squatters on several occasions, but to no avail. When federal lands were officially opened for sale in Illinois in 1814, for example, there were already 13,000 settlers, forcing Congress to reverse itself and grant them all preemption rights. Finally, in the Land Act of 1820, Congress set the price of land at $1.25 an acre, the minimum purchase at eighty acres (in contrast to the 640-acre minimum in 1785), and a down payment of $100 in cash. This was the most liberal land law yet passed in American history, but the cash requirement still favored speculators, who had more cash than most small farmers.

There were four major migration routes. In upstate New York, the Mohawk and Genesee Turnpike led New England migrants to Lake Erie, where they traveled by boat to northern Ohio. In the Middle States region, the turnpike from Philadelphia to Pittsburgh led to the Ohio River, as did the National Road that began in Baltimore and led to Wheeling. In the South, the Wilderness Road through the Cumberland Gap led to Kentucky, and passes in the mountains of North and South Carolina led to Tennessee. The Federal Road skirted the southern edge of the Appalachians and allowed farmers from South Carolina and eastern Georgia to move directly into Alabama and Mississippi. In this way, geography facilitated lateral westward movement (Northerners tended to migrate to the Old Northwest, Southerners to the Old Southwest). Except in southern Ohio and parts of Kentucky and Tennessee, there was very little contact between regional cultures. New Englanders carried their values and lifestyles

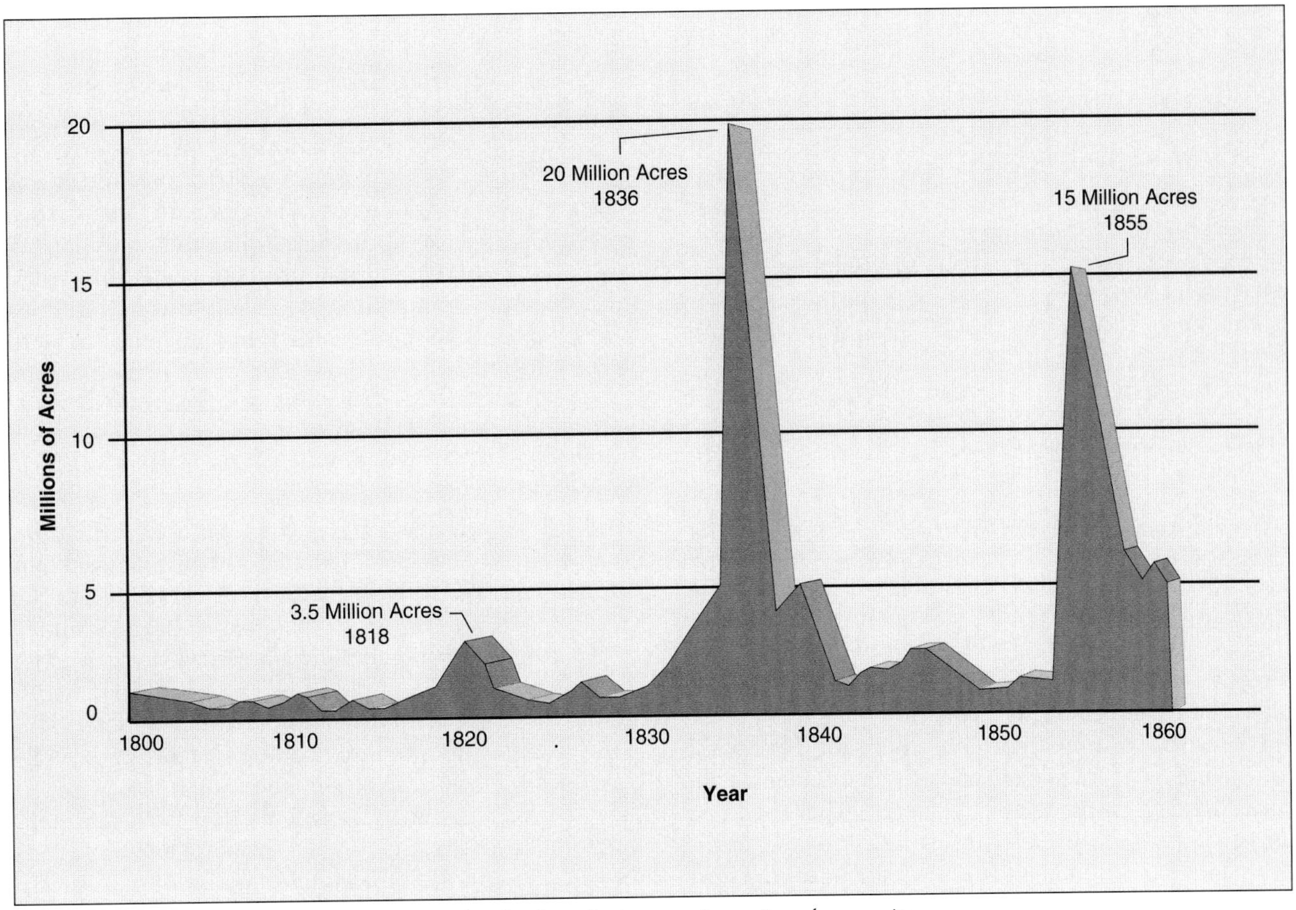

Western Land Sales *Surges in western land sales reflect surges in westward expansion. Western land sales following the War of 1812 reached an unprecedented 3.5 million acres, but that was small in comparison with what was to come in the 1830s and 1850s. Not all land sales reflected actual settlement, however, and speculation in western lands was rampant. Collapse of the postwar speculative boom contributed to the Panic of 1819, and the abrupt end to the boom of the 1830s led to the Panic of 1837.*

Source: Robert Riegel and Robert Athearn, *America Moves West* (New York: Holt, Rinehart, 1964).

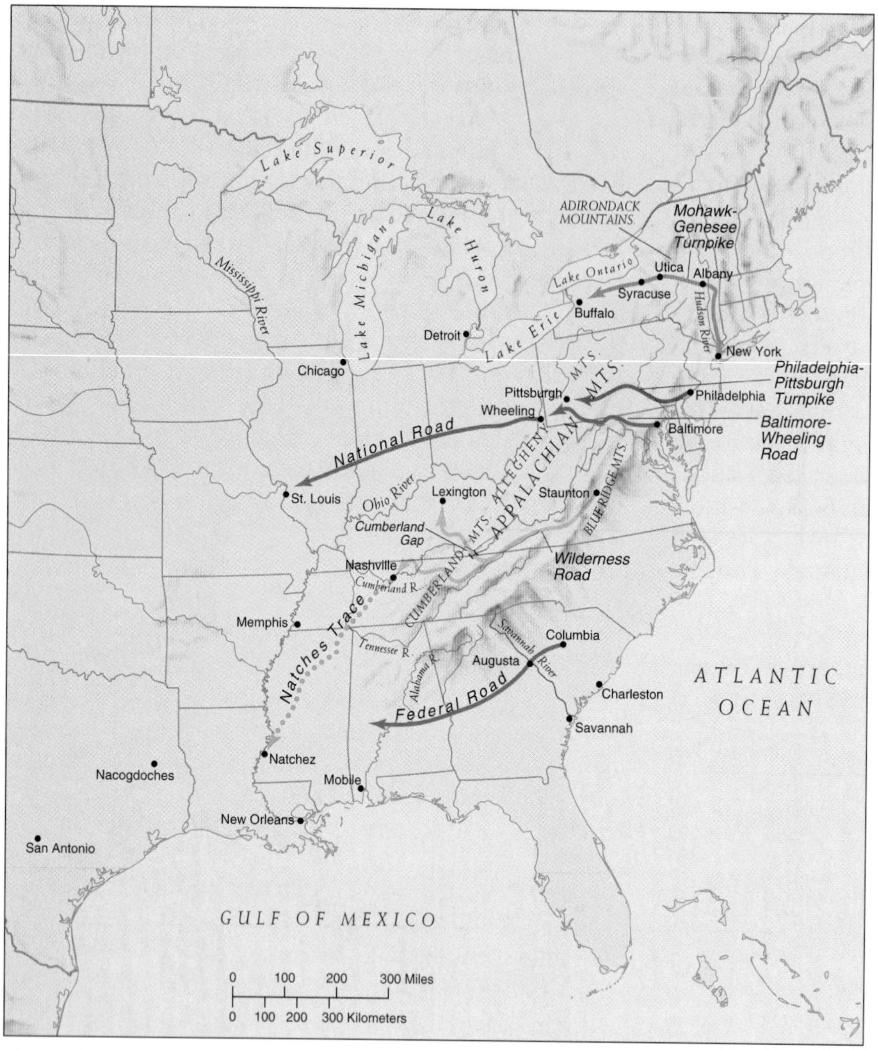

Major Migration Routes, 1800–1820 *The barrier of the Appalachian Mountains permitted only a few routes to the west. Settlers from the northern states took the Genesee Turnpike, Middle States migrants favored the Philadelphia-Pittsburgh Turnpike and the National Road, and Southerners used the Wilderness and Federal Roads. Because most westward movement was lateral, regional mixing among western settlers was rare. New Englanders carried their attitudes West, and Southerners did the same.*

Source: Donald Meinig, *The Shaping of America*, Vol. 2, *Continental America* (New Haven: Yale University Press, 1994).

directly west and settled largely with their own communities; Southerners did the same.

One section of northern Ohio along Lake Erie, for example, had been Connecticut's western land claim since the days of its colonial charter. Rather than give up the land when the Northwest Territory was established in 1787, Connecticut held onto the Western Reserve (as it was known) and encouraged its citizens to move there. Group settlement was common. General Moses Cleaveland of the Revolutionary War led one of the first groups of Yankees, fifty-two in all. In 1795 they settled the community that bears his name (though not his spelling of it). Many other groups followed, naming towns such as Norwalk after those they had left in Connecticut. These New Englanders brought to the Western Reserve their religion (Congregational), their love of learning (tiny Norwalk soon boasted a three-story academy), and their adamant opposition to slavery.

Western migration in the South was very different. Just as on other frontiers, pioneers hacked wagon roads through the wilderness, encountered resistance from Indian peoples, and cleared the land for settlements and farms. But on this frontier, the hands on the ax handle were likely to be black, the people clearing the land doing it not for themselves but to create plantations for slave owners. More than half of the migrants to the Old Southwest after 1812 were involuntary—enslaved African Americans.

Even before the war, plantation owners in the Natchez district of Mississippi had made fortunes growing cotton, which they shipped to Britain from New Orleans. After the war, as cotton growing expanded, hopeful slave owners from older parts of the South (Virginia, North and South Carolina, Georgia), flooded into the region. The movement was like a gold rush, characterized by high hopes, land speculation, and riches—for a few. Most of the settlers in the Old Southwest were small farm families living in forest clearings. Most did not own slaves, but they hoped to, for ownership of slaves was the means to wealth. Quickly, the lifestyle and values of older southern states were replicated on this new frontier.

This western transplantation of distinctive regional cultures explains why, although by 1820 western states accounted for more than a third of all states (eight out of twenty-three), the West did not form a third, unified political region. Although there were common western issues—in particular, the demand for better roads and other transportation routes—in general, communities in the Old Northwest shared New England political attitudes, whereas those in the Old Southwest shared southern attitudes.

Camp Meeting. Color lithograph by Kennedy and Lucas, after painting by A. Rider, ca. 1835, negative number 26275. Collection of the New York Historical Society, New York City.

The rural and community nature of the Second Great Awakening is captured in this illustration. The preacher exhorts the large audience, which responds with emotion. Many of the most enthusiastic converts were women, who gained a new feeling of moral and social consequence through their religious experience.

The Second Great Awakening on the Frontier

The religious movement known as the Second Great Awakening began quietly in the 1790s in New England, but by 1800 it had spread through the Protestant churches of the entire country. It was most dramatic on the frontier, where church organization was naturally weak. The great institution of western Protestantism became the camp meeting, an outdoor gathering that included many sects and might go on for days. The greatest of the early camp meetings took place at Cane Ridge, Kentucky, in 1801, when an estimated 20,000 people came together for a week of preaching and singing. This was a remarkable assembly considering that the largest town in the West at the time had fewer than 2,000 inhabitants. Preachers shouted from the stand, and in the flickering firelight of evening hundreds of people, overcome with religious enthusiasm, fell to speaking in tongues or jerking uncontrollably. "Many things transpired there," one observer wrote, "that had the same effects as miracles on infidels and unbelievers."

Organized religion became one of the most important institutions within the continuing westward migration. Camp meetings frequently provided the first occasion for the new settlers of an area to come together, and religious meetinghouses were often the first public buildings erected in a community. In the absence of resident ministers, preaching was provided by Methodist circuit riders or perhaps a Baptist farmer who heard "the call" and had himself licensed as a lay preacher. On the frontier as well as in the East, women were often in the majority among church members. They thus played an important role in an institution that was fundamental to the planting of new American communities.

The Election of 1816 and the Era of Good Feelings

In 1816 James Monroe, the last of the Virginia Dynasty, was easily elected president over his Federalist opponent, Rufus King (183 to 34 electoral votes). This was the last election in which Federalists ran a candidate. Monroe had no opponent in 1820 and was reelected nearly unanimously (231 to 1). The triumph of the Democratic Republicans over the Federalists seemed complete. But although the Democratic Republicans kept their name, they had accepted so many Federalist political principles that it was not easy to tell which party had actually triumphed.

Tall, dignified, dressed in the old-fashioned style of knee breeches and white-topped boots that Washington had worn, Monroe looked like a traditional figure. But his politics reflected changing times. Soon after his inauguration, the president made a goodwill tour of the country, the first president since Washington to do so. Reflecting the new geography of the nation, he went the farthest west any president had yet traveled to visit the frontier post of Detroit. When he visited Boston, as recently as 1815 the heart of a secession-minded Federalist region, he received an enthusiastic welcome, prompting the Federalist *Columbian Centinel* to proclaim an "Era of Good Feelings." The phrase has been applied to Monroe's presidency (1817–25) ever since.

Monroe sought a government of national unity, and he chose men from North and South, Democratic Republicans and Federalists, for his cabinet. He selected John Quincy Adams, a former Federalist, as his secretary of state, virtually assuring that Adams, like his father, would become president. To balance Adams, Monroe picked John C. Calhoun of South Carolina, a prominent War Hawk, as secretary of war. And Monroe supported the American System, a program of national economic development that became identified with Westerner Henry Clay, Speaker of the House of Representatives.

In supporting the American System, Monroe was following President Madison, who had proposed the program in his message to Congress of December 1815. Madison and Monroe broke with Jefferson's agrarianism to embrace much of the Federalist program for economic development, including the chartering of a national bank, a tax on imported goods to protect American manufacturers, and a national system of roads and canals. All three of these had first been proposed by Alexander Hamilton in the 1790s (see Chapter 8). At the time they had met with bitter Democratic Republican opposition. The support that Madison and Monroe gave to Hamilton's ideas following the War of 1812 was a crucial sign of the dynamism of the American commercial economy. Many Democratic Republicans now acknowledged that the federal government had a role to play in fostering the economic and commercial conditions in which both yeoman farmer and merchant could succeed. This active support for capitalist development explained why so many former Federalists were willing to join Monroe's party of national unity.

In 1816 Congress chartered the Second Bank of the United States for twenty years. Located in Philadelphia, the bank had a capital of $35 million, of which the government contributed $7 million. The bank was to provide large-scale financing that the smaller state banks could not handle and to create a strong national currency. Because they feared concentrated economic power, Democratic Republicans had allowed the charter of the original Bank of the United States, founded in 1791, to expire in 1811. The Democratic Republican about-face in 1816 was a sign that the strength of commercial interests had grown to rival that of farmers, whose distrust for central banks persisted.

The Tariff of 1816 was the first substantial protective tariff in American history. In 1815, British manufacturers, who had been excluded for eight years (from the Embargo Act of 1807 to the end of the War of 1812), flooded the United States market with their products. American manufacturers complained that the British were dumping goods below cost to prevent the growth of American industries. Congress responded with a tariff on imported woolens and cottons, on iron, leather, hats, paper, and sugar. The measure had southern as well as northern support, although in later years differences over the passage of higher tariffs would become one of the most persistent sources of sectional conflict.

The third item in the American System, funding for roads and canals—internal improvements, as they came to be known—was more controversial. Monroe and Madison both supported genuinely national (that is, interstate) projects such as the National Road from Cumberland, Maryland to Vandalia, Illinois. Congressmen, however, aware of the urgent need to improve transportation in general and scenting the political advantages that could accrue to them from directing funds to their districts, proposed spending federal money on local projects. Both Madison and Monroe vetoed such local proposals, believing them to be unconstitutional. Thus it was that some of the most famous projects of the day, such as the Erie Canal, which lay wholly within New York state, and the early railroads, were financed by state or private money.

The support of Madison and Monroe for measures initially identified with their political opposition was an indicator of their realism. The three aspects of the American System—bank, tariff, roads—were all parts of the basic infrastructure that the American economy needed in order to develop. Briefly, during the Era of Good Feelings, politicians agreed about the need for all three. Later, each would be a source of heated partisan argument.

The Diplomacy of John Quincy Adams

The diplomatic achievements of the Era of Good Feelings were due almost entirely to the efforts of one man, John Quincy Adams, Monroe's secretary of state. Adams set himself the task of tidying up the borders of the United States. Two accords with Britain—the Rush-Bagot Treaty of 1817 and the Convention of 1818—fixed the border between the United States and Canada at the 49th parallel and resolved conflicting U.S. and British claims to Oregon with an agreement to occupy it jointly for ten (eventually twenty) years. The American claim to Oregon (present-day British Columbia, Washington, Oregon, northern Idaho, and parts of Montana) was based on China trader Robert Gray's discovery of the Columbia River in 1792 and on the Lewis and Clark expedition of 1804–06. The British Hudson's Bay Company, however, had land-based fur-trading operations in the region, and established a major base at Fort Vancouver on the Columbia River in 1825.

Adams's major diplomatic accomplishment was the Adams-Onís or Transcontinental Treaty of 1819, in which he skillfully wrested concessions from the faltering Spanish empire. In 1818 General Andrew Jackson led an American force on a mission purportedly to end raids on the Florida border by Seminole Indians against American settlements. Exceeding his orders, Jackson invaded Florida itself, and Spain, preoccupied with revolts throughout its Latin American empire, was unable to repulse him. Jackson's success made it clear that the United States could easily snatch Florida from Spain by force. Adams convinced Spain not only to cede Florida but also to drop all previous claims it had to the Louisiana Territory and Oregon. In return, the United States relinquished claims on Texas and assumed responsibility for the $5 million in claims U.S. citizens had against Spain. Although many Westerners believed Adams should have been able to obtain Texas as well as Florida, the Transcontinental Treaty was hailed at the time as a success. It proved an important spur to American expansionism and highlighted Americans' growing confidence in foreign affairs.

That growing confidence was also apparent in Adams's culminating diplomatic success. In 1821, Mexico achieved its independence from Spain; by 1822, Argentina, Chile, and Colombia were independent as well. Adams picked his way through these remarkable changes in Latin America to the policy that bears his president's name, the Monroe Doctrine. The

United States was the first country outside Latin America to recognize the independence of Spain's former colonies. Many Americans enthusiastically supported the Latin American revolts and were proud to think that they were modeled on the American Revolution, as the Latin American liberator, Simón Bolívar, claimed.

But then the European powers (France, Austria, Russia, and Prussia) began talk of a plan to help Spain recover the lost colonies. What was the United States to do? The British, suspicious of the European powers, proposed a British-American declaration against European intervention in the hemisphere. Others might have been flattered by an approach from the British empire, but Adams would have none of it. Showing the national pride that was so characteristic of the era, Adams insisted on an independent American policy. He therefore drafted for the president the hemispheric policy that the United States has followed ever since.

On December 2, 1823, the president presented the Monroe Doctrine to Congress and the world. He called for the end of colonization of the Western Hemisphere by European nations (this was aimed as much at Russia and its Pacific coast settlements as at other European powers). Intervention by European powers in the affairs of the independent New World nations would be considered by the United States a danger to its own peace and safety. Finally, Monroe pledged that the United States would not interfere in the affairs of European countries or in the affairs of their remaining New World colonies.

All of this was a very large bark from a very small dog. In 1823, the United States lacked the military and economic force to back up its grand statement. In fact, what kept the European powers out of Latin America was British opposition to European intervention, enforced by the Royal Navy. But the Monroe Doctrine was to take on quite another aspect at the end of the century, when the United States did have the power to enforce it. The Monroe Doctrine was more immediately useful in Adams's last diplomatic achievement, the Convention of 1824, in which Russia gave up its claim to the Oregon

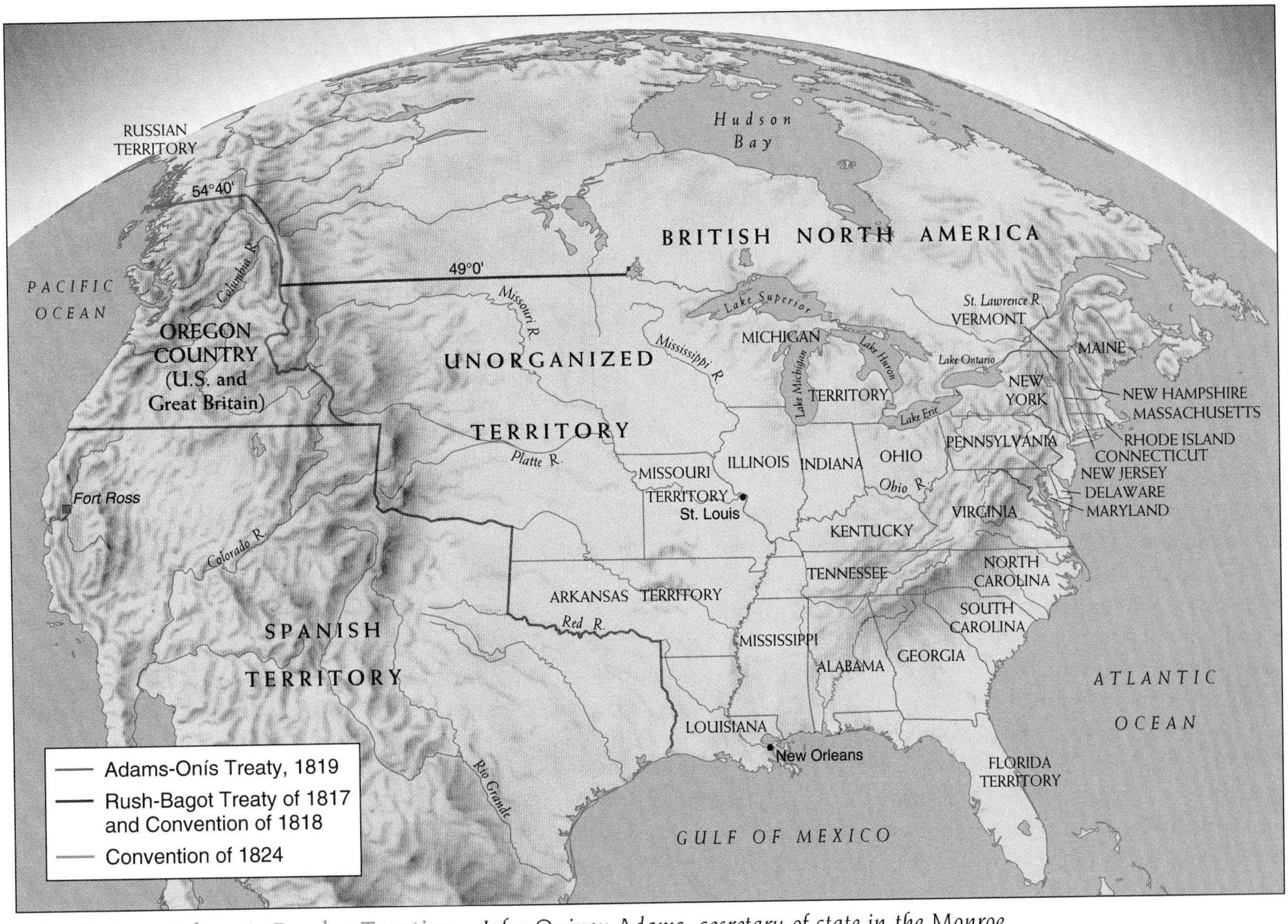

John Quincy Adams's Border Treaties *John Quincy Adams, secretary of state in the Monroe administration (1817–25), solidified the nation's boundaries in several treaties with Britain and Spain. The Rush-Bagot Treaty of 1817 and the Conventions of 1818 and 1824 settled the northern boundary with Canada and the terms of a joint occupancy of Oregon. The Adams-Onís Treaty of 1819 added Florida to the United States and settled the disputed border between the American Louisiana Territory and Spanish possessions in the West.*

Territory and accepted 54° 40′ as the southern border of Russian America. Thus Adams contained another possible threat to American continental expansion.

This string of diplomatic achievements—the treaties with Russia, Britain, and Spain and the Monroe Doctrine—represented a great personal triumph for the stubborn, principled John Quincy Adams. A committed nationalist and expansionist, he showed that reason and diplomacy were in some circumstances more effective than force. Adams's diplomatic achievements were a fitting end to the period dominated by the Virginia Dynasty, the trio of enlightened revolutionaries who did so much to shape the new nation.

The Panic of 1819

Across this impressive record of political and economic nation building fell the shadow of the Panic of 1819. A delayed reaction to the end of the War of 1812 and the Napoleonic Wars, the panic forced Americans to come to terms with their economic place in a peaceful world. As British merchant ships resumed trade on routes they had abandoned during the wars, the American shipping boom ended. And as European farm production recovered from the wars, the international demand for American foodstuffs declined and American farmers and shippers suffered.

Domestic economic conditions made matters worse. The western land boom that began in 1815 turned into a speculative frenzy. Land sales, which had totaled 1 million acres in 1815, mushroomed to 3.5 million in 1818. Some lands in Mississippi and Alabama, made valuable by the international demand for cotton, were selling for $100 an acre. Many settlers bought on credit, aided by loans from small and irresponsible "wildcat" state banks. A number of speculators, carried away by the excitement of it all, also bought large tracts of land on credit and promoted them heavily. This was not the first—or the last—speculative boom in western lands. But it ended like all the rest—with a sharp contraction of credit, begun on this occasion by the Second Bank of the United States, which in 1819 forced state banks to foreclose on many bad loans. Many small farmers were ruined, and six years of depression followed.

In response to farmer protests, Congress passed a relief act in 1821 that extended the payment period for western lands, and some state legislatures passed "stay laws" that prevented banks from executing foreclosures. Nonetheless, many small banks failed, taking down their creditors with them. Many western farmers blamed the faraway Bank of the United States for their troubles. In the 1830s Andrew Jackson would build a political movement on their resentment.

Urban workers suffered both from the decline in international trade and from manufacturing failures caused by competition from British imports. As urban workers lobbied for local relief (there was no federal welfare), they found themselves deeply involved in urban politics, where they could express their resentment against the merchants and owners who had laid them off. Thus developed another component of Andrew Jackson's new political coalition.

Another confrontation arose over the tariff. Southern planters, hurt by a decline in the price of cotton, began to actively protest the protective tariff, which kept the price of imported goods high even when cotton prices were low. Manufacturers, hurt by British competition, lobbied for even higher rates, which they achieved in 1824 over southern protests. Southerners then began to express doubts about the fairness of a political system in which they were always outvoted.

The Panic of 1819 was a symbol of this transitional time. It showed how far the country had moved since 1800 from Jefferson's republic of yeoman farmers toward a nation dominated by commerce. And the anger and resentment expressed by the groups harmed by the depression—farmers, urban workers, and southern planters—were portents of the politics of the upcoming Jackson era.

The Missouri Compromise

In the Missouri Crisis of 1819–21, the nation confronted the momentous issue that had been buried in the general enthusiasm for expansion: As America moved west, would the largely southern system of slavery expand as well? Until 1819, this question was decided regionally. As residents of the northern states moved west, the territory into which they expanded (the Old Northwest) was free of slavery. As southerners moved into Alabama, Mississippi, and Louisiana (the Old Southwest), they brought their slaves with them. This regional difference had been mandated by Congress in the Northwest Ordinance of 1787, which explicitly banned slavery in the northern section of trans-Appalachia but made no mention of it elsewhere. Because so much of the expansion into the Old Northwest and Southwest was lateral (Northerners stayed in the north, Southerners in the south), there was little conflict over sectional differences. In 1819, however, the sections collided—in Missouri.

In 1819, Missouri applied for admission to the Union as a slave state. To the slave-owning Kentuckians and Tennesseans who were the territory's major settlers, this extension of slavery seemed natural and inevitable. But Illinois, also an adjacent state, prohibited slavery. The northern states, all of which had abolished slavery by 1819, looked askance at the extension of slavery northward.

In addition to the moral issue of slavery, the Missouri question raised the political issue of sectional balance. Northern politicians did not want to admit another slave state. To do so would tip the balance of power in the Senate, where the 1819 count of slave and free states was eleven apiece. For their part, Southerners believed they needed an advantage in the Senate; because of faster population growth in the North, they were already outnumbered (105 to 81) in the House of Representatives. But above all, Southerners did not believe Congress had the power to limit the expansion of slavery. They were alarmed that Northerners were considering national legislation on the matter. Slavery, in southern eyes, was a question of property and therefore a matter for state rather than federal legislation. Thus, from the very beginning the expansion of slavery raised constitutional issues.

The urgency of these considerations among politicians in 1819 illustrates how delicate matters of sectional balance had already become. Indeed, the aging politician of Monticello, Thomas Jefferson, immediately grasped the seriousness of the question of the expansion of slavery. As he prophetically wrote to a friend, "This momentous question like a fire bell in the night, awakened and filled me with terror. I considered it at once the [death] knell of the Union."

In 1819 Representative James Tallmadge Jr. of New York began more than a year of congressional controversy when he demanded that Missouri agree to the gradual end of slavery as the price of entering the Union. At first, the general public paid little attention, but religious reformers (Quakers prominent among them) organized a number of antislavery rallies in northern cities that made politicians take notice. Former Federalists in the North who had seen their party destroyed by the achievements of Jefferson and his successors in the Virginia Dynasty eagerly seized on the Missouri issue. This was the first time that the growing northern reform impulse

The Missouri Compromise *Before the Missouri Compromise of 1820, the Ohio River was the dividing line between the free states of the Old Northwest and the slaveholding states of the Old Southwest. The compromise stipulated that Missouri would enter the Union as a slave state (balanced by Maine, a free state), but slavery would be prohibited in the Louisiana Territory north of 36° 30´ (Missouri's southern boundary). This awkward compromise lasted until 1846 when the Mexican-American War reopened the issue of the expansion of slavery.*

CHRONOLOGY

1790s	Second Great Awakening begins
1800	Thomas Jefferson elected president
1802	Russian-American Company headquarters established at Sitka, Alaska
1803	Louisiana Purchase *Marbury v. Madison* Ohio admitted to the Union
1804	Lewis and Clark expedition begins Thomas Jefferson reelected president Russians reestablish Sitka following the Tlingit Revolt
1807	*Chesapeake-Leopard* incident Embargo Act
1808	James Madison elected president
1809	Tecumseh forms military alliance among Northwest Confederacy peoples
1811	Battle of Tippecanoe
1812	War of 1812 begins James Madison reelected president Louisiana admitted to the Union
1814	Hartford Convention Treaty of Ghent
1815	Battle of New Orleans
1816	James Monroe elected president Congress charters Second Bank of the United States Indiana admitted to the Union
1817	Mississippi admitted to the Union
1818	Illinois admitted to the Union Andrew Jackson invades Florida
1819	Panic of 1819 Adams-Onís Treaty Alabama admitted to the Union
1819–20	Missouri Crisis and Compromise
1820	James Monroe reelected president Maine admitted to the Union
1821	Missouri admitted to the Union as a slave state
1823	Monroe Doctrine

had intersected with sectional politics. It was also the first time that southern threats of secession were made openly in Congress.

The Senate debate over the admission of Missouri, held in the early months of 1820, was the nation's first extended debate over slavery. Observers noted the high proportion of free African Americans among the listeners in the Senate gallery. They, like Thomas Jefferson, realized that the fate of the Union and the fate of the black race in America were inseparable. But the full realization that the future of slavery was central to the future of the nation would not become apparent to the general public until the 1850s.

In 1820, Congress achieved compromise over the sectional differences. Henry Clay forged the first of the many agreements that were to earn him the title of "the Great Pacificator" (peacemaker). A glance at the map shows the state of Missouri as an awkward intrusion into an otherwise slave-free area, a visual break in the smooth westward continuation of sectionalism. This visual impression is reflected in the Missouri Compromise itself, which was difficult to arrange and had an awkward air about it. The compromise maintained the balance between free and slave states: Maine (which had been part of Massachusetts) was admitted as a free state in 1820 and Missouri as a slave state in the following year. A policy was also enacted with respect to slavery in the rest of the Louisiana Purchase: slavery was prohibited north of 36° 30′ north latitude—the southern boundary of Missouri—and permitted south of that line. This meant that the vast majority of the Louisiana Territory would be free. In reality, then, the Missouri Compromise could be only a temporary solution, because it left open the question of how the balance between slave and free states would be maintained. The seriousness of the sectional struggle over the Missouri question also directed popular attention to the changing nature of national politics.

CONCLUSION

In complex ways a developing economy, geographical expansion, and even a minor war helped shape American unity. Locally, small, settled, face-to-face communities in both the North and the South began to send their more mobile, expectant members to new occupations in urban centers or west to form new settlements, displacing Indian communities in the process.

The westward movement was the novel element in the American national drama. Europeans believed that large size and a population in motion bred instability and political disintegration. Thomas Jefferson thought otherwise, and the Louisiana Purchase was the gamble that confirmed his guess. The westward population movement dramatically changed the political landscape and Americans' view of themselves. Few of those changes, though, were fully apparent in 1820.

Expansion would not create the settled communities of yeoman farmers Jefferson had hoped for. Rather, it would breed a nation of restless and acquisitive people and a new kind of national democratic politics that reflected their search for broader definitions of community.

REVIEW QUESTIONS

1. What economic and political problems did the United States face as a new nation in a world dominated by war between Britain and France? How successful were the efforts by the Jefferson, Madison, and Monroe administrations to solve these problems?
2. The anti-European cast of Jefferson's republican agrarianism made it appealing to many Americans who wished to believe in their nation's uniqueness, but how realistic was it?
3. Some Federalists opposed the Louisiana Purchase, warning of the dangers of westward expansion. What are arguments for and against expansion?
4. What contradictions in American Indian policy did the confrontations between Tecumseh's alliance and soldiers and settlers in the Old Northwest reveal? Can you suggest solutions to them?
5. What did the War of 1812 accomplish?
6. What were the issues that made it impossible for the Era of Good Feelings to last?

RECOMMENDED READING

Frank Bergon, ed., *The Journals of Lewis and Clark* (1989). A handy abridgment of the fascinating history of the expedition. (For more intensive study, Gary Moulton's six-volume unabridged edition of the expedition journals is unsurpassed.)

John Boles, *The Great Revival, 1787–1805* (1972). The standard work on the Second Great Awakening.

George Drago, *Jefferson's Louisiana: Politics and the Clash of Legal Traditions* (1975). Provides an illuminating example of the cultural flexibility of the federal system.

R. David Edmunds, *Tecumseh and the Quest for Indian Leadership* (1984). A sympathetic portrait.

Joseph J. Ellis, *American Sphinx: The Character of Thomas Jefferson* (1998). An engaging exploration of Jefferson's many contradictions.

John Mack Faragher, *Sugar Creek* (1987). The fullest examination of the lives of pioneers in the Old Northwest.

Donald Hickey, *The War of 1812: A Forgotten Conflict* (1989). Takes a fresh look at the events and historiography of the war.

Drew McCoy, *The Elusive Republic: Political Economy in Jeffersonian America* (1980). The most useful discussion of the ties between expansion and republican agrarianism.

Glover Moore, *The Missouri Controversy, 1819–1821* (1953). The standard account.

Curtis P. Nettels, *The Emergence of a National Economy, 1775–1815* (1962). A useful overview.

Merrill Peterson, *Thomas Jefferson and the New Nation* (1970). A good one-volume political biography of Jefferson. (The major biography, by Dumas Malone, is a multivolume work.)

James Ronda, *Lewis and Clark among the Indians* (1984). An innovative look at the famous explorers through the eyes of the Indian peoples they encountered.

ADDITIONAL BIBLIOGRAPHY

American Communities from Coast to Coast

James Gibson, *Imperial Russia in Frontier America* (1976)
Marcel Giraud, *A History of French Louisiana, 1698–1715* (1974)
Carey McWilliams, *North from Mexico: The Spanish-Speaking People of the United States* (1948)
Douglas Monroy, *Thrown among Strangers: The Making of Mexican Culture in Frontier California* (1990)
Barbara Sweetland Smith and Redmond Barnett, eds., *Russian America* (1990)
David Weber, *The Spanish Frontier in North America* (1993)

The National Economy

Robert G. Albion, *The Rise of New York Port, 1815–1860* (1939)
W. Eliot Brownlee, *Dynamics of Ascent: A History of the American Economy* (1979)
Stuart Bruchey, *The Roots of American Economic Growth, 1607–1861* (1965)
Samuel Eliot Morison, *Maritime History of Massachusetts: 1783–1860* (1921)
Douglass C. North, *The Economic Growth of the United States, 1790–1860* (1966)

The Jefferson Presidency

Thomas P. Abernathy, *The Burr Conspiracy* (1954)
Henry Adams, *The United States in 1800* (1955)
Noble E. Cunningham, *The Jeffersonian Republicans and Power: Party Operations, 1801–1809* (1963)
Richard E. Ellis, *The Jeffersonian Crisis: Courts and Politics in the Young Republic* (1971)
David Hackett Fischer, *The Revolution of American Conservatism: The Federalist Party in the Era of Jeffersonian Democracy* (1965)
Charles G. Haines, *The Role of the Supreme Court in American Government and Politics, 1789–1835* (1944)
Linda K. Kerber, *Federalists in Dissent: Imagery and Ideology in Jeffersonian America* (1970)
Burton Spivak, *Jefferson's English Crisis: Commerce, Embargo, and the Republican Revolution* (1979)
Robert W. Tucker and David Hendrickson, *Empire of Liberty: The Statecraft of Thomas Jefferson* (1990)
G. Edward White, *The Marshall Court and Cultural Change, 1815–1835*, abridged ed. (1991)
Robert H. Wiebe, *The Opening of American Society: From the Adoption of the Constitution to the Eve of Disunion* (1984)
James S. Young, *The Washington Community: 1800–1828* (1966)

Renewed Imperial Rivalry

Robert F. Berkhofer Jr., *Salvation and Savage: An Analysis of Protestant Missions and American Indian Response, 1787–1862* (1965)
Henry Warner Bowden, *American Indians and Christian Missions: Studies in Cultural Conflict* (1981)
Gregory Evans Dowd, *A Spirited Resistance: The North American Indian Struggle for Unity, 1745–1815*
Reginald Horsman, *Expansion and American Indian Policy, 1783–1812* (1967)
Dorothy Jones, *License for Empire: Colonialism by Treaty in Early America* (1982)
Drew R. McCoy, *The Last of the Fathers: James Madison and the Republican Legacy* (1989)
Francis Paul Prucha, *The Great Father: The United States Government and the American Indians*, 2 vols. (1984)
Bernard Sheehan, *Seeds of Extinction: Jeffersonian Philanthropy and the American Indian* (1973)

The War of 1812

Reginald Horsman, *The Causes of the War of 1812* (1962)
Steven Watts, *The Republic Reborn: War and the Making of Liberal America, 1790–1820* (1987)

Defining the Boundaries

John Boles, *Religion in Antebellum Kentucky* (1976)
Andrew Cayton, *The Frontier Republic: Ideology and Politics in the Ohio Country, 1789–1812* (1986)
———, *Frontier Indiana* (1996)
Paul Conklin, *Cane Ridge: America's Pentecost* (1990)
George Dangerfield, *The Era of Good Feelings* (1952)
Anita Shafer Goodstein, *Nashville, 1780–1860: From Frontier to City* (1989)
Harlan Hatcher, *The Western Reserve: The Story of New Connecticut in Ohio* (1991)
Walter LaFeber, ed., *John Quincy Adams and the American Continental Empire* (1965)
Ernest R. May, *The Making of the Monroe Doctrine* (1975)
Malcolm J. Rohrbough, *The Land Office Business* (1968)
———, *The Trans-Appalachian Frontier: Peoples, Societies, and Institutions, 1775–1850* (1978)
William Ganson Rose, *Cleveland: The Making of a City* (1990)
Richard Slotkin, *Regeneration through Violence: The Mythology of the American Frontier* (1973)
Richard C. Wade, *The Urban Frontier: The Rise of Western Cities, 1790–1850* (1973)
Kenneth J. Winkle, *The Politics of Community: Migration and Politics in Antebellum Ohio* (1988)

Biography

Harry Ammon, *James Monroe: The Quest for National Identity* (1971)
Leonard Baker, *John Marshall: A Life in Law* (1974)
Irving Brant, *James Madison* (1950–61)
Dumas Malone, *Jefferson the President: First Term, 1801–1805* (1970)
———, *Jefferson the President: Second Term, 1805–1809* (1974)

CHAPTER TEN

THE GROWTH OF DEMOCRACY

1824–1840

George Caleb Bingham, *Stump Speaking*, from the Art Collection of NationsBank

Chapter Outline

THE NEW DEMOCRATIC POLITICS
The Expansion and Limits of Suffrage
The Election of 1824
Organizing Popular Politics
The Election of 1828

THE JACKSON PRESIDENCY
A Popular Figure
The Spoils System and the New Politics
The Nation's Leader vs. Sectional Spokesmen
A Strong Executive

INTERNAL IMPROVEMENTS: BUILDING AN INFRASTRUCTURE
The Transportation Revolution
Canals and Steamboats
Railroads
The Legal Infrastructure
Commercial Agriculture in the Old Northwest
Effects of the Transportation Revolution

JACKSON AND HIS OPPONENTS: THE RISE OF THE WHIGS
The Nullification Crisis
Indian Removal
The Bank War
Jackson's Reelection in 1832
Whigs, Van Buren, and the Election of 1836
The Panic of 1837

THE SECOND AMERICAN PARTY SYSTEM
Whigs and Democrats
The Campaign of 1840
The Whig Victory Turns to Loss: The Tyler Presidency

AMERICAN ARTS AND LETTERS
The Spread of the Written Word
Creating an American Culture
Artists and Builders

AMERICAN COMMUNITIES
Martin Van Buren Forges a New Kind of Political Community

When Martin Van Buren left Albany for Washington in the fall of 1821 to take up his new position as junior senator from New York, he wrote complacently: "I left the service of the state [of New York] for that of the federal government with my friends in full and almost unquestioned possession of the state government in all its branches, at peace with each other and overflowing with kindly feelings towards myself." Thus did Van Buren sum up more than ten years of intense activity in New York State politics in which he and his allies, nicknamed the Bucktails (for the Indian-inspired insignia, the tail of a buck, that members wore on their hats), created one of the first modern democratic political parties. How could it be, Washington politicians asked, that this short, invariably pleasant but rather nondescript man had triumphed over the renowned DeWitt Clinton?

Tall, handsome, arrogant DeWitt Clinton, governor of New York from 1817 to 1823 (and again from 1825 until his death in 1828), had been swept into office on a tide of enthusiasm for his plan to build a canal the length of the state. Clinton soon gained legislative approval for the project—the Erie Canal—the most ambitious and most successful canal project in an era of canal building. An aristocrat in wealth, connections, and attitude, Clinton represented old style politics. During his first terms as governor he ran the New York Democratic Republican Party as though it were his personal property, dispensing patronage to relatives and friends (many of whom were Federalists) on the basis of their loyalty to him rather than their political principles.

Martin Van Buren was a new kind of politician. Born in the small, Dutch-dominated town of Kinderhook, New York, Van Buren was the son of a tavern keeper, not a member of the wealthy elite. He grew up with an enduring resentment of the aristocratic landowning families such as the Van Schaacks and the Van Rensselaers (and, by extension, the Clintons) who disdained him when he was young. Masking his anger with charming manners, Van Buren took advantage of the growing strength of the Democratic Republican Party in New York State to wrest control of it from Clinton and forge it into a new kind of political organization. Clinton's use of patronage to reward friends at the expense of young party loyalists infuriated Van Buren and other rising politicians. Two years after Clinton became governor, Van Buren wrote bitterly to a friend: "A man to be a sound politician and in any degree useful to his country must be guided by higher and steadier considerations than those of personal sympathy and private regard. . . . In the name of all that is holy, where is the evidence of that towering mind and those superior talents which it has been the business of puffers and toad eaters to attribute to [Clinton]?"

By 1819, Van Buren had gathered together enough other disgruntled Democratic Republicans to form the Bucktail faction and openly challenge Clinton. Two years later, at the state constitutional convention of 1821 (where they made up three fourths of the delegates), the Bucktails sealed their victory. Meeting in Albany to revise the out-of-date constitution of 1777, the convention voted to streamline the organization of state government and sharply curtail the patronage powers of the governor. To cement these changes, delegates enacted nearly total manhood suffrage: all adult male citizens who paid state or local taxes, served in the militia, or worked on state roads—more than four-fifths of the adult male population—were now eligible to vote directly for state legislators, governor, and members of Congress.

This dramatic democratization of politics reflected the state's changing population. Already the bustling port of New York was the nation's largest city, and the state's commercial opportunities were attracting shrewd Yankee traders from New England "whose laws, customs and usages," conservative senator Rufus King complained, "differ from those of New York." The old ruling families, failing to recognize the new commercial and social values of the newcomers, were losing their grip on politics. Rising politicians like Van Buren and other Bucktails, in contrast, found opportunity in these changing conditions. Attuned to popular feeling, they responded to the state's growing and increasingly diverse population by creating a new kind of political community. A political party, they maintained, should be a democratic organization expressing the will of all its members, not an organization dominated by an elite group like Clinton's and bound together only by family ties and political favors. All party members, including leaders, would have to abide by majority rule. Party loyalty, rather than personal opinion or friendship, would be the bond that kept the party together and, rather than aristocratic background, the principal requirement for party leadership. "The first man we see step to the rear," wrote Bucktail Silas Wright Jr., still smarting from the factionalism and favoritism of the Clinton years, "we cut down."

By the time he departed for Washington in the fall of 1821, Van Buren left in Albany a closely knit group of friends and allies who practiced these new political principles. Party decisions, reached by discussion in legislative caucus and publicized by the party newspaper, the *Albany Argus*, were binding on all members and enforced by patronage decisions. The group, dubbed the Albany Regency, ran New York State politics for twenty years. For all those years Martin Van Buren was in Washington, where he was a major architect of the new democratic politics of mass participation that has been called the Second American Party System. This new movement created, for the first time in American history, national communities of political partisans. Van Buren understood how to create these new communities. Organization and discipline were essential not for their own sake but because they allowed the political leader to reach out to public opinion. "Those who have wrought great changes in the world," Van Buren wrote, " never succeeded by gaining over chiefs; but always by exciting the multitude. The first is the resource of intrigue and produces only secondary results, the second is the resort of genius and transforms the face of the universe." The sources and expression of the new politics were linked to wider economic and cultural factors that encouraged national cohesion.

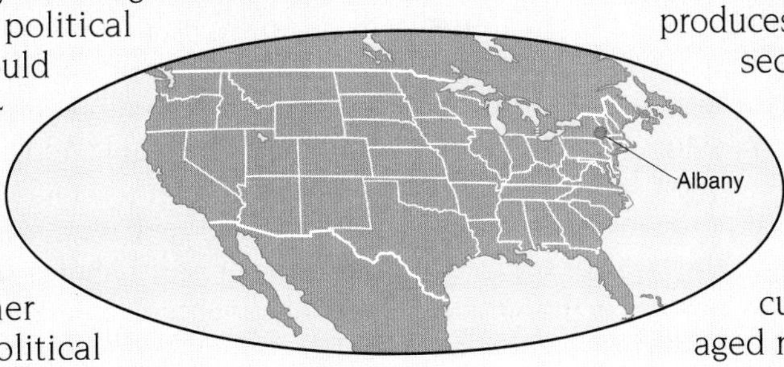

Key Topics

- The role of Andrew Jackson's presidency in affirming and solidifying the new democratic politics
- The part played by the transportation revolution in unifying the nation
- Establishment of the basic two-party pattern of American political democracy
- The creation of a distinctive American cultural identity by writers and artists

THE NEW DEMOCRATIC POLITICS

The early years of the nineteenth century were a time of extraordinary growth and change for the new republic. The changes pulled the nation in two contradictory directions, toward both sectionalism and nationalism.

The two major sections of the country, the North and the South, had always had different social systems, and from the time of the first Continental Congress they had also always disagreed as to the nature of the political compromises they needed to make. Economic development in the early nineteenth century increased the difference between the sections as the South committed itself to cotton growing and the slave system and the North moved rapidly to a commercial, industrializing economy. Although both North and South were still economically interconnected, the two sections were on very different paths. Had the United States of America still consisted only of the thirteen original states, North-South compromises might well have broken down by the 1820s and split the nation into two parts.

Westward expansion, however, provided a nationalizing force. Because of developments in transportation, in 1840 the larger United States was more closely knit than the original thirteen states had been in 1787. And the nine new states west of the Appalachians that entered the Union between 1800 and 1840—making up one-third of the membership of the U.S. Senate—contributed their own regional perspective to national politics. Although settlement patterns tended to align people in what is now called the Old Northwest (Ohio, Indiana, Illinois, Wisconsin, and Michigan) with New England and those in the Old Southwest (Mississippi and Alabama) and the slave states of the Louisiana Purchase (Louisiana, Arkansas, and Missouri) with the South, Westerners as a whole shared common concerns and attitudes that national politicians from the two older areas could not ignore if they wished to build strong political allegiances in the new region. The political effect of westward expansion in the period 1820–40 was to modify although not to eliminate the basic sectional differences between North and South. But the most dramatic effect of westward expansion was the encouragement it gave to democratic politics.

The Expansion and Limits of Suffrage

Before 1800 most of the original thirteen states limited the vote to property owners or taxpayers, or less than half the white male population. In DeWitt Clinton's New York and other states the wealthy held the levers of political power. In national politics as well, in spite of occasional revolts from below such as the Whiskey Rebellion of 1794 (see Chapter 8), political control remained in the hands of the traditional elite until the end, in 1825, of the Virginia Dynasty of presidents.

Westward expansion changed the nature of American politics. Mobility itself promoted change by undermining the traditional authority structures in the older states. "Old America seems to be breaking up and moving westward," an observer commented in 1817. Rapid westward expansion bolstered the national pride that Americans felt in their successful republican revolution and fostered a spirit of self-reliance. As Andrew Jackson, recruiting troops for the War of 1812, boasted, "We are the free born sons of America; the citizens of the only republic now existing in the world; and the only people on earth who possess rights, liberties, and property which they dare call their own."

The new western states extended the right to vote to all white males over the age of twenty-one. Kentucky entered the Union with universal manhood suffrage in 1792, Tennessee (1796), and Ohio (1803) with low taxpayer qualifications that approached universal suffrage. Soon older states such as New Jersey (1807) and Maryland (1810) dropped their property qualification for voting. By 1820, most of the older states had followed suit. Some states liberalized voting in the hopes of dissuading disgruntled nonvoters from moving west or because it seemed unfair to recruit men to fight in the War of 1812 but not allow them to vote. In most states, however, the

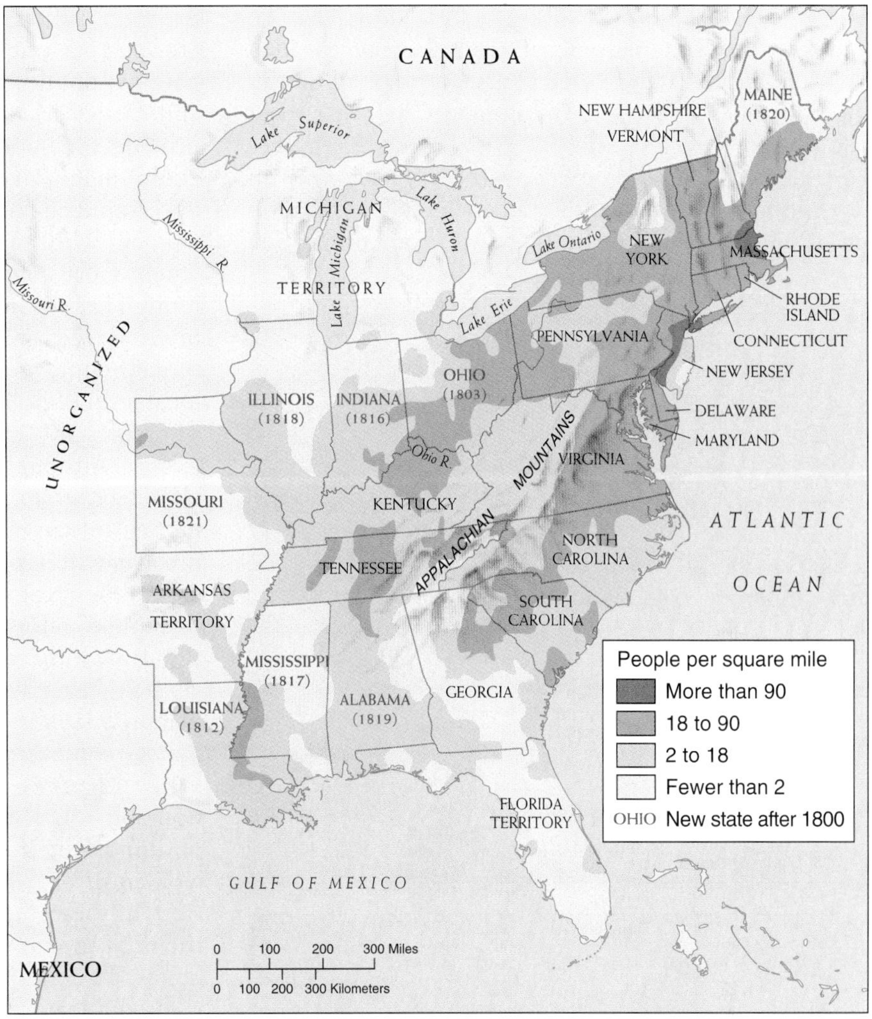

Population Trends: Westward Expansion, 1830 *Westward population movement, a trickle in 1800, had become a flood by 1830. Between 1800 and 1830 the U.S. white and African American population more than doubled (from 5.3 million to 12.9 million), but the trans-Appalachian population grew tenfold (from 370,000 to 3.7 million). By 1830 more than a third of the nation's inhabitants lived west of the original thirteen states.*

driving force behind reform was competition for votes between parties or factions of parties (such as the Bucktails and the Clintonians in New York).

In Connecticut, the Democratic Republicans, appealing to young, democratically minded but propertyless young men, first challenged the state's controlling Federalists in 1802 and finally in 1817 achieved suffrage for all men who paid taxes or served in the militia (that is, nearly everyone). In South Carolina, the rivalry was geographical, pitting the more numerous up-country residents who supported Jefferson's Democratic Republicans against the wealthy Federalist slave-owning political elite of the low country who controlled the state legislature. A compromise agreement of 1808 allocated votes to the lower house by population (favoring the up-country), and to the upper house by wealth (favoring the low country). This redistribution of power led directly to a demand for universal white manhood suffrage, which became law (with a two-year residency requirement) in South Carolina in 1810. There were laggards—Rhode Island, Virginia, and Louisiana did not liberalize their voting qualifications until later—but by 1840, more than 90 percent of adult white males in the nation could vote. And they could vote for more officials: governors and (most important) presidential electors were now elected by direct vote, rather than chosen by small groups of state legislators.

Universal white manhood suffrage, of course, was far from true universal suffrage: The right to vote remained barred to most of the nation's 500,000 free African Americans and to women of any race. Only in five New England states (Maine, New Hampshire, Vermont, Massachusetts, and Rhode Island) could free African American men vote before 1865. In most of the other northern states the right of free African American men to vote was limited, first by custom and later by law. In 1821 in New York, for example, the same Bucktail-dominated legislature that voted to extend the franchise to most white men also restricted it among African American men to those with property valued at $250 or more, a very high amount at the time. As a result, only 68 of the nearly 13,000 African Americans in New York City qualified to vote in 1825.

Free African Americans were denied the vote in all southern states—and surprisingly, in the new western states as well. The Ohio constitution of 1802 denied African Americans the rights to vote, to hold public office, and to testify against white men in court cases. Later restrictions barred black men from serving in the state militia and on juries. The constitutions of other western states—Illinois, Indiana, Michigan, Iowa, Wisconsin, and, later, Oregon—attempted to solve the "problem" of free African Americans by simply denying them entry into the state at all.

The denial of suffrage to white women stemmed from the patriarchal belief that men headed households and represented the interests of all household members. Even wealthy single women who lived alone were considered subordinate to male relatives and denied the right to vote. (New Jersey was an exception to this rule until it amended its constitution in 1807 to withdraw the franchise from propertied women.) Although unable to vote, women of the upper classes had long played important informal roles in national politics. Presidents' wives like Abigail Adams and Dolley Madison were famous for their ability to provide the social settings in which their husbands could quietly conduct political business. Another unrecognized group of skilled politicians were the women who ran the Washington boardinghouses where most congressmen lived during the legislative term. These women, longtime Washington residents, often served as valuable sources of information and official contacts for their boarders. At the state and local level of politics as well, women—often the wives of politicians—engaged in political activities.

Although the extension of suffrage to all classes of white men seemed to indicate that women had no role in public affairs, in fact women's informal involvement in politics grew along with the increasing pace of political activity. At the same time, however, as "manhood" rather than property became the qualification for voting, men began to ignore women's customary political activity and to regard their participation as inappropriate, an attitude that politically active women increasingly resented.

Thus, in this period famous for democratization and "the rise of the common man" the exclusion of important groups—African American men, and women of all races—marked the limits of liberalization. It is also true that nowhere else in the world was the right to vote so widespread as it was in the United States. The extension of suffrage to the common man marked a major step beyond the republicanism advocated by the Revolutionary generation. Thomas Jefferson had envisaged a republic of property-owning yeoman farmers. Now, however, propertyless farm workers and members of the laboring poor in the nation's cities could vote as well. European observers were curious about the democratization of voting: Could "mob rule" possibly succeed? And how would it affect traditional politics? The election of 1824 provided the first outline of the answer.

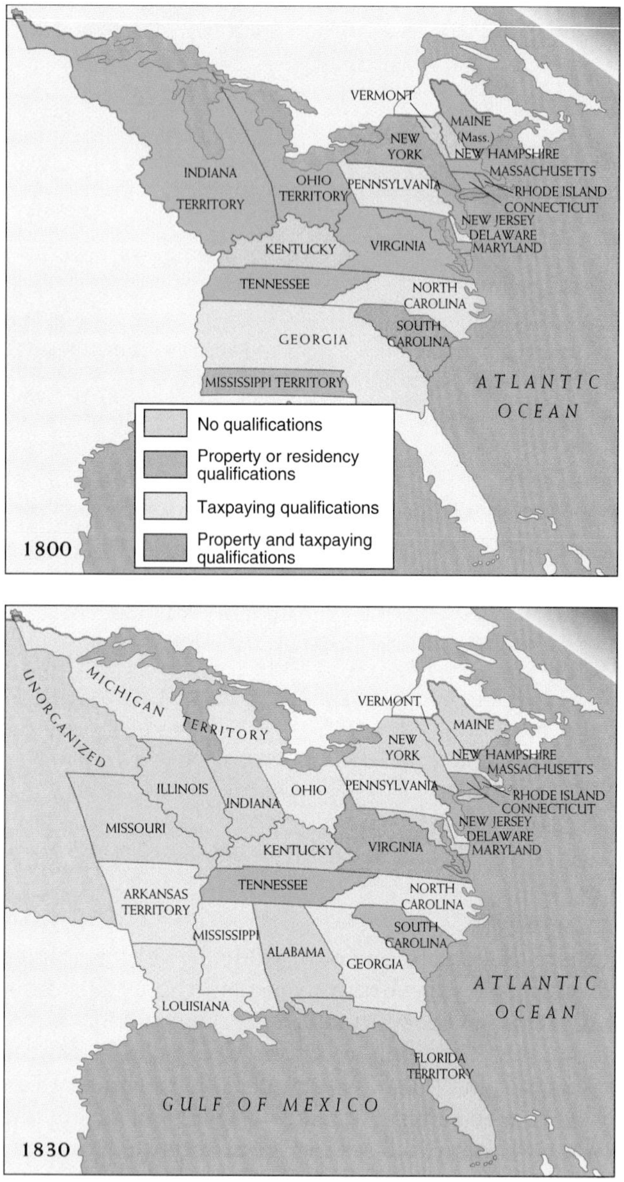

The Growth of Universal White Manhood Suffrage

Kentucky was the first western state to enact white male suffrage without tax or property qualifications. Other western states followed, and by 1820 most of the older states had dropped their suffrage restrictions as well. By 1840, more than 90 percent of the nation's white males could vote. But although voting was democratized for white men, restrictions on free African American male voters grew tighter, and women were excluded completely.

The Election of 1824

The 1824 election marked a dramatic end to the political truce that James Monroe had established in 1817. In that "Era of Good Feelings," one big political party, the expanded Democratic Republicans, had absorbed the remaining Federalists. This brief moment of unanimity did not survive the Panic of 1819 and the Missouri Crisis (see Chapter 9). Thus five candidates, all of them members of the Democratic Republican Party, ran for president in the elections of 1824. The candidate chosen by the usual method of congressional caucus was William H. Crawford of Georgia. The traditional stepping stone to the presidency, however, had been the office of secretary of state, giving a strong claim to John Quincy Adams of Massachusetts, who held that position in President Monroe's administration. Adams was nominated by his state legislature, as were two other candidates, Henry Clay of Kentucky and Andrew Jackson of Tennessee. The fifth candidate, John C. Calhoun of South Carolina, Monroe's secretary of war, withdrew before the election to run for vice president. Each candidate was clearly identified with a region: Adams with New England, Crawford and Calhoun with the South, Clay and Jackson with the West. Jackson, a latecomer to the race, was at first not taken seriously because his record as a legislator was lackluster and his political views unknown. His reputation as a military hero, however, enabled him to run as a national candidate despite his regional identification. He won 43 percent of the popular vote and more electoral votes—99—than any other candidate. The runner-up, John Quincy Adams, won 31 percent of the popular vote and 84 electoral votes. But neither had an electoral majority, leaving it up to the House of Representatives, as in the election of 1800, to pick the winner.

After some political dealing, Henry Clay threw his support to Adams and the House elected Adams president. This was customary and proper: the Constitution gave the House the power to decide, and Clay had every right to advise his followers how to vote. But when Adams named Clay his secretary of state, the traditional stepping-stone to the highest office, Jackson's supporters promptly accused them of a "corrupt bargain." Popular opinion, the new element in politics, supported Jackson. John Quincy Adams served four miserable years as president, knowing that Jackson would challenge him, and win, in 1828.

The legislative accomplishments of Adams's presidency were scanty. Adams's ambitious proposals for national development were rebuffed by a hostile Congress, although he did succeed in obtaining funding for an extension of the National Road west from Wheeling—significantly, an issue on which he could count on western votes. Congress stalled Adams's request to send American delegates to a conference in Panama called by the Latin American liberator Simón Bolívar, in part because Southerners feared attendance might lead to recognition of the revolutionary black republic of Haiti. Thus Adams's desire to lead the nation from a position above politics was frustrated by a political opposition that he thought illegitimate but that was in reality an early portent of the emerging two-party system.

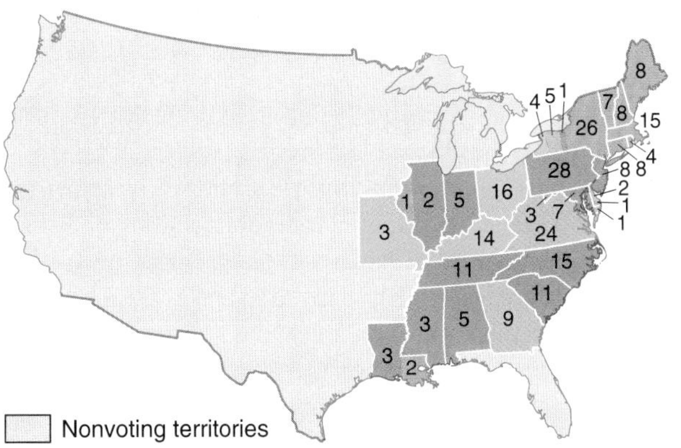

	Electoral Vote (%)	Popular Vote (%)
Andrew Jackson (Democratic Republican)	99 (38)	153,544 (43)
JOHN QUINCY ADAMS (Democratic Republican)	**84 (32)**	**108,740 (31)**
William H. Crawford (Democratic Republican)	41 (16)	46,618 (13)
Henry Clay (Democratic Republican)	37 (14)	47,136 (13)

The Election of 1824 *The presidential vote of 1824 was clearly sectional. John Quincy Adams carried his native New England and little else, Henry Clay carried only his own state of Kentucky and two adjoining states, and Crawford's appeal was limited to Virginia and Georgia. Only Andrew Jackson moved beyond the regional support of the Old Southwest to wider appeal and the greatest number of electoral votes. Because no candidate had a majority, however, the election was thrown into the House of Representatives, which chose Adams.*

Organizing Popular Politics

As the election of 1824 showed, hand-in-hand with the spread of universal manhood suffrage went a change in popular attitudes that spelled the end of personal, elitist politics. The triumph of Van Buren and the Bucktails in New York in 1821 was one example of this sort of change, but politicians in other states shared Van Buren's vision of tightly organized, broad-based political groups. John C. Calhoun of South Carolina was first elected to his state legislature in 1808, the year that the iron political grip of the low-country planters was weakened. Calhoun, himself from the up-country, depended throughout his political career on the up-country voters who achieved universal white manhood suffrage in 1810. In Virginia a group known as the Richmond Junto had control of state politics by 1816, and in Tennessee the Nashville Junto, masterminded by John Overton, held sway by 1822. In New Hampshire, Isaac Hill's Concord Regency was firmly in control by 1825. Each of these organizations, to a greater or lesser extent, aspired to the same discipline and control as the Albany Regency aspired to, and each had wider aspirations. The Nashville Junto led the way by nominating Andrew Jackson for president in 1824.

The crucial element in the success of the new party system, as Van Buren realized, was its mass appeal.

Just as the religion of the day emphasized emotion over reason, so too the new political parties appealed to popular enthusiasms. The techniques of mass campaigns—huge political rallies, parades, and candidates with wide "name recognition" such as military heroes—were quickly adopted by the new political parties. So were less savory techniques such as the distribution of lavish food and (especially) drink at polling places, which frequently turned elections into rowdy, brawling occasions. These mass campaigns were something new. In 1834, the French visitor Michel Chevalier witnessed a mile-long nighttime parade in support of Andrew Jackson. Stunned by the orderly stream of banners lit by torchlight, the portraits of George Washington, Thomas Jefferson, and Jackson, and the enthusiastic cheering of the crowd, Chevalier wrote, "These scenes belong to history. They are the episodes of wondrous epic which will bequeath a lasting memory to posterity, that of the coming of democracy."

As Chevalier noted, the spirit that motivated the new mass politics was democratic pride in participation. The new politics placed great emphasis on party loyalty. Just as professional politicians such as Van Buren were expected to be loyal, so the average voter was encouraged to make a permanent commitment to a political party. The party provided some of the same satisfactions that popular sports offer today: excitement, entertainment, and a sense of belonging. In effect, political parties functioned as giant national men's clubs. They made politics an immediate and engrossing topic of conversation and argument for men of all walks of life. In this sense, the political party was the political manifestation of a wider social impulse toward community. But the glue that held political parties together went beyond the appeal of a particular leader or loyalty to one's friends. Political parties were based on genuine differences of political opinion. The task of politicians, as Van Buren recognized, was to emphasize those differences in ways that forged support not just for one election but for permanent, national communities of political interest.

Politics, abetted by the publication of inexpensive party newspapers, was a great topic of conversation among men in early nineteenth-century America, as Richard Caton Woodville's 1845 painting Politics in an Oyster House *suggests.*

The Election of 1828

The election of 1828 was the first to demonstrate the power and effectiveness of the new party system. With the help of Martin Van Buren, his campaign manager, Andrew Jackson rode the wave of the new democratic politics to the presidency. Jackson's party, the Democratic Republicans (they soon dropped "Republicans" and became simply the Democrats), spoke the language of democracy, and they opposed the special privilege personified for them by President John Quincy Adams and his National Republican (as distinguished from "Democratic Republican") Party. Neither Jackson nor Adams campaigned on his own—that was considered undignified. But the supporters of both candidates campaigned vigorously, freely, and negatively. Jackson's supporters portrayed the campaign as a contest between "the democracy of the country, on the one hand, and a lordly purse-proud aristocracy on the other." In their turn, Adams's supporters depicted Jackson as an illiterate backwoodsman, a murderer (he had killed several men in duels), and an adulterer (apparently unwittingly, he had married Rachel Robards before her divorce was final).

Jackson's running mate for vice president was John C. Calhoun of South Carolina. Although this choice assured Jackson of valuable southern support, it also illustrated the transitional nature of politics, for Calhoun was currently serving as vice president to John Quincy Adams, Jackson's opponent. That Calhoun was able easily to lend his support to a rival faction was a holdover from the old elite and personal politics that would soon be impossible in the new democratic political system.

Jackson won 56 percent of the popular vote (well over 80 percent in much of the South and West) and a decisive electoral majority of 178 votes to Adams's 83. The vote was interpreted as a victory for the common man. But the most important thing about

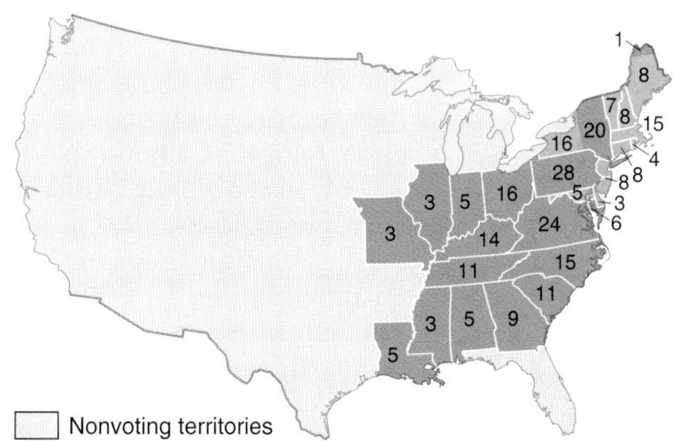

	Electoral Vote (%)	Popular Vote (%)
ANDREW JACKSON (Democrat)	**178 (68)**	**647,286 (56)**
John Quincy Adams (National Republican)	83 (32)	508,064 (44)

The Election of 1828 *Andrew Jackson's victory in 1828 was the first success of the new national party system. The coalition of state parties that elected him was national, not regional. Although his support was strongest in the South and West, his ability to carry Pennsylvania and parts of New York demonstrated his national appeal.*

Jackson's victory was the coalition that achieved it. The new democratically based political organizations—the Richmond and Nashville Juntos, the Albany and Concord Regencies, with help from Calhoun's organization in South Carolina—worked together to elect him. Popular appeal, which Jackson the military hero certainly possessed, was not enough to ensure victory. To be truly national, a party had to create and maintain a coalition of North, South, and West. The Democrats were the first to do this.

THE JACKSON PRESIDENCY

Andrew Jackson's election ushered in a new era in American politics, an era that historians have called "the Age of the Common Man." Jackson himself, however, was no "common man": he was a military hero, a rich slave owner, and an imperious and decidedly undemocratic personality. "Old Hickory," as Jackson was affectionately called, was tough and unbending, just like hickory itself, one of the hardest of woods. Yet he had a mass appeal to ordinary people unmatched—and indeed unsought—by earlier presidents. The secret to Jackson's extraordinary appeal lies in the changing nature of American society. Jackson was the first to respond to the ways in which westward expansion and the extension of the suffrage were changing politics at the national as well as the local and state levels.

A Popular Figure

Jackson was born in 1767 and raised in North Carolina. During the American Revolution he was captured and beaten by the British, an insult he never forgot. As a young man without wealth or family support, he moved west to the frontier "station" of Nashville, Tennessee, in 1788. There he made his career as a lawyer and his considerable wealth as a slave-owning planter. He had a touchy sense of pride and honor that led him into many duels. As he showed in his campaigns against the "Five Civilized Tribes" in the Old Southwest during the War of 1812, he was ruthless toward Indians. He first became a national hero with his underdog win against the British in the battle of New Orleans. In the popular mind, his fierce belligerence came to symbolize pioneer independence. The fact that he had little political experience, which would have made his nomination impossible under the traditional system of politics, was not a hindrance in the new age of popular politics.

On March 4, 1829, Andrew Jackson was inaugurated as president of the United States. Jackson himself was still in mourning for his beloved wife Rachel, whose recent death he attributed to the slanders of the campaign. But everyone else was celebrating. The small community of Washington was crowded with strangers, many of them Westerners and common people who had come especially for Jackson's inauguration. Their celebrating dismayed the city's more respectable citizens. Jackson's brief Inaugural Address was almost drowned out by the cheering of the crowd, and after the ceremony the new president was mobbed by well-wishers. The same unrestrained enthusiasm was evident at a White House reception, where the crowd was large and disorderly. People stood on chairs and sofas to catch glimpses of Jackson and shoved and pushed to reach the food and drink, which was finally carried out to the lawn. In the rush to follow, some people exited through windows rather than the doors. All in all, a disapproving observer noted, this behavior indicated the end of proper government and the beginning of "the reign of King Mob." Indeed, Jackson's administration was different from all those before it.

The Spoils System and the New Politics

Jackson began his term rewarding party loyalists by giving them positions in the national government. Although Jackson himself spoke loftily of democratizing the holding of public office, New York Bucktail William Marcy put the matter more bluntly: there was "nothing wrong in the rule, that to the victor belong the spoils of the enemy." Hence the expression "spoils system" to describe the practice of awarding government appointments to loyalists of the winning party. This attitude toward public office was one of the strongest points of difference between the new politics and the old.

Until 1829, presidential inaugurations had been small, polite, and ceremonial occasions. Andrew Jackson's popularity, however, brought a horde of well-wishers to Washington for his inaugural. Conservative critics, dismayed by the disorderly crowd at Jackson's frontier-style open house at the White House, feared "the reign of King Mob" had begun.

What Jackson did was to transfer a common state practice to the national level and to set a precedent that was followed in national politics until passage of the Pendleton Act of 1883, which began the reform of the civil service system. Jackson opened up all federal positions to party loyalists, and his opponents quickly found examples of corruption and inefficiency among the new officeholders. It is doubtful, though, if any alternative to the spoils system—such as the elite, independent civil service that the British were developing at the time—would have been consistent with the democratic spirit of American politics in the 1820s.

In fact, although the spoils system upset Jackson's opponents more than most of his other controversial actions, the number of officeholders he replaced was rather small—only about 10 percent (of a total of 10,093 offices). As was true in so many other cases, it was not so much the appointments themselves as the manner in which Jackson made them—brooking no argument, not even from supporters—that opponents found so aggravating.

The Nation's Leader vs. Sectional Spokesmen

Despite his western origins, Jackson was a genuinely national figure. He was more interested in asserting strong national leadership than promoting sectional compromise. He believed that the president, who symbolized the popular will of the people, ought to dominate the government. As he put it in his first annual message, "the first principle of our system [is that] the majority is to govern." This was new. Voters were much more accustomed to thinking of politics in sectional terms. Jackson faced a Congress full of strong and immensely popular sectional figures. Three stood out: Southerner John C. Calhoun, Northerner Daniel Webster, and Westerner Henry Clay.

Intense, dogmatic, and uncompromising, John C. Calhoun of South Carolina had begun his political career as an ardent nationalist and expansionist in his early days as a War Hawk before the War of 1812. Since the debate over the Missouri Compromise in 1820, however, Calhoun had wholeheartedly identified with southern interests, first and foremost among which was the expansion and preservation of slavery. As the South's minority position in Congress became clear over the years, Calhoun's defense of southern economic interests and slavery became more and more rigid. Not for nothing did he earn his nickname "the Cast-Iron Man."

Senator Daniel Webster of Massachusetts was the outstanding orator of the age. Large, dark, and stern, Webster delivered his speeches in a deep, booming voice that, listeners said, "shook the world." He was capable of pathos as well, bringing tears to the eyes of those who heard him say, while defending Dartmouth College before the Supreme Court (in the case of the same name), "It is a small college, sir, but there are those who love it." Webster, a lawyer for business interests, became the main spokesman for the new northern commercial interests, supporting a high protective tariff, a national bank, and a strong federal government. Webster's fondness for comfortable living, and especially brandy, made him less effective as he grew older, but then, as a contemporary of his remarked, "No man could be as great as Daniel Webster looked."

In contrast with the other two, Henry Clay of Kentucky, spokesman of the West, was charming, witty, and always eager to forge political compromises. Clay held the powerful position of Speaker of the House of Representatives from 1811 to 1825 and later served several terms in the Senate. A spellbinding storyteller and well known for his ability to make a deal, Clay worked to incorporate western desires for cheap and good transportation into national politics. It was he who promoted the political agenda known as the American System: a national bank, a protective tariff, and the use of substantial federal funds for internal improvements such as roads, canals, and railroads (see Chapter 9). Clay might well have forged a political alliance between the North and the West if not for the policies of President Jackson, his fellow Westerner and greatest rival. Jackson's preeminence thwarted Clay's own ambition to be president.

The prominence and popularity of these three politicians show that sectional interests remained strong even under a president as determined as Jackson to override them and disrupt "politics as usual" by imposing his own personal style.

A Strong Executive

The mob scene that accompanied Jackson's inauguration was more than a reflection of the popular enthusiasm for Old Hickory. It also signaled a higher level of controversy in national politics. Jackson's personal style quickly stripped national politics of the polite and gentlemanly aura of cooperation it had acquired during the Era of Good Feelings and that Adams had vainly tried to maintain. Jackson had played rough all his life, and he relished controversy. His administration (1829–37) had plenty of it.

Andrew Jackson dominated his administration. Except for Martin Van Buren, whom he appointed secretary of state, he mostly ignored the heads of government departments who made up his official cabinet. Instead he consulted with an informal group, dubbed the "Kitchen Cabinet," made up of Van Buren and old western friends. The Kitchen Cabinet did not include John C. Calhoun, the vice president, or either of the other two great sectional representatives, Henry Clay and Daniel Webster. Jackson never forgave Clay for his role in the "corrupt bargain" of 1825, and he saw Daniel Webster as a representative of his favorite political target, the privileged elite.

Jackson used social distance to separate himself from other politicians. When Jackson's secretary of war, John Henry Eaton, married a beautiful woman of flamboyant reputation, he transgressed the social code of the time. It was rumored that Peggy Eaton had been John's mistress and that there were other men in her past. She was, in nineteenth-century thinking, a fallen woman and unfit for polite society. The respectable ladies of Washington shunned her. But Jackson, aroused by memories of the slanders against his own wife, defended Peggy Eaton and urged his cabinet members to force their wives to call on her. When, to a woman, they refused, Jackson called the husbands henpecked. This episode chilled the social life of cabinet members and their families and drove a wedge between Jackson and Calhoun, whose wife was a leader in the anti-Eaton group. Although Jackson claimed to be motivated only by chivalry, he wanted to keep his distance from Calhoun, and this episode helped him do it. Ironically, it may never have occurred had Jackson not been a widower. His wife Rachel would surely have sided with Mrs. Calhoun in upholding the moral code of the time.

Jackson freely used the tools of his office to strengthen the executive branch of government at the expense of the legislature and judiciary. By using the veto more frequently than all previous presidents combined (twelve vetoes compared with nine by the first six presidents), Jackson forced Congress to constantly consider his opinions. Even more important, Jackson's "negative activism" restricted federal activity, thereby allowing more power to remain in state hands.

In one of his most famous and unexpected actions, the veto of the Maysville Road Bill of 1830, Jackson refused to allow federal funding of a southern spur of the National Road in Kentucky, claiming such funding should be left to the state. Like Presidents James Madison and James Monroe before him, Jackson believed that federal funding for extensive and expensive transportation measures was unconstitutional because it infringed on the "reserved powers" the Constitution left to the states. The veto was unexpected because it disappointed Jackson's strongest supporters, Westerners who wanted better transportation. But by addressing his veto message to a popular audience, not just to Congress, and by dramatically portraying federal funding as a threat to the popular political principle of states' rights (and by making it clear that he was not opposed to federal funding of all internal improvements), Jackson actually gained political support. He also had the satisfaction of defeating a measure central to the American System proposed by his western rival, Henry Clay.

INTERNAL IMPROVEMENTS: BUILDING AN INFRASTRUCTURE

Despite the ongoing constitutional debate over who should fund internal improvements, no one argued that they should not be funded at all. On the contrary, ordinary people and politicians of all persuasions agreed that both federal and state governments had an important role in encouraging economic growth and in fostering the development of a national market. And that role included subsidizing the costs of the basic infrastructure—the canals and railroads—that would tie the national market together.

The Transportation Revolution

Between 1800 and 1840 the United States experienced truly revolutionary improvements in transportation. More than any other development, these improvements encouraged Americans to look beyond their local communities to broader ones and to foster the enterprising commercial spirit for which they became so widely known.

Improved transportation had dramatic effects both on individual mobility and on the economy. By 1840 it was easier for people to move from one locale to another, but even more remarkably people now had easy access in their own cities and towns to commercial goods made in distant centers. Thus even for people who remained in one place, horizons were much broader in 1840 than they had been forty years before. The difference lay in better roads, in improvements in water transport, and in the invention and speedy development of railroads.

In 1800, travel by road was difficult for much of the year. Mud in the spring, dust in the summer, and snow in the winter all made travel by horseback or carriage uncomfortable, slow, and sometimes dangerous. Over the years, localities and states tried to improve local roads or contracted with private turnpike companies to build, maintain, and collect tolls on important stretches of road. In general, however, local roads remained poor.

The federal government demonstrated its commitment to the improvement of interregional transportation by funding the National Road in 1808, at the time the greatest single federal transportation expense (its eventual cost was $7 million). Built of gravel on a stone foundation, it crossed the Appalachian Mountains at Cumberland, Maryland, thereby opening up the West. Built in stages—to Wheeling, Virginia (now West Virginia), by 1818, to Columbus, Ohio, by 1833, to Vandalia, Illinois, almost at the Mississippi River, by 1850—the National Road tied the East and the West together, providing strong evidence of the nation's commitment to both expansion and cohesion and helping to foster a national community.

Although the federal commitment was great, the states actually spent more than the federal government on internal improvements—canals and railroads as well as roads. In the 1820s, state spending for internal improvements totaled $26 million. Half of this amount was incurred by two states, New York and Pennsylvania, but even smaller states such as South Carolina spent $2 million, largely on canals. In the next decade, state spending for canals, railroads, and turnpikes soared to $108 million. States and towns, especially in newly populated areas of the West, competed against each

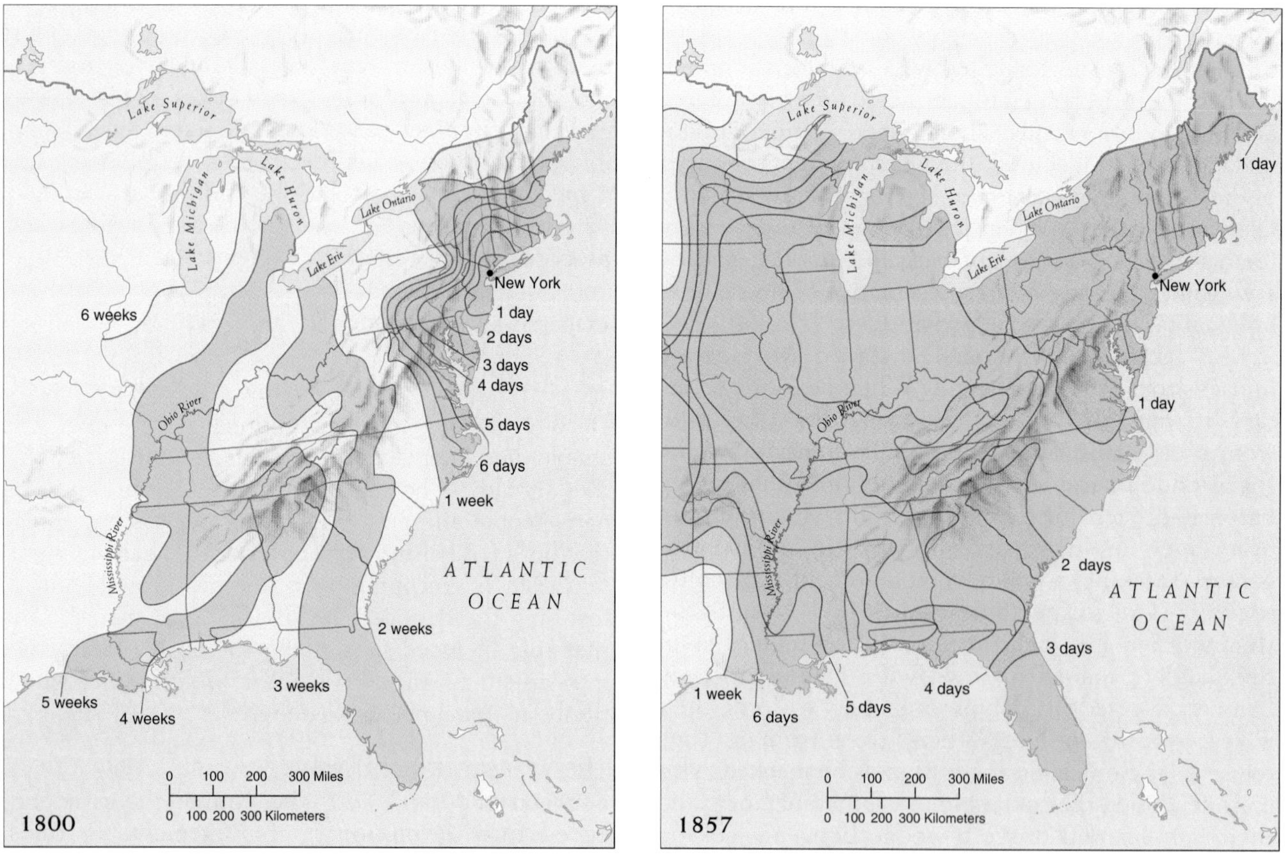

Travel Times, 1800 and 1857 *The transportation revolution dramatically reduced travel times and vastly expanded everyone's horizons. Improved roads, canals, and steamboats and the introduction of railroads made it easier for Americans to move than ever before, and made even those who did not move less isolated. Better transportation linked the developing West to the eastern seaboard and fostered a national identity and pride.*

Thomas Coke Ruckle, *Fairview Inn or Three Mile House on Old Frederick Road*, c. 1829?, watercolor on paper. Collection of the Maryland Historical Society, Baltimore, Maryland.

This 1829 painting of Fairview Inn on the National Road just three miles west of Baltimore illustrates the importance of good transportation. The busy traffic attests to commercial activity and to confidence in westward expansion—the canvas-covered wagons were able to travel as far west as Ohio on the National Road at the time.

other in giving land, subsidies, and other forms of encouragement to road, canal, and railroad companies to provide transportation to their particular localities. Some of these commitments were overly generous and led to financial difficulty: by 1842, nine states (Arkansas, Florida, Illinois, Indiana, Louisiana, Maryland, Michigan, Mississippi, and Pennsylvania) had defaulted on some of their transportation loans, and Ohio and New York were forced to suspend dividends to investors.

Canals and Steamboats

However much they helped the movement of people, the National Road and other roads were unsatisfactory in a commercial sense. Shipment of bulky goods like grain was too slow and expensive by road. Waterborne transportation was much cheaper and still the major commercial link among the Atlantic seaboard states and in the Mississippi-Ohio River system. But before the 1820s most water routes were north-south or coastal (Boston to Charleston, for example); east-west links were urgently needed. Canals turned out to be the answer.

The Erie Canal—the most famous canal of the era—was the brainchild of New York governor DeWitt Clinton, who envisioned a link between New York City and the Great Lakes through the Hudson River and a 364-mile-long canal stretching from Albany to Buffalo. When Clinton proposed the canal in 1817 it was derisively called "Clinton's Ditch"; the longest then existing American canal was only 27 miles long and had taken nine years to build. Nevertheless, Clinton convinced the New York legislature to approve a bond issue for the canal, and investors (New York and British merchants) subscribed to the tune of $7 million, an immense sum for the day.

Building the canal—40 feet wide, 4 feet deep, 364 miles long, with 83 locks and more than 300 bridges along the way—was a vast engineering and construction challenge. What came to be called Yankee ingenuity showed at every step of the way, from the creation of stump pullers to remove trees from the route, to substitutes for cement (previously imported from England), and to the widespread use of Dupont blasting powder, the forerunner of dynamite (which was not invented for another forty years).

Manpower was another concern. In the early stages nearby farmers worked for $8 a month, but when malaria hit the workforce in the summer of 1819, many went home. They were replaced by 3,000 Irish contract laborers, who were much more expensive—50 cents a day plus room and board—but more reliable (if they survived). Local people regarded the Irish workers as different and frightening, but the importation of foreign contract labor for this job was a portent of the future. Much of the heavy construction work on later canals and railroads was performed by immigrant labor.

DeWitt Clinton had promised, to general disbelief, that the Erie Canal would be completed in less than ten years, and he made good on his promise. The canal was the wonder of the age. On October 26, 1825, Clinton declared it open in Buffalo and sent the first boat, the *Seneca Chief*, on its way to New York at the incredible speed of four miles an hour. (Ironically, the Seneca Indians, for whom the boat was named, had been "removed" from the path of the canal and confined to a small reservation.) The boat reached New York City on November 4, where it was greeted with elaborate ceremonies, including one in which vials of water from the great rivers of the world—the Nile, Ganges, Mississippi, Rhine, and Danube—were emptied into New York harbor to symbolize the opening of commerce between the heart of America and the world.

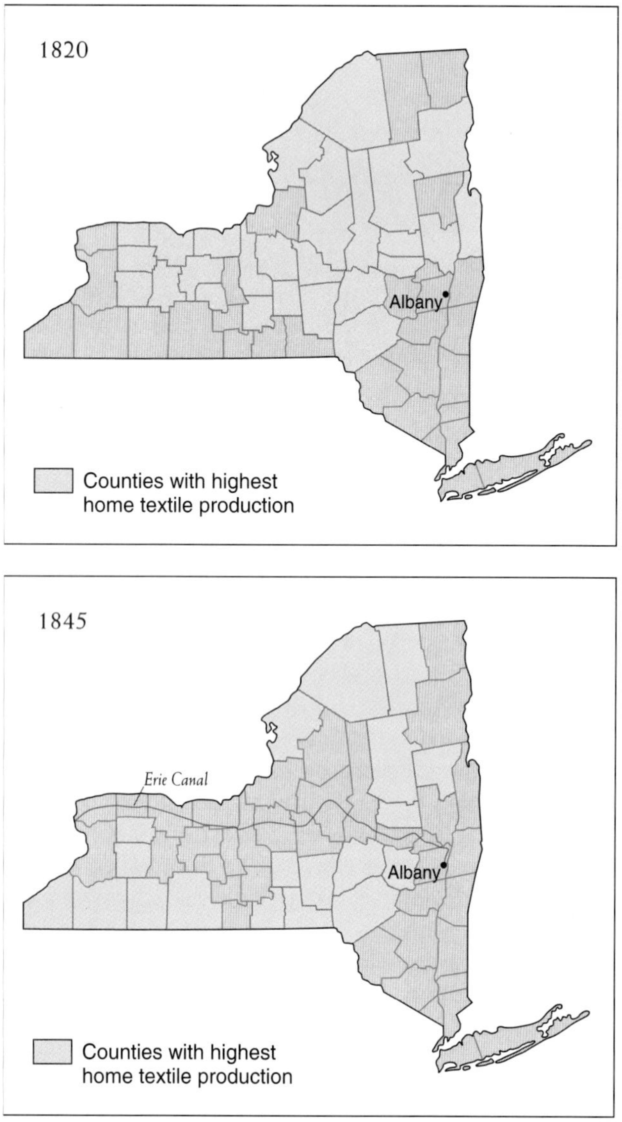

The Impact of the Erie Canal on Household Textile Manufacture *In 1820 the household manufacture of woolen cloth for home use was widespread in New York State, but in 1845, twenty years after the Erie Canal opened, many fewer counties were producing significant quantities of fabric. Because they could now buy cheap manufactured textiles, New York women living near the canal were freed from the time-consuming task of making cloth for their families.*

Source: Arthur Harrison Cole, *The American Wool Manufacture* (Cambridge, Mass.: Harvard University Press, 1926), p. 280.

This grand gesture was appropriate. The Erie Canal provided easy passage to and from the interior, both for people and for goods. It drew settlers like a magnet from the East and, increasingly, from overseas: by 1830, 50,000 people a year were moving west on the canal to the rich farmland of Indiana, Illinois, and territory farther west. Earlier settlers now had a national, indeed an international, market for their produce. Moreover, farm families began purchasing household goods and cloth, formerly made at home. Indeed, one of the most dramatic illustrations of the canal's impact is a rapid decline in the production of homespun cloth. In 1825, the year the Erie Canal opened, New York homesteads produced 16.5 million yards of textiles. By 1835 this figure had shrunk by almost half—8.8 million yards—and by 1855 it had dropped to less than 1 million.

Towns along the canal—Utica, Rochester, Buffalo—became instant cities, each an important commercial center in its own right. Perhaps the greatest beneficiary was the city of New York, which quickly established a commercial and financial supremacy no American city could match. The Erie Canal decisively turned New York's merchants away from Europe and toward America's own heartland, building both interstate commerce and a feeling of community. As the famous song put it,

You'll always know your neighbor,
You'll always know your pal,
If you've ever navigated
On the Erie Canal.

The phenomenal success of the Erie Canal prompted other states to construct similar waterways to tap the rich interior market. Between 1820 and 1840, $200 million was invested in canal building, three-quarters of it provided by state governments. The Blackstone Canal linked Worcester, Massachusetts, with Providence, Rhode Island; the Pennsylvania Main Line Canal ran all the way from Philadelphia to Pittsburgh; and many other canals were built in Maine, Maryland, Ohio, Indiana, and Illinois. None of these waterways achieved the success of the Erie, which collected $8.5 million in tolls in its first nine years. And the port cities they were meant to benefit—Philadelphia and Baltimore, for example—never threatened New York's commercial supremacy. Nevertheless, the spurt of canal building ended the geographical isolation of much of the country. For example, Ohio's canal system opened up the American interior by linking the Ohio River to Lake Erie in the north and to the Pennsylvania canals to the east.

An even more important improvement in water transportation, especially in the American interior, was the steamboat. Robert Fulton first demonstrated the commercial feasibility of steamboats in 1807, and they were soon operating in the East. Redesigned with more efficient engines and shallower, broader hulls, steamboats transformed commerce on the country's great inland river system: the Ohio, the Mississippi, the Missouri, and their tributaries. Steamboats were extremely dangerous, however; boiler explosions, fires, and sinkings were common. Public outrage at these conditions led to one of the first uses of federal regulatory power in the public interest. The first Steamboat Act, passed in 1838 and strengthened in 1852, set standards for the construction, equipment, and operation of steamboat boilers, required measures to prevent fire and collisions, and established an inspection system to make sure the new regulations were carried out. Although steamboats were privately owned and operated, the public that they served insisted on the need for safety standards to promote the wider community welfare.

Mary Keys, American (active 1832) *Lockport on the Erie Canal*, 1832. Watercolor on paper 15¼ x 20½ inches. Munson-Williams-Proctor Institute Museum of Art, Utica, NY 55.45.

Mary Keys, a local artist, painted this watercolor in 1832 illustrating one of the Erie Canal's engineering triumphs, the famous "combined" locks—two sets of five locks rising side by side for 60 feet—at Lockport. One observer boasted, "Here the great Erie Canal has defied nature."

Dangerous as they were, steamboats greatly stimulated trade in the nation's interior. There had long been downstream trade on flatboats along the Mississippi River system, but it was limited by the return trip overland on the arduous and dangerous Natchez Trace. For a time, steamboats actually increased the down-river flatboat trade, because boatmen could now make more round trips in the same amount of time, traveling home by steamboat in speed and comfort.

The increased river- and canal-borne trade, like the New England shipping boom of a generation earlier, stimulated urban growth and all kinds of commerce. Cities such as Cincinnati, already notable for its rapid growth, experienced a new economic surge. A frontier outpost in 1790, Cincinnati was by the 1830s a center of steamboat manufacture and machine tool production as well as a central shipping point for food for the southern market. Even in sleepy agricultural villages like Mark Twain's hometown of Hannibal, Missouri, the steamboat was a powerful symbol of energy and international commerce. As Twain recounts in "Old Times on the Mississippi," the steamboat brought the town to life:

> A negro drayman, famous for his quick eye and prodigious voice, lifts up the cry, "S-t-e-a-m-boat a comin'!"...The town drunkard stirs, the clerks wake up, a furious clatter of drays follows, every house and store pours out a human contribution, and all in a twinkling the dead town is alive and moving. Drays, carts, men, boys, all go hurrying from many quarters to a common center, the wharf....Then such a scramble as there is to get aboard, and to get ashore, and to take in freight and to discharge freight, all at one and the same time; and such a yelling and cursing as the mates facilitate it all with! Ten minutes later the steamer is under way again....After ten more minutes the town is dead again, and the town drunkard asleep by the skids once more.

Railroads

Remarkable as all these transportation changes were, the most remarkable was still to come. Railroads, new in 1830 (when the Baltimore and Ohio Railroad opened with 13 miles of track), grew to an astounding 31,000 miles by 1860. By that date, New England and the Old Northwest had laid a dense network of rails, and several lines had reached west beyond the Mississippi. The South, the least industrialized section of the nation, had fewer railroads. "Railroad mania" surpassed even canal mania as investors—as many as one-quarter of them British—rushed to profit from the new invention.

Early railroads, like the steamboat, had to overcome many technological and supply problems with far-reaching economic effects. For example, locomotives, to generate adequate power, had to be heavy. Heavy locomotives, in turn, required iron rather than wooden rails. The resulting increased demand forced America's iron industry to modernize (at first, railroad iron was imported from England). Heavy engines also required a solid gravel roadbed and strong wooden ties. Arranging steady supplies of both and the labor to lay them was a construction challenge on a new scale. The demand for locomotives and the need to service them fostered the development of a specialized industry, represented by Philadelphia's Baldwin Locomotive Works.

Finally, there were problems of standardization and production quality. Because so many early railroads were short and local, intended simply to connect nearby towns, builders used any gauge (track width) that served their purposes. Thus gauges varied from place to place, forcing long-haul passengers and freight to change trains frequently. For each change, commercial shippers were burdened with the cost of unloading goods from one train and loading them on another. At one time, the trip from Philadelphia to Charleston involved eight gauge changes. Add to this that the early railroads—often hurriedly and poorly built by private companies trying to save money—were prone to frequent breakdowns and accidents, and its not surprising to learn that traveling by ship between Philadelphia and Charleston long remained more pleasant than traveling by rail.

For some years after the introduction of the railroad, canal boats and coastal steamers carried more freight and at lower cost. It was not until the 1850s that consolidation of local railroads into larger systems began in earnest. But already it was clear that this youngest transportation innovation would have far-reaching social consequences.

The Legal Infrastructure

Accompanying the transportation revolution was a series of decisions by federal courts asserting broad federal powers over interstate commerce. The effect of these decisions was to vastly encourage commercial enterprise. By preventing states from interfering with interstate commerce, the government assured entrepreneurs the freedom and security to operate in the risky new national market. Two key decisions were handed down by Chief Justice John Marshall (who had been on the bench since 1801). In *Dartmouth College v. Woodward* (1819) the Supreme Court prevented states from interfering in contracts, and in *Gibbons v. Ogden* (1824) it enjoined the state of New York from giving a monopoly over a steamboat line to Robert Fulton, inventor of the vessel. Although Fulton's invention was protected by a federal patent, its commercial application was not. Patenting thus encouraged technology, but not at the expense of competition. A decision handed down by Marshall's successor, Roger Taney, *Charles River Bridge v. Warren Bridge* (1837), again supported economic opportunity by denying a monopoly. All three cases involved federal reversal of decisions made at the state level, illustrating how the Supreme Court, under Marshall's leadership, strengthened the power of the federal government and thus fostered national policy rather than localism.

At the state level, another crucial commercial protection was the passage of laws concerning incorporation of businesses that had grown too large for individual proprietorship, family ownership, or limited partnership. Businesses that needed to raise large amounts of capital by attracting many investors found the contractual protections provided by incorporation to be essential. The protection investors wanted most was limited liability—the assurance that they would lose no more than what they had invested in a corporation if it were sued or went bankrupt. Initially transportation companies and banks benefited the most from state charters of incorporation. They were less commonly used by merchants and manufacturers until later in the century. Incorporation increased the powers of government, for it made businesses subject to state regulation. Nevertheless, the net effect of state incorporation laws was to encourage large-scale economic activity and to hasten the commercialization of rural areas.

Commercial Agriculture in the Old Northwest

The impact of the transportation revolution and of technological innovation on rural people (who in spite of the growth of cities still constituted more than two-thirds of the American population) went far beyond the breaking down of rural isolation. Every advance in transportation—better roads, canals, steamboats, railroads—made it easier for farmers to get their produce to market. Improvements in agricultural machinery increased the amount of acreage a farmer could cultivate. These two developments, added to the availability of rich, inexpensive land in the heartland, moved American farmers permanently away from subsistence agriculture and into production for sale.

The impact of the transportation revolution on the Old Northwest was particularly marked. Settlement of the region, ongoing since the 1790s, accelerated. In the 1830s, after the opening of the Erie Canal, migrants from New England streamed into northern Ohio, Illinois, Indiana, southern Wisconsin, and Michigan and began to reach into Iowa.

Cyrus McCormick is shown demonstrating his reaper to skeptical farmers. When they saw that the machine cut four times as much wheat a day as a hand-held scythe, farmers flocked to buy McCormick's invention. Agricultural practices, little changed for centuries, were revolutionized by machines like this.

Government policy strongly encouraged western settlement. The easy terms of federal land sales were an important inducement: terms eased from an initial rate of $2.00 per acre for a minimum of 320 acres in 1800, to $1.25 an acre for 80 acres in 1820. Still, this was too much for most settlers to pay all at once. Some people simply squatted, taking their chances that they could make enough money to buy the land before someone else bought it. Less daring settlers relied on credit, which was extended by banks, storekeepers, speculators, promoters, and, somewhat later, railroads, which received large grants of federal lands.

The very need for cash to purchase land involved western settlers in commercial agriculture from the beginning. Farmers, and the towns and cities that grew up to supply them, needed access to markets for their crops. Canals, steamboats, and railroads ensured that access, immediately tying the individual farm into national and international commercial networks. The long period of subsistence farming that had characterized colonial New England and the early Ohio Valley frontier was superseded by commercial agriculture stimulated by the transportation revolution.

Commercial agriculture in turn encouraged regional specialization. Ohioans shipped corn and hogs first by flatboat and later by steamboat to New Orleans. Cincinnati, the center of the Ohio trade, earned the nickname "Porkopolis" because of the importance of its slaughterhouses. By 1840, the national center of wheat production had moved west of the Appalachians to Ohio. Wheat flowed from the upper Midwest along the Erie Canal to eastern cities and increasingly to Europe. Because in each new western area yields were higher than in earlier ones, farmers in older regions were forced to shift away from wheat to other crops. The constant opening of new farmland encouraged mobility and wasteful soil practices. Many farmers were disinclined to make a permanent commitment to their land, but rather counted on rising land prices and short-term crop profits to improve their financial situation. Prepared to move on when the price was right, they regarded their farmland not as a permanent investment but as a speculation.

At the same time, farmers who grew wheat or any other cash crop found themselves at the mercy of far-off markets, which established crop prices; distant canal or railroad companies, which set transportation rates; and the state of the national economy, which determined the availability of local credit. This direct dependence on economic forces outside the control of the local community was something new. So, too, was the dependence on technology, embodied in expensive new machines that farmers often bought on credit.

New tools made western farmers unusually productive. John Deere's steel plow (invented in 1837) cut plowing time in half, making cultivation of larger acreages possible. Seed drills were another important advance. But the most remarkable innovation was Cyrus McCormick's reaper, patented in 1834. Earlier, harvesting had depended on manpower alone. A man could cut two or three acres of wheat a day with a cradle scythe, but with the horse-drawn reaper he could cut twelve acres. Impressed by these figures, western farmers rushed to buy the new machines, confident that increased production would rapidly pay for them. In most years, their confidence was justified. But in bad years, farmers found that their new levels of debt could mean failure and foreclosure. They were richer but more economically vulnerable than they had been before.

Effects of the Transportation Revolution

The effects of the transportation revolution were many. The new ease of transportation undergirded economic growth by making distant markets accessible. The startling successes of innovations such as canals and railroads attracted large capital investments, including significant amounts from foreign investors ($500 million between 1790 and 1861) that fueled further

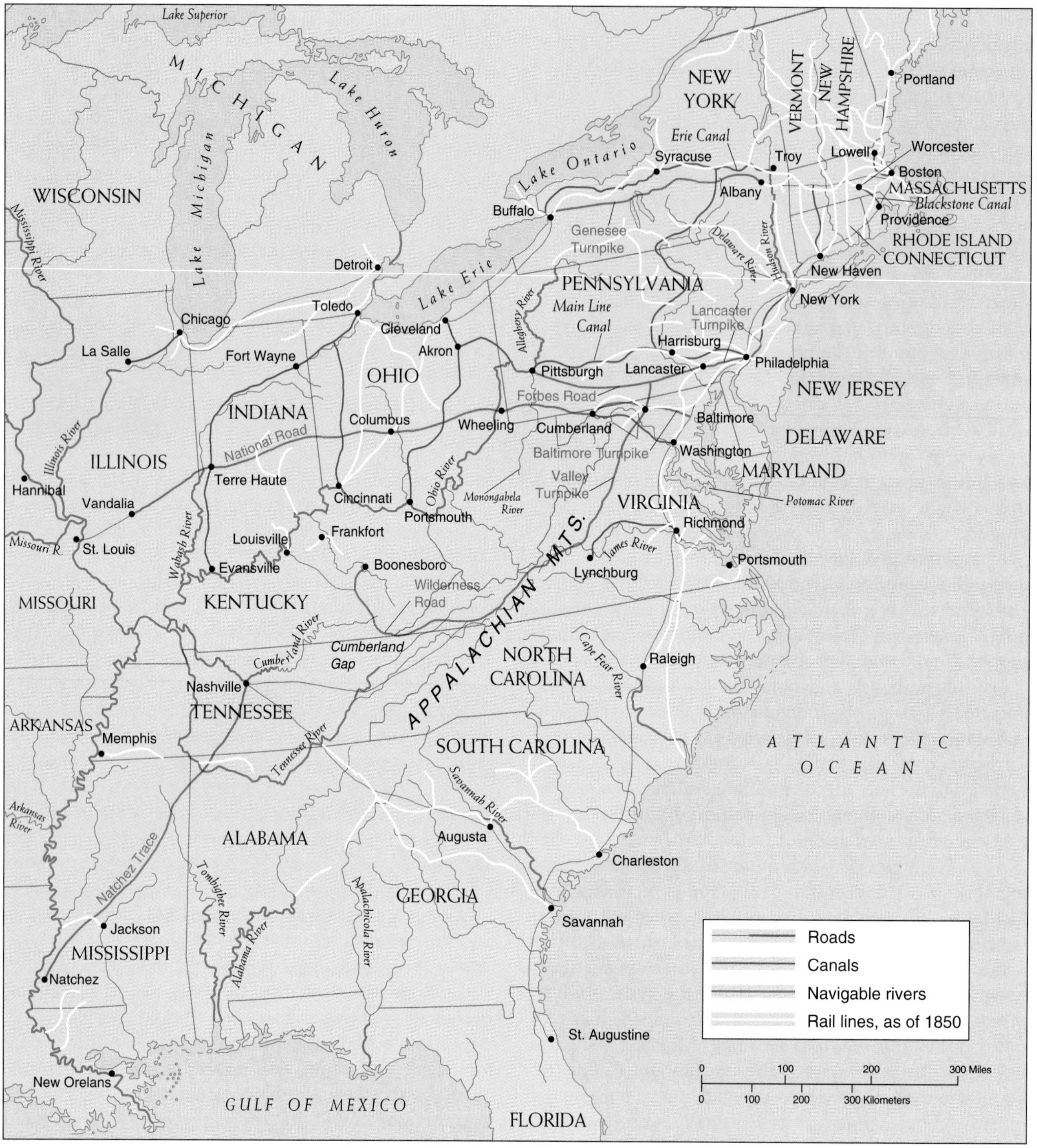

Commercial Links: Rivers, Canals, Roads, 1830, and Rail Lines, 1850 *By 1830, the United States was tied together by a network of roads, canals, and rivers. This "transportation revolution" fostered a great burst of commercial activity and economic growth. Transportation improvements accelerated the commercialization of agriculture by getting farmers' products to wider, nonlocal markets. Access to wider markets likewise encouraged new textile and other manufacturers to increase their scale of production. By 1850, another revolutionary mode of transportation, the railroad, had emerged as a vital link to the transportation infrastructure.*

growth. In turn, the transportation revolution fostered an optimistic, risk-taking mentality in the United States that stimulated invention and innovation. More than anything, the transportation revolution allowed people to move with unaccustomed ease. Already a restless people compared with Europeans, Americans took advantage of new transport to move even more often—and farther away—than they had before.

There were other, less directly economic effects. Every east-west road, canal, and railroad helped to reorient Americans away from the Atlantic and toward the heartland. This new focus was decisive in the creation of national pride and identity. Transportation improvements such as the Erie Canal and the National Road linked Americans in larger communities of interest beyond the local community in which they lived. Other results were less positive. The technological triumphs of canal building and rail laying fostered a brash spirit of conquest over nature that was to become part of the American myth of the frontier. Furthermore, although every new transportation or communication link broke down local and regional isolation and helped to build a spirit of pride in the nation, it also refocused attention on questions of national politics. The new transportation system caused a subtle political shift, for it strengthened the influence of the North by improving the North's ties with the West more than those of the South. In this way, the new modes of communication and transportation served to heat up the politics of the era.

JACKSON AND HIS OPPONENTS: THE RISE OF THE WHIGS

As transportation improvements, increased commercialization, and the new politics drew the people of the United States out of localism into larger networks, fundamental questions about national unity arose. What was the correct balance between local interests—the rights of the states—and the powers of the central government? The men who wrote the federal Constitution in Philadelphia in 1787 had not been able to reach agreement on this question. Because the Constitution deliberately left the federal structure ambiguous, all subsequent sectional disagreements automatically became constitutional issues that carried a threat to national unity. The great issues of Jackson's presidency expressed this continuing tension between nationalism and sectionalism. Jackson's responses to them created such controversy that a permanent opposition—another political party, known as the Whigs—was born.

The Nullification Crisis

The political issue that came to symbolize the divergent sectional interests of North and South, pitting the rights of individual states against the claims of a federal majority, was the protective tariff. The first substantial protective tariff was enacted in 1816 after northern manufacturing interests clamored for protection from the ruthless British competition that followed the War of 1812 (see Chapter 9). As a group, wealthy southern planters were opposed to tariffs, both because tariffs raised the cost of the luxury goods they imported from Europe and because they believed in the principle of free trade, fearing that American tariffs would cause other countries to retaliate with tariffs against southern cotton. Most southern congressmen, assured that the 1816 tariff was a temporary postwar recovery measure, voted for it. But it was not temporary. As the North industrialized and new industries demanded protection, tariff bills in 1824 and 1828 raised rates still higher and protected more items. Southerners protested, but they were outvoted in Congress by northern and western representatives, who agreed both on the need to protect industry and on the tariff as a way to raise federal revenue.

The 1828 tariff, nicknamed "the Tariff of Abominations," was a special target of southern anger, because Jackson's supporters in Congress had passed it in order to increase northern support for him in the presidential campaign of that year. It imposed especially high tariffs on imported textiles and iron that ranged from a third to half their total value. Southerners in Congress lacked the votes to block the tariff and faced the bleak prospect that their economic interests would always be ignored by the majority. Southern opponents of the tariff insisted that it was not a truly national measure but a sectional one that helped only some groups while harming others. Thus it was unconstitutional because it violated the rights of some of the states.

South Carolina, Calhoun's home state, reacted the most forcefully to the tariff of 1828. Of the older southern states, South Carolina had been the hardest hit by the opening of the new cotton lands in the Southwest, which had drained both population and commerce from the state. One index of South Carolina's changed status was the declining position of Charleston. In 1800 it was still as important a seaport as New York and Boston, but by the 1820s it had been eclipsed by all the major northern ports as well as by Mobile and New Orleans, then the major ports for exporting cotton. To these economic woes were added the first real fears about national attitudes toward slavery. South Carolinians, who had always had close personal ties with slave owners in the Caribbean islands, were shaken by the news that the British Parliament, bowing to popular pressure at home, was planning to emancipate all the slaves in the British West Indies. If Congress had the power to impose tariffs that were harmful to some states, South Carolinians asked, what would prevent it from enacting legislation like Britain's, depriving Southerners of their slaves and, thus, of their livelihood?

The result of these fears was a renewed interest in the doctrine of nullification, a topic that became the subject of widespread discussion in South Carolina in 1828. The doctrine upheld the right of a state to declare a federal law null and void and to refuse to enforce it within the state. This was not a new argument. Thomas Jefferson and James Madison had used it in the Kentucky and Virginia Resolves of 1798, which they wrote in opposing the Alien and Sedition Acts (see Chapter 8). The Hartford Convention of 1814–15, at which Federalists protested grievances related to the War of 1812, had adopted the same position (see Chapter 9). At issue in each case was the power of the state against that of the federal government. Now the same constitutional issue emerged again, this time, linked to the most intractable sectional issue, the South's determination to protect the institution of slavery.

South Carolina had an important supporter of nullification in the person of John C. Calhoun, who wrote a widely circulated defense of the doctrine, the *Exposition and Protest,* in 1828. Because Calhoun was soon to serve as Andrew Jackson's vice president, he wrote the *Exposition* anonymously. He hoped to use his influence with Jackson to gain support for nullification, but he was disappointed.

Where Calhoun saw nullification as a safeguard of the rights of the minority, Jackson saw it as a threat to national unity. As the president said at a famous exchange of toasts at the annual Jefferson Day dinner in 1830, "Our Federal Union, it must be preserved." In response to Jackson, Calhoun offered his own toast: "The Union—next to our liberty most dear. May we always remember that it can only be preserved by distributing equally the benefits and burdens of the Union." The president and the vice president were thus in open disagreement on a matter of crucial national importance. The outcome was inevitable: Calhoun lost all influence with Jackson, and two years later he took the unusual step of resigning the vice presidency. Martin Van Buren was elected to the office for Jackson's second term. Calhoun, his presidential aspirations in ruins, became a senator from South Carolina, and in that capacity participated in the last act of the nullification drama.

In 1832 the nullification controversy became a full-blown crisis. In passing the tariff of 1832, Congress (in spite of Jackson's urging) retained high taxes on woolens, iron, and hemp, although it reduced duties on other items. South Carolina responded with a special convention and an Ordinance of Nullification, in which it rejected the tariff and refused to collect the taxes it required. The state further issued a call for a volunteer militia and threatened to secede from the Union if Jackson used force against it. Jackson responded vehemently, denouncing the nullifiers—"Disunion by armed force is treason"—and obtaining from Congress a Force Bill authorizing the federal government to collect the tariff in South Carolina at gunpoint if necessary. Intimidated, the other southern states refused to follow South Carolina's lead. More quietly, Jackson also asked Congress to revise the tariff. Henry Clay, the Great Pacificator, swung into action and soon, with Calhoun's support, had crafted the Tariff Act of 1833. This measure appeared to meet southern demands by pledging a return to the tariff rate of 1816 (an average of 20 percent) by 1842 through a series of very small annual decreases for nine years, followed by a large cut in the final year. (In fact, in 1842 Congress quickly voted a return to higher tariff rates.) In 1833 the South Carolina legislature, unwilling to act without the support of other southern states, quickly accepted this face-saving compromise and repealed its nullification of the tariff of 1832. In a final burst of bravado, the legislature nullified the Force Bill, but Jackson defused the crisis by ignoring this second nullification.

The nullification crisis was the most serious threat to national unity that the United States had ever experienced. South Carolinians, by threatening to secede, had forced concessions on a matter they believed of vital economic importance. They—and a number of other Southerners—believed that the resolution of the crisis illustrated the success of their uncompromising tactics. Most of the rest of the nation simply breathed a sigh of relief, echoing Daniel Webster's sentiment, spoken in the heat of the debate over nullification, "Liberty and Union, now and forever, one and inseparable!" Most Americans firmly believed that although every effort should be made to address sectional concerns, national unity and majority rule came first. But another event of the Jackson years, Indian removal, clearly showed how unfair majority rule could be when the minority was not strong enough to force a compromise.

Indian Removal

The official policy of the United States government from the time of Jefferson's administration was to promote the assimilation of Indian peoples by encouraging them to adopt white ways. To Indian groups who resisted "civilization" or who needed more time to adapt, Jefferson offered the alternative of removal from settled areas in the East to the new Indian Territory west of the Mississippi River. Following this logic, at the end of the War of 1812 the federal government signed removal treaties with a number of Indian nations of the Old Northwest, thereby opening up large tracts of land for white settlement (see Chapter 9). In the Southwest, however, the "Five Civilized Tribes"—the Cherokees, Chickasaws, Choctaws, Creeks, and Seminoles—remained. By the 1830s, under constant pressure from settlers, each of the five tribes had ceded most of its lands, but sizable self-governing groups lived in

Georgia, Alabama, Mississippi, and Florida. All of these (except the Seminoles) had moved far in the direction of coexistence with whites, and they resisted suggestions that they should voluntarily remove themselves.

The Cherokees took the most extensive steps to adopt white ways. Their tribal lands in northwestern Georgia boasted prosperous farms, businesses, grain and lumber mills, and even plantations with black slaves. Intermarriage with whites and African Americans had produced an influential group of mixed bloods within the Cherokee nation, some of whom were eager to accept white ways. Schooled by Congregationalist, Presbyterian, and Moravian missionaries, the Cherokees were almost totally literate in English. They took special pride in the alphabet for their own language that was developed by the Cherokee scholar Sequoyah, and in 1828 they began publishing a tribal newspaper, the *Cherokee Phoenix*, in both Cherokee and English. A year earlier the tribe abolished its traditional form of government and established a constitutional republic.

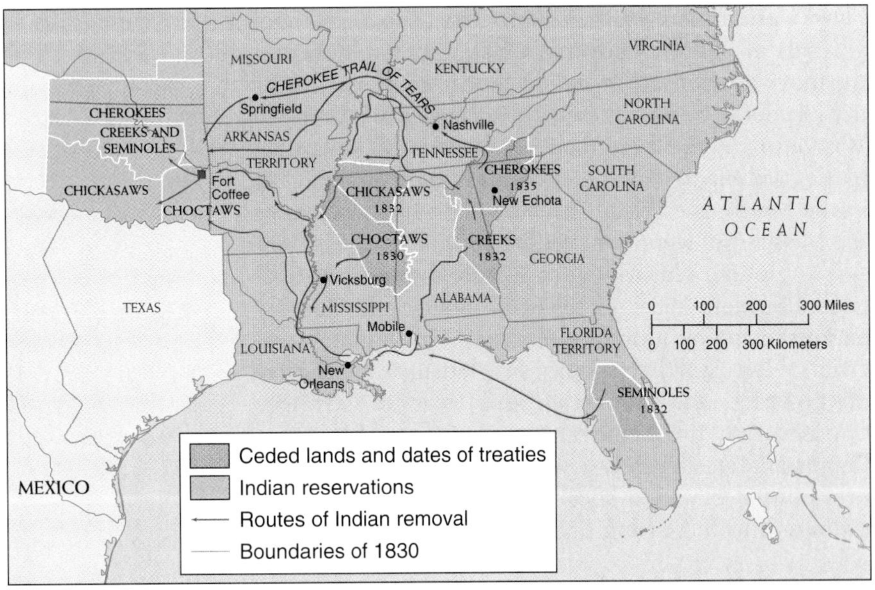

Southern Indian Cessions and Removals, 1830s *Pressure on the five major southern Indian peoples—the Cherokees, Chickasaws, Choctaws, Creeks, and Seminoles—that began during the War of 1812 culminated with their removal in the 1830s. Some groups from every tribe ceded their southern homelands peacefully and moved to the newly established Indian Territory west of Arkansas and Missouri. Some, like the Seminoles, resisted by force. Others, like the Cherokees, resisted in the courts but finally lost when President Andrew Jackson refused to enforce a Supreme Court decision in their favor. The Cherokees, the last to move, were forcibly removed by the U.S. Army along "the Trail of Tears" in 1838.*

Despite the evidence of the Cherokees' successful adaptation to the dominant white culture, in the 1820s the legislatures of Georgia, Alabama, and Mississippi, responding to pressures from land-hungry whites, voted to invalidate federal treaties granting special self-governing status to Indian lands. Because the federal government, not the states, bore responsibility for Indian policy, these state actions constituted a sectional challenge to federal authority. In this instance, however, unlike the Nullification Crisis, the resisting states had presidential support. Living up to his reputation as a ruthless Indian fighter, Jackson determined on a federal policy of wholesale removal of the southern Indian tribes.

In 1830, at President Jackson's urging, the U.S. Congress passed the hotly debated Indian Removal Act, which appropriated funds for relocation, by force if necessary. When Jackson increased the pressure by sending federal officials to negotiate removal treaties with the southern tribes, most reluctantly signed and prepared to move. The Cherokees, however, fought their removal by using the white man's weapon—the law. At first they seemed to have won: in *Cherokee Nation v. Georgia* (1831) and *Worcester v. Georgia* (1832) Chief Justice John Marshall ruled that the Cherokees, though not a state or a foreign nation, were a "domestic dependent nation" that could not be forced by the state of Georgia to give up its land against its will. However, when President Jackson heard the Supreme Court's decision, he is reputed to have said, "John Marshall has made his decision. Now let him enforce it." Ignoring the decision, Jackson continued his support for removal.

Faced by the Cherokees' de facto defeat, what could the other Indian tribes do? Some Seminoles of Florida chose to fight. Aided by runaway slaves and by their unsurpassed knowledge of their homeland, the Florida Everglades, some Seminole bands fought a guerrilla war that lasted into the 1840s before the U.S. military gave up and allowed them to remain. The majority of Seminoles and members of other tribes were much less fortunate: most of the Choctaws moved west in 1830; the last of the Creeks were forcibly moved by the military in 1836, and the Chickasaws a year later. And in 1838, in the last and most infamous removal, resisting Cherokees were driven west to Oklahoma along what came to be known as "the Trail of Tears." A 7,000-man army escorting them watched thousands (perhaps a quarter of the 16,000 Cherokees) die along the way. Another futile effort to resist removal, the Black Hawk "war," occurred in the Old Northwest. In 1832, Sac and Fox Indians, led by Black

Hawk, attempted to move back to their old tribal grounds in Illinois following removal, but settlers saw the move as an invasion and demanded military protection. Federal troops chased the Black Hawk band to Wisconsin, where more than 300 Indians died in a final battle, and Black Hawk himself was taken prisoner. As in the South, the last of the remaining Indians east of the Mississippi were removed by the end of the 1830s.

Indian removal was a deeply divisive national issue. President Jackson's sweeping policy undoubtedly expressed the opinion of most Southerners and Westerners. But northern opinion, led by Protestant missionaries and reform groups, was so strongly opposed that the Removal Act passed the House of Representatives by only 3 votes (out of 200). Jackson's presidential claim to speak for popular opinion was running into increasing opposition.

The Bank War

The last major event of Jackson's presidency, his refusal to renew the charter of the Second Bank of the United States, had lasting political consequences. Jackson's opponents, already angry about his earlier actions, were so infuriated by the bank episode that they formed the permanent opposition party known as the Whigs. It was from the heat of the Bank War that the now characteristic American two-party system emerged.

The first Bank of the United States had been chartered by Congress in 1791, at Alexander Hamilton's urging. Federalists supported it, Jeffersonians opposed it and allowed its charter to expire in 1811. But after the War of 1812 almost all Democratic Republicans came to appreciate the stability provided by a central bank. Thus in 1816 Congress granted a twenty-year charter to the Second Bank of the United States. Like its predecessor, the Bank played a powerful role in the expanding American economy, encouraging the growth of strong and stable financial interests and curbing less stable and irresponsible ones.

Also, like its predecessor, the Bank was not a government agency but a private institution, the majority of whose directors were appointed by the government. Its stockholders were some of the nation's richest men (New York's John Jacob Astor and Philadelphia's Stephen Girard among them). The bank was directed by the erudite and aristocratic Nicholas Biddle of Philadelphia. Biddle, a friend of Thomas Jefferson and an avid amateur scientist, was the editor of the journals of Lewis and Clark.

The Bank, which with thirty branches was the nation's largest, performed a variety of functions: it held the government's money (about $10 million), sold government bonds, and made commercial loans. But its most important function was the control it exercised over state banks. At the time, America lacked a national currency. The money in circulation was a mixture of paper money (U.S. notes and the notes of state banks) and gold and silver coins (specie, or hard currency), many of them of foreign origin. Because state banks tended to issue more paper money than they could back with hard currency, the Bank always demanded repayment of its loans to them in coin. This policy forced state banks to maintain adequate reserves, curbed inflationary pressures (overprinting of banknotes), and restricted speculative activities such as risky loans. In times of recession, the bank eased the pressure on state banks, demanding only partial payment in coin. Thus the Bank acted as a currency stabilizer by helping to control the money supply. It brought a semblance of order to what we today would consider a chaotic money system—coins of various weights and a multitude of state banknotes, many of which were discounted (not accepted at full face value) in other states.

This figurehead of Andrew Jackson, carved in 1834 for the navy frigate Constitution, captures the unmoveable resolve that made Jackson so popular early in his presidency and so reviled during the Bank War.

Museum of the City of New York (M52.11)

The concept of a strong national bank was supported by the majority of the nation's merchants and businessmen and was a key element in Henry Clay's American System. Nevertheless, the Bank had many opponents. The objections arose from both sectional and political resentments. A number of state bank directors felt overshadowed by the central bank's size and power. Western land speculators, and many western farmers, chafed at the bank's tight control over the currency reserves of state banks, claiming it was harmful to western development. Both western farmers and urban workers had bitter memories of the Panic of 1819, which the Bank had caused (at least in part) by sharply contracting credit. To some people, the economic power of the Bank was frightening; they feared that monied elites would use it to their own advantage. Although the rapid growth of the national economy made some sort of control necessary, many ordinary people were uneasy not only about the Bank but about banks of all kinds. They believed that a system based on paper currency would be manipulated by bankers in unpredictable and dangerous ways. Among those who held that opinion was Andrew Jackson, who had hated and feared banks ever since the 1790s, when he had lost a great deal of money in a speculative venture.

Early in his administration, Jackson hastened to tell Nicholas Biddle, "I do not dislike your Bank any more than all banks." By 1832, Jackson's opinion had changed and he and Biddle were locked in a personal conflict that harmed not only the national economy but the reputations of both men. Biddle, urged on by Henry Clay and Daniel Webster, precipitated the conflict by making early application for rechartering the Bank. Congress approved the application in July 1832. Clay and Webster, though well aware of Jackson's antibank feelings, believed the president would not risk a veto in an election year. They were wrong. Jackson immediately decided on a stinging veto, announcing to Van Buren, "The bank...is trying to kill me, but I will kill it!"

And kill it he did that same July, with one of the strongest veto messages in American history. Denouncing the Bank as unconstitutional, harmful to states' rights, and "dangerous to the liberties of the people," Jackson presented himself as the spokesman for the majority of ordinary people and the enemy of special privilege. Asserting that the Bank's "exclusive privileges" were benefiting only the rich, Jackson claimed to speak for the "humble members of society—the farmers, mechanics and laborers"—and to oppose injustice and inequality. Nor did Jackson's veto message speak only of the sharp division between social classes. It also aroused sectional and national feelings by its allusions to the many British and eastern bank stockholders who were profiting from the debts of poor Southerners and Westerners. In short, the veto spoke directly to many of the fears and resentments that Americans felt at this time of exceptionally rapid economic and social change. Jackson's message was a campaign document, written to appeal to voters. Most of the financial community was appalled, believing both the veto and the accompanying message to be reckless demagoguery.

Jackson's Reelection in 1832

Nevertheless, Jackson's veto message was a great popular success, and it set the terms for the presidential election of 1832. Henry Clay, the nominee of the anti-Jackson forces, lost the battle for popular opinion. Democrats successfully painted Clay as the defender of the Bank and of privilege. His defeat was decisive: he drew only 49 electoral votes, to Jackson's 219. A handful of votes went to the first third party in American history, the short-lived Anti-Masonic Party. This party played on the resentments of the newly enfranchised "common man" against the traditional political elite, many of whom (including both Jackson and Clay) were members of the Masonic order, a fraternal society with secret rituals and special customs. The Anti-Masonic Party did make one lasting contribution to the political process. It was the first to hold a national nominating convention, an innovation quickly adopted by the other political parties.

Although the election was a triumph for Jackson, the Bank War continued. It was to have serious effects on the economy and on political principle. The Bank charter did not expire until 1836, but Jackson, declaring that "the hydra of corruption is only scotched, not dead," decided to kill the Bank by transferring its $10 million in government deposits to favored state banks ("pet banks," critics called them). Cabinet members objected, but Jackson ignored them. Two secretaries of the treasury refused to carry out Jackson's orders and were abruptly removed. Jackson then found a more pliant man, Roger Taney, for the job. (Jackson later rewarded him with the post of chief justice of the Supreme Court.) Henry Clay led an unprecedented vote of censure in the Senate, but in the House loyal Democrats prevented a censure vote. To all of these protests, Jackson responded that the election had given him a popular mandate to act against the Bank. The president was the direct representative of the people, he claimed, and could act upon the popular will, regardless of the opinion of Congress or even the cabinet. Short of impeachment, there was nothing Congress could do to prevent Jackson from acting on his expansive—and novel—interpretation of presidential powers.

Whigs, Van Buren, and the Election of 1836

But there was someone outside Congress with power to respond: the Bank's director, Nicholas Biddle. "This worthy President thinks that because he has scalped Indians...he is to have his way with the Bank," Biddle commented. "He is mistaken." As the government withdrew its deposits, Biddle abruptly called in the Bank's commercial loans, thereby causing a sharp panic and recession in the winter of 1833–34. Merchants, businessmen, and southern planters were all furious—at Jackson. His opponents, only a loose coalition up to this time, coalesced into a formal opposition party that called itself the Whigs. Evoking the memory of the Patriots who had resisted King George III in the American Revolution, the new party called on everyone to resist tyrannical "King Andrew." Just as Jackson's own calls for popular democracy had appealed to voters in all regions, so his opponents overcame their sectional differences to unite in opposition to his economic policies and arbitrary methods.

The Whigs first tested their strength against Vice President Martin Van Buren, Jackson's designated successor, in the presidential election of 1836. Still not completely free of the methods and attitudes of traditional politics, the Whigs ran four sectional candidates: William Henry Harrison of Ohio, Hugh Lawson White of Tennessee, W. P. Mangum of North Carolina, and Daniel Webster of Massachusetts. The Whigs hoped the combined votes for these regional candidates would deny Van Buren a majority and force the election into the House of Representatives, where they hoped to win. The strategy failed, but not by much: although Van Buren captured 170 electoral votes to the Whigs' 124, the popular vote was much closer, 50.9 percent to 49.1 percent. A shift of only 2,000 votes in Pennsylvania would have thrown the election into the House of Representatives, vindicating the Whig strategy. The Whig defeat drove home the weakness of the traditional sectional politics, but the closeness of the popular vote showed that the basis for a united national opposition did exist. In 1840, the Whigs would prove that they had learned this lesson.

The Panic of 1837

Meanwhile, the consequences of the Bank War continued. The recession of 1833–34 was followed by a wild speculative boom, caused as much by foreign investors as by the expiration of the Bank. Many new state banks were chartered that were eager to give loans, the price of cotton rose rapidly, and speculation in western lands was feverish (in Alabama and Mississippi, the mid-1830s were known as "the Flush Times"). A government surplus of $37 million distributed to the states in 1836 made the inflationary pressures worse. Jackson became alarmed at the widespread use of paper money (which he blamed for the inflation), and in July 1836 he issued the Specie Circular, announcing that the government would accept payment for public lands only in hard currency. At the same time, foreign investors, especially British banks, affected by a world recession, called in their American loans. The sharp contraction of credit led to the Panic of 1837 and a six-year recession, the worst the American economy had yet known. Ironically, Andrew Jackson, whose bad experience with speculation had led him to destroy the Bank of the United States, set in motion the events that caused the boom and bust he so feared. And he left his successor, Martin Van Buren, an impossible political legacy.

In 1837, 800 banks suspended business, refusing to pay out any of their $150 million in deposits. The collapse of the banking system led to business closures and outright failures. Nationwide, the unemployment rate is estimated to have reached more than 10 percent. In the winter of 1837–38 in New York City alone, one-third of all manual laborers were unemployed and an estimated 10,000 were living in abject poverty. New York laborers took to the streets. Four or five thousand protesters carrying signs reading "Bread, Meat, Rent, Fuel!" gathered at City Hall on February 10, 1838, then marched to the warehouse of a leading merchant, Eli Hart. Breaking down the door, they took possession of the thousands of barrels of flour Hart had stored there rather than sell at what the mob considered a fair price. Policemen and state militia who tried to prevent the break-in were beaten by the angry mob.

Nor were the working class and the poor the only victims. Among the many hurt by the panic was Philip Hone, former mayor of New York and once a man of considerable wealth. Hone lost two-thirds of his own fortune and was unable to help his three grown sons when they lost their jobs. "Business of all kinds [is] completely at a stand," Hone noted in 1840, wondering "how the poor man manages to get a dinner for his family." The Panic of 1837 lasted six long years, causing widespread misery. Not until 1843 did the economy show signs of recovery.

In neither 1837 nor 1819 did the federal government take any action to aid victims of economic recession. No banks were bailed out, no bank depositors were saved by federal insurance, no laid-off workers got unemployment payments. Nor did the government undertake any public works projects or pump money into the economy. All of these steps, today seen as essential to prevent economic collapse and to alleviate human suffering, were unheard of in 1819 and 1837. Soup kitchens and charities were mobilized in major cities, but only by private, volunteer groups, not by local or state governments. Panics and depressions were believed to be natural stages in the business cycle, and government intervention was considered unwarranted—although it was perfectly acceptable for government to intervene to promote growth. As a result, workers, farmers, and members of the new business middle class suddenly realized that participation in America's booming economy was very dangerous. The rewards could be great, but so could the penalties.

Martin Van Buren (quickly nicknamed "Van Ruin") spent a dismal four years in the White House presiding over bank failures, bankruptcies, and massive unemployment. Van Buren, who lacked Jackson's compelling personality, could find no remedies to the

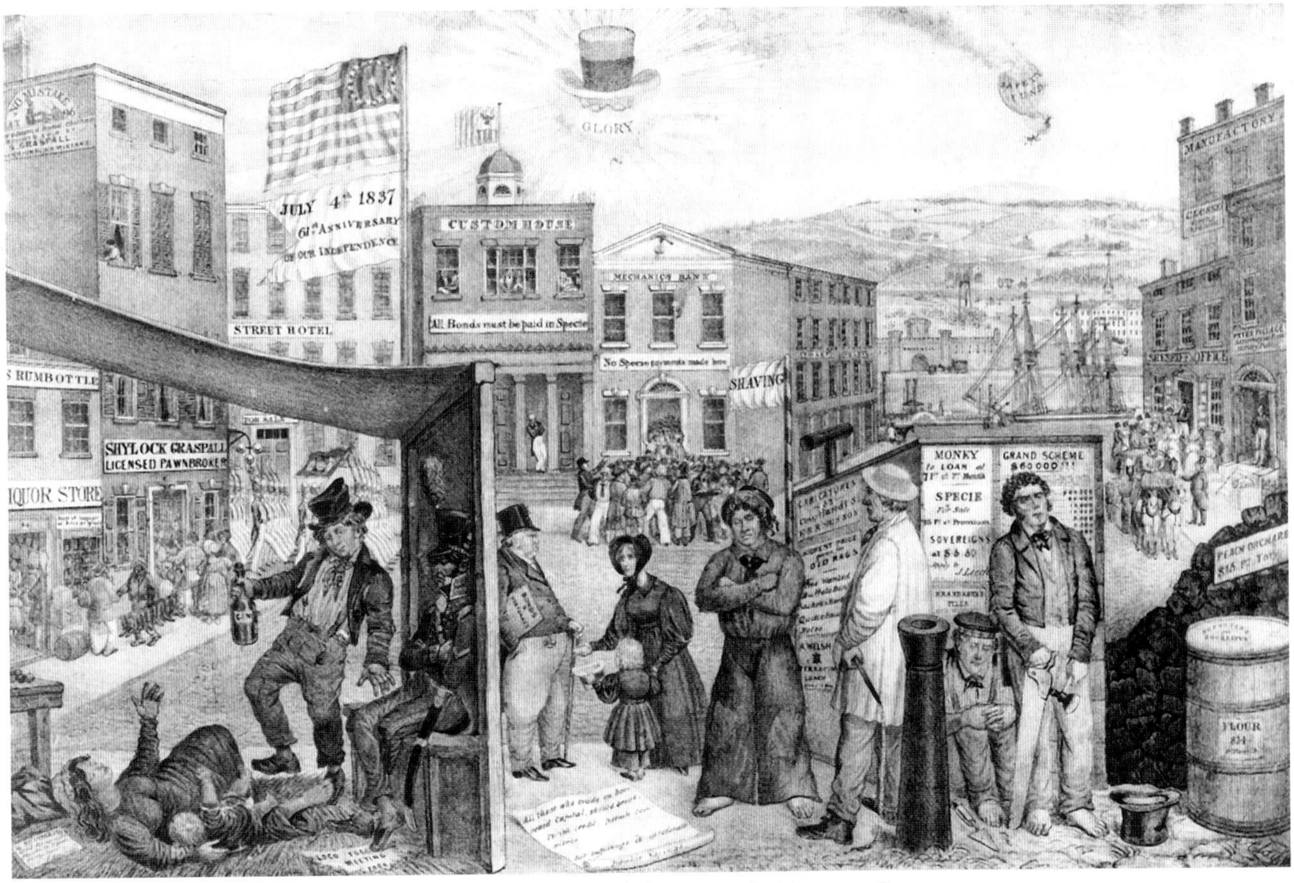

This contemporary cartoon bitterly depicts the terrible effects of the Panic of 1837 on ordinary people—bank failures, unemployment, drunkenness, and destitution—which the artist links to the insistence of the rich on payment in specie (as Jackson had required in the Species Circular of 1836). Over the scene waves the American flag, accompanied by the ironic message, "61st Anniversary of our Independence."

depression. His misfortune gave the opposition party, the newly formed Whigs, their opportunity.

THE SECOND AMERICAN PARTY SYSTEM

The First American Party System, the confrontation between the Federalists and the Jeffersonian Democratic Republicans that began in the 1790s, had been widely viewed as an unfortunate factional squabble that threatened the common good of the republic (see Chapter 8). By the 1830s, with the expansion of suffrage, politics and the reality of continuing political disagreements had come to be taken as a fact of life. The political struggles of the Jackson era, coupled with the dramatic social changes caused by expansion and economic growth, created the basic pattern of American politics: two major parties, each with at least some appeal among voters of all social classes and in all sections of the country. That pattern, which we call "the Second American Party System," remains to this day.

Whigs and Democrats

There were genuine differences between the Whigs and the Democrats, but they were not sectional differences. Instead, the two parties reflected just-emerging class and cultural differences. The Democrats, as they themselves were quick to point out, had inherited Thomas Jefferson's belief in the democratic rights of the small, independent yeoman farmer. Because most of the country was rural, it is not surprising that the Democrats had nationwide appeal, especially in the South and West, the most rural regions. As a result of Jackson's presidency, Democrats came to be identified with independence and a distaste for interference, whether from the government or from economic monopolies such as the Bank of the United States. They favored expansion, Indian removal, and the freedom to do as they chose on the frontier. In the politics of the time, these were conservative values. They reflected the opposition of most Democratic voters to the rapid social and economic changes that accompanied the transportation revolution.

Overview

The Second American Party System

Democrats	First organized to elect Andrew Jackson to the presidency in 1828. The Democratic Party spoke for Jeffersonian democracy, expansion, and the freedom of the "common man" from interference from government or from financial monopolies like the Bank of the United States. It found its power base in the rural South and West and among some northern urban workers. The Democratic Party was the majority party from 1828 to 1860.
Whigs	Organized in opposition to Andrew Jackson in the early 1830s. Heir to Federalism, the Whig Party favored a strong role for the national government in the economy (for example, it promoted Henry Clay's American System) and supported active social reform. Its power base lay in the North and Northwest among voters who benefited from increased commercialization and among some southern planters and urban merchants. The Whigs won the elections of 1840 and 1848.

The Whigs were themselves often the initiators and beneficiaries of economic change and were more receptive to it. Heirs of the Federalist belief in the importance of a strong federal role in the national economy (see Chapter 8), they supported the elements of Henry Clay's American System: a strong central government, the Bank of the United States, a protective tariff, and internal improvements. In fact, when it came to improvements, the Whigs wanted to improve people as well as roads. Religion was an important element in political affiliation, and many Whigs were members of evangelical reforming denominations. Reformers believed that everyone, rich and poor, was capable of the self-discipline that would lead to a good life. Thus Whigs favored government intervention in both economic and social affairs, calling for education and social reforms such as temperance that aimed to improve the ordinary citizen. Many rich men were Whigs, but so were many poorer men who had a democratic faith in the perfectibility of all Americans. The Whigs' greatest strength was in New England and the northern part of the West (the Old Northwest), the areas most affected by commercial agriculture and factory work.

Yet neither party was monolithic. As has continued to be true of American political parties, both the Democrats and the Whigs were a coalition of interests affected by local and regional factors. The job of the party leader, as the Democrats' Martin Van Buren had been among the first to realize, was to forge the divergent local party interests into a winning national majority. Although Jackson's appeal was strongest in the rural South and West, the Democrats also appealed to some workers in northern cities. Reflecting the emerging issues of class and ethnicity, these Democrats, many of them immigrants, voted against the wealthier, native-born Americans, who were mostly Whigs. Urban workers cared little about rural issues, and they were less committed to the slave system than many Southerners, but they shared with Democrats from other regions a dislike of big business. On the other hand, a number of southern planters, who had close ties to merchant and banking interests, and residents of the South's commercial cities were attracted to the Whig policy of a strong federal role in economic development, though they were less active than many northern Whigs in advocating sweeping social reform.

The Campaign of 1840

In 1840, the Whigs set out to beat the Democrats at their own game. Passing over the ever-hopeful Henry Clay, the Whigs nominated a man as much like Andrew Jackson as possible, the aging Indian fighter William Henry Harrison, former governor of the Indiana Territory from 1801 to 1812. In an effort to duplicate Jackson's winning appeal to the South as well as the West, the Whigs balanced the ticket by nominating a Southerner, John Tyler, for vice president. The campaign slogan was "Tippecanoe and Tyler too" (Tippecanoe was the site of Harrison's famous victory over Tecumseh's Indian confederation in 1811). As if this were not enough, Whigs made Harrison out to be a humble man who would be happy to live in a log cabin, although he actually lived in a large and comfortable house. Thus began another long-lived political legend. The Whigs reached out to ordinary people with torchlight parades, barbecues, songs, coonskin caps, bottomless jugs of (hard) cider, and claims that Martin Van Buren, Harrison's hapless opponent, was a man of privilege and aristocratic tastes. Nothing could be further from the truth: Van Buren was the son of a tavern keeper. But Van Buren, a short man who lacked a commanding presence, had always dressed meticulously, and now even his taste in coats and ties was used against him.

The Whig campaign tactics, added to the popular anger at Van Buren because of the continuing depression, gave Harrison a sweeping electoral victory, 234 votes to 60. Even more remarkable, the campaign achieved the greatest voter turnout up to that time (and rarely equaled since), 80 percent.

The Whig Victory Turns to Loss: The Tyler Presidency

Although the Whig victory of 1840 was a milestone in American politics, the triumph of Whig principles was short-lived. William Henry Harrison, who was sixty-eight, died of pneumonia a month after his inauguration. For the first time in American history the vice president stepped up to the presidency. Not for the last time, important differences between the dead president and his successor reshaped the direction of American politics.

John Tyler of Virginia was a former Democrat who had left the party because he disagreed with Jackson's autocratic style. The Whigs had sought him primarily for his sectional appeal and had not inquired too closely into his political opinions, which turned out to be anti-Whig as well as anti-Jackson. President Tyler vetoed a series of bills embodying all the elements of Henry Clay's American System: tariffs, internal improvements, a new Bank of the United States. In exasperation, congressional Whigs read Tyler out of the party, and his entire cabinet of Whigs resigned. To replace them, Tyler appointed former Democrats like himself. Thus the Whig triumph of 1840, one of the clearest victories in American electoral politics, was negated by the stalemate between Tyler and the Whig majority in Congress. The Whigs were to win only one more election, that of 1848.

Although the circumstances that robbed the Whigs of their victory were accidental, the Tyler debacle laid bare the great division that the two-party system was intended to hide: the sectional difference between the North and the South. The Whigs were a short-lived national party because they could not bridge that gap. And by the 1850s not even the Democrats could remain united.

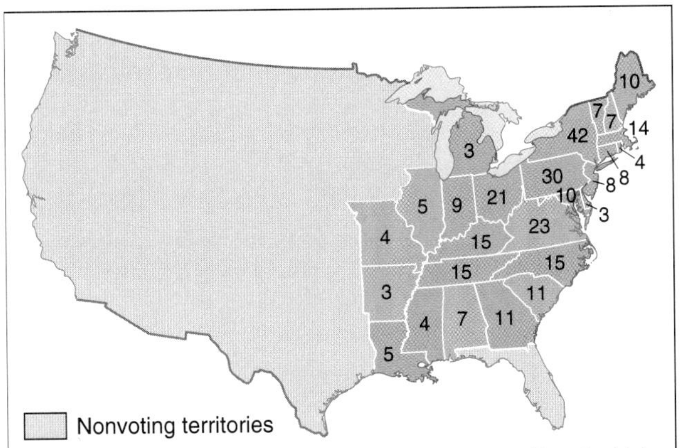

	Electoral Vote (%)	Popular Vote (%)
WILLIAM HENRY HARRISON (Whig)	**234 (80)**	**1,275,016 (53)**
Martin Van Buren (Democrat)	60 (20)	1,129,102 (47)

The Election of 1840 *The Whigs triumphed in the election of 1840 by beating the Democrats at their own game. Whigs could expect to do well in the commercializing areas of New England and the Old Northwest, but their adopted strategy of popular campaigning worked well in the largely rural South and West as well, contributing to Harrison's victory. The Whigs' choice of John Tyler as vice-presidential candidate, another strategy designed to appeal to southern voters, backfired when Harrison died and Tyler, who did not share Whig principles, became America's first vice president to succeed to the presidency.*

AMERICAN ARTS AND LETTERS

Jackson's presidency was a defining moment in the development of an American identity. His combination of western belligerency and combative individualism was the strongest statement of American distinctiveness since Thomas Jefferson's agrarianism. Did Jackson speak for all of America? The Whigs did not think so. And the definitions of American identity that were beginning to emerge in popular culture and in intellectual circles were more complex than the message coming from the White House. Throughout the nation, however, there was a widespread interest in information and literature of all kinds. The Age of the Common Man would prove to be the period when American writers and painters found the national themes that allowed them to produce the first distinctively American literature and art.

The Spread of the Written Word

The transportation revolution improved communication. The number of newspapers, magazines, and books grew rapidly, helping broaden people's horizons beyond their own community. A print revolution began in 1826 when a reform organization, the American Tract Society, installed the country's first steam-powered press. Three years later the new presses had turned out 300,000 Bibles and 6 million religious tracts, or pamphlets. The greatest growth, however, was in newspapers that reached a mass audience. The number of newspapers soared from 376 newspapers in 1810 to 1,200 in 1835. This rise paralleled the growth of interest in politics, for most newspapers were published by political parties and were

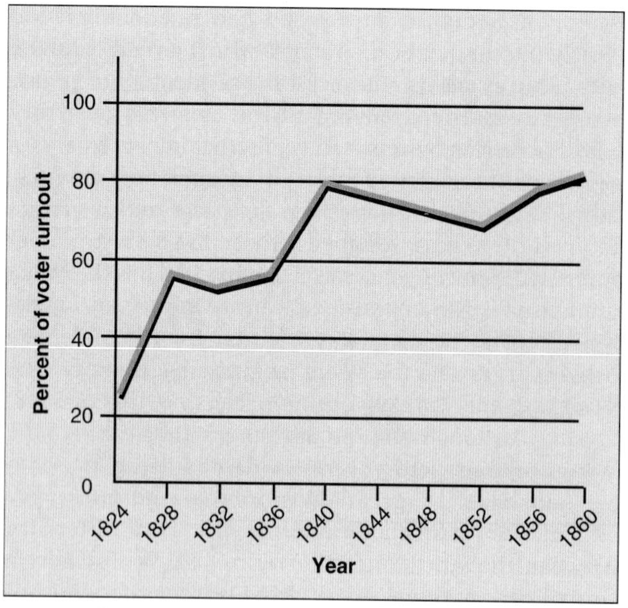

Pre–Civil War Voter Turnout *The turnout of voters in presidential elections more than doubled from 1824 to 1828, the year Andrew Jackson was first elected. Turnout surged to 80 percent in 1840, the year the Whigs triumphed. The extension of suffrage to all white men and heated competition between two political parties with nationwide membership turned presidential election campaigns into events with great popular appeal.*

openly partisan. Packed with articles that today would be considered libelous and scandalous, newspapers were entertaining and popular reading. For western readers, the popular Crockett almanacs offered a mix of humorous stories and tall tales attributed to Davy Crockett (the boisterous Tennessee "roarer" who died defending the Alamo in 1836) along with meteorological and climate information. Throughout the country, religious literature was still the most widely read, but a small middle-class audience existed for literary magazines and, among women especially, for sentimental magazines and novels.

Accompanying all these changes in print communication was an invention that outsped them all: the telegraph, so innovative that its inventor spent years fruitlesssly seeking private funds to back its application. Finally, with financing from the federal government, Samuel F. B. Morse sent his first message from Washington to Baltimore in 1844. Soon messages in Morse code would be transmitted instantaneously across the continent. The impact of this revolutionary invention, the first to separate the message from the speed at which a human messenger could travel, was immediate. The timeliness of information available to the individual, from important national news to the next train's arrival time, vastly increased. Distant events gained new and exciting immediacy. Everyone's horizon and sense of community was widened.

Creating an American Culture

For all the improvements in communication, the United States was a provincial culture, still looking to Britain for values, standards, and literary offerings, and still mocked by the British. In a famous essay in the *Edinburgh Review* in 1820, Sidney Smith bitingly inquired, "In the four quarters of the globe, who reads an American book? or goes to an American play? or looks at an American picture or statue? What does the world yet owe to American physicians or surgeons? What new substances have their chemists discovered?" The answer was nothing—yet.

In the early years of the nineteenth century, eastern seaboard cities actively built the cultural foundation that would nurture American art and literature. Philadelphia's American Philosophical Society, founded by Benjamin Franklin in 1743, boasted a distinguished roster of scientists, including Thomas Jefferson—concurrently its president and president of the United States—and Nicholas Biddle, Jackson's opponent in the Bank War. Culturally, Boston ran a close second to Philadelphia, founding the Massachusetts General Hospital (1811) and the Boston Athenaeum (1807), a gentlemen's library and reading room containing "the works of learning and science in all languages; particularly such rare and expensive publications as are not generally to be obtained in this country." The *North American Review*, published in Boston, emerged as the country's most

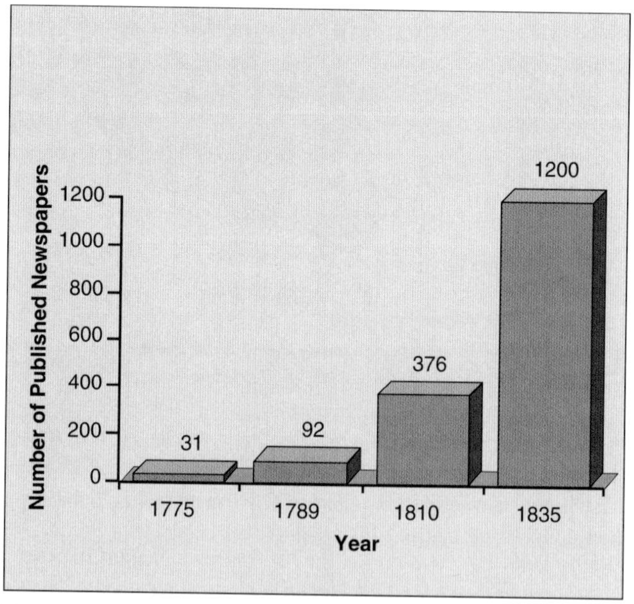

The Burgeoning of Newspapers *Newspapers have a long history in the United States. Even before the American Revolution the colonies boasted 37 newspapers (see Chapter 6), and within little more than a decade that number had nearly tripled. Toward the end of the century, however, the number of newspapers expanded rapidly, by 1835 numbering more than 30 times that of 1775.*

The Boston Athenaeum was one of Boston's leading cultural institutions. The library, shown in this engraving, was probably the finest in the country in the early nineteenth century.

important and long-lasting intellectual magazine. Devoted to keeping its readers in touch with European intellectual developments, the *Review* had a circulation of 3,000 in 1826, about the same as similar British journals. Southern cities were much less successful in supporting culture. Charleston had a Literary and Philosophical Society (founded in 1814), but the widely dispersed residences of the southern elite made urban cultural institutions difficult to sustain. Thus, unwittingly, the South ceded cultural leadership to the North.

The cultural picture was much spottier in the West. A few cities, such as Lexington, Kentucky, and Cincinnati, Ohio, had civic cultural institutions, and some transplanted New Englanders maintained connections with New England culture. A group of pioneers in Ames, Ohio, for example, founded a "coonskin library" composed of books purchased from Boston and paid for in coonskins. But most pioneers were at best uninterested and at worst actively hostile to traditional literary culture. This was neither from lack of literacy nor from failure to read. Newspaper and religious journals both had large readerships in the West: The Methodist *Christian Advocate,* for example, reached 25,000 people yearly (compared with the *North American Review*'s 3,000). The frontier emphasis on the practical was hard to distinguish from anti-intellectualism. As writer Hugh Henry Brackenridge lamented from Pittsburgh, it was not "the want of learning I consider as a defect, but the contempt of it."

Thus in the early part of the nineteenth century, the gap between the intellectual and cultural horizons of a wealthy Bostonian and a frontier farmer in Michigan widened. Part of the unfinished task of building a national society was the creation of a national culture that could fill this gap. For writers and artists, the challenge was to find distinctively American themes.

Of the eastern cities, New York produced the first widely recognized American writers. In 1819, Washington Irving published *The Sketch Book,* thus immortalizing Rip Van Winkle and the Headless Horseman. Within a few years James Fenimore Cooper's Leatherstocking novels (of which *The Last of the Mohicans,* published in 1826, is the best known) achieved wide success in both America and Europe. Cooper's novels featured a heroic frontiersman, Natty Bumppo (modeled on Daniel Boone) who observes favorably the nobility of the Indians even as he participates in their defeat by the forces of civilization. Cooper's novels established the long American experience of westward expansion, of which the conquest of the Indians was a vital part, as a serious and distinctive American literary theme.

It was New England, however, that claimed to be the forge of American cultural independence from Europe. As Ralph Waldo Emerson proclaimed in "The American Scholar," a lecture he delivered in 1837 to the Harvard faculty, "Our day of dependence, our long apprenticeship to the learning of other lands, draws to a close." He went on to encourage American writers to find inspiration in the ordinary details of daily life. The stuff of literature, he declared, were to be found in "the familiar, the low...the milk in the pan; the ballad in the street; the news of the boat." Immensely popular, Emerson was the star of the lyceum circuit, a lecture network that sent speakers on cultural subjects to all parts of the country. He gave more than 1,500 lectures in twenty states between 1833 and 1860. "The American Scholar," his most famous lecture, carried a message of cultural self-sufficiency that Americans were eager to hear.

Asher Durand, a member of the Hudson River School of landscape painting, produced this work, Kindred Spirits, *in 1849 as a tribute to Thomas Cole, the school's leader. Cole is one of the figures depicted standing in a romantic wilderness.*

Artists and Builders

Artists were as successful as novelists in finding American themes. Thomas Cole, who came to America from England in 1818, found great inspiration in the American landscape, painting scenes of New York State's Catskill and Adirondack Mountains that reflect the influence of the British romantic school of landscape painting. With these works, Cole founded the Hudson River school of American painting. The frankly nationalistic style and subject matter of this school are reflected in the comment of New Yorker Philip Hone: "Every American is bound to prove his love of country by admiring Cole."

The western painters—realists such as Karl Bodmer and George Catlin as well as the romantics who followed them, like Albert Bierstadt and Thomas Moran—drew on the dramatic western landscape and its peoples. Their art was an important contribution to the American sense of the land and to the nation's identity. Catlin, driven by a need to document Indian life before it disappeared, spent eight years among the tribes of the upper Missouri River. Then he assembled his collection—more than 500 paintings in all—and toured the country from 1837 to 1851 in an unsuccessful attempt to arouse public indignation about the plight of the western Indian nations. Another unusual western painter, John James Audubon, could at first find no publisher in this country for his striking and sometimes grotesque etchings of American birds. George Caleb Bingham, an accomplished genre painter, produced somewhat tidied-up scenes of real-life American workers, such as flatboatmen on the Missouri River. All these painters found much to record and to celebrate in American life. Ironically, the inspiration for the most prevalent theme, the American wilderness, was profoundly endangered by the rapid western settlement of which the nation was so proud.

The haste and transiency of American life are nowhere so obvious as in the architectural record of this era, which is sparse. The monumental neoclassical style (complete with columns) that Jefferson had recommended for official buildings in Washington continued to be favored for public buildings elsewhere and by private concerns trying to project an imposing image, such as banks. A few southern planters built impressive mansions, and there were odd experiments such as the prison built in Philadelphia in the 1820s that was designed to look like a medieval castle. The effect of this building on the imagination, one admiring commentator remarked, was "peculiarly impressive, solemn and instructive."

But in general Americans were in too much of a hurry to build for the future, and in balloon-frame construction they found the perfect technique for the present. Balloon-frame structures—which consist of a basic frame of wooden studs fastened with crosspieces top and bottom—could be put up quickly, cheaply, and without the help of a skilled carpenter. Covering the frame with wooden siding was equally simple, and the

CHRONOLOGY

1817	Erie Canal construction begins
1818	National Road completed to Wheeling
1819	*Dartmouth College v. Woodward*
1821	Martin Van Buren's Bucktails defeat DeWitt Clinton in New York
1824	*Gibbons v. Ogden* John Quincy Adams elected president by the House of Representatives
1825	Erie Canal opens
1826	First American use of the steam-powered printing press
1828	Congress passes "Tariff of Abominations" Andrew Jackson elected president John C. Calhoun publishes *Exposition and Protest* anonymously
1830	Jackson vetoes Maysville Road Bill Congress passes Indian Removal Act Baltimore and Ohio Railroad opens
1832	Nullification Crisis begins Jackson vetoes renewal of Bank of the United States charter Jackson reelected president
1833	National Road completed to Columbus, Ohio
1834	Cyrus McCormick patents the McCormick reaper Whig party organized
1836	Jackson issues Specie Circular Martin Van Buren elected president
1837	*Charles River Bridge v. Warren Bridge* John Deere invents steel plow Ralph Waldo Emerson first presents "The American Scholar" Panic of 1837
1838	Cherokee removal along the "Trail of Tears"
1840	Whig William Henry Harrison elected president
1841	John Tyler assumes presidency at the death of President Harrison
1844	Samuel F. B. Morse operates first telegraph

resultant dwelling was as strong, although not as well insulated, as a house of solid timber or logs. Balloon-frame construction was first used in Chicago in the 1830s, where it created the city almost instantly. The four-room balloon-frame house, affordable to many who could not have paid for a traditionally built dwelling, became standard in that decade. This was indeed housing for the common man and his family.

CONCLUSION

Andrew Jackson's presidency witnessed the building of a strong national party system based on nearly universal white manhood suffrage. At the same time that the nation expanded politically (nine new western states were admitted between 1800 and 1840), construction of new roads, canals, and railroads and other improvements in transportation and communication created the infrastructure that united the nation physically. Sectionalism and localism seemed to have been replaced by a more national consciousness that was clearly expressed in the two national political parties, the Whigs and the Democrats. The Second American Party System created new democratic political communities united by common political opinions. Culturally, American writers and artists began to establish a distinctive American identity in the arts. But as the key battles of the Jackson presidency—the Nullification Crisis, Indian removal, the Bank War—attested, the forces of sectionalism resisted the strong nationalizing tendencies of the era. As the next two chapters will show, economic and social forces continued to force the South and the North apart.

REVIEW QUESTIONS

1. What reasons might a person of the 1820s and 1830s give for opposing universal white manhood suffrage? Suffrage for free African American men? For women of all races?
2. Opponents believed that Andrew Jackson was unsuited in both political experience and temperament to be president of the United States, yet his presidency is considered one of the most influential in American history. Explain the changes in political organization and attitude that made his election possible.
3. Both the Nullification Crisis and Indian Removal raised the constitutional issue of the rights of a minority in a nation governed by majority rule. What rights, in your opinion, does a minority have, and what kinds of laws are necessary to defend those rights?
4. Why was the issue of government support for internal improvements so controversial? Who benefited from the transportation revolution? Who lost ground?
5. What were the key differences between Whigs and Democrats? What did each party stand for? Who were their supporters? What were the links between each party's programs and party supporters?
6. What distinctive American themes did the writers, artists, and builders of the 1820s and 1830s express in their works? Are they still considered American themes today?

RECOMMENDED READING

Donald B. Cole, *Martin Van Buren and the American Political System* (1984). An excellent study of Van Buren's key role in the transformation of politics.

Donald B. Cole, *The Presidency of Andrew Jackson* (1993). In this recent work, Jackson is seen as just as influential, but less commanding and more ambiguous in his political attitudes than in earlier studies.

Daniel Feller, *The Jacksonian Promise* (1995). A recent overview of the period 1815–1840 that stresses the optimism and enterprising spirit of the era rather than the anxiety some other historians have discerned.

Ronald P. Formisano, *The Transformation of Political Culture: Massachusetts Parties, 1790s–1840s* (1983). One of many detailed studies that have contributed to our understanding of the development of the second party system.

William W. Freehling, *Prelude to Civil War* (1966). An examination of the Nullification Crisis that stresses the centrality of slavery to the dispute.

Paul W. Gates, *The Farmer's Age: Agriculture, 1815–1860* (1966). The standard source on the growth of commercial agriculture.

Jean V. Matthews, *Toward a New Society: American Thought and Culture, 1800–1830* (1991). A valuable survey of American attitudes toward religion, politics, science, nature, and culture in the early nineteenth century.

Robert Remini, *Andrew Jackson and the Source of American Freedom* (1981). An account of Jackson's White House years by his major biographer.

Carol Sheriff, *The Artificial River: The Erie Canal and the Paradox of Progress, 1817–1862* (1996). Shows how the building of the canal changed personal lives and fostered religious beliefs in human perfectability.

Alan Taylor, *William Cooper's Town: Power and Persuasion on the Frontier of the Early American Republic* (1995). The Pulitzer Prize-winning study of the founding and development of Cooperstown, New York, by the father of novelist James Fenimore Cooper. An engrossing study of the effects of the democratization of politics.

George Rogers Taylor, *The Transportation Revolution, 1815–1860* (1951). The indispensable book on all aspects of the American economy during this period.

Harry L. Watson, *Liberty and Power: The Politics of Jacksonian America* (1990). An excellent recent overview of Jacksonian politics.

ADDITIONAL BIBLIOGRAPHY

The New Democratic Politics and the Jackson Presidency

William L. Anderson, *Cherokee Removal: Before and After* (1991)

Ralph S. Cotterill, *The Southern Indians* (1954)

John Ehle, *Trail of Tears* (1988)

Richard E. Ellis, *The Union at Risk* (1987)

Paul Goodman, *Towards a Christian Republic: Antimasonry and the Great Tradition in New England, 1826–1836* (1988)

Michael D. Green, *The Politics of Indian Removal* (1982)
Lucy Maddox, *Removals: Nineteenth-Century American Literature and the Politics of Indian Affairs* (1991)
Michael Rogin, *Fathers and Children: Andrew Jackson and the Destruction of American Indians* (1975)
Ronald N. Satz, *American Indian Policy in the Jacksonian Era* (1975)
Arthur M. Schlesinger Jr., *The Age of Jackson* (1945)
John Ward, *Andrew Jackson: Symbol for an Age* (1955)
Chilton Williamson, *American Suffrage: From Property to Democracy, 1760–1860* (1960)

Internal Improvements

Allan G. Bogue, *From Prairie to Corn Belt: Farming on the Illinois and Iowa Frontier* (1968)
Clarence Danhof, *Changes in Agriculture: The Northern United States, 1820–1870* (1969)
E. M. Dodd, *American Business Corporations until 1860* (1954)
Albert Fishlow, *American Railroads and the Transformation of the Ante-Bellum Economy* (1965)
Robert W. Fogel, *Railroads and American Economic Growth: Essays in Econometric History* (1964)
Carter Goodrich, *Government Promotion of American Canals and Railroads, 1800–1890* (1960)
John Denis Haeger, *The Investment Frontier: New York Businessmen and the Economic Development of the Old Northwest* (1981)
Oscar Handlin and Mary Handlin, *Commonwealth: A Study of the Role of Government in the American Economy: Massachusetts, 1774–1861* (1947)
Louis Hartz, *Economic Policy and Democratic Thought: Pennsylvania, 1776–1860* (1948)
Erik F. Hiates, James Mak, and Gary M. Walton, *Western River Transportation: The Era of Early Internal Development, 1800–1860* (1975)
Morton J. Horwitz, *The Transformation of American Law, 1780–1860* (1977)
Philip Jordan, *The National Road* (1948)
Karl Raitz,ed., *The National Road* (1995)
Harry N. Scheiber, *The Ohio Canal Era: A Case Study of Government and the Economy, 1820–1861* (1969)
Ronald E. Shaw, *Canals for a Nation: The Canal Era in the United States, 1790–1860* (1990)
Ronald Shaw, *Erie Water West: History of the Erie Canal* (1966)
Peter Temin, *Iron and Steel in Nineteenth-Century America* (1964)
———, *The Jacksonian Economy* (1965)
Peter Way, *Common Labour: Workers and the Digging of North American Canals, 1780-1860* (1993)

The Rise of the Whigs and the Second American Party System

John Ashworth, *Agrarians and Aristocrats: Party Ideology in the United States, 1837–1846* (1983)
R. G. Gunderson, *The Log Cabin Campaign* (1957)
Bray Hammond, *Banks and Politics in America* (1957)
Daniel W. Howe, *The Political Culture of the American Whigs* (1980)
Lawrence F. Kohl, *The Politics of Individualism: Parties and the American Character in the Jacksonian Era* (1989)
Richard P. McCormick, *The Second American Party System: Party Formation in the Jacksonian Era* (1966)
James Roger Sharp, *The Jacksonians versus the Banks: Politics in the United States after the Panic of 1837* (1970)
Joel H. Sibley, *The Partisan Imperative: The Dynamics of American Politics before the Civil War* (1985)
Harry L. Watson, *Jacksonian Politics and Community Conflict: The Emergence of the Second American Party System in Cumberland County, North Carolina* (1981)

American Arts and Letters

John L. Brooke, *Knowledge Is Power: The Diffusion of Information in Early America, 1700–1865* (1989)
Cathy N. Davidson, *Revolution and the Word: The Rise of the Novel in America* (1986)
William J. Gilmore, *Reading Becomes a Necessity of Life: Material and Cultural Life in Rural New England, 1780–1835* (1989)
Neil Harris, *The Artist in American Society: The Formative Years, 1790–1860* (1966)
Nathan O. Hatch, *The Democratization of American Christianity* (1989)
Barbara Novak, *Nature and Culture: American Landscape Painting 1825–1875* (1982)
Albert Von Frank, *The Sacred Game: Provincialism and Frontier Consciousness in American Literature, 1630–1860* (1985)
Gwendolyn Wright, *Building the Dream: A Social History of Housing in America* (1981)

Biography

Irving H. Bartlett, *Daniel Webster* (1978)
Richard Current, *Daniel Webster and the Rise of National Conservatism* (1955)
———, *John C. Calhoun* (1963)
Robert V. Remini, *Henry Clay: Statesman for the Union* (1991)
Leonard L. Richards, *The Life and Times of Congressman John Quincy Adams* (1986)
C. M. Wiltse, *John C. Calhoun: Nullifier, 1829–1839* (1949)

CHAPTER ELEVEN

THE SOUTH AND SLAVERY

1790s–1850s

Taylor, *An American Slave Market*, 1852. Oil on canvas. Chicago Historical Society.

Chapter Outline

KING COTTON AND SOUTHERN EXPANSION

The Cotton Gin and Expansion into the Old Southwest

The Question of Slavery

The Internal Slave Trade

The Economics of Slavery

Cotton Culture

TO BE A SLAVE

The Maturing of the American Slave System

The Challenge to Survive

From Cradle to Grave

House Servants

Artisans and Skilled Workers

Field Work

THE AFRICAN AMERICAN COMMUNITY

Slave Families

African American Religion

Freedom and Resistance

Slave Revolts

Free African Americans

YEOMEN AND POOR WHITE PEOPLE

Yeomen

Poor White People

Yeoman Values

PLANTERS

Small Slave Owners

The Old Planter Elite

The Natchez "Nabobs"

Plantation Life

The Plantation Mistress

Coercion and Violence

THE DEFENSE OF SLAVERY

Developing Proslavery Arguments

After Nat Turner

Changes in the South

AMERICAN COMMUNITIES

Natchez-under-the-Hill

The wharfmaster had just opened the public auction of confiscated cargoes in the center of Natchez when a great cry was heard. An angry crowd of flatboatmen, Bowie knives in hand, was storming up the bluffs from the Mississippi shouting, as the local newspaper reported, "threats of violence and death upon all who attempted to sell and buy their property." It was November 1837, and the town council had just enacted a restrictive tax of $10 per flatboat, a measure designed to rid the wharf district known as Natchez-under-the-Hill of the most impoverished and disreputable of the riverboatmen. The council had made its first confiscation of cargo after nine captains refused to pay this tax. As the boatmen approached, merchants and onlookers shrank back in fear. But the local authorities had called out the militia, and a company of farmers and planters now came marching into the square with their rifles primed and lowered. "The cold and sullen bayonets of the Guards were too hard meat for the Arkansas toothpicks," reported the local press, and "there was no fight." The boatmen sullenly turned back down the bluffs. It was the first confrontation in the "Flatboat Wars" that erupted as Mississippi ports tried to bring their troublesome riverfronts under regulation.

The first European to take notice of this "land abundant in subsistence" was a member of Hernando de Soto's expedition in the sixteenth century. The area was "thickly peopled" by the Natchez Indians, he wrote. It was not until the French established the port of Fort Rosalie in the 1720s, however, that Europeans settled in the area. The French destroyed the highly organized society of the Natchez Indians in the 1730s and the port became a major Mississippi River trading center. From Fort Rosalie, the French conducted an extensive frontier trade that brought peoples of different races together, leading to intermarriage and the growth of a mixed-race population. French traders bought deerskins, for which there was a large export market, from Choctaw, Chickasaw, and Creek hunters. During the same period, some Africans who had been imported by the French to work as slaves on plantations found roles in the French-Indian trade as boatmen, hunters, soldiers, and interpreters.

When the Spanish took control of the territory in 1763 they laid out the new town of Natchez high on the bluffs, safe from Mississippi flooding. Fort Rosalie, rechristened Natchez-under-the-Hill, continued to flourish as the produce grown by American farmers in Kentucky and Tennessee moved downriver on flatboats. Thus Americans became the newest additions to the ethnic diversity of this well-established trading center. When Americans took possession of Mississippi in 1798, the district surrounding the port became the most important center of settlement in the Old Southwest. Once again this abundant land of rich, black soil became thickly peopled, but this time with cotton planters and their African American slaves.

Under-the-Hill gained renown as the last stop for boatmen before New Orleans. Minstrel performers sang of their exploits:

Den dance de boatmen dance,
O dance de boatmen dance,
O dance all night till broad daylight,
An go home wid de gals in de morning.

According to one traveler, "They feel the same inclination to dissipation as sailors who have long been out of port." There were often as many as 150 boats drawn up at the wharves. The crowds along the riverfront, noted John James Audubon, who visited in the 1820s, "formed a medley which it is beyond my power to describe." Mingling among American rivermen of all descriptions were trappers and hunters in fur caps, Spanish shopkeepers in bright smocks, French gentlemen from New Orleans in velvet coats, Indians wrapped in their trade blankets, African Americans both free and slave—a pageant of nations and races. Clapboard shacks and flatboats dragged on shore and converted into storefronts served as grog shops, card rooms, dance halls, and hotels. Whorehouses with women of every age and color abounded.

On the bluffs, meanwhile, the town of Natchez had become the winter home to the southwestern planter elite. They built their mansions with commanding views of the river. A visitor attending a ball at one of these homes was dazzled by the display: "Myriads of wax candles burning in wall sconces, sparkling chandeliers, entrancing music, the scent of jasmine, rose and sweet olive, the sparkle of wine mellowed by age, the flow of wit and brilliant repartee, all were there." Sustaining this American aristocracy was the labor of thousands of enslaved men and women, who lived in the squalid quarters behind the great house and worked the endless fields of cotton. It was they who made possible the greatest accumulations of wealth in early-nineteenth-century America.

The Natchez planters, their wealth and confidence growing with cotton's growing dominance of the local economy, found Under-the-Hill an increasing irritant. "A gentleman may game with a gambler by the hour," one resident remembered, "and yet despise him and refuse to recognize him afterward." The Under-the-Hill elite, however—gamblers, saloon keepers, and pimps—disturbed this social boundary when they began staying at hotels and even building town houses in Natchez town. And in the wake of the slave revolt led by Nat Turner in Virginia in 1831 in which fifty-five white people were killed, the planters began to feel increasingly threatened by the racial mingling of the riverfront.

In the late 1830s the Natchez elite was jolted by rumors that their slaves were conspiring to murder them during Fourth of July celebrations while Under-the-Hill desperadoes looted their mansions. The rumors reinforced the growing conviction among planters that they could no longer tolerate the polyglot community of the riverfront. The measures that ultimately provoked the flatboatmen's threats in November 1837 soon followed.

In response to these threats, the planters issued an extralegal order giving all the gamblers, pimps, and whores of Under-the-Hill twenty-four hours to evacuate the district. As the Mississippi militia sharpened their bayonets, panic swept the wharves, and that night dozens of flatboats loaded with a motley human cargo headed for the more tolerant community of New Orleans. Other river ports issued similar orders of expulsion. "The towns on the river," one resident remembered, "became purified from a moral pestilence which the law could not cure." Three years later a great tornado hit Under-the-Hill, leveling the shacks that had served so long as a rendezvous for the rivermen, and gradually the Mississippi reclaimed the bottom.

These two communities—Natchez, home to the rich slave-owning elite, and Natchez-under-the-Hill, the bustling polyglot trading community—epitomize the paradox of the American South in the early nineteenth century. Enslaved African Americans grew the region's most lucrative crop, cotton. On the resulting profits, aristocratic Southerners built a sumptuous and distinctive lifestyle for themselves. The boatmen and traders of Natchez-under-the-Hill who brought the cotton and other products to market were vital to the planters' prosperity. But the polyglot racial and social mixing of Natchez-under-the-Hill threatened the system of control, built on a rigid distinction between free white people and enslaved black people, by which the planters maintained slavery. Because the slave owners could not control the boatmen, they expelled them. This defensive reaction—to seal off the world of slavery from the wider commercial world—exposed the vulnerability of the slave system at the very moment of its greatest commercial success.

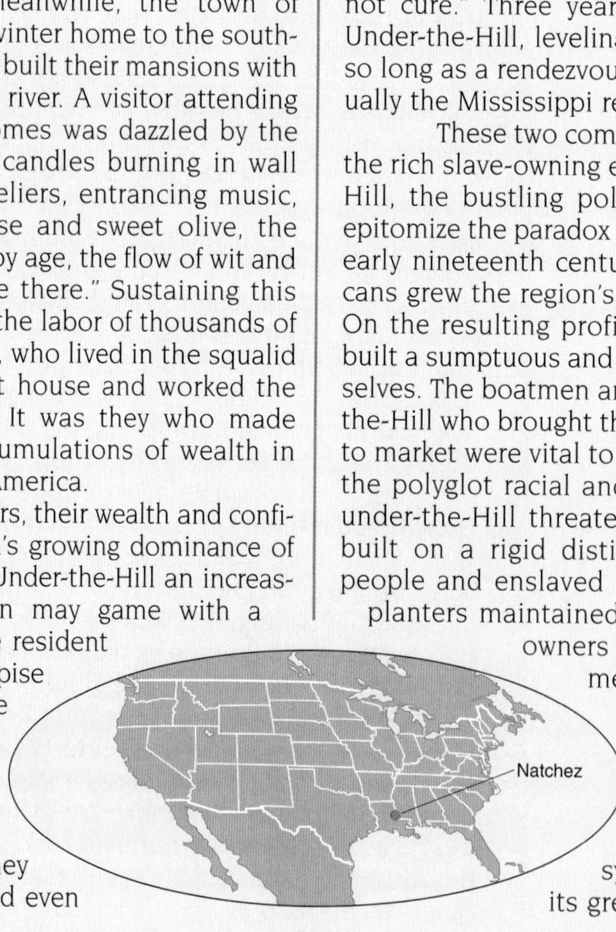

KEY TOPICS

- The domination of southern life by the slave system
- The economic implications of "King Cotton"
- The creation of African American communities under slavery
- The social structure of the white South and its increasing defensiveness

KING COTTON AND SOUTHERN EXPANSION

Slavery had long dominated southern life. African American slaves grew the great export crops of the colonial period—tobacco, rice, and indigo—on which slave owners' fortunes were made, and their presence shaped southern society and culture (see Chapter 4). Briefly, in the early days of American independence, the slave system waned, only to be revived by the immense profitability of cotton in a newly industrializing world. Cotton became the dominant crop in a rapidly expanding South that included not only the original states of Maryland, Delaware, Virginia, North and South Carolina, and Georgia, but Kentucky, Tennessee, Missouri, Alabama, Mississippi, Louisiana (the Old Southwest), Arkansas, Florida, and Texas as well. The overwhelming economic success of cotton and of the slave system on which it depended created a distinctive regional culture quite different from that developing in the North.

The Cotton Gin and Expansion into the Old Southwest

Short-staple cotton had long been recognized as a crop ideally suited to southern soils and growing conditions. But it had one major drawback: the seeds were so difficult to remove from the lint that it took an entire day to hand-clean a single pound of cotton. The invention in 1793 that made cotton growing profitable was the result of collaboration between a young Northerner named Eli Whitney, recently graduated from Yale College, and Catherine Greene, a South Carolina plantation owner and widow of Revolutionary War General Nathanael Greene, who hired Whitney to tutor her children. Whitney built a prototype cotton engine, dubbed "gin" for short, a simple device consisting of a hand-cranked cylinder with teeth that tore the lint away from the seeds. At Greene's suggestion, the teeth were made of wire. With the cotton gin it was possible to clean more than fifty pounds of cotton a day. Soon large and small planters in the inland regions of Georgia and South Carolina had begun to grow cotton. By 1811, this area was producing 60 million pounds of cotton a year, and exporting most of it to England.

Other areas of the South quickly followed South Carolina and Georgia into cotton production. New land was wanted because cotton growing rapidly depleted the soil. The profits to be made from cotton growing drew a rush of southern farmers into the so-called black belt—an area stretching through western

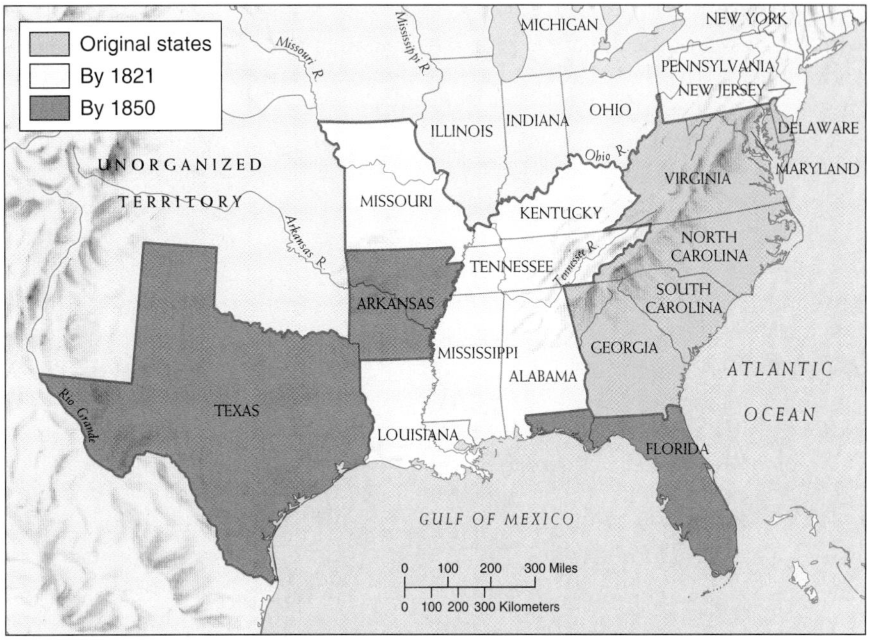

The South Expands, 1790–1850 *This map shows the dramatic effect cotton production had on southern expansion. From the original six states of 1790, westward expansion, fueled by the search for new cotton lands, added another six states by 1821, and three more by 1850.*

Georgia, Alabama, and Mississippi that was blessed with exceptionally fertile soil. Following the War of 1812, southerners were seized by "Alabama fever." In one of the swiftest migrations in American history, white southerners and their slaves flooded into western Georgia and the areas that would become Alabama and Mississippi (the Old Southwest). On this frontier, African American pioneers (albeit involuntary ones) cleared the forests, drained the swamps, broke the ground, built houses and barns, and planted the first crops.

This migration caused the population of Mississippi to double (from 31,306 to 74,448) and that of Alabama to grow sixteenfold (from 9,046 to 144,317) between 1810 and 1820. This and subsequent western land booms dramatically changed the population of the original southern states as well. Nearly half of all white South Carolinians born after 1800 eventually left the state, usually to move west. By 1850 there were more than 50,000 South Carolina natives living in Georgia, almost as many in Alabama, and 26,000 in Mississippi.

Southerners had historically taken the lead in westward expansion. Backcountry residents of Virginia and North Carolina were the first to venture over the Appalachians, and Virginians and Carolinians were the major settlers of the first two trans-Appalachian states, Kentucky (1792) and Tennessee (1796). John C. Calhoun of South Carolina and Henry Clay of Kentucky had been two of the most prominent expansionist War Hawks in Congress before the War of 1812. Like the simultaneous expansion into the Old Northwest, settlement of the Old Southwest took place at the expense of the region's Indian population (see Chapter 9). Beginning with the defeat of the Creeks at Horseshoe Bend in 1814 and ending with the Cherokee forced migration along "the Trail of Tears" in 1838, the "Five Civilized Tribes"—the Cherokees, Chickasaws, Choctaws, Creeks, and Seminoles—were forced to give up their lands and move to Indian Territory (see Chapter 10).

Steamboats at New Orleans await loads of cotton, the nation's major export. Just as the giant bales crowd the wharf, so too the culture created by "King Cotton" dominated southern life.

On the southern frontier, as on the northern frontier, the killing, confinement, and removal of Indian peoples was the result of white expansion and settlement motivated by the hunger for land and profit. In the South, however, there was an additional motivation, rooted in slavery, for Indian removal: there was simply no room in the southern social order for anything other than white and black, master and slave. Literate, slave-owning "redskins" confused this simple picture: they were too "civilized" to be like slaves, but the wrong color to be masters. Thus southern Indian removal, like southern expansion, was dictated by the needs of the slave system.

Following "the Alabama Fever" of 1816–20, several later surges of southern expansion (1832–38, and again in the mid–1850s) carried cotton planting over the Mississippi River into Louisiana and deep into Texas. Each surge ignited feverish speculative frenzies, remembered in terms like "the Flush Times" for the heated rush of the 1830s. In the minds of the mobile, enterprising Southerners who sought their fortunes in the West, cotton profits and expansion went hand in hand. But the expansion of cotton meant the expansion of slavery.

The Question of Slavery

Cotton growing was well suited to the southern plantation system of agriculture. That system was characterized by large plantings of a single crop tended by gangs of workers who performed the same operation (planting, hoeing, or picking) under the supervision of an overseer. The southern labor system shifted from white indentured servitude to African slavery during the colonial period because servants would not perform plantation work for others when they could farm their own land (see Chapter 4). White Southerners believed that only African slaves could be forced to work day after day, year after year, at the rapid and brutal pace required in the cotton fields of large plantations in the steamy southern summer. As the production of cotton climbed higher every year in response to a seemingly inexhaustible international demand, so too did the demand for slaves and the conviction of Southerners that slavery was an economic necessity.

At the very moment that the South was committing its future to cotton, however, and assuring the persistence of slavery there, opinion about slavery was changing. Britain outlawed the international slave trade in 1807 and the United States took the same step in 1808. In the preceding quarter century, all the northern states had abolished slavery or passed laws for gradual emancipation (see Chapter 7). Between 1776 and 1786 all the states except South Carolina and Georgia either banned or

The immense size of the internal slave trade made sights like this commonplace on southern roads. Groups of slaves, chained together in gangs called coffles, were marched from their homes in the Upper South to cities in the Lower South, where they were auctioned to new owners.

heavily taxed the international slave trade, and it was only at the insistence of these two states that the Constitutional Convention prohibited Congress from passing a federal law to outlaw the slave trade for twenty years. All the southern states banned the importation of foreign slaves after the successful slave revolt in Haiti in 1791; Southerners feared that Caribbean revolutionaries might incite their own slaves to rebellion.

Attitudes changed again following the invention of the cotton gin in 1793 and the realization of the riches to be made from cotton. Slave smuggling became so rampant that South Carolina officially reopened the trade in 1804. For the next four years, Charleston boomed as one of the world's largest slaving ports: at least 40,000 Africans were imported. It was clear, however, that national opinion found the international slave trade abhorrent, and on January 1, 1808, the earliest date permitted by the Constitution, a bill to abolish the importation of slaves became law. Although a small number of slaves continued to be smuggled from Africa, the growth of the slave labor force after 1808 depended primarily on natural increase. And the ban on foreign importations vastly increased the importance of the internal slave trade.

The Internal Slave Trade

The cotton boom caused a huge increase in the domestic slave trade. Plantation owners in the Upper South (Delaware, Kentucky, Maryland, Virginia, and Tennessee) sold their slaves to meet the demand for labor in the new and expanding cotton-growing regions of the Old Southwest. In every decade after 1820 at least 150,000 slaves were uprooted either by slave trading or planter migration to the new areas, and in the expansions of the 1830s and the 1850s, the number reached a quarter of a million. Cumulatively, between 1820 and 1860 nearly 50 percent of the slave population of the Upper South took part against their will in southern expansion.

Purchased by slave traders from owners in the Upper South, slaves were gathered together in notorious "slave pens" like the ones in Richmond and Charleston and then moved south by train or boat. In the interior, they were carried as cargo on steamboats on the Mississippi River, hence the phrase "sold down the river." Often slaves moved on foot, chained together in groups of fifty or more known as "coffles." Coffles were a common sight on southern roads, and one difficult to reconcile with the notion of slavery as a benevolent institution. Arriving at a central market in the Lower South like Natchez, New Orleans, or Mobile, the slaves, after being carefully inspected by potential buyers, were sold at auction to the highest bidder.

Although popular stereotype portrayed slave traders as unscrupulous outsiders who persuaded kind and reluctant masters to sell their slaves, the historical truth is much harsher. Traders, far from being shunned by slave-owning society, were often respected community members. One Charleston trader, Alexander McDonald, served as both an alderman and a bank president and was described as "a man of large means and responsible for all his engagements" who had "the confidence of the public." Similarly, the sheer scale of the slave trade makes it impossible to believe that slave owners only reluctantly parted with their slaves at times of economic distress. Instead, it is clear that many owners sold slaves and separated slave families not out of necessity but to increase their profits. The sheer size and profitability of the internal slave trade made a mockery of Southern claims for the benevolence of the slave system.

The Economics of Slavery

The rapid growth of cotton production was an international phenomenon, prompted by events occurring far from the American South. The insatiable demand for cotton was a result of the technological and social changes that we know today as the industrial revolution. Beginning early in the eighteenth century, a series of inventions resulted in the mechanized spinning and weaving of cloth in the world's first factories in the north of England. The ability of these factories to produce unprecedented amounts of cotton cloth revolutionized the world economy. The invention of the cotton gin came at just the right time. British textile manufacturers were eager to buy all the cotton that the South could produce.

Was the southern plantation system profitable? Clearly, in the years before 1860, southern farmers believed so. The figures for cotton production support this conclusion: from 720,000 bales in 1830, to 2.85 million bales in 1850, to nearly 5 million in 1860. By the time of the Civil War, cotton accounted for almost 60 percent of American exports, representing a total value of nearly $200 million a year.

Cotton's central place in the national economy and its international importance led Senator James Henry Hammond of South Carolina to make a famous boast in 1858:

> Without firing a gun, without drawing a sword, should they make war on us, we could bring the whole world to our feet.... What would happen if no cotton was furnished for three years?... England would topple headlong and carry the whole civilized world with her save the south. No, you dare not to make war on cotton. No power on the earth dares to make war upon it. Cotton is King.

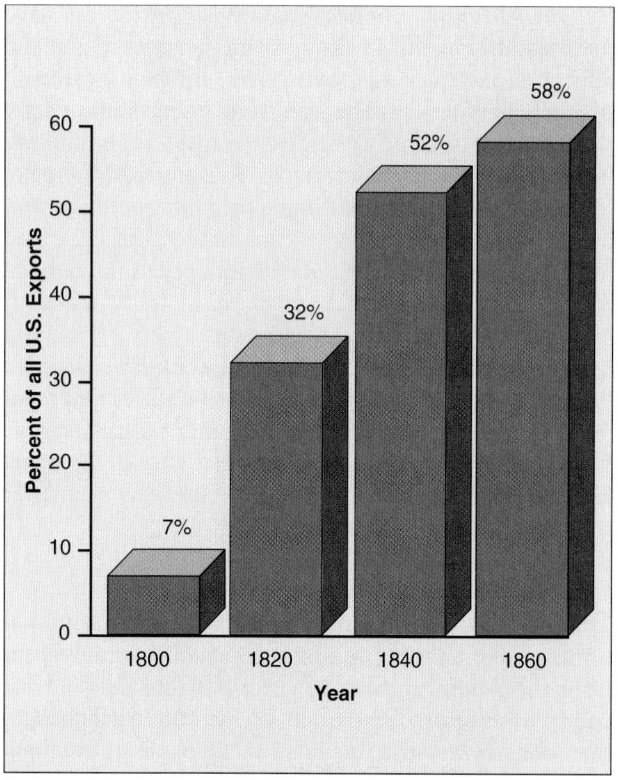

Cotton Exports as a Percentage of All U.S. Exports, 1800–1860 *One consequence of the growth of cotton production was its importance in international trade. The growing share of the export market, and the great value (nearly $200 million in 1860) led southern slave owners to believe that "Cotton Is King." The importance of cotton to the national economy entitled the South to a commanding voice in national policy, many Southerners believed.*

Indeed, the export of cotton from the South was the dynamic force in the developing American economy in the period 1790–1840. Just as the international slave trade had been the dynamic force in the Atlantic economy of the eighteenth century (see Chapter 4), southern slavery financed northern industrial development in the nineteenth century.

The connection between southern slavery and northern industry was very direct. Most mercantile services associated with the cotton trade (insurance, for example) were in northern hands and, significantly, so was shipping. This economic structure was not new. In colonial times, New England ships dominated the African slave trade. Some New England families—like the Browns of Providence who made fortunes in the slave trade—invested some of their profits in the new technology of textile manufacturing in the 1790s. Other merchants—such as the Boston Associates who financed the cotton textile mills at Lowell—made their money from cotton shipping and brokerage. Thus as cotton boomed, it provided capital for the new factories of the North.

Cotton Culture

Northerners, who were caught up in rapid industrialization and urbanization, failed to recognize their economic connection to the South and increasingly regarded it as a backward region. Senator from New York William H. Seward, on his first visit to Virginia, found ample justification for his antislavery convictions:

> It was necessary that I should travel in Virginia to have any idea of a slave state.... An exhausted soil, old and decaying towns, wretchedly-neglected roads, and in every respect, an absence of enterprise and improvement, distinguish the region through which we have come, in contrast to that in which we live. Such has been the effect of slavery.

Concentration on plantation agriculture did divert energy and resources from the South's cities. At a time when the North was experiencing the greatest spurt of urban growth in the nation's history, southern cities did not keep pace. Charleston, for example, one of America's five largest cities in 1800, had a population of only 41,000 in 1860, compared with Boston's 177,840 and Baltimore's 212,418. The one exception was New Orleans, the great port at the mouth of the extensive Mississippi River transportation system. In 1860 New Orleans was the nation's fifth largest city, with a population of 169,000. The nine other leading cities were all northern or western. Most of the South remained rural: less than 3 percent of Mississippi's population lived in cities of more than 2,500 residents, and only 10 percent of Virginia's did.

The South also lagged behind the North in industrialization and in canals and railroads. In 1860, only 15 percent of the nation's factories were located in the South. Noteworthy exceptions were the iron industry near Richmond, which in 1860 boasted four rolling mills, fourteen foundries, and various machine shops employing 1,600 mechanics, and William Gregg's cotton textile mills in Graniteville, just east of Augusta, Georgia. Similarly, the South was initially left behind by the transportation revolution. In 1850, only 26 percent of the nation's railroads were in the South, increasing to still only 35 percent in 1860.

The failure of the South to industrialize at the northern rate was not a matter of ignorance but of choice. Southern capital was tied up in land and slaves, and Southerners, buoyed by the world's insatiable demand for cotton, saw no reason to invest in economically risky railroads, canals, and factories. Nor were they eager to introduce the disruptive factor of free wage labor into the tightly controlled slave system. Cotton was safer. Cotton was King.

Thus the cotton boom created a distinctive regional culture. Although cotton was far from being the only crop (the South actually devoted more acreage to corn than to cotton in 1860), its vast profitability affected all aspects of society. In the first half of the nineteenth century, King Cotton reigned supreme over an expanding domain as Southerners increasingly tied their fortunes to the slave system of cotton production. As a British tourist to Mobile wryly noted in the 1850s, the South was a place where "people live in cotton houses and ride in cotton carriages. They buy cotton, sell cotton, think cotton, eat cotton, drink cotton, and dream cotton. They marry cotton wives, and unto them are born cotton children." The South was truly in thrall to King Cotton.

TO BE A SLAVE

The slave population, estimated at 700,000 by 1790, grew to more than 4 million. After 1808 (when official American participation in the international slave trade ceased) the growth occurred because of natural increase—that is, births within the slave population. In spite of the burden of slavery, a distinctive African American community, which had first emerged in the eighteenth century (see Chapter 4), flourished in the years before the Civil War.

The Maturing of the American Slave System

Dependence on King Cotton meant dependence on slave labor. In 1850, 55 percent of all slaves were engaged in cotton growing. Another 20 percent labored to produce other crops: tobacco (10 percent), rice, sugar, and hemp. About 15 percent of all slaves were domestic servants, and the remaining 10 percent worked in mining, lumbering, industry, and construction.

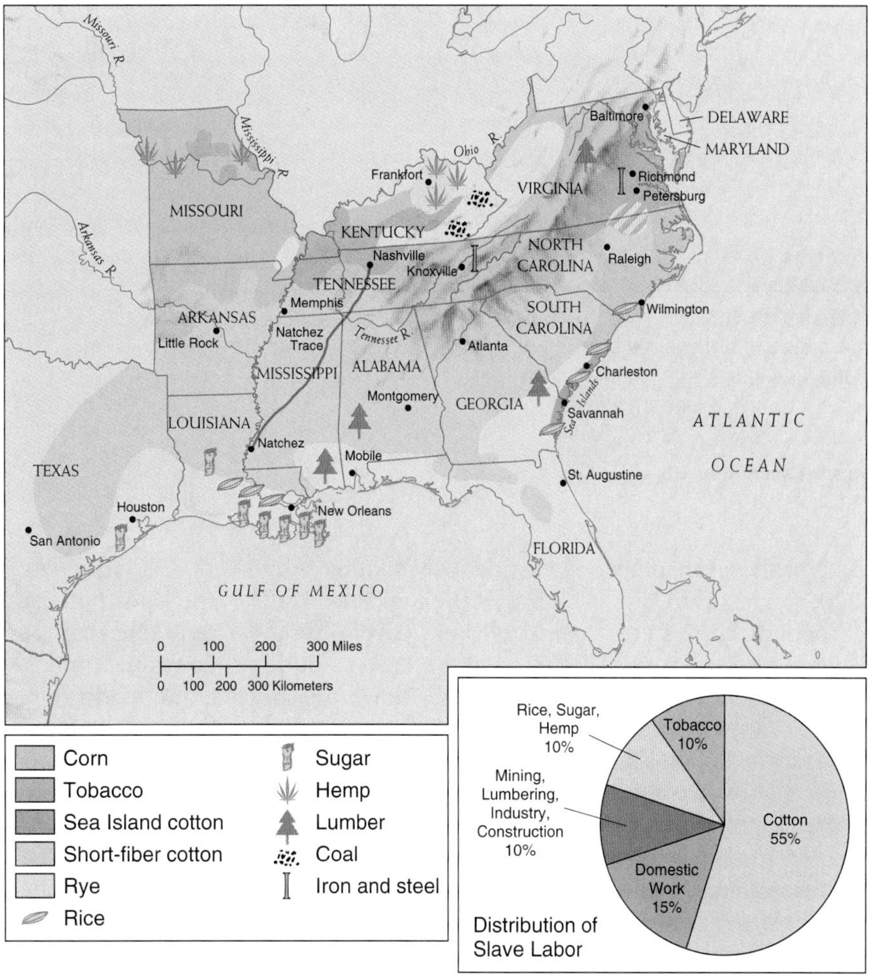

Agriculture, Industry, and Slavery, 1850 *The distribution of the slave population in the South was determined by agricultural and industrial patterns. In 1850, 55 percent of all slaves worked in cotton, 10 percent in tobacco, and another 10 percent in rice, sugar, and hemp. Ten percent worked in mining, lumbering, industry, and construction, and 15 percent worked as domestic servants. Slaves were not generally used to grow corn, the staple crop of the yeoman farmer.*

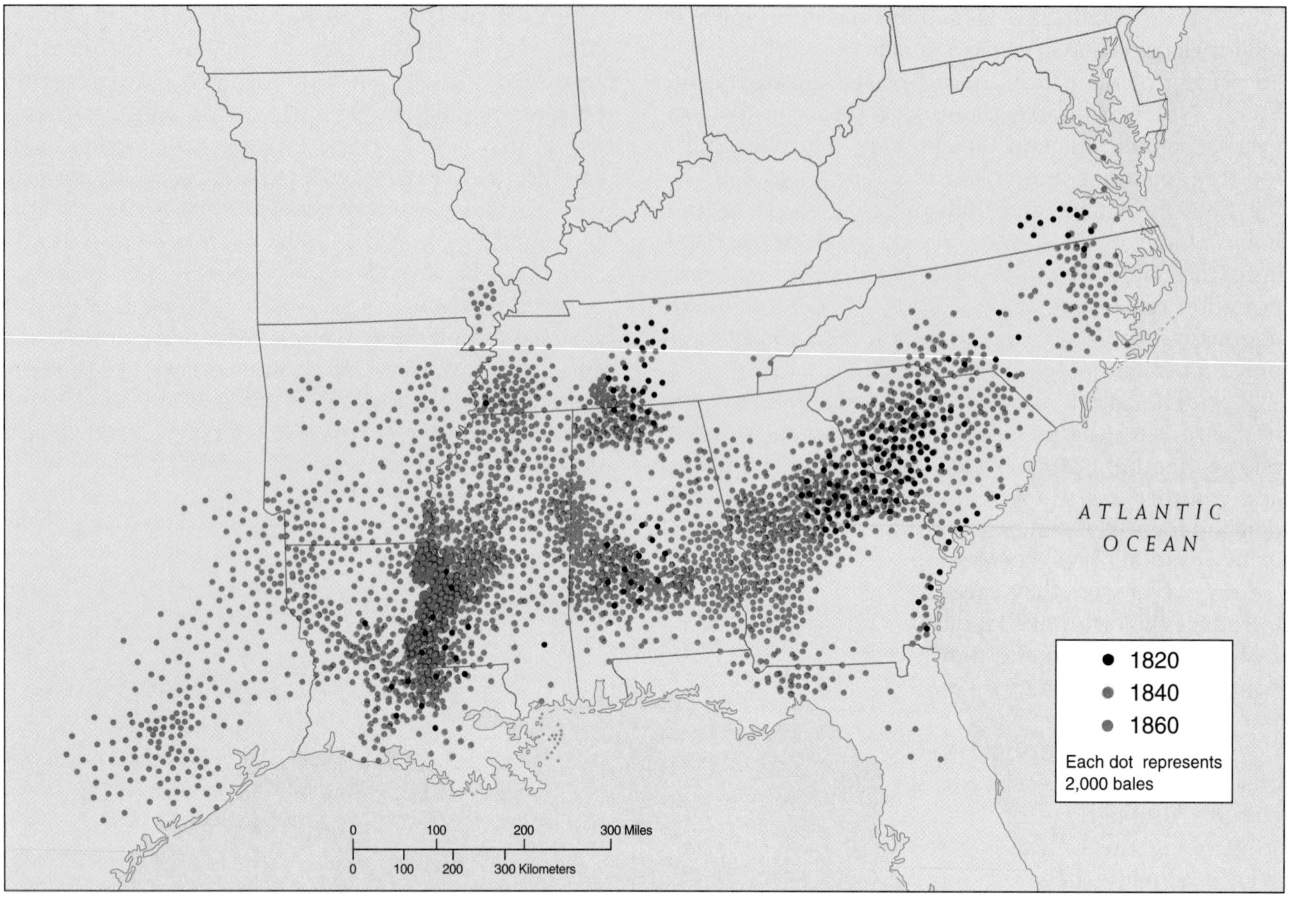

Cotton Production, 1820–1860 *In the forty-year period from 1820 to 1860, cotton production grew dramatically both in quantity and in extent. The westward expansion that cotton production encouraged in the 1830s and 1850s is reflected in the symbols for 1840 and 1860, and the growing concentration of cotton production in the black belt (so-called for its rich soils) of the Lower South is clearly evident.*

Source: Sam Bowers Hilliard, *Atlas of Antebellum Southern Agriculture* (Baton Rouge: Louisiana State University Press, 1984), pp. 67–71.

Slavery had become distinctively southern: by 1820, as a result of laws passed after the Revolution, all of the northern states had abolished slaveholding. Slaves were increasingly clustered in the Lower South, as Upper South slave owners sold slaves downriver or migrated westward with their entire households. An estimated 1 million slaves migrated involuntarily to the Lower South between 1820 and 1860. Moreover, as expansion to the Southwest accelerated, so did the demand for slaves in the newly settled regions, thus fueling the internal slave trade.

Slaves were not distributed equally among southern slave owners. More than half of all slave owners owned five slaves or fewer, but 75 percent of all slaves lived in groups of ten or more. This disproportionate distribution could have a major impact on a slave's life, for it was a very different matter to be the single slave of a small farmer as opposed to a member of a 100-person black community on a large plantation.

Finally, of all the New World slave societies, the one that existed in the American South was the only one that grew by natural increase rather than the constant importation of captured Africans. This fact alone made the African American community of the South different from the slave societies of Cuba, the Caribbean islands, and Brazil. The first thing to understand, then, are the circumstances of survival.

The Challenge to Survive

The primary challenge facing African Americans was survival. The very young were at risk: mortality rates for slave children under five were twice those for their white counterparts. The reason was clear: pregnant black women were inadequately nourished, worked too hard, or were too frequently pregnant, giving birth to six to eight children at year-and-one-half intervals. When the British actress Fanny Kemble came to live on her husband's Georgia plantation in 1837, what

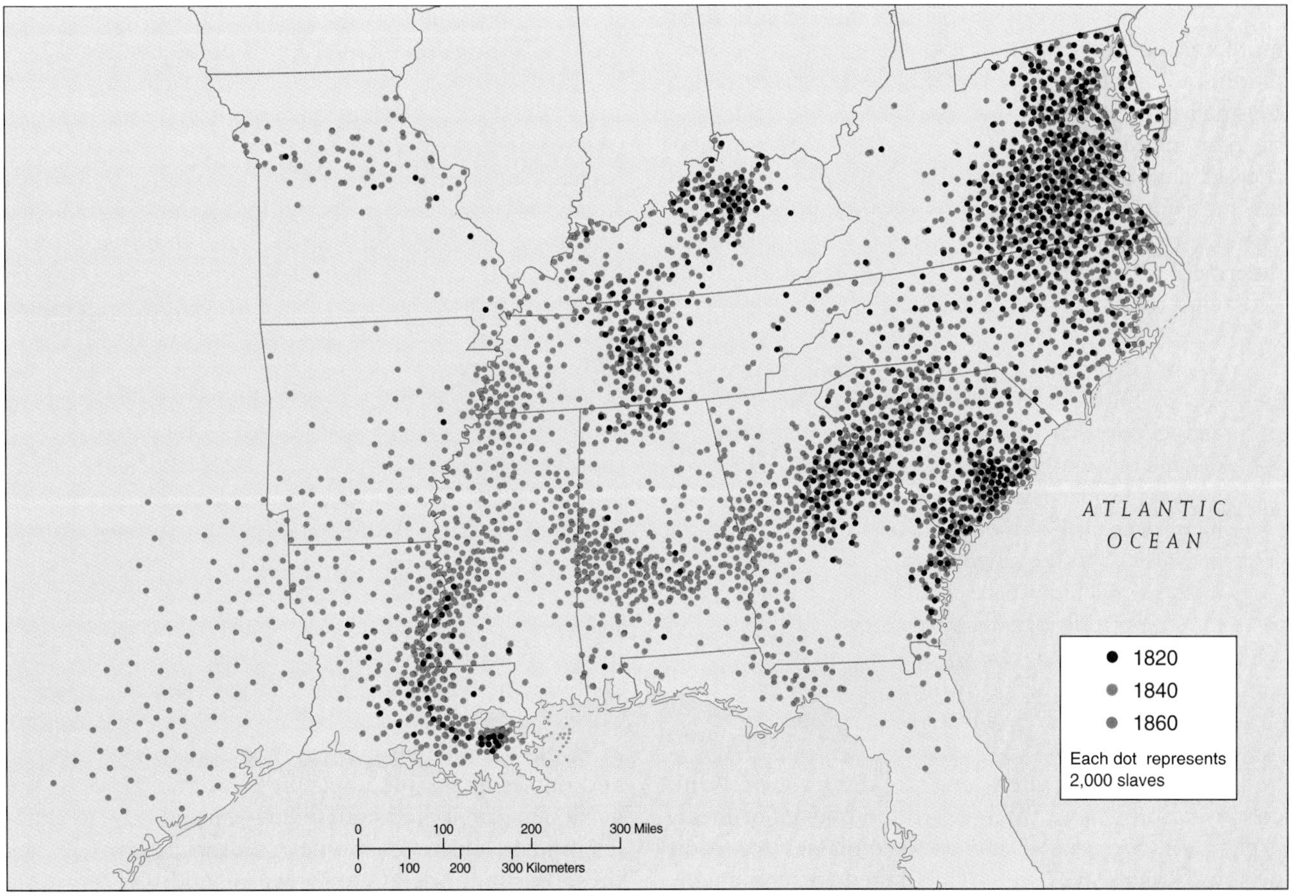

Slave Population, 1820–1860 *The growth of cotton production caused a redistribution of the enslaved African American population in the South. Although slaves were still used to grow tobacco in Virginia and rice in coastal South Carolina, after 1830 an increasing number were sold "down the river" to work new cotton plantations in the Lower South. Thus although U.S. participation in the international slave trade was outlawed in 1808, the domestic trade in slaves flourished.*

Source: Sam Bowers Hilliard, *Atlas of Antebellum Southern Agriculture* (Baton Rouge: Louisiana State University Press, 1984), pp. 29–34.

shocked her more deeply than any other aspect of the slave system was the treatment of pregnant black women. Sensing her sympathy, pregnant slave women came to Kemble to plead for relief from field work, only to be brusquely ordered back to the fields by the overseer and Kemble's husband.

Health remained a lifelong issue for slaves. Malaria and infectious diseases such as yellow fever and cholera were endemic in the South. White people as well as black died, as the life expectancy figures for 1850 show: 40–43 years for white people and 30–33 years for African Americans. Slaves were more at risk because of the circumstances of slave life: poor housing, poor diet, and constant, usually heavy work. Sickness was chronic: 20 percent or more of the slave labor force on most plantations were sick at any one time. Many owners believed sick slaves were only "malingering." Because of the poor medical knowledge of the time, they failed to realize that adequate diet, warm housing, and basic sanitation might have prevented the pneumonia and dysentery that killed or weakened many slaves, and that exacted an especially high toll on very young children.

From Cradle to Grave

Slavery was a lifelong labor system, and the constant and inescapable issue between master and slave was how much work the slave would—or could be forced to—do. Southern white slave owners claimed that by housing, feeding, and clothing their slaves from infancy to death they were acting more humanely than northern industrialists who employed people only during their working years. But in spite of occasional instances of manumission—the freeing of a slave—the child born of a slave was destined to remain a slave.

Children lived with their parents (or with their mother if the father was a slave on another farm or plantation) in housing provided by the owner. Slaves owned by small farmers usually had only a bed or mattress to sleep on in the attic or a back room. Larger slave owners housed slaves in one-room cabins with dirt floors and few furnishings (a table, stools, a cooking pot and a few dishes, a bed or corn-shuck mattresses). Fanny Kemble described, with some horror, the one-room slave cabins she found on her husband's plantation:

> These cabins consist of one room, about twelve feet by fifteen, with a couple of closets smaller and closer than the state-rooms of a ship, divided off from the main room and each other by rough wooden partitions, in which the inhabitants sleep. They have almost all of them a rude bedstead, with the gray moss of the forests for mattress, and filthy, pestilential-looking blankets for covering. Two families (sometimes eight and ten in number) reside in one of these huts, which are mere wooden frames pinned, as it were, to the earth by a brick chimney outside.

Masters supplied food to their slaves. One common ration for a week was three pounds of meat, a quart of corn meal, and some molasses for each person. Often slaves were encouraged to supplement their diet by keeping their own gardens, and by hunting—though not, of course, with guns. Slaves were also provided with clothes, usually of rough homespun cloth: two shirts, two pairs of pants, and a pair of shoes a year for men, and enough cloth for women to make an equal number of smocks for themselves and their children yearly. This clothing was barely adequate, and in severe winters slaves suffered badly.

From birth to about age seven, slave children played with one another and with white children, observing and learning how to survive. They saw the penalties: black adults, perhaps their own parents, whipped for disobedience; black women, perhaps their own sisters, violated by white men. And they might see one or both parents sold away as punishment or for financial gain. They would also see signs of white benevolence: special treats for children at holidays, appeals to loyalty from the master or mistress, perhaps friendship with a white child. One former slave recalled:

> Yessum, when they used to have company in the big house, Miss Ross would bring them to the door to show them us children. And, my blessed, the yard would be black with us children, all string up there next the doorstep looking up in they eyes. Old Missus would say, "Ain't I got a pretty crop of little niggers coming on?"

The children would learn slave ways of getting along: apparent acquiescence in white demands; pilfering; malingering, sabotage, and other methods of slowing the relentless work pace. Fanny Kemble, an accomplished actress, was quick to note the pretense in the "outrageous flattery" she received from her husband's slaves. But many white Southerners genuinely believed that their slaves were both less intelligent and more loyal than they really were. An escaped slave, Jermain Loguen, recalled with some distaste the charade of "servile bows and counterfeit smiles...and other false expressions of gladness" with which he placated his master and mistress. Frederick Douglass, whose fearless leadership of the abolitionist movement made him the most famous African American of his time, wryly noted, "As the master studies to keep the slave ignorant, the slave is cunning enough to make the master think he succeeds."

Most slaves spent their lives as field hands, working in gangs with other slaves under a white overseer, who was usually quick to use his whip to keep up the work pace. But there were other occupations. In the "big house" there were jobs for women as cooks, maids, seamstresses, laundresses, weavers, and nurses. Black men became coachmen, valets, and gardeners, or skilled craftsmen—carpenters, mechanics, and blacksmiths. Some children began learning these occupations at age seven or eight, often in an informal apprentice system. Other children, both boys and girls, were expected to take full care of younger children while the parents were working. Of course black children had no schooling of any kind: in most of the southern states, it was against the law to teach a slave to read, although indulgent owners often rewarded their "pet" slaves by teaching them in spite of the law. At age twelve, slaves were considered full grown and put to work in the fields or in their designated occupation. As Mary Raines, a former slave in South Carolina, recalled, "I was a strong gal, went to de field when I's twelve years old, hoe my acre of cotton, 'long wid de grown ones, and pick my 150 pounds of cotton."

House Servants

At first glance, working in the big house might seem to have been preferable to working in the fields. Physically it was much less demanding, and house slaves were often better fed and clothed. They also had much more access to information, for white people, accustomed to servants and generally confident of their loyalty, often forgot their presence and spoke among themselves about matters of interest to the slaves: local gossip, changes in laws or attitudes, policies toward disobedient or rebellious slaves. As Benjamin Russel, a former slave in South Carolina, recalled:

> How did we get the news? Many plantations were strict about this, but the greater the precaution the alerter became the slave, the wider they opened their ears and the more eager they became for outside information. The sources were: girls that waited on the tables, the ladies' maids and the drivers; they would pick up everything they heard and pass it on to the other slaves.

For many white people, one of the worst surprises of the Civil War was the eagerness of their house slaves to flee. Considered by their masters the best treated and the most loyal, these slaves were commonly the first to leave or to organize mass desertions. Even the Confederacy's first family, President Jefferson Davis and his wife Varina, were chagrined by the desertion of their house servants in 1864.

From the point of view of the slave, the most unpleasant thing about being a house servant (or the single slave of a small owner) was the constant presence of white people. There was no escape from white supervision. Many slaves who were personal maids and children's nurses were required to live in the big house and rarely saw their own families. Cooks and other house servants were exposed to the tempers and whims of all members of the white family, including the children, who prepared themselves for lives of mastery by practicing giving orders to slaves many times their own age. And house servants, more than any others, were forced to act grateful and ingratiating. The demeaning images of Uncle Tom and the ever-smiling mammy derive from the roles slaves learned as the price of survival. At the same time, genuine intimacy was possible, especially between black nurses and white children. But these were bonds that the white children were ultimately forced to reject as the price of joining the master class.

Artisans and Skilled Workers

A small number of slaves were skilled workers: weavers, seamstresses, carpenters, blacksmiths, mechanics. More slave men than women achieved skilled status (partly because many jobs considered appropriate for women, like cooking, were not thought of as skilled). Solomon Northup, a northern free African American kidnapped into slavery, explained in his 1853 narrative, *Twelve Years a Slave,* that he had been forced to do a variety of work. He had had three owners and had been hired out repeatedly as a carpenter and as a driver of other slaves in a sugar mill; he had also been hired out to clear land for a new Louisiana plantation and to cut sugar cane. Black people worked as lumberjacks (of the 16,000 lumber workers, almost all were slaves), as miners, as deckhands and stokers on Mississippi riverboats, as stevedores loading cotton on the docks of Charleston, Savannah, and New Orleans, and in the handful of southern factories. Because slaves were their masters' property, the wages of the slave belonged to the owner, not the slave.

The extent to which slaves made up the laboring class was most apparent in cities. A British visitor to Natchez in 1835 noted slave "mechanics, draymen, hostelers, labourers, hucksters and washwomen and the heterogeneous multitude of every other occupation." In the North, all these jobs were performed by white workers. In part because the South failed to attract as much immigrant labor as the North, southern cities offered both enslaved and free black people opportunities in skilled occupations such as blacksmithing and carpentering that free African Americans in the North were denied.

Field Work

A full 75 percent of all slaves were field workers. Field hands, both men and women, worked from "can see to can't see" (sunup to sundown) summer and winter, and frequently longer at harvest, when eighteen-hour days were common. On most plantations, the bell sounded an hour before sunup, and slaves were expected to be on their way to the fields as soon as it was light. The usual pattern of working in groups of twenty to twenty-five harked back to African communal systems of agricultural work. Many work gangs had black drivers in addition to white overseers. Work continued till noon, and after an hour or so for lunch and rest the slaves worked nearly until dark. In the evening the women prepared dinner at the cabins and everyone snatched a few hours of socializing before bedtime. Work days were shorter in the winter, perhaps only ten hours.

Work was tedious in the hot and humid southern fields, and the overseer's whip was never far away. Cotton growing was hard work: plowing and planting, chopping weeds with a heavy hoe, and picking the ripe cotton from the stiff and scratchy bolls at the rate of 150 pounds a day. In the rice fields, slaves worked knee-deep in water. On sugar plantations, harvesting the cane and getting it ready for boiling was exceptionally heavy work. A strong, hardworking slave—a "prime field hand"—was valuable property, worth at least $1,000 to the master. Slaves justifiably took pride in their strength, as observed by a white Northerner traveling in Mississippi in 1854 who came across a work gang happy to be going home early because of rain:

> First came, led by an old driver carrying a whip, forty of the largest and strongest women I ever saw together...they carried themselves loftily, each having a hoe over the shoulder, and walking with a free, powerful stride. Behind them came the ...[plowhands and their mules], thirty strong, mostly men, but a few of them women....A lean and vigilant white overseer, on a brisk pony, brought up the rear.

That, of course, is only one side of the story. Compare Solomon Northup's memory of cotton picking:

> It was rarely that a day passed by without one or more whippings. The delinquent [who had not picked enough cotton] was taken out, stripped, made to lie upon the ground, face downwards, when he received a punishment proportioned to his offence. It is the literal, unvarnished truth, that the crack of the lash, and the shrieking of the slaves, can be heard from dark till bed time, on [this] plantation, any day almost during the entire period of the cotton-picking season.

Slaves aged fast in this regime. Poor diet and heavy labor undermined health. When they were too old to work, they took on other tasks within the black community, such as caring for young children. Honored by the slave community, the elderly were tolerated by white owners, who continued to feed and clothe them until their deaths. Few actions show the hypocrisy of southern paternalism more clearly than the speed with which white owners evicted their elderly slaves in the 1860s when the end of the slave system was in sight.

THE AFRICAN AMERICAN COMMUNITY

Surely no group in American history has faced a harder job of community building than the black people of the antebellum South. Living in intimate, daily contact with their oppressors, African Americans nevertheless created an enduring culture of their own, a culture that had far-reaching and lasting influence on all of southern society (see Chapter 4). Within their own communities, African American values and attitudes, and especially their own forms of Christianity, played a vital part in shaping a culture of endurance and resistance.

Few African Americans were unfortunate enough to live their lives alone among white people. Over half of all slaves lived on plantations with twenty or more other slaves, and others, on smaller farms, had links with slaves on nearby properties. Urban slaves were able to make and sustain so many secret contacts with other African Americans in cities or towns that slave owners wondered whether slave discipline could be maintained in urban settings. There can be no question that the bonds among African Americans were what sustained them during the years of slavery.

In law, slaves were property, to be bought, sold, rented, worked, and otherwise used (but not abused or killed) as the owner saw fit. But slaves were also human beings, with feelings, needs, and hopes. Even though most white Southerners believed black people to be members of an inferior, childish race, all but the most brutal masters acknowledged the humanity of their slaves. Furthermore, as a practical matter, white owners had long since learned that unhappy or rebellious slaves were poor workers. White masters learned to live with the two key institutions of African American community life: the family and the African American church.

Slave Families

No southern state recognized slave marriages in law. Most owners, though, not only recognized but encouraged them, sometimes even performing a kind of wedding ceremony for the couple. James Henry Hammond conducted a special ceremony for his slaves, to whom he gave $5.00 for a first marriage and $3.50 for a second marriage. Masters sometimes tried to arrange marriages, but slaves usually found their own mates, sometimes on their own plantation, sometimes elsewhere. Masters encouraged marriage among their slaves, believing it made the men less rebellious, and for economic reasons they were eager for women to have children. Thomas Jefferson, always a clear thinker, put the matter bluntly: "I consider a [slave] woman who [gives birth to] a child every two years as more profitable than the best man on the farm.... What she produces is an addition to the capital." Whatever marriages meant to the masters, to slaves they were a haven of love and intimacy in a cruel world and the basis of the African American community. Husbands and wives had a chance, in their own cabins, to live their own lives among loved ones. The relationship between slave husband and wife was different from that of the white husband and wife. The patriarchal system dictated that the white marriage be unequal, for the man had to be dominant and the woman dependent and submissive. Slave marriages were more equal, for husband and wife were both powerless within the slave system. Both knew that neither could protect the other from abuse at the hands of white people.

Husband and wife cooperated in loving and sheltering their children and teaching them survival skills. Above all, family meant continuity. Parents made great efforts to teach their children the family history. As Alex Haley's *Roots* illustrated, many African American families today maintain strong oral traditions dating back to their African origins. Parents did their best to surround children with a supportive and protective kinship network.

The strength of these ties is shown by the many husbands, wives, children, and parents who searched for each other after the Civil War when slavery came to an end. Observing African Americans' postwar migrations, a Freedmen's Bureau agent commented that "every mother's son among them seemed to be in search of his mother; every mother in search of her children." As the ads in black newspapers indicate, some family searches went on into the 1870s and 1880s, and many ended in failure.

Given the vast size of the internal slave trade, fear of separation was constant—and real. Far from being a rare event prompted only by financial necessity, separations of slave families were common. One in every five slave marriages was broken, and one in every three children sold away from their families. These figures clearly show that slave owners' support for slave marriages was secondary to their desire for profits. The scale of the trade was a strong indication of the economic reality that underlay their protestations of paternalism.

In the face of constant separation, slave communities attempted to act like larger families. Following practices developed early in slavery, children were taught to respect and learn from all the elders, to call all adults of a certain age "aunt" or "uncle," and to call children of their own age "brother" or "sister" (see Chapter 4). Thus, in the absence of their own family, separated children could quickly find a place and a source of comfort in the slave community to which they had been sold.

This emphasis on family and on kinship networks had an even more fundamental purpose. The kinship of the entire community, where old people were respected and young ones cared for, represented a conscious rejection of white paternalism. The slaves' ability, in the most difficult of situations, to structure a community that expressed their values, not those of their masters, was extraordinary. Equally remarkable was the way in which African Americans reshaped Christianity to serve their needs.

African American Religion

Slaves brought religions from Africa but were not allowed to practice them, for white people feared religion would create a bond among slaves that might lead to rebellion. African religions managed to survive in the slave community in forms that white people considered "superstition" or "folk belief," such as the medicinal use of roots by conjurers. Religious ceremonies survived, too, in late-night gatherings deep in the woods where the sound of drumming, singing, and dancing could not reach white ears (see Chapter 4). In the nineteenth century, these African traditions allowed African Americans to reshape white Christianity into their own distinctive faith.

Most masters of the eighteenth century made little effort to Christianize their slaves, afraid they might take the promises of universal brotherhood and equality too literally. The Great Awakening, which swept the South after the 1760s, introduced many slaves to Christianity, often in mixed congregations with white people (see Chapter 5). The transformation was completed by the Second Great Awakening, which took root among black and white Southerners in the 1790s. The number of African American converts, preachers, and lay teachers grew rapidly, and a distinctive form of Christianity took shape.

Five generations of one family on a South Carolina plantation are gathered together for this 1862 picture, providing living evidence of the importance of kinship in the building of African American communities.

Free African Americans founded their own independent churches and denominations. The first African American Baptist and Methodist churches were founded in Philadelphia in 1794 by the Reverend Absalom Jones and the Reverend Richard Allen. In 1816, the Reverend Allen joined with African American ministers from other cities to form the African Methodist Episcopal (AME) denomination. By the 1830s, free African American ministers like Andrew Marshall of Savannah and many more enslaved black preachers and lay ministers preached, sometimes secretly, to slaves. Their message was one of faith and love, of deliverance, of the coming of the promised land.

African Americans found in Christianity a powerful vehicle to express their longings for freedom and justice. But why did their white masters allow it? Some white people, themselves converted by the revivals, doubtless believed that they should not deny

African cultural patterns persisted in the preference for night funerals and for solemn pageantry and song, depicted in British artist John Antrobus's Plantation Burial, *ca.* 1860. *Like other African American customs, the community care of the dead contained an implied rebuke to the masters' care of the living slaves.*

their slaves the same religious experience. But the evangelical religion of the early nineteenth century was also a powerful form of social control. Southern slave owners, seeking to counteract the appeal of African American religion, expected their Christianity to make their slaves obedient and peaceful. Forbidding their slaves to hold their own religious gatherings, owners insisted that their slaves attend white church services. Slaves were quick to realize the owners' purpose. As a former Texas slave recalled: "We went to church on the place and you ought to heard that preachin'. Obey your massa and missy, don't steal chickens and eggs and meat, but nary a word 'bout havin' a soul to save." On many plantations, slaves attended religious services with their masters every Sunday, sitting quietly in the back of the church or in the balcony as the minister preached messages justifying slavery and urging obedience. But at night, away from white eyes, they held their own prayer meetings. Another former Texas slave recalled:

> [We] used to have a prayin' ground down in the hollow and sometimes we come out of the field, between eleven and twelve at night, scorchin' and burnin' up with nothin' to eat, and we wants to ask the good Lawd to have mercy. We put grease in a snuff pan or bottle and make a lamp. We takes a pine torch, too, and goes down to the hollow to pray. Some gits so joyous they starts to holler loud and we has to stop up they mouth [so the whites won't hear].

In churches and in spontaneous religious expressions, the black community made Christianity its own. Fusing Christian texts with African elements of group activity such as the circle dance, the call-and-response pattern, and, above all, group singing, black people created a unique community religion full of emotion, enthusiasm, and protest. Nowhere is this spirit more compelling than in the famous spirituals: "Go Down Moses," with its mournful refrain "Let my people go"; the rousing "Didn't My Lord Deliver Daniel...and why not every man"; the haunting "Steal Away." Some of these spirituals became as well known to white people as to black people, but only African Americans seem to have appreciated the full meaning of their subversive messages.

Nevertheless, this was not a religion of rebellion, for that was unrealistic for most slaves. Black Christianity was an enabling religion: it helped slaves to survive, not as passive victims of white tyranny but as active opponents of an oppressive system that they daily protested in small but meaningful ways. In their faith, African Americans expressed a spiritual freedom that white people could not destroy.

Freedom and Resistance

Whatever their dreams, most slaves knew they would never escape. Freedom was too far away. Almost all successful escapes in the nineteenth century (approximately 1,000 a year) were from the Upper South (Delaware, Maryland, Virginia, Kentucky, Missouri). A slave in the Lower South or the Southwest simply had too far to go to reach freedom. In addition, white Southerners were determined to prevent escapes. Slave patrols were a common sight on southern roads. Any black person without a pass from his or her master was captured (usually roughly) and returned home to certain punishment. But despite almost certain recapture, slaves continued to flee and to help others do so. Escaped slave Harriet Tubman of Maryland, who made nineteen rescue missions freeing 300 slaves in all, had extraordinary determination and skill. As a female runaway, she was unusual, too: most escapees were young men, for women often had small children they were unable to take and unwilling to leave behind.

Much more common was the practice of "running away nearby." Slaves who knew they could not reach freedom still frequently demonstrated their desire for liberty or their discontent over mistreatment by taking unauthorized leave from their plantation. Hidden in nearby forests or swamps, provided with food smuggled by other slaves from the plantation, the runaway might return home after a week or so, often to rather mild punishment. Although in reality most slaves could have little hope of gaining freedom, even failed attempts at rebellion shook the foundations of the slave system and thus temporary flight by any slave was a warning sign of discontent that a wise master did not ignore.

Slave Revolts

The ultimate resistance, however, was the slave revolt. Southern history was dotted with stories of former slave conspiracies and rumors of current plots (see Chapter 4). Every white Southerner knew about the last-minute failure of Gabriel Prosser's insurrection in Richmond in 1800 and the chance discovery of Denmark Vesey's plot in Charleston in 1822. But when in 1831, Nat Turner actually started a rebellion in which a number of white people were killed, southern fears were greatly magnified.

Gabriel Prosser, a literate blacksmith, had gathered more than a thousand slaves for an assault on Richmond. Although the attempt was aborted at the last minute and Prosser and thirty-five others were caught and hanged, white people were especially frightened to learn that Prosser had organized under a banner proclaiming "Death or Liberty" and had hoped for help from the independent black people of Haiti. The notion of an international force of revolutionary slaves demanding their freedom was a fundamental challenge to slave owners' assumptions about their own liberty and power.

Denmark Vesey's conspiracy raised fears among white people concerning African American religion and free black people. Vesey was a well-traveled former seaman who lived in Charleston and worked as a carpenter. Free, well read, and eloquent, he was a lay preacher at Charleston's African Methodist Episcopal Church, where he drew on quotations from the Bible and from the congressional debates during the Missouri Crisis (1819–20) to make a forceful argument against slavery. His co-conspirator, Gullah Jack, was a "conjure-man" who drew on the African religious traditions that flourished among the slaves in the South Carolina low country. Vesey and Gullah Jack drew up a plan to evade the lax city patrol and steal weapons from the Charleston arsenal and horses from livery stables. Then, while mounted and armed slaves beat back white counterattacks in the streets of Charleston, house slaves would capture their owners and murder any who tried to escape. Vesey's aim was to seize Charleston and ultimately to sail to the free black Caribbean nation of Haiti.

Vesey and Gullah Jack recruited at least eighty country and city slaves into the conspiracy, including several trusted house slaves of South Carolina governor Thomas Bennett. Two weeks before the date fixed for the insurrection, the plot was betrayed by a house servant who reported the two slaves who had tried to recruit him into the conspiracy. The accused slaves laughed at the charge and coolly managed to convince the authorities that there was no plot. But two days before the revolt, another house servant confessed, and this time the authorities believed him. In the frantic roundup that followed, thirty-five black people were hanged (Vesey among them) and thirty-seven others sold down the river. But some rebels were not caught because their fellow conspirators died without betraying them. Charlestonians had to live with the knowledge that some of their city's most trusted black servants had conspired to kill their masters—and might still plan to do so.

In the wake of the Vesey conspiracy, Charlestonians turned their fear and anger outward. Planter Robert J. Turnbull wrote bitterly, "By the Missouri question, our slaves thought, there was a charter of liberties granted them by Congress....[The Vesey conspiracy] will long be remembered, as

Harriet Tubman escaped in 1849 from slavery in Maryland, and returned nineteen times to free almost 300 other slaves. Here Tubman (at left), the most famous "conductor" on the Underground Railroad, is shown with some of those she led to freedom.

This drawing shows the moment, almost two months after the failure of his famous and bloody slave revolt, when Nat Turner was accidentally discovered in the woods near his home plantation. Turner's cool murder of his owner and methodical organization of his revolt deeply frightened many white Southerners.

amongst the choicest fruits of that question in Congress." White people attempted to seal off the city from dangerous outside influences. The AME Church (where radical ideas such as the Missouri question had been discussed) was destroyed, and in December 1822 the South Carolina legislature passed a bill requiring that all black seamen be seized and jailed while their ships were in Charleston harbor. Initially most alarmed about free black people from Haiti, Charlestonians soon came to believe that northern free black seamen were spreading antislavery ideas among their slaves.

The most famous slave revolt—Nat Turner's revolt in Southampton County, Virginia—was a partial success. A literate man, Nat Turner was, like Denmark Vesey, a lay preacher, but unlike Vesey he was also a slave. It was Turner's intelligence and strong religious commitment that made him a leader in the slave community and, interestingly, these very same qualities led his master, Joseph Travis, to treat him with kindness even though Turner had once run away for a month after being mistreated by an overseer. Turner began plotting his revolt after a religious vision in which he saw "white spirits and black spirits engaged in battle"; "the sun was darkened—the thunder rolled in the Heavens, and blood flowed in streams." Turner and five other slaves struck on the night of August 20, 1831, first killing Travis, who, Turner said, "was to me a kind master, and placed the greatest confidence in me; in fact, I had no cause to complain of his treatment of me."

Moving from plantation to plantation and killing a total of fifty-five white people, the rebels numbered sixty by the next morning, when they fled from a group of armed white men. More than forty blacks were executed after the revolt, including Turner, who was captured accidentally after he had hidden for two months in the woods. Thomas R. Gray, a white lawyer to whom Turner dictated a lengthy confession before his death, was impressed by Turner's composure. "I looked on him," Gray said, "and my blood curdled in my veins." If intelligent, well-treated slaves such as Turner could plot revolts, how could white Southerners ever feel safe?

Gabriel's Rebellion, the Denmark Vesey plot, and Nat Turner's Revolt were the most prominent examples of organized slave resistance, but they were far from the only ones. Conspiracies and actual or rumored slave resistance began in colonial times (see Chapter 4) and never ceased. These plots exposed the truth white Southerners preferred to ignore: Only force kept Africans and African Americans enslaved, and because no system of control could ever be total, white Southerners could never be completely safe from the possibility of revolt. Nat Turner brought white Southerners' fears to the surface. After 1831, the possibility of slave insurrection was never far from their minds.

Free African Americans

Another source of white disquiet was the growing number of free African Americans. By 1860 nearly 250,000 free black people lived in the South. For most, freedom dated from before 1800, when antislavery feeling among slave owners in the Upper South was widespread and cotton cultivation had yet to boom. In Virginia, for example, the number of manumitted (freed) slaves jumped tenfold in twenty years (see Chapter 7). But a new mood became apparent in 1806 when Virginia tightened its lenient manumission law: now the freed person was required to leave the state within a year or be sold back into slavery. After 1830 manumission was virtually impossible throughout the South.

Most free black people lived in the countryside of the Upper South, where they worked as tenant farmers or farm laborers. Urban African Americans were much more visible. Life was especially difficult for female-headed families because only the most menial work—street peddling and laundry work, for example—was available to free black women. The situation for African American males was somewhat better. Although they were discriminated against in employment and in social life, there were opportunities for skilled black craftsmen in trades such as blacksmithing and carpentering.

Cities such as Charleston, Savannah, and Natchez were home to flourishing free African American communities that formed their own churches and fraternal orders. In Natchez, a free black barber, William Johnson, owned several barber shops, a small farm, and an estate valued at $25,000 in 1851 that included fifteen slaves. Johnson had a white attorney and friends among the city's leading politicians, and he lived in a white neighborhood. Half a dozen other free African Americans in Natchez were similarly prosperous, and they, too, were slave owners. This tiny elite kept a careful social distance from most of Natchez's approximately 1,000 free black people (one-quarter of all free African Americans in Mississippi in 1840), who were miserably poor. This free black elite treated white people with great tact and deference.

Free African Americans had reason to be careful, for their position was increasingly precarious. Throughout the South in the 1830s, state legislatures tightened black codes—laws concerning free black people. Free African Americans could not carry firearms, could not purchase slaves (unless they were members of their own family), and were liable to the criminal penalties meted out to slaves (that is, whippings and summary judgments without a jury trial). They could not testify against whites, hold office, vote, or serve in the militia. In other words, except for the right to own property, free blacks had no civil rights. Following the cleanup of the alarming race mixing in Natchez-under-the-Hill, the Natchez elite focused on free African Americans. In 1841, whites mounted a campaign to deport from the state any free black person who adopted "the practices of the rogue, the incendiary, and the abolitionist." Many poor free African Americans were deported from Natchez that summer and in the following years. William Johnson, whose own security was not threatened, aided some poor black people by quietly helping them obtain attestations of good character from white planters. For

One of the ways Charleston attempted to control its African American population was to require all slaves to wear badges showing their occupation. After 1848, free black people also had to wear badges, which were decorated, ironically, with a liberty cap.

all of his (comparative) wealth, as a black man he could do nothing openly to help his own people.

As this episode shows, white people increasingly feared the influence free black people might have on slaves, for free African Americans were a living challenge to the slave system. Their very existence disproved the basic southern equations of white equals free, and black equals slave. No one believed more fervently in those equations than the South's largest population group, white people who did not own slaves.

YEOMEN AND POOR WHITE PEOPLE

The pervasive influence of the slave system in the South is reflected in the startling contrast of two facts: two-thirds of all Southerners did not own slaves, yet slave owners dominated the social and political life of the region. Who were the two-thirds of white Southerners who did not own slaves, and how did they live? Throughout the south, slave owners occupied the most productive land: tobacco-producing areas in Virginia and Tennessee, coastal areas of South Carolina and Georgia where rice and cotton grew, sugar lands in Louisiana, and large sections of the cotton-producing black belt, which stretched westward from South Carolina to Texas. Small farmers, usually without slaves, occupied the rest of the land. This land ranged from adequate to poor, from depleted, once-rich regions in Virginia to the Carolina hill country and the pine barrens of Mississippi.

Yeomen

The word "yeoman," originally a British term for a farmer who works his own land, is often applied to independent farmers of the South, most of whom lived on family-sized farms. Although yeoman farmers sometimes owned a few slaves, in general they and their families worked their land by themselves. Typical of the yeoman-farmer community was northwestern Georgia, once home to the Creeks and Cherokees, but now populated by communities of small farmers who grew enough vegetables to feed their families, including corn, which they either ate themselves or fed to hogs. In addition, these farmers raised enough cotton every year (usually no more than one or two bales) to bring in a little cash. At least 60 percent owned their own farms, but some were wealthier than others. Isaac Cobb of Carroll County owned 700 acres of land on which he grazed cattle, sheep, and hogs. On 200 of these acres, twelve slaves helped him produce 2,000 bushels of grain and twelve bales of cotton. In contrast, Richard White, of the same county, used only family labor to farm 50 acres devoted to food and grains and the grazing of a few cattle, sheep, and hogs. These two men, and thousands like them, were the yeomen Thomas Jefferson celebrated—economically independent yet intimately tied to a larger but still very local group.

The local community was paramount. Farm men and women depended on their relatives and neighbors for assistance in large farm tasks such as planting, harvesting, and construction. Events requiring lots of hands like logrollings, corn shuckings, and quilting bees were community events. Farmers repaid this help, and obtained needed goods, through complex systems of barter with other members of the community. In their organization, southern farm communities were no different from northern ones, with one major exception—slavery. In the South, one of the key items in the community barter system was the labor of slaves, who were frequently loaned out to neighbors by small slave owners such as Isaac Cobb to fulfill an obligation to another farmer.

Where yeomen and large slave owners lived side by side, as in the Georgia black belt where cotton was the major crop, slavery again provided a link between richer and poorer. Large plantation owners often bought food for their slaves from small local farmers, ground the latter's corn in the plantation mill, ginned their cotton, and transported and marketed it as well. But although planters and much smaller yeomen were part of a larger community network, in the black belt the large slave owners were clearly dominant. Only in their own up-country communities did yeomen feel truly independent.

The goal of yeoman farm families was economic independence. Their mixed farming and grazing enterprises, supported by kinship and community ties, afforded them a self-sufficiency epitomized by Carl G. von Iwonski's painting of this rough but comfortable log cabin in New Braunfels, Texas.

Poor White People

Not all small farmers were on an equal footing. One-third of the farmers in the Georgia up-country were tenant farmers. Some were farmers' sons, striking out on their own while waiting to inherit their fathers' land. But others were poor whites with little hope of improving their condition. From 30 to 50 percent of all southern white people were landless, a proportion similar to that in the North. But the existence of slavery affected the opportunities for southern poor white people. Slaves made up the permanent, stable work force in agriculture and in many skilled trades. Many poor white people led highly transient lives in search of work, such as farm labor at harvest time, which was only temporary. Others were tenant farmers working under share-tenancy arrangements that kept them in debt to the landowner. Although they farmed poorer land with less equipment than landowning farmers, most tenant farmers grew enough food to sustain their families. Like the yeomen, but with more difficulty, tenant farmers aspired to independence.

Relationships between poor whites and black slaves were complex. White men and women often worked side by side with black slaves in the fields and were socially and sexually intimate with enslaved and free African Americans. White people engaged in clandestine trade to supply slaves with items like liquor that slave owners prohibited, helped slaves to escape, and even (in an 1835 Mississippi case) were executed for their participation in planning a slave revolt. At the same time, the majority of poor white people insisted, sometimes violently, on their racial superiority over blacks. For their part, many African American slaves, better dressed, better nourished, and healthier, dismissed them as "poor white trash." But the fact was that the difficult lives of poor whites, whom one contemporary described as "a third class of white people," served to blur the crucial racial distinction between independent whites and supposedly inferior, dependent black people on which the system of slavery rested. Like the boatmen whom the Natchez slave owners viewed with such alarm, poor white people posed a potential threat to the slave system.

Yeoman Values

In 1828 and 1832, southern yeomen and poor white men voted overwhelmingly for Andrew Jackson. They were drawn variously to his outspoken policy of ruthless expansionism, his appeals to the common man, and his rags-to-riches ascent from poor boy to rich slave owner. It was a career many hoped to emulate. The dominance of the large planters was due at least in part to the ambition of many yeomen, especially those with two or three slaves, to expand their holdings and become rich. These farmers, enthusiastic members of the lively democratic politics of the South, supported the leaders they hoped to join.

But for a larger group of yeomen, independence and not wealth was most important. Many southern yeomen lived apart from large slaveholders, in the up-country regions where plantation agriculture was unsuitable. The very high value southern yeomen placed on freedom grew directly from their own experience as self-sufficient property-owning farmers in small, family-based communities. This was a way of life that southern "plain folk" were determined to preserve. It made them resistant to the economic opportunities and challenges that capitalism and industrialization posed for northern farmers, which southern yeomen perceived as encroachments on their freedom.

The irony was that the freedom yeomen so prized rested on slavery. White people could count on slaves to perform the hardest and worst labor, and the degradation of slave life was a daily reminder of the freedom they enjoyed in comparison. Slavery meant that all white people, rich and poor, were equal in the sense that they were all free. This assumption of white skin privilege had formed in the eighteenth century as slavery became the answer to the South's labor problem (see Chapter 4). The democratization of politics in the early nineteenth century and the enactment of nearly universal white manhood suffrage perpetuated the belief in white skin privilege, even though the gap between rich and poor white people was widening.

Southern yeomen did not blindly follow the rich slave owners who were their political leaders. Rather, they supported a freedom they believed they would not have under any other system. But southern unanimity on this point, which looked so strong, was actually very fragile. Anything that appeared to threaten slavery threatened the entire southern social structure, trapping Southerners in ever more rigid and defensive positions.

PLANTERS

Remarkably few slave owners fit the popular stereotype of the rich and leisured plantation owner with hundreds of acres of land and hundreds of slaves. Only

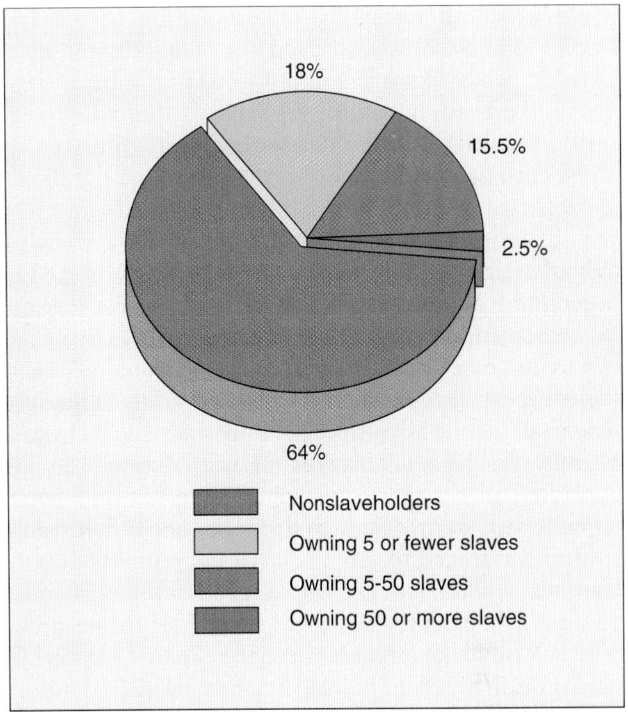

Slaveholding and Class Structure in the South, 1830

The great mass of the southern white population were yeoman farmers. In 1830, slave owners made up only 36 percent of the southern white population; owners of more than fifty slaves constituted a tiny 2.5 percent. Yet they and the others who were middling planters dominated politics, retaining the support of yeomen who prized their freedom as white men above class-based politics.

Source: U.S. Bureau of the Census.

36 percent of southern white people owned slaves in 1830, and only 2.5 percent owned fifty slaves or more. Just as yeomen and poor whites were diverse, so, too, were southern slave owners.

Small Slave Owners

The largest group of slave owners were small yeomen taking the step from subsistence agriculture to commercial production. To do this in the South's agricultural economy, they had to own slaves. But upward mobility was difficult. Owning one or two slaves increased farm production only slightly, and it was hard to accumulate the capital to buy more. One common pattern was for a slave owner to leave one or two slaves to farm while he worked another job (this arrangement usually meant that his wife had unacknowledged responsibility for their supervision). In other cases, small farmers worked side by side with their slaves in the fields. In still other cases, owners hired out their slaves to larger slave owners.

In every case, the owner was economically vulnerable: a poor crop or a downturn in cotton prices could wipe out his gains and force him to sell his slaves. When times improved, he might buy a new slave or two and try again, but getting a secure footing on the bottom rung of the slave owner ladder was very difficult. The roller-coaster economy of the early nineteenth century did not help matters, and the Panic of 1837 was a serious setback to many small farmers.

John Flintoff was an aspiring slave owner who moved from North Carolina to Mississippi in 1841, hoping to make his fortune. Working as an overseer on his uncle's land, Flintoff began his career as a slave owner by buying three slave children (one was seven years old), the cheapest slaves available. Over the years he bought nine in all. While an overseer, Flintoff married and began a family. But he was unsuccessful as an overseer. As he confessed in his diary, "managing negroes and large farms is soul destroying." In 1853 his uncle fired him. Flintoff was forced to sell his slaves and return to North Carolina, where, with the help of his in-laws, he bought 124 acres of land. Assisted by several slaves he grew corn, wheat, and tobacco—not the wonderfully profitable cotton of which he had dreamed. By 1860, Flintoff was modestly successful; wealthy enough to send his son to college and to free his wife from routine farm chores. As he boasted, his wife "has lived a Lady."

For a smaller group of slave owners, the economic struggle was not so hard. Middle-class professional men—lawyers, doctors, and merchants—frequently managed to become large slave owners because they already had capital (the pay from their professions) to invest in land and slaves. Sometimes they received payment for their services not in money but in slaves. These owners were the most likely to own skilled slaves—carpenters, blacksmiths, other artisans—and to rent them out for profit. By steady accumulation, the most successful members of this middle class were able to buy their way into the slave-owning elite and to confirm that position by marrying their sons or daughters into the aristocracy.

Here the career of Andrew Jackson of Tennessee is instructive. Jackson, an orphan, had no family money. He began a profitable career as a prosecutor in Nashville in the 1790s, frequently taking small plots of land as payment for his services. In 1796, the year he was elected Tennessee's delegate to the U.S. House of Representatives, he owned 10 slaves. In 1798 Jackson owned 15 slaves. He widened his economic activities, buying land, partnership in a store, a plantation for himself (the Hermitage), and a racetrack. Then came some bad years—the mercantile business failed, and debts on land came due—and Jackson was soon preoccupied with military matters. But he continued to accumulate slaves: 44 by 1820, 95 by 1828 (the year he was elected president), 150 a few years later, and almost 200 by the time of his death in 1845.

The Old Planter Elite

The slave-owning elite, those 2.5 percent who owned fifty slaves or more, enjoyed the prestige, the political leadership, and the lifestyle to which many white Southerners aspired. Almost all great slave owners inherited their wealth. They were rarely self-made men, although most tried to add to the land and slaves they had inherited. Men of wealth and property had led southern politics since colonial times, but increasingly after 1820 it was men from the middle classes who were most often elected to political office. As the nation moved toward universal manhood suffrage, planters tried to learn how to appeal to the popular vote, but most never acquired "the common touch." It was the smaller slave owners who formed a clear majority in every southern state legislature before 1860.

The eastern seaboard had first given rise to a class of rich planters in the colonial period, as attested by the plantations of William Byrd and Robert "King" Carter of Virginia and the cultured life of the planter elite, centered in Charleston, that had established itself in the South Carolina low country and Sea Islands.

One such planter was Thomas Chaplin, descended from an indentured servant who arrived in 1672 from the British sugar-producing island of Barbados. In 1839 he married Mary McDowell, granddaughter of a rich Charleston merchant, and in 1840 they moved into the old family house on the 376-acre Tombee Plantation on St. Helena Island near Beaufort, South Carolina. Master of sixty to seventy slaves, Chaplin grew sea-island cotton (a long-staple variety), potatoes, and corn and raised beef and mutton. Although St. Helena land was rich and fertile, the climate bred mosquito-borne malaria, epidemic from mid-May until November. Most planters and their families lived in Charleston or the healthier up-country during the "sickly season," and few poorer white people lived on St. Helena at all. As a consequence, by 1845 black people outnumbered white people eight to one on the island (2,000 African Americans to 250 whites). St. Helena and the other Sea Islands of South Carolina were unique in the relative autonomy of their black population and the persistence of African customs and language.

Soon after he took possession of Tombee Plantation, Chaplin was forced to sell off more than half his slaves to settle family debts and lawsuits. Land rich but labor poor, Chaplin fretted in 1850: "So many mouths to feed & so few to work that it is impossible for me to get along." Although completely dependent on his black labor force, Chaplin was indifferent to them as individuals. Unlike many planters, Chaplin refused to attend slave weddings, dismissing them as "tomfoolery," and only grudgingly did he permit his slaves to choose husbands and wives from other plantations. He complained unceasingly about the high rate of infant mortality among slaves, going so far as to accuse mothers of killing their own babies. He failed to realize that overwork and poor nutrition (counteracted only in part by the constant pilfering from his storehouses and barns) were to blame. Unlike most planters, Chaplin never hired an overseer for the work in his fields, but after 1852 he increasingly left the details of management to a black slave driver.

The Natchez "Nabobs"

As Southerners and slave owning spread westward, membership in the elite broadened to include the new wealth of Alabama, Mississippi, Louisiana, and Texas. The rich planters of the Natchez community were popularly called "nabobs" (from a Hindi word for Europeans who had amassed fabulous wealth in India). Frederick Stanton, owner of Stanton Hall in Natchez, was a physician who had immigrated from Northern Ireland. The source of his wealth was not medicine but the cotton commission (brokerage) business. At the time of his death he owned 444 slaves and 15,109 acres of land on six Louisiana and Mississippi plantations that produced more than 3,000 bales of cotton a year. Another great Natchez family, the Surgets, of French origin, traced their wealth further back, to a Spanish land grant of 2,500 acres to Pierre Surget. In the 1850s his grandsons Frank and James Surget controlled some 93,000 acres in Mississippi, Arkansas, and Louisiana (half of it plantation land and half bought on speculation, for resale). Each brother sold 4,000 bales of cotton a year, and between them they owned upwards of 1,000 slaves. Each also owned palatial mansions in Natchez—Cherry Hill and Clifton.

The extraordinary concentration of wealth in Natchez—in 1850 it was the richest county in the nation—fostered a self-consciously elite lifestyle that derived not from long tradition but from suddenly acquired riches. Fastidious Northerners such as Thomas Taylor, a Pennsylvania Quaker who visited Natchez in 1847, noted: "Many of the chivalric gentry whom I have been permitted to see dashing about here on highbred horses, seem to find their greatest enjoyment in recounting their bear hunts, 'great fights,' and occasional exploits with revolvers and Bowie knives—swearing 'terribly' and sucking mint juleps & cherry cobblers with straws."

Plantation Life

The urban life of the Natchez planters was unusual. Many wealthy planters, especially those on new lands in the Old Southwest, lived in isolation on their plantations with their families and slaves. Through family networks, common boarding school experience, political activity, and frequent visiting, the small planter elite consciously worked to create and maintain a distinctive lifestyle that was modeled on that of the English aristocracy, as Southerners understood it. This

William H. Brown, *Hauling the Whole Week's Picking* (detail), 1842. Watercolor. The Historic New Orleans Collection.

This scene is part of a larger mural, created by artist William Henry Brown in 1842, which depicts everyday life at Nitta Yuma, a Mississippi cotton plantation. The elegant white woman, here seen elaborately dressed to go riding, depended for her leisure status on the work of African American slaves, such as this one feeding her horse.

entailed a large estate, a spacious, elegant mansion, and lavish hospitality. For men, the gentlemanly lifestyle meant immersion in masculine activities such as hunting, soldiering, or politics and a touchy concern with "honor" that could lead to duels and other acts of bravado. Women of the slave-owning elite, in contrast, were expected to be gentle, charming, and always welcoming of relatives, friends, and other guests.

But this gracious image was at odds with the economic reality. Large numbers of black slaves had to be forced to work to produce the wealth of the large plantations. Each plantation, like the yeoman farm but on a larger scale, aimed to be self-sufficient, producing not only the cash crop but most of the food and clothing for both slaves and family. There were stables full of horses for plowing, transportation, and show. There were livestock and vegetable gardens to be tended, and carpentering, blacksmithing, weaving, and sewing to be done. A large plantation was an enterprise that required many hands, many skills, and a lot of management. Large plantation owners might have overseers or black drivers to supervise field work, but frequently they themselves had direct financial control of daily operations. Even if they were absentee landlords (like, for example, Thomas Chaplin in South Carolina and the richest of the Natchez elite), planters usually required careful accounts from their overseers and often exercised the right to overrule their decisions.

A paternalistic ideology infused the life of large plantations that permitted the planter elite to rationalize their use of slaves and the submissiveness they demanded of wives. According to this ideology, each plantation was a family composed of both black and white. The master, as head of the plantation, was head of the family, and the mistress was his "helpmate." The master was obligated to provide for all of his family, both black and white, and to treat them with humanity. In return, slaves were to work properly and do as they were told, as children would. Most elite slave owners spoke of their position of privilege as a duty and a burden. (Their wives were even more outspoken about the burdensome aspects of supervising slave labor, which they bore more directly than their husbands.) John C. Calhoun spoke for many slave owners when he described the plantation as "a little community" in which the master directed all operations so that the abilities and needs of every member, black and white, were "perfectly harmonized." Convinced of their own benevolence, slave owners expected not only obedience but gratitude from all members of their great "families."

The Plantation Mistress

Southern paternalism not only laid special burdens on plantation mistresses but put restrictions on their lives and activities not experienced by northern women of the same social rank. For example, although northern women like southern women were barred from public life and taught that their proper role was domestic and family-based, in the North, women came clearly to control the domestic "sphere" and to carry domestic concerns outside the family and into a wide range of activities that addressed various social reforms. Such autonomous behavior was out of the question for plantation mistresses, who were locked by the paternalistic model into positions that bore heavy responsibility but carried no real authority. The difficulties experienced by these in some ways quite privileged women illustrate the way the slave system affected every aspect of the personal life of slave owners.

Plantation mistresses spent most of their lives tending family members—including slaves—in illness and in childbirth, and supervising their slaves' performance of such daily tasks as cooking, housecleaning, weaving, and sewing. In addition, the plantation mistress often had to spend hours, even days, of behind-the-scenes preparation for the crowds of guests she was expected to welcome in her role as elegant and gracious hostess.

Despite the reality of the plantation mistress's daily supervision of an often extensive household, she did not rule it: her husband did. The plantation master was the source of authority to whom wife, children, and slaves were expected to look for both rewards and punishments. A wife who challenged her husband or sought more independence from him threatened the entire paternalistic system of control. After all, if she were not dependent and obedient, why should slaves be? In addition, although many southern women were deeply affected by evangelical religion and exhortations to care for those in need, their response was personal rather than social. Enlisting in reform movements like their northern counterparts would have been far too threatening to the system of slave control to be tolerated in the South, for it might have led slaves to believe that their lives, too, could be improved.

In addition to their strictly defined family roles, many southern women also suffered deeply from isolation from friends and kin. Sometimes the isolation of life on rural plantations could be overcome by long visits, but women with many small children and extensive responsibilities found it difficult to leave. Plantation masters, on the other hand, often traveled widely for political and business reasons. John C. Calhoun, for example, who spoke so earnestly about the plantation community, spent much less time than his wife on the family plantation, Fort Hill. He spent years in Washington as a politician while Floride Calhoun, who had accompanied him in his early career, remained at Fort Hill after the first five of their ten children were born.

Plantation women in the Old Southwest, many of whom had moved unwillingly and now were far from their families on the eastern seaboard, were particularly lonely. "I seldom see any person aside from our own family, and those employed upon the plantation," Mary Kendall wrote. "For about three weeks I did not have the pleasure of seeing one white female face, there being no white family except our own upon the plantation." The irony is that she was surrounded by women, but the gap between the white mistress and her black slaves was generally unbridgeable.

Although on every plantation black women served as nursemaids to young white children and as lifelong maids to white women, usually accompanying them when they moved as brides into their own homes, there are few historical examples of genuine sympathy and understanding of black women by white women of the slave-owning class. Few of the latter seemed to understand the sadness, frustration, and despair often experienced by their lifelong maids, who were forced to leave their own husbands and children to serve in their mistresses' new homes. A number of southern women did rail against "the curse of slavery," but few meant the inhumanity of the system; most were actually complaining about the extra work entailed by housekeeping with slaves. As one plantation mistress explained, "Slaves are a continual source of more trouble to housekeepers than all other things, vexing them, and causing much sin. We are compelled to keep them in ignorance and much responsibility rests on us." Years later many former slaves remembered their mistresses as being kinder than their masters, but fully a third of such accounts mention cruel whippings and other punishments by white women.

Coercion and Violence

There were generous and benevolent masters, but most large slave owners believed that constant discipline and coercion were necessary to make slaves work hard. Some slave owners used their slaves with great brutality. Owners who killed slaves were occasionally brought to trial (and usually acquitted), but no legal action was taken in the much more frequent cases of excessive punishment, general abuse, and rape.

One of the most common violations of the paternalistic code of behavior (and of southern law) was the sexual abuse of female slaves by their masters. Usually, masters forcibly raped their women slaves at will, and slave women had little hope of defending themselves from these attacks. Sometimes, however, long-term intimate relationships between masters and slaves developed. James Henry Hammond kept two slave mistresses, Sally Johnson and her daughter Louisa, for twenty years and fathered several children by each of them. Hammond's instructions to his (white) son Harry, written in 1856, about the future of his mistresses and slave children tell us much about the boundaries of the slave system: "In the last will I made I left to you...Sally Johnson the mother of Louisa & all the children of both....I cannot free these people & send them North. It would be cruelty to them....Do not let Louisa or any of my children...be the slaves of strangers. Slavery in the family will be their happiest earthly condition."

It was rare for slave owners to publicly acknowledge fathering slave children or to free these children, and black women and their families were helpless to protest their treatment. Equally silenced was the master's wife, who for reasons of modesty as well as her subordinate position was not supposed to notice either her husband's infidelity or his flagrant crossing of the color lines. As Mary Boykin Chesnut, wife of a South Carolina slave owner, vehemently confided to her diary: "God forgive us, but ours is a monstrous system....Like the patriarchs of old, our men live all in one house with their wives and their concubines, and the mulattoes one sees in every family partly resemble the white children. Any lady is ready to tell you who is the father of all the mulatto children in everybody's household but her own. Those, she seems to think, drop from the clouds."

An owner could do what he chose on his plantation, and his sons grew up expecting to do likewise.

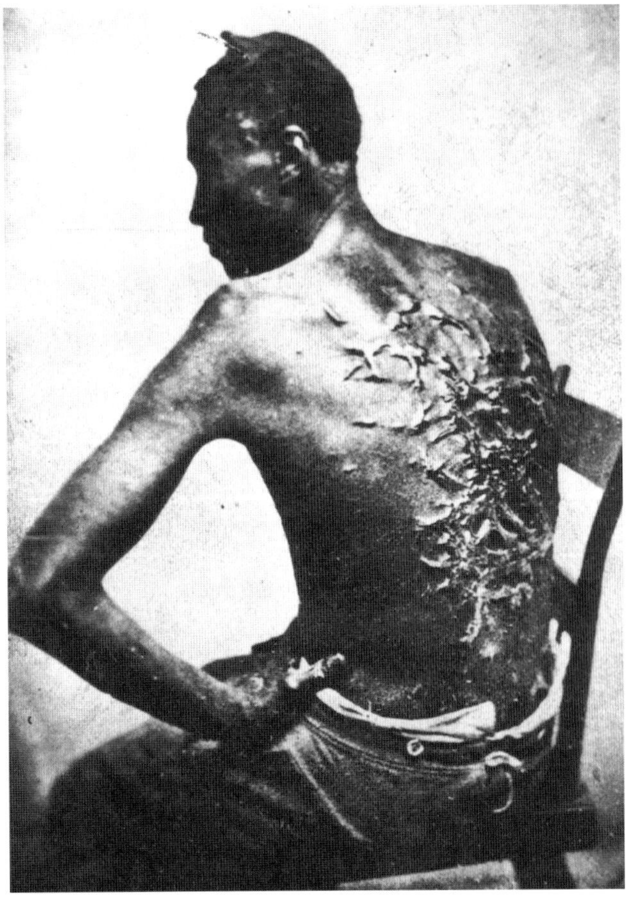

This Louisiana slave named Gordon was photographed in 1863 after he had escaped to Union lines during the Civil War. He bears the permanent scars of the violence that lay at the heart of the slave system. Few slaves were so brutally marked, but all lived with the threat of beatings if they failed to obey.

Unchecked power is always dangerous, and it is not surprising that it was sometimes misused. Perhaps the most surprising thing about the southern slave system is how much humanity survived despite the intolerable conditions. For that, most of the credit goes not to white paternalism but to African Americans and the communities they created under slavery.

THE DEFENSE OF SLAVERY

"Slavery informs all our modes of life, all our habits of thought, lies at the basis of our social existence, and of our political faith," announced South Carolina planter William Henry Trescot in 1850, explaining why the South would secede from the Union before giving up slavery. Slavery bound white and black Southerners together in tortuous ways that eventually led, as Trescot had warned, to the Civil War.

Population figures tell much of the story of the complex relationship between whites and blacks: of the

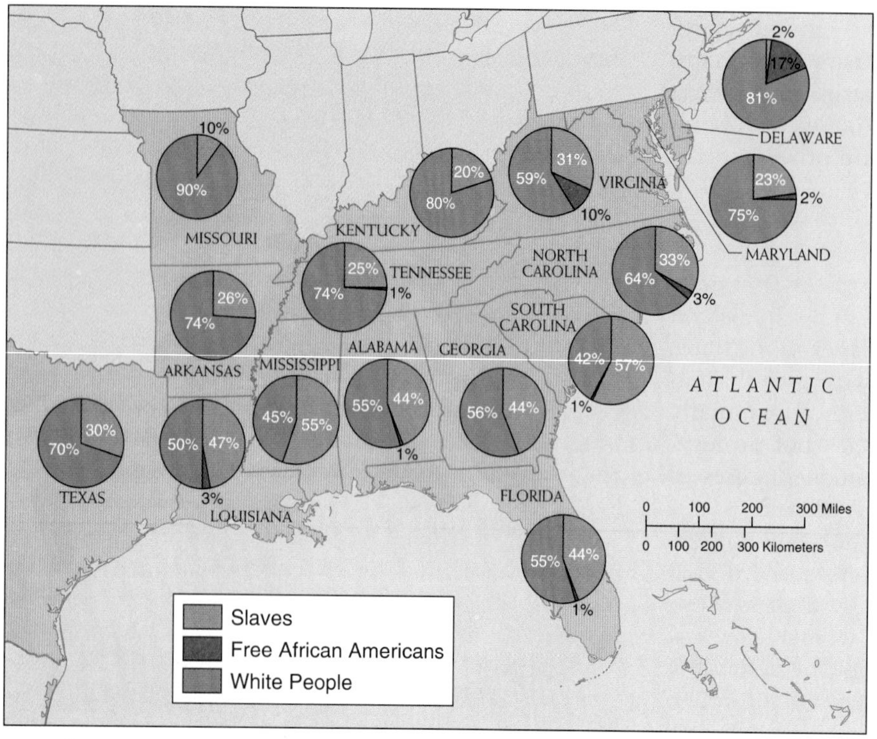

Population Patterns in the South, 1850 *In South Carolina and Mississippi the enslaved African American population outnumbered the white population; in four other Lower South states the percentage was above 40 percent. These ratios frightened many white Southerners. White people also feared the free black population, though only three states in the Upper South and Louisiana had free black populations of over 3 percent. Six states had free black populations that were so small (less than 1 percent) as to be statistically insignificant.*

12 million people who lived in the South in 1860, 4 million were slaves. Indeed, in the richest agricultural regions, such as the Sea Islands of South Carolina and Georgia and parts of the black belt, black people outnumbered whites. These sheer numbers of African Americans reinforced white people's perpetual fears of black retaliation for the violence exercised by the slave master. Every rumor of slave revolts, real or imagined, kept those fears alive. The basic question was this: What might slaves do if they were not controlled? Thomas Jefferson summed up this dilemma: "We have the wolf by the ears; and we can neither hold him nor safely let him go. Justice is in one scale, and self-preservation in the other."

Developing Proslavery Arguments

In the flush of freedom following the American Revolution, a number of slave owners in the Upper South freed their slaves, and Thomas Jefferson, ever the optimist, claimed that "a total emancipation with the consent of the masters" could not be too far in the future. Nevertheless, southern legislatures were unwilling to write steps toward emancipation into law, preferring to depend on the charity of individual slave owners. Once the cotton boom began in the 1790s, this charity was rarely exercised and Jefferson's vision of peaceful emancipation faded. On the contrary, Southerners increasingly sought to justify slavery.

Southern apologists had several conventional lines of defense. They found justifications for slavery in the Bible and in the histories of Greece and Rome, both slave-owning societies. The strongest defense was a legal one: the Constitution allowed slavery. Though never specifically mentioned in the final document, slavery had been a major issue between North and South at the Constitutional Convention in 1787. In the end, the delegates agreed that seats in the House of Representatives would be apportioned by counting all of the white population and three-fifths of the black people (Article I, Section 2, Paragraph 3); they included a clause requiring the return of runaway slaves who had crossed state lines (Article IV, Section 2, Paragraph 3); and they agreed that Congress could not abolish the international slave trade for twenty years (Article I, Section 9, Paragraph 1). There was absolutely no question: the Constitution did recognize slavery.

The Missouri Crisis of 1819–20 alarmed most Southerners, who were shocked by the evidence of widespread antislavery feeling in the North. South Carolinians viewed Denmark Vesey's conspiracy, occurring only two years after the Missouri debate, as an example of the harm that irresponsible northern antislavery talk could cause. After Nat Turner's revolt in 1831, Governor John Floyd of Virginia blamed the uprising on "Yankee peddlers and traders" who supposedly told slaves that "all men were born free and equal." Thus northern antislavery opinion and the fear of slave uprisings were firmly linked in southern minds.

After Nat Turner

In 1831 the South began to close ranks in defense of slavery. Several factors contributed to this regional solidarity. Nat Turner's revolt was important, linked as it was in the minds of many Southerners with antislavery agitation from the North. Militant abolitionist William

Lloyd Garrison began publishing the *Liberator*, the newspaper that was to become the leading antislavery organ, in 1831. The British gave notice that they would soon abolish slavery on the sugar plantations of the West Indies, an action that seemed to many Southerners much too close to home. Emancipation for West Indian slaves came in 1833. Finally, 1831 was the year before the Nullification Crisis (see Chapter 10) was resolved. Although the other southern states did not support the hotheaded South Carolinians who called for secession, they did sympathize with the argument that the federal government had no right to interfere with a state's special interest (namely, slavery). Following the crisis, other southern states joined with South Carolina in the belief that the only effective way to prevent other federal encroachment was militant and vehement defense of slavery.

In the 1830s, southern states began to barricade themselves against "outside" antislavery propaganda. In 1835, a crowd broke into a Charleston post office, made off with bundles of antislavery literature, and set an enormous bonfire, to fervent state and regional acclaim. By 1835, every southern legislature had tightened its laws concerning control of slaves. For example, they tried to blunt the effect of abolitionist literature by passing laws forbidding slaves to learn how to read. In only three border states—Kentucky, Tennessee, and Maryland—did slave literacy remain legal. By 1860, it is estimated, only 5 percent of all slaves could read. Slaves were forbidden to gather for dances, religious services, or any kind of organized social activity without a white person present. They were forbidden to have whiskey because it might encourage them toward revolt. The penalty for plotting insurrection was death. Other laws made manumission illegal and placed even more restrictions on the lives of free black people (as in Natchez). In many areas slave patrols were augmented and became more vigilant in restricting African American movement and communication between plantations.

In 1836, Southerners introduced a "gag rule" in Washington to prevent congressional consideration of abolitionist petitions. Attempts were made to stifle all open debate about slavery within the South; dissenters were pressured to remain silent or to leave. A few, such as James G. Birney and Sarah and Angelina Grimké of South Carolina, left for the North to act on their antislavery convictions, but most chose silence. Among those under the greatest pressure to conform were Christian ministers, many of whom professed to believe that preaching obedience to slaves was a vital part of making slavery a humane system.

In addition to fueling fears of slave rebellions, the growing abolitionist sentiment of the 1830s raised the worry that southern opportunities for expansion would be cut off. Southern politicians painted melodramatic pictures of a beleaguered white South hemmed in on all sides by "fanatic" antislavery states, while at home Southerners were forced to contemplate what might happen when they had "to let loose among them, freed from the wholesome restraints of patriarchal authority...an idle, worthless, profligate set of free negroes" whom they feared would "prowl the...streets at night and [haunt] the woods during the day armed with whatever weapons they could lay their hands on."

Finally, southern apologists moved beyond defensiveness to develop proslavery arguments. One of the first to do this was James Henry Hammond, elected a South Carolina congressman in 1834. In 1836 Hammond delivered a major address to Congress in which he denied that slavery was evil. Rather, he claimed, it had produced "the highest toned, the purest, best organization of society that has ever existed on the face of the earth." One wonders what Hammond's slaves, especially Sally and Louisa Johnson, would have thought of this argument.

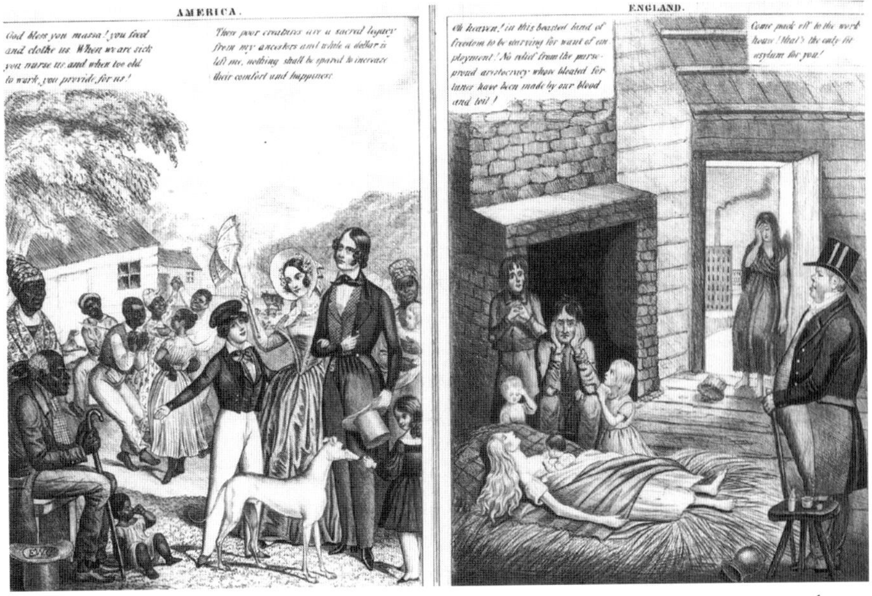

This 1841 proslavery cartoon contrasts healthy, well-cared-for African American slaves with unemployed British factory workers living in desperate poverty. The comparison between contented southern slaves and miserable northern "wage slaves" was frequently made by proslavery advocates.

CHRONOLOGY

1790s	Second Great Awakening Black Baptist and African Methodist Episcopal churches founded
1793	Cotton gin invented
1800	Gabriel Prosser's revolt discovered in Virginia
1806	Virginia tightens law on manumission of slaves
1808	Congress prohibits U.S. participation in the international slave trade
1816–20	"Alabama Fever": migration to the Old Southwest
1819–20	Missouri Crisis
1822	Denmark Vesey's conspiracy in Charleston
1831	Nat Turner's revolt in Virginia William Lloyd Garrison begins publishing antislavery newspaper, the *Liberator*
1832	Nullification Crisis
1832–38	"Flush Times": second wave of westward expansion
1832	Virginia legislature debates and defeats a measure for gradual emancipation
1833	Britain frees slaves throughout the empire, including the West Indies
1835	Charleston crowd burns abolitionist literature Tightening of black codes completed by southern legislatures
1836	Congress passes "gag rule" to prevent discussion of antislavery petitions James Henry Hammond announces to Congress that slavery is not evil
1854	George Fitzhugh publishes *Sociology for the South*, a defense of slavery
1857	Hinton Helper publishes *The Impending Crisis*, an attack on slavery
1858	James Henry Hammond's "King Cotton" speech

In 1854 another southern spokesman, George Fitzhugh, asserted that "the negro slaves of the South are the happiest, and, in some sense, the freest people in the world" because all the responsibility for their care was borne by concerned white masters. Fitzhugh contrasted southern paternalism with the heartless individualism that ruled the lives of northern "wage slaves." Northern employers did not take care of their workers, Fitzhugh claimed, because "selfishness is almost the only motive of human conduct in free society, where every man is taught that it is his first duty to change and better his pecuniary situation." In contrast, Fitzhugh argued, southern masters and their slaves were bound together by a "community of interests."

Changes in the South

In spite of these defensive and repressive proslavery measures, which made the South seem monolithic in northern eyes, there were some surprising indicators of dissent. Most came from up-country nonslaveholders. One protest occurred in the Virginia state legislature in 1832, when nonslaveholding delegates, alarmed by the Nat Turner rebellion, forced a two-week debate on the merits of gradual abolition. In the final vote, abolition was defeated 73 to 58. Although the subject was never raised again, this debate was a startling indicator of frequently unvoiced doubts about slavery that existed in the South.

But slavery was not a static system. From the 1830s on, financial changes increasingly underlined class differences between southern whites. It was harder to become a slaveholder: from 1830 to 1860 slave owners declined from 36 to 25 percent of the population. In 1860 the average slaveholder was ten times as wealthy as the average nonslaveholder. A major reason for the shrinking number of slave owners and their increased wealth was the rapidly increasing price of slaves: a "prime field hand" was worth more than $1,500 in 1855. Such prices caused the internal slave trade to flourish: during the 1850s slave owners from the Upper South sold some 250,000 slaves to the Lower South for handsome profits. Such a difference in the extent of slaveholding between Upper and Lower South threatened regional political unity and provoked concern. One remedy suggested in South Carolina was to reopen the international slave trade!

Economic changes adversely affected poor whites and yeomen as well. Increased commercialization of agriculture (other than cotton) led to higher land prices that made it harder for poor whites to buy or rent land. Extensive railroad building in up-country regions during the boom of the 1850s ended the isolation of many yeomen, exposing them for the first time to the temptations and dangers of the market economy. While slave owners grew increasingly worried about threats from the abolitionist and capitalist North, yeomen worried about local threats to their independence from banks, railroads, and activist state governments. In North Carolina, disputes between slave owners and nonslaveholders erupted in print in 1857, when Hinton Helper published an attack on slavery in a book titled *The Impending Crisis*. His protest was an indicator of the growing tensions between the haves and the have-nots in the South. Equally significant, though, Helper's book was published in New York, where he was forced to move once his views became known.

In spite of these signs of tension and dissent, the main lines of the southern argument were drawn in the 1830s and remained fixed thereafter. The defense of slavery stifled debate within the South, prevented a search for alternative labor systems, and narrowed the possibility of cooperation in national politics. In time, it made compromise impossible.

CONCLUSION

The amazing growth of cotton production after 1793 transformed the South and the nation. Physically, the South expanded explosively westward: in all, seven southern and southwestern states were admitted to the Union between 1800 and 1845. Cotton production fastened the slave system of labor upon the region. Although the international slave trade was abolished in 1808, the internal slave trade flourished, with devastating effects on African American families. Nationally, the profitable cotton trade fueled economic development and provided much of the original capital for the infant factory system of the North. Cotton production was based on the labor of African American slaves, who built strong communities under extremely difficult circumstances. The cohesion of African American families and the powerful faith of African American Christianity were the key community elements that bred a spirit of endurance and resistance. White Southerners, two-thirds of whom did not own slaves, denied their real dependence on slave labor by claiming equality in white skin privilege, while slave owners boasted of their own paternalism. But the extreme fear generated by a handful of slave revolts, the exaggerated reaction to the race mixing of Natchez-under-the Hill, and the growing number of free African Americans in many areas gave the lie to white claims of benevolence. In the 1830s, the South defensively closed ranks against real and perceived threats to the slave system. In this sense, the white South was nearly as trapped as the African American slaves they claimed to control. And in defending the slave system, the South was increasingly different from the dynamic capitalist free labor system that was gaining strength in the North.

REVIEW QUESTIONS

1. How did cotton production after 1793 transform the social and political history of the South? How did the rest of the nation benefit? In what way was it an "international phenomenon"?
2. What were the two key institutions of the African American slave community? How did they function, and what beliefs did they express?
3. The circumstances of three very different groups—poor whites, educated and property-owning American Indians, and free African Americans—put them outside the dominant southern equation of white equals free and black equals slave. Analyze the difficulty each group encountered in the slave-owning South.
4. Who were the yeoman farmers? What was their interest in slavery?
5. Southern slaveholders claimed that their paternalism justified their ownership of slaves, but paternalism implied obligations as well as privileges. How well do you think slaveholders lived up to their paternalistic obligations?
6. How did slaveowners justify slavery? How did their defense change over time?

RECOMMENDED READING

Ira Berlin, *Slaves without Masters* (1974). A full portrait of the lives of free black people in the South before the Civil War.

Charles C. Bolton, *Poor Whites of the Antebellum South: Tenants and Laborers in Central North and Northeast Mississippi* (1994). A careful consideration of a hitherto "invisible" population.

B. A. Botkin, ed., *Lay My Burden Down: A Folk History of Slavery* (1945). One of the first of many volumes drawing on the words of former slaves concerning their memories of slavery.

Orville Vernon Burton, *In My Father's House Are Many Mansions: Family and Community in Edgefield, South Carolina* (1985). A detailed community study that considers the farms, families, and everyday relations of white and black people in the period 1850–80.

Thomas D. Clark and John D. W. Guice, *Frontiers in Conflict: The Old Southwest, 1795–1830* (1989). Considers the Indian nations and their removal, white settlement, and the economic development of the region.

Catherine Clinton, *The Plantation Mistress: Woman's World in the Old South* (1982). Illustrates how slavery shaped the lives of elite white women. The exclusive focus on white women, however, neglects the black women with whom they lived on a daily basis.

Drew Gilpin Faust, *James Henry Hammond and the Old South* (1982). This outstanding biography uses the complex and interesting story of one man's life and ambitions to tell a larger story about southern attitudes and politics.

Lacy K. Ford Jr., *Origins of Southern Radicalism: The South Carolina Upcountry, 1800–1860* (1988). One of a growing number of studies of up-country nonslaveholders and their commitment to liberty and equality.

Eugene Genovese, *Roll, Jordan, Roll: The World the Slaves Made* (1974). The landmark book that redirected the attention of historians from slaves as victims to the slave community as an active participant in the paternalism of the southern slave system.

Steven Hahn, *The Roots of Southern Populism: Yeoman Farmers and the Transformation of the Georgia Upcountry, 1850–1890* (1983). One of the first studies of the changing world of southern yeomen.

Bruce Levine, *Half Slave and Half Free: The Roots of Civil War* (1992). A useful survey of the different lines of development of the northern and southern economies and the political conflicts between the regions.

Stephanie McCurry, *Masters of Small Worlds: Yeoman Households, Gender Relations, and the Political Culture of the Antebellum South Carolina Low Country* (1995). A study of yeomen that links their prized political and economic independence with their strong patriarchal control over their own families.

James Oakes, *The Ruling Race: A History of American Slaveholders* (1982). Oakes disagrees with Genovese's characterization of paternalism and sees slave owners instead as entrepreneurial capitalists. Especially useful for distinguishing the various classes of slave owners.

Peter J. Parish, *Slavery: History and Historians* (1989). A useful survey and synopsis of a large literature.

Brenda Stevenson, *Life in Black and White: Family and Community in the Slave South* (1996). A careful study of families, black and white, in Louden County, Virginia, that illustrates the difficulties both free and enslaved African American families faced.

Michael Tadman, *Speculators and Slaves: Masters, Traders, and Slaves in the Old South* (1989). Examines the extent, organization, and values of the internal slave trade.

ADDITIONAL BIBLIOGRAPHY

King Cotton

Peter A. Coclanis, *The Shadow of a Dream: Economic Life and Death in the South Carolina Low Country, 1670–1920* (1989)

Robert W. Fogel and Stanley Engerman, *Time on the Cross: The Economics of American Negro Slavery* (1974)

Joseph P. Reidy, *From Slavery to Agrarian Capitalism in the Cotton Plantation South:Central Georgia, 1800-1880* (1992)

Harold D. Woodman, *Slavery and the Southern Economy* (1966)

Gavin Wright, *The Political Economy of the Cotton South: Households, Markets, and Wealth in the Nineteenth Century* (1978)

Slavery and African American Communities

John Blassingame, *The Slave Community*, rev. ed. (1979)

Randolph B. Campbell, *An Empire for Slavery: The Peculiar Institution in Texas, 1821–1865* (1989)

Charles T. Davis and Henry Louis Gates Jr., eds., *The Slave's Narrative* (1985)

Carl N. Degler, *Neither White nor Black: Slavery and Race Relations in Brazil and the United States* (1971)

Charles B. Dew, *Bond of Iron: Master and Slave at Buffalo Forge* (1994)

Merton L. Dillon, *Slavery Attacked: Southern Slaves and Their Allies, 1619–1865* (1990)

Douglas Egerton, *Gabriel's Rebellion:The Virginia Slave Conspiracies of 1800 and 1802* (1993)

Paul D. Escott, *Slavery Remembered: A Record of Twentieth-Century Slave Narratives* (1979)

Barbara Field, *Slavery on the Middle Ground: Maryland during the Nineteenth Century* (1985)
Eugene D. Genovese, *From Rebellion to Revolution: Afro-American Slave Revolts in the Making of the Modern World* (1979)
Claudia D. Goldin, *Urban Slavery in the American South, 1820–1860* (1976)
Nathan Huggins, *Black Odyssey: The Afro-American Ordeal in Slavery* (1977)
Michael P. Johnson and James L. Roark, *Black Masters: A Free Family of Color in the Old South* (1984)
———, *No Chariot Down: Charleston's Free People of Color on the Eve of the Civil War* (1984)
Charles Joyner, *Down by the Riverside: A South Carolina Slave Community* (1984)
Peter Kolchin, *American Slavery, 1619–1877* (1993)
Lawrence W. Levine, *Black Culture and Black Consciousness: Afro-American Folk Thought from Slavery to Freedom* (1977)
Ann Patton Malone, *Sweet Chariot: Slave Family and Household Structure in Nineteenth-Century Louisiana* (1992)
Melton McLaurin, *Celia: A Slave* (1991)
Stephen B. Oates, *The Fires of Jubilee: Nat Turner's Fierce Rebellion* (1975)
Albert Raboteau, *Slave Religion: The "Invisible Institution" in the Antebellum South* (1978)
Willie Lee Rose, *A Documentary History of Slavery in North America* (1976)
Kenneth Stampp, *The Peculiar Institution* (1956)
Robert Starobin, *Industrial Slavery in the Old South* (1970)
Sterling Stuckey, *Slave Culture: Nationalist Theory and the Foundation of Black America* (1987)
David E. Swift, *Black Prophets of Justice: Activist Clergy before the Civil War* (1989)
Thomas L. Webber, *Deep Like Rivers: Education in the Slave Quarters, 1831–1865* (1978)
Deborah Gray White, *Arn't I a Woman?* (1985)

Yeomen, Planters, and the Defense of Slavery

David T. Bailey, *Shadow on the Church: Southwestern Evangelical Religion and the Issue of Slavery, 1783–1860* (1985)
Carol Bleser, ed., *In Joy and in Sorrow: Women, Family, and Marriage in the Victorian South, 1830–1900* (1991)
Dickson D. Bruce, *Violence and Culture in the Antebellum South* (1979)
Joan Cashin, *A Family Venture: Men and Women on the Southern Frontier* (1991)
Bill Cecil-Fronsman, *Common White: Class and Culture in Antebellum North Carolina* (1992)
Jane T. Censer, *North Carolina Planters and Their Children, 1800–1860* (1984)
Bruce Collins, *White Society in the Antebellum South* (1985)
William J. Cooper, *The South and the Politics of Slavery, 1829–1856* (1978)
———, *Liberty and Slavery: Southern Politics to 1860* (1983)
Daniel Dupre, *Transforming the Cotton Frontier: Madison County, Alabama, 1800–1840* (1997)
Clement Eaton, *The Freedom of Thought Struggle in the Old South* (1964)
Drew Gilpin Faust, ed. *The Ideology of Slavery: Proslavery Thought in the Antebellum South, 1830–1860* (1981)
Drew Gilpin Faust, *Southern Stories: Slaveholders in Peace and War* (1992)
Elizabeth Fox-Genovese, *Within the Plantation Household* (1988)
John Hope Franklin, *The Militant South 1800–1861* (1956)
George M. Frederickson, *White Supremacy: A Comparative Study in American and South African History* (1981)
———, *The Black Image in the White Mind: The Debate on Afro-American Character and Destiny, 1817–1914* (1971)
Jean Friedman, *The Enclosed Garden: Women and Community in the Evangelical South, 1830–1900* (1985)
J. William Harris, *Plain Folk and Gentry in a Slave Society: White Liberty and Black Slavery in Augusta's Hinterlands* (1985)
Suzanne Lebsock, *The Free Women of Petersburg: Status and Culture in a Southern Town, 1784–1860* (1984)
Donald G. Mathews, *Religion in the Old South* (1977)
John McCardell, *The Idea of a Southern Nation: Southern Nationalists and Southern Nationalism, 1830–1860* (1979)
Christopher Morris, *Becoming Southern:The Evolution of a Way of Life, Warren County and Vicksburg, Mississippi, 1770–1860* (1995)
James Oakes, *Slavery and Freedom: An Interpretation of the Old South* (1990)
Frank Owsley, *Plain Folk in the South* (1949)
Anne F. Scott, *The Southern Lady, from Pedestal to Politics, 1830–1930* (1970)
Steven Stowe, *Intimacy and Power in the Old South: Ritual in the Lives of the Planters* (1987)
Bertram Wyatt-Brown, *Southern Honor: Ethics and Behavior in the Old South* (1982)

CHAPTER TWELVE

INDUSTRY AND THE NORTH

1790s–1840s

Unidentified artist, *Middlesex Company Woolen Mills of Lowell, Mass.*, ca. 1848. Oil on canvas. Museum of American Textile History, North Andover, Mass.

Chapter Outline

PREINDUSTRIAL WAYS OF WORKING

Rural Life: The Springer Family
The Family Labor System
Urban Artisans and Workers
Patriarchy in Family, Work, and Society
The Social Order

THE MARKET REVOLUTION

The Accumulation of Capital
The Putting-Out System
British Technology and American Industrialization
Slater's Mill
The Lowell Mills
Family Mills
"The American System of Manufactures"
Other Factories

FROM ARTISAN TO WORKER

Personal Relationships
Mechanization and Women's Work
Time, Work, and Leisure
The Cash Economy
Free Labor
Early Strikes

A NEW SOCIAL ORDER

Wealth and Class
Religion and Personal Life
The New Middle-Class Family
Family Limitation
Motherhood
Sentimentalism
Transcendentalism and Self-Reliance

AMERICAN COMMUNITIES

Women Factory Workers Form a Community in Lowell, Massachusetts

In the 1820s and 1830s, young farm women from all over New England flocked to Lowell to work a twelve-hour day in one of the first cotton textile factories in America. Living six to eight to a room in nearby boardinghouses, the women of Lowell earned an average of $3 a week. Some also attended inexpensive nighttime lectures or classes. Lowell, considered a model factory town, drew worldwide attention. As one admirer of its educated workers said, Lowell was less a factory than a "philanthropic manufacturing college."

The Boston investors who financed Lowell were businessmen, not philanthropists, but they wanted to keep Lowell free of the dirt, poverty, and social disorder that made English factory towns notorious. Built in 1823, Lowell boasted six neat factory buildings grouped around a central clock tower, the area pleasantly landscaped with flowers, shrubs, and trees. Housing was similarly well ordered: a Georgian mansion for the company agent; trim houses for the overseers; row houses for the mechanics and their families; and boardinghouses, each supervised by a responsible matron, for the workforce that made Lowell famous—young New England farm women.

The choice of young women as factory workers seemed shockingly unconventional. In the 1820s and 1830s, young unmarried women simply did not live alone; they lived and worked with their parents until they married. In these years of growth and westward expansion, however, America was chronically short of labor, and the Lowell manufacturers were shrewd enough to realize that young farm women were an untapped labor force. For farmers' sons, the lure of acquiring their own farms in the West was much stronger than factory wages, but for their sisters, escaping from rural isolation and earning a little money was an appealing way to spend a few years before marriage. To attract respectable young women, Lowell offered supervision both on the job and at home, with strict rules of conduct, compulsory religious services, cultural opportunities such as concerts and lectures, and cash wages.

When they first arrived in Lowell, the young women were often bewildered by the large numbers of townspeople and embarrassed by their own rural clothing and ways of speech. The air of the mill was hot, humid, and full of cotton lint, and the noise of the machinery—"The buzzing and hissing and whizzing of pulleys and rollers and spindles and flyers"—was constant. Very quickly, however, other women workers—often their own sisters or neighbors who had preceded them to the mill—helped them adjust. It was company policy for senior women to train the newcomers. The work itself was simple, consisting largely of knotting broken threads on spinning machines and power looms. Most women enjoyed the work. They were not bothered by the long hours; farm people were accustomed to long days. One woman wrote home: "The work is not disagreeable. It tried my patience sadly at first, but in general I like it very much. It is easy to do, and does not require very violent exertion, as much of our farm work does."

The most novel aspect of textile mills was a rigid work schedule. Power-driven machinery operated at a sustained, uniform pace throughout every mill; human workers had to learn to do the same. Each mill published elaborate schedules and imposed fines and penalties on latecomers. It was this kind of precise work schedule that represented the single largest change from preindustrial work habits; it was the hardest for workers to adjust to. Moreover, each mill positioned one or two overseers on every floor to make sure the pace was maintained. Men held these positions, and they earned more than the women who made up most of the workforce; this arrangement was unquestioned.

Why did young women come to Lowell? Some worked out of need and some to add to their family's income, but most regarded Lowell as opportunity. It was escape from rural isolation and from parental supervision, a chance to buy the latest fashions and learn "city ways," to attend lectures and concerts, to save for a dowry or to pay for an education. As writer Lucy Larcom, one of the most famous workers, said, the young farm women who came to Lowell sought "an opening into freer life." Working side by side and living in company boardinghouses with six to twelve other women, some of whom might be relatives or friends from home, the Lowell women built a close, supportive community for themselves.

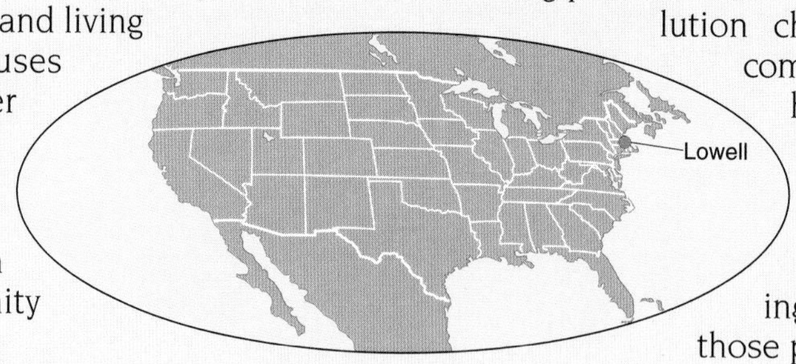

The owners of Lowell made large profits. They also drew praise for their carefully managed community with its intelligent and independent workforce. But their success was short-lived. In the 1830s, because of competition and poor economic conditions, the owners imposed wage cuts and work speedups that their model workforce did not take lightly. Although the Lowell women had been brought together under a system of paternalistic control, the close bonds they forged in the boardinghouses gave them the courage and solidarity to "turn out" in spontaneous protests, which were, however, unsuccessful in reversing the wage cuts. By 1850 the "philanthropic manufacturing college" was no more. The original Lowell workforce of New England farm girls had been replaced by poor Irish immigrants of both sexes, who tended more machines for much less pay than their predecessors. Now Lowell was simply another mill town.

The history of Lowell epitomizes the process by which the North (both New England and the Middle Atlantic states) began to change from a society composed largely of self-sufficient farm families (Jefferson's "yeoman farmers") to one of urban wageworkers in an industrial economy. Industrialization did not occur overnight. Large factories were not common until the 1880s, but by that decade most workers had already experienced a fundamental change in their working patterns. Once under way, the market revolution changed the very basis of community: how people worked, how they thought, how they lived. In the early years of the nineteenth century, northern communities led this transformation, fostering attitudes far different from those prevalent in the South.

Key Topics

- Preindustrial ways of working and living
- The nature of the market revolution
- The effects of industrialization on workers in early factories
- Ways the market revolution changed the lives of ordinary people
- The emergence of the middle class

PREINDUSTRIAL WAYS OF WORKING

The Lowell mill was a dramatic example of the changes factories imposed on people's accustomed ways of working and interacting with each other. To fully understand the novelty of these changes in long-established patterns of work, it is important to understand traditional ways of working on farms—where 97 percent of all Americans lived in 1800—and in cities.

Rural Life: The Springer Family

The young family of Thomas and Elizabeth Springer began farming near the city of Wilmington in Mill Creek, Delaware, in the 1790s. Although no single family can represent all of the nation's farmers, a close look at the Springers can help to identify traditional patterns and the seeds of commercial change. The Springers, who had two infant daughters, owned 129 acres of farmland, 104 of which Thomas Springer had bought from his father for less than the market price. At twenty-nine, Springer, to whom family wealth had given a substantial advantage, owned four African American slaves: Ace, a young man; Sara and Amelia, young girls; and Will, aged sixty. Ace was in the process of buying his freedom, something he could not have done further south.

Although Delaware remained a slave state until the Civil War, as the case of Ace suggests, it developed differently from states further south. By 1861, only 2 percent of the state's population was still enslaved. In part this decline reflected the strong antislavery feeling that many residents of Delaware shared with people in the neighboring free state of Pennsylvania. But it was primarily because farmers like Thomas Springer found their soil was not suitable for growing cotton, the crop that fastened slavery on the states of the deep south (see Chapter 11).

The Springers had access to a commercial market for their crops. From their herd of thirty or forty sheep and at least fifteen milking cows, the Springers provided Wilmington butchers with some livestock, and they sold wool, milk, and butter in local markets. They also raised oats, hay, and Indian corn to feed the livestock, as well as wheat and vegetables for both family use and commercial sale. They may have sold some of the wheat to Wilmington merchants for transshipment to Philadelphia and then Europe, but in general the Springers, like most preindustrial farm families, planted and produced a diverse range of crops for their own use. Only after their own needs were met did they sell their surplus on the commercial market.

It was Elizabeth Springer who, with the help of the female slaves and perhaps female relatives, was in charge of spinning the wool and collecting the dairy cows' milk that was intended for sale, and she was also responsible for preparing all the farm meals and preserving the vegetables and fruits grown for the family. Both the Springers, who had family living nearby, and all the neighboring farmers who made up the larger community shared their labor with each other in a barter system. They helped each other construct houses and barns, pick apples, thresh wheat, cut firewood, and prune trees. Neighbor women assisted one another in childbirth. Thus the Springers, like their neighbors, produced goods for their own use, for a community network, and for a larger, cash market, in that order. This kind of community network of barter and mutual obligation characterized traditional farming families throughout the nation. But because of the thriving market in nearby Wilmington, the Springers already, in a small way, had begun the transition from traditional to commercial agriculture.

The Family Labor System

In the traditional, predindustrial economy, people like the Springers did most of their work at or near their homes. One kind of traditional work was the labor of caring for the home itself and for its members, including spinning, weaving, and sewing clothes for everyone. These jobs, which fell to the women of the family, were time-consuming, multistage activities that occupied much of the year. Mothers introduced their daughters to the easiest tasks, such as carding wool, at a young age, and taught them the more difficult skills of spinning and weaving as they grew older. This infor-

In the 1840s Edward Hicks painted his childhood home, rendering an idealized image of rural harmony that owes more to faith in republican agrarianism than to the artist's accurate memory. The prosperous preindustrial farm depicted was similar to the Springers' farm described in the text in its mixed yield—sheep, cattle, dairy products, and field crops—and in its employment of an African American farm worker, shown plowing.

mal family apprenticeship system was echoed in the barn and field tasks sons learned from their fathers. In this way one generation passed along essential skills to the next generation.

On the rocky farms of New England, where farm surpluses were rare and a home-produced item was cheaper and easier to obtain than an item from Britain or even Boston, many farmers worked off the farm at some other job. Sometimes an entire family developed a skill such as shoemaking that they could practice over the long New England winters. Much of what families crafted was for local and immediate use, not for a distant market. Among New England farmers, the need to find several jobs bred ingenuity and flexibility. As Noah Webster observed in 1785, "Every man is in some measure an artist—he makes a variety of utensils, rough indeed, but such as will answer his purpose—he is a husbandsman [farmer] in summer and mechanic in winter."

Two other notable characteristics of rural home production were slated soon to disappear. First, things had no fixed prices, and money rarely exchanged hands. People usually paid for a home-crafted item or a neighbor's help with a particular task in foodstuffs or a piece of clothing or by helping the neighbor with a job he needed to have done. Thus goods and services originating in the home were part of the complicated reciprocal arrangements among community residents who knew each other well. The "just price" for an item was set by agreement among neighbors, not by some impersonal market. Another characteristic of traditional rural work was its relatively slow, unscheduled, task-oriented pace. There was no fixed production schedule or specified period of time for task completion. People did their jobs as they needed to be done, along with the daily household routine. "Home" and "work" were not separate locations or activities, but intermixed.

Urban Artisans and Workers

In urban areas, skilled craftsmen had controlled preindustrial production since the early colonial period. Trades were perpetuated through a formal system of apprenticeship in which a boy went to work in the shop of a master, usually at the age of twelve or fourteen. Over the next three to seven years the young apprentice learned all aspects of the craft, gaining increasing responsibility and status as the day approached when he could strike out on his own. During that time, the master not only taught the apprentice his trade but housed, fed, and clothed him. Usually the apprentice lived with the master craftsman and was treated more like a member of the family than an employee. Thus the family-learning model used on farms was formalized in the urban apprenticeship system. At the end of the contract period the apprentice became a journeyman craftsman. Journeymen worked for wages in the shop of a master craftsman until they had enough capital to set up shop for themselves. Generally, they could not afford to marry until they achieved master status.

Like farmers, urban artisans usually kept long hours—sunup to sundown was common—but the pace of work varied enormously with the time of year and the number of orders. And work was frequently interrupted by family activities and neighborliness. Most cities were densely settled, and one bumped into one's neighbors all the time. Sales, business contracts, meals, and other occasions were often accompanied by a friendly drink of rum or other spirits. There was no clear separation between work and leisure.

Although women as well as men did task-oriented skilled work, the formal apprenticeship system was exclusively for men. Because it was assumed that women would marry, most people thought that all girls needed to learn were domestic skills. Women who needed or wanted work, however, found a small niche of respectable occupations as domestic servants, laundresses, or seamstresses, often in the homes of the wealthy, or as cooks in small restaurants or street food vendors. Some owned and managed boardinghouses. Prostitution, another common female occupation (especially in seaport cities) was not respectable.

Patriarchy in Family, Work, and Society

Like the farm family, an entire urban household was commonly organized around one kind of work. Usually the family lived at the shop or store, and all family members worked with the craftsman at his trade. A printer's wife, for example, would be capable of keeping most of the shop's functions going in the printer's absence and of supervising the work of apprentices and her children. Some artisans, like blacksmiths, needed shops separate from their homes but probably relied on their children to fetch and carry and to help with some of the work. Others, like bakers, who generally had to get up in the middle of the night to perform their work, relied on their wives to sell their products during the day.

Every small community had artisans such as blacksmiths and wheelwrights who did such essential work as shoeing horses and mending wagons for local farmers. Artist John Neagle's heroic image of the blacksmith Pat Lyon presents him as the very model of honest industry.

In both rural and urban settings, working families were organized along strictly patriarchal lines. The man had unquestioned authority to direct the lives and work of family members and apprentices and to decide on occupations for his sons and marriages for his daughters. His wife had many crucial responsibilities—feeding, clothing, child rearing, taking care of apprentices, and all the other domestic affairs of the household—but in all these duties she was subject to the direction of her husband. Men were heads of families and bosses of artisanal shops; although entire families were engaged in the enterprise, the husband and father was the trained craftsman, and assistance by the family was informal and generally unrecognized.

The patriarchal organization of the family was reflected in society as a whole. Legally, men had all the power: neither women nor children had property or legal rights. For example, a married woman's property belonged to her husband, a woman could not testify on her own behalf in court, and in the rare cases of divorce the husband kept the children, for they were considered his property. When a man died, his son or sons inherited his property. It was customary to allow widows the use of one-third of the property, but unfilial sons could deprive their mothers of support if they chose. Some widows successfully continued a family business, and some single daughters received inheritances from rich fathers, but these were exceptions. The basic principle was that the man, as head of the household, represented the common interests of everyone for whom he was responsible—women, children, servants, apprentices. He thus controlled everything of value, and he alone could vote for political office.

The Social Order

In this preindustrial society everyone, from the smallest yeoman farmer to the largest urban merchant, had a fixed place in the social order. The social status of artisans was below that of wealthy merchants but decidedly above that of common laborers. Yeoman farmers, less grand than large landowners, ranked above tenant farmers and farm laborers. Although men of all social ranks mingled in their daily work, they did not mingle as equals, for great importance was placed on rank and status, which were distinguished by dress and manner. Although by the 1790s many artisans who owned property were voters and vocal participants in urban politics, few directly challenged the traditional

WEALTH IN BOSTON, 1687–1848

Percent of the Population	Percent of Wealth Held 1687	1771	1833	1848
Top 1 percent	10%	16%	33%	37%
Top 10 percent	42	65	75	82
Lowest 80 percent	39	29	14	4

This table tracing the distribution of wealth in Boston reflects the gains made by merchants during the international shipping boom of 1790–1807 and the way in which intermarriage between wealthy families consolidated these gains.

authority of the rich and powerful to run civic affairs. The rapid spread of universal white manhood suffrage after 1800 democratized politics (see Chapter 10). At the same time, economic changes undermined the preindustrial social order.

Beginning to upset this social order were a few wealthy artisans in seacoast cities like New York. Cabinetmaker Duncan Phyfe, who gave his name to a distinctive style of furniture, is one example. Phyfe, immigrating from Scotland, opened his first shop in 1792. By 1815 he had an elegant salesroom, three workshops employing up to 100 journeymen, and a fortune of $500,000, much of it from real estate investments. Another successful New York artisan, Stephen Allen, began as an apprentice sailmaker. Allen made his fortune when he arranged to bypass the traditional middlemen and buy his materials directly from wholesalers. His sailmaking operation made a profit of $100,000 between 1802 and 1825, and when he retired he was elected mayor of New York, customarily a position reserved for gentlemen. These New York artisans, and others like them in other cities, owed much of their success to the ever-expanding effects of the economic upheaval known as the market revolution.

THE MARKET REVOLUTION

The market revolution, the most fundamental change American communities ever experienced, was the outcome of three interrelated developments: rapid improvements in transportation (see Chapter 10), commercialization, and industrialization. Improved transportation allowed both people and goods to move with new ease and speed. Commercialization involved the replacement of household self-sufficiency and barter with the production of goods for a cash market. And industrialization involved the use of power-driven machinery to produce goods once made by hand. Taken together, these three developments rapidly joined most ordinary Americans into a commercial market that supplied them with abundant quantities of inexpensive manufactured goods.

The Accumulation of Capital

In the northern states, the business community was composed largely of merchants in the seaboard cities: Boston, Providence, New York, Philadelphia, and Baltimore. Many had made substantial profits in the international shipping boom of the period 1790–1807 (as discussed in Chapter 9). During those years, the proportion of American trade carried in American ships jumped from 59 percent to 92 percent, and earnings to American merchants rose from $5.9 million to $42.1 million.

Such extraordinary opportunities attracted enterprising people. Established merchants like Philadelphia's Robert Morris opened up new markets such as the China trade, but there was room for newcomers as well. John Jacob Astor, who had arrived penniless from Germany in 1784, made his first fortune in the Pacific Northwest fur trade with China and eventually dominated the fur trade in the United States through his American Fur Company. Astor made a second fortune in New York real estate, and when he retired in 1834 with $25 million he was reputed to be the wealthiest man in America. Many similar stories of success, though not so fabulous as Astor's, demonstrated that risk-takers might reap rich rewards in international trade.

But the early years of the nineteenth century posed difficulties for international trade. Following the 1807 Embargo Act only the most daring American merchants were willing to risk restrictions and the chance of capture to reap exceptional profits. More cautious men perceived opportunity in the potentially huge domestic American market, deprived of cheap British goods by war in Europe (and later, the War of 1812) and underserved by the traditional family-centered, slow-paced, and localized system of skilled craftsmanship. Mobilizing the capital available within the business community, merchants began to control, transform, and increase American home-based production.

Some of the nation's wealthiest men turned to local investments. In Providence, Rhode Island, Moses Brown and his son-in-law William Almy began to invest some of the profits the Brown family had reaped from a worldwide trade in iron, candles, rum, and African slaves in the new manufacture of cotton textiles. Philadelphia merchant and banker Stephen

Girard, who had made his fortune in the West Indies trade, invested in the Lehigh Valley coalfields and in the canals and railroads that linked the coalfields to Philadelphia. Cincinnati merchants banded together to finance the building of the first steamboats to operate on the Ohio River. And even in rural towns, local merchants and shopkeepers invested in the work of local craftsmen.

Much of the capital for the new investments came from banks, both those in seaport cities that had been established for the international trade and those, like the Lynn, Massachusetts, Mechanics Bank, founded in 1814 by a group of Lynn's Quaker merchants, that served local clients. An astonishing amount of capital, however, was raised through family connections. In the late eighteenth century, members of the business communities in the seaboard cities had begun to consolidate their position and property by intermarriage. In Boston, such a strong community developed that when Francis Cabot Lowell needed $300,000 in 1813 to build the world's first automated cotton mill in Waltham, Massachusetts (the prototype of the Lowell mills), he had only to turn to his family network.

Although much of the original capital for American manufacturing, such as Almy and Brown's collaboration with Samuel Slater, came from the shipping boom of 1790–1807, southern cotton provided the capital for continuing development. Because Northerners built the nation's ships, controlled the shipping trade, and provided the nation's banking, insurance, and financial services, the astounding growth in southern cotton exports enriched northern merchants almost as much as southern planters. In 1825, for example, of the 204,000 bales of cotton shipped from New Orleans, about one-third (69,000) were transshipped through the northern ports of New York, Philadelphia, and Boston. Southerners complained that their combined financial and shipping costs diverted forty cents of every dollar paid for their cotton to northerners. Profits from cotton shipping provided some of the funds the Boston Associates made available to Francis Cabot Lowell. In another example, New York merchant Anson Phelps invested the profits he made from cotton shipping in iron mines in Pennsylvania and metalworks in Connecticut. Although imperfectly understood at the time, the truth is that the development of northern industry was paid for by southern cotton produced by enslaved African American labor.

The Putting-Out System

Initially, the American business community invested not in machinery and factories but in the "putting-out system" of home manufacture, thereby expanding and transforming it. In this significant departure from preindustrial work, people still produced goods at home but under the direction of a merchant, who "put out" the raw materials to them, paid them a certain sum per finished piece, and sold the completed item to a distant market.

A crucial aspect of the new putting-out system was the division of labor. In the preindustrial system, an individual worker or his household made an entire item—a shoe, for example. Now an unskilled worker often made only a part of the finished product in large quantities for low per-piece wages.

The change in the shoe industry in Lynn, Massachusetts, shows how the putting-out system transformed American manufacturing. Long a major center of the shoe industry, Lynn, in 1800, produced 400,000 pairs of shoes—enough for every fifth person in the country. The town's 200 master artisans and their families, including journeymen and apprentices, worked together in hundreds of small home workshops called "ten-footers" (from their size, about ten feet square). The artisans and journeymen cut the leather, the artisans' wives and daughters did the binding of the upper parts of the shoe, the men stitched the shoe together, and children and apprentices helped where needed. In the early days, the artisan commonly bartered his shoes for needed products. For example, in 1773, a Lynn shopkeeper wrote to Providence merchant Nicholas Brown (Moses Brown's brother) offering to trade 100 pairs of shoes for 100 pounds of tea! Sometimes an artisan sold his shoes to a larger retailer in Boston or Salem, and sometimes a sea captain arranged to lend an artisan money for the raw materials and then sold the finished shoes at every port his ship visited. Although production of shoes in Lynn increased yearly from 1780 to 1810 as markets widened, shoes continued to be manufactured in traditional artisanal ways.

The investment of merchant capital in the shoe business changed everything. In Lynn, a small group of Quaker shopkeepers and merchants, connected by family, religious, and business ties, took the lead in reorganizing the trade. Financed by the bank they founded in 1814, Lynn capitalists like Micajah Pratt built large, two-story central workshops to replace the scattered ten-footers. Pratt employed a few skilled craftsmen to cut leather for shoes, but he put out the rest of the shoemaking to less-skilled workers who were no longer connected by family ties. Individual farm women and children sewed the uppers, which, when completed, were soled by farm men and boys. Putting-out workers were paid on a piecework basis; the men and boys earned more than the women and children but much less than a master craftsman or a journeyman. This arrangement allowed the capitalist to employ much more labor for the same investment than with the traditional artisan workshop. Shoe production increased enormously: the largest central shop in 1832 turned out ten times more shoes

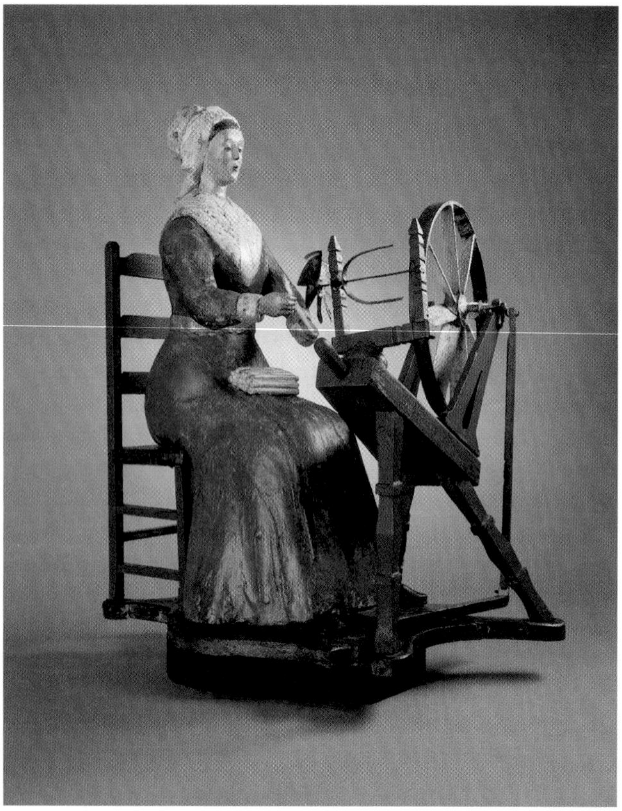

Woman at Spinning Wheel, ca. 1850–70. Carved and painted wood and iron. Photographed by Ken Burris. Shelburne Museum, Shelburne, Vermont.

This carved and painted figure, designed as a whirligig and trade sign, shows a woman at a spinning wheel. Until cotton textile mills industrialized this work, spinning was one of the most time-consuming tasks that women and young girls did at home.

than the largest shopkeeper had sold in 1789. Gradually the putting-out system and central workshops replaced artisan's shops. Some artisans became wealthy owners of workshops, but most became wage earners, and the apprenticeship system eventually disappeared.

The putting-out system moved the control of production from the individual artisan households to the merchant capitalists, who could now control labor costs, production goals, and shoe styles to fit certain markets. For example, the Lynn trade quickly monopolized the market for cheap boots for southern slaves and western farmers, leaving workshops in other cities to produce shoes for wealthier customers. This specialization of the national market—indeed, even thinking in terms of a national market—was new. Additionally, and most important from the capitalist's point of view, the owner of the business controlled the workers and could cut back or expand the labor force as economic and marketplace conditions warranted. The unaccustomed severity of economic slumps like the Panics of 1819 and 1837 made this flexibility especially desirable.

While the central workshop system prevailed in Lynn and in urban centers like New York City, the putting-out system also fostered a more dispersed form of home production. By 1810 there were an estimated 2,500 so-called outwork weavers in New England, operating handlooms in their own homes. Other crafts that rapidly became organized according to the putting-out system were flax and wool spinning, straw braiding, glove making, and the knitting of stockings. For example, the palm-leaf hat industry that supplied farm laborers and slaves in the South and West relied completely on women and children, who braided the straw for the hats at home part-time. Absorbed into families' overall domestic routines, the outwork activity seemed small, but the size of the industry itself was surprising: in 1837, 33,000 Massachusetts women braided palm-leaf hats, whereas only 20,000 worked in the state's cotton textile mills. They were producing for a large national market, made possible by the dramatic improvements in transportation that occurred between 1820 and 1840.

Although the putting-out system meant a loss of independence for artisans such as those in Lynn, New England farm families liked it. From their point of view, the work could easily be combined with domestic work, and the pay was a new source of income that they could use to purchase mass-produced goods—among them shoes, boots, hats, buttons, stockings, suspenders, horsewhips, machine-made textiles, and men's work clothes—rather than spend the time required to make these things themselves. It was in this way that farm families moved away from the local barter system and into a larger market economy. The longer-term consequences of industrial capitalism—the destruction of the artisan tradition and the undermining of the patriarchal family—took some years to emerge. For example, apprentices were still taken on in the Lynn shoemaking trade until 1840.

British Technology and American Industrialization

Important as were the transportation revolution and the commercialization made possible by the putting-out system, the third component of the market revolution, industrialization, brought the greatest changes to personal lives. Begun in Britain in the eighteenth century, industrialization was the result of a series of technological changes in the textile trade. Mechanization moved the production of cotton and woolen yarn out of the home to the "manufactory" ("factory" for short), where power-driven machines did the work. In marked contrast to the putting-out system, in which capitalists had dispersed work into many individual households, industrialization required workers to concentrate in factories and pace themselves to the rhythms of power-driven machinery.

Many British people, especially the elite, looked on factories with horror. In England, the first factory workers were orphaned children, women, and poor Irish immigrants. These people flooded into ill-prepared rural factory towns. Horrified at the dirt and squalor of these towns, and by the relentless pace of the machinery, British poet William Blake condemned the entire concept of industrialization, writing ominously of "dark, satanic mills." If this was progress, he wanted no part of it.

Some Americans, most notably Thomas Jefferson, shared these sentiments, basing their dream of American development on the independent yeoman farmer rather than on industrialization. But conditions in New England favored rapid industrialization. New England had swift rivers that could power factory machinery, and it had wealthy merchants looking for new ways to invest their capital. Some of these merchants, whose fortunes derived from shipping southern cotton to textile factories in England, quickly realized that the manufacturing could be done in New England—if Americans could learn the secrets of British industrial technology.

Slater's Mill

The simplest and quickest way for America to industrialize was to copy the British, but the British, well aware of the value of their machinery, enacted laws forbidding its export and even the emigration of skilled workers. Over the years, however, Americans managed to lure a number of British artisans to the United States.

In 1789 Samuel Slater, who had just finished an apprenticeship in the most up-to-date cotton spinning factory in England, disguised himself as a farm laborer and slipped out of England without even telling his mother good-bye. In Providence, Rhode Island, he met Moses Brown and William Almy, who had been trying without success to duplicate British industrial technology. Having carefully committed the designs to memory before leaving England, Slater promptly built copies of the latest British machinery for Brown and Almy. Slater's mill, as it became known, began operation in 1790. It was the most advanced cotton mill in America. Although Slater was a skilled mechanic and improved on the original British machines, it is nonetheless true that American industrialization owed its start to technology that the British had not wished to share.

Following British practice, Slater drew his workforce primarily from among young children (ages seven to twelve) and women, whom he paid much less than the handful of skilled male workers he hired to keep the machines working. The yarn spun at Slater's mill was then put out to local home weavers, who turned it into cloth on handlooms. As a result, home weaving flourished in areas near the mill, giving families a new opportunity to make money at a task with which they were already familiar. In 1790, home weavers had no way of knowing that their profitable occupation would soon be challenged by power looms in factories.

Many others followed Slater's lead, and the rivers of New England were soon dotted with mills wherever waterpower could be tapped. Embargo and war sheltered American factories from British competition from 1807 to 1815, but when the War of 1812 ended, the British cut prices ruthlessly in an effort to drive the newcomers out of business. In 1816 Congress passed the first tariff, aimed largely against British cotton textiles, in response to the clamor by New England manufacturers for protection for their young industry. Interestingly, the issue of tariff protection, usually regarded as a sectional issue between North and South (see "The Nullification Crisis" in Chapter 10) initially aroused controversy in New England, where many seaport merchants opposed it because they saw it as a threat to the international free trade from which they had so richly profited.

This early nineteenth-century watercolor shows Slater's mill, the first cotton textile mill in the United States, which depended on the waterpower of Pawtucket Falls for its energy. New England was rich in swiftly flowing streams that could provide power to spinning machines and power looms.

The Lowell Mills

Another way to deal with British competition was to beat the British at their own game. With the intention of designing better machinery, a young Bostonian, Francis Cabot Lowell, made an apparently casual tour of British textile mills in 1810. Lowell, the founder of the Lowell mills described in the opening of this chapter, made a good impression on his English hosts, who were pleased by his interest and his intelligent questions. They did not know that each night, in his hotel room, Lowell made sketches from memory of the machines he had inspected during the day.

Lowell was more than an industrial spy, however. When he returned to the United States, he went to work with a Boston mechanic, Paul Moody, to improve on the British models. Lowell and Moody not only made the machinery for spinning cotton more efficient, but they also invented a power loom. This was a great advance, for now all aspects of textile manufacture, from the initial cleaning and carding (combing) to the production of finished lengths of cloth, could be gathered together in the same factory. Such a mill required a much larger capital investment than a small spinning mill such as Slater's, but Lowell's family network gave him access to the needed funds. In 1814 he opened the world's first integrated cotton mill in Waltham, near Boston. It was a great success: in 1815, the Boston Associates (Lowell's partners) made profits of 25 percent, and their efficiency allowed them to survive the intense British competition. Many smaller New England mills did not survive, even with the tariff protection voted in 1816. The lesson was clear: size mattered.

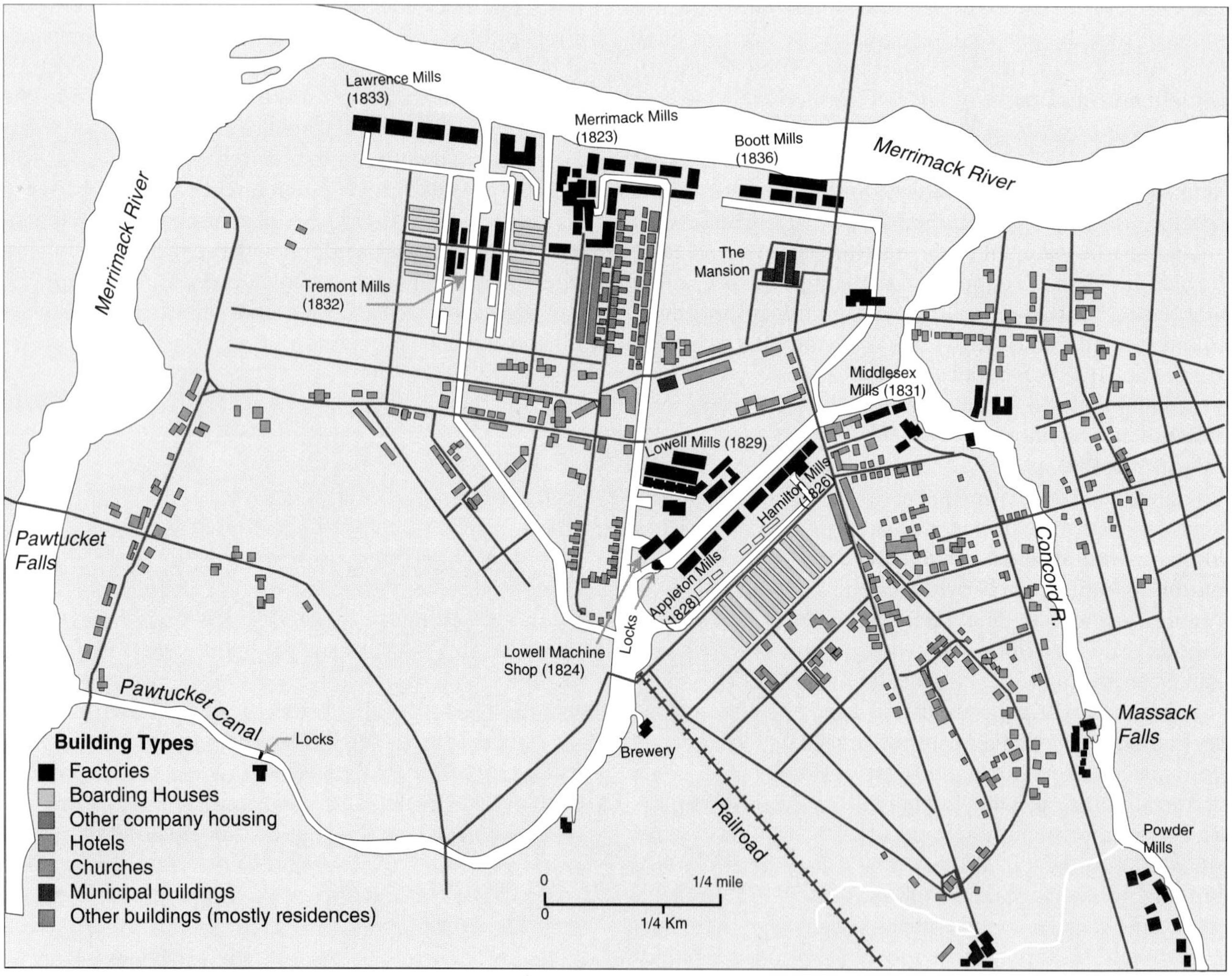

Lowell, Massachusetts, 1832 *This town plan of Lowell, Massachusetts, in 1832 illustrates the comprehensive relationship the owners envisaged between the factories and the workforce. The mills are located on the Merrimack River, while nearby are the boardinghouses for the single young female workers, row houses for the male mechanics and their families, and houses for the overseers. Somewhat farther away is the mansion of the company agent.*

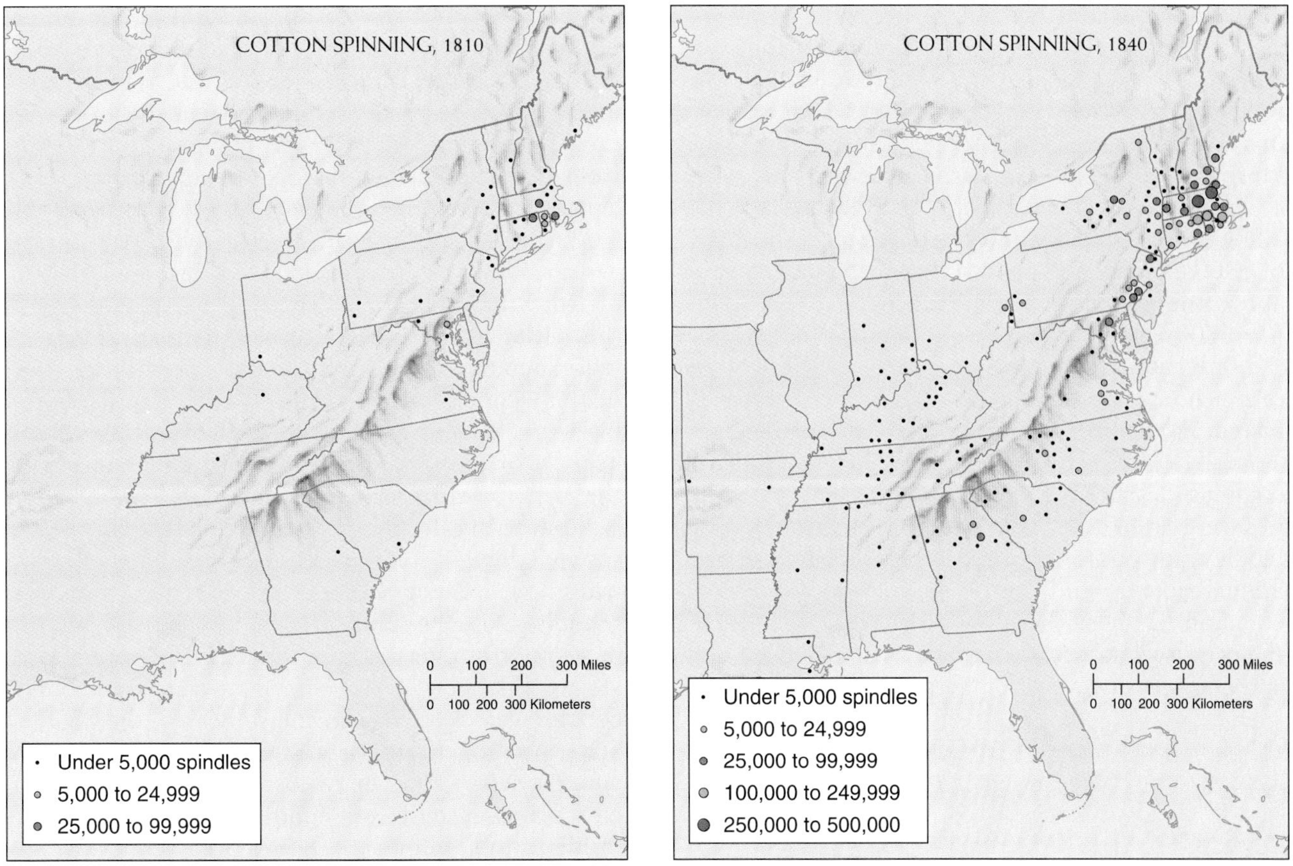

The Growth of Cotton Textile Manufacturing, 1810–1840 *Although cotton textile manufacturing spread to other parts of the country after 1810, New England never lost its early lead. By 1839, the extent of industrialization in New England far outstripped that of other regions. Although much of New England was still rural, more and more residents were drawn into the market economy. Nationally, the proportion of wage laborers rose from 12 percent in 1800 to 40 percent in 1860. The majority of them were New Englanders who had made the transition from artisan to worker.*

Source: *Atlas of the Historical Geography of the United States*, © Carnegie Institute of Washington, Plate 186.

The Boston Associates took the lesson to heart, and when they moved their enterprise to a new location in 1823, they thought big. They built an entire town at the junction of the Concord and Merrimack Rivers where the village of East Chelmsford stood, renaming it Lowell in memory of Francis, who had died, still a young man, in 1817. As the opening of this chapter describes, the new industrial community boasted six mills and company housing for all the workers. In 1826 the town had 2,500 inhabitants; ten years later the population was 17,000.

Family Mills

Lowell was unique. No other textile mill was ever such a showplace. None was as large, integrated so many tasks, or relied on such a homogeneous workforce. Its location in a new town was also unusual. Much more common in the early days of industrialization were small rural spinning mills, on the model of Slater's first mill, built on swiftly running streams near existing farm communities. Although the economic benefits to local residents were considerable, the presence of the mills and mill workers brought rural communities troubling new issues of authority and diversity.

Because the owners of smaller mills often hired entire families, their operations came to be called family mills. The employment pattern at these mills followed that established by Slater at his first mill in 1790. Children aged eight to twelve, whose customary job was doffing (changing) bobbins on the spinning machines, made up 50 percent of the workforce. Women and men each made up about 25 percent of the workforce, but men had the most skilled and best-paid jobs.

The engagement of an entire family in a particular line of work was hardly new; both farm and artisan families were accustomed to working at a family enterprise. And unless a family member was very highly skilled, more than one worker per family was a necessity. To take one example, in the Rockdale mills, located on Chester Creek in Delaware, wages in the 1840s ranged from $1 a week for unskilled children to $12 a week for skilled workers. Unskilled adult laborers earned between $2.50 and $3.50 a week, or between $110 and $150 a year, allowing for sickness and temporary layoffs. Wages of $300 a year were necessary to keep a family safely above the poverty line. Single workers, who had to pay $70 to $100 a year for room and board, were at a disadvantage compared with a family, who could rent a house for $25 a year and survive on an estimated $200 a year for food.

Relations between these small rural mill communities and the surrounding farming communities were often difficult, as the history of the towns of Dudley and Oxford, Massachusetts, shows. Samuel Slater, now a millionaire, built three small mill communities near these towns in the early years of the century. Each consisted of a small factory, a store, and cottages and a boardinghouse for workers. Slater or one of his sons ran the mills personally; they were not absentee owners. Most of Slater's workers came from outside the Dudley-Oxford area. They were a mixed group—single young farm women of the kind Lowell attracted, the poor and destitute, and workers from other factories looking for better conditions. They rarely stayed long: almost 50 percent of the workforce left every year.

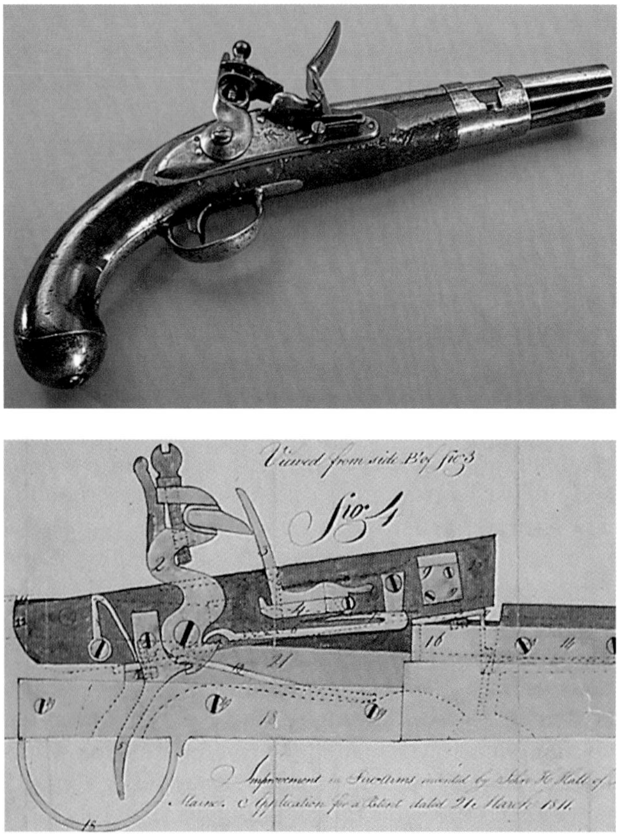

In 1816 Connecticut gunsmith Simeon North did what Eli Whitney had only hoped to do. North produced the first gun with interchangeable parts. North's invention, taken up and improved by the national armories at Springfield and Harpers Ferry, formed the basis of the American system of manufactures.

Slater's mills provided a substantial amount of work for local people, putting out to them both the initial cleaning of the raw cotton and the much more lucrative weaving of the spun yarn. But in spite of this economic link, relations between Slater and his workers on one side and the farmers and shopkeepers of the Dudley and Oxford communities on the other were stormy. They disagreed over the building of mill dams (essential for the mill power supply, they sometimes flooded local fields), over taxes, over the upkeep of local roads, and over schools. Slater, hoping to save money and exercise more control over his mill workers' time, wanted to set up his own school for factory children. The debates were so constant, and so heated, that in 1831 Slater petitioned the Massachusetts General Court to create a separate town, Webster, that would encompass his three mill communities. For their part, the residents of Dudley and Oxford became increasingly hostile to Slater's authoritarian control, which they regarded as undemocratic. Their dislike carried over to the workers as well. Disdaining the mill workers for their poverty and transiency, people in the rural communities began referring to them as "operatives," making them somehow different in their work roles from themselves. Industrial work thus led to new social distinctions. Even though the people of Dudley and Oxford benefited from the mills, they did not fully accept the social organization on which their new prosperity rested, nor did they feel a sense of community with those who did the work that led to their increased well-being.

"The American System of Manufactures"

Not all American industrial technology was copied from British inventions, for there were many homegrown inventors. Indeed, calling Americans "mechanic[s] by nature," one Frenchman observed that "in Massachusetts and Connecticut there is not a labourer who had not invented a machine or tool." By the 1840s, to take but one example, small towns like St. Johnsbury, Vermont, boasted many small industries based on local inventions such as those by Erastus Fairbanks in scales and plows, Lemuel Hubbard in pumps, and Nicanor Kendall in guns. But perhaps most important was the pioneering American role in the development of standardized parts.

The concept of interchangeable parts, realized first in gun manufacturing, was so unusual that the British soon dubbed it "the American system of manufactures." In this system, a product such as a gun was broken down into its component parts and an exact mold was made for each. All pieces made from the same mold (after being hand filed by inexpensive unskilled laborers) matched a uniform standard. As a result, repairing a gun that malfunctioned required only installing a replacement for the defective part rather than laboriously making a new part or perhaps an entirely new gun.

Eli Whitney, the co-inventor of the cotton gin, was the first to take up the challenge of interchangeable parts, and in 1798 he contracted with the government to make 10,000 rifles in twenty-eight months, an incredibly short period had he been planning to produce each rifle by hand in the traditional way. Whitney's ideas far outran his performance. It took him ten years to fulfill his contract, and even then he had not managed to perfect the production of all the rifle parts. Two other New Englanders, Simeon North and John Hall, created milling machines that could grind parts to the required specifications and brought the concept to fruition, North in 1816 and Hall in 1824. Subsidized by the government to make rifles for the national armory at Harpers Ferry, Virginia, Hall wrote triumphantly to the secretary of war, "I have succeeded in an object which has hitherto baffled...all the endeavors of those who have heretofore attempted it—I have succeeded in establishing methods of fabricating arms exactly alike." When the system of interchangeable machine-made parts was adopted by the other national armory, at Springfield, Massachusetts, the Springfield rifle got its name.

America's early lead in interchangeable parts was a substantial source of national pride. As American gunmaker Samuel Colt boasted, "There is nothing that cannot be made by machine." Standardized production quickly revolutionized the manufacture of items as simple as nails and as complicated as clocks. By 1810 a machine had been developed that could produce 100 nails a minute, cutting the cost of nail making by two-thirds. Finely made wooden and brass clocks, previously made (expensively) by hand, were replaced by mass-produced versions turned out in the Connecticut factories of Eli Terry, Seth Thomas, and Chauncey Jerome and sold nationwide by Yankee peddlers. Now ordinary people could keep precise time rather than estimate time by the sun, and factories could require workers to come to work on time. The need of railroads for precise timekeeping gave further support to the new system of manufacture.

Like the factory system itself, the American system spread slowly. For example, Isaac Singer's sewing machine, first patented in 1851, was not made with fully interchangeable parts until 1873, when the company was already selling 230,000 machines a year. The sewing machine revolutionized the manufacture of clothing, which up to this time had been made by women for their families at home and by hand.

American businesses mass-produced high-quality goods for ordinary people earlier than manufacturers in Britain or any other European country were able to do. The availability of these goods was a practical demonstration of American beliefs in democracy and equality. As historian David Potter has perceptively remarked: "European radical thought is prone to demand that the man of property be stripped of his carriage and his fine clothes. But American radical thought is likely to insist, instead, that the ordinary man is entitled to mass-produced copies, indistinguishable from the originals."

Other Factories

Although cotton textile mills were the first and best known of the early factories, some factories produced other items, among them metal and iron. Like the textile mills, many of these factories were rural because they depended on natural water sources for power or because they needed to be near their raw materials, such as iron ore. And like the early textile mills, these first heavy industries initially coexisted with the traditional artisanal system.

The rapid development of the steamship industry in Cincinnati illustrates both the role of merchant capital and the coexistence of old and new production methods. The first steamboat appeared on the Ohio River in 1811, and Cincinnati's merchants, who had heretofore invested their profits in land and real estate speculation, were quick to see its advantages. Cincinnati's first steamboat, financed by local merchant capital, was commissioned in 1816. It proved so successful that by 1819 one-quarter of all western steamboats were being built in Cincinnati. By 1826, Cincinnati's steamship industry had grown to include four iron foundries employing 54 men, five steam engine and finishing factories employing 126 people, and three boatyards with 200 workers. At the same time, much of the detail work on the steamboat was performed by traditional artisans such as cabinetmakers, upholsterers, tinsmiths, and blacksmiths, who did record-breaking amounts of work in their small, independent shops. In this way, new factory methods and industrial techniques were often coupled with old craft techniques.

The new concepts of specialization and standardization and the increased production they brought about were basic to the system of industrial capitalism. In turn, the system led to vast increases in wealth and in living standards for many—eventually most—of the inhabitants of industrial nations. But for many workers

Steamboats transformed commerce on western rivers and helped to make the fortune of Cincinnati, which became a center of steamboat manufacture. This Currier and Ives print of 1855 shows the Mayflower, *one of the most elegant and handsome steamboats on the Mississippi River.*

in early-nineteenth-century America, the transition from the old method of production to the new one did not come without a price.

FROM ARTISAN TO WORKER

The changes wrought by the market revolution had major and lasting effects on ordinary Americans. The proportion of wage laborers in the nation's labor force rose from 12 percent in 1800 to 40 percent by 1860. Most of these workers were employed in the North, and almost half were women, performing outwork in their homes. The young farm woman who worked at Lowell for a year or two, then returned home; the master craftsman in Lynn who expanded his shop with the aid of merchant capital; the home weaver who prospered on outwork from Slater's mill—all were participating, often unknowingly, in fundamental personal and social changes.

Personal Relationships

The putting-out system, with its division of each craft into separate tasks, effectively destroyed artisan production and the apprenticeship system. For example, in New York by the mid-1820s, tailors and shoemakers were teaching apprentices only a few simple operations, in effect using them as helpers. Printers undercut the system by hiring partly trained apprentices as journeymen. In almost every trade, apprentices no longer lived with the master's family, and their parents received cash payment for the child's work. Thus in effect the apprenticeship system was replaced by child labor.

Artisans who helped to destroy the older system did so unwillingly, in response to harsh new competition caused by improvements in transportation. For example, in the 1850s Philadelphia's 7,000 shoemakers, shut out of the cheap shoe market by the success of the shoe manufacturers of Lynn, turned to the specialty markets of ladies' shoes and expensive men's shoes and boots. But even in this luxury market, the pressure of cheaper competition forced them to accept the central shop and the putting-out system rather than the individual artisanal shop. To compete, they had to change and adopt the same new labor organization as their rivals.

Although the breakdown of the family work system undoubtedly harmed independent urban artisans, it may have had a liberating effect on the women and children of farm families. About a third of the Lowell women workers did not return to their farm homes, instead remaining in town and marrying urban men or continuing to work. And of the women who did return home, fewer than half married farmers. There is no doubt that working at Lowell provided these women with new options. Women and children who earned wages by doing outwork at home may have found their voices strengthened by this evidence of their power and worth. Patriarchal control over family members was no longer absolute.

The breakdown of the patriarchal relationship between the master craftsman and his workers became an issue in the growing political battle between the North and the South over slavery. Southern defenders of slavery compared their cradle-to-grave responsibility to their slaves with northern employers' "heartless" treatment of their "wage slaves." Certainly the new northern employer assumed less responsibility for individual workers than had the traditional artisan. Although the earliest textile manufacturers, like those at Lowell, provided housing for their workers, workers soon became responsible for their own food and housing. Moreover, northern employers felt no obligation to help or care for old or disabled workers. Southerners were right: this was a heartless system. But Northerners were also right: industrialization was certainly freer than the slave system, freer even than the hierarchical craft system, although it sometimes offered only the freedom to starve.

Mechanization and Women's Work

Industrialization posed a major threat to the status and independence of skilled male workers. In trade after trade, mechanization meant that most tasks could be performed by unskilled labor. For example, the textile mills at Lowell and elsewhere hired a mere handful of skilled mechanics; most of the rest of the workers were unskilled and lower paid. In fact, the work in the textile mills was so simple that children came to form a large part of the workforce. By 1850 in New York City, many formerly skilled trades, including shoemaking, weaving, silversmithing, pottery making, and cabinetmaking, were filled with unskilled, low-paid workers who did one specialized operation or tended machinery. Many former artisans were reduced to performing wage labor for others. Because women were so frequently hired in the putting-out system, male workers began to oppose female participation in the workforce, fearing that it would lower their own wages.

Mechanization changed the nature of women's work in other ways as well. The industrialization of textiles—first in spinning, then in weaving—relieved women of a time-consuming home occupation. To supplement family income, women now had the choice of following textile work into the factory or finding other kinds of home work. At first, these were attractive options, but negative aspects soon developed, especially in the nation's cities.

The 1820s saw the birth of the garment industry. In New York City, employers began hiring women to sew ready-made clothing, at first rough, unfitted clothing for sailors and southern slaves, but later overalls and shirts for Westerners and finer items such as men's shirts. Most women performed this work at low piecework rates in their homes. Although by 1860 Brooks Brothers, the famous men's clothing firm, had 70 "inside" workers in a model central workshop, the firm relied primarily on putting out sewing to 3,000 women who worked at home.

Soon the low pay and seasonal nature of the industry became notorious. Two basic problems were overcrowding of the market and low wages. Women were pushed into the garment trade because they were barred from many occupations considered inappropriate for them, and the oversupply of workers led to wage cutting. To make matters worse, most people believed that "respectable" women did not do factory work (Lowell in its "model" years was the exception that proved the rule), and this disparagement fostered low pay and poor working conditions.

Manufacturers in the garment trade made their profits not from efficient production but by obtaining intensive labor for very low wages. The lower the piece rate, the more each woman, sewing at home, had to produce to earn enough to live. The invention of the sewing machine only made matters worse. Manufacturers dropped their piecework rates still lower, and some women found themselves working fifteen to eighteen hours a day, producing more than they ever had, but earning the same pay.

Time, Work, and Leisure

Preindustrial work had a flexibility that factory work did not, and it took factory workers a while to get accustomed to the constant pace of work. Long hours did not bother them, for they were accustomed to

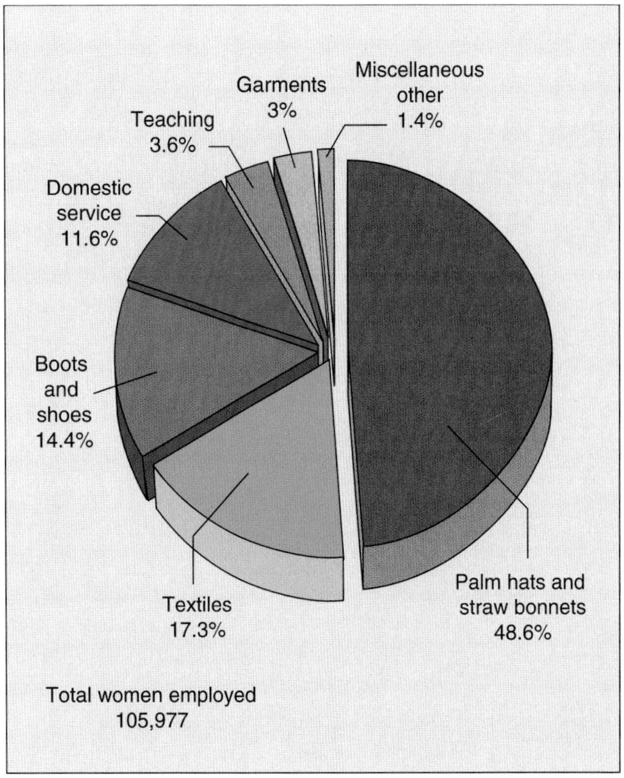

Occupations of Women Wage Earners in Massachusetts, 1837 *This chart shows how important outwork was for women workers. Textile work in factories occupied less than 20 percent of women, while outwork in palm-leaf hats, straw bonnets, and boots and shoes accounted for over half of the total workforce. Teaching was a new occupation for women in 1837. The small percentage of 3.6 would grow in the future.*

Source: Based on Thomas Dublin, *Transforming Women's Work* (Ithaca, N.Y.: Cornell University Press, 1991), table 1.1, p. 20.

twelve-hour workdays and six-day weeks on the farm and in the shop. But in the early days of Slater's mill in Rhode Island, workers sometimes took a few hours off to go berry picking or to attend to other business. And when Slater insisted on a twelve-hour day that required candles for night work, one upset father demanded that his children be sent home at sunset, the traditional end of the workday.

Factory workers gradually adjusted to having their lives regulated by the sound of the factory bell, but they did not necessarily become the docile "hands" the owners wanted. Absenteeism was common, accounting for about 15 percent of working hours, and there was much pilfering. Workers were beginning to think of themselves as a separate community whose interests differed from those of owners, and the tyranny of time over their work was certainly one reason for this.

Another adjustment required by the constant pace was that time now had to be divided into two separate activities—work and leisure. In preindustrial times work and leisure were blended for farmers and artisans. The place of work—often the home—and the pace made it possible to stop and have a chat or a friendly drink with a visitor. Now, however, the separation of home and workplace and the pace of production not only squeezed the fun out of the long workday but left a smaller proportion of time for leisure activities.

For many workingmen, the favored spot for after-hours and Sunday leisure became the local tavern. Community-wide celebrations and casual sociability, still common in rural areas, began to be replaced in cities by spectator sports—horse racing, boxing, and (beginning in the 1850s) baseball—and by popular entertainments such as plays, operas, minstrel shows, concerts, and circuses. Some of these diversions, such as plays and horse racing, appealed to all social classes, but others, like parades, rowdy dance halls, and tavern games like quoits and ninepins were favored working-class amusements. The effect of these changes was to make working-class amusements more distinct, and visible, than they had been before.

The Cash Economy

Another effect of the market revolution was the transformation of a largely barter system into a cash economy. For example, a farm woman might pay in butter and eggs for a pair of shoes handmade for her by the local shoemaker. A few years later that same woman, now part of the vast New England outwork industry, might buy new footwear with the cash she had earned from braiding straw for hats, making gloves, or sewing shirts at home. Moreover, the shoes would have been commercially manufactured, perhaps in Lynn. In this way, in hundreds of thousands of small transactions, community economic ties were replaced by distant, sometimes national ones.

The rise of the cash economy also changed the relationships among workers and their employers. In some cases the pay envelope was the only direct contact between factory worker and (often absentee) owner. For workers, this change was both unsettling and liberating. On the minus side, workers were no longer part of a settled, orderly, and familiar community. On the plus side, they were now free to labor wherever they could, at whatever wages their skills or their bargaining power could command. That workers took their freedom seriously is evidenced by the very high rate of turnover in the New England textile mills. By the 1830s, at both the small family mills and the model mills at Lowell, almost half the workforce left every year.

But if moving on was a sign of increased freedom of opportunity for some workers, for others it was an unwanted consequence of the market revolution. In New England, for example, many quite prosperous artisans and farmers faced disruptive competi-

TIME TABLE OF THE LOWELL MILLS,

To take effect on and after Oct. 21st, 1851.

The Standard time being that of the meridian of Lowell, as shown by the regulator clock of JOSEPH RAYNES, 43 Central Street

	From 1st to 10th inclusive.				From 11th to 20th inclusive.				From 21st to last day of month.			
	1stBell	2dBell	3dBell	Eve.Bell	1stBell	2d Bell	3d Bell	Eve.Bell	1stBell	2dBell.	3dBell	Eve.Bell.
January,	5.00	6.00	6.50	*7.30	5.00	6 00	6.50	*7.30	5.00	6.00	6.50	*7.30
February,	4.30	5.30	6.40	*7.30	4.30	5.30	6.25	*7.30	4.30	5.30	6.15	*7.30
March,	5.40	6.00		*7.30	5.20	5.40		*7.30	5.05	5.25		6.35
April,	4.45	5.05		6.45	4.30	4.50		6.55	4.30	4.50		7.00
May,	4 30	4.50		7·00	4.30	4.50		7.00	4.30	4.50		7 00
June,	"	"		"	"	"		"	"	"		"
July,	"	"		"	"	"		"	"	"		"
August,	"	"		"	"	"		"	"	"		"
September,	4.40	5.00		6.45	4.50	5.10		6.30	5.00	5.20		*7.30
October,	5.10	5.30		*7.30	5.20	5.40		*7.30	5.35	5.55		*7.30
November,	4.30	5.30	6.10	*7.30	4.30	5.30	6.20	*7.30	5.00	6.00	6.35	*7.30
December,	5.00	6.00	6.45	*7.30	5.00	6.00	6.50	*7.30	5.00	6·00	6.50	*7.30

* Excepting on Saturdays from Sept. 21st to March 20th inclusive, when it is rung at 20 minutes after sunset.

YARD GATES,

Will be opened at ringing of last morning bell, of meal bells, and of evening bells; and kept open Ten minutes.

MILL GATES.

Commence hoisting Mill Gates, Two minutes before commencing work.

WORK COMMENCES,

At Ten minutes after last morning bell, and at Ten minutes after bell which "rings in" from Meals.

BREAKFAST BELLS.

During March "Ring out"........at....7.30 a. m.........."Ring in" at 8:05 a. m.
April 1st to Sept. 20th inclusive.....at....7 00 " " .... " " at 7.35 " "
Sept. 21st to Oct. 31st inclusive.....at....7.30 " " .... " " at 8.05 " "
Remainder of year work commences after Breakfast.

DINNER BELLS.

"Ring out"..........................12.30 p. m.........."Ring in".... 1.05 p. m.

In all cases, the *first* stroke of the bell is considered as marking the time.

B. H. Penhallow, Printer, 28 Merrimack Street.

This timetable from the Lowell Mills illustrates the elaborate time schedules that the cotton textile mills expected their employees to meet. For workers, it was difficult to adjust to the regimentation imposed by clock time, in contrast to approximate times common to preindustrial work.

tion from factory goods and western commercial agriculture. They could remain where they were only if they were willing to become factory workers or commercial farmers. Often the more conservative choice was to move west and try to reestablish one's traditional lifestyle on the frontier.

Free Labor

At the heart of the industrializing economy was the notion of free labor. Originally, "free" referred to individual economic choice—that is, to the right of workers to move to another job rather than be held to a position by customary obligation or the formal contract of apprenticeship or journeyman labor. But "free labor" soon came to encompass as well the range of attitudes—hard work, self-discipline, and a striving for economic independence—that were necessary for success in a competitive, industrializing economy. These were profoundly individualistic attitudes, and owners cited them in opposing labor unions and the use of strikes to achieve wage goals. As the *Cincinnati Gazette* put it in 1857: "We are not speaking of leaving work—that all men have the right to do; but of combining to interrupt and arrest the machinery. The first is a plain, individual right. The last is a conspiracy against the interest, and even the safety of the public." Owners opposed government action, such as proposals for legislation mandating a ten-hour day, on the same grounds: it denied workers wishing to work a twelve-hour day the opportunity to do so!

For their part, many workers were inclined to define freedom more collectively, arguing that their just grievances as free American citizens were not being heard. As a group of New Hampshire female workers rhetorically asked, "Why [is] there...so much want, dependence and misery among us, if forsooth, we are freemen and freewomen?" Or, as the Lowell strikers of 1836 sang as they paraded through the streets:

> *Oh! Isn't it a pity, such a pretty girl as I,*
> *Should be sent to the factory to pine away and die?*
> *Oh! I cannot be a slave,*
> *I will not be a slave,*
> *For I'm so fond of liberty*
> *That I cannot be a slave.*

Early Strikes

Rural women workers led some of the first strikes in American labor history. Because young women formed the majority of the workforce in early textile mills like Lowell, their participation in spontaneous protests is not surprising. What was surprising was that women, whose public role and activities were limited at the time, were the ones who led these protests. In 1824, in one of the first of these actions, women workers at a Pawtucket, Rhode Island, textile mill led their coworkers, female and male, out on strike to protest wage cuts and longer hours.

More famous were the strikes that the women at the model mill at Lowell led. The first serious trouble came in 1834, when 800 women participated in a spontaneous turnout to protest a wage cut of 25 percent. The owners were shocked and outraged by the strike, considering it both unfeminine and ungrateful. The workers, however, were bound together by a sense of sisterhood and were protesting not just the attack on their economic independence but the blow to their position as "daughters of freemen still." Nevertheless the wage cuts were enforced, as were more cuts in 1836, again in the face of a turnout. Many women simply packed their clothes in disgust and returned home to the family farm.

Like these strikes, most turnouts by factory workers in the 1830s—male or female—were unsuccessful. Owners, claiming that increasing competition made wage cuts inevitable, were always able to find new workers—Irish immigrants, for example—who would work at lower wages. The preindustrial notion of a community of interest between owner and workers had broken down.

Collective labor action by the women workers of Lowell underlined that point. In 1845 they formed the first chapter of the New England Female Labor Reform Association. The chapter soon had over 400 members, and other chapters sprang up in mill towns such as Fall River, Dover, Nashua, and Manchester. The Lowell chapter, led by Sarah Bagley, submitted a petition to the Massachusetts legislature demanding a law limiting the workday to ten hours, which the Lowell owners were unwilling to consider. The ten-hour day, a major labor goal throughout the nation, had first been demanded by skilled male workers in Boston in 1825. When the Massachusetts legislature ignored the Lowell petition on the grounds that many of the signers were nonvoters (because they were women), Bagley broke with customary notions of female propriety and challenged the legislature in a formal address: "For the last half century, it has been deemed a violation of woman's sphere to appear before the public as a speaker: but when our rights are trampled upon and we appeal in vain to our legislator, what are we to do?...Shall not our voice be heard...shall it be [said] to the daughters of New England that they have not political rights?"

The answer seemed at first to be yes. The Massachusetts legislature continued adamantly to ignore the ten-hour-day proposal even when presented with another petition in 1846 that had 10,000 signatures, 4,000 from Lowell women. But in 1847, legislators in New Hampshire, responding to a petition from women workers in Nashua who had refused to work after "lighting up" (after dark), made theirs the first state to enact a ten-hour-day law. Maine followed in 1848 and Pennsylvania in 1849. For the first time, thanks to women's pioneering role in factory protests, a group of workers had obtained state legislation improving their working conditions.

A NEW SOCIAL ORDER

The market revolution reached into every aspect of life, down to the most personal family decisions. It also fundamentally changed the social order, creating a new middle class with distinctive habits and beliefs.

Wealth and Class

There had always been social classes in America. Since the early colonial period planters in the South and merchants in the North had comprised a wealthy elite. Somewhere below the elite but above the mass of people were the "middling sort": a small professional group that included lawyers, ministers, schoolteachers, doctors, public officials, some prosperous farmers, prosperous urban shopkeepers and innkeepers, and a few wealthy artisans such as Boston silversmith Paul Revere. "Mechanics and farmers"—artisans and yeoman farmers—made up another large group, and the laboring poor, consisting of ordinary laborers, servants, and marginal farmers were below them. At the very bottom were the paupers—those dependent on public charity—and the enslaved. This was the "natural" social order that fixed most people in the social rank to which they were born. Although many a male servant in early America aspired to become a small farmer or artisan, he did not usually aspire to become a member of the wealthy elite, nor did serving maids often marry rich men.

The market revolution ended the old social order, creating the dynamic and unstable one we recognize today: upper, middle, and working classes, whose members all share the hope of climbing as far up the social ladder as they can. This social mobility was new, and it fascinated French observer Alexis de Tocqueville: "The first thing that strikes one in the United States is the innumerable crowd of those striving to escape from their original social condition." In the early nineteenth century the upper class remained about the same in size and composition. In the seacoast cities, as the example of Francis Cabot Lowell showed, the elite was a small, intermarried group, so distinctive in its superior cultural style that in Boston its members were nicknamed "Brahmins" (after the highest caste in India). The expanding opportunities of the market revolution enriched this already rich class: by the 1840s, the top 1 percent of the population owned about 40 percent of the nation's wealth. At the other extreme, fully one-third of the population possessed little more than the clothes they wore and some loose change.

WEALTH IN NEW YORK CITY, 1828–1845

Percent of the Population	Percent of Wealth Held 1828	1845
Top 1 percent	40%	50%
Top 4 percent	63	80

The impact of the market revolution on New York City, the nation's largest seaport, is shown by the dramatic increase in wealth of the already wealthy elite in a period of less than 20 years.

The major transformation came in the lives of the "middling sort." As discussed earlier, the market revolution downgraded many independent artisans but elevated others, like Duncan Phyfe and Stephen Allen of New York, who became wealthy businessmen and manufacturers. Other formerly independent artisans or farmers (or more frequently, their children) joined the rapidly growing ranks of managers and white-collar workers such as accountants, bank tellers, clerks, bookkeepers, and insurance agents. Occupational opportunities shifted dramatically in just one generation. In Utica, New York, for example, 16 percent of the city's young men held white-collar jobs in 1855, compared with only 6 percent of their fathers. At the same time, 15 percent fewer younger men filled artisanal occupations than older men.

These new, white-collar workers owed not only their jobs but their lifestyles to the new structure and organization of industry. The new economic order demanded certain habits and attitudes of workers: sobriety, responsibility, steadiness, and hard work. Employers, for their part, were expected to maintain both physical and psychological distance from their workers and to rein in employees' traditional spontaneity and boisterous sociability. Historian Paul Johnson has sketched this change in lifestyle in his study of the city of Rochester: "In 1825 a northern businessman dominated his wife and children, worked irregular hours, consumed enormous amounts of alcohol, and seldom voted or went to church. Ten years later the same man went to church twice a week, treated his family with gentleness and love, drank nothing but water, worked steady hours and forced his employees to do the same." Rochester, a town transformed by the opening of the Erie Canal in 1825, grew from 300 in 1815 to 10,000 in 1830. In this pressure-cooker environment, new middle-class attitudes like that of Johnson's businessman were formed.

The Tea Party *painted by Henry Sargent in 1821 depicts an elegant gathering of what were known as the* Boston Brahmins*—a small and wealthy group of* New England elite. *Intermarriage tended to concentrate wealth in this group and to separate them from the "middling sort."*

Religion and Personal Life

Religion, which had undergone dramatic changes since the 1790s, played a key role in the emergence of the new attitudes. The Second Great Awakening (see Chapter 9) had supplanted the orderly and intellectual Puritan religion of early New England. The new evangelistic religious spirit, which stressed the achievement of salvation through personal faith, was more democratic and more enthusiastic than the earlier faith. The old concern with sin survived in dramatic sermons that vividly portrayed hellfire and damnation, but the way to salvation was broader. The concept of original sin, the cornerstone of Puritan belief, was replaced by the optimistic belief that a willingness to be saved was enough to ensure salvation. Conversion and repentance were now community experiences, often taking place in huge revival meetings in which an entire congregation focused on the sinners about to be saved. But although continued support from the community was important, the converted bore a heavy personal responsibility to demonstrate their faith in their own daily lives through morally respectable behavior. In this way the new religious feeling fostered individualism and self-discipline.

The Second Great Awakening had its greatest initial success on the western frontier in the 1790s, but by the 1820s evangelical religion was reaching a new audience: the people whose lives were being changed by the market revolution and who needed help in adjusting to the demands made by the new economic conditions. In 1825 in Utica, New York, and other towns along the recently opened Erie Canal, evangelist Charles G. Finney began a series of dramatic revival meetings. His spellbinding message reached both rich and poor, converting members of all classes to the new evangelistic religion. In 1830, made famous by these gatherings, Finney was invited by businessmen to preach in Rochester. Finney preached every day for six months—three times on Sundays—and his wife, Lydia, made home visits to the unconverted and mobilized the women of Rochester for the cause. Under the Finneys' guidance and example, prayer meetings were held in schools and businesses, and impromptu religious services were held in people's homes. As one person recalled, "You could not go upon the streets and hear any conversation, except upon religion."

Evangelism rapidly became the religion of the new middle class. Men soon found that evangelism's stress on self-discipline and individual achievement helped them adjust to new business conditions. Moreover, it gave them a basis for demanding the same behavior from their workers. Businessmen now argued that traditional paternalism had no role in the new business world. Because achievement depended on individual character, each worker was responsible for making his own way.

Master artisans, themselves successful businessmen, often took the lead in reforming the habits of younger workers. Stephen Allen, the New York sailmaker who became mayor, attributed his success to long workdays, avoidance of debt, and "employing the utmost economy in all my concerns." Another New York artisan, master baker Thomas Mercein, took advantage of the opening of the Apprentices' Library, founded by the General Society of Mechanics and Tradesmen in 1820, to preach a similar message. "Cherish, I beseech you, a deep-rooted abhorrence of the alluring but fatal paths of vice and dissipation," Mercein told the apprentices. "Industry, ardour, sobriety, and perseverance in your different pursuits will lead to a successful competition in the world."

The New Middle-Class Family

The market revolution and the new evangelism also affected women's family roles. To begin with, the "softer," more emotional aspects of the new religious approach often especially appealed to women, and it was they who made certain that their families joined them in conversion. And as men increasingly concentrated their energies on their careers and occupations, women assumed major new responsibilities for rearing the children and inculcating in them the new attitudes necessary for success in the business world.

As the work roles of middle-class men and women diverged, so did social attitudes about appropriate male and female characteristics and behavior. Men were expected to be steady, industrious, responsible, and painstakingly attentive to their business. They had little choice: in the competitive, uncertain, and rapidly changing business conditions of the early nineteenth century, these qualities were essential for men who hoped to hold their existing positions or to get ahead. In contrast, women were expected to be nurturing, gentle, kind, moral, and selflessly devoted to their families. They were expected to operate within the "woman's sphere"—the home. Neither this division of responsibilities nor the distinction between men's and women's desirable characteristics and behavior was completely new; they were implicit in much earlier thinking about appropriate gender roles. But now clearly defined gender roles became a matter of social importance.

The unsettling demands of the market revolution forced a dramatic change in family life. When the master craftsman became a small manufacturer, or the small subsistence farmer began to manage a large-scale commercial operation, production moved away from both the family home and its members. Husbands and fathers became managers of paid workers—or workers themselves—and although they were still considered the heads of their households, they spent most of the day away from their homes and families. The husband was no longer the undisputed head of a family unit that combined work and personal life. Their wives, on the other hand, remained at home, where they were still responsible for cooking, cleaning, and other domestic tasks but no longer contributed directly to what had previously been the family enterprise. Instead, women took on a new responsibility, that of providing a quiet, well-ordered, and relaxing refuge from the pressures of the industrial world. As Utica author John Mather Austin advised in his manual, *A Voice to the Married*, the husband should regard his home as "an elysium to which he can flee and find rest from the stormy strife of a selfish world."

The invention of photography made possible family portraits that earlier were too expensive for all but the wealthiest. This portrait of the Edward Miner Gallaudet family, photographed by Mathew Brady in the 1860s, exhibits the gender differences expected in the middle-class family: strong, self-reliant men and softer, more clinging women.

Women's magazines like Sarah Josepha Hale's *Ladies' Magazine* gave homemakers some help in creating this refuge for their husbands and families, describing "patterns of virtue, of piety, of intelligence and usefulness in private life." By 1850 this magazine, which Hale merged in 1837 with *Godey's Lady's Book*—a magazine that concentrated on fashion—offered 70,000 readers a popular mixture of advice, recipes, and patterns for everything from simple embroidery to ballgowns to "model cottages," as the new suburban ideal middle-class homes were called.

A sure sign that traditional methods were inadequate for new needs was the appearance of housekeeping guides such as Catharine Beecher's book *Treatise on Domestic Economy*. First published in 1841, this book became the standard guide for a generation of middle-class American women. In it, Beecher combined innovative ideas for household design—she introduced important principles of organization for the kitchen in particular—with medical information, child-rearing advice, recipes, and much discussion of the mother's moral role in the family. Beecher's attempt to help women modernize their traditional housekeeping tasks within the context of their newly defined family role clearly filled a need: her book and the Bible were the only books that many pioneer women carried west.

The maintenance or achievement of a middle-class lifestyle required the joint efforts of husband and wife. More cooperation between them was called for than in the preindustrial, patriarchal family. The nature of the new, companionate marriage that evolved in response to the market revolution was reflected most clearly in decisions concerning children.

Family Limitation

Middle-class couples chose to have fewer children than their predecessors. Children who were being raised to succeed in the middle class placed considerable demands on family resources: they required more care, training, and education than children who could be put to work at traditional tasks at an early age. The dramatic fall in the birth rate during the nineteenth century (from an average of seven children per woman in 1800 to four in 1900) is evidence of conscious decisions about family limitation, first by members of the new middle class and later by working-class families. Few couples used mechanical methods of contraception such as the condom, partly because these were difficult to obtain and partly because most people associated their use with prostitution and the prevention of venereal disease rather than with family planning. Instead, people used birth control methods that relied on mutual consent: coitus interruptus (withdrawal before climax), the rhythm method (intercourse only during the woman's infertile period), and, most often, abstinence or infrequent intercourse. Medical manuals suggested that couples consider ending their sex life after they had reached the desired number of children.

When mutual efforts at birth control failed, married women often sought a surgical abortion, a new technique that was much more reliable than the folk remedies women had always shared among themselves. Surgical abortions were widely advertised after 1830, and widely used, especially by middle-class married women seeking to limit family size. Some historians estimate that one out of every four pregnancies was aborted in the years 1840–60 (about the same rate as in 1990). The rising rate of abortion by married women (in other words, its use as birth control) prompted the first legal bans; by 1860, twenty states had outlawed the practice. Even in the absence of accurate statistics, it is clear that dangerous illegal abortions continued, especially among unmarried women who believed they lacked alternatives.

Accompanying the interest in family limitation was a redefinition of sexuality. Doctors generally recommended that sexual urges be controlled, but they believed that men would have much more difficulty exercising such control than women, partly because, they also believed, women were uninterested in sex. (Women who were visibly interested ran the risk of being considered immoral or "fallen," and thereupon shunned by the middle class.) Medical manuals of the period suggested that it was the task of middle-class women to help their husbands and sons restrain their sexuality by appealing to their higher, moral natures. Although it is always difficult to measure the extent to which the suggestions in advice books were applied in actual practice, it seems that many middle-class women accepted this new and limited definition of their sexuality because of their desire to limit the number of pregnancies.

Many women of the late eighteenth century wanted to be free of the medical risks and physical debility that too-frequent childbearing brought, but they had little chance of achieving that goal until men became equally interested in family limitation. The rapid change in attitudes toward family size that occurred in the early nineteenth century has been repeated around the world as other societies undergo the dramatic experience of industrialization. It is a striking example of the ways economic changes affect our most private and personal decisions.

Motherhood

New responsibilities toward children led to another major redefinition of women's roles. Child rearing had been shared in the preindustrial household, boys learning farming or craft skills from their fathers while girls learned domestic skills from their mothers. The children of the new middle class, however, needed a new kind of upbringing, one that involved a long period of nurturing in the beliefs and personal habits necessary for success. Mothers assumed primary responsibility for this training, in part because fathers were too busy but also because people believed that women's superior qualities of gentleness, morality, and loving watchfulness were essential to the task.

Fathers retained a strong role in major decisions concerning children, but mothers commonly turned to other women for advice on daily matters. Through their churches, women formed maternal associations for help in raising their children to be religious and responsible. In Utica, New York, for example, these extremely popular organizations enabled women to form strong networks sustained by mutual advice and by publications such as *Mother's Magazine*, issued by the Presbyterian Church, and *Mother's Monthly Journal*, put out by the Baptists.

Middle-class status required another sharp break with tradition. As late as 1855, artisanal families expected all children over fifteen to work. Middle-class families, on the other hand, sacrificed to keep their sons in school or in training for their chosen professions, and they often housed and fed their sons until the young men had "established" themselves financially and could marry.

This watercolor, The Happy Home, *illustrates the importance of domesticity for middle class families and the powerful new role for women as they used their moral influence in childrearing.*

Mothers continued to be concerned about their children's character and morality, as women's activities in the great religious revivals of the 1830s showed. They also took the lead in an important informal activity: making sure their children had friends and contacts that would be useful when they were old enough to consider careers and marriage. Matters such as these, rarely considered by earlier generations living in small communities, now became important in the new middle-class communities of America's towns and cities.

Contrary to the growing myth of the self-made man, middle-class success was not a matter of individual achievement. Instead it was usually based on a family strategy in which women's efforts were essential. The reorganization of the family described in this section was successful: from its shelter and support emerged generations of ambitious, responsible, and individualistic middle-class men. But although boys were trained for success, this was not an acceptable goal for their sisters. Women were trained to be the nurturing, silent "support system" that undergirded male success. And women were also expected to ease the tensions of the transition to new middle-class behavior by acting as models and monitors of traditional values.

Sentimentalism

The individualistic competitiveness engendered by the market revolution caused members of the new middle class to place extraordinary emphasis on sincerity and feeling. So-called sentimentalism sprang from nostalgia for the imagined trust and security of the familiar, face-to-face life of the preindustrial village. Sermons, advice manuals, and articles now thundered warnings to young men of the dangers and deceits of urban life, and especially of fraudulent "confidence men and painted ladies" who were not what they seemed. Middle-class women were expected to counteract the impersonality and hypocrisy of the business world by the example of their own morality and sincere feeling.

For guidance in this new role women turned to a new literary form, the sentimental novel. In contrast to older forms like sermons and learned essays, the novel was popular, accessible, and emotionally engrossing. Although denounced by ministers and scholars as frivolous, immoral, and subversive of authority, the novel found a ready audience among American women. Publishers of novels found a lucrative market, one that increased from $2.5 million in 1820 to $12.5 million in 1850. By 1850, *Harper's Magazine* estimated, four-fifths of the reading public were women, and they were reading novels written by women.

To be a "lady novelist" was a new and rather uncomfortably public occupation for women. Several authors, such as Susan Warner, were driven to novel writing when their fathers lost their fortunes in the Panic of 1837. Novel writing could be very profitable: Warner's 1850 novel *The Wide Wide World* went through fourteen editions in two years, and works by other authors such as Lydia Maria Child, Catherine Sedgwick, and E.D.E.N. Southworth sold in the thousands of copies. Sentimental novels concentrated on private life. Religious feeling, antipathy toward the dog-eat-dog world of the commercial economy, and the need to be prepared for unforeseen troubles were common themes. Although the heroines usually married happily at the end of the story, few novels concentrated on romantic love. Most of these domestic novels, as they were known, presented readers with a vision of responsibility and community based on moral and caring family life.

Although sentimentalism originally sprang from genuine fear of the dangers individualism posed to community trust, it rapidly hardened into a rigid code of etiquette for all occasions. Moments of genuine and deep feeling, such as death, were smothered in elaborate rules concerning condolences, expressions of grief, and appropriate clothing. A widow, for example, was expected to wear "deep mourning" for a year—dresses of dull black fabrics and black bonnets covered with long, thick black veils—and in the following year "half mourning"—shiny black silk dresses, perhaps with trim of gray, violet, or white, and hats without veils. Thus sentimentalism rapidly became concerned not with feelings but social codes. Transformed into a set of rules about genteel manners to cover all occasions, sentimentalism itself became a mark of middle-class status. And it became one of the tasks of the middle-class woman to make sure her family conformed to the social code and associated only with other respectable families. In this way, women forged and enforced the distinctive social behavior of the new middle class.

Transcendentalism and Self-Reliance

As the new middle class conformed to the rules of sentimental behavior, it also sought a more general intellectual reassurance. Middle-class men, in particular, needed to feel comfortable about their public assertions of individualism and self-interest. One source of reassurance was the philosophy of transcendentalism and its well-known spokesman, Ralph Waldo Emerson. Originally a Unitarian minister, Emerson quit the pulpit in 1832 and became what one might call a secular minister. Famous as a writer and lecturer, he popularized transcendentalism, a romantic philosophical theory claiming that there was an ideal, intuitive reality transcending ordinary life. The best place to achieve that individual intuition of the Universal Being, Emerson suggested, was not in church or in society but alone in the natural world. As he wrote in "Nature" (1836), "Standing on the bare ground—my head bathed by the blithe air, and uplifted into infinite space—all mean egotism vanishes. I become a transparent Eyeball; I am nothing; I see all; the currents of the Universal Being circulate through me; I am part and parcel of God." The same assertion of individualism rang through Emerson's stirring polemic "Self-Reliance" (1841). Announcing that "Whoso would be a man, must be a nonconformist," Emerson urged that "Nothing is at last sacred but the integrity of your own mind." Inspirational but down-to-earth, Emerson was just the philosopher to inspire young businessmen of the 1830s and 1840s to achieve success in a responsible manner.

Emerson's younger friend, Henry David Thoreau, pushed the implications of individualism further than the more conventional Emerson. Determined to live the transcendental ideal of association with nature, Thoreau lived in solitude in a primitive cabin for two years at Walden Pond, near Concord, Massachusetts, confronting "the essential facts of life." His experience was the basis for *Walden* (1854), a penetrating criticism of the spiritual cost of the market revolution. Denouncing the materialism that led "the mass of men [to] lead lives of quiet desperation," Thoreau recommended a simple life of subsistence living that left time for spiritual thought. Margaret Fuller, perhaps the most intellectually gifted of the transcendental

Emerson's romantic glorification of nature included the notion of himself as a "transparent eyeball," as he wrote in "Nature" in 1836. A contemporary produced this cartoon.

CHRONOLOGY

1790	Samuel Slater's first mill opens in Rhode Island
1793	Cotton gin invented
1798	Eli Whitney contracts with the federal government for 10,000 rifles, which he undertakes to produce with interchangeable parts
1807	Embargo Act excludes British manufactures
1810	Francis Cabot Lowell tours British textile factories First steamboat on the Ohio River
1812	Micajah Pratt begins his own shoe business in Lynn, Massachusetts
1813	Francis Cabot Lowell raises $300,000 to build his first cotton textile factory at Waltham, Massachusetts
1815	War of 1812 ends; British competition in manufactures resumes
1816	First protective tariff
1820s	Large-scale outwork networks develop in New England
1823	Lowell mills open
1824	John Hall successfully achieves interchangeable parts at Harpers Ferry armory Women lead strike at Pawtucket textile mill
1825	Erie Canal opens
1830	Charles G. Finney's Rochester revivals
1834	First strike at Lowell mills
1836	Ralph Waldo Emerson lecture "Nature" published
1841	Catharine Beecher's *Treatise on Domestic Economy* published
1845	New England Female Labor Reform Association formed
1847	New Hampshire passes first ten-hour-day law

circle, was patronized by Emerson because she was a woman. She expressed her sense of women's wasted potential in her pathbreaking work *Woman in the Nineteenth Century* (1845). Intellectually and emotionally, however, Fuller achieved liberation only when she moved to Europe and participated in the liberal Italian revolution of 1848. The romantic destiny she sought was tragically fulfilled when she, her Italian husband, and their child died in a shipwreck off the New York coast as they returned to America in 1850.

Although Thoreau and Fuller were too radical for many readers, Emerson's version of the romantic philosophy of transcendentalism, seemingly so at odds with the competitive and impersonal spirit of the market revolution, was in fact an essential component of it. Individualism, or, as Emerson called it, self-reliance, was at the heart of the personal transformation required by the market revolution. Sentimentalism, transcendentalism, and evangelical religion all helped the new middle class to forge values and beliefs that were appropriate to their social roles.

CONCLUSION

The market revolution involved three transformations: improvements in transportation, commercialization, and industrialization. Each began at different times. The transportation revolution (discussed in Chapter 10), usually dated from 1825 (the year of the opening of the Erie Canal), accelerated with the building of railroads in the 1830s and 1840s. Commercialization began earlier, around 1805, as a consequence of the reorganization of manufacturing through the putting-out system by northern entrepreneurs. After 1805, the cash purchase of items manufactured elsewhere slowly eroded local barter arrangements. American industrialization began with Samuel Slater's small cotton spinning mill in Rhode Island in 1790, but the most famous early example was the mill town of Lowell, whose factories opened in 1823. These three transformations, taken together, constituted the market revolution that, by changing the ways people worked, changed how they thought.

For most people the changes were gradual. Until midcentury, the lives of rural people were still determined largely by community events, although the spread of democratic politics and the availability of newspapers and other printed material increased their connection to a larger world. Wage earners made up only 40 percent of the working population in 1860, and factory workers made up an even smaller percentage.

The new middle class was most dramatically affected by the market revolution. All aspects of life, including intimate matters of family organization, gender roles, and the number and raising of children, changed. New values—evangelical religion, sentimentalism, and transcendentalism—helped the members of the new middle class in their adjustment. As the next chapter describes, the nation's cities were the first arena where old and new values collided.

REVIEW QUESTIONS

1. What changes in preindustrial life and work were caused by the market revolution?
2. This chapter argues that when people begin doing new kinds of work, their beliefs and attitudes change. Give three examples of such changes described in the chapter. Can you think of other examples?
3. Discuss the opinion offered by historian David Potter that mass production has been an important democratizing force in American politics. Do you agree? Why or why not?
4. Consider the portrait of the nineteenth-century middle-class family offered in this chapter and imagine yourself as a member of such a family. What new aspects of family relations would you welcome? Which would be difficult? Why?

RECOMMENDED READING

Christopher Clark, *The Roots of Rural Capitalism: Western Massachusetts, 1780–1860* (1990). The most thorough examination to date of how the commercial spirit changed rural life.

Alan Dawley, *Class and Community: The Industrial Revolution in Lynn* (1976). A pathbreaking study of the shift from artisanal to wage labor.

Thomas Dublin, *Women at Work: The Transformation of Work and Community in Lowell, Massachusetts, 1826–1860* (1979). A careful look at the female workers of Lowell and their changing conditions.

Thomas Dublin, *Transforming Women's Work: New England Lives in the Industrial Revolution* (1994). A thoughtful study of the effects of women's outwork.

Karen Halttunen, *Confidence Men and Painted Women: A Study of Middle-Class Culture in America* (1982). Explores the development and importance of sentimentalism to the new middle class.

David Houndshell, *From the American System to Mass Production, 1800–1932* (1984). Shows how not only Eli Whitney but an entire network of New England "mechanics" contributed to the invention of interchangeable parts.

Paul Johnson, *A Shopkeeper's Millennium: Society and Revivals in Rochester, New York, 1815–1837* (1978). A study of the changing relationship between masters and workers in Rochester.

Bruce Laurie, *Artisans into Workers: Labor in Nineteenth-Century America* (1989). Using many specific examples, traces the changes in labor described in this chapter.

Jonathan Prude, *The Coming of Industrial Order: Town and Factory Life in Rural Massachusetts, 1810–1860* (1983). A major source of information on family mills.

Steven J. Ross, *Workers on the Edge: Work, Leisure and Politics in Industrializing Cincinnati, 1788–1890* (1985). Studies the growth of wage labor in a major western city.

Mary Ryan, *The Making of the Middle Class* (1981). A study of Utica, New York, that was the first to clearly discern the role of women in the family strategies of the new middle class.

Charles Sellers, *The Market Revolution: Jacksonian America 1815–1846* (1991). A synthesis of the political, religious, and economic change of the period.

Christine Stansell, *City of Women: Sex and Class in New York, 1789–1860* (1983). Exceptionally useful in exploring the range of women's work and the social dynamics of rapidly growing New York City.

ADDITIONAL BIBLIOGRAPHY

The Market Revolution

Thomas C. Cochran, *Frontiers of Change: Early Industrialism in America* (1981)

Robert F. Dalzell Jr., *Enterprising Elite: The Boston Associates and the World They Made* (1987)

L. C. Hunter, *A History of Industrial Power in the United States, 1780–1930*, vol. 1: *Waterpower in the Century of the Steam Engine* (1979)

David J. Jeremy, *Transatlantic Industrial Revolution: The Diffusion of Textile Technology between Britain and America* (1981)

Benjamin W. Labaree, *Patriots and Partisans, The Merchants of Newburyport, 1764–1815* (1962)

Walter Licht, *Industrializing America: The Nineteenth Century* (1995)

Diane Linstrom, *Economic Development in the Philadelphia Region, 1810–1850* (1978)

Merritt R. Smith, *Harpers Ferry Armory and the New Technology* (1977)

Barbara Tucker, *Samuel Slater and the Origins of the American Textile Industry, 1790–1860* (1984)

Caroline F. Ware, *Early New England Cotton Manufacturing* (1931)

From Artisan to Worker

Mary H. Blewett, *Men, Women, and Work: Class, Gender, and Protest in the New England Shoe Industry, 1780–1910* (1988)

John L. Brooke, *The Heart of the Commonwealth: Society and Political Culture in Worcester County, Massachusetts, 1713–1861* (1989)

Robert Doherty, *Society and Power: Five New England Towns, 1800–1860* (1977)

Paul G. Faler, *Mechanics and Manufacturers in the Early Industrial Revolution: Lynn, Massachusetts* (1981)

Michael H. Glickstein, *Concepts of Free Labor in Antebellum America* (1991)

Susan E. Hirsch, *Roots of the American Working Class: The Industrialization of Crafts in Newark, 1800–1860* (1978)

Joan M. Jensen, *Loosening the Bonds: Mid-Atlantic Farm Women, 1750–1850* (1986)

Jack Larkin, *The Reshaping of Everyday Life, 1790–1840* (1988)

Bruce Laurie, *Working People of Philadelphia, 1800–1850* (1980)

Scott C. Martin, *Killing Time: Leisure and Culture in Southwestern Pennsylvania, 1800–1850* (1995)

Howard Rock, *Artisans of the New Republic: Tradesmen of New York City in the Age of Jefferson* (1979)

W. J. Rorabaugh, *The Craft Apprentice: From Franklin to the Machine Age in America* (1986)

Charles G. Steffan, *The Mechanics of Baltimore: Workers and Politics in the Age of Revolution, 1763–1812* (1984)

A New Social Order

Jeanne Boydston, *Home and Work* (1990)

Nancy E. Cott, *The Bonds of Womanhood: "Woman's Sphere" in New England, 1780–1835* (1977)

Betty G. Farrell, *Elite Families: Class and Power in Nineteenth Century Boston* (1993)

Clyde Griffen and Sally Griffen, *Natives and Newcomers: The Ordering of Opportunity in Mid-Nineteenth-Century Poughkeepsie* (1978)

James C. Mohr, *Abortion in America: The Origins and Evolution of National Policy, 1800–1900* (1978)

Edward Pessen, *Riches, Class, and Power before the Civil War* (1973)

James Reed, *From Private Vice to Public Virtue: The Birth Control Movement and American Society since 1830* (1978)

Anthony F. C. Wallace, *Rockdale: The Growth of an American Village in the Early Industrial Revolution* (1977)

Middle-Class Culture

Barbara A. Bardes and Suzanne Gossett, *Declarations of Independence: Women and Political Power in Nineteenth-Century American Fiction* (1990)

Nina Baym, *Woman's Fiction: A Guide to Novels by and about Women in America* (1978)

———, *Feminism and American Literary History* (1992)

Paul F. Boller, *American Transcendentalism, 1830–1860* (1974)

John F. Kasson, *Rudeness and Civility: Manners in Nineteenth-Century America* (1990)

Mary Kelley, *Private Women, Public Stage: Literary Domesticity in Nineteenth-Century America* (1984)

F. O. Matthiessen, *American Renaissance* (1941)

Walter Benn Michaels and Donald E. Pease, eds., *The American Renaissance Reconsidered* (1985)

Leonard Neufeldt, *The Economist: Henry Thoreau and Enterprise* (1989)

Russell Nye, *Society and Culture in America, 1830–1860* (1974)

Lewis Perry, *Intellectual Life in America* (1984)

Ann Rose, *Transcendentalism as a Social Movement* (1981)

Shirley Samuels, ed., *The Culture of Sentiment: Race, Gender, and Sentimentality in Nineteenth-Century America* (1992)

Jane Tompkins, *Sensational Designs: The Cultural World of American Fiction, 1790–1860* (1986)

Joyce W. Warren, *The (Other) American Traditions: Nineteenth-Century Women Writers* (1993)

Biography

Paul Blanchard, *Margaret Fuller: From Transcendentalism to Revolution* (1978)

Walter Harding, *Thoreau: Man of Concord* (1960)

Joel Porte, *Representative Man: Ralph Waldo Emerson in His Time* (1979)

R. D. Richardson Jr., *Henry Thoreau: A Life of the Mind* (1986)

CHAPTER THIRTEEN

COMING TO TERMS WITH THE NEW AGE

1820s–1850s

The Bootblack, by George Henry Yewell, 1852, oil on canvas, 14 x 12 inches, Collection of the New York Historical Society.

AMERICAN COMMUNITIES

Seneca Falls: Women Reformers Respond to the Market Revolution

Chapter Outline

URBAN AMERICA

The Preindustrial City
The Growth of Cities
Patterns of Immigration
Class Structure in the Cities
Sanitation and Living Patterns
Ethnic Neighborhoods
Urban Popular Culture
Civic Order
Urban Life of Free African Americans

THE LABOR MOVEMENT AND URBAN POLITICS

The Union Movement
Big-City Machines

SOCIAL REFORM MOVEMENTS

Evangelism, Reform, and Social Control
Education and Women Teachers
Temperance
Moral Reform, Asylums, and Prisons
Utopianism and Mormonism

ANTISLAVERY AND ABOLITIONISM

The American Colonization Society
African Americans' Fight against Slavery
Abolitionists
Abolitionism and Politics

THE WOMEN'S RIGHTS MOVEMENT

The Grimké Sisters
Women's Rights

In the summer of 1848, a small advertisement appeared in an upstate New York newspaper announcing a "convention to discuss the social, civil, and religious condition and rights of woman," to be held at Seneca Falls on the 19th and 20th of July.

Charlotte Woodward, a nineteen-year-old glove maker who did outwork in her rural home, saw the advertisement and persuaded six friends to join her in the 40-mile journey to the convention. "At first we travelled quite alone," she recalled. "But before we had gone many miles we came on other wagon-loads of women, bound in the same direction. As we reached different crossroads we saw wagons coming from every part of the country, and long before we reached Seneca Falls we were a procession."

To the surprise of the convention organizers, almost 300 people—men as well as women—attended the two-day meeting. The focus of their discussions was the Declaration of Sentiments, a petition for women's rights modeled on the Declaration of Independence. "We hold these truths to be self-evident," it announced: "That all men and women are created equal." As the Declaration of Independence detailed the oppressions King George III had imposed on the colonists, the Declaration of Sentiments detailed, in a series of resolutions, the oppressions men had imposed on women. Men had deprived women of legal rights, of the right to own their own property, of custody of their children in cases of divorce, of the right to higher education (at that time only Oberlin College and Mount Holyoke Female Seminary admitted women), of full participation in religious worship and activity, and of the right to vote. After discussion, the attendees approved all the resolutions, and all but the last of them, which a minority found too radical, unanimously. "Why Lizzie, thee will make us ridiculous!" Quaker Lucretia Mott had exclaimed when Elizabeth Cady Stanton proposed the voting rights measure. Indeed the newspapers reporting on the convention thought the demand for the vote was ridiculously unfeminine. But the group that assembled in Seneca Falls was undeterred. Buoyed by the success of this first women's rights convention, they promptly planned another one three weeks later in New York's largest upstate city, Rochester, to reach new supporters and to develop strategies to implement their resolutions.

The fight for women's rights was only one of many reform movements that emerged in the United States in the wake of the economic and social disruptions of the market revolution. The Seneca Falls region was itself deeply affected by that revolution. A farming frontier in 1800, it had been drawn into national commerce in 1828 when it was reached by an offshoot of the Erie Canal. It was drawn even further into the modern age when the railroad arrived in 1841. A village of 200 in 1824, Seneca Falls had grown to a town of over 4,000 by 1842. It was now a center for flour milling (in 1845, the nine mills in the town produced a total of 2,000 barrels of flour a day) and manufacturing, and a hub of the outwork network of which Charlotte Woodward was a part. Swamped by newcomers (among them a growing number of poor Irish Catholics), the inhabitants of Seneca Falls struggled to maintain a sense of community. They formed volunteer organizations of all kinds—religious, civic, social, educational, recreational. And they became active participants in reform movements seeking to counteract the effects of industrialization, rapid growth, and the influx of newcomers.

Many reformers belonged to liberal religious groups with wide social perspectives. Perhaps a third of those attending the women's rights convention, for example, were members of the Wesleyan Methodist Society of Seneca Falls, which had broken with the national Methodist organization because it would not take a strong stand against slavery. Another quarter were Progressive Quakers of the nearby town of Waterloo, who had broken with their national organization for the same reason. Both groups were outspoken in their belief in the moral equality of all humankind and in their commitment to social activism. The Wesleyans, for example, resolved in 1847 that "we cannot identify our Christian and moral character with societies where women and colored persons are excluded." Seneca Falls had been the site of a "Temperance Reformation" in the early 1840s, and many attendees at the Women's Rights convention were also active in the temperance movement, a more limited but extremely popular reform cause dedicated to promoting abstinence from alcohol.

The idea for the Women's Rights convention emerged during a meeting in early July, 1848, between Lucretia Mott—a Philadelphia Quaker and the nation's best-known woman reformer—and Elizabeth Cady Stanton of Seneca Falls, wife of a well-known antislavery orator and niece of a leading reform philanthropist. Reflecting her many concerns, Mott had just finished a tour of the new penitentiary at Auburn and a nearby Indian reservation and was visiting her sister in Waterloo. Stanton called for tea to renew her acquaintance with Mott, and it was in this context of friendship and shared concern for reform that the two began planning the convention that was held two weeks later.

Stanton and her family had moved from Boston, where, she remembered, they had "near neighbors, a new home with all the modern conveniences, and well-trained servants." Living in a house on the outskirts of Seneca Falls, her three children suffering from malaria, she had none of those things. "I now fully understood," she mused,

> the practical difficulties most women had to contend with.... The general discontent I felt with woman's portion as wife, mother, housekeeper, physician and spiritual guide, the chaotic conditions into which everything fell without her constant supervision, and the wearied anxious look of the majority of women impressed me with a strong feeling that some active measures should be taken to remedy the wrongs of society in general, and of women in particular.

As she and Mott spoke of the changes that would be necessary to allow women to care for their families but have energy left over to reform "the wrongs of society," the idea of a women's rights convention was born. The women's rights movement that took shape from this convention proved exceptionally long-lasting. Stanton, soon to form a working partnership with former temperance worker Susan B. Anthony, devoted the rest of her life to women's rights.

But what of Charlotte Woodward, a local farm girl, unaware of the national reform community? Why was she there? In this age of hopefulness and change she wanted a better life for herself. She was motivated, she said, by "all the hours that I sat and sewed gloves for a miserable pittance, which, after it was earned, could never be mine." By law and custom her father, as head of the household, was entitled to her wages. "I wanted to work," she explained, "but I wanted to choose my task and I wanted to collect my wages." The reforming women of Seneca Falls, grouped together on behalf of social improvement, had found in the first women's rights convention a way to speak for the needs of working women such as Charlotte Woodward

All over the North, in communities like Seneca Falls as well as in cities like New York , Americans gathered together in reform organizations to try to solve the problems that the market revolution posed for work, family life, personal and social values, and urban growth. Through these organizations local women and men became participants in wider communities of concern.

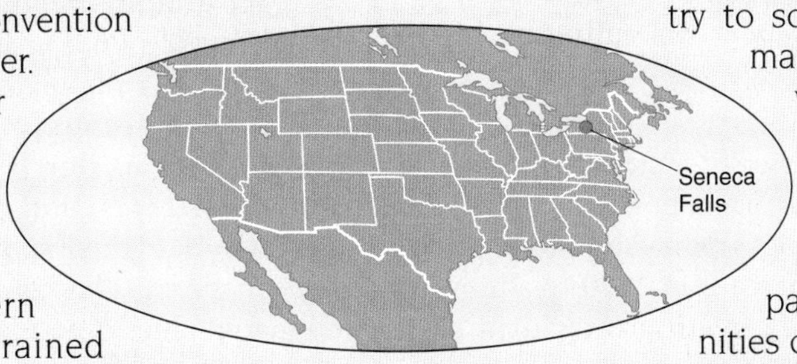

KEY TOPICS

- **The new social problems that accompanied urbanization and immigration**
- **The responses of reformers**
- **The origins and political effects of the abolitionist movement**
- **The involvement of women in reform efforts**

URBAN AMERICA

Although the market revolution affected all aspects of American life, nowhere was its impact so noticeable as in the cities. It was within the urban environment, with its stimulating, frightening confusion of rapid physical growth, occupational and ethnic change, and economic competition, that new American political and social forms began to emerge.

The Preindustrial City

The preindustrial cities of eighteenth-century America were small and compact. They were "walking cities," in which people mostly got around on foot. Philadelphia, for example, which had been laid out by William Penn himself in 1682, was an orderly grid of streets bordered by neat row houses in a dense, small-scale housing pattern that fostered neighborliness.

In these cities, rich and poor lived side by side. Merchants lived next door to their businesses, and in the busy streets and public places they daily rubbed elbows with their employees and with artisans and laborers. The wealthy enjoyed unquestioned authority. Merchants sat on the city council, which had broad powers to regulate the public markets, to set prices for basic foodstuffs, to grant licenses to artisans and traders, and to encourage community harmony. The same wealthy men organized charity and relief for the poor in hard times, often walking door to door in their neighborhood to solicit donations. Wealthy men were active in neighborhood volunteer fire departments and in the volunteer watch societies that prevented crime and kept neighborhood order. When larger disturbances such as bread riots broke out, the mayor and other city officials were expected to appear and disperse the mob by force of their own authority.

The Growth of Cities

The market revolution dramatically increased the size of America's cities, with the great seaports leading the way. The proportion of America's population living in cities increased from only 7 percent in 1820 to almost 20 percent in 1860, a rate of growth greater than at any other time in the country's history.

The nation's five largest cities in 1850 were the same as in 1800, with one exception. New York, Philadelphia, Baltimore, and Boston still topped the list, but New Orleans had edged out Charleston (see Chapter 9). The rate of urban growth was extraordinary. All four Atlantic seaports grew at least 25 percent each decade between 1800 and 1860, and often much more. New York, which grew from 60,000 in 1800 to 202,600 in 1830 and to more than 1 million in 1860, emerged as the nation's most populous city, its largest port, and its financial center. Between 1820 and 1830, the decade in which the Erie Canal added commerce with the American interior to the city's long-standing role in international trade, New York's population grew 64 percent.

Philadelphia, which had been the nation's largest city in 1800, was half the size of New York in 1850. Nevertheless, its growth was substantial—from 70,000 in 1800 to 389,000 in 1850 and to 565,529 in 1860. Philadelphia became as much an industrial as a commercial city. Old artisanal industries such as hand-loom weaving, tailoring, and shoe manufacture coexisted with new industries such as the huge Baldwin locomotive works, foundries, and chemical companies.

Baltimore, with 212,418 residents in 1860 was about half the size of Philadelphia. The city's merchants, hoping to counter the threat posed by the Erie Canal to their trade links with the trans-Appalachian West, financed the nation's first important railroad, the Baltimore and Ohio, which began operation in 1830. Although Baltimore remained the east coast center of the tobacco trade with Europe, by 1850 its major partner in foreign trade was Brazil, to which it shipped flour and from which it imported coffee.

Boston, in colonial times, had dominated the triangular trade linking Britain and the West Indies. By 1860, with a population of 177,840, the city had emerged as the center of a new triangular trade: the ships of Boston merchants carried New England cotton cloth, shoes, and other manufactured goods to the South, delivered southern cotton to British and European ports, and returned to Boston with European manufactured goods. Boston still dominated the China trade as well.

New Orleans, fed by the expansion of cotton throughout the South and commercial agriculture in the Mississippi Valley, had a population of 168,675 in 1860. In the 1850s, New Orleans handled about half the nation's cotton exports and by 1860, its exports—$5 million in 1815—had risen to $107 million.

The market revolution oriented the attention of each of these major seaports away from the oceans and toward trade with the nation's interior. Prosperous merchants in these cities now depended on American exports rather than European imports for their profits.

Another result of the market revolution was the appearance of "instant" cities at critical points on the new transportation network. Utica, New York, once a frontier trading post, was transformed by the opening of the Erie Canal into a commercial and manufacturing center. By 1850 the city's population had reached 22,000. Chicago, on the shores of Lake Michigan, was transformed by the coming of the railroad into a major junction for water and rail transport. The city, which emerged as a fur trading center around Fort Dearborn, an army post built in 1803, had become, by the 1850s, a hub of trade boasting grain storage facilities, slaughterhouses, and warehouses of all kinds. Farm implement manufacturers such as Cyrus McCormick built manufacturing plants there to serve the needs of Midwest farmers. By 1860 Chicago had a population of 100,000, making it the nation's eighth largest city (after Cincinnati and St. Louis).

Patterns of Immigration

One of the key aspects of urban growth was a surge in immigration to the United States that began in the 1820s and accelerated dramatically after 1830 (see "Immigration and Community: The Changing Face of Ethnicity in the United States, 1800–1860," on page 380). From an annual figure of about 20,000 in 1831, immigration ballooned to a record 430,000 in 1854 before declining in the years prior to the Civil War. The proportion of immigrants in the population jumped from 1.6 percent in the 1820s to 11.2 percent in 1860. In the nation's cities the proportion was vastly larger: by 1860, nearly half of New York's population (48 percent) was foreign-born.

Most of the immigrants to the United States during this period came from Ireland and Germany. Political unrest and poor economic conditions in Germany and the catastrophic Potato Famine of 1845–1850 in Ireland was responsible for an enormous surge in immigration from those countries between 1845 and 1854. The starving, desperate "Famine Irish" who crowded into eastern seaports were America's first large refugee group. Between them, the Germans and the Irish represented the largest influx of non-English immigrants the country had known (many Americans found the Irish dialect as strange as a foreign language). They were also the poorest: most of the Irish arrived destitute. In addition most of the Irish and half of the Germans were Catholics, an unwelcome novelty to many Protestant Americans.

Many German immigrants made their way to agricultural communities in Ohio, Indiana, Missouri, and Texas, but many others, and most Irish immigrants, settled in America's major cities. Few immigrants found life in the United States pleasant or easy. In addition to the psychological difficulties of leaving a home and familiar ways behind, most immigrants endured harsh living and working conditions. One common immigrant response was to construct ethnic neighborhoods and communities for mutual support. For their inhabitants, these Irish and German neighborhoods were a positive response that eased the difficulties of adaptation to American circumstances. But native-born Americans, unprepared for the "foreignness" and poverty of many new immigrants, reacted with hostility to immigrant clustering, and indeed, to the immigrants themselves. Because the immigrant influx widened the social gap between rich and poor and dramatically altered living patterns, immigration contributed to the social problems that America's urban centers faced—and were unable to solve—in the early nineteenth century.

Class Structure in the Cities

Although per capita income in America is estimated to have doubled between 1800 and 1850, the gap between rich and poor increased and became glaringly apparent in the nation's cities. The benefits of the market revolution were unequally distributed: by the 1840s the top 1 percent of the population owned about 40 percent of the nation's wealth, while, at the other extreme, one-third of the population owned virtually nothing. In the cities, then, there was a very small group of wealthy people worth more than $5,000 (about 3 percent of the population), a very large group of poor people worth $100 or less (nearly 70 percent), and a middle class with incomes in between (25–30 percent).

Differences in income affected every aspect of urban life. Very poor families, including almost all new immigrants, performed unskilled labor in jobs whose future was uncertain at best, lived in cheap rented housing, moved frequently, and depended on more than one income to survive. Artisans and skilled workers with incomes of $500 or more could live adequately, though often in cramped quarters that also served as their shops. A middle-class family with an income of more than $1,000 a year could live comfortably in a house of four to six rooms complete with carpeting, wallpaper, and good furniture. The very rich

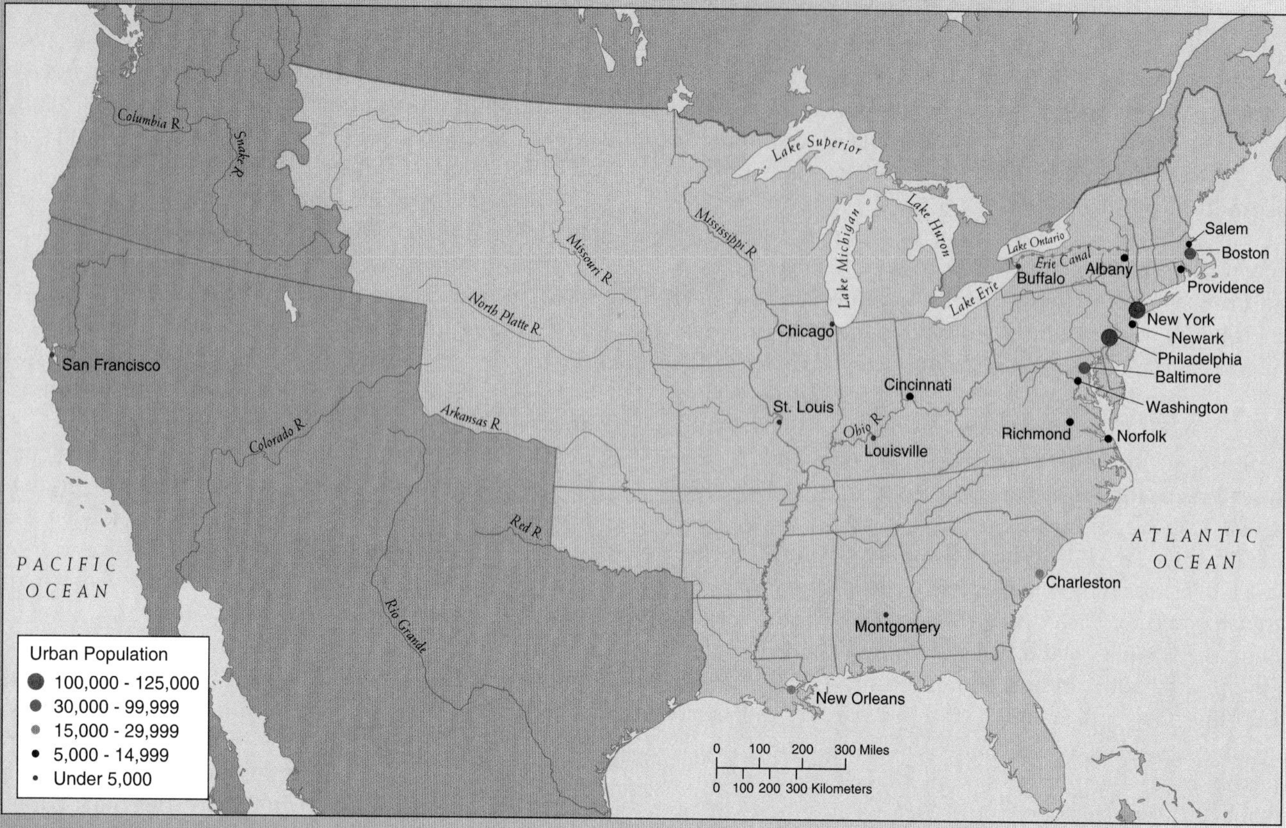

American Cities, 1820

Source: *Statistical Abstract of the United States*

The Growth of Cities, 1820–1860

The cities of North America grew more rapidly between 1820 and 1860 than at any other time in the nation's history. Eastern seaport cities remained the largest, but New York grew to twice the size of the second largest city, Philadelphia. New York's growth, due in large part to the increase in trade following the opening of the Erie Canal, illustrates

built mansions and large town houses and staffed them with many servants. In the summer they left the cities for country estates or homes at seaside resorts such as Newport, Rhode Island, which attracted wealthy families from all over the country.

Sanitation and Living Patterns

Early-nineteenth-century cities lacked municipal water supplies, sewers, and garbage collection. People drank water from wells, used outdoor privies that often contaminated the water supply, and threw garbage and slop out the door to be foraged by roaming herds of pigs. Clearly, this was a recipe for disease, and every American city suffered epidemics of sanitation-related diseases such as yellow fever, cholera, and typhus. Philadelphia's yellow fever epidemic of 1793 caused 4,000 deaths and stopped all business with the outside world for more than a month.

Yet the cities were slow to take action. In response to the yellow fever epidemic Philadelphia completed a city water system in 1801, but users had to pay a fee, and only the richest subscribed in the early days. Neither New York nor Boston had a public water system until the 1840s. Garbage collection remained a private service, and cities charged property owners for the costs of sewers, water mains, and street paving. Poorer areas of the cities could not afford the costs.

Provision of municipal services forced residential segregation. Richer people clustered in neighborhoods that had the new amenities. One of New York's first wealthy areas, Gramercy Park, was developed in 1831 by a speculator who transformed what had been Gramercy Farm into "an ornamental private square or park, with carriageways and footwalks." Only purchasers of the surrounding lots had keys to the park; everyone else was

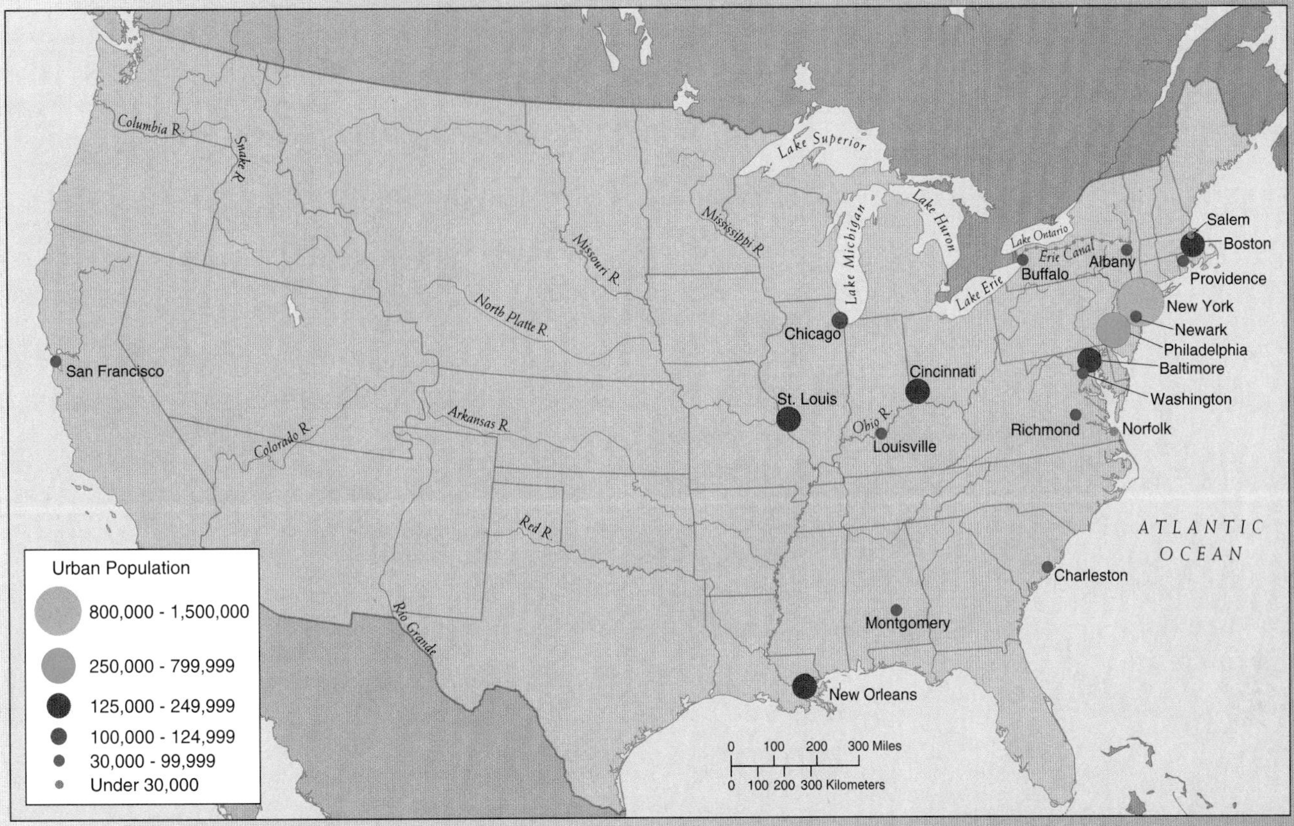

American Cities, 1860

Source: *Statistical Abstract of the United States*

the importance of trade between port cities and the nation's interior. Inland river cities like Cincinnati and St. Louis and the great Mississippi seaport of New Orleans grew rapidly. San Francisco, Louisville, and Buffalo—still villages in 1820—grew also, but Chicago, which rapidly emerged as a hub for both water and rail transport, surpassed them all.

excluded. By the 1850s the middle class began to escape cities completely by moving to the new "streetcar suburbs," named for the new mode of urban transportation that connected these nearby areas to the city itself.

As the middle class left the city, the poor clustered in bad neighborhoods that became known as slums. The worst New York slum in the nineteenth century was Five Points, a stone's throw from city hall. There immigrants, free black people, and criminals were crammed into rundown buildings known in the slang of the time as "rookeries." Notorious gangs of thieves and pickpockets with names such as the Plug Uglies and the Shirt Tails dominated the district. Starvation and murder were commonplace.

Five Points was grim even in comparison with the notorious slums of London. As knowledgeable an Englishman as the author Charles Dickens exclaimed on a visit to the district in 1842, "All that is loathsome, drooping and decayed is here...Where dogs would howl to lie, women, and men and boys slink off to sleep, forcing the dislodged rats to move away in quest of better lodgings." With the influx of European immigrants after 1830, middle-class Americans increasingly saw slums as the home of strange and foreign people, who deserved less than American-born citizens. In this way, residential patterns came to embody larger issues of class and citizenship.

Ethnic Neighborhoods

To poverty-stricken Irish immigrants, these same slums represented not only family ties and familiar ways but community support as they learned how to survive in new surroundings. Isolated partly by their own beliefs (for Catholics fully reciprocated the hatred and fear

The Five Points neighborhood in lower Manhattan illustrates the segregated housing patterns that emerged as New York City experienced rapid growth. Immigrants, free African Americans, the poor and criminals were crowded together in New York's most notorious slum, while wealthier people moved to more prosperous neighborhoods.

Protestants showed them), Irish immigrants created their own communities in Boston and New York, their major destinations. They raised the money to erect Catholic churches with Irish priests. They established parochial schools with Irish nuns as teachers and sent their children to them in preference to the openly anti-Catholic public schools. They formed mutual aid societies based on kinship or town of origin in Ireland. Men and women formed religious and social clubs, lodges, and brotherhoods and their female auxiliaries. Irishmen manned fire and militia companies as well. This dense network of associations served the same purpose that social welfare organizations do today: providing help in time of need and offering companionship in a hostile environment.

Germans who settled in urban areas also built their own ethnic enclaves—"Little Germanies"—in which they sought to duplicate the rich cultural life of German cities. In general, German immigrants were skilled workers and not as poor as the Irish. Like the Irish, however, the Germans formed church societies, mutual benefit societies, and fire and militia companies to provide mutual support. Partly because their communities were more prosperous than those of the Irish, the Germans also formed a network of leisure organizations: singing societies, debating and political clubs, concert halls like New York's Beethoven Hall, theaters, *turnvereins* (gymnastics associations), and beer gardens. They published German-language newspapers as well.

Ethnic clustering, then, allowed new immigrants to hold onto aspects of their culture that they valued and to transplant them to American soil. Many native-born Americans, however, viewed ethnic neighborhoods with deep suspicion. The Boston *American* expressed the sentiments of many in 1837 when it remarked:

> our foreign population are too much in the habit of retaining their own national usages, of *associating too* exclusively *with each other,* and living in groups together. *It would be the part of wisdom, to ABANDON AT ONCE ALL USAGES AND ASSOCIATIONS WHICH MARK THEM AS FOREIGNERS, and to become in feeling and custom, as well as in privileges and rights, citizens of the United States.*

Urban Popular Culture

The size, diversity, and changing working conditions in American cities bred a new urban popular culture with New York, the largest city, leading the way. In the period 1820–60, urban workers experienced the replacement of artisanal labor by wagework, two serious depressions (1837–43 and 1857), and vastly increased competition from immigrant labor. In response to these pressures, working-class amusements became rougher and rowdier. Taverns that served as neighborhood centers of drink and sociability were also frequent centers of brawls and riots. Community groups such as fire engine companies that had once included men of all social classes now attracted rough young laborers who formed their own youth gangs and defended "their" turf against other gangs. Some trades, such as that of butcher, became notorious for starting fights in taverns and grog shops.

Theaters, which had been frequented by men of all social classes, provided another setting for violence. Few women, except for the prostitutes who met their customers in the third tier of the balcony, attended. In the 1820s, a long-standing tradition of small-scale rioting by poorer patrons against unpopular actors began to change into more serious violence. The Astor Place Riot of 1849 began as a theater riot against a British actor but escalated into a pitched battle between the mob and the militia that left twenty-two dead.

By the 1830s, middle-class and upper-class men withdrew to more respectable theaters to which they could bring their wives and daughters. Workers found new amusements in theaters such as the Lafayette Circus that featured dancing girls and horseback riders as well as theatrical acts. Another popular urban working-class amusement was the blackface minstrel show. White actors (often Irish) blacked their faces and entertained audiences with songs (including the famous "Dixie," written by an Irishman as a blackface song), dances, theatrical skits, and antiblack political jokes. Cruel stereotypes such as Zip Coon, an irresponsible free black man, and Jim Crow, a slow-witted slave, entertained white audiences. Historians have speculated that the popularity of blackface expressed not only white racism but also nostalgia for the freer behavior of preindustrial life that was now impossible for white workers but that

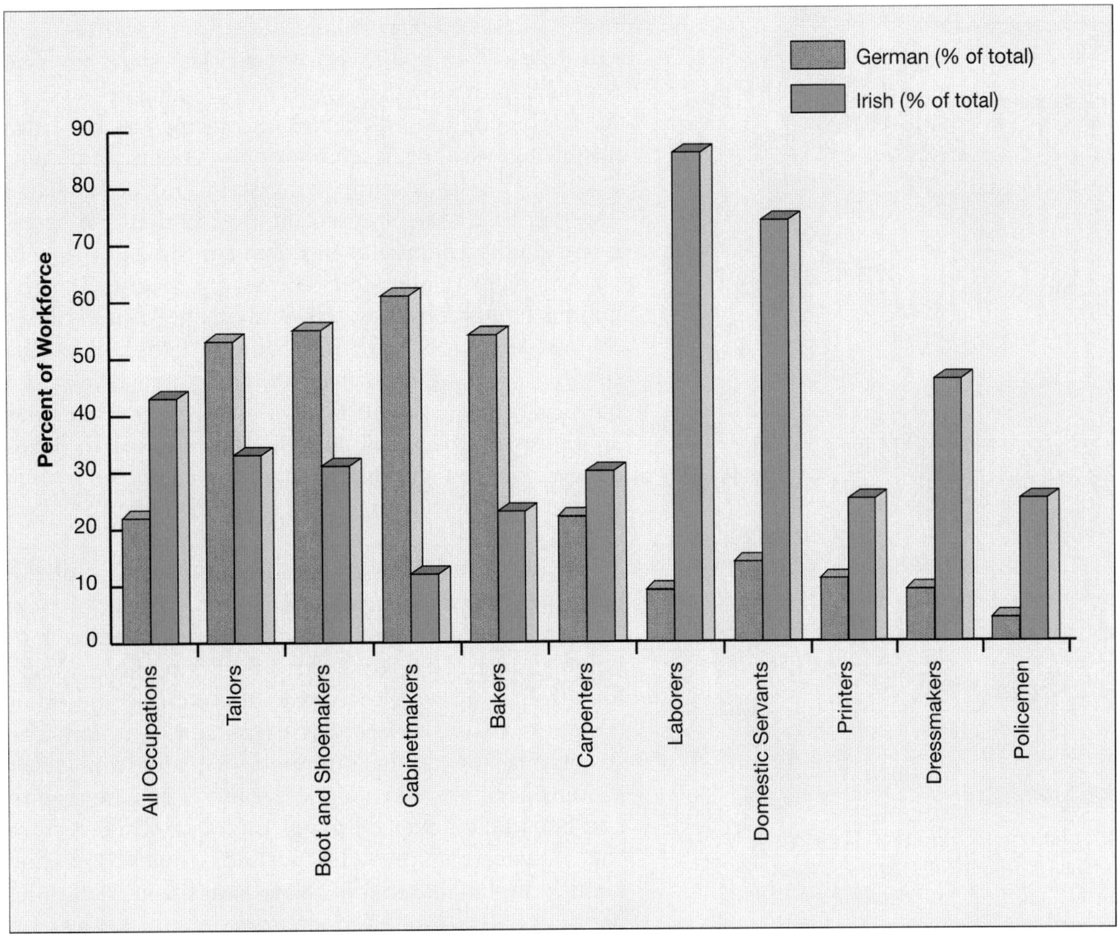

Participation of Irish and German Immigrants in the New York City Workforce for Selected Occuptations, 1855

Source: Robert Ernst, *Immigrant Life in New York City* 1825-1863 (Syracuse: Syracuse University Press, 1994).

they imagined African American slaves continued to enjoy in carefree dependency.

The new working-class culture flourished especially on the Bowery, a New York City street filled with artisanal workshops, small factories, shops with cheap goods, dance halls, theaters, ice cream parlors, and oyster bars. Here working-class youth, the "Bowery b'hoys" (slang pronunciation of "boy") and "gals," found Saturday night amusements and provided it for themselves with outrageous clothing and behavior. The deliberately provocative way they dressed was in effect a way of thumbing their noses at the more respectable classes. The costumes worn by the characters in one long-running series of melodramas staged by the Bowery Theater imitated this style. Mose, the hero of the series, dressed more like a pirate captain than a worker, and his gal Lise wore a bright-colored, body-hugging dress that challenged the discreet, sober fashions worn by middle-class women.

This 1848 playbill promotes A Glance at New York, *which featured two well-known working-class figures, Mose, the Bowery B'hoy, and his gal, Lise. His exaggerated clothing and hairstyle and her flashy colors were deliberate parodies aimed at New York's respectable middle class for the benefit of the rowdy working-class culture that grew up in the Bowery district of the city in the 1830s.*

Another challenge to middle-class respectability came from the immensely popular "penny papers" (so called from their price), the *New York Morning Post* and the *New York Sun*, which began appearing in 1833. These papers, with lurid headlines such as "Double Suicide," and "Secret Tryst," and "Bloody Murder," fed the same popular appetite for scandal, as did other popular reading such as the *Police Gazette* magazine, pamphlets about murder trials, swindlers, and pirates, and temperance dime novels such as *Franklin Evans; or, The Inebriate* written in 1842 by the struggling young newspaperman, Walter (later Walt) Whitman. Urban journalist, Democratic Party activist, and poet, Whitman distilled his passionate love for the variety and commonness of the American people in *Leaves of Grass*, a book of free-verse poems published in 1855. Regarded at the time as scandalous because of its frank language, Whitman's poetry nevertheless captured the driving energy and democratic spirit of the new urban popular culture. In a rather more sinister way, so did the writings of Edgar Allan Poe, who found the inspiration for his gothic horror stories such as "The Murders in the Rue Morgue" (1841) and "The Mystery of Marie Roget" (1842) not in Europe (as his titles might suggest) but in contemporary American crimes.

This fascination with urban violence led one observer to comment cynically in 1859 that "No narrative of human depravity or crime can shock or horrify an American reader." But Alexis de Tocqueville, the famous French observer who visited the United States in 1831–32 wrote with foreboding, "I look upon the size of certain American cities, and especially on the nature of their population, as a real danger." Here was an expression of a new fear in American urban life—concern about civic order.

Civic Order

Tocqueville's fears for civic order echoed that of the urban middle class, who now found menacing even traditions of lower-class amusement that dated back to colonial times. New York City's tradition of New Year's Eve "frolics," in which laborers, apprentices, and other members of the lower classes paraded through the streets playing drums, trumpets, whistles, and other noisemakers, was an example. By the 1820s the revelry had been taken over by gangs of young workers from the lower classes who called themselves the Callithumpian Band. On New Year's Eve 1828, the band, 4,000 strong and equipped with drums, tin kettles, rattles, horns, and whistles, marched through the city. On their way they overturned carts and broke windows in the commercial district, in some wealthy homes near Battery Park, and in an African American church. They then marched to the City Hotel, where middle-class couples were just leaving a ball, and obstructed traffic. The indignant couples watched helplessly as several hundred watchmen called to disperse the mob cautiously declined to do so. In the following year, the traditional New Year's Eve parade was banned by the city government.

The prosperous classes were frightened by the urban poor and by working-class rowdyism. They resented having to avoid many parts of the city that were unsafe for them, and they disliked even more the disturbances in "their" parts of the city, as this irritable notation in the diary of merchant Philip Hone indicates: "Riot, disorder, and violence increase in our city, every night is marked by some outrage committed by gangs of young ruffians who prowl the streets insulting females, breaking into the houses of unoffending publicans [tavern keepers], making night hideous by yells of disgusting inebriety, and—unchecked by the city authorities—committing every sort of enormity with apparent impunity."

In colonial days, civic disturbances had been handled informally: members of the city watch asked onlookers for such assistance as was necessary to keep the peace. New York City's first response in the 1820s and 1830s to increasing civic disorder was to hire more city watchmen and to augment them with constables and marshals. When riots occurred, the militia were called, and deaths were increasingly common as they forcibly restrained mobs. Finally, in 1845, the city created a permanent police force with a mandate to keep the poor in order. There had been substantial opposition to the idea of this first professional police force in the United States on the grounds that it infringed personal liberty, but as middle-class fear of what became known as "the dangerous classes" grew, police protection came to seem necessary. Here was an indication that the harmonious preindustrial urban community no longer existed.

But even with police forces in place, the pressures of rapid urbanization, immigration, and the market revolution proved to be more than America's cities could contain. The violence was more than just rowdyism and socially disapproved behavior. Beginning in the 1830s, a series of urban riots broke out against the two poorest urban groups: Catholics and free black people. As if their miserable living conditions were not enough, Irish immigrants were met with virulent anti-Catholicism. In 1834 rioters burned an Ursuline convent in Charlestown, Massachusetts; in 1844 a Philadelphia mob attacked priests and nuns and vandalized Catholic churches; in 1854 a mob destroyed an Irish neighborhood in Lawrence, Massachusetts. Often the Irish replied in kind—for example, in the 1806 riot in New York when they counterattacked a mob that disrupted their Christmas Eve mass in a Catholic church on Augustus Street. But the most common targets of urban violence were free African Americans.

Urban Life of Free African Americans

By 1860, there were nearly half a million free African Americans in the United States, constituting about 11 percent of the country's total black population. More than half of all free African Americans lived in the North, mostly in cities, where they competed with immigrants and native-born poor white people for jobs as day laborers and domestic servants. Their relative social position is reflected in statistics on per capita annual income in Boston in the 1850s—$91 for black people and $131 for Irish immigrants compared to $872 for the population at large. Philadelphia and New York had the largest black communities: 22,000 African Americans in Philadelphia and 12,500 in New York (another 4,313 lived just across the East River in Brooklyn). There were much smaller but still significant black communities in the New England cities of Boston, Providence, and New Haven and in Ohio cities like Cincinnati.

Free African Americans in northern cities faced residential segregation (except for the domestic servants who lived in with white families), pervasive job discrimination, segregated public schools, and severe limitations on their civil rights. In addition to these legal restrictions there were matters of custom: African Americans of all economic classes endured daily affronts, such as exclusion from public concerts, lectures, and libraries and segregation or exclusion from public transportation. For example, in Massachusetts—which had the reputation of being more hospitable to black people than any other northern state—the famed African American abolitionist Frederick Douglass was denied admission to a zoo on Boston Common, a public lecture and revival meeting, a restaurant, and a public omnibus, all within the space of a few days.

In common with Irish and German immigrants, African Americans created defenses against the larger hostile society by building their own community structures. They formed associations for aiding the poorest members of the community, for self-improvement, and for socializing. Tired of being insulted by the white press, African American communities supported their own newspapers. The major community organization was the black Baptist or African Methodist Episcopal (AME) church, which served, as one historian put it, as "a place of worship, a social and cultural center, a political meeting place, a hiding place for fugitives, a training ground for potential community leaders, and one of the few places where blacks could express their true feelings."

Free African Americans suffered many forms of discrimination, but as this 1850 daguerreotype of an unknown woman shows, they sought to achieve the same levels of education and economic comfort as other Americans.

Employment prospects for black men deteriorated from 1820 to 1850. Those who had held jobs as skilled artisans were forced from their positions, and their sons denied apprenticeships, by white mechanics and craftsmen who were themselves suffering from the effects of the market revolution. Limited to day labor, African Americans found themselves in direct competition with the new immigrants, especially the Irish, for jobs. On the waterfront, black men lost their jobs as carters and longshoremen to the Irish. One of the few occupations to remain open to them was that of seaman. More than 20 percent of all American sailors in 1850 were black, and over the years their ranks included an increasing number of runaway slaves. The pay was poor and the conditions miserable, but many black men found more equality aboard ship than they did ashore. Mothers, wives, and daughters were left ashore to work as domestic servants (in competition with Irishwomen), washerwomen, and seamstresses.

Free African Americans remained committed to their enslaved brethren in the South. In New York, for example, black communities rioted four times—in 1801, 1819, 1826, and 1832—against slave catchers taking escaped slaves back to slavery. But even more frequently, free African Americans were themselves targets of urban violence. An 1829 riot in Cincinnati sent a thousand black people fleeing to Canada in fear for their lives; a three-day riot in Providence in 1831 destroyed an African American district; and an 1834 New York riot destroyed a church, a school, and a dozen homes. Philadelphia, "the City of Brotherly Love," had the worst record. Home to the largest free African American community in the North, Philadelphia was repeatedly rocked by antiblack riots in the period between 1820 and 1859. A riot in 1834 destroyed two churches and thirty-one homes and left one African American dead and many injured. In 1842, a predominantly Irish mob attacked black marchers celebrating Jamaican Emancipation Day. The marchers counterattacked, wounding three Irish boys and provoking widespread arson, which firemen refused to put out for fear of the mob. The disturbance ended only when the mayor called out seven companies of the militia. Other cities had similar stories. Urban riots of all kinds had cost 125 lives by 1840, by 1860 more than 1,000.

THE LABOR MOVEMENT AND URBAN POLITICS

Universal white manhood suffrage and the development of mass politics (see Chapter 10), coupled with the rapid growth of cities, changed urban politics. The traditional leadership role of the wealthy elite waned, and members of the wealthiest class gradually withdrew from direct participation in urban politics. In New York City, elite political leaders had disappeared by 1845. In their place were professional politicians whose job it was to make party politics work. In New York and in other large cities, this change in politics was spurred by working-class activism.

The Tradition of Artisanal Politics

The nation's urban centers had long been strongholds of craft associations for artisans and skilled workers. These organizations, and their parades and celebrations, were recognized parts of the urban community. Groups of master craftsmen marching in community parades with signs such as "By Hammer and Hand All Arts Do Stand" were visible symbols of the strength and solidarity of workers' organizations.

Also traditional were riots and demonstrations by workers (usually journeymen or apprentices, not the master artisans themselves) over matters as political and far-reaching as the American Revolution or as practical and immediate as the price of bread. In fact, protests by urban workers had been an integral part of the older social order controlled by the wealthy elite. In the eighteenth century, when only men of property could vote, such demonstrations usually indicated widespread discontent or economic difficulty among workers. They served as a warning signal that the political elite rarely ignored.

By the 1830s the status of artisans and independent craftsmen in the nation's cities had changed. As discussed in Chapter 12, the artisanal system was crumbling, undercut by competition between cities (the result of the transportation revolution) and by the growth of the putting-out system. Furthermore, the rapid influx of immigrants changed the character of the labor force. New York provides a particularly dramatic example. The city's rapid growth as a manufacturing center was based on the labor of Irish and German immigrant workers, who made up 65 percent of the workforce by 1855. Germans clustered primarily in the skilled trades, while the Irish performed most of the low-paid labor. Indeed, 86 percent of day laborers were Irishmen, while Irishwomen made up 74 percent of the domestic servants.

This seal of the General Society of Mechanics and Tradesmen illustrates in its motto—"By Hammer and Hand All Arts Do Stand"—the personal and community pride artisans took in their work.

There was no safety net for workers who lost their jobs—no unemployment insurance or welfare—and no public regulation of wages and conditions of work. The first protests against these harsh conditions came from the women workers at the new cotton textile factories in Lowell and elsewhere. The members of urban workers' associations, increasingly angry over their declining status in the economic and social order, also became—tentatively at first, but then with growing conviction—active defenders of working-class interests.

What was new was the open antagonism between workers and employers. The community of interest between masters and workers in preindustrial times broke down. Workers realized they had to depend on other workers, not employers, for support. In turn, employers and members of the middle class began to take urban disorders much more seriously than their grandfathers might have done.

The Union Movement

Urban worker protest against changing conditions quickly took the form of party politics. The Workingmen's Party was founded in Philadelphia in 1827, and chapters quickly formed in New York and Boston as well. Using the language of class warfare—"two distinct classes...those that live by their own labor and they that live upon the labor of others"—the "Workies" campaigned for the ten-hour day and the preservation of the small artisanal shop. They also called for the end of government-chartered monopolies—banks were high on the list—and for a public school system and cheap land in the West. Although the Workies themselves did not survive as a party, Jacksonian Democrats were quick to pick up on some of their themes. The Democrats attracted many workers' votes in 1832, the year Andrew Jackson campaigned against the "monster" Bank of the United States.

Both major parties competed for the votes of urban workers. In New York City in 1835 a radical antimonopoly branch of the Democratic Party known officially as the Equal Rights Party attracted some worker support. For their part, the Whigs wooed workers by assuring them that Henry Clay's American System, and tariff protection in particular, would be good for the economy and for workers' jobs. Nevertheless, neither major political party really spoke to the primary need of workers—for well-paid, stable jobs that assured them independence and respect. Unsatisfied with the response of political parties, workers turned to labor organization to achieve their goals.

Between 1833 and 1837 a wave of strikes in New York City cut the remaining ties between master craftsmen and the journeymen who worked for them. In 1833, journeymen carpenters struck for higher wages. Workers in fifteen other trades came to their support, and within a month the strike was won. The lesson was obvious: if skilled workers banded together across craft lines, they could improve their conditions. The same year, representatives from nine different craft groups formed the General Trades Union of New York. By 1834 similar groups had sprung up in over a dozen cities—Boston, Louisville, and Cincinnati among them. In New York alone, the GTU helped organize almost forty strikes between 1833 and 1837, and it encouraged the formation of more than fifty unions. In 1834 also, representatives of several local GTUs met in Baltimore and organized the National Trades Union. In its founding statement the NTU criticized the "unjustifiable distribution of the wealth of society in the hands of a few individuals," which had created for working people "a humiliating, servile dependency, incompatible with...natural equality."

Naturally, employers disagreed with the NTU's criticism of the economic system. Convinced that unions were dangerous, New York employers took striking journeymen tailors to court in 1836. Judge Ogden Edwards pronounced the strikers guilty of conspiracy and declared unions un-American. He assured the strikers that "the road of advancement is open to all" and that they would do better to strive to be masters themselves rather than "conspire" with their fellow workers. The GTU responded with a mass rally at which Judge Edwards was burned in effigy. A year later, stunned by the effects of the Panic of 1837, the GTU collapsed. The founding of these general unions, a visible sign of a class-based community of interest among workers, is generally considered to mark the beginning of the American labor movement. However, these early unions included only white men in skilled trades who made up only a small percentage of all workers. The majority of workers—men in unskilled occupations, all free African Americans, and all women—were excluded.

Big-City Machines

Although workers were unable to create strong unions or stable political parties that spoke for their economic interests, they were able to shape urban politics. As America's cities experienced unprecedented growth, the electorate mushroomed. In New York, for example,

By 1855, half the voters in New York City were foreign-born. This 1858 engraving of an Irish bar in the Five Points area appeared in the influential Harper's Weekly. *It expressed the dislike of temperance reformers for immigrants and their drinking habits and the dismay of political reformers that immigrant saloons and taverns were such effective organizing centers for urban political machines.*

the number of voters grew from 20,000 in 1825 to 88,900 in 1855. Furthermore, by 1855 half of the voters were foreign-born. At the time, America was the only country in the world where propertyless white men had the vote. The job of serving this largely working-class electorate and making the new mass political party work at the urban level fell to a new kind of career politician—the boss—and a new kind of political organization—the machine.

Just as the old system of elite leadership had mirrored the social unity of eighteenth-century cities, so the new system of machine politics reflected the class structure of the rapidly growing nineteenth-century cities. Feelings of community, which had arisen naturally out of the personal contact that characterized neighborhoods in earlier, smaller cities, now were cultivated politically. The existence of distinct ethnic neighborhoods fostered political organization. Because immigrants clustered in neighborhoods, their impact on politics could be concentrated and manipulated. Legally, three years' residence in the United States was required before one could apply for citizenship, but there was clear evidence of swifter naturalization in large cities with effective political organizations. In New York, for example, the Irish-dominated districts quickly became Democratic Party strongholds. Germans, who were less active politically than the Irish, nevertheless voted heavily for the new Republican Party in the 1850s. Between them, these two new blocs of immigrant voters destroyed the Whig Party that had controlled New York politics before the immigrants arrived.

In New York City, the Tammany Society, begun in the 1780s as a fraternal organization of artisans, slowly evolved into the key organization of the new mass politics. (Named after the Delaware chief mentioned in Chapter 3, the society met in a hall called the Wigwam and elected "sachems" as their officers.) Tammany, which was affiliated with the national Democratic Party, reached voters by using many of the techniques of mass appeal made popular earlier by craft organizations—parades, rallies, current songs, and party newspapers.

Along with these new techniques of mass appeal went new methods of organization: a tight system of political control beginning at the neighborhood level with ward committees and topped by a chairman of a citywide general committee. At the citywide level, ward leaders—bosses—bartered the loyalty and votes of their followers for positions on the city payroll for party members and community services for their neighborhood. This was machine politics. Through it workers, although they lacked the political or organizational strength to challenge the harmful effects of the market revolution, could use their numbers to ameliorate some of its effects at the local level. Machine politics served to mediate increasing class divisions and ethnic diversity as well. The machines themselves offered personal ties and loyalties—community feeling—to recent arrivals in the big cities (increasingly, immigrants from Europe) and help in hard times to workers who cast their votes correctly.

In America's big cities the result was apparent by midcentury: the political "machine" controlled by the "boss"—the politician who represented the interests of his group and delivered their votes in exchange for patronage and favors.

Critics said that big-city machines were corrupt, and indeed they often were. Antagonism between reformers, who were usually members of the upper and middle classes, and machine politicians, who spoke for the working class, was evident by the 1850s. This antagonism was to become chronic in American urban politics. One result of the market revolution was the political expression, in a democratic society, of the conflict of interests between owners and workers.

SOCIAL REFORM MOVEMENTS

The passion for reform that had become such an important part of the new middle-class thinking was focused on the problems of the nation's cities. As the opening of this chapter describes, the earliest response to the dislocations caused by the market revolution was community-based and voluntary. Middle-class people tried to deal with social changes in their communities by joining organizations devoted to reforms such as temperance, education, prisons and asylums, women's rights, abolitionism, and, above all, the spread of evangelical religion. The reform message was vastly amplified by inventions such as the steam printing press, which made it possible to publish reform literature in great volume. Soon there were national networks of reform groups.

Alexis de Tocqueville commented on the vast extent of American voluntary associations and their many purposes. "In no country in the world," he noted, "has the principle of association been more successfully used, or more unsparingly applied to a multitude of different objects, than in America." The widespread reform movements of the era depended on the energy and hope of communities of like-minded people.

Evangelism, Reform, and Social Control

Evangelical religion was fundamental to social reform. Men and women who had been converted to the enthusiastic new faith assumed personal responsibility for making changes in their own lives. Personal reform quickly led to social reform; recall, for example, the northern businessman described in Chapter 12 who gave up drinking alcohol and insisted that his employees do the same. Religious converts were encouraged in their social activism by such leading revivalists as Charles G. Finney, who preached a doctrine of "perfectionism," claiming it was possible for all Christians to personally understand and live by God's will and thereby become "as perfect as God." Furthermore, Finney predicted, "the complete reformation of the whole world" could be achieved if only enough converts put their efforts into moral reform. This new religious feeling was intensely hopeful: members of evangelistic religions really did expect to convert the world and create the perfect moral and religious community on earth.

Much of America was swept by the fervor of moralistic reform, and it was the new middle class, who applied new notions of morality to the movement, that set the agenda for reform. Reform efforts arose from the recognition that the traditional methods of small-scale local relief were no longer adequate. In colonial times, families (sometimes at the request of local government) had housed and cared for the ill or incapacitated. Small local almshouses and prisons had housed the poor and the criminal. Reformers now realized that large cities had to make large-scale provisions for social misfits and that institutional rather than private efforts were needed. This thinking was especially true of the institutional reform movements that began in the 1830s, such as the push for insane asylums. At this time, of course, the federal government provided no such relief.

A second characteristic of the reform movements was a belief in the basic goodness of human nature. All reformers believed that the condition of the unfortunate—the poor, the insane, the criminal—would improve in a wholesome environment. Thus insane asylums were built in rural areas, away from the noise and stress of the cities, and orphanages had strict rules that were meant to encourage discipline and self-reliance. Prison reform carried this sentiment to the extreme. On the theory that bad social influences were largely responsible for crime, some "model" prisons completely isolated prisoners from one another, making them eat, sleep, work, and do required Bible reading in their own cells. The failure of these prisons to achieve dramatic changes for the better in their inmates (a number of isolated prisoners went mad, and some committed suicide) or to reduce crime was one of the first indications that reform was not a simple task.

A third characteristic of the reform movements was their moralistic dogmatism. Reformers were certain they knew what was right and were determined to see their improvements enacted. It was a short step from developing individual self-discipline to imposing discipline on others. The reforms that were proposed thus took the form of social controls. Lazy, sinful, intemperate, or unfit members of society were to be reformed for their own good, whether they wanted to be or not. This attitude was bound to cause controversy; by no means did all Americans share the reformers' beliefs, nor did those for whom it was intended always take kindly to being the targets of the reformers' concern.

Indeed, some aspects of the social reform movements were harmful. The evangelical Protestantism of the reformers promoted hostility to Catholic immigrants from Ireland and Germany beginning in the 1830s. The temperance movement, in particular, targeted immigrants for their free drinking habits. Seeking uniformity of behavior rather than tolerance, the reformers thus helped to promote the virulent nativism that infected American politics between 1840 and 1860 (see Chapter 15 and "Immigration and Community: The Changing Face of Ethnicity in America, 1800–1865" on page 380).

Regional and national reform organizations quickly grew from local projects to deal with social problems such as drinking, prostitution, mental illness, and crime. In 1828, for example, Congregationalist minister Lyman Beecher joined other ministers in forming a General Union for Promoting the Observance of the Christian Sabbath; the aim was to prevent business on Sundays. To achieve its goals, the General Union adopted the same methods used by political parties: lobbying, petition drives, fund-raising, and special publications. These and other efforts, Beecher said, were all for the purpose of establishing "the moral government of God."

In effect, the sabbath reformers engaged in political action but remained aloof from direct electoral politics, stressing their religious mission. In any case, their goal was controversial. Workingmen (who usually worked six days a week) were angered when the General Union forced the Sunday closure of their favorite taverns and were quick to vote against the Whigs, the party most sympathetic to reform thinking. Other reforms likewise muddied the distinction between political and social activity. It is not surprising that women, who were barred from electoral politics but not from moral and social activism, were major supporters of reform.

Education and Women Teachers

Women became deeply involved in reform movements through their churches. It was they who did most of the fund-raising for the home missionary societies that were beginning to send the evangelical message worldwide—at first by ministers alone, later by married couples. Nearly every church had a maternal association, where mothers gathered to discuss ways to raise

Catharine Beecher, a member of one of America's leading families of religious reformers, advocated teaching as a suitable employment for young single women because it called for the nurturing skills and moral values she claimed all women possessed.

their children as true Christians. These associations reflected a new and more positive definition of childhood. The Puritans had believed that children were born sinful and that their wills had to be broken before they could become godly. Early schools reflected these beliefs: teaching was by rote, and punishment was harsh and physical. Educational reformers, however, tended to believe that children were born innocent and needed gentle nurturing and encouragement if they were to flourish. At home, mothers began to play the central role in child rearing. Outside the home, women helped spread the new public education pioneered by Horace Mann, secretary of the Massachusetts State Board of Education.

Although literacy had long been valued, especially in New England, schooling since colonial times had been a private enterprise and a personal expense. Town grammar schools, required in Massachusetts since 1647, had been supported primarily by parents' payments, with some help from local property taxes. In 1827, Massachusetts pioneered compulsory education by legislating that public schools be supported by public taxes. Soon schooling for white children between the ages of five and nineteen was common, although, especially in rural schools, the term might be only a month or so long. Uniformity in curriculum and teacher training, and the grading of classes by ability—measures pioneered by Horace Mann in the 1830s—quickly caught on in other states. In the North and West (the South lagged far behind), more and more children went to school, and more and more teachers, usually young single women, were hired to teach them.

The spread of public education created the first real career opportunity for women. Horace Mann insisted that to learn well, children needed schools with a pleasant and friendly atmosphere. One important way to achieve that atmosphere, Mann recommended, was to group children by ages rather than combining everyone in the traditional ungraded classroom and to pay special attention to the needs of the youngest pupils. Who could better create the friendly atmosphere of the new classroom than women? The great champion of teacher training for women was Catharine Beecher, daughter of Lyman, who clearly saw her efforts as part of the larger work of establishing "the moral government of God." Arguing that women's moral and nurturing nature ideally suited them to be teachers, Beecher campaigned tirelessly on their behalf. Since "the mind is to be guided chiefly by means of the affections," she argued, "is not woman best fitted to accomplish these important objects?"

By 1850 women were dominant in primary school teaching, which had come to be regarded as an acceptable occupation for educated young women during the few years between their own schooling and marriage. For some women, teaching was a great adventure; they enthusiastically volunteered to be "schoolmarms" on the distant western frontiers of Wisconsin and Iowa. Still others thought globally. The young women who attended Mary Lyon's Mount Holyoke Female Seminary in Massachusetts, founded in 1837, hoped to be missionary teachers in distant lands. For others, a few years of teaching was quite enough. Low pay (half of what male schoolteachers earned) and community supervision (women teachers had to board with families in the community) were probably sufficient to make almost any marriage proposal look appealing.

Temperance

Reformers believed not only that children could be molded but that adults could change. The largest reform organization of the period, the American Society for the Promotion of Temperance founded in 1826, boasted more than 200,000 members by the mid-1830s. Dominated by evangelicals, local chapters used revival methods—lurid temperance tracts detailing the evils of alcohol, large prayer and song meetings, and heavy group pressure—to encourage young men to stand up, confess their bad habits, and

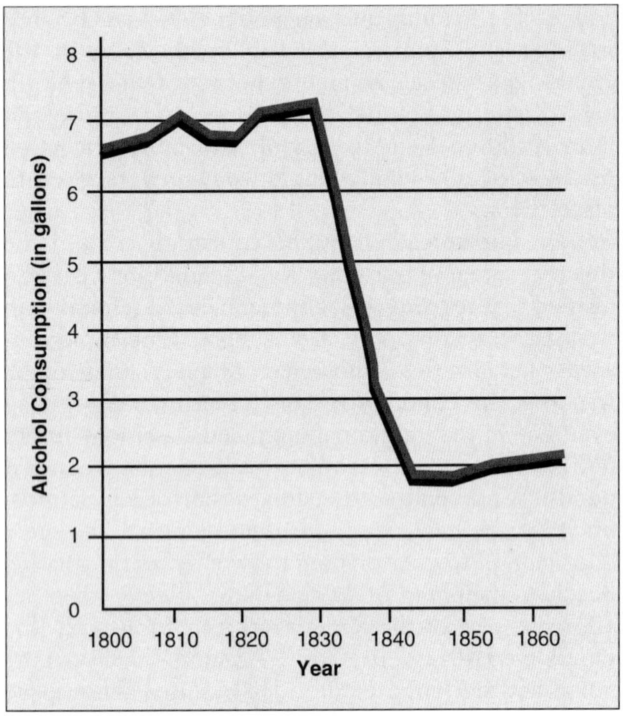

Per Capita Consumption of Alcohol, 1800–1860
The underlying cause for the dramatic fall in alcohol consumption during the 1830s was the changing nature of work brought about by the market revolution. Contributing factors were the shock of the Panic of 1837 and the untiring efforts of temperance reformers.

Source: W. J. Rorabaugh, *The Alcoholic Republic: An American Tradition* (New York: Oxford University Press, 1979).

"take the pledge" (not to drink). Here again, women played an important role.

Excessive drinking was a national problem, and it appears to have been mostly a masculine one, for respectable women did not drink in public. (Many did, however, drink alcohol-based patent medicines. Lydia Pinkham's Vegetable Compound, marketed for "female complaints," was 19 percent alcohol.) Men drank hard liquor—whiskey, rum, and hard cider—in abundance. Traditionally, drinking had been a basic part of men's working lives. It concluded occasions as formal as the signing of a contract and accompanied such informal activities as card games. Drink was a staple offering at political speeches, rallies, and elections. In the old artisanal workshops, drinking had been a customary pastime. Much of the drinking was well within the bounds of sociability, but the widespread use (more than seven gallons of hard liquor per capita in 1830—more than twice as much as today's rate) must have encouraged drunkenness.

There were many reasons to support temperance. Heavy-drinking men hurt their families economically by spending their wages on drink. Women had no recourse: the laws of the time gave men complete financial control of the household, and divorce was difficult as well as socially unacceptable. Excessive drinking also led to violence and crime, both within the family and in the larger society.

But there were other reasons as well. The new middle class, preoccupied with respectability and morality, found the old easygoing drinking ways unacceptable. As work patterns changed, employers banned alcohol at work and increasingly considered drinking men not only unreliable but immoral. Temperance became a social and political issue. Whigs, who embraced the new morality, favored it; Democrats, who in northern cities consisted increasingly of immigrant workers, were opposed. Both German and Irish immigrants valued the social drinking that occurred in beer gardens and saloons and were hostile to temperance reform.

The Panic of 1837 affected the temperance movement. Whereas most temperance crusaders in the 1820s had been members of the middle class, the long depression of 1837–43 prompted artisans and skilled workers to give up or at least cut down substantially on drinking. Forming associations known as Washington Temperance Societies, these workers spread the word that temperance was the workingman's best chance to survive economically and to maintain his independence. Their wives, gathered together in Martha Washington Societies, were frequently even more committed to temperance than their husbands. While the men's temperance groups were often deeply involved in working-class politics, the women's groups stressed the harm that alcoholism could do to homes and families and provided financial help to distressed women and children.

Campaigns against alcohol were frequent and successful. By the mid-1840s alcohol consumption had been more than halved, to less than two gallons per capita, about the level of today. Concern over drinking would remain constant throughout the nineteenth century and into the twentieth.

Moral Reform, Asylums, and Prisons

Alcohol was not the only "social evil" that reform groups attacked. Another was prostitution, which was common in the nation's port cities. The customary approach of evangelical reformers was to "rescue" prostitutes, offering them the salvation of religion, prayer, and temporary shelter. The success rate was not very high. As an alternative to prostitution, reformers usually offered domestic work, a low-paying and restrictive occupation that many women scorned. Nevertheless, campaigns against prostitution, generally organized by women, continued throughout the nineteenth century.

One of the earliest and most effective antiprostitution groups was the Female Moral Reform Society. Founded by evangelical women in New York in 1834 (the first president was Lydia Finney), it boasted 555 affiliates throughout the country by 1840. It was surprising that so many respectable women were willing to acknowledge the existence of something so disreputable as prostitution. Even more surprising was the speed with which the societies realized that prostitution was not so much a moral as an economic issue. The societies rapidly moved to organize charity and work for poor women and orphans. They also took direct action against the patrons of prostitutes by printing their names in local papers, and they successfully lobbied the New York state legislature for criminal penalties against the male clients as well as the women themselves.

Another dramatic example of reform was the asylum movement, spearheaded by a woman evangelist, Dorothea Dix. In 1843, Dix horrified the Massachusetts state legislature with the results of her several years of study into the conditions to which insane women were subjected. She described in graphic detail how the women were incarcerated with ordinary criminals, locked up in "cages, closets, stalls, pens! Chained, naked, beaten with rods, and lashed into obedience!" Dix's efforts led to the establishment of a state asylum for the insane in Massachusetts and to similar institutions in other states. Between 1843 and 1854 Dix traveled more than 30,000 miles to publicize the movement for humane treatment of the insane. By 1860 twenty-eight states had public institutions for the insane.

Other reformers were active in related causes, such as prison reform and the establishment of orphanages, homes of refuge, and hospitals. Model penitentiaries were built in Auburn and Ossining (known as "Sing Sing"), New York, and in Philadelphia and Pittsburgh. Characterized by strict order and discipline, these prisons were supposed to reform rather than simply incarcerate their inmates, but their regimes of silence and isolation caused despair more often than rehabilitation.

Utopianism and Mormonism

Amid all the political activism and reform fervor of the 1830s, a few people chose escape into utopian communities and new religions. The upstate New York area along the Erie Canal was the seedbed for this movement, just as it was for evangelical revivals and reform movements like the Seneca Falls convention. The area was so notable for its reform enthusiasms that it has been termed "the Burned-Over District," a reference to the waves of reform that swept through like forest fires.

Apocalyptic religions tend to spring up in places experiencing rapid social change. The Erie Canal region, which experienced the full impact of the

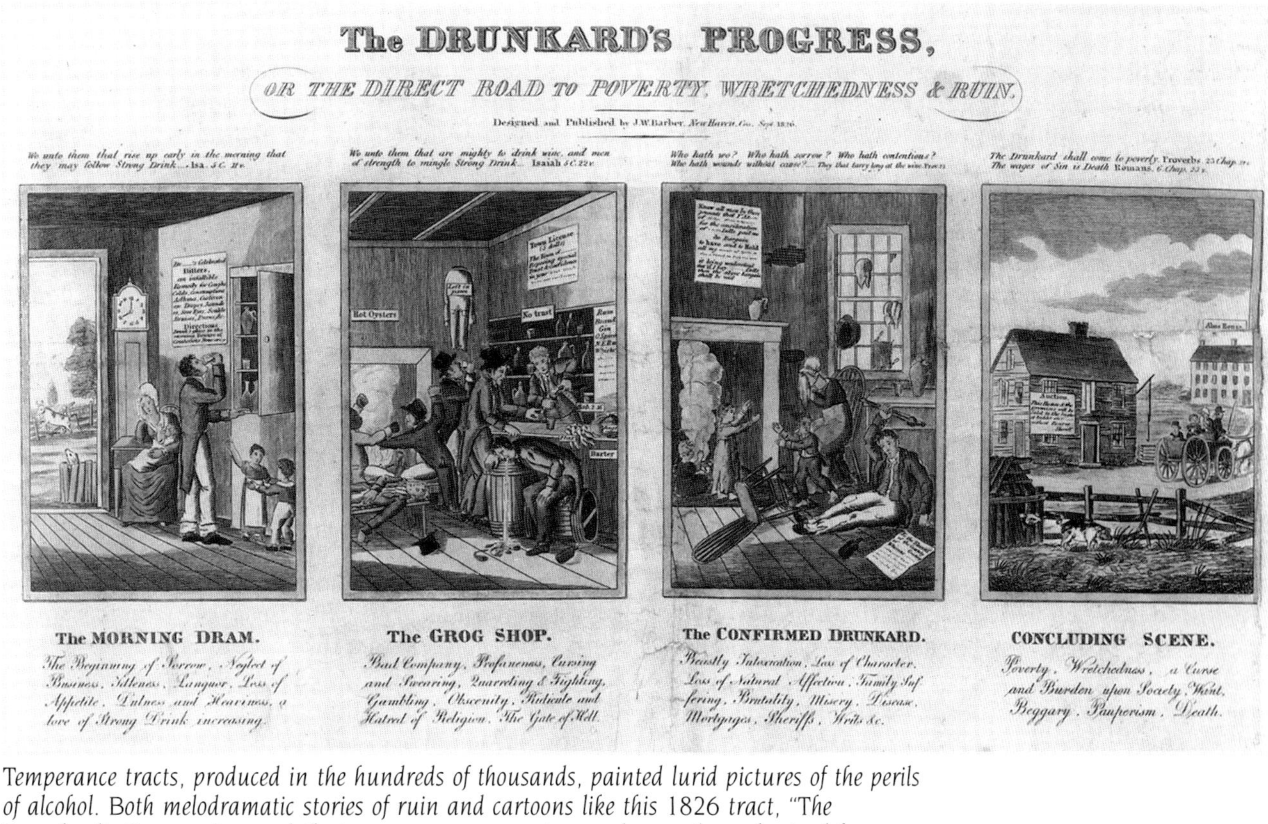

Temperance tracts, produced in the hundreds of thousands, painted lurid pictures of the perils of alcohol. Both melodramatic stories of ruin and cartoons like this 1826 tract, "The Drunkard's Progress," spread the temperance message in popular, easily understood forms.

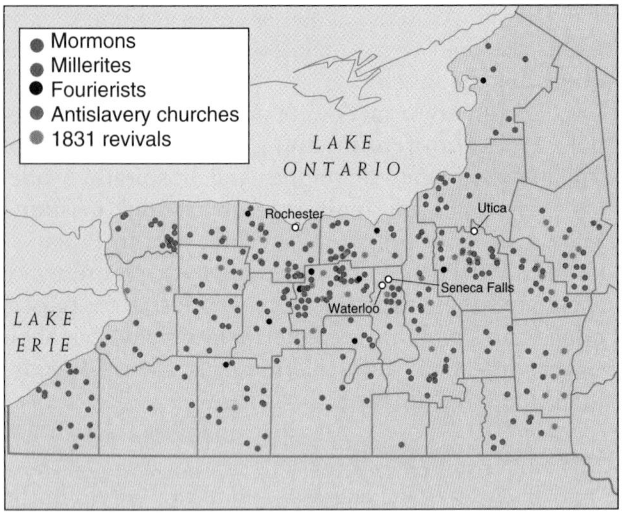

Reform Movements in the Burned-Over District
The so-called Burned-Over District, the region of New York State most changed by the opening of the Erie Canal, was a seedbed of religious and reform movements. The Mormon Church originated there and Utopian groups and sects like the Millerites and the Fourierists thrived. Charles G. Finney held some of his most successful evangelical revivals in the district. Antislavery feeling was common in the region, and the women's rights movement began at Seneca Falls.

Source: Whitney Cross, *The Burned-Over District* (1950; reprint, New York: Hippocrene Books, 1981).

market revolution in the early nineteenth century, was such a place. A second catalyst is hard times, and the prolonged depression that began with the Panic of 1837 led some people to embrace a belief in imminent catastrophe. The Millerites (named for their founder, William Miller) believed that the Second Coming of Christ would occur on October 22, 1843. In anticipation, members of the church sold their belongings and bought white robes for their ascension to heaven. When the Day of Judgment did not take place as expected, most of Miller's followers drifted away. But a small group persisted. Revising their expectations, they formed the core of the Seventh-Day Adventist faith, which is still active today.

The Shakers, founded by "Mother" Ann Lee in 1774, were the oldest utopian group. An offshoot of the Quakers, the Shakers espoused a radical social philosophy that called for the abolishment of the traditional family in favor of a family of brothers and sisters joined in equal fellowship. Despite its insistence on celibacy, the Shaker movement grew between 1820 and 1830, eventually reaching twenty settlements in eight states with a total membership of 6,000. The Shaker's simple and highly structured lifestyle, their isolation from the changing world, and their belief in equality drew new followers, especially among women. In contrast, another utopian community, the Oneida Community, became notorious for its sexual freedom. Founded by John Humphrey Noyes in 1848, the Oneida community, like the Shaker community, viewed itself as one family. But rather than celibacy, members practiced "complex marriage," a system of highly regulated group sexual activity. Only "spiritually advanced" males (Noyes himself and a few others) could father children, who were raised communally. These practices gave the sect a notorious reputation as a den of "free love" and "socialism," preventing Noyes from increasing its membership beyond 200.

Still other forthrightly socialist communities flourished briefly. New Harmony, Indiana, founded by the famous Scottish industrialist Robert Owen in 1825, was to be a manufacturing community without poverty and unemployment. The community survived only three years. Faring little better were the "phalanxes," huge communal buildings structured on the socialist theories of the French thinker Charles Fourier. Based on his belief that there was a rational way to divide work, Fourier suggested, for example, that children would make the best garbage collectors because they didn't mind dirt! And Louisa May Alcott (who later wrote *Little Women* and many other novels and stories) lived with her family at Fruitlands in Massachusetts, which had begun as a rural community of transcendentalists. The rapid failure of these socialist communities was due largely to inadequate planning and organization. Another reason may have been, as Alcott suggested in her satirical reminiscence, *Transcendental Wild Oats,* that the women were left to do all the work while the men philosophized. Nevertheless, it is striking that at a time when so many voluntary associations successfully organized the activities of their members so few cooperative communities succeeded.

The most successful of the nineteenth-century communitarian movements was also a product of the Burned-Over District. In 1830, a young man named Joseph Smith founded the Church of Jesus Christ of Latter-Day Saints based on the teachings of the *Book of Mormon,* which he claimed to have received from an angel in a vision.

Initially, Mormonism, as the new religion became known, seemed little different from the many other new religious groups and utopian communities of the time. But under the benevolent but absolute authority of its patriarch, Joseph Smith, it rapidly gained distinction for its extraordinary communitarianism. Close cooperation and hard work made the Mormon community successful, attracting both new followers and the animosity of neighbors, who resented Mormon exclusiveness and economic success. The Mormons were harassed in New York and driven west to Ohio and then Missouri. Finally they seemed to find an ideal home in Nauvoo, Illinois, where in 1839 they built a model community, achieving almost complete self-government and isolation from non-Mormon neighbors. But in 1844, dissension within the community over Joseph Smith's new doctrine of polygamy (marriage between one man and more than one woman, simultaneously) gave outsiders a chance to intervene. Smith and his brother were arrested peacefully but were killed by a mob from which their jailers failed to protect them.

The beleaguered Mormon community decided to move beyond reach of harm. Led by Brigham Young, the Mormons migrated in 1846 to the Great Salt Lake in present-day Utah. After several lean years (once, a grasshopper plague was stopped by the providential arrival of sea gulls, who ate the insects), the Mormon method of communal settlement proved successful. Their hopes of isolation were dashed, however, by the California Gold Rush of 1849.

ANTISLAVERY AND ABOLITIONISM

The antislavery feeling that was to play such an important role in the politics of the 1840s and 1850s also had its roots in the religious reform movements that began in the 1820s and 1830s. Three groups—free African Americans, Quakers, and militant white reformers—worked to bring an end to slavery, but each in different ways. Their efforts eventually turned a minor reform movement into the dominant political issue of the day.

Antislavery activity was not new. For free African Americans the freedom of other black people had always been a major goal, but in order to achieve legal change they needed white allies. In 1787 antislavery advocates had secured in the Constitution a clause specifying a date after which American participation in the international slave trade could be made illegal, and Congress outlawed it in 1808. By 1800 slavery had been abolished or gradual emancipation enacted in most northern states. In 1820 the Missouri Compromise prohibited slavery in most of the Louisiana Purchase lands. None of these measures, however, addressed the continuing reality of slavery in the South.

The American Colonization Society

The first attempt to "solve" the problem of slavery was a plan for gradual emancipation of slaves (with compensation to their owners) and their resettlement in Africa. This plan was the work of the American Colonization Society, formed in 1817 by northern religious reformers (Quakers prominent among them) and a number of southern slave owners, most from the Upper South and the border states (Kentuckian Henry Clay was a supporter). Northerners were especially eager to send the North's 250,000 free black people back to Africa, describing them, in the words of the society's 1829 report, as "notoriously ignorant, degraded and miserable, mentally diseased, [and] broken-spirited," a characterization that completely ignored the legal and social discrimination they faced. Some northern members of the society also supported laws disenfranchising and restricting the rights of free African Americans. The American Colonization Society was remarkably ineffective; by 1830, it had managed to send only 1,400 black people to a colony in Liberia, West Africa. Critics pointed out that more slaves were born in a week than the society sent back to Africa in a year.

Hannah Harrison Cohoon, *Tree of Life*, 1845, tempera on paper. From the collection of Hancock Shaker Village, Pittsfield, Mass.

Shaker Hannah Cohoon's 1845 painting of the Tree of Life*—her effort to reproduce a vision she had seen while in a religious trance—communicates the intense spirituality of Shaker life.*

African Americans' Fight against Slavery

Most free African Americans rejected colonization, insisting instead on a commitment to the immediate end of slavery and the

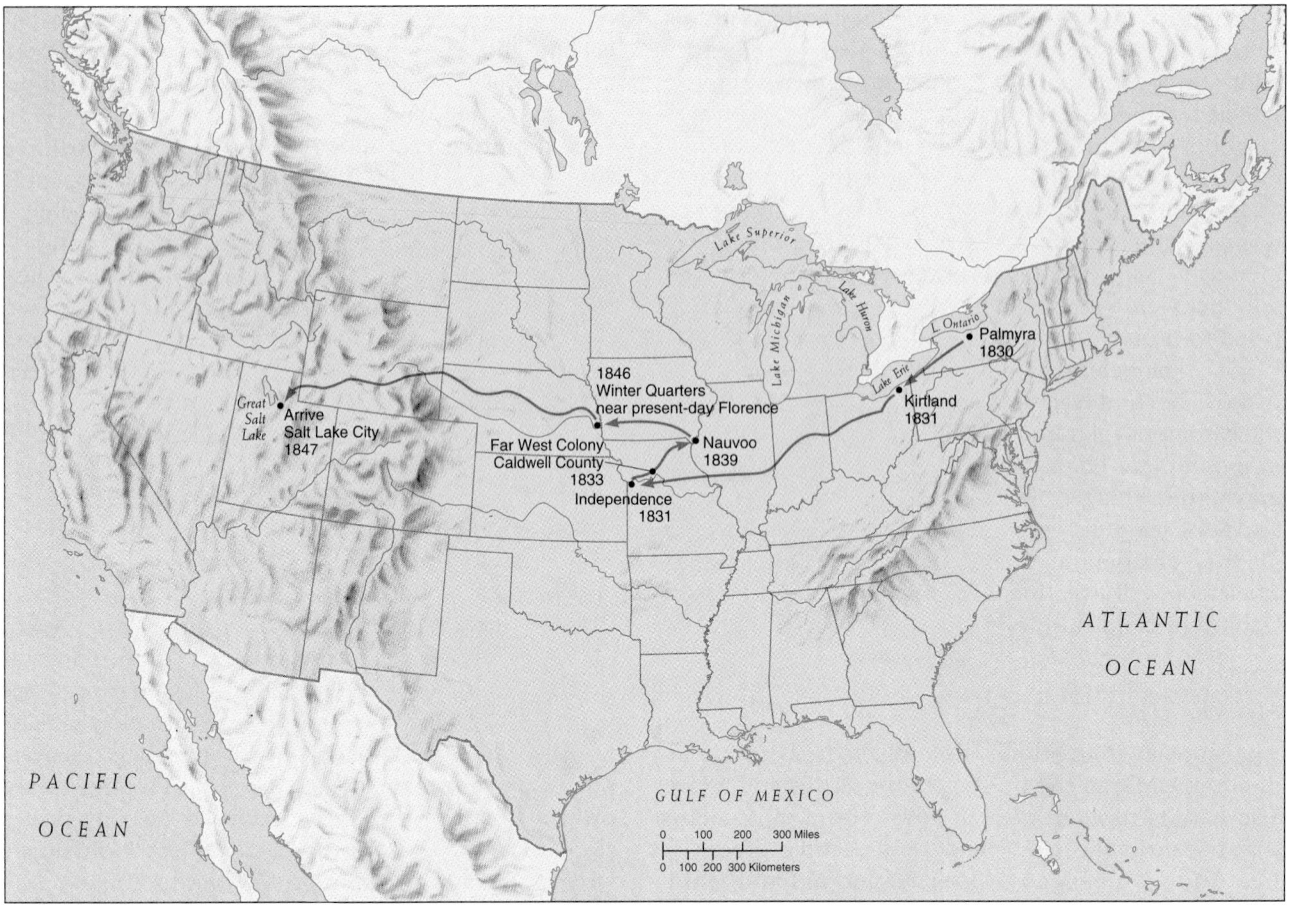

The Mormon Migration, 1830—1847 *The Mormon church and community, founded by Joseph Smith of Palmyra, New York, in 1830, aroused intense opposition. Two early settlements, one in Kirtland, Ohio, and another near Independence, Missouri, were driven out in 1838. The Mormons regrouped and prospered in Nauvoo, Illinois, until the mob murder of Joseph Smith in 1844. Their escape to the west began in 1846, first to Winter Quarters, Nebraska, and finally to the desolate Great Salt Lake region of Utah, where the Mormons hoped to be free of outside interference.*

equal treatment of black people in America. "We are natives of this country," an African American minister in New York pointed out. Then he added bitterly, "We only ask that we be treated as well as foreigners." By 1830 there were at least fifty black abolitionist societies in the North. These organizations held yearly national conventions, where famous African American abolitionists like Frederick Douglass, Harriet Tubman, and Sojourner Truth spoke. The first African American newspaper, founded in 1827 by John Russwurm and Samuel Cornish, announced its antislavery position in its title, *Freedom's Journal.*

In 1829 David Walker, a free African American in Boston, wrote a widely distributed pamphlet, *Appeal to the Colored Citizens of the World,* that encouraged slave rebellion. "We must and shall be free...in spite of you," Walker warned whites. "And woe, woe will be it to you if we have to obtain our freedom by fighting." White Southerners blamed pamphlets such as these and the militant articles of African American journalists for stirring up trouble among southern slaves, and in particular for Nat Turner's revolt in 1831. The vehemence of white southern reaction testifies to the courage of that handful of determined free African Americans who persisted in speaking for their enslaved brothers and sisters long before most white Northerners even noticed.

Abolitionists

The third and best-known group of antislavery reformers was headed by William Lloyd Garrison. In 1831 Garrison broke with the gradualist persuaders of the American Colonization Society and began publishing his own paper, the *Liberator.* In the first issue Garrison declared, "I am in earnest—I will not equivocate—I will not excuse—I will not retreat a single inch—AND I WILL BE HEARD." Garrison, the embodiment of moral indignation, was totally incapable of compromise. His approach was to mount a sweeping crusade condemning slavery as sinful and demanding its immediate abolishment. Garrison's crusade, like evangelical religion, was personal and moral. In reality, Garrison did not expect that all slaves would be freed immediately, but he did want and expect everyone to acknowledge the immorality of slavery. On the other hand, Garrison took the truly radical step of demanding full social equality for African Americans, referring to them individually as "a man and a brother" and "a woman and a sister." Garrison's determination electrified the antislavery movement, but his inability to compromise limited his effectiveness as a leader.

Garrison's moral vehemence radicalized northern antislavery religious groups. Theodore Weld, an evangelical minister, joined Garrison in 1833 in forming the American Anti-Slavery Society. The following year, Weld encouraged a group of students at Lane Theological Seminary in Cincinnati to form an antislavery society. When the seminary's president, Lyman Beecher, sought to suppress it, the students moved en masse to Oberlin College in northern Ohio, where they were joined by revivalist Charles Finney, who became president of the college. Oberlin soon became known as the most liberal college in the country, not only for its antislavery stance but for its acceptance of African American students and of women students as well.

Moral horror over slavery engaged many Northerners deeply in the abolitionist movement. They flocked to hear firsthand accounts of slavery by Frederick Douglass and Sojourner Truth, and by the white sisters from South Carolina, Angelina and Sarah Grimké. Northerners eagerly read slave narratives and books such as Theodore Weld's 1839 *American Slavery As It Is* (based in part on the recollections of Angelina Grimké, whom Weld had married) that provided graphic details of abuse. Lyman Beecher's daughter, Harriet Beecher Stowe, was to draw on the

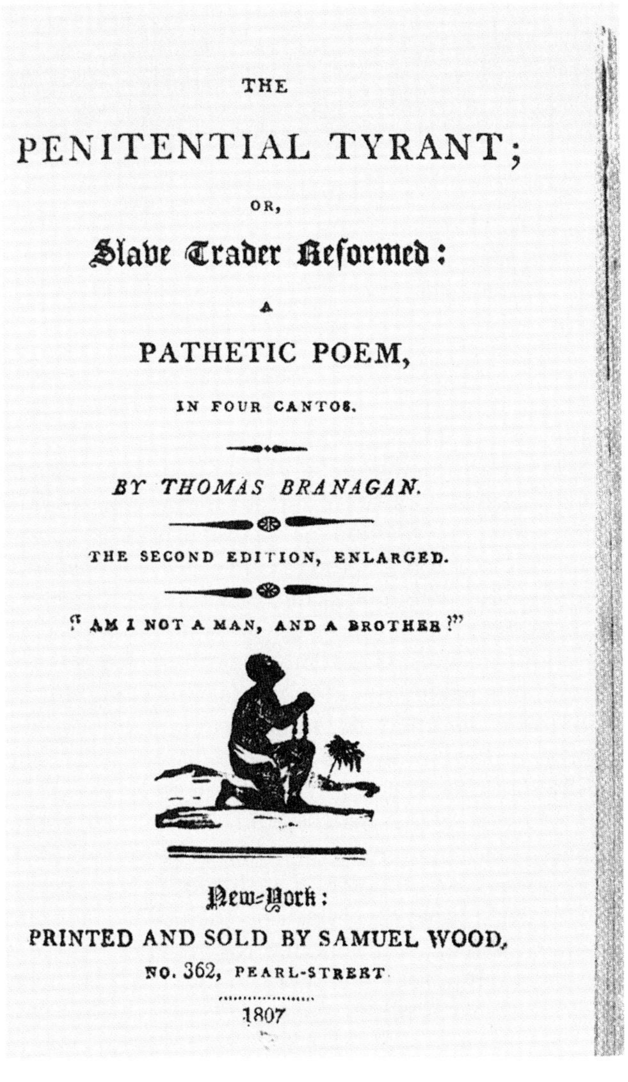
THE

PENITENTIAL TYRANT;

OR,

Slave Trader Reformed:

A

PATHETIC POEM,

IN FOUR CANTOS.

BY THOMAS BRANAGAN.

THE SECOND EDITION, ENLARGED.

"AM I NOT A MAN, AND A BROTHER?"

New-York:

PRINTED AND SOLD BY SAMUEL WOOD,

NO. 362, PEARL-STREET.

1807

The different dates on these two widely used antislavery images are important. The title page of Thomas Branagan's 1807 book includes a then already commonly used image of a male slave. The engraving of a chained female slave was made by Patrick Reason, a black artist, in 1835. The accompanying message, "Am I Not a Woman and a Sister?" spoke particularly to white female abolitionists in the North, who were just becoming active in antislavery movements in the 1830s.

The Philadelphia Anti-Slavery Society was one of the largest and best-known local chapters of the American Anti-Slavery Society, founded in 1833. The national society depended on local chapters to collect signatures for petitions, organize local meetings, and raise the money to print and distribute more than a million pieces of antislavery literature. The Philadelphia chapter, founded in 1832, included a number of Quakers, among whom Lucretia Mott (second from right in the front row) was prominent.

Grimké-Weld book for her immensely popular antislavery novel, *Uncle Tom's Cabin*, published in 1852.

The style of abolitionist writings and speeches was similar to the oratorical style of the religious revivalists. Northern abolitionists believed that a full description of the evils of slavery would force southern slave owners to confront their wrongdoing and lead to a true act of repentance—freeing their slaves. They were confrontational, denunciatory, and personal in their message, much like the evangelical preachers. Southerners, however, regarded abolitionist attacks as libelous and abusive.

Abolitionists adopted another tactic of revivalists and temperance workers when, to enhance their powers of persuasion, they began to publish great numbers of antislavery tracts. In 1835 alone they mailed more than a million pieces of antislavery literature to southern states. This tactic also drew a backlash: southern legislatures banned abolitionist literature, encouraged the harassment and abuse of anyone distributing it, and looked the other way when (as in South Carolina) proslavery mobs seized and burned it. The Georgia legislature even offered a $5,000 reward to anyone who would kidnap William Lloyd Garrison and bring him to the South to stand trial for inciting rebellion. Most seriously, most southern states reacted by toughening laws concerning emancipation, freedom of movement, and all aspects of slave behavior. Hoping to prevent the spread of the abolitionist message, most southern states reinforced laws making it a crime to teach a slave how to read. Ironically, then, the immediate impact of abolitionism in the South was to stifle dissent and make the lives of slaves harder (see Chapter 11).

Even in the North, controversy over abolitionism was common. Some places were prone to anti-abolitionist violence. The Ohio Valley, settled largely by Southerners, was one such place, as were northern cities experiencing the strains of rapid growth, such as Philadelphia. Immigrant Irish, who found themselves pitted against free black people for jobs, were often violently antiabolitionist. A tactic that abolitionists borrowed from revivalists—holding large and emotional meetings—opened the door to mob action. Crowds of people often disrupted such meetings, especially those addressed by Theodore Weld, whose oratorical style earned him the title of "the Most Mobbed Man in the United States." William Lloyd Garrison was stoned, dragged through the streets, and on one occasion almost hanged by a Boston mob. In the three-day New York riot of 1834, abolitionist Arthur Tappan's home and store were sacked at the same time that black churches and homes were damaged and free blacks attacked. In 1837, antislavery editor Elijah P. Lovejoy of Alton, Illinois, was killed and his press destroyed. In 1838, a mob threatened a meeting of the Philadelphia Female Anti-Slavery Society one night and, the next night, burned down the hall in which they had met.

Abolitionism and Politics

Abolitionism began as a social movement but soon intersected with sectional interests and became a national political issue. In the 1830s, massive abolitionist petition drives gathered a total of nearly 700,000 petitions requesting the abolition of slavery and the slave trade in the District of Columbia but were rebuffed by Congress. At southern insistence and with President Andrew Jackson's approval, Congress passed a "gag rule" in 1836 that prohibited discussion of antislavery petitions.

Many Northerners viewed the gag rule and censorship of the mails, which Southerners saw as necessary defenses against abolitionist frenzy, as alarming threats to free speech. First among them was Massachusetts representative John Quincy Adams, the only former president ever to serve in Congress after leaving the executive branch. Adams so publicly and persistently denounced the gag rule as a violation of the constitutional right to petition that it was repealed in 1844. Less well-known Northerners like the thousands of women who canvassed their neighborhoods with petitions made personal commitments to abolitionism that they did not intend to abandon.

John Quincy Adams was also a key figure in the abolitionists' one undoubted victory, the fight to free the fifty-three slaves on the Spanish ship *Amistad* and return them to Africa. Although the Africans successfully mutinied against the *Amistad's* crew in 1839, when the ship was found in American waters a legal battle over their "ownership" ensued, during which the Africans themselves were held in jail. Prominent abolitionists, most notably Lewis Tappan, financed the legal fight which went all the way to the Supreme Court, where Adams won the case for the *Amistad* defendants against the American government, which supported the Spanish claim.

Although abolitionist groups raised the nation's emotional temperature, they failed to achieve the moral unity they had hoped for, and they began to splinter. One perhaps inevitable but nonetheless distressing split was between white and black abolitionists. Frederick Douglass and William Lloyd Garrison parted ways when Douglass, refusing to be limited to a simple recital of his life as a slave, began to make specific suggestions for improvements in the lives of free African Americans. When Douglass chose the path of political action, Garrison denounced him as "ungrateful." Douglass and other free African Americans worked under persistent discrimination, even from antislavery whites; some of the latter refused to hire black people or to meet with them as equals. For example, some Philadelphia Quaker meetings, though devoted to the antislavery cause, maintained segregated seating for black people in their churches. While many white reformers eagerly pressed for civil equality for African Americans, they did not accept the idea of social equality. On the other hand, black and white "stations" worked closely in the risky enterprise of passing fugitive slaves north over the famous Underground Railroad, as the various routes by which slaves made their way to freedom were called. Contrary to abolitionist legend, however, it was free African Americans, rather than white people, who played the major part in helping the fugitives.

Among white abolitionists, William Lloyd Garrison remained controversial, especially after 1837, when he espoused a radical program that included women's rights, pacifism, and the abolition of the prisons and asylums that other reformers were working to establish. In 1840 the abolitionist movement formally split. The majority moved toward party politics (which Garrison abhorred), founding the Liberty Party and choosing James G. Birney (whom Theodore Weld had converted to abolitionism) as their presidential candidate. Thus the abolitionist movement, which began as an effort at moral reform, took its first major step into politics, and this step in turn led to the formation of the Republican Party in the 1850s and to the Civil War.

For one particular group of antislavery reformers, the abolitionist movement opened up new possibilities for action. Through their participation in antislavery activity, some women came to a vivid realization of the social constraints on their activism.

THE WOMEN'S RIGHTS MOVEMENT

American women, without the vote or a role in party politics, found a field of activity in social reform movements. There was scarcely a reform movement in which women were not actively involved. Often men

Women's gatherings, like the first women's rights convention in Seneca Falls in 1848 and this meeting of strikers in Lynn in 1860, were indicators of widespread female activism.

were the official leaders of such movements, and some women—especially those in the temperance, moral reform, and abolitionist movements—formed all-female chapters to define and implement their own policies and programs.

The majority of women did not participate in these activities, for they were fully occupied with housekeeping and child rearing (families with five children were the average). A few women—mostly members of the new middle class, who could afford servants—had the time and energy to look beyond their immediate tasks. Touched by the religious revival, these women enthusiastically joined reform movements. Led thereby to challenge social restrictions, some, like the Grimké sisters, found that their commitment carried them beyond the limits of what was considered acceptable activity for women.

The Grimké Sisters

Sarah and Angelina Grimké, members of a prominent South Carolina slaveholding family, rejected slavery out of religious conviction and moved north to join a Quaker community near Philadelphia. In the 1830s, these two sisters found themselves drawn into the growing antislavery agitation in the North. Because they knew about slavery firsthand, they were in great demand as speakers. At first they spoke to "parlor meetings" of women only, as was considered proper. But interested men kept sneaking into the talks, and soon the sisters found themselves speaking to mixed gatherings. The meetings got larger and larger, and soon the sisters realized that they had become the first female public speakers in America. In 1837 Angelina Grimké became the first woman to address a meeting of the Massachusetts state legislature (Sarah Bagley, the Lowell worker, was the second).

The sisters challenged social norms on two grounds. The antislavery movement was widely disapproved, and many famous male orators were criticized by the press and mobbed at meetings. The Grimké sisters were criticized for speaking because they were women. A letter from a group of ministers cited the Bible in reprimanding the sisters for stepping out of "woman's proper sphere" of silence and subordination. Sarah Grimké answered the ministers in her 1838 *Letters on the Equality of the Sexes and the Condition of Women,* claiming that "men and women were CREATED EQUAL. . . .Whatever is right for a man to do, is right for woman." She followed with this ringing assertion: "I seek no favors for my sex. I surrender not our claim to equality. All I ask of our brethren is, that they will take their feet from off our necks and permit us to stand upright on that ground which God designed us to occupy."

Not all female assertiveness was as dramatic as Sarah Grimké's, but women in the antislavery movement found it a constant struggle to be heard. Some solved the problem of male dominance by forming their own groups, like the Philadelphia Female Anti-Slavery Society. In the antislavery movement and other reform groups as well, men accorded women a secondary role, even when—as was frequently the case—women constituted a majority of the members.

Women's Rights

The Seneca Falls Convention of 1848, the first women's rights convention in American history, was an outgrowth of almost twenty years of female activity in social reform. Every year after 1848 women gathered to hold women's rights conventions and to work for political, legal, and social equality. Over the years, in response to persistent lobbying, states passed property laws more favorable to women and altered divorce laws to allow women to retain custody of

CHRONOLOGY

1817	American Colonization Society founded
1820s	Shaker colonies grow
1825	New Harmony founded, fails three years later
1826	American Society for the Promotion of Temperance founded
1827	Workingmen's Party founded in Philadelphia *Freedom's Journal* begins publication Public school movement begins in Massachusetts
1829	David Walker, *Appeal to the Colored Citizens of the World*, published
1830	Joseph Smith founds Church of Jesus Christ of Latter-Day Saints (Mormon Church) Charles G. Finney's revivals in Rochester
1831	William Lloyd Garrison begins publishing antislavery newspaper, the *Liberator*
1832	Immigration begins to increase
1833	American Anti-Slavery Society founded by Garrison and Theodore Weld
1834	First Female Moral Reform Society founded in New York National Trades Union formed
1836	Congress passes "gag rule" to prevent discussion of antislavery petitions
1837	Antislavery editor Elijah P. Lovejoy killed Angelina Grimké addresses Massachusetts legislature Sarah Grimké, *Letters on the Equality of the Sexes and the Condition of Women* Panic begins seven-year recession
1839	Theodore Weld publishes *American Slavery As It Is*
1840s	New York and Boston complete public water systems
1840	Liberty Party founded
1843	Millerites await the end of the world Dorothea Dix spearheads asylum reform movement
1844	Mormon leader Joseph Smith killed by mob
1845	New York creates city police force Beginning of Irish Potato Famine and heavy Irish immigration
1846	Mormons begin migration to the Great Salt Lake
1848	Women's Rights Convention at Seneca Falls John Noyes founds Oneida Community

children. Teaching positions in higher education opened up to women, as did jobs in some other occupations, and women gained the vote in some states, beginning with Wyoming Territory in 1869. In 1920, seventy-two years after universal woman suffrage was first proposed at Seneca Falls, women's right to vote was at last guaranteed in the Nineteenth Amendment to the Constitution.

Historians have only recently realized how much the reform movements of this "Age of the Common Man" were due to the efforts of the "common woman." Women played a vital role in all the social movements of the day. In doing so they implicitly challenged the popular notion of separate spheres for men and women—the public world for him, home and family for her. The separate spheres argument, although it heaped praise on women for their allegedly superior moral qualities, was meant to exclude them from political life. The reforms discussed in this chapter show clearly that women reformers believed they had a right and a duty to propose solutions for the moral and social problems of the day. Empowered by their own religious beliefs and activism, the Seneca Falls reformers spoke for all American women when they demanded an end to the unfair restrictions they suffered as women.

CONCLUSION

Beginning in the 1820s, the market revolution changed the size and social order of America's preindustrial cities and towns. Immigration, dramatically rapid population growth, and changes in working life and class structure created a host of new urban problems ranging from sanitation to civic order. These changes occurred so rapidly that they seemed overwhelming. Older, face-to-face methods of social control no longer worked. To fill the gap, new kinds of associations—the political party, the religious crusade, the reform cause, the union movement—sprang up. These associations were new manifestations of the deep human desire for social connection, for continuity, and—especially in the growing cities—for social order. A striking aspect of these associations was the uncompromising nature of the attitudes and beliefs on which they were based. Most groups were formed of like-minded people who wanted to impose their will on others. Such intolerance boded ill for the future. If political parties, religious bodies, and reform groups were to splinter along sectional lines (as happened in the 1850s), political compromise would be very difficult. In the meantime, however, Americans came to terms with the market revolution by engaging in a passion for improvement. As a perceptive foreign observer, Francis Grund, noted, "Americans love their country not as it is but as it will be."

REVIEW QUESTIONS

1. What impact did the new immigration of the 1840s and 1850s have on American cities?
2. Why did urbanization produce so many problems?
3. What motivated the social reformers of the period? Were they benevolent helpers or dictatorial social controllers? Study several reform causes and discuss similarities and differences among them.
4. Abolitionism differed little from other reforms in its tactics, but the effects of antislavery activism were politically explosive. Why was this so?

RECOMMENDED READING

Arthur Bestor, *Backwoods Utopias* (1950). The standard work on utopian communities.

Paul Boyer, *Urban Masses and Moral Order in America, 1820–1920* (1978). Interprets reform as an effort to reestablish the moral order of the preindustrial community.

Amy Bridges, *A City in the Republic: Antebellum New York and the Origins of Machine Politics* (1984). An innovative look at the transition from elite political control to machine politics.

Paul A. Gilje, *The Road to Mobocracy: Popular Disorder in New York City, 1763–1834* (1987). Provides an interesting and entertaining description of the many varieties of civic disorder of the day.

Oscar Handlin, *Boston's Immigrants: A Study in Acculturation* (rev. ed., 1959). A pathbreaking exploration of conflict and adaptation among Boston's Irish community.

Daniel Walker Howe, "The Evangelical Movement and Political Culture in the North during the Second Party System," *Journal of American History*, 78:1 (March 1991). An award-winning article that explores the connections among religion, politics, and reform.

Leon Litwack, *North of Slavery: The Negro in the Free States, 1790–1860* (1961). The standard source on free black people in the North.

Eric Lott, *Love and Theft: Blackface Minstrelsy and the American Working Class* (1993). Explores the complicated relationships between working-class amusements and racial attitudes.

Steven Mintz, *Moralists and Modernizers: America's Pre-Civil War Reformers* (1995). A brief but inclusive study of reforms and reformers.

David Roediger, *The Wages of Whiteness* (1991). Explores the links between artisanal republicanism, labor organization, and white racism.

David Rothman, *The Discovery of the Asylum: Social Order and Disorder in the New Republic* (1971). Explores institutional reforms.

Kathryn Sklar, *Catharine Beecher: A Study in American Domesticity* (1973). An absorbing "life and times" that explores the possibilities and limits of women's roles in the early nineteenth century.

Sean Wilentz, *Chants Democratic: New York City and the Rise of the American Working Class, 1788–1850* (1983). An important book, rooted in social history, that reveals how workers acted upon their understanding of republicanism in confronting the changes wrought by the market revolution.

ADDITIONAL BIBLIOGRAPHY

Immigration

Kathleen Neils Conzen, *Immigrant Milwaukee, 1836–1860* (1976)
Hasia Diner, *Erin's Daughters in America* (1983)
Jay P. Dolan, *The Immigrant Church: New York's Irish and German Catholics, 1815–1865* (1975)
Oscar Handlin, *The Uprooted* (1951; 2nd ed. 1973)
Noel Ignatiev, *How the Irish Became White* (1995)
Kerby A. Miller, *Emigrants and Exiles: Ireland and the Irish Exodus to North America* (1985)
Stanley Nadel, *Little Germany: Ethnicity, Religion, and Class in New York City, 1845–1880* (1990)
LaVern J. Rippley, *The German-Americans* (1976)
Dennis P. Ryan, *Beyond the Ballot Box: A Social History of the Boston Irish, 1845–1917* (1989)

Urban and Labor

Oliver E. Allen, *The Tiger: The Rise and Fall of Tammany Hall* (1995)
W. Jeffrey Bolster, *Black Jacks: African American Seamen in the Age of Sail* (1997)
Michael Feldberg, *The Philadelphia Riots of 1844: A Study of Ethnic Conflict* (1975)
Herbert G. Gutman, *Work, Culture, and Society in Industrializing America: Essays in American Working-Class History* (1976)
James Oliver Horton, *Free People of Color: Inside the African American Community* (1993)
James Oliver Horton and Lois E. Horton, *Black Bostonians: Family Life and Community Struggle in the Antebellum North* (1979)
David Montgomery, *Citizen Worker: The Experience of Workers in the United States with Democracy and the Free Market during the Nineteenth Century* (1993)
Gary B.Nash, *Forging Freedom: Philadelphia's Black Community, 1720–1840* (1988)
Edward Pessen, *Most Uncommon Jacksonians: The Radical Leaders of the Early Labor Movement* (1967)
Mary Ryan, *Civic Wars: Democracy and Public Life* (1997)
Amy Gilman Srebnick, *The Mysterious Death of Mary Roberts, Sex and Culture in the Nineteenth Century* (1995)
Sam Bass Warner, *The Private City: Philadelphia in Three Periods of Its Growth* (1968)

Religion, Reform, and Utopianism

Lawrence Cremin, *American Education: The National Experience, 1783–1861* (1981)
Whitney R. Cross, *The Burned-Over District: The Social and Intellectual History of Enthusiastic Religion in Western New York, 1800–1850* (1950)
Jed Dannenbaum, *Drink and Disorder: Temperance Reform in Cincinnati from the Washingtonian Revival to the WCTU* (1984)
Barbara Epstein, *The Politics of Domesticity: Women, Evangelism, and Temperance in Nineteenth Century America* (1981)
Michael Fellman, *The Unbounded Frame: Freedom and Community in Nineteenth-Century American Utopianism* (1973)
Lori D. Ginzberg, *Women and the Work of Benevolence: Morality, Politics, and Class in the Nineteenth-Century United States* (1990)
Klaus J. Hansen, *Mormonism and the American Experience* (1981)
Carl F. Kaestle, *Pillars of the Republic: Common Schools and American Society, 1780–1860* (1983)
Louis J. Kern, *An Ordered Love: Sex Roles and Sexuality in Victorian Utopias—The Shakers, the Mormons, and the Oneida Community* (1981)
W. J. Rorabaugh, *The Alcoholic Republic: An American Tradition* (1979)
Ann C. Rose, *Transcendentalism as a Social Movement, 1830–1850* (1981)
Timothy L. Smith, *Revivalism and Social Reform: American Protestantism on the Eve of the Civil War* (1980)

Abolitionism

R.J.M. Blackett, *Building an Antislavery Wall: Black Americans in the Abolitionist Movement, 1830–1860* (1983)
David Brion Davis, *The Problem of Slavery in the Age of Revolution, 1770–1823* (1975)
Louis Gerteis, *Morality and Utility in American Antislavery Reform* (1987)
Howard Jones, *Mutiny on the Amistad* (1987).
Jean Fagan Yellin, *Women and Sisters: The Antislavery Feminists in American Culture* (1989)

Women's Rights

Carl N. Degler, *At Odds: Women and the Family in America from the Revolution to the Present* (1980)
Ellen C. Dubois, *Feminism and Suffrage: The Emergence of an Independent Women's Movement in America, 1848–1869* (1978)
Keith Melder, *Beginnings of Sisterhood: The American Women's Rights Movement, 1800–1850* (1977)
Sandra S. Weber, *Special History Study, Women's Rights National Historical Park, Seneca Falls, New York* (1985)

Biography

Robert H. Abzug, *Passionate Liberator, Theodore Dwight Weld and the Dilemma of Reform* (1980)
Frederick Douglass, *The Narrative of the Life of Frederick Douglass, An American Slave* (1845)
Elisabeth Griffith, *In Her Own Right: The Life of Elizabeth Cady Stanton* (1984)
Nathan I. Huggins, *Slave and Citizen: The Life of Frederick Douglass* (1980)
Gerda Lerner, *The Grimké Sisters from South Carolina: Pioneers for Women's Rights and Abolition* (1967)
John L. Thomas, *The Liberator: William Lloyd Garrison* (1963)

IMMIGRATION & COMMUNITY

The Changing Face of Ethnicity in America

1800–1860

Between 1790 and 1820, the rate of immigration to the United States was low, held in check by the Napoleonic Wars in Europe. It began to pick up in the 1820s, increased sharply in the 1830s, and reached a record 430,000 in 1854. As immigration increased, the ethnic composition of the immigrant stream changed. Most of the new immigrants were Irish, driven from home by the Potato Famine of 1845, and German, driven by economic and political unrest in the German Principalities.

Until the 1880s, the task of receiving immigrants fell completely on cities and states, not the federal government. New York City, by far the largest port of entry, did not even establish an official reception center until 1855, when Castle Garden, at the bottom of Manhattan Island (near present-day Battery Park), was so designated.

The influx of mostly poor, mostly Catholic foreigners provoked nativist hostility among many Protestant, native-born Americans, including many leaders of the major reform movements. It would be a mistake, however, to think that immigration was unwelcome to everyone. Industries needed willing workers, and western states were eager for settlers. In 1852 Wisconsin appointed a commissioner of emigration with responsibility for attracting Europeans to the state. Soon Iowa and Minnesota joined Wisconsin in advertising widely in Europe for settlers.

Immigrant labor fueled the nation's expanding economy and helped turn wilderness into farmland. Many of the changes in industry and transportation that accompanied the market revolution would have been impossible without immigrants. Irish contract workers, for example, were essential to the completion of the Erie Canal in 1825. And Irish women and men kept the mills at Lowell operating when the mill operators, facing increasing competition, sought cheaper labor to replace their original labor force of farm women.

Irish immigration to the United States dated from colonial times. Many of Ireland's young people, with no hope of owning land at home, had long looked to America for better opportunities. But in 1845 Ireland's green fields of potato plants turned black with blight, and for five years a catastrophic famine ravaged the land. The Irish had two choices: starve or leave. One million people died, and another 1.5 million emigrated, most to the United States. The Famine Irish were America's first major refugee group. Starving, suffering from disease (thousands died of typhus during the voyage), and destitute, hundreds of thousands disembarked in the east-coast ports of New York, Philadelphia, Boston, and Baltimore. Lacking the money to go inland, they remained in the cities. Crowded together in miserable housing, desperate for work at any wages, foreign in their religion and pastimes (drinking and fighting, their critics said), tenaciously nationalistic and bitterly anti-British, they created ethnic enclaves of a kind new to American cities.

The largest number of Irish immigrants settled in New York. Fewer settled in Boston, but that city, smaller and more homogeneous than New York, was overwhelmed by the influx. By 1850, a quarter of Boston's population was Irish. The home of Puritanism and the center of American intellectualism, Boston was not welcoming. All over the city in places of business and in homes normally eager for domestic servants the signs went up: "No Irish Need Apply." The Irish were able to get only the worst and poorest-paying jobs and could afford housing only in an area of East Boston that was described by a health committee in 1849 as "a perfect hive of human beings, without comforts and mostly without common necessaries; in many cases, huddled together like brutes, without regard to sex or age or sense of decency."

Despite poverty and local hostility, the Irish created within their neighborhoods an impressive network of Catholic churches and schools, mutual aid societies, and religious and social clubs. And almost from the moment of their arrival, the Irish sent huge sums of money back to Ireland so that relatives could join them in America. For however bad the conditions in the adopted country, they were better than those in Ireland. As one newcomer wrote, "There is a great many ill conveniences here, but no empty bellies."

Irish immigrants changed American urban politics. In Boston, they quickly took over the local Democratic Party, opposing that city's traditional, Whig-dominated power structure. Irish political strength lay at the neighborhood level. Many politicians were saloonkeepers, for the saloon was the secular center of Irish society—much to the horror of temperance reformers. One Irish saloonkeeper, Patrick Joseph Kennedy, founded one of America's most famous political dynasties. Barely a century after Patrick's birth into a poor immigrant family in Boston, his grandson John Fitzgerald Kennedy was elected the first Irish Catholic president of the United States.

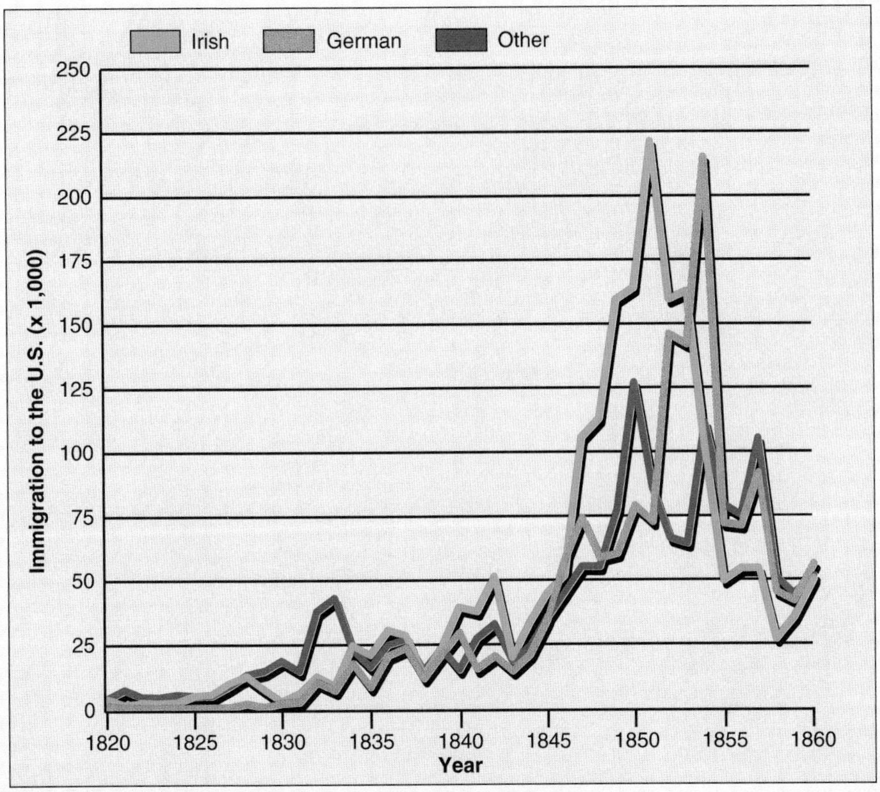

Immigration to the United States, 1820–1860

The typical German immigrant was a small farmer or artisan dislodged by the same market forces that were at work in America: the industrialization of manufacturing and the commercialization of farming. The first two major ports of embarkation for the Germans were Bremen (in northern Germany) and Le Havre (in northern France), which were also the main ports for the importation of American tobacco and cotton. The tobacco boats bore the Bremen passengers to Baltimore, and the cotton ships took them to New Orleans, a major entry point for European immigrants until the Civil War. From these ports, many Germans made their way up the Mississippi and Ohio valleys, where they settled in Milwaukee, Pittsburgh, Cincinnati, and St. Louis and on farms in Ohio, Indiana, Missouri, and Texas. In Texas the nucleus of a German community began with a Mexican land grant in the 1830s. Few Germans settled in the South.

German agricultural communities took a distinctive form that fostered cultural continuity. Immigrants formed predominantly German towns by clustering, or taking up adjoining land. A small cluster could support German churches, German-language schools, and German customs and thereby attract other Germans, some directly from Europe and some from other parts of the United States. Non-German neighbors often sold out and moved on, but the Germans stayed and passed on their land to succeeding generations. They used soil conservation practices that were unusual for the time. German cluster communities still endure in Texas, the Midwest, and the Pacific Northwest, and more American farm families are today of German origin than of any other background.

Large German populations settled in "little Germanies" in New Orleans, St. Louis, Cincinnati, and Milwaukee, and in the eastern cities of New York, Philadelphia, and Baltimore. There they developed a flourishing community culture, with German language schools, theater groups, and a German-language press. In the summer, entire families frequented beer gardens, where there was always music, in the semi-rural outskirts of the cities. At first the Germans were greeted with hostility (temperance societies were especially unhappy about the beer gardens), but by 1860, German culture, with its emphasis on music, intellectual interests, and love of nature, had become widely influential. Among its contributions to American life were not only beer (then a new drink to most Americans) but gymnasiums and candle-lit Christmas trees. Germans also had an important impact on American public education, which was then in its formative years. The first kindergarten in America was founded by Margarethe Schurz in Watertown, Wisconsin, where she and her husband, Carl Schurz, settled in 1856. German ideas were also influential in the development of music programs, gymnastics, vocational training, and high schools.

Other areas attracting immigrants in the early nineteenth century were Gold Rush California, which drew, among others, numbers of Chinese, and Utah Territory, where the Mormon Church recruited many former English factory workers to its new Zion. In Texas and Mexico, a high proportion of residents were listed as foreign-born in 1860 who were in fact native-born Mexicans who had become foreigners only by virtue of the conquest of their homeland by the United States in the Mexican-American war.

The Chinese who came to California in the 1850s following the Gold Rush worked in the mines, most as independent prospectors. Other miners disliked their industriousness and their clanishness. One reporter noted groups of twenty or thirty "Chinamen, stools, tables,

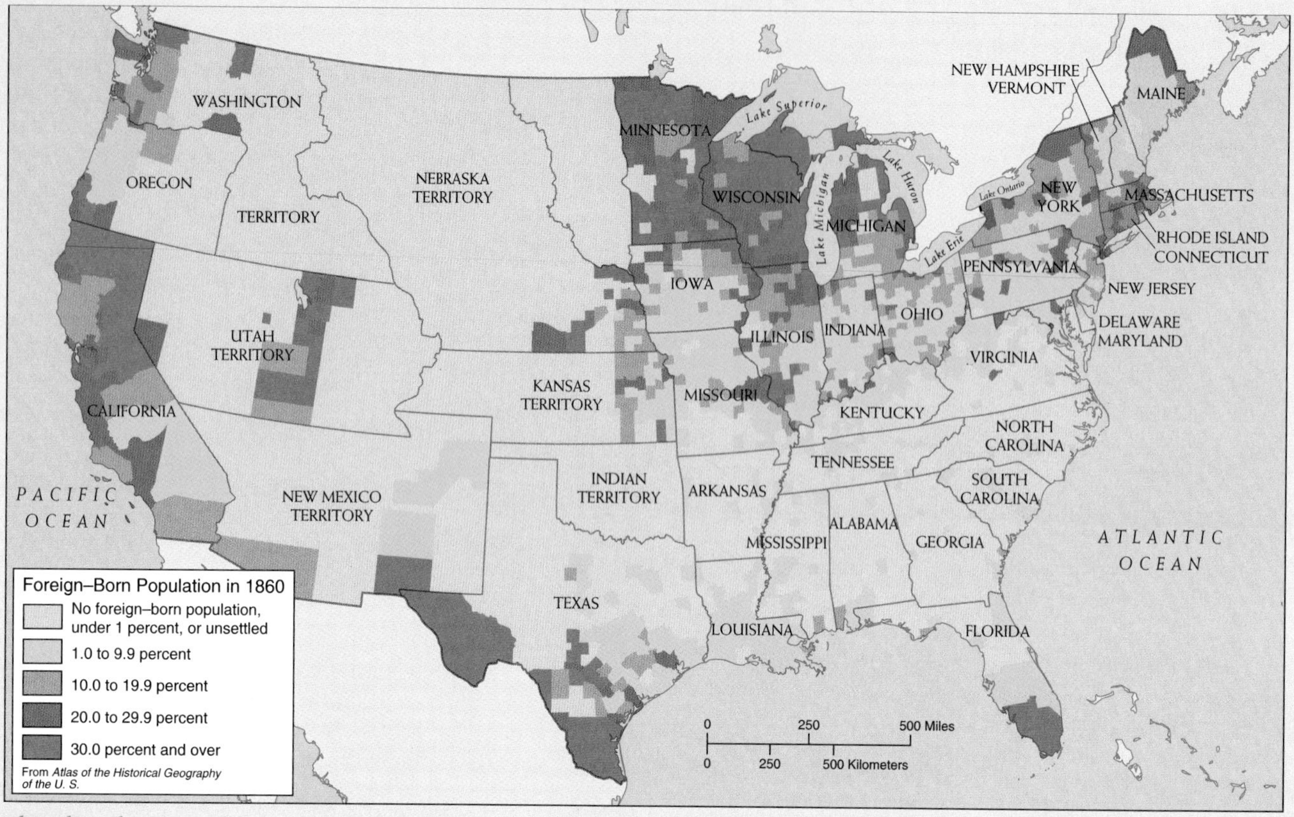

The distribution of foreign-born residents of the United States in 1860.

cooking utensils, bunks, etc., all huddled up together in indiscriminate confusion, and enwreathed with dense smoke, inhabiting close cabins, so small that one would not be of sufficient size to allow a couple of Americans to breathe in it." In 1852 the California legislature enacted a Foreign Miner's Tax aimed at the Chinese. By the time the tax was repealed in 1870, it had cost Chinese miners five million dollars. By the mid-1860s, Chinese workers made up 90 percent of the laborers building the Central Pacific Railroad, replacing more expensive white laborers and sowing the seeds of the long-lasting hostility of American workers toward Chinese. In the meantime, however, San Francisco's Chinatown, the oldest Chinese ethnic enclave in America, became a well established, thriving community. In the years to come, as hostility against the Chinese broke into violence, Chinatowns in San Francisco and elsewhere served a vital function as safe refuges for the Chinese who remained in the United States.

IN THEIR OWN WORDS

The unprecedented immigration of the 1840s and 1850s evoked the first organized nativist (antiforeign) movement in American history. As immigration swelled the country's previously small Catholic population, Protestant ministers became alarmed. One of them was Reverend Lyman Beecher, who equated Catholicism with the antidemocratic powers of Europe and suggested that Catholic immigrants followed their bidding. Despite his disclaimer, Beecher viewed immigration as a religious as well as a political threat.

> Catholic Europe is throwing swarm on swarm [of immigrants] upon our shores. There is evidently a supervision abroad—and one here—by which they come, and set down together, in city or country, as a Catholic body, and are led or followed quickly by a Catholic priesthood, who maintain over them in the land of strangers and unknown tongues an ascendency as absolute as they are able to exert in Germany itself.
>
> In the beginning this eruption of revolutionary Europe was not anticipated, and we opened our doors wide to the influx and naturalization of foreigners. But it is becoming a terrific inundation; it has increased upon our native population from five to thirty-seven percent, and is every year advancing. It seeks, of course, to settle down upon the unoccupied territory of the West, and may at no distant day equal, and even outnumber the native population.
>
> But what if this emigration, self-moved and slow in the beginning, is now rolling its broad tide at the bidding of the powers of Europe hostile to free

institutions, and associated in holy alliance to arrest and put them down? Is this a vain fear? Are not the continental powers alarmed at the march of liberal opinions, and associated to put them down?...A tenth part of the suffrage of the nation,...condensed and wielded by the Catholic powers of Europe, might decide our elections, perplex our policy, inflame and divide the nation, break the bond of our union, and throw down our free institutions....

I have no fear of the Catholics, considered simply as a religious denomination, and unallied to the church and state establishments of the European governments hostile to republican institutions.

Let the Catholics mingle with us as Americans, and come with their children under the full action of our common schools and republican institutions, and the various powers of assimilation, and we are prepared cheerfully to abide the consequences. If in these circumstances the Protestant religion cannot stand before the Catholic, let it go down, and we will sound no alarm, and ask no aid, and make no complaint. It is no ecclesiastical quarrel to which we would call the attention of the American nation.[1]

Compelled by the Potato Famine to migrate to America, many Irish felt an enduring longing for their homeland, as the following song of lament reflects.

Farewell to thee, Erin mavourneen,
Thy valleys I'll tread nevermore;
This heart that now bleeds for thy sorrows,
Will waste on a far distant shore.
The green sods lie cold on my parents,
A cross marks the place of their rest,—
The wind that moans sadly above them,
Will waft their poor child to the West.[2]

Few personal memoirs from Irish immigrants of this period survive, but the combined effects of the Famine Exodus and the hostile American reception were felt in later generations, as William Alfred's memoir of his great-grandmother, Anna Maria Gavin, attests.

Of Ireland she rarely spoke, save to recall that she was often hungry there and that for her main meal she often ate cress out of the brooks on oaten bread with a bit of lard. Although she always used to say she had no desire to return to Ireland to live, she lived out of a trunk to her dying day, and taught her children to do the same. I myself, till well on in my twenties, felt that Ireland, which I had never seen, was my true country. When, over eighty, she died, it did not seem strange six months afterward to receive a clipping from an Irish newspaper, which read: "Died in Exile: Anna Maria Gavin Egan."

Of her first years here, she never tired of speaking. She and her mother landed at Castle Garden and walked up Broadway to City Hall, with bundles of clothes and pots and featherbeds in their arms. The singing of the then exposed telegraph wires frightened them, as did the bustle of the people in the streets. They lost their fear when they met an Irish policeman who directed them to a rooming house on Baxter Street.

Her training as a "manty-maker" (mantua-maker, in other words, dressmaker) gave her an advantage over other girls of her age. She got a job fast. On her way from work the first year, she nightly passed a house in whose tall, lit first-floor windows sat the most beautiful women she had ever seen, dressed to the nines, their hair as trimly curled, their faces painted fresh as new French china dolls. After weeks of gawking, she built up the courage to hazard a smile. "Come up here...," one of the women called to her, "and we'll wipe that smile off your face."[3]

On the other edge of the continent in California, another new immigrant group, the Chinese, were making their presence felt. By 1852 there were nearly 25,000 Chinese in California, attracted by the Gold Rush. They did not always, at first, encounter hostility, as the following report in a California paper of 1852 suggests.

Quite a large number of the Celestials [Chinese] have arrived among us of late, enticed thither by the golden romance that has filled the world. Scarcely a ship arrives that does not bring an increase to this worthy integer of our population. [Soon] the China boys will vote at the same polls, study at the same schools and bow at the same altar as our own countrymen.[4]

German Beer Halls, like this one pictured on New York's Bowery, offered music and contact with nature as well as beer from the owners' own breweries. Much to the dismay of American temperance reformers, German immigrants viewed beer halls and gardens as gathering places for the entire family.

Gift of Mrs. Robert M. Littlejohn, Museum of the City of New York. 33.169.1

Samuel Waugh's The Bay and Harbor of New York, *painted in 1855, shows the newly opened Castle Garden, the city's first official reception center for immigrants, receiving a boatload of newcomers from Ireland and perhaps from Germany. Note the anti-Irish caricatures, including the trunk on the right labeled "Pat Murfy for Ameriky." A Chinese junk rides at anchor in the harbor, a reminder that not all immigration in this period was from Europe.*

Another newspaper report described the emerging Chinatown of San Francisco.

> The majority of the houses were of Chinese importation and were stores, stocked with hams, tea, dried fish, dried ducks, and other Chinese eatables, besides copper pots and kettles, fans, shawls, chessmen, and all sorts of curiosities. Suspended over the doors were brilliantly-colored boards covered with Chinese writings, and with several yards of red ribbon streaming from them; while the streets thronged with Celestials, chattering vociferously as they rushed about from store to store.[5]

The large German immigrant population was more geographically dispersed than either the Irish or the Chinese. Their experience is also better documented with firsthand accounts, because many more German immigrants than Irish sent letters home to family members and wrote reminiscences. Many German immigrants brought farming skills with them to America and put them to use, often in company with kin and friends, in rural ethnic clusters. Wilhelmina Stille, her brother Wilhelm Stille, and her fiance Wilhelm Krumme settled together along the Ohio River near Wheeling, Virginia (now West Virginia). The following letter, written in October 1838, is from Wilhelmina Stille to her mother.

> We got married on August 10th. We've bought 80 acres of land and our brother has too, they are next to one another but his is so much better it cost 400 talers and ours 300 talers, we paid 200 talers of it since we didn't have any more. So we're asking you, dear mother and brothers in the name of the Lord, send me the rest of my money, please don't fail me because we have nowhere else to turn. I also want to tell you that my brother Wilhelm left his boss last fall and went down the river on a boat that was loaded with all kinds of goods, flour, potatoes, string beans, cabbage, onions, apples and two others had a quarter of it each. The city is called Neuoliens [New Orleans] which is 15 hundred miles away it's in South America there they can't grow such things. When he got back he started to work on his land, he's built himself a house and has already cleared 3 acres of farmland. We live 3 hours away from Wilingen [Wheeling] right on the road and are very happy for I have a happy marriage and live in peace.[6]

Another German immigrant, Carl Blümer, settled in Santa Fé before the Mexican-American War. As the following letter of October 31, 1852, suggests, he and his brother August were caught up in some of the dramatic events of America's westward expansion.

> My dearest, my eternally beloved mother:
> Your reproach, my dear mother, is justified; years have passed without my writing to you; I don't

want to try to excuse myself, only to the extent that I knew for certain that August [his brother] had sent you all my news until he left for California. Mother! Mother! Brother August is no more! August came here, to Santa Fé, in the spring of 1849; but he only stayed with me for a few months, and went from here to California, thinking and hoping to make a fortune more quickly there. He arrived safely in California; went to the gold mines and wrote his *last* letter to me from the gold mines in Mariposa, in California, in the winter of 1849. Then I didn't hear anything from him for a long time, until I finally received a letter the following year from his brother-in-law, who informed me that he had died in August 1850 in the gold mines on the Yuba River in California. He fell ill with abdominal ailments, and he passed away, calm and composed, after about a month. A German, who worked with him, wrote that he was buried decently. Peace be to his ashes in a foreign land, in an unknown place! His spirit will hover about us in love!...

I myself, my dear mother, have almost always been well, in this country, since 1836; the climate here is one of the nicest, at least the healthiest, on earth. I've been married for about 4 years; my wife is a Mexican, the youngest daughter of a good but poor family; she is named Felisiana Quintana y Alarid. She is pretty about 26 years old. She presented me with a daughter as a first-born child, whom we baptized Carlota, (Charlotte). My second is a boy; named Carlos (Karl or Charles) and is about 15 months old. My business here has almost always been as a merchant; about a year ago I gave up my trading company and am mostly employed in the service of the government. Since the United States of North America took possession of this country, as a result of the war, since the year 1846, I have always had one or other government post; *Treasurer* I have had since 1846 and I still have; my yearly salary is 500 dollars, about 700 Prussian talers. Felisiana sends you, dear mother, her filial love and devotion, and all of you a dear and sisterly kiss.

Farewell!/Forever/ Your true son
and your true brother and uncle, Carl Blümer[7]

Carl Schurz, who emigrated from Germany in 1852 when the nativist political movement was at its height, gained great prominence in the United States, becoming a general in the Union Army, a senator from Missouri, and secretary of the interior in the administration of Rutherford B. Hayes. In this letter to a German friend, he reflects with pride on some of his accomplishments in his adopted country.

Here in America I lived for several years quietly and unobtrusively in an ideally happy family circle until at last in the year '56, when the movement against slavery developed magnificently, I found myself drawn into public life. I knew that I should accomplish something. America is the country for ambitious capability, and the foreigner who studies its conditions thoroughly, and with full appreciation, can procure for himself an even greater field of activity than the native. My success surprised even myself; I found my boldest expectations outdone. I flung myself with all my heart into the Antislavery Movement and thus showed the Americans something new....It is said that I made Lincoln President. That is certainly not true; but the fact that people say it indicates that I did contribute something toward raising the wind which bore Lincoln into the presidential chair and thus shook the slave system to its very foundations.[8]

Study Questions

1. Why did immigrant groups of the 1830s through the 1850s generate more controversy than earlier groups?
2. Many immigrants regarded ethnic neighborhoods as essential to their economic and cultural survival, but many native-born Americans regarded them as hindrances to complete adoption of "American" customs and attitudes. What is your opinion?
3. In what ways did Irish, German, and Chinese immigrants participate in the social, political, economic, and cultural life of the United States?
4. Do you see any validity in the arguments of nativists like Lyman Beecher?

Sources

1. Lyman Beecher, *Plea for the West* (1835)
2. "The Emigrant's Farewell," *Boston Pilot,* August 16, 1862
3. William Alfred, "An Irish Integrity," in Thomas C. Wheeler, ed., *The Immigrant Experience: The Anguish of Becoming American* (1972)
4. *Daily Alta California* (San Francisco), May 12, 1852, quoted in Ronald Takaki, *A Different Mirror: A History of Multicultural America* (1993)
5. Thomas Chinn, H.M. Lai, and Philip Choy, *A History of the Chinese in California* (1969)
6. Walter D. Kamphoefner, Wolfgang Helbich, and Ulrike Summer, eds., *News from the Land of Freedom: German Immigrants Write Home* (1991)
7. *Ibid.*
8. Letter from Carl Schurz to Theodor Petrasch, Bonn, September 24, 1863, quoted in A.E. Zucker, ed. *The Forty-Eighters, Political Refugees of the German Revolution of 1848* (1950)

CHAPTER FOURTEEN

THE TERRITORIAL EXPANSION OF THE UNITED STATES

1830s–1850s

Samuel Chamberlain, *General Wool Crossing the Military Plaza*, San Antonio, c. 1856. San Jacinto Museum of History Association.

Chapter Outline

EXPLORING THE WEST
The Fur Trade
Government-Sponsored Exploration
Expansion and Indian Policy
THE POLITICS OF EXPANSION
Manifest Destiny, an Expansionist Ideology
The Overland Trails
Oregon
The Santa Fé Trade
Mexican Texas
Americans in Texas
The Texas Revolt
The Republic of Texas
Texas Annexation and the Election of 1844
THE MEXICAN-AMERICAN WAR
Origins of the War
Mr. Polk's War
The Press and Popular War Enthusiasm
CALIFORNIA AND THE GOLD RUSH
Russian-Californio Trade
Early American Settlement
Gold!
Mining Camps
THE POLITICS OF MANIFEST DESTINY
The "Young America" Movement
The Wilmot Proviso
The Free-Soil Movement
The Election of 1848

AMERICAN COMMUNITIES
Texans and Tejanos
"Remember the Alamo!"

For thirteen days in February and March 1836, a force of 187 Texans held the mission fortress known as the Alamo against a siege by 5,000 Mexican troops under General Antonio López de Santa Anna, president of Mexico. Santa Anna had come north to subdue rebellious Texas, the northernmost part of the Mexican province of Coahuila y Texas, and to place it under central authority. On March 6 he ordered a final assault, and in brutal fighting that claimed over 1,500 Mexican lives, his army took the mission. All the defenders were killed, including Commander William Travis and the well-known frontiersmen Jim Bowie and Davy Crockett. It was a crushing defeat for the Texans, but the cry "Remember the Alamo!" rallied their remaining forces, which, less than two months later, routed the Mexican army and forced Santa Anna to grant Texas independence from Mexico. Today the Alamo, in San Antonio, is one of the most cherished historic shrines in the United States.

But memory is selective: some things tend to be forgotten. Within a generation of the uprising few remembered that many *Tejanos*, Spanish-speaking people born in Texas, had joined with American settlers fighting for Texas independence. The Americans were concentrated in the central and eastern portions of the huge Texas territory, where during the 1820s the Mexican government had authorized several colonies managed by *empresarios* (land agents) like Stephen F. Austin. These settler communities consisted mostly of farmers from the Mississippi Valley, who introduced slavery and cotton growing to the rich lands of coastal and upland Texas.

The Tejano community, descended from eighteenth-century Spanish and Mexican settlers, included wealthy *rancheros* who raised cattle on the shortgrass prairies of south Texas, as well as the cowboys known as *vaqueros* and the *peónes*, or poor tenant farmers. Although there was relatively little contact between the Americans and Tejanos, their leaders interacted in San Antonio, the center of regional government. The Tejano elite welcomed the American immigrants and were enthusiastic about their plans for the economic development of Texas. Many Americans married into elite Tejano families, who hoped that by thus assimilating and sharing power with the Americans they could not only maintain but strengthen their community.

The Mexican state, however, was politically and socially unstable during these first years after its successful revolt against Spain in 1821. Liberals favored a loose federal union, conservatives a strong central state. As a northern frontier province, Texas did not have the benefits of statehood; as a result most Tejanos found themselves taking the liberal side in the struggle, opting for more local control over government activities. When, in 1828, the conservative centralists came to power in Mexico City and decided the Americans had too much influence in Texas, many Tejanos rose up with the Americans in opposition. In 1832 the Tejano elite of San Antonio and many prominent rancheros went on record in favor of provincial autonomy and a strong role for the Americans.

One of the leaders of the San Antonio community was the wealthy ranchero Juan Nepomuceno Seguín. As Santa Anna's army approached from the south, Seguín recruited a company of Tejano volunteers and joined the American force inside the walls of the Alamo. During the siege, Commander Travis sent Seguín and some of his men for reinforcements. Stopped by Mexican troops on his way across the lines, Seguín called out, "¡*Somos paisanos*!" (We are countrymen), confusing the guards just long enough for Seguín and his men to make their escape despite the hail of gunfire that quickly ensued. Seguín returned from his unsuccessful mission to find the burned bodies of the Alamo defenders, including seven San Antonio Tejanos. "*Texas será libre*!" Seguín called out as he directed the burial of the Alamo defenders—"Texas shall be free!" In April, Seguín led a regiment of Tejanos in the decisive battle of San Jacinto that won independence for Texas.

At first Tejanos were pleased with independence and played an important political role in the new Republic of Texas. The liberal Lorenzo de Zavala was chosen vice president, and Seguín became the mayor of San Antonio. But soon things began to change, illustrating a recurring pattern in the American occupation of new lands—a striking shift in the relations between different cultures in frontier areas. Most commonly, in the initial stage newcomers blended with native peoples, creating a "frontier of inclusion." The first hunters, trappers, and traders on every American frontier—west of the Appalachians, in the Southwest, and in the Far West—married into the local community and tried to learn native ways. Outnumbered Americans adapted to local societies as a matter of simple survival.

A second, unstable stage occurred when the number of Americans increased and they began occupying more and more land or, as in California, "rushing" in great numbers to mine gold, overrunning native communities. The usual result was warfare and the rapid growth of hostility and racial prejudice—all of which was largely absent in earlier days. A third stage—that of stable settlement—occurred when the native community had been completely "removed" or isolated. In this "frontier of exclusion," racial mixing was rare. Generally, when Europeans pushed American Indians onto reservations they cut themselves off from sources of human history that could have helped them more fully understand the country into which they had moved. And in Texas, American settlers—initially invited in by Mexicans and Tejanos—developed an anti-Mexican passion, regarding all Spanish-speakers as Mexican enemies rather than Tejano allies.

Unscrupulous Americans exploited these prejudices to acquire Tejano property. If the rancheros were "sufficiently scared," one wrote, they would "make an advantageous sale of their lands," and if "two or three hundred of our troops should be stationed here, I have no doubt but a man could make some good speculations." Tejanos were attacked and forced from their homes; some of their villages were burned to the ground. "On the pretext that they were Mexicans," Seguín wrote, Americans treated Tejanos "worse than brutes...My countrymen ran to me for protection against the assaults or exactions of these adventurers." But even in his capacity as mayor Seguín could do little, and in 1842 he and his family, like hundreds of other Tejano families, fled south to Mexico in fear for their lives.

Thus the Tejanos became symbols of a romanticized past rather than full participants in the building of western communities. Spanish-speaking communities in Texas, and later in New Mexico and California, like the communities of Indians throughout the West, became conquered peoples. "White folks and Mexicans were never made to live together," a Texas woman told a traveler a few years after the revolution. "The Mexicans had no business here," she said, and the Americans might "just have to get together and drive them all out of the country." The descendants of the first European settlers of the American Southwest had become foreigners in the land their people had lived in for two centuries.

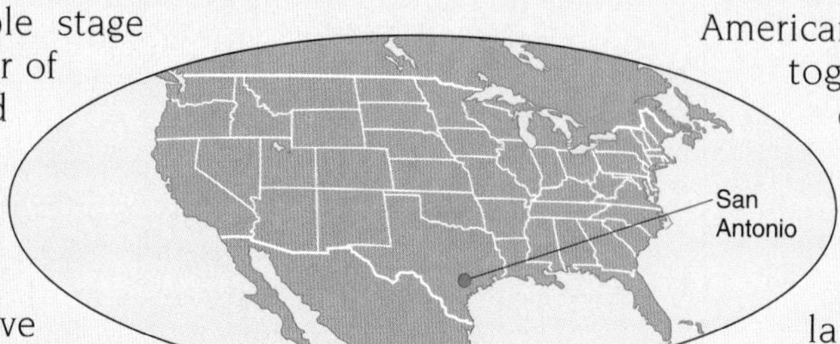

KEY TOPICS

- **Continental expansion and the concept of Manifest Destiny**
- **The contrasting examples of frontier development in Oregon, Texas, and California**
- **How the political effects of expansion heightened sectional tensions**

EXPLORING THE WEST

There seemed to be no stopping the expansion of the American people. By 1840 they had occupied all of the land east of the Mississippi River and had organized all of it (except for Florida and Wisconsin) into states. Of the ten states admitted to the Union between 1800 and 1840, all but one were west of the Appalachian Mountains. Less than sixty years after the United States gained its independence, the majority of its population lived west of the original thirteen states.

The speed and success of this expansion were a source of deep national pride that whetted appetites for more. Many Americans looked eagerly westward to the vast unsettled reaches of the Louisiana Purchase: to Texas, Santa Fé, and trade with Mexico, and even to the Far West, where New England sea captains had been trading for furs since the 1790s. By 1848 the United States had gained all of these coveted western lands. This chapter examines the way the United States became a continental nation, forming many frontier communities in the process. Exploring the vast continent of North America and gaining an understanding of its geography took several centuries and the efforts of many people.

The Fur Trade

The fur trade, which flourished from the 1670s to the 1840s, was an important spur to exploration on the North American continent. In the 1670s the British Hudson's Bay Company and its French Canadian rival, Montreal's North West Company, began exploring beyond the Great Lakes in the Canadian West in search of beaver pelts. Traders and trappers for both companies depended on the goodwill and cooperation of the native peoples of the region, in particular the Assiniboins, Crees, Gros Ventres, and Blackfeet, all of whom moved freely across what later became the U.S.-Canadian border. From the marriages of European men with native women arose a distinctive mixed-race group, the *métis* (see Chapter 5). In 1821 the Hudson's Bay Company absorbed its Montreal rival and ran the fur trade from trading posts in the far Canadian North such as Norway House, Cumberland House, and Fort George. British, French Canadian, and métis employees of the Hudson's Bay Company also trapped and explored throughout the Canadian West and in the Oregon Country, then jointly occupied by the British and Americans (see Chapter 9).

Not until the 1820s were American companies able to challenge British dominance of the trans-Mississippi fur trade. In 1824, William Henry Ashley of the Rocky Mountain Fur Company instituted the "rendezvous" system. This was a yearly trade fair, held deep in the Rocky Mountains (Green River and Jackson Hole were favored locations), to which trappers brought their catch of furs. There they traded them for goods transported by the fur companies from St. Louis: traps, guns, ammunition, tobacco, beads and fabrics (for later trade with Indian peoples), and alcohol. These yearly fur rendezvous were modeled on traditional Indian trade gatherings such as the one at the Mandan villages on the upper Missouri and the huge gathering that took place every year at Celilo Falls on the Columbia River during the annual salmon run. Like its Indian model, the fur rendezvous was a boisterous, polyglot, many-day affair at which trappers of many nationalities—Americans and Indian peoples, French Canadians and métis, as well as Mexicans from Santa Fé and Taos—gathered to trade, drink, and gamble.

For the "mountain men" employed by the American fur companies, the rendezvous was their only contact with American society. The rest of the year they spent deep in the mountains trapping beaver and living in some sort of relationship with local Indian peoples. Some lived in a constant state of danger, always alert to the possibility of attack by parties of local people. But most trappers sought accommodation and friendship: nearly half of them contracted long-lasting marriages with Indian women, who not only helped in the trapping and curing of furs but also acted as vital diplomatic links between the white and Indian worlds. Contemporaries often viewed the mountain men—tough, bearded, leather-clad, fluent in Indian tongues—as half-savage, but we should perhaps see them as an example of successful adaptation to frontier life. Indeed, one

The artist Alfred Jacob Miller, a careful observer of the western fur trade, shows us a mountain man and his Indian wife in his 1837 Bourgeois Walker and His Wife. *Both Walker and his wife worked together to trap and prepare beaver pelts for market.*

legendary trapper became a Crow chief: the African American Jim Beckwourth, who married a Crow woman and was accepted into her tribe.

For all its adventure, the American fur trade was short-lived. By the 1840s, the population of beaver in western streams was virtually destroyed, and the day of the mountain man was over. But with daring journeys like that of Jedediah Smith, the first American to enter California over the Sierra Nevada mountains, the mountain men had helped forge a clear picture of western geography. Soon permanent settlers would follow the trails they had blazed.

Government-Sponsored Exploration

The federal government played a major role in the exploration and development of the West. Thomas Jefferson decisively influenced American westward expansion with the Louisiana Purchase of 1803. When he dispatched the Lewis and Clark expedition the next year it may have been largely to satisfy his own intense scientific and geographic curiosity about the West, but he also instructed Meriwether Lewis and William Clark to draw the western Indians into the American trading network, away from the British.

The exploratory and scientific aspects of the Lewis and Clark expedition set a precedent for many government-financed quasi-military expeditions. In 1806 and 1807, Lieutenant Zebulon Pike led an expedition to the Rocky Mountains in Colorado. Major Stephen Long's exploration and mapping of the Great Plains in the years 1819–20 was part of a show of force meant to frighten British fur trappers out of the West. Then, in 1843 and 1844, another military explorer, John C. Frémont, mapped the overland trails to Oregon and California. In the 1850s, the Pacific Railroad surveys explored possible transcontinental railroad routes. The tradition of government-sponsored western exploration continued after the Civil War in the famous geological surveys, the best known of which is the 1869 Grand Canyon exploration by Major John Wesley Powell.

Beginning with Long's expedition, the results of these surveys were published by the government, complete with maps, illustrations, and, after the Civil War, photographs. These publications fed a strong popular appetite for pictures of the breathtaking scenery of the Far West and information about its inhabitants. Artists like Karl Bodmer, who accompanied a private expedition by the scientifically inclined German prince Maximilian in the years 1833–34, produced stunning portraits of American Indians. Over the next three decades Thomas Moran, Albert Bierstadt, and other landscape artists traveled west with government expeditions and came home to paint grand (and sometimes fanciful) pictures of Yosemite Valley and Yellowstone (later designated among the first national parks). All these images of the American West made a powerful contribution to the emerging American self-image. American pride in the land—the biggest of this, the longest of that, the most spectacular of something else—was founded on the images brought home by government surveyors and explorers.

In the wake of the pathfinders came hundreds of government geologists and botanists as well as the surveyors who mapped and plotted the West for settlement according to the Land Ordinance of 1785. The basic pattern of land survey and sale established by these measures (see Chapter 7) was followed all the way to the Pacific Ocean. The federal government sold the western public lands at low prices and, to veterans of the War of 1812, gave away land in the Old Northwest. And following policies established in the Old Northwest (see Chapter 9), the federal government also shouldered the expense of Indian removal, paying

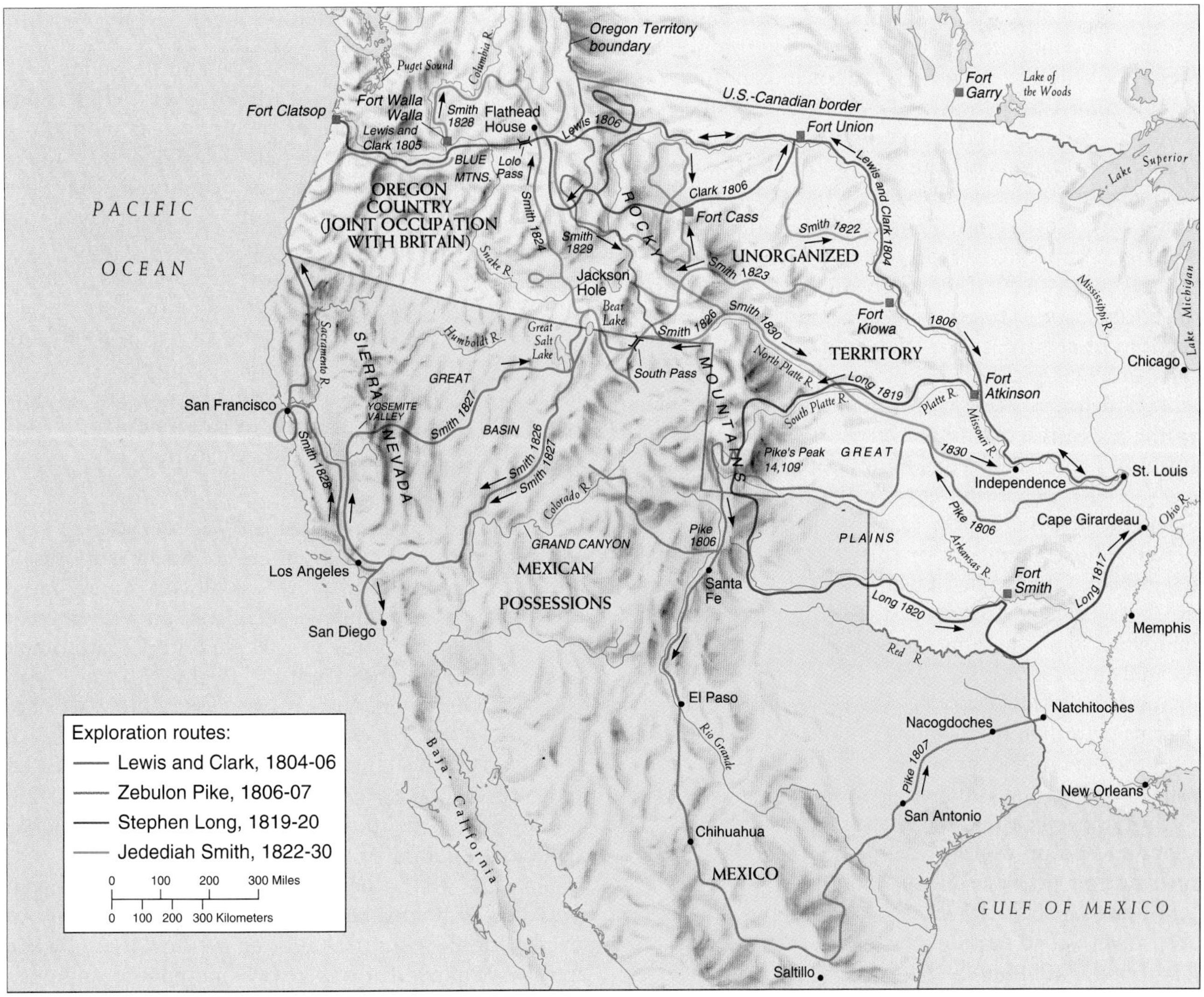

Exploration of the Continent, 1804–1830 *Lewis and Clark's "voyage of discovery" of 1804–06 was the first of many government-sponsored western military expeditions. Crossing the Great Plains in 1806, Lieutenant Zebulon Pike was captured by the Spanish in their territory and taken to Mexico but returned in 1807 via Texas. Major Stephen Long, who crossed the Plains in 1819–20, found them "arid and forbidding." Meanwhile fur trappers, among them the much-traveled Jedediah Smith, became well acquainted with the West as they hunted beaver for their pelts.*

the soldiers or the officials who fought or talked Indian peoples into giving up their lands and making long-term commitments to compensate the Indian people themselves. The government also supported the forts and soldiers whose task was to maintain peace between settlers and Indian peoples in newly opened areas.

Expansion and Indian Policy

While American artists were painting the way of life of western Indian peoples, eastern Indian tribes were being removed from their homelands to Indian Territory (present-day Oklahoma, Kansas, and Nebraska), west of Arkansas, Missouri, and Iowa on the eastern edge of the Great Plains, a region widely regarded as unfarmable and popularly known as the Great American Desert. The justification for this western removal, as Thomas Jefferson had explained early in the century, was the creation of a space where Indian people could live undisturbed by white people while they slowly adjusted to "civilized" ways. But the government officials who negotiated the removals failed to predict the tremendous speed at which white people would settle the West.

As a result, encroachment on Indian Territory was not long in coming. The territory was crossed by the Santa Fé Trail, established in 1821; in the 1840s the northern part was crossed by the heavily traveled

Overland Trails to California, Oregon, and the Mormon community in Utah. In 1854, the government abolished the northern half of Indian Territory, establishing the Kansas and Nebraska Territories in its place and opening them to immediate white settlement. The tribes of the area—the Potawatomis, Wyandots, Kickapoos, Sauks, Foxes, Delawares, Shawnees, Kaskaskias, Peorias, Piankashaws, Weas, Miamis, Omahas, Otos, and Missouris—signed treaties accepting either vastly reduced reservations or allotments. Those who accepted allotments—sections of private land—often sold them, under pressure, to white people. Thus many of the Indian people who had hoped for independence and escape from white pressures in Indian Territory lost both their autonomy and their tribal identity.

The people in the southern part of Indian Territory, in what is now Oklahoma, fared somewhat better. Those members of the southern tribes—the Cherokees, Chickasaws, Choctaws, Creeks, and Seminoles—who had survived the trauma of forcible removal from the Southeast in the 1830s quickly created impressive new communities. The five tribes divided up the territory and established self-governing nations with their own schools and churches. The societies they created were not so different from the American societies from which they had been expelled. The five tribes even carried slavery west with them: an elite economic group established plantations and shipped their cotton to New Orleans like other Southerners. Until after the Civil War, these southern tribes were able to withstand outside pressures and remain the self-governing communities that treaties had assured them they would be.

The removal of the eastern tribes did not solve "the Indian Problem," the term many Americans used to describe their relationship with the first occupants of the land. West of Indian Territory were the nomadic and warlike Indians of the Great Plains: the Sioux, Cheyennes, Arapahoes, Comanches, and Kiowas. Beyond them were the seminomadic tribes of the Rocky Mountains—the Blackfeet, Crows, Utes, Shoshonis, Nez Percé, and Salish peoples—and, in the Southwest, the farming cultures of the Pueblos, Hopis, Acomas, Zunis, Pimas, and Papagos and the migratory Apaches and Navajos. Even farther west were hundreds of small tribes in California and the Pacific Northwest. Clearly, all of these people could not be "removed," for where could they go? The first western pioneers ignored the issue. Beginning in the 1840s, they simply passed through the far western tribal lands on their way to establish new frontiers of settlement in California and Oregon. Later, after the Civil War, the government would undertake a series of Indian wars that ultimately left the remaining Indian peoples penned up on small reservations.

THE POLITICS OF EXPANSION

America's rapid expansion had many consequences, but perhaps the most significant was that it reinforced Americans' sense of themselves as pioneering people. In the 1890s Frederick Jackson Turner, America's most famous historian, observed that the repeated experience of settling new frontiers across the continent had shaped Americans into a uniquely adventurous, optimistic, and democratic people. Other historians have disagreed with Turner, but there is no question that his view of the frontier long ago won the battle for popular opinion. Ever since the time of Daniel Boone, venturing into the wilderness has held a special place in the American imagination, seen almost as an American right.

Manifest Destiny, an Expansionist Ideology

How did Americans justify their restless expansionism? After all, the United States was already a very large country with much undeveloped land. To push beyond existing boundaries was to risk war with Great Britain, which claimed the Pacific Northwest, and with Mexico, which held what is now Texas, New Mexico, Arizona, Utah, Nevada, California, and part of Colorado. If the United States prevailed it would be reducing 75,000 Spanish-speaking people and 150,000 Indian people to subject status. Undertaking such a conquest required a rationale.

In 1845 newspaperman John O'Sullivan provided it. It was, he wrote, "our manifest destiny to overspread the continent allotted by Providence for the free development of our yearly multiplying millions." Sullivan argued that Americans had a God-given right to bring the benefits of American democracy to other, more backward peoples—meaning Mexicans and Indians—by force, if necessary. The notion of manifest destiny summed up the powerful combination of pride in what America had achieved and missionary zeal and racist attitudes toward other peoples that lay behind the thinking of many expansionists. Americans were proud of their rapid development: the surge in population, the remarkable canals and railroads, the grand scale of the American enterprise. Why shouldn't it be even bigger? Almost swaggering, Americans dared other countries—Great Britain in particular—to stop them.

Behind the bravado was concern about the economic future of the United States. After the devastating Panic of 1837 (see Chapter 10), many politicians became convinced that the nation's prosperity depended on vastly expanded trade with Asia. Senator Thomas Hart Benton of Missouri had been advocating trade with India by way of the Missouri and Columbia Rivers since the 1820s (not the easiest of routes, as Lewis and Clark had shown). Soon Benton and others were pointing out

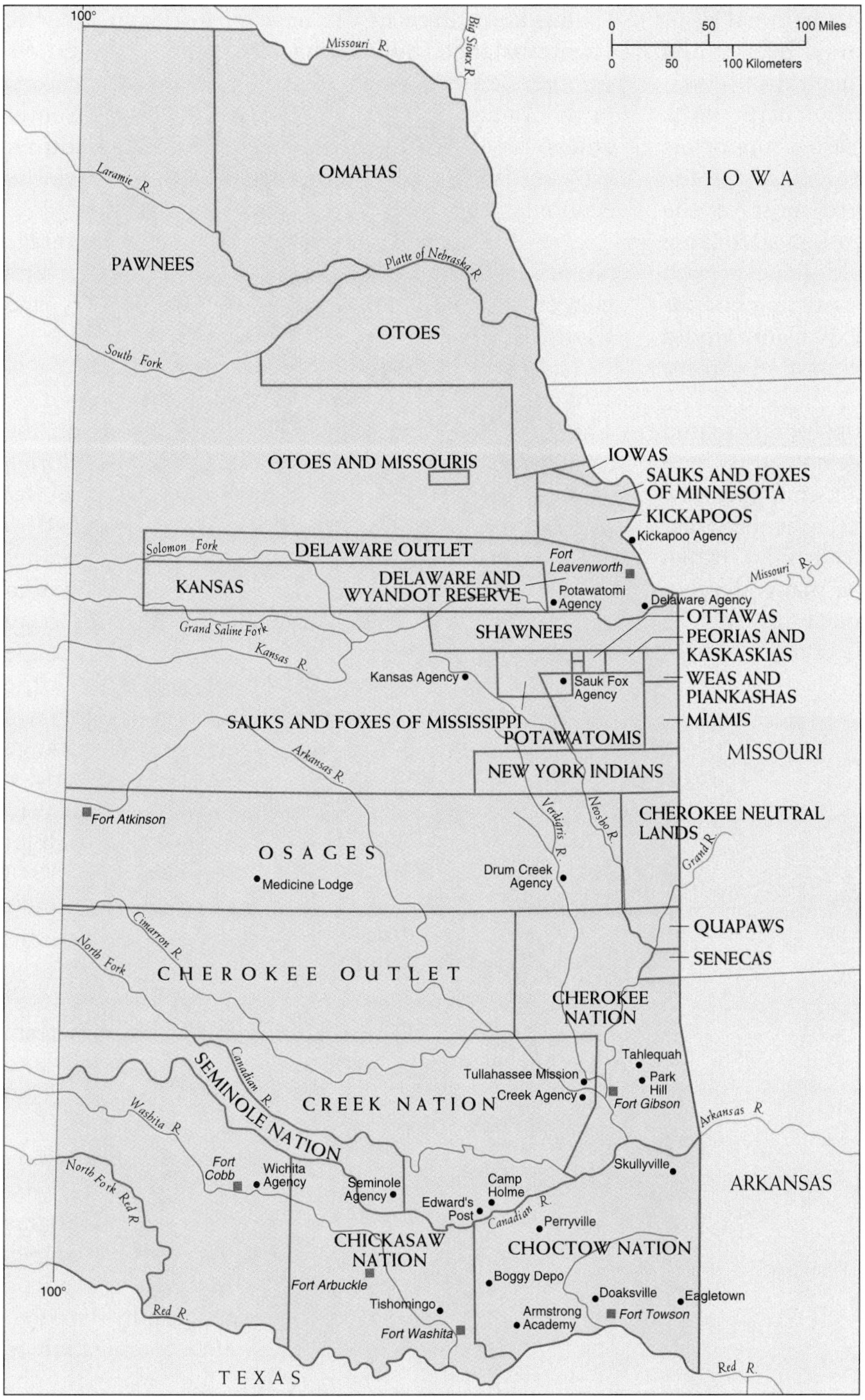

Indian Territory before the Kansas-Nebraska Act of 1854

Indian Territory lay west of Arkansas, Missouri, and Iowa and east of Spanish Territory. Most of the Indian peoples who lived there in the 1830s and the 1840s had been "removed" from east of the Mississippi River. The southern part (now Oklahoma) was inhabited by peoples from the Old Southwest: the Cherokees, Chickasaws, Choctaws, Creeks, and Seminoles. North of that (in what is now Kansas and Nebraska) lived peoples who had been removed from the Old Northwest. All these Indian peoples had trouble adjusting not only to a new climate and a new way of life but to the close proximity of some Indian tribes who were their traditional enemies.

how greatly Pacific trade would increase if the United States held the magnificent harbors of the west coast, among them Puget Sound in the Oregon Country held jointly with Britain and the bays of San Francisco and San Diego, both in Mexican-held California.

In one sense, manifest destiny was evangelical religion on a larger scale. The same revivalist fervor that Charles G. Finney had sparked in Rochester in 1830 had a continental echo: missionaries were among the first to travel to the Far West to Christianize Indian people. Just as many of Finney's eastern converts mounted reform movements aimed at changing the lives of workers, so did the western missionaries attempt to "civilize" the Indian peoples. They believed that the only way to do so was to destroy their cultures and to surround them with good American examples.

Expansionism was also tied to national politics. O'Sullivan, whose "manifest destiny" became the expansionist watchword, was not a neutral observer: he was the editor of the *Democratic Review*, a party newspaper. Most Democrats were wholehearted supporters of expansion, whereas many Whigs (especially in the North) opposed it. Whigs welcomed most of the changes wrought by industrialization but advocated strong government policies that would guide growth and development within the country's existing boundaries; they feared (correctly) that expansion would raise the contentious issue of the extension of slavery to new territories.

On the other hand, many Democrats feared the industrialization that the Whigs welcomed. Where the Whigs saw economic progress, Democrats saw economic depression (the Panic of 1837 was the worst the nation had experienced), uncontrolled urban growth, and growing social unrest. For many Democrats, the answer to the nation's social ills was to continue to follow Thomas Jefferson's vision of establishing agriculture in the new territories in order to counterbalance industrialization (see Chapter 9). Another factor in the political struggle over expansion in the 1840s was that many Democrats were Southerners, for whom the continual expansion of cotton-growing lands was a matter of social faith as well as economic necessity.

These were politicians' reasons. The average farmer moved west for many other reasons: land hunger, national pride, plain and simple curiosity, and a sense of adventure.

The Overland Trails

The 2,000-mile trip on the Overland Trails from the banks of the Missouri River to Oregon and California usually took seven months, sometimes more. Travel was slow, dangerous, tedious, and exhausting. Forced to lighten their loads as animals died and winter weather threatened, pioneers often arrived at their destination with little food and few belongings. Uprooted from family and familiar surroundings, pioneers faced the prospect of being, in the poignant and much-used biblical phrase, "strangers in a strange land." Yet despite the risks, settlers streamed west: 5,000 to Oregon by 1845 and about 3,000 to California by 1848 (before the discovery of gold). Some arrived by ship, but this was more expensive than the overland journey, which itself was not cheap: a wagon, a team of oxen, food, clothing, and essential tools cost between $500 and $1,000.

Pioneers had many motives for making the trip. Glowing reports from Oregon's Willamette Valley, for example, seemed to promise economic opportunity and healthy surroundings, an alluring combination to farmers in the malaria-prone Midwest who had been hard hit by the Panic of 1837. But rational motives do not tell the whole story. Many men were motivated by a sense of adventure, by a desire to experience the unknown, or, as they put it, to "see the elephant." Women were more likely to think of the trip as *A Pioneer's Search for an Ideal Home*, the title that Phoebe Judson chose for

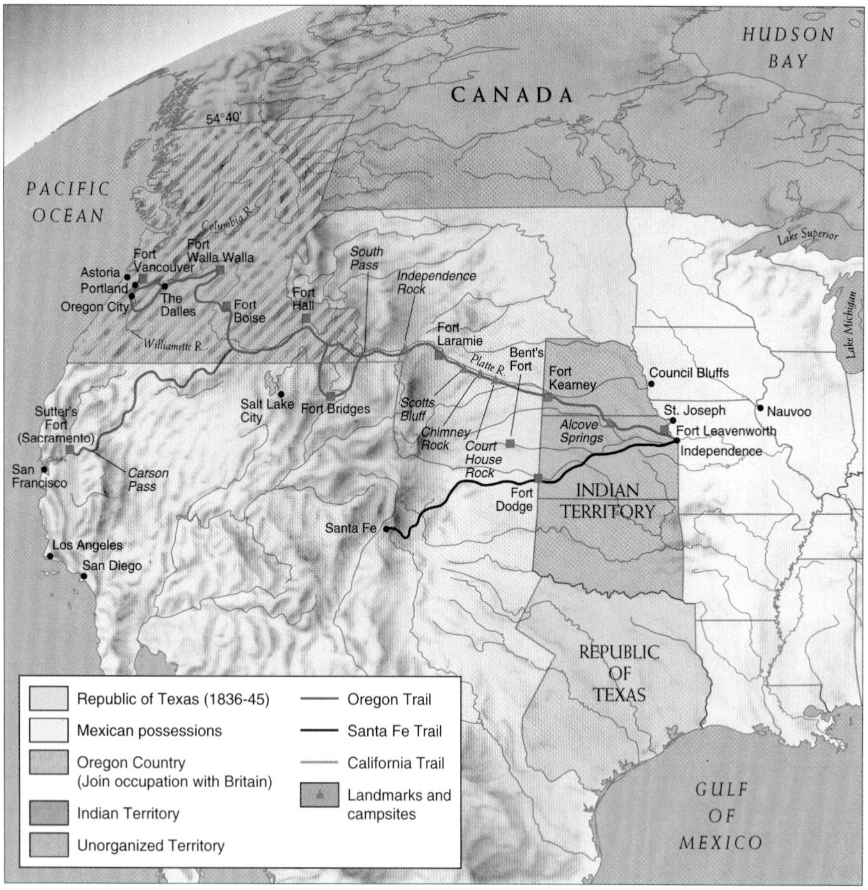

The Overland Trails, 1840 *All the great trails west started at the Missouri River. The Oregon, California, and Mormon Trails followed the Platte River into Wyoming, crossed South Pass, and divided in western Wyoming. The much harsher Santa Fé Trail stretched 900 miles southwest across the Great Plains. All of the trails crossed Indian Territory and, to greater or lesser extent, Mexican possessions as well.*

her account of her family's 1852 trip to Oregon.

Few pioneers traveled alone, partly because they feared Indian attack (which was rare) but largely because they needed help fording rivers or crossing mountains with heavy wagons. Most Oregon pioneers traveled with their families but usually also joined a larger group, forming a "train." In the earliest years, when the route was still uncertain, trains hired a "pilot," generally a former fur trapper. Often the men of the wagon train drew up semimilitary constitutions, electing a leader. Democratic as this process appeared, not everyone was willing to obey the leader, and many trains experienced dissension and breakups along the trail. But in essence all pioneers—men, women, and children—were part of a new, westward-moving community in which they had to accept both the advantages and disadvantages of community membership.

J. Goldsborough Bruff, one of thousands who rushed to California for gold in 1849, sketched many events in his Overland Trail journey. Here he depicts several wagons being ferried over the Platte River. The need for individuals to cooperate is obvious. Less obvious in this sketch is the danger: most river crossing points lacked ferries, and both people and livestock often drowned trying to ford them.

Joseph Goldsborough Bruff, *Ferriage of the Platte above the Mouth of Deer Creek, July 20, 1849*. The Henry E. Huntington Library and Art Gallery, San Marino, Calif.

Wagon trains started westward as soon as the prairies were green (thus ensuring feed for the livestock). The daily routine was soon established. Men took care of the moving equipment and the animals, while the women cooked and kept track of the children. Slowly, at a rate of about fifteen miles a day, the wagon trains moved west along the Platte River, crossing the Continental Divide at South Pass in present-day Wyoming. West of the Rockies the climate was much drier. The long, dusty stretch along the Snake River in present-day southern Idaho finally gave way to Oregon's steep and difficult Blue Mountains and to the dangerous rafting down the Columbia River, in which many drowned and all were drenched by the cold winter rains of the Pacific Northwest. California-bound migrants faced even worse hazards: the complete lack of water in the Humbolt Sink region of northern Nevada and the looming Sierra Nevadas, which had to be crossed before the winter snows came. (Members of the ill-fated Donner party, snowbound on the Nevada side of that range in 1846–47, resorted to cannibalism before they were rescued.)

In addition to the ever-present tedium and exhaustion, wagon trains were beset by such trail hazards as illness and accident. Danger from Indian attack, which all pioneers feared, was actually very small. Before the 1849 California Gold Rush, conflicts between wagon trains and Indians claimed the lives of only thirty-four white people (twenty-four in one wagon train) and twenty-five Indians. In subsequent years, as thousands of gold rushers flocked west, the deaths increased, but, significantly, more Indians than white people died. It appears that unprovoked white attacks on Indians were more common than the reverse.

In contrast, cholera killed at least a thousand people a year in 1849 and the early 1850s when it stalked sections of the trail along the Platte River. Spread by contaminated water, cholera caused vomiting and diarrhea, which in turn led to extreme dehydration and death, often in one night. In the afflicted regions, trailside graves were a frequent and grim sight. Drownings were not uncommon, nor were accidental ax wounds or shootings, and children sometimes fell out of wagons and were run over. The members of the wagon train community did what they could to arrange decent burials, and they provided support for survivors: men helped widows drive their wagons onward, women nursed and tended babies whose mothers were dead, and at least one parentless family, the seven Sager children, were brought to Oregon in safety.

By 1860 almost 300,000 people had traveled the Overland Trails to Oregon or California. Ruts from the wagon wheels can be seen in a number of places along the route even today. In 1869 the completion of the transcontinental railroad marked the end of the wagon train era (although many people made shorter trips to other western locations by wagon). In retrospect, the pioneers remembered their journey as more dangerous and less tedious than it actually was. The stories that came down to their grandchildren told of a heroic adventure. These "pioneers' tales" were not the truth as it had

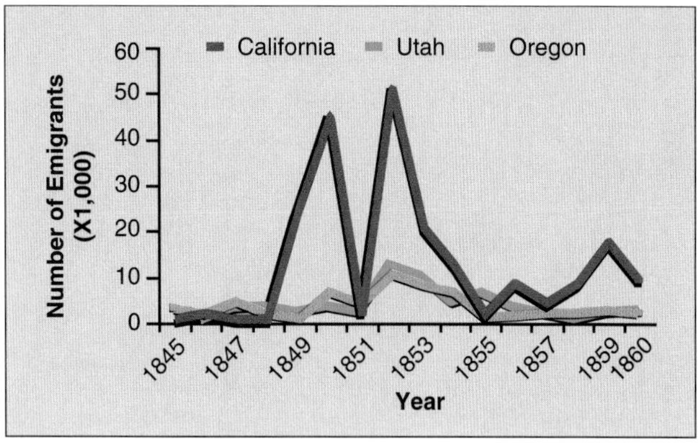

Overland Emigration to Oregon, California, and Utah, 1840–1860 *Before 1849 the westward migration consisted primarily of family groups going to Oregon or Utah. The discovery of gold in California dramatically changed the migration: through 1854 most migrants were single men "rushing" to California, which remained the favored destination up until 1860. Over the twenty-year period from 1840 to 1860 the Overland Trails were transformed from difficult and dangerous routes to well-marked and well-served thoroughfares.*

Source: John Unruh Jr., *The Plains Across* (Champaign-Urbana: University of Illinois Press, 1979), pp. 119–20.

really happened but an effort to find the true heroism in an important episode by making a good story out of it.

Oregon

The American settlement of Oregon provides a capsule example of the stages of frontier development. The first contacts between the region's Indian peoples and Europeans were commercial. Spanish, British, Russian, and American ships traded for sea otter skins from the 1780s to about 1810. Subsequently land-based groups scoured the region for beaver skins as well. In this first "frontier of inclusion" there were frequent, often sexual contacts between Indians and Europeans.

Both Great Britain and the United States claimed the Oregon Country by right of discovery, but in the Convention of 1818 the two nations agreed to occupy it jointly, postponing a final decision on its disposition. In reality, the British clearly dominated the region. In 1824 the Hudson's Bay Company consolidated Britain's position by establishing a major fur trading post at Fort Vancouver, on the banks of the Columbia River. Like all fur-trading ventures, the post exemplified the racial mixing of a "frontier of inclusion." Fort Vancouver housed a polyglot population of eastern Indians (Delawares and Iroquois), local Chinook Indians, French and métis from Canada, British traders, and Hawaiians. Discovered by British Captain James Cook in 1778, Hawaii was visited by the first American ship in 1790. The island kingdom quickly became a favorite stop for American and British traders in sea otter furs destined for China and later for New England whaling ships. Hawaiian men, famous for their sailing skills, often joined the crews of American and British ships and served, as at Fort Vancouver, as workers in the fur trade. But the effect of the fur trade on native tribes in Oregon was catastrophic; suffering the fate of all Indian peoples after their initial contact with Europeans, they were decimated by European diseases.

The first permanent European settlers in Oregon were retired fur trappers and their Indian wives and families. They favored a spot in the lush and temperate Willamette Valley that became known as French Prairie, although the inhabitants were a mixed group of Americans, British, French Canadians, Indian peoples, and métis. The next to arrive were Protestant and Catholic missionaries, among them Methodist Jason Lee in 1834, Congregationalists Marcus and Narcissa Whitman in 1837, Franciscan priests Frances Blanchet and Modeste Demers in 1838, and Jesuit Pierre-Jean De Smet in 1840. None of these missionaries was very successful. Epidemics had taken the lives of many of the region's peoples, and those who were left were disinclined to give up their nomadic life and settle down as the missionaries wanted them to do.

Finally, in the 1840s, came the Midwest farmers who would make up the majority of Oregon's permanent settlers, carried on the wave of enthusiasm known as "Oregon fever" and lured by free land and patriotism. By 1845 Oregon boasted 5,000 American settlers, most of them living in the Willamette Valley and laying claim to lands to which they had as yet no legal right because neither Britain nor the United States had concluded land treaties with Oregon's Indian peoples. Their arrival signaled Oregon's shift from a "frontier of inclusion" to a "frontier of exclusion."

For these early settlers, life was at first very difficult. Most arrived in late autumn, exhausted from the strenuous overland journey. They could not begin to farm until the spring, and so they depended on the earlier settlers for their survival over the winter. Ironically, in the earliest years American settlers got vital help from the Hudson's Bay Company, even though its director, John McLoughlin, had been ordered by the British government not to encourage American settlement. McLoughlin disregarded his orders, motivated both by sympathy for the plight of the newcomers and by a keen sense of the dangers his enterprise would face if he were outnumbered by angry Americans.

The handful of American settlers in Oregon found themselves in possession of a remote frontier. One of the first things they did was to draw up their own constitution. When the first Oregon settlers (including a number of former mountain men) met in the summer of 1843 to draft a constitution, they prohibited African Americans (both free and enslaved) from settling in the territory. By avoiding the divisive issue of slavery, they hoped to build community feeling between white settlers from the North and the South. In spite of the law, some Southerners did bring their slaves to Oregon with them, but when an early free African American pioneer, George Bush, came to Oregon, he deliberately settled north of the Columbia River, in what later became Washington Territory. Thus Oregon got African American slaves that it did not want and lost a free man who became renowned for his willingness to cooperate with others and his community spirit.

The influx of American settlers and their efforts to establish their own government created strains between the United States and Britain. Campaigning for the presidency in 1844, James K. Polk coined the belligerent slogan "Fifty-four Forty or Fight," suggesting that the United States would go to war if it didn't get control of all the territory south of latitude 54°40′, the border between Russian Alaska and British Canada. In office, however, Polk was willing to compromise. In June, 1846, Britain and the United States concluded a treaty establishing the forty-ninth parallel as the U.S.-Canada border but leaving the island of Vancouver in British hands. The British then quietly wound up their declining fur trade in the region. In 1849 the Hudson's Bay Company closed Fort Vancouver and moved its operations to Victoria, thus ending the Pacific Northwest's largely successful experience with joint occupancy. Oregon's Donation Land Claim Act of 1850 codified the practice of giving 320 acres to each white male age eighteen or over and 640 acres to each married couple to settle in the territory (African Americans, Hawaiians, and American Indians were excluded).

The white settlers realized that they had to forge strong community bonds if they hoped to survive on their distant frontier. Cooperation and mutual aid were the rule. Until well into the 1850s, residents organized yearly parties that traveled back along the last stretches of the Oregon Trail to help straggling parties making their way to the territory. Kinship networks were strong and vital: many pioneers came to join family who had migrated before them. Although most settlers lived on their own land claims rather than in towns, neighborly cooperation was crucial. Food sharing and mutual labor were essential in the early years, when crop and livestock loss to weather or natural predators was common. Help, even to total strangers, was customary in times of illness or death.

Although this community feeling did not extend to Indian groups as a whole, relations with the small and unthreatening disease-thinned local Indian tribes were generally peaceful until 1847, when Cayuse Indians killed the missionaries Marcus and Narcissa Whitman. Their deaths triggered a series of "wars" against the remaining native people. A "frontier of exclusion" had been achieved. Nonetheless the process by which Oregon became part of the United States (it was admitted as a state in 1859) was relatively peaceful, especially when compared to American expansion into the Spanish provinces of New Mexico and Texas.

James Warre, *American Settlement of Oregon City*, 1846. Watercolor. Courtesy American Antiquarian Society.

This watercolor of tiny Oregon City in 1846 suggests how small the American population of the Oregon Territory was when its status was being decided in America's favor. With just 953 inhabitants in 1850, Oregon City was the largest city in the territory.

The Santa Fé Trade

Santa Fé, first settled by colonists from Mexico in 1609 and the center of the Spanish frontier province of New Mexico, had long attracted American frontiersmen and traders. But Spain had forcefully resisted American penetration. For example, Lieutenant Zebulon Pike's Great Plains and Rocky Mountain exploration of 1806–07 ended ignominiously with his capture by Spanish soldiers.

When Mexico gained its independence from Spain in 1821, this exclusionary policy changed. American traders were now welcome in Santa Fé, but the trip over the legendary Santa Fé Trail from Independence,

Missouri, was a forbidding 900 miles of arid plains, deserts, and mountains. On the Santa Fé trail, unlike the Oregon Trail, there was serious danger of Indian attack, for neither the Comanches nor the Apaches of the southern high plains tolerated trespassers. In 1825, at the urging of Senator Benton and others, Congress voted federal protection for the Santa Fé Trail, even though much of it lay in Mexican territory. The number of people venturing west in the trading caravans increased yearly because the profits were so great (the first American trader to reach Santa Fé, William Becknell, realized a thousand percent profit). By the 1840s a few hundred American trappers and traders (called *extranjeros*, or foreigners) lived permanently in New Mexico. In Santa Fé, some American merchants married daughters of important local families, suggesting the start of the inclusive stage of frontier contact.

Settlements and trading posts soon grew up along the long Santa Fé Trail. One of the most famous was Bent's Fort, on the Arkansas River in what is now eastern Colorado, which did a brisk trade in beaver skins and buffalo robes. Like most trading posts, it had a multiethnic population. In the 1840s the occupants included housekeeper Josefa Tafoya of Taos, whose husband was a carpenter from Pennsylvania; an African American cook; a French tailor from New Orleans; Mexican muleteers; and a number of Indian women, including the two Cheyenne women who were the (successive) wives of William Bent, cofounder of the fort. The three small communities of Pueblo, Hardscrabble, and Greenhorn, spinoffs of Bent's Fort, were populated by men of all nationalities and their Mexican and Indian wives. All three communities lived by trapping, hunting, and a little farming. This racially and economically mixed existence was characteristic of all early trading frontiers, but another western frontier, the American agricultural settlement in Texas, was different from the start.

Alfred Jacob Miller painted the busy life of Fort Laramie, a multiracial trading fort, in 1837. Bent's Fort, another multiracial trading center, would have looked much like this.

Mexican Texas

In 1821, when Mexico gained its independence from Spain, there were 2,240 *Tejano* (Spanish-speaking) residents of Texas. Established in 1716 as a buffer against possible French attack on New Spain, the main Texas settlements of Nacogdoches, Goliad, and San Antonio remained small, far-flung frontier outposts (see Chapter 5). As was customary throughout New Spain, communities were organized around three centers: missions and *presidios* (forts), which formed the nucleus of towns, and the large cattle-raising *ranchos* on which rural living depended. As elsewhere in New Spain, society was divided into two classes: the *ricos* (rich), who claimed Spanish descent, and the mixed-blood *pobres* (poor). Tejano town life was traditionally hierarchical, dominated by the ricos who were connected by blood or marriage with the great ranching families. The most colorful figures on the ranchos were mestizo (mixed-blood) vaqueros, renowned for their horsemanship; Americanization of their name made "buckaroos" of the American cowboys to whom they later taught their skills. Most Tejanos were neither ricos nor vaqueros but small farmers or common laborers who led hardscrabble frontier lives. But all Tejanos, rich and poor, faced the constant threat of raids by Comanche Indians.

The Comanches exemplified the revolutionary changes brought about in the lives of Plains Indians by the reintroduction of horses into the American continent (see Chapter 5). "A Comanche on his feet is out of his element...but the moment he lays his hands upon his horse," said artist George Catlin, "I doubt very much whether any people in the world can surpass [him]." Legendary warriors, the Comanches raided the small Texas settlements at will and even struck deep into Mexico itself. Once they raided so far south that they saw brightly plumed birds (parrots) and "tiny men with tails" (monkeys); apparently they had reached the tropical Yucatán. The nomadic Comanches followed the immense buffalo herds on which they depended for food and clothing. Their relentless raids on the Texas settlements rose from a determination to hold onto this rich buffalo territory, for the buffalo provided all that they wanted. They had no interest in being converted by mission priests or incorporated into mixed-race trading communities.

Painted by George Catlin about 1834, this scene, Comanche Village, *shows how the everyday life of the Comanches was tied to buffalo. The women in the foreground are scraping buffalo hide, and buffalo meat can be seen drying on racks. The men and boys may be planning their next buffalo hunt.*

Americans in Texas

In 1821, seeking to increase the strength of its buffer zone between the heart of Mexico and the marauding Comanches, the Mexican government granted Moses Austin of Missouri an area of 18,000 square miles within the territory of Texas. Moses died shortly thereafter, and the grant was taken up by his son Stephen F. Austin, who became the first American *empresario* (land agent). From the beginning the American settlement of Texas differed markedly from that of other frontiers. Elsewhere, Americans frequently settled on land to which Indian peoples still held title, or, as in the case of Oregon, they occupied lands to which other countries also made claim. In contrast, the Texas settlement was fully legal: Austin and other empresarios owned their lands as a result of formal contracts with the Mexican government. In exchange, Austin agreed that he and his colonists would become Mexican citizens and would adopt the Catholic religion. It is difficult to say which of these two provisions was the more remarkable, for most nineteenth-century Americans defined their Americanness in terms of citizenship and the Protestant religion.

Additionally, in startling contrast with the usual frontier free-for-all, Austin's community was populated with handpicked settlers, Austin insisting that "no frontiersman who has no other occupation than that of hunter will be received—no drunkard, no gambler, no profane swearer, no idler." Neither Austin nor later empresarios had any trouble finding Americans to apply, for the simple reason that Mexican land grants were magnificent: a square league (4,605 acres) per family. Soon Americans (including African American slaves, to whose presence the Mexican government turned a blind eye) outnumbered Tejanos by nearly two to one: in 1830 there were an estimated 7,000 Americans and 4,000 Tejanos living in Texas.

The Austin settlement of 1821 was followed by others, twenty-six in all, concentrating in the fertile river bottoms of east Texas (along the Sabine River) and south central Texas (the Brazos and the Colorado). These large settlements were highly organized farming enterprises whose principal crop was cotton, grown by African American slave labor, which was sold in the international market. By the early 1830s, Americans in Texas were exporting an estimated $500,000 worth of goods yearly to New Orleans, two-thirds of it cotton.

Austin's colonists and those who settled later were predominantly Southerners who viewed Texas as a natural extension of settlement in Mississippi and Louisiana. These settlers created enclaves (self-contained communities) that had little contact with Tejanos or Indian peoples. In fact, although they lived in Mexican territory, most Americans never bothered to learn Spanish. Nor, in spite of Austin's promises, did they become Mexican citizens or adopt the Catholic religion. Yet because of the nature of agreements made by the empresarios, the Americans could not set up local American-style governments like the one created by settlers in Oregon. Like the immigrants who flooded into east coast cities (see Chapter 13) the Americans in Texas were immigrants to another country—but one they did not intend to adapt to.

The one exception to American exclusiveness occurred in San Antonio, the provincial government center. There, just as in Santa Fé, a handful of wealthy Americans married into the Tejano elite with ease. One such marriage in San Antonio linked wealthy Louisianan James Bowie, the legendary fighter for whom the Bowie knife is named, and Ursula Veramendi, daughter of the vice governor of Texas. With the marriage, Bowie became a wealthy, honored, and well-connected Mexican citizen. Only after the death of his wife and children in a cholera epidemic in 1833 did Bowie support the cause of Anglo-Texan independence, going on to fight—and die—at the Alamo.

The great ranchos excited the admiration of many Americans, who later made cattle raising a major western industry. In these early days in Texas, Americans watched and learned as Tejanos rounded up range cattle, branded them, and drove more than 20,000 each year to Nacogdoches for the U.S. market. Praise for Tejano horsemanship was unstinting: they are "not surpassed perhaps by any other people in the Globe," enthused one American immigrant. Tejano customs, especially multiday celebrations that mixed religious ceremonies, feasting, horse racing, and elaborate *fandangos* (dances), offered striking evidence of the richly textured community life created by Tejanos of all social classes.

For a brief period Texas was big enough to hold three communities: Comanche, Tejano, and American. The nomadic Comanches rode the high plains of northern and western Texas, raiding settlements primarily for horses. The Tejanos maintained their ranchos and missions mostly in the South, while American farmers occupied the eastern and south central sections. Each group would fight to hold its land: the Comanches, their rich hunting grounds, the Mexicans, their towns and ranchos; and the newcomers, the Americans, their rich land grants.

The Texas Revolt

The balance between the three communities in Texas was broken in 1828, when centrists gained control of the government in Mexico City and, in a dramatic shift of policy, decided to exercise firm control over the northern province. As the Mexican government restricted American immigration, outlawed slavery, levied customs duties and taxes, and planned other measures, Americans seethed and talked of rebellion. Bolstering their cause were as many as 20,000 additional Americans, many of them openly expansionist, who flooded into Texas after 1830. These most recent settlers did not intend to become Mexican citizens. Instead, they planned to take over Texas. What ensued was reminiscent of the American Revolution, at least in the eyes of some Americans. But for all the invocations of the Revolution, the real issue in Texas was conquest.

Whereas many of the older American settlers in Texas found much that was admirable, or at least understandable, in Spanish Mexican culture, many of the post-1830 immigrants were vehemently anti-Mexican. Many had grievances: failure to obtain a land grant, restrictions on trade because of Mexican customs regulations, difficulties in understanding Hispanic law, which differed markedly from the Anglo-American legal tradition. Above all, in the eyes of many Americans, there was the matter of race. Statements of racial superiority were commonplace, and even Stephen Austin wrote in 1836 that he saw the Texas conflict as one of barbarism on the part of "a mongrel Spanish-Indian and negro race, against civilization and the Anglo-American race." Most recent American migrants to Texas had come from the South, and racist statements of this sort made political compromise with the Mexican government, a step favored by many of the older American settlers, impossible.

Between 1830 and 1836, in spite of the mediation efforts of Austin (who was imprisoned for eighteen months by the Mexican government for his pains), the mood on both the Mexican and the American-Texan sides became more belligerent. In the fall of 1835 war finally broke out, and a volunteer American Texan and Tejano army seized Goliad and San Antonio, in the heart of Mexican Texas, from the small Mexican army that was sent to quell them. Believing they had won, the Americans were caught off guard by a major counterattack led by the Mexican general and president Antonio López de Santa Anna. As described in the opening of this chapter, on March 6, 1836, Santa Anna and his forces overwhelmed the 187 men who refused to surrender—or to escape from—the Alamo in San Antonio. At Santa Anna's orders, the women at the Alamo—one American woman and several Tejanas—and an African American slave named Joe were spared so that Texans could hear their eyewitness accounts. From those accounts the legend of the Alamo was born.

From San Antonio, Santa Anna divided his army and led part of it in pursuit of the remaining army of American and Tejano volunteers commanded by General Sam Houston. On April 21, 1836, at the San Jacinto River in eastern Texas, Santa Anna thought he had Houston trapped at last. Confident of victory against the exhausted Texans, Santa Anna's army rested in the afternoon, failing even to post sentries. Although Houston advised against it, Houston's men voted to attack immediately rather than wait till the next morning. Shouting "Remember the Alamo!" for the first time, the Texans completely surprised their opponents and won an overwhelming victory. On May 14, 1836, Santa Anna signed a treaty fixing the southern boundary of the newly independent Republic of Texas at the Rio Grande. The Mexican Congress, however, repudiated the treaty and refused to recognize Texan independence. It also rejected the offer by President Andrew Jackson to solve the matter through purchase.

The Republic of Texas

Despite the military triumph of the Americans who had proclaimed the Republic of Texas, the land between the Rio Grande and the Nueces River remained disputed territory. In the eyes of the Mexicans, the American insistence on the Rio Grande boundary was little more than a blatant effort to stake a claim to New Mexico, an older and completely separate Spanish settlement. An effort by the Republic of Texas in 1841 to capture Santa Fé was easily repulsed.

The Republic of Texas was unexpectedly rebuffed in another quarter as well. The U.S. Congress refused to grant it statehood when, in 1837, Texas applied for admission to the Union. Petitions opposing the admission of a fourteenth slave state (there were then thirteen free states) poured into Congress.

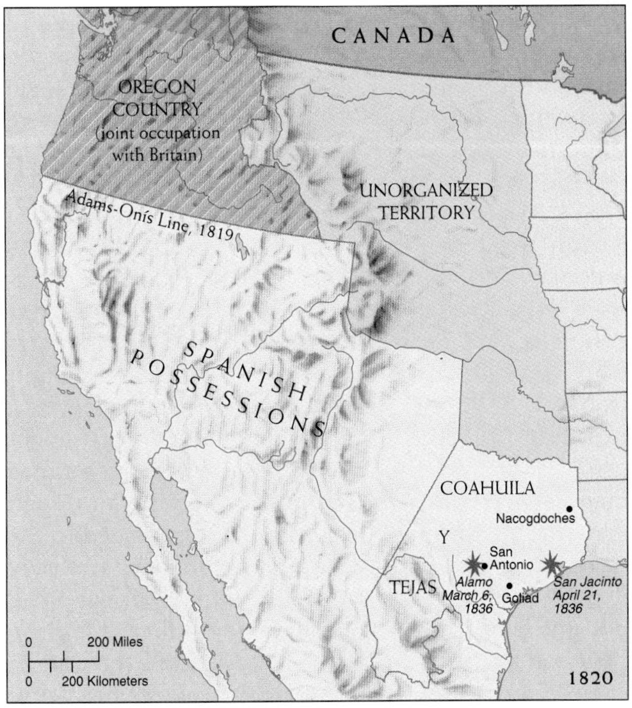

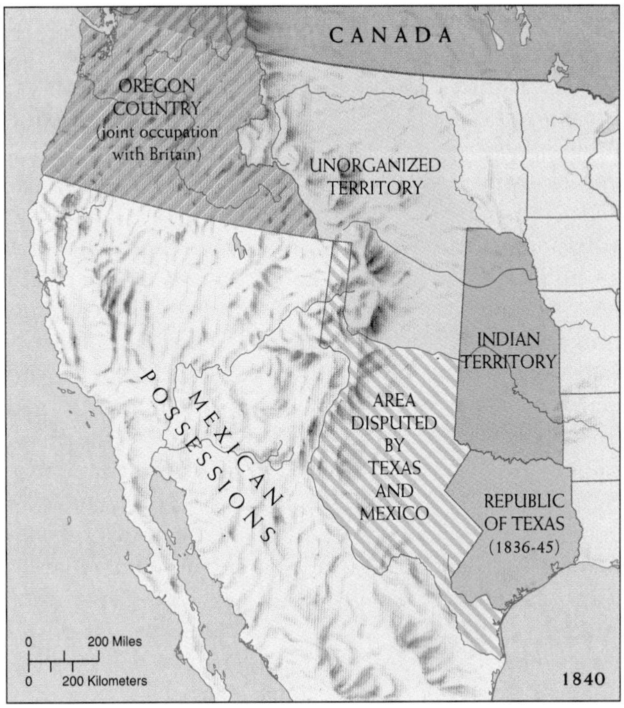

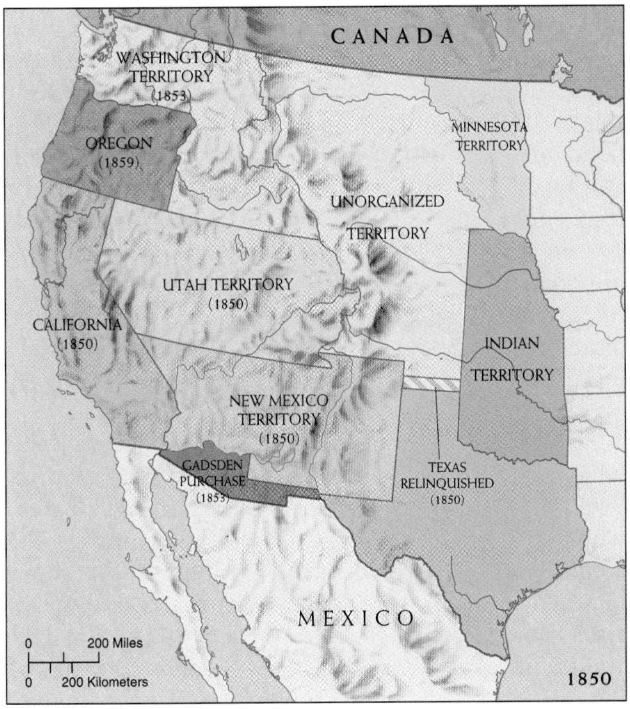

Texas: From Mexican Province to U.S. State *In the space of twenty years, Texas changed shape three times. Initially part of the Mexican province of Coahuila y Tejas, it became the Republic of Texas in 1836, following the Texas Revolt, and was annexed to the United States in that form in 1845. Finally, in the Compromise of 1850 following the Mexican-American War, it took its present shape.*

Congressman John Quincy Adams of Massachusetts, known as the conscience of New England, led the opposition to the admission of Texas. Adams was (and is still) the only former president to subsequently serve in Congress, and his unprecedented position gave immense authority to his opinions. Congress debated and ultimately dropped the Texas application. Although President Jackson was sympathetic to the Texan cause, he knew that he did not have the power to quell the controversy that the admission of Texas would arouse. But he did manage to extend diplomatic recognition to the Republic of Texas, on March 3, 1837, less than twenty-four hours before he left office. Breaking the good news to Texas agents at the White House, Jackson offered toasts to the Republic of Texas and to its president, his old friend Sam Houston.

Sam Houston must often have wondered whether the presidency of the Republic of Texas was an honor worth having. The unresolved conflict with Mexico put heavy stress on American-Tejano relations. Immediately after the revolt, many Tejano residents fled to Mexico, and American squatters moved in to claim their lands. In some regions, vigilantes forced Tejanos to leave. San Antonio, however, the most important city of Mexican Texas, saw an accommodation between the old elite and the new American authorities. Although they slowly lost political power, members of the Tejano elite were not immediately dispossessed of their property. As before, ambitious Anglos married into the Tejano elite. The intermarriages made it easier for the Tejano elite to adjust to the changes in law and commerce that the Americans quickly enacted. But following a temporary recapture of San Antonio by Mexican forces in 1842, positions hardened. Many more of the Tejano elite fled to Mexico, and Americans discussed banishing or imprisoning all Tejanos until the border issue was settled. This was, of course, impossible. Culturally, San Antonio remained a Mexican city long after the Americans had declared independence. The Americans in the Republic of Texas were struggling to reconcile American ideals of democracy with the reality of subordinating those with a prior claim, the Tejanos, to the status of a conquered people.

Ethnocentric attitudes quickly triumphed. Tejanos and other Mexicans were soon being blamed by Americans for their own subordination. Senator Edward Hannegan of Indiana was one of the most outspoken: "Mexico and the United States are peopled by two distinct and utterly unhomogeneous races," he announced in 1847. "In no reasonable period could we amalgamate." In the same year, the *Democratic Review*, completely ignoring the Spanish discovery and conquest of the Americas, offered the following rationalization: "Had Mexico been settled by a vigorous race of Europeans...that would have turned its advantages to account, developed its wealth, increased its commerce and multiplied its settlements, she would not now be in danger of losing her lands by emigration from the North."

American control over the other Texas residents, the Indians, was also slow in coming. Although the coastal Indian peoples were soon killed or removed, the Comanches still rode the high plains of northern and western Texas. West of the Rio Grande, equally fierce Apache bands were in control. Both groups soon learned to distrust American promises to stay out of their territory, and they did not hesitate to raid and to kill trespassers. Not until after the Civil War and major campaigns by the U.S. Army were these fierce Indian tribes conquered.

Texas Annexation and the Election of 1844

Martin Van Buren, who succeeded Andrew Jackson as president in 1837, was too cautious to raise the Texas issue during his term of office. But Texans themselves continued to press for annexation to the United States while at the same time seeking recognition and support from Great Britain. The idea of an independent and expansionist republic on its southern border that might gain the support of America's traditional enemy alarmed many Americans. Annexation thus became an urgent matter of national politics. This issue also added to the troubles of a governing Whig Party that was already deeply divided by the policies of John Tyler, who had become president by default when William Harrison died in office (see Chapter 10). Tyler raised the issue of annexation in 1844, hoping thereby to ensure his reelection, but the strategy backfired. Presenting the annexation treaty to Congress, Secretary of State John Calhoun awakened sectional fears by connecting Texas with the urgent need of southern slave owners to extend slavery.

In a storm of antislavery protest, Whigs rejected the treaty proposed by their own president and ejected Tyler himself from the party. In his place they chose Henry Clay, the party's longtime standard-bearer, as their presidential candidate. Clay took a noncommittal stance on Texas, favoring annexation, but only if Mexico approved. Since Mexico's emphatic disapproval was well known, Clay's position was widely interpreted as a politician's effort not to alienate voters on either side of the fence.

In contrast, in the Democratic Party wholehearted and outspoken expansionists seized control. Sweeping aside their own senior politician, Van Buren, who like Clay tried to remain uncommitted, the Democrats nominated their first "dark horse" candidate, James K. Polk of Tennessee. Southerners and Westerners among the Democrats—including such notables as Robert Walker of Mississippi, Stephen Douglas of Illinois, and Lewis Cass of Michigan—beat the drum of manifest destiny, promising that expansion meant a glorious extension of democracy. They enthusiastically endorsed Polk's platform, which called for "the re-occupation of Oregon and the re-annexation of Texas at the earliest practicable period."

Polk won the 1844 election by the narrow margin of 40,000 popular votes (although he gained 170 electoral votes to Clay's 105). An ominous portent for the Whigs was the showing of James G. Birney of the Liberty Party, who polled 62,000 votes, largely from northern antislavery Whigs. Birney's third-party campaign was the first political sign of the growing strength of antislavery opinion. Nevertheless, the 1844 election was widely interpreted as a mandate for expansion. Thereupon John Tyler, in one of his last actions as president, pushed through Congress a joint resolution (which did not require the two-thirds approval by the Senate necessary for treaties) for the annexation of Texas. Three months later the Texas congress approved annexation, and thus nine years after its founding the Republic of Texas disappeared. Florida had just been approved for statehood as well, and when Texas entered the Union in December 1845 it was the twenty-eighth state and the fifteenth slave state.

THE MEXICAN–AMERICAN WAR

James K. Polk lived up to his campaign promises. In 1846 he peacefully added Oregon south of the forty-ninth parallel to the United States; in 1848, following the Mexican-American War, he acquired Mexico's northern provinces of California and New Mexico as well. Thus, with the annexation of Texas, the United States, in the short space of three years, had added 1.5 million square

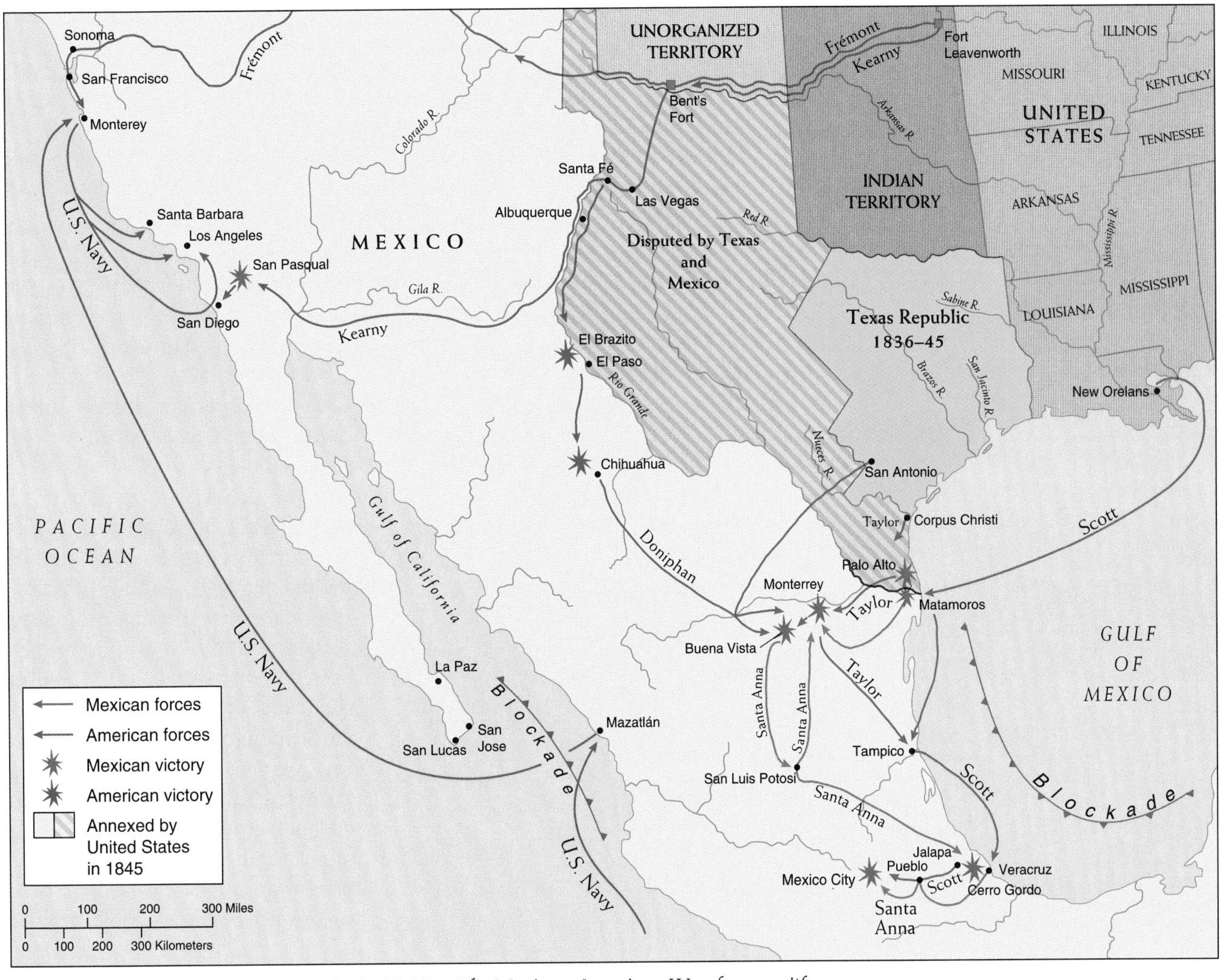

The Mexican-American War, 1846–1848 *The Mexican-American War began with an advance by U.S. forces into the disputed area between the Nueces River and the Rio Grande in Texas. The war's major battles were fought by General Zachary Taylor in northern Mexico and General Winfield Scott in Vera Cruz and Mexico City. Meanwhile Colonel Stephen Kearny secured New Mexico and, with the help of the U.S. Navy and John C. Frémont's troops, California.*

miles of territory, an increase of nearly 70 percent. Polk was indeed "the manifest destiny" president.

Origins of the War

In the spring of 1846, just as the controversy over Oregon was drawing to a peaceful conclusion, tensions with Mexico grew more serious. As soon as Texas was granted statehood in 1845, the Mexican government broke diplomatic relations with the United States. In addition, because the United States accepted the Texas claim of all land north of the Rio Grande, it found itself embroiled in a border dispute with Mexico. In June 1845, Polk sent General Zachary Taylor to Texas, and by October a force of 3,500 Americans were on the Nueces River with orders to defend Texas in the event of a Mexican invasion.

Polk had something bigger than border protection in mind. He coveted the continent clear to the Pacific Ocean. At the same time that he sent Taylor to Texas, Polk secretly instructed the Pacific naval squadron to seize the California ports if Mexico declared war. He also wrote the American consul in Monterey, Thomas Larkin, that a peaceful takeover of California by its residents—Spanish Mexicans and Americans alike—would not be unwelcome. When, in addition, the federally commissioned explorer John C. Frémont and a band of armed men appeared in California in the winter of 1845–46, Mexican authorities became alarmed and ordered him to leave. After withdrawing briefly to Oregon, Frémont returned to California and was on hand in Sonoma in June to assist in the Bear Flag Revolt, in which a handful of American settlers, declaring that they were playing "the Texas game," announced California's independence from Mexico.

Meanwhile, in November 1845, Polk followed up his warlike gestures by sending a secret envoy, John Slidell, to Mexico with an offer of $30 million or more for the Rio Grande border in Texas and Mexico's provinces of New Mexico and California. When the Mexican government refused even to receive Slidell, an angry Polk ordered General Taylor and his forces south to the Rio Grande, into the territory that Mexicans considered their soil. In April 1846 a brief skirmish between American and Mexican soldiers broke out in the disputed zone. Polk seized on the event, sending a war message to Congress: "Mexico has passed the boundary of the United States, has invaded our territory and shed American blood upon American soil.... War exists, and, notwithstanding all our efforts to avoid it, exists by the act of Mexico herself." This last claim of President Polk's was, of course, contrary to fact. On May 13, 1846, Congress declared war on Mexico.

Mr. Polk's War

From the beginning, the Mexican-American War was politically divisive. Whig critics in Congress, among them a gawky young congressman from Illinois named Abraham Lincoln, questioned Polk's account of the border incident. They accused the president of misleading Congress and of maneuvering the country into an unnecessary war. It is with these suspicions that the history of Congressional concern over the way presidents have exercised their war powers begins. The issue would again be prominent, for example, more than a hundred years later during the Vietnam War and in the Reagan years. As the Mexican-American War dragged on and casualties and costs mounted—13,000 Americans and 50,000 Mexicans died and the United States spent $97 million—opposition increased, especially among northern antislavery Whigs. More and more people came to the opinion that the war was nothing more than a plot by Southerners to expand slavery. Many Northerners asked why Polk had been willing to settle for only a part of Oregon but was so eager to pursue a war for slave territory. Thus expansionist dreams served to fuel sectional antagonisms.

General Winfield Scott's amphibious attack on the Mexican coastal city of Vera Cruz in March 1847 was a considerable military feat that was greeted with wide popular acclaim in the United States. Popular interest in the battles of the Mexican-American War was fed by illustrations such as this in newspapers and magazines.

The northern states witnessed both mass and individual protests against the war. In Massachusetts, the legislature passed a resolution condemning Polk's declaration of war as unconstitutional, and philosopher-writer Henry David Thoreau went to jail rather than pay the taxes he believed would support the war effort. Thoreau's dramatic gesture was undercut by his aunt, who paid his fine after he had spent only one night in jail. Thoreau then returned to his cabin on Walden Pond, where he wrote his classic essay "Civil Disobedience," justifying the individual's moral right to oppose an immoral government. In the early twentieth century, the Indian nationalist Mohandas Gandhi used Thoreau's essay to justify his campaign of "passive resistance" against British imperial rule in India. In turn, Martin Luther King and others used Gandhi's model of civil disobedience as a basis for their activities in the civil rights movement of the 1950s and 1960s.

Whigs termed the war with Mexico "Mr. Polk's War," but the charge was not just a Whig jibe. Although he lacked a military background, Polk assumed the overall planning of the war's strategy (a practice that the critical Mr. Lincoln was to follow in the Civil War). By his personal attention to the coordination of civilian political goals and military requirements, Polk gave a new and expanded definition to the role of the president as commander in chief during wartime. In 1846 Polk sent General Taylor south into northeastern Mexico and Colonel Stephen Kearny to New Mexico and California. Taylor captured the northern Mexico cities of Palo Alto in May and Monterrey in September 1846. Meanwhile, Kearny marched his men 900 miles to Santa Fé, which surrendered peacefully. Another march of roughly the same distance brought him by fall to southern California, which he took with the help of naval forces and Frémont's irregular troops.

The northern provinces that Polk had coveted were now secured, but contrary to his expectations, Mexico refused to negotiate. In February 1847, General Santa Anna of Alamo fame attacked American troops led by General Taylor at Buena Vista but was repulsed by Taylor's small force. A month later, in March 1847, General Winfield Scott launched an amphibious attack on the coastal city of Veracruz and rapidly captured it. Americans celebrated these twin victories joyously, but they were to be the last easy victories of the war. It took Scott six months of brutal fighting against stubborn Mexican resistance on the battlefield and harassing guerrilla raids to force his way to Mexico City. American troops reacted bitterly to their high casualty rates, retaliating against Mexican citizens with acts of murder, robbery, and rape. Even General Scott himself admitted that his troops had "committed atrocities to make Heaven weep and every American of Christian morals blush for his country." In September, Scott took Mexico City, and Mexican resistance came to an end.

Territory Added, 1845–1853 *James K. Polk was elected president in 1844 on an expansionist platform. He lived up to most of his campaign rhetoric by gaining the Oregon Country (to the forty-ninth parallel) peacefully from the British, Texas by the presidential action of his predecessor John Tyler, and present-day California, Arizona, Nevada, Utah, New Mexico, and part of Colorado by war with Mexico. In the short space of three years, the size of the United States grew by 70 percent. In 1853, the Gadsden Purchase added another 30,000 square miles.*

With the American army went a special envoy, Nicholas Trist, who delivered Polk's terms for peace. In the Treaty of Guadalupe Hidalgo, signed February 2, 1848, Mexico ceded its northern provinces of California and New Mexico (which included present-day Arizona, Utah, Nevada, and part of Colorado) and accepted the Rio Grande as the boundary of Texas. The United States agreed to pay Mexico $15 million and assume about $2 million in individual claims against that nation.

When Trist returned to Washington with the treaty, however, Polk was furious. He had actually recalled Trist after Scott's sweeping victory, intending to send a new envoy with greater demands, but Trist had ignored the recall order. "All Mexico!" had become the phrase widely used by those in favor of further expansion, Polk among them. But two very different groups opposed further expansion. The first group, composed of northern Whigs, included such notables as Ralph Waldo Emerson, who grimly warned, "The United States will conquer Mexico, but it will be as the man swallows arsenic, which brings him down in turn. Mexico will poison us." The second group was composed of Southerners who realized that Mexicans could not be kept as conquered people but would have to be offered territorial government as Louisiana had in 1804. Senator John C. Calhoun of South Carolina, leading the opposition, warned against admitting "colored and mixed-breed" Mexicans "on an equality with people of the United States." "We make a great mistake, sir," he argued on the floor of the Senate, "when we suppose that all people are capable of self-government." Bowing to these political protests, Polk reluctantly accepted the treaty. A later addition, the $10 million Gadsden Purchase of parts of present-day New Mexico and Arizona, added another 30,000 square miles to the United States in 1853. This purchase, made to facilitate a southern transcontinental railroad route through arid borderland, was a far cry from the rich heartland of Mexico that Polk had hoped to annex.

The Press and Popular War Enthusiasm

The Mexican-American War was the first war in which regular, on-the-scene reporting by representatives of the press caught the mass of ordinary citizens up in the war's daily events. Thanks to the recently invented telegraph, newspapers could get the latest news from their reporters, who were among the world's first war correspondents. The "penny press," with more than a decade's experience of reporting urban crime and scandals, was quick to realize that the public's appetite for sensational war news was apparently insatiable. For the first time in American history, accounts by journalists, and not the opinions of politicians, became the major shapers of popular attitudes toward a war. From beginning to end, news of the war stirred unprecedented popular excitement.

The reports from the battlefield united Americans in a new way: they became part of a temporary but highly emotional community linked by newsprint and buttressed by public gatherings. In the spring of 1846, news of Zachary Taylor's victory at Palo Alto prompted the largest meeting ever held in the cotton textile town of Lowell, Massachusetts. In May 1847, New York City celebrated the twin victories at Veracruz and Buena Vista with fireworks, illuminations, and a "grand procession" estimated at 400,000 people. Generals Taylor and Scott became overnight heroes, and in time both became presidential candidates. Exciting, sobering, and terrible, war news had a deep hold on the popular imagination. It was a lesson newspaper publishers never forgot.

Woodville, *War News from Mexico*, oil on canvas. Manovgian Foundation on loan to the National Gallery of Art, Washington, D.C.

The unprecedented immediacy of the news reporting of the Mexican-American War, transmitted for the first time by telegraph, is captured here by Richard Caton Woodville in War News from Mexico (1848). *By including an African American man and child, the artist is also voicing a political concern about the effect of the war on slavery.*

CALIFORNIA AND THE GOLD RUSH

In the early 1840s California was inhabited by many seminomadic Indian tribes whose people numbered approximately 50,000. There were also some 7,000 Californios, descendants of the Spanish Mexican pioneers who had begun to settle in 1769. The American presence in California at first consisted of a few traders and settlers who often intermarried with Californios. Even American annexation at the end of the Mexican-American War changed little for the handful of Americans on this remote frontier. But then came the Gold Rush of 1849, which changed California permanently.

Russian-Californio Trade

The first outsiders to penetrate the isolation of Spanish California were not Americans but Russians. Because the distance between California and Mexico City was so great, the Spanish had found it difficult to maintain the elaborate system of twenty-one missions first established in the eighteenth century (see Chapter 5). Nevertheless, Spanish officials in Mexico insisted on isolation, forbidding the colonists to trade with other nations. Evading Spanish regulations, Californios conducted a small illegal trade in cattle hides with American merchant ships (for the shoes made in the workshops of Massachusetts), and

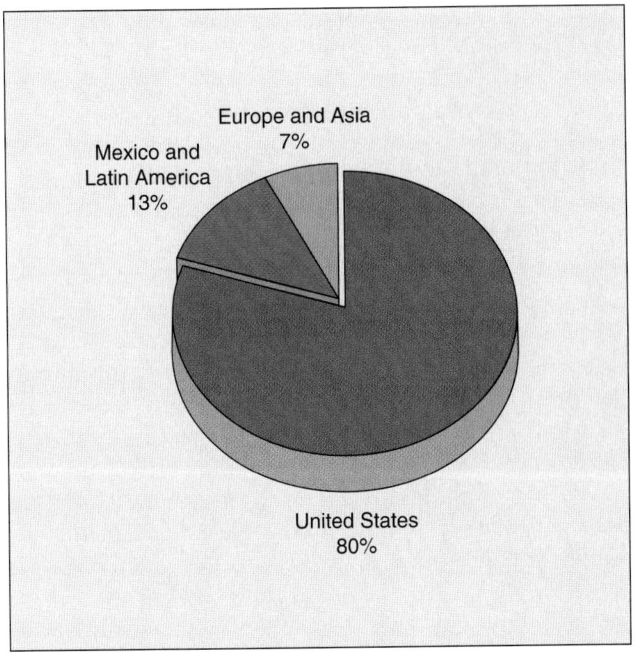

Where the Forty-Niners Came From *Americans drawn to the California Gold Rush of 1849 encountered a more diverse population than most had previously known. Nearly as novel to them as the 20 percent from foreign countries was the regional variety from within the United States itself.*

a much larger trade with the Russian American Fur Company in Sitka, Alaska. A mutually beneficial barter of California food for iron tools and woven cloth from Russia was established in 1806. This arrangement became even brisker after the Russians settled Fort Ross (near present-day Mendocino) in 1812, and led in time to regular trade with Mission San Rafael and Mission Sonoma. That the Russians in Alaska, so far from their own capital, were better supplied with manufactured goods than the Californios is an index of the latter's isolation.

When Mexico became independent in 1821, the California trade was thrown open to ships of all nations. Nevertheless, Californios continued their special relationship with the Russians, exempting them from the taxes and inspections that they required of Americans. However, agricultural productivity declined after 1832, when the Mexican government ordered the secularization of the California missions, and the Russians regretfully turned to the rich farms of the Hudson's Bay Company in the Pacific Northwest for their food supply. In 1841, they sold Fort Ross, and the Russian-Californio connection came to an end.

Early American Settlement

It was Johann Augustus Sutter, a Swiss who had settled in California in 1839, becoming a Mexican citizen, who served as a focal point for American settlement in the 1840s. Sutter held a magnificent land grant in the Sacramento Valley. At the center of his holdings was Sutter's Fort, a walled compound that was part living quarters and part supply shop for his vast cattle ranch, which was run largely on forced Indian labor. In the 1840s, Sutter offered valuable support to the handful of American overlanders who chose California over Oregon, the destination preferred by most pioneers. Most of these Americans, keenly aware that they were interlopers in Mexican territory, settled near Sutter in California's Central Valley, away from the Californios clustered along the coast.

The 1840s immigrants made no effort to intermarry with the Californios or to conform to Spanish ways. They were bent on taking over the territory. In June 1846 these Americans banded together at Sonoma in the Bear Flag Revolt (so called

California in the Gold Rush *This map shows the major gold camps along the Mother Lode in the western foothills of the Sierra Nevada mountains. Gold seekers reached the camps by crossing the Sierra Nevadas near Placerville on the Overland Trail or by sea via San Francisco. The main area of Spanish-Mexican settlement, the coastal region between Monterey and Los Angeles, was remote from the gold fields.*

Source: Warren A. Beck and Ynez D. Haase, *Historical Atlas of California* (Norman: University of Oklahoma Press, 1974), map 50.

Frank Marryat, *The Bar of A Gambling Saloon*, published 1855. Lithograph. Collection of the New York Historical Society, New York City.

This drawing of the bar of a gambling saloon in San Francisco in 1855 shows the effects of the Gold Rush on California. Men from all parts of the world are gathered at this elegant bar in the large cosmopolitan city of San Francisco, which had been only a small trading post before gold was discovered in 1849.

because their flag bore a bear emblem), declaring independence from Mexico. The American takeover of California was not confirmed until the Treaty of Guadalupe Hidalgo in 1848. In the meantime, California was regarded by most Americans merely as a remote, sparsely populated frontier, albeit one with splendid potential. Polk and other expansionists coveted the magnificent harbors in San Diego and San Francisco as the basis for Pacific trade with Asia, but in 1848 this prospect was still only a dream.

Gold!

In January 1848 carpenter James Marshall noticed small flakes of gold in the millrace at Sutter's Mill (present-day Coloma). Soon he and all the rest of John Sutter's employees were panning for gold in California's streams. The news, which they had hoped to keep secret, spread, and before long it seemed that all the men in California were at the mines. When explorer John Frémont returned to San Francisco in June 1848, he found it almost deserted because of the "gold fever."

In the autumn of 1848, the east coast heard the first rumors about the discovery of gold in California. The reports were confirmed in mid-November when an army courier arrived in Washington carrying a tea caddy full of gold dust and nuggets. The spirit of excitement and adventure so recently aroused by the Mexican-American War was now directed toward California, the new El Dorado. Thousands left farms and jobs and headed west, by land and by sea, to make their fortune. Later known as "forty-niners" for the year the gold rush began in earnest, these people came from all parts of the United States—and indeed, from all over the world. They transformed what had been a quiet ranching paradise into a teeming and tumultuous community in search of wealth in California's rivers and streams.

Eighty percent of the forty-niners were Americans. They came from every state. The Gold Rush was an eye-opening expansion of their horizons for the many who had known only their hometown folks before. The second largest group of migrants were from nearby Mexico and the west coast of Latin America (13 percent). The remainder came from Europe and Asia.

The presence of Chinese miners surprised many Americans. Several hundred Chinese arrived in California in 1849 and 1850, and in 1852 more than 20,000 landed in San Francisco hoping to share in the wealth of Gum Sam (Golden Mountain). Most came, like the Americans, as temporary sojourners, intending to return home as soon as they made some money. Again, like most of the American miners, the majority of Chinese were men who left their wives at home. Dressed in their distinctive blue cotton shirts, baggy pants, and broad-brimmed hats, and with long queues hanging down their backs, hardworking Chinese miners soon became a familiar sight in the gold fields, as did the presence of "Chinatowns." The distinctive appearance of the Chinese, added to the threat of economic competition that they posed, quickly aroused American hostility. A special tax was imposed on foreign miners in 1852, and in the 1870s, Chinese immigration was sharply curtailed.

In 1849, as the gold rush began in earnest, San Francisco, the major entry port and supply point, sprang to life. From a settlement of 1,000 in 1848 it grew to a city of 35,000 in 1850. This surge suggested that the real money to be made in California was not in panning for gold but from feeding, clothing, housing, provisioning, and entertaining the miners. Among the first to learn that lesson was the German Jewish immigrant Levi Strauss, who sold so many tough work pants to miners that his name became synonymous with his product. And Jerusha Marshall, who opened a twenty-room boardinghouse in the city, candidly wrote to her eastern relatives: "Never was there a better field for making money than now presents itself in this place.... We are satisfied to dig our gold in San Francisco." From these "instant" beginnings San Francisco stabilized to become a major American city. Meanwhile, the white population of California had jumped from an estimated pre-Gold Rush figure of 11,000 to more than 100,000 by 1852. California was admitted as a state in 1850.

Mining Camps

Most mining camps, like San Francisco, boomed almost instantly to life, but unlike San Francisco, they were empty again within a few years. In spite of the aura of glamour that surrounds the names of the famous camps—Poker Flat, Angels Camp, Whiskey Bar, Placerville, Mariposa—they were generally dirty and dreary places. Most miners lived in tents or hovels, unwilling to take time from mining to build themselves decent quarters. They cooked monotonous meals of beans, bread, and bacon or, if they had money, bought meals at expensive restaurants and boardinghouses (where the table might be no more than a plank over two flour barrels). Many migrants traveled to the mines with relatives or fellow townspeople. But often they split up in California—each man with his own idea of where he could find gold the easiest—and ended up on their own. They led a cheerless, uncomfortable, and unhealthy existence, especially during the long, rainy winter months, with few distractions apart from the saloon, the gambling hall, and the prostitute's crib.

Most miners were young, unmarried, and unsuccessful. Only a small percentage ever struck it rich in California. Gold deposits that were accessible with pick and shovel were soon exhausted, and the deeper deposits required capital and machinery. Some of the workings at the Comstock Lode in Virginia City, Nevada, a later mining center, were half a mile deep. But many men were ashamed to come home until they had "made their pile." Increasingly, as they stayed on in California, they had to give up the status of independent miners and become wage earners for large mining concerns.

As in San Francisco, a more reliable way to earn money in the camps was to supply the miners. Every mining community had its saloonkeepers, gamblers, prostitutes, merchants, and restauranteurs. Like the miners themselves, these people were transients, always ready to pick up and move at the word of a new gold strike. The majority of women in the early mining camps were prostitutes. Some grew rich or married respectably, but most died young of drugs, venereal disease, or violence. Most of the other women were hardworking wives of miners, and in this predominantly male society they made good money doing domestic work: keeping boardinghouses, cooking, doing laundry. Even the wives of professional men who in the East might have been restrained by propriety succumbed to the monetary opportunities and kept boardinghouses.

Partly because few people put any effort into building communities—they were too busy seeking gold—violence was endemic in mining areas, and much of it was racial. Discrimination, especially against Chinese, Mexicans, and African Americans, was common. Frequently miners' claims were "jumped": thieves would rob them of the gold they had accumulated, kill them, or chase them away, and then file their own claim for the victims' strike. Or unscrupulous miners might use the law to their advantage to secure the claims of others without violence—for example by taking advantage of the prohibitively high mining tax on foreigners.

In the end, most mining camps were at best temporary communities. The gold "played out" and people moved on, leaving ghost towns behind. By the

Chinese first came to California in 1849 attracted by the Gold Rush. Frequently, however, they were forced off their claims by intolerant whites. Rather than enjoy an equal chance in the gold fields they were often forced to work as servants or in other menial occupations.

mid-1850s, the immediate effects of the Gold Rush had passed. California had a booming population, a thriving agriculture, and a corporate mining industry. The Gold Rush also left California with a population that was larger, more affluent, and (in urban San Francisco) more culturally sophisticated than that in other newly settled territories. It was also significantly more multicultural than the rest of the nation, for many of the Chinese and Mexicans, as well as immigrants from many European countries, remained in California after the Gold Rush subsided. But the Gold Rush left some permanent scars, and not just on the foothills landscape: the virtual extermination of the California Indian peoples, the dispossession of many Californios who were legally deprived of their land grants, and the growth of racial animosity toward the Chinese in particular. The major characteristics of the mining frontier, evident first in the California Gold Rush and repeated many times thereafter in similar "rushes" in Colorado, Montana, Idaho, South Dakota, and Arizona, were a lack of stable communities and a worsening of racial tensions.

THE POLITICS OF MANIFEST DESTINY

In three short years, from 1845 to 1848, the territory of the United States grew an incredible 70 percent and became a continental nation. This expansion and the concept of manifest destiny that justified it quickly became the dominant issues in national politics.

The "Young America" Movement

One source of the belief in manifest destiny was national pride—the conviction that American democracy was so superior it would lead inevitably to the expansion of the nation. The swift victory in the Mexican-American War and the "prize" of California gold seemed to confirm that conviction. European events in 1848 also served to foster American pride. In that year a series of democratic revolutions—in Italy, France, Germany, Hungary, and parts of the Austrian Empire—swept the Continent. Expansionists assumed that American democracy and manifest destiny were the models for these liberal revolutions. When Lajos Kossuth, the famed Hungarian revolutionary, visited the United States in 1851, he was given a hero's welcome, and Daniel Webster complacently assured him that "we shall rejoice to see our American model upon the lower Danube."

In an even more confident gesture, President Franklin Pierce dispatched Commodore Matthew Perry across the Pacific to Japan, a nation famous for its insularity and hostility to outsiders. The mission resulted in 1854 in a commercial treaty that opened Japan to American trade. Perry's feat caused a newspaper in tiny Olympia, Washington, to boast, "We shall have the boundless Pacific for a market in manifest destiny. We were born to command it."

But efforts closer to home by the Young America movement, as expansionist Democrats styled themselves, were more controversial. Victory in the Mexican-American War and the evident weakness of the

Details of Perry's ship and military parade from Japanese print, Ukiyo-e school, *Landing of Commodore Perry in Japan.*

This Japanese painting shows Commodore Matthew Perry landing in Japan in 1854. The commercial treaty Perry signed with the Japanese government, which opened a formerly closed country to American trade, was viewed in the United States as another fruit of manifest destiny.

OVERVIEW

EXPANSION CAUSES THE FIRST SPLITS IN THE SECOND AMERICAN PARTY SYSTEM

1844	Whigs reject President John Tyler's move to annex Texas and expel him from the Whig Party.
	Southern Democrats choose expansionist James K. Polk as their presidential candidate, passing over Martin Van Buren, who is against expansion.
	Liberty Party runs abolitionist James Birney for president, attracting northern antislavery Whigs.
1846	The Wilmot Proviso, proposing to ban slavery in the territories that might be gained in the Mexican-American War, splits both parties: southern Whigs and Democrats oppose the measure; northern Whigs and Democrats support it.
1848	The new Free-Soil Party runs northern Democrat Martin Van Buren for president, gaining 10 percent of the vote from abolitionists, antislavery Whigs, and some northern Democrats. This strong showing by a third party causes Democrat Lewis Cass to lose the electoral votes of New York and Pennsylvania, allowing the Whig Zachary Taylor to win.

Mexican government whetted the appetite of some southern expansionists for more territory. But most American politicians were cautious about further gains. When in the spring of 1848 Polk recommended American intervention in the civil war in the Mexican province of Yucatán, Congress rebuffed him. Senator John C. Calhoun, harking back to Polk's manipulation of Congress in 1846, cautioned, "I did hope that the experience of the Mexican War—that precipitate and rash measure which has cost the country so dearly in blood and treasure—would have taught the administration moderation and caution." In the winter of 1848, rumors swept Washington that Polk had offered Spain up to $100 million for Cuba (compared with the $15 million paid for Mexico's provinces of California and New Mexico). The nation was spared a raging political battle when Spain spurned all offers.

Thus the Mexican-American War was divisive even after it was won. A small group of expansionists, most from the South, wanted more, in spite of clear evidence that most Americans had had enough. Throughout the 1850s, these expansionists continued to covet Mexico, Central America, and Cuba. Adventures in these directions, all organized by Southerners intent on acquiring new lands for cotton, further inflamed the festering sectional differences of the 1850s that are discussed in Chapter 15.

The Wilmot Proviso

In 1846, almost all the northern members of the Whig Party opposed Democratic president James Polk's belligerent expansionism on antislavery grounds. Northern Whigs correctly feared that expansion would reopen the issue of slavery in the territories. "We appear...to be rushing upon perils headlong, and with our eyes all open," Daniel Webster warned in 1847. His remedy? "We want no extension of territory; we want no accession of new states. The country is already large enough." But the outpouring of enthusiasm for the Mexican-American War drowned Webster's words and convinced most Whig congressmen that they needed to vote military appropriations for the war in spite of their misgivings.

Ironically it was not the Whigs but a freshman Democratic congressman from Pennsylvania, David Wilmot, who opened the door to sectional controversy over expansion. In August 1846, only a few short months after the beginning of the Mexican-American War, Wilmot proposed, in an amendment to a military appropriations bill, that slavery be banned in all the territories acquired from Mexico. He was ready, Wilmot said, to "sustain the institutions of the South as they exist. But sir, the issue now presented is not whether slavery shall exist unmolested where it is now, but whether it shall be carried to new and distant regions, now free, where the footprint of a slave cannot be found." In the debate and voting that followed, something new and ominous occurred: southern Whigs joined southern Democrats to vote against the measure, while Northerners of both parties supported it. Sectional interest had triumphed over party loyalty. Wilmot's Proviso triggered the first breakdown of the national party system and reopened the debate about the place of slavery in the future of the nation.

The Wilmot Proviso was so controversial that it was deleted from the necessary military appropriations bills during the Mexican-American War. But in 1848, following the Treaty of Guadalupe Hidalgo, the question of the expansion of slavery could no longer be avoided or postponed. Antislavery advocates from the North argued with proslavery Southerners in a debate that was much more prolonged and more bitter than the Missouri Crisis of 1819. Civility quickly wore thin: threats were uttered and fistfights broke out on the floor of the House of Representatives. The Wilmot Proviso posed a fundamental challenge to both parties. Neither the Democrats nor the Whigs could take a strong stand on the amendment because neither party could get its northern and southern wings to agree. Decisive action, for or against, was a serious threat to party unity. Webster's fear that expansion would lead to sectional conflict had become a reality.

The Free-Soil Movement

Why did David Wilmot propose this controversial measure? Wilmot, a northern Democrat, was propelled not by ideology but by the pressure of practical politics. The dramatic rise of the Liberty Party, founded in 1840 by abolitionists, threatened to take votes away from both the Whig and the Democratic parties. The Liberty Party won 62,000 votes in the 1844 presidential election, all in the North. This was more than enough to deny victory to the Whig candidate, Henry Clay. Neither party could afford to ignore the strength of this third party.

The Liberty Party took an uncompromising stance against slavery. As articulated by Ohio's Salmon P. Chase, the party platform called for the "divorce of the federal government from slavery." The party proposed to prohibit the admission of slave states to the Union, end slavery in the District of Columbia, and abolish the interstate slave trade that was vital to the expansion of cotton growing into the Old Southwest (see Chapter 11). Liberty Party members also favored denying office to all slaveholders (a proposal that would have robbed all the southern states of their senators) and forbidding the use of slave labor on federal construction projects. In short, the party proposed to quickly strangle slavery. The popularity of this radical program among northern voters in 1844 was an indication of the moral fervor of abolitionism (see Chapter 13).

But Liberty Party doctrine was too uncompromising for the mass of northern voters, who immediately realized that the southern states would leave the Union before accepting it. Still, as the 1844 vote indicated, many Northerners opposed slavery. From this sentiment the Free-Soil Party was born. The free-soil argument was a calculated adjustment of abolitionist principles to practical politics. It shifted the focus from the question of the morality of slavery to the ways in which slavery posed a threat to northern expansion. The free-soil doctrine thus established a direct link between expansion, which most Americans supported, and sectional politics.

Free-soilers were willing to allow slavery to continue in the existing slave states because they supported the Union, not because they approved of slavery. They were unwilling, however, to allow the extension of slavery to new and unorganized territory. If the South were successful in extending slavery, they argued, northern farmers who moved west would find themselves competing at an economic disadvantage with large planters using slave labor. Free-soilers also insisted that the northern values of freedom and individualism would be destroyed if the slave-based southern labor system were allowed to spread. To free-soilers, the South was composed of little more than corrupt aristocrats, degraded slaves, and a large class of poor whites who were deprived of opportunity because they did not understand the value of honest labor.

Finally, many free-soilers really meant "antiblack" when they said "antislavery." They proposed to ban all African American people from the new territories (a step that four states—Indiana, Illinois, Iowa, and Oregon—took but did not always enforce). William Lloyd Garrison promptly denounced the free-soil doctrine as "whitemanism," a racist effort to make the territories white. There was much truth to his charge, but there was no denying that the free-soil doctrine was popular. Although abolitionists were making headway in their claim for moral equality regardless of skin color, most Northerners were unwilling to consider social equality for African Americans, free or slave. Banning all black people from the western territories seemed a simple solution.

Finally, the free-soil movement was a repudiation of the sectional compromise of 1820. If the Missouri Compromise line were carried westward to the Pacific Ocean, as Secretary of State James Buchanan proposed in 1848, much of present-day New Mexico and Arizona and the southern half of California would have been admitted as slave states, and everything to the north would have been free. Free-soilers opposed this arrangement. Their opposition in 1848 to the Missouri Compromise line indicated how influential antislavery feeling was becoming in the North.

The Election of 1848

A swirl of emotions—pride, expansionism, sectionalism, abolitionism, free-soil sentiment—surrounded the election of 1848. The Treaty of Guadalupe Hidalgo had been signed earlier in the year, and the vast northern Mexican provinces of New Mexico and California and the former

Republic of Texas had been incorporated into the United States. But the issues raised by the Wilmot Proviso remained to be resolved, and every candidate had to have an answer to the question of whether slavery should be admitted in the new territories.

Lewis Cass of Michigan, the Democratic nominee for president (Polk, in poor health, declined to run for a second term), proposed to apply the doctrine of popular sovereignty to the crucial slave–free issue. This democratic-sounding notion of leaving the decision to the citizens of each territory was based on the Jeffersonian faith in the common man's ability to vote both his own self-interest and the common good. In fact, however, popular sovereignty was an admission of the nation's failure to resolve sectional differences. It simply shifted decision making on the crucial issue of the expansion of slavery from national politicians to the members of territorial legislatures, who, belonging to different parties, were in as much disagreement as members of Congress and just as unable to resolve it.

In 1848, the Whigs once again adopted the campaign strategy that had worked so successfully for them in the presidential election of 1840. They nominated a hero of the Mexican-American War, General Zachary Taylor, who ran on his military exploits. In this poster, every letter of Taylor's name is decorated with scenes from the recent war, which had seized the popular imagination in a way no previous conflict had done. Emphasizing Taylor's reputation as a national hero (and therefore above petty politics), the Whigs were able to evade the question of whether or not he favored the extension of slavery into the territories.

As Cass stated it, the doctrine of popular sovereignty was deliberately vague about when a territory would choose its status. Would it do so during the territorial stage? at the point of applying for statehood? Clearly, this question was crucial, for no slave owner would invest in new land if the territory could later be declared free, and no abolitionist would move to a territory that was destined to become a slave state. Cass hoped his ambiguity on this point would win him votes in both North and South. Even so, sectional differences ran so deep that the Democrats found it necessary to print two campaign biographies of Cass. The biography circulated in the North touted Cass's doctrine of popular sovereignty as the best way to keep slavery out of the territories; the biography in the South implied the opposite.

For their part, the Whigs passed over perennial candidate Henry Clay and turned once again to a war hero, General Zachary Taylor. Taylor, a Louisiana slaveholder, refused to take a position on the Wilmot Proviso, allowing both northern and southern voters to hope that he agreed with them. Privately, Taylor opposed the expansion of slavery. In public, he evaded the issue by running as a war hero and a national leader who was above sectional politics.

The deliberate vagueness of the two major candidates displeased many northern voters. An uneasy mixture of disaffected Democrats (among them David Wilmot) and Whigs joined former Liberty Party voters to support the candidate of the Free-Soil Party, former president Martin Van Buren. Van Buren, angry at the Democratic Party for passing him over in 1844 and displeased with the growing southern dominance of the Democratic Party, ran as a spoiler. He knew he could not win the election, but he could divide the Democrats. In the end, Van Buren garnered 10 percent of the vote (all in the North). The vote for the Free-Soil Party cost Cass the electoral votes of New York and Pennsylvania, and General Taylor won the election with only 47 percent of the popular vote. This was the second election after 1840 that the Whigs had won by running a war hero who could duck hard questions by claiming to be above politics. Uncannily, history was to repeat itself: Taylor, like William Henry Harrison, died before his term was completed, and the chance he offered to maintain national unity—if ever it existed—was lost.

CHRONOLOGY

1609	First Spanish settlement in New Mexico
1670s	British and French Canadians begin fur trade in western Canada
1716	First Spanish settlements in Texas
1769	First Spanish settlement in California
1780s	New England ships begin sea otter trade in Pacific Northwest
1790	First American ship visits Hawaii
1803	Louisiana Purchase
1804–06	Lewis and Clark expedition
1806	Russian-Californio trade begins
1806–07	Zebulon Pike's expedition across the Great Plains to the Rocky Mountains
1819–20	Stephen Long's expedition across the Great Plains
1821	Hudson's Bay Company gains dominance of western fur trade
	Mexico seizes independence from Spain
	Santa Fé Trail opens, soon protected by U.S. military
	Stephen F. Austin becomes first American empresario in Texas
1824	First fur rendezvous sponsored by Rocky Mountain Fur Company
	Hudson's Bay Company establishes Fort Vancouver in Oregon Country
1830	Indian Removal Act moves eastern Indians to Indian Territory
1833–34	Prince Maximilian and Karl Bodmer visit Plains Indians
1834	Jason Lee establishes first mission in Oregon Country
1835	Texas revolts against Mexico
1836	Battles of the Alamo and San Jacinto
	Republic of Texas formed
1843–44	John C. Frémont maps trails to Oregon and California
1844	Democrat James K. Polk elected president on an expansionist platform
1845	Texas annexed to the United States as a slave state
	John O'Sullivan coins the phrase "manifest destiny"
1846	Oregon question settled peacefully with Britain
	Mexican-American War begins
	Bear Flag Revolt in California
	Wilmot Proviso
1847	Cayuse Wars begin in Oregon
	Americans win battles of Buena Vista, Veracruz, and Mexico City
1848	Treaty of Guadalupe Hidalgo
	Free-Soil Party captures 10 percent of the popular vote in the North
	General Zachary Taylor, a Whig, elected president
1849	California Gold Rush

CONCLUSION

In the decade of the 1840s, westward expansion took many forms, from relatively peaceful settlement in Oregon, to war with Mexico over Texas, to the sheer overwhelming numbers of gold rushers who changed California forever. Most of these frontiers—in Oregon, New Mexico, and California—began as frontiers of inclusion in which a small number of Americans were eager for trade, accommodation, and intermarriage with the original inhabitants. Texas, with its agricultural enclaves, was the exception to this pattern. Yet on every frontier, as the number of American settlers increased, so did the sentiment for exclusion, so that by 1850, whatever their origins, the far-flung American continental settlements were more similar than different and the success of manifest destiny seemed overwhelming.

The election of 1848, virtually a referendum on manifest destiny, yielded ironic results. James K. Polk, who presided over the unprecedented expansion, did not run for a second term, and thus the Democratic Party gained no electoral victory to match the military one. The electorate that had been so thrilled by the war news voted for a war hero—who led the antiexpansionist Whig Party. The election was decided by Martin Van Buren, the Free-Soil candidate who voiced the sentiments of the abolitionists, a reform group that had been insignificant just a few years before. The amazing expansion achieved by the Mexican-American War—America's manifest destiny—made the United States a continental nation but stirred up the issue that was to tear it apart. Sectional rivalries and fears now dominated every aspect of politics. Expansion, once a force for unity, now divided the nation into Northerners and Southerners, who could not agree on the community they shared—the federal Union.

REVIEW QUESTIONS

1. Define and discuss the concept of manifest destiny.
2. Trace the different ways in which the frontiers in Oregon, Texas, and California moved from frontiers of inclusion to frontiers of exclusion.
3. Take different sides (Whig and Democrat) and debate the issues raised by the Mexican-American War.
4. Referring back to Chapter 13, compare the positions of the Liberty Party and the Free-Soil Party. Examine the factors that made the free-soil doctrine politically acceptable to many, and abolitionism so controversial.

RECOMMENDED READING

Arnoldo De Leon, *The Tejano Community, 1836–1900* (1982). Traces the changing status of Tejanos after Texas came under the control of American Texans.

John Mack Faragher, *Women and Men on the Overland Trail* (1979). One of the first books to consider the experience of women on the journey west.

William Goetzman, *Exploration and Empire: The Explorer and the Scientist in the Winning of the American West* (1966). Considers the many government-sponsored explorations of the West.

Thomas R. Hietala, *Manifest Design: Anxious Aggrandizement in Late Jacksonian America* (1985). An interesting reassessment of manifest destiny from the perspective of party politics.

Julie Roy Jeffrey, *Converting the West: A Biography of Narcissa Whitman* (1991). Makes a clear connection between the missionary Whitman's evangelical upbringing and her failure to understand the culture of Oregon's Cayuse Indians.

Robert W. Johannsen, *To the Halls of the Montezumas: The Mexican War in the American Imagination* (1985). A lively book that explores the impact of the Mexican-American War on public opinion.

Paul D. Lack, *The Texas Revolutionary Experience: A Political and Social History, 1835–1836* (1992). A political and social history that stresses the chaotic and discordant nature of the Texas Revolt.

Janet Lecompte, *Pueblo, Hardscrabble, Greenhorn: The Upper Arkansas, 1832–1856* (1978). A social history that portrays the racial and ethnic diversity of the trading frontier.

Michael Morrison, *Slavery and the American West: The Eclipse of Manifest Destiny and the Coming of the Civil War* (1997). In a study of competing ideas over the future of the West, the author stresses the links between expansion and sectional disagreements.

Malcolm Rohrbough, *Days of Gold: The California Gold Rush and the American Nation* (1997). A lively history that emphasizes the effects of this "great American epic" on the national self-image.

David J. Weber, *The Mexican Frontier, 1821–1846: The American Southwest under Mexico* (1982). A fine study of the history of the Southwest before American conquest. The author is a leading borderlands historian.

Richard White, *"It's Your Misfortune and None of My Own": A History of the American West* (1991). A major reinterpretation that focuses on the history of the region itself rather than on the westward expansion of Americans. Pays much more attention to Spanish Mexicans and Indian peoples than earlier texts.

ADDITIONAL BIBLIOGRAPHY

Exploration, the Fur Trade, and Expansion

Jennifer S. H. Brown, *Strangers in Blood: Fur Trade Company Families in Indian Country* (1980)
William H. Goetzmann, *Army Exploration in the American West, 1803–1863* (1959)
William H. Goetzmann and William N. Goetzmann, *The West of the Imagination* (1986)
Norman A. Graebner, *Empire on the Pacific: A Study in American Continental Expansion* (1955)
LeRoy R. Hafen, ed., *The Mountain Men and the Fur Trade of the Far West,* 10 vols. (1968–72)
Reginald Horsman, *Race and Manifest Destiny* (1981)
Theodore J. Karaminski, *Fur Trade and Exploration: Opening of the Far Northwest, 1821–1852* (1983)
Patricia Nelson Limerick, *The Legacy of Conquest: The Unbroken Past of the Unbroken West* (1987)
Frederick Merk, *Manifest Destiny and Mission in American History: A Reinterpretation* (1963)
———, *History of the Westward Movement* (1978)
Dale Morgan, *Jedediah Smith and the Opening of the West* (1982)
Peter Nabakov, ed., *Native American Testimony: An Anthology of Indian and White Relations* (1978)
James P. Ronda, *Astoria and Empire* (1990)
Henry Nash Smith, *Virgin Land: The American West as Symbol and Myth* (1950)
Edward H. Spicer, *Cycles of Conquest: The Impact of Spain, Mexico, and the United States on the Indians of the Southwest, 1533–1960* (1981)
Robert A.Trennert, *Alternative to Extinction: Federal Indian Policy and the Beginnings of the Reservation System, 1846–1851* (1975)
Sylvia Van Kirk, *"Many Tender Ties": Women in Fur Trade Society in Western Canada, 1670–1870* (1980)
Albert K. Weinberg, *Manifest Destiny: A Study of Nationalist Expansionism in American History* (1957)
Peter Booth Wiley with Korogi Ichiro, *Yankees in the Land of the Gods: Commodore Perry and the Opening of Japan* (1990)
David J. Wishart, *The Fur Trade of the American West, 1807–1840: A Geographic Synthesis* (1979)

California and Oregon

John W. Caughey, *The California Gold Rush* (1975)
Malcolm Clark Jr., *Eden Seekers: The Settlement of Oregon, 1818–1862* (1981)
Douglas H. Daniels, *Pioneer Urbanites: A Social and Cultural History of Black San Francisco* (1980)
James R. Gibson, *Farming the Frontier: The Agricultural Opening of Oregon Country, 1786–1846* (1985)
Albert L. Hurtado, *Indian Survival on the California Frontier* (1988)
Julie Roy Jeffrey, *Frontier Women: Civilizing The West?, 1840–1860* (1998)
David Johnson, *Founding the Far West: California, Oregon, and Nevada, 1840–1890* (1992)
Alvin Josephy, *The Nez Perce and the Opening of the Northwest* (1965)
Rodman W. Paul, *California Gold: The Beginning of Mining in the Far West* (1974)
Leonard Pitt, *The Decline of the Californios: A Social History of the Spanish-Speaking Californians, 1846–1890* (1966)
James J. Rawls, *Indians of California: The Changing Image* (1984)
Kevin Starr, *Americans and the California Dream, 1850–1915* (1973)
John I. Unruh Jr., *The Plains Across: Overland Emigrants and the Trans-Mississippi West, 1840–1860* (1979)

Texas and the Mexican-American War

K. Jack Bauer, *The Mexican War, 1846–1848* (1974)
William C. Binkley, *The Texas Revolution* (1952)
Gene M. Brack, *Mexico Views Manifest Destiny* (1976)
Donald E. Chipman, *Spanish Texas, 1519–1821* (1992)
Seymour Conner and Odie Faulk, *North America Divided: The Mexican War, 1846–1848* (1971)
Arnoldo De Leon, *They Called Them Greasers: Anglo Attitudes toward Mexicans in Texas, 1821–1900* (1983)
John S. D. Eisenhower, *So Far from God: The U.S. War with Mexico 1846–1848* (1989)
Neil Harlow, *California Conquered: War and Peace on the Pacific, 1846–1850* (1982)
Ernest McPherson Lander Jr., *Reluctant Imperialist: Calhoun, South Carolina, and the Mexican War* (1980)
Timothy Matovina, *Tejano Religion and Ethnicity: San Antonio, 1921–1860* (1995)
Frederick Merk, *Slavery and the Annexation of Texas* (1972)
David Montejano, *Anglos and Mexicans in the Making of Texas, 1836–1986* (1987)
Chaplain W. Morrison, *Democratic Politics and Sectionalism: The Wilmot Proviso Controversy* (1967)
Stanley Noyes, *Los Comanches: The Horse People, 1751–1845* (1994)
David Pletcher, *The Diplomacy of Annexation: Texas, Oregon, and the Mexican War* (1973)
Joseph G. Raybeck, *Free Soil: The Election of 1848* (1970)
Andreas V. Reichstein, *Rise of the Lone Star: The Making of Texas* (1989)
John H. Schroeder, *Mr. Polk's War: American Opposition and Dissent, 1846–1848* (1971)
Joel H. Sibley, *The Shrine of Party: Congressional Voting Behavior, 1841–1852* (1967)
Otis A. Singletary, *The Mexican War* (1960)
Jésus F. de la Teja, *San Antonio de Béxar: A Community on New Spain's Northern Frontier* (1995)

Biography

Marquis James, *The Raven: The Story of Sam Houston* (1929)
Charles G. Sellers, *James K. Polk: Jacksonian, 1795–1843* (1957)
———, *James K. Polk: Continentialist, 1843–1846* (1966)

APPENDIX

THE DECLARATION OF INDEPENDENCE

When in the course of human events it becomes necessary for one people to dissolve the political bands which have connected them with another and to assume, among the powers of the earth, the separate and equal station to which the laws of nature and of nature's God entitle them, a decent respect to the opinions of mankind requires that they should declare the causes which impel them to the separation.

We hold these truths to be self-evident, that all men are created equal; that they are endowed by their Creator with certain unalienable rights; that among these are life, liberty, and the pursuit of happiness. That, to secure these rights, governments are instituted among men, deriving their just powers from the consent of the governed; that, whenever any form of government becomes destructive of these ends, it is the right of the people to alter or to abolish it, and to institute a new government, laying its foundation on such principles, and organizing its powers in such form, as to them shall seem most likely to effect their safety and happiness. Prudence, indeed, will dictate that governments long established should not be changed for light and transient causes; and, accordingly, all experience hath shown that mankind are more disposed to suffer, while evils are sufferable, than to right themselves by abolishing the forms to which they are accustomed. But when a long train of abuses and usurpations, pursuing invariably the same object, evinces a design to reduce them under absolute despotism, it is their right, it is their duty, to throw off such government and to provide new guards for their future security. Such has been the patient sufferance of these colonies, and such is now the necessity which constrains them to alter their former systems of government. The history of the present King of Great Britain is a history of repeated injuries and usurpations, all having, in direct object, the establishment of an absolute tyranny over these States. To prove this, let facts be submitted to a candid world:

He has refused his assent to laws the most wholesome and necessary for the public good.

He has forbidden his governors to pass laws of immediate and pressing importance, unless suspended in their operation till his assent should be obtained; and, when so suspended, he has utterly neglected to attend to them.

He has refused to pass other laws for the accommodation of large districts of people, unless those people would relinquish the right of representation in the legislature, a right inestimable to them and formidable to tyrants only.

He has called together legislative bodies at places unusual, uncomfortable, and distant from the depository of their public records, for the sole purpose of fatiguing them into compliance with his measures.

He has dissolved representative houses, repeatedly for opposing, with manly firmness, his invasions on the rights of the people.

He has refused, for a long time after such dissolutions, to cause others to be elected; whereby the legislative powers, incapable of annihilation, have returned to the people at large for their exercise; the state remaining, in the meantime, exposed to all the danger of invasion from without and convulsions within.

He has endeavored to prevent the population of these States; for that purpose, obstructing the laws for naturalization of foreigners, refusing to pass others to encourage their migration hither, and raising the conditions of new appropriations of lands.

He has obstructed the administration of justice by refusing his assent to laws for establishing judiciary powers.

He has made judges dependent on his will alone for the tenure of their offices and the amount and payment of their salaries.

He has erected a multitude of new offices and sent hither swarms of officers to harass our people and eat out their substance.

He has kept among us, in time of peace, standing armies, without the consent of our legislatures.

He has affected to render the military independent of, and superior to, the civil power.

He has combined with others to subject us to a jurisdiction foreign to our Constitution and unacknowledged by our laws, giving his assent to their acts of pretended legislation—

For quartering large bodies of armed troops among us;

For protecting them, by mock trial, from punishment for any murders which they should commit on the inhabitants of these States;

For cutting off our trade with all parts of the world;

For imposing taxes on us without our consent;

For depriving us, in many cases, of the benefit of trial by jury;

For transporting us beyond seas to be tried for pretended offences;

For abolishing the free system of English laws in a neighboring province, establishing therein an arbitrary government, and enlarging its boundaries, so as to render it at once an example and fit instrument for introducing the same absolute rule into these colonies;

For taking away our charters, abolishing our most valuable laws, and altering, fundamentally, the powers of our governments.

For suspending our own legislatures and declaring themselves invested with power to legislate for us in all cases whatsoever.

He has abdicated government here by declaring us out of his protection and waging war against us.

He has plundered our seas, ravaged our coasts, burnt our towns, and destroyed the lives of our people.

He is, at this time, transporting large armies of foreign mercenaries to complete the works of death, desolation, and tyranny already begun with circumstances of cruelty and perfidy scarcely paralleled in the most barbarous ages, and totally unworthy the head of a civilized nation.

He has constrained our fellow citizens, taken captive on the high seas, to bear arms against their country, to become the executioners of their friends and brethren, or to fall themselves by their hands.

He has excited domestic insurrections amongst us and has endeavored to bring on the inhabitants of our frontiers, the merciless Indian savages, whose known rule of warfare is an undistinguished destruction of all ages, sexes, and conditions.

In every stage of these oppressions, we have petitioned for redress in the most humble terms; our repeated petitions have been answered only by repeated injury. A prince whose character is thus marked by every act which may define a tyrant is unfit to be the ruler of a free people.

Nor have we been wanting in attention to our British brethren. We have warned them, from time to time, of attempts made by their legislature to extend an unwarrantable jurisdiction over us. We have reminded them of the circumstances of our emigration and settlement here. We have appealed to their native justice and magnanimity, and we have conjured them, by the ties of our common kindred, to disavow these usurpations, which would inevitably interrupt our connections and correspondence. They, too, have been deaf to the voice of justice and consanguinity. We must, therefore, acquiesce in the necessity which denounces our separation, and hold them, as we hold the rest of mankind, enemies in war, in peace, friends.

We, therefore, the representatives of the United States of America, in general Congress assembled, appealing to the Supreme Judge of the world for the rectitude of our intentions, do, in the name and by the authority of the good people of these colonies, solemnly publish and declare, that these united colonies are, and of right ought to be, free and independent states: that they are absolved from all allegiance to the British Crown, and that all political connection between them and the state of Great Britain is, and ought to be, totally dissolved; and that, as free and independent states, they have full power to levy war, conclude peace, contract alliances, establish commerce, and to do all other acts and things which independent states may of right do. And, for the support of this declaration, with a firm reliance on the protection of Divine Providence, we mutually pledge to each other our lives, our fortunes, and our sacred honor.

THE CONSTITUTION OF THE UNITED STATES OF AMERICA

We the people of the United States, in order to form a more perfect union, establish justice, insure domestic tranquillity, provide for the common defense, promote the general welfare, and secure the blessings of liberty to ourselves and our posterity, do ordain and establish this Constitution for the United States of America.

Article I

Section 1. All legislative powers herein granted shall be vested in a Congress of the United States, which shall consist of a Senate and House of Representatives.

Section 2. 1. The House of Representatives shall be composed of members chosen every second year by the people of the several States, and the electors in each State shall have the qualifications requisite for electors of the most numerous branch of the State legislature.

2. No person shall be a representative who shall not have attained to the age of twenty-five years, and been seven years a citizen of the United States, and who shall not, when elected, be an inhabitant of that State in which he shall be chosen.

3. Representatives and direct taxes[1] shall be apportioned among the several States which may be included within this Union, according to their respective numbers, which shall be determined by adding to the whole number of free persons, including those bound to service for a term of years, and excluding Indians not taxed, three fifths of all other persons.[2] The actual enumeration shall be made within three years after the first meeting of the Congress of the United States, and within every subsequent term of ten years, in such manner as they shall by law direct. The number of representatives shall not exceed one for every thirty thousand, but each State shall have at least one representative; and until such enumeration shall be made, the State of New Hampshire shall be entitled to choose three, Massachusetts eight, Rhode Island and Providence Plantations one, Connecticut five, New York six, New Jersey four, Pennsylvania eight, Delaware one, Maryland six, Virginia ten, North Carolina five, South Carolina five, and Georgia three.

4. When vacancies happen in the representation from any State, the executive authority thereof shall issue writs of election to fill such vacancies.

5. The House of Representatives shall choose their speaker and other officers; and shall have the sole power of impeachment.

Section 3. 1. The Senate of the United States shall be composed of two senators from each State, chosen by the legislature thereof,[3] for six years; and each senator shall have one vote.

2. Immediately after they shall be assembled in consequence of the first election, they shall be divided as equally as may be into three classes. The seats of the senators of the first class shall be vacated at the expiration of the second year, of the second class at the expiration of the fourth year, and of the third class at the expiration of the sixth year, so that one third may be chosen every second year; and if vacancies happen by resignation, or otherwise, during the recess of the legislature of any State, the executive thereof may make temporary appointments until the next meeting of the legislature, which shall then fill such vacancies.[4]

3. No person shall be a senator who shall not have attained to the age of thirty years, and been nine years a citizen of the United States, and who shall not, when elected, be an inhabitant of that State for which he shall be chosen.

4. The Vice President of the United States shall be President of the Senate, but shall have no vote, unless they be equally divided.

5. The Senate shall choose their other officers, and also a president pro tempore, in the absence of the Vice President, or when he shall exercise the office of the President of the United States.

6. The Senate shall have the sole power to try all impeachments. When sitting for that purpose, they shall be on oath or affirmation. When the President of the United States is tried, the chief justice shall preside: and no person shall be convicted without the concurrence of two thirds of the members present.

7. Judgment in cases of impeachment shall not extend further than to removal from office, and disqualification to hold and enjoy any office of honor, trust or profit under the United States: but the party convicted shall nevertheless be liable and subject to indictment, trial, judgment and punishment, according to law.

Section 4. 1. The times, places, and manner of holding elections for senators and representatives, shall be prescribed in each State by the legislature thereof; but the Congress may at any time by law make or alter such regulations, except as to the places of choosing senators.

2. The Congress shall assemble at least once in every year, and such meeting shall be on the first Monday in December, unless they shall by law appoint a different day.

Section 5. 1. Each House shall be the judge of the elections, returns and qualifications of its own members, and a majority of each shall constitute a quorum to do business; but a smaller number may adjourn from day to day, and may be authorized to compel the attendance of absent members, in such manner, and under such penalties as each House may provide.

2. Each House may determine the rules of its proceedings, punish its members for disorderly behavior, and, with the concurrence of two thirds, expel a member.

3. Each House shall keep a journal of its proceedings, and from time to time publish the same, excepting such parts as may in their judgment require secrecy; and the yeas and nays of the members of either House on any ques-

[1]See the Sixteenth Amendment.

[2]See the Fourteenth Amendment.

[3]See the Seventeenth Amendment.

[4]See the Seventeenth Amendment.

tion shall, at the desire of one fifth of those present, be entered on the journal.

4. Neither House, during the session of Congress, shall, without the consent of the other, adjourn for more than three days, nor to any other place than that in which the two Houses shall be sitting.

Section 6. 1. The senators and representatives shall receive a compensation for their services, to be ascertained by law, and paid out of the Treasury of the United States. They shall in all cases, except treason, felony, and breach of the peace, be privileged from arrest during their attendance at the session of their respective Houses, and in going to and returning from the same; and for any speech or debate in either House, they shall not be questioned in any other place.

2. No senator or representative shall, during the time for which he was elected, be appointed to any civil office under the authority of the United States, which shall have been created, or the emoluments whereof shall have been increased, during such time; and no person holding any office under the United States shall be a member of either House during his continuance in office.

Section 7. 1. All bills for raising revenue shall originate in the House of Representatives; but the Senate may propose or concur with amendments as on other bills.

2. Every bill which shall have passed the House of Representatives and the Senate, shall, before it become a law, be presented to the President of the United States; If he approves he shall sign it, but if not he shall return it, with his objections, to that House in which it shall have originated, who shall enter the objections at large on their journal, and proceed to reconsider it. If after such reconsideration two thirds of that House shall agree to pass the bill, it shall be sent, together with the objections, to the other House, by which it shall likewise be reconsidered, and if approved by two thirds of that House, it shall become a law. But in all such cases the votes of both Houses shall be determined by yeas and nays, and the names of the persons voting for and against the bill shall be entered on the journal of each House respectively. If any bill shall not be returned by the President within ten days (Sundays excepted) after it shall have been presented to him, the same shall be a law, in like manner as if he had signed it, unless the Congress by their adjournment prevent its return, in which case it shall not be a law.

3. Every order, resolution, or vote to which the concurrence of the Senate and the House of Representatives may be necessary (except on a question of adjournment) shall be presented to the President of the United States; and before the same shall take effect, shall be approved by him, or being disapproved by him, shall be repassed by two thirds of the Senate and House of Representatives, according to the rules and limitations prescribed in the case of a bill.

Section 8. The Congress shall have the power

1. To lay and collect taxes, duties, imposts, and excises, to pay the debts and provide for the common defense and general welfare of the United States; but all duties, imposts, and excises shall be uniform throughout the United States.

2. To borrow money on the credit of the United States;

3. To regulate commerce with foreign nations, and among the several States, and with the Indian tribes;

4. To establish a uniform rule of naturalization, and uniform laws on the subject of bankruptcies throughout the United States;

5. To coin money, regulate the value thereof, and of foreign coin, and fix the standard of weights and measures;

6. To provide for the punishment of counterfeiting the securities and current coin of the United States;

7. To establish post offices and post roads;

8. To promote the progress of science and useful arts, by securing for limited times to authors and inventors the exclusive right to their respective writings and discoveries;

9. To constitute tribunals inferior to the Supreme Court;

10. To define and punish piracies and felonies committed on the high seas, and offenses against the law of nations;

11. To declare war, grant letters of marque and reprisal, and make rules concerning captures on land and water;

12. To raise and support armies, but no appropriation of money to that use shall be for a longer term than two years;

13. To provide and maintain a navy;

14. To make rules for the government and regulation of the land and naval forces;

15. To provide for calling forth the militia to execute the laws of the Union, suppress insurrections and repel invasions;

16. To provide for organizing, arming, and disciplining the militia, and for governing such part of them as may be employed in the service of the United States, reserving to the States respectively, the appointment of the officers, and the authority of training the militia according to the discipline prescribed by Congress;

17. To exercise exclusive legislation in all cases whatsoever, over such district (not exceeding ten miles square) as may, by cession of particular States, and the acceptance of Congress, become the seat of the government of the United States, and to exercise like authority over all places purchased by the consent of the legislature of the State in which the same shall be, for the erection of forts, magazines, arsenals, dockyards, and other needful buildings; and

18. To make all laws which shall be necessary and proper for carrying into execution the foregoing powers, and all other powers vested by this Constitution in the government of the United States, or any department or officer thereof.

Section 9. 1. The migration or importation of such persons as any of the States now existing shall think proper to admit, shall not be prohibited by the Congress prior to the year one thousand eight hundred and eight, but a tax or duty may be imposed on such importation, not exceeding ten dollars for each person.

2. The privilege of the writ of habeas corpus shall not be suspended, unless when in cases of rebellion or invasion the public safety may require it.

3. No bill of attainder or ex post facto law shall be passed.

4. No capitation, or other direct, tax shall be laid, unless in proportion to the census or enumeration hereinbefore directed to be taken.[5]

5. No tax or duty shall be laid on articles exported from any State.

6. No preference shall be given by any regulation of commerce or revenue to the ports of one State over those of another: nor shall vessels bound to, or from, one State be obliged to enter, clear, or pay duties in another.

7. No money shall be drawn from the treasury, but in consequence of appropriations made by law; and a regular statement and account of the receipts and expenditures of all public money shall be published from time to time.

8. No title of nobility shall be granted by the United States: and no person holding any office of profit or trust under them, shall, without the consent of the Congress, accept of any present, emolument, office, or title, of any kind whatever, from any king, price, or foreign State.

Section 10. 1. No State shall enter into any treaty, alliance, or confederation; grant letters of marque and reprisal; coin money; emit bills of credit; make any thing but gold and silver coin a tender in payment of debts; pass any bill of attainder, ex post facto law, or law impairing the obligation of contracts, or grant, any title of nobility.

2. No State shall, without the consent of the Congress, lay any imposts or duties on imports or exports, except what may be absolutely necessary for executing its inspection laws: and the net produce of all duties and imposts laid by any State on imports or exports, shall be for the use of the treasury of the United States; and all such laws shall be subject to the revision and control of the Congress.

3. No State shall, without the consent of the Congress, lay any duty of tonnage, keep troops, or ships of war in time of peace, enter into any agreement or compact with another State, or with a foreign power, or engage in war, unless actually invaded, or in such imminent danger as will not admit of delay.

Article II

Section 1. 1. The executive power shall be vested in a President of the United States of America. He shall hold his office during the term of four years, and, together with the Vice President, chosen for the same term, be elected, as follows:

2. Each State shall appoint, in such manner as the legislature thereof may direct, a number of electors, equal to the whole number of senators and representatives to which the State may be entitled in the Congress: but no senator or representative, or person holding any office of trust or profit under the United States, shall be appointed an elector.

The electors shall meet in their respective States, and vote by ballot for two persons, of whom one at least shall not be an inhabitant of the same State with themselves. And they shall make a list of all the persons voted for, and of the number of votes for each; which list they shall sign and certify, and transmit sealed to the seat of the government of the United States, directed to the president of the Senate. The president of the Senate shall, in the presence of the Senate and House of Representatives, open all the certificates, and the votes shall then be counted. The person having the greatest number of votes shall be the President, if such number be a majority of the whole number of electors appointed; and if there be more than one who have such majority, and have an equal number of votes, then the House of Representatives shall immediately choose by ballot one of them for President; and if no person have a majority, then from the five highest on the list the said House shall in like manner choose the President. But in choosing the President, the votes shall be taken by States, the representation from each State having one vote; a quorum for this purpose shall consist of a member or members from two thirds of the States, and a majority of all the States shall be necessary to a choice. In every case after the choice of the President, the person having the greatest number of votes of the electors shall be the Vice President. But if there should remain two or more who have equal votes, the Senate shall choose from them by ballot the Vice President.[6]

3. The Congress may determine the time of choosing the electors, and the day on which they shall give their votes; which day shall be the same throughout the United States.

4. No person except a natural born citizen, or a citizen of the United States, at the time of the adoption of this Constitution, shall be eligible to the office of President; neither shall any person be eligible to the office who shall not have attained to the age of thirty-five years, and been fourteen years a resident within the United States.

5. In case of the removal of the President from office, or of his death, resignation, or inability to discharge the powers and duties of the said office, the same shall devolve on the Vice President, and the congress may by law provide for the case of removal, death, resignation or inability, both of the President and Vice President, declaring what officer shall then act as President, and such officer shall act accordingly until the disability be removed, or a President shall be elected.

6. The President shall, at stated times, receive for his services a compensation which shall neither be increased nor diminished during the period for which he shall have been elected, and he shall not receive within that period any other emolument from the United States, or any of them.

7. Before he enter on the execution of his office, he shall take the following oath or affirmation:—"I do

[5]See the Sixteenth Amendment.

[6]Superseded by the Twelfth Amendment.

solemnly swear (or affirm) that I will faithfully execute the office of President of the United States, and will to the best of my ability, preserve, protect and defend the Constitution of the United States."

Section 2. 1. The President shall be commander in chief of the army and navy of the United States, and of the militia of the several States, when called into the actual service of the United States; he may require the opinion in writing, of the principal officer in each of the executive departments, upon any subject relating to the duties of their respective offices, and he shall have power to grant reprieves and pardons for offenses against the United States, except in cases of impeachment.

2. He shall have power, by and with the advice and consent of the Senate, to make treaties, provided two thirds of the senators present concur; and he shall nominate, and by and with the advice and consent of the Senate, shall appoint ambassadors, other public ministers and consuls, judges of the Supreme Court, and all other officers of the United States, whose appointments are not herein otherwise provided for, and which shall be established by law; but the Congress may by law vest the appointment of such inferior officers, as they think proper, in the President alone, in the courts of laws, or in the heads of departments.

3. The President shall have power to fill up all vacancies that may happen during the recess of the Senate, by granting commissions which shall expire at the end of their next session.

Section 3. He shall from time to time give to the Congress information of the state of the Union, and recommend to their consideration such measures as he shall judge necessary and expedient; he may, on extraordinary occasions, convene both Houses, or either of them, and in case of disagreement between them with respect to the time of adjournment, he may adjourn them to such time as he shall think proper; he shall receive ambassadors and other public ministers; he shall take care that the laws be faithfully executed, and shall commission all the officers of the United States.

Section 4. The President, Vice President, and all civil officers of the United States, shall be removed from office on impeachment for, and conviction of, treason, bribery, or other high crimes and misdemeanors.

Article III

Section 1. The judicial power of the United States shall be vested in one Supreme Court, and in such inferior courts as the Congress may from time to time ordain and establish. The judges, both of the Supreme and inferior courts, shall hold their offices during good behavior, and shall, at stated times, receive for their services, a compensation, which shall not be diminished during their continuance in office.

Section 2. 1. The judicial power shall extend to all cases, in law and equity, arising under this Constitution, the laws of the United States, and treaties made, or which shall be made, under their authority;—to all cases of admiralty and maritime jurisdiction;—to controversies to which the United States shall be a party;[7]—to controversies between two or more States;—between a State and citizens of another State;—between citizens of different States;—between citizens of the same State claiming lands under grants of different States, and between a State, or the citizens thereof, and foreign States, citizens or subjects.

2. In all cases affecting ambassadors, other public ministers and consuls, and those in which a State shall be party, the Supreme Court shall have original jurisdiction. In all the other cases before mentioned, the Supreme Court shall have appellate jurisdiction, both as to law and fact, with such exceptions, and under such regulations as the Congress shall make.

3. The trial of all crimes, except in cases of impeachment, shall be by jury; and such trial shall be held in the State where the said crimes shall have been committed; but when not committed within any State, the trial shall be such place or places as the congress may by law have directed.

Section 3. 1. Treason against the United States shall consist only in levying war against them, or in adhering to their enemies, giving them aid and comfort. No person shall be convicted of treason unless on the testimony of two witnesses to the same overt act, or on confession in open court.

2. The Congress shall have power to declare the punishment of treason, but no attainder of treason shall work corruption of blood, or forfeiture except during the life of the person attained.

Article IV

Section 1. Full faith and credit shall be given in each State to the public acts, records, and judicial proceedings of every other State. And the Congress may by general laws prescribe the manner in which such acts, records and proceedings shall be proved, and the effect thereof.

Section 2. 1. The citizens of each State shall be entitled to all privileges and immunities of citizens in the several States.[8]

2. A person charged in any State with treason, felony, or other crime, who shall flee from justice, and be found in another State, shall on demand of the executive authority of the State from which he fled, be delivered up to be removed to the State having jurisdiction of the crime.

3. No person held to service or labor in one State under the laws thereof, escaping into another, shall, in consequence of any law or regulation therein, be discharged from such service or labor, but shall be delivered up on claim of the party to whom such service or labor may be due.[9]

Section 3. 1. New States may be admitted by the Congress into this Union; but no new State shall be formed or erected within the jurisdiction of any other State, nor any State be formed by the junction of two or more States, or parts of States, without the consent of the legislatures of the States concerned as well as of the Congress.

---

[7]See the Eleventh Amendment.

[8]See the Fourteenth Amendment, Sec. 1.

[9]See the Thirteenth Amendment.

2. The Congress shall have power to dispose of and make all needful rules and regulations respecting the territory or other property belonging to the United States; and nothing in this Constitution shall be so construed as to prejudice any claims of the United States, or of any particular State.

Section 4. The United States shall guarantee to every State in this Union a republican form of government, and shall protect each of them against invasion; and on application of the legislature, or of the executive (when the legislature cannot be convened) against domestic violence.

Article V

The Congress, whenever two thirds of both Houses shall deem it necessary, shall propose amendments to this Constitution, or, on the application of the legislatures of two thirds of the several States, shall call a convention for proposing amendments, which in either case shall be valid to all intents and purposes, as part of this Constitution, when ratified by the legislatures of three fourths of the several States, or by conventions in three fourths thereof, as the one or the other mode of ratification may be proposed by the Congress; Provided that no amendment which may be made prior to the year one thousand eight hundred and eight shall in any manner affect the first and fourth clauses in the ninth section of the first article; and that no State, without its consent, shall be deprived of its equal suffrage in the Senate.

Article VI

1. All debts contracted and engagements entered into, before the adoption of this Constitution, shall be as valid against the United States under this Constitution, as under the Confederation.[10]

2. This Constitution, and the laws of the United States which shall be made in pursuance thereof; and all treaties made, or which shall be made, under the authority of the United States, shall be the supreme law of the land; and the judges in every State shall be bound thereby, any thing in the Constitution or laws of any State to the contrary notwithstanding.

3. The senators and representatives before mentioned, and the members of the several State legislatures, and all executive and judicial officers, both of the United States and of the several States, shall be bound by oath or affirmation to support this Constitution; but no religious test shall ever be required as a qualification to any office or public trust under the United States.

Article VII

The ratification of the conventions of nine States shall be sufficient for the establishment of this Constitution between the States so ratifying the same.

Done in Convention by the unanimous consent of the States present the seventeenth day of September in the year of our Lord one thousand seven hundred and eighty-seven, and of the independence of the United States of America the twelfth. In witness whereof we have hereunto subscribed our names.

[Names omitted]

* * *

Articles in addition to, and amendment of, the Constitution of the United States of America, proposed by Congress, and ratified by the legislatures of the several States, pursuant to the fifth article of the original Constitution.

Amendment I [First ten amendments ratified December 15, 1791]

Congress shall make no law respecting an establishment of religion, or prohibiting the free exercise thereof; or abridging the freedom of speech, or of the press; or the right of the people peaceably to assemble, and to petition the government for a redress of grievances.

Amendment II

A well regulated militia, being necessary to the security of a free State, the right of the people to keep and bear arms, shall not be infringed.

Amendment III

No soldier shall, in time of peace be quartered in any house, without the consent of the owner, nor in time of war, but in a manner to be prescribed by law.

Amendment IV

The right of the people to be secure in their persons, houses, papers, and effects, against unreasonable searches and seizures, shall not be violated, and no warrants shall issue, but upon probable cause, supported by oath or affirmation, and particularly describing the place to be searched, and the persons or things to be seized.

Amendment V

No person shall be held to answer for a capital or otherwise infamous crime, unless on a presentment or indictment of a grand jury, except in cases arising in the land or naval forces, or in the militia, when in actual service in time of war or public danger; nor shall any person be subject for the same offense to be twice put in jeopardy of life or limb; nor shall be compelled in any criminal case to be a witness against himself, nor be deprived of life, liberty, or property, without due process of law; nor shall private property be taken for public use, without just compensation.

Amendment VI

In all criminal prosecutions, the accused shall enjoy the right to a speedy and public trial, by an impartial jury of the State and district wherein the crime shall have been committed, which district shall have been previously ascertained by law, and to be informed of the nature and cause of the accusation; to be confronted with the witnesses against him; to have compulsory process for obtaining witnesses in his favor, and to have the assistance of counsel for his defense.

[10]See the Fourteenth Amendment, Sec. 4.

Amendment VII

In suits at common law, where the value in controversy shall exceed twenty dollars, the right of trial by jury shall be preserved, and no fact tried by a jury shall be otherwise reexamined in any court of the United States, than according to the rules of the common law.

Amendment VIII

Excessive bail shall not be required, nor excessive fines imposed, nor cruel and unusual punishments inflicted.

Amendment IX

The enumeration in the Constitution of certain rights shall not be construed to deny or disparage others retained by the people.

Amendment X

The powers not delegated to the United States by the Constitution, nor prohibited by it to the States, are reserved to the States respectively, or to the people.

Amendment XI [January 8, 1798]

The judicial power of the United States shall not be construed to extend to any suit in law or equity, commended or prosecuted against one of the United States by citizens of another State, or by citizens or subjects of any foreign State.

Amendment XII [September 25, 1804]

The electors shall meet in their respective States, and vote by ballot for President and Vice President, one of whom, at least, shall not be an inhabitant of the same State with themselves; they shall name in their ballots the person voted for as President, and in distinct ballots, the person voted for as Vice President, and they shall make distinct lists of all persons voted for as President and of all persons voted for as Vice President, and of the number of votes for each, which lists they shall sign and certify, and transmit sealed to the seat of the government of the United States, directed to the President of the Senate;—The President of the Senate shall, in the presence of the Senate and House of Representatives, open all the certificates and the votes shall then be counted;—The person having the greatest number of votes for President, shall be the President, if such number be a majority of the whole number of electors appointed; and if no person have such majority, then from the persons having the highest numbers not exceeding three on the list of those voted for as President, the House of Representatives shall choose immediately, by ballot, the President. But in choosing the President, the votes shall be taken by States, the representation from each State having one vote; a quorum for this purpose shall consist of a member or members from two thirds of the States, and a majority of all the States shall be necessary to a choice. And if the House of Representatives shall not choose a President whenever the right of choice shall devolve upon them, before the fourth day of March next following, then the Vice President shall act as President, as in the case of the death or other constitutional disability of the President. The person having the greatest number of votes as Vice President shall be the Vice President, if such number be a majority of the whole number of electors appointed, and if no person have a majority, then from the two highest numbers on the list, the Senate shall choose the Vice President; a quorum for the purpose shall consist of two thirds of the whole number of Senators, and a majority of the whole number shall be necessary to a choice. But no person constitutionally ineligible to the office of President shall be eligible to that of Vice President of the United States.

Amendment XIII [December 18, 1865]

Section 1. Neither slavery nor involuntary servitude, except as a punishment for crime whereof the party shall have been duly convicted, shall exist within the United States, or any place subject to their jurisdiction.

Section 2. Congress shall have power to enforce this article by appropriate legislation.

Amendment XIV [July 28, 1868]

Section 1. All persons born or naturalized in the United States, and subject to the jurisdiction thereof, are citizens of the United States and of the State wherein they reside. No State shall make or enforce any law which shall abridge the privileges or immunities of citizens of the United States; nor shall any State deprive any person of life, liberty, or property, without due process of law; nor deny to any person within its jurisdiction the equal protection of the laws.

Section 2. Representatives shall be apportioned among the several States according to their respective numbers, counting the whole number of persons in each State, excluding Indians not taxed. But when the right to vote at any election for the choice of electors for President and Vice President of the United States, representatives in Congress, the executive and judicial officers of a State, or the members of the legislature thereof, is denied to any of the male inhabitants of such State, being twenty-one years of age, and citizens of the United States, or in any way abridged, except for participating in rebellion, or other crime, the basis of representation there shall be reduced in the proportion which the number of such male citizens shall bear to the whole number of male citizens twenty-one years of age in such State.

Section 3. No person shall be a senator or representative in Congress, or elector of President and Vice President, or hold any office, civil or military, under the United States, or under any State, who having previously taken an oath, as a member of Congress, or as an officer of the United States, or as a member of any State legislature, or as an executive or judicial officer of any State, to support the Constitution of the United States, shall have engaged in insurrection or rebellion against the same, or given aid or comfort to the enemies thereof. But Congress may by a vote of two thirds of each House, remove such disability.

Section 4. The validity of the public debt of the United States, authorized by law, including debts incurred for payment of pensions and bounties for services in suppressing insurrection or rebellion, shall not be questioned.

But neither the United States nor any State shall assume or pay any debt or obligation incurred in aid of insurrection or rebellion against the United States, or any claim for the loss or emancipation of any slave; but all such debts, obligations, and claims shall be held illegal and void.

Section 5. The Congress shall have the power to enforce, by appropriate legislation, the provisions of this article.

Amendment XV [March 30, 1870]

Section 1. The right of citizens of the United States to vote shall not be denied or abridged by the United States or by any State on account of race, color, or previous condition of servitude.

Section 2. The Congress shall have power to enforce this article by appropriate legislation.

Amendment XVI [February 25, 1913]

The Congress shall have power to lay and collect taxes on incomes, from whatever source derived, without apportionment among the several States, and without regard to any census or enumeration.

Amendment XVII [May 31, 1913]

The Senate of the United States shall be composed of two senators from each State, elected by the people thereof, for six years; and each senator shall have one vote. The electors in each State shall have the qualifications requisite for electors of the most numerous branch of the State legislature.

When vacancies happen in the representation of any State in the Senate, the executive authority of such State shall issue writs of election to fill such vacancies: *Provided,* That the legislature of any State may empower the executive thereof to make temporary appointments until the people fill the vacancies by election as the legislature may direct.

This amendment shall not be so construed as to affect the election or term of any senator chosen before it becomes valid as part of the Constitution.

Amendment XVIII[11] *[January 29, 1919]*

After one year from the ratification of this article, the manufacture, sale, or transportation of intoxicating liquors within, the importation thereof into, or the exportation thereof from the United States and all territory subject to the jurisdiction thereof for beverage purposes is thereby prohibited.

The Congress and the several States shall have concurrent power to enforce this article by appropriate legislation.

This article shall be inoperative unless it shall have been ratified as an amendment to the Constitution by the legislatures of the several States, as provided in the constitution, within seven years from the date of the submission hereof to the States by Congress.

[11]Repealed by the Twenty-first Amendment.

Amendment XIX [August 26, 1920]

The right of citizens of the United States to vote shall not be denied or abridged by the United States or by any State on account of sex.

Congress shall have the power to enforce this article by appropriate legislation.

Amendment XX [January 23, 1933]

Section 1. The terms of the President and Vice President shall end at noon on the 20th day of January and the terms of Senators and Representatives at noon on the 3d day of January, of the years in which such terms would have ended if this article had not been ratified; and the terms of their successors shall then begin.

Section 2. The Congress shall assemble at least once in every year, and such meeting shall begin at noon on the 3d day of January, unless they shall by law appoint a different day.

Section 3. If, at the time fixed for the beginning of the term of President, the President-elect shall have died, the Vice President-elect shall become President. If a President shall not have been chosen before the time fixed for the beginning of his term, or if the President-elect shall have failed to qualify, then the Vice President-elect shall act as President until a President shall have qualified; and the Congress may by law provide for the case wherein neither a President-elect nor a Vice President-elect shall have qualified, declaring who shall then act as President, or the manner in which one who is to act shall be selected, and such person shall act accordingly until a President or Vice President shall have qualified.

Section 4. The Congress may by law provide for the case of the death of any of the persons from whom, the House of Representatives may choose a President whenever the right of choice shall have devolved upon them, and for the case of the death of any of the persons from whom the Senate may choose a Vice President whenever the right of choice shall have devolved upon them.

Section 5. Sections 1 and 2 shall take effect on the 15th day of October following the ratification of this article.

Section 6. This article shall be inoperative unless it shall have been ratified as an amendment to the Constitution by the legislatures of three-fourths of the several States within seven years from the date of its submission.

Amendment XXI [December 5, 1933]

Section 1. The Eighteenth Article of amendment to the Constitution of the United States is hereby repealed.

Section 2. The transportation or importation into any State, Territory, or possession of the United States for delivery or use therein of intoxicating liquors in violation of the laws thereof, is hereby prohibited.

Section 3. This article shall be inoperative unless it shall have been ratified as an amendment to the Constitution by conventions in the several States, as provided in the Constitution, within seven years from the date of the submission thereof to the States by the Congress.

Amendment XXII [March 1, 1951]

No person shall be elected to the office of the President more than twice, and no person who has held the office of President, or acted as President, for more than two years of a term to which some other person was elected President shall be elected to the office of the President more than once.

But this article shall not apply to any person holding the office of President when this article was proposed by the Congress, and shall not prevent any person who may be holding the office of President, or acting as President, during the term within which this article becomes operative from holding the office of President or acting as President during the remainder of such term.

This article shall be inoperative unless it shall have been ratified as an amendment to the Constitution by the legislatures of three-fourths of the several States within seven years from the date of its submission to the States by the Congress.

Amendment XXIII [March 29, 1961]

Section 1. The District constituting the seat of Government of the United States shall appoint in such manner as the Congress may direct.

A number of electors of President and Vice President equal to the whole number of Senators and Representatives in Congress to which the District would be entitled if it were a State, but in no event more than the least populous State; they shall be in addition to those appointed by the States, but they shall be considered, for the purposes of the election of President and Vice President, to be electors appointed by a State; and they shall meet in the District and perform such duties as provided by the twelfth article of amendment.

Section 2. The Congress shall have power to enforce this article by appropriate legislation.

Amendment XXIV [January 23, 1964]

Section 1. The right of citizens of the United States to vote in any primary or other election for President or Vice President, for electors for President or Vice President, or for Senator or Representative in Congress, shall not be denied or abridged by the United States or any State by reason of failure to pay any poll tax or other tax.

Section 2. The Congress shall have power to enforce this article by appropriate legislation.

Amendment XXV [February 10, 1967]

Section 1. In case of the removal of the President from office or of his death or resignation, the Vice President shall become President.

Section 2. Whenever there is a vacancy in the office of the Vice President, the President shall nominate a Vice President who shall take office upon confirmation by a majority of both Houses of Congress.

Section 3. Whenever the President transmits to the President pro tempore of the Senate and the Speaker of the House of Representatives his written declaration that he is unable to discharge the powers and duties of his office, and until he transmits to them a written declaration to the contrary, such powers and duties shall be discharged by the Vice President as Acting President.

Section 4. Whenever the Vice president and a majority of either the principal officers of the executive departments or of such other body as Congress may by law provide, transmit to the President pro tempore of the Senate and the Speaker of the House of Representatives their written declaration that the President is unable to discharge the powers and duties of his office, the Vice President shall immediately assume the powers and duties of the office as Acting President.

Thereafter, when the President transmits to the President pro tempore of the Senate and the Speaker of the House of Representatives his written declaration that no inability exists, he shall resume the powers and duties of his office unless the Vice President and a majority of either the principal officers of the executive departments or of such other body as Congress may by law provide, transmit within four days to the President pro tempore of the Senate and the Speaker of the House of Representatives their written declaration that the President is unable to discharge the powers and duties of his office. Thereupon Congress shall decide the issue, assembling within forty-eight hours for that purpose if not in session. If the Congress, within twenty-one days after receipt of the latter written declaration, or, if Congress is not in session, within twenty-one days after Congress is required to assemble, determines by two-thirds vote of both Houses that the President is unable to discharge the powers and duties of his office, the Vice President shall continue to discharge the same as Acting President; otherwise, the President shall resume the powers and duties of his office.

Amendment XXVI [June 30, 1971]

Section 1. The right of citizens of the United States who are eighteen years of age or older to vote shall not be denied or abridged by the United States or by any State on account of age.

Section 2. The Congress shall have power to enforce this article by appropriate legislation.

Amendment XXVII[12] [May 7, 1992]

No law, varying the compensation for services of the Senators and Representatives, shall take effect until an election of Representatives shall have intervened.

---

[12]James Madison proposed this amendment in 1789 together with the ten amendments that were adopted as the Bill of Rights, but it failed to win ratification at the time. Congress, however, had set no deadline for its ratification, and over the years—particularly in the 1980s and 1990s—many states voted to add it to the Constitution. With the ratification of Michigan in 1992 it passed the threshold of 3/4ths of the states required for adoption, but because the process took more than 200 years, its validity remains in doubt.

PRESIDENTS AND VICE PRESIDENTS

1. George Washington (1789)
   John Adams (1789)
2. John Adams (1797)
   Thomas Jefferson (1797)
3. Thomas Jefferson (1801)
   Aaron Burr (1801)
   George Clinton (1805)
4. James Madison (1809)
   George Clinton (1809)
   Elbridge Gerry (1813)
5. James Monroe (1817)
   Daniel D. Thompkins (1817)
6. John Quincy Adams (1825)
   John C. Calhoun (1825)
7. Andrew Jackson (1829)
   John C. Calhoun (1829)
   Martin Van Buren (1833)
8. Martin Van Buren (1837)
   Richard M. Johnson (1837)
9. William H. Harrison (1841)
   John Tyler (1841)
10. John Tyler (1841)
11. James K. Polk (1845)
    George M. Dallas (1845)
12. Zachary Taylor (1849)
    Millard Fillmore (1849)
13. Millard Fillmore (1850)
14. Franklin Pierce (1853)
    William R. King (1853)
15. James Buchanan (1857)
    John C. Breckinridge (1857)
16. Abraham Lincoln (1861)
    Hannibal Hamlin (1861)
    Andrew Johnson (1865)
17. Andrew Johnson (1865)
18. Ulysses S. Grant (1869)
    Schuyler Colfax (1869)
    Henry Wilson (1873)
19. Rutherford B. Hayes (1877)
    William A. Wheeler (1877)
20. James A. Garfield (1881)
    Chester A. Arthur (1881)
21. Chester A. Arthur (1881)
22. Grover Cleveland (1885)
    T. A. Hendricks (1885)
23. Benjamin Harrison (1889)
    Levi P. Morgan (1889)
24. Grover Cleveland (1893)
    Adlai E. Stevenson (1893)
25. William McKinley (1897)
    Garret A. Hobart (1897)
    Theodore Roosevelt (1901)
26. Theodore Roosevelt (1901)
    Charles Fairbanks (1905)
27. William H. Taft (1909)
    James S. Sherman (1909)
28. Woodrow Wilson (1913)
    Thomas R. Marshall (1913)
29. Warren G. Harding (1921)
    Calvin Coolidge (1921)
30. Calvin Coolidge (1923)
    Charles G. Dawes (1925)
31. Herbert C. Hoover (1929)
    Charles Curtis (1929)
32. Franklin D. Roosevelt (1933)
    John Nance Garner (1933)
    Henry A. Wallace (1941)
    Harry S. Truman (1945)
33. Harry S. Truman (1945)
    Alben W. Barkley (1949)
34. Dwight D. Eisenhower (1953)
    Richard M. Nixon (1953)
35. John F. Kennedy (1961)
    Lyndon B. Johnson (1961)
36. Lyndon B. Johnson (1963)
    Hubert H. Humphrey (1965)
37. Richard M. Nixon (1969)
    Spiro T. Agnew (1969)
    Gerald R. Ford (1973)
38. Gerald R. Ford (1974)
    Nelson A. Rockefeller (1974)
39. James E. Carter Jr. (1977)
    Walter F. Mondale (1977)
40. Ronald W. Reagan (1981)
    George H. Bush (1981)
41. George H. Bush (1989)
    James D. Quayle III (1989)
42. William J. Clinton (1993)
    Albert Gore (1993)

PRESIDENTIAL ELECTIONS

Year	Number of States	Candidates	Party	Popular Vote*	Electoral Vote†	Percentage of Popular Vote
1789	11	GEORGE WASHINGTON	No party designations		69	
		John Adams			34	
		Other Candidates			35	
1792	15	GEORGE WASHINGTON	No party designations		132	
		John Adams			77	
		George Clinton			50	
		Other Candidates			5	
1796	16	JOHN ADAMS	Federalist		71	
		Thomas Jefferson	Democratic-Republican		68	
		Thomas Pinckney	Federalist		59	
		Aaron Burr	Democratic-Republican		30	
		Other Candidates			48	
1800	16	THOMAS JEFFERSON	Democratic-Republican		73	
		Aaron Burr	Democratic-Republican		73	
		John Adams	Federalist		65	
		Charles C. Pinckney	Federalist		64	
		John Jay	Federalist		1	
1804	17	THOMAS JEFFERSON	Democratic-Republican		162	
		Charles C. Pinckney	Federalist		14	
1808	17	JAMES MADISON	Democratic-Republican		122	
		Charles C. Pinckney	Federalist		47	
		George Clinton	Democratic-Republican		6	
1812	18	JAMES MADISON	Democratic-Republican		128	
		DeWitt Clinton	Federalist		89	
1816	19	JAMES MONROE	Democratic-Republican		183	
		Rufus King	Federalist		34	
1820	24	JAMES MONROE	Democratic-Republican		231	
		John Quincy Adams	Democratic-Republican		1	
1824	24	JOHN QUINCY ADAMS	Democratic-Republican	108,740	84	30.5
		Andrew Jackson	Democratic-Republican	153,544	99	43.1
		William H. Crawford	Democratic-Republican	46,618	41	13.1
		Henry Clay	Democratic-Republican	47,136	37	13.2
1828	24	ANDREW JACKSON	Democrat	647,286	178	56.0
		John Quincy Adams	National-Republican	508,064	83	44.0
1832	24	ANDREW JACKSON	Democrat	687,502	219	55.0
		Henry Clay	National-Republican	530,189	49	42.4
		William Wirt	Anti-Masonic	33,108 (combined with John Floyd)	7	2.6 (combined with John Floyd)
		John Floyd	National-Republican		11	

*Percentage of popular vote given for any election year may not total 100 percent because candidates receiving less than 1 percent of the popular vote have been omitted.

†Prior to the passage of the Twelfth Amendment in 1904, the electoral college voted for two presidential candidates; the runner-up became Vice-President. Data from *Historical Statistics of the United States, Colonial Times to 1957* (1961), pp. 682–683, and *The World Almanac.*

PRESIDENTIAL ELECTIONS
(continued)

Year	Number of States	Candidates	Party	Popular Vote	Electoral Vote	Percentage of Popular Vote
1836	26	MARTIN VAN BUREN	Democrat	765,483	170	50.9
		William H. Harrison	Whig	739,795	73	49.1
		Hugh L. White	Whig		26	
		Daniel Webster	Whig		14	
		W. P. Mangum	Whig		11	
1840	26	WILLIAM H. HARRISON	Whig	1,274,624	234	53.1
		Martin Van Buren	Democrat	1,127,781	60	46.9
1844	26	JAMES K. POLK	Democrat	1,338,464	170	49.6
		Henry Clay	Whig	1,300,097	105	48.1
		James G. Birney	Liberty	62,300		2.3
1848	30	ZACHARY TAYLOR	Whig	1,360,967	163	47.4
		Lewis Cass	Democrat	1,222,342	127	42.5
		Martin Van Buren	Free-Soil	291,263		10.1
1852	31	FRANKLIN PIERCE	Democrat	1,601,117	254	50.9
		Winfield Scott	Whig	1,385,453	42	44.1
		John P. Hale	Free-Soil	155,825		5.0
1856	31	JAMES BUCHANAN	Democrat	1,832,955	174	45.3
		John C. Frémont	Republican	1,339,932	114	33.1
		Millard Fillmore	American ("Know Nothing")	871,731	8	21.6
1860	33	ABRAHAM LINCOLN	Republican	1,865,593	180	39.8
		Stephen A. Douglas	Democrat	1,382,713	12	29.5
		John C. Breckinridge	Democrat	848,356	72	18.1
		John Bell	Constitutional Union	592,906	39	12.6
1864	36	ABRAHAM LINCOLN	Republican	2,206,938	212	55.0
		George B. McClellan	Democrat	1,803,787	21	45.0
1868	37	ULYSSES S. GRANT	Republican	3,013,421	214	52.7
		Horatio Seymour	Democrat	2,706,829	80	47.3
1872	37	ULYSSES S. GRANT	Republican	3,596,745	286	55.6
		Horace Greeley	Democrat	2,843,446	*	43.9
1876	38	RUTHERFORD B. HAYES	Republican	4,036,572	185	48.0
		Samuel J. Tilden	Democrat	4,284,020	184	51.0
1880	38	JAMES A. GARFIELD	Republican	4,453,295	214	48.5
		Winfield S. Hancock	Democrat	4,414,082	155	48.1
		James B. Weaver	Greenback-Labor	308,578		3.4
1884	38	GROVER CLEVELAND	Democrat	4,879,507	219	48.5
		James G. Blaine	Republican	4,850,293	182	48.2
		Benjamin F. Butler	Greenback-Labor	175,370		1.8
		John P. St. John	Prohibition	150,369		1.5
1888	38	BENJAMIN HARRISON	Republican	5,447,129	233	47.9
		Grover Cleveland	Democrat	5,537,857	168	48.6
		Clinton B. Fisk	Prohibition	249,506		2.2
		Anson J. Streeter	Union Labor	146,935		1.3

*Because of the death of Greeley, Democratic electors scattered their votes.

PRESIDENTIAL ELECTIONS
(continued)

Year	Number of States	Candidates	Party	Popular Vote	Electoral Vote	Percentage of Popular Vote
1892	44	GROVER CLEVELAND	Democrat	5,555,426	277	46.1
		Benjamin Harrison	Republican	5,182,690	145	43.0
		James B. Weaver	People's	1,029,846	22	8.5
		John Bidwell	Prohibition	264,133		2.2
1896	45	WILLIAM MCKINLEY	Republican	7,102,246	271	51.1
		William J. Bryan	Democrat	6,492,559	176	47.7
1900	45	WILLIAM MCKINLEY	Republican	7,218,491	292	51.7
		William J. Bryan	Democrat; Populist	6,356,734	155	45.5
		John C. Woolley	Prohibition	208,914		1.5
1904	45	THEODORE ROOSEVELT	Republican	7,628,461	336	57.4
		Alton B. Parker	Democrat	5,084,223	140	37.6
		Eugene V. Debs	Socialist	402,283		3.0
		Silas C. Swallow	Prohibition	258,536		1.9
1908	46	WILLIAM H. TAFT	Republican	7,675,320	321	51.6
		William J. Bryan	Democrat	6,412,294	162	43.1
		Eugene V. Debs	Socialist	420,793		2.8
		Eugene W. Chafin	Prohibition	253,840		1.7
1912	48	WOODROW WILSON	Democrat	6,296,547	435	41.9
		Theodore Roosevelt	Progressive	4,118,571	88	27.4
		William H. Taft	Republican	3,486,720	8	23.2
		Eugene V. Debs	Socialist	900,672		6.0
		Eugene W. Chafin	Prohibition	206,275		1.4
1916	48	WOODROW WILSON	Democrat	9,127,695	277	49.4
		Charles E. Hughes	Republican	8,533,507	254	46.2
		A. L. Benson	Socialist	585,113		3.2
		J. Frank Hanly	Prohibition	220,506		1.2
1920	48	WARREN G. HARDING	Republican	16,143,407	404	60.4
		James M. Cox	Democrat	9,130,328	127	34.2
		Eugene V. Debs	Socialist	919,799		3.4
		P. P. Christensen	Farmer-Labor	265,411		1.0
1924	48	CALVIN COOLIDGE	Republican	15,718,211	382	54.0
		John W. Davis	Democrat	8,385,283	136	28.8
		Robert M. La Follette	Progressive	4,831,289	13	16.6
1928	48	HERBERT C. HOOVER	Republican	21,391,993	444	58.2
		Alfred E. Smith	Democrat	15,016,169	87	40.9
1932	48	FRANKLIN D. ROOSEVELT	Democrat	22,809,638	472	57.4
		Herbert C. Hoover	Republican	15,758,901	59	39.7
		Norman Thomas	Socialist	881,951		2.2
1936	48	FRANKLIN D. ROOSEVELT	Democrat	27,752,869	523	60.8
		Alfred M. Landon	Republican	16,674,665	8	36.5
		William Lemke	Union	882,479		1.9
1940	48	FRANKLIN D. ROOSEVELT	Democrat	27,307,819	449	54.8
		Wendell L. Willkie	Republican	22,321,018	82	44.8
1944	48	FRANKLIN D. ROOSEVELT	Democrat	25,606,585	432	53.5
		Thomas E. Dewey	Republican	22,014,745	99	46.0

PRESIDENTIAL ELECTIONS
(continued)

Year	Number of States	Candidates	Party	Popular Vote	Electoral Vote	Percentage of Popular Vote
1948	48	HARRY S. TRUMAN	Democrat	24,105,812	303	49.5
		Thomas E. Dewey	Republican	21,970,065	189	45.1
		J. Strom Thurmond	States' Rights	1,169,063	39	2.4
		Henry A. Wallace	Progressive	1,157,172		2.4
1952	48	DWIGHT D. EISENHOWER	Republican	33,936,234	442	55.1
		Adlai E. Stevenson	Democrat	27,314,992	89	44.4
1956	48	DWIGHT D. EISENHOWER	Republican	35,590,472	457*	57.6
		Adlai E. Stevenson	Democrat	26,022,752	73	42.1
1960	50	JOHN F. KENNEDY	Democrat	34,227,096	303†	49.9
		Richard M. Nixon	Republican	34,108,546	219	49.6
1964	50	LYNDON B. JOHNSON	Democrat	42,676,220	486	61.3
		Barry M. Goldwater	Republican	26,860,314	52	38.5
1968	50	RICHARD M. NIXON	Republican	31,785,480	301	43.4
		Hubert H. Humphrey	Democrat	31,275,165	191	42.7
		George C. Wallace	American Independent	9,906,473	46	13.5
1972	50	RICHARD M. NIXON‡	Republican	47,165,234	520	60.6
		George S. McGovern	Democrat	29,168,110	17	37.5
1976	50	JIMMY CARTER	Democrat	40,828,929	297	50.1
		Gerald R. Ford	Republican	39,148,940	240	47.9
		Eugene McCarthy	Independent	739,256		
1980	50	RONALD REAGAN	Republican	43,201,220	489	50.9
		Jimmy Carter	Democrat	34,913,332	49	41.2
		John B. Anderson	Independent	5,581,379		
1984	50	RONALD REAGAN	Republican	53,428,357	525	59.0
		Walter F. Mondale	Democrat	36,930,923	13	41.0
1988	50	GEORGE BUSH	Republican	48,901,046	426	53.4
		Michael Dukakis	Democrat	41,809,030	111	45.6
1992	50	BILL CLINTON	Democrat	43,728,275	370	43.2
		George Bush	Republican	38,167,416	168	37.7
		H. Ross Perot	United We Stand, America	19,237,247		19.0
1996	50	BILL CLINTON	Democrat	45,590,703	379	49.0
		Robert Dole	Republican	37,816,307	159	41.0
		H. Ross Perot	Reform	7,874,283		8.0

*Walter B. Jones received 1 electoral vote.

†Harry F. Byrd received 15 electoral votes.

‡Resigned August 9, 1974: Vice President Gerald R. Ford became President.

ADMISSION OF STATES INTO THE UNION

State	Date of Admission	State	Date of Admission
1. Delaware	December 7, 1787	26. Michigan	January 26, 1837
2. Pennsylvania	December 12, 1787	27. Florida	March 3, 1845
3. New Jersey	December 18, 1787	28. Texas	December 29, 1845
4. Georgia	January 2, 1788	29. Iowa	December 28, 1846
5. Connecticut	January 9, 1788	30. Wisconsin	May 29, 1848
6. Massachusetts	February 6, 1788	31. California	September 9, 1850
7. Maryland	April 28, 1788	32. Minnesota	May 11, 1858
8. South Carolina	May 23, 1788	33. Oregon	February 14, 1859
9. New Hampshire	June 21, 1788	34. Kansas	January 29, 1861
10. Virginia	June 25, 1788	35. West Virginia	June 20, 1863
11. New York	July 26, 1788	36. Nevada	October 31, 1864
12. North Carolina	November 21, 1789	37. Nebraska	March 1, 1867
13. Rhode Island	May 29, 1790	38. Colorado	August 1, 1876
14. Vermont	March 4, 1791	39. North Dakota	November 2, 1889
15. Kentucky	June 1, 1792	40. South Dakota	November 2, 1889
16. Tennessee	June 1, 1796	41. Montana	November 8, 1889
17. Ohio	March 1, 1803	42. Washington	November 11, 1889
18. Louisiana	April 30, 1812	43. Idaho	July 3, 1890
19. Indiana	December 11, 1816	44. Wyoming	July 10, 1890
20. Mississippi	December 10, 1817	45. Utah	January 4, 1896
21. Illinois	December 3, 1818	46. Oklahoma	November 16, 1907
22. Alabama	December 14, 1819	47. New Mexico	January 6, 1912
23. Maine	March 15, 1820	48. Arizona	February 14, 1912
24. Missouri	August 10, 1821	49. Alaska	January 3, 1959
25. Arkansas	June 15, 1836	50. Hawaii	August 21, 1959

DEMOGRAPHICS OF THE UNITED STATES

POPULATION GROWTH

Year	Population	Percent Increase
1630	4,600	
1640	26,600	478.3
1650	50,400	90.8
1660	75,100	49.0
1670	111,900	49.0
1680	151,500	35.4
1690	210,400	38.9
1700	250,900	19.2
1710	331,700	32.2
1720	466,200	40.5
1730	629,400	35.0
1740	905,600	43.9
1750	1,170,800	29.3
1760	1,593,600	36.1
1770	2,148,100	34.8
1780	2,780,400	29.4
1790	3,929,214	41.3
1800	5,308,483	35.1
1810	7,239,881	36.4
1820	9,638,453	33.1
1830	12,866,020	33.5
1840	17,069,453	32.7
1850	23,191,876	35.9
1860	31,443,321	35.6
1870	39,818,449	26.6
1880	50,155,783	26.0
1890	62,947,714	25.5
1900	75,994,575	20.7
1910	91,972,266	21.0
1920	105,710,620	14.9
1930	122,775,046	16.1
1940	131,669,275	7.2
1950	150,697,361	14.5
1960	179,323,175	19.0
1970	203,235,298	13.3
1980	226,545,805	11.5
1990	248,709,873	9.8
1996	265,557,000	6.8

Source: *Historical Statistics of the United States* (1975); *Statistical Abstract by the United States* (1991, 1997).

Note: Figures for 1630–1780 include British colonies within limits of present United States only; Native American population included only in 1930 and thereafter.

WORKFORCE

Year	Total Number Workers (1000s)	Farmers as % of Total	Women as % of Total	% Workers in Unions
1810	2,330	84	(NA)	(NA)
1840	5,660	75	(NA)	(NA)
1860	11,110	53	(NA)	(NA)
1870	12,506	53	15	(NA)
1880	17,392	52	15	(NA)
1890	23,318	43	17	(NA)
1900	29,073	40	18	3
1910	38,167	31	21	6
1920	41,614	26	21	12
1930	48,830	22	22	7
1940	53,011	17	24	27
1950	59,643	12	28	25
1960	69,877	8	32	26
1970	82,049	4	37	25
1980	108,544	3	42	23
1990	117,914	3	45	16
1995	124,900	3	46	15

Source: *Historical Statistics of the United States* (1975); *Statistical Abstract of the United States* (1991, 1996).

VITAL STATISTICS
(per thousands)

Year	Births	Deaths	Marriages	Divorces
1800	55	(NA)	(NA)	(NA)
1810	54.3	(NA)	(NA)	(NA)
1820	55.2	(NA)	(NA)	(NA)
1830	51.4	(NA)	(NA)	(NA)
1840	51.8	(NA)	(NA)	(NA)
1850	43.3	(NA)	(NA)	(NA)
1860	44.3	(NA)	(NA)	(NA)
1870	38.3	(NA)	9.6 (1867)	0.3 (1867)
1880	39.8	(NA)	9.1 (1875)	0.3 (1875)
1890	31.5	(NA)	9.0	0.5
1900	32.3	17.2	9.3	0.7
1910	30.1	14.7	10.3	0.9
1920	27.7	13.0	12.0	1.6
1930	21.3	11.3	9.2	1.6
1940	19.4	10.8	12.1	2.0
1950	24.1	9.6	11.1	2.6
1960	23.7	9.5	8.5	2.2
1970	18.4	9.5	10.6	3.5
1980	15.9	8.8	10.6	5.2
1990	16.7	8.6	9.8	4.7
1994	15.0	8.8	9.1	4.6

Source: *Historical Statistics of the United States* (1975); *Statistical Abstract of the United States* (1991, 1997).

RACIAL COMPOSITION OF THE POPULATION
(in thousands)

Year	White	Black	Indian	Hispanic	Asian
1790	3,172	757	(NA)	(NA)	(NA)
1800	4,306	1,002	(NA)	(NA)	(NA)
1820	7,867	1,772	(NA)	(NA)	(NA)
1840	14,196	2,874	(NA)	(NA)	(NA)
1860	26,923	4,442	(NA)	(NA)	(NA)
1880	43,403	6,581	(NA)	(NA)	(NA)
1900	66,809	8,834	(NA)	(NA)	(NA)
1910	81,732	9,828	(NA)	(NA)	(NA)
1920	94,821	10,463	(NA)	(NA)	(NA)
1930	110,287	11,891	(NA)	(NA)	(NA)
1940	118,215	12,866	(NA)	(NA)	(NA)
1950	134,942	15,042	(NA)	(NA)	(NA)
1960	158,832	18,872	(NA)	(NA)	(NA)
1970	178,098	22,581	(NA)	(NA)	(NA)
1980	194,713	26,683	1,420	14,609	3,729
1990	205,710	30,486	2,065	22,354	7,458
1996	219,749	30,503	2,288	28,269	9,743

Source: U.S. Bureau of the Census, *U.S. Census of Population: 1940*, vol. II, part 1, and vol. IV, part 1; *1950*, vol. II, part 1; *1960*, vol. I, part 1; *1970*, vol. I, part B; and *Current Population Reports*, P25-1095 and P25-1104; *Statistical Abstract of the United States* (1997); and unpublished data.

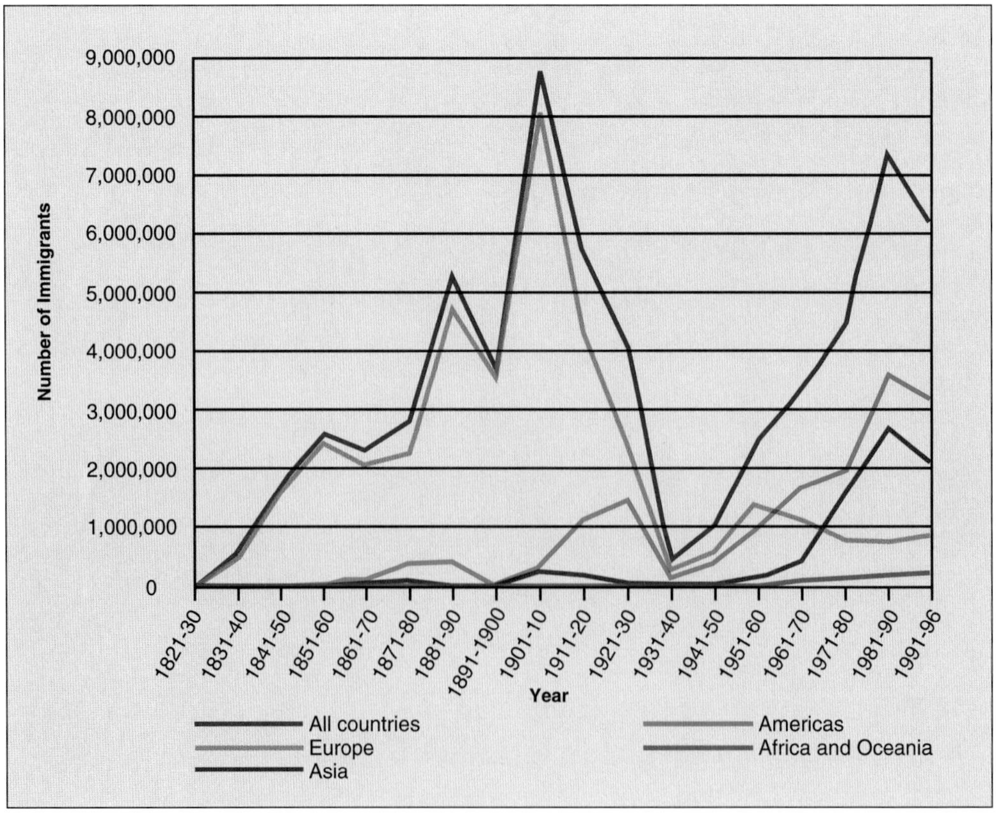

Immigration to the United States since 1820

Source: *Statistical Yearbook of the Immigration and Naturalization Service*, 1996.

Photo and Text Credits

Chapter 1: Photos: Cahokia Mounds State Historic Site, xxxii (vols. I, II, A, B, C)/xlviii (combined edition); Jerry Jacka/Arizona State Museum, University of Arizona, 6; Denver Museum of Natural History, 7; American Museum of Natural History, 11; National Museum of the American Indian/Smithsonian Institution, 13; Helga Teiwes, Arizona State Museum, 13; David Hiser/David Muench Photography, Inc., 14; George Gerster/Comstock, 15; Rota/American Museum of Natural History, 20 Text: "Emergence Song" (excerpt) from William Brandon, *The Magic World: American Indian Songs and Poems*. Copyright © 1971 by William Brandon. Reprinted with the permission of William Morrow and Company, Inc., 5; Winnebago song, "This Newly Created World," from the Winnebago Medicine Rite as recorded in Raul Radin, *The Road to Life and Death: A Ritual Drama of the American Indians* (Bollinger Series V), p. 254. Copyright 1945 and © renewed 1972 by Princeton University Press. Reprinted with the permission of the publishers., 10

Chapter 2: Photos: The Granger Collection, 25; Art Resource, Musee Conde, Chantilly/Giraudon, Art Resource, NY, 29; From THE SHIP, AN ILLUSTRATED HISTORY by Bjorn Landstrom, Copyright © 1961 by Bokforlaget Forum AB. Used by permission of Doubleday, a division of Bantam Doubleday Dell Publishing Group, Inc., 31; The Granger Collection, 32; The British Library, 34; Library of Congress, 35; The British Library, 36; Jacques Le Moyne, "Rene de Loudonniere and Chief Athore," 1564, watercolor, The New York Public Library, NY, 41; Capitaine de la Nation, *Codex Canadienses*, artist Louis Nicolas, from the collection of Gilcrease Museum, Tulsa, OK, 42; The Bridgeman Art Library, 43; The Granger Collection, 44 Text: "The African, Indian and European Population of the Americas" from Colin McEvedy and Richard Jones, *Atlas of World Population History*. Copyright © 1978 by Colin McEvedy and Richard Jones. Reprinted with the permission of Penguin Putnam, Inc., 39

Chapter 3: Photos: Jerry Jacka Photography, 49; New York Public Library, 53; (left) "Princeton University Library," Manuscripts Division. Department of Rare Books and Special Collections. Princeton University Library, 55; Library of Congress, 55; Library of Congress, 56; Library of Congress, 60; The John Carter Brown Library, at Brown University, 61; The Fine Arts Museum of San Francisco, 62; The New York Historical Society, 65; The Historical Society of Pennsylvania, 66; Courtesy, American Antiquarian Society, 68

Chapter 4: Photos: The British Library, 73; Library of Congress, 77; The Bridgeman Art Library, 79; Library of Congress, 81; The Granger Collection, New York, 82; American Antiquarian Society, 83; The Maryland Historical Society, 85; Carolina Art Association/Gibbes Museum of Art, 86; Colonial Williamsburg Foundation, 90; The Philbrook Museum of Art, 91; Michael Holford/The Victoria and Albert Museum, 93; The Saint Louis Art Museum, 96; Virginia Museum of Fine Arts, 99 Text: "Estimated Number of Africans Imported to British North America," from R.C. Simmons, *The American Colonies: From Settlement to Independence* (London:Longman, 1976). Copyright © 1976 by R.C. Simmons. Reprinted with the permission of The Peters Fraser and Dunlop Group Limited, 80

Chapter 5: Photos: Colonial Williamsburg Foundation, 103; The Historical Society of Pennsylvania, 106; Jack W. Dykinga & Associates, 110; United States Geological Survey, 112; William Johnson/Stock, Boston, 113; Henry Glassie, Pattern in the Material Folk Culture of the Eastern United States, 114; (left) Courtesy, American Antiquarian Society, 118; Library of Congress, 118; Schalkwijk/Art Resource, NY, 121; American Antiquarian Society, 124; John Carter Brown Library, Brown University, 127 Text: "Distribution of Assessed Taxable Wealth in Eighteenth-Century Chester County, Pennsylvania," Copyright © 1968 by Peter N. Stearns. Reprinted with the permission of the publishers. 122; "Wealth Held by Richest 10 Percent of the Population: Northern and Southern Colonies Compared, 1770," Copyright © by Princeton University Press, renewed 1993 by Jackson Turner Main. Reprinted with the permission of Princeton University Press, 122

Chapter 6: Photos: The Granger Collection, 132; National Gallery of Canada, 138; Treaty, dated 13 July 1765, between Sir William Johnson and representatives of the Delaware, Shawnee, and Mingo nations. On parchment, 16" x 24.5". Photo by Carmelo Guadagno. Photograph courtesy of National Museum of the American Indian/Smithsonian Institution. Neg. 39369, 140; Massachusetts Historical Society, 142; Museum of Fine Arts, Boston, 144; Library of Congress, 145; The Granger Collection, 146; Library of Congress, 147; Library of Congress, 149; Christie's Images, 150; Connecticut Historical Society, 154; The Granger Collection, 156; The Granger Collection, 158

Chapter 7: Photos: Sam Holland, South Carolina State House, 162; Anne S. K. Brown Military Collection, Brown University Library, 166; Museum of Fine Arts, Boston, 167; The Granger Collection, 168; (top) Gilbert Stuart. "The Mohawk Chief Joseph Brant," 1786. Oil on canvas, 30" x 25". New York State Historical Association, Cooperstown, NY, 172; The Bostonian Society/Old State House, 172; Library of Congress, 176; Data available from U.S. Geological Survey, EROS Data Center, Sioux Falls, SD, 181; Corbis-Bettmann, 185; Library of Congress, 186; Art Resource, NY, 189

Chapter 8: Photos: The Granger Collection, 193; Print and Picture Collection, The Free Library of Philadelphia, 197; Collection of The New York Historical Society, 200; "The Republican Court," 1861, by Daniel P. Huntington. Oil on canvas. Gift of the Crescent Boys' Club. Brooklyn Museum of Art, 201; Indiana Historical Society Library (negative no. C2584), 205; "General George Washington Reviewing the Western Army...," by Francis Kemmelmeyer, after 1794. Oil on paper backed with linen. Dimensions 18 1/8" x 23 1/8". Courtesy of Winterthur Museum, 206; Collection of The New York Historical Society, 210; The Granger Collection, 212; Pennsylvania Academy of the Fine Arts, 213; Library of Congress, 214; Courtesy of American Antiquarian Society, 216; Library Company of Philadelphia, 217 Text: "Housing Values," Copyright © 1985 by Social Science History Association. Reprinted with the permission of Duke University Press, 215

Immigration & Community, to 1800: Photos: The Granger Collection, 225; The Granger Collection, 226 Text: "The Ancestry of the British Colonial Population" from Thomas L. Purvis, "The European Ancestry of the United States Population" in *William and Mary Quarterly*, 61 (1984): 85–101. Copyright © 1984 by the Institute of Early American History and Culture. Reprinted with the permission of the publishers., 223

Chapter 9: Photos: Henry Ford Museum & Greenfield Village, 228; Friedrich H. von Kittlitz, A View of the Russian Capital, 1827, from F.P. Litke. Alaska and Polar Regions, Department, Elmer E. Rasmusen Library Rare books, University of Alaska, Fairbanks, 232; Launching of ship "Fame" from Becket's Shipyard, Essex, Massachusetts, 1802, oil on canvas, by George Ropes. Mark Sexton, Peabody Essex Museum, 236; top, Library of Congress, 237; Library of Congress, 237; Museum of Early Southern Decorative Arts, 238; Thomas Gilcrease Institute of American History and Art, 243; Field Musuem of Natural History, 245; Library of Congress, 245; Library of Congress, 249; Library of Congress, 250; The New York Historical Society, 253

Chapter 10: Photos: NationsBank, 261; Walters Art Gallery, 268; Library of Congress, 270; The Maryland Historical Society, 273; Munson-Williams-Proctor Institute, 275; Chicago Historical Society, 277; Museum of the City of New York, 282; Library of Congress, 285; "Collection of the

Boston Athenaeum," 289; New York Public Library, 290 Text: "The Impact of the Erie Canal on Household Textile Manufacture" from Arthur Harrison Cole, The American Wool Manufacture. Copyright 1926 by the President and Fellows of Harvard College. Reprinted with the permission of Harvard University Press, 274

Chapter 11: Photos: Chicago Historical Society, 294; Library of Congress, 298; Wilson S. Armistead, University of Michigan Press, 299; Library of Congress, 307; The Historic New Orleans Collection, 308; Sophia Smith Collection, Smith College, 309; Library of Congress, 310; American Numismatic Society of New York, (left and right), 311; Daughters of the Republic of Texas, Yanaguana Society Collection, 312; The Historic New Orleans Collection, 315; National Archives, 317; Library of Congress, 319

Chapter 12: Photos: American Textile History Museum, 324; Abby Aldrich Rockefeller Folk Art Center, Williamsburg, VA, 328; Museum of Fine Arts, Boston, 329; Library of Congress, 332; Rhode Island Historical Society, 333; James L. Amos, National Geographic Society, (top & bottom) 336; High-Pressure Steamboat Mayflower, 1855, color lithograph by N. Currier. The Bettmann Archive. Corbis-Bettmann, 338; Baker Library, Graduate School of Business Administration, Harvard University, 340; Musuem of Fine Arts, Boston, 343; Mathew Brady/Brown Brothers, 344; The New York Historical Society, 346; Library of Congress, 347

Chapter 13: Photos: The New York Historical Society, 351; The Granger Collection, 358; Library of Congress, 360; Zelsa P. Mackay Collection, Courtesy George Eastman House, 362; "Seabury Champlin's June 3, 1791 Certificate of Membership in NY Mechanic Society," Abraham Godwin, print. Courtesy Winterthur Museum, 363; Frank and Marie-Therese Wood Print Collections, The Picture Bank, 364; The Schlesinger Library, Radcliffe College, 367; Library of Congress, 369; Hannah Harrison, Hancock Shaker Village, 371; Library of Congress (left & right), 373; Sophia Smith Collection, Smith College, 374; Lynn Historical Society, 376

Immigration & Community, 1800–1860: Photos: Dover Publications, Inc., 383; Museum of the City of New York, 384

Chapter 14: Photos: San Jacinto Museum of History Association, 386; Walters Art Gallery, 390; Henry E. Huntington Library and Art Gallery, 395; American Antiquarian Society, 397; The Walters Art Gallery, Baltimore, 398; Art Resource, NY, 399; Brown University Library, 404; National Gallery of Art, 406; The New York Historical Society, 408; California State Library, 409; Bigelow Collection, Museum of Fine Arts, Boston, 410; Steven Laschever/Museum of American Political Life/University of Hartford, 413 Text: "Overland Emigration to Oregon, California, and Utah, 1840-1860" from John Unruh, Jr., *The Plains Across: The Overland Emigrants and the Trans-Mississippi West, 1840-60*. Copyright © 1979 by the Board of Trustees of the University of Illinois. Reprinted with the permission of the University of Illinois Press., 396; "California in the Gold Rush," from Warren A. Beck and Ynez D. Haase, *Historical Atlas of California*. Copyright © 1974 by the University of Oklahoma Press. Reprinted with the permission of the publishers., 407

Chapter 15: Photos: The Granger Collection, 417; Harriet Beecher Stowe Center, Hartford, CT, Stowe-Day Foundation, 422; Courtesy American Antiquarian Society, 423; Library of Congress, 424; The Granger Collection, 431; Corbis-Bettmann, 432; New York Public Library, 434; Library of Congress, 435; Museum of the City of New York, 436; The Granger Collection, 437; Library of Congress, 440; United States Senate, 443

Chapter 16: Photos: Armen Shamalian Photographers, Art Resource, NY, 447; Courtesy Museum of Fine Arts, Boston, 451; The Picture Bank, 455; Alexander Gardner, National Archives, 456; Library of Congress, 458; Valentine Museum Library, (left) 459; Library of Congress, 459; Reproduced from Pauli Murray, *Proud Shoes: The Story of an American Family*, HarperCollins Publishers, Inc., 1987, 466; Center of Military History, U.S. Army, 468; The Metropolitan Museum of Art, 469; Culvery Pictures, Inc., 471; Thomas C. Roche, Library of Congress, 475; Army Military History Institute, 476; Library of Congress, 477

Chapter 17: Photos: The Metropolitan Museum of Art, 481; National Archives, 485; Chicago Historical Society, 486; The Granger Collection, 488; The Susan B. Anthony House, Rochester, NY, 492; The Picture Bank/Harper's Weekly, 495; Library of Congress, 498; Library of Congress, 499; The University of North Carolina, (left) 501; Rutherford B. Hayes Presidential Center, 501; The Granger Collection, New York, 505; The Picture Bank, Frank and Marie-Therese Wood Print Collection, 507

Chapter 18: Photos: Christie's Images, 513; National Anthropological Archives, 518; Marion Koogler McNay Art Museum, 519; Timothy O'Sullivan, Amon Carter Museum, 522; Witte Museum, 525; Harper's Weekly, 527; Nebraska State Historical Society, Solomon D. Butcher Collection, 531; Library of Congress, 532; The Metropolitan Museum of Art, 537; Library of Congress, 538; Photo courtesy of State Historical Society of Iowa, Iowa City, 541; Edward Truman/The Denver Public Library, Western History Collection, 542 Text: "Oklahoma Territory" from John W. Morrois, Charles R. Goins, and Edwin C. McReynolds, *Historical Atlas of Oklahoma*, Third Edition. Copyright © 1965, 1976, 1986 by the University of Oklahoma Press. Reprinted with the permission of the publishers., 515; History and the Land feature and "Ethnic Composition of North Dakota, 1900," from John R. Shortridge, "The Great Plains" in Mary Kupiec Cayton, Elliott J. Gorn, and Peter W. Williams, *Encyclopedia of American Social History II*. Copyright © 1993 by Charles Scribner's Sons. Reprinted with the permission of Scribner's, an imprint of Simon & Schuster Macmillan. 528–529

Chapter 19: Photos: The Granger Collection, 547; U.S. Department of the Interior, National Park Service, Edison National Historic Site, 551 Chicago Historical Society, 553; Color engraving by J. Keppler from Puck, February 23, 1881, Collection of The New York Historical Society, New York City, 554; The Denver Public Library, Western History Collection, 556; Museum of the City of New York, 563; National Archives, 565; Terra Museum of American Art, 568; The Granger Collection, 570; Rhode Island School of Design, 573 Text: "U.S. Economy, 1873-1900" from Bernard Bailyn et al., *The Great Republic*, Third Edition. Copyright © 1985 by D.D. Heath and Company. Reprinted with the permission of Houghton Mifflin Company., 557

Chapter 20: Photos: Vermont State House, 578; Sally Anderson-Bruce/Museum of American Political Life, 583; Library of Congress, 585; Library of Congress, 588; Library of Congress, 590; The Granger Collection, New York, 594; National Archives, 596; Library of Congress, 601; Library of Congress, 603; Library of Congress, 604

Chapter 21: Photos: San Diego Museum of Art, 609; Lewis W. Hine/George Eastman House, 614; Henry Street Settlement, 615; Museum of the City of New York, 618;The Toledo Museum of Art, 622; Brown Brothers, 624; UPI/Corbis-Bettmann, 626; Collection of The American Labor Museum, Botto House National Landmark, 629; Planned Parenthood ® Federation of America, Inc. At, 810 Seventh Avenue, New York, NY, 10019., 631; Schomburg Center for Research in Black Culture, 632; California Historical Society, 635; Theodore Roosevelt Collection, Harvard College Library/The Houghton Library, Harvard University, 636

Chapter 22: Photos: Corbis-Bettmann, 642; The Granger Collection, 646; Culver Pictures, Inc., 649; Wallace Kirkland Papers, Jane Addams Memorial Collection, Special Collections, The University Library, University of Illinois at Chicago, 651; The Granger Collection; 652; Library of Congress, 653; National Archives, 654; National Archives, 655; Virginia War Museum/War Memorial Museum of Virginia, 659; Library of Congress, 661; Stock Montage Inc./ Historial Pictures Collection, 665;

Pemco Webster & Stevens Collection, Museum of History and Industry, Seattle, WA, 666; Art Resource, NY 667

Chapter 23: Photos: The Equitable Life Assurance Society of the United States, 673; A&P Food Stores, LTD, 678; Brown Brothers, 679; Ford Motor Company, Detroit, 680; Culver Pictures, Inc., 683; Gaslight Advertising Archives, Inc., Commack, NY, 685; The Granger Collection, 688; Corbis-Bettmann, 689; Bracken Library, Ball State University Libraries, Archives and Special Collections, W.A. Swift Photo Collection, 695; AP/Wide World Photos, 696; Library of Congress, 699; Reiss, Winold. Portrait of Langston Hughes (1902-1967 Poet) © 1925. National Portrait Gallery, Washington, DC, USA, Art Resource, NY, 701; "Copyright, 1928, Los Angeles Times. Reprinted by permission." Los Angeles Times Syndicate International, 702

Immigration & Community, 1860–1930: Photos: UPI/Lewis W. Hine, Corbis-Bettmann, 711; Jacob A. Riss/Museum of the City of New York, 713

Chapter 24: Photos: SuperStock, Inc., 714; Brown Brothers, 718; Dorothea Lange/The Oakland Museum, 720; Whitney Museum of American Art, 721; Cartoon by Covarrubias from *Vanity Fair* depicting Franklin D. Roosevelt's first-term inauguration on March 4, 1933. Conde Nast/Franklin D. Roosevelt Library, Hyde Park, NY, 724; Terry Dintenfass Gallery, 730; The Granger Collection, 732; Library of Congress, 736; Walker Evans/Library of Congress, 738; Whitney Museum of American Art, 739; Frank Driggs Collection, 741; UPI/Corbis-Bettmann, 743

Chapter 25: Photos: Christie's Images, 748; National Archives, 754; Franklin D. Roosevelt Library, 755; The Granger Collection, 759; Corbis-Bettmann, 761; Japanese American National Museum, 763; Graydon Wood/Philadelphia Museum of Art, 764; AP/Wide World Photos, 765; National Archives, 769; Center of Military History, U.S. Army, 771; Robert Capa/Corbis-Bettmann, 776; Imperial War Museum, London, 779; Corbis-Bettmann, 780 Text: "Gallup Polls: European War and World War I, 1938-1940" from *The Gallup Poll: Public Opinion, 1935-1974*. Reprinted with the permission of Random House, Inc., 753; "Effects of War Spending, 1940-1945" from Robert L. Heilbroner, *The Economic Transformation of America*. Copyright © 1977 by Harcourt Brace and Company. Reprinted with the permission of the publisher., 757; Langston Hughes, "Beaumont to Detroit: 1943" from *The Collected Poems of Langston Hughes*, edited by Arnold Rampersad and David Roessel. Originally published in *Common Ground* (Autumn 1943). Copyright © 1994 by the Estate of Langston Hughes. Reprinted with the permission of Alfred A. Knopf, Inc. and Harold Ober Associates, Inc., 764

Chapter 26: Photos: Michael Barson, 785; UPI/Corbis-Bettmann, 789; Brown Brothers, 793; AP/Wide World Photos, 797; UPI/Corbis-Bettmann, 799; Michael Barson/Archive Photos, 803; Hank Walker/Time Life Syndication, 804; Corbis-Bettmann, 806; National Archives, 809; AP/Wide World Photos, 812

Chapter 27: Photos: Saatchi Collection, London/A.K.G., Berlin/SuperStock, Inc., 817; Bernard Hoffman/*Life Magazine*/© 1950 Time Ind., Time Life Syndication, 821; Williger, FPG International LLC, 822; UPI/Corbis-Bettmann, 826; Archive Photos, 828; Motorola, Inc., 831; Globe Photos, Inc., 832; A. Wagg/FPG International LLC, 834; AP/Wide World Photos, 838; Corbis-Bettmann, 839; NASA Headquarters, 841; Photo. No. ST-A26-18-62 in the John F. Kennedy Library, 843; AP/Wide World Photos, 844 Text: Allen Ginsberg, "Howl" (excerpt) from *Collected Poems, 1947-1980*. Copyright © 1955, 1958, and renewed 1983, 1986 by Allen Ginsberg. Reprinted with the permission of HarperCollins Publishers, Inc., 833

Chapter 28: Photos: Romare Bearden Foundation/Licensed by VAGA, New York, NY, 848; Frank Driggs Collection,852; Dan McCoy/Black Star, (left) 853; Corbis-Bettmann, 853; UPI/Corbis-Bettmann, 856; John G. Moebes/Greensboro New & Record, 857; UPI/Corbis-Bettmann, 860; Bill Hudson/AP/Wide World Photos, 863; AP/Wide World Photos, 864; George Ballis/Take Stock, 867; John Launois/Black Star, 868; Matt Herron/Media Image Resource Alliance, 869; Benson Latin American Collection, University of Texas at Austin, 872; Corbis-Bettmann, 873

Chapter 29: Photos: Library of Congress, 878; Philip Jones Griffiths/Magnum Photos, Inc., 883; Jeffrey Blankfort/Jeroboam, Inc., 884; Bernie Boston, 885; Archive Photos, 888; Jeffrey Blankfort/Jeroboam, Inc., 895; Matt Herron/Media Image Resource Alliance, 897; Corbis-Bettmann, 901; Corbis-Bettmann, 908 Text: Bob Dylan, "The Times They are a-Changin'" (excerpt). Copyright © 1963, 1964 by Warner Bros. Music, renewed 1991 by Special Rider Music. All rights reserved. International copyright secured. Reprinted with the permission of Special Rider Music., 885

Chapter 30: Photos: Robert McElroy/Woodfin Camp & Associates, 917; Guido Alberto Rossi/The Image Bank, 921; Corbis-Bettmann, 925; Centro Cultural de la Raza, 928; Everett Collection, Inc., 931; AP/Wide World Photos, 932; Corbis-Bettmann, 937; SIPA Press, 939

Chapter 31: Photos: Tsing-Fang Chen/SuperStock, Inc., 945; Dennis Brack/Black Star, 948; Dennis Brack/ Black Star, 953; Corbis-Bettmann, 958; (left) Photo Network for Michael Philip Manheim, 959; Alberto Guido Rossi/The Image Bank, 959; Lynn Johnson/Black Star, 960; Joyce Dopkeen/*The New York Times*, January 31, 1993, 962; A. Berliner/Liaison Agency, Inc., 963; Lisa Quinones/Black Star, 965; Peter Turnley/Black Star, 972; Patrick Downs/Los Angeles Times Syndicate, 973; Lloyd Francis, Jr./Black Star, 1992, San Jose Mercury News/Black Star, 974; Sygma, 976; Reuters/Mike Segar/Archive Photos, 978; Joe Marquette/AP/Wide World Photos, 980

Immigration & Community, since 1930: Photos: Ed Bohon/The Stock Market, 989; Charles Gupton/The Stock Market, 991

INDEX

A

Abenaki Indians, 67
Abernathy, Ralph, 856, 861
Abolitionism, 318–19, 320, 371–75
Abortion, 345, 933–34
Aboukir Bay, battle of (1798), 210
Abraham Lincoln Brigade, 738
Abrams v. *United States*, 663
Acadia, 53, 54, 95, 111, 136, 137, 206, 232
Acculturation, 90–91
Acheson, Dean, 795, 803, 805
Ackerman, Nathan, 720
Acoma (pueblo), 18, 52
Acosta, Joseph de, 3
Acquired immune deficiency syndrome (AIDS), 965–66
Acres of Diamonds (Conwell), 554
Act of Trade and Navigation (1651), 64
Adams, Abigail, 133, 155, 166–67, 184, 187, 266
Adams, Charles Francis, 440–41, 606
Adams, Charles Francis, Jr., 506
Adams, Henry, 231
Adams, John, 133–34, 152, 159, 167, 184, 188, 237; in American Revolution, 169, 177; Boston Massacre trial, 149; Constitutional Convention and, 196; Declaration of Independence and, 158; presidency of, 209–10, 211; at Second Continental Congress, 155, 156; as vice-president, 200, 201
Adams, John Quincy, 250; *Amistad* trial and, 375; diplomacy of, 254–56; election of 1824, 267; election of 1828, 268; as Massachusetts representative, 375, 402; presidency of, 250, 254–56, 267; as secretary of state, 253
Adams, Samuel, 133, 144, 147, 148, 149, 150, 152, 199, 213
Adams–Onís Treaty of 1819, 255
Addams, Jane, 611, 614, 651, 654
Address to the Negroes of the State of New York (Hammon), 186
Adena culture, 15
Administration of Justice Act (1774), 152
Advertising, 553, 685, 830, 832
Affirmative action, 926, 928
Afghanistan, Soviet invasion of, 939
AFL. *See* American Federation of Labor (AFL)
Africa: agriculture in, 77, 305; European conquest of, 83; Portuguese explorations of, 31; slave trade and, 74, 78–83
African Americans: *See also* Civil rights movement (1957–1962); Reconstruction (1863–1877); Segregation; Slavery; as abolitionists, 371–72; American Revolution and, 171, 173, 174–75, 185–87; Black Power movement, 895–98; churches, 494; in Civil War, 465–67, 471, 476; community structures of, 361; cowboys, 526–27, 538; economic autonomy after Civil War, 494–97; education of, 494, 500, 571, 617; family, 493–94; free, 99–100, 186, 307–8, 310–11, 361–62, 371–72, 431; freedom in Reconstruction period, meaning of, 492–98; in Great Depression, 743–44; Great Migration and, 664–65, 680; institutions, 186; labor, 556, 565, 760; McCarthyism and, 804; middle-class status of, 925; in military, 655, 665, 768–70; music of, 89–90, 91, 701, 819, 827–28; New Deal and, 743–44; in New South, 565; politics and, 497–98, 499, 927; in Progressive Era, 631–33; race riots, 664–65, 763–64, 769, 891–92; racial violence in 1890s, 596–97; racism and, 595, 617, 631–32, 655, 693; religion and, 89, 307–8, 362, 494; Republican Party and, 498; return to South, 920; in sports, 575, 687; in the twenties, 700–701; unemployment rates in late '70s, 926; in unions, 760; in Vietnam War, 887, 897; voting rights, 265, 487, 490, 497, 596, 617, 853; women, 565, 768–69, 920; in World War I, 664–65; in World War II, 758, 763–64, 768–70; writers, 186–87, 738
African Marine Fund, 186
African Methodist Episcopal (AME) Church, 307, 310, 361, 494
African National Congress, 907
Agent Orange, 882
Age of Anxiety, 805–8
Age of Capital, 504–6
Age of Reason, The (Paine), 216
Age of the Common Man, 269, 287, 377
Agnew, Spiro T., 903, 910
Agrarian republic (1790–1824), 228–59; Adams (John Quincy) presidency, 250, 254–56; Atlantic ports, 234–35, 236; coast-to-coast expansion and, 231–35; Indian policy in, 243–47; international trade in, 235–37; Jefferson presidency and, 237–43; Lewis and Clark expedition and, 229–30; Mississippi River, 232–33; Missouri Compromise, 250, 256–58; national economy, development of, 235–37; Panic of 1819, 250, 256; Russian settlement, 231–32; Second Great Awakening and, 253; trans–Appalachian settlement, 233–34; War of 1812 and, 247–49; westward expansion, 244–45, 250–58
Agrarian Tradition, 13
Agribusiness, 534–35, 920–21
Agricultural Adjustment Administration (AAA), 724–25, 731, 741
Agricultural colleges, 571
Agriculture: *See also* Plantation system; Slavery; African communal systems of, 305; in California, 534–35; crop-lien system, 502–4; development of, 10–22; Dust Bowl of the 1930s and, 730–33; ecological impact of, 535–36; family farm, 62, 531–32; farmers' organizations, 585–87, 589; in Great Depression, 719, 732, 744; on Great Plains, 529–36; Homestead Act and, 529–30; laborers/migrant workers in, 555, 698–99, 732, 744; market production in, 533–34; Mexican immigration and, 698–99; in Middle Ages, 28, 29; Mormon, 523; Native American, 542; New Deal programs, 724–25, 728, 731, 741; oil shortage and, 918–19; in Old Northwest, 276–77; preindustrial rural life, 327–28; production technologies, 532–33; in Reconstruction South, 495–97, 502–4; regional specialization in, 277; as revolution, 11–12; sharecropping system, 483, 495, 497, 503; tenant farmers, 99, 312–13, 532; in trans–Mississippi West, 529–33; in the twenties, 681–82, 698–99; West African, 77; in World War II, 758
Agriculture, Department of, 457, 533, 581, 634, 758
Aguinaldo, Emilio, 604
AIDS, 965–66
Aid to Families with Dependent Children program (AFDC), 980
Ailes, Roger, 969–70
Air pollution, 564
Akerman, Amos T., 502
Akwamu, Gold Coast state of, 82
Alabama, 298; civil rights movement in, 857–58, 862–64, 869–71; Montgomery bus boycott, 849–50, 856; Reconstruction era in, 482–83; Selma campaign, 869–71
"Alabama Fever" of 1816–1820, 298
Alamo, the (1836), 387–88, 400, 712–13
Alaska, 231–32, 407, 599
Albany Argus, 263
Albany Conference of 1754, 135
Albany (Georgia) movement (1961–1962), 861–62
Albright, Madeleine, 978
Alcohol consumption: prohibition and, 620–21, 661, 692–93; temperance movement and, 364, 367–68, 369, 588
Alcott, Louisa May, 370
Aleutian Islands, 7
Aleut people, 7, 231
Aleut Revolt (1762), 231
Alfred, William, 383
Algonquian Indians, 21–22, 26, 54, 60, 95, 113
Alianza Federal de Mercedes, 901
Alien Act (1798), 210, 249
Alien Act (1918), 669
Alienation in the twenties, 701–3
Alien Enemies Act (1798), 210
All-American Canal, 733
Allen, Ethan, 156
Allen, Richard, 307, 955
Allen, Stephen, 330, 342, 344
Allende, Salvador, 907
Alliance for Progress, 842
All in the Family (TV program), 931
Allis Chalmers Company, 627
Almy, William, 330, 331, 333
Altenburg, Myrtle, 660
Altgeld, John Peter, 558–59, 591, 606, 614
Amalgamated Clothing Workers, 729
Amalgamated Iron, Steel and Tin Workers, 591
America First Committee, 752
American Anti-Slavery Society, 373
American Bar Association (ABA), 585
American Board of Commissioners for Foreign Missions, 243–44
"American Century," 788–89
American China Development Company, 601
American Civil Liberties Union, 696, 763
American Colonization Society, 371
American Crisis, The (Paine), 216
American Dictionary of the English Language (Webster), 217
American Enterprise Institute, 931
American Equal Rights Association, 491
American Expeditionary Force (AEF), 656
American Federation of Labor (AFL), 559, 627–28, 643, 644, 658, 694, 729
American Federation of Labor–Congress of Industrial Organization (AFL–CIO), 919
American Historical Association, 584–85
American Horse, Chief, 542
American Independent Party, 904
American Indian Defense Association, 734
American Indian Movement (AIM), 901–2
American Indians. *See* Native Americans
American (Know-Nothing) Party, 431–32, 433
American League against War and Fascism, 752
American Liberty League, 726
American Medical Association (AMA), 584, 663, 698, 826
American Missionary Association (AMA), 494
American Philosophical Society, 288
"American plan," 678
American Political Tradition (Hofstadter), 808
American Protective Association, 693
American Protective League, 663–64
American Railway Union (ARU), 591
American Red Cross, 651, 653, 654, 663
American Renaissance, 420–21, 562
American Revolution, 163–75; *See also* Pre-revolutionary period; African Americans and, 171, 173,

American Revolution (cont.)
174–75, 185–87; beginnings of, 156–59; campaign for New York and New Jersey, 168–69; casualties, 166; demobilization after, 178–79; economy in, 187–89; financing, 156, 176–77; first engagements of, 153–54; French and Spanish alliance, politics in, 170–71; Loyalists in, 167–68, 175; Native Americans and, 172–73, 179, 182; Northern campaigns of 1777, 169–70; Patriot forces in, 164, 165–67; peace talks, 177; in South, 157, 173–75; Valley Forge, 163–64, 169; war at sea, 171; Yorktown strategy, 175
American Servicemen's Union, 887
Americans for Democratic Action (ADA), 798, 799
American Slavery (Weld), 373
American Society for the Promotion of Temperance, 367–68
American Spelling Book (Webster), 216, 217
American System, 253–54, 282
American system of manufactures, 336–37
American Telephone & Telegraph (AT&T), 684
American Tract Society, 287
American Union against Militarism, 651
American Woman Suffrage Association (AWSA), 491, 588
Amerindians. *See* Native Americans
Ames, Fisher, 241
Amherst, Jeffery, 139, 140
Amistad (ship), 375
Ammons, Elias, 627
Amusement parks, 571
Anaconda Copper Mining Company, 522
Anaconda Plan, 460, 461
Anasazi people, 14, 16, 18
Ancient Society (Morgan), 539
Anderson, Benedict, 134
Anderson, Mary, 697
Anderson, Maxwell, 736
Anderson, Sherwood, 629, 702, 737
Andersonville prison camp, 467–68
Andrews, Eliza, 493
Andropov, Yuri, 955
Andros, Edmund, 69
Angel Island detention center, 711
Anglican church, 113, 114, 115, 125, 185
Anglican culture, 125
Anglo-Dutch wars, 65, 94
Angola, Portuguese colony of, 79
Annan, Kofi, 978
Annapolis Convention, 196
Anson, "Cap," 575
Anthony, Susan B., 353, 465, 491–92
Anthracite coal, 551
Antibiotics, 826
Anti-Catholicism, 361, 432, 709
Anti-communism. *See* Cold War era
Antietam, battle of (1862), 461
Anti-Federalists, 198, 199, 200
Anti-immigrant sentiment, 431, 971
Anti-Imperialist League, 605–6
Anti-Masonic Party, 283
Antiprostitution movement, 368–69
Anti-Saloon League, 620
Antitrust legislation, 554, 627, 633–34
Antiwar demonstrations, 887
Antiwar movements: Spanish–American War, 604–5; Vietnam War, 883–88, 904; World War I, 651, 653–54
Antrobus, John, 308
Anza, Juan Bautista de, 110
A'ongonte. *See* Williams, Eunice (daughter)
Apache Indians, 3, 7, 19, 51, 87, 398, 519–20
Appalachian highlands, backcountry of, 114–15, 204–5
Appeal to the Colored Citizens of the World, 372
Applied Christianity (Gladden), 592
Appomattox, surrender at (1865), 460, 477
Apprenticeship, 328–29, 338
Apprentices' Library, 344
Arapahoe Indians, 229
Arawaks, 3
Arbenz Guzmán, Jácobo, 837
Arbuckle, Roscoe "Fatty," 683
Archaeology of early America, 4, 6–7
Archaic period, 1–23; Adena culture, 15; agriculture, 10–16; Cahokia, 1, 2, 13, 17; Clovis technology, 5–6; Desert Culture, 7–9, 12; division of labor, 10, 12; forest communities, 10; forest efficiency, 9–10; Hopewell culture, 15; hunting, 6–7, 12–13; modes of subsistence in, 7; Mogollon people, 13; Old Cordilleran Culture, 9; regional cultures, 6–10; religion, 12–13; Woodland culture, 14–17
Architecture: balloon-frame construction, 290–91; of Gilded Age, 567; Jefferson on, 215; log construction, 114, 115; nationalism in, 213–14; New England, 113; nineteenth-century urban, 562–63; skyscrapers, 562, 680; of Washington, D.C., 214; wood construction, 113
Area Redevelopment Act (1963), 840
Arizona, 18, 109; Bisbee deportation, 643; secession in Civil War of, 452
Arkansas, school desegregation in, 855
Armed forces. *See* Military, the
Arminianism, 125–26
Arminius, Jacobus, 126
Armour, Philip Danforth, 550
Arms control, 691, 955–56
Arms race, 796, 841, 956
Armstrong, John F., 504
Army Nurse Corps, 768
Arnhem, battle of (1944), 776
Arnold, Benedict, 157, 167–68
ARPANET, 946
Art: Ashcan realist school, 622; early nineteenth century, 290–91; founding of art museums, 568; nationalism in, 213–14; New Deal programs, 735–37; in post-revolutionary period, 213–15; Renaissance, 30; western, 537, 538–39
Art Decoration (Spofford), 568
Arthur, Chester A., 583
Arthur Mervyn (Brown), 218
Articles of Confederation, 175, 176–77, 196, 197
Artisanal politics, 362–63
Artisans, 117, 305, 328–29, 338
Ashantis, 77
Ashcan realist school, 622
Ashe, Arthur, 966
Ashley, William Henry, 389
Asia: Cold War in, 795–96; Native American migration from, 3–5, 7; trade with, 29, 392–93
Asian American Political Alliance (AAPA), 902
Asian Americans, 988; *See also* Chinese Americans; Japanese Americans; civil rights and, 874–75; immigration, 408, 409, 874, 970–71, 987–88; protest movements by, 902–3
Assemblies, power of, 123
Assembly line, 679
Assiniboin Indians, 229
Association of Community Organizations for Reform Now (ACORN), 928
"Associative state," 690
Astor, John Jacob, 282, 330
Astor Place Riot (1849), 359
Aswan High Dam, 836
Asylum movement, 369
Atchison, David, 430, 431
Atchison, Topeka, and Santa Fe Railroad, 505
Athapascans (Na-Dene people), 7
Atlanta, Georgia, 474, 476, 858, 859
Atlantic Charter (1941), 754, 779
Atlantic Ocean, clockwise circulation of winds and currents, 32
Atlantic ports, 234–35, 236
Atomic bomb, 749–50, 780–82, 805
Atomic diplomacy, 796
Attucks, Crispus, 148
Atwater, Lee, 969–70
Audubon, John James, 290, 296
Austin, John Mather, 344
Austin, Moses, 399
Austin, Stephen F., 387, 399
Austin, Texas, 399
Austin, Warren, 789
Automobiles and automobile industry, 658, 679–80, 715–16, 759, 823
Ayer, Francis Wayland, 553
Aztecs, 2, 11, 33–34, 35

B

B–17 Flying Fortress, 774–75
Babbitt (Lewis), 702–3
Babcock, Orville E., 508
Baby and Child Care (Spock), 807
Baby boom, 806, 807
Backcountry, 114–15, 204–5
Bacon, Francis, 29
Bacon, Nathaniel, 68
Bacon's Rebellion, 66, 68, 84
Baez, Joan, 884, 885
Bagley, Sarah, 341, 376
Baker, Ella, 859
Baker, Ernest Hamlin, 659
Baker, Newton D., 654
Baker, Ray Stannard, 618
Bakke, Allan, 926
Bakker, Jim, 932
Bakongos, 77
Balanced Budget and Emergency Deficit Reduction Act (1985), 966–67
Balance of power, 239
Balboa, Vasco Nuñez de, 33
Baldwin, Harrison, 801
Baldwin, James, 842
Ball, Lucille, 802
Ballard, Martha, 117
Balloon-frame construction, 290–91
Baltimore, Lords, 56–57
Baltimore, Maryland, 354
Banjo, 90, 91
Bankhead–Jones Tenancy Act (1937), 725
Bank holiday (1933), 723
Bank of Massachusetts, 187
Bank of New York, 187
Bank of North America, 177, 187
Bank of the United States, 202, 203, 282; Second, 254, 256, 282–83
Banks, Dennis, 901
Banks, Nathaniel P., 485
Banks and banking: *See also* Economy; Bank of North America, 177, 187; Bank War, 282–83; collapse of 1837, 284; collapse of 1893, 590; Federal Reserve Banks, 638; in Great Depression, 719, 723–24; market revolution and, 331; post-revolutionary, 187; Second Bank of United States, 254, 256, 282–83
Banneker, Benjamin, 186, 214
Baptist Association, 186
Baptist Church, 113, 114, 127, 346, 422
Baraka, Imamu Amiri, 833, 891
Barbados, 64, 76, 155
Barlow, Joel, 216
Barnard, Evan G., 514, 515
Barnes, A.A., 604
Barnett, Ross, 862
Barnum, P.T., 214
Barracoons, 80
Barry, Leonora M., 558, 588
Barry, Marion, 858
Barter system, 328, 340, 532
Barton, Clara, 468
Baruch, Bernard M., 657, 796
Baruch, Dorothy, 827
Baseball, 574–75, 686–87
Bastille, storming of, 203

Bataan Peninsula, "Death March" on (1942), 771
Batista, Fulgencio, 843
Baton Rouge, Louisiana, 171
Battle of Bunker's Hill, The (Trumbull), 214
Bay of Pigs, 842–43
Bay Psalm Book, The, 62
Bear Flag Revolt (1846), 404, 407–8
Beatles, 885
Beats, 832–33
Beauregard, P.G.T., 450, 452
Beaver Wars, 65
Bebop, 852
Becard de Granville, Charles, 42
Becknell, William, 398
Beckwourth, Jim, 390
Beecher, Catharine, 345, 367
Beecher, Edward, 448
Beecher, Lyman, 366, 373, 382–83, 421
Begin, Menachem, 937
Belknap, William W., 508
Bell, Alexander Graham, 550
Bell, John, 438, 440
Bellamy, Edward, 579, 585, 589, 592
Bellow, Saul, 736
Bellows, George, 629
Bellows, Henry, 449
"Beloved Community," 858
Benjamin, Asher, 215
Benjamin, Judah P., 458
Bennett, Thomas, 309
Bent, William, 398
Benton, Thomas Hart, 392, 398
Bent's Fort, 398
Bering, Vitus, 231
Beringia, 4, 5, 6, 7
Berkeley, William, 68
Berkman, Alexander, 669
Berle, Adolf A., 723
Berlin, Irving, 766
Berlin Airlift (1949), 793, 794
Berlin crisis (1948), 793–94
Berlin Wall, 971–72
Bernard, Francis, 147–48
Bernstein, Carl, 908
Berrigan, Daniel and Philip, 887
Berry, Chuck, 828
Bethlehem Shipbuilding Company, 658
Bethune, Mary McLeod, 744
Bevel, James, 869
Beveridge, Albert J., 597, 598
Bible, the, 125
Bickerdyke, Mary Ann, 448–49, 468
Biddle, Nicholas, 282, 283, 288
Bierstadt, Albert, 290, 390, 537
Big bands, 741
Big Business, labor in age of, 555–59
Big Foot, 541
"Big stick" approach of Roosevelt, 645
Bikel, Theodore, 895
Bikini Islands, atomic testing on, 796
Bill for Establishing Religious Freedom, 185
Bill of Rights, 184, 200; of 1689, 69
Bills of attainder, 167
Billy the Kid, 528
Biloxi, 87
Bingham, George Caleb, 290
Birmingham, Alabama, 862–64
Birney, James G., 319, 375, 402, 423
Birth control, 345, 630–31, 688, 698
Birth of a Nation, The (film), 694
Birth rate: baby boom, 806, 807; colonial, 119–20; nineteenth-century fall in, 345
Bisbee, Arizona, deportation of strikers from, 643
Bison (buffalo), American, 6–7, 39, 399, 518, 526, 535
Black Baptist churches, 494
Black belt, 297–98
Black Cat, Chief, 229–30
Black codes, 487–88, 494–95
Black consciousness, 868–69
Black Death, 29, 30
Black Elk, 542
Black Elk Speaks, 902
Blackface, 359–60
Black Hawk, 243
Black Hawk "war," 281–82
Black Hills, discovery of gold in, 519
Black Hoof, 246
Black Kettle, Chief, 519
Blacklisting in 1950s, 831
Black Muslims. *See* Nation of Islam (NOI)
Black Panther Party for Self-Defense, 897
Black Power, 895–98
Blacks. *See* African Americans
"Black Sox" scandal (1920), 686, 687
"Black Tuesday" (October 29, 1929), 717
Blackwell, Henry, 491
Blaine, James G., 599–600
Blake, William, 333
Blanchet, Frances, 396
Blatch, Harriot Stanton, 697
"Bleeding Kansas," 430–31
Bliss, W.D.P., 592
Blitzkrieg, 752–53
Blood type, native American, 4
"Bloody Sunday," 870
Bloudy Tenent of Persecution, The (Williams), 113
Blue laws, 573
Blues music, 686
Blum, Abraham, 711
Blümer, Carl, 384–85
Boardinghouses, 569
Board of Commissioners of the Customs, 146
Board of Indian Commissioners, 539
Bodmer, Karl, 290, 390
Boesky, Ivan, 967
Bogart, Humphrey, 802
Bohemians, 561, 628–29
Boland Amendment, 955, 957
Bolívar, Simón, 255, 267
Bolshevik Revolution (1917), 663, 668–69
Bomb shelters, 805
Bonaparte, Joseph, 241
Bond, Julian, 858
Bonhomme Richard (ship), 171
Bonny, African state of, 82
Bonus Army, 722
Book of Mormon, 370
Book of Trades, The, 118, 226
Booksellers, colonial, 125
Boom-and-bust business cycle, 557
Boomtowns, 523
Boone, Daniel, 216
Booth, John Wilkes, 477
Borah, William, 667
Border states in Civil War, 452
Bornu, kingdom of, 80
Boston, Massachusetts: Back Bay district, 562; Battle of Bunker Hill, 157; colonial, 63, 123; in 1800, 234–35; founding of, 60; Fugitive Slave Act and, 427; Irish immigrants in, 380–81; nineteenth century, growth in, 354; occupation of (1768), 148; police strike (1919), 665, 689
Boston *American*, 358
Boston Associates, 334–35
Boston Athenaeum, 288, 289
Boston Brahmins, 342, 343
Boston Evening Post, 147
Boston Gazette, 145
Boston Massacre (1770), 148–49
Boston Pamphlet, 149
Boston Port Bill, 151
Boston Tea Party, 150–51
Botha, Pieter William, 907
Boulder Dam (Hoover Dam), 733
Bourbon "family compact" of monarchies, 170
Bourne, Randolph, 654
Bowen, Louise, 630
Bowery, the, 360
Bowie, James, 387, 399–400
Boxer Rebellion (1899), 601
Boynton, Amelia, 869
Bozeman Trail, 519
Bracero program, 758, 871, 986
Brackenridge, Hugh Henry, 195, 204, 213, 216, 289
Braddock, Edward, 137
Bradford, Cornelia Smith, 117
Bradford, William, 59
Bradley, Omar N., 811, 812
Bradley, Tom, 927
Bradstreet, Anne, 62
Brady, "Diamond Jim," 567
Brady, Mathew, 344
"Brain trust" of Roosevelt, 723
Branagan, Thomas, 373
Brandeis, Louis, 620, 637
Brando, Marlon, 829
Brandywine Creek, battle of (1777), 169
Brant, Joseph, 172–73, 213
Brazil, sugar production in, 76
Breckinridge, John C., 438–40
Brest-Litovsk, Treaty of (1918), 668
Brewster, Mary, 610
Brezhnev, Leonid, 906, 955
Briefe and True Report of the Newfound Land of Virginia (Harriot), 45
Britain. *See* England; Great Britain
Britain, battle of (1940), 752–53, 773–74
British Board of Trade, 135
British West Indies, 171, 279, 319
Brooklyn Bridge, 562–63
Brooks, Preston, 434
Brotherhood of Carpenters and Joiners, 627
Brotherhood of Professional Base Ball Players, 575
Brotherhood of Sleeping Car Porters, 701, 763
Broun, Heywood, 687
Brown, Charles Brockden, 218
Brown, Dee, 902
Brown, Edmund G., 949
Brown, John, 431, 434, 437–38
Brown, Moses, 330, 331, 333
Brown, Nicholas, 331
Brown, William Henry, 315
Brown, William Hill, 218
Brown Berets, 900
Brown University, 884
Brown v. *Board of Education*, 854–55, 866
Bruce, Blanche K., 499
Bruff, J. Goldsborough, 395
Bryan, William Jennings, 594–95, 604, 636, 696
Brzezinski, Zbigniew, 938, 939
Bubonic plague, 29, 30
Buchanan, James, 412, 422, 428, 433, 434, 441, 523
Buchanan, Patrick, 977, 980
Bucktail faction, 263, 267
Budd, Charles Jay, 636
Budget deficit under Reagan, 952
Buell, Don Carlos, 462
Buffalo, 6–7, 39, 399, 518, 526, 535
Buffalo Bill, the King of the Border Men (Judson), 538
Bulge, Battle of the (1944), 776
Bull market of 1920s, 717
Bull Run, first battle of (1861), 452–53
Bull Run, second battle of (1862), 461
Bunau-Varilla, Philippe, 645
"Bundling," 62
Bundy, McGeorge, 841
Bunker Hill, Battle of (1775), 157
Bureaucracies, rise of, 30
Bureau of American Ethnology, 539
Bureau of Indian Affairs (BIA), 517, 518, 734
Bureau of Reclamation, 733
Bureau of Standards, 690
Burger, Warren E., 906
Burgoyne, John, 169

Burial ceremony, slave, 89
Burke, Clifford, 743
Burke, Edmund, 153
"Burned-Over District," 369–70
Burns, Anthony, 427
Burr, Aaron, 211, 212
Burroughs, William, 833
Bush, George, 397, 940, 958, 969, 970
Bushnell, Nolan, 959
Business: *See also* Corporations; Economy; Industrialization; Big Business, 555–59; crisis of 1890s, 589–92; in Eisenhower administration, 820–21; financial collapse of 1893, 590; horizontal combination in, 553–54; incorporation laws, 276; triumph of, 550–55; in the twenties, 688–92; vertical integration of, 553, 555, 690; World War I and, 657, 658; World War II and, 758; youth market in 1950s, 827
Business cycle, boom-and-bust, 557
Busing, school, 925
Butler, Andrew, 434
Butler, Benjamin F., 464, 485
Butler v. *United States*, 741
Byrd, William, 314
Byrnes, James F., 756

C

Cabeza de Vaca, Alvar Núñez, 37
Cabinet, 201
Cable cars, 563
Cable television, 963
Cabot, John, 42
Cabrillo, Juan, 109–10
Caesar's Column (Donnelly), 589
Cahill, Holger, 737
Cahokia, 1–2, 13, 15, 17, 19
Cajuns, 137, 232
Calhoun, Floride, 316
Calhoun, John C., 247, 253, 267, 270, 271, 280, 298, 316, 402, 406, 411; Compromise of 1850 and, 424, 425; election of 1828 and, 268; on states' rights, 422–23
California, 406–10; admission to Union, 425; agribusiness in, 534–35; Bear Flag Revolt, 404, 407–8; Dust Bowl refugees in, 732; gold rush (1849), 381, 382, 383–84, 395, 407, 408–10, 516, 522; Indian revolt (1775), 110–11; missions in, 232; Overland Trails to, 392, 394–96; Proposition 187, 988; Russian-Californio trade, 406–7; settlement of, 109–10, 407–8
California Citrus Growers' Association, 534
Calley, William L., Jr., 905
Callithumpian Bank, 360–61
Calvert family, 56–57, 69
Calvin, John, 40, 58
Calvinism, 114, 127
Cambodia, invasion of (1969), 904
Camden, South Carolina, 174
Caminetti Act (1893), 523
Campaign finance, 981
Camp David Accords (1978), 937–38
Camp meetings, 253
Campus protest, 884–86
Canada: American expeditionary force against (1775), 157; as annexation target, 599; colony of, 53, 54, 123; immigrants from, 986; prerevolutionary conquest of, 137–39; Second Continental Congress and, 155; War of 1812 campaign against, 248
Canada Act (1791), 206
Canadian Company, 53
Canals, 254, 262, 272, 273–75, 278, 279, 355, 636
Cane Ridge, Kentucky, camp meeting at, 253
Cannon, James, 704
Capital, accumulation of, 330–31
Capitalism, 612; welfare, 677–78
Capitol building, architecture of, 214
Capone, Al "Scarface," 687, 693
Capra, Frank, 740
Captivity narrative, 125
Caravel, 31
Caribbean Basin Initiative (CBI), 954–55
Carib people, 34
Carlos III of Spain, King, 205
Carmichael, Stokely, 894, 895–97
Carnegie, Andrew, 550, 554–55, 564, 604, 632, 676
Carnegie Steel Company, 570, 591
Carolina, colony of, 54
Caroline, Fort, 40–41
Carpetbaggers, 498–99
Carranza, Venustiano, 648, 649
Carson, Kit, 463, 543
Carson, Rachel, 929
Carter, Jimmy, 914, 936–40, 952; election of 1976, 923–24; foreign policy under, 936–40; Iran hostage crisis, 939, 940; "malaise speech" of, 938; presidency of, 924, 925; Three Mile Island and, 914
Carter, Robert "King," 314
Carter, Rosalynn, 924
Cartier, Jacques, 42
Casablanca Conference (1943), 774
Casa de Contratación, 95
Casey, Robert, 958
Cash economy, 340–41
Cass, Lewis, 402, 413, 428
Cassina plant, 20
Castle Garden, 380, 384
Castor, John, 83
Castro, Fidel, 843–44, 940
Castro, Sal, 900
Catalan Atlas, 77
Catherine of Aragon, 40
Catholic Church. *See* Roman Catholic Church
Catlin, George, 290, 398
Catt, Carrie Chapman, 654, 660, 661
Cattle industry, 521, 526–28
Cayuga Indians, 21
Cayuse Indians, 397
Celebrity, cult of (1920s), 683, 686–87
Censorship, Hollywood and, 683
Census (1790), 222
Centennial Exposition of 1876, 550
Centers for Disease Control (CDC), 965
Central America, 33, 954–55
Central Intelligence Agency (CIA), 801, 833, 835–37, 843, 907, 936, 955
Central Pacific Railroad, 457, 504–5, 556
Central Park, 571
Central Valley Project (CVP), 733
Century of Dishonor, A (Phillips), 540
Chaco Canyon, 14
Chamber of Commerce, 658, 678
Chambers, Whittaker, 802
Champlain, Lake, 169
Champlain, Samuel de, 53, 58
Chancellorsville, battle of (1863), 473
Chaney, James, 867
Chaplin, Charlie, 675, 802
Chaplin, Thomas, 314–15
Chapman, John Jay, 584
Charles, Ray, 766
Charles I of England, King, 56, 58, 64
Charles II of England, King, 64, 65, 69, 113
Charles IV of Spain, King, 241
Charles River Bridge v. *Warren Bridge*, 276
Charleston, South Carolina, 64, 92, 94; aftermath of Civil War in, 485; American Revolution in, 157; colonial, 85; culture of, 289; decline of, 279, 300; in 1800, 234; slavery in, 83; trade, 98; Vesey conspiracy in, 309–10
Charlotte Temple (Rowson), 218
Charter governments, abolition of, 69
Chase, Salmon P., 412, 422, 426, 455, 470, 475
Chautauqua campgrounds, 569
Cheever, John, 736, 823
Chernenko, Konstantin, 955
Cherokee Indians, 4, 20, 68, 115, 137, 138, 140, 172, 243, 280, 281, 392, 514, 516–17
Cherokee Nation v. *Georgia*, 281, 517
Cherokee Phoenix, 281
Chesapeake Algonquian Confederacy, 56
Chesapeake colonies, 54–58, 115; *See also* Maryland; Bacon's Rebellion in, 66, 68, 84
Chesnut, Mary Boykin, 317, 441, 450, 452, 474, 475, 476
Chester, Pennsylvania, 451
Chevalier, Michel, 268
Cheyenne Indians, 4, 229, 543
Chiang Kai-shek, 795
Chicago, Illinois: Democratic convention (1968), 894–95; fire of 1871, 562; growth in nineteenth century, 355; Haymarket square tragedy, 558–59; meat-packing industry in, 548–49, 551; Memorial Day Massacre (1937), 729; race riots (1919), 665
Chicago World's Fair (1893), 597–98
Chicano nationalism, 899–901
Chichimec Indians, 34
Chickasaw Indians, 20, 37, 68, 87, 107, 140, 172, 243, 280, 281, 392, 514
Child, Lydia Maria, 347
Childhood, middle-class, 569
Child labor, 333, 335, 336, 338, 566, 614
Children: child care in World War II, 761–62; immigrant, 226; middle-class child rearing, 345–46; settlement of Great Plains and, 531; slave, 302, 304; in textile industry, 333, 335, 336
Children's Bureau, 614, 636, 662, 762
Chin, Frank, 902
China: Boxer Rebellion, 601; communist revolution in, 795–96; Japanese invasion of, 751; Nixon and, 905–6, 907; Open Door policy and, 601, 646–47, 648; pre–World War I investments in, 647; trade, 236, 601
China Lobby, 796
Chinese Americans: California gold rush and, 382, 383–84, 408, 409; discrimination against, 556–57; immigrants, 382, 383–84, 709, 711, 987–88, 990–91
Chinese Eastern Railway, 668
Chinese Exclusion Act (1882), 556–57, 558, 709, 711
Chinweizu, 83
Chippewas, 21
Chisholm v. *Georgia*, 202
Choctaw Indians, 20, 68, 87, 137, 140, 172, 243, 280, 281, 392, 514
Cholera, 395, 400
Christian Advocate, 289
Church, Frank, 883
Church and state, relationship between, 185
Churches, African American, 494
Churchill, Winston, 754, 774, 779, 790–91
Church of England, 113, 114, 115, 125, 185
Church of Jesus Christ of Latter-Day Saints (Mormonism), 370–71, 372, 425, 523–24
CIA. *See* Central Intelligence Agency (CIA)
Cigarette-making machine, 551
Cigarette smoking, advertising for, 685
Cincinnati, Ohio, 233, 234, 337, 338
Cincinnati Gazette, 341
Circle dance, 89
Circuit Courts of Appeals Act (1891), 585
Cities and towns: *See also specific cities*; *See also* Urbanization; African Americans in, 361–62; civil order in, 360–61; class structure in, 355–56; colonial, 117, 121–22; company towns, 626–27; environment and, 563–64; ethnic neighborhoods and, 357–58; ghettos, 625–26, 709; Great Migration, 664–65, 680; on Great Plains, 531; growth of, 236, 274, 354–57; housing, 355–56, 562, 570; immigrants in, 380, 708–9; immigration patterns and, 355; industrial, 559–64; "instant", 355;

metropolitan expansion in 1990s, 981–83; migration to, 891; nativism and, 709; political progressives and urban reform in, 616; politics in, 362–65, 615–16; popular culture in, 358–60; preindustrial, 354; public space, 572–73; restoration of (1970s), 928–29; riots in, 361, 362, 431, 471, 891–92; sanitation and living patterns in, 356–57; slums, 357; in the South, 300; in the twenties, 681; urban decay, 890–91; urbanization, 354–62; urban landscape, 562–63
Citizen Genêt affair, 203–4
Citizens' Protective League, 644
City manager, 616
Civic order, 360–61
Civic participation, 880
Civic virtue, 219
Civil authority, military subordination to, 179
"Civil Disobedience" (Thoreau), 405
Civilian Conservation Corps (CCC), 724, 725, 757
Civil rights: after World War II, 581–82; in World War II, 763–64
Civil Rights Acts: of 1866, 483, 488, 489, 500, 509; of 1875, 502, 596; of 1957, 866; of 1964, 865, 866, 903, 920; of 1968, 901
Civil Rights Cases (1883), 502, 596
Civil Rights Congress, 804
Civil rights movement (1957–1962), 855–71; Albany (Georgia) movement (1961–1962), 861–62; Asian Americans and, 874–75; in Birmingham, Alabama, 862–64; Freedom Rides, 860–61; Freedom Summer (Mississippi, 1964), 867–68; Johnson and, 865, 869, 871; Kennedy and, 859–60, 861, 864–65; King and, 850, 852–53, 856–57, 858, 859, 861, 870–71, 894; legislation, 866; Malcolm X and, 868–69, 895; Mexican Americans and, 871–72; Native Americans and, 873–74; origins of, 851–55; presidential election of 1960 and, 859–60; Puerto Ricans and, 872–73; sit-ins, 857–58; SNCC and, 858–59; Voting Rights Act (1965), 866, 870–71; Washington March (1963), 864–65
Civil Service Reform Association, 584
Civil service system, 270, 506, 584–85, 799
Civil War, 447–77, 484–85; African Americans and, 465–67, 471, 476; Appomattox, surrender at, 460, 477; army life in, 467–68; border states in, 452; Bull Run, battles of, 452–53, 461; casualties of, 452–53; Confederacy and, 442–43, 457, 458–59, 469, 472; through 1862, 459–64; ending of, 472–77; end of slavery and, 464–67; Fort Sumter and, 450–51; on home front, 469–72; house slaves during, 306; major battles (1861–1863), 461, 462; mobilization for, 450–55; Native Americans and, 462–63, 514; naval war, 463–64; in Northern Virginia, 461; overall strategy of, 460; parallels with Revolutionary War, 453; Peninsular campaign, 461, 462, 463, 467; secession of the South and, 440–41; Shiloh, 461–62, 468; strengths of North and South in, 453–55; in Trans-Mississippi West, 462–63; turning point, 460, 472–73; wartime politics, 469–70
Claiborne, William, 241
Clairton, Pennsylvania, 961
Clans, Native American, 12
Clansman, The (Dixon), 631
Clark, Fort, 230
Clark, George Rogers, 173, 180
Clark, Jim, 869
Clark, Kenneth B., 854
Clark, Ramsey, 892
Clark, Tom C., 800, 801
Clark, William, 229–30, 245–46, 390
Class. *See* Social class
Classical antiquity, revived interest in, 29–30
Clay, Henry, 247, 253, 270–71, 280, 298, 363, 371, 402; Compromise of 1850 and, 424, 425; election of 1824 and, 267; election of 1832 and, 283; election of 1844 and, 413; Missouri Compromise and, 258
Clayton, Will, 788–89
Clayton Antitrust Act (1914), 638
Cleaveland, Moses, 252
Clemenceau, Georges, 666
Cleveland, Grover, 536, 583, 589, 591, 593–94, 601
Cliff dwellings, Anasazi, 14
Climate, 6, 16–17
Clinton, Bill, 173–74, 175, 977–81
Clinton, DeWitt, 247, 262, 273, 274
Clinton, Henry, 168, 171
Clinton, Hillary Rodham, 978
Clipper ships, 236
Closing Circle (Commoner), 929–30
Clovis technology, 5–6
Coal industry, 551, 682
Coalition of Labor Union Women, 920
Cobb, Isaac, 311
Cobo, Bernabé, 3, 4
Cocaine, 964
Cochise, 519–20
Cody, "Buffalo Bill," 538
Coffee, 36
Coffles, 299
Cohn, Roy, 804
Cohoon, Hannah, 371
Coinage Act (1873), 593
Colbert, Jean-Baptiste, 94
Cold Harbor, battle of (1864), 476
Cold War era, 786–815, 834–35; Age of Anxiety, 805–8; in Asia, 795–96; atomic diplomacy, 796; Bay of Pigs and, 842–43; containment policy, 791–96, 811; costs of, 935; Cuban missile crisis and, 843–44; division of Europe, 790–91; Eisenhower and, 833; at home, 800–808; immigration in, 986; Kennedy and, 841–44; Korean War and, 808–14, 833; major policies of, 792; propaganda films in, 802, 803; Red Scare, 801–2; spy cases, 802–3; Suez crisis, 837; television and politics in, 831–32; Truman and, 796–800; U-2 incident, 835; United Nations (UN) and, 789–90; at University of Washington, 786–87; youth culture in, 826–29
Cole, Leslie, 779
Cole, Thomas, 290
Coleman, James S., 829
Colfax, Louisiana, 501
Colfax, Schuyler, 506
College Entrance Examination Board, 623
College football, 687
College of New Jersey, 126
Colleges and universities, 494, 533, 571–72, 825, 880, 897, 902; *See also* Education
Collier, John, 622, 734–35
Collier-Burns Act (1947, California), 824
Collins, Judy, 885
Colombia, 645
Colonial America, 49–71; *See also* Pre-revolutionary period; Carolina, 54; Chesapeake, 54–58, 115; economic growth in, 97–98, 121–23; English colonies, 54–64; Enlightenment and, impact of, 124–25; French crescent, 106, 111–12; frontier heritage in, 117–19; Great Awakening in, 126–29; indentured servitude in, 57, 118–19; Indian America, 106–8; Jamestown, 54–55; Maryland, 56–57; Massachusetts Bay colony, 59–60; Middle colonies, 113–15; New England, 58–64, 112–13; New France, 52, 53–54, 69, 104, 111, 120, 121; New Mexico, 52–53, 87, 109; New Netherland, 64–65; Pennsylvania, 65–66, 114; Plymouth Colony, 59; population growth in, 119–20, 222; Puritans in, 58, 59–63, 66, 67–68, 112–13, 125; regions of, 106–16; religious decline in, 125–26; Restoration Colonies, 64–66; Santa Fé, in seventeenth century, 50–51; slavery in, 73–100; social and political patterns in, 119–23; social class in, 120–21; South, the, 115–16; Spanish, 50–53, 106, 108–11; tobacco in, 55–56, 84–85; traditional culture in, 116–17; transformation in British, 123–29; war in, 66–70; women in, 58, 61–63, 117
Colonization, 26–48; English, 43–45; European expansionism and, 28–33; French, 39–42; Roanoke Island, 26–27; Spanish, 33–39
Colorado Fuel and Iron Company, 627
Colorado River, 733, 734
Colorado Volunteer Infantry Regiment, 462
Colorado Volunteers, 519
Colored Farmers' Alliance and Cooperative Union, 586
Colt, Samuel, 337
Columbia Broadcasting System (CBS), 684, 740
Columbian Centinel, 253
Columbia River, dams on, 733
Columbia University, 886
Columbus, Christopher, 3, 23, 28, 31–33, 36, 76
Comanche Indians, 398–99, 400, 516
Comedies, film, 739
Commerce Department, 690
Commercial broadcasting, 684
Commission form of government, 616
Commission on Training Camp Activities, 661
Committee for Tarring and Feathering, 150
Committee of Safety, 153
Committee of Style, 198
Committee of the People, 189
Committee on an Appeal for Human Rights, 858
Committee on Equal Employment Opportunity, 860
Committee on Public Information (CPI), 653, 685
Committee on Un-American Activities, 765, 786
Committees of Correspondence, 149, 152, 154, 155
Committees of Observation and Safety, 153, 155
Committee to Re-Elect the President (CREEP), 908
Commoner, Barry, 929–30
Commons, John R., 619
Common Sense (Paine), 157–58, 216
Commonwealth of Independent States, 972; *See also* Soviet Union
Communal cultures, 117
Communications, 141–42, 288; *See also* Newspapers
Communications Decency Act (1995), 947
Communism: *See also* Cold War era; collapse of, 971–72; containment policy and, 791–96, 811; Reagan and, 953–56; Red Scares, 669, 694, 801–2; refugees fleeing, 986
Communist Party, 669, 727, 738
Communities Organized for Public Service (COPS), 928
Community Action Program (CAP), 889
Community Development Act (1974), 928
Community Development Corporations (CDCs), 929
Company towns, 626–27
Composers' Forum Laboratory, 736
Comprehensive AIDS Revenue Emergency Act, 966
Comprehensive Community Health Centers, 889
Compromise of 1850, 424–28
Compromise of 1877, 509
Compulsory education, 367, 623
Comstock, Henry, 522
Comstock Lode of silver, 409, 522
Concentration camps, Nazi, 778–79
Concord, 154
Concord Regency, 267
Conestoga, massacre at (1763), 140
Confederacies, Indian, 20, 21, 22
Confederacy, 458–59; *See also* Civil War; cotton diplomacy of, 457, 458; Davis as president of, 305, 443, 450, 458, 459, 461, 471, 472, 476, 477; establishment of, 442–43; finances of, 458–59; readmission of Confederate states, 490; strengths of, compared to North, 453–55
Confederate Army, desertions from, 469, 472

Confederation Congress, 175–82, 188
Congregationalist Church, 113, 244; *See also* Puritans
Congress, U.S.: *See also* New Deal; *specific legislation*; antitrust legislation, 554; Cold War–era legislation, 800–801; Confederation, 175–82, 188; first Continental, 133–34, 152–53; immigration legislation, 659, 694, 709–10, 792, 801, 875, 971; Indian policies, 243–47, 280–82, 298, 391–92, 517; powers of, 176; Reconstruction and, 488–90; second Continental, 155–59
Congressional elections: of 1866, 489; of 1894, 594; of 1930, 722; of 1934, 726; of 1942, 757, 779; of 1946, 798; of 1994, 979
Congressional Reconstruction, 489–90
Congress of Industrial Organizations (CIO), 729; AFL–CIO, 919
Congress of Racial Equality (CORE), 764, 852, 860
Connecticut, 166; abolition of slavery in, 186; colony of, 63, 70, 113; Foxwoods gambling casino in, 962; New Light politicians in, 128
Connecticut River Valley, 60
Connecticut Wits, 216
Connor, Eugene "Bull," 862–63
Conquistadors, 33
Consciousness-raising (CR) groups, 898
Conservation, 634–36
Conservatism, 945–85; courts and, 977; in government agencies, 950–51; New Right, 931–34; paradoxes of Reagan-Bush years, 976–77; Reaganomics, 949–51; Reagan presidency, 945–58; religious, 931–32; revival of, in 1970s, 931–35
Considerations on the Keeping of Negroes (Woolman), 87
Considerations on the Propriety of Imposing Taxes (Dulany), 143
Conspicuous consumption, 567–68
Constitution, U.S., 196–200; Bill of Rights and, 184, 200; Constitutional Convention and, 196–98; as defense for slavery, 318; Eighteenth Amendment to, 661, 692; Eleventh Amendment to, 202; Fifteenth Amendment to, 490, 502, 509; First Amendment to, 200, 215, 947; Fourteenth Amendment to, 483, 489, 502, 509, 619, 854; Nineteenth Amendment to, 377, 661; Progressive challenge to conservative view of, 619; ratification of, 198–200; Sixteenth Amendment of, 638; Thirteenth Amendment to, 465, 486; Twelfth Amendment of, 212; Twenty-First Amendment to, 693
Constitutional Convention (1787), 196–98
Constitutional conventions, southern (1867–1869), 499–500
Constitutional Union Party, 438
Constitutions, state, 183–84
Construction industry, 676; *See also* Architecture
Consumer-based industries, 676
Consumption, 567–68, 570, 677, 685–86, 806
Containment policy, 791–96, 811
Continental Army, 163–64, 165, 166, 178
Continental Congress, 170; first, 133–34, 152–53; second, 155–59
Contraband Relief Association, 464
Contrabands, escaped slaves as, 464
Contraception. *See* Birth control
"Contract with America," 979
Contras, 955, 957
Convention: of 1800, 211; of 1818, 254, 255, 396; of 1824, 255–56
Convict labor, 566
Conwell, Russell, 554
Cook, James, 396
Cooke, Jay, 456
Coolidge, Calvin, 665, 674, 682, 688, 689–90
Cooper, Gary, 802
Cooper, James Fenimore, 289–90
Cooper, Peter, 593
Cooperative commonwealth, idea of, 579–80
Cooperatives, 558, 586
Copernicus, 124
Copland, Aaron, 736
Copley, John Singleton, 144, 167, 213
Copperheads (Peace Democrats), 469–70
Copper mining, 643–44
Coquette, The (Foster), 218
Coral Sea, battle of the (1942), 776
Coram, Thomas, 86
Corbin, Margaret, 167
Cornish, Samuel, 372
Cornwallis, Charles, 169, 174–75
Coronado, Francisco Vásquez de, 39, 52
Corporations, 276, 505, 522–23, 658, 676–77, 690; *See also* Business; Industrialization; *specific corporations*
Cortés, Hernán, 34, 35, 36, 110
Cortina, Juan, 525
Cotton, 235; Civil War and, 455; industry, 564, 565, 566–67; slavery and, 297–301; southern dependence on, 503–4; textile manufacturing and, 94, 325–26, 333–36; westward expansion and, 252, 302
Cotton diplomacy, 457, 458
Cotton gin, 235, 297–98, 299
"Cotton Whigs," 430
Coughlin, Charles E., 726
Council of Economic Advisers (CEA), 797, 840
Council of Revision, 197, 198
Council of the Indies, 39, 123
Council on Religion and Homosexuality, 899
Counterculture, 884–85
Country Builder's Assistant, The (Benjamin), 215
Country music, 686
Coureurs de bois, 53
Courts. *See* Judiciary; Supreme Court, U.S.
Covenant Chain, 67, 69, 135
Cowboys, 526–27, 528, 538
Cowpens, battle at (1781), 175
Cox, Archibald, 910
Cox, James M., 669
Coxey, Jacob Sechler, 590
Coxey's Army, 590
Crack cocaine, 964
Craft system, European, 117, 118
Craft unions, 559
Craft workers, 556
Crawford, William H., 266
Crazy Horse, 519
Crédit Mobilier scandal, 506
Cree Indians, 21
Creek Indians, 20, 68, 94, 107, 108, 137, 140, 172, 243, 245, 248, 249, 280, 281, 392, 514
Creek Rebellion (1813–1814), 245
Creek War (1812–1814), 248
Creel, George, 653
Creoles, 88, 90
Crèvecoeur, Hector St. Jean de, 227
Crèvecoeur, Michel-Guillaume Jean de, 216, 227
Crime: drug trade, 964–65; in gold mining camps, 409; juvenile delinquency, 762, 829; in 1970s, 927; organized, 692–93
Crittenden, John J., 452
CROATOAN, 26, 27
Crockett, Davy, 288, 387, 831
Cromwell, Oliver, 61, 64
Crop lien system, 502–4
Crops, 1, 2, 10, 36; *See also specific crops*
Crow Indians, 229
Crusade for Justice, 901
Crusades, 29
Cuba, 87, 602–3, 842–44
Cuban–American Treaty of 1903, 603
Cuban immigrants, 561
Cuban missile crisis (1962), 843–44
Cuban Revolution (1959), 842–43
Cubberley, Elwood, 622
Cugoano, Ottobah, 80
Cullen, Countee, 701
Culpeper's Rebellion, 68
Culture(s): *See also* Mass culture; Popular culture; African-American, 75, 89–90; American, marketing of, 964; anglican, 125; in colonial America, 103–29; communal, 117; cotton, 300–301; democracy and, 287–91; electronic, 946–47, 963–64; in Gilded Age, 567–75; of Great Depression, 735–41; "Me Decade," 934–35; Native American regional, beginnings of, 6–10; of 1950s, 825–33; oral, 116; post-revolutionary, 213–19; pre–Civil War, 420–22; working class, 358, 359–61; youth, 826–29
Culture of Narcissism, The (Lasch), 934
Cumming, Kate, 468
Cumming v. *Richmond County Board of Education*, 596–97
Cuomo, Mario, 952
Currency: *See also* Money supply; in American Revolution, 176–77; Bank War and, 282–83; creation of national, 456–57; laws, 188–89
Curtis, Edward Sheriff, 539
Curtis, William, 493
Curtis Act (1898), 515
Custer, George Armstrong, 519
Cyberspace regulation, 947
Czechoslovakia, in World War II, 751–52

D

Dabney, Robert Lewis, 484
da Gama, Vasco, 31
Daley, Richard, 879, 889, 894–95
Dallas, Texas, Kennedy assassination in, 844–45
Dalrymple, Oliver, 534
Dams, 636, 733
Dana, Charles, 466
Danbury Hatters' Case, 627
Dare, Virginia, 26
Darrow, Clarence, 696
Dartmouth College v. *Woodward*, 276
Darwin, Charles, 696
Daugherty, Harry M., 689
Daughters of Bilitis, 899
Daughters of Liberty, 147
Davidson, Donald, 703
Davis, Harry P., 683–84
Davis, Henry W., 485
Davis, Jefferson, 305, 443, 450, 458, 459, 461, 471, 472, 476, 477
Davis, John W., 690
Davis, Katherine Bement, 688
Davis, Miles, 852
Dawes, Charles, 691
Dawes, William, 155
Dawes Plan, 691
Dawes Severalty Act (1887), 540–41, 542
Dawkins, Henry, 127
D–Day (1944), 775, 776
Dean, James, 829
Death of General Wolfe (West), 213
DeBow's Review, 495
Debs, Eugene V., 591–92, 637, 663, 669–70
Debs v. *United States*, 663
Debt, national, 952
Declaration and Resolves, 153
Declaration of Independence, 158–59, 168
Declaration of Sentiments, 352
Declaration of the Causes and Necessities of Taking Up Arms, 156
Declaratory Act, 145, 151
Deere, John, 277, 532
Deerfield raid, 104–5
Defense budget. *See* Military spending
Defense Department, 801
Deganawida, Chief, 21
de Gaulle, Charles, 775–76
de Kooning, Willem, 736
Delaware: colony of, 66; rural life in, 327; as Union state, 452
Delaware Indians, 3, 22, 66, 107, 115, 136, 140, 205, 243, 246

Delaware Prophet, 139
Delaware River, Washington's crossing of, 169
Dell, Floyd, 629
Deloria, Vine, Jr., 902
DeLuca, Allesandro, 562
Demers, Modest, 396
Democracy, 262–91; cultural growth and, 287–91; election of 1824, 266–67; election of 1828, 268–69; infrastructure building and, 271–79; Jackson presidency and, 269–71, 279–83; limits of, 595–97; new democratic politics, 263, 264–69; post-Revolution debate over, 183; Second American Party System, 263, 285–87; suffrage, expansion and limits of, 263, 264–66; Van Buren and, 262–63, 284; Whigs, rise of, 279–87
Democracy and Education (Dewey), 619
Democratic Party, 285, 286, 365; *See also* Congressional elections; Political parties; Presidential elections; *See also* Presidential elections; in Civil War, 469; expansionism in West and, 394; Ku Klux Klan and, 695; machines, 615; overview of, 433
Democratic Republicans, 208–9, 211, 212, 237, 247, 254, 263, 267
Democratic Societies, 204, 207, 208
Demos, John, 105
Demsey, Jack, 687
Dennis, Dave, 867
Department stores, 552–53
Depression: *See also* Great Depression; of 1873, 507–8; in 1890s, 590; post–revolutionary, 187–88
Derrian, Pat, 936
Descartes, René, 124
Deseret, 523
Desert Culture, Native American, 7–9, 12
Desertions, in Civil War, 469, 472
Desert Paiutes, 11
De Smet, Pierre–Jean, 396
de Soto, Hernán, 37, 295
Destruction of the Indies, The (Las Casas), 34–36
Detroit, Michigan, 112, 248, 892
Dewey, George, 603
Dewey, John, 619, 653, 703
Dewey, Thomas E., 779, 799, 812–14, 851
DeWitt, John L., 762
Dewson, Molly, 742–43
Días, Bartolomeu, 31
Díaz, Adolfo, 692
Díaz, Porfirio, 648
DiBaradino, Frank, 710
Dickens, Charles, 357
Dickinson, Emily, 420
Dickinson, John, 146, 152, 156
Diem, Ngo Dinh, 837–38, 842
Dien Bien Phu, 837
Dies, Martin, 801
Diet, slave, 88, 90
Diet for a Small Planet (Lappe), 929
Diggs, Annie, 589
Dine, 3
Dingley tariff of 1897, 595
Diplomacy, 457, 458, 644, 646–47, 796, 835; *See also* Foreign policy
DiPrima, Diane, 833
Direct primary, 617
Discovery Settlement, and Present State of Kentucke (Filson), 216
Disease: in American Revolution, 163; in Civil War, 467; on immigrants' voyage to U.S., 225, 380; meat-packing industry and, 549; Native Americans and, 34, 35, 37, 59, 60–61, 107, 140, 230; among pioneers heading west, 395; among slaves, 81, 82, 303; urban sanitation and, 356, 563, 564; in World War I, 661–63; in World War II, 762
Disney, Walt, 740
Displaced Persons Act (1948), 986, 988
District of Columbia, 202
Division of labor, 10, 12
Divorce rate, 926
Dix, Dorothea, 369, 468
Dixiecrat party, 799
Dixon, Thomas, 631
Documentaries, 737, 738
Dodge, Mabel, 629
Dole, Robert, 923, 980
Dole, Sanford B., 601
Dollar diplomacy, 646–47
Dom Affonso of the Kongo, King, 82–83
Domesticated animals, 36
Dominican Republic, 645
Dominion of New England, 69
Domino theory, 837–38
Donation Land Claim Act of 1850, 397
Donnelly, Ignatius, 589
Donovan, William, 756
Doolittle, Amos, 154
Dos Passos, John, 702
Douglas, Stephen A., 402, 428, 433; Civil War and, 469; Compromise of 1850 and, 424, 425; election of 1860 and, 438–39, 440; Kansas-Nebraska Act and, 429–31; Lecompton constitution and, 436; Lincoln-Douglas debates, 418–19
Douglas, Walter, 643–44
Douglass, Frederick, 304, 361, 372, 373, 375, 420, 421, 427, 435, 467, 487, 491, 598
Dower, 117
Downing, Lucy Winthrop, 62
Draft: Civil War, 459, 470–71; Vietnam War, 887; World War I, 654–55; World War II and, 753
Dragging Canoe (Tsiyu-Gunsini), Chief, 172
Drake, Francis, 44–45, 56
Drayton Hall mansion, 116
Dred Scott v. *Sandford*, 434–35
Dreier, Mary, 626
Dresden, Germany, bombing of, 775
Drew, Charles, 769–70
Drexel Burnham Lambert, 967
Drought Relief Service, 731
Drugs, 964–65
Duane, James, 152
Duarte, José Napoleón, 955
Du Bois, W.E.B., 606, 632–33, 667, 804
Dukakis, Michael, 969
Duke, James Buchanan, 553
Dulany, Daniel, 143
Dulles, Allen, 835, 841
Dulles, John Foster, 834, 837
Dumbarton Oaks, 789
Dun and Bradstreet, 567
Dunbar, Paul Laurence, 853
Dunmore, Lord, 152, 157, 173
Dunmore's War, 140–41
Duong Van Minh, 989
Du Pont Corporation, 658, 677
Duquesne, Fort, 137, 138
Durand, Asher, 290
Dust Bowl (1935–1940), 535, 681, 730–33
Dustin, Hannah, 119
Dutch. *See* Netherlands
Dutch Reformed church, 244
Dylan, Bob, 885
Dynamic Sociology (Ward), 619
Dysentery, 81, 163

E

Eagleton, Thomas, 908
Eakins, Thomas, 573
Earhart, Amelia, 698
Earl, Ralph, 154
Earp, Wyatt, 528
Earth Day, 929
East Germany, 971
East India Company, 95, 150, 151
Eastland, James, 861
Eastman, Max, 629
East St. Louis, Illinois, riot (1917), 664, 665
Eaton, John Henry, 271
Ecological impact of agriculture, 535–36
Economic Opportunity Act (1964), 888
Economic Recovery Tax Act (1981), 950
Economy: *See also* Industrialization; Panic; Recession; in American Revolution, 187–89; American System, 253–54, 282; cash, 340–41; in Civil War, 470–71; under Clinton, 980–81; colonial, 61, 97–98, 121–23; defense contracts and, 951; downturn of 1974 and 1975, 916; in 1830s, 284–85; under Eisenhower, 821–23; family farm, 62; Great Depression and weaknesses in, 718–19; under Kennedy, 840–41; national, development of, 235–37; in 1980s, 958–62, 966–68; post–World War II, 788–89, 797, 805–7; pre–Civil War, 420; under Reagan, 951–52; in Reconstruction period, 484; of South in 1970s, 920; Soviet, 956; stagflation, 916–22; supply-side theory, 949–50; in the twenties, 688–92; in World War I, 657–58; in World War II, 757–58
Ederle, Gertrude, 687
Edict of Nantes, 40, 64
Edinburgh Review, 288
Edison, Thomas Alva, 550
Edmunds Act (1882), 524
Edmunds-Tucker Act (1887), 524
Education: *See also* Colleges and universities; African American, 494, 500, 571, 617; in Cold War, 807–8; in colonial New England, 61–62; compulsory, 367, 623; in Gilded Age, 571–72; high schools, 571; industrial, 571; "land-grant" colleges, 533; Native American, 541; in 1950s, 835; nineteenth-century reform of, 366–67; post–World War II growth of, 825; in Progressive Era, 619, 622–23; segregation and, 500, 617; Sputnik and, 822–23, 835; standardization of, 622–23; vocational, 623; of women, 61–62, 367, 572, 807; in World War II, 762
Education, Department of, 584
Edwards, Jonathan, 126
Edwards, Ogden, 365
Edward VI of England, King, 43
Efficiency, concept of, 614
Efficiency experts, 626
Eighteenth Amendment, 661, 692
Einstein, Albert, 749
Eisenhower, Dwight D.: Cold War and, 833; election of 1952, 812–14; foreign policy, 833–39; leadership style, 820; Little Rock crisis and, 855; on military-industrial complex, 833, 838–39; presidency, 820–23; in World War II, 767, 779
El Alamein, battle of (1942), 774
El Alianzo Hispano-Americano, 525–26
Elections. *See* Congressional elections; Presidential elections
Electoral Commission, 509
Electricity, TVA and, 725–26
Electronic culture, 946–47, 963–64
Eleventh Amendment, 202
Eliot, John, 3, 67
Eliot, T.S., 703, 736
Elizabeth I of England, 43–45
Ellicott, Andrew, 214
Ellis, Havelock, 687
Ellis Island, 624, 709
Ellison, Ralph, 736, 738
Ellsberg, Daniel, 907–8
El Salvador, Reagan administration and, 955
Ely, Richard, 619
Emancipation Proclamation, 465, 486
Embargo Act (1807), 242–43, 330
Emergency Banking Act (1933), 723, 725
Emergency Needs of Women, 742
Emergency Relief Act (1932), 722

Emergency Relief Appropriation Act (1935), 727, 728
Emerson, John, 434
Emerson, Ralph Waldo, 290, 347, 405–6, 437
Employment. *See* Labor
Employment Act (1946), 797
Empress of China (ship), 236
Encomienda system, 33, 34, 120
Energy, Department of, 916
Energy, sources of, 551
Energy crisis (1973), 916–17, 918–19
Enforcement Acts (1870, 1871), 501–2
England: in American Revolution, 168–75; Anglo-Dutch wars, 65, 94; Bacon's Rebellion, 66, 68, 84; cotton diplomacy and, 457; emancipation of slaves in British West Indies, 279; exploration and colonization, 40, 42, 43–45; Glorious Revolution, 66, 69; impressment into British navy, 242; Indian America and, 107; King George's War, 95; King William's War, 66, 69–70, 94, 107, 119; mercantilist policy, 94, 95–97, 235; Queen Anne's War, 94, 95; slave trade and, 44, 79; social change in sixteenth century, 43–44; War of Jenkins's Ear, 94–95
English Board of Trade, 69–70
English Civil War (1642), 61
English colonies, 54–64; Chesapeake, 54–58; cultural transformation of, 123–29; indentured servants in, 57; New England, 58–64; population of, 57, 120; regulation in, 95–97; social class in, 120–21; spread of settlement (1650–1700), 67
English Peasants' Revolt (1381), 30
English Separatists, 59
Enlightenment, 124–25, 126, 185
Entails, law of, 184–85
Environment: commercial agriculture and, 535–36; endangered, 929–31; mining and, 523; pollution of, 563–64, 734; Progressive Era and, 634–36
Environmentalism, 634–36, 929–30
Environmental Protection Agency (EPA), 906, 930
EPIC (End Poverty in California), 726
Equal Employment Opportunity Commission, 865, 920
Equality (Bellamy), 579
Equal Pay Act (1963), 840
Equal protection, segregation and, 854
Equal Rights Amendment (ERA), 697, 923, 933
Equal Rights Party, 363
Equiano, Olaudah, 77–78, 79, 80, 81, 90, 100
Era of Good Feelings, 250, 253
Erdman Act (1898), 595
Erhard, Werner, 934
Erie Canal, 262, 273–74, 275, 279, 355, 356, 369–70, 380, 508
Erie Indians, 21
Erie Railroad, 554
Españoles, 120
Espionage Act (1917), 663–65
Espy, Sarah R., 440
Essay on Liberty of the Press, An (Hay), 215
Essay on the Principle of Population (Malthus), 238
Estonian refugees, 988–89
Ethnicity: *See also* Immigration; specific ethnicities; in colonial America, 222–27; ethnic neighborhoods, 357–58, 624; in meat-packing industry, 548; settlement in West and, 529; suburbanization and, 824, 825
Etiquette, 347
Ettor, Joseph, 628
Eugenicists, 693
Europe: *See also specific countries*; World War I; World War II; expansionism of, 28–45; Marshall Plan and, 792–93; in Middle Ages, 28, 29; post–World War II division of, 790–91; Renaissance, 29–30
Evangelism, 343–44, 365–67, 598–99, 931–32
Evans, Hiram W., 694
Evans, John, 519
Evans, Walker, 737, 738
Evergood, Philip, 730
Evolution, theory of, 696
Executive Orders: No. 8802, 763, 866; No. 9066, 762; No. 9835, 801; No. 9981, 866
Exodusters, 495
Expansionism. *See* Europe; Imperialism; Westward expansion
Exploration, European (1492–1591), 30–45
Exposition and Protest (Calhoun), 280

F

Factions, dangers of, 208
Factory system, 238, 332–33, 336–37
Factory towns, 325–26
Fairbanks, Erastus, 336
Fair Deal, 799–800
Fair Employment Practices Committee, 763, 765
Fair Labor Standards Act (1938), 743, 745
Fall, Albert, 689
Fallen Timbers, battle of (1794), 194–95, 205, 207, 234, 246
Falwell, Jerry, 932
Families with Dependent Children (AFDC), 889
Family: African American, 493–94; excessive drinking and, 367–68; family labor system, 327–28, 338; Great Plains settlement and, 531; limitation on size of, 345; middle class, 344–45; in New France, 112; patriarchy in, 329; Puritan, 61; slave, 75, 88–89, 304, 306–7; two-income, 805–7; in World War II, 761–62
Family Assistance Plan, 906
Family farm, 62, 531–32
Family Limitation, 631
Family mills, 335–36
Famines in Middle Ages, 29
Farm Bureau, 658
Farmer-labor unity, 589
Farmers' Alliance, 586–89
Farmer's Holiday Association, 722
Farming. *See* Agriculture
Farmington, Connecticut, 166
Farnham, Marynia, 807
Farragut, David, 460, 462
Fashion in World War II, 766
Faubus, Orval, 855
Fauset, Jessie, 701
Federal Art Project (FAP), 730, 736–37
Federal Board for Vocational Education, 623
Federal Bureau of Investigation (FBI), 663, 756, 786, 893
Federal Communications Commission, 740, 830
Federal courts, 201–2
Federal Emergency Relief Administration (FERA), 724, 725
Federal Employees Loyalty and Security Program (1947), 792, 801
Federal Highway Act (1956), 822, 824
Federal Housing Administration (FHA), 821, 890
Federalist, The (Madison, Hamilton, and Jay), 199, 208
Federalist Gazette of the United States, 216
Federalists, 198, 208–9, 210, 211, 212, 237; *See also* Presidential elections
Federal Music Project (FMP), 736
Federal Project No. 1, 735–36
Federal Reserve Act (1913), 638
Federal Reserve Banks, 638
Federal Reserve Board, 658
Federal Theater Project (FTP), 736
Federal Trade Commission (FTC), 638
Federal Writers Project, 736, 757
Federation of Mexican Workers Unions, 700
Fellowship of Reconciliation (FOR), 691, 852
Female Moral Reform Society, 368–69
Feminine Mystique, The (Friedan), 823, 898
Feminism, 218–19, 697–98, 823; *See also* Women; Women's movement
Feminization of poverty, 926
Fenno, John, 216
Ferdinand and Isabella, 31, 32, 33
Fermi, Enrico, 749
Ferraro, Geraldine, 952
Fertility: colonial, 119–20; post–World War II, 806, 807
Feudalism, 28
Field, Stephen J., 619
Fifteenth Amendment, 490, 502, 509
Fifty-Fourth Massachusetts Colored Infantry, 465, 467
Filibusters, 428
Fillmore, Millard, 425, 433
Film *noir*, 808
Filson, John, 216
Financial services, development of, 236–37
Finney, Charles G., 343, 366, 373
Finney, Lydia, 343, 369
First Amendment, 200, 215, 947
First American Party System, 285
First Reconstruction Act (1867), 489, 497
Fish resources, exploitation of, 41–42
Fiske, John, 693
Fitzgerald, F. Scott, 702
Fitzgerald, Robert, 465–67, 474
Fitzgerald, Zelda, 687
Fitzhugh, George, 320
Five Civilized Tribes, 243, 280–81, 514; *See also* Cherokee Indians; Chickasaw Indians; Choctaw Indians; Creek Indians; Seminole Indians
Five Nation Iroquois Confederacy, 53
Five Points, New York City, 357
Five-Power Treaty (1922), 691
Flacks, Richard, 880
Flanagan, Hallie, 736
Flappers of the twenties, 687, 688
"Flatboat Wars," 295
Flathead Indians, 542
Fletcher, Alice Cunningham, 539
Flint, Michigan, 715–16
Flintoff, John, 314
Florentine Codex, 11, 35
Florida: colony of, 40–41, 108, 139, 155; Indians of, 19–20; Jackson's invasion of, 254; maroon colonies in, 91–92; naming of, 37; slavery in, 87
Floyd, John, 318
Flying Cloud (ship), 236
Flynn, Elizabeth Gurley, 628
Foch, Ferdinand, 656
Folklore, African, 90
Follow Through, 889
Folsom technology, 6–7
Food and Drug Administration (FDA), 634
Food and Fuel Act (1917), 657
"Food for Freedom" program, 758
Food riots (1863), 472
Football, college, 687
Foragers, desert, 7–8, 11–12
Forbes, Charles R., 689
Forbes, Steve, 980
Ford, Betty, 923
Ford, Gerald, 910, 922
Ford, Henry, 550, 657, 679, 680, 752
Ford Motor Company, 658, 679, 759
Ford River Rouge factory, protest at (1932), 722
Foreign Miner's Tax (1852), 382
Foreign policy: *See also specific presidents*; under Carter, 936–38; under Clinton, 978; under Eisenhower, 833–39; Good Neighbor policy, 599–600; isolationism, 752, 753; under Jefferson, 242–43; under Kennedy, 841–44; under McKinley, 602–4; under Monroe, 254–55; in 1970s, 935–40; under Nixon, 905–6, 907; Open Door policy, 601, 646–47, 648; pre-World War I, 645–49; under Reagan, 953–58; Spanish–American War, 601–5; under Taft, 646–47; under Truman, 791–96, 808–11; in the twenties, 691–92; under Washington, 203–8; under Wilson, 648–49
Forest efficiency, 9–10

Forest Management Act (1897), 536
Forests, national, 535–36
Fort Gibson, battle at (1863), 462
Fort Jackson, Treaty of (1814), 248, 250
Fort Laramie, Treaty of (1868), 519, 540
Fort McIntosh, Treaty of (1785), 182
Fort Pillow, Tennessee, massacre at (1863), 466
Fortress Monroe, Virginia, 464
Fort Stanwix, Treaty of (1768), 140
Fort Stanwix, Treaty of (1784), 182
Fort Wayne, Treaty of (1809), 246
"Forty–niners," 407, 408
Fosdick, Raymond, 661
Fossils, early American, 4
Foster, Andrew "Rube," 687
Foster, Hannah Webster, 218
Four Bears, Chief, 230
Four Corners, 14
Fourier, Charles, 370
Fourteen Points, 666
Fourteenth Amendment, 483, 489, 502, 509, 619, 854
Fox, Charles James, 152
Fox, George, 114
Fox, William, 682
Fox Indians, 107, 281–82
Foxwoods Casino, Connecticut, 962
France: *See also* New France; World War I; World War II; American Revolution and, 170–71, 177; British blockade of (1793–1794), 206–7; colonization by, 39–42; cotton diplomacy in Civil War and, 457; Franco-American alliance of 1778, 203; in French and Indian War, 135–41; French Resistance in World War II, 775–76; fur trade, 41–42, 53–54; immigration from, 222, 223–24; in Indochina, 837; Louisiana Purchase and, 239–41; Napoleonic Wars, 242, 248, 249; Reign of Terror, 203; revolution in, 203–4, 216, 236; sugar plantations, 76–77; XYZ affair, 209–10
Franciscan missionaries, 50, 52–53, 109, 110, 396
Franco, Francisco, 738, 751
Frankfurter, Felix, 723
Franklin, Ann Smith, 117
Franklin, Benjamin, 117, 118, 119, 121, 222; American culture and, 288; in American Revolution, 169, 170, 177; colonial newspapers and, 142; Constitutional Convention and, 197, 198; Declaration of Independence and, 158; on Great Awakening, 126; in House of Commons, 146; Hutchinson and, 150; Paxton Boys and, 140; Plan of Union, 135; *Poor Richard's Almanac*, 125; as Postmaster, 141, 156
Franklin, James, 142
Franklin Evans, or the Inebriate (Whitman), 360
Franz Ferdinand, Archduke, 650
Fraternal societies, 570
Fredricksburg, battle of (1862), 461
Freed, Alan, 828
Freedmen, 482–83, 487, 497
Freedmen's Bureau, 474, 486, 488, 494, 495
Freedmen's Bureau Act (1865), 495
Freedom Rides, 860–61
Freedom's Journal, 372
Freedom Summer (Mississippi, 1964), 867–68
Free labor, notion of, 341
Free silver issue, 593–94
Free-Soil Party, 412, 413, 423–24, 430–31, 433
Free speech, wartime restrictions on, 663
Free speech movement, 884
Frémont, John C., 390, 403, 404, 433, 455
French and Indian War, 135–41
French Canadian immigrants, 561
French crescent, 106, 111–12
French Revolution (1789), 203–4, 216, 236
Freneau, Philip, 213, 216
Freud, Sigmund, 688
Frick, Henry C., 591
Friedan, Betty, 823, 898
Friends of Oder, 208
Fries, John, 211
Frobisher, Martin, 45
Frontier heritage, 117–19
Frontiers, 137, 396, 520–28, 530–31; *See also* Westward expansion
Fruitlands, Massachusetts, 370
Fugitive Slave Act (1850), 426–28, 464
Fugitive slaves, 75, 91–92, 109, 308–9
Fugitives (scholarly group), 703
Fulbright, J. William, 844, 883
Fuller, Margaret, 347–48
Fulton, Robert, 275, 276
Fundamental Orders, 63
Fur trade, 41–42, 53–54, 106, 107, 231, 236, 389–90, 397

G

Gabrielson, Guy, 804
Gadsden, Christopher, 152, 153
Gadsden Purchase (1853), 406, 524
Gage, Thomas, 148, 152, 153, 155, 157
Gag rule, 319, 375
Galileo, 124
Gallatin, Albert, 210, 211
Gallaudet, Edward Miner, 344
Galloway, Joseph, 152
Galton, Francis, 620
Gambling, Indian tribes and, 961–63
Gandhi, Mohandas, 405, 856, 858
Gang labor system, 75
Gangster films, 739
Garfield, James A., 583, 584
Garment industry, 339, 556, 626
Garrison, William Lloyd, 318–19, 372–76, 412
Garvey, Marcus, 701, 868
Gary, Elbert, 657, 666
Gates, Horatio, 169, 174, 175, 178
Gavin, Anna Maria, 383
Gay Activist Alliance, 899
Gay Liberation Front (GLF), 899
Gay liberation movement, 899
Gay Men's Health Crisis, 966
Gay Pride marches, 899
Geeche dialect, 90
Gemeinschaft and *Gesellschaft*, 620
General Agreement on Tariffs and Trade (GATT), 793, 978–79
General Court of Massachusetts Bay Colony, 60, 62, 63, 112, 113
General Federation of Women's Clubs, 630, 669
General Land Revision Act (1891), 535
General Motors, 658, 677, 679, 715
General Society of Mechanics and Tradesmen, 344
General Trades Union of New York, 365
General Union for Promoting the Observance of the Christian Sabbath, 366
Generational conflict, 883–88
Genêt, Edmond, 203–4
Genocide of Spanish conquest, 35
Gente de razón, 120
Gentility, middle class and, 568–69
Geological surveys of West, 390, 537
George, David Lloyd, 666
George, Henry, 534, 587–88
George III of England, King, 143, 145, 151, 153, 156, 157, 175
Georgia: civil rights movement in, 858, 859; in Civil War, 474, 476; colony of, 74–75, 86, 155; slavery in, 74–75
Georgia Constitutionalist, 435
German immigrants, 224–26, 355, 358, 359, 363, 365, 380, 381, 384–85; culture of, 381
Germany: Berlin crisis (1948), 793–94; Nazis in, 751, 775–76; post-World War II division of, 790; reparations, 667, 690–91; reunification of, 972; World War I and, 650–52, 656–57; World War II and, 771–78
Geronimo, 520
Gettysburg, battle of (1863), 460, 473
Ghent, Treaty of (1814), 249
Ghettos, 625–26, 709
Ghost Dance, 541–42
Ghost towns, 523
Gibbons v. *Ogden*, 276
GI Bill of Rights (1944), 787, 807, 822, 825
Gibson, Charles Dana, 653
Gibson, Josh, 687
Gifford, Walter S., 721
GI Forum, 871
Gilbert, Humphrey, 44, 45
Gilded Age, 567–75
Gilder, George, 950
Gillespie, Dizzy, 852
Gillette, George, 873
Gingrich, Newt, 979–80
Ginsberg, Allen, 832–33
Girard, Stephen, 282, 330–31
Girls Friendly Societies, 593
Gish, Lillian, 752
Giton, Judith, 223–24
Gladden, Washington, 592
Glasnost, 955–56
Global warming trend, 6
Glorieta Pass, battle of (1862), 462
"Glorious Ninety-two," 148
Glorious Revolution, 66, 69
Gnadenhutten, massacre at (1782), 194
Godey's Lady's Book, 345
Godkin, E.L., 508, 606
Gold: in Black Hills, 519; California Gold Rush, 381, 382, 383–84, 395, 407, 408–10, 516, 522; search for in New World, 32–33, 36
Gold, Michael, 738
Goldman, Emma, 629, 631, 669
Gold Standard Act (1900), 595
Goldwater, Barry, 869, 949
Goldwyn, Samuel, 682
Gompers, Samuel, 559, 590, 596, 606, 627, 644, 658, 678
Gone with the Wind (Mitchell), 737
Gonzales, Corky, 901
Goodman, Andrew, 867
Goodman, Benny, 741
Goodman, Paul, 832
Good Neighbor Policy, 599–600
Gorbachev, Mikhail, 956–57, 971
Gordon, Richard, 823
Gordon, Thomas, 142
Gorman, Howard, 735
Gorton, Samuel, 63
Gospel of Wealth, The (Carnegie), 555
Gospel of work, 555
Gossip column, 684
Gould, Jay, 505, 550, 554
Government: *See also* Politics; balance of power in, 239; civil service reform, 506, 584–85, 799; colonial, 123; commission form of, 616; era of divided, 979–81; exploration of West sponsored by, 390; under Jefferson, 238–39; machinery of politics, 583–84; post–Civil War growth of, 581–83; post-revolutionary, formation of, 196–200; spoils system, 269–70, 584–85; in the twenties, 688–92; urban, structural reforms in, 616
Government-business partnership, 658
Graduated income tax, 636
Graduate studies, 571–72; *See also* Colleges and universities
Grady, Henry Woodfin, 564
Graham, Billy, 807, 931
Gramercy Park, New York City, 356–57
Gramm-Rudmann Act (1985), 966–67
Grand Banks, fish in, 41–42
Grand Coulee Dam, 733
Grandfather clauses, 596

"Grand Tory ride," 167, 168
Grange, Harold E. "Red," 687
Grange movement, 585–86
Grant, Madison, 693
Grant, Ulysses S., 460; in Civil War, 449, 461–62, 473–74, 476; election of 1868, 490; election of 1872, 506–7; presidency, 502, 518, 593, 604; as secretary of war, 489
Grapes of Wrath (Steinbeck), 737
Grass-roots politics, 927–31
Gray, Robert, 236, 254
Gray, Thomas R., 310
Great Atlantic and Pacific Tea Company (A&P), 552, 677, 678
Great Awakening, 126–29, 185, 307; Second, 253, 343
Great Britain: *See also* England; American Civil War and, 457, 458; factory system in, 238, 332–33; immigration from, 222–23, 224; imperial crisis in pre-revolutionary period, 141–49; Napoleonic Wars and, 242, 248, 249; Oregon Country and, 396; post-revolutionary hostility, 205–6; Suez crisis (1956), 837; in War of 1812, 245, 247–49, 264; in the West, 205–6; in World War I, 650, 651, 655; in World War II, 753–54, 770, 774, 775
Great Compromise, 198
Great Depression, 717–22; *See also* New Deal; arts and, 735–37; banks in, 719, 723–24; bull market and, 717; culture of, 735–41; documentaries of, 737, 738; economic weaknesses and, 718–19; in Flint, Michigan, 715–16; Hollywood in, 738–39; Hoover and, 721–22; left wing politics in, 737–38; minorities in, 743–44, 986; presidential election of 1932 and, 722; radio, golden age of, 740; swing music, 740–41; unemployment in, 719–21, 744; Wall Street crash, 717–18
Great Gatsby, The (Fitzgerald), 702
Great Migration: African American, 664–65, 680; Puritan, 59–60
Great Northern Railroad, 505
Great Plains, 39, 392, 529–36, 730–33
Great Serpent Mound (Ohio), 15, 16
Great Society, 880, 888–90
Great Swamp Fight, 67
Great Uprising of 1877, 587
Great War. *See* World War I
Great White Fleet, 600
Greece, post–World War II aid for, 791
Greeley, Horace, 442, 464, 506–7, 530
Green, James K., 483
Green, William, 678
Greenback-Labor Party, 593
Greenbacks, 456–57, 593
Green berets, 841–42
Greene, Catherine, 167, 297
Greene, Nathanael, 165, 169, 175, 297
Greensboro, Alabama, 482–83
Greensboro, North Carolina, 857–58
Greenville, Treaty of (1795), 194–95, 207
Greenwich Village radicals, 628–29
Greenwood, John, 96
Gregg, William, 301
Grenada, 155, 955
Grenville, George, 143, 145
Grier, Robert C., 435
Griffith, D.W., 694
Grimké, Sarah and Angelina, 319, 373, 376
Griswold, Roger, 210
Grizzly bear, 535
Group Theater, 738
Groves, Leslie, 750
Grund, Francis, 378
Guadalcanal, 777–78
Guadalupe Hidalgo, Treaty of (1848), 405, 408, 412, 524
Guatemala, 837
Guilford Court House, 175
Gullah dialect, 90
Gullah Jack, 309
Gutiérrez, Bernardo, 241

H

Habeas corpus, writ of, 452
Hahn, William, 635
Haig, Alexander, 951
Haight-Ashbury, San Francisco, 884
Haiti, 77, 240, 267
Hakluyt, Richard, 44, 111
Hale, Edward Everett, 593
Hale, Sarah Josepha, 345
Hale County, Alabama, 482–83
Haley, Alex, 306
Half-Way Covenant (1662), 125
Hall, John, 337
Hamburg, Germany, bombing of, 775
Hamer, Fannie Lou, 867, 868
Hamilton, Alexander, 179, 207; Adams and, 211; American System and, 253–54; conflict with Jefferson, 203; Constitutional Convention and, 198; on factions, 208; *The Federalist* and, 199, 200; fiscal program of, 202–3; industrialization and, 238; "loose constructionist" position of, 203; nationalism and, 196–97; newspaper published by, 216; as Treasury secretary, 201
Hamilton, Charles V., 897
Hamilton, Henry, 173
Hammon, Jupiter, 186
Hammond, James Henry, 300, 306, 317, 319, 424, 437, 455
Hampton Roads conference (1865), 476
Hancock, John, 148
Handsome Lake, 246
Hanegan, Edward, 402
Hanson, Ole, 665, 669
Harding, Warren G., 663, 669–70, 676, 688–89, 694
Hard Labor, Treaty of (1768), 140
Harlan, John Marshall, 596
Harlem, 700–701
Harlem Renaissance, 701
Harmar, Josiah, 205
Harpers Ferry raid (1859), 437–38
Harper's Magazine, 346
Harper's Weekly, 506
Harrington, Michael, 888, 924
Harriot, Thomas, 26, 27, 45, 55
Harris, David, 441
Harrison, Benjamin, 536, 583
Harrison, William Henry, 246, 248, 284, 286, 287
Hart, Eli, 284
Hartford, Connecticut, 63
Hartford Convention (1814–1815), 249, 280
Harvard College, 61, 124, 126
Harvester, 532, 533
Hat Act of 1732, 96
Hatcher, Richard, 927
Hausas, 77
Hawai'i, 396, 600–601
Hawkins, John, 44, 45, 79
Hawthorne, Nathaniel, 420
Hay, George, 215
Hay, John, 601, 646, 648
Hayden, Casey, 867
Hayden, Tom, 880
Hayes, Rutherford B., 385, 508–9, 528, 583, 584, 587
Haymarket Square tragedy (1886), 558–59
Hays, Wayne, 895
Hays, Will, 683
Hays (later McCauley), Mary Ludwig, 167
Haywood, William D. "Big Bill," 628, 629, 644
Headright grants, 56
Head Start, 889
Health, Education and Welfare, Department of, 821
Health care and medicine, 467, 698, 826, 964–66, 977–78; *See also* Disease
Hearst organization, 685
Heller, Walter, 840–41
Helms, Jesse, 932
Helper, Hinton, 321
Hemingway, Ernest, 702
Hendrick, Iroquois chief, 135
Henry, Patrick, 134, 143, 149, 152, 154, 185, 196
Henry IV of France, 40
Henry VIII of England, King, 40, 43
Henry Street Settlement House, 516, 610–11, 615
Henry "the Navigator," Prince, 30–31
Hepburn Act (1906), 634
Heritage Foundation, 931
Heroes of America, 472
Hessian mercenaries, 168
Hetch Hetchy Valley, 635
Hiawatha, 21
Hickel, Walter, 930
Hickok, "Wild Bill," 528
Hicks, Edward, 328
Hicks, Granville, 738
Hidalgo, Miguel, 241
Hidatsa Indians, 229
Higginson, Thomas Wentworth, 427, 438, 465–66, 606
Higher education. *See* Colleges and universities
Higher Education Act (1963), 840
Highway system, interstate, 822
Hill, Isaac, 267
Hill, James J., 505
Hillard, George, 427
Hillman, Sidney, 729
Hillsborough, Lord, 147–48
Hine, Lewis, 614, 736
Hippies, 884
Hiroshima, bombing of (1945), 780, 782
Hispanic-American Alliance, 525–26
Hispaniola, 76
Hiss, Alger, 802
History of the Rise, Progress, and Termination of the American Revolution (Warren), 217
History of the Standard Oil Company (Tarbell), 618
Hitler, Adolf, 751–53, 771, 773, 775, 776
Hmongs, 971
Hobby, Oveta Culp, 821
Ho Chi Minh, 837, 842
Hoffman, Abbie, 894
Hofstadter, Richard, 808
Hohokam people, 13–14, 17
Hollow Horn Bear, Chief, 540–41
Hollywood, 675–76, 682–83, 738–39, 766, 801–2, 808, 831; *See also* Movie industry
Holmes, Oliver Wendell, Jr., 619–20, 663
Holocaust, 778–79
Home front: in Civil War, 469–72; in World War I, 657–63; in World War II, 760–66, 986
Homelessness, 966–67
Home rule, 509
Homestead Act (1862), 457, 529–30
Homestead Strike (1892), 591
Homosexuals, 770, 804, 899
Honduras, 646
Hone, Philip, 284, 290, 361
Hood, John Bell, 474
Hooker, Joseph "Fighting Joe," 472
Hooker, Thomas, 63
Hoover, Herbert: election of 1928, 704–5; Great Depression and, 721–22; presidency, 688, 690; Wall Street crash and, 718; in World War I, 657
Hoover, J. Edgar, 787, 800, 804, 807, 893
Hoover Dam (Boulder Dam), 733
Hopewell culture, 15
Hopi Indians, 4, 18, 51, 516, 544
Hopkins, Harry, 724, 727
Horizontal combination, 553–54
Horses, 36–37, 107, 108
Horseshoe Bend, battle of (1814), 245, 248
Housekeeping guides, 345
House of the Seven Gables, The (Hawthorne), 421

House servants, slaves as, 304–5
House Un-American Activities Committee (HUAC), 802
Housework, 568–69
Housing: balloon-frame construction, 290–91; class structure in cities and, 355–56; in factory town, 325; in Harlem in the twenties, 700; log construction, 114, 115; of Mexican immigrants, 699; in 1950s, 821–22; post–Civil War urban, 562–63; post–World War II, 799; slave, 304; tenements, 562, 570; wood construction, 113; in World War I, 659; in World War II, 761
Housing Act (1949), Title I of, 890
Housing survey (1798), 215
Houston, Sam, 400, 402
Houston, Texas, 680
Howard, Merrimon, 495
Howard, Oliver O., 495
Howe, Frederic C., 616, 621
Howe, Julia Ward, 491
Howe, Richard, 169
Howe, Samuel Gridley, 438
Howe, William, 157, 168, 169
Howl (Ginsberg), 833
How the Other Half Lives (Riis), 618
Hubbard, Lemuel, 336
Hudson, Henry, 58
Hudson, Rock, 966
Hudson River school of painting, 290
Hudson's Bay, 95
Hudson's Bay Company, 69, 95, 389, 396, 397
Huerta, Victoriano, 648
Hughes, Charles Evans, 652, 691
Hughes, Langston, 700, 701, 738, 764
Huguenots, French, 40, 64, 222, 223–24
Hull, William, 248
Hull House, 614
Humanism, 30
Human potential movement, 934
Human sacrifice, 17
Humphrey, Hubert H., 839, 868, 894, 895, 904
Hungary, 834, 971
Hunt, E. Howard, 907, 908
Hunter-gatherers, 4
Huntington, Collis P., 505
Huntington, Daniel, 201
Hunting traditions, Native American, 6–7, 12–13
Huron Indians, 21, 53, 65, 112, 136
Hurston, Zora Neale, 701, 736
Hussein, Saddam, 973
Hutchinson, Anne, 63, 113
Hutchinson, Thomas, 144, 149–50, 168
Hutterites, 530
Hyde, Henry, 934
Hyde Amendment, 934
Hydrogen bombs, 796
Hylton v. U.S., 202

I

Ibos, 77, 90
Ice Age, 4, 5
Ickes, Harold, 726, 744, 798
Identity, politics of, 895–902
If Christ Came to Chicago (Stead), 593
If Jesus Came to Boston (Hale), 593
Illegal immigration, 988, 990
Illinois: *See also* Chicago, Illinois; Lincoln-Douglas debates in, 418–19; riots in (1917), 664, 665
Illinois Central Railroad, 506
Imbangala, kingdom of, 82
Immigration: *See also Specific immigrant groups*; chain migration, 987–88; in colonial period, 222–27; from 1800 to 1860, 380–85; from 1860 to 1930, 555, 708–13; illegal, 988, 990; immigrants in company towns, 626–27; nativism and anti-immigrant feeling, 380, 382, 431–32, 595, 699; from 1930 to 2000, 986–91; in 1990s, 970–71; in Progressive Era, 623–24; quota system, 710; restrictions in the twenties, 693–94; settlement of Great Plains and, 530; in seventeenth century, 120; urban ethnic communities, 569–71; urbanization and patterns of, 355; urban population growth and, 559–62
Immigration Act: of 1882, 709; of 1891, 709; of 1917, 659, 710; of 1921, 694
Immigration and Nationality Act: of 1952, 792, 801, 874, 987; of 1965, 874, 971, 987
Immigration and Naturalization Service, 988
Immigration Reform and Control Act (1986), 971, 988
Immigration Restriction League, 693
Impeachment, Johnson and, 489–90
Impending Crisis, The (Helper), 321
Imperialism, 597–605
"Implied" powers, 203
Impressment into British navy, 242
Ince, Thomas, 651
Inchon, campaign at (1950), 809
Incidents in the Life of a Slave Girl (Jacobs), 427
Income. *See* Wealth
Income tax, 636, 658, 950
Incorporation, customs of, 567
Incorporation laws, 276
Indentured servants, 57, 118–19, 222, 225–26
Indianapolis Recorder, 606
Indian Bureau, 543
Indian Confederacy, 246
Indian Education and Civilization (Senate report), 539
Indian Gaming Regulatory Act (1988), 961
Indian Intercourse Act (1790), 204–5, 242
Indian Removal Act (1830), 281, 282, 516
Indian Reorganization Act (1934), 541, 735
Indian Rights Association, 540
"Indians," origins of term, 3; *See also* Native Americans
Indian Territory, 391–92, 393, 514, 517
Indian Wars, 518–20
Indigo culture, 85–86
Individualism, 347, 612
Industrial cities, 559–64
Industrial education, 571
Industrialization, 325–49; accumulation of capital and, 330–31; American system of manufactures, 336–37; British technology and, 332–33; cash economy and, 340–41; free labor notion, 341; hazards of industrial work, 557; Jefferson's opposition to, 238; market revolution, 330–38; mass production, 679; mechanization and women's work, 339; new social order and, 342–48; in New South, 564–65; personal relationships and, 338–39; preindustrial ways of working and, 327–30; productivity in 1970s, 917–19; putting-out system, 331–32; in Reconstruction North, 504–6; social distinctions in industrial work, 336; in South, 301, 564–65; southern slavery and northern, 300; strikes and, 341–42; textile industry, 333–36; time, work, and leisure in, 339–40; westward relocation of industry, 550
Industrial relations, 619
Industrial revolution: British, 92; second, 551, 552, 676
Industrial Workers of the World (IWW), 628, 630, 643, 644, 659, 669
Industry: *See also* Business; Industrialization; *specific industries*; ailing, in the twenties, 681–82; microelectronic, 959–60; rise of, 550–55
Inequality, social, 121–23
Inflation, 187, 470, 472, 917, 924
Influence of Sea Power upon American History (1660–1873), The (Mahan), 600
Influenza epidemic (1918–1919), 662–63
Infrastructure, 271–79, 301
INF Treaty, 956
In His Steps (Sheldon), 593
Initiative, 617
Inquisition, 123–24
Insane asylums, 366
Insurance, 678
Intellectual trends, 619–20, 700–703
Interchangeable parts, concept of, 336–37
Intercolonial cooperation, 149–50
Intercontinental exchange, 36–37
Interesting Narrative of the Life of Olaudah Equiano, The (Equiano), 79
Interior, Department of the, 581, 636
Internal Security Act (1950), 792, 801
International Association of Machinists, 627
International Bank for Reconstruction and Development (World Bank), 788–89
International Brotherhood of Teamsters, 727
International Court of Justice, 789–90
International Ladies Garment Workers Union (ILGWU), 625–26
International Longshoremen's Association (ILA), 727
International Monetary Fund (IMF), 788–89
Internment, Japanese American, 762–63
Interstate carriers, segregation on, 861
Interstate commerce, 276
Interstate Commerce Commission (ICC), 582–83, 634
Interstate highway system, 822
Intolerable Acts (1774), 133, 134, 151–52
Inuit people, 231
Inupiat (Eskimos), 7
Investment overseas in 1920s, 691–92
Iran, 835–36; hostage crisis, 939, 940
Iran-Contra scandal, 956–58
Iran-Iraq war (1980–1988), 957
Ireland: English invasion of, 44; immigrants from, 273, 355, 358, 359, 363, 365, 380–81, 383; Potato Famine (1845–1850), 355, 380, 383
Iron Act (1750), 96
Ironclad vessels, 463–64
Iron curtain, 791; *See also* Cold War era
Iron industry, 301, 564
Iron making, West African, 77
Iron Teeth, 518, 519
Iroquois, 21, 105
Iroquois Confederacy, 21, 65, 67, 135, 136, 137
Iroquois Five Nations, 106–7
Iroquois Indians, 113, 136, 140, 173, 179, 182
Irrigation in California, 535
Irving, Washington, 289
Isabella and Ferdinand, 31, 32
Isolationism, 752, 753
Israel, 836–37, 916
Italian immigrants, 561, 708, 709, 710–11
Italy, World War II and, 775
Iwo Jima, Battle of (1944), 778
IWW. *See* Industrial Workers of the World (IWW)

J

J. Walter Thompson agency, 685
Jackson, Andrew, 245, 313; election of 1828, 267, 268; inauguration of, 269, 270; Indian policy of, 280–82, 517; invasion of Florida, 254; Kitchen Cabinet, 271; national leadership of, 270; political coalition of, 256; presidency of, 269–71, 279–83; reelection in 1832, 283; as slave owner, 314; Texas and, 400; War of 1812 and, 248, 249, 264
Jackson, Helen Hunt, 540
Jackson, Henry, 940
Jackson, Jesse, 897, 952, 953
Jackson, Jimmy Lee, 869–70
Jackson, Mahalia, 819
Jackson, Michael, 963
Jackson, Rachel, 269, 271
Jackson, Robert, 790
Jackson, Thomas "Stonewall," 473
Jackson, William H., 537
Jacobs, Harriet, 427
Jamaica, 76, 155
James, Duke of York, 65
James, Henry, 562
James, William, 604
James I of England, King, 54, 56, 58

James II of England, King, 69
Jamestown colony, 54–55
Japan: atomic bombing of, 780–82; Manchuria, invasion of, 751; militarist–imperialist leaders in 1930s, 751; post–World War II occupation of, 795; Russo-Japanese War, 646; in World War II, 755, 770–71, 776–78, 780–82
Japanese American Citizens League, 763, 902
Japanese Americans, 624–25, 708, 770; wartime internment of, 762–63
Jarvis, John Wesley, 243
Jaworski, Leon, 910
Jay, John, 152, 177, 179–80, 184, 199, 202, 207
Jay Cooke and Company, 507
Jay's Treaty (1794), 181, 207–8
Jazz, 686, 852
Jazz Singer, The, 683
Jefferson, Thomas, 149, 211, 306; on architecture, 215; conflict with Hamilton, 203; Constitutional Convention and, 196; Declaration of Independence and, 158; in election of 1800, 212; foreign policy of, 242–43; on immigration, 222, 226–27; Inaugural Address of 1801, 208, 215, 217–18, 238–39, 242; inauguration of 1801, 237; Indian policy of, 243–46, 280; on industrialization, 333; judiciary under, 239; legislation on Western Territory drafted by, 181–82; Lewis and Clark expedition and, 229, 230; Louisiana Purchase and, 229, 239–41; national government under, diminishment of, 238–39; political philosophy of, 237–38; presidency of, 201, 237–43; protest against Whiskey Tax and, 195; on race, 99, 100; reform by, 184–85; on republicanism, 142; at Second Continental Congress, 155, 156; as secretary of state, 201; on slave music and dance, 90; slavery issue and, 185, 306; "strict constructionist" position of, 202–3; as vice president, 209
Jenckes, Thomas A., 584
Jerdone, Francis, 89
Jerome, Chauncey, 337
Jesuit missionaries, 54, 105, 109, 111
Jews: discriminatory treatment in Middle Ages, 28–29; immigrants, 560–61, 626, 708, 711; *pogroms*, 708; in World War II, 752, 778–79
Jews without Money (Gold), 738
Jim Crow laws, 596, 853
João I of Portugal, 30
Job Corps, 888, 889
Jobs, Steve, 959
Jobs or Income Now (JOIN), 879
John Brown's raid (1959), 437–38
Johnson, Andrew, 486–87, 489–90
Johnson, Anthony, 83
Johnson, Cave, 428
Johnson, Frank, 870
Johnson, Hiram, 617, 636
Johnson, Hugh, 726
Johnson, James Weldon, 665, 701
Johnson, Lady Bird, 844
Johnson, Lyndon Baines, 839, 844, 845, 860; civil rights and, 865, 869, 871; credibility gap of, 882–83; Great Society program of, 880, 888–90; Vietnam War and, 881–83, 893
Johnson, Magic, 966
Johnson, Maynard, 927
Johnson, Paul, 342
Johnson, Sally, 317
Johnson, Thomas L., 616
Johnson, William, 311
Johnson-Reed Immigration Act (1924), 694
Johnston, Albert Sidney, 462
Johnston, Joe, 473
Joint Committee on Reconstruction, 488
Jolson, Al, 683
Jones, Absalom, 186, 307
Jones, Jim, 934
Jones, John Paul, 171
Jones, LeRoi (Imamu Amiri Baraka), 833, 891
Jones, Paula, 979
Jones, Samuel "Golden Rule," 616
Jones, Spike, 766
Jones Act (1917), 872
Joplin, Janis, 885
Joplin, Scott, 573
Jornada del Muerto, 52
Joseph, Chief, 520
Journalism, 617–19, 684–85; *See also* Newspapers
Juárez, Benito, 457
Judicial review, 239
Judiciary, 198, 201–2, 239, 627–28; *See also* Supreme Court, U.S.
Judiciary Act (1789), 201–2, 239
Judson, Edward Zane Carroll, 538
Judson, Phoebe, 394–95
Julian, George W., 487
Jungle, The (Sinclair), 618
Justice Department, 644, 860
Juvenile delinquency, 762, 829

K

Kachinas, 18
Kahnawake community, 105, 107, 112
Kalabari, African state of, 82
Kamikaze pilots, 778
Kansas: admission to union, 436; "Bleeding Kansas," 430–31; Lecompton constitution, 435–36
Kansas and Nebraska Territories, 392, 430, 517
Kansas Nebraska Act (1854), 393, 429–31, 433
Kansas Pacific Railroad, 526
Kaskaskia, 112, 173
Katz, Bruce, 947
Katzenbach, Nicholas, 881
KDKA, 684
Kearny, Stephen, 403, 405
Keckley, Elizabeth, 464
Keep America Out of War Congress, 752
Kefauver, Estes, 831
Kelley, Florence, 611, 614, 626, 630, 654, 697
Kelley, Oliver H., 585
Kellogg-Briand Pact (1928), 691
Kemble, Fanny, 302–3, 304
Kendall, Mary, 316
Kendall, Nicanor, 336
Kenna, Michael "Hinky Dink," 584
Kennan, George, 791–92, 805, 809
Kennedy, Jacqueline, 844
Kennedy, John F., 381, 839–45; assassination of, 844–45, 865; Bay of Pigs, 842–43; civil rights and, 859–60, 861, 864–65; Cold War and, 841–44; Cuban missile crisis, 843–44; election of 1960, 839–40; New Frontier liberalism, 840–41; political career of, 839
Kennedy, Joseph P., 839
Kennedy, Patrick Joseph, 380
Kennedy, Robert F., 839, 859, 860, 862, 874, 894
Kent State University, 904
Kentucky, as Union state, 452
Kentucky Resolve, 211, 249, 280
Kerensky, Alexander, 668
Kerner, Otto, 892
Kerner Commission, 892
Kerouac, Jack, 832–33
Kerr, Clark, 884
Key, Ellen, 687–88
Key, Francis Scott, 249
Key, Mary, 275
Keynes, John Maynard, 727, 950
Khomeini, Ayatollah Ruholla, 940
Khrushchev, Nikita, 834–35, 844
Kickapoo Indians, 22
Kim Il Sung, 809
Kindergartens, 381, 571, 622–23
King, B.B., 819
King, Coretta Scott, 859, 865
King, Lonnie, 858
King, Martin Luther, Jr., 405, 856–57; in Albany, Georgia, 861; assassination of, 894; Atlanta sit-in and, 858, 859; in Birmingham, 862–63; bus boycott and, 850; Poor People's Campaign, 894; in Selma, 870–71; Southern Christian Leadership Conference, 856–57; Vietnam War and, 893–94
King, Mary, 867
King, Rodney, 975
King, Rufus, 253, 263
King George's War (1744–1748), 95
King Philip's War, 66, 67–68, 125
Kings Mountain, battle at (1780), 175
Kingston, Maxine Hong, 902
King William's War (1689–97), 66, 69–70, 94, 107, 119
Kino, Eusebio, 109, 110, 111
Kinship system: *See also* Family; African American, 75, 89, 306–7, 664; Native American, 12; in New France, 112; in West Africa, 77
Kiowa Indians, 229
Kirkpatrick, Jean, 954
Kissinger, Henry A., 904, 935, 937
Kitchen Cabinet, 271
Kitchin, Claude, 651
Kivas, 13, 14, 51
Knickerbocker Base Ball Club, 575
Knights of Labor, 558, 565, 579, 588, 589
Knights of the Golden Circle, 470
Know-Nothings. *See* American (Know-Nothing) Party
Knox, Henry, 189, 201
Knox, Philander C., 646, 647
Kodiak Island, 231
Koop, C. Everett, 966
Korean Americans, 976, 987–88
Korean War, 808–14, 833
Korematsu v. *U.S.*, 763
Kossuth, Lajos, 410
Kristallnacht, 752
Krug, J.A., 873
Krutch, Joseph Wood, 703
Ku Klux Klan, 483, 490, 500–501; in the twenties, 694–95
Ku Klux Klan Act (1871), 483, 502
Kupferberg, Tuli, 895
Kursk, battle of (1943), 774
Kuwait, Iraqi invasion of (1990), 973
Kwanzaa, 898

L

Labor: *See also* Industrialization; Labor movement; Working women; African American, 362, 494–97, 556, 565, 760; Big Business and, 555–59; changing status of, 555–57; child, 333, 335, 336, 338, 566, 614; convict, 566; division between leisure and work, 340; factory work schedule, 326; family labor system, 327–28, 338; federal employment growth (1871–1901), 581–82; mobilization against wage system, 557–59; in New South, 565–66; pace of urban versus rural, 328; putting-out system, 331–32; unskilled, 504; in World War I, 658–59, 665–66; in World War II, 758–59
Labor Day, 559
Labor Department, Women's Bureau of, 660
Labor-Management Relations Act. *See* Taft-Hartley Act (1947)
Labor movement: American Federation of Labor (AFL), 559, 627–28, 643, 644, 658, 694, 729; artisanal politics, 362–63; farmer-labor unity, 589; farmers and, 585–87; Industrial Workers of the World and, 628, 630, 643, 644, 659, 669; labor solidarity in 1890s, 590–92; New Deal and, 729; organizing, 585–89; in Progressive Era, 627–29; union movement, 363–64; urban politics and, 362–65; western mining industry and, 523; women's alliances and, 588–89; workers' search for power, 587–88

Labor unions. *See* Union(s)
Laclède, Pierre, 233
Lacrosse, 20–21
Ladies' Magazine, 345
La Flesche, Suzette (Bright Eyes), 539
La Follette, Robert M., 616–17, 619, 667, 690
Lakota Indians, 3, 518
Lamb, William, 586
Land: *See also* Westward expansion; colonial shortages of, 122–23; Dawes Severalty Act and, 540–41, 542; frontier heritage, 119; homesteading, 457, 529–30; land sales, 390–91; post–Civil War redistribution of, 485–86, 494–97, 498, 500; speculation, 194–95
Land Act of 1820, 251
"Land-grant" colleges, 533
Landis, Kenesaw Mountain, 686
Landis, Paul, 827
Landon, Alfred M., 729
Land Ordinance (1785), 180, 182, 250, 390
Lands Claims Commission, 534
Lange, Dorothea, 720, 737
Language: African American, 90; Native American, 21
L'Anse aux Meadows, Newfoundland, 28
Laos, 842
Lappe, Frances Moore, 929
La Raza Unida Party (LRUP), 901
Larcom, Lucy, 326
Lardner, Ring, Jr., 687, 802, 811
Larkin, Thomas, 404
La Salle, Robert Sieur de, 54, 87
Las Casas, Bartolomé de, 34–35
Lasch, Christopher, 934
Las Corras Blancas, 525
Lasswell, Harold, 756
Lathrop, Julia C., 662
Latin America, 599, 600, 692, 842
Latrobe, Benjamin Henry, 85
La Villa Real de la Santa Fé de San Francisco. *See* Santa Fé, New Mexico
Law and Order Leagues, 587
Lawrence, Amos, 428, 430
Lawrence, Kansas, 430–31, 434, 462
Lawrence, Massachusetts, 628
Lawson, James, 858, 859
Lea, Luke, 518–19
Leadbelly (Huddie Ledbetter), 788
Leadership Conference on Civil Rights, 865
League of Nations, 666, 667
League of the Ho-De-No-Sau-Nee, or Iroquois (Morgan), 539
League of United Latin American Citizens (LULAC), 871–72
League of Women Voters, 697; *See also* National American Woman Suffrage Association
Lear, Norman, 931
Leary, Timothy, 885
Lease, Mary E., 588
Leatherstocking novels, 289–90
Leavenworth, Fort, 767
Leaves of Grass (Whitman), 360
Lecompton Constitution, 435–36
Lee, Arthur, 133
Lee, Fort, 169
Lee, Jason, 396
Lee, "Mother" Ann, 370
Lee, Richard Henry, 149, 158, 175, 182
Lee, Robert E., 455, 458, 460, 461, 469, 472, 476
Lee, Russell, 737
Legal Defense and Education Fund, 851–52
Legal infrastructure, 276
Legal Services Program, 889
Legends of trans–Mississippi West, 537–38
Leisler, Jacob, 69
Leisure activities, 340, 568, 569, 571, 572–73, 621–22
LeMay, Curtis, 904
Lemke, William, 726
Lemlich, Clara, 626
le Moyne, Jacques, 20, 41
Lend-Lease Program, 754, 774
L'Enfant, Pierre Charles, 214, 239
Lenin, V.I., 668
Lenni Lenape, 3
Leopard (ship), 242
Leo XIII, Pope, 593
Lester, Julius, 869
LeSueur, Meridel, 738
Letter on Tolerance (Locke), 113
Letters from a Farmer in Pennsylvania (Dickinson), 146
Letters from an American Farmer (Crèvecoeur), 216, 227
Letters on the Equality of the Sexes and the Condition of Women (Grimké), 376
Letters to Mothers (Sigourney), 431
Levitt, William, 822
Levittown, 822
Lewis, Andrew L. "Drew," Jr., 950
Lewis, John L., 729, 760, 858, 861, 864, 869
Lewis, Meriwether, 229–30, 245–46, 390
Lewis, Sinclair, 702–3
Lewis and Clark expedition, 229–30, 240, 241, 390–91
Lexington and Concord, battles of, 153–54
Leyte Gulf, Battle of (1944), 778
Liberal Republicans, 506–7
Liberator (newspaper), 319
Liberia, 371
Liberty Bonds, 657
Liberty Party, 375, 402, 412, 433
Liberty (sloop), 148
Liddy, G. Gordon, 907, 908
Life magazine, 806, 807, 827
Life of Washington (Weems), 217
Liliuokalani, Queen, 601
Limited Nuclear Test-Ban Treaty (1962), 844
Lincoln, Abraham, 217; assassination of, 477; Civil War and, 449, 452; diplomacy under, 457; *Dred Scott* decision and, 435; economic policy of, 456–57; election of 1860, 438–40, 441; election of 1864, 475–76; emancipation of slaves, 464–65; First Inaugural Address, 444, 450; on free labor versus slavery, 504; inauguration of, 443–44; Lincoln-Douglas debates, 418–19; national currency, creation of, 456–57; as party leader, 455; political challenges to, 469–70; presidency of, 455–57; Reconstruction plan, 485–86; secession and, 441–42; Second Inaugural Address, 477; War Department expansion and, 456
Lincoln, Mary Todd, 452, 464
Lincoln-Douglas debates, 418–19
Lindbergh, Charles A., 687, 752
Lindsay, John, 899
Lindstrom, Walter, 710
Lippmann, Walter, 629, 703, 791–92, 814
Lisbon, Portugal, 30
Literacy, 125, 217, 218, 366–67
Literary Digest, 730
Literature: of beats, 832–33; children's, 569; of Cold War era, 808; early nineteenth century, 288–90; of Great Depression, 737; "Indian Renaissance" in, 902; New Deal and, 736; of 1950s, 832–33; post-revolutionary, 215–18; pre–Civil War, 420–21; suburban life image and, 823; of the twenties, 702–3; westerns, 537–38; women authors in nineteenth century, 346–47; in World War II, 766
Little, Malcolm. *See* Malcolm X
Little Bighorn, battle of, 519, 541
Little Rock, Arkansas, 855
Little Turtle, Chief, 194–95, 205, 207, 246
Livingston, Robert R., 158, 184
Local government, growth of, 581
Lochner v. *New York*, 619
Locke, Alain, 700–701
Locke, John, 113, 124, 142
Lodge, Henry Cabot, 652, 667–68, 693
Loew, Marcus, 674
Loewe v. *Lawler*, 627
Log construction, 114, 115
Loguen, Jermain, 304
Lonely Crow, The (Riesman), 825
Long, Huey, 727
Long, Stephen, 390, 391
Long Island, battle of (1776), 168
Long lots, French colonial, 112
Longworth, Alice Roosevelt, 689
Longworth, Nicholas, 689
Looking Backward (Bellamy), 579
Los Alamos, New Mexico, 749–50
Los Angeles, California, 232; ethnic and racial divisions in, 824, 975–76; founding of, 110; Hollywood, 675–76, 682–83, 738–39, 766, 801–2, 808, 831; post–World War II, 824; riot (1992), 974, 975–76
Los Angeles Times, 628
Lost Colony. *See* Roanoke Island
"Lost generation," 702
Louisburg, fortress of, 95, 136, 137
Louis XVI of France, King, 203
Louisiana: *See also* New Orleans, Louisiana; colony of, 109, 111, 112, 137; cuisine of, 90; Long as governor, 727; slavery in, 87
Louisiana Purchase, 229, 238, 239–41
Louisiana Territory, 240, 241
Louisville Democrat, 435
Love, Nat, 538
Love Canal, 929
Lovejoy, Elijah P., 375
Lowell, Francis Cabot, 331, 334, 335, 342
Lowell, Josephine, 630
Lowell, Massachusetts, 325–26, 334–35, 341
Loyalists, 167–68, 175
Loyall Nine, 144
Loyalty programs, 787, 801
Luce, Henry, 788, 796
Ludlow Massacre (1914), 627
Luis, José, 990
Lumber industry, 565
Lundberg, Ferdinand, 807
Lusitania, sinking of (1915), 651
Luther, Martin, 40
Lutheran church, 114
Lynchings, 596–97
Lynd, Robert and Helen, 679
Lynn, Massachusetts, 331
Lyon, Mary, 367
Lyon, Matthew, 210, 212

M

MacArthur, Douglas, 722; dismissal of, 811–12; in Korean War, 809–11; occupation of Japan, 795; in World War II, 755, 767, 771–72, 777, 778
McCain, Franklin, 858
McCarran, Pat, 801
McCarran Act. *See* Internal Security Act (1950)
McCarran-Walter Immigration Act. *See* Immigration and Nationality Act (1952)
McCarthy, Eugene, 894
McCarthy, Joseph R., 800, 803–5, 831
McCarthyism, 803–5
McClellan, George B., 461, 463, 467, 475
McCloskey, Paul "Pete," 929
McClure, S.S., 618
McClure's, 618
McCormick, Anne O'Hare, 698
McCormick, Cyrus, 277, 355, 470, 532, 585
McCoy, Joseph G., 526, 538
McDonald, Alexander, 299
Macdonald, Dwight, 832
McFarlane, Robert, 957
McGovern, George, 798, 883, 908
McGrath, J. Howard, 805
McHenry, Fort, 249
McHenry, James, 198
Machine industry, 676
Machine politics, 364–65, 584, 615–16

Mckay, Claude, 701
McKay, Donald, 236
Mackinac, 112
McKinley, William, 595, 601–4, 633, 710
McKinley tariff of 1890, 593
McLaurin v. *Oklahoma State Regents*, 854, 866
MacLeish, Archibald, 740
McLoughlin, John, 396
McNamara, John and James, 628
McNamara, Robert, 841, 844
McNary-Haugen Farm Relief bill (1927), 681–82
McNeill, George E., 555, 592
Macon's Bill Number 2 (1810), 243
Macune, Charles W., 586
Madeira, colony of, 76
Madero, Francisco, 648
Madison, Dolley, 249, 266
Madison, James, 239; Annapolis Convention and, 196; Constitutional Convention and, 198; election of 1808, 243; *Federalist, The*, 199, 208; as floor leader in House of Representatives, 202; foreign policy and, 203; political parties and, 209; presidency of, 247; on slavery, 198; War of 1812 and, 247
Madonna, 963
Magazines, 288–89, 345, 569, 618, 629, 630–31
Mahan, Alfred Thayer, 600
Mail-order houses, 551–52
Maine: admission to Union, 258; colony of, 64
Maine, USS, 603
Maize, 10, 15, 36
Malcolm X, 868–69, 895
Mali Empire, 77
Mallory, Stephen R., 458
Malthus, Thomas, 119, 238
Mammals, in Archaic period, 4, 6
Manchuria, 751
Mandan Indians, 229, 245
Mandingos, 77
Mangum, W.P., 284
Manhattan Project, 749
Manifest Destiny, 392–94, 410–13
Man in the Grey Flannel Suit (Wilson), 825
Mann, Horace, 367
Mann Act (1910), 621
Manpower Retraining Act (1963), 840
Mansa Musa, 77
Mansfield, Mike, 883
Manteo (Indian), 26
Manufactures, American system of, 336–37
Manumission, 186, 303
Mao Zedong, 795
Marbury, William, 239
Marbury v. *Madison*, 239
March on Washington (1963), 864–65
March on Washington Movement, 763
March to the Sea, Sherman's (1864), 460, 474–75
Marcos, Ferdinand, 903, 907
Marcy, William, 269
Margin accounts, 717
Margold, Nathan, 735
Marine Corps Women's Reserve, 768
Market production in agriculture, 533–34
Market research, 685, 827
Market revolution, 330–38, 380
Maroon colonies, 91–92
Marriage, 184; post–World War II, 805–6; slave, 88, 89, 306, 493; in World War II, 761
Marsh, Reginald, 739
Marshall, Andrew, 307
Marshall, Burke, 860
Marshall, George C., 768, 793, 812
Marshall, James, 408
Marshall, Jerusha, 408
Marshall, John, 239, 276, 281
Marshall, Thurgood, 851, 854, 860
Marshall Plan, 792–93
Martha Washington Societies, 368
Martí, José, 602
Martín, Enrico, 3
Martin, Joseph Plumb, 164
Martinique, 77
Marx, Karl, 668
Marxism, 738
Maryland: colony of, 56–57; constitution of, 183–84; House of Delegates, 57; ratification of Articles of Confederation, 176; as Union state, 452
Mary of England, Queen, 43
*M*A*S*H* (TV), 811
Mason, George, 88, 184, 196–97, 200
Mason, John, 428
Massachusetts: *See also* Boston, Massachusetts; abolition of slavery in, 186; colony of, 61–62, 113; education in, 61–62, 367; House of Representatives, 147, 148, 153; ratification of Constitution, 199; Shays' Rebellion in, 189, 196
Massachusetts Bay colony, 59–60
Massachusetts circular letter, 147–48
Massachusetts General Court, 60, 62, 63, 112, 113
Massachusetts General Hospital, 288
Massachusetts Government Act, 151–52
Massachusetts (Indians), 22, 60
Massasoit, 59, 60, 67
Mass culture in the 1920s, 674–76, 682–88, in 1950s, 829–31, 832
Masses, The (magazine), 629
Masson, Paul, 534
Mass-production system, 679
Mass transportation systems, 563
Maternity and Infancy Act (1921), 662
Mather, Cotton, 119, 124, 128
Mattachine Society, 899
Maximilian, Austrian archduke, 457
Mayans, 11
Mayflower, 59
Mayflower Compact, 59, 117
Mayhew, Thomas, 67
Maysville Road Bill (1830), 271
Mazarin, Jules, 111
Mazowiecki, Tadeusz, 971
Mbundus, 77
Meade, George Gordon, 460, 473
Measles, 81
Meat Inspection Act (1906), 634
Meat-packing industry, 548–49, 551, 634
Mechanics Bank, 331
"Me Decade," 934–35
Media. *See* Newspapers; Radio broadcasting; Television
Medicare and Medicaid, 826, 889
Medicine. *See* Health care and medicine
Medicine Lodge Treaty (1867), 518, 519, 540
Mellon, Andrew, 689, 718
Melville, Herman, 420, 421
Memminger, Christopher, 458
Memorial Day Massacre (1937), 729
Memphis, Tennessee, popular music in, 818–19
Mencken, H.L., 696, 702
Mendez v. *Westminster*, 871
Menéndez de Avilés, Don Pedro, 41
Menomini Indians, 11
Mercantilism, 94, 95–97, 235
Mercein, Thomas, 344
Merchant class, 29–30
Meredith, James, 862
Meridian, Mississippi, 501
Merriam Report (1928), 734–35
Merrimac (ship), 464
Mesa Verde, Colorado, 14
Mesoamerica, civilizations of, 10–11
Mestizos, 39, 121
Metacomet (King Philip), 67, 68
Methodist church, 127, 422
Métis (mestizos), 112, 389
Mexican Americans, 988; *barrios*, 986; *bracero* program, 758, 986; Chicano nationalism, 899–901; civil rights movement and, 871–72; in Great Depression, 744; illegal aliens, 990; immigration of, 625, 659, 698–700, 712–13, 732–33, 758, 970, 986, 990; in local political office, 927–28; in military, 765; in the twenties, 698–700; in World War I, 659; zoot-suit riots, 764–65
Mexican–American War (1846–1848), 403–6, 411, 524
Mexican American Youth Organization (MAYO), 901
Mexicanos, 524–26
Mexican Revolution (1911), 648, 649
Mexico: pre–World War I policies toward, 648–49; struggle for independence, 241
Mexico, Valley of, 10
Mexico City, 108
M'Fingal (Trumbull), 216
Miami, Fort, 194–95, 206, 207
Miami Indians, 22, 205, 234, 243, 246
Miami River valley, 234
Michigan, 112, 248, 715–16
Michigan, University of, 885–86
Michilimackinac, Fort, 139–40
Micmacs, 21, 42
Microelectronic industry, 959–60
Middle Ages, 28, 29
Middle class: colonial, 121; family life of, 344–45; in Gilded Age, 568–71; industrialization and, 342–48; post–World War II, 805; religion of, 343–44; sentimentalism of, 346–47; social reform movement and, 366; suburbanization and, 821–25; temperance movement and, 367–68; transcendentalism and, 347–48; women, 344–47, 568–69, 630–31
Middle colonies, culture of region, 113–15
Middle East, Reagan administration and, 956–57
Middle Passage, 81–82, 89
Middletown (Lynd and Lynd), 679
Midway, battle of (1942), 776–77
Midwifery, 117
Migrant farm workers, 698–99
Migration: Native American, from Asia, 3–5, 7; into Old Southwest, 298; routes westward, 251–52; theories of transoceanic, 3; trans-Appalachian, 231, 233–34
Military, the: African Americans in, 655, 665, 768–70; buildup under Reagan, 950; in Civil War, 453–55, 468–69, 470–71; desegregation of, 799; draft for, 459, 470–71, 654–55, 764, 887; homosexuals in, 770, 804; Native Americans in, 770; racism in, 655; service as "Americanizing" experience, 770; subordination to civil authority, 179; women in, 768–69; in World War I, 654–57; in World War II, 765, 766–71
Military contracts, 758, 951
Military-industrial complex, 825, 833, 838–39
Military spending, 800, 811, 833–34, 841
Militias, 165–67, 168, 175
Milken, Michael, 967
Miller, Alfred Jacob, 390
Miller, Arthur, 808
Miller, William, 194, 370
Millerites, 370
Millett, Kate, 898
Milliken's Bend, battle of (1863), 466
Mills, C. Wright, 825
Mill towns, 566–67
Mims, Fort, 248
Mingo Creek, Pennsylvania, 194–95, 196
Mingo Creek Democratic Society, 194, 195, 204
Mining: communities, 521, 522–23; copper, 643–44; gold, in California, 408, 409; industry, 506, 522–23; mining camps, 409–10; silver, 36, 522; strikes, 591, 627, 643–44
Minkins, Shadrach, 427
Minneapolis Central Labor Union, 727
Minorities. *See* African Americans; *specific ethnic groups*
Minstrel tradition, 359–60, 631–32
Mirandola, Pico della, 30
Missionaries, 243, 245; foreign missions, 598–99;

Franciscan, 50, 52–53, 109, 110, 396; Jesuit, 54, 105, 109, 111; in West, 393, 396
Mission Indians, 68
Mission system, Spanish, 110–11, 232
Mississippi, 298; *See also* Natchez, Mississippi; civil rights movement and, 867–68; Civil War in, 461–62; Ku Klux Klan in, 501
Mississippian society, 2, 15–16, 19
Mississippi Freedom Democratic Party (MFDP), 867–68
Mississippi River, 1, 232–33
Mississippi Valley, 1, 2, 109
Mississippi Valley Cotton Planters' Association, 564
Missouri: admission to Union, 245; in Civil War, 452
Missouri Compromise, 250, 256–58; *Dred Scott* decision and, 434–35
Missouri Crisis (1819–1820), 250, 256, 309, 318
Missouri v. *ex. rel. Gaines*, 854, 866
Mitchell, George, 901
Mitchell, Margaret, 737
Mitchum, Robert, 808
Mittelberger, Gottlieb, 224–26
Mobile, Alabama, 87, 171
Moby Dick (Melville), 421
Model T, 679
Modern Chivalry (Brackenridge), 216
Modern Woman: The Lost Sex (Lundberg & Farnham), 807
Mogollon culture, 13
Mohawk Indians, 4, 21
Mojados ("wetbacks"), 871
Molasses Act of 1733, 97
Moley, Raymond, 723
Momaday, N. Scott, 902
Monarchies, 30, 170
Monarchists, British, 142
Mondale, Walter, 923, 940, 952
Money supply: *See also* Currency; colonial monetary regulations, 96; free silver issue, 593–94; post-revolutionary inflation, 187; Second Bank of United States and, 282, 283
Monitor (ironclad ship), 464
Monk, Thelonius, 852
Monmouth, battle of (1778), 171
Monongahela Valley, 194, 960–61
Monroe, James, 240, 253–54
Monroe Doctrine, 254–55, 457; Roosevelt Corollary to, 645–46
Montagnais Indians, 21
Montaigne, Michel Eyquem de, 29
Montcalm, Marquis de, 138
Montesquieu, Baron de la Brède de, 199
Montgomery, Richard, 157
Montgomery bus boycott (1955), 849–50, 856
Montgomery convention (1861), 443
Montgomery Improvement Association (MIA), 850
Montgomery Ward, 552, 553
Monticello, 237
Montreal, Canada, 54, 138, 157
Moody, Paul, 334
Moon, Sun Myung, 934
Moon landing (1969), 907
Moore, Amzie, 770
Moore, Milcah Martha, 147
Moore's Creek Bridge, Battle of (1776), 157
Moralism/morality, 366, 649, 687–88
Moral Majority, Inc., 932
Moral reform movement, 368–69
Moran, Thomas, 91, 290, 390, 537
Moravians, 243, 246
Morelos, José María, 241
Morgan, Albert, 499
Morgan, J.P., 555, 633
Morgan, Lewis Henry, 539
Morgan v. *Virginia*, 851–52, 866
Morgenthau, Henry, 744, 756
Morison, Peter A., 930
Morison, Samuel Eliot, 808
Mormonism, 370–71, 372, 381, 425, 523–24
Morrill, Justin, 571
Morrill Federal Land Grant Act (1862), 457, 533, 571
Morrill Tariff Act (1861), 457
Morris, Gouverneur, 184
Morris, Robert, 177, 197, 236, 330
Morristown, New Jersey, 169
Morse, Samuel F.B., 288
Moscow, siege of (1941), 774
Mose, Fort (Florida), 87
Moses, Bob, 867
Moskowitz, Belle, 703
Mossadegh, Mohammed, 835–36, 940
Mostel, Zero, 802
Motherhood, middle class, 345–46
Mother's Magazine, 346
Mother's Monthly Journal, 346
Motion Picture Producers and Distributors of America, 683
Motion pictures. *See* Movie industry
Mott, Lucretia, 352–53, 375
Moultrie, Fort, 157
Moundbuilding, 15, 16, 19
"Mountain men," 389–90
Mount Holyoke Female Seminary, 352, 367
Movie industry, 621–22, 674–75, 682–83, 688, 738–39, 801–2, 808, 829, 831
Moynihan, Daniel Patrick, 906, 927
MTV (Music Television), 963–64
Muckraking, 617–19
Muhammad, Elijah, 868
Muir, John, 634–35
Mulattoes, 39, 83, 99
Muller v. *Oregon*, 620
Munich conference (1938), 751–52
Munn v. *Illinois*, 586
Murphy, Edgar Gardner, 631
Murphy, Frank, 716
Murray, John, 140
Murray, Judith Sargent, 218, 219
Murray, Pauli, 467, 764
Murray, Philip, 798
Murrow, Edward R., 831
Musicals, movie, 739
Music and dance: African American, 89–90, 91, 701, 819, 827–28; bebop, 852; counterculture, 885; in Gilded Age, 570–71, 573; in Great Depression, 740–41; jazz, 686, 852; in Memphis, 818–19; music videos, 963–64; in 1950s, 818–19; in 1970s, 934; radio broadcasting and, 684; rock 'n' roll, 818–19, 827–28; swing era, 740–41; in the twenties, 686, 687, 701; in World War II, 766
Muskie, Edmund, 904
Muslim civilization, contact with, 29
Mussolini, Benito, 751, 755, 775
Mutual acculturation in the South, 90–91
Mutual aid societies (*mutualistas*), 699–700
My Lai Massacre (1968), 905

N

Na-Dene people, 7
Nagasaki, bombing of (1945), 782
Nantes, Edict of (1598), 40
Napoleon Bonaparte, 239–40, 241, 242
Napoleonic Wars, 242, 248, 249
Narraganset Indians, 22, 59, 61, 67, 113
Narrative of the Life of Frederick Douglass (Douglass), 421
Narváez, Pánfilo de, 37
Nash, Diane, 858
Nashville, Tennessee, 858
Nashville Junto, 267
Nasser, Gamal Abdel, 836–37
Nast, Thomas, 506
Natchez, Mississippi, 171, 295–96, 311, 315
Natchez Indians, 19, 87, 107, 295
Natchez Trace, 234
Nathan, Maud, 630
National Aeronautics and Space Administration (NASA), 841
National American Woman Suffrage Association, 589, 597, 654, 660–61, 669, 697; *See also* League of Women Voters
National Association for the Advancement of Colored People (NAACP), 611, 632–33, 665, 701, 764, 851
National Association of Colored Women, 597
National Association of Manufacturers, 627, 678
National bank, 282–83
National Board of Censorship (NBC), 621–22
National Board of Health, 564
National Broadcasting Company (NBC), 684, 740
National Child Labor Committee, 614
National Colored Farmers' Alliance, 589
National Commission on Neighborhoods, 929
National Committee for a Sane Nuclear Policy (SANE), 838
National Congress of American Indians (NCAI), 873–74
National Conservation Commission, 634
National Conservative Political Action Committee, 931–32
National Consumers' League (NCL), 614, 626, 630, 697
National Defense Act (1916), 651
National Defense Education Act (1958), 823, 825, 835
National Education Association, 571, 623
National Farmers' Alliance and Industrial Union, 586
National forests, creation of, 535–36
National Gazette, 216
National Guard, creation of, 587
National Housing Act: of 1937, 745; of 1949, 799
National Housing Agency, 761
National Indian Gaming Association, 963
National Indian Youth Council (NIYC), 874
National Industrial Recovery Act (1933), 725, 726, 727
National Institute of Mental Health, 826
National Institutes of Health, 826
Nationalism, 579–80; in art and architecture, 213–14; black cultural, 897–98; Chicano, 899–901; emergence of American, 141–42; post-revolutionary, 196, 201
National Labor Relations Act (1935), 715, 728, 742, 798, 799
National Labor Relations Board, 715, 728, 919
National Labor Union (NLU), 558
National Land Company, 530
National League, formation of, 575
National Mineral Act (1866), 506
National Municipal League, 616
National Negro Business League, 632
National Negro Conference (1909), 611, 633
National Negro Congress, 763
National Organization for Women (NOW), 898
National Origins Act (1929), 710
National parks, 535, 536, 537, 634–35
National Park Service, 635
National party system, crisis in, 429–34
National pastimes in Gilded Age, 573–75; *See also* Leisure activities
National progressivism, 633–38
National Reclamation Act (1902), 535, 536, 733
National Recovery Administration (NRA), 726, 741
National Republican Party, 268
National Road, 254, 267, 271, 272, 273, 279
National Security Act (1947), 792, 800–801
National Security Council (NSC), 801; NSC-68, 792, 811
National Security League, 651
National Socialists (Nazis), 751, 775–76, 778–79, 986; *See also* World War II
National states, rise of, 30
National Trades Union, 365
National Union for Social Justice, 726
National War Labor Board (NWLB), 658, 677–78, 756, 760
National Welfare Rights Organization (NWRO), 926

National Woman's Loyal League, 491
National Woman's Party (NWP), 660, 661, 697
National Woman Suffrage Association (NWSA), 491–92, 588–89
National Women's Alliance, 589
National Youth Administration, 757
Nation of Islam (NOI), 868
Native American Rights Fund (NARF), 874, 902
Native Americans, 1–23; *See also* Archaic period; *specific tribes*; in agrarian republic (1790–1824), 243–47; American Revolution and, 172–73, 179, 182; blood types, 4; in Chesapeake region, 54–55; civil rights movement and, 873–74; Civil War and, 462–63, 514; death rates among, 927; Deerfield raid, 104–5; disease and, 34, 35, 37, 59, 60–61, 107, 140, 230; Dunmore's War and, 140–41; education of, 541; endurance and rejuvenation, 542–44; ethnographic studies of, 538–39; European struggle over the West and, 139–41; French and Indian War, 135–41; gambling casinos and, 961–63; Ghost Dance, 541–42; horses and, 36–37, 107, 108; Indian America, region of, 106–8; Indian removal policy, 280–82, 298, 391–92, 516; Indian Wars, 518–20; Jackson and, 280–82, 517; under Jefferson, 243–46, 280; King Philip's War and, 66, 67–68, 125; Lewis and Clark expedition and, 229–30; massacre at Gnadenhutten (1782), 194; in the military, 770; mission system and, 110–11, 232; New Deal for, 734–35; in New England, 60–61, 113; in New France, 53; in New Mexico, 52–53; in Northeast, 21–22; Oklahoma Land Rush and, 514–15; Paxton Boys massacre, 140; photography and study of, 539; population, 17, 18, 36, 107; pre 1500, 1–23; Puritans and, 60–61; in Queen Anne's War, 95; Red Power movement, 900, 901–2; reform policy and politics, 539–41; regional cultures, beginnings of, 6–10; religion, 12–13; relocation programs for, 873; reservations, 517–18, 520, 542, 543, 735; runaway slaves and, 91; settlement of continent, 3–6; slavery of, 85, 87; slave trade, 68–69; in South, 19–21; in Southwest, 13–14, 17–19; stereotypical view of, 2; Supreme Court rulings on, 281, 517; termination policy and, 873–74, 961; transformation of societies of, 539–45; trans-Mississippi West development and, 516–20, 539–45; treaties with, 205; tribal names, origins of some, 4; tribal sovereignty of, 961–63; warfare among, 16–17; War of 1812 and, 248; wars in the South, 68–69; Washington presidency and, 204–5; westward expansion and, 234, 245, 246; in World War II, 758
Nativism, 382–83, 431–32, 595, 699, 709
Nat Turner's Revolt, 310
Naturalization Act: of 1740, 222; of 1798, 210, 222–23
"Nature" (Emerson), 347
Naumkeag. *See* Salem, Massachusetts
Navajo Indians, 7, 19, 51, 463, 543–44, 735
Naval war: in American Revolution, 171; in Civil War, 463–64; in War of 1812, 248–49; in World War I, 655; in World War II, 774, 776–78
Navigation Acts (1651–1696), 69, 96
Navy, creation of, 157
Navy Nurse Corps, 768
Nazis (National Socialists), 751, 775–76, 778–79, 986
Negro Family: The Case for National Action (Moynihan), 927
Negro Leagues, 575
Negro National League, 687
Negro Youth Council, 804
Neighborhood Playhouse, 611
Neighborhood Youth Corps, 889
Nelson, Gaylor, 929
Nelson, Willie, 935
Nemattanew, 56
Nembe, African state of, 82
Neolin (Delaware Prophet), 139
"Neolithic Revolution," 11
Netherlands, 58–59; Anglo-Dutch Wars, 65, 94; New Netherland colony, 64–65; slave trade and, 76, 79
Neutrality: neutral shipping rights, 242, 243; Washington's proclamation of (1793), 204; World War I and, 650–52
Neutrality Acts (1935, 1936, 1937, 1939), 752, 753
Nevelson, Louise, 736
Nevers, Ernie, 687
New Amsterdam, 64–65
Newburgh, New York, 178–79
New Deal, 722–35; *See also* Great Depression; Roosevelt, Franklin D.; confidence restoration and, 723–24; critics of, 726–27; first, 722–26; First Hundred Days, 724–26; labor movement and, 729; legislation, 724–28; minorities and, 743–44; New Deal coalition, 716, 729–30, 799; presidential election of 1936 and, 728, 729–30; recession in, 744–45; second, 726–35; Second Hundred Days, 727–29; Supreme Court packing and, 741–42; in the West, 730–35; women's network, 742–43
New England: southern slavery and industrialization of, 300; textile industry in, 682
New England colonies: community life in, 61–63; culture of region, 112–13; dissent in, 63–64; early contacts in, 58–59; English colonies, 58–64; fur trade and, 236; government of, 112–13; Great Awakening in, 127; Indians and, 60–61; King Philip's War and, 66, 67–68; Massachusetts Bay Colony, 59–60; Plymouth Colony, 59; Puritans in, 58, 59–63, 66, 67–68, 112–13, 125; shipbuilding industry, 97; slave trade in, 79, 97; urban development in, 122–23
New-England Courant, 142
New England Emigrant Aid Society, 430–31
New England Female Labor Reform Association, 341
New England Freedmen's Aid Society, 474
Newfoundland, 95
New France, 52, 53–54, 69, 104, 111, 120, 121
New Frontier liberalism, 840–41
New Hampshire: abolition of slavery in, 186; colony of, 64
New Harmony, Indiana, 370
New Immigrants (1860–1930), 708–13
New Jersey: colony of, 65; constitution of, 184; revolutionary campaign for, 168–69; slavery in, 87
New Jersey Plan, 197–98
Newlands Reclamation Act (1902), 635
New Lights, 127, 128
Newman, Pauline, 626
New Mexico, colony of, 52–53, 87, 109
New Nationalism, 636, 637
New Netherland, 64–65
New Orleans, battle of (1815), 248, 249
New Orleans, Louisiana, 138, 206, 234; American Revolution and, 171, 177; capture of (1862), 462; founding of, 87; French legacy in, 232–33; growth of, 300, 354
Newport, Rhode Island, 87–88, 171, 567
New Right, 931–34
New South, 564–67, 631
New Spain, 108, 120, 121, 123, 171, 205–6, 232
Newspapers: antislavery, 319; chains, 685; colonial, 141–42; ethnic, 709; growth of (1810–1835), 287–88; Indian, 281; "penny papers," 360, 406; political party, 268; post-revolutionary liberty of press, 216; in the twenties, 684–85
New Sweden, 115
Newton, Huey P., 897
Newton, Isaac, 124
New York: colony of, 65, 67, 113–14; constitution of, 184; in 1800, 234; Erie Canal and, 262, 273–74, 275, 279, 355, 356, 369–70, 380, 508; growth in nineteenth-century, 354; ratification of Constitution, 199; revolutionary campaign for, 168–69; slavery in, 87
New York Bureau of Municipal Research, 616
New York City: bohemian community, 628–29; Central Park, 571; colonial, 114; depression of 1873 and, 507–8; draft riots in Civil War, 471; garment industry, 626; Harlem, 700–701; Irish immigrants in, 380; labor movement in, 587–88; Lower East Side, 610–11, 615; machine politics in, 615–16; police force, creation of, 361; politics in nineteenth-century, 364–65; popular culture in, 358–59; riot of 1834, 375; slave uprising in (1712), 92; strikes in (1833–1837), 363–64; Tammany Hall, 584, 587, 616, 703; as temporary capital, 200; Tompkins Square Riot (1874), 587; wealth in (1828–1845), 342
New York Sons of Liberty, 151
New York State Factory Investigation Commission, 626
New York Stock Exchange, 507
Nez Percé Indians, 520
Nez Percé Treaty (1863), 540
Ng, Wing, 990–91
Niagara movement, 632, 633
Nicaragua, 646, 692, 938, 955
Nicholas II, Czar, 668
Nickelodeons, 682
Niebuhr, Reinhold, 798
Nimitz, Chester, 777
Nineteenth Amendment, 377, 661
Nixon, E.D., 850
Nixon, Richard M.: *See also* Watergate scandal; Checkers speech, 814, 832; dirty tricks under, 907–10; domestic policy of, 906–7; election of, 903; election of 1960 and, 839–40; fiscal policy of, 906; foreign policy of, 905–6, 907; Hiss case and, 802; presidency, 903–7; resignation of, 908, 910; Southern strategy of, 903–4; Supreme Court and, 906; as vice-president, 837, 838; as vice–presidential candidate, 812, 814, 831–32; Vietnam War and, 904–5
Noble, Elizabeth, 737
No Man's Land, 514–15
Nonimportation, associations of, 146–47
Non-Importation Act (1806), 242
Non-Intercourse Act (1809), 243
Non-violent resistance, 856
Norfolk, Virginia, 157
Normal schools, 572
Norris, George W., 725
North, Frederick, Lord, 149, 151, 153, 170, 171, 175
North, Oliver, 957–58
North, Simeon, 336, 337
North, the: *See also* Civil War; Great Migration to, 664–65; investment in New South, 564–65; Reconstruction in, 504–9; revolutionary campaigns of 1777, 169–70; slavery and, 87–88, 423–24
North Africa, World War II in, 774
North American Free Trade Agreement (NAFTA), 978–79
North American Review, 288–89
Northampton, Massachusetts, 126
North Atlantic Treaty Organization (NATO), 792, 794–95
North Carolina: colonial, 64; Culpeper's Rebellion, 68; declaration of independence (1776), 158; ratification of Constitution, 199; secession of, 452
Northeast Territory, 179–82
Northern Farmers' Alliance, 586
Northern Flint (maize), 15
Northern Pacific Railroad, 507
Northern Securities Company, 633
Northern Securities v. *U.S.*, 634
North Korea, 809
Northup, Solomon, 305, 306, 427
North West Company, 389
Northwest Confederation, 243, 246
Northwest Indians, 544
Northwest Ordinance (1787), 180–81, 182, 256, 529
Northwest Territory, 180–81

Notes on the State of Virginia (Jefferson), 226–27
Novak, Anna, 721
Nova Scotia, 155
Novels, 218, 289–90, 346–47, 537–38; *See also* Literature
Noyes, John Humphrey, 370
NSC-68, 792, 811
Nuclear arms race, 796
Nuclear power: mobilizations against, 915; Three Mile Island, 914–15
Nuclear Regulatory Commission, 914
Nuclear weapons, 749–50, 780–82, 805
Nullification crisis, 249, 279–80
Nuremberg Laws, 752
Nuremberg trials (1945–1946), 789–90
Nurses and nursing, 468–69, 571, 610, 611, 768
Nye, Gerald P., 752

O

Oakley, Annie, 538
Oak Ridge, Tennessee, 758
Oberlin College, 352, 373
Occupational Safety and Health Administration, 906
Ochoa, Estevan, 525
Ochoa, Victor Orozco, 928
Ochs, Phil, 885
O'Connor, Basil, 723
Odets, Clifford, 738
Office of Economic Opportunity (OEO), 888
Office of Inter-American Affairs, 765
Office of Price Administration (OPA), 756
Office of Strategic Services (OSS), 756
Office of War Information (OWI), 756, 759
Office of War Mobilization (OWM), 756
Oglethorpe, James Edward, 86
O'Hara, Charles, 175
Ohio, 15, 16; *See also* Cincinnati, Ohio; canal system, 274–75; French and Indian War in, 136
Ohio Company, 136, 137, 140, 182
Ohio Indians, 137, 139, 173, 179, 182
Oil crisis (1973), 916–17, 918–19
Oil industry, 506
Ojibwas, 21
Okinawa, invasion of (1945), 778
Oklahoma Land Rush, 514–15
Old Cordilleran Culture, 9
Old Lights, 127
Old Northwest, 264, 276–77
Old South Church (Boston), 150
Old Southwest, 264, 297–98
Oligopoly, 677
Oliphant v. *Suquamish Indian Tribe*, 927
Olive Branch Petition, 156, 157
Oliver, Andrew, 144
Olmsted, Frederick Law, 449, 562
Olney, Richard C., 590
Olympic Games boycott (1984), 954
Omaha Act (1882), 539
Omnibus Reconciliation Act (1981), 950
Oñate, Juan de, 52–53
Oneida Community, 370
Oneida Indians, 21, 173, 179
O'Neill, Eugene, 703
O'Neill, George, 934
O'Neill, Nena, 934
Onondagas, 21
"On the Equality of the Sexes" (Wollstonecraft), 218
On the Road (Kerouac), 833
OPEC, 916, 919
Opechancanough, 55, 56
Open Door policy, 601, 646–47, 648
Open Marriage: A New Life Style for Couples (O'Neill & O'Neill), 934
Open shop, 627, 678
Operation Breadbasket, 897
Operation Desert Shield, 973
Operation Desert Storm, 973–74
Operation Ranch Hand, 882
Operation Rolling Thunder, 882, 885
Operation Torch, 774
Operation Wetback, 871–72
Oppenheimer, J. Robert, 750, 786
Oraibi, Arizona, 18
Oral cultures, 116
Ordinance of Nullification, 280
Oregon, 254, 255–56, 396–97; Overland Trails to, 394–96; settlement of, 396–97
Organization Man (Whyte), 825
Organization of Afro-American Unity, 869
Organization of Petroleum Exporting Countries (OPEC), 916, 919
Organized crime, prohibition and, 692–93
Organized labor. *See* Labor movement; Union(s)
Origin of Species, The (Darwin), 696
Orlando, Vittorio, 666
Orozco, José Clemente, 737
Orrick, John, 482
Orwell, George, 770
Ostend Manifesto, 428
O'Sullivan, John, 392, 394, 515
Oswald, Lee Harvey, 845
Oswego, fort of, 138
Otis, Harrison Gray, 628
Otis, James, Jr., 143, 144, 148, 167
Ottawa Indians, 112, 139–40
Our Girls Cooperative Manufacturing Company, 558
Outsourcing, 917–18
Outwork system, 332, 556
Overland Trails, 392, 394–96
Overton, John, 267
Owen, Robert, 370

P

Pacific, imperialism in, 599–601
Pacific Northwest, Spanish in, 232
Pacific Railroad surveys, 390
Pacific Railway Act (1862), 504
Packard, Vance, 832
Packingtown, Chicago, 548–49
Pahlavi, Shah Mohammed Reza, 836, 940
Paige, Satchel, 687
Paine, Thomas, 157–58, 216
Painting. *See* Art
Palace of Governors (Santa Fé), 50, 51
Palestine Liberation Organization (PLO), 939
Palmer, A. Mitchell, 669
Palmer, Potter, 567
Pan-African Congress, 667
Panama, Isthmus of, 33
Panama, Republic of, 645
Panama Canal, 645, 936
Pan-American Conference (1889–1890), 600
Panetta, Leon, 950
Panic: of 1819, 250, 256; of 1837, 284–85, 368, 392, 394; of 1857, 436–37; of 1873, 587
Pan-Indian strategy, 246–47, 248
Pantheism, 13
Panyaring (kidnapping), 80
Paoli, battle of (1777), 169
Papago people, 13, 17
Parent-Teacher Association, 669
Paris, France, 775–76
Paris, Treaty of: of 1763, 138; of 1783, 177, 187, 205
Paris Peace Agreement (1973), 905
Parke, Robert, 224
Parker, Alton B., 634
Parker, Charlie, 852
Parker, Junior, 819
Parker, Theodore, 438
Parker, William H., 892
Parks: national, 536, 537; urban, 572–73
Parks, Rosa, 849
Parliament, English, 133, 143–45
Parsons, Talcott, 807
Party system. *See* Political parties
Passaic, New Jersey, 709
Passing of the Great Race, The (Grant), 693
Paternalism, 315–16, 326
Paterson, New Jersey, 629
Paterson, William, 197
Patriarchy, 329, 338–39, 898
Patriots in American Revolution, 164, 165–67
Patronage system, 239, 262–63
Patrons of Husbandry. *See* Grange movement
Patterson, Joseph M., 684
Patton, George S., 779
Patuxet Indians, 59
Paul, Alice, 660, 697
Pawnee Indians, 4, 516
Pawtuckets, 60
Paxton Boys, 140
Payne, Alexander Spotswood, 99
Payne, John Robert Dandridge, 99
Peace Corps, 840
Peace Democrats (Copperheads), 469–70
Peace movement of 1960s, 883–88
Peace of Utrecht (1713), 94
Peale, Charles Wilson, 213–14
Peale, Norman Vincent, 823
Pea Ridge, battle at (1862), 462
Pearl Harbor, 754, 755
Pendleton, George H., 584
Pendleton Civil Service Reform Act (1883), 270, 584
Penn, William, 65, 70, 114, 222, 223
Pennsylvania: abolition of slavery in, 186; backcountry, 114–15; colony of, 65–66, 114, 223; constitution of, 183–84; founding of, 65–66; ratification of Constitution, 199; Whiskey Rebellion in, 194–95, 207
Pennsylvania Gazette, 142
Pennsylvania Railroad, 505
"Penny press," 360, 406
Pensacola, Florida, 108, 171
Pension Act (1890), 581–82
Pentagon, 800
Pentagon Papers, 907–8
People's Party. *See* Populism
People the Best Governors, The, 183
Pepperell, William, 168
Pequot Indians, 22, 61, 113
Pequot War (1637), 61, 67
Peralta, Pedro de, 53
Perfectionism, doctrine of, 366
Perkins, Frances, 626, 703, 729, 743
Perot, H. Ross, 977
Perry, David, 141
Perry, J.H., 23
Perry, Matthew, 410
Perry, Oliver H., 248
Pershing, John J., 648–49, 656
Persian Gulf war (1991), 972–75
Peter, Paul, and Mary, 885
Petersburg, siege of (1864), 476
Peter the Great, Tsar, 231
Phelps, Anson, 331
Phelps-Dodge mining company, 643–44
Philadelphia, Pennsylvania: in American Revolution, 169–70; antiblack riots (1820–1859), 362; colonial, 66, 114; Constitutional Convention at, 196–98; in 1800, 234; founding of, 65; immigrants in, 711–12; nineteenth-century growth in, 354; slavery in, 87; yellow fever epidemic of 1793, 356
Philadelphia Anti-Slavery Society, 374, 375
Philadelphia Female Anti-Slavery Society, 376
Philadelphia Negro, The (Du Bois), 632
Philip II of Spain, King, 45
Philippines, 603–4, 770–71, 796–97
Philippine Sea, battle of the (1944), 778
Phillips, David Graham, 618
Phillips, Wendell, 437, 540
Phillips, William, 430
Phonograph, 686
Photography, 475, 539, 737

Phyfe, Duncan, 330, 342
Pickett, George, 473
Pickett's Charge (1863), 473
Pickford, Mary, 683
Piecework, 339
Piedmont region, 84, 566–67
Pierce, Franklin, 427, 428, 433
Pierce, William, 931
Pike, Zebulon, 390, 391, 397
Pilgrims, 59
Pima Indians, 5, 13, 17, 18, 110, 542
Pinchot, Gifford, 634–35
Pinckney, Charles Cotesworth, 212, 242, 243
Pinckney, Elizabeth Lucas, 85
Pinckney, Thomas, 208
Pinckney's Treaty (1796), 208, 232
Pioneers, 394–97
Pioneer's Search for an Ideal Home, A (Judson), 394–95
Pitcher, Molly, 167
Pitt, Fort, 138, 140
Pitt, William, 137, 145, 153, 170
Pittsburgh, Pennsylvania, 195
Pittsburgh Gazette, 216
Plague, 59
Plains Indians, 516; use of horse by, 107, 108
Plano, Texas, 981–82
Plano technology, 7
Plantation system, 74–75, 88, 115–16, 235; economics of, 299–300; plantation life, 315–17; sugar, 76–77; tobacco, 84–85
Planter class, 98, 296, 313–17, 485–86
Platt, Orville H., 603
Pleistocene epoch, 4, 6–7
"Pleistocene Overkill," 6
Plessy v. *Ferguson*, 596, 852
Plow, Deere's "singing", 532
"Plumbers, the," 907
Plunkitt, George Washington, 615
Plymouth Colony, 59
Pocahontas, 55
Poe, Edgar Allan, 360
Poems on Various Subjects, Religious and Moral (Wheatley), 186–87
Poindexter, John, 957, 958
Point Loma, California, community, 580
Poland, 752, 971
Police force, creation of, 361
Police Gazette, 360
Poliomyelitis vaccine, 826
Political machines, 364–65, 584, 615–16
Political parties, 208–13; *See also* Congressional elections; Presidential elections; *specific parties*; crisis in national party system (1850s), 429–34; mass campaign techniques, 268; in Reconstruction South, 498–502; rise of, 208–9; Second American Party System, 263, 285–87; slavery and, 422; as state or local organizations, 583–84
Politics: African Americans and, 497–98, 499, 927; artisanal, 362–63; in Civil War, 469–70; colonial, 119–23, 142; of emancipation, 464–65; grass-roots, 927–31; Great Awakening, 128–29; in Great Depression, 737–38; growth of democracy and new, 263, 264–69; of identity, 895–902; Irish immigrants in, 380–81; labor movement and, 587; late nineteenth-century, 583–85; machine, 364–65, 584, 615–16; of manifest destiny, 410–13; mass, 267–68; mass participation, 263; newspapers and interest in, 287–88; of Reconstruction, 484–92, 498–504; of reform, 589, 593–97; spoils system in, 269–70, 584–85; in states during revolution, 182–89; television and, 831–32, 964; urban, 362–65; women and, 266, 742–43
Polk, James K., 397, 402, 403, 404–6, 411, 524
Pollock, Jackson, 736
Pollution, 564, 891; air, 564; water, 563–64, 734
Polygamy, Mormon, 425, 523–24
Polygyny in West Africa, 77
Ponce de León, Juan, 37
Pontiac, Chief, 139–40
Poor People's Campaign, 894
Poor Richard's Almanac, 125
Pope, John, 461
Popé (Franciscan priest), 51
Popular culture, 358–60, 570–71, 631–32, 765–66, 808, 964
"Popular Front" period, 738
Popular sovereignty, 413, 435–36
Population: colonial, 36, 84, 85, 119–20; in 1800, 219; in 1850, 421; Native American, 17, 18, 36, 107; percent by ancestry (1500–1975), 39; slave, 85, 301; urban, 559–62, 693
Population density, 17, 18
Populism, 589, 590, 593, 594–95, 597
Porter, David, 477
Port Huron Statement, The, 879–80
Portolá, Gaspar de, 110
Port Royal, 69, 95, 464
Portugal: explorations, 30–31; slave trade and, 76, 77
Potatoes, 10, 36
Potawatomie Creek, massacre at (1856), 431, 434
Potawatomi Indians, 22, 112, 243, 246
Potlatch ceremonies, 544
Potsdam Conference (1945), 780, 790
Potter, David, 337
Pound, Ezra, 703
Poverty: cause of, 889; feminization of, 926; homelessness, 966–67; in 1970s, 924–27; percentage in, 968–69; war on, 888–92
Poverty Point, Louisiana, 2, 15
Powderly, Terence V., 558, 579
Powell, Adam Clayton, Jr., 851
Powell, Bud, 852
Powell, Colin, 974
Powell, John Wesley, 390
Power Elite, The (Mills), 825
Power loom, invention of, 334
Power of Sympathy, The (Brown), 218
Powers, Francis Gary, 835
Powhatan, 22, 54–55
Prairie du Chien, 112
Pratt, Micajah, 331
Predestination, Calvinist theology of, 125
Preface to Morals, A (Lippmann), 703
Pregnancy, teenage, 926
Preindustrial city, 354
Preindustrial ways of working, 327–30
Premarital sex, 688, 884–85
Prentiss, Benjamin, 448
Pre-revolutionary period, 132–59; American nationalism, emergence of, 141–42; Boston Tea Party, 150–51; British imperial crisis in, 141–49; Continental Congress, first, 133–34, 152–53; Continental Congress, second, 155–59; Declaration of Independence, 158–59, 168; intercolonial cooperation in, 149–50; Lexington and Concord, battles of, 153–54; rebellion in, 149–59; republicanism in, 142; Seven Years War in America, 135–41, 142, 232
Presbyterian Church, 113, 114, 244, 346, 422
Preservationists, urban, 928
Preservation of environment, 634–36
Presidency, 200–201
Presidential activism, 633–38
Presidential Commission on the Status of Women, 840
Presidential elections: of 1796, 209; of 1800, 211–13; of 1804, 242; of 1808, 243; of 1812, 247; of 1816, 253–54; of 1824, 266–67; of 1828, 268–69; of 1832, 283; of 1836, 283–84; of 1840, 286–87; of 1844, 402–3; of 1848, 412–13; of 1852, 428; of 1856, 432–34; of 1860, 438–40, 441; of 1864, 475–76; of 1868, 490, 582; of 1872, 506–7, 582; of 1876, 508–9, 582; of 1880, 582, 584; of 1884, 582; of 1888, 582; of 1892, 582, 589, 593; of 1896, 582, 594–95; of 1900, 582; of 1908, 636; of 1912, 636–37; of 1916, 651–52; of 1920, 669–70; of 1924, 690; of 1928, 703–5, 707; of 1932, 722; of 1936, 728, 729–30; of 1940, 753; of 1944, 779–80; of 1948, 798–99; of 1952, 811–14, 820, 832; of 1960, 839–40, 859–60; of 1964, 869; of 1976, 923–24; of 1980, 940–41, 949; of 1984, 952–53; of 1988, 969–70; of 1992, 976–77; of 1996, 979–83
President's Committee on Civil Rights, 851
President's Emergency Committee for Unemployment, 721
President's Organization for Unemployment Relief (POUR), 721
Presidios, 109
Presley, Elvis, 818–19, 827, 828, 831
Presotta, Rose, 716
Press, the: *See also* Newspapers; colonial, 141–42; liberty of, 215–18
Price, Hickman, 681
Primary, direct, 617
Princeton, New Jersey, 169
Princeton University, 126
Print revolution, 287–88
Prisoners of war (POW), World War II, 770–71
Prisons, 366, 369
Pritchett, Laurie, 861
Proclamation of Amnesty and Reconstruction, 485
Prodigy, 947
Production: control shifted from artisan to capitalist, 333; mass-production system, 679; standardized, 337
Production lines, 551
Professional Air Traffic Controllers Organization (PATCO) strike, 950
Professionalism, civil service reform and, 584–85
Professional training, 571
Progress and Poverty (George), 587
Progressive diplomacy, 644
Progressive Era (1900–1917), 609–38; education standardization in, 622–23; environmental activism in, 634–36; intellectual trends in, 619–20; journalism in, 617–19; labor movement in, 627–29; leisure in, redemption of, 621–22; national progressivism, 633–38; political progressives and urban reform in, 616; presidential activism in, 633–36; presidential election of 1912, 636–37; prohibition movement, 620–21; prostitution in, 621; racism in, 631–33; social control and its limits in, 620–23; social reform in, 614–20; states in, 616–17; themes of, 612–14; trustbusting in, 633–34; urban machine in, 615–16; Wilson's first term, 637–38; women and, 614–15, 630–31; working-class communities in, 623–29
Prohibition, 620–21, 661, 692–93
Promysbleniki (fur trappers), 231
Property ownership, expectation of, 119
Proposition 13 (California), 931
Proposition 187 (California), 971
"Proprietary colonies," 57
Proslavery arguments, 318–20
Prosser, Gabriel, 309
Prostitution, 368–69, 527, 621
Protestant Association, 69
Protestantism, 40, 253, 612
Protestant Reformation, 40, 43, 126–29
Protest movements of 1960s, 891–94, 896; American Indian Movement (AIM), 901–2; anti–Vietnam War, 883–88; by Asian Americans, 902–3; Black Power, 895–98; by Chicanos, 899–901; Free speech movement, 884; gay liberation movement, 899; SDS, 879–80, 883; women's liberation movement, 898–99
Providence, Rhode Island, 63
Public education. *See* Education
Public health, 661–63, 762; *See also* Health care and medicine
Public space in Gilded Age, 572–73

Public Works Administration (PWA), 725, 726, 733, 744
Puebla, battle of (1862), 526
Pueblo Bonito (Chaco Canyon), 14
Pueblo Indians, 14, 18–19, 50–53, 109
Pueblo Revolt, 87
Puerto Ricans, 872–73, 986
Pullman, George, 591
Pullman Palace Car Company, 591
Pullman strike (1894), 591–92
Pure Food and Drug Act (1906), 634
Puritans, 58, 59–63, 66, 67–68, 112–13, 125
Putnam, Frederick Ward, 598
Putting-out system, 331–32
Puzzled America (Anderson), 737
Pyle, Ernie, 768

Q

Quakers, 65, 87, 113, 114, 234, 243, 246, 353, 370, 371, 518
Quality circles, 918
Quantrill, William, 462
Quapaw Indians, 542
Quartering Act, 152
Quayle, Dan, 970
Quebec, 53, 112, 155
Quebec, Battle of (1759), 138
Quebec Act (1774), 152
Quebec City, 54
Queen Anne's War, 94, 95
Quincy, Josiah, Jr., 149
Quotas, immigration, 694

R

Race riots, 664–65, 763–64, 769, 891–92
Racial Darwinism, 631
Racial violence, 596–97
Racism: in 1890s, 595; Mexican immigrants and, 699; in military, 655; in Progressive Era, 631–33; reform campaigns and, 617; scientific, 693, 709
Rader, Melvin, 786
Radical Reconstruction, 498
Radical Republicans, 485, 487–89
Radio broadcasting, 658, 674, 683–84, 687, 740, 830
Radio Corporation of America (RCA), 658, 677
Ragtime, 570–71, 573
Railroad car, refrigerated, 549
Railroads, 278, 279; expansion in Reconstruction period, 504–6; Great Plains settlement and, 530; in Reconstruction South, 500; routes, 521; standardization of, 276; strikes against, 504, 587; transcontinental, 395, 429, 457, 504–6, 516, 550; transportation revolution and, 275–76; in the twenties, 682
Railroad Telegrapher, 606
Raines, Mary, 304
Raleigh, Walter, 26–27, 44, 45
Raleigh Tavern, 152
Rancherias, 18
Rand, Ayn, 802
Randolph, A. Philip, 701, 763, 864
Randolph, Edmund, 197, 198, 201
Randolph, John, 243
"Range wars" of 1870s, 528
Rankin, Jeannette, 755
Ransom, John Crowe, 703
Rape of slaves, 317
Rappe, Virginia, 683
Raskob, John J., 704, 717
Ray, James Earl, 894
Reagan, Ronald, 802, 923, 940–41; as California governor, 949; Central American policy under, 954–55; communism and, 953–56; economy under, 951–52; foreign policy, 953–58; as great communicator, 948–49; Iran-Contra scandal and, 956–58; military buildup under, 950; presidency, 945–58; spending cuts under, 950; tax cuts under, 950; terrorism and, 956–57
Reagan Doctrine, 954
Reagonomics, 949–51
Reaper, 532–33
Reason, Patrick, 373
Recall, 617
Recession: of 1833–1834, 284; in 1930s, 744–45
Reconquista (Reconquest), 31
Reconstruction (1863–1877), 484–509, 510; Congressional, 489–90; constitutional amendments (1865–1870), 486, 489, 490, 491; crop lien system and, 502–4; impeachment crisis, 489–90; Johnson and, 486–87; Lincoln's plan for, 485–86; meaning of freedom and, 492–98; in North, 504–9; politics of, 484–92; Radical Republicans and, 487–89; Republican Party and, 498–99; resistance to, 500–502; in South, 482–83, 484–85, 498–504; woman suffrage and, 490–92
Reconstruction Acts (1867, 1868), 482, 498
Reconstruction Finance Corporation (RFC), 721–22
Recording industry, 686
Red Cloud, 518, 519
Red Eagle, 248
Redeemed Captive Returning to Zion, The (Williams), 104, 125
Red Power movement, 900, 901–2
Red Record, A (Wells), 597
Redress and Reparations Movement, 902
Red River War (1874–1875), 520
Red Scares, 669, 694, 801–5
Red Shirts, 565
Red Sticks, 248
Red Strings, 472
Reeb, James J., 870
Reed, James, 667
Reed, John, 629
Reese, Brister, 483
Reese, Fred, 869
Referendum, 617
Reform. *See* Social reform movements
Reformation, Protestant, 40, 43, 126–29
Reform politics, 589, 593–97
Refugee Relief Act (1953), 986
Refugees, 380, 986, 988
Reggan, John, 458
Regional specialization in agriculture, 277
Regulation: British colonial, 95–97; under Eisenhower administration, 820–21; in Progressive Era, 621–22, 633–34
Reich, Charles, 885
Reid, Whitelaw, 564
Religion: African American, 89, 307–8, 362, 494; American Revolution and, 185; apocalyptic, 369–70; in Cold War, 807; decline in colonial America, 125–26; disagreements about slavery, 422; efforts to Christianize Indians, 243–44; evangelism, 343–44, 365–67, 598–99, 931–32; fundamentalism in the twenties, 695–96; Great Awakening, 126–29, 185, 307; liberal religious groups, 353; of middle class, 343–44; in Middle colonies, 114; Native American, 12–13; in New England, 63, 113; Second Great Awakening, 253, 343; of slaves, 89; social gospel movement, 592–93, 612; suburban life and, 823
Relocation programs, Indian, 873
Remington, Frederic, 538–39
Renaissance, 29–30
Reparations, World War I, 667, 690–91
"Report on Manufactures" (Hamilton), 203
"Report on the Public Credit" (Hamilton), 202
Representative government, 123, 143
Reproduction, colonial patterns of, 116–17
Republican agrarianism, 237–38
Republicanism, 142, 199
Republican Party, 365; *See also* Congressional elections; Political parties; Presidential elections; founding of, 432–34; freedmen in, 483; Liberal Republicans, 506–7; Lincoln presidency and, 457; overview of, 433; post–World War II, 798; in Reconstruction South, 498–502; Roosevelt and split in, 636; slavery and, 419
Reservations, Indian, 517–18, 520, 542, 543, 735
Reserve Officer Training Corps, 767–68
Resettlement Administration (RA), 728, 731
Resistance in the Army (RITA), 887
Restoration Colonies, 64–66
Retirees in Sunbelt, 920
Reuther, Walter, 798, 865
Revels, Hiram R., 499
Revenue Act (1962), 841
Revere, Paul, 68, 149, 155, 342
Revivalism. *See* Great Awakening
Revolutionary war. *See* American Revolution
Revolutions of 1848, 410
Reykjavík, 956
Rhee, Syngman, 809
Rhode Island: abolition of slavery in, 186; colony of, 63, 70; Constitutional Convention and, 196; currency law in, 188–89; rejection of Constitution, 199; slavery in, 87–88
Rhode Island State Gazette, 142
Ribault, Jean, 40–41
Ribicoff, Abraham, 895
Rice, Grantland, 687
Rice production, 36, 74–75, 85–86
Richardson, H.H., 567
Richelieu, Armand Jean du Plessis, 111
Richmond Enquirer, 438
Ridgway, Matthew, 809
Riesman, David, 825
Rifles, 467
Rights, states', 422–23, 435, 458, 484; *See also* Civil rights movement (1957–1962); Women's movement
Rights of Man, The (Paine), 216
Riis, Jacob, 618
Riley, Benjamin F., 440
Riley, James Whitcomb, 592
Ring shout, 89
Riots, 382, 472; race, 664–65, 763–64, 769, 891–92; urban, 361, 362, 431, 471, 891–92; zoot-suit, 764–65
Rivera, Diego, 737
Roads, 254, 272–73, 278, 822; National Road, 254, 267, 271, 272, 273, 279
Roanoke Island, 26–27, 45
"Roaring Twenties," 682, 687–88
Roberts, Percy, 495
Robertson, Pat, 932, 977
Robeson, Paul, 701, 804
Robinson, Jackie, 852
Robinson, Jo Ann, 850
Robinson, Ruby Doris, 867
Rochambeau, Comte de, 175
Roche, Thomas C., 475
Rochester, New York, 342, 343
Rockefeller, John D., 506, 550, 553, 554, 676
Rockefeller, John D., Jr., 627
Rockefeller, Nelson, 922
Rockingham, Lord, 145, 170, 175
Rockne, Knute, 687
Rock 'n' roll, 818–19, 827–28
Rocky Mountain Fur Company, 389
Rocky Mountains, 392, 537
Rocky Mountain School, 537
Roebling, John, 562
Roebling, Washington, 562
Roe v. Wade, 933–34
Roger, Ginger, 802
Rogers, Edith Nourse, 768
Rolfe, John, 55
Roman Catholic Church, 123–24; abortion and, 933–34; authority of, 28, 29, 30; in Maryland colony, 57; in Mexicanos community, 526; mission system and, 110–11; nativism and anti-Catholic feelings, 432, 709; Quebec Act and,

Roman Catholic Church *(cont.)*
152; slavery and, 86–87; social gospel movement and, 593
Rome-Berlin Axis, 751
Romero, Oscar, 955
Rommel, Edwin, 774
Roosevelt, Eleanor, 723, 742, 743, 789, 798, 840
Roosevelt, Franklin D., 737; *See also* New Deal; Atlantic Charter and, 754; atomic bomb and, 749; biographical information on, 722–23; "Black Cabinet" of, 744; court packing and, 741–42; death of, 779; election of 1932, 722; election of 1936, 730; fireside chats of, 723; as governor, 723; polio of, 723; postwar diplomatic plans of, 790; race issues and, 763; World War II and, 753–58, 774, 778–79
Roosevelt, James, 722
Roosevelt, Kermit, 835
Roosevelt, Sara Delano, 722
Roosevelt, Theodore, 537, 539, 587, 644; foreign policy of, 645–46; muckrakers and, 618; New Nationalism of, 636, 637; presidency, 632, 633–36; Spanish-American War and, 603, 606
Roosevelt Corollary to Monroe Doctrine, 645–46
Root, Elihu, 645
Roots (Haley), 306
Root-Takahira Agreement, 646
Rorty, James, 737
Rosenberg, Julius and Ethel, 802–3
Rosenfeld, Morris, 626
Rosenman, Samuel, 723
"Rosie the Riveter," 759
Ross, Edward A., 620
Ross, Fort, 232
Rostow, Walt, 842
Roth, Herbert, 603
Rothapfel, Samuel L. "Roxy," 674
Rothstein, Arthur, 737
Rough Riders, 603
Rowlandson, Mary, 125
Rowson, Susanna Haswell, 218
Roxy Theater, 674
Royal African Company, 79, 84, 95
Royal governors, 123
Royal Proclamation (1763), 140, 141
Rukeyser, Muriel, 736
Rum, production of, 97
Runaway slaves, 75, 91–92, 109, 308–9
Running Bulls, Battle of (1937), 716
Rupert's Land, 69
Rush, Benjamin, 219
Rush-Bagot Treaty of 1817, 254, 255
Rusk, Dean, 841, 887
Russel, Benjamin, 304–5
Russell, Charles, 538
Russia: *See also* Soviet Union; Alaskan settlement, 231–32; Bolshevik Revolution, 663, 668–69; immigrants from, 708, 712
Russian American Fur Company, 231, 407
Russian-Californio trade, 406–7
Russo–Japanese War, 646
Russwurm, John, 372
Rustin, Bayard, 856, 864
Ruth, George Herman "Babe," 686, 687
Rutledge, Edward, 169
Ryan, Robert, 808
Ryswick, Treaty of, 69

S

Sabbath reformers, 366
Sacajawea, 230
Sac Indians, 243, 281–82
Sacramento River Commission, 523
Sadat, Anwar el–, 937
Safer, Morley, 882
Sagres Point, institute at, 30, 31
St. Augustine, Florida, 41, 87, 94, 108–9
St. Bartholomew's Day Massacre (1572), 40
St. Clair, Arthur, 182, 194–95, 205, 207
St. Domingue. *See* Haiti
St. Lawrence Valley, 42
St. Louis, Missouri, 233
St. Thomas's African Episcopal Church, 186
Salcedo, Manuel, 241
Salem, Massachusetts, 59, 62–63, 113
Salinger, J.D., 808
Salisbury, Harrison, 883
Salk, Jonas, 826
Saloons, 548
Sampson, Deborah, 167
San Antonio, Texas, 109, 241, 399, 402, 625
Sanborn, Franklin, 438
Sanchez, David, 900
Sandburg, Carl, 549
Sand Creek Massacre (1864), 519
Sanders, Carl, 862
San Diego, California, 110
Sandinista Liberation Front, 938
Sandino, Augustino, 692
San Francisco, California, 110, 408–9; Chinatown, 382, 384
San Francisco State College, 902
San Gabriel, Mission, 110
Sanger, Margaret, 629, 630–31, 688, 698
Sangre de Cristo Mountains, 50
Sanitary Commission, 468
Sanitary Fairs, 470
Sanitation, 356–57, 449, 563–64
San Jacinto, battle of (1836), 388, 400
Santa Anna, Antonio López de, 387, 400, 405
Santa Cruz, Mission, 110
Santa Fé, New Mexico, 19, 50–51, 397
Santa Fe Ring, 524–25
Santa Fé Trail, 391–92, 397–98
Santee Sioux, 463
Santo Domingo, 604–5
San Xavier de Bac, Mission, 109, 110
Saratoga, British defeat at (1777), 169, 170
Sargent, Henry, 343
"Saturday Night Massacre," 910
Sauer, Carl, 27
Sault Ste. Marie, 112
Savio, Mario, 884
Saybrook Platform (1708), 125
Scalawags, 499
Scalping, practice of, 17
Scarlet Letter, The (Hawthorne), 420
Schecter v. *United States*, 741
Schenck v. *United States*, 663
Schiff, Jacob, 610
Schlafly, Phyllis, 932, 933
Schlesinger, Arthur, Jr., 804
Schmidt, C.B., 530
Schneiderman, Rose, 626, 712
Schonholtz, Ray, 929
School and Society, The (Dewey), 619
School busing, 925
Schreyvogel, Charles, 538
Schumacher, E.F., 930
Schuman, William, 736
Schurz, Carl, 381, 385, 419, 440
Schurz, Margarethe, 381
Schwarzkopf, Norman, 974
Schwerner, Michael, 867
Scientific management, 626
Scientific racism, theories of, 693, 709
Scopes, John T., 696
Scots-Irish Presbyterians, 127, 222, 224
Scott, Winfield, 403, 404, 405, 406, 428, 460, 461
Seale, Bobby, 897
Seamen, black, 362
Sears, Roebuck and Company, 552
Seattle strike of 1919, 665, 666, 669
Seattle (Suquamish leader), 518
Secession of the South, 440–41
Second American Party System, 263, 285–87
Second Bank of the United States, 254, 256, 282–83
Second Great Awakening, 253, 343
Second industrial revolution, 676
"Secret Six," 438
Sectional balance, political issue of, 256–57
Sectional compromise, 208
Securities and Exchange Commission (SEC), 967
Sedgwick, Catherine, 347
Sedition Act: of 1798, 210–11, 216; of 1918, 663–64
Segregation, 596, 617; *See also* Civil rights movement (1957–1962); in education, 500, 617; of Mexican Americans, 871; in the military, 655, 665, 769–70; in the South, 852–53; Supreme Court on, 596, 850, 871
Seguín, Juan Nepomuceno, 388
Seigneurial class, 53, 120, 152
Sekes, 77
Selective Service Act (1940), 654, 753
Selective Service System, 767, 887
"Self–Reliance" (Emerson), 347
Selma, Alabama, 869–71
Seminole Indians, 91, 108, 243, 280, 281, 392
Seneca Falls Convention (1848), 352–53, 376
Seneca Indians, 21, 246
Sentimentalism, 346–47
"Separate but equal" doctrine, 596
Sequoyah, 281
Serapis (ship), 171
Serra, Junípero, 110, 111, 171
Service sector, 968–69, 982
Settle, Thomas, 499
Settlement house movement, 610–11, 615
Settlement of continent, Native American, 3–6
Seven Days Battles (1862), 461, 468, 469
Seventh-Day Adventists, 370
Seven Years War in America, 135–41, 142, 143, 144, 232
Seward, William Henry, 300, 424, 428, 435, 438, 455, 457, 465, 470, 599
Sewer systems, 563–64
Sewing machine, invention of, 339
Sexual behavior: campaign against venereal disease and, 661–62; in nineteenth-century, 345; Puritan, 62; in the sixties, 884–85; in the twenties, 687–88
Sexual Politics (Millett), 898
Seymour, Horatio, 490
Shackamaxon Treaty (1682), 66
Shahn, Ben, 737
Shakers, 370, 371
Shaman, 13
Shame of the Cities, The (Steffen), 618
Sharecropping system, 483, 495, 497, 503
Share Our Wealth Society, 727
Share wage system, 495–96
Shattuck, Job, 189
Shaw, Robert Gould, 465
Shawnee Indians, 22, 115, 136, 140, 205, 234, 243, 246
Shays, Daniel, 189
Shays' Rebellion, 189, 196
Sheen, Fulton J., 823
Sheldon, Charles M., 593
Shelikhov, Gregory, 231
Sheppard-Towner Act (1921), 698
Sherman, Roger, 158
Sherman, William Tecumseh, 449, 464, 473–75, 476, 485, 520; "March to the Sea," 460, 474–75
Sherman Antitrust Act (1890), 554, 627, 633–34
Sherman Silver Purchase Act (1890), 593–94
Shiloh, battle of (1862), 461–62, 468
Shipbuilding industry, 97, 236, 463–64
Shipping trade, 235–37, 242, 243, 331
Shoe industry, 331–32
Shoshonis, 8–9
Shuttlesworth, Fred, 862
Sibley, Henry H., 462
Siegenthaler, John, 861
Sierra Club, 635
Sigourney, Lydia, 431

Silent Spring (Carson), 929
Silicon Valley, 921, 959–60
Silko, Leslie, 902
Silverhorn, 519
Silver mines, 36, 522
Simon, Sidney, 771
Simon, William E., 916
Sims, Thomas, 427
Sinclair, Upton, 618, 634, 726
Singer, Isaac, 337
Sioux Indians, 3, 230, 463, 516, 518, 519, 541–42
Sirhan Sirhan, 894
Sit-down strikes, 729
Sit-ins, 857–58
Sitka, Russian settlement of, 231–32
Sitting Bull, 519
Six-Day War (1967), 916
Sixteenth Amendment, 638
Sketch Book, The, 289
Skin color, status of, 99–100; *See also* African Americans
Skoaquik (Snaketown), 13–14
Skycrapers, 562, 680
Slater, Samuel, 331, 333, 336
Slaughterhouse cases (1873), 502
Slave codes, 88
"Slave power," 423
Slave revolt of 1831, 296
Slavery, 294–321; abolitionism and, 318–19, 320, 371–75; beginnings of, 76–78; British emancipation of slaves, 279; changing attitudes toward, 298–99; in Chesapeake region, 57; Civil War and end of, 464–67; coercion and violence in, 75, 91–92, 317; community life in, 75, 88–89, 306–11; Compromise of 1850 and, 424–26; conditions of, 301–6; Constitutional Convention and guarantee for southern, 198; cotton production and, 297–301; culture and, 75, 89–90; daily life in, 88; defense of, 317–21, 338–39; distribution of slaves, 301, 302; *Dred Scott* decision, 434–35; economics of, 299–300; *encomienda* as form of, 33, 34; family in, 75, 88–89, 306–7; freedom and, 98–100, 308–9, 492–98; Free-Soil movement and, 412; in French Louisiana, 87; in Georgia, 74–75; health issues, 303; Indian, 85, 87; Jefferson and, 185, 306; John Brown's raid and, 437–38; Lincoln-Douglas debates, 418–19; in lower South, 85–86; maturing of system of, 301–4; Missouri Compromise and issue of, 256–57, 258; mortality rates in, 302–3; in North, 87–88, 186; occupations in, 304–6; Oregon and, 397; planters and, 313–17; political parties and, 208, 422; population, 85, 301; prohibition in Northwest Territory, 182; religion and, 89; runaway slaves, 75, 91–92, 109, 308–9; slave revolts, 92, 309–10; social structure of slave colonies, 98–99; in Spanish colonies, 86–87; states' rights and, 422–23; structure of empire and, 92–98; sugar and, 75, 76–77; in tobacco colonies, 84–85; violence and resistance, 75, 91–92, 308–9; West African, 77–78; Wilmot Proviso and, 411–12, 413, 422; yeomen and, 311–13
Slave ships, 81–82
Slave trade, 74, 78–83; after American Revolution, 186; arrival in New World, 82; demography of, 78; economic importance of, 92–94; effects on Africa of, 82–83; end of, 426; English participation in, 44, 79; estimated number of Africans imported to British North America, 80; Indian, 68–69; internal, 299, 307, 320–21; Middle Passage, 81–82, 89; nationalities of slavers, 79; in New England, 97; origins of, 76; outlawing of, 298–99; Portuguese establishment of, 31; profits in, 93; shock of enslavement, 79–81
Sloan, Alfred P., 677, 679
Sloan, John, 622, 629
Slovik, Eddie, 768
Slums, 357, 610–11
Small Is Beautiful (Schumacher), 930
Smallpox, 34, 35, 60–61, 81, 140, 230
Smiley, Glenn, 856
Smith, Adam, 92
Smith, Al, 616, 626, 703–4, 726, 729
Smith, Bessie, 686, 701
Smith, Gaddis, 936
Smith, Gerrit, 438
Smith, Hoke, 617
Smith, Howard K., 839
Smith, Jedediah, 390, 391
Smith, John, 54–55, 59
Smith, Joseph, 370, 371, 523
Smith, Margaret Chase, 804
Smith, Perry H., 567
Smith, Sidney, 288
Smith, Venture, 80
Smith-Hughes Act (1917), 623
Smithsonian Institution, 1
Smyth, Ellison Alger, 565
Snaketown, 13–14
Snyder, Gary, 833
Soap operas, 740
Social class: in cities, 355–56; class conflicts, 504; in colonial America, 120–21; emergence of, 10–11; industrialization and, 342–48; preindustrial social order, 329–30; seigneurial class, 53, 120, 152; in the South, 98–99, 296, 313–17, 320–21, 472, 485–86; wealth and, 342
Social control, 620–23
Social Control (Ross), 620
Social Darwinism, 555, 612, 619, 709
Social gospel movement, 592–93, 612
Socialist Party, 592, 628, 631, 637, 669
Social reform movements, 365–77; abolitionism, 318–19, 320, 371–75; antiprostitution movement, 368–69; asylum movement, 369; in education, 366–67; evangelism and, 365–67; moral reform, 368–69; Mormonism, 370–71, 372, 381, 425, 523–24; prison reform, 366, 369; in Progressive Era, 614–20; state reforms, in revolution, 184–85; temperance, 364, 367–68, 369, 588; utopianism, 369–70, 579; women's rights, 375–77
Social Register, 567
Social Security Act (1935), 727–28, 742, 743, 744
Social Security system, 728, 799, 889
Social welfare spending, in 1960s, 889–90
Society for Individual Rights, 899
Society of Friends. *See* Quakers
Society of Propagating the Gospel among Indians, 243
Sociological jurisprudence, 620
Sociology, field of, 620
Soil Conservation Service (SCS), 732
Sokoloff, Nikolai, 736
Somoza, Anastasio, 938
Songhai, kingdom of, 77, 82
Sons of Liberty, 144, 148, 151, 204, 470
Sorensen, Theodore, 841
Soulé, Pierre, 428
Souls of Black Folk, The (Du Bois), 632
South, the: *See also* Civil War; Confederacy; American Revolution in, 157, 173–75; in Civil War, 453–55, 463–64, 471–72; cotton production and expansion of, 297–306; culture of region, 115–16; economic changes in 19th century, 321; economy in 1970s, 920; Indian cessions and removals (1830s), 281; mutual acculturation in, 90–91; Native Americans in, 19–21; population patterns in, 318; Reconstruction in, 482–83, 484–85, 498–504; reentry to Union, 486–87; retiree migration to, 920–21, 922; secession of, 438, 440–41, 442; segregation in, 852–53; slavery in. *See* Slavery; social class in, 98–99, 296, 313–17, 320–21, 472, 485–86; textile industry in, 682; war in colonial, 68–69; War of 1812 in, 248
South Carolina: colonial, 64, 85; nullification crisis and, 279–80; rice belt, 74; universal white manhood suffrage in, 183; wars with Native Americans, 68–69
Southeast Asia Treaty Organization (SEATO), 837
Southern Argus, 497
Southern Baptist Convention, 422
Southern Christian Leadership Conference (SCLC), 856–57, 862
Southern Farmers' Alliance, 586
Southern Tenant Farmers Union (STFU), 724–25
South Korea, 809
Southwest, 13–14, 17–19, 524–26
Southworth, E.D.E.N., 347
Sovereignty and Goodness of God (Rowlandson), 125
Soviet economy, modernizing of, 956
Soviet Union: *See also* Cold War era; Afghanistan, invasion of, 939; Cuban missile crisis and, 843–44; dissolution of, 972; *glasnost* and, 955–56; Hungarian revolt and (1956), 834; in World War II, 772–74
Soyer, Isaac, 721
Space program, 822–23, 835, 841
Spain: American Revolution and, 170–71, 177; expansionism, 33–39; exploration, 31–33; hostility toward new United States, 205–6, 207; slavery in colonies, 86–87; slave trade and, 82
Spalding, Albert, 574–75, 580
Spanish-American War, 601–5
Spanish Armada, 45
Spanish borderlands, 106, 108–11
Spanish Civil War (1936), 738, 751
Spanish colonies, 50–53
Spaulding, Elbridge G., 457
Speaker of the House, 210
Specie Circular, 284
Spectator sports, 340
Spencer, Herbert, 619
"Spheres of influence," 779
Spice trade, 29
Spiritual, African American, 308
Spock, Benjamin, 807
Spofford, Harriet, 568
Spoils system, 269–70, 584–85
Sports, 340, 573–75, 684, 686–87
Spotsylvania, battle of (1864), 476
Spratt, L.W., 443
Springer, Thomas and Elizabeth, 327
Springfield, Massachusetts, 189
Springfield rifle, 337
Springsteen, Bruce, 934
Sputnik satellite, 822–23, 835
Spy cases, post–World War II, 802–3
Squanto, 59
Stagflation, 916–22
Stalin, Josef, 775, 779, 790–91, 834
Stalingrad, battle of (1942), 774
Stamp Act (1765), 133, 134, 143–45, 146, 151
Stamp Act Congress (1765), 133, 144
Standardized production, 337
Standard Oil Company, 506, 553
Standish, Miles, 60
Stanford, Leland, 505
Stanford-Binet intelligence test, 655
Stanton, Edwin M., 456, 475, 489
Stanton, Elizabeth Cady, 352–53, 465, 491–92, 588
Stanton, Frederick, 315
Stanwyck, Barbara, 802
Star-Spangled Banner, 249
State constitutions, 183–84
State Department, 800
State legislatures, 183
States' declarations of rights, 184
States' rights, 422–23, 435, 458, 484
States' Rights ("Dixiecrat") party, 799
Stead, W.T., 593
Steamboat Act (1838, 1852), 276
Steamboats, 275, 337, 338

Stearns, George, 438
Steel industry, 551, 591, 665–66, 960
Steffen, Lincoln, 618
Stein, Gertrude, 702
Steinbeck, John, 737
Stephens, Alexander, 428, 436, 443, 458, 472
Stephenson, David C., 695
Stevens, Isaac, 518
Stevens, John L., 601
Stevens, John Paul, 947
Stevens, Thaddeus, 487
Stevenson, Adlai E., Jr., 812, 843, 845
Stewart, William M., 505
Stieglitz, Alfred, 629
Stille, Wilhelmina, 384
Stilwell, Joseph, 776, 795
Stimson, Henry, 768, 780
Stock market, 590, 677, 717–18, 744, 967; *See also* Economy
Stockyards, 549
Stone, Lucy, 491
Stone Age, 4, 7, 10
Stonewall Riot (1969), 899
Stono Rebellion (1739), 92
Stowe, Harriet Beecher, 373–74, 421–22
Strategic Arms Limitation Treaty: SALT I, 906, 936; SALT II, 935, 936
Strategic Defense Initiative (SDI), 951, 953, 956
Strauss, Levi, 408
Strikes: automobile, 715–16; crisis of 1890s and, 590–92; early, 341–42; garment industry, 625–26; Great Uprising of 1877, 587; mining, 591, 627, 643–44; in New York City (1833–1837), 363–64; PATCO, 950; post–World War I, 665–66, 669; post–World War II (1946), 797; railroad, 504, 587; silk workers, 629; sit-down, 715–16, 729; steel, 665–66; student, 886, 897; textile, 628; in World War II, 759–60
Strong, Ellen Ruggles, 468
Strong, George Templeton, 440, 468, 471
Strong, Josiah, 559, 598, 599, 604
Stryker, Roy, 737
Stuart, Gilbert, 172, 205, 213
Student Nonviolent Coordinating Committee (SNCC), 858–59
Student Peace Union, 838
Student protest, 879–80, 883–88, 897, 899–901
Students for a Democratic Society (SDS), 879–80, 883
Student strikes, 897
Student Volunteers for Foreign Missions, 599
Submarine warfare, 650–51, 652, 774
Submerged Lands Act (1953), 820
Suburbanization, 681, 821–25
Subversive Activities Control Board, 801
Subways, 563
Suez Canal crisis (1956), 837
Suffrage. *See* Voting rights
Sugar, 36, 75, 76–77, 93, 565
Sugar Act, 134, 143, 151
Sullivan, Louis H., 562
Sullivan, Timothy D. "Big Tim," 615–16, 626
Summer camps, 569
Summit diplomacy, 835
Sumner, Charles, 434
Sumner, William Graham, 619
Sumter, Fort (1861), 450–51
Sunbelt, migration to, 920–21, 922
Supply Priorities and Allocation Board (SPAB), 756
Supply-side economics, 949–50, 952
Supreme Court, U.S.: *See also Specific decisions and cases*; on affirmative action, 926; antitrust cases, 595, 634, 687; civil rights and, 502, 596, 850, 851–52, 854, 871; court packing by FDR, 741–42; on cyberspace regulation, 947; *Dred Scott* decision, 434–35; on Espionage and Sedition Acts, 663; establishment of, 202; on Hyde Amendment, 934; on Indian policy, 281, 517; on interstate commerce, 276; on Japanese American internment, 763; on judicial review, 239; Lincoln and, 452; NIRA ruling, 728; Nixon and, 906; on polygamy, 524; in Progressive Era, 619–20, 634; right to review, 585; on state regulation, 586; on trade associations, 690; unions and, 678
Suquamish Indians, 518, 927
Surget family, 315
Susquehannock Indians, 68
Sutter, Fred, 644
Sutter, Johann Augustus, 407
Sweatt v. *Painter*, 866
Sweden, immigrants from, 710
Swift, Gustavus, 553
Swift, Jonathan, 142
Swift, Morrison, 606
Swing music, 740–41
Sylvis, William, 558
Syphilis, 36

T

Tabloids, 684–85
Tadoussac, village of, 42
Tafoya, Josefa, 398
Taft, Robert A., 752, 811, 812
Taft, William Howard, 604, 632, 636–37, 645, 646–47, 658
Taft-Hartley Act (1947), 798, 799
Taino Indians, 32, 35
Takagi, Harry, 874
Talbot, Marion, 630
Tallmadge, James, Jr., 257
Tammany, Chief, 66
Tammany Hall, 584, 587, 616, 703
Tammany Society, 365
Tamsarre, Anton, 988–89
Taney, Roger B., 276, 283, 434–35, 452
Tappan, Arthur, 375
Tappan, Lewis, 375
Tarawa, battle of (1943), 778
Tarbell, Ida, 553, 618, 653
Tariffs, 256; of 1789, 202; of 1816, 254; of 1824, 279; of 1828 (Tariff of Abominations), 279; of 1832, 280; of 1833, 280; Dingley (1897), 595; in late nineteenth century, 583; McKinley (1890), 593; tariff protection issue, 333; Wilson-Gorman (1894), 602
Tarring and feathering, 167
Task system, 75, 86
Tate, Allen, 703
Taxation: colonial, 143–49, 151; growth of local, 581; income, 636, 658, 950; under Lincoln, 456–57; Whiskey Tax, 194–95, 206
Taylor, Frederick Winslow, 556, 626
Taylor, Maxwell, 842
Taylor, Robert, 802
Taylor, Thomas, 315
Taylor, Zachary, 403, 404, 405, 406, 413, 425
Taylor Grazing Act (1934), 731
Tea Act (1773), 149, 150, 151
Teachers, women as, 366–67
Teach-ins, 886
Teapot Dome scandal, 689
Technology: *See also* Transportation; agricultural, 277, 532–33; of Archaic period, 5–7; British industrial, 332–33; revolution in, 550–51
Tecumseh, 245, 246–47, 248, 249
Teenagers. *See* Youth
Tejanos, 387–88, 398–400, 402
Telegraph, 288
Televangelists, 932, 964
Television, 829–32, 839, 882, 964, 970, 974
Teller, Henry, 603
Temperance movement, 364, 367–68, 369, 588
Temple mounds, 1, 2
Tenant farmers, 99, 312–13, 532
Tenements, 562, 570
Tennent, Gilbert, 126
Tennent, William, 126
Tennessee: in Civil War, 466; Scopes trial in, 696; secession of, 452
Tennessee Valley Authority (TVA), 725–26
Tenochtitlán, 33
Ten Percent Plan, 485
Tenskwatawa (The Prophet), 245, 246
Tenure of Office Act (1867), 489
Teotihuacan, 10–11
"Termination" policy, 873–74, 961
Terrorism, 956–57
Terry, Eli, 337
Tet Offensive (1968), 892–93
Texas, 241, 387–88, 398–403; admission of, 401–2; the Alamo (1836), 387–88; annexation of, 402–3; Compromise of 1850 and, 426; Mexican, 398–99; Mexican immigrants in, 712–13; Republic of, 388, 401–2; revolt in (1836), 400; secession of, 462; settlement of, 109, 388, 399–400
Textile industry, 325–26, 333–36, 682; in New South, 564, 565, 566–67; putting-out system, 331–32; strikes, 628
Thames, battle of the (1813), 245, 248
Thayer, Eli, 430
Theater, 359, 571
Third International (Comintern), 668
Third-party movement, 589
Thirteenth Amendment, 465, 486
This Side of Paradise (Fitzgerald), 702
Thomas, J. Parnell, 801–2
Thomas, M. Carey, 697
Thomas, Norman, 752
Thomas, Seth, 337
Thoreau, Henry David, 347, 405, 420, 437
Thornburgh, Richard, 914
Thorndike, E.L., 623
Thornton, William, 214
Three-fifths rule, 198
Three Mile Island, Pennsylvania, 914–15
Thurmond, J. Strom, 799, 851
Ticonderoga, Fort, 156–57, 169
Tidewater region, 84, 85
Tijerina, Reies López, 901
Tilden, Bill, 687
Tilden, Samuel J., 508
Tillman, Benjamin, 631
Timber Culture Act (1873), 535
Timbuktu, 77
Timucua Indians, 41
Tingley, Katherine, 580
Tippecanoe, battle of (1811), 246–47, 286
Title VII, 920
Tlingit Indians, 231
Tobacco, 30, 55–56, 84–85, 116, 235
Tocqueville, Alexis de, 360, 365, 536
Toleration Act (1689), 113, 115
Toltec Empire, 11, 33
Tombee Plantation (St. Helena Island), 314–15
Tompkins Square Riot (1874), 587
Tonkin, Gulf of, 881
Tönnies, Ferdinand, 620
Toombs, Robert, 423, 428, 438, 458
Tordesillas, Treaty of (1494), 39, 45
Tories, 167, 183
Toussaint L'Ouverture, François, 240
Tower, John, 958
Town meetings, 112, 117, 151
Townsend, Francis E., 727
Townshend, Charles, 145–46
Townshend Revenue Acts, 145–46, 147, 149, 151
Trade: *See also* Slave trade; in agrarian republic period, 235–37; with Asia, 29, 392–93; China, 236, 601; colonial, 92, 97, 98, 141; drug, 964–65; fur, 41–42, 53–54, 106, 107, 231, 236, 389–90, 397; imports in 1970s, impact of, 917; NAFTA and, 978–79; Native American trade networks,

16; Open Door policy and, 601; reexport, 236, 242; Russian-Californio, 406–7; Santa Fé, 397; shipping, 235–37, 242, 243, 331; spice, 29; trade deficit with Great Britain (1784–1786), 187, 188; triangular, 98
Trade associations, expansion of national, 690
Trading monopolies, 95–97
"Trail of Tears," 281
Trans-Appalachian settlement, 231, 233–34
Transborder peoples, 986
Transcendentalism, 347–48
Transcendental meditation (TM), 934
Transcendental Wild Oats (Alcott), 370
Transcontinental Treaty (1819), 254
Trans-Mississippi West, 513–45; cattle industry in, 526–28; Civil War in, 462–63; ethnography of, 538–39; farming communities in, 529–33; frontier settlement, 520–26, 530–31; landscape of West, 536–39; legends of, 537–38; mining communities, 521, 522–23; Mormon settlements, 523–24; Native Americans and, 516–20, 539–45; Oklahoma Land Rush, 514–15; Southwest settlements, 524–26
Transportation: *See also* Railroads; agriculture in Old Northwest and, 276–77; American System and, 253–54; automobiles, 658, 679–80, 715–16, 759, 823; canals, 254, 262, 272, 273–75, 278, 279, 355, 636; steamboats, 275, 337, 338; mass transportation systems, 563; revolution, 271–79; roads, 254, 267, 271, 272–73, 278, 279, 822; slavery and growth of, 93; in South, 301; steamboats, 275, 337, 338; subways and trolleys, 563
Trans-Siberian Railway, 668
Travis, Joseph, 310
Travis, William, 387
Treason, 167
Treasury, Department of the, 581
Treatise on Domestic Economy (Beecher), 345
Trenchard, John, 142
Trench warfare, 656–57
Trenton, New Jersey, 169
Trescot, William Henry, 317
Tres Riches Heures, 29
Triangle Shirtwaist Company fire (1911), 626
Triangular trade, 98
Tribal council, 12
Tribal Government Tax Status Act (1983), 961
Triple Alliance (Central Powers), 650
Triple Entente (Allies), 650
Trist, Nicholas, 405
Trolleys, electric, 563
Trotter, William Monroe, 633, 667
Truman, Harry S.: atomic bomb and, 780–82; civil rights and, 851; Cold War and, 796–814; containment policy and, 791–96; election of 1948, 798–99; Fair Deal and, 799–800; Korean conflict and, 808–11; presidency, 796–814
Truman Doctrine, 791–92
Trumbull, John, 214, 216
Trumbull, Lyman, 505–6
Trustbusting, 633–34
Truth, Sojourner, 372, 373
Tsuzuki, Byron Takashi, 763
Tubb, Ernest, 766
Tuberculosis, 549, 611
Tubman, Harriet, 309, 310, 372, 426
Tugwell, Rexford G., 723, 728–29
Tukekas, Old Chief, 520
Tunney, Gene, 687
Turkey, post–World War II aid for, 791
Turnbull, Robert J., 309–10
Turner, Frederick Jackson, 392, 597
Turner, Henry M., 465
Turner, Nat, 296, 309, 310, 318, 372
Turner, Stansfield, 936
Turner Diaries (Pierce), 931
Tuscarora Indians, 68, 173
Tuskegee Institute, 571
Twain, Mark, 276, 604, 607
Tweed, William Marcy, 506, 584
"Tweed Ring," 508
Twelfth Amendment, 212
Twelve Years a Slave (Northup), 305, 427
Twenties, the, 673–707; African Americans in, 700–701; agriculture and ailing industries in, 681–82; automobile industry and, 679–80; bull market of, 717; cities and suburbanization in, 681; economy in, 688–92; election of 1928, 703–5, 707; feminism in, 697–98; foreign policy in, 691–92; government in, 688–92; immigration restrictions in, 693–94; intellectuals and alienation in, 701–3; Ku Klux Klan in, 694–95; mass culture in, rise of, 675–76, 682–88; Mexican immigration in, 698–700; modern corporation and, 676–77; new morality in, 687–88; postwar prosperity in, 676–82; prohibition in, 692–93; religious fundamentalism in, 695–96; resistance to change in, 692–96; second industrial revolution in, 676; welfare capitalism and, 677–78
Twenty-First Amendment, 693
Two-income family, 805–7
Tydings, Millard E., 804
Tyler, John, 286, 287, 402, 403
Typhoid fever, 163, 563

U

U–2 incident (1960), 835
U–boats, 651, 655
Ulises criollo (Vasconcelos), 712
Uncle Tom's Cabin (Stowe), 375, 421–22
Underclass, 926–27
Underground Railroad, 309, 375
Underwood-Simmons Act (1913), 638
Unemployed Councils, 727
Unemployment: in depression of 1873, 507–8; financial collapse of 1893 and, 590; in Great Depression, 719–21, 744
Unidentified flying object (UFO) sightings, 808
Unification Church, 934
Union(s), 363–64; *See also specific unions*; African Americans in, 760; American Federation of Labor (AFL), 559, 627–28, 643, 644, 658, 694, 729; biracial cooperation in, 851; craft, 559; Industrial Workers of the World (IWW), 628, 630, 643, 644, 659, 669; mining industry, 523, 627; in New Deal coalition, 716; in 1970s, 919; in 1930s, 729; open shop, 627, 678; strikes in 1890s and, 591–92; in the twenties, 678, 682; women in, 588; in World War I, 658–59; in World War II, 760
Union Army, 451, 453, 464, 469, 470–71; *See also* Civil War
Union League, 482, 497–98
Union of Russian Workers, 669
Union Pacific Railroad Company, 457, 504, 554
United Automobile Workers (UAW), 715, 729, 759
United Fruit Company, 553, 646, 837
United Latin American Citizens (LULAC), 700
United Mine Workers, 627, 682, 729
United Nations (UN), 789–90, 809
U.S. Children's Bureau, 614, 636, 662, 762
U.S. Foreign Debt Commission, 691
U.S. Forest Service, 535, 536, 634
United States Industrial Commission, 595
U.S. Office of Education, 762
U.S. Patent Office, 533
U.S. Public Health Service, 662
U.S. Rubber Company, 760
United States Sanitary Commission, 449, 470, 491
U.S. Steel Corporation, 555, 564, 628, 658
U.S. v. *Cruikshank*, 502
United States v. *John*, 961
U.S. v. *Reese*, 502
United States v. *Reynolds*, 524
United States v. *Wheeler*, 874, 927, 961
Universal Doctrine of Human Rights, 789
Universal Negro Improvement Association, 701
Universal white manhood suffrage, 212–13, 263, 264–65, 266, 330
University of California at Berkeley, 884, 902
University of Mississippi, 862
University of Washington, 786–87
University of Wisconsin, 886
Up from Slavery (Washington), 632
Uprising of the 20,000, 625–26
Uptown, Chicago, Illinois, 879–80
Upward Bound, 889
Urban civilizations, Mesoamerican, 10–11
Urbanization. *See* Cities and towns
Urban Renewal Act, 879
Urbina, Rosa Maria, 990
Urey, Harold C., 796
Utah, 425; *See also* Mormonism; admission to Union, 425
Ute Indians, 8
Utopianism, 369–70, 579

V

Vallandigham, Clement, 470
Valley Forge, 163–64, 169
Van Buren, Martin, 262–63, 267, 268, 280, 284–87, 402, 413
Vance, Cyrus R., 936, 938, 940
Vandenberg, Arthur H., 791, 796
Vanderbilt, Cornelius, 505
Van Devanter, Wilis, 742
Van Kleeck, Mary, 660
Vardaman, James, 617
Vasconcelos, José, 712
Vaudeville, 573
Vaughn, Robert, 55
Veblen, Thorstein, 567
Venereal disease, campaign against, 661–62
Veramendi, Ursula, 400
Vergennes, Comte de, 170, 171, 177
Vermont: abolition of slavery in, 186; settlement of, 140
Verrazano, Giovanni da, 42
Versailles peace conference (1918), 666
Versailles Treaty (1919), 667–68, 751
Vertical integration, 553, 555, 690
Vesey, Denmark, 309–10, 318
Vespucci, Amerigo, 33
Vessey, John, 953
Veterans Bureau, 582
Veterans of Foreign Wars, 887
Veto power, 201
Vice-admiralty courts, 146
Vicksburg, battle of (1863), 460, 473
Videocassette recorders (VCR), 963
Vietnam, Democratic Republic of, 905
Vietnam Veterans against the War, 887
Vietnam War, 881–83; African Americans in, 887, 897; air attacks, 882; antiwar movement, 883–88, 904; domestic agenda and, 880; domino theory and, 837; foundations for, 837–38; generational opposition to, 883–88; Johnson and, 881–83, 893; Kennedy and, 842; King and, 893–94; military in, 887–88, 905; My Lai Massacre, 905; Nixon and, 904–5; refugees at end of, 989; television and, 882; Tet Offensive (1968), 892–93; veterans of, 887, 888
Vigilantism, 195, 643–44, 663–64
Villa, Francisco "Pancho," 648–49
Vincennes, capture of (1779), 173
Virginia: American Revolution and reform in, 184–85; backcountry, 115; Bacon's Rebellion, 66, 68, 84; Civil War in northern, 461; colony of, 54, 98; Harpers Ferry raid, 437–38; House of Burgesses, 98, 147, 149; House of Delegates, 184; Jamestown colony, 54–55; John Smith's map of, 55; ratification of Constitution, 199–200; Roanoke colony, 26–27, 45; secession of, 452

Virginia Company, 54–55, 56, 59
Virginia Declaration of Rights, 184, 200
Virginia Dynasty, 237, 253; *See also* Jefferson, Thomas; Madison, James; Monroe, James
Virginia (ironclad ship), 463–64
Virginian, The (Wister), 538
Virginia Plan, 197
Virginia Resolve, 211, 249, 280
Virginia Slave Code, 84
Virginia Stamp Act Resolutions, 143–44
Virtual communities, 946–47
Vision of Columbus, The (Barlow), 216
Vison, Fred, 854
VISTA (Volunteers in Service to America), 889
Vittorio Emmanuel, King, 775
Vizcaíno, Sebastián, 110
V–J Day, 787
Vocational education, 623
Voice to the Married, A (Austin), 344
Volstead Act (1919), 692
Vorse, Mary Heaton, 629
Voter registration, 867
Voter turnout: declining, 922; in election of 1856, 434; in election of 1860, 440; pre–Civil War, 288
Voting rights: African American, 265, 487, 490, 497, 596, 617, 853; democracy and changes in, 263, 264–66; universal white manhood suffrage, 212–13, 263, 264–65, 266, 330; for women, 184, 185, 266, 377, 490–92, 660–61, 662
Voting Rights Act (1965), 866, 870–71

W

Wade, Benjamin F., 485, 490
Wade-Gayles, Gloria, 819
Wage labor, rise of, 338–40, 341–42
Wage system, 494–96, 555, 557–59, 565–66
WAGE (Women Act to Gain Equality), 920
Wagner, Robert F., 616, 626, 728
Wagner Act. *See* National Labor Relations Act (1935)
Wagner-Steagall Act. *See* National Housing Act (1937)
Wagon trains, 395–96
Waite, David, 594
Waiting for Lefty (Odets), 738
Wald, Lillian D., 610, 611, 626, 651, 654
Walden (Thoreau), 347, 420
Waldo, Albigense, 163
Waldorf-Astoria hotel, 568
Walker, David, 372
Walker, Leroy P., 458
Walker, Margaret, 736
Walker, Moses "Fleet," 575
Walker, Reid A., 963
Walker, Robert, 402
Walker, William, 428
Wallace, A.S., 440
Wallace, George, 863, 864, 870, 904
Wallace, Henry A., 732, 753, 798–99, 804
Wallace, Mike, 892
Walpole, Robert, 94, 96, 123
Walsh, Frank, 658
Walsh, Lawrence, 958
Wampanoag Indians, 59, 60, 67, 113
Wanchese (Indian), 26, 27
War bonds, 756
Ward, Clara, 819
Ward, Lester Frank, 619
Ware v. *Hylton*, 202
War for independence. *See* American Revolution
War Hawks, 247–48, 298
War Industries Board (WIB), 657
War Manpower Commission (WMC), 756, 759, 762
Warner, Susan, 347
War of 1812, 245, 247–49, 264
War of Jenkins's Ear, 94–95
War of the League of Augsburg, 69
War of the Spanish Succession (Queen Anne's War), 94, 95
War of the Worlds (radio show), 740
War on poverty, 888–92
War Powers Act (1941), 756
War Production Board, 758
War Relocation Authority, 762
Warren, Earl, 845, 854, 855
Warren, Mercy Otis, 167, 198, 216, 217
Warren, Robert Penn, 703
War Resisters' League, 856
Warsaw, Jewish ghetto of, 775
Warsaw Pact, 795
Washington, Booker T., 571, 632, 633
Washington, D.C.: architecture of, 214; Bonus Army in, 722; in Civil War, 455; contrabands in, 464; in 1800, 239; March on (1963), 864–65; War of 1812 and burning of, 249
Washington, Fort, 169
Washington, George, 152, 196, 237; in American Revolution, 157, 163–64, 165, 166, 168, 169, 175, 178–79; Annapolis Convention and, 196; Constitutional Convention and, 197; Farewell Address, 195, 208; fiscal program, 202–3; foreign policy, 203–8; French and Indian War, 137; inauguration of (1789), 200; as landlord, 194–95; presidency of, 200–208; at Second Continental Congress, 155–56; slavery issue and, 186; at Valley Forge, 163–64; western expansion and, 140; Whiskey Rebellion and, 206
Washington, Martha, 167
Washington Temperance Societies, 368
Washington Territory, 397
Waste Land, The (Eliot), 703
Water, Muddy, 819
Watergate scandal, 904–11
Waterloo, battle of (1815), 240
Water pollution, 563–64, 734
Water supply, 535, 563–64; New Deal in West and, 733–34
Water transportation. *See* Canals; Steamboats; Shipbuilding industry
Watie, Stand, 462
Watkins, Ida, 681
Watson, Henry, 482
Watson, Sereno, 441
Watson, Tom, 595, 597
Watt, James, 950
Waugh, Samuel, 384
WAVES, 768, 769
Wayne, Anthony, 194–95, 207
Wealth: distribution of, 122, 342, 355, 690, 718–19, 924–26, 967–68; gospel of, 554–55
Wealth and Poverty (Gilder), 950
Weather Bureau, 533
Weaver, James Baird, 589, 593
Weaver, Robert, 744
Webb, Alex, 482, 497
Webb family, 422
Webster, Daniel, 270, 271, 284, 410, 411, 424, 425
Webster, Noah, 217, 328
Weems, Mason Locke (Parson Weems), 216–17
Weinberger, Caspar, 951, 958
Weissmuller, Johnny, 687
Weld, Theodore, 373, 375, 422
Welfare capitalism, 677–78
Welfare Reform Act, 980
Welfare system, 820, 889–90, 925, 926
Welles, Orson, 736, 740, 802
Wells, H.G., 740
Wells, Ida B., 596–97, 598
Wesleyan Methodist Society of Seneca Falls, 353
West, Benjamin, 138, 213
West Africa, slavery in, 77–78
Western Federation of Miners (WFM), 591, 628
Western literary genre, 216, 537–38
Western Reserve, 179, 252
Westmoreland, William, 882, 893
West Point, New York, 171
West Virginia, 452
Westward expansion, 250–58; *See also* Native Americans; Railroads; Trans–Mississippi West; American Revolution and, 173; American sovereignty and, 208; California, 406–10; cattle industry and, 521, 526–28; Dust Bowl (1935–1940) in, 730–33; exploration, 389–92; Gadsden Purchase (1853), 406, 524; geological surveys and, 390, 537; Lewis and Clark expedition, 229–30, 240, 241, 390–91; Louisiana Purchase, 229, 238, 239–41; Manifest Destiny, 392–94, 410–13; Mexican–American War, 403–6, 411, 524; migration routes, 251–52; Missouri Compromise and, 250, 256–58; Native Americans and, 243–47, 516–20, 539–45; New Deal and, 730–35; Overland Trails, 392, 394–96; politics of, 392–403; pre-revolutionary struggle for, 139–41; Santa Fé trade, 397; Southerners and, 298; surge after War of 1812, 250–52; Texas, 387–88, 398–403; trans-Appalachian settlement, 231, 233–34; War of 1812 and, 247–49
"Wetback" (*mojados*), 871
Wheatley, Phillis, 186–87
Wheat production, 531, 534, 681
Wheeler, Burton K., 742
Wheeler, Edward L., 538
Wheeler, Harry, 644
Wheeler, Judith P., 930
Where Life Is Better (Rorty), 737
Whig Party, 142, 183, 286, 394, 433; "Cotton Whigs", 430; election of 1836 and, 283–84; Kansas Nebraska Act and, 430; Mexican–American War and, 405; rise of, 279–87; Tyler and, 287
Whip Inflation Now (WIN), 922
Whirling Thunder, 243
Whiskey Rebellion, 194–95, 196, 200, 206, 207, 211, 216, 219
Whiskey Ring, 508
Whiskey Tax (1791), 194–95, 206
White, Hugh Lawson, 284
White, John, 26, 27, 44, 45
White, Richard, 311
White, William Allen, 689, 704, 729
White Angel Bread Line (Lange), 720
White Collar (Mills), 825
White collar workers, 342
Whitefield, George, 126
"White flight," 890, 925
White supremacy, 595–97, 694
Whitman, Marcus, 396, 397
Whitman, Narcissa, 396, 397
Whitman, Slim, 818
Whitman, Walt, 360, 420, 468–69
Whitney, Eli, 297, 337
Whole Earth 'Lectronic Link (WELL), 946–47
Whyte, William H., 825
Wide Wide World, The (Warner), 347
Wilderness, battle of the (1864), 476
Wild West shows and legends, 537–38
Wilkening, Ruby, 749
Wilkins, Roy, 859
Wilkinson, James, 180
Willamette Valley, Oregon, 394, 396
Willard, Frances E., 588, 593
William and Mary, College of, 124
William of Orange, 69
Williams, Eunice (daughter), 105, 119
Williams, Eunice (mother), 104
Williams, Gail, 947
Williams, John, 104–5, 125
Williams, Nancy, 494
Williams, Nat D., 819
Williams, Roger, 63, 113
Williams, Stephen, 105
Williamsburg, Virginia, 186

Willkie, Wendell L., 753
Wills, Helen, 687
Wilmington, Delaware, 327
Wilmot, David, 411
Wilmot Proviso (1846), 411–12, 413, 422
Wilson, Charles, 820, 833
Wilson, Pete, 971
Wilson, Sloan, 825
Wilson, William Julius, 925
Wilson, Woodrow, 644, 710; election of 1912, 636–37; election of 1916, 651–52; foreign policy of, 648–49; Fourteen Points, 666; labor movement and, 644; League of Nations and, 666, 667; moralism of, 649; New Freedom campaign, 637; presidency, 627, 637–38; World War I and, 650–70
Wilson-Gorman tariff (1894), 602
Winchell, Walter, 684
Wines, California, 534
Wingina, Chief, 26, 27
Winnebagos, 10
Winthrop, John, 58, 59, 60, 62, 124
Wisconsin, progressive reform in, 616–17, 619
Wisconsin Territory, 434
Wister, Owen, 538
Witchcraft scares, 62–63
Wobblies. *See* Industrial Workers of the World (IWW)
Wolcott, Marion Post, 737
Wolfe, James, 138, 141
Wolfe, Tom, 934, 964
Wollstonecraft, Mary, 218
Wolofs, 77
Woman in the Nineteenth Century (Fuller), 348
Woman Rebel, 630–31
Woman's Christian Temperance Union (WCTU), 588, 620, 661
Woman's Peace Party, 651, 654, 691
Woman suffrage. *See* Voting rights
Women: *See also* Working women; African American, 565, 768–69, 920; in American Revolution, 166–67, 178, 184; antilynching movement and, 596–97; army nurses, 468–69; birth control and, 345, 630–31, 688, 698; in cattle industry, 527; in Civil War, 448–49, 451, 468–69; in Clinton administration, 978; colonial, 58, 61–63, 117; in company towns, 626; education of, 61–62, 367, 572, 807; Equal Rights Amendment and, 697, 923, 933; feminization of poverty, 926; Great Plains settlement and, 531, 532; Indian rights and, 540; intellectual, 218–19; in Ku Klux Klan, 694–95; land speculators, 529; Mexican immigrant, 525, 698–99; middle class, 344–47, 568–69, 630–31; in the military, 768–69; missionaries, 598–99; motherhood and, 345–46; Nationalist movement and, 579; Native American, status of, 12; network in New Deal, 742–43; novelists, 346–47; patriarchical organization and, 329; on plantations, 315, 316–17; politics and, 266, 742–43; post-revolutionary, 217, 218–19; post–World War II, 805–7; progressive reform and, 614–15; prostitution and, 358–59, 527, 621; Quaker, 114; sentimentalism and, 346–47; slave, 306, 317; in SNCC, 867; social gospel movement and, 593; temperance movement and, 588, 620, 661; in the twenties, 687, 688, 697–98; at Valley Forge, 163; voting rights, 184, 185, 266, 377, 490–92, 660–61, 662; in World War I, 659–60; in World War II, 758–59, 768–69
Women in Industry Service (WIS), 660
Women's Airforce Service Pilots, 768
Women's Army Auxiliary Corps (WAAC), 768
Women's Army Corps (WAC), 768
Women's Bureau, 660
Women's Central Association of Relief (WCAR), 449
Women's club movement, 630
Women's Committee of the Council of National Defense, 654
Women's Educational and Industrial Union, 571
Women's Emergency Brigade, 716
Women's International League for Peace and Freedom, 838
Women's magazines, 345
Women's movement, 375–77, 588–89, 610–11, 630–31, 669, 697, 840, 898–99; Seneca Falls Convention and, 352–53, 376
Women's National Indian Association (WNIA), 540
Women's Political Council (WPC), 850
Women's Strike for Equality, 899
Women's studies programs, 898
Women's Trade Union League, 626, 697
Women's Union Missionary Society of Americans for Heathen Lands, 598–99
Women workers. *See* Working women
Wood, James Madison, 807
Wood, Robert E., 752
Woodland culture, 14–17
Woodstock Nation, 885
Woodville, Richard Caton, 268
Woodward, Bob, 908
Woodward, Charlotte, 352–53
Woodward, Ellen, 742
Wool Act (1699), 96
Woolman, John, 87
Woolworth, Frank and Charles, 552
Worcester v. *Georgia*, 281
Work, gospel of, 555
Work day, 341–42, 558
Workers. *See* Labor; Labor movement; Working women
Workers Loyalty League, 644
Working class, 358, 359–61, 569–71, 623–29; *See also* Labor movement
Workingmen's Party (Workies), 363
Working women: in Great Depression, 720–21; in Knights of Labor, 588; legislation on, 840; mechanization and women's work, 339; in 1970s, 920; in 1950s, 806–7; patriarchal organization and, 329; strikes by, 341–42, 376; as teachers, 366–67; in textile industry, 325–26, 333; in the twenties, 697–98; wage system and, 556; women's alliances, 588–89; in World War I, 659–60; in World War II, 758–59
Workplace equality, 920
Works Progress Administration (WPA), 727, 728, 731, 735, 744, 757
World Court, 691
World's fair (Chicago, 1893), 597–98
World Trade Organization, 978
World War I, 643–72; aftermath of, 690–91; alliances in, 650; anti-German campaign, 652, 653; casualties of, 657; cost of, 657; end of, 666–70; entry into, 644, 652–53; Espionage and Sedition Acts in, 663–64; Fourteen Points, 666; Great Migration and racial tensions in, 664–65; on homefront, 657–63; labor and, 658–59, 665–66; mobilization for, 653–57; neutrality and, 650–52; onset of, 649–50; peace conference, 666–67; pre-war foreign policy, 645–49; reparations after, 667, 690–91; repression and reaction in, 663–66; Russian Revolution and, 668–69; submarine warfare, 650–51, 652; Versailles Treaty, 667–68, 751; vigilante justice in, 643–44; women and, 659–60
World War II, 748–82; armed forces, 766–71; declaration of, 755; economic conversion in, 757–58; in Europe, 772–73; holocaust, 778–79; homefront in, 760–66, 986; last stages of, 778–82; mobilization for, 756–60, 766–69; in North Africa, 774; onset of, 751–55; overseas occupation in, 770; Pacific Theater, 770–72, 776–78; Pearl Harbor, 754, 755; personnel and bombs, 773; prisoners of war in, 770–71; progress of, 771–78; submarine warfare, 774
Wounded Knee, battle of (1890), 541–42
Wounded Knee, South Dakota, 901–2
Wovoka, 541
Wright, Richard, 736, 738
Wright, Silas, Jr., 263
Wright, Wilbur and Orville, 550
Wrigley, William K., 687
WU (Women United), 920

X

XYZ affair, 209–10

Y

Yale College, 124
Yalta Conference (1945), 779–80
Yamasee Indians, 68
"Yankee Doodle," 148
"Yankees," origin of term, 141
Yellow fever, 81, 356, 564
Yellowstone National Park, 535, 537
Yeltsin, Boris, 972
Yeomen farmers, 311–14
Yezierska, Anzia, 736
Yippies (Youth International Party), 894
Yom Kippur War (1973), 916
Yoneda, Karl G., 762
York (Toronto), burning of (1813), 248
Yorktown, battle of (1781), 175
Yorubas, 77
Yosemite Act: of 1864, 537; of 1890, 634
Yosemite Park, 634–35
Young, Andrew, 938–39
Young, Brigham, 370, 523
Young, Coleman, 927
Young, Owen D., 677
Young, Robert, 752
"Young America" movement, 410–11, 428
Young Men's Christian Association (YMCA), 569, 599
Young Women's Christian Association (YWCA), 569, 593, 599
Youth: counterculture, 884–85; culture, 826–29; delinquency, 762, 829; rock 'n' roll music and, 818–19, 827–28; teenage pregnancy, 926
Youth International Party (Yippies), 894
Yucatan Peninsula, 10, 11
Yukon River basin, fossils in, 4–5
Yuman people, 17–18
Yuppies, 964

Z

Zapata, Emiliano, 649
Zavala, Lorenzo de, 388
Zenger, John Peter, 141
Zhou Enlai, 810
Zimmermann, Arthur, 652
Zoot-suit riots, 764–65
Zukor, Adolph, 682
Zuni Indians, 516
Zwerg, James, 861